Physics for the IB Diploma

Fourth edition

K. A. Tsokos

CAMBRIDGE UNIVERSITY PRESS
Cambridge, New York, Melbourne, Madrid, Cape Town, Singapore, São Paulo

Cambridge University Press
The Edinburgh Building, Cambridge CB2 2RU, UK

www.cambridge.org
Information on this title: www.cambridge.org/9780521604055

First, second and third editions © K.A. Tsokos 1998, 1999, 2001
Fourth edition © Cambridge University Press 2005

First published by K.A. Tsokos 1998
Second edition 1999
Third edition 2001
Fourth edition published by Cambridge University Press 2005

Printed in the United Kingdom at the University Press, Cambridge

A catalogue record for this publication is available from the British Library

ISBN-13   978-0-521-60405-5 paperback
ISBN-10   0-521-60405-2 paperback

ACKNOWLEDGEMENTS
We are grateful to the following for permission to reproduce photographs:

Anglo-Australian Observatory/David Malin Images, pp. 465, 502, 543(c); © Bettmann/CORBIS,
pp. 257, 535 *bl*; Jeremy Burgess/Science Photo Library, p. 470(a); CERN, p. 396(b); Harold
Edgerton/Science Photo Library, p. 89; Lick Observatory OP, University of California/Science
Photo Library, p. 535*tl*; Richard Megna/Fundamental Photos/Science Photo Library, p. 297;
NOAO/Science Photo Library, p. 543(a), (b); Popperfoto.com, p. 258; Science Museum/Science
and Society Picture Library, p. 395; Science Photo Library, pp. 76, 552.

Cover design courtesy of Michael Dunning/Science Photo Library

Contents

For Alexios and Alkeos

Preface

Physics is a fundamental science and those who study it will gain an understanding of the basic laws that govern everything from the very small subatomic scale to the very large cosmic scale. The study of physics provides us with an unparalleled power of analysis that is useful in the study of the other sciences, engineering and mathematics, as well as in daily life.

The fourth edition of *Physics for the IB Diploma* is a text that has been written with the needs of the IB student in mind. It covers the new syllabus that was examined for the first time in May 2003. The fourth edition covers the entire IB syllabus, including all options at both standard level (SL) and higher level (HL). It includes a chapter on the role of physics in the theory of knowledge (TOK) along with many discussion questions for TOK. The questions and problems at the end of each chapter have been expanded and there are answers at the end of the book for all those involving calculation (and for some others too). Each chapter opens with a list of objectives, which include the important formulae that will be covered in the chapter.

Part I of the book covers the core material and the additional higher level (AHL) material. The title and running heads of each chapter clearly indicate whether the chapter is part of the core or AHL. Part II covers the optional subjects. Two options available only to standard level students (Option A, Mechanics, and Option B, Atomic and Nuclear Physics) are the same as the corresponding AHL material and therefore these two options are not presented separately. Another standard level option, Option C, Energy, includes an entire chapter from AHL

Thermal Physics, namely Thermodynamics. Thermodynamics is presented in Chapter 3.4. Option E, The History and Development of Physics, is presented in Part II as a separate set of chapters but much of the material is common to both core and AHL material; those parts of the syllabus are not repeated in Option E. Instead, there are references to the appropriate sections in Part I.

The division of this book into chapters and sections follows the syllabus published by the International Baccalaureate Organization (IBO) as closely as possible. This does not mean, however, that this particular order should be followed. Within reason, the sections are fairly independent of each other and so alternative teaching sequences may be followed. It must also be stressed that this book is not an official guide to the IB syllabus nor is this book connected with the IBO in any way.

The book contains many example questions and answers that are meant to make the student more comfortable with solving problems. Some are more involved than others. There are also questions at the end of each chapter, which the student should attempt to answer to test his or her understanding. Even though the IB does not require calculus for physics, I have used calculus, on occasion, in the text and in the questions for the benefit of those students taking both physics and mathematics at higher level. They can apply what they are learning in mathematics in a concrete and well-defined context. However, calculus is not essential for following the book. It is assumed that a student starting a physics course at this level knows the basics of trigonometry and is comfortable with simple algebraic manipulations.

In questions and examples I have not resisted the temptation to use 10 m s^{-2} as the numerical value of the acceleration due to gravity. I have followed the conventions of symbols used by the IBO in the *Physics Data Booklet* with one major exception. The *Data Booklet* uses the symbol s for displacement. Almost universally, the symbol s is reserved for distance and so s stands for distance in this book, not displacement. Also, I have chosen to call initial velocities, speeds, etc. by v_0 rather than the IBO's u.

I wish to thank my wife Ellie Tragakes for her great help and support with this book. I also want to thank the editors of this book, Una Yeung and Andrew Coleman, and the proofreader, Geoff Amor, for their invaluable help and their great professionalism. Without them this edition would not have been possible.

K. A. Tsokos

Athens

January 2005

A note to the reader

The main text of each chapter contains a number of different features, which are clearly identified by the use of headings or by other typographical means, as outlined below.

Learning outcomes
These are provided as bullet lists at the beginning of each chapter and indicate what you will have learned or be able to do when you have finished studying the chapter.

Important results, laws, definitions and significant formulae
Particularly important material, such as important results, laws, definitions and significant formulae, appear in a shaded box.

Example questions
These occur in nearly all of the chapters. They are indicated by the heading 'Example question(s)' and all have a full answer. It is a good idea to attempt to solve these problems before reading the answers. There are over 500 such example questions in this book.

Material for higher level students
This material is highlighted in a shaded box that is labelled 'HL only'.

Material that is outside the IB syllabus
Some material is included that is outside the IB syllabus and will not be examined in the IB exams. It is included here for two reasons. The first is that I believe that it clarifies syllabus material and in some cases it does so in essential ways. The second is that it gives the interested student a more rounded view of the subject that is not bounded by the rigid syllabus content. Such material is highlighted in a shaded box that is labelled 'Supplementary material'.

Questions
Each chapter ends with a numbered set of questions and problems to solve. Answers to all those that involve calculation are given at the end of the book. Answers are also provided for some other questions where it is useful for students to be able to check their answers.

Part 1

Core and AHL

The realm of physics

Physics is an experimental science in which measurements made must be expressed in units. In the International System of units used throughout this book, the SI system, there are seven fundamental units, which are defined in this chapter. All quantities are expressed in terms of these units directly or as a combination of them.

Objectives

By the end of this chapter you should be able to:
- appreciate the order of magnitude of various quantities;
- perform simple order-of-magnitude calculations *mentally*;
- state the *fundamental units* of the SI system.

Orders of magnitude and units

How many molecules are there in the sun? This may sound like a very difficult question with which to start a physics textbook, but very basic physics can give us the answer. Before we try to work out the answer, guess what you think the answer is by giving a power of 10. The number of molecules in the sun is 10 to the power . . . ?

To answer the question we must first have an idea of the mass of the sun. You may know this, or you can easily look it up (to save you doing this for this example, we can tell you that it is about 10^{30} kg). Next, you will need to know what the chemical composition of the sun is. It is made up of 75% hydrogen and 25% helium, but as we are only making a rough estimate, we may assume that it is made out of hydrogen entirely. The molar mass of hydrogen is 2 g mol^{-1} and so the sun contains $10^{33}/2$ mol = 5×10^{32} mol. The number of molecules in one mole of any substance is given by the Avogadro constant, which is about 6×10^{23}, so the sun has around $5 \times 10^{32} \times 6 \times 10^{23} = 3 \times 10^{56}$ molecules. How close was your guess?

The point of this exercise is that, first, we need units to express the magnitude of physical quantities. We must have a consistent set of units we all agree upon. One such set is the International System (SI system), which has seven basic or fundamental units. The units of all other physical quantities are *combinations* of these seven. These units are presented later in this section. The second point is that we have been able to answer a fairly complicated sounding question without too much detailed knowledge – a few simplifying assumptions and general knowledge have been enough. The third point you may already have experienced. How close was your guess for the number of molecules in the sun? By how much did your exponent differ from 56? Many of you will have guessed a number around 10^{1000} and that is way off. The number 10^{1000} is a huge number – you cannot find anything real to associate with such a number. The mass of the universe is about 10^{53} kg and so repeating the calculation above we find that the number of hydrogen molecules in the entire universe (assuming it is all hydrogen) is about 10^{79} – a big number to be sure but nowhere near 10^{1000}. Part of learning physics is to appreciate the magnitude of things – whether they are masses, times, distances, forces or just pure numbers such as the number of hydrogen molecules in the universe. Hopefully, you will be able to do that after finishing this course.

The SI system

The seven basic SI units are:

1. The *metre* (m). This is the unit of distance. It is the distance travelled by light in a vacuum in a time of 1/299 792 458 seconds.

2. The *kilogram* (kg). This is the unit of mass. It is the mass of a certain quantity of a platinum–iridium alloy kept at the Bureau International des Poids et Mesures in France.

3. The *second* (s). This is the unit of time. A second is the duration of 9 192 631 770 full oscillations of the electromagnetic radiation emitted in a transition between the two hyperfine energy levels in the ground state of a caesium-133 atom.

4. The *ampere* (A). This is the unit of electric current. It is defined as that current which, when flowing in two parallel conductors 1 m apart, produces a force of 2×10^{-7} N on a length of 1 m of the conductors.

5. The *kelvin* (K). This is the unit of temperature. It is $\frac{1}{273.16}$ of the thermodynamic temperature of the triple point of water.

6. The *mole* (mol). One mole of a substance contains as many molecules as there are atoms in 12 g of carbon-12. This special number of molecules is called Avogadro's number and equals 6.02×10^{23}.

7. The *candela* (cd). This is a unit of luminous intensity. It is the intensity of a source of frequency 5.40×10^{14} Hz emitting $\frac{1}{683}$ W per steradian.

The details of these definitions should not be memorized.

In this book we will use all of the basic units except the last one. Some of these definitions probably do not make sense right now – but eventually they will.

Physical quantities other than those above have units that are combinations of the seven fundamental units. They have *derived* units. For example, speed has units of distance over time, metres per second (i.e. m/s or, preferably, m s^{-1}). Acceleration has units of metres per second squared (i.e. m/s^2, which we write as m s^{-2}). In other words, we treat the symbols for units as algebraic quantities. Similarly, the unit of force is the newton (N). It equals the combination kg m s^{-2}. Energy, a very important quantity in physics, has the joule (J) as its unit. The joule is the combination N m and so equals (kg m s^{-2} m), or kg m^2 s^{-2}. The quantity power has units of energy per unit of time and so is measured in J s^{-1}. This combination is called a watt. Thus, 1 W = (N m s^{-1}) = (kg m s^{-2} m s^{-1}) = kg m^2 s^{-3}.

Occasionally, small or large quantities can be expressed in terms of units that are related to the basic ones by powers of 10. Thus, a nanometre (symbol nm) is 10^{-9} m, a microgram (μg) is 10^{-6} g = 10^{-9} kg, a gigaelectron volt (GeV) equals 10^9 eV, etc. The most common prefixes are given in Table 1.1.

Power	Prefix	Symbol	Power	Prefix	Symbol
10^{-18}	atto-	a	10^1	deka-	da*
10^{-15}	femto-	f	10^2	hecto-	h*
10^{-12}	pico-	p	10^3	kilo-	k
10^{-9}	nano-	n	10^6	mega-	M
10^{-6}	micro-	μ	10^9	giga-	G
10^{-3}	milli-	m	10^{12}	tera-	T
10^{-2}	centi-	c	10^{15}	peta-	P*
10^{-1}	deci-	d	10^{18}	exa-	E*

*Rarely used.

Table 1.1 Common prefixes.

When we write an equation in physics, we have to make sure that the units of the quantity on the left-hand side of the equation are the same as the units on the right-hand side. If the units do not match, the equation cannot be right. For example, the period T (a quantity with units of time) of a pendulum is related to the length of the pendulum l (a quantity with units of length) and the acceleration due to gravity g

(units of acceleration) through

$$T = 2\pi \sqrt{\frac{l}{g}}$$

The units on the right-hand side must reduce to units of time. Indeed, the right-hand side units are

$$\sqrt{\frac{m}{m\,s^{-2}}} = \sqrt{s^2} = s$$

as required (note that 2π is a dimensionless constant). The fact that the units on both sides of an equation must match actually offers a powerful method for guessing equations.

For example, the velocity of a wave on a string is related to the length l and mass m of the string, and the tension force F the string is subjected to. How exactly does the velocity depend on these three variables? One guess is to write

$$v = cF^x l^y m^z$$

where c is a numerical constant (a pure number without units) and x, y and z are numbers to be determined. There could be some confusion here because m stands for mass but we also use the symbol m for the metre. To avoid this we will use the notation $[M]$ to stand for the unit of mass, $[L]$ for the unit of length, $[T]$ for the unit of time, etc. Then, looking at the units of the last equation we have that

$$\frac{[L]}{[T]} = \left([M][L][T]^{-2}\right)^x [L]^y [M]^z$$

$$[L][T]^{-1} = [M]^{x+z}[L]^{x+y}[T]^{-2x}$$

The two equations match if the exponents of $[L]$, $[M]$ and $[T]$ match – that is, if

$$x + z = 0$$
$$x + y = 1$$
$$-2x = -1$$

These equations imply that

$$x = \frac{1}{2}, \quad y = \frac{1}{2} \quad \text{and} \quad z = -\frac{1}{2}$$

In other words, the original formula becomes

$$v = cF^{1/2}l^{1/2}m^{-1/2} = c\sqrt{\frac{Fl}{m}}$$

Obviously this method cannot give the value of the dimensionless constant c. To do that we have to learn some physics!

Tables 1.2–1.4 give approximate values for some interesting sizes, masses and time intervals.

Expressing a quantity as a plain power of 10 gives what is called the 'order of magnitude' of that quantity. Thus, the mass of the universe

	Length/m
Distance to edge of observable universe	10^{26}
Distance to the Andromeda galaxy	10^{22}
Diameter of the Milky Way galaxy	10^{21}
Distance to nearest star	10^{16}
Diameter of solar system	10^{13}
Distance to sun	10^{11}
Radius of the earth	10^{7}
Size of a cell	10^{-5}
Size of a hydrogen atom	10^{-10}
Size of a nucleus	10^{-15}
Size of a proton	10^{-17}
Planck length	10^{-35}

Table 1.2 Some interesting sizes.

	Mass/kg
The universe	10^{53}
The Milky Way galaxy	10^{41}
The sun	10^{30}
The earth	10^{24}
Boeing 747 (empty)	10^{5}
An apple	0.25
A raindrop	10^{-6}
A bacterium	10^{-15}
Mass of smallest virus	10^{-21}
A hydrogen atom	10^{-27}
An electron	10^{-30}

Table 1.3 Some interesting masses.

	Time/s
Age of the universe	10^{17}
Age of the earth	10^{17}
Time of travel by light to nearby star	10^{8}
One year	10^{7}
One day	10^{5}
Period of a heartbeat	1
Period of red light	10^{-15}
Time of passage of light across a nucleus	10^{-24}
Planck time	10^{-43}

Table 1.4 Some interesting time intervals.

has an order of magnitude of 10^{53} kg and the mass of the Milky Way galaxy has an order of magnitude of 10^{41} kg. The ratio of the two masses is then simply 10^{12}.

Fundamental interactions

There are four basic or fundamental interactions in physics. However, in 1972, the electromagnetic and weak interactions were unified into one – the electroweak interaction. In this sense, then, we may speak of just three fundamental interactions (see Figure 1.1).

Gravitational   Gravitational

Electromagnetic

Weak (nuclear force)   Electroweak

Colour (or strong nuclear force) Colour

Figure 1.1 The fundamental interactions of physics. Since 1972, the electromagnetic and weak interactions have been shown to be part of a generalized interaction called the electroweak interaction.

Example questions

Let us close this chapter with a few problems similar to the one we started with. These problems are sometimes known as Fermi problems, after the great physicist Enrico Fermi, who was a master in this kind of estimation.

Q1

How many grains of sand are required to fill the earth? (This is a classic problem that goes back to Aristotle.)

Answer

The radius of the earth is about 6400 km, which we may approximate to 10 000 km. The volume of the earth is thus approximately $8 \times (10 \times 10^{6})^{3}$ m$^{3} \approx 8 \times 10^{21}$ m^{3}. We are assuming a cubical earth of side equal to twice the radius. This is a simplifying assumption. The true volume is $\frac{4}{3}\pi R^{3} = 1.1 \times 10^{21}$ m^{3}, which agrees with our estimate (we are only interested in the power of 10 not the number in front). The diameter of a grain of sand varies of course but we will take 1 mm as a fair estimate. Then the number of grains of sand required to fill the earth is

$$\frac{8 \times 10^{21} \text{ m}^{3}}{(1 \times 10^{-3})^{3} \text{ m}^{3}} = 8 \times 10^{30} \approx 10^{31}$$

Q2

Estimate the speed with which human hair grows.

Answer

I cut my hair every 2 months and the barber cuts a length of about 2 cm. The speed is thus

$$\frac{2 \times 10^{-2}}{2 \times 30 \times 24 \times 60 \times 60} \text{ m s}^{-1} \approx \frac{10^{-2}}{3 \times 2 \times 36 \times 10^{4}}$$
$$\approx \frac{10^{-6}}{6 \times 40} = \frac{10^{-6}}{240}$$
$$\approx 4 \times 10^{-9} \text{ m s}^{-1}$$

Q3

If all the people on earth were to hold hands in a straight line, how long would the line be? How many times would it wrap around the earth?

Answer

Assume that each person has his or her hands stretched out to a distance of 1.5 m and that the population of earth is 6×10^{9} people. Then the length would be $6 \times 10^{9} \times 1.5$ m $= 9 \times 10^{9}$ m. The circumference of the earth is $2\pi R \approx 6 \times 6 \times 10^{6}$ m $\approx 4 \times 10^{7}$ m and so the line would wrap $\frac{9 \times 10^{9}}{4 \times 10^{7}} \approx 200$ times around the equator.

Q4 ▬▬▬▬▬▬▬▬▬▬▬▬▬▬▬

How many revolutions do the wheels of a car make before it is junked?

Answer

We assume that the car runs 250 000 km before it is junked and that the wheels have a radius of 30 cm. Then the number of revolutions is

$$\frac{2.5 \times 10^8}{2\pi \times 0.3} \approx \frac{2.5}{2 \times 1}10^8 \approx 10^8$$

Q5 ▬▬▬▬▬▬▬▬▬▬▬▬▬▬▬

What depth of car tyre wears off with each turn? (This is another classic problem.)

Answer

We assume that a depth of 5 mm wears off every 60 000 km. (These numbers are 'standard' for people who own cars.) Then, for a wheel of radius 30 cm the number of revolutions is (see previous problem) $\frac{6 \times 10^7}{2\pi \times 0.3} \approx \frac{6}{2 \times 1}10^7 \approx 3 \times 10^7$ and so the wear per revolution is $\frac{5}{3 \times 10^7}$ mm/rev $\approx 10^{-7}$ mm/rev.

Questions

Have a look through these questions and answer any that you can. However, don't worry about any you can't answer; leave them for now and come back to them when you reach the end of the course.

1 How long does light take to travel across a proton?

2 How many hydrogen atoms does it take to make up the mass of the earth?

3 What is the age of the universe expressed in units of the Planck time?

4 What is the radius of the earth (6380 km) expressed in units of the Planck length?

5 How many heartbeats are there in the lifetime of a person (75 years)?

6 What is the mass of our galaxy in terms of a solar mass?

7 What is the diameter of our galaxy in terms of the astronomical unit, i.e. the distance between the earth and the sun?

8 The molar mass of water is 18 g mol^{-1}. How many molecules of water are there in a glass of water (of volume 0.3 L)?

9 Assuming that the mass of a person is made up entirely of water, how many molecules are there in a human body (of mass 60 kg)?

10 Assuming the entire universe to be made up of hydrogen gas, how many molecules of hydrogen are there?

11 Give an order-of-magnitude estimate of the density of a proton.

12 How long does light from the sun take to arrive on earth?

13 How many apples do you need to make up the mass of an average elephant?

14 How many bricks are used to build an average two-storey family house?

15 (a) How many metres are there in 5.356 nm?
(b) How many in 1.2 fm?
(c) How many in 3.4 mm?

16 (a) How many joules of energy are there in 4.834 MJ?
(b) How many in 2.23 pJ?
(c) How many in 364 GJ?

17 (a) How many seconds are there in 4.76 ns?
(b) How many in 24.0 ms?
(c) How many in 8.5 as?

18 What is the velocity of an electron that covers a distance of 15.68 mm in 87.50 ns?

19 An electron volt (eV) is a unit of energy equal to 1.6×10^{-19} J. An electron has a kinetic energy of 2.5 eV.
(a) How many joules is that?
(b) What is the energy in eV of an electron that has an energy of 8.6×10^{-18} J?

20 What is the volume in cubic metres of a cube of side 2.8 cm?

21 What is the side in metres of a cube that has a volume of 588 cubic millimetres?

22 One inch is 2.54 cm and one foot has 12 inches. The acceleration due to gravity is about 9.8 m s^{-2}. What is it in feet per square second?

23 One fluid ounce is a volume of about 2.96×10^{-5} m^3. What is the side, in inches, of

a cube whose volume is 125 fluid ounces? (One inch is 2.54 cm.)

24 A horsepower (hp) is a unit of power equal to about 746 W. What is the power in hp of a 224 kW car engine?

25 Give an order-of-magnitude estimate for the mass of:
   (a) an apple;
   (b) this physics book;
   (c) a soccer ball.

26 Give an order-of-magnitude estimate for the time taken by light to travel across the diameter of the Milky Way galaxy.

27 A white dwarf star has a mass about that of the sun and a radius about that of the earth. Give an order-of-magnitude estimate of the density of a white dwarf.

28 A sports car accelerates from rest to 100 km per hour in 4.0 s. What fraction of the acceleration due to gravity is the car's acceleration?

29 Give an order-of-magnitude estimate for the number of electrons in your body.

30 Give an order-of-magnitude estimate for the gravitational force of attraction between two people 1 m apart.

31 Give an order-of-magnitude estimate for the ratio of the electric force between two electrons 1 m apart to the gravitational force between the electrons.

32 The frequency f (a quantity with units of inverse seconds) of oscillation of a mass m attached to a spring of spring constant k (a quantity with units of force per length) is related to m and k. By writing $f = cm^x k^y$ and matching units on both sides show that $f = c\sqrt{\frac{k}{m}}$, where c is a dimensionless constant.

33 Without using a calculator *estimate* the value of the following expressions and then compare with the exact value using a calculator:
   (a) $\dfrac{243}{43}$;
   (b) 2.80×1.90;
   (c) $\dfrac{312 \times 480}{160}$;
   (d) $\dfrac{8.99 \times 10^9 \times 7 \times 10^{-6} \times 7 \times 10^{-6}}{(8 \times 10^2)^2}$;
   (e) $\dfrac{6.6 \times 10^{-11} \times 6 \times 10^{24}}{(6.4 \times 10^6)^2}$.

Uncertainties and errors

This chapter introduces the basic methods of dealing with experimental error and uncertainty in measured physical quantities. Physics is an experimental science and often the experimenter will perform an experiment to test the prediction of a given theory. No measurement will ever be completely accurate, however, and so the result of the experiment will be presented with an experimental error. Thus, in comparing the results of an experiment with the prediction of the theory being tested, the experimenter will have to decide if the disagreement between theory and experiment is due to failure of the theory or whether the disagreement falls within the bounds of experimental error and so can be tolerated.

Objectives

By the end of this chapter you should be able to:
*   state the *various types of errors* that may arise in the measurement of a physical quantity;
*   state the difference between *accuracy* and *precision*;
*   draw a *line of best fit*;
*   appreciate the importance of *significant digits*.

Errors of measurement

There are two *main* types of error of measurement or observation. They can be grouped into *random* and *systematic* even though in many cases it is not possible to sharply distinguish between the two. We may say that random errors are almost always the fault of the observer whereas systematic errors are due to both the observer and the instrument being used. In practice, all errors are a combination of the two.

A random error is characterized by the fact that it is revealed by repeated measurements (the measurements *fluctuate* about some value – they are sometimes larger and sometimes smaller) whereas a systematic error is not. Random errors can be reduced by averaging over repeated measurements, whereas errors that are systematic cannot.

We may also consider a third class of errors called *reading errors*. This is a familiar type of error that has to do with the fact that it is often difficult to read the instrument being used with absolute precision. This type of reading error is inherent in the instrument being used and *cannot be improved upon by repeated measurements*. If a length is measured using a ruler whose smallest division is a millimetre and the end of the object to be measured falls in between two divisions on the ruler, it is easy to determine that the length is, say, between 14.5 cm and 14.6 cm, but there is some guesswork involved in stating that the length is 14.54 cm. Some people would accept 14.5 cm as the length (if in the judgement of the observer the length is closer to 14.5 cm than to 14.6 cm) and take as the uncertainty in the measurement *the smallest subdivision in the instrument* – 1 mm in the case of the ruler. They would then state their measurement as (14.5 ± 0.1) cm. Others accept *half the length of the smallest subdivision as an estimate of the error.* Thus, in the case of the ruler the error would be ± 0.5 mm $= \pm 0.05$ cm. The experimenter may then state the length as (14.54 ± 0.05) cm. Others still claim they can read a millimetre ruler to ± 0.02 cm. The safest approach is to be conservative and accept the smallest sub-division as the estimate of the reading error. When reading a digital instrument, we take as the reading error *the smallest division* of the instrument. So a digital voltmeter that records voltage to three decimal places, for example 2.248 V, will have a reading error of ± 0.001 V.

In some sense, though, even a reading error can be thought to be a random error. If you were asked to measure, using a ruler, the length of 20 identical, precisely made rods (but you did not know that they were identical) you would most likely come up with 20 measurements that would not all be the same. If you are an experienced and careful observer, your 20 measurements should not differ much from each other. Then it would make sense to state the error in each of your measurements as a reading error of ± 0.05 cm. But if you are not careful, the 20 measurements will differ substantially from each other. The error must then be treated as a random error as described next.

Random errors

If a measurement is repeated many times, it can be expected that the measurement will be too large as often as it will be too small. So, if an average of these measurements is taken, the error will tend to cancel. The experimental result of the measurement of a given quantity x will thus be the average of the individual measurements, i.e.

$$\bar{x} = \frac{x_1 + x_2 + \cdots + x_N}{N}$$

where N is the total number of measurements. We then define the deviation of each individual measurement from the average by $\Delta x_i = x_i - \bar{x}$. If the absolute magnitudes of all these deviations are smaller than the reading error, then we can quote the experimental result as

$$\bar{x} \pm \text{reading error}$$

However, if the deviations from the mean are larger in magnitude than the reading error, the experimental error in the quantity x will have to include random errors as well. To estimate the random error we calculate the quantity

$$e = \sqrt{\frac{(\Delta x_1)^2 + (\Delta x_2)^2 + \cdots + (\Delta x_N)^2}{N - 1}}$$

which is called the unbiased estimate of the standard deviation of the N measurements x_i. (With graphic calculators this can be done quite easily and quickly.) The result of the experiment is then expressed as

$$\bar{x} \pm e$$

To illustrate these points consider the measurement of a length using a ruler. The reading error according to one observer is ± 0.02 cm. The experimenter produces a table of results and, after computing the average of the measurements, the deviation and its square are also inserted in the table – see Table 2.1.

Length/cm (± 0.02 cm)	Deviation Δx/cm	$(\Delta x)^2$/cm^2
14.88	0.09	0.0081
14.84	0.05	0.0025
15.02	0.23	0.0529
14.57	−0.22	0.0484
14.76	−0.03	0.0009
14.66	−0.13	0.0169

Table 2.1 A table of results.

The average is 14.79 cm and the standard deviation of these measurements is 0.1611 cm. The random error is larger than the reading error and so it must be included in the result. The result of the measurement is thus expressed as 14.8 ± 0.2 cm. This is a much more realistic statement than simply quoting the average and the reading error, 14.79 ± 0.02 cm. Note that it does not make sense to quote the average to more than one decimal point as the error makes even the first decimal point uncertain. Note also that once a large number of measurements are accumulated, further measurements do not appreciably change the estimate of the error. Thus, it is of little use to take, say, 50 measurements of the length of the object in the example above.

Note also, finally, that even the calculation of a standard deviation is not all that necessary. The largest deviation from the mean in Table 2.1 is 0.23 cm, which we may round to 0.2 cm and accept that as a rough estimate of the error.

Systematic errors

The most common source of a systematic error is an incorrectly *calibrated* instrument. For example, consider a digital force sensor. When the sensor is to be used for the first time, it must be calibrated. This means that we must apply a force whose value we are confident we know, say 5.0 N, and then adjust the sensor so that it too reads 5.0 N. If we apply the 5.0 N force and then adjust the instrument to read 4.9 N, the instrument will be incorrectly calibrated. It will also be incorrectly calibrated if the sensor is adjusted to read 5.0 N when the 'known' force that we apply is not really 5.0 N. If we use this sensor to verify Newton's second law, we would expect to get a straight-line graph through the origin if we plot the net force on the body versus its acceleration. Since

all measurements of the force will be off by the same amount, the straight line will not pass through the origin. The systematic error in the force would then be the vertical intercept (see Figure 2.1a).

A systematic error will also arise if we use an instrument that has a *zero error*. For example, if an ammeter shows a current of 0.1 A even before it is connected to a circuit, it has a zero error. It must be adjusted to read zero. If the adjustment is not done, every measurement of current made with this ammeter will be larger than the true value of the current by 0.1 A. Thus, if this ammeter is used to investigate the voltage–current characteristic of an ohmic resistor, we will not get the expected straight line through the origin but a straight line that misses the origin. The systematic error in the current would then be the horizontal intercept (see Figure 2.1b).

Systematic errors are not always easy to estimate but sometimes the direction of the error is. Thus, suppose that an experimenter assumes that no friction is present in an experiment on an air track, where the velocity of an object sliding on it is measured after having travelled a certain distance. A small amount of friction will slow down the object and so the velocity measurements will be consistently lower than their true values. It is difficult though to estimate by how much.

A systematic error will also arise if the experimenter makes the same error for all the measurements she takes. For example, consider measuring a length with a ruler. The ruler is aligned with the object to be measured and the experimenter must then position her eye directly above the ruler. If, however, the experimenter consistently stands to the side, as shown in Figure 2.2, the measured value will always be larger than the true length. If she stands on the other side, the measured value will always be smaller than the true length.

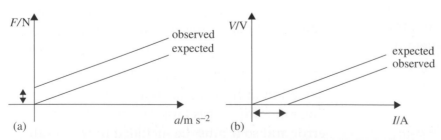

Figure 2.1 The types of systematic error that arise from incorrectly calibrated instruments and instruments that have a zero error.

Figure 2.2 An example of a systematic error that is due to the observer.

A similar systematic error would occur in measuring the volume of a liquid inside a graduated tube if the tube is not exactly vertical. The measured values would always be *larger* than the true value.

Accuracy and precision

In everyday language, the words 'accuracy' and 'precision' are usually taken to mean the same thing, but this is not the case in physics.

▶ Measurements are *accurate* if the systematic error is small. They are *precise* if the random error is small (see Figure 2.3).

Figure 2.3 The meaning of accurate and precise measurements. Four different sets of six measurements each are shown.

Measurements of a physical quantity can be accurate but not precise, or precise but not accurate. Consider, for example, measurements of voltage taken with a high-quality digital voltmeter that suffers from a systematic error. The voltmeter allows us to record the voltage to many significant figures and repeated measurements of the same voltage give essentially the same reading. These measurements are very precise but they are not accurate, since the systematic error in the readings means that they are not representative of the true voltage. Similarly,

readings can be accurate in that their average gives the correct reading, but if individual readings differ wildly from each other, they are not precise.

Significant digits

Let us multiply the numbers 24 and 328. The answer is 7872. However, if these numbers are the result of a measurement, then at the very least we would expect that the last digit of each is uncertain. In other words, the first number could be anything from 23 to 25 and the other from 327 to 329. The product could thus range from 7251 to 8225. Thus, it makes no sense to retain so many digits in our answer for the product of 7872. The first number has been given to two significant digits, the second to three. Thus, the answer for the product must be given to no more than two significant digits – that is, as 7900 or 7.9×10^3. Keeping only two significant digits in the answer for the product ensures that the process of multiplication does not introduce, incorrectly, additional significant figures.

The rules for significant figures are as follows.

The leftmost non-zero digit is significant and is in fact the most significant digit in the number. If the number has no decimal point, the rightmost non-zero digit is significant and is in fact the least significant. If the number does have a decimal point, the least significant digit is the rightmost digit (which may be zero). The number of significant digits of a number is the number of digits from the most to the least significant. Thus, 0.345 has 3 as the most significant digit and 5 as the least. The number thus has three significant digits. In the number 0.000 0006 the most and least significant digit is 6 and so we have one significant digit. The number 5460 has three significant digits (no decimal point hence the last zero does not count), 54 has two and 300 000 has one. Similarly, 3.450 has four significant digits, 54.0 has three and 0.000 500 has three.

> ▶ In multiplication or division (or raising a number to a power or taking a root) the result must have as many significant digits as those of the number with the least significant digits entering the operation.

Line of best fit

If we have reason to suspect that the data points we have plotted fall on a straight line, we must draw the best straight line through the points. This means using a ruler and choosing that line which goes through as many data points as possible in such a way that the distances between the line and the points on one side of it are, on average, the same as the distances between the line and points on the other side of it.

Thus, suppose that in an experiment to verify Hooke's law, data for the tension and extension of a spring are collected and plotted as shown in Figure 2.4. The experimenter has included vertical uncertainty bars representing an uncertainty of ± 10 N in the values of the tension (the length of the vertical bar is thus 20 N). Uncertainties in the extension could also be shown by placing horizontal bars at the positions of the data points, but we will not do this here.

The experimenter then draws the line of best fit through the data points and obtains a straight line in the graph shown in Figure 2.5. The line of best fit will ideally pass through the error bars of all the data points. *Note that we never join points by straight-line segments.* The slope of this line is 200 N m^{-1} and this represents the spring constant.

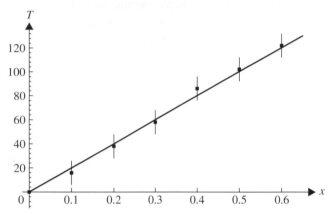

Figure 2.5 The line of best fit through the data points.

In many experiments it will be necessary to obtain the slope (gradient) of the graph. Here the slope of this line is 200 N m^{-1} and represents the spring constant. To find the slope one must use the line of best fit and not data points (see Figure 2.6). We must take two points on the line of best fit, which must be chosen to be as far apart as possible and then apply the formula

$$\text{slope} = \frac{\Delta y}{\Delta x}$$

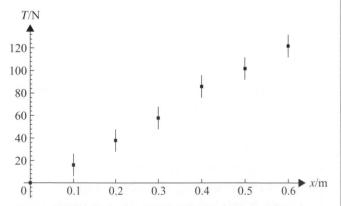

Figure 2.4 Data points plotted together with uncertainties in the values for the tension.

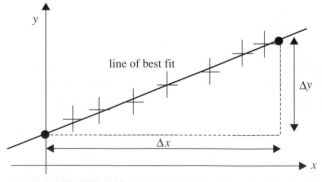

Figure 2.6 Finding the slope of a straight line uses the line of best fit and two widely separated points on the line of best fit.

Questions

1 A student measured a given quantity many times and got the results shown in Figure 2.7. The true value of the quantity is indicated by the dotted line. Should she continue accumulating more data in the hope of getting a result that agrees with the true value?

Figure 2.7 For question 1.

2 In the data of question 1, is the source of error systematic or random?

3 In an experiment to measure current and voltage across a device, the following data was collected: $(V, I) = \{(0.1, 26), (0.2, 48), (0.3, 65), (0.4, 90)\}$. The current was measured in mA and the voltage in mV. The uncertainty in the current was ± 4 mA. Plot the *current versus the voltage* and draw the line of best fit through the points. Does the line pass through the origin?

4 In a similar experiment, the following data was collected for current and voltage: $(V, I) = \{(0.1, 27), (0.2, 44), (0.3, 60), (0.4, 78)\}$ with an uncertainty of ± 4 mA in the current. Plot the *current versus the voltage* and draw the line of best fit. Can it be claimed that the line passes through the origin?

5 In yet another experiment, the following data was collected for current and voltage: $(V, I) = \{(0.1, 29), (0.2, 46), (0.3, 62), (0.4, 80)\}$, with uncertainty of ± 4 mA in the current. Plot the *current versus the voltage* and draw the line of best fit. Can it be claimed that the line passes through the origin? The experimenter is convinced that the straight line fitting the data should go through the origin. What can allow for this?

6 The velocity of an object after a distance x is given by $v^2 = 2ax$ where a is the constant acceleration. Figure 2.8 shows the results of an experiment in which velocity and distance travelled were measured. Draw a smooth curve through the points. Estimate the acceleration, and the velocity of the object after a distance of 2.0 m.

Figure 2.8 For question 6.

Mathematical and graphical techniques

This chapter is an introduction to the basic techniques of graphical analysis in physics, in particular how to graph variables in order to obtain straight-line graphs.

Objectives

By the end of this chapter you should be able to:

- find the *change in a variable* given the changes in other variables related to it;
- *transform the variables of an equation* so that a *linear* relationship and graph are obtained;
- extract relevant information from a graph;
- understand the need for *assumptions* in simplifying various situations.

Multiplicative changes

Given an equation that relates one variable, say y, to one or more other variables, it is essential that we learn how the value of y changes when one (or more) of the other variables change multiplicatively. Consider as a simple first example the equation

$$y = cx$$

where c is a constant. How does the value of y change if x is tripled? Obviously, the value of y is also tripled since y and x are directly proportional to each other. More formally, let us call y' the new value of y; then $y' = c(3x) = 3(cx) = 3y$. That is, the value of y is tripled as expected. The answer in this case is simple since the direct proportionality of the variables is clear. When the variables are not so simply related, the answer can still be easily found. Suppose that we are given the variation with tension T of frequency f

$$f = \frac{1}{2L}\sqrt{\frac{T}{\mu}}$$

(the other variables in this equation are constants). How does the frequency change if the tension is tripled? Again we call the new value of the frequency f' and then

$$f' = \frac{1}{2L}\sqrt{\frac{3T}{\mu}}$$

$$= \sqrt{3}\left(\frac{1}{2L}\sqrt{\frac{T}{\mu}}\right)$$

$$= \sqrt{3}\,f$$

that is, the value of the frequency is increased by a factor of root 3. Equivalently we could have written

$$\frac{f'}{f} = \frac{\frac{1}{2L}\sqrt{\frac{3T}{\mu}}}{\frac{1}{2L}\sqrt{\frac{T}{\mu}}}$$

$$= \sqrt{3}$$

since all the common variables cancel out.

Similarly, the average kinetic energy of the molecules of a gas depends on absolute temperature through

$$\tfrac{1}{2}mc^2 = \tfrac{3}{2}kT$$

If the temperature is doubled what happens to the speed c? Taking ratios

$$\frac{\frac{1}{2}m(c')^2}{\frac{1}{2}mc^2} = \frac{\frac{3}{2}k(2T)}{\frac{3}{2}kT} = 2$$

$$\Rightarrow \frac{(c')^2}{c^2} = 2$$

$$\Rightarrow c' = \sqrt{2}c$$

The speed increases by $\sqrt{2}$.

The pressure, volume, temperature and number of molecules of an ideal gas are related by

$$pV = NkT$$

where k is a constant. If the pressure of a gas is doubled while the temperature is halved and the number of molecules is left unchanged, what will be the new volume of the gas?

In this case the ratio method gives

$$\frac{(2p)V'}{pV} = \frac{Nk\left(\frac{T}{2}\right)}{NkT} = \frac{1}{2}$$

$$\Rightarrow \frac{2V'}{V} = \frac{1}{2}$$

$$\Rightarrow V' = \frac{V}{4}$$

Straight-line graphs

The easiest graph to deal with is that of the straight line: $y = mx + c$. In this form, the constant m represents the slope (also known as the gradient) of the straight line and c the

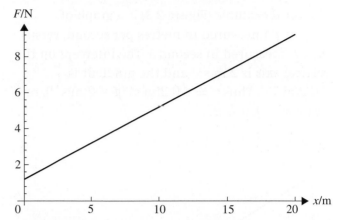

Figure 3.1 The straight-line graph of tension versus extension.

intercept on the y (vertical) axis. Figures 3.1–3.3 show three examples of straight-line graphs. Figure 3.1 represents a force F (plotted on the vertical axis and measured in newtons, N) as a function of distance x (measured in metres, m). We can read off the intercept on the F axis as 1.2 N. The gradient can be measured to be 0.4 N m^{-1}. Note that the units for the gradient must be given. Thus, the equation of this line is $F = 0.4(\text{N m}^{-1})x + 1.2$ N. It is usually convenient not to mention units in the equation of the line so that we can write the simpler $F = 0.4x + 1.2$, but it is then crucial to note that x must be expressed in metres so that F ends up being expressed in newtons.

Figure 3.2 shows distance x on the vertical axis (measured in metres) plotted as a function of time t (measured in seconds). The intercept on the vertical axis is -1.6 m and the gradient is 0.6 m s^{-1}. Thus, the equation of this line is $x = 0.6(\text{m s}^{-1})t - 1.6$ m, or simply $x = 0.6t - 1.6$.

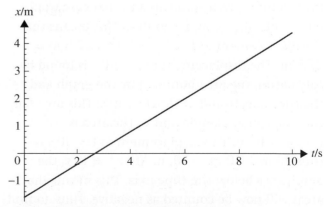

Figure 3.2 Graph of distance versus time.

The third example (Figure 3.3) is a graph of velocity v (measured in metres per second) versus time t (measured in seconds). The intercept on the vertical axis is 2 m s^{-1} and the gradient is -0.2 m s^{-2}. Thus $v = -0.2(\text{m s}^{-2})t + 2(\text{m s}^{-1})$, or just $v = -0.2t + 2$.

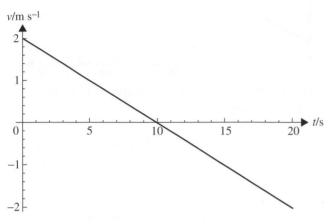

Figure 3.3 Graph of velocity versus time.

As we will see in our study of motion in mechanics, the area under a velocity–time graph represents the displacement *change* of the moving object.

Suppose that initially the object is at a displacement of 20 m from the origin. To find the displacement of the object 5 s after the start we need to find the area that is bounded by the graph and the time axis from $t = 0$ s to $t = 5$ s. This shape is a trapezoid and its area is $\left(\frac{2+1}{2}\right) \times 5 = 7.5$ m. Note that the units of the area in this graph are units of distance, since we multiply a velocity (m s^{-1}) by time (s). (If the vertical axis represented a force measured in newtons and the horizontal axis distance measured in metres, the area in that case would have units of N $\times$ m, i.e. joules.) This means that the displacement at $t = 5$ s is 20 m + 7.5 m = 27.5 m. The displacement at $t = 10$ s is found by calculating the area bounded by the graph and the time axis from $t = 0$ to $t = 10$ s. This area has the shape of a triangle and so the area is $\left(\frac{2 \times 10}{2}\right) = 10$ m. The displacement at $t = 10$ s is thus 20 m + 10 m = 30 m. After $t = 10$ s, the graph goes below the time axis. This means that areas will now be counted as negative. Thus, to find the displacement at $t = 15$ s we proceed as follows:

first find the area from $t = 0$ to $t = 10$ s, which is 10 m. Then find the area from $t = 10$ s to $t = 15$ s. It is -7.5 m. The area from $t = 0$ to $t = 15$ s is thus 10 m $- 7.5$ m $= 2.5$ m. The displacement at $t = 15$ s is thus 20 m + 2.5 m = 22.5 m.

Getting a linear graph

In an experiment it is more than likely that when a measured quantity y is plotted against another measured quantity x on which it depends, a straight-line graph will not result. Thus, suppose that the expected theoretical relationship between the variables is $y = ax^2 + b$, as in Figure 3.4.

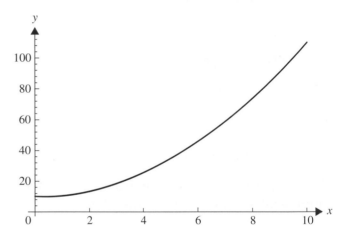

Figure 3.4 Graph of the parabola $y = ax^2 + b$.

Then if we call the variable $x^2 = w$, the expected relationship becomes $y = aw + b$, which is the equation of a standard straight line with gradient a and intercept b. Hence, we must plot y versus w (i.e. x^2) to get a straight line (see Figure 3.5).

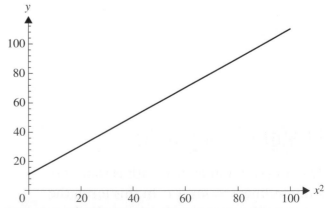

Figure 3.5 By graphing against the variable x^2 we get a straight line.

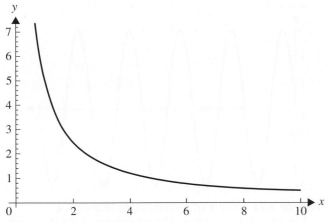

Figure 3.6 Graph of the hyperbola $xy = c$.

Similarly if the expected relationship is $xy = c$ (Figure 3.6), we call $\frac{1}{x} = w$ in which case the expected relationship is $y = \frac{c}{x} = cw$, which again is a straight line going through the origin with gradient c. Thus we must plot y versus $\frac{1}{x}$ to get a straight line (Figure 3.7).

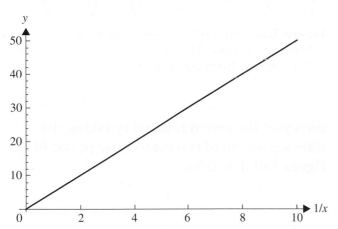

Figure 3.7 We get a straight line by plotting against the variable $\frac{1}{x}$.

If y and x are related by $y = ae^x + b$, a straight line is obtained by plotting y versus e^x. The gradient is then a and the intercept b. If the relationship is $y = \frac{a}{x^2+b}$, we rewrite it as $\frac{1}{y} = \frac{x^2+b}{a}$ so that a graph of $\frac{1}{y}$ versus x^2 is a straight line. Finally, a relationship such as $y^2 = cx^3$ yields a straight line when y^2 is plotted against x^3.

Interpreting graphs

Given a graph, we should be able to extract information from it and use that information to give a description of what is going on. In Figure 3.8 the velocity is decreasing uniformly from an initial value of 20 m s^{-1}. The velocity becomes zero at 2 s and then becomes negative. The graph could represent the motion of an object thrown vertically up with an initial velocity of 20 m s^{-1}. The time of 2 s then represents the time when the object reaches its highest point.

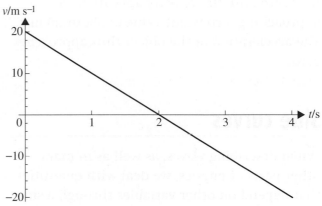

Figure 3.8 The velocity is decreasing uniformly and becomes zero at 2 s. The object then changes its direction of motion.

In Figure 3.9, displacement is graphed against time for a given motion. The object is at displacement zero at time zero and becomes a maximum at 2 s. The object returns to its initial position after 4 s.

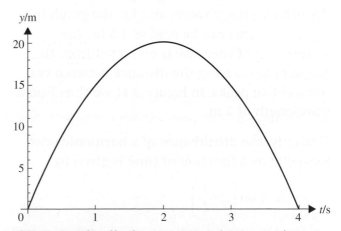

Figure 3.9 The displacement reaches a maximum at 2 s and becomes zero at 4 s.

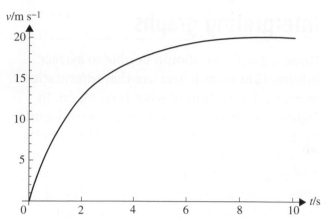

Figure 3.10 The velocity is becoming constant and so the acceleration becomes zero.

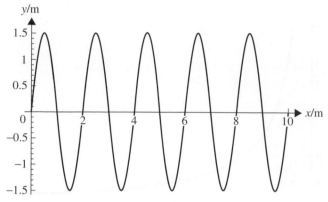

Figure 3.11 Graph of a harmonic wave as a function of position. The wavelength of the wave can be determined from this graph.

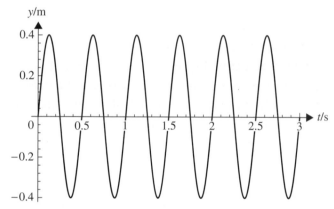

Figure 3.12 Graph of a harmonic wave as a function of time. The period of the wave can be determined from this graph.

In Figure 3.10, the velocity appears to be approaching a constant value of about 20 m s^{-1}. The acceleration of the object thus approaches zero.

Sine curves

When describing waves, as well as in many other parts of physics, we deal with quantities that depend on other variables through a sine function, $y = C \sin(ax + b)$, with C, a and b being constants. For example, the disturbance of a harmonic wave at a distance x at a specific instant of time can be shown to be

$$y = A \sin\left[2\pi \frac{x}{\lambda}\right]$$

where the constants A and λ are known as the amplitude and wavelength of the wave. The amplitude is thus the largest possible disturbance (i.e. y value) and for the graph in Figure 3.11 this can be read as 1.5 m. The wavelength of the wave is extracted from the graph by measuring the distance between two consecutive peaks. In Figure 3.11 we thus find a wavelength of 2 m.

Similarly, the disturbance of a harmonic wave looked at as a function of time is given by

$$y = A \sin\left[2\pi \frac{t}{T}\right]$$

where A is again the amplitude (in Figure 3.12 it has a value of 0.4 m) and T is the period of

the wave. The period is found by taking the time separation of two consecutive peaks; in Figure 3.12, $T = 0.5$ s.

Making assumptions

When we solve a physics problem, we always make assumptions that simplify the problem. Sometimes we are careful to list our assumptions and sometimes not.

For example, in most of the chapters on mechanics we will be solving problems involving 'bodies' in motion acted upon by forces. The 'bodies' can be anything from human beings to leaves, bricks, cars or planets. However, we will always be treating them as *point particles*, because this simplifies the problem. We will mostly ignore frictional forces unless told otherwise, because again this simplifies the problem. But we must always be aware that our solution has been derived under various assumptions and so the real solution might differ if the effects of the factors we neglected are taken into account. We also, usually, assume that strings (and springs) have no mass – the famous physics strings. This makes life easier and the assumption is good provided the other bodies in the problem really have masses much larger than that of the string.

When studying thermal physics we usually don't take into account the fact that thermal energy is always lost to the surroundings no matter how careful we have been to prevent that. If you were asked to calculate the number of atoms in your body, you would have to make a simplifying assumption otherwise the problem is hopelessly difficult – pretending that all your mass is made of out of water is such a simplifying assumption. You must then justify why it is a good simplifying assumption. In dealing with gases we assume that the gas is ideal. This is a good assumption for the air in a football but not a very good one for the material of a star that is about to become a white dwarf!

In the chapters on electricity you will learn about Coulomb's law, which allows us to find the force between two spherical charges. We cannot use this law to find the force between two plane sheets of charge though. Using Coulomb's law will only be an estimate of the force, not a precise calculation of it. Under certain conditions (which we must identify) this estimate may be a very good approximation to the real answer. In other cases it might not be. In electric circuits we usually assume that connecting wires and ammeters have no resistance. If a device used in the circuit has a resistance of a few tens of ohms, this assumption is good. But if the device has a very low resistance, comparable to that of the connecting wires and the ammeter, the

assumption is not good. Similarly, voltmeters are assumed to have an infinite resistance. This means, in practice, a resistance much larger than the rest of the resistors in the circuit. If the largest resistor in the circuit is 100 ohms and the voltmeter has a resistance of 100 000 ohms the assumption is good. But if you are dealing with 100 000 ohm resistors the assumption of an infinite voltmeter resistance breaks down.

So, part of learning physics involves identifying assumptions in a problem and being able to explain whether the assumptions are justified or not.

Questions

1 The pressure of an ideal gas is 4 atm. If the only change is to increase the temperature by a factor of 4, what will the new pressure of the gas be? (Use $pV = NkT$.)

2 The kinetic energy of a mass m is given by $\frac{1}{2}mv^2$. If the speed v is doubled, by what factor does the energy change?

3 The kinetic energy ($E_k = \frac{1}{2}mv^2$) of a body doubles. By what factor did the speed increase?

4 A constant force F brings a body of mass m and initial speed v to rest over a distance d. If the initial speed doubles, over what distance will the same force stop the same body? (Use $v^2 = \frac{2Fd}{m}$.)

5 The electric force between two charges Q_1 and Q_2 a distance r apart is given by $F = k\frac{Q_1 Q_2}{r^2}$, where k is a constant.
   (a) If both charges double, by what factor does the force between them increase?
   (b) If both charges double but the force between them stays the same, by what factor did their separation change?

6 The frequency of a standing wave on a string of fixed length L kept under tension T is given by $f = \frac{\sqrt{cT}}{2L}$, where c is a constant. By what factor should the tension be changed so that the frequency triples?

7 The period of a pendulum of length L is given by $T = 2\pi\sqrt{\frac{L}{g}}$, where g is a constant. If the

period doubles, by what factor did the length change?

8 The frequency of oscillation of a mass m attached to a spring is given by $f = \frac{1}{2\pi}\sqrt{\frac{k}{m}}$, where k is a constant. If the frequency increases by a factor of 4, by what factor did the mass change?

9 The power radiated by a body kept at a temperature T is given by $P = kT^4$, where k is a constant. If the temperature is doubled, by what factor does the power increase?

10 The period of a planet around the sun is given by $T^2 = kR^3$, where k is a constant and R is the mean distance of the planet from the sun. A planet orbits the sun at a distance from the sun that is twice the distance of earth from the sun. What is the period of this planet. (The earth's period is one year.)

11 When a strong wind creates waves on a pond, a piece of cork floating in the water oscillates so that its distance from the bottom of the pond is given by the graph in Figure 3.13.

depth/m

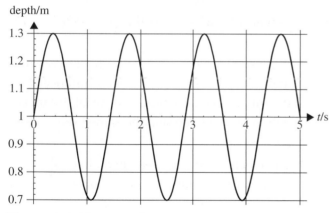

Figure 3.13 For question 11.

(a) What is the depth of the pond?
(b) What is the frequency of the wave travelling on the pond?
(c) What is the amplitude of the wave?

12 The image of an object a distance a from a lens is formed at a distance b from the lens, where a and b are related through the equation $\frac{1}{a} + \frac{1}{b} = \frac{1}{f}$ and f is the (constant) focal length of the lens.

(a) If a set of data for a and b is collected, how should it be plotted in order to give a straight line?
(b) How can the focal length of the lens be measured from the graph?

13 The pressure of a fixed quantity of gas at constant volume is related to temperature in kelvin by

$$\frac{P}{T} = \text{constant}$$

(a) What does a graph of pressure versus temperature give?
(b) If the temperature is expressed in degrees Celsius ($T(K) = T(°C) + 273$) what does a graph of pressure versus temperature give?

14 The period of a planet around the sun is related to the mean distance of the planet from the sun through Kepler's third law

$$T^2 = \text{constant} \times R^3$$

If a student plots the period T on the vertical axis, what must be plotted on the horizontal axis in order that the resulting graph is a straight line?

15 The kinetic energy of a mass m moving in a straight line with speed v is given by $E_k = \frac{1}{2}mv^2$, where the speed is related to acceleration a (assumed constant) and distance travelled d through $v^2 = 2ad$. What would a graph of E_k versus d give?

16 In the photoelectric effect, light of frequency f falling on a metallic surface causes the emission of electrons of kinetic energy E_k. Einstein's formula relates these through

$$E_k = hf - \phi$$

where ϕ and h are constants. ϕ depends on the surface used whereas h is a universal constant. A graph of E_k versus f gives a straight line.

(a) How can ϕ be measured from the graph?
(b) How can h be measured?
(c) In a second experiment with a different surface, a second straight line is obtained. What do the two lines have in common?

Vectors and scalars

Quantities in physics are either scalars (i.e. they just have magnitude) or vectors (i.e. they have magnitude and direction). The tools for dealing with vectors are presented in this chapter.

Objectives

By the end of this chapter you should be able to:
• describe the difference between *vector* and *scalar quantities* and give examples of each;
• *add* and *subtract vectors* by a *graphical technique*, such as the parallelogram rule;
• find the *components of a vector* along a given set of axes;
• reconstruct the *magnitude* and *direction* of a vector from its given components;
• solve problems with vectors.

Vectors

Some quantities in physics, such as time, distance, mass, speed, temperature, etc., just need one number to specify them. These are called *scalar* quantities. For example, it is sufficient to say that the mass of a body is 10 kg or that the temperature today is 18°C. On the other hand, many quantities are fully specified only if, in addition to a number, a direction is given. Examples are velocity, acceleration, force, etc. These are called *vector* quantities. For example, when describing the velocity of an object, it is necessary to specify both the magnitude of velocity (speed) and the direction in which the object is moving. Table 4.1 lists some examples of vectors and scalars.

A vector is represented by a straight line with an arrow at one end, as shown in Figure 4.1a. The direction of the arrow represents the direction of the vector and the length of the line represents the magnitude of the vector. To

Vectors	Scalars
Displacement	Distance
Velocity	Speed
Acceleration	Mass
Force	Time
Weight	Density
Electric field	Electric potential
Magnetic field	Energy
Gravitational field	Gravitational potential
Torque	Temperature
Area	Volume
Momentum	Electric charge
Angular velocity	Work

Table 4.1 Examples of vectors and scalars.

say that two vectors are the same means that both magnitude and direction are the same. Two vectors with the same direction are not necessarily along the same line. As long as they are parallel to each other and have the same

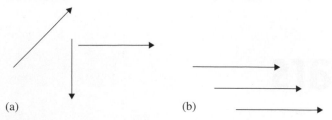

(a) (b)

Figure 4.1 (a) Representation of vectors by arrows. (b) These three vectors are equal to each other.

magnitude, they are the same. Thus, the vectors in Figure 4.1b are all equal to each other. This ability to shift a vector around parallel to itself (called parallel transport) is very important in what follows.

Vectors are represented symbolically either with an arrow on top of the symbol for the vector or in bold type. Thus, both $\vec{a}$ and **a** represent a vector, and its magnitude is denoted by $|\vec{a}|$, $|\mathbf{a}|$ or just a.

Two vectors that have the same magnitude but are opposite to each other in direction are the negatives of one another (see Figure 4.2).

Figure 4.2 Two opposite vectors that are equal in magnitude.

Multiplication of a vector by a scalar

A vector can be multiplied by a scalar (i.e. a number) in a simple way. If the vector $\vec{a}$ is multiplied by the number k, then the resulting vector $k\vec{a}$ has the same direction as $\vec{a}$ if $k > 0$ and opposite to $\vec{a}$ if $k < 0$. The magnitude of the vector $k\vec{a}$ is simply $k|\vec{a}|$. Thus, if the vector $\vec{a}$ has a magnitude of 10 units, multiplying $\vec{a}$ by the number -0.5 results in a vector of magnitude 5 units in the opposite direction to $\vec{a}$. (See Figure 4.3.)

Figure 4.3 Multiplication of vectors by a scalar.

Addition of vectors

Figure 4.4 shows vectors $\vec{a}$ and $\vec{b}$. We want to find the vector that equals $\vec{a} + \vec{b}$. Adding two or more vectors together gives the vector sum, which is the combined effect of the vectors acting on a body. Thus, if two forces act on a mass, their vector sum is the one force whose effect on the mass is the same as the effects of the two forces together. For this reason, the sum of a number of vectors is called the net vector or the resultant vector.

There are two equivalent graphical methods for adding two vectors. The first is the parallelogram method (see Figure 4.4):

1 Shift $\vec{b}$ parallel to itself so that its beginning point coincides with the beginning point of $\vec{a}$.

2 Complete the parallelogram whose two sides are $\vec{a}$ and $\vec{b}$.

3 Draw the diagonal of the parallelogram which starts at the beginning of $\vec{a}$ and $\vec{b}$. This diagonal is $\vec{a} + \vec{b}$.

The second method is the head-to-tail method (see Figure 4.5):

1 Shift $\vec{b}$ parallel to itself so that its beginning point touches the end point of $\vec{a}$.

2 Join the beginning point of $\vec{a}$ to the end point of $\vec{b}$. This is vector $\vec{a} + \vec{b}$.

You might ask if we would have obtained a different answer if, instead, we had shifted $\vec{a}$ to

Figure 4.4 Adding two vectors involves shifting one of them parallel to itself so as to form a parallelogram with the two vectors as the two sides. The diagonal represents the sum.

Figure 4.5 One of the vectors is shifted parallel to itself until its beginning point coincides with the end of the other vector. The sum is then the arrow that joins the only beginning point to the only end point.

the end of $\vec{b}$ and then joined the beginning of $\vec{b}$ to the end of $\vec{a}$. Check that you get the same answer if you do this. This is a way of seeing that $\vec{a} + \vec{b} = \vec{b} + \vec{a}$.

Example questions

Q1 ▰▰▰▰▰▰▰▰▰▰▰▰▰▰▰▰

Add together two vectors: the first has a magnitude of 100 units and is directed east, the other has a magnitude of 50 units directed at 45° to the first.

Answer

See Figure 4.6. First we make a scale representing 10 units of the vector magnitude with 1 cm on paper. Measuring the diagonal we find a length of 13.85 cm, implying a sum of 138.5 units. Using a protractor we find that $\theta = 14.2°$.

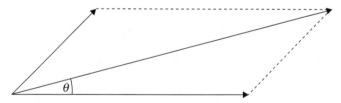

Figure 4.6 (Not to scale).

Q2 ▰▰▰▰▰▰▰▰▰▰▰▰▰▰▰▰

A velocity vector of magnitude $1.2 \, \text{m s}^{-1}$ is horizontal. A second velocity vector of magnitude $2 \, \text{m s}^{-1}$ must be added to the first so that the sum is vertical in direction. What is the direction of the second vector and what is the magnitude of the sum?

Answer

See Figure 4.7. Again we need a scale. Representing $1 \, \text{m s}^{-1}$ by 2 cm, we see that the $1.2 \, \text{m s}^{-1}$ corresponds to 2.4 cm and $2 \, \text{m s}^{-1}$ to

4 cm. First draw the horizontal vector; mark the vertical direction and using a compass (or a ruler) mark a distance of 4 cm from A. It intersects the vertical line at B. AB must be one of the sides of the parallelogram we are looking for. Thus, measure a distance of 2.4 cm horizontally from B to C and join O to C. This is the direction in which the second velocity vector must be pointing. Measuring the diagonal (i.e. the vector representing the sum) we find 3.85 cm, which represents $1.93 \, \text{m s}^{-1}$. Using a protractor we find that the $2 \, \text{m s}^{-1}$ velocity vector makes an angle of about 25° with the vertical.

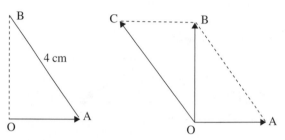

Figure 4.7 (Not to scale).

Q3 ▰▰▰▰▰▰▰▰▰▰▰▰▰▰▰▰

A person walks 5 km east, followed by 3 km north and then another 4 km east. Where does he end up?

Answer

The walk consists of three steps and we may represent each one by a vector (see Figure 4.8). The first step is a vector of magnitude 5 km directed east. The second is a vector of magnitude 3 km directed north and the last step is represented by a vector of 4 km directed east. The person will end up at a place that is given by the vector sum of these three vectors, that is **OA + AB + BC**, which equals the vector **OC**. By measurement or by simple geometry, the distance from O to C is 9.5 km and the angle to the horizontal is 18.4°.

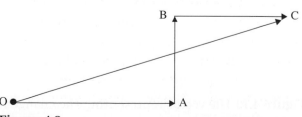

Figure 4.8.

Subtraction of vectors

We are given two vectors $\vec{a}$ and $\vec{b}$. We want to find $\vec{a} - \vec{b}$. Since $\vec{a} - \vec{b}$ is the same as $\vec{a} + (-\vec{b})$, all we have to do is find the vector $-\vec{b}$ and add that to $\vec{a}$ (see Figure 4.9).

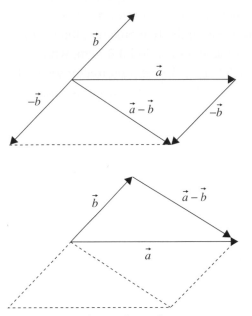

Figure 4.9 Subtraction of vectors.

We have the important result that:

> ▶ The vector $\vec{a} - \vec{b}$ is the vector from the tip of vector $\vec{b}$ to the tip of vector $\vec{a}$.

This is very useful because in physics we are often interested in finding the *change* in a vector. For example, consider a body whose velocity changes from $\vec{v}_1$ to $\vec{v}_2$. The vector representing the change in the velocity is the vector $\overrightarrow{\Delta v} = \vec{v}_2 - \vec{v}_1$, which is the vector joining the tip of $\vec{v}_1$ to the tip of $\vec{v}_2$ (see Figure 4.10).

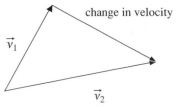

Figure 4.10 The vector representing the change in velocity, $\vec{v}_2 - \vec{v}_1$.

Example question

Q4

A body moves in a circle of radius 3 m with a constant speed of 6.0 m s^{-1}. The velocity vector is at all times tangent to the circle. The body starts at A and proceeds to B and then C. Find the change in the velocity vector between A and B and between B and C. (See Figure 4.11.)

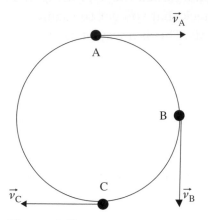

Figure 4.11.

Answer

From A to B we have to find the difference $\vec{v}_B - \vec{v}_A$. The vectors are shown in Figure 4.12.

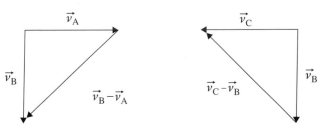

Figure 4.12.

The vector $\vec{v}_B - \vec{v}_A$ is directed south-west and its magnitude is (by the Pythagorean theorem)

$$\sqrt{v_A^2 + v_B^2} = \sqrt{6^2 + 6^2}$$
$$= \sqrt{72}$$
$$= 8.49 \text{ m s}^{-1}$$

The vector $\vec{v}_C - \vec{v}_B$ has the same magnitude as $\vec{v}_B - \vec{v}_A$ but is directed north-west.

Components of a vector

Suppose that we use perpendicular axes x and y and draw vectors on this x–y plane. We take the origin of the axes as the starting point of the vector. (Other vectors whose beginning points are not at the origin can be shifted parallel to themselves until they, too, begin at the origin.) Given a vector $\vec{a}$ we define its *components along the axes* as follows. From the tip of the vector draw lines parallel to the axes and mark the point on each axis where the lines intersect the axes (Figure 4.13).

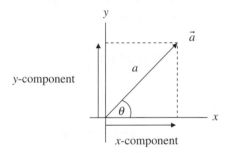

Figure 4.13 The components of a vector.

The x and y components of $\vec{a}$ are called a_x and a_y. They are given by

$$a_x = a \cos\theta$$
$$a_y = a \sin\theta$$

where a is the magnitude of the vector $\vec{a}$ and θ is the angle between the vector and the positive x-axis. Some care must be taken in identifying the correct angle that goes in these formulae. The angle is properly measured from the positive x-axis to the vector, in the counter-clockwise direction (see Figure 4.14).

Figure 4.14 The angle of a vector is measured from the positive x-axis to the vector, in the counter-clockwise direction.

Example question

Q5

Find the components of the vectors in Figure 4.15. The magnitude of $\vec{a}$ is 10 units and that of $\vec{b}$ is 20 units.

Figure 4.15.

Answer

The relevant angle for $\vec{a}$ is $180° + 45° = 225°$ and that for $\vec{b}$ is $330°$. Thus

$$a_x = 10.0 \cos 225°$$
$$= -7.07$$
$$a_y = 10.0 \sin 225°$$
$$= -7.07$$
$$b_x = 20.0 \cos 330°$$
$$= 17.3$$
$$b_y = 20.0 \sin 330°$$
$$= -10.0$$

As we see, the components of a vector can be negative as well as positive. It is somewhat less precise, but in practice more convenient, not to have to deal with negative components. Consider the vector shown in Figure 4.16.

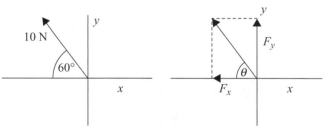

Figure 4.16 Any angle can be used to find the magnitude of the components.

Its x component is clearly negative, $F_x = 10 \cos 120° = -5\,\text{N}$. We could state, however, that the x component of the vector is 5 N in the negative x direction. This is equivalent to stating that $F_x = -5$ N. It has the advantage that by using trigonometry, we can find the numerical value of the component by choosing the most convenient angle in the problem (here the angle of 60°). We do not have to deal with the awkward 'the counter-clockwise angle from the positive x-axis' (here the angle of 120°). In any case treating the components as positive or negative is a question of convenience and up to you, provided you are clear about what are you are doing.

Example question

Q6

Find the components of the vector $\vec{W}$ along the axes shown in Figure 4.17.

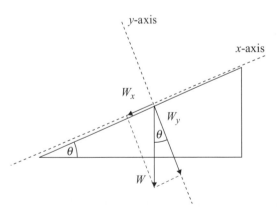

Figure 4.17.

Answer

See Figure 4.18. Notice that the angle between the vector $\vec{W}$ and the y-axis is θ.

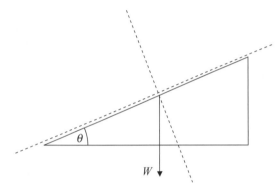

Figure 4.18.

Then by simple trigonometry

$W_x = W \sin \theta$ (W_x is opposite the angle θ so the sine is used)

$W_x = W \cos \theta$ (W_y is adjacent to the angle θ so the cosine is used)

An additional notation for vectors is to give the x and y components as an ordered pair so that, for example, $\vec{a} = (2, 1)$ denotes a vector with x component equal to 2 and y component equal to 1.

Reconstructing the vector from its components

Knowing the components of a vector allows us to reconstruct it (i.e. to find the magnitude and direction of the vector). Suppose that we are given that the x and y components of a vector are F_x and F_y. We need to find the magnitude of the vector $\vec{F}$ and the angle (θ) it makes with the x-axis (see Figure 4.19). The magnitude is found by using the Pythagorean theorem and the angle by using the definition of tangent.

$$F = \sqrt{F_x^2 + F_y^2}, \qquad \theta = \arctan \frac{F_y}{F_x}$$

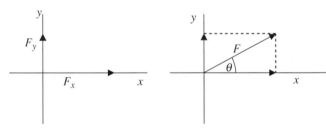

Figure 4.19 Given the components of a vector we can find its magnitude and direction.

As an example, consider the vector whose components are $F_x = 4$ and $F_y = 3$. Then the magnitude is simply

$$F = \sqrt{F_x^2 + F_y^2} = \sqrt{4^2 + 3^2} = \sqrt{25} = 5$$

and the direction is found from

$$\theta = \arctan \frac{F_y}{F_x} = \arctan \frac{3}{4} = 36.87°$$

Here is another example. We need to find the magnitude and direction of the vector with components $F_x = -2$ and $F_y = -4$. From Figure 4.20, it follows that the vector lies in the third quadrant.

The magnitude is

$$F = \sqrt{F_x^2 + F_y^2} = \sqrt{(-2)^2 + (-4)^2}$$
$$= \sqrt{20} = 4.47$$

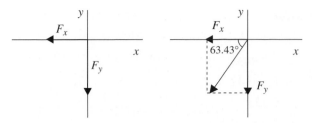

Figure 4.20 The vector is in the third quadrant. We expect the angle it makes with the positive x-axis to be between 180 and 270 degrees.

The direction is found from

$$\theta = \arctan \frac{F_y}{F_x} = \arctan \frac{-4}{-2} = \arctan 2$$

The calculator gives $\theta = \tan^{-1} 2 = 63.43°$. Here we must be careful. Our vector is in the third quadrant, so the angle it makes with the positive x-axis must be between 180° and 270°. We now realize that there is another angle whose tangent is 2. It is the angle $180° + 63.43° = 243.43°$ and this is what we want. Thus, in finding the direction, first make a diagram to see what quadrant your vector lies in so that you know what angles to expect. Never blindly take what the calculator gives. Of course if you denote the angle as in Figure 4.20, you still give a complete description of the vector and that is fine.

As a final example consider the vector with $F_x = 5$ and $F_y = -4$. It lies in the fourth quadrant. Its magnitude is $F = \sqrt{5^2 + (-4)^2} = 6.4$ and its direction is $\theta = \arctan\frac{-4}{5} = -38.66°$. The calculator gives the angle from the x-axis to the vector in the clockwise direction. We are expecting an angle between 270 and 360 degrees. The angle is $360° - 38.66° = 321.34°$.

Adding vectors by components

Adding vectors whose components are given is straightforward. If $\vec{a} = (a_x, a_y)$ and $\vec{b} = (b_x, b_y)$, then $\vec{c} = \vec{a} + \vec{b}$ implies that $\vec{c}$ has components

$$c_x = a_x + b_x, \quad c_y = a_y + b_y$$

For example, if $\vec{a} = (1, 1)$ and $\vec{b} = (-3, 2)$ then $\vec{a} + \vec{b} = (1 - 3, 1 + 2) = (-2, 3)$; that is, the x component of the sum is the sum of the x

components of the individual vectors and so on. Similarly if $\vec{d} = \vec{a} - \vec{b}$, then

$$d_x = a_x - b_x = 4, \quad d_y = a_y - b_y = -1$$

Example questions

Q7

$\vec{a} = (1, 1)$, $\vec{b} = (1, -1)$. Find the magnitude of $\vec{a}$ and $\vec{b}$ and the magnitude of $\vec{a} + \vec{b}$.

Answer

$a = \sqrt{2}$
$b = \sqrt{2}$
$\vec{a} + \vec{b} = (2, 0)$

so the magnitude is 2.

Q8

$\vec{a} = (1, 3)$, $\vec{b} = (2, -2)$. Find the vector $\vec{c}$ such that $\vec{a} + \vec{b} + \vec{c} = 0$.

Answer

$\vec{c} = -(\vec{a} + \vec{b})$
$\quad = -(3, 1)$
$\quad = (-3, -1)$.

If the components are not given, then we have to find them.

Figure 4.21 shows two vectors $\vec{F}_1$ and $\vec{F}_2$ of magnitude 10 and 14, respectively. Vector $\vec{F}_1$ makes an angle of 60° with the x-axis and vector $\vec{F}_2$ an angle of 30°. We want to find the magnitude and direction of the vector $\vec{F}_1 + \vec{F}_2$.

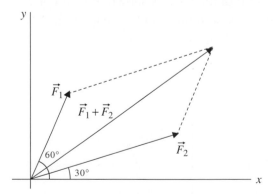

Figure 4.21 Finding the sum of two vectors using components. (Not to scale.)

The components of the vectors are

$$F_{1x} = F_1 \cos 60°$$
$$= 5.0$$

$$F_{1y} = F_1 \sin 60°$$
$$= 8.660$$
$$F_{2x} = F_2 \cos 30°$$
$$= 12.124$$
$$F_{2y} = F_2 \sin 30°$$
$$= 7.0$$

Hence the components of the vector $\vec{F} = \vec{F}_1 + \vec{F}_2$ are

$$F_x = F_{1x} + F_{2x}$$
$$= 17.124$$
$$F_y = F_{1y} + F_{2y}$$
$$= 15.660$$

The vector $\vec{F} = \vec{F}_1 + \vec{F}_2$ thus has magnitude

$$F = \sqrt{F_x{}^2 + F_y{}^2}$$
$$= \sqrt{17.124^2 + 15.660^2}$$
$$= 23.2$$

The direction of $\vec{F} = \vec{F}_1 + \vec{F}_2$ is given by

$$\tan \theta = \frac{F_y}{F_x}$$
$$= \frac{15.660}{17.124}$$
$$= 0.9145$$

so that

$$\theta = \arctan 0.9145$$
$$= 42.4°$$

Example question

Q9

Find the sum of the vectors shown in Figure 4.22. $\vec{F}_1$ has magnitude 8 units and $\vec{F}_2$ magnitude 12 units. Their directions are as indicated.

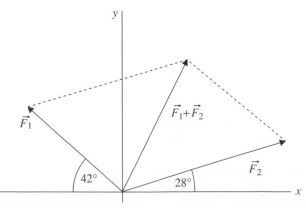

Figure 4.22 (Not to scale).

Answer

$$F_{1x} = -F_1 \cos 42°$$
$$= -5.945$$
$$F_{1y} = F_1 \sin 42°$$
$$= 5.353$$
$$F_{2x} = F_2 \cos 28°$$
$$= 10.595$$
$$F_{2y} = F_2 \sin 28°$$
$$= 5.634$$

The sum $\vec{F} = \vec{F}_1 + \vec{F}_2$ then has components

$$F_x = F_{1x} + F_{2x}$$
$$= 4.650$$
$$F_y = F_{1y} + F_{2y}$$
$$= 10.987$$

Thus, the magnitude of the sum is

$$F = \sqrt{4.650^2 + 10.987^2}$$
$$= 11.9$$

and its direction is

$$\theta = \arctan \frac{10.987}{4.65}$$
$$= 67.1°$$

Questions

1 A body is acted upon by the two forces shown in Figure 4.23. In each case draw the one force whose effect on the body is the same as the two together.

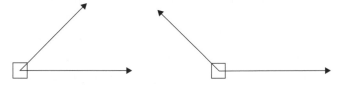

Figure 4.23 For question 1.

2 Vector A has a magnitude of 12 units and makes an angle of 30° with the positive x-axis. Vector B has a magnitude of 8 units and makes an angle of 80° with the positive x-axis. Using a graphical method, find the magnitude and direction of the vectors
   (a) $\vec{A} + \vec{B}$
   (b) $\vec{A} - \vec{B}$
   (c) $\vec{A} - 2\vec{B}$.

3 Repeat the previous problem, this time using components.

4 A person walks 5.0 km due east, then 3.0 km due north and finally stops after walking an additional 2.0 km due north-east. How far and in what direction relative to her starting point is she?

5 Find the magnitude and direction of the vectors with components:
(a) $A_x = -4.0\,\text{cm}$, $A_y = -4.0\,\text{cm}$
(b) $A_x = 124\,\text{km}$, $A_y = -158\,\text{km}$
(c) $A_x = 0$, $A_y = -5.0\,\text{m}$
(d) $A_x = 8.0\,\text{N}$, $A_y = 0$.

6 The components of vectors $\vec{A}$ and $\vec{B}$ are as follows: $(A_x = 2, A_y = 3)$, $(B_x = -2, B_y = 5)$. Find the magnitude and direction of the vectors:
(a) $\vec{A}$;
(b) $\vec{B}$;
(c) $\vec{A} + \vec{B}$;
(d) $\vec{A} - \vec{B}$;
(e) $2\vec{A} - \vec{B}$.

7 Vectors $\vec{A}$ and $\vec{B}$ have components $(A_x = 3, A_y = 4)$, $(B_x = -1, B_y = 5)$. Find the magnitude and direction of the vector $\vec{C}$ such that $\vec{A} - \vec{B} + \vec{C} = 0$.

8 The displacement vector of a moving object has components $(r_x = 2, r_y = 2)$ initially. After a certain time the displacement vector has components $(r_x = 4, r_y = 8)$. What vector represents the change in the displacement vector?

9 Figure 4.24 shows the velocity vector of a particle moving in a circle with speed $10\,\text{m s}^{-1}$ at two separate points. The velocity vector is tangential to the circle. Find the vector representing the *change* in the velocity vector.

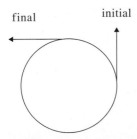

final   initial

Figure 4.24 For question 9.

10 In a certain collision, the momentum vector of a particle changes direction but not magnitude. Let $\vec{p}$ be the momentum vector of a particle suffering an elastic collision and changing direction by $30°$. Find, in terms of $p\,(=|\vec{p}|)$, the magnitude of the vector representing the change in the momentum vector.

11 Points P and Q have coordinates $P = (x_1, y_1)$, $Q = (x_2, y_2)$.
(a) Find the components of the vector from P to Q.
(b) What are the components of the vector from Q to P?
(c) What is the magnitude of the vector from the origin to P?

12 The velocity vector of an object moving on a circular path has a direction that is tangent to the path (see Figure 4.25). If the speed (magnitude of velocity) is constant at $4.0\,\text{m s}^{-1}$ find the change in the velocity vector as the object moves (a) from A to B and (b) from B to C. (c) What is the change in the velocity vector from A to C? How is this related to your answers to (a) and (b)?

Figure 4.25 For question 12.

13 A molecule with a velocity of $352\,\text{m s}^{-1}$ collides with a wall as shown in Figure 4.26 and bounces back with the same speed.
(a) What is the change in the molecule's velocity?
(b) What is the change in the speed?

Figure 4.26 For question 9.

14 Find the components of the vectors shown along the axes indicated by a + in Figure 4.27. Take the magnitude of each vector to be 10 units.

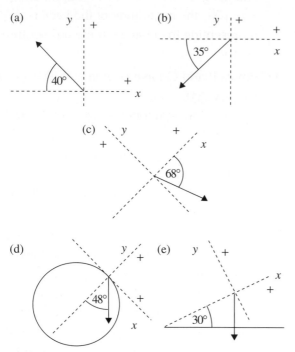

Figure 4.27 For question 14.

15 Vector A has a magnitude of 6.00 units and is directed at 30° to the positive x-axis. Vector B has a magnitude of 6.00 units and is directed at 120° to the positive x-axis. Find the magnitude and direction of vector C such that $\vec{A} + \vec{B} + \vec{C} = 0$. Place the three vectors so that one begins where the previous ends. What do you observe?

16 Plot the following pairs of vectors on a set of x- and y-axes. The angles given are measured counter-clockwise from the positive x-axis. Then, using the algebraic component method, find their sum in magnitude and direction:

(a) 12 N at 20° and 14 N at 50°

(b) 15 N at 15° and 18 N at 105°

(c) 20 N at 40° and 15 N at 310° (i.e. −50°).

Graphical analysis and uncertainties

This chapter introduces the basic methods of dealing with logarithmic and exponential functions in physics. It also introduces the basic methods for calculating the uncertainty in a quantity, which is a function of other measured quantities. The uncertainty in measured quantities will produce an uncertainty in a number obtained using the measured quantities.

Objectives

By the end of this chapter you should be able to:
*   deal with logarithmic functions, semi-logarithmic and logarithmic plots;
*   find the *error* in a calculated quantity in terms of the errors of the dependent quantities;
*   find the error in the *slope* and *intercept* of a straight-line graph.

Logarithmic functions

Semi-logarithmic plots

The exponential function $y = e^x$ plays a significant role in many areas of physics. The activity (number of decays per unit time) as a function of time for a radioactive element behaves as $A = A_0 e^{-\lambda t}$, where λ is known as the decay constant. The current through a diode varies with applied voltage as $I = I_0 e^{kV/T}$, where T is the temperature in kelvin and k is a constant. When the exponential is negative, we speak of a decay problem, whereas positive exponentials represent growth problems.

Time, t/min	Activity/Bq
0	120
1	93
2	73
3	57
4	44
5	35
6	27
7	21
8	16
9	13
10	10

Table 5.1 Experimental data.

Let us concentrate on the radioactive decay problem. Consider the data in Table 5.1, which was collected in an experiment.

The graph of activity versus time is an exponential decay curve as expected. This is shown in Figure 5.1.

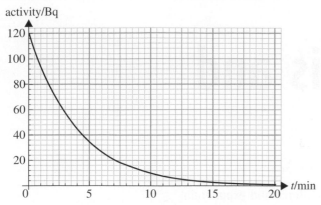

Figure 5.1 The exponential decay curve.

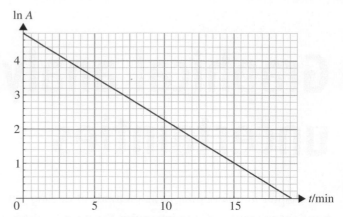

Figure 5.2 The exponential decay curve becomes linear if we plot the logarithm of activity versus time.

The half-life can be determined from this graph by finding the time at which the activity is 60 decays per minute (i.e. half its original value). From the graph, this is found to be about 2.8 minutes. It is more convenient, however, to plot a different graph so that a straight line is obtained.

> ▶ Since $A = A_0 e^{-\lambda t}$, it follows by taking natural logarithms that
>
> $\ln A = \ln A_0 - \lambda t$
>
> and thus a graph of $\ln A$ versus time is a straight line with slope equal to the negative decay constant, and the vertical intercept is the logarithm of the initial activity. This is called a semi-logarithmic plot as it involves the logarithm of only one of the variables.

Such a graph can be made by using a calculator to compute the natural logarithm of each activity value and plotting the logarithm against time, as in Figure 5.2.

Finding the slope of this straight line as usual, we obtain:

$$\text{slope} = -\frac{4.8}{19} \approx -0.25 \, \text{min}^{-1}$$

Thus, the decay constant is $0.25 \, \text{min}^{-1}$. Using the known relationship between the decay

constant and the half-life

$$\lambda T_{1/2} = \ln 2$$

it follows that the half-life is

$$T_{1/2} = \frac{\ln 2}{\lambda}$$
$$= \frac{0.693}{0.25}$$
$$= 2.8 \, \text{min}$$

The vertical intercept is about 4.8 and equals $\ln A_0$. Hence, the initial activity is found to be

$$4.8 = \ln A_0$$
$$\Rightarrow A_0 = e^{4.8}$$
$$\approx 121 \, \text{Bq}$$

Logarithmic plots

Consider now a variable that depends on another through a power.

If $y = kx^n$, then $\ln y = \ln k + n \ln x$, which means that a graph of $\ln y$ versus $\ln x$ gives a straight line with slope n and vertical intercept equal to $\ln k$.

Thus, consider the following data for the maximum current I that can flow in a wire of diameter D (see Table 5.2 and Figure 5.3).

This is a curve of unknown equation. Suspecting a power relationship between the

I/A	D/mm
0	0
1	2.2
2	3.5
3	4.6
4	5.57
5	6.47
6	7.31
7	8.1
8	8.86
9	9.59
10	10.29

Table 5.2 The maximum current that can flow in a particular wire.

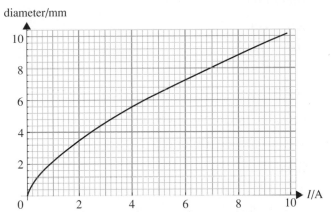

Figure 5.3 A plot of diameter versus current gives a curve of unknown equation.

diameter D and the current I, we take natural logarithms of both variables and plot $\ln D$ versus $\ln I$ (Figure 5.4). (Note that the zero on the vertical axis has been suppressed.)

We find the slope in the usual way:

$$\text{slope} = \frac{2 - 1}{1.8 - 0.3} = 0.67$$

Thus, $D = kI^{0.67}$. The constant k can also be determined by finding the intercept of the line with the vertical axis. The intercept is 0.8 and so $\ln k = 0.80 \Rightarrow k = e^{0.80} \approx 2.2$. Finally, $D = 2.2I^{0.67}$, where the current is in amps and the diameter in mm.

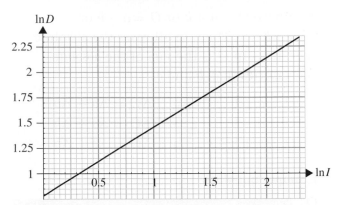

Figure 5.4 A plot of $\ln D$ versus $\ln I$ gives a straight line.

Propagation of errors

Suppose that in an experiment quantities a, b, c, etc., are measured, each with an error Δa, Δb, Δc, etc. That is $a = a_0 \pm \Delta a$, $b = b_0 \pm \Delta b$, $c = c_0 \pm \Delta c$, etc., where the subscript zero indicates the mean value of the quantity. Thus, if a mass is measured to be $4.5 \text{ kg} \pm 0.1 \text{ kg}$, $m_0 = 4.5 \text{ kg}$, and $\Delta m = 0.1 \text{ kg}$.

> ▶ If $a = a_0 \pm \Delta a$, the quantity Δa is called the *absolute uncertainty* or error in the measurement of the quantity a and the ratio $\frac{\Delta a}{a_0}$ is the *fractional* or *relative uncertainty* or error. The quantity $\frac{\Delta a}{a_0} \times 100\%$ gives the percentage error in the quantity a.

Thus, in the measurement of mass, the absolute error is 0.1 kg and the fractional or relative error is $0.1/4.5 = 0.02$ or 2%.

If we wish to calculate a quantity Q in terms of a, b, c, etc., an error in Q will arise as a result of the individual errors in a, b and c. That is, the errors in a, b and c propagate to Q. How do we find the error in Q given the errors in a, b, c, etc.?

There are two cases to consider and we will give the results without proof.

Addition and subtraction

The first case involves the operations of addition and/or subtraction. For example, we might have $Q = a + b$ or $Q = a - b$ or $Q = a + b - c$. Then, in all cases the absolute uncertainty in Q is the *sum* of the *absolute* uncertainties in a, b and c.

$$Q = a + b \quad \Rightarrow \quad \Delta Q = \Delta a + \Delta b$$
$$Q = a - b \quad \Rightarrow \quad \Delta Q = \Delta a + \Delta b$$
$$Q = a + b - c \quad \Rightarrow \quad \Delta Q = \Delta a + \Delta b + \Delta c$$

Example question

Q1

The side a of a square is measured to be 12.4 cm $\pm$ 0.1 cm. Find the error in a calculation of the perimeter S of the square.

Answer

Here we have addition and so the error in S is

$$\Delta S = \Delta a + \Delta a + \Delta a + \Delta a$$
$$= 4\Delta a$$
$$= 0.4 \text{ cm}$$

Thus

$$S = 49.6 \text{ cm} \pm 0.4 \text{ cm}$$

Considerable errors result if the small difference of two large numbers is taken. If $Q = a - b$, and $a = 538.7 \pm 0.4$ and $b = 537.3 \pm 0.4$, then $Q = 1.4 \pm 0.8$. The fractional error in this case is 0.57 or 57%. The error in the quantities a and b is small compared with the mean values of a and b but huge compared with the difference.

Multiplication, division, powers and roots

Suppose now that the quantity to be calculated involves a multiplication such as in $Q = ab$, a division as in $Q = \frac{a}{b}$ or $Q = \frac{ab}{c}$, or a power $Q = a^n$, or a root $Q = \sqrt[n]{a}$. In all these cases the fractional uncertainty in Q is the *sum* of the *fractional* uncertainties of a, b and c.

$$Q = ab \quad \Rightarrow \quad \frac{\Delta Q}{Q_0} = \frac{\Delta a}{a_0} + \frac{\Delta b}{b_0}$$
$$Q = \frac{a}{b} \quad \Rightarrow \quad \frac{\Delta Q}{Q_0} = \frac{\Delta a}{a_0} + \frac{\Delta b}{b_0}$$
$$Q = \frac{ab}{c} \quad \Rightarrow \quad \frac{\Delta Q}{Q_0} = \frac{\Delta a}{a_0} + \frac{\Delta b}{b_0} + \frac{\Delta c}{c_0}$$

$$Q = a^n \quad \Rightarrow \quad \frac{\Delta Q}{Q_0} = |n|\frac{\Delta a}{a_0}$$
$$Q = \sqrt[n]{a} \quad \Rightarrow \quad \frac{\Delta Q}{Q_0} = n\frac{\Delta a}{a_0}$$

Example questions

Q2

The sides of a rectangle are measured to be $a = 2.5$ cm $\pm$ 0.1 cm and $b = 5.0$ cm $\pm$ 0.1 cm. Find the area A of the rectangle.

Answer

The fractional uncertainty in a is

$$\frac{\Delta a}{a} = \frac{0.1}{2.5}$$
$$= 0.04$$

or 4%

That in b is

$$\frac{\Delta b}{b} = \frac{0.1}{5.0}$$
$$= 0.02$$

or 2%

Thus, the fractional uncertainty in the area is

$0.04 + 0.02 = 0.06$ or 6%

Since

$$A_0 = 2.5 \times 5.0$$
$$= 12.5 \text{ cm}^2$$

and

$$\frac{\Delta A}{A_0} = 0.06$$
$$\Rightarrow \Delta A = 0.06 \times 12.5$$
$$= 0.75 \text{ cm}^2$$

Hence

$$A = 12.5 \text{ cm}^2 \pm 0.8 \text{ cm}^2$$

Q3

A mass is measured to be $m = 4.4 \pm 0.2$ kg and its speed 18 ± 2 m s^{-1}. Find the kinetic energy of the mass.

Answer

The kinetic energy is $E_k = \frac{1}{2}mv^2$ (i.e. $E_{k0} = 713$ J) and from

$$\frac{\Delta E_k}{E_{k0}} = \frac{\Delta m}{m_0} + 2\frac{\Delta v}{v_0}$$

it follows that $\Delta E_k = 191$ J; that is
$E_k = 713 \pm 191$ J or just $E_k = 700 \pm 200$ J.

Q4

The length of a simple pendulum is increased by 4%. What is the fractional increase in the pendulum's period?

Answer

The period is related to the length through $T = 2\pi\sqrt{\frac{L}{g}}$. Thus $\frac{\Delta T}{T_0} = \frac{1}{2}\frac{\Delta L}{L_0}$ and since $\frac{\Delta L}{L_0} = 4\%$ we have $\frac{\Delta T}{T_0} = \frac{1}{2} \times 4\% = 2\%$.

Q5

A body radiates according to the black-body law $P = cT^4$, where T is the temperature and c is a constant. If the temperature of the body is increased by 3%, how does the radiated power change?

Answer

$$\frac{\Delta P}{P} = 4\frac{\Delta T}{T} = 4 \times 3\% = 12\%.$$

Other functions

Suppose, finally, that the calculated quantity Q depends on a variable a through a sine, $Q = \sin a$. If a is measured to be $58° \pm 2°$ what is the error in Q? Using calculus (and being very careful to change from degrees to radians before we differentiate) we can show that, approximately,

$$\Delta Q = \cos a\, \Delta a$$
$$= \cos 58° \times 2° \times \frac{\pi}{180°}$$
$$= 0.0185$$
$$\approx 0.02$$

It is easier in practice, however, to find the largest and smallest values of Q through
$$Q_{max} = \sin(58° + 2°)$$
$$= 0.8660$$
$$Q_{min} = \sin(58° - 2°)$$
$$= 0.8290$$

so we can deduce that the error is half of the difference

$$\Delta Q = \tfrac{1}{2}(0.8660 - 0.8290)$$
$$= 0.0175$$
$$\approx 0.02$$

The mean value of Q is
$$Q_{mean} = \sin 58°$$
$$= 0.8480$$
$$\approx 0.85$$
and so
$$Q = 0.85 \pm 0.02$$

This method can be applied to any other functional form relating Q to a.

Uncertainties in the slope and intercept

Having decided the line of best fit for a given set of data that are expected to fall on a straight line, it is usually necessary to calculate the slope and intercept of that straight line. However, since the data points are the result of measurements in an experiment, they are subject to experimental uncertainties. Thus, let us return to the example of Chapter 1.2. In an experiment to verify Hooke's law, data for the tension and extension of a spring are collected and plotted as shown in Figure 5.5. The experimenter has included vertical uncertainty bars representing an uncertainty of ± 10 N in the values of the tension in Figure 5.5 (the length of the vertical bar is thus 20 N).

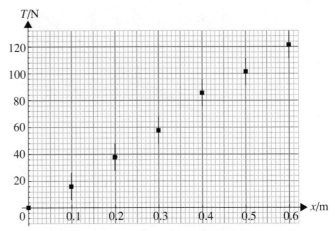

Figure 5.5 Data points plotted together with uncertainties in the values for the tension.

The experimenter then draws the line of best fit through the data points and obtains a straight line, as shown in Figure 5.6. The slope of this line is 200 N m^{-1} and this represents the spring constant. What is the uncertainty in the slope and intercept?

Figure 5.6 The line of best fit through the data points.

A simple way to estimate these uncertainties is by drawing two extreme straight lines as in Figure 5.7 and finding the slope of each. Both straight lines are made to pass through a point that is halfway in the range of the x values: in this case the point with $x = 0.3$ m. The first line is then drawn so as to have the largest slope and still fit the data (this means it will pass at the extremes of the vertical error bars). The second line is made to have the least slope and still fit the data. The two slopes are then measured.

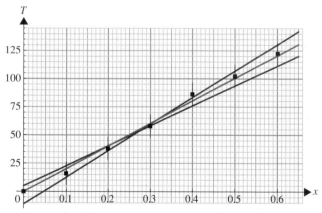

Figure 5.7 The uncertainty in the slope can be estimated by drawing two extreme additional graphs through the centre point.

Measurement of the two slopes gives 235 N m^{-1} and 177 N m^{-1}; that is, errors of $+35$ N m^{-1} and -23 N m^{-1}. Taking the *average* of these two errors gives 29 N m^{-1}, so we may state that the spring constant is 200 ± 30 N m^{-1}. The same procedure allows an estimate of the vertical intercept. The line of best fit gives an intercept

of zero. The line with the largest slope has an intercept of -11 N and the line of least slope has an intercept of $+5$ N. The *average* of the *absolute* values of these errors is $(11 + 5)/2 = 8$ and so the intercept is calculated to be 0 ± 8 N.

Questions

1 A circle and a square have the same perimeter. Which shape has the largest area?

2 A sphere and a cube have the same surface area. Which shape has the largest volume?

3 What is the approximate value of $1 - \cos x$ when x is small?

4 The natural logarithm of the voltage across a capacitor of capacitance $C = 5\,\mu$F as a function of time is shown in Figure 5.8. The voltage is given by the equation $V = V_0 e^{-t/RC}$, where R is the resistance of the circuit. Find
(a) the initial voltage;
(b) the time for the voltage to be reduced to half its initial value;
(c) the resistance of the circuit.

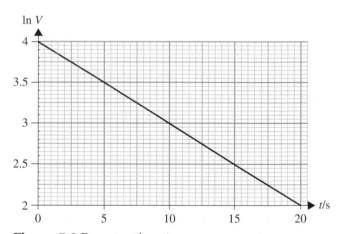

Figure 5.8 For question 4.

5 Figure 5.9 shows how the velocity of a steel ball depends on time as it falls through a viscous medium. Find the equation that gives the velocity as a function of time.

6 Table 5.3 shows the mass M of several stars and their corresponding luminosity L (power emitted). By plotting the luminosity versus the mass on logarithmic paper, find the

Figure 5.9 For question 5.

relationship between these quantities, assuming a power law of the kind $L = kM^\alpha$, giving the numerical value of the parameter α.

Mass M (in solar masses)	Luminosity L (in terms of the sun's luminosity)
1	1
3	42
5	238
12	4700
20	26500

Table 5.3 For question 6.

7 Table 5.4 shows the data collected in an experiment.

Assuming the suspected relationship between the variables is $y = cx^{2.5}$, plot the data in order to get a straight line and then find the value of the constant c.

x	1.0	2.0	3.0	4.0	5.0	6.0
y	2.0	11.3	31.2	64.0	111.8	176.4

Table 5.4 For question 7.

8 The variable y depends on x through $y = ke^{x^2}$. How should these two variables be plotted in order to get a straight-line graph?

9 Two forces are measured to be 120 ± 5 N and 60 ± 3 N. Find the sum and difference of the two forces, giving the uncertainty in each case.

10 The quantity Q depends on the measured values a and b in the following ways:

(a) $Q = a/b$, $a = 20 \pm 1$, $b = 10 \pm 1$;

(b) $Q = 2a + 3b$, $a = 20 \pm 2$, $b = 15 \pm 3$;

(c) $Q = a - 2b$, $a = 50 \pm 1$, $b = 24 \pm 0.5$;

(d) $Q = a^2$, $a = 10.0 \pm 0.3$;

(e) $Q = a^2/b^2$, $a = 100 \pm 5$, $b = 20 \pm 2$.

In each case find the value of Q and its uncertainty.

11 The centripetal force is given by $F = \frac{mv^2}{r}$. If the mass is measured to be 2.8 ± 0.1 kg, the velocity 14 ± 2 m s^{-1} and the radius 8.0 ± 0.2 m, find the force on the mass, including the uncertainty.

12 The mass of a rectangular block is measured to be 2.2 kg with an uncertainty of 0.2 kg. The sides are measured as 60 ± 3 mm, 50 ± 1 mm and 40 ± 2 mm. Find the density of the cube in kilograms per cubic metre, giving the uncertainty in the result.

13 The radius r of a circle is measured to be 2.4 cm $\pm$ 0.1 cm.

(a) What is the error in the area of the circle?

(b) What is the error in the circumference?

14 The radius r of a sphere is measured to be 22.7 cm $\pm$ 0.2 cm.

(a) What is the error in the surface area of the sphere?

(b) What is the error in the volume?

15 The sides of a rectangle are measured as 4.4 ± 0.2 cm and 8.5 ± 0.3 cm. Find the area and perimeter of the rectangle.

16 The period of a simple pendulum depends on length through $T = 2\pi\sqrt{\frac{L}{g}}$. If the length is increased by a factor of 2, by what factor does the period change?

17 In the previous question, if the length of the pendulum is increased by 2%, what is the fractional increase in the period?

18 If the length of a pendulum is measured with a fractional uncertainty of 0.5% and the period with a fractional uncertainty of 0.6%, what is the fractional uncertainty in the measured value of the acceleration due to gravity?

Kinematic concepts

Motion is a fundamental part of physics and this chapter introduces the basic quantities used in the description of motion. Even the simplest of motions, such as a leaf falling from a tree, can be a fairly complicated thing to analyse. To learn how to do that requires that we sharpen our definitions of everyday concepts such as speed, distance and time. As we will see, once we master motion in a straight line, more complicated types of motion such as circular and parabolic motion will follow easily.

Objectives

By the end of this chapter you should be able to:
- describe the difference between *distance* and *displacement*;
- state the definitions of *velocity, average velocity, speed* and *average speed*;
- solve problems of *motion in a straight line with constant velocity, $x = x_0 + vt$*;
- appreciate that different observers belonging to different *frames of reference* can give differing but equally valid descriptions of motion;
- use graphs in describing motion;
- understand that the slope of a displacement–time graph is the velocity and that the area under a velocity–time graph is the change in displacement.

Displacement and velocity

Consider the motion of a point particle that is constrained to move in a straight line, such as the one in Figure 1.1. Our first task is to choose a point on this line from which to measure distances. This point can be chosen arbitrarily and we denote it by O.

When we say that the distance of a point P from O is 3 m, we mean that the point in question could be 3 m to the left or right of O. To distinguish the two points we introduce the

Figure 1.1 To measure distance we need an origin to measure distances from.

concept of *displacement*. The displacement of a point from O will be a quantity whose numerical value will be the distance and its sign will tell us if the point is to the right or left of O. Thus a displacement of −4 m means the point is at a distance of 4 m to the left of O, whereas a displacement of 5 m means a distance of 5 m to the right of O. Displacement is a vector; for the case of motion in a straight line, the displacement vector is very simple. It can be determined just by giving its magnitude and its sign. We will use the convention that positive displacements correspond to the right of O, negative to the left. (This is entirely arbitrary and we may choose any side of the origin as the positive displacement; this takes care of cases where it is not obvious what 'right' means.) We will use the symbol x for displacement in a straight line (we reserve the symbol $\vec{r}$ for displacements in more than one dimension) and s for distance (from the Latin *spatium*). Displacement, being a vector, is represented graphically by an arrow that begins at O and ends at the point of interest. (See Figure 1.2.)

Figure 1.2 Displacement can be positive (point A) or negative (point B).

We will use the capital letter S to stand for the total distance travelled, and Δx for the change in displacement. The change in displacement is defined by

Δx = final displacement − initial displacement

If the motion consists of many parts, then the change in displacement is the sum of the displacements in each part of the motion. Thus, if an object starts at the origin, say, and changes its displacement first by 12 m, then by −4 m and then by 3 m, the change in displacement is $12 - 4 + 3 = 11$ m. The final displacement is thus $11 + 0 = 11$ m.

Example questions

Q1
A mass initially at O moves 10 m to the right and then 2 m to the left. What is the final displacement of the mass?

Answer
$\Delta x = +10$ m $- 2$ m $= 8$ m. Hence the final displacement is 0 m $+ 8$ m $= 8$ m.

Q2
A mass initially at O, first moves 5 m to the right and then 12 m to the left. What is the total distance covered by the mass and what is its change in displacement?

Answer
The total distance is 5 m + 12 m = 17 m. The change in displacement is $+5$ m $- 12$ m $= -7$ m. The mass now finds itself at a distance of 7 m to the left of the starting point.

Q3
An object has a displacement of −5 m. It moves a distance to the right equal to 15 m and then a distance of 10 m to the left. What is the total distance travelled and final displacement of the object? What is the change in displacement of the object?

Answer
The distance travelled is 15 m + 10 m = 25 m. The object now finds itself at a distance of 0 m from O and thus its displacement is zero. The original displacement was $x = -5$ m and thus the change in displacement is $\Delta x = 0$ m $-(-5$ m$) = +5$ m.

Speed

If an object covers a total distance S in a total time T, the average speed of the object is defined by

$$\bar{v} = \frac{S}{T}$$

Suppose that you drive your car for a given amount of time, say 50 minutes. The odometer of the car shows that in those 50 minutes a distance of 30 km was covered. The average speed for this motion is

$$\bar{v} = \frac{30\,\text{km}}{50\,\text{min}} = 0.60\,\frac{\text{km}}{\text{min}}$$
$$= 0.60\,\frac{1000\,\text{m}}{60\,\text{s}} = 10\,\text{m s}^{-1}$$

Using the concept of the average speed is only a crude way of describing motion. In the example above, the car could, at various times, have gone faster or slower than the average speed of 10 m s^{-1}. Cars are equipped with an instrument called a speedometer, which shows the speed of the car at a particular instant in time. We call the speedometer reading the instantaneous speed or just speed. Speed is defined by measuring the distance the car (or whatever it is that is moving) covers in a very short interval of time (see Figure 1.3). If this distance is δs and the time interval δt then the *instantaneous speed* is

$$v = \frac{\delta s}{\delta t}$$

Figure 1.3 Speed at a given time t is defined in terms of the small distance δs travelled in a small interval of time δt right after t.

Note that, by definition, speed is always a positive number.

A word on notation

If Q is any physical quantity, we will use ΔQ to denote the change in Q:

$$\Delta Q = Q_{\text{final}} - Q_{\text{initial}}$$

The symbol Δ will thus represent a *finite* change in a quantity. The symbol δQ represents an *infinitesimal* change in Q. Thus, δQ plays roughly the same role as the calculus quantity $\mathrm{d}Q$. So the definition of instantaneous speed $\frac{\delta s}{\delta t}$ is to be understood as the *calculus quantity* $\frac{\mathrm{d}s}{\mathrm{d}t}$: that is, the derivative of distance with respect to time. Equivalently, we may understand it as

$$\frac{\delta s}{\delta t} = \lim_{\Delta t \to 0} \frac{\Delta s}{\Delta t}$$

If a quantity Q depends on, say, time in a linear way, then the graph showing the variation of Q with t will be a straight line. In that case (and only in that case)

$$\frac{\delta Q}{\delta t} = \frac{\Delta Q}{\Delta t}$$

and each of these quantities represent the (constant) gradient of the graph.

In order to avoid a proliferation of deltas, we will mostly use the capital delta; when infinitesimal quantities are involved, we will simply state it explicitly.

Example question

Q4

A car of length 4.2 m travelling in a straight line takes 0.56 s to go past a mark on the road. What is the speed of the car?

Answer

From $v = \frac{\Delta s}{\Delta t}$, we find $v = 7.5$ m s^{-1}. This is taken as the speed of the car the instant the middle point of the car goes past the mark on the road.

Velocity

Average speed and instantaneous speed are positive quantities that do not take into account the direction in which the object moves. To do that we introduce the concept of velocity. The average velocity for a motion is defined as the change in displacement of the object divided by the total time taken. (Recall that the change in displacement, Δx, means final minus initial displacement.)

$$\bar{v} = \frac{\Delta x}{\Delta t}$$

Similarly, the **instantaneous velocity** at some time t, or just velocity, is defined by the ratio of the change in displacement, δx, divided by the time taken, δt.

$$v = \frac{\delta x}{\delta t}$$

(See Figure 1.4.)

Figure 1.4 The definition of velocity at time t involves the small displacement change δx in the small time interval δt right after t.

We are using the same symbol for speed and velocity. It will always be clear which of the two we are talking about.

Unlike speed, which is always a positive number, velocity can be positive or negative. Positive velocity means the object is *increasing its displacement* – that is, it moves toward the 'right' by our convention. Negative velocity signifies motion in which the displacement is *decreasing* – that is, toward the 'left'. Thus, it is important to realize that the quantity δx can be positive or negative. (It is worthwhile to note that the magnitude of velocity is speed but the magnitude of average velocity is not related to average speed.)

Example questions

Q5

A car starts out from O in a straight line and moves a distance of 20 km towards the right, and then returns to its starting position 1 h later. What is the average speed and the average velocity for this trip?

Answer

The total distance covered is 40 km. Thus, the average speed is 40 km h^{-1}. The change in displacement for this trip is 0 m because

$$\text{displacement} = \text{final} - \text{initial}$$
$$= 0 \text{ m} - 0 \text{ m}$$
$$= 0 \text{ m}$$

So the average velocity is zero.

Q6

A car moves in exactly the same way as in example question 1, but this time it starts out not at O but a point 100 km to the right of O. What is the average speed and the average velocity for this trip?

Answer

The distance travelled is still 40 km and hence the average speed is the same, 40 km h^{-1}. The change in displacement is given by

$$\text{displacement} = \text{final} - \text{initial}$$
$$= 100 \text{ km} - 100 \text{ km}$$
$$= 0 \text{ km}$$

Hence the average velocity is zero as before. This example shows that the starting point is irrelevant. We have the freedom to choose the origin so that it is always at the point where the motion starts.

Q7

A car 4.0 m long is moving to the left. It is observed that it takes 0.10 s for the car to pass a given point on the road. What is the speed and velocity of the car at this instant of time?

Answer

We can safely take 0.10 s as a small enough interval of time. We are told that in this interval of time the distance travelled is 4.0 m and so the speed is 40 m s^{-1}. The velocity is simply -40 m s^{-1}, since the car is moving to the left.

Motion with uniform velocity (or just *uniform motion*) means motion in which the velocity is constant. This implies that the displacement changes by equal amounts in equal intervals of time (no matter how small or large). Let us take the interval of time from $t = 0$ to time t.

> ▶ If the displacement at $t = 0$ is x_0 and the displacement at time t is x, then it follows that
>
> $$v = \frac{\Delta x}{\Delta t}$$
> $$= \frac{x - x_0}{t - 0}$$
> $$\Rightarrow x = x_0 + vt$$
>
> This formula gives the displacement x at time t in terms of the constant velocity v and the initial displacement x_0. Note that t in this formula stands for the time for which the object has been moving.

Example questions

Q8

The initial displacement of a body moving with a constant velocity 5 m s^{-1} is -10 m. When does the body reach the point with displacement 10 m? What distance does the body cover in this time?

Answer

From

$$x = x_0 + vt$$
$$\Rightarrow 10 = -10 + 5t$$
$$\Rightarrow t = 4 \, \text{s}$$

So the distance travelled is 20 m.

Q9

Bicyclist A starts with initial displacement zero and moves with velocity 3 m s^{-1}. At the same time, bicyclist B starts from a point with displacement 200 m and moves with velocity -2 m s^{-1}. When does A meet B and where are they when this happens?

Answer

The formula giving the displacement of A is

$$x_A = 0 + 3t$$

and that for B is

$$x_B = 200 + (-2)t$$
$$= 200 - 2t$$

When they meet they have the same displacement, so

$$x_A = x_B$$
$$\Rightarrow 3t = 200 - 2t$$
$$\Rightarrow 5t = 200$$
$$\Rightarrow t = 40 \, \text{s}$$

Their common displacement is then 120 m.

Q10

Object A starts from the origin with velocity 3 m s^{-1} and object B starts from the same place with velocity 5 m s^{-1}, 6 seconds later. When will B catch up with A?

Answer

We take object A to start its motion when the clock shows zero. The displacement of A is then given by

$$x_A = 3t$$

and that of B by

$$x_B = 5(t - 6)$$

The formula for B is understood as follows. When the clock shows that t seconds have gone by, object B has only been moving for $(t - 6)$

seconds. When B catches up with A, they will have the same displacement and so

$$3t = 5(t - 6)$$
$$\Rightarrow 2t = 30$$
$$\Rightarrow t = 15 \, \text{s}$$

The displacement then is 45 m.

Frames of reference

We are used to measuring velocities with respect to observers who are 'at rest'. Thus, velocities of cars, aeroplanes, clouds and falling leaves are all measured by observers who are at rest on the surface of the earth. However, other observers are also entitled to observe and record a given motion and they may reach different results from the observer fixed on the surface of the earth. These other observers, who may themselves be moving with respect to the fixed observer on earth, are just as entitled to claim that they are 'at rest'. There is in fact no absolute meaning to the statement 'being at rest' – a fact that is the starting point of Einstein's theory of special relativity. No experiment can be performed the result of which will be to let observers know that they are moving with constant velocity and that they are not at rest. Consider two observers: observer A is fixed on the earth; observer B moves past A in a box without windows. B cannot, by performing experiments within his box (he cannot look outside) determine that he is moving, let alone determine his velocity with respect to A.

An observer who uses measuring tapes and stopwatches to observe and record motion is called a *frame of reference*. Consider the following three frames of reference: the first consists of observer A on the ground; the second consists of observer B, who is a passenger in a train sitting in her seat; the third consists of observer C, a passenger on the train who walks in the direction of the motion of the train at 2 m s^{-1}, as measured by the passenger sitting in her seat. The train moves in a straight line with constant velocity of 10 m s^{-1}, as measured by the observer on the ground. The three observers describe their situation as follows: A says he is at rest, that B moves forward at 10 m s^{-1} and that C moves forward at 12 m s^{-1}. This is because in 1 s the train moves forward a distance of 10 m but, in this same second, C has walked an additional distance of 2 m making him 12 m away from A. Thus A measures a velocity of 12 m s^{-1} for C. Observer B says that she is at rest. As far as B is concerned, A is moving backwards (the station is being left behind) with a velocity of -10 m s^{-1}, and C is moving forward at a velocity of 2 m s^{-1}. Observer C claims he is at rest. As far as he is concerned, A is moving backwards at -12 m s^{-1} and B at -2 m s^{-1}.

Example question

Q11

A cart moves in a straight line with constant speed. A toy cannon on the cart is pointed vertically up and fires a ball. Ignoring air resistance, where will the ball land?

Answer

The ball will land back into the cannon. For an observer moving along with the cannon, this is obvious. This observer considers herself to be at rest; so the ball will move vertically up and then fall vertically down into the cannon. As far as an observer on the ground is concerned, the cart moves forward with a certain velocity but so does the ball. The horizontal component of velocity of the cannon is the same as that of the ball, which means that the ball is at all times vertically over the cannon.

This introduces the concept of relative velocity. Let two observers P and Q have velocities $\vec{v}_P$ and $\vec{v}_Q$ as measured by the *same* frame of reference. Then the relative velocity of P with respect to Q, denoted by $\vec{v}_{PQ}$, is simply $\vec{v}_{PQ} = \vec{v}_Q - \vec{v}_P$.

(Note that we are subtracting vectors here.) This definition makes use of the fact that by subtracting the vector velocity $\vec{v}_Q$ it is as if we make Q be at rest, so that we can refer to the velocity of P. In the example of the cannon

above, the relative velocity in the horizontal direction between the cannon and the ball is zero. This is why it falls back into the cannon.

Example questions

Q12

A car (A) moves to the left with speed 40 km h^{-1} (with respect to the road). Another car (B) moves to the right with speed 60 km h^{-1} (also with respect to the road). Find the relative velocity of B with respect to A.

Answer

The relative velocity of B with respect to A is given by the difference

60 km h^{-1} $-$ (-40 km h^{-1}) $= 100$ km h^{-1}.

Note that we must put in the negative sign for the velocity of A.

Q13

Rain comes vertically down and the water has a velocity vector given in Figure 1.5a (as measured by an observer fixed on the surface of the earth). A girl runs towards the right with a velocity vector as shown. (Again as measured by the observer fixed on the earth.) Find the velocity of the rain relative to the running girl.

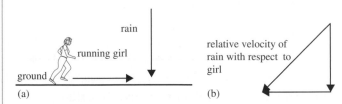

Figure 1.5.

Answer

We are asked to find the difference in the vector velocities of rain minus girl and this vector is given by Figure 1.5b. The rain thus hits the girl from the front.

Q14

This is the same as example question 9, which we did in the last section. We will do it again using the concept of relative velocity. Bicyclist A starts with initial displacement zero and moves with velocity 3 m s⁻¹. At the same time, bicyclist B starts from a point with displacement 200 m and moves with velocity -2 m s⁻¹. When does A meet B and where are they when this happens?

Answer

The velocity of B relative to A is

$$v_{BA} = v_B - v_A$$
$$= -3 - 2$$
$$= -5 \text{ m s}^{-1}$$

When B meets A, the displacement of B becomes zero, since A thinks of herself sitting at the origin. Thus

$$0 = 200 - 5t$$
$$\Rightarrow t = 40s$$

Graphs for uniform motion

In uniform motion, if we make a graph of velocity versus time we must get a horizontal straight line. Figure 1.6 shows the v–t graph for motion with constant velocity v.

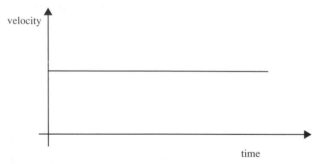

Figure 1.6 Uniform velocity means that the velocity–time graph is a horizontal straight line.

If we wanted to find the displacement from $t = 0$ to time t, the answer would be given by the formula $x = x_0 + vt$. The same answer can, however, also be obtained directly from the graph: vt is simply the area under the graph, as shown in Figure 1.7.

This means that the area under the graph gives the change in displacement. This area added to the initial displacement of the mass gives the final displacement at time t.

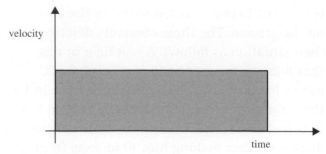

Figure 1.7 The area under the curve in a velocity–time graph gives the displacement change.

A graph of displacement versus time for *uniform motion* also gives a straight line (Figure 1.8).

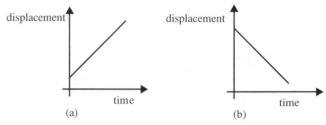

(a)   (b)

Figure 1.8 The displacement–time graph for uniform motion is a straight line: (a) motion to the right, (b) motion to the left.

This is the graph of the equation $x = x_0 + vt$. Comparing this with the standard equation of a straight line, $y = mx + c$, we see that the slope of this graph gives the velocity. We can also deduce this from the definition of velocity, $\frac{\Delta x}{\Delta t}$. But $\frac{\Delta x}{\Delta t}$ is also the definition of the slope of the straight-line x–t graph, hence the slope is the velocity. In Figure 1.8a the slope is positive, which means, therefore, that the velocity is positive, and the mass is moving to the right. In Figure 1.8b the mass is moving at constant velocity to the left.

▶ The slope of a displacement–time graph gives the velocity.

The time when the graph intersects the time axis is the time the moving object goes past point O, the point from which distances and displacements are measured.

The corresponding velocity–time graph for negative velocity is shown in Figure 1.9.

Figure 1.9 The velocity–time graph for uniform motion towards the left.

The area 'under' the curve is below the time axis and is counted as negative. This is consistent with the fact that negative velocity takes the moving object towards the left and thus towards negative displacements.

Consider now the graph of displacement versus time in Figure 1.10. We may extract the following information from it. The initial displacement is −10 m. The object moves with a positive velocity of 2 m s^{-1} for the first 10 s of the motion and with a negative velocity of 2 m s^{-1} in the next 5 s. The object is at the origin at 5 s and 15 s. The change in displacement is +10 m and the total distance travelled is 30 m. The average speed is thus 2 m s^{-1} and the average velocity is 0.67 m s^{-1}. Make sure you can verify these statements.

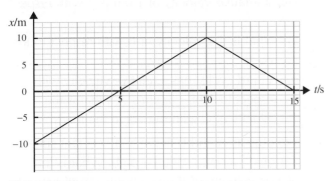

Figure 1.10.

> ▶ We can thus summarize our findings for uniform motion in a straight line: The graph of displacement versus time is a straight line whose slope is the velocity. The graph of velocity versus time is a horizontal straight line and the area under the graph gives the change in displacement. The displacement after time t is given by the formula
> $x = x_0 + vt$.

Example question

Q15

A mass starts out from O with velocity 10 m s^{-1} and continues moving at this velocity for 5 s. The velocity is then abruptly reversed to −5 m s^{-1} and the object moves at this velocity for 10 s. For this motion find:

(a) the change in displacement;
(b) the total distance travelled;
(c) the average speed;
(d) the average velocity.

Answer

The problem is best solved through the velocity–time graph, which is shown in Figure 1.11.

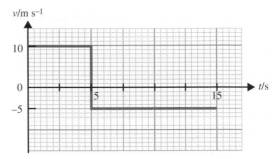

Figure 1.11.

The initial displacement is zero. Thus, after 5 s the displacement is 10 × 5 m = 50 m (area under first part of the curve). In the next 10 s the displacement changes by −5 × 10 = −50 m. The change in displacement is thus 0 m. The object moved toward the right, stopped and returned to its starting position. The distance travelled was 50 m in moving to the right and 50 m coming back giving a total of 100 m. The average velocity is zero, since the change in displacement is zero. The average speed is 100 m/15 s = 6.7 m s^{-1}.

Questions

1 A plane flies 3000.0 km in 5.00 h. What is its average speed in metres per second?

2 A car must be driven a distance of 120.0 km in 2.5 h. During the first 1.5 h the average speed was 70 km h^{-1}. What must the average speed for the remainder of the journey be?

3 A person walks a distance of 3.0 km due south and then a distance of 2.0 km due east. If the walk lasts for 3.0 h find

(a) the average speed for the motion;

(b) the average velocity.

4 Find the displacement–time graph for an object moving in a straight line whose velocity–time graph is given in Figure 1.12. The displacement is zero initially. You do not have to put any numbers on the axes.

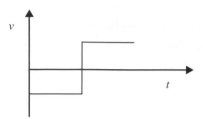

Figure 1.12 For question 4.

5 An object moving in a straight line according to the velocity–time graph shown in Figure 1.13 has an initial displacement of 8.00 m.

(a) What is the displacement after 8.00 s?

(b) What is the displacement after 12.0 s?

(c) What is the average speed and average velocity for this motion?

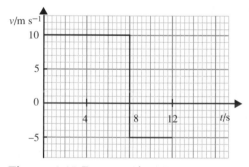

Figure 1.13 For question 5.

6 Two cyclists, A and B, have displacements 0 km and 70 km, respectively. At $t = 0$ they begin to cycle towards each other with velocities 15 km h^{-1} and 20 km h^{-1}, respectively. At the same time, a fly that was sitting on A starts flying towards B with a velocity of 30 km h^{-1}. As soon as the fly reaches B it immediately turns around and flies towards A, and so on until A and B meet.

(a) What will the displacement of the two cyclists and the fly be when all three meet?

(b) What will be the distance travelled by the fly?

7 A particle of dust is bombarded by air molecules and follows a zigzag path at constant speed v.

(a) Assuming each step has a length d, find the distance travelled by the dust particle in time t.

(b) What is the length of the displacement vector after N steps where N is large? Assume that each step is taken in a random direction on the plane. (This problem assumes you are familiar with the scalar product of two vectors.)

8 Two cars are moving on the same straight-line road. Car A moves to the right at velocity 80 km h^{-1} and car B moves at 50 km h^{-1} to the left. Both velocities are measured by an observer at rest on the road.

(a) Find the relative velocity of car B with respect to car A.

(b) Find the relative velocity of car A with respect to car B.

9 A cyclist A moves with speed 3.0 m s^{-1} to the left (with respect to the road). A second cyclist, B, moves on the same straight-line path as A with a relative velocity of 1.0 m s^{-1} with respect to A.

(a) What is the velocity of B with respect to the road?

(b) A third cyclist has a relative velocity with respect to A of -2.0 m s^{-1}. What is the velocity of C with respect to the road?

10 Two objects A and B move at a constant speed of 4 m s^{-1} along a circular path. What is the relative velocity of B (magnitude and direction) with respect to A when the objects are in the positions shown in Figure 1.14?

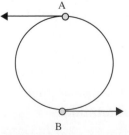

Figure 1.14 For question 10.

11 Find the velocity of the two objects whose displacement–time graphs are shown in Figure 1.15.

(a)

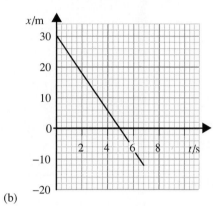

(b)

Figure 1.15 For question 11.

12 An object moving in a straight line has a displacement–time graph as shown in Figure 1.16.

(a) Find the average speed for the trip.

(b) Find the average velocity for the trip.

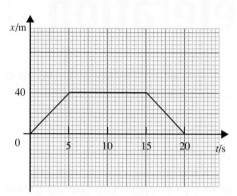

Figure 1.16 For question 12.

Motion with constant acceleration

To complete our description of motion we need the concept of acceleration. This concept and its use are introduced here.

Objectives

By the end of this chapter you should be able to:

- recognize situations of accelerated motion and to define *acceleration* as $a = \frac{\Delta v}{\Delta t}$;
- *describe a motion given a graph for that motion;*
- understand that the *slope of a displacement–time graph is the velocity;*
- understand that the *slope of a velocity–time graph is the acceleration* and the *area under a velocity–time graph is the change in displacement;*
- understand that the *area under an acceleration–time graph is the change in velocity;*
- analyse motion from *ticker tape, stroboscopic* pictures and *photogate* data;
- solve problems of kinematics for motion in a straight line with constant acceleration using

$$v = v_0 + at$$
$$x = x_0 + v_0 t + \tfrac{1}{2}at^2$$
$$x = \left(\frac{v + v_0}{2}\right)t$$
$$v^2 = v_0^2 + 2ax$$

(It must be emphasized that these formulae *only* apply in the case of motion in a straight line with constant acceleration.)

Acceleration

To treat situations in which velocity is not constant we need to define acceleration a. If the velocity changes by Δv in a very short interval of time Δt then

$$a = \frac{\Delta v}{\Delta t}$$

is the definition of the **instantaneous acceleration**. We will mostly be interested in situations where the acceleration is constant, in which case the instantaneous acceleration and the average acceleration are the same thing. Such a motion is called *uniformly accelerated motion*. In this case the intervals Δv and Δt do not have to be infinitesimally small. Then

$$a = \frac{\Delta v}{\Delta t}$$

$$= \frac{v - v_0}{t - 0}$$

where t is the total time taken for the trip, v the final velocity and v_0 the initial velocity.

> ▶ In this case, by rewriting the last equation we find
>
> $$v = v_0 + at$$
>
> This is the formula that gives the velocity at a time of t seconds after the start of the motion in terms of the (constant) acceleration a and the initial velocity.

If we put $a = 0$ in this formula, we find that $v = v_0$ at all times. The velocity does not change since there is no acceleration.

Example question

Q1

An object starting with an initial velocity of 2.0 m s^{-1} undergoes constant acceleration. After 5.0 s its velocity is found to be 12.0 m s^{-1}. What is the acceleration?

Answer

From $v = v_0 + at$ we find

$$12 = 2 + a \times 5$$

$$\Rightarrow a = 2.0 \text{ m s}^{-2}$$

> ▶ For motion in a straight line, *positive* acceleration means that the velocity is *increasing* whereas negative acceleration implies a decreasing velocity.

In solving problems it is sometimes confusing to decide whether the acceleration is positive or negative. The only criterion is whether the acceleration increases or decreases the *velocity* (and not speed). In the top part of Figure 2.1 the velocity is increasing and so the acceleration is positive. (The direction of positive velocities is taken to be toward the right.) In the bottom part the velocity is decreasing and thus the acceleration is negative.

Figure 2.1 In the top part the acceleration is positive. In the bottom part the acceleration is negative.

Similarly, in the top part of Figure 2.2 the velocity is increasing (-15 m s^{-1} is larger than -20 m s^{-1}) and so the acceleration is positive. In the bottom part the velocity is decreasing (-8 m s^{-1} is less than -5 m s^{-1}) and so the acceleration is negative. In the second case note that the *speed* (i.e. the magnitude of velocity) is increasing even though the acceleration is negative.

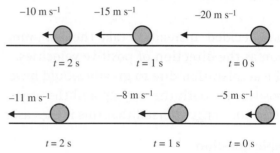

Figure 2.2 In the top diagram the acceleration is positive. In the bottom it is negative.

Acceleration due to gravity

We encounter a very special acceleration when an object is dropped or thrown. This is an acceleration that acts on all objects and has the same magnitude for all bodies independently of their mass. This assumes conditions of free fall – that is, only gravity is acting on the body. Air resistance, friction and other forces are assumed absent. Under these conditions (as will be discussed in detail in later chapters) all objects experience the same acceleration. On earth the magnitude of this acceleration is about 9.8 m s^{-2}, a number we will often approximate to 10.0 m s^{-2} for convenience. We always use the symbol g for the *magnitude* of the acceleration due to gravity. Consider a body falling freely under gravity. We take, as is customary, the upward direction to be the direction of positive velocities. On the way up the velocity is decreasing, hence we state that the acceleration due to gravity is negative. On the way down the velocity is still decreasing (-12.0 m s^{-1} is less than -2 m s^{-1}) and so the acceleration due to gravity is negative on the way down as well as on the way up (see Figure 2.3). (On the way down the *speed* is increasing.)

Figure 2.3 Motion in a vertical straight line under gravity. If the upward direction is the positive direction for velocity, then the acceleration due to gravity is negative for both the way up as well as the way down.

If we had decided, instead, to take the *downward* direction as the direction of positive velocities, then the acceleration due to gravity would have been positive for both the way up and the way down. Can you verify yourself that this is the case?

Example question

Q2

An object initially at $x = 12$ m has initial velocity of -8 m s^{-1} and experiences a constant acceleration of 2 m s^{-2}. Find the velocity at $t = 1$ s, 2 s, 3 s, 4 s, 5 s, 6 s and 10 s.

Answer

Applying the equation $v = v_0 + at$ we get the results shown in Table 2.1.

Time/s	1	2	3	4	5	6	10
Velocity/m s^{-1}	-6	-4	-2	0	2	4	12

Table 2.1.

This means that the body stops instantaneously at $t = 4$ s and then continues moving. We do not need to know the initial position of the body to solve this problem. Note also that the acceleration is positive and hence the velocity must be increasing. This is indeed the case as shown in Table 2.1 (e.g. -4 m s^{-1} is larger than -6 m s^{-1}). However, the speed decreases from $t = 0$ s to $t = 4$ s and increases from $t = 4$ s onwards.

In motion with constant positive acceleration the graph showing the variation of velocity with time is one of the three in Figure 2.4.

This represents a mass moving towards the right with increasing velocity. This is the graph of the equation $v = v_0 + at$.

The first graph of Figure 2.5 represents a mass that starts moving to the right (velocity is

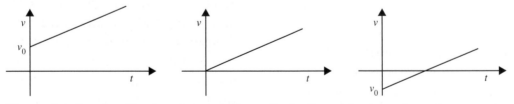

Figure 2.4 Graphs showing the variation of velocity with time when the acceleration is constant and positive. In the graphs above, the only difference is that the initial velocity v_0 is positive, zero and negative, respectively.

Figure 2.5 Graphs showing the variation of velocity with time when the acceleration is constant and negative. In the graphs above, the only difference is that the initial velocity v_0 is positive, zero and negative, respectively.

positive) but is decelerating (negative acceleration). At a specific time the mass stops instantaneously and begins moving again towards the left (negative velocity).

> ▶ The acceleration can be found from the velocity–time graph by taking the slope of the graph. We see this directly by comparing $v = v_0 + at$ and the standard equation for a straight line, $y = c + mx$.
>
> If the acceleration is not uniform, the velocity–time graph will not be a straight line. The acceleration at a given point is found by first drawing a tangent to the curve at the point of interest. The slope of the tangent is the acceleration at that point.

In the case of uniform motion (no acceleration) the area under a velocity–time graph gave the change in displacement. We would like to know if a similar result holds in the case of accelerated motion as well.

To do this we will make use of what we learned in uniform motion together with a little trick. Consider the velocity–time graph of an accelerated motion in Figure 2.6. The trick consists of approximating this motion with another motion in four steps. We will assume that during each of the steps the velocity is constant. The velocity then changes abruptly to a new constant value in the next step. The approximation is shown in the figure. Clearly, this is a very crude approximation of the actual motion.

Figure 2.6 The velocity is assumed to increase abruptly and then remain constant for a period of time.

We can improve the approximation tremendously by taking more and thinner steps, as shown in Figure 2.7.

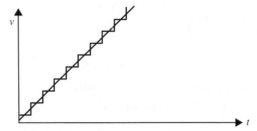

Figure 2.7 The approximation is made better by considering more steps.

Clearly, the approximation can be made as accurate as we like by choosing more and more (and thus thinner and thinner) steps.

The point of the approximation is that during each step the velocity is constant. In each step, the displacement increases by the area under the step, as we showed in the case of uniform motion. To find the total change in displacement for the entire trip we must thus add up the areas under all steps. But this gives the area under the original straight line! So we have managed to show that:

> ▶ Even in the case of accelerated motion, the change in displacement is the area under the velocity–time graph, just as in uniform motion. (See Figure 2.8.)
>
>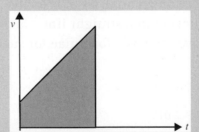

Figure 2.8 The area under the graph is the change in displacement.

Using this result we can now find a formula for the displacement after time t. We are given a velocity–time graph with constant acceleration (a straight-line graph in a v–t diagram).

We want to find the area under the line from $t = 0$ to a time of t s. Since the area we have is the shape of a trapezoid, the area is the sum of two parallel bases times height divided by two:

$$\text{area} = \left(\frac{v + v_0}{2}\right)$$

This actually gives a useful formula for displacement for motion with constant acceleration. Assuming zero initial displacement

$$x = \left(\frac{v + v_0}{2}\right)t$$

This is useful when we know the initial and final velocities but not the acceleration.

However, we do know that $v = v_0 + at$ and so the area (i.e. the change in displacement after time t) is

$$\text{area} = \frac{v_0 + at + v_0}{2} \times t$$
$$= v_0 t + \tfrac{1}{2}at^2$$

Thus, the displacement after time t is this area added to the initial displacement, that is

$$x = x_0 + v_0 t + \tfrac{1}{2}at^2$$

(We see that when the acceleration is zero, this formula becomes identical to the one we derived earlier for constant velocity, namely $x = x_0 + v_0 t$.) Note that this formula says that when $t = 0, x = x_0$ as it should.

In the previous section an analysis of velocity–time graphs for motion in a straight line allowed us to derive the basic formulae for such motion:

$$v = v_0 + at$$
$$x = x_0 + v_0 t + \tfrac{1}{2}at^2$$

or

$$x = \left(\frac{v + v_0}{2}\right)t$$

All of these involve time. In some cases, it is useful to have a formula that involves velocity and displacement without any reference to time. This can be done by solving the first

equation for time

$$t = \frac{v - v_0}{a}$$

and using this value of time in the second equation:

$$x = x_0 + v_0 \frac{v - v_0}{a} + \frac{1}{2}a\frac{(v - v_0)^2}{a^2}$$
$$2a(x - x_0) = 2v_0 v - 2v_0^2 + v^2 + v_0^2 - 2vv_0$$

i.e.

$$v^2 = v_0^2 + 2a(x - x_0)$$

If the initial displacement is zero, then this reduces to the simpler

$$v^2 = v_0^2 + 2ax$$

Example questions

Q3
A mass has an initial velocity of 10.0 m s^{-1}. It moves with acceleration -2.00 m s^{-2}. When will it have zero velocity?

Answer

We start with

$$v = v_0 + at$$

$$v = 0 \quad \text{and so}$$

$$0 = v_0 + at$$

Putting in the numbers we get

$$0 = 10 + (-2.00)t$$

so $t = 5.00$ s.

Q4
What is the displacement after 10.0 s of a mass whose initial velocity is 2.00 m s^{-1} and moves with acceleration $a = 4.00$ m s^{-2}?

Answer

We assume that the initial displacement is zero so that $x_0 = 0$.

$$x = x_0 + v_0 t + \tfrac{1}{2}at^2$$

so

$$x = 0 + 2 \times 10 + \tfrac{1}{2} \times 4 \times 10^2$$
$$= 220 \text{ m}$$

Q5

A car has an initial velocity of $v_0 = 5.0$ m s^{-1}. When its displacement increases by 20.0 m, its velocity becomes 7.0 m s^{-1}. What is the acceleration?

Answer

Again take $x_0 = 0$ so that

$$v^2 = v_0^2 + 2ax$$

So $7^2 = 5^2 + 2a \times 20$
therefore
$a = 0.60$ m s^{-2}

Q6

A body has initial velocity $v_0 = 4.0$ m s^{-1} and a velocity of $v = 12$ m s^{-1} after 6.0 s. What displacement did the body cover in the 6.0 s?

Answer

We may use

$$x = \left(\frac{v + v_0}{2}\right) t$$

to get

$$x = \left(\frac{12 + 4}{2}\right) 6$$
$$= 48 \text{ m}$$

This is faster than using $v = v_0 + at$ in order to find the acceleration as

$12 = 4 + 6a$
$\Rightarrow a = 1.333$ m s^{-2}

and then

$$x = v_0 t + \tfrac{1}{2}at$$
$$= 4 \times 6 + \tfrac{1}{2} \times 1.333 \times 36$$
$$= 48 \text{ m}$$

The two examples that follow involve motions that start at different times.

Q7

Two balls start out moving to the right with constant velocities of 5 m s^{-1} and 4 m s^{-1}. The slow ball starts first and the other 4 s later. How far from the starting position are they when they meet?

Answer

See Figure 2.9.

Figure 2.9.

Let the two balls meet t s after the first ball starts moving. The displacement of the slow ball is $x = 4t$ m and that travelled by the fast ball $5(t - 4)$ m. The factor $t - 4$ is there since after t s the fast ball has actually been moving for only $t - 4$ s. These two displacements are equal when the two balls meet and thus $4t = 5t - 20$, or $t = 20$ s. The common displacement is thus 80 m.

Q8

A mass is thrown upwards with an initial velocity of 30 m s^{-1}. A second mass is dropped from directly above, a height of 60 m from the first mass, 0.5 s later. When do the masses meet and how high is the point where they meet?

Answer

See Figure 2.10. We choose the upward direction to be positive for velocities and displacements. The masses experience an acceleration of -10 m s^{-2}, the acceleration due to gravity. Since the motion is along a *vertical* straight line, we use the symbol y for displacement rather than x.

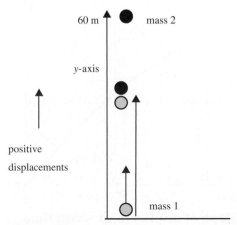

Figure 2.10.

The first mass moves to a displacement given by $y_1 = 30t - 5t^2$. The second moves to a displacement of $y_2 = 60 - 5(t - 0.5)^2$. The displacements are the same when the masses meet. Thus

$$30t - 5t^2 = 60 - 5(t - 0.5)^2$$
$$\Rightarrow t = 2.35 \text{ s}$$

The common displacement at this time is 42.9 m.

Graphs of acceleration versus time

In a graph of acceleration versus time the area under the graph gives the change in velocity. In Figure 2.11 the area from time zero to 4 s is 12 m s^{-1} and thus the velocity after 4 s is 12 m s^{-1} plus whatever initial velocity the object had.

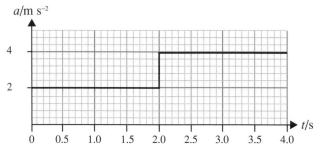

Figure 2.11 The area under an acceleration–time graph is the change in velocity.

Graphs of displacement versus time

In motion with constant acceleration, a graph of displacement versus time is a parabola. Consider a ball that is dropped from rest from a height of 20 m. The graph of displacement versus time is shown in Figure 2.12.

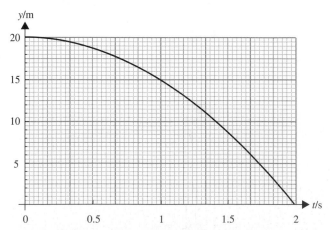

Figure 2.12 Graph of displacement versus time. The object hits the floor at 2 s.

Q9

An object with initial velocity 20 m s^{-1} and initial displacement of -75 m experiences an acceleration of -2 m s^{-2}. Draw the displacement–time graph for this motion for the first 20 s.

Answer

The displacement is given by $x = -75 + 20t - t^2$ and this is the function we must graph. The result is shown in Figure 2.13.

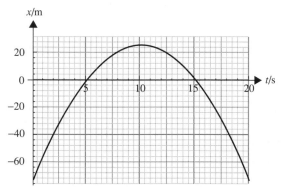

Figure 2.13.

At 5 s the object reaches the origin and overshoots it. It returns to the origin 10 s later ($t = 15$ s). The furthest it gets from the origin on the right side is 25 m. The velocity at 5 s is 10 m s^{-1} and at 15 s it is -10 m s^{-1}. At 10 s the velocity is zero.

In general, if the velocity is not constant, the graph of displacement with time will be a curve. Drawing the tangent at a point on the curve and finding the slope of the tangent gives the velocity at that point.

Measuring speed and acceleration

The speed of an object is determined experimentally by measuring the distance travelled by the object in an interval of time. Dividing the distance by the time taken gives the average speed. To get as close an approximation to the instantaneous speed as possible, we must make the time interval as small as possible. We can measure speed electronically by attaching a piece of cardboard of known length to the object so that a single photogate will record the time taken for that known length to go through the photogate, as in Figure 2.14. The ratio of the cardboard length to time taken is the speed of the object when it is halfway through the photogate.

length of cardboard

photogate

timer

Figure 2.14 Measuring speed with a photogate.

Speed can also be measured with a tickertape, an instrument that makes marks on a paper tape at regular intervals of time (usually 50 marks per second). If one end of the tape is attached to the moving object and the other end goes through the marker, then to find the speed at a particular point we would measure the distance between two consecutive marks (distance travelled by the object) and divide by the time taken (1/50 s). In Figure 2.15 the dotted lines are supposed to be 0.5 cm apart. Then the top tape represents uniform motion with speed

$$v = \frac{0.5}{1/50} \text{ cm s}^{-1}$$
$$= 25 \text{ cm s}^{-1}$$
$$= 0.25 \text{ m s}^{-1}$$

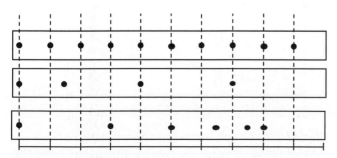

Figure 2.15 Measuring speed with a tickertape.

In the second tape the moving object is accelerating. The distance between the first two dots is about 0.75 cm so the average speed

between those two dots is

$$v = \frac{0.75}{1/50} \text{ cm s}^{-1}$$
$$= 0.375 \text{ m s}^{-1}$$

The distance between dots 2 and 3 is 1.25 cm and so the average speed between those dots is

$$v = \frac{1.25}{1/50} \text{ cm s}^{-1}$$
$$= 0.625 \text{ m s}^{-1}$$

Between dots 3 and 4 the distance is 1.5 cm and so

$$v = \frac{1.5}{1/50} \text{ cm s}^{-1}$$
$$= 0.750 \text{ m s}^{-1}$$

We may thus take the average speed between $t = 0$ s and $t = 1/50$ s to be 0.375 m s^{-1}, between $t = 1/50$ s and $t = 2/50$ s to be 0.625 m s^{-1} and between $t = 2/50$ s and $t = 3/50$ s to be 0.750 m s^{-1}. Thus the average acceleration in the first 1/50 s is 12.5 m s^{-2} and in the next 1/50 s it is 6.25 m s^{-2}. The acceleration is thus not constant for this motion.

The third tape shows decelerated motion.

Related to the tickertape method is that of a stroboscopic picture (see Figure 2.16). Here the moving body is photographed in rapid succession with a constant, known interval of time between pictures. The images are then developed on the same photograph, giving a multiple exposure picture of the motion. Measuring the distances covered in the known time interval allows a measurement of speed.

Figure 2.16 Measuring speed with a stroboscope.

Once measurement of speed is possible, acceleration can also be determined. To measure the acceleration at a specific time, t, one must first measure the velocity a short interval of time before t, say $t - T/2$ and again a short time after t, $t + T/2$ (see Figure 2.17). If the values of velocity found are respectively u and v, then

$$a = \frac{v - u}{T}$$

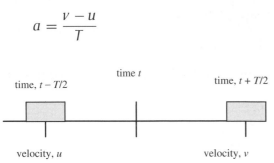

Figure 2.17 Measuring acceleration requires knowing the velocity at two separate points in time.

More on graphs

In kinematics the most useful graph is that of velocity versus time ($v-t$). The slope of such a graph gives the acceleration and the area under the graph gives the change in displacement. Let's examine this in detail. Consider the following problem, which is hard to solve with equations but is quite easy using a $v-t$ graph. Two masses, A and B, are to follow the paths shown in Figure 2.18. The paths are the same length, but one involves a hill and the other a valley.

Figure 2.18 Which mass gets to the end first? They both travel the same distance.

Which mass will get to the end first? (Remember, the distance travelled is the same.) We know that the first mass will slow down as it climbs the hill and then speed up on the way down until it reaches its original speed on the level part. The second mass will first speed up on the way down the hill and slow down to its original speed when it reaches the level part. Let us make the $v-t$ graph for each mass. The graphs for A and B must look like Figure 2.19.

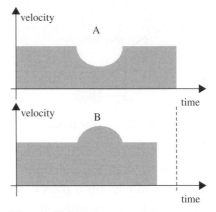

Figure 2.19.

It is then obvious that since the areas under the two curves must be the same (same displacement) the graph for B must stop earlier: that is, B gets to the end first. The same conclusion is reached more quickly if we notice that the average speed in case B is higher and so the time taken is less since the distance is the same.

Consider the following question. The graph of velocity versus time for two objects is given in Figure 2.20. Both have the same initial and final velocity. Which object has the largest average velocity?

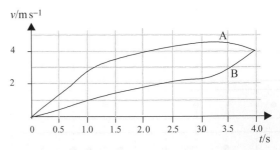

Figure 2.20 Graph showing the variation of velocity with time for two motions that have the same initial and final velocity.

Average velocity is the ratio of total displacement divided by time taken. Clearly, object A has a larger displacement (larger area under curve). Thus, it has a larger average velocity. The point is that you *cannot* say that average velocity is half of the sum of initial and final velocities. (Why? Under what circumstances *can* you say it?)

Consider finally the graph in Figure 2.21, which shows the variation of the displacement of an object with time. We would like to obtain the graph showing the variation of the velocity with time.

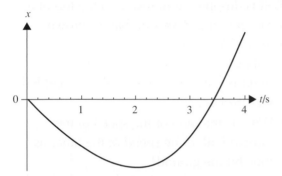

Figure 2.21 Graph showing the variation of displacement with time.

Our starting point is that *velocity is the slope of the displacement–time graph*. We see that initially the slope is negative, it becomes less negative and at $t = 2$ s it is zero. From then on the slope becomes increasingly positive. This leads to the velocity–time graph in Figure 2.22.

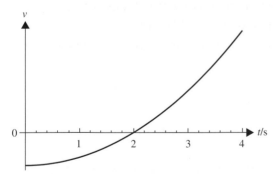

Figure 2.22 Graph showing the variation of velocity with time for the motion in Figure 2.21.

The *slope of the velocity–time graph is acceleration* and from the graph we see that the slope is initially zero but then becomes more and more positive. Hence, the acceleration–time graph must be something like Figure 2.23.

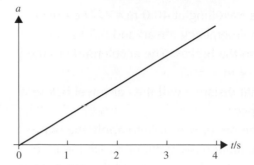

Figure 2.23 Graph showing the variation of acceleration with time for the motion in Figure 2.21.

Questions

In the graphs in this section, the point where the axes cross is the origin unless otherwise indicated.

1 The initial speed of a car moving on a straight road is 2.0 m s^{-1} and becomes 8.0 m s^{-1} after travelling for 2.0 s under constant acceleration. What is the acceleration?

2 A plane starting from rest takes 15.0 s to take off after speeding over a distance of 450.0 m on the runway with constant acceleration. With what velocity does it take off?

3 The acceleration of a car is assumed constant at 1.5 m s^{-2}. How long will it take the car to accelerate from 5.0 m s^{-1} to 11 m s^{-1}?

4 A car accelerates from rest to 28 m s^{-1} in 9.0 s. What distance does it travel?

5 A body has an initial velocity of 12 m s^{-1} and is brought to rest over a distance of 45 m. What is the acceleration of the body?

6 A body at the origin has an initial velocity of -6.0 m s^{-1} and moves with an acceleration of 2.0 m s^{-2}. When will its displacement become 16 m?

7 A body has an initial velocity of 3.0 m s^{-1} and after travelling 24 m the velocity becomes 13 m s^{-1}. How long did this take?

8 What deceleration does a passenger of a car experience if his car, which is moving at 100.0 km h^{-1}, hits a wall and is brought to rest in 0.100 s? Express the answer in m s^{-2}.

9 A car is travelling at 40.0 m s^{-1}. The driver sees an emergency ahead and 0.50 s later slams on the brakes. The acceleration of the car is -4 m s^{-2}.

(a) What distance will the car travel before it stops?

(b) If the driver was able to apply the brakes instantaneously without a reaction time, over what distance would the car stop?

(c) Calculate the difference in your answers to (a) and (b).

(d) Assume now that the car was travelling at 30.0 m s^{-1} instead. Without performing any calculations, would the answer to (c) now be less than, equal to or larger than before? Explain your answer.

10 A ball is thrown upwards with a speed of 24.0 m s^{-1}.

(a) When is the velocity of the ball 12.0 m s^{-1}?

(b) When is the velocity of the ball -12.0 m s^{-1}?

(c) What is the displacement of the ball at those times?

(d) What is the velocity of the ball 1.50 s after launch?

(e) What is the maximum height reached by the ball?

(Take the acceleration due to gravity to be 10.0 m s^{-2}.)

11 A stone is thrown vertically upwards with an initial speed of 10.0 m s^{-1} from a cliff that is 50.0 m high.

(a) When does it reach the bottom of the cliff?

(b) What speed does it have just before hitting the ground?

(c) What is the total distance travelled by the stone?

(Take the acceleration due to gravity to be 10.0 m s^{-2}.)

12 A rock is thrown vertically down from the roof of a 25.0 m high building with a speed of 5.0 m s^{-1}.

(a) When does the rock hit the ground?

(b) With what speed does it hit the ground?

(Take the acceleration due to gravity to be 10.0 m s^{-2}.)

13 A window is 1.50 m high. A stone falling from above passes the top of the window with a speed of 3.00 m s^{-1}. When will it pass the bottom of the window? (Take the acceleration due to gravity to be 10.0 m s^{-2}.)

14 A ball is dropped from rest from a height of 20.0 m. One second later a second ball is thrown vertically downwards. If the two balls arrive on the ground at the same time, what must have been the initial velocity of the second ball?

15 A ball is dropped from rest from the top of a 40.0 m building. A second ball is thrown downward 1.0 s later.

(a) If they hit the ground at the same time, find the speed with which the second ball was thrown.

(b) What is the ratio of the speed of the thrown ball to the speed of the other as they hit the ground?

(Take the acceleration due to gravity to be 10.0 m s^{-2}.)

16 Two balls are dropped from rest from the same height. One of the balls is dropped 1.00 s after the other. What distance separates the two balls 2.00 s after the second ball is dropped?

17 An object moves in a straight line with an acceleration that varies with time as shown in Figure 22.4. Initially the velocity of the object is 2.00 m s^{-1}.

(a) Find the maximum velocity reached in the first 6.00 s of this motion.

(b) Draw a graph of the velocity versus time.

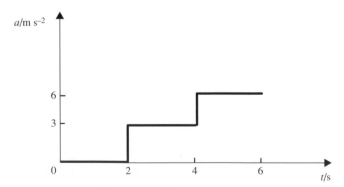

Figure 2.24 For question 17.

18 Figure 2.25 shows the variation of velocity with time of an object. Find the acceleration at 2.0 s.

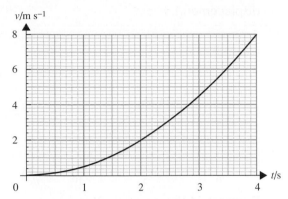

Figure 2.25 For question 18.

19 Figure 2.26 shows the variation of the displacement of a moving object with time. Draw the graph showing the variation of the velocity of the object with time.

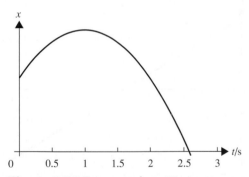

Figure 2.26 For question 19.

20 Figure 2.27 shows the variation of the displacement of a moving object with time. Draw the graph showing the variation of the velocity of the object with time.

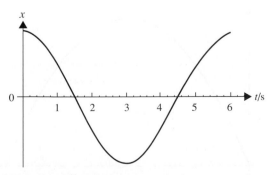

Figure 2.27 For question 20.

21 Figure 2.28 shows the variation of the displacement of a moving object with time. Draw the graph showing the variation of the velocity of the object with time.

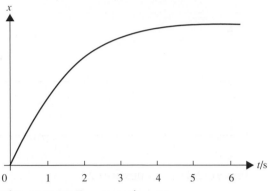

Figure 2.28 For question 21.

22 Figure 2.29 shows the variation of the displacement of a moving object with time. Draw the graph showing the variation of the velocity of the object with time.

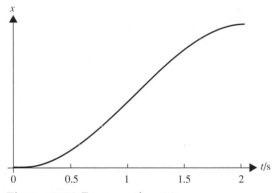

Figure 2.29 For question 22.

23 Figure 2.30 shows the variation of the displacement of a moving object with time. Draw the graph showing the variation of the velocity of the object with time.

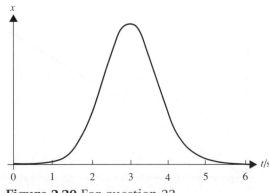

Figure 2.30 For question 23.

24 Figure 2.31 shows the variation of the velocity of a moving object with time. Draw the graph showing the variation of the displacement of the object with time.

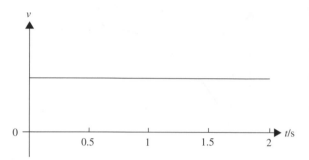

Figure 2.31 For question 24.

25 Figure 2.32 shows the variation of the velocity of a moving object with time. Draw the graph showing the variation of the displacement of the object with time.

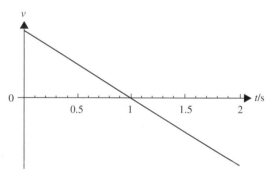

Figure 2.32 For question 25.

26 Figure 2.33 shows the variation of the velocity of a moving object with time. Draw the graph showing the variation of the displacement of the object with time (assuming a zero initial displacement).

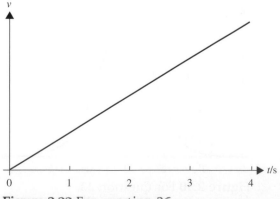

Figure 2.33 For question 26.

27 Figure 2.34 shows the variation of the velocity of a moving object with time. Draw the graph showing the variation of the displacement of the object with time (assuming a zero initial displacement).

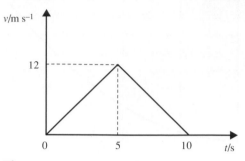

Figure 2.34 For question 27.

28 Figure 2.35 shows the variation of the velocity of a moving object with time. Draw the graph showing the variation of the acceleration of the object with time.

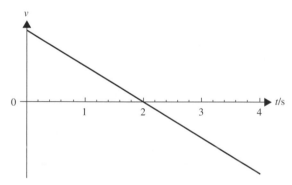

Figure 2.35 For question 28.

29 Figure 2.36 shows the variation of the velocity of a moving object with time. Draw the graph showing the variation of the acceleration of the object with time.

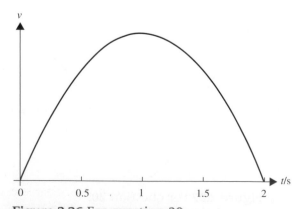

Figure 2.36 For question 29.

30 Your brand new convertible Ferrari is parked 20.0 m from its garage when it begins to rain. You do not have time to get the keys so you begin to push the car towards the garage. If the maximum acceleration you can give the car is 2.0 m s^{-2} by pushing and 3.0 m s^{-2} by pulling back on the car, find the least time it takes to put the car in the garage. (Assume that the car, as well as the garage, are point objects.)

31 Figure 2.37 shows the displacement versus time of an object moving in a straight line. Four points on this graph have been selected.
   (a) Is the velocity between A and B positive, zero or negative?
   (b) What can you say about the velocity between B and C?
   (c) Is the acceleration between A and B positive, zero or negative?
   (d) Is the acceleration between C and D positive, zero or negative?

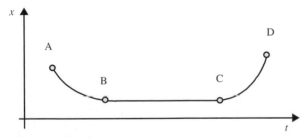

Figure 2.37 For question 31.

32 A hiker starts climbing a mountain at 08:00 in the morning and reaches the top at 12:00 (noon). He spends the night on the mountain and the next day at 08:00 starts on the way down following exactly the same path. He reaches the bottom of the mountain at 12:00. Prove that there must be a time between 08:00 and 12:00 when the hiker was at the same spot along the route on the way up and on the way down.

33 Make velocity–time sketches (no numbers are necessary on the axes) for the following motions.
   (a) A ball is dropped from a certain height and bounces off a hard floor. The speed just before each impact with the floor is the same as the speed just after impact. Assume that the time of contact with the floor is negligibly small.
   (b) A cart slides with negligible friction along a horizontal air track. When the cart hits the ends of the air track it reverses direction with the same speed it had right before impact. Assume the time of contact of the cart and the ends of the air track is negligibly small.
   (c) A person jumps from a hovering helicopter. After a few seconds she opens a parachute. Eventually she will reach a terminal speed and will then land.

34 A cart with a sail on it is given an initial velocity and moves toward the right where, from some distance away, a fan blows air at the sail (see Figure 2.38). The fan is powerful enough to stop the cart before the cart reaches the position of the fan. Make a graph of the velocity of the cart as a function of time that best represents the motion just described. List any assumptions you made in drawing your graph.

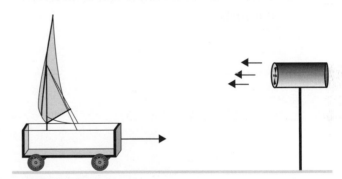

Figure 2.38 For question 34.

35 A stone is thrown vertically up from the edge of a cliff 35.0 m from the ground. The initial velocity of the stone is 8.00 m s^{-1}. (See Figure 2.39.)

Figure 2.39 For question 35.

(a) How high will the stone get?

(b) When will it hit the ground?

(c) What velocity will it have just before hitting the ground?

(d) What distance will the stone have covered?

(e) What is the average speed and average velocity for this motion?

(f) Make a graph to show the variation of velocity with time.

(g) Make a graph to show the variation of displacement with time.

(Take the acceleration due to gravity to be 10.0 m s^{-2}.)

36 A ball is thrown upward from the edge of a cliff with velocity 20.0 m s^{-1}. It reaches the bottom of the cliff 6.0 s later.

(a) How high is the cliff?

(b) With what speed does the ball hit the ground?

37 A rocket accelerates vertically upwards from rest with a constant acceleration of 4.00 m s^{-2}. The fuel lasts for 5.00 s.

(a) What is the maximum height achieved by this rocket?

(b) When does the rocket reach the ground again?

(c) Sketch a graph to show the variation of the velocity of the rocket with time from the time of launch to the time it falls to the ground.

(Take the acceleration due to gravity to be 10.0 m s^{-2}.)

38 A hot air balloon is rising vertically at constant speed 5.0 m s^{-1}. A sandbag is released and it hits the ground 12.0 s later.

(a) With what speed does the sandbag hit the ground?

(b) How high was the balloon when the sandbag was released?

(c) What is the relative velocity of the sandbag with respect to the balloon 6.0 s after it was dropped?

(Assume that the balloon's velocity increased to 5.5 m s^{-1} after releasing the sandbag. Take the acceleration due to gravity to be 10.0 m s^{-2}.)

The concept of force

Two basic ingredients of mechanics are the concepts of mass and force. A force can deform, stretch, rotate or compress a body and is intimately connected to the acceleration it can produce on a body (the relation between acceleration and force will be the detailed subject of a later chapter). Mass is a measure of the amount of material in a body, measured in kilograms; in classical mechanics the mass of an object is a constant. There are different kinds of forces in nature; the most common force of everyday life is the force of gravitation – the force with which the earth pulls us towards the centre of the earth. We give this force a special name: the weight of a body. We don't fall to the centre of the earth because the ground on which we stand exerts another force on us, upwards – a force due to the contact between ourselves and the ground. The origin of this force is electromagnetic. This is also the force that keeps us alive (atoms exist and bind into molecules because of this force), and prevents the chair on which you are sitting from collapsing, and so on. These are the only forces that affect our daily lives. It turns out that the electromagnetic force is just one very special aspect of a more general force, called the electroweak force. The other aspect of this force (the weak nuclear force) is responsible for decay processes inside atomic nuclei. Finally, the colour force, or strong nuclear force, keeps the quarks bound inside protons and neutrons. Physicists hope that the electroweak force and the nuclear force will one day be shown to be different aspects of one more general force (the 'unified force') but this has not yet been accomplished. An even more speculative expectation is that the gravitational force, too, will be shown to be part of an even more unified force, whose different aspects we see as the three different forces today. But none of these attempts for a complete unification has been achieved yet. Apart from the gravitational, electroweak and colour force, no other forces, or interactions, are known at the present time.

Objectives

By the end of this chapter you should be able to:
- state the difference between *mass* and *weight*;
- define gravitational field strength and give its units ($N\ kg^{-1}$ or $m\ s^{-2}$);
- draw vectors representing forces acting on a given body;
- identify situations in which frictional forces develop and draw those frictional forces;
- use Hooke's law correctly, $T = kx$.

Forces and their direction

A force is a vector quantity. Its direction is very important and it is crucial to be able to identify the direction of a given force. What follows is a list of the forces we will be dealing with in this and later chapters, as well as a discussion of their properties and direction. The unit of force is the newton; this will be properly defined when we discuss the second law of mechanics.

Weight

This force is the result of the gravitational attraction between the mass in question and the mass of the earth. (If the body finds itself on a different planet then its weight is defined as the gravitational attraction between its mass and that planet's mass.) The **weight** of a body is the gravitational force experienced by that body, which on earth is given by the formula

$$W = mg$$

where

- m is the mass of the body measured in kilograms

- g is the gravitational field strength of the earth, which is a property of the gravitational field of the earth (see Chapter 2.10). Its units are newton per kilogram, N kg^{-1}. The gravitational field strength is also known as 'the acceleration due to gravity'. The units of g are thus also m s^{-2}.

If m is in kg and g in N kg^{-1} or m s^{-2} then W is in newtons, N. On the *surface* of the earth, $g = 9.81$ N kg^{-1} – a number that we will often approximate by the more convenient 10 N kg^{-1}. This force is always directed vertically downward, as shown in Figure 3.1.

earth

Figure 3.1 The weight of an object is always directed vertically downward.

The mass of an object is the same everywhere in the universe, but its weight depends on the *location* of the body. For example, a mass of 70 kg has a weight of 687 N on the surface of the earth ($g = 9.81$ N kg^{-1}) and a weight of 635 N at a height of 250 km from the earth's surface (where $g = 9.07$ N kg^{-1}). However, on the surface of Venus, where the gravitational field strength is only 8.9 N kg^{-1}, the weight is 623 N.

Tension

A string that is taut is said to be under tension. The force that arises in any body when it is stretched is called **tension**. This force is the result of electromagnetic interactions between the molecules of the material making up the string. A tension force in a string is created when two forces are applied in opposite directions at the ends of the string (see Figure 3.2).

Figure 3.2 A tension force in a string.

To say that there is tension in a string means that an arbitrary point on the string is acted upon by two forces (the tension T) as shown in Figure 3.3. If the string hangs from a ceiling and a mass m is tied at the other end, tension develops in the string. At the point of support at the ceiling, the tension force pulls down *on the ceiling* and at the point where the mass is tied the tension acts upwards *on the mass*.

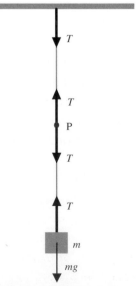

Figure 3.3 The tension is directed along the string.

In most cases we will idealize the string by assuming it is massless. This does not mean that the string *really* is massless, but rather that its mass is so small compared with any other masses in the problem that we can neglect it. In that case, the tension T is the same at all points on the string. The direction of the tension force is along the string. Further examples of tension forces in a string are given in Figure 3.4. A string or rope that is not taut has zero tension in it.

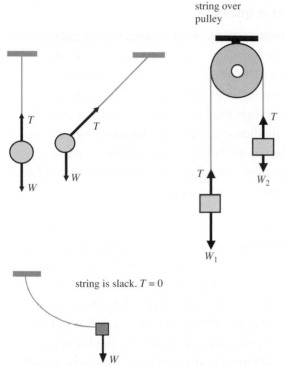

string over pulley

string is slack. $T = 0$

Figure 3.4 More examples of tension forces.

Normal reaction (contact) forces

If a body touches another body, there is a *force of reaction* or *contact force* between the two bodies. This force is perpendicular to the body exerting the force. Like tension, the origin of this force is also electromagnetic. In Figure 3.5 we show the reaction force on several bodies.

Drag forces

Drag forces are forces that oppose the motion of a body through a fluid (a gas or a liquid). Typical examples are the air resistance force experienced by a car (see Figure 3.6) or plane, or the resistance force experienced by a steel marble dropped into a jar of honey. Drag forces

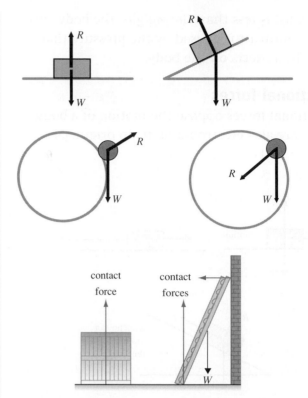

Figure 3.5 Examples of reaction forces, R.

are directed opposite to the velocity of the body and in general depend on the speed of the body. The higher the speed, the higher the drag force.

Figure 3.6 The drag force on a moving car.

Upthrust

Any object placed in a fluid experiences an upward force called upthrust (see Figure 3.7). If the upthrust force equals the weight of the body, the body will float in the fluid. If the

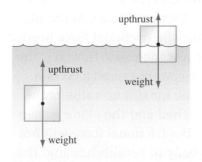

Figure 3.7 Upthrust.

upthrust is less than the weight, the body will sink. Upthrust is caused by the pressure that the fluid exerts on the body.

Frictional forces

Frictional forces oppose the motion of a body. They are also electromagnetic in origin. (See Figure 3.8.)

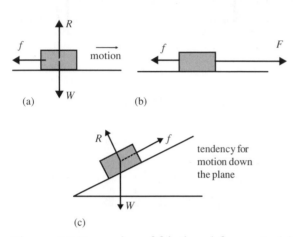

(a)

(b)

(c)

Figure 3.8 Examples of frictional forces. In (a) and (b) the motion to the right is opposed by a frictional force to the left. In (c) the body does not move but has a tendency to move down the plane. A frictional force directed up the plane opposes this tendency.

Friction arises whenever one body slides over another. In this case we speak of sliding or kinetic friction. Friction also arises whenever there is just a tendency for motion, not necessarily motion itself, such as when a block rests on an inclined plane or if a block on a level road is pulled by a small force that does not result in motion. In this case, we speak of static friction. Suppose that the plane on which the block rests is slowly elevated (Figure 3.8c). The block will tend to move to the left. This motion will be opposed by a frictional force. As the plane is elevated even more, the frictional force needed to keep the block at rest increases. However, the static frictional force cannot exceed a certain maximum value. If the maximum value of the frictional force is reached and the plane is then elevated a bit more, the frictional force will not be able to keep the body in equilibrium and the block will slide down. As soon as the body begins

to slide, the frictional force opposing the motion becomes the kinetic friction force. The kinetic friction force is always less than the maximum value of the static friction force. This is a well-known phenomenon of everyday life. It takes a lot of force to get a heavy piece of furniture to start moving (you must exceed the maximum value of the static friction force), but once you get it moving, pushing it along becomes easier (you are now opposed by the smaller kinetic friction force).

Example question

Q1
A brick of weight 50 N rests on a horizontal surface. The maximum frictional force that can develop between the brick and the surface is 30 N. When the brick slides on the surface, the frictional force is 10 N. A horizontal force F is applied to the brick, its magnitude increasing slowly from zero. Find the frictional force on the brick for various values of F.

Answer

The maximum frictional force is 30 N. This means that as long as F is less than 30 N, the frictional force equals F and the brick stays where it is. If F becomes slightly more than 30 N, the frictional force cannot match it and thus the brick will move. But as soon as the brick moves, the frictional force will drop to the kinetic value 10 N, for all values of $F > 30$ N. We can summarize these results as shown in Table 3.1.

F	0 N	12 N	28 N	29 N	30 N	30.01 N	40 N
f	0 N	12 N	28 N	29 N	30 N	10 N	10 N
	no motion	no motion	no motion	no motion	no motion	motion	motion

Table 3.1.

Frictional forces between the road and the tyres are what allow a car to take a turn. Although, generally, frictional forces oppose the motion of a body, in some cases frictional forces are responsible for motion. A typical example is the wheels of a car. The engine forces the wheels to turn. The wheels exert a force on the ground and so the ground exerts an equal and opposite force on the wheels, making them move forward. This will become clearer when we look at Newton's third law in a later chapter.

Free-body diagrams

A free-body diagram is a diagram showing the magnitude and direction of all the forces acting on a chosen body. The body is shown on its own, free of its surroundings and of any other bodies it may be in contact with. In Figure 3.9 we show three situations in which forces are acting; below each is the corresponding free-body diagram for the shaded bodies.

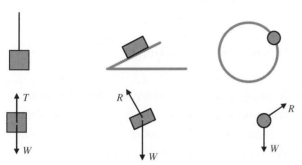

Figure 3.9 Free-body diagrams for the bodies in dark grey.

In any mechanics problem, it is important to be able to draw correctly the free-body diagrams for all the bodies of interest. It is also important that the length of the arrow representing a given force is proportional to the magnitude of the force.

Hooke's law

If we try to extend a spring, a force pulls the spring back to its original length; if we try to compress a spring, again a force tries to pull the spring back to its original length (see Figure 3.10). The force in the spring, the tension, has a simple relationship to the amount by which the spring is extended or compressed.

If this amount is x, then the tension T is proportional to x (see Figure 3.11). This statement is known as Hooke's law. This means

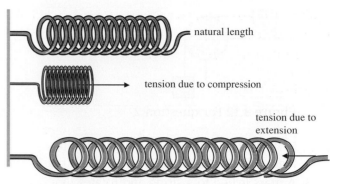

Figure 3.10 The tension in a spring is proportional and opposite to the extension.

that the more we want to extend or compress the spring, the bigger the force required to pull or push it with. In equation form it says that $T = kx$, where k is the constant of proportionality known as the spring constant. It varies from spring to spring. Its units are those of force over extension: N m^{-1}.

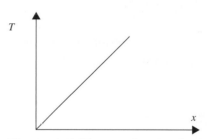

Figure 3.11 The tension in the spring is linearly proportional to the extension.

The extension or compression of the spring must not be too large, otherwise Hooke's law isn't applicable. The range of extensions (or compressions) for which Hooke's law is satisfied is known as the elastic limit; beyond the elastic limit the relationship between tension and extension is more complicated.

Questions

1 A mass swings at the end of a string like a pendulum. Draw the forces on the mass at:
   (a) its lowest position;
   (b) its highest position.

2 A mass rests on a rough table and is connected by a string that goes over a pulley

Figure 3.12 For question 2.

to a second hanging mass, as shown in Figure 3.12. Draw the forces on each mass.

3 A mass is tied to a string and rotates in a vertical circle, as shown in Figure 3.13. Draw the forces on the mass when the string is horizontal.

Figure 3.13 For question 3.

4 A bead rolls on the surface of a sphere, having started from the top, as shown in Figure 3.14. Draw the forces on the bead:
(a) at the top;
(b) at the point where it is about to leave the surface of the sphere.

Figure 3.14 For question 4.

5 A mass hangs at the end of a vertical spring which is attached to the ceiling. Draw the forces on:
(a) the hanging mass;
(b) the ceiling.

6 Look at Figure 3.15. In which case is the tension in the string largest?

Figure 3.15 For question 6.

7 A force of 125 N is required to extend a spring by 2.8 cm. What force is required to stretch the same spring by 3.2 cm?

8 A mass hangs attached to three strings, as shown in Figure 3.16. Draw the forces on:
(a) the hanging mass;
(b) the point where the strings join.

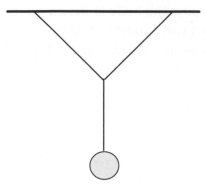

Figure 3.16 For question 8.

9 A spring is compressed by a certain distance and a mass is attached to its right end, as shown in Figure 3.17. The mass rests on a rough table. What are the forces acting on the mass?

Figure 3.17 For question 9.

10 A block rests on an elevator floor as shown, as shown in Figure 3.18. The elevator is held in place by a cable attached to the ceiling. Draw the forces on:
(a) the block;
(b) the elevator.

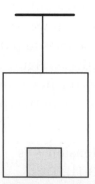

Figure 3.18 For question 10.

Newton's first law and equilibrium

Mechanics rests on Newton's three laws. The first law is discussed in this chapter. The first law leads to a study of systems in equilibrium, which is a state in which the net force on the system is zero.

Objectives

By the end of this chapter you should be able to:
- relate situations in which the acceleration is zero to equilibrium situations in which the net force is zero;
- find the net force on a body using the methods of vector addition;
- solve problems of equilibrium.

Newton's first law

In ancient times, Aristotle had maintained that a force is what is required in order to keep a body in motion. The higher the speed, the larger the force needed. Aristotle's idea of force is not unreasonable and is in fact in accordance with experience from everyday life: it does require a force to push a piece of furniture from one corner of a room to another. What Aristotle failed to appreciate is that everyday life is plagued by friction. An object in motion comes to rest because of friction and thus a force is required if it is to keep moving. This force is needed in order to cancel the force of friction that opposes the motion. In an idealized world with no friction, a body that is set into motion does not require a force to keep it moving. Galileo, 2000 years after Aristotle, was the first to realize that the state of no motion and the state of motion with constant speed in a straight line are indistinguishable from each other. Since no force is present in the case of no motion, no forces are required in the case of motion in a straight line with constant speed either. Force is related, as you will see, to changes in velocity (i.e. accelerations).

Newton's first law (generalizing statements of Galileo) states the following:

▶ When no forces act on a body, that body will either remain at rest or continue to move along a straight line with constant speed.

A body that moves with acceleration (i.e. changing speed or changing direction of motion) must have a force acting on it. An ice hockey puck slides on ice with practically no friction and will thus move with constant speed in a straight line. A spacecraft leaving the solar system with its engines off has no force acting on it and will continue to move in a straight line at constant speed (until it encounters another body that will attract or hit it). Using the first law, it is easy to see if a force is acting on a body. For example, the earth rotates around the sun and thus we know at once that a force must be acting on the earth.

Newton's first law is also called the law of *inertia*. Inertia is the reluctance of a body to change its state of motion. Inertia keeps the body in the same state of motion when no forces act on the body. When a car accelerates forward, the passengers are thrown back into their seats. If a car brakes abruptly, the passengers are thrown forward. This implies that a mass tends to stay in the state of motion it was in before the force acted on it. The reaction of a body to a change in its state of motion (acceleration) is inertia.

A well-known example of inertia is that of a magician who very suddenly pulls the tablecloth off a table leaving all the plates, glasses, etc., behind on the table. The inertia of these objects makes them 'want' to stay on the table where they are. Similarly, if you pull very suddenly on a roll of kitchen paper you will tear off a sheet. But if you pull gently you will only succeed in making the paper roll rotate.

Inertial frames of reference

A system on which no forces act is called an inertial frame of reference. Inertial reference frames played a crucial role in the history of physics: observers belonging to different inertial frames will come up with the same laws of physics. For example, an observer at rest on the surface of the earth is an (approximate) inertial reference frame. (We say approximate, since the earth rotates about its axis as well as around the sun – but these motions produce small accelerations and over a short interval of time we can neglect them.) A passenger on a

train that moves with constant velocity relative to an observer on the earth is also an inertial reference frame. The two observers will discover the same laws of physics by performing experiments in their respective frames. There is no experiment that the observer on the train can perform whose result will be to determine that the train is moving. Nor will he ever discover laws of physics that are different from the ones discovered by the observer on the ground.

Equilibrium

When the net force on a body is zero, the body is said to be in **equilibrium**. If a body is displaced slightly from its equilibrium position, the net force on the body may or may not be zero. If it is still zero, the position of equilibrium is called a neutral equilibrium position. An example is a mass resting on a horizontal table, as in Figure 4.1.

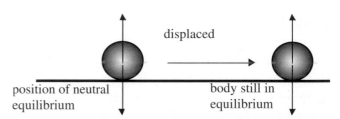

Figure 4.1 In a position of neutral equilibrium the net force on a body is zero. A displacement results in another equilibrium position.

On the other hand, if after displacing the body from its equilibrium position the net force is no longer zero, then we distinguish two kinds of equilibrium in the original position. If the net force in the displaced position tends to move the body back towards the initial equilibrium position, then we speak of stable equilibrium. If, on the other hand, the force on the body tends to make it move even further from the initial position, we speak of unstable equilibrium (see Figure 4.2)

Figure 4.2 In unstable equilibrium the net force on the body is zero, but a small displacement results in motion away from the equilibrium position. In stable equilibrium, the motion is back towards the equilibrium position.

Note that an equilibrium position can be both stable and unstable at the same time. For example, a mass on a surface that resembles a saddle is in equilibrium if placed at the centre of the saddle. The equilibrium is stable or unstable depending on the direction in which the mass is then displaced.

Equilibrium of a point particle means that the net force on the point is zero. To find the net force we must use the methods of vector addition, and here we will exclusively use the component method. We choose a set of axes whose origin is the point body in question and find the components of all the forces on the body. As promised in Chapter 1.4, we will use only positive components. Then the sum of the x components to the 'right' must equal the sum of the x components to the 'left', and the sum of the y components 'up' must equal the sum of the y components 'down'. Let us look at a simple example. A block of weight 10.0 N rests on a horizontal table. What is the normal reaction on the block from the table? Figure 4.3 shows the forces on the block, which is assumed to be a point object. The dotted lines represent the axes along which we will take components. There are no forces with

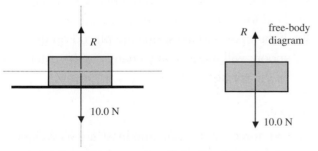

Figure 4.3 The forces acting on a block resting on a table.

horizontal components. In the vertical direction the component of R is simply R in the 'up' direction. The 10.0 N force has a component of 10.0 N in the 'down' direction. Equating the up with the down components we find $R = 10.0$ N.

Let us look at a slightly less trivial example. A 20.0 N weight hangs from strings as shown in Figure 4.4. We want to find the tension in each string.

Figure 4.4 Free-body diagrams for joining point and hanging mass.

We call the tensions in the three strings T, R and S. The point where the strings meet is in equilibrium and so the net force from these three tensions is zero. Getting components along the horizontal and vertical directions we have:

$$T_x = 0$$
$$T_y = T \text{ 'down'}$$
$$R_x = R \cos 30°$$
$$\quad = 0.866R \text{ 'left'}$$
$$R_y = R \sin 30°$$
$$\quad = 0.500R \text{ 'up'}$$
$$S_x = S \cos 45°$$
$$\quad = 0.707S \text{ 'right'}$$
$$S_y = S \sin 45°$$
$$\quad = 0.707S \text{ 'up'}$$

We thus have

$$0.866R = 0.707S$$
$$0.707S + 0.500R = T$$

Equilibrium of the hanging mass demands, however, that $T = 20.0$ N. Thus we can find $R = 14.6$ N and $S = 17.9$ N.

Example questions

Q1

A mass $m = 10.0$ kg hangs from two strings which are attached to the ceiling as shown in Figure 4.5. What is the tension in each string?

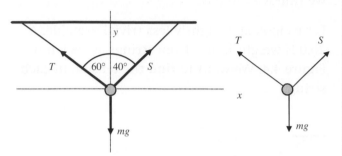

Figure 4.5.

Answer

The three forces acting on m are as shown, with T and S being the tensions in the two strings. Taking components about horizontal and vertical axes through m we find (here we will make use of only positive components) $T_x = T \cos 30° = 0.87T$ to the left, $T_y = T \sin 30° = 0.50T$ up, $S_x = S \cos 50° = 0.64S$ to the right, $S_y = S \sin 50° = 0.77S$ up. The weight mg is already along one of the axes: it has a component $mg = 100$ N down. Equilibrium thus demands (net force has zero x and y components)

$$0.87T = 0.64S$$
$$0.50T + 0.77S = 100$$

from which we find $T = 65.3$ N and $S = 87.9$ N.

Q2

A block of weight 50.0 N rests on a rough horizontal table and is attached by strings to a hanging mass of weight 12.0 N, as shown in Figure 4.6. Find the force of friction between the block and the table if the block on the table is in equilibrium.

Answer

The diagram shows the forces acting on the block and the mass as well as the tensions at the point where the three strings join. Since that point is in equilibrium, the net force on it is zero. Taking components of the forces R, S and 12.0 N along horizontal and vertical axes we find:

$$R_x = R \text{ 'left'}$$
$$R_y = 0$$

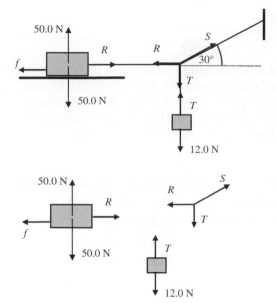

Figure 4.6.

$$S_x = S \cos 30°$$
$$= 0.866 S \text{ 'right'}$$
$$S_y = S \sin 30°$$
$$= 0.500 S \text{ 'up'}$$

Equilibrium then demands that

$$R = 0.866 S$$
$$0.500 S = T$$
$$= 12.0$$

since $T = 12.0$ N by the equilibrium of the hanging mass. We can thus find $S = 24.0$ N and so $R = 20.8$ N. Demanding now equilibrium for the block on the table, we see that the frictional force must equal R, i.e. 20.8 N.

Q3

A mass of 125 g is attached to a spring of spring constant $k = 58$ N m^{-1} that is hanging vertically.
(a) Find the extension of the spring.
(b) If the mass and the spring are placed on the moon, will there be any change in the extension of the spring?

Answer

(a) The forces on the hanging mass are its weight and the tension of the spring. Since we have equilibrium, the two forces are equal in magnitude. Therefore

$$kx = mg$$

$$x = \frac{mg}{k}$$

$$= \frac{0.125 \times 10}{58}$$

$$= 2.2 \, cm$$

(b) The extension will be less, since the acceleration of gravity is less.

Questions

1 What is the net force on each of the bodies shown in the diagrams in Figure 4.7? The only forces acting are the ones shown. Indicate direction by 'right', 'left', 'up' and 'down'.

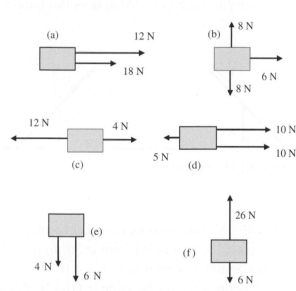

Figure 4.7 For question 1.

2 Find the magnitude and direction of the net force in Figure 4.8.

Figure 4.8 For question 2.

3 In Figure 4.9, what must *F* and θ be such that the three forces give a net force of zero?

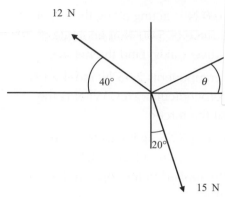

Figure 4.9 For question 3.

4 Why is it impossible for a mass to hang attached to two horizontal strings as shown in Figure 4.10?

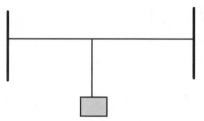

Figure 4.10 For question 4.

5 A mass is hanging from a string that is attached to the ceiling. A second piece of string (identical to the first) hangs from the lower end of the mass. (See Figure 4.11.)

Figure 4.11 For question 5.

Which string will break if:
(a) the bottom string is slowly pulled with ever increasing force;
(b) the bottom string is very abruptly pulled down?

6 A force of 10.0 N is acting along the negative x-axis and a force of 5.00 N at an angle of 20° with the positive x-axis. Find the net force.

7 A force has components 2.45 N and 4.23 N along two perpendicular axes. What is the magnitude of the force?

8 A weight of mass 12.5 kg hangs from very light pulleys as shown in Figure 4.12. What force must be applied to the rope so that the mass stays at rest?

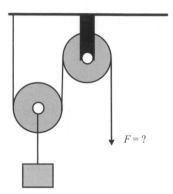

Figure 4.12 For question 8.

9 A mass of 2.00 kg rests on a rough horizontal table. The maximum frictional force between the mass and the table is 12 N. The block is attached to a hanging mass by a string that goes over a smooth pulley. What is the largest mass that can hang in this way without forcing the block to slide? (See Figure 4.13.)

Figure 4.13 For question 9.

10 A mass of 5.00 kg hangs attached to three strings as shown in Figure 4.14. Find the tension in each string. (Hint: Consider the equilibrium of the point where the strings join.)

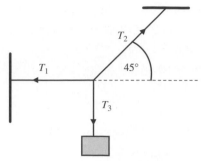

Figure 4.14 For question 10.

11 A rod of mass 5.00 kg is first pulled and then pushed at constant velocity by a force at 45° to the horizontal as shown in Figure 4.15. Assuming that in both cases the frictional force is horizontal and equal to 0.4 times the normal reaction force on the rod, find the force F in each case. What does this imply?

Figure 4.15 For question 11.

12 A 455 N crate is being pulled at constant velocity by a force directed at 30° to the horizontal as shown in Figure 4.16. The frictional force on the crate is 1163 N. What is the magnitude of the pulling force?

Figure 4.16 For question 12.

13 (a) A 2598 kg aeroplane is moving horizontally in a straight line at constant velocity. What is the upward force on the aeroplane?

(b) The plane is now diving (again at constant velocity) making an angle of 10° to the horizontal. Find the lift force on the plane assuming that it is normal to the velocity of the plane.

14 A mass M is connected with a string to a smaller mass m. The mass M is resting on an inclined plane and the string goes over a pulley at the top of the plane so that the mass m is hanging vertically, as shown in Figure 4.17. What must the angle of the plane be in order to have equilibrium?

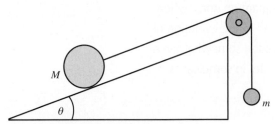

Figure 4.17 For question 14.

15 A mass m is attached to two identical springs of spring constant k. The other end of each spring is attached to the ceiling so that each makes an angle θ with the vertical, as shown in Figure 4.18. If the mass is in equilibrium, what is the extension of each spring?

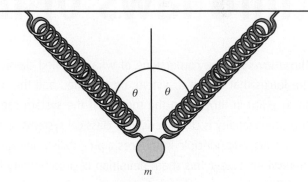

Figure 4.18 For question 15.

CHAPTER 2.5

Newton's second and third laws of mechanics

These laws are the cornerstone of what is called classical physics. They imply that, once the forces that act on a system are specified and the motion of the system is known at some point in time, then the motion of the system can be predicted at all future times. This predictability is characteristic of classical systems as opposed to quantum ones, where the uncertainty principle introduces a probabilistic interpretation on the future evolution of the system. Lately, this sharp definition of predictability has been eroded somewhat even for classical systems: chaotic behaviour can imply a loss of predictability in some cases.

This is the front page from Newton's book called *Principia* (Principles) in which he outlined his theories of the laws that governed the motion of objects.

Objectives

By the end of this chapter you should be able to:

- recognize situations of equilibrium, i.e. situations where *the net force and hence the acceleration are zero*;
- state the difference between *gravitational mass* and *inertial mass*;
- draw the forces on the body of interest and apply Newton's second law on that body, $F_{net} = m_i a$;
- recognize that the net force on a body is in the *same direction as the acceleration* of that body;
- identify pairs of forces that come from Newton's third law.

Newton's second law

This fundamental law asserts that:

> ▶ The net force on a body is proportional to that body's acceleration and is in the same direction as the acceleration. Mathematically
>
> $$\vec{F} = m_i \vec{a}$$
>
> where the constant of proportionality, m_i, is the *inertial mass* of the body.

Inertial and gravitational mass

The inertial mass, m_i, is measured in kilograms (kg).

The proper definition of **inertial mass** is:

> inertial mass = net force on a body divided by the acceleration of the body

In Chapter 2.3 we were introduced to the concept of the weight (i.e. the gravitational force) W of an object and stated that $W = mg$. It is not obvious that the mass that appears in the formula for weight should be the same as the inertial mass of Newton's second law. These two masses are in fact distinguished by their different names, inertial and gravitational mass. We may thus state that the weight is given by $W = m_g g$, where the constant m_g is the **gravitational mass** of the body: that is

> gravitational mass = gravitational force on a body divided by the acceleration due to gravity

Inertial and gravitational masses are the same, as the following example shows. Consider an application of Newton's second law to the case of a body that is allowed to fall freely without friction, air resistance, etc. (see Figure 5.1).

The diagram shows the net force on the freely falling body, which happens to be its weight, $W = m_g g$. By Newton's second law, the net force equals the inertial mass times the acceleration,

Figure 5.1 A mass falling to the ground acted upon by gravity.

and so

$$m_g g = m_i a$$
$$\Rightarrow a = \frac{m_g}{m_i} g$$

that is, the acceleration of the freely falling body is not exactly g as we thought. Experiments going back to Galileo, however, show us that indeed all bodies fall in vacuum with the same acceleration (the acceleration due to gravity) irrespective of their density, their mass, their shape and the material from which they are made. This *experimental fact* implies that the inertial and gravitational masses must be the same. Albert Einstein has shown that it is a natural consequence of his general theory of relativity (see Option G on relativity) that inertial and gravitational mass are the same. In what follows, inertial mass, gravitational mass and mass will be taken to mean the same thing.

> ▶ The equation $F = ma$ defines the unit of force, the newton (symbol N). One newton is the force required to accelerate a mass of 1 kg by 1 m s^{-2} in the direction of the force.

It is important to realize that the second law speaks of the net force on the body. Thus, if a number of individual forces act on a body, we must first find the net force by vector addition.

A simple everyday example of the second law is that when you jump from some height you bend your knees on landing. This is because by bending your knees you stretch out the time it takes to reduce your speed to zero, and thus your acceleration (deceleration) is least. This means that the force from the ground on to you is least.

Example questions

Q1

A man of mass $m = 70$ kg stands on the floor of an elevator. Find the force of reaction he experiences from the elevator floor when:
(a) the elevator is standing still;
(b) the elevator moves up at constant speed 3 m s^{-1};
(c) the elevator moves up with acceleration 4 m s^{-2};
(d) the elevator moves down with acceleration 4 m s^{-2}.

Answer

Two forces act on the man: his weight mg vertically down and the reaction force R from the floor vertically up.

(a) There is no acceleration and so by Newton's second law the net force on the man must be zero. Hence

$R = mg$
 $= 700$ N

(b) There is no acceleration and so again

$R = mg$
 $= 700$ N

(c) There is acceleration upwards. Hence

$R - mg = ma$

so

$R = mg + ma$
 $= 700$ N $+ 280$ N
 $= 980$ N

(d) We again have acceleration, but this time in the downward direction. Hence

$mg - R = ma$

so

$R = mg - ma$
 $= 700$ N $- 280$ N
 $= 420$ N

Note: In (c) the acceleration is up, so we find the net force in the upward direction. In (d) the acceleration is down, so we find the net force in

the downward direction. Newton's law in all cases involves accelerations and forces in the same direction.

Q2

A man of mass 70 kg is moving *upward* in an elevator at a constant speed of 3 m s^{-1}. The elevator comes to rest in a time of 2 s. What is the reaction force on the man from the elevator floor during the period of deceleration?

Answer

The acceleration experienced by the man is -1.5 m s^{-2}. So

$R - mg = ma$
$\Rightarrow R = mg + ma$
 $= 700 + (-105) = 595$ N

If, instead, the man was moving *downward* and then decelerated to rest, we would have

$mg - R = ma$
$\Rightarrow R = mg - ma$
 $= 700 - (-105) = 805$ N

Both cases are easily experienced in daily life. When the elevator goes up and then stops we feel 'lighter' during the deceleration period. When going down and about to stop, we feel 'heavier' during the deceleration period. The feeling of 'lightness' or 'heaviness' has to do with what reaction force we feel from the floor.

Q3

A hot air balloon of mass 150 kg is tied to the ground with a rope (of negligible mass). When the rope is cut, the balloon rises with an acceleration of 2 m s^{-2}. What was the tension in the rope?

Answer

The forces on the balloon originally are its weight, the upthrust and the tension (see Figure 5.2).

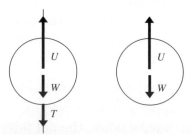

Figure 5.2.

Initially we have equilibrium and so $U = W + T$. After the rope is cut the net force is $U - W$ and so

$$U - W = ma$$
$$= 150 \times 2$$
$$= 300 \text{ N}$$

From the first equation

$$T = U - W = 300 \text{ N}$$

The next examples show how Newton's second law is applied when more than one mass is present.

Q4

Two blocks of mass 4.0 and 6.0 kg are joined by a string and rest on a frictionless horizontal table (see Figure 5.3). If a force of 100 N is applied horizontally on one of the blocks, find the acceleration of each block.

Figure 5.3.

Answer

Method 1: The net force on the 6.0 kg mass is $100 - T$ and on the 4.0 kg mass just T. Thus, applying Newton's second law separately on *each* mass

$$100 - T = 6a$$
$$T = 4a$$

Solving for a (by adding the two equations side by side) gives $a = 10 \text{ m s}^{-2}$ and the tension is thus

$$T = 4.0 \times 10$$
$$= 40 \text{ N}$$

Note: The free-body diagram makes it clear that the 100 N force acts *only* on the body to the right. It is a common mistake to say that the body to the left is also acted upon by the 100 N force.

Method 2: We may consider the two bodies as one of mass 10 kg. This is denoted by the dotted

line in Figure 5.4. The net force on the body is 100 N. Note that the tensions are irrelevant now since they cancel out. (They did not in Method 1 as they acted on *different* bodies. Now they act on the *same* body. They are now *internal* forces and these are irrelevant.)

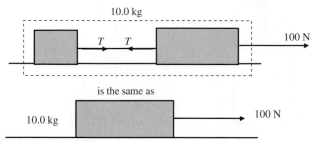

Figure 5.4.

Applying Newton's second law on the single body we have

$$100 = 10a$$
$$\Rightarrow a = 10 \text{ m s}^{-2}.$$

But to find the tension we must break up the combined body into the original two bodies. Newton's second law on the 4.0 kg body gives

$$T = 4a = 40 \text{ N}$$

(the tension on this block is the net force on the block). If we used the other block, we would see that the net force on it is $100 - T$ and so

$$100 - T = 6 \times 10$$
$$= 60$$

giving $T = 40 \text{ N}$ as before.

Q5

(Atwood's machine) Two masses of $m = 4.0 \text{ kg}$ and $M = 6.0 \text{ kg}$ are joined together by a string that passes over a pulley. The masses are held stationary and suddenly released. What is the acceleration of each mass?

Answer

Intuition tells us that the larger mass will start moving downward and the small mass will go up. So if we say that the larger mass's acceleration is a, then the other mass's acceleration will also be a in magnitude but, of course, in the opposite direction. The two accelerations are the same because the string cannot be extended.

Method 1: The forces on each mass are weight mg and tension T on m and weight Mg and tension T on M (see Figure 5.5).

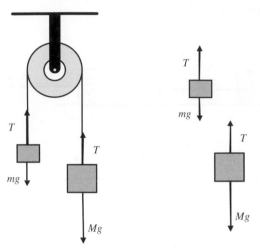

Figure 5.5.

Newton's second law applied to each mass states

$$T - mg = ma \qquad (1)$$
$$Mg - T = Ma \qquad (2)$$

Note these equations carefully. Each says that the net force on the mass in question is equal to that mass times that mass's acceleration. In the first equation we find the net force in the upward direction, because that is the direction of acceleration. In the second we find the net force downward, since that is the direction of acceleration in that case. We want to find the acceleration, so we simply add up these two equations side by side to find

$$Mg - mg = (m + M)a$$

hence

$$a = \frac{M - m}{M + m} g$$

(Note that if $M \gg m$, the acceleration tends to g (why?).) This shows clearly that if the two masses are equal then there is no acceleration. This is a convenient method for measuring g: Atwood's machine effectively 'slows down' g so the falling mass has a much smaller acceleration from which g can then be determined. Putting in the numbers for our example we find $a = 2.0$ m s^{-2}. Having

found the acceleration we may, if we wish, also find the tension in the string, T. Putting the value for a in formula (1) we find

$$T = m\frac{M - m}{M + m} g + mg$$
$$= 2\frac{Mm}{M + m} g$$
$$= 48 \text{ N}$$

(If $M \gg m$, the tension tends to $2mg$ (why?).)

Method 2: We treat the two masses as one body and apply Newton's second law on this body (but this is trickier than in the previous example) – see Figure 5.6.

Figure 5.6.

In this case the net force is $Mg - mg$ and, since this force acts on a body of mass $M + m$, the acceleration is found as before from $F = \text{mass} \times$ acceleration. Note that the tension T does not appear in this case, being now an internal force.

Q6

In Figure 5.7, a block of mass M is connected to a smaller mass m through a string that goes over a pulley. Ignoring friction, find the acceleration of each mass and the tension in the string.

Figure 5.7.

Answer

Method 1: The forces are shown in Figure 5.7. Thus

$$mg - T = ma$$
$$T = Ma$$

from which (adding the two equations side by side)

$$a = \frac{mg}{m+M}$$

(If $M \gg m$ the acceleration tends to zero (why?).)
If $M = 8.0$ kg and $m = 2.0$ kg, this gives
$a = 2.0$ m s^{-2}. Hence

$$T = \frac{Mmg}{m+M}$$
$$= 16.0 \text{ N}$$

Method 2: Treating the two bodies as one results in the situation shown in Figure 5.8.

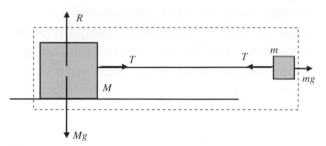

Figure 5.8.

The net force on the mass $M + m$ is mg. Hence

$$mg = (M+m)a$$
$$\Rightarrow a = \frac{mg}{m+M}$$

The tension can then be found as before.

Q7

Consider finally 100 blocks each of mass $m = 1.0$ kg that are placed next to each other in a straight line, as shown in Figure 5.9.

Figure 5.9.

A force $F = 100$ N is applied to the block at the left. What force does the 60th block exert on the 61st (see Figure 5.10)?

free-body diagram for the last 40 blocks

Figure 5.10.

Answer

To answer the question, we treat the 100 blocks as one body, in which case the net force on the system is 100 N. Since the mass is 100 kg, the acceleration of each block is 1 m s^{-2}.

Let T be the required force. It is the net force on the body inside the dotted line of mass 40 kg. Since this force accelerates a mass of 40 kg by 1 m s^{-2}, $T = ma = 40$ N.

Terminal velocity

When a body moves through a fluid (a gas or liquid), it experiences an opposing force that depends on the speed of the body. If the speed is small, the opposing force is proportional to the speed, whereas for larger speeds the force becomes proportional to the square of the speed. Consider, for example, a body falling through air. The forces on the body are its weight, mg, and the opposing force, which we assume is proportional to the speed, $F = kv$. Initially the speed is small, so the body falls with an acceleration that is essentially that due to gravity. As the speed increases, so does the opposing force and hence, after a while, it will become equal to the weight. In that case the acceleration becomes zero and the body continues to fall with a *constant* velocity, called *terminal velocity*. Figure 5.11 shows a body falling from rest and acquiring a terminal velocity of 50 m s^{-1} after about 25 s. The acceleration of the body is initially that due to gravity but becomes zero after about 25 s.

$$mg = kv_T \quad \Rightarrow \quad v_T = \frac{mg}{k}$$

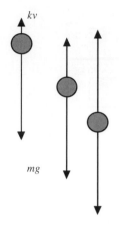

$$mg = kv_T \Rightarrow v_T = \frac{mg}{k}$$

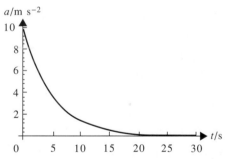

Figure 5.11 The opposing force grows as the speed increases and eventually becomes equal to the weight. From that point on, the acceleration is zero and the body has achieved its terminal velocity.

The inclined plane

The motion of a body along a straight line that is kept at an angle to the horizontal (inclined plane) is an important application of Newton's laws. The following is an example. A mass of $m = 2.0$ kg is held on a frictionless inclined plane of 30°. What is the acceleration of the mass if it is released?

There are two forces acting on the mass (see Figure 5.12).

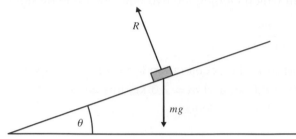

Figure 5.12 A mass on an inclined plane.

The two forces are: its weight vertically down of magnitude mg, and the reaction from the plane, which is perpendicular to the plane, of magnitude R. We can find the components of these two forces along two mutually perpendicular axes, one being along the plane (see Figure 5.13). The force R is already along one of the axes so we don't bother with that. But mg is not.

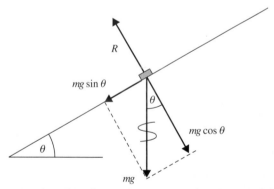

Figure 5.13 We take components along axes that lie along the plane and normally to the plane.

The magnitude of the component of mg along the plane is $mg \sin \theta$, where $\theta = 30°$ is the angle of the incline. This component lies down the plane. The other component is $mg \cos \theta$, in the direction perpendicular to the plane. In that direction there is no acceleration, hence the net force there is zero: that is, $R - mg \cos \theta = 0$. This tells us that $R = mg \cos \theta$. In the direction along the plane, there is a single unbalanced force, namely $mg \sin \theta$, and therefore by Newton's second law, this force will equal mass times acceleration in that same direction: that is

$$mg \sin \theta = ma$$

where a is the unknown acceleration. Hence, we find

$$a = g \sin \theta$$

This is an important result and we will make use of it many times. Note that the acceleration does not depend on the mass. For the numerical values of this problem we find $a = 5.0 \text{ m s}^{-2}$.

You may wonder why we took as our axes the ones along and perpendicular to the inclined plane. The answer is that we did not have to choose these axes. Any other set would have done. This choice, however, is the most convenient, because it exploits the fact that the acceleration will take place along the plane, so we choose that direction as one of our axes. If we had chosen another set of axes, say a horizontal and a vertical one, then we would find acceleration along both of these axes. Acceleration, of course, is a vector and if we combined these two accelerations, we would find the same acceleration (in magnitude and direction) as above. Try to work out the details.

An accelerometer

Consider a mass that is hanging from a string of length L, which is attached to the ceiling of a train. What will be the angle the string makes with the vertical if (a) the train moves forward with a constant speed of 3 m s^{-1}, or (b) moves forward with an acceleration of 4 m s^{-2}? If the train moves with constant speed in the horizontal direction, the acceleration in this direction is zero. Hence the net force in the horizontal direction must also be zero. The only forces on the mass are its weight vertically down, and the tension T of the string along the string. So, to produce zero force in the horizontal direction the string must be vertical. In case (b) there is acceleration in the horizontal direction and hence there must also be a net force in this

direction. The string will therefore make an angle θ with the vertical (see Figure 5.14).

Figure 5.14 When the forces are not in the direction of acceleration, we must take components.

In this case we take components of the forces on the mass along the horizontal and vertical directions. In the horizontal direction we have only the component of T, which is $T \sin \theta$, and in the vertical direction we have $T \cos \theta$ upward and mg downward. Therefore

$$T \sin \theta = ma \quad \text{and} \quad T \cos \theta = mg$$

Hence, $a = g \tan \theta$. Note that the mass does not enter into the expression for a. This is actually a crude device that can be used to measure acceleration – an accelerometer.

Newton's third law

Newton's third law states that:

> ▶ If body A exerts a force F on body B, then body B exerts an equal but opposite force on body A. (See Figure 5.15.)

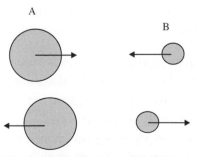

Figure 5.15 The two bodies exert equal and opposite forces on each other.

Make sure you understand that these equal and opposite forces act on *different* bodies. Thus, you cannot use this law to claim that it is impossible to ever have a net force on a body because for every force on it there is also an equal and opposite force. Here are a few examples of this law:

- You stand on roller-skates facing a wall. You push on the wall and you move away from it. This is because you exerted a force on the wall and in turn the wall exerted an equal and opposite force on you, making you accelerate away.

- You are about to step off a boat onto the dock. Your foot exerts a force on the dock, and in turn the dock exerts a force on you (your foot) in the opposite direction making you (and the boat) move away from the dock. (You probably fall in the water!)

- A helicopter hovers in air. Its rotors exert a force downward on the air. Thus, the air exerts the upward force on the helicopter that keeps it from falling.

- A book of mass 2 kg is allowed to fall feely. The earth exerts a force on the book, namely the weight of the book of about 20 N. Thus, the book exerts an equal and opposite force on the earth – a force upward equal to 20 N.

Be careful with situations where two forces are equal and opposite but have nothing to do with the third law. For example, a block of mass 3 kg resting on a horizontal table has two forces acting on it. Its weight of 30 N and the reaction from the table that is also 30 N. These two forces are equal and opposite, but they are acting on the same body and so have nothing to do with Newton's third law. (We have seen in the last bullet point above the force that pairs with the weight of the block. The one that pairs with the reaction force is a downward force on the table.)

Newton's third law also applies to cases where the force between two bodies acts at a distance: that is, the two bodies are separated by a certain distance. For example, two electric charges will exert an electric force on each other and any two masses will attract each other with the gravitational force. These forces must be equal and opposite. (See Figure 5.16.)

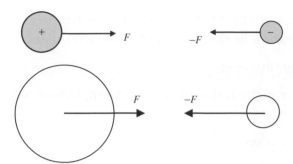

Figure 5.16 The two charges and the two masses are different but the forces are equal and opposite.

Questions

1 (a) Under what circumstances would a constant force result in an increasing acceleration on a body?
  (b) Under what circumstances would a constant force result in zero acceleration on a body?

2 A car of mass 1354 kg finds itself on a muddy road. If the force from the engine pushing the car forward exceeds 575 N, the wheels slip (i.e. they rotate without rolling). What is the maximum acceleration that the car can move with on this road?

3 The net force on a mass of 1.00 kg initially at rest is 1.00 N and acts for 1.00 s. What will the velocity of the mass be at the end of the 1.00 s interval of time?

4 A mass of 2.00 kg is acted upon by two forces of 4.00 N and 10.0 N. What is the smallest and largest acceleration these two forces can produce on the mass?

5 A man of mass m stands in an elevator. Find the reaction force from the elevator floor on the man when:
  (a) the elevator is standing still;
  (b) the elevator moves up at constant speed v;
  (c) the elevator accelerates down with acceleration a;
  (d) the elevator accelerates down with acceleration $a = g$.
  (e) What happens when $a > g$?

6 A bird is in a glass cage that hangs from a spring scale. Compare the readings of the scale in the following cases.
  (a) The bird is sitting in the cage.

(b) The bird is hovering in the cage.

(c) The bird is moving upward with acceleration.

(d) The bird is accelerating downward.

(e) The bird is moving upward with constant velocity.

7 Get in an elevator and stretch out your arm holding your heavy physics book. Press the button to go up. What do you observe happening to your stretched arm? What happens as the elevator comes to a stop at the top floor? What happens when you press the button to go down and what happens when the elevator again stops? Explain your observations carefully using the second law of mechanics.

8 A block of mass 2.0 kg rests on top of another block of mass 10.0 kg that itself rests on a frictionless table (see Figure 5.17). The largest frictional force that can develop between the two blocks is 16 N. Calculate the largest force with which the bottom block can be pulled so that both blocks move together without sliding on each other.

Figure 5.17 For question 8.

9 Figure 5.18 shows a person in an elevator pulling on a rope that goes over a pulley and is attached to the top of the elevator. Identify all the forces shown and for each find the reaction force (according to Newton's third law). On what body does each reaction force act?

Figure 5.18 For questions 9 and 10.

10 Take the mass of the elevator shown in Figure 5.18 to be 30.0 kg and that of the person to be 70.0 kg. If the elevator accelerates upwards at 0.500 m s^{-2}, find the reaction force on the person from the elevator floor.

11 A small passenger car and a fully loaded truck collide head-on. Which vehicle experiences the greater force?

12 What force does a man of mass 80.0 kg exert on the earth as he falls freely after jumping from a table 1 m high from the surface of the earth?

13 Three blocks rest on a horizontal frictionless surface, as shown in Figure 5.19. A force of 20.0 N is applied horizontally to the right on the block of mass 2.0 kg. Find the individual forces acting on each mass. Identify action–reaction pairs.

Figure 5.19 For question 13.

14 A (massless) string hangs vertically from a support in the ceiling. A mass of 10.0 kg is attached to the other end of the string. What is the force the string exerts on the support?

15 A block of mass 15.0 kg rests on a horizontal table. A force of 50.0 N is applied vertically downward on the block. Calculate the force that the block exerts on the table.

16 A block of mass 10.0 kg rests on top of a bigger block of mass 20.0 kg, which in turn rests on a horizontal table (see Figure 5.20). Find the individual forces acting on each block. Identify action–reaction pairs according to Newton's third law.

Figure 5.20 For question 16.

17 If a vertical downward force of 50.0 N acts on the top block in Figure 5.20, what are the forces on each block now.

18 A massless string has the same tension throughout its length. Can you explain why?

19 Look back at Figure 5.18. The person has a mass of 70.0 kg and the elevator a mass of 30.0 kg. If the force the person exerts on the elevator floor is 300.0 N, find the acceleration of the elevator ($g = 10$ m s^{-2}).

20 (a) Calculate the tension in the string joining the two masses in Figure 5.21.
   (b) If the position of the masses is interchanged, will the tension change?

Figure 5.21 For question 20.

21 One hundred equal masses $m = 1.0$ kg are joined by strings as shown in Figure 5.22. The first mass is acted upon by a force $F = 100$ N. What is the tension in the string joining the 60th mass to the 61st?

Figure 5.22 For question 21.

22 A mass of 3.0 kg is acted upon by three forces of 4.0 N, 6.0 N and 9.0 N and is in equilibrium. Convince yourself that these forces can indeed be in equilibrium. If the 9.0 N force is suddenly removed, what will the acceleration of the mass be?

23 What is the tension in the string joining the two masses in Figure 5.23? What is the acceleration of each mass?

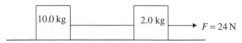

Figure 5.23

24 Two bodies are joined by a string and are pulled up an inclined plane that makes an angle of 30° to the horizontal, as shown in Figure 5.24. Calculate the tension in the string when:
   (a) the bodies move with constant speed;
   (b) the bodies move up the plane with an acceleration of 2.0 m s^{-2}.
   (c) What is the value of F in each case?

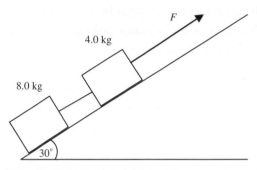

Figure 5.24 For question 24.

25 The velocity–time graph in Figure 5.25 is a student's graph for the vertical motion of a person who jumps from a helicopter and a few seconds later opens a parachute.
   (a) Using the laws of mechanics *carefully* explain the shape of the curve. (When does the parachute open? When does the air resistance force reach its maximum value? Is the air resistance force constant?)
   (b) How would you improve on the student's graph?

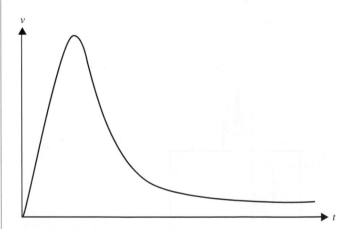

Figure 5.25 For question 25.

Linear momentum

This chapter introduces the concept of momentum and, by using Newton's second and third laws, the law of momentum conservation is derived. This law is the basis for analysing collisions.

Objectives

By the end of this chapter you should be able to:

*   state the definition of *momentum* ($\vec{p} = m\vec{v}$) and appreciate that momentum is a *vector* quantity;
*   state the definition of *average net force* in terms of momentum, $\vec{F}_{net} = \frac{\Delta p}{\Delta t}$;
*   state the definition of *impulse* as the change in momentum and understand that the *area under a force–time graph* is the impulse of the force;
*   derive the *law of conservation of momentum* using Newton's second and third laws;
*   identify situations in which *momentum is conserved* and solve related problems.

The concept of momentum

Momentum is a very important and useful concept in mechanics.

▶ The momentum of a body of mass m and velocity $\vec{v}$ is defined to be

$$\vec{p} = m\vec{v}$$

Momentum is a vector quantity whose direction is the same as that of the velocity of the body. The unit of momentum is kg m s^{-1} or, equivalently, N s.

In terms of momentum, Newton's second law of mechanics can be stated as

$$\vec{F}_{net} = \frac{\Delta \vec{p}}{\Delta t}$$

that is, the (average) net force on a body equals the *rate of change* of the body's momentum.

If the mass of the body is *constant*, this reduces to the familiar $\vec{F}_{net} = m\vec{a}$. This is because in that case

$$
\begin{aligned}
\vec{F}_{net} &= \frac{\Delta \vec{p}}{\Delta t} \\
&= \frac{m\vec{v}_f - m\vec{v}_i}{\Delta t} \\
&= m\frac{\vec{v}_f - \vec{v}_i}{\Delta t} \\
&= m\frac{\Delta \vec{v}}{\Delta t} \\
&= m\vec{a}
\end{aligned}
$$

The advantage of the formulation of Newton's second law in terms of momentum is that it can be used also in cases where the mass of the body is *changing* (such as, for example, in the motion of a rocket).

Example questions

Q1

A 0.100 kg ball moving at 5 m s^{-1} bounces off a vertical wall without a change in its speed (see Figure 6.1). If the collision with the wall lasted for 0.1 s, what force was exerted on the wall?

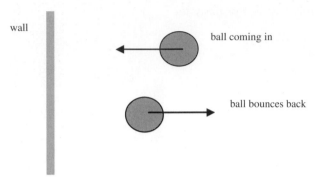

wall

ball coming in

ball bounces back

Figure 6.1.

Answer

The momentum of the ball changed from −0.5 N s to 0.5 N s in 0.1 s (note the signs: momentum is a vector). The magnitude of the average force on the ball is thus

$$|\vec{F}_{net}| = \left|\frac{\Delta \vec{p}}{\Delta t}\right|$$

$$= \frac{0.5 - (-0.5)\,N\,s}{0.1\,s} = 10\,N$$

This is also the force exerted by the ball on the wall by Newton's third law.

Q2

A 0.50 kg ball bounces vertically off a hard surface. A graph of velocity versus time is shown in Figure 6.2. Find the magnitude of the momentum change of the ball during the bounce. The ball stayed in contact with floor for 0.15 s. What average force did the ball exert on the floor?

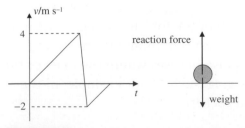

Figure 6.2.

Answer

The initial momentum is $0.50 \times 4 = 2$ N s. The final is $0.50 \times (-2) = -1$ N s. The magnitude of the change is therefore 3 N s. The forces on the ball during contact are its weight and the reaction from the floor. Thus

$$|\vec{F}_{net}| = R - mg$$

$$= \left|\frac{\Delta \vec{p}}{\Delta t}\right|$$

$$= \frac{3.0\,N\,s}{0.15\,s}$$

$$= 20\,N$$

so

$$R = 20 + 5$$
$$= 25\,N$$

Q3

Bullets of mass 30 g are being fired from a gun with a speed of 300 m s^{-1} at a rate of 20 per second. What force is being exerted on the gun?

Answer

Using the definition of force involving rate of change of momentum as above, we see that the momentum of one bullet changes from zero before it is fired to mv after it has been fired. If there are ΔN bullets being fired in time Δt, then the magnitude of the momentum change per second is

$$\frac{\Delta p}{\Delta t} = \frac{\Delta N}{\Delta t} mv$$

$$= 20\,s^{-1} \times 0.030\,kg \times 300\,m\,s^{-1}$$

$$= 180\,N$$

Q4

Mass falls at a rate of μ kg s^{-1} onto a conveyor belt which moves at constant speed v (see Figure 6.3). What force must be exerted on the belt to make it turn at constant speed?

Figure 6.3.

Answer

The horizontal momentum of the falling mass increases from zero when it first hits the belt to mv. The rate of increase of momentum is thus μv and this is the force on the belt, $F = \mu v$.

Q5

A helicopter rotor whose length is $R = 5.0$ m pushes air downwards with a speed v. Assuming that the density of air is constant at $\rho = 1.20$ kg m^{-3} and the mass of the helicopter is 1200 kg, find v. You may assume that the rotor forces the air in a circle of radius R (spanned by the rotor) to move with the downward speed v.

Answer

The momentum of the air under the rotor is mv, where m is the mass of air in a circle of radius 5.0 m. In time Δt the mass is enclosed in a cylinder of radius R and height $v\Delta t$. Thus, the momentum of this mass is $\rho\pi R^2 v^2 \Delta t$ and its rate of change is $\rho\pi R^2 v^2$. This is the force on the helicopter upwards, which must equal the helicopter's weight of 12 000 N. So

$$\rho\pi R^2 v^2 = Mg$$

$$\Rightarrow v = \sqrt{\frac{Mg}{\rho\pi R^2}}$$

Thus, $v = 11.3$ m s^{-1}.

Impulse

Newton's second law, in terms of momentum change, states that the *average* net force on a body (here we use magnitudes of forces and momenta) is given by

$$\bar{F}_{net} = \frac{\Delta p}{\Delta t}$$

If Δt is infinitesimally small, this gives the instantaneous force on the body. If not, it gives the *average* force on the body, $\bar{F}$. We may then write

$$\Delta p = \bar{F}\Delta t$$

Figure 6.4 shows a ball in contact with a tennis racket. The magnitude of the impulse delivered

to the ball is Δp and equals the product of the magnitude of the average force on the ball times the interval of time for which the contact lasts.

Figure 6.4 The momentum of the ball changes as a result of the collision with the tennis racket. This means there is a force on the ball while it is in contact with the racket.

The quantity $\Delta p = \bar{F}\Delta t$ is called the *impulse* of the force and has the following interpretation in terms of a graph that shows the variation of the force with time (see Figure 6.5).

▶ Impulse is the area under the curve of a force–time graph and equals the *total* momentum change of the mass.

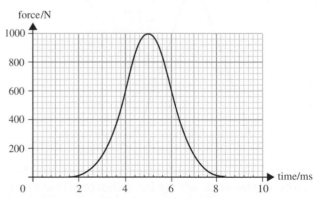

Figure 6.5 The area under the force–time graph gives the total momentum change of the body the force acts upon.

In the graph of Figure 6.5 the area is about 2.5 N s (can you verify this?) and the force acts for about 6.0 ms. This means that during the 6.0 ms the momentum of the body changed by

2.5 N s. The maximum force that acted on the body was 1000 N and the average force

$$\bar{F} = \frac{\Delta p}{\Delta t}$$
$$= \frac{2.5}{6.0 \times 10^{-3}} \text{ N}$$
$$\approx 470 \text{ N}$$

Consider, then, a body of mass m that moves with velocity v and is brought to rest by a non-constant force F. The change in the momentum of the body is $\Delta p = 0 - mv = -mv$. (We may ignore the sign if we are interested only in the magnitude of the momentum change.) Let us examine two possibilities. In the first case, the force brings the body to rest over a longer period of time compared with the second. The graphs of force versus time might be as shown in Figure 6.6. The thick curve represents the force that brings the body to rest over a short time. This force is larger, on average, than the force that brings the body to rest over a longer time interval. The areas under the curves are the same since they both represent the change in the momentum of the body, which is mv in both cases.

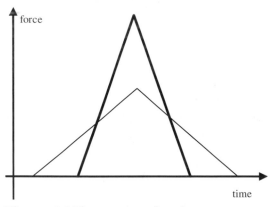

Figure 6.6 The areas under the two curves are the same so the force acting for a shorter time must be larger on average.

These graphs can be thought of as idealizations of the forces experienced by a driver of a car that is brought suddenly to rest in a crash. (What are more realistic graphs?) A driver not wearing a safety belt will quickly come to rest after hitting the steering wheel or the windscreen and will experience a large force. A driver wearing a safety belt in a car with an air-bag, however, will come to rest over a longer period of time since the belt and the air-bag start bringing him to rest earlier and allow him to move forward a bit while coming to rest. The force he experiences is thus correspondingly smaller.

Example questions

Q6 ▬▬▬▬▬▬▬▬▬▬▬▬▬▬▬▬▬▬▬

A ball of mass 0.250 kg moves on a frictionless horizontal floor and hits a vertical wall with speed 5.0 m s^{-1}. The ball rebounds with speed 4.0 m s^{-1}. If the ball was in contact with the wall for 0.150 s, find the average force that acted on the ball.

Answer

The magnitude of the change in the ball's momentum is (remember that momentum is a vector)

$$\Delta p = p_f - p_i$$
$$= 0.250 \times 4.0 - (-0.250 \times 5.0)$$
$$= 1.0 - (-1.25)$$
$$= 2.25 \text{ N s}$$

Hence

$$F_{ave} = \frac{\Delta p}{\Delta t}$$
$$= \frac{2.25 \text{ N s}}{0.150 \text{ s}}$$
$$= 15 \text{ N}$$

Q7 ▬▬▬▬▬▬▬▬▬▬▬▬▬▬▬▬▬▬▬

The force in example question 6 is assumed to vary with time as shown in Figure 6.7.
Deduce the *maximum* force that acted on the ball.

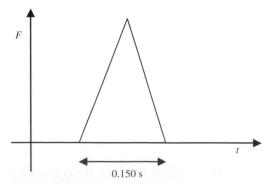

Figure 6.7.

A second, harder, ball of identical mass to the first also bounces off the wall with the same initial and final speed, but since it is harder it stays in contact with the wall for only 0.125 s. What is the maximum force exerted by the wall on this ball?

Answer

The area under the curve is the total change in the ball's momentum, which we found to be $\Delta p = 2.25$ N s. The area is a triangle and so

$\frac{1}{2} \times F_{max} \times 0.150 = 2.25$

$\Rightarrow F_{max} = 30$ N

The area under the force–time graph in the case of the harder ball will be the same. Thus

$\frac{1}{2} \times F_{max} \times 0.125 = 2.25$

$\Rightarrow F_{max} = 36$ N

Q8

A force of 1000.0 N acts on a body of 40.0 kg initially at rest for a time interval of 0.0500 s. What is the velocity of the mass?

Answer

The impulse is

$F\Delta t = 1000 \times 0.05$ N s

$= 50.0$ N s

and this equals the amount by which the body's momentum increases. The velocity is thus

$\frac{50}{40}$ m s$^{-1} = 1.25$ m s^{-1}

Q9

A force F varies with time according to $F = 4 + 12t$, where F is in newtons and t in seconds. The force acts on a block of mass $m = 2.00$ kg, which is initially at rest on a frictionless horizontal surface. F makes an angle of 30° with the horizontal (see Figure 6.8). When will the force lift the body from the table? What will the velocity of the body be at that instant?

Figure 6.8.

Answer

The block will leave the table when the normal reaction force R becomes zero.

$R + F \sin 30° = mg$

so

$F = 40$ N when $R = 0$.

This happens when $t = 3.0$ s. The horizontal component of F is

$(4 + 12t) \cos 30° = 3.64 + 10.39t$

The change in the body's momentum in the horizontal direction is the area under the F_x versus t graph from $t = 0$ to $t = 3.0$ s. This area is 57.7 N s. Thus, the horizontal component of velocity is 28.8 m s^{-1}. The vertical component is zero.

The law of conservation of momentum

Given a system of two masses say m_1 and m_2 with velocities $\vec{v}_1$ and $\vec{v}_2$, the total momentum of the system is defined as the vector sum of the individual momenta

$$P_{total} = m_1\vec{v}_1 + m_2\vec{v}_2$$

Example questions

Q10

Two masses of 2.0 kg and 3.0 kg move to the right with speeds of 4.0 m s^{-1} and 5.0 m s^{-1}, respectively. What is the total momentum of the system?

Answer

$P = (2 \times 4 + 3 \times 5)$ N s

$= 23$ N s

Q11

A mass of 2.0 kg moves to the right with a speed of 10.0 m s^{-1} and a mass of 4.0 kg moves to the left with a speed of 8.0 m s^{-1}. What is the total momentum of the system?

swer

$$= (2 \times 10 - 4 \times 8)\,\text{N s}$$

$$= -12\,\text{N s}$$

The minus sign means that the direction of this total momentum is to the left.

Consider now two bodies A and B of masses m_A and m_B on a horizontal frictionless table. The forces on each mass are the weight and the normal reaction force from the table, which equals the weight. Thus, the net force on each mass is zero. If these masses have some initial velocity, then by Newton's first law they continue moving with that same velocity until a force acts on them. If the bodies move in such a way that they will collide at some point in time, then at the point of collision a force will be exerted on each body. As a result of this force, each mass will change its velocity and thus its momentum. If we consider the two bodies together as a system, then the net force on the system is zero. As we mentioned already, the weight of each mass is cancelled by the reaction force and the only force that remains is the force during the collision. However, from Newton's third law, the force that body A experiences must be equal and opposite to that which B experiences. Thus, even though there is a net force acting on each mass for the duration of the collision, the net force on the *system* of the two masses is zero. We see that at all times the net external force on the *system* is zero. (See Figure 6.9.)

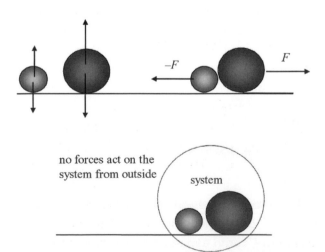

no forces act on the system from outside

system

Figure 6.9 The total momentum of an isolated system is conserved.

A system in which no external forces act is called an *isolated* system. Isolated systems have the property that the total momentum stays the same at all times. If the system consists of a number of bodies (in our example, two) then the total momentum is defined as the sum of the individual momenta of the bodies in the system. If, before the collision, the bodies A and B had velocity vectors $\vec{v}_A$ and $\vec{v}_B$, then the total momentum of the system is

$$\vec{P}_{\text{total}} = m_A\vec{v}_A + m_B\vec{v}_B$$

We should remind ourselves that momentum is a vector and thus when we say that the total momentum is the sum of the individual momenta we mean the *vector sum*.

If, as a result of the collision, the two bodies now have velocity vectors $\vec{u}_A$ and $\vec{u}_B$, then the total momentum is now

$$\vec{P}_{\text{total}} = m_A\vec{u}_A + m_B\vec{u}_B$$

and equals the total momentum before the collision. The individual momenta have changed as a result of the collision but their vector sum is the same. This is the law of conservation of linear momentum.

When no external forces act on a system, the total momentum of the system is conserved (i.e. stays the same).

Example questions

Q12

Let a mass of 3.0 kg be standing still and a second mass of 5.0 kg come along and hit it with velocity 4.0 m s^{-1}. Suppose that the smaller mass moves off with a speed of 3.0 m s^{-1}. What happens to the larger mass? (See Figure 6.10.)

Answer

The system of the two masses is an isolated system as we discussed above. Thus, momentum will be conserved. Before the collision the total momentum of the system was $(3.0 \times 0 + 5.0 \times 4.0)\,\text{N s} = 20\,\text{N s}$. This must also be the total momentum after the collision. But after the collision the total

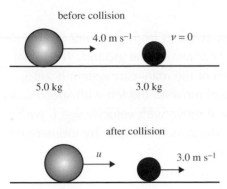

Figure 6.10.

momentum is $(3.0 \times 3.0 + 5.0 \times u)$ N s where u is the unknown speed of the larger mass. Thus $20 = 9.0 + 5.0u$ and so $u = 2.2$ m s^{-1}.

Q13

Two masses of 2.0 kg and 4.0 kg are held with a compressed spring between them. If the masses are released, the spring will push them away from each other. If the smaller mass moves off with a speed of 6.0 m s^{-1}, what is the speed of the other mass? (See Figure 6.11.)

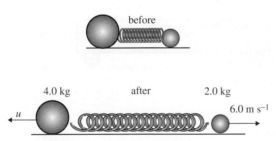

Figure 6.11.

Answer

Here our system consists of the two masses and the spring. There are no external forces here, since gravity is cancelled by the upward reaction forces from the table where the masses rest. The only force is the elastic force of the spring with which it pushes the masses away. But this is not an external force so total momentum will stay the same. The spring exerts equal and opposite forces on each mass. Before the masses start moving apart, the total momentum is zero, since nothing moves. After the masses move away, the total momentum is

$(2 \times 6 - 4 \times u)$ N s, where u is the unknown speed of the heavy mass. Note the minus sign. The masses are moving in opposite directions, so one of the velocities (and also one of the momenta) is negative. Thus, $12 - 4u = 0$ and so $u = 3.0$ m s^{-1}.

Q14

A ball is released from some height above the earth's surface. Treat the ball as the entire system under consideration. As the ball falls, is the momentum of the system conserved?

Answer

No, because there is an external force acting on the ball, namely its weight.

Q15

A ball is released from some height above the earth's surface. Treat the ball and the earth as the entire system under consideration. As the ball falls, is the momentum of the system conserved?

Answer

Yes, because there are no external forces on the system. The earth exerts a force on the ball but the ball exerts an equal and opposite force on the earth. Hence the net force on the earth–ball system is zero.

(This means that as the ball falls, the earth moves up a bit!)

Proof of momentum conservation

We will now prove the law of momentum conservation for an isolated system consisting of two bodies A and B. It is easy to generalize to systems with more than two bodies. Let the two bodies have masses m_a and m_b with velocities before the collision $\vec{v}_a$ and $\vec{v}_b$. As a result of the collision the two bodies change their velocities to $\vec{u}_a$ and $\vec{u}_b$. Let $\vec{F}$ stand for the force that A experiences during the collision, which lasted a time Δt. (See Figure 6.12.)

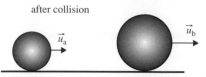

after collision

Figure 6.12 Diagram used for proof of the law of conservation of momentum.

Then, by Newton's second law

$$\vec{F} = \frac{\Delta \vec{p}_a}{\Delta t}$$

$$= \frac{m_a \vec{u}_a - m_a \vec{v}_a}{\Delta t}$$

The force experienced by B is $-\vec{F}$ (Newton's third law) and so

$$-\vec{F} = \frac{\Delta \vec{p}_b}{\Delta t}$$

$$= \frac{m_b \vec{u}_b - m_b \vec{v}_b}{\Delta t}$$

Thus

$$m_a \vec{u}_a - m_a \vec{v}_a = -(m_b \vec{u}_b - m_b \vec{v}_b)$$
$$\Rightarrow m_a \vec{v}_a + m_b \vec{v}_b = m_a \vec{u}_a + m_b \vec{u}_b$$

which states precisely that the total momentum before and after the collision is the same.

Example questions

Q16

(a) A man of mass m stands on a cart of mass M that rests on a horizontal frictionless surface. If the man begins to walk with velocity v *with respect to the cart*, how will the cart move? See Figure 6.13.

(b) What happens when the man gets to the edge of the cart and stops walking?

Figure 6.13.

Answer

(a) Let us look at things from the point of view of an observer at rest on the ground. The initial momentum of the man–cart system is zero. The cart will move to the left with speed u, so the man will move with velocity $v - u$ *with respect to the ground*. Hence, by momentum conservation

$$0 = m(v - u) - Mu$$
$$\Rightarrow u = \frac{mv}{M + m}$$

(b) When the man stops, the cart will stop as well, so the total momentum of the man–cart system remains zero.

Q17

A cart of mass M moves with constant velocity v on a frictionless road (see Figure 6.14). Rain is falling vertically on to the road and begins to fill the cart at a steady rate of μ kg per second. Find the velocity of the cart t seconds later.

Figure 6.14.

Answer

We look at things from the point of view of an observer on the ground. After a time of t s the mass of the cart is $M + \mu t$. Momentum is conserved as there are no external forces. So if u is the velocity after time t, we must have

$$Mv = (M + \mu t)u$$
$$\Rightarrow u = \frac{M}{M + \mu t}v$$

HL only

Q18

A cart of mass M is filled with water and moves with velocity v on a frictionless road. Water begins to leak from a small hole in the base of the cart and falls out at a rate of μ kg per second. (See Figure 6.15.) What happens to the velocity of the cart?

Figure 6.15.

Answer

We look at things from the point of view of *an observer on the ground* and take as our system the cart plus *all* the water (including that which is falling out). The falling water still moves with the same velocity to the right as far as the ground observer is concerned, and since there are no external forces, momentum is conserved and there can be no change of velocity.

We can also get the same answer if we take as our system the cart and the water *inside* the cart. As far as the ground observer is concerned, the water leaves the cart with a horizontal velocity v to the right. Thus, there is a force on the cart directed to the *left* of magnitude μv. Hence, the observer deduces that, since net force = rate of change of momentum,

$$-\mu v = \frac{\delta M}{\delta t}v + M\frac{\delta v}{\delta t}$$
$$= -\mu v + M\frac{\delta v}{\delta t}$$
$$\Rightarrow \delta v = 0$$

Two-dimensional collisions

Consider a stationary body of mass 12 kg that is hit by a 4.0 kg mass moving at 12 m s^{-1}. The collision is not head-on, and the bodies move at an angle to the original direction of motion of the 4.0 kg body as shown in Figure 6.16 (the view is from the top). How can we find the speeds of the two bodies after the collision?

Figure 6.16.

Momentum is a vector and is conserved. This means that

x-component of total momentum before
= *x*-component of total momentum after

y-component of total momentum before
= *y*-component of total momentum after

Thus

$$4 \times 12 = 4 \times v \cos 60° + 12 \times u \cos 30°$$
$$0 = 4 \times v \sin 60° - 12 \times u \sin 30°$$

and so

$$2 \times v + 10.392 \times u = 48$$
$$3.464 \times v - 6 \times u = 0$$

Solving simultaneously gives

$$v = 6.0 \text{ m s}^{-1}$$
$$u = 3.5 \text{ m s}^{-1}.$$

Questions

1 The momentum of a ball increased by 12.0 N s as a result of a force that acted on the ball for 2.00 s. What was the average force on the ball?

2 A 0.150 kg ball moving horizontally at 3.00 m s^{-1} collides normally with a vertical wall and bounces back with the same speed.
   (a) What is the impulse delivered to the ball?
   (b) If the ball was in contact with the wall for 0.125 s, find the average force exerted by the ball on the wall.

3 The bodies in Figure 6.17 suffer a head-on collision and stick to each other afterwards. Find their common velocity.

Figure 6.17 For question 3.

4 Two masses of 2.00 kg and 4.00 kg are kept on a frictionless horizontal table with a compressed spring between them. If the masses are released, the larger mass moves away with velocity 3.50 m s^{-1}. What is the velocity of the other mass?

5 A 70.0 kg person stands at the back of a 200.0 kg boat of length 4.00 m that floats on stationary water. She begins to walk toward the front of the boat. When she gets to the front, how far back will the boat have moved? (Neglect the resistance of the water.)

6 A ball of mass 250 g rolling on a horizontal floor with a speed 4.00 m s^{-1} hits a wall and bounces with the same speed, as shown in Figure 6.18.
   (a) What is the magnitude and direction of the momentum *change* of the ball?
   (b) Is momentum conserved here? Why or why not?

Figure 6.18 For question 6.

7 A mass of 0.500 kg moving at 6.00 m s^{-1} strikes a wall normally and bounces back with a speed of 4.00 m s^{-1}. If the mass was in contact with the wall for 0.200 s find:
   (a) the change of momentum of the mass;
   (b) the average force the wall exerted on the mass.

8 A person holds a book stationary in their hand and then releases it.
   (a) As the book falls, is its momentum conserved?
   (b) What does the law of conservation of momentum say for this example?

9 A binary star system consists of two stars that are orbiting a common centre, as shown in Figure 6.19. The only force acting on the stars is the gravitational force of attraction in a direction along the line joining the stars.
   (a) Explain carefully why the total momentum of the binary star is constant.

Figure 6.19 For question 9.

   (b) Explain why the two stars are always in diametrically opposite positions.
   (c) Hence explain why the two stars have a common period of rotation and why the inner star is the more massive of the two.

10 (a) A fan on a floating barge blows air at high speed toward the right, as shown in Figure 6.20a. Will the barge move? Explain your answer.
   (b) A sail is now put up on the barge so that the fan blows air toward the sail, as shown in Figure 6.20b. Will the barge move? Explain your answer.

(a)   (b)

Figure 6.20 For question 10.

11 If you jump from a height of 1.0 m from the surface of the earth, the earth actually moves up a bit as you fall.
   (a) Explain why.
   (b) *Estimate* the distance the earth moves, listing any assumptions you make.
   (c) Would the earth move more, less or the same if a heavier person jumps?

12 A time-varying force whose graph versus time is shown in Figure 6.21 acts on a body of mass 3.00 kg.
   (a) Find the impulse of the force.
   (b) Find the velocity of the mass at 17 s, assuming the initial velocity was zero.
   (c) What should the initial velocity be if the mass had to stop at 17 s?

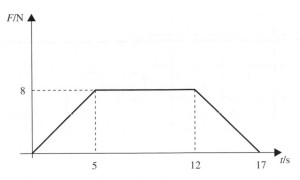

Figure 6.21 For question 12.

13 A rocket in space where gravity is negligible has a mass (including fuel) of 5000 kg. If it is desired to give the rocket an average acceleration of 15.0 m s^{-2} during the first second of firing the engine and the gases leave the rocket at a speed of 1500 m s^{-1} (relative to the rocket), how much fuel must be burned in that second?

14 Two masses moving in a straight line towards each other collide as shown in Figure 6.22. Find the velocity (magnitude and direction) of the larger mass after the collision.

Figure 6.22 For question 14.

15 Two cars of masses 1200 kg and 1400 kg collide head-on and stick to each other. The cars are coming at each other from opposite directions with speeds of 8.0 m s^{-1} and 6 m s^{-1}, respectively. With what velocity does the wreck move away from the scene of the accident?

16 A 0.350 kg mass is approaching a moving rod with speed 8.00 m s^{-1}. The ball leaves the rod at right angles with a speed of 12.0 m s^{-1} as shown in Figure 6.23. What impulse has been imparted to the ball?

Figure 6.23 For question 16.

17 Two cars A and B of mass 1200 kg and 1300 kg, respectively, collide at an intersection and stick to each other as a result of the collision as shown in Figure 6.24. Find the speeds of A and B before the collision.

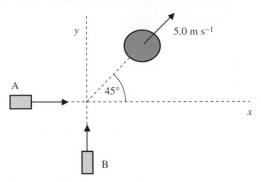

Figure 6.24 For question 17.

18 A boy rides on a scooter pushing on the road with one foot with a horizontal force that depends on time, as shown in the graph in Figure 6.25. While the scooter rolls, a constant force of 25 N opposes the motion. The combined mass of the boy and scooter is 25 kg.

(a) Find the speed of the boy after 4.0 s, assuming he started from rest.
(b) Draw a graph to represent the variation of the boy's speed with time.

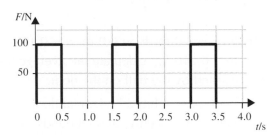

Figure 6.25 For question 18.

19 A student stands on a plate that is connected to a force sensor that measures the force exerted by the student on the plate. The student then jumps straight up. Figure 6.26 is an idealized version of the reading of the sensor as a function of time. Using this graph find the following:

(a) the mass of the student;

(b) the acceleration of the student at 0.6 s;

(c) the time the student leaves the plate;

(d) the maximum height the student jumps to.

(e) What would be a more *realistic* graph of force versus time?

Figure 6.26 For question 19.

20 A ball of mass m is dropped from a height of h_1 and rebounds to a height of h_2. The ball is in contact with the floor for a time interval of τ.

(a) Show that the average net force on the ball is given by

$$F = m \frac{\sqrt{2gh_1} + \sqrt{2gh_2}}{\tau}$$

(b) If $h_1 = 8.0$ m, $h_2 = 6.0$ m, $\tau = 0.125$ s, $m = 0.250$ kg, calculate the average force exerted by the ball on the floor.

21 A ball of mass m hits a horizontal floor normally with speed v_1 and rebounds with speed v_2. The ball stayed in contact with the floor for a time of τ s. Show that the average force on the ball from the floor during the collision is given by $\frac{m(v_1+v_2)}{\tau} + mg$. Find an expression for the average *net* force on the ball.

22 Figure 6.27 shows the variation with time of the force exerted on a body of mass 4.0 kg that is initially at rest. Find:

(a) the acceleration of the mass at 4 s;

(b) the velocity of the mass at 5 s;

(c) the acceleration of the mass at 8 s;

(d) the velocity of the mass at 10 s.

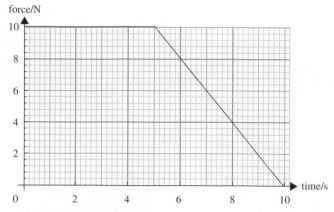

Figure 6.27 For question 22.

HL only

23 You have a mass of 60.0 kg and are floating weightless in space. You are carrying 100 coins each of mass 0.10 kg.

(a) If you throw all the coins at once with a speed of 5.0 m s^{-1} in the same direction, with what velocity will you recoil?

(b) If instead you throw the coins one at a time with a speed of 5.0 m s^{-1} *with respect to you,* discuss whether your final speed will be different from before. (Use your graphics display calculator to calculate the speed in this case.)

24 Figure 6.28 shows the variation with time of the force exerted on a ball as the ball came into contact with a spring.

(a) For how long was the spring in contact with the ball?

(b) *Estimate* the magnitude of the change in momentum of the ball.

(c) What was the *average* force that was exerted on the ball?

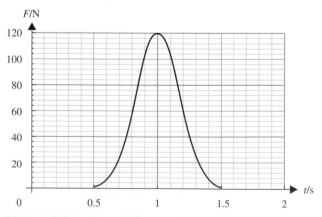

Figure 6.28 For question 24.

Work, energy and power

The topic of mechanics continues in this chapter with the fundamental concept of work done by a force, as well as the concepts of energy and power. Applications of the law of conservation of energy are discussed.

Objectives

By the end of this chapter you should be able to:

- state the definition of *work done by a force*, $W = Fs \cos \theta$, appreciate the significance of the angle appearing in the formula and understand that this formula can only be used when the force is *constant*;
- understand that the *work done by a varying* force is given by the *area under the graph* of force versus displacement;
- state the definitions of *kinetic energy*, $E_k = \frac{1}{2}mv^2$ (also $E_k = \frac{p^2}{2m}$), *gravitational potential energy*, $E_p = mgh$, and *elastic potential energy*, $E_e = \frac{1}{2}kx^2$.
- appreciate that gravitational potential energy can be calculated by measuring heights from an *arbitrary* level;
- understand that, when frictional forces are absent, the total energy $E = E_k + E_p + E_e = \frac{1}{2}mv^2 + mgh + \frac{1}{2}kx^2$ is conserved;
- use the work–kinetic energy relation that states that the work done by the net force is the *change in kinetic energy*;
- understand that, in the presence of *external forces*, the work done is the change in the mechanical energy, $W = \Delta E$;
- state the definition of *power*, $P = \frac{\Delta W}{\Delta t}$, and its very useful form in mechanics, $P = Fv$;
- calculate the *efficiency* of simple machines;
- understand that in all collisions *momentum is always conserved*, but that *kinetic energy* is only conserved in *elastic* collisions.

Work done by a force

Consider a *constant* force $\vec{F}$ acting on a body of mass m as shown in Figure 7.1. The body moves a distance s along a straight line.

The force is always acting upon the body as it moves. Note that the force moves its point of application by a distance s. We define a quantity

called the **work** *done by the force* $\vec{F}$ by

$$W = Fs \cos \theta$$

where θ is the angle between the force and the direction along which the mass moves. (The cosine here can be positive, negative or zero; thus work can be positive, negative or zero. We will see what that means shortly.)

Figure 7.1 A force moving its point of application performs work.

> The work done by a force is the product of the force times the distance moved by the object in the direction of the force.
>
> The unit of work is the joule. One joule is the work done by a force of 1 N when it moves a body a distance of 1 m in the direction of the force. $1\,\text{J} = 1\,\text{N m}$.

Example question

Q1

A mass is being pulled along a level road by a rope attached to it in such a way that the rope makes an angle of 40.0° with the horizontal. The force in the rope is 20.0 N. What is the work done by this force in moving the mass a distance of 8.00 m along the level road?

Answer

Applying the definition of work done, we have

$W = Fs \cos \theta$

where $F = 20.0\,\text{N}$, $s = 8.00\,\text{m}$ and $\theta = 40°$. Thus

$W = 20 \times 8 \times \cos 40°$

$\quad = 123\,\text{J}$

If the force is not constant or the motion does not take place in a straight line, or both, we must be careful. First consider the case of a force of constant magnitude when the motion is not along a straight line.

Example questions

Q2

Find the work done by the tension in a string, as a mass attached to the end of the string performs circular motion (see Figure 7.2).

Answer

This is a case where the force, although constant in magnitude, changes in direction. However, the

Figure 7.2.

angle between the force and *any small* displacement of the mass as it revolves around the circle is 90° and since cos 90° = 0, the work done is zero.

Q3

A force of constant magnitude 25 N acts on a body that moves along a curved path. The direction of the force is along the velocity vector of the body, i.e. it is *tangential to the path*. Find the work after the mass moves a distance of 50 m along the curved path.

Answer

The diagram on the left of Figure 7.3 shows the path of the body. The diagram on the right is an enlargement of part of the path. We see that the work done when the body travels a *small distance* Δs is

$F \Delta s \cos 0° = F \Delta s$

Breaking up the entire path into small bits in this way, and adding the work done along each bit, we find that the *total* work done is $W = Fs$, where s is the distance travelled along the curved path.

Figure 7.3.

If the force is not constant in magnitude, we must be supplied with the graph that shows the variation of the magnitude of the force with distance travelled. Then we have the following important result:

> The area under the graph that shows the variation of the magnitude of the force with distance travelled is the work done.

We can apply this result to the case of the tension in the spring. Since $T = kx$, where k is the spring constant and x the extension (or compression) of the string, the graph of force versus position is as shown in Figure 7.4.

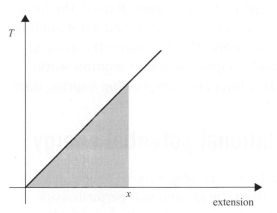

Figure 7.4 The area under a force–distance graph gives the total work performed by the non-constant force.

To find the work done in extending the spring from its natural length ($x = 0$) to extension x, we need to calculate the area of the triangle whose base is x and height is $T = kx$. Thus

$$\text{area} = \tfrac{1}{2}kx \times x$$
$$= \tfrac{1}{2}kx^2$$

The work to extend a spring from its natural length by an amount x is thus

$$W = \tfrac{1}{2}kx^2$$

It follows that the work done when extending a spring from an extension x_1 to an extension x_2 is

$$W = \tfrac{1}{2}k\left(x_1^2 - x_2^2\right)$$

Work done by gravity

We will now concentrate on the work done by a very special force, namely the weight of a mass. Remember that weight is mass times acceleration due to gravity and is directed vertically down. Thus, if a mass is displaced

horizontally, the work done by mg is zero, since in this case the angle is $90°$:
$W = mgd \cos 90° = 0$. (See Figure 7.5.)

Figure 7.5 The force of gravity is normal to this horizontal displacement so no work is being done.

Note that we are not implying that it is the weight that is forcing the mass to move along the table. We are calculating the work done by a particular force (the weight) if the mass (somehow) moves in a particular way.

If the body falls a vertical distance h, then the work done by W is $+mgh$. The force of gravity is parallel to the displacement, as in Figure 7.6a.

If the mass is thrown vertically upwards to a height h from the launch point, then the work done by W is $-mgh$ since now the angle between direction of force (vertically down) and displacement (vertically up) is $180°$. The force of gravity is parallel to the displacement but opposite in direction, as in Figure 7.6b.

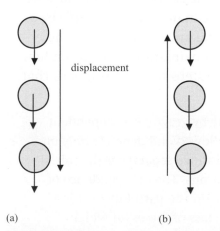

Figure 7.6 The force of gravity is parallel to the displacement in (a) and anti-parallel (i.e. parallel but opposite in direction) in (b).

Consider now the case where a mass moves along some arbitrary path, as shown in Figure 7.7.

Figure 7.7 The work done by gravity is independent of the path followed.

The path consists of horizontal and vertical segments. We now ask about the work done by the weight of the mass. The work done by mg will be equal to the sum of the work done along each horizontal and vertical step. But mg does no work along the horizontal steps since the angle between the force and the displacement in that case will be 90° and $\cos 90° = 0$. We are thus left with the vertical steps only. The work done along each step will be $\pm mg\,\Delta h$, where Δh is the step height. The plus sign is used when we go down a step and the minus sign when we go up a step. (In Figure 7.7 the mass will be forced to go up twice and down eight times.) Thus, what counts is the net number of steps going down (six in our figure). But, this adds up to the vertical distance separating the initial and final position. Hence, the work done by mg is mgh.

If the start and finish positions are joined by an arbitrary smooth curve rather than a 'staircase', the result is still the same. This is because we can always approximate a smooth curve by a series of horizontal and vertical steps; the quality of the approximation depends on how small we take the steps to be. This means that:

> ▶ The work done by gravity is independent of the path followed and depends only on the vertical distance separating the initial and final positions. The independence of the work done on the path followed is a property of a class of forces (of which weight is a prominent member) called *conservative forces*.

Work done in holding something still

If you try to hold up a heavy object, such as a chair, you will soon get tired. However, the force with which you are holding the chair does zero work since there is no displacement. This is somewhat unexpected. We normally associate getting tired with doing work. Indeed, the forces inside the muscles of the arm and hand holding the chair do work. This is because the muscles stretch and compress and that requires work, just as stretching and compressing a spring does.

Gravitational potential energy

As we just saw, the weight mg of a mass m a height h from the ground will perform work mgh if this mass moves from its position down to the ground. The ability to do this work is there because the mass just happens to be at a height h from the ground. The ability to do work is called energy. When the force in question is the weight (which depends on gravity), we call this energy *gravitational* **potential energy**:

$$E_p = mgh$$

Any mass has gravitational potential energy by virtue of its position. But what determines h? Obviously, we have to choose a reference level from which we will measure heights. But we can choose any level we like. A mass $m = 2$ kg sitting on a table 1 m from the floor will have $E_p = 2 \times 10 \times 1 = 20$ J if the reference level is the floor, but will have $E_p = 0$ if the reference level is the table. If the reference level is chosen to be the ceiling, 2 m above the table, then $E_p = -2 \times 10 \times 2 = -40$ J. (See Figure 7.8.)

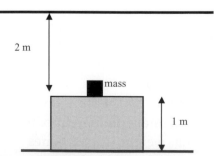

Figure 7.8 The mass has different potential energies depending on the reference level chosen.

So, the same mass will have different gravitational potential energy depending on what reference level we choose. This might seem to make E_p a useless quantity. But if you are patient, you will see that this is not the case.

Potential energy can be understood in the following way. Consider a mass resting on a horizontal floor. If an external force equal to mg is applied to the mass vertically up and the mass moves without acceleration to a position h metres higher than the floor, the work done *by the external force* is mgh. What has become of this work? This work has gone into gravitational potential energy of the mass. This energy is stored as potential energy in the new position of the mass. Similarly, if a spring is initially unstretched and an external force stretches it by an amount x, then the work done by this external force is $\frac{1}{2}kx^2$. This work is stored as elastic potential energy in the (now stretched) spring.

▶ This is a general result for all kinds of potential energies: when an *external* force changes the state of a system without acceleration and does work W in the process, the work so performed is stored as potential energy in the new state of the system.

Example question

Q4

A mass of 10 kg rests on top of a vertical spring whose base is attached to the floor. The spring compresses by 5 cm. What is the spring constant of the spring? How much energy is stored in the spring?

Answer

The mass is at equilibrium so

$$mg = kx$$

$$\Rightarrow k = \frac{mg}{x}$$

$$= \frac{100}{0.05}$$

$$= 2000\,\mathrm{N\,m}^{-1}$$

The stored energy is

$$E_e = \frac{1}{2}kx^2$$

$$= \frac{1}{2} \times 2000\,(0.05)^2$$

$$= 2.5\,\mathrm{J}$$

The work–kinetic energy relation

What effect does the work done have on a body? When a body of mass m is acted upon by a *net* force F, then this body experiences an acceleration $a = \frac{F}{m}$ in the direction of F. Suppose that this body had speed v_0 when the force was first applied to it and that the speed after moving a distance x (in the direction of the net force) becomes v_f, as shown in Figure 7.9.

Figure 7.9 A force accelerates a mass, increasing its kinetic energy.

We know from kinematics that

$$v_f^2 = v_0^2 + 2ax$$

so replacing the acceleration by F/m we find

$$v_f^2 = v_0^2 + 2\frac{F}{m}x$$

$$\Rightarrow Fx = \frac{1}{2}mv_f^2 - \frac{1}{2}mv_0^2$$

But Fx is the work done on the mass. This work equals the change in the quantity $E_k = \frac{1}{2}mv^2$, a quantity called the **kinetic energy** of the mass. We thus see that the net work done on a mass results in a change of the kinetic energy of the object. This is a very useful result with applications in many areas of physics.

▶ The work done by the *net* force on a body is equal to the change in the kinetic energy of the body

work done by net force $= \Delta E_k$

Example questions

Q5

A mass of 5.00 kg moving with an initial velocity of 12.0 m s⁻¹ is brought to rest by a horizontal force over a distance of 12.0 m. What is the force?

Answer

The change in the kinetic energy of the mass is (final minus initial)

$$0 - \frac{1}{2}mv^2 = -\frac{1}{2} \times 5.00 \times 144$$
$$= -360\,\text{J}$$

The work done by the force f is

$$-fs = -12\,f$$

Hence

$$-12\,f = -360$$
$$\Rightarrow f = 30.0\,\text{N}$$

(There is a minus sign in the work done by f because the force is acting in a direction opposite to the motion and $\cos 180° = -1$.)

Q6

An electron is acted upon by an electric force that accelerates it from rest to a kinetic energy of 5.0×10^{-19} J. If this is done over a distance of 3.0 cm, find the electric force.

Answer

The work done by the electric force is the change in kinetic energy (the electric force is the only force acting and so it is the net force) and equals the product of force times distance. Hence

$$F \times 0.03 = 5.0 \times 10^{-19}$$
$$\Rightarrow F = 1.7 \times 10^{-17}\,\text{N}$$

Q7

A mass m hangs from two strings attached to the ceiling such that they make the same angle with the vertical (as shown in Figure 7.10). The strings are shortened very slowly so that the mass is raised a distance h above its original position. What is the work done by the tension in each string as the mass is so raised?

Figure 7.10.

Answer

The net work done is zero since the net force on the mass is zero. The work done by gravity is $-mgh$ and thus the work done by the two equal tension forces is $+mgh$. The work done by each is thus $mgh/2$.

Q8

A mass m hangs vertically at the end of a string of length L. A force F is applied to the mass horizontally so that it slowly moves to a position a distance h higher, as shown in Figure 7.11. What is the work done by the force F? (Note: F is not constant.)

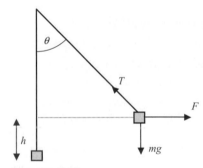

Figure 7.11.

Answer

The answer is obtained at once by noting that since the mass is in equilibrium at all times the net force is zero and hence the work done by the net force is zero. But T does zero work since it is always normal to the direction in which the mass moves (along the arc of a circle). The weight does work $-mgh$ and thus the work done by F must be $+mgh$.

Conservation of energy

We have already seen that, when a net force F performs work W on a body, then the kinetic energy of the body changes by W (here the subscripts 'i' and 'f' stand for 'initial' and 'final')

$$W = \Delta E_k$$
$$= \tfrac{1}{2}mv_f^2 - \tfrac{1}{2}mv_i^2$$

Consider now the case where the only force that does work on a body is gravity. This corresponds to motions in which the body is either in free fall (gravity is the only force acting) or the body is sliding on a frictionless surface (we now have the normal reaction force acting here as well as gravity but this force does zero work since it is normal to the direction of motion). Suppose that the vertical height of the body when the velocity is v_i is H, and the velocity becomes v_f at a height of h from the reference level (see Figure 7.12).

v_i start

finish

H

v_f

h

Figure 7.12 The total energy at the top and bottom (and at any point in between) of the incline is the same.

The work done by gravity is simply $mg(H-h)$ and so

$$mg(H-h) = \tfrac{1}{2}mv_f^2 - \tfrac{1}{2}mv_i^2$$

This can be rearranged as

$$mgh + \tfrac{1}{2}mv_f^2 = mgH + \tfrac{1}{2}mv_i^2$$

which shows that in the motion of this body the sum of the kinetic and potential energies of the mass stays the same. Calling the quantity $mgh + \tfrac{1}{2}mv^2$ the total energy of the mass, then the result we derived states that the total energy E of the mass stays the same at all times, i.e. the total energy is conserved,

$$E_i = E_f$$

As the mass comes down the plane, its potential energy decreases but its kinetic energy increases in such a way that the sum stays the same. We have proven this result in the case in which gravity is the only force doing work in our problem. Consider now the following example questions.

Example questions

Q9

Find the speed of the mass at the end of a pendulum of length 1.00 m that starts from rest at an angle of 10° with the vertical.

Answer

Let us take as the reference level the lowest point of the pendulum (Figure 7.13). Then the total energy at that point is just kinetic, $E_k = \tfrac{1}{2}mv^2$, where v is the unknown speed. At the initial point the total energy is just potential, $E_p = mgh$, where

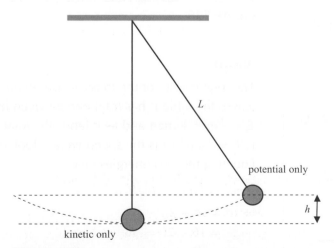

L

potential only

h

kinetic only

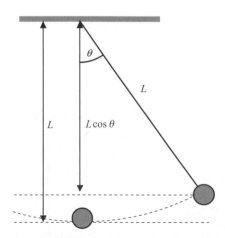

θ

L

L

L

$L\cos\theta$

Figure 7.13.

h is the vertical difference in height between the two positions, that is

$$h = 1.00 - 1.00 \cos 10°$$
$$= 0.015 \text{ m}$$

(see Figure 7.13)

Thus

$$\tfrac{1}{2}mv^2 = mgh$$
$$v = \sqrt{2gh}$$
$$= 0.55 \text{ m s}^{-1}$$

Note how the mass has dropped out of the problem. (At positions other than the two shown, the mass has both kinetic and potential energy.)

Q10

A mass rolls up an incline of angle 28° with an initial speed of 3.0 m s^{-1}. How far up the incline will the mass get?

Answer

Let the furthest the mass will get be a height h from the floor, as shown in Figure 7.14. At this point the kinetic energy must be zero since otherwise the mass would have climbed higher. Then the total energy at this point is just $E = mgh$. The total energy at the initial position is

$$E = \tfrac{1}{2}mv^2$$

and so

$$h = \frac{v^2}{2g}$$

giving $h = 0.45$ m. The distance moved along the plane is thus

$$\frac{0.45}{\sin 28°} = 0.96 \text{ m}.$$

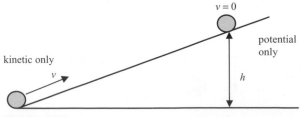

Figure 7.14.

Q11

What must the minimum speed of the mass in Figure 7.15 be at the initial point such that the mass makes it over the barrier of height h?

Figure 7.15.

Answer

To make it over the barrier the mass must be able to reach the highest point. Any speed it has there will then make it roll over. Thus, at the very least, we must be able to get the ball to the highest point with zero speed. Then the total energy would be just $E = mgh$ and the total energy at the starting position is $E = \tfrac{1}{2}mv^2$. Thus, the speed must be bigger than $v = \sqrt{2gh}$. Note that if the initial speed u of the mass is larger than $v = \sqrt{2gh}$, then when the mass makes it to the other side of the barrier its speed will be the same as the starting speed u.

Q12

A mass rolls off a 1.0 m high table with a speed of 4.0 m s^{-1}, as shown in Figure 7.16. With what speed does it strike the floor?

Figure 7.16.

Answer

The total energy of the mass is conserved. As it leaves the table it has total energy given by $E = \tfrac{1}{2}mv^2 + mgh$ and as it lands the total energy is $E = \tfrac{1}{2}mu^2$ (u is the speed we are looking for). Equating the two energies gives

$$\tfrac{1}{2}mu^2 = \tfrac{1}{2}mv^2 + mgh$$
$$\Rightarrow u^2 = v^2 + 2gh$$
$$= 16 + 20 = 36$$
$$\Rightarrow u = 6.0 \text{ m s}^{-1}$$

Q13

A ball is thrown vertically upward with a speed of 4.0 m s^{-1} from a height of 1.0 m from the floor, as shown in Figure 7.17. With what speed does the ball strike the floor?

4.0 m s^{-1}

1.0 m

Figure 7.17.

Answer

Working in precisely the same way as in the previous example we find

$$\frac{1}{2}mu^2 = \frac{1}{2}mv^2 + mgh$$
$$\Rightarrow u^2 = v^2 + 2gh$$
$$= 16 + 20$$
$$= 36$$
$$\Rightarrow u = 6.0 \text{ m s}^{-1}$$

(The answer is the same as that for example question 12 – why?)

If, in addition to the weight, there are spring tension forces acting in our system, then the previous discussion generalizes to again lead to

$$E_i = E_f$$

where now the total mechanical energy includes elastic potential energy as well, that is

$$E = \frac{1}{2}mv^2 + mgh + \frac{1}{2}kx^2$$

Example question

Q14

A body of mass 0.40 kg is held next to a compressed spring as shown in Figure 7.18. The spring constant is $k = 250$ N m^{-1} and the compression of the spring is 12 cm. The mass is then released. Find the speed of the body when it is at a height of 20 cm from the horizontal.

spring

20 cm

Figure 7.18.

Answer

Initially the total mechanical energy of the system is only the elastic potential energy of the spring

$$E = \frac{1}{2}kx^2$$
$$= \frac{1}{2} \times 250 \times 0.12^2$$
$$= 1.8 \text{ J}$$

At a height of 20 cm from the floor, the total mechanical energy consists of kinetic and gravitational energies only. The spring has decompressed and so has no elastic potential energy. Then

$$E = \frac{1}{2}mv^2 + mgh$$
$$= \frac{1}{2}(0.4)v^2 + (0.4)(10)(0.20)$$
$$= 0.2v^2 + 0.8$$

Thus

$$0.2v^2 + 0.8 = 1.8$$
$$\Rightarrow 0.2v^2 = 1.0$$
$$\Rightarrow v^2 = 5$$
$$\Rightarrow v = 2.2 \text{ m s}^{-1}$$

Frictional forces

In the presence of friction and other resistance forces, the *mechanical energy* of a system (i.e. the sum of kinetic, gravitational potential and elastic potential energies) will not be conserved. These forces will, in general, decrease the total mechanical energy of the system. Similarly, external forces, such as forces due to engines, may increase the mechanical energy of a system. In these cases we may write

$$W = \Delta E$$

where W stands for the total work done by the *external forces* and ΔE is the change in the mechanical energy of the system. By external forces we mean forces *other* than weight and spring tension forces.

This equation is easily understood in the following way. If there are no external forces, then $W = 0$, $\Delta E = 0$ and the total mechanical energy stays the same: it is conserved.

If, on the other hand, external forces do act on the system, then the work they do goes into changing the mechanical energy. If the work done is negative (resistance forces), the mechanical energy decreases. If the work done is positive (pulling forces), the mechanical energy increases.

Example question

Q15 ▮▮▮▮▮▮▮▮▮▮▮▮

A body of mass 2.0 kg (initially at rest) slides down a curved path of total length 16 m as shown in Figure 7.19. When it reaches the bottom, its speed is measured and found to equal 6.0 m s^{-1}. Show that there is a force resisting the motion. Assuming the force to have constant magnitude, determine what that magnitude is.

Figure 7.19.

Answer

Without any resistance forces, the speed at the bottom is expected to be

$$v = \sqrt{mgh}$$
$$= \sqrt{2.0 \times 10 \times 5.0}$$
$$= 10 \text{ m s}^{-1}$$

The measured speed is less than this and so there is a resistance force. The total mechanical energy

at the top is

$$E_{\text{top}} = mgh$$
$$= 2.0 \times 10 \times 5.0$$
$$= 100 \text{ J}$$

At the bottom it is

$$E_{\text{bottom}} = \tfrac{1}{2}mv^2$$
$$= \tfrac{1}{2} \times 2.0 \times (6.0)^2$$
$$= 36 \text{ J}$$

The total energy decreased by 64 J – this must be the work done by the resistance force. Thus

$$fs = 64 \text{ J}$$
$$\Rightarrow f = \frac{64}{16}$$
$$= 4.0 \text{ N}$$

We have seen that in the presence of external forces the total mechanical energy of a system is not conserved. The change in the total energy is the work done by the external forces. Another way of looking at this is to say the change in the mechanical energy has gone into other forms of energy *not included* in the mechanical energy, such as thermal energy ('heat') and sound. In this way *total energy* (which now includes the other forms as well as the mechanical energy) *is* conserved. This is the general form of the law of conservation of energy, one of the most important principles of physics.

▶ The total energy cannot be created or destroyed but can only be transformed from one form into another.

Power

When a machine performs work, it is important to know not only how much work is being done but also how much work is performed within a given time interval. A cyclist performs a lot of work in a lifetime of cycling, but the same work is performed by a powerful car engine in a much shorter time. **Power** is the rate at which work is being performed.

► When a quantity of work ΔW is performed within a time interval Δt the ratio

$$P = \frac{\Delta W}{\Delta t}$$

is called the power developed. Its unit is joule per second and this is given the name watt (W): $1\,W = 1\,J\,s^{-1}$.

Another common unit for power when it comes to machines and car engines is the horsepower, hp, a non-SI unit that equals 746 W.

Consider a constant force F, which acts on a body of mass m. The force does an amount of work $F\,\Delta x$ in moving the body a small distance Δx along its direction. If this work is performed in time Δt, then

$$P = \frac{\Delta W}{\Delta t}$$
$$= F\frac{\Delta x}{\Delta t}$$
$$= F v$$

where v is the instantaneous speed of the mass. This is the power produced in making the body move at speed v. As the speed increases, the power necessary increases as well. Consider an aeroplane moving at constant speed on a straight-line path. If the power produced by its engines is P, and the force pushing it forward is F, then P, F and v are related by the equation above. But since the plane moves with no acceleration, the total force of air resistance must equal F. Hence the force of air resistance can be found simply from the power of the plane's engines and the constant speed with which it coasts.

Example questions

Q16

What is the minimum power required to lift a mass of 50.0 kg up a vertical distance of 12 m in 5.0 s?

Answer

The work performed to lift the mass is

$mgh = 50.0 \times 10 \times 12$
$= 6.0 \times 10^3\,J$

The power is thus

$$\frac{6.0 \times 10^3}{5.0} = 1200\,W$$

This is only the minimum power required. In practice, the mass has to be accelerated from rest, which will require additional work and hence more power.

Q17

A helicopter rotor whose length is R pushes air downwards with a speed v. Assuming that the density of air is constant and equals ρ and the mass of the helicopter is M, find v. You may assume that the rotor forces the air in a circle of radius R (spanned by the rotor) to move with the downward speed v. Hence find the power developed by the engine. How does this power depend on the linear size of the helicopter?

Answer

The momentum of the air under the rotor is mv, where m is the mass of air in a circle of radius R. In time ΔT the mass is enclosed in a cylinder of radius R and height $v\Delta T$. Thus, the momentum of this mass is $\rho\pi R^2 v^2 \Delta t$ and its rate of change is $\rho\pi R^2 v^2$. This is the force on the helicopter upwards, which must equal the helicopter's weight of Mg. Thus

$$Mg = \rho\pi R^2 v^2$$
$$\Rightarrow v = \sqrt{\frac{Mg}{\rho\pi R^2}}$$

The power required from the helicopter engine is thus

$$P = Fv$$
$$= Mg\sqrt{\frac{Mg}{\rho\pi R^2}}$$

To find the dependence on a typical linear size L of the helicopter, note that the weight depends on L as L^3 and so

$$P \propto L^3 \sqrt{\frac{L^3}{L^2}} \propto L^{7/2}$$

This implies that if the length of a helicopter is 16 times that of a model helicopter, its required power will be $16^{7/2} = 16\,384$ times larger than that for the model.

Efficiency

Suppose that a mass is being pulled up along a rough inclined plane with *constant* speed. Let the mass be 15 kg and the angle of the incline 45°. The constant frictional force opposing the motion is 42 N.

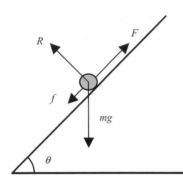

Figure 7.20.

The forces on the mass are shown in Figure 7.20 and we know that

$$R = mg \cos \theta$$
$$= 106.1 \text{ N}$$

$$F = mg \sin \theta + f$$
$$= 106.1 + 42$$
$$= 148.1 \text{ N}$$

since the mass has no acceleration. Let the force raise the mass a distance of 20 m along the plane. The work done by the force F is

$$W = 148.1 \times 20$$
$$= 2960 \text{ J}$$

The force effectively raised the 15 kg a vertical height of 14.1 m and so increased the potential energy of the mass by $mgh = 2121$ J. The efficiency with which the force raised the mass is thus

$$\eta = \frac{\text{useful work}}{\text{actual work}}$$
$$= \frac{2121}{2960}$$
$$= 0.72$$

Example question

Q18

A 0.50 kg battery-operated toy train moves with constant velocity 0.30 m s⁻¹ along a level track. The power of the motor in the train is 2.0 W and the total force opposing the motion of the train is 5.0 N.

(a) What is the efficiency of the train's motor?
(b) Assuming the efficiency and the opposing force stay the same, calculate the speed of the train as it climbs an incline of 10.0° to the horizontal.

Answer

(a) The power delivered by the motor is 2.0 W. Since the speed is constant, the force developed by the motor is also 5.0 N. The power used in moving the train is $Fv = 5.0 \times 0.30 = 1.5$ W. Hence the efficiency is

$$\eta = \frac{1.5 \text{ W}}{2.0 \text{ W}}$$
$$= 0.75$$

(b) The net force pushing the train up the incline is

$$F = mg \sin \theta + 5.0$$
$$= 0.50 \times 10 \times \sin 10° + 5.0$$
$$= 5.89 \text{ N}$$

Thus

$$\eta = \frac{5.89 \times v}{2.0 \text{ W}}$$
$$= 0.75$$
$$\Rightarrow v = \frac{2.0 \times 0.75}{5.89}$$
$$= 0.26 \text{ m s}^{-1}$$

Kinetic energy and momentum

We have seen in Chapter 2.6 on momentum that, in a collision or explosion where no external forces are present, the total momentum of the system is conserved. You can easily convince yourself that in the three collisions illustrated in Figure 7.21 momentum is conserved. The incoming body has mass 8.0 kg and the other a mass of 12 kg.

Figure 7.21 Momentum is conserved in these three collisions.

In the first collision the bodies have stuck together and move as one. In the second the incoming body has slowed down as a result of the collision and the heavy body moves faster. In the third the incoming body has bounced back.

Let us examine these collisions from the point of view of energy.

In all cases the total kinetic energy before the collision is

$$E_k = \tfrac{1}{2} \times 8 \times 10^2 = 400 \, \text{J}$$

The total kinetic energy after the collision in each case is:

case 1 $E_k = \tfrac{1}{2} \times 20 \times 4^2 = 160 \, \text{J}$

case 2 $E_k = \tfrac{1}{2} \times 8 \times 1^2 + \tfrac{1}{2} \times 12 \times 6^2 = 220 \, \text{J}$

case 3 $E_k = \tfrac{1}{2} \times 8 \times 2^2 + \tfrac{1}{2} \times 12 \times 8^2 = 400 \, \text{J}$

We thus observe that *whereas momentum is conserved in all cases,* kinetic energy is not. When kinetic energy is conserved (case 3), the collision is said to be *elastic*. When it is not (cases 1 and 2), the collision is *inelastic*. In an inelastic collision, kinetic energy is lost. When the bodies stick together after a collision (case 1), the collision is said to be *totally inelastic* and in this case the maximum possible kinetic energy is lost.

The lost kinetic energy gets transformed into other forms of energy, such as thermal energy, deformation energy (if the bodies are permanently deformed as a result of the collision) and sound energy.

Example questions

Q19

A moving body of mass m collides with a stationary body of double the mass and sticks to it. What fraction of the original kinetic energy is lost?

Answer

The original kinetic energy is $\tfrac{1}{2}mv^2$, where v is the speed of the incoming mass. After the collision the two bodies move as one with speed u that can be found from momentum conservation:

$$mv = (m + 2m)u$$

$$\Rightarrow u = \frac{v}{3}$$

The total kinetic energy after the collision is therefore

$$\frac{1}{2}(3m)\left(\frac{v}{3}\right)^2 = \frac{mv^2}{6}$$

and so the lost kinetic energy is

$$\frac{mv^2}{2} - \frac{mv^2}{6} = \frac{mv^2}{3}$$

The fraction of the original energy that is lost is thus

$$\frac{mv^2/3}{mv^2/2} = \frac{2}{3}$$

Q20

A body at rest of mass M explodes into two pieces of masses $M/4$ and $3M/4$. Calculate the ratio of the kinetic energies of the two fragments.

Answer

Here it pays to derive a very useful expression for kinetic energy in terms of momentum. Since

$$E_k = \frac{mv^2}{2}$$

it follows that

$$E_k = \frac{mv^2}{2} \times \frac{m}{m}$$

$$= \frac{m^2 v^2}{2m}$$

$$= \frac{p^2}{2m}$$

The total momentum before the explosion is zero, so it is zero after as well. Thus, the two fragments must have *equal and opposite momenta*. Hence

$$\frac{E_{light}}{E_{heavy}} = \frac{p^2/(2M_{light})}{p^2/(2M_{heavy})}$$

$$= \frac{M_{heavy}}{M_{light}}$$

$$= \frac{3M/4}{M/4}$$

$$= 3$$

The problem of least time

In Figure 7.22 a number of paths join the starting position A to the final position B.

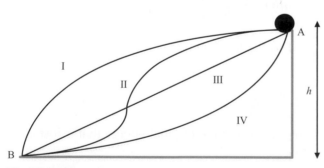

Figure 7.22.

A mass m at A will start with a tiny speed and move down to B. As we saw, the speed at B will be the same no matter what path the mass follows. The speed will equal $\sqrt{2gh}$ in all cases. This does not mean, however, that the time taken is the same for all paths. Finding the path joining A to B such that a mass takes the least

time is a famous problem in physics and requires the development of a branch of calculus called the calculus of variations. It is called the brachistochrone (least time) problem. The answer is that the curve joining A to B must be a cycloid. This is the curve traced out by a point on the rim of a wheel as the wheel rolls. In Figure 7.22, curve IV resembles a cycloid most. This problem was posed to both Newton and Leibniz (the inventors of calculus) by the Swiss mathematician Bernoulli. When Bernoulli saw the solutions given by the two men, he is supposed to have said of Newton 'one can always tell a lion by its claws'.

Questions

1 A horizontal force of 24 N pulls a body a distance of 5.0 m along its direction. Calculate the work done by the force.

2 A block slides along a rough table and is brought to rest after travelling a distance of 2.4 m. The frictional force is assumed constant at 3.2 N. Calculate the work done by the frictional force.

3 A block is pulled as shown in Figure 7.23 by a force making an angle of 20° to the horizontal. Find the work done by the pulling force when its point of application has moved 15 m.

Figure 7.23 For question 3.

4 A block of mass 4.0 kg is pushed to the right by a force $F = 20.0$ N. A frictional force of 14.0 N is acting on the block while it is moved a distance of 12.0 m along a horizontal floor. The forces acting on the mass are shown in Figure 7.24.
   (a) Calculate the work done by each of the four forces acting on the mass.
   (b) Hence find the net work done.
   (c) By how much does the kinetic energy of the mass change?

Figure 7.24 For question 4.

5 A weight lifter slowly lifts a 100 kg mass from the floor up a vertical distance of 1.90 m and then slowly lets it down to the floor again.
  (a) Find the work done by the weight of the mass on the way up.
  (b) Find the work done by the force exerted by the weight lifter when lifting the weight up.
  (c) What is the total work done by the weight on the way up and the way down?

6 A block of mass 2.0 kg and an initial speed of 5.4 m s^{-1} slides on a rough horizontal surface and is eventually brought to rest after travelling a distance of 4.0 m. Calculate the frictional force between the block and the surface.

7 A spring of spring constant $k = 200$ N m^{-1} is slowly extended from an extension of 3.0 cm to an extension of 5.0 cm. How much work is done by the extending force?

8 A spring of spring constant $k = 150$ N m^{-1} is compressed by 4.0 cm. The spring is horizontal and a mass of 1.0 kg is held to the right end of the spring. If the mass is released, with what speed will it move away?

9 Look at Figure 7.25.
  (a) What is the minimum speed v the mass must have in order to make it to position B? What speed will the mass have at B?
  (b) If $v = 12.0$ m s^{-1}, what will the speed be at A and B?

Figure 7.25 For question 9.

10 A mass is released from rest from the position shown in Figure 7.26. What will its speed be as it goes past positions A and B?

Figure 7.26 For question 10.

11 The speed of the 8.0 kg mass in position A in Figure 7.27 is 6.0 m s^{-1}. By the time it gets to B the speed is measured to be 12.0 m s^{-1}.

Figure 7.27 For question 11.

What is the frictional force opposing the motion? (The frictional force is acting along the plane.)

12 A toy gun shoots a 20.0 g ball when a spring of spring constant 12.0 N m^{-1} decompresses. The amount of compression is 10.0 cm (see Figure 7.28). With what speed does the ball exit the gun, assuming that there is no friction between the ball and the gun? If, instead, there is a frictional force of 0.05 N opposing the motion of the ball, what will the exit speed be in this case?

Figure 7.28 For question 12.

13 A variable force F acts on a body of mass $m = 2.0$ kg initially at rest, moving it along a straight horizontal surface. For the first 2 m the force is constant at 4 N. In the next 2 m it is constant at 8 N. In the next 2 m it drops from 8 N to 2 N uniformly. It then increases uniformly from 2 N to 6 N in the next 2 m.

It then remains constant at 6 N for the next 4 m.

(a) Draw a graph of the force versus distance.
(b) Find the work done by this force.
(c) What is the final speed of the mass?

14 A body of mass 12.0 kg is dropped vertically from rest from a height of 80.0 m. Ignoring any resistance forces during the motion of this body, draw graphs to represent the variation with distance fallen of
(a) the potential energy;
(b) the kinetic energy.
For the same motion draw graphs to represent the variation with time of
(c) the potential energy;
(d) the kinetic energy.
(e) Describe qualitatively the effect of a constant resistance force on each of the four graphs you drew.

15 A 25.0 kg block is very slowly raised up a vertical distance of 10.0 m by a rope attached to an electric motor in a time of 8.2 s. What is the power developed in the motor?

16 The engine of a car is developing a power of 90.0 kW when it is moving on a horizontal road at a constant speed of 100.0 km h^{-1}. What is the total horizontal force opposing the motion of the car?

17 The motor of an elevator develops power at a rate of 2500 W.
(a) At what speed can a 1200 kg load be raised?
(b) In practice it is found that the load is lifted more slowly than indicated by your answer to (a). Suggest reasons why this is so.

18 A load of 50.0 kg is raised a vertical distance of 15 m in 125 s by a motor.
(a) What is the power necessary for this?
(b) The power supplied by the motor is in fact 80 W. Calculate the efficiency of the motor.
(c) If the same motor is now used to raise a load of 100.0 kg and the efficiency remains the same, how long would that take?

19 For cars having the same shape but different size engines it is true that the power developed by the car's engine is proportional to the third power of the car's maximum speed. What does this imply about the speed dependence of the wind resistance force?

20 The top speed of a car whose engine is delivering 250 kW of power is 240 km h^{-1}. Calculate the value of the resistance force on the car when it is travelling at its top speed on a level road.

21 Describe the energy transformations taking place when a body of mass 5.0 kg:
(a) falls from a height of 50 m without air resistance;
(b) falls from a height of 50 m with constant speed;
(c) is being pushed up an incline of 30° to the horizontal with constant speed.

22 An elevator starts on the ground floor and stops on the 10th floor of a high-rise building. The elevator picks up a constant speed by the time it reaches the 1st floor and decelerates to rest between the 9th and 10th floors. Describe the energy transformations taking place between the 1st and 9th floors.

23 A car of mass 1200 kg starts from rest, accelerates uniformly to a speed of 4.0 m s^{-1} in 2 s and continues moving at this constant speed in a horizontal straight line for an additional 10 s. The brakes are then applied and the car is brought to rest in 4 s. A constant resistance force of 500 N is acting on the car during its entire motion.
(a) Calculate the force accelerating the car in the first 2 s of the motion.
(b) Calculate the average power developed by the engine in the first 2 s of the motion.
(c) Calculate the force pushing the car forward in the next 10 s.
(d) Calculate the power developed by the engine in those 10 s.
(e) Calculate the braking force in the last 4 s of the motion.
(f) Describe the energy transformations that have taken place in the 16 s of the motion of this car.

24 A mass of 6.0 kg moving at 4.0 m s^{-1} collides with a mass of 8.0 kg at rest on a frictionless surface and sticks to it. How much kinetic energy was lost in the collision?

25 Two masses of 2.0 kg and 4.0 kg are held in place, compressing a spring between them. When they are released, the 2.0 kg moves away with a speed of 3.0 m s^{-1}. What was the energy stored in the spring?

26 A block of mass 0.400 kg is kept in place so it compresses a spring of spring constant 120 N m^{-1} by 15 cm (see Figure 7.29). The block rests on a rough surface and the frictional force between the block and the surface when the block begins to slide is 1.2 N.

Figure 7.29 For question 26.

(a) What speed will the block have when the spring returns to its natural length?
(b) What percentage is this of the speed the mass would have had in the absence of friction?

27 Two bodies are connected by a string that goes over a pulley, as shown in Figure 7.30. The lighter body is resting on the floor and the other is being held in place a distance of 5.0 m from the floor. The heavier body is then released. Calculate the speeds of the two bodies as the heavy mass is about to hit the floor.

4.0 kg

5.0 m

2.0 kg

Figure 7.30 For question 27.

28 A mass m of 4 kg slides down a frictionless incline of $\theta = 30°$ to the horizontal.
(a) Plot a graph of the kinetic and potential energies of the mass as a function of time.
(b) Plot a graph of the kinetic and potential energies of the mass as a function of distance travelled along the incline.
(c) On each graph, plot the sum of the potential and kinetic energies. The mass starts from rest from a height of 20 m.

29 Show that an alternative formula for kinetic energy is $E_k = \frac{p^2}{2m}$, where p is the momentum of the mass m. This is very useful when dealing with collisions.

30 A body of mass M, initially at rest, explodes and splits into two pieces of mass $M/3$ and $2M/3$, respectively. Find the ratio of the kinetic energies of the two pieces. (Use the formula from the previous problem.)

31 A mass m is being pulled up an inclined plane of angle θ by a rope along the plane.
(a) What is the tension in the rope if the mass moves up at constant speed v?
(b) What is the work done by the tension when the mass moves up a distance of d m along the plane?
(c) What is the work done by the weight of the mass?
(d) What is the work done by the normal reaction force on the mass?
(e) What is the net work done on the mass?

HL only

32 A mass $m = 2.0$ kg is attached to the end of a string of length $L = 4.5$ m. The other end of the string is attached to the ceiling. The string is displaced from the vertical by an angle $\theta_0 = 50°$ and then released. What is the tension in the string when the string makes an angle $\theta = 20°$ with the vertical?

33 A car of mass 1200 kg is moving on a horizontal road with constant speed 30 m s^{-1}. The engine is then turned off and the car will eventually stop under the action of an air

resistance force. Figure 7.31 shows the variation of the car's speed with time after the engine has been turned off.

Figure 7.31 For question 33.

(a) Calculate the average acceleration of the car in the first and second 10 s intervals.

(b) Explain why it takes longer to reduce the speed from 20.0 m s^{-1} to 10.0 m s^{-1} compared with from 30.0 m s^{-1} to 20.0 m s^{-1}.

(c) The average speed in the first 10 s interval is 21.8 m s^{-1} and in the second it is 13.5 m s^{-1}. Use this information and your answer in (a) to deduce that the air resistance force is proportional to the square of the speed.

(d) Calculate the distance travelled by the car in the first and second 10 s intervals.

(e) Calculate the work done by the resistance force in the first and second 10 s intervals.

34 A bungee jumper of mass 60 kg jumps from a bridge 24 m above the surface of the water. The rope is 12 m long and is assumed to obey Hooke's law.

(a) What should the spring constant of the rope be if the woman is to just reach the water?

(b) The same rope is used by a man whose mass is more than 60 kg. Explain why the man will not stop before reaching the water. (Treat the jumper as a point and ignore any resistance to motion.)

35 For the bungee jumper of mass 60 kg in question 34, calculate:

(a) the speed of the jumper when she has fallen by 12 m;

(b) the maximum speed attained by the jumper during her fall.

(c) Explain why the maximum speed is reached after falling more than a distance of 12 m (the unstretched length of the rope).

HL only

(d) Sketch a graph to show the variation of the speed of the jumper with distance fallen.

36 A carriage of mass 800 kg moving at 5.0 m s^{-1} collides with another carriage of mass 1200 kg that is initially at rest. Both carriages are equipped with buffers. The graph in Figure 7.32 shows the velocities of the two carriages before, during and after the collision.

Figure 7.32 For question 36.

Use the graph to:

(a) show that the collision has been elastic;

(b) calculate the average force on each carriage during the collision;

(c) calculate the impulse given to the heavy carriage.

(d) If the buffers on the two carriages had been stiffer, the time of contact would have been less but the final velocities would be unchanged. How would your answers to (b) and (c) change?

(e) Calculate the kinetic energy of the two carriages at the time during the collision when both have the same velocity and compare your answer with the final kinetic energy of the carriages. How do you account for the difference?

HL only

37 Show that in an elastic, head-on collision of a particle of mass m with a stationary particle of mass M the fraction of the original kinetic energy transferred to M is

$$\frac{4Mm}{(m+M)^2}$$

38 Two masses of 3.0 kg and 8.0 kg collide head-on elastically. Before the collision the 8.0 kg mass is at rest and the 3.0 kg moves at speed 10.0 m s⁻¹. Find the velocities after the collision.

39 Two masses of 6.0 kg and 4.0 kg are constrained to move on a frictionless horizontal ring as shown in Figure 7.33.

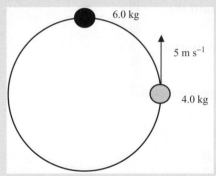

Figure 7.33 For question 39.

Initially the heavy mass is at rest and the other moves in a counter-clockwise direction with speed 5.0 m s⁻¹. At $t = 0$ s the two masses collide elastically. With what velocities do the masses move after the collision? At what points on the circle do subsequent collisions take place?

HL only

40 A mass m moves with a speed v on a horizontal table towards a wedge of mass M, as shown in Figure 7.34. How high on the wedge will m get if:
   (a) the wedge is firmly fixed on the table;
   (b) the wedge is free to move on the table without friction?

Figure 7.34 For question 40.

41 A battery toy car of mass 0.250 kg is made to move up an inclined plane which makes an angle of 30° with the horizontal. The car starts from rest and its motor provides a constant acceleration of 4 m s⁻² for 5 s. The motor is then turned off.
   (a) Find the distance travelled in the first 5 s.
   (b) Find the furthest the car gets on the inclined plane.
   (c) When does the car return to its starting place?
   (d) Make a graph of the velocity as a function of time.
   (e) On the same axes, make a graph of the kinetic energy and potential energy of the car as a function of the distance travelled.
   (f) In which periods in the car's motion is its mechanical energy conserved?
   (g) What is the average power developed by the car's motor?
   (h) What is the maximum power developed by the motor?

Circular motion

Our discussion of motion so far has been restricted to motion in a straight line. In this chapter, we examine the more complicated motion of an object along a circular path.

Objectives

By the end of this chapter you should be able to:
- understand that acceleration is present when the *magnitude of the velocity*, or its *direction*, or *both change*;
- understand that in motion on a circle with constant speed there is *centripetal acceleration* of constant magnitude, $a_c = \frac{v^2}{r}$, directed at the centre of the circle;
- recognize situations in which a force is acting in a direction *toward the centre of a circle*;
- solve problems involving applications of Newton's second law to motion on a circle, $F_{net} = ma_c = \frac{mv^2}{r}$.

Circular motion and centripetal acceleration

We now examine the case of motion on a circle. Consider the object in Figure 8.1, which rotates on a circle of radius R in the counter-clockwise direction, with constant speed v.

Let T be the time taken to complete one full revolution. We call T the *period* of the motion. Since the speed is constant and the object covers a distance of $2\pi R$ in a time of T s, it

follows that

$$v = \frac{2\pi R}{T}$$

We may also note that the object sweeps out an angle of 2π radians in a time equal to the period, so we define the angular speed of the object by

$$\text{angular speed} = \frac{\text{angle swept}}{\text{time taken}}$$

that is

$$\omega = \frac{2\pi}{T}$$

The units of angular speed are radians per second or just s^{-1}.

It is important to note right away that the speed may be constant but the velocity is not. It keeps changing direction. (The velocity vector is at a tangent to the circle – see Figure 8.2.) Since the velocity changes, we have acceleration.

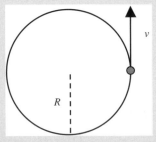

Figure 8.1 An object moving on a circle of radius R.

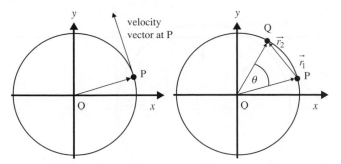

Figure 8.2 The velocity vector is tangent to the circular path.

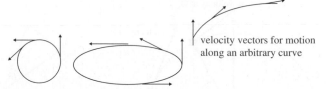

Figure 8.3 The velocity vector is tangential to the path.

What follows is a *derivation* of the expression for acceleration in circular motion. You may want to skip it and go directly to the result just before the end of this section (p. 120).

The position vector at time t_1 is given by $\vec{r}_1$ and at a later time t_2 by the vector $\vec{r}_2$. Note that since we chose the origin of our coordinate axes to be at the centre of the circle, the displacement vector of the moving object always has the same magnitude, equal to the radius of the circle. Thus, what changes as the object moves is the direction of the displacement vector, not its magnitude. The velocity of the object is defined as

$$\vec{v} = \frac{\Delta \vec{r}}{\Delta t}$$

where $\Delta \vec{r}$ is a vector representing the difference $\vec{r}_2 - \vec{r}_1$, and the time difference $\Delta t = t_2 - t_1$ is assumed to be as small as possible. It is clear that the vector $\Delta \vec{r}$ is the vector from P to Q. Similarly, the speed of the object is the distance travelled, which is the length of the arc Δs divided by Δt. But remember that the time interval $\Delta t = t_2 - t_1$ must be taken to be as small as possible. As this time difference becomes infinitesimal, $\Delta \vec{r}$ becomes tangential to the circle at point P.

▶ This means that the direction of the velocity for motion on a circle has a direction that is at a tangent to the circle. This is a general result. The direction of velocity is always at a tangent to the path (see Figure 8.3).

The magnitude of the velocity is the magnitude of $\Delta \vec{r}$ divided by Δt. The speed, on the other hand, is the ratio of Δs, the distance travelled, to Δt. Thus, the magnitudes of velocity and speed appear to be different. But recall again that Δt must be infinitesimal, which implies that the difference in the length of Δs and that of $\Delta \vec{r}$ becomes negligible. Thus, the magnitude of velocity is the speed.

▶ Similarly, for acceleration

$$\vec{a} = \frac{\Delta \vec{v}}{\Delta t}$$

where $\Delta \vec{v}$ is a vector. Thus, we have acceleration every time the velocity *vector* changes. This vector will change if:
- its magnitude changes;
- the direction changes;
- both magnitude and direction change.

For motion in a circle with constant *speed*, it is the direction of the velocity vector that changes. We must thus find the difference $\vec{v}_Q - \vec{v}_P$. (Note that the magnitude of the velocity vectors at P and Q are the same – they equal the constant speed v of the moving object.)

In Figure 8.4 the velocity vector at Q has been moved parallel to itself so that it starts at the same point as the velocity vector at P. The difference is thus as shown. The magnitude of this vector can be found from simple trigonometry. From the sine rule

$$\frac{\Delta v}{\sin \theta} = \frac{v}{\sin\left(\frac{\pi}{2} - \frac{\theta}{2}\right)}$$

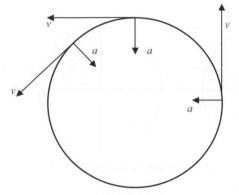

Figure 8.4 The velocity vector changes direction in circular motion, hence we have acceleration.

Figure 8.5 The centripetal acceleration vector is normal to the velocity vector.

Recall now that the points P and Q are separated only infinitesimally from each other and so the angle θ is very small. Thus, $\sin\theta \approx \theta$ and $\sin(\frac{\pi}{2} - \frac{\theta}{2}) \approx 1$ (the angle must be expressed in radians). Further, $\theta = \frac{\Delta s}{R}$ and $\Delta s = v\Delta t$. Substituting, we find

$$\Delta v = \frac{vv\,\Delta t}{R}$$
$$\Rightarrow a_c = \frac{v^2}{R}$$

This gives us the magnitude of the acceleration vector for motion around a circle of radius R with constant speed v. As we see, the magnitude of the acceleration vector is constant, if v is constant. But what about its direction? As Δt gets smaller and smaller, the angle θ gets smaller and smaller, which means that the vector $\Delta\vec{v}$, which is in the direction of acceleration, becomes perpendicular to $\vec{v}$. This means that the acceleration vector is normal to the circle and directed towards the centre of the circle. It is a **centripetal acceleration**.

▶ A body moving along a circle of radius R with speed v experiences centripetal acceleration that has magnitude given by $a_c = \frac{v^2}{R}$ and is directed toward the centre of the circle. (See Figure 8.5.)

If the magnitude of the velocity changes, we have **tangential acceleration**. This is a vector directed along the velocity vector if the speed is increasing and opposite to the velocity vector if the speed is decreasing. The magnitude of the tangential acceleration is given by

$$a_t = \frac{\Delta v}{\Delta t}$$

where v is the speed and Δt is infinitesimally small.

When the velocity direction and magnitude are changing, we have both centripetal acceleration and tangential acceleration. The total acceleration is then the vector sum of the vectors representing these accelerations.

Example questions

Q1

A mass moves along a circle of radius 2.0 m with constant speed. It makes one full revolution in 3.0 s. What is the acceleration of the mass?

Answer

The acceleration is v^2/R so we need to know v. But since the mass covers a distance of $2\pi R$ in a time $T = 3.0$ s, we must have

$$v = \frac{2\pi R}{T}$$
$$= \frac{2 \times 3.14 \times 2.0}{3.0}\,\text{m s}^{-1}$$
$$= 4.2\,\text{m s}^{-1}$$

Hence $a = 8.8$ m s^{-2}.

Q2

The radius of the earth is $R = 6.4 \times 10^6$ m. What is the centripetal acceleration experienced by someone on the equator?

Answer

A mass on the equator covers a distance of $2\pi R$ in a time $T = 1$ day. Thus

$v = 4.6 \times 10^2 \, \text{m s}^{-1}$

and so

$a = 3.4 \times 10^{-2} \, \text{m s}^{-2}$

This is quite small compared with the acceleration due to gravity.

Q3

A mass moves in a circle with constant speed in a counter-clockwise direction, as in Figure 8.6a. What is the direction of the velocity change when the mass moves from A to B?

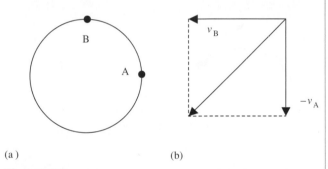

(a)   (b)

Figure 8.6.

Answer

The velocity at A is vertical and at B it points to the left. The change in the velocity vector is $\vec{v}_B - \vec{v}_A$ and this difference of vectors is directed as shown in Figure 8.6b.

Centripetal forces

If we know that a body moves in a circle, then we know at once that a net force must be acting on the body, since it moves with acceleration. If the speed is constant, the direction of the acceleration is towards the centre of the circle and therefore that is also the direction of the net force. It is a **centripetal force**. Consider a car that moves on a circular level road of radius r with constant speed v. Friction between the

wheels and the road provides the necessary force directed towards the centre of the circle that enables the car to take the turn. (See Figure 8.7.)

Figure 8.7 A car will skid outwards (i.e. will cover a circle of larger radius) if the friction force is not large enough.

Example questions

Q4

A mass is tied to a string and moves with constant speed in a horizontal circle. The string is tied to the ceiling, at a point higher than the mass. Draw the forces on the mass.

Answer

The common mistake here is to put a horizontal force pointing toward the centre and call it the centripetal force. When you are asked to find forces on a body, the list of forces that are available include the weight, reaction forces (if the body touches another body), friction (if there is friction), tension (if there are strings or springs), resistance forces (if the body moves in air or a fluid), electric forces (if electric charges are involved), etc. Nowhere in this list is there an entry for a centripetal force.

Think of the word centripetal as simply an adjective that *describes* forces already acting on the body, *not* as a new force. In this example, the only forces on the mass are the weight and the tension. If we decompose the tension into horizontal and vertical components, we see that the weight is equal and opposite to the vertical component of the tension. This means that the only force left on the body is the horizontal component of the tension. We may now call this force the centripetal force. But this is not a new force. It is simply the component of a force that is already acting on the body. (See Figure 8.8.)

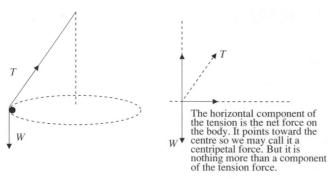

Figure 8.8.

Q5

A mass m is tied to a string and *made* to move in a vertical circle of radius R with constant speed v. Find the tension in the string at the lowest and highest points.

Answer

The forces are as shown in Figure 8.9. At the lowest point, the net force is $T_1 - mg$ and so

$$T_1 - mg = m\frac{v^2}{r}$$

giving

$$T_1 = mg + m\frac{v^2}{r}$$

At the highest point, the net force is $mg + T_2$ and so

$$T_2 = m\frac{v^2}{r} - mg$$

This shows that the string goes slack unless $v^2 > gr$.

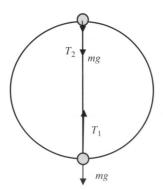

Figure 8.9 The tension in the string is different at different positions of the mass.

It is important to note that, since a centripetal force is at right angles to the direction of motion, the work done by the force is zero. (Recall that $W = Fs\cos\theta$, and here the angle is a right angle.)

It is a common mistake in circular motion problems to include a force pushing the body *away* from the centre of the circle: a **centrifugal force**. It is important to stress that no such force exists. A body in circular motion cannot be in equilibrium and so no force pushing away from the centre is required.

Supplementary material

Angular momentum

Consider a point mass m which rotates about some axis with speed v as shown in Figure 8.10.

Figure 8.10 A mass rotating counter-clockwise in a circle has an angular momentum pointing out of the page.

We define the magnitude of the angular momentum of the mass m by

$$L = mvr$$

(Angular momentum is a vector but we will not make use of its vector nature here.) If the mass moves along a path other than a circle, then the angular momentum is given by

$$L = mvb$$

where b is the *perpendicular* distance of the axis from the direction of velocity. In Figure 8.11 the axis goes into the page through P. Since $b = r\sin\theta$ it follows that $L = mvr\sin\theta$, where θ is the angle between the velocity vector and the vector from the axis to the position of the mass. The units of angular momentum are J s.

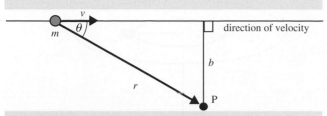

Figure 8.11 A mass has angular momentum about an axis through P.

Example question

Q6

Find the angular momentum of two masses, each of 2.0 kg, that are separated by 5.0 m and rotate about an axis along the perpendicular bisector of the line joining them with speed $v = 7.5$ m s^{-1} (see Figure 8.12).

5.0 m

Figure 8.12.

Answer

$L = 2mvr = 75$ J s.

Questions

1 A mass moves on a circular path of radius 2.0 m at constant speed 4.0 m s^{-1} (see Figure 8.13).
   (a) What is the magnitude and direction of the *average* acceleration during a quarter of a revolution (from A to B)?
   (b) What is the centripetal acceleration of the mass?

B

A

Figure 8.13 For question 1.

2 A body of mass 1.00 kg is tied to a string and rotates on a horizontal, frictionless table.
   (a) If the length of the string is 40.0 cm and the speed of revolution is 2.0 m s^{-1}, find the tension in the string.
   (b) If the string breaks when the tension exceeds 20.0 N, what is the largest speed the mass can rotate at?
   (c) If the breaking tension of the string is 20.0 N but you want the mass to rotate at 4.00 m s^{-1}, what is the shortest length string that can be used?

3 An astronaut rotates at the end of a test machine whose arm has a length of 10.0 m, as shown in Figure 8.14. If the acceleration she experiences must not exceed $5g$ ($g = 10$ m s^{-2}), what is the maximum number of revolutions per minute of the arm?

10 m

Figure 8.14 For question 3.

4 A wheel of radius R rotates making f revolutions per second. The quantity f is known as the frequency of the motion. Show that $1/f$ is the time to complete one revolution, called the period T of the motion. Show that the centripetal acceleration of a point at the rim of the wheel is

$a = 4\pi^2 R f^2$

5 The earth (mass $= 5.98 \times 10^{24}$ kg) rotates around the sun in an orbit that is approximately circular, with a radius of 1.5×10^{11} m.
   (a) Find the orbital speed of the earth around the sun.
   (b) Find the centripetal acceleration experienced by the earth.
   (c) Find the magnitude of the gravitational force exerted on the earth by the sun.

6 (a) What is the angular speed of a mass that completes a 3.5 m radius circle in 1.24 s?
   (b) What is the frequency of the motion?

7 What is the centripetal acceleration of a mass that moves in a circle of radius 2.45 m making 3.5 revolutions per second?

8 What would be the length of the day if the centripetal acceleration at the equator were equal to the acceleration due to gravity? ($g = 9.8\,\mathrm{m\,s^{-2}}$.)

9 A loop-the-loop machine has radius R of 18 m (see Figure 8.15).
   (a) What is the minimum speed at which a cart must travel so that it will safely loop the loop?
   (b) What will the speed at the top be in this case?

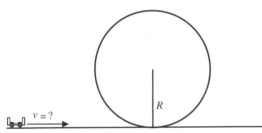

Figure 8.15 For question 9.

10 Calculate the centripetal force on the earth as it rotates around the sun. The mass of the earth is about $6.0 \times 10^{24}\,\mathrm{kg}$. The earth orbits the sun in a circular orbit of radius $1.5 \times 10^{11}\,\mathrm{m}$ in one year.

11 What is the centripetal acceleration of a point on the earth at 50° latitude as a result of the earth's rotation about its axis? Express the answer as a fraction of g, the acceleration due to gravity. What angle to the true vertical would a mass hanging at the end of a string make? Take g to be exactly $9.8\,\mathrm{m\,s^{-2}}$.

12 A horizontal disc has a hole through its centre. A string passes through the hole and connects a mass m on top of the disc to a bigger mass M that hangs below the disc. Initially the smaller mass is rotating on the disc in a circle of radius r. What must the speed of m be such that the big mass stands still? (See Figure 8.16.)

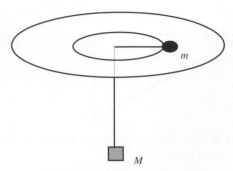

Figure 8.16 For question 12.

13 A mass of 5.00 kg is tied to two strings of equal length, which are attached to a vertical pole at points 2.0 m apart. As the pole rotates about its axis, the strings make a right angle with each other, as shown in Figure 8.17.

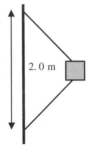

Figure 8.17 For question 13.

If the mass makes 2 revolutions per second, find:
(a) the tension in each string;
(b) the speed of revolution that makes the lower string go slack;
(c) If the mass now rotates at half the speed you found in part (b), find the angle the top string makes with the vertical.

14 A mass moves counter-clockwise along a vertical circle of radius 4.00 m. At positions A and B, where the radii make an angle of 45° with the horizontal (see Figure 8.18), the mass has speed 4.0 m s^{-1}. At A the speed of the mass is increasing at a rate of 3.0 m s^{-2} whereas at B the speed is decreasing at a rate of 3.0 m s^{-2}. Thus, the acceleration of the mass in each position consists of the centripetal acceleration (which is directed toward the centre) and a tangential acceleration whose magnitude is the rate of change of speed. Find the magnitude and direction of the acceleration vector of the mass at positions A and B.

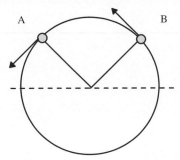

Figure 8.18 For question 14.

15 In an amusement park ride a cart of mass 300 kg and carrying four passengers each of mass 60 kg is dropped from a vertical height of 120 m along a path that leads into a loop-the-loop machine of radius 30 m. The cart then enters a straight stretch from A to C where friction brings it to rest after a distance of 40 m. (See Figure 8.19.)

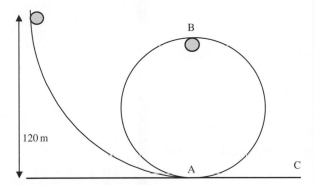

Figure 8.19 For question 15.

(a) Find the velocity of the cart at A.
(b) Find the reaction force from the seat of the cart onto a passenger at B.
(c) What is the acceleration experienced by the cart from A to C (assumed constant)?

16 A mass of 5.0 kg is attached to a string of length 2.0 m which is initially horizontal. The mass is then released. Figure 8.20 shows the mass when the string is in a vertical position.
(a) Find the speed of the mass when the string is in the vertical position.
(b) Find the acceleration of the mass.
(c) Draw the forces on the mass.
(d) Find the tension in the string.

initial position of mass

Figure 8.20 For question 16.

17 A neutron star has a radius of 50.0 km and completes one revolution every 25 ms. Calculate the centripetal acceleration experienced at the equator of the star.

18 In an amusement park a box is attached to a rod of length 25 m and rotates in a vertical circle. The park claims that the centripetal acceleration felt by the occupants sitting firmly in the box is $4g$. How many revolutions per minute does the machine make?

19 A marble rolls from the top of a big sphere as shown in Figure 8.21. What is the angle θ when the marble is about to leave the sphere? Assume a zero speed at the top.

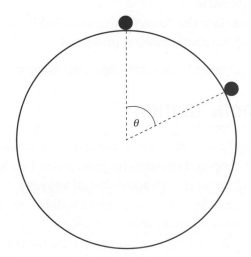

Figure 8.21 For question 19.

Projectile motion

Galileo is credited with the discovery of the secrets of parabolic motion. He did experiments with falling bodies, from which he deduced the acceleration due to gravity and its independence of the body's mass, and discovered that projectiles follow parabolic paths. Examples of parabolic motion include the paths of a stone thrown into the air at an angle, a bullet shot from a gun and water sprayed from a hose. The basic fact here is that every object that falls freely under the action of the earth's gravity experiences an acceleration g directed vertically down. In what follows, it is assumed that the earth is flat. This means that we only consider a small part of the earth's surface so that it is approximately flat, in which case the acceleration due to gravity is pointing normally to the horizontal ground.

Objectives

By the end of this chapter you should be able to:
* understand parabolic motion as a *combination of two simultaneous straight-line motions*, one horizontal and one vertical;
* understand that in parabolic motion there is an acceleration in the vertical direction (due to gravity) but none in the horizontal direction;
* derive expressions for maximum height (by setting $v_y = 0$) and maximum range ($y = 0$) reached by imposing appropriate conditions on the equations;
* solve problems of *parabolic motion*;
* draw the *velocity* and *acceleration vectors* of the projectile at various points on its path;
* appreciate the convenience afforded by the *law of conservation of energy* in some parabolic motion problems.

Parabolic motion

Let us begin by looking at what happens when an object is thrown horizontally from some height h above the ground with some initial velocity. Experience tells us that the object will follow a curved path and will eventually fall to the ground. What we want to know is how far the object travels, how long it takes to fall to the ground, the precise shape of the curved path, etc.

Figure 9.1 shows the positions of two objects every 0.2 s: the first was simply allowed to drop from rest, the other was launched horizontally with no vertical component of velocity. We see that the displacements in the y (i.e. vertical) direction are covered *in the same time*.

How do we understand this fact? A simple way is to make use of the concept of relative velocity. Consider two bodies, one dropped from rest and the other launched horizontally with velocity v. From the point of view of a stationary observer on the ground, body B falls vertically whereas body A follows a parabolic path. Consider now the description of the same situation from the

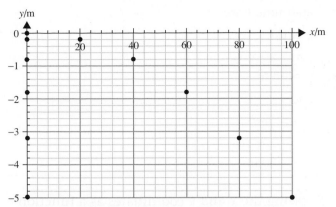

Figure 9.1 A body dropped from rest and one launched horizontally cover the same vertical displacement in the same time.

point of view of another observer on the ground who moves with velocity $v/2$ with respect to the ground. From the point of view of this observer, body A has velocity $v/2$ and body B has velocity $-v/2$. The motions of the two bodies are therefore *identical* (except for direction). So this observer will determine that the two bodies reach the ground at the *same time*. Since time is absolute in Newtonian physics, the two bodies

must reach the ground at the same time as far as any other observer is concerned as well. (See Figure 9.2.)

This means that the motion of the body launched horizontally can be analysed quite simply because we can separate the vertical motion from the horizontal motion. Let v_0 be the initial velocity of the object in the horizontal direction. Since there is no acceleration in this direction, the horizontal velocity component at all times will be equal to v_0

$$v_x = v_0$$

and the displacement in the horizontal direction will be given by

$$x = v_0 t$$

In the vertical direction, the object experiences an acceleration g in the vertically down direction. Thus, the velocity in the vertical direction will be given by

$$v_y = -gt$$

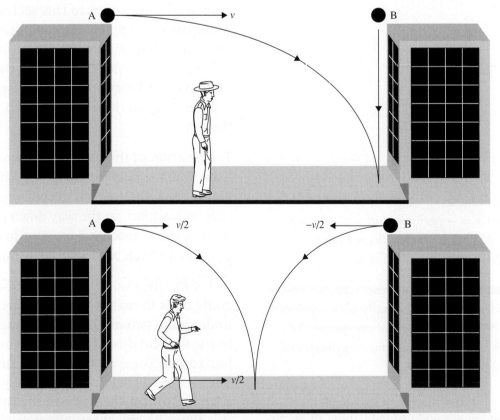

Figure 9.2 The motions of the ball projected horizontally and the ball dropped vertically from rest are identical from the point of view of the moving observer. The two balls will thus reach the ground at the same time.

(we are assuming that positive velocity means the body moves upward; the acceleration due to gravity is then negative, or $-g$) and the displacement is given by

$$y = -\frac{1}{2}gt^2$$

The point of launch is assumed to be the origin, as in Figure 9.3, so that the initial displacement is zero, $x = 0$, $y = 0$.

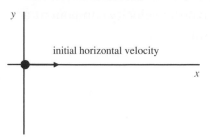

Figure 9.3.

Example questions

Q1

An object is launched horizontally from a height of 20.0 m above the ground, as shown in Figure 9.4. When will it hit the ground?

Figure 9.4.

Answer

The object will hit the ground when $y = -20.0$ m, and thus from $y = -\frac{1}{2}gt^2$ we find $-20 = -5t^2$, giving $t = 2.0$ s. Note that we do not need to know the actual velocity of launch.

Q2

An object is launched horizontally with a velocity of 12 m s^{-1}. What is the vertical component of velocity after 2.0 s? What are the coordinates of the object after 4.0 s?

Answer

The horizontal component of velocity is 12 m s^{-1} at all times. From $v_y = -gt$, the vertical component is $v_y = -20$ m s^{-1}. The coordinates

after time t are

$$x = v_0 t$$
$$= 12.0 \times 4.0$$
$$= 48 \text{ m}$$

and

$$y = -\frac{1}{2}gt^2$$
$$= -5 \times 16$$
$$= -80 \text{ m}$$

Knowing the x and y coordinates as a function of time allows us to find the shape of the curved path followed by an object launched horizontally: from $x = v_0 t$ we solve for time $t = \frac{x}{v_0}$ and substituting in $y = -\frac{1}{2}gt^2$ we find

$$y = -\frac{1}{2}g\left(\frac{x}{v_0}\right)^2$$

which is the equation of a parabola.

Launch at an arbitrary angle

In the previous section we studied the horizontal launch of a projectile. In this section we will study the more general case of launch at an arbitrary angle. Figure 9.5 shows an object thrown at an angle of $\theta = 30°$ to the horizontal with initial velocity vector $\vec{v}_0$, whose magnitude is 20 m s^{-1}, and the path it follows through the air.

The position of the object is shown every 0.2 s. Note how the dots get closer together as the object rises (the speed is decreasing) and how they move apart on the way down (the speed is increasing). It reaches a maximum height of 5.1 m and travels a horizontal distance of 35 m.

As before, the easiest way to analyse what is going on is to realize that the object is actually undergoing two motions simultaneously – one in the vertical direction and another in the horizontal. Thus, if the object begins at point O (see Figure 9.6) at $t = 0$ and subsequently finds itself at point P, then we can say that during this time the object actually moved a horizontal displacement OX and a vertical displacement OY. Note that the time taken to cover the

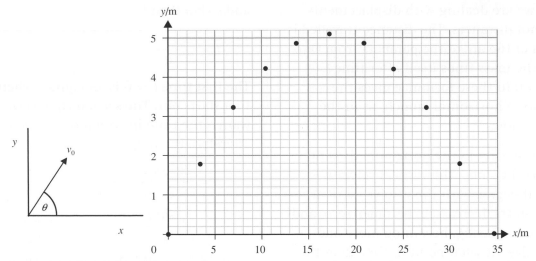

Figure 9.5 An object is launched at an arbitrary angle to the horizontal. The path followed is parabolic.

displacement OX is the same as the time taken to cover OY. OX and OY are just the components of the displacement vector of the mass at P.

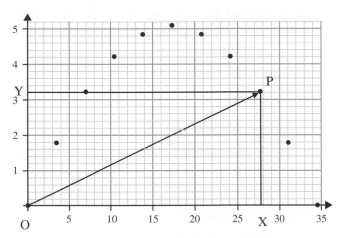

Figure 9.6 The position vector of a point P as an object executes parabolic motion.

The point of doing things this way is that we have succeeded in reducing the motion in the plane into two motions taking place at the same time on straight lines. Since we know all about straight-line motion, it means we also know all about motion in a plane.

Let us then throw an object into the air with velocity vector $\vec{v}_0$ (of magnitude v_0) at an angle θ to the horizontal. The suffix zero in $\vec{v}_0$ is to remind us that this is the initial velocity of the object. The component of initial velocity in the horizontal direction is simply $v_0 \cos\theta$.

▶ At any future time, the horizontal velocity component will be the same, that is

$$v_x = v_0 \cos\theta$$

since there is no acceleration horizontally. If we call the displacement in the horizontal direction x, then after a time of t s goes by

$$x = v_0 t \cos\theta$$

On the other hand, in the vertical direction there is acceleration, namely the acceleration due to gravity, g. (In our formulae, the acceleration will be taken to be negative. A positive velocity means that the mass is moving up. On the way up, the velocity decreases and so the acceleration is negative. On the way down, the velocity is getting more and more negative and so the acceleration must again be taken to be negative.)

▶ The initial velocity in the vertical direction is $v_0 \sin\theta$, so the vertical velocity component at any time t after launch is given by

$$v_y = v_0 \sin\theta - gt$$

The displacement in the vertical direction, y, after time t seconds is given by

$$y = v_0 t \sin\theta - \tfrac{1}{2}gt^2$$

Note that we are dealing with displacements here and not distances. The distance travelled is the length of the arc of the parabola from O to wherever the mass finds itself after time t. Setting $\theta = 0$ in these formulae gives the formulae for a horizontal launch, as in the previous section.

Unlike the velocity in the horizontal direction, which stays the same, the vertical velocity is changing. It begins with the value $v_0 \sin \theta$ at time zero, starts decreasing, becomes zero, and then keeps decreasing, becoming more and more negative. At what point in time does the vertical velocity component become zero? Setting $v_y = 0$ we find

$$0 = v_0 \sin \theta - gt$$
$$\Rightarrow t = \frac{v_0 \sin \theta}{g}$$

The time when the vertical velocity becomes zero is, of course, the time when the mass attains its maximum height. What is this height? Going back to the equation for the vertical component of displacement we find that when

$$t = \frac{v_0 \sin \theta}{g}$$

y is given by

$$y_{max} = v_0 \frac{v_0 \sin \theta}{g} \sin \theta - \frac{1}{2} \left(\frac{v_0 \sin \theta}{g} \right)^2$$
$$= \frac{v_0^2 \sin^2 \theta}{2g}$$

This is the formula for the maximum height attained by the mass. You should not remember it by heart but rather you should be able to derive it.

What about the maximum displacement in the horizontal direction (sometimes called the range)? At this point the vertical component of displacement is zero. Setting $y = 0$ in the formula for y gives

$$0 = v_0 t \sin \theta - \frac{1}{2} g t^2$$
$$= t \left(v_0 \sin \theta - \frac{1}{2} g t \right)$$

and so $t = 0$ and

$$t = \frac{2 v_0 \sin \theta}{g}$$

The first time $t = 0$ is, of course, when the mass first starts out. The second time is what we want – the time in which the range is covered. Therefore the range is

$$x = \frac{2 v_0^2 \sin \theta \cos \theta}{g}$$
$$= \frac{v_0^2 \sin 2\theta}{g}$$

Note, incidentally, that the time it takes to cover the range is twice the time needed to reach the maximum height. This suggests that the motion is symmetric about the highest point.

The maximum value of $\sin 2\theta$ is 1 and this happens when $2\theta = 90°$ (i.e. $\theta = 45°$); in other words, we obtain the maximum range with a launch angle of 45°. This equation also says that there are two different angles of launch that give the same range for the same initial speed. These two angles add up to a right angle (can you see why?).

Example questions

Q3 ▓▓▓▓▓▓▓▓▓▓▓▓▓▓▓▓▓▓▓▓▓▓▓▓▓▓▓▓
A mass is launched with a speed of 10 m s^{-1} at
(a) 30° to the horizontal;
(b) 0° to the horizontal;
(c) 90° to the horizontal.
Find the x- and y-components of the initial velocity in each case.

Answer

(a) $v_x = v_0 \cos \theta$
$\quad\quad = 10 \times \cos 30°$
$\quad\quad = 8.66$ m s^{-1}
$\quad v_y = v_0 \sin \theta$
$\quad\quad = 10 \times \sin 30°$
$\quad\quad = 5$ m s^{-1}

(b) $v_x = 10$ m s^{-1}
$\quad v_y = 0$ m s^{-1}

(c) $v_x = 0$
$\quad v_y = 10$ m s^{-1}

Q4

Sketch graphs to show the variation with time of the horizontal and vertical components of velocity of the projectile of example question 3(a).

Answer

See Figure 9.7.

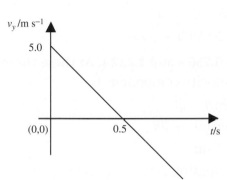

Figure 9.7.

Q5

A mass is launched at 30° to the horizontal with initial speed 25.0 m s^{-1}. What is the maximum height obtained?

Answer

The vertical velocity is given by

$$v_y = v_0 \sin \theta - gt$$

and becomes zero at the highest point. Thus

$$t = \frac{v_0 \sin \theta}{g}$$
$$= 1.25 \text{ s}$$

and so maximum height = 7.82 m by substituting in the formula for y.

Q6

After what time does the mass in the previous example question move a horizontal distance of 3.0 m?

Answer

$$x = v_0 t \cos \theta$$

and so

$$t = \frac{3.0}{25.0 \times \cos 30°}$$
$$= 0.14 \text{ s}$$

Q7

For the same mass as in example questions 5 and 6, when is the height of the mass 4.0 m?

Answer

From

$$y = v_0 t \sin \theta - \tfrac{1}{2} g t^2$$

we find

$$4.0 = 25t \times 0.5 - 5t^2$$

and so $y = 4.00$ m when $t = 0.38$ s and $t = 2.1$ s. There are two solutions here since the mass attains the height of 4 m twice: on its way up and on its way down.

Q8

A projectile is launched horizontally from a height of 45 m above the ground. As it hits the ground, the velocity makes an angle of 60° to the horizontal. Find the initial velocity of launch.

Answer

The time it takes to hit the ground is found from $y = -\tfrac{1}{2} g t^2$ (here $\theta = 0$ since the launch is horizontal) and so

$$-45 = -5t^2$$
$$\Rightarrow t = 3 \text{ s}$$

Thus, when the projectile hits the ground

$$v_y = 0 - 10 \times 3$$
$$= -30 \text{ m s}^{-1}$$

Hence

$$\tan 60° = \left| \frac{v_y}{v_x} \right|$$

$$\Rightarrow v_x = \frac{30}{\tan 60°}$$
$$= 17 \text{ m s}^{-1}$$

The shape of the path

(The proof is not required for examination purposes.) The last thing that remains to be done here is to figure out the shape of the path the object follows in the air. We can do this very easily by concentrating on the formulae for displacement in the x and y directions:

$$x = v_0 t \cos\theta$$
$$y = v_0 t \sin\theta - \tfrac{1}{2}gt^2$$

Using the first equation we solve for time to find $t = \frac{x}{v_0 \cos\theta}$ and substituting in the expression for y we find

$$y = v_0 \sin\theta \left(\frac{x}{v_0 \cos\theta}\right) - \frac{1}{2}g\left(\frac{x}{v_0 \cos\theta}\right)^2$$
$$y = x\tan\theta - \frac{g}{2v_0^2 \cos^2\theta}x^2$$

which is the equation of a parabola.

Use of energy conservation

In some problems we are asked to find the speed of a projectile at some point along its path. If speed is all that is being asked for, a very simple method using the law of conservation of energy can be used. Consider the following example. A ball is launched at 12 m s^{-1} at an angle of 60° to the horizontal. It lands on the roof of a building 5 m high (see Figure 9.8). What is the speed of the ball on landing?

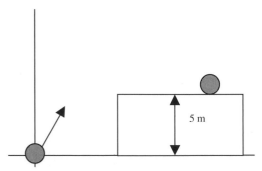

Figure 9.8 A ball is launched at ground level and lands on the roof of a building.

Let us use conservation of energy first. At launch, the total energy of the mass is $E = \tfrac{1}{2}mv^2$ and on landing it is $E = \tfrac{1}{2}mu^2 + mgh$.

Equating the two results in

$$\tfrac{1}{2}mu^2 + mgh = \tfrac{1}{2}mv^2$$
$$\Rightarrow u^2 = v^2 - 2gh$$

This gives

$$u^2 = 144 - 2 \times 10 \times 5$$
$$= 44$$
$$\Rightarrow u = 6.63 \text{ m s}^{-1}$$

Another method of solution uses the equations of projectile motion and is much more complicated. We must find the vertical component of velocity when the vertical displacement of the ball is 5 m: we use $y = v_0 t \sin\theta - \tfrac{1}{2}gt^2$ to find the time when the vertical displacement becomes 5 m. The result is found from:

$$5 = 12t\sin 60° - 5t^2$$
$$\Rightarrow 5t^2 - 10.392t + 5 = 0$$

The roots are 0.756 s and 1.322 s. At these times, the vertical velocity component is

$$v_y = v_0\sin\theta - gt$$
$$= 12\sin 60° - 10t$$
$$= \pm 2.83 \text{ m s}^{-1}$$

The speed on landing is thus given by

$$u = \sqrt{v_y^2 + v_x^2}$$
$$= \sqrt{2.83^2 + 6^2}$$
$$= 6.63 \text{ m s}^{-1}$$

The advantage of the energy conservation method is clear.

Questions

1 An arrow is shot horizontally towards point O, which is at a distance of 20.0 m. It hits point P 0.10 s later. (See Figure 9.9.)
   (a) What is the distance OP?
   (b) What was the arrow's initial velocity?

Figure 9.9 For question 1.

2 A ball rolls off a table with a horizontal speed 2.0 m s^{-1}. If the table is 1.3 m high, how far from the table will the ball land?

3 A ball is kicked horizontally with a speed of 5.0 m s^{-1} from the roof of a house 3 m high.
 (a) When will the ball hit the ground?
 (b) What will the speed of the ball be just before hitting the ground?

4 An object is launched horizontally with a speed of 8.0 m s^{-1} from a point 20 m from the ground.
 (a) How long will it take the object to land on the ground?
 (b) What is the speed of the object 1 s after launch?
 (c) What angle does the velocity make with the horizontal 1 s after launch?
 (d) With what velocity does the object hit the ground?

5 Two objects are thrown horizontally with the same speed (4.0 m s^{-1}) from heights of 4.0 m and 8.0 m, as shown in Figure 9.10. What distance will separate the two objects when both land on the ground?

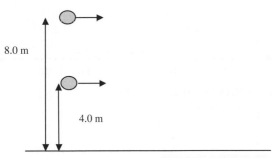

Figure 9.10 For question 5.

6 With what speed should the object at 4.0 m height in Figure 9.10 be launched if it is to land at the same point as the object launched from 8.0 m at 4.0 m s^{-1}?

7 A plane flying at a constant speed of 50.0 m s^{-1} and a constant height of 200 m drops a package of emergency supplies to a group of hikers. If the package is released just as the plane flies over a huge fir tree, find at what distance from the tree the package will land.

8 The longest distance an athlete can throw the discus is L. How high would the same athlete be able to throw the discus vertically? (Assume, unrealistically, that the speed of throwing is the same in both cases and ignore air resistance.)

9 In a loop-the-loop cart, as shown in Figure 9.11, a passenger drops their keys when at the highest point. The cart is moving at 6 m s^{-1} and is 8 m from the ground. Where will the keys land?

Figure 9.11 For question 9.

10 For an object thrown at an angle of 40° to the horizontal at a speed of 20 m s^{-1}, draw graphs of:
 (a) horizontal velocity against time;
 (b) vertical velocity against time;
 (c) acceleration against time.

11 What is the highest point reached by an object thrown with speed 4.0 m s^{-1} at 40° to the horizontal?

12 A stone is thrown with initial speed 6.0 m s^{-1} at 35° to the horizontal. What is the direction of the velocity vector 1 s later?

13 An object is thrown with speed 20.0 m s^{-1} at an angle of 50° to the horizontal. Draw graphs to show the variation with time of:
 (a) the horizontal displacement;
 (b) the vertical displacement.

14 An object of mass 4.0 kg is thrown with speed 20.0 m s^{-1} at an angle of 30° to the horizontal. Draw graphs to show the variation with time of:
 (a) the gravitational potential energy of the body;
 (b) the kinetic energy of the body.

15 A cruel hunter takes aim horizontally at a monkey that is hanging from the branch of a tree, as shown in Figure 9.12. The monkey lets go of the branch as soon as the hunter pulls the trigger. Treating the monkey and the bullet as point particles, determine if the bullet will hit the monkey.

Figure 9.12 For question 15.

16 A ball is launched horizontally from a height of 20 m above ground on earth and follows the path shown in Figure 9.13. Air resistance and other frictional forces are neglected. The position of the ball is shown every 0.20 s.
   (a) Determine the horizontal component of velocity of the ball.
   (b) Draw the net force on the ball at $t = 1$ s.
   (c) The ball is now launched under identical conditions on the surface of a planet where the acceleration due to gravity is 20 m s^{-2}. Draw the position of the ball on Figure 9.13 at time intervals of 0.20 s.

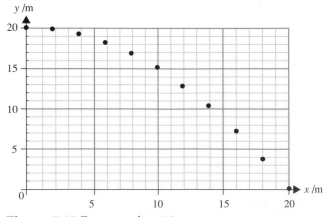

Figure 9.13 For question 16.

17 A ball is launched from the surface of a planet. Air resistance and other frictional forces are neglected. The position of the ball is shown every 0.20 s in Figure 9.14. Use this diagram to determine:
   (a) the components of the initial velocity of the ball;
   (b) the angle to the horizontal the ball was launched at;
   (c) the acceleration due to gravity on this planet.
   (d) Draw two arrows on Figure 9.14 to represent the velocity and acceleration vectors of the ball at $t = 1$ s.
   (e) The ball is now launched under identical conditions from the surface of a *different* planet where the acceleration due to gravity is twice as large. Draw the path of the ball on Figure 9.14.

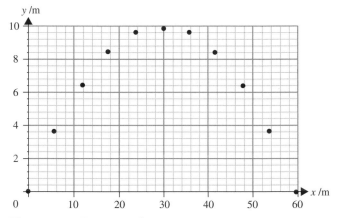

Figure 9.14 For question 17.

> **HL only**
>
> **18** A soccer ball is kicked so that it has a range of 30 m and reaches a maximum height of 12 m. What velocity (magnitude and direction) did the ball have as it left the footballer's foot?

19 A stone is thrown with a speed of 20.0 m s^{-1} at an angle of 48° to the horizontal from the edge of a cliff 60.0 m above the surface of the sea. Calculate the speed with which the stone hits the sea.

20 A projectile is launched with speed v_0 at the foot of an inclined plane at an angle of θ to the horizontal, as shown in Figure 9.15. The inclined plane makes a smaller angle ϕ with the horizontal. Show that the projectile will land a distance d up the plane given by

$$d = \frac{2v_0^2 \cos\theta \, \sin(\theta - \phi)}{g\cos^2\phi}$$

Figure 9.15 For question 20.

21 A ball is kicked with a velocity of 5.0 m s^{-1} up an inclined plane that makes an angle of 30° to the horizontal. The ball's velocity makes an angle of 25° to the base of the incline. (See Figure 9.16.) What is the shape of its path? Explain. Find how high on the incline the ball will get.

Figure 9.16 For question 21.

22 The maximum height reached by a projectile is 20 m. The direction of the velocity 1.0 s after launch is 20°; find the speed of launch.

Gravitation

This chapter will introduce you to one of the fundamental laws of physics: Newton's law of gravitation. The law of gravitation makes it possible to calculate the orbits of the planets around the sun, and predicts the motion of comets, satellites and entire galaxies. The details of the motion of the planets were discovered by observation by Kepler, whose three laws can be seen to be a direct consequence of the gravitational law of attraction and Newton's laws of mechanics. Kepler's laws were published in 1619 in a book called the *Harmony of the World*, whereas Newton's law of gravitation was published in his monumental *Philosophiae Naturalis Principia Mathematica*, on 5 July 1686. In ancient times, Ptolemy constructed an involved system in which the sun and the planets orbited the earth in perfectly circular paths. When observations did not agree with the assumed circular paths, Ptolemy and his successors asserted that planets move along additional smaller circular paths at the same time that they complete the orbit. This elaborate theory of epicycles has no foundation in physical principles and is a good example of attempts to explain physical phenomena without an understanding of the underlying principles. The Ptolemaic world view prevailed for centuries until Copernicus, early in the sixteenth century, asserted that the sun was at the centre of the motion of the planets in the solar system. Newton's law of gravitation has had great success in dealing with planetary motion but cannot account for some small irregularities, such as the precession of the orbit of Mercury and the bending of light near very massive bodies. In 1915, Einstein introduced the general theory of relativity, which replaced Newton's theory of gravity and resolved the difficulties of the Newtonian theory.

Objectives

By the end of this chapter you should be able to:

- appreciate that there is an attractive force between any two point masses that is directed along the line joining the two masses, $F = G\frac{M_1 M_2}{r^2}$;
- state the definitions of *gravitational potential energy*, $E_p = -G\frac{M_1 M_2}{r}$, *gravitational potential*, $V = -G\frac{M}{r}$, and *gravitational field strength*, $g = G\frac{M}{r^2}$;
- understand that the work done as a mass m is moved across two points with *gravitational potential difference* ΔV is $W = m\Delta V$;
- solve problems of *orbital motion* using the equation for orbital speed at a distance r from a body of mass M: $v = \sqrt{\frac{GM}{r}}$;
- understand the meaning of *escape speed*, and solve related problems using the equation for escape speed from a body of mass M and radius R: $v_{esc} = \sqrt{\frac{2GM}{R}}$;
- understand the term *weightlessness*.

Newton's law of gravitation

We have seen that Newton's second law implies that, whenever a mass moves with acceleration, a force must be acting on it. An object falling freely under gravity is accelerating at 9.8 m s^{-2} and thus experiences a net force in the direction of the acceleration. This force is, as we know, the weight of the mass. Similarly, a planet that revolves around the sun also experiences acceleration and thus a force is acting on it. Newton hypothesized that the force responsible for the falling apple is the same as the force acting on a planet as it revolves around the sun. The conventional weight of a body is nothing more than the gravitational force of attraction between that body and the earth.

> ▶ Newton proposed that the attractive force of gravitation between two *point* masses is given by the formula
>
> $$F = G\frac{M_1 M_2}{r^2}$$
>
> where M_1 and M_2 are the masses of the attracting bodies, r the separation between them and G a new constant of physics called Newton's constant of universal gravitation. It has the value $G = 6.667 \times 10^{-11}$ N m^2 kg^{-2}. The direction of the force is along the line joining the two masses.

This formula applies to point masses, that is to say masses which are very small (in comparison with their separation). In the case of objects such as the sun, the earth, and so on, the formula still applies since the separation of, say, the sun and a planet is enormous compared with the radii of the sun and the planet. In addition, Newton proved that for bodies which are *spherical* and of uniform density one can assume that the entire mass of the body is concentrated at the centre – as if the body *is* a point mass.

Figure 10.1 shows the gravitational force between two masses. The gravitational force is always attractive.

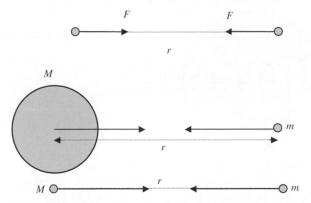

Figure 10.1 The mass of the spherical body to the left can be thought to be concentrated at the centre.

The force on each mass is the same. This follows both from the formula as well as from Newton's third law.

Example questions

Q1

Find the force between the sun and the earth.

Answer

The average distance between the earth and the sun is $R = 1.5 \times 10^{11}$ m. The mass of the earth is 5.98×10^{24} kg and that of the sun 1.99×10^{30} kg. Thus

$$F = 3.5 \times 10^{22} \text{ N}$$

Q2

If the distance between two bodies is doubled, what happens to the gravitational force between them?

Answer

Since the force is inversely proportional to the square of the separation, doubling the separation reduces the force by a factor of 4.

We said that the force we ordinarily call the weight of a mass (i.e. mg) is actually the force of gravitational attraction between the earth of mass M_e and the mass of the body in question. The mass of the earth is assumed to be concentrated at its centre and thus the distance that goes in Newton's formula is the radius of the earth, R_e (see Figure 10.2).

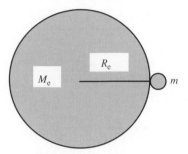

Figure 10.2 The gravitational force due to a spherical uniform mass is the same as that due to an equal point mass concentrated at the centre.

Therefore, we must have that

$$G\frac{M_e m}{R_e^2} = mg$$

$$\Rightarrow g = \frac{GM_e}{R_e^2}$$

This is an extraordinary result. It relates the acceleration of gravity to the mass and radius of the earth. Thus, the acceleration due to gravity on the surface of Jupiter is

$$g = \frac{GM_J}{R_J^2}$$

Example questions

Q3

Find the acceleration due to gravity (the gravitational field strength) on a planet 10 times as massive as the earth and with radius 20 times as large.

Answer

From

$$g = \frac{GM}{R^2}$$

we find

$$g = \frac{G(10M_e)}{(20R_e)^2}$$

$$= \frac{10GM_e}{400R_e^2}$$

$$= \frac{1}{40}\frac{GM_e}{R_e^2}$$

$$= \frac{1}{40}g_e$$

Thus $g = 0.25$ m s^{-2}.

Q4

Find the acceleration due to gravity at a height of 300 km from the surface of the earth.

Answer

$$g = \frac{GM_e}{(R_e + h)^2}$$

where $R_e = 6.38 \times 10^6$ m is the radius of the earth and h the height from the surface. We can now put the numbers in our calculator to find $g = 8.94$ m s^{-2}.

The order-of-magnitude arithmetic without a calculator is as follows:

$$g = \frac{GM_e}{(R_e + h)^2}$$

$$= \frac{6.67 \times 10^{-11} \times 5.98 \times 10^{24}}{(6.68 \times 10^6)^2}$$

$$\approx \frac{7 \times 6}{50} \times 10$$

$$\approx \frac{42}{5}$$

$$\approx 8 \text{ m s}^{-2}$$

Orbital motion

The law of gravitation combined with Newton's second law of mechanics allows an understanding of the motion of planets around the sun as well as the motion of satellites around the earth. The motion of an object that is attracted and bound to a much heavier mass is, according to the law of gravitation, necessarily an ellipse or a circle. This follows because the law of gravitation is an inverse square law: $F = \frac{GMm}{r^2}$. No other form of the law of gravitation (except for a Hooke's law type force, $F = kr$) would lead to closed orbits as observed for the planets. Elliptical orbits with the sun at the focus of the ellipse is what Kepler deduced (Kepler's first law) by analysing the observations made by Tycho Brahe. Newton's law of gravitation and his second law of mechanics provide a theoretical understanding of Kepler's conclusions.

Orbital speed

Consider a planet of mass m in a circular orbit of radius r around the sun, as shown in Figure 10.3. The force on the planet is the gravitational force between the mass of the sun and the mass of the planet, that is

$$F = \frac{GMm}{r^2}$$

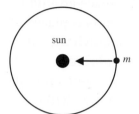

Figure 10.3.

Equating the force with the product of mass times acceleration (the acceleration here is centripetal) we get

$$\frac{GMm}{r^2} = m\frac{v^2}{r}$$

$$\Rightarrow v^2 = \frac{GM}{r}$$

This formula gives the velocity of the planet when it is in an orbit of radius r. For satellites, M stands for the mass of the earth, and this formula shows that the closer the satellite is to the earth, the larger its speed has to be (Figure 10.4 shows this relationship as a graph).

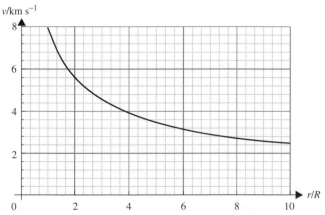

Figure 10.4 The speed of a satellite in circular orbit around the earth. The distances are from the earth's centre in terms of the earth's radius.

Note that the speed does not depend on the satellite's mass.

Example question

Q5 ▬▬▬▬▬▬▬

Evaluate the speed of a satellite in orbit at a height of 500 km from the earth's surface and a satellite that just grazes the surface of the earth. (Take the radius of the earth to be 6.38×10^6 m.)

Answer

The speed is given by

$$v^2 = \frac{GM}{r}$$

$$= \frac{6.67 \times 10^{-11} \times 5.98 \times 10^{24}}{6.88 \times 10^6}$$

$$\Rightarrow v = 7.6 \times 10^3 \text{ m s}^{-1}$$

For a grazing orbit, using the same method

$$v = 7.9 \times 10^3 \text{ m s}^{-1}$$

Period of motion

If the time taken for one revolution of the satellite or planet is T, then we must have $v = \frac{2\pi r}{T}$. So, substituting in the formula for speed we find

$$\left(\frac{2\pi r}{T}\right)^2 = \frac{GM}{r}$$

$$\Rightarrow T^2 = \frac{4\pi^2}{GM}r^3$$

▶ Applied to planets (now M stands for the mass of the sun), this law states that the period of a planet around the sun is proportional to the 3/2 power of the orbit radius: this is simply Kepler's third law of planetary motion.

For elliptical orbits, R should be replaced by the semi-major axis of the ellipse or (approximately) by the average distance of the planet from the sun.

Weightlessness

Consider an astronaut of mass m in a spacecraft *in orbit* around the earth a distance r from the earth's centre (see Figure 10.5).

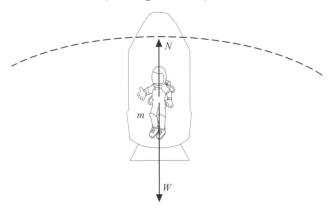

Figure 10.5.

The forces on the astronaut are the reaction force N from the floor and his weight W (i.e. the gravitational force from the earth). The net force on the astronaut is

$$G\frac{Mm}{r^2} - N$$

and so

$$G\frac{Mm}{r^2} - N = m\frac{v^2}{r}$$

$$\Rightarrow N = G\frac{Mm}{r^2} - m\frac{v^2}{r}$$

$$= \frac{m}{r}\left(G\frac{M}{r} - v^2\right)$$

But the speed of the astronaut is given by $v^2 = \frac{GM}{r}$, which implies that $N = 0$. Thus, the astronaut experiences no reaction forces from the floor and so 'feels' weightless.

Looked at in a simpler way, the astronaut is falling freely but *so is the spacecraft*, hence there are no reaction forces. At a distance of 300 km from the earth's surface, gravity is not negligible. There is s a force of gravity on the astronaut but no reaction force from the spacecraft floor.

Gravitational field strength

Physicists (and philosophers) since the time of Newton, including Newton himself, wondered how a mass 'knows' about the presence of another mass nearby that will attract it. By the nineteenth century, physicists had developed the idea of a 'field', which was to provide the answer to the question. A mass M is said to create a *gravitational field* in the space around it. This means that when another mass is placed at some point near M, it 'feels' the gravitational field in the form of a gravitational force. (Similarly, an electric charge will create around it an electric field and another charge will react to this field by having an electric force on it.)

We define **gravitational field strength** as follows.

▶ The gravitational field strength at a certain point is the force per unit mass experienced by a small point mass m at that point. The force experienced by a small point mass m placed at distance r from a mass M is

$$F = G\frac{Mm}{r^2}$$

So the gravitational field strength (F/m) of the mass M is

$$g = G\frac{M}{r^2}$$

The units of gravitational field strength are N kg^{-1}.

If M stands for the mass of the earth, then the gravitational field strength is nothing more than the acceleration due to gravity at distance r from the centre of the earth.

The usefulness of the definition of the gravitational field strength is that it tells us something about the gravitational effects of a given mass without actually having to put a second mass somewhere and find the force on it.

The gravitational field strength is a vector quantity whose direction is given by the direction of the force a point mass would experience if placed at the point of interest. The gravitational field strength around a single point mass M is radial, which means that it is the same for all points equidistant from the mass and is directed towards the mass. The same is true outside a uniform spherical mass. This is illustrated in Figure 10.6.

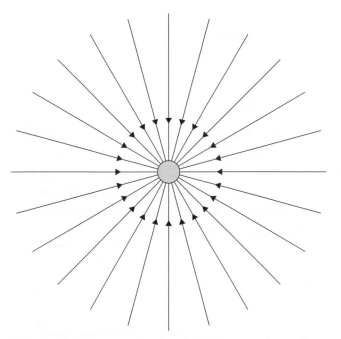

Figure 10.6 The gravitational field around a point (or spherical) mass is radial.

This is to be contrasted to the assumption of a constant gravitational field strength, which would result in the situation illustrated in Figure 10.7. The assumption of constant acceleration of gravity (as, for example, when we treated projectile motion) corresponds to this case.

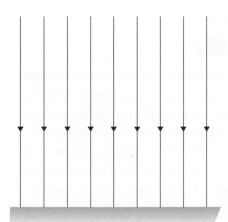

Figure 10.7 The gravitational field above a flat mass is uniform.

Example questions

Q6 ▄▄▄▄▄▄▄▄▄▄▄▄▄

Two stars have the same density but star A has double the radius of star B. Determine the ratio of the gravitational field strength at the surface of each star.

Answer

The volume of star A is 8 times that of star B since the radius of A is double. Hence the mass of A is 8 times that of B. Thus

$$\frac{g_A}{g_B} = \frac{GM_A/R_A^2}{GM_B/R_B^2}$$

$$= \frac{M_A}{M_B}\frac{R_B^2}{R_A^2}$$

$$= 8 \times \frac{1}{4}$$

$$= 2$$

Q7 ▄▄▄▄▄▄▄▄▄▄▄▄▄

Show that the gravitational field strength at the surface of a planet of density ρ has a magnitude given by $g = \frac{4G\pi\rho R}{3}$.

Answer

We have

$$g = \frac{GM}{R^2}$$

Since

$$M = \rho\frac{4\pi R^3}{3}$$

it follows that

$$g = \frac{G4\pi\rho R^3}{3R^2}$$

$$= \frac{4G\pi\rho R}{3}$$

Gravitational potential energy

Consider a mass M placed somewhere in space, and a second mass m that is a distance R from M. The two masses have gravitational potential energy, which is stored in their gravitational field. This energy is there because work had to be done in order to move one of the masses, say m, from a position very far away (infinity) to the position near the other mass. (See Figure 10.8.)

The work that was done by the agent moving the mass went into potential energy.

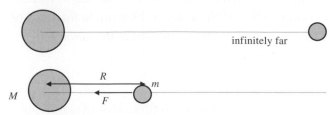

Figure 10.8 Work is being done in bringing the small mass from infinity to a given position away from the big mass. This work is stored as potential energy.

Supplementary material

The gravitational force is not constant but decreases as the separation of the masses increases, so we cannot straightforwardly compute the work done. Using calculus, the total work done in moving the mass from infinity to R is

$$W = \int_{\infty}^{R} \frac{GMm}{r^2} dr$$

$$W = -\frac{GMm}{r} \Big|_{\infty}^{R}$$

$$W = -\frac{GMm}{R}$$

▶ This work is energy that is stored in the gravitational field of the two masses and is called the gravitational potential energy of the two masses when they are separated by a distance R:

$$E_p = -\frac{GMm}{R}$$

A satellite's total energy as it orbits the earth is the sum of its kinetic and gravitational potential energies:

$$E = \tfrac{1}{2}mv^2 - \frac{GMm}{r}$$

This expression simplifies if we use Newton's law of gravitation and the second law of

mechanics

$$G\frac{Mm}{r^2} = m\frac{v^2}{r}$$

$$\Rightarrow v^2 = \frac{GM}{r}$$

$$\Rightarrow E_k = \frac{GMm}{2r}$$

so that

$$E = -\frac{GMm}{2r}$$

or

$$E = -\tfrac{1}{2}mv^2$$

Figure 10.9 shows the kinetic energy $E_k = \frac{GMm}{2r}$, potential energy $E_p = -\frac{GMm}{r}$ and total energy $E = -\frac{GMm}{2r}$ of a mass of 1 kg in orbit around the earth, as a function of distance from the earth's centre. This distance is measured in terms of the earth's radius R.

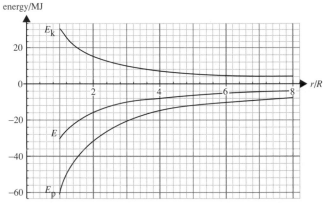

Figure 10.9 Graphs of the kinetic, potential and total energy of a mass of 1 kg in circular orbit around the earth.

Example question

HL only

Q8

This problem is known as 'the satellite paradox'. A satellite in low orbit experiences air resistance. Suppose that, as a result of this, the radius of the satellite's orbit decreases by a small amount (small compared with the actual orbit radius) equal to δr. Show that the speed of the satellite *increases* by

$$\delta v = \frac{\delta r}{2}\sqrt{\frac{GM}{r^3}}$$

Calculate the change in the kinetic and potential energy of the satellite and hence explain how a resistance force such as air resistance results in an *increase* of the satellite's speed.

Hint: If x is 'small' $\frac{1}{1+x} \approx 1 - x$.

Answer

The satellite's energy is

$$E = -\frac{GMm}{2r}$$

or

$$E = -\tfrac{1}{2}mv^2$$

Using the second version it follows that

$$\delta E = -mv\,\delta v$$

If the radius decreases, the energy becomes

$$E' = -\frac{GMm}{2(r - \delta r)}$$

$$= -\frac{GMm}{2r\left(1 - \frac{\delta r}{r}\right)}$$

$$\approx -\frac{GMm}{2r}\left(1 + \frac{\delta r}{r}\right)$$

$$= -\frac{GMm}{2r} - \frac{GMm}{2r^2}\delta r$$

that is, the total energy decreases as it should. The decrease is

$$\delta E = -\frac{GMm}{2r^2}\delta r$$

Hence

$$-\frac{GMm}{2r^2}\delta r = -mv\,\delta v$$

$$\Rightarrow \delta v = \frac{GM}{2vr^2}\delta r$$

$$= \frac{GM}{2\sqrt{\frac{GM}{r}}r^2}\delta r$$

$$= \frac{\delta r}{2}\sqrt{\frac{GM}{r^3}}$$

The kinetic energy increase can be found from

$$E_k = \tfrac{1}{2}mv^2$$

$$\Rightarrow \delta E_k = mv(\delta v)$$

$$= m\sqrt{\frac{GM}{r}}\frac{\delta r}{2}\sqrt{\frac{GM}{r^3}}$$

$$= \frac{GMm}{2r^2}\delta r$$

and the change in potential energy from

$$E_p = -\frac{GMm}{r - \delta r}$$

$$= -\frac{GMm}{r\left(1 - \frac{\delta r}{r}\right)}$$

$$\approx -\frac{GMm}{r}\left(1 + \frac{\delta r}{r}\right)$$

$$\Rightarrow \delta E_p = -\frac{GMm}{r^2}\delta r$$

We see that the speed increases, which increases the kinetic energy, but the potential energy decreases by more. Thus, the total energy decreases. The decrease in total energy must equal the work done by the air-resistance force.

Related to the concept of gravitational potential energy is that of **gravitational potential**, V. The gravitational potential is a field, because it is defined at every point in space, but unlike the gravitational field strength, it is a *scalar* quantity.

▶ The gravitational potential at a point P in the gravitational field is the work done per unit mass in bringing a small point mass m from infinity to point P. If the work done is W, then the gravitational potential is the ratio of the work done to the mass m, that is

$$V = \frac{W}{m}$$

The gravitational potential due to a *single* mass M a distance r from the centre of M is

$$V = -\frac{GM}{r}$$

The units of gravitational potential are J kg^{-1}.

If we know that a mass, or an arrangement of masses, produces a gravitational potential V at some point in space, then putting a mass m at that point means that the gravitational potential energy of the mass will be $E_p = mV$.

If a mass m is positioned at a point in a gravitational field where the gravitational potential is V_1 and is then moved to another point where the gravitational potential is V_2, then the work that is done on the mass is

$$W = m(V_2 - V_1)$$
$$= m\Delta V$$

Example questions

Q9

The graph in Figure 10.10 shows the variation of the gravitational potential due to a planet with distance r. Using the graph estimate:

(a) the gravitational potential energy of an 800 kg spacecraft that is at rest on the surface of the planet;

(b) the work done to move this spacecraft from the surface of the planet to a distance of four planet radii from the surface of the planet.

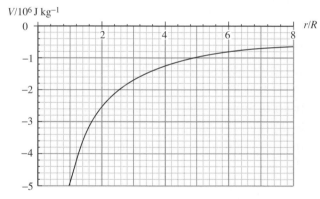

Figure 10.10.

Answer

(a) On the surface of the planet $r = R$, or $r/R = 1$, and from the graph $V = -5 \times 10^6 \, J\,kg^{-1}$. Hence

$$E_p = mV$$
$$= 800 \times (-5 \times 10^6)$$
$$= -4 \times 10^9 \, J$$

(b) When the distance from the *surface* is four planet radii, $r/R = 5$ and the potential there is $V = -1 \times 10^6 \, J\,kg^{-1}$. Hence

$$W = m\Delta V$$
$$= 800 \times (-1 \times 10^6 + 5 \times 10^6)$$
$$= 3.2 \times 10^9 \, J$$

Q10

Figure 10.11 shows the variation of the gravitational potential due to a planet and its moon with distance r from the centre of the planet. The centre-to-centre distance between the planet and the moon is d. The planet's centre is at $r = 0$ and the centre of the moon is at $r = d$. What is the minimum energy required so that a 500 kg probe at rest on the planet's surface will arrive on the moon?

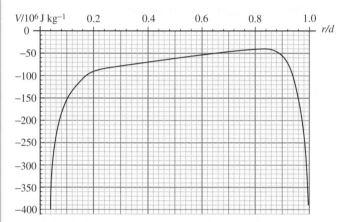

Figure 10.11.

Answer

The probe will arrive at the moon provided it has enough energy to get to the peak of the curve. Once there, the moon will pull it in. On the surface of the planet $V = -390 \times 10^6 \, J\,kg^{-1}$. At the peak the potential is $V = -40 \times 10^6 \, J\,kg^{-1}$. Hence

$$W = m\Delta V$$
$$= 500 \times (-40 \times 10^6 + 390 \times 10^6).$$
$$= 1.75 \times 10^{11} \, J$$

Escape velocity

The total energy of a mass m moving near a large, stationary mass M is

$$E = \tfrac{1}{2}mv^2 - \frac{GMm}{r}$$

where v is the speed of the mass when at a distance r from M. (If M is also free to move, then the total energy would have to include a term $\frac{1}{2}Mu^2$, where u is be the speed of M. This complicates things so we assume that M is held fixed.) The only force acting on m is the gravitational force of attraction between M and m. Suppose that the mass m is launched with a speed v_0 away from M. Will m escape from the pull of M and move very far away from it? To move very far away means that the distance between M and m is so large that it is practically infinite. Then the law of energy conservation states that

$$\tfrac{1}{2}mv_0^2 - \frac{GMm}{R} = \tfrac{1}{2}mv_\infty^2$$

The left-hand side of this equation represents the total energy E (kinetic plus potential) of the mass m at the point of launch, a distance R from the centre of M, and the right-hand side is the total energy of the mass at infinity, where the potential energy is zero. Thus, if the mass m is to escape from the pull of M, it must have a total energy that is either zero or positive. If $E = 0$, then the mass m makes it to infinity and just about stops there, $v_\infty = 0$. If $E > 0$, then m not only gets to infinity but is also moving there with speed v_∞, given by the expression above. If, on the other hand, $E < 0$, then the mass cannot make it to infinity; it is forever trapped by the pull of M.

- $E > 0$: mass escapes and never returns;
- $E < 0$: mass moves out a certain distance but returns – mass is trapped;
- $E = 0$: the critical case separating the other two – mass just barely escapes.

This is a general result: whenever the total energy of a mass is negative, that mass is trapped by the attraction of whatever is causing the total energy to be negative. Here it is gravity that is responsible. Later on we will see that the total energy of the electron in its orbit around the atomic nucleus is also negative. There it is the electrical force that is responsible for $E < 0$. The quarks inside protons also have $E < 0$. The strong nuclear force is the reason for that.

Back to gravitation again. What must the smallest launch velocity be for a mass to escape the pull of the earth?

▶ From the expression above we find that the smallest v is that for which $v_\infty = 0$ (i.e. $E = 0$). In this case

$$\tfrac{1}{2}mv^2 - \frac{GMm}{R} = 0$$

$$\Rightarrow v = \sqrt{\frac{2GM}{R}}$$

This is the minimum velocity that a mass launched from the surface of the earth must have in order to reach infinity and stop there. This is called the escape velocity, v_{esc}, from the earth. Note that the escape velocity is independent of the mass of the body escaping.

Using the fact that $g = \frac{GM_e}{R_e^2}$ we see that the escape velocity can be rewritten as

$$v_{esc} = \sqrt{2gR_e}$$

where g is the acceleration due to gravity at the surface of the earth. The numerical value of this escape velocity is about 11.2 km s^{-1}.

The order-of-magnitude arithmetic without a calculator is as follows:

$$v = \sqrt{\frac{2GM}{R}}$$

$$= \sqrt{\frac{2 \times 6.67 \times 10^{-11} \times 5.98 \times 10^{24}}{6.38 \times 10^6}}$$

$$\approx \sqrt{\frac{2 \times 7 \times 6 \times 10^7}{6}}$$

$$= \sqrt{2 \times 7 \times 10^7}$$

$$= \sqrt{140 \times 10^6}$$

$$\approx 12 \times 10^3 \text{ m s}^{-1}$$

In practice, in order to escape, a mass must overcome not only the pull of the earth but also the pull of the sun and the big planets. This means that the escape velocity from the earth is somewhat larger than 11.2 km s^{-1}. This discussion does not apply to powered objects such as rockets; it applies only to objects launched from the earth like cannon balls. In other words, it applies to *ballistic* motion.

Example questions

Q11

The inevitable example! What must the radius of a star of mass M be such that the escape velocity from the star is equal to the speed of light, c?

Answer

Using

$$v = \sqrt{\frac{2GM}{R}}$$

with $v = c$, we find

$$R = \frac{2GM}{c^2}$$

Since nothing can exceed the speed of light, the result above states that if the radius of the star is equal to or less than the value above, nothing can escape from the star. It is a black hole. The interesting thing about this formula is that it correctly gives the radius of the black hole even though Newton's law of gravitation, which we used, does not apply! When dealing with very massive objects, Newton's law has to be replaced by Einstein's law of gravitation. Surprisingly, though, the answer is the same. This radius is called the Schwarzschild radius of the star.

Q12

Compute the Schwarzschild radius of the earth and the sun.

Answer

For the sun

$$R = \frac{2GM}{c^2}$$
$$= \frac{2 \times 6.67 \times 10^{-11} \times 2 \times 10^{30}}{\left(3 \times 10^8\right)^2} \text{ m}$$
$$\approx 3 \times 10^3 \text{ m}$$

Similarly, for the earth $R_e = 8.86$ mm. This shows that both the earth and the sun are far from being black holes!

Supplementary material

The binary star system

(This section is not required for examination purposes but will be useful to those who study the astrophysics option.)

Two stars can orbit around each other in what is called a binary star system. The orbit of each star can be an ellipse but we will consider here the much simpler case of circular orbits. Consider two stars of mass M_1 and M_2. They attract each other with the gravitational force

$$F = G\frac{M_1 M_2}{d^2}$$

where d is the separation of their centres of mass (see Figure 10.12).

Figure 10.12 The two stars in the binary star system attract each other.

The centre of mass of the two stars is not acted upon by any external forces and is thus moving in a straight line with constant speed. Without loss of generality, we may consider the speed to be zero, in which case it follows that the two masses orbit the common centre of mass. Taking the orbits to be circular, the orbit radii (i.e. the distances of each mass from the centre of mass) are given by

$$R_1 = \frac{M_2 d}{M_1 + M_2}$$
$$R_2 = \frac{M_1 d}{M_1 + M_2}$$

See Figures 10.13 and 10.14.

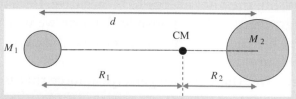

Figure 10.13 The two stars orbit their centre of mass.

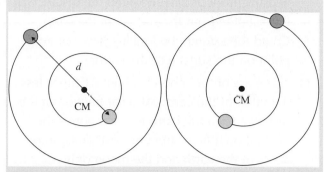

Figure 10.14 The orbits of the two stars.

The speeds of rotation can be found from

$$G\frac{M_1 M_2}{d^2} = M_1 \frac{v_1^2}{R_1}$$

$$\Rightarrow v_1^2 = G\frac{M_2 R_1}{d^2}$$

$$G\frac{M_1 M_2}{d^2} = M_2 \frac{v_2^2}{R_2}$$

$$\Rightarrow v_2^2 = G\frac{M_1 R_2}{d^2}$$

and thus

$$v_1^2 = G\frac{M_2}{d^2}\frac{M_2 d}{M_1 + M_2}$$

$$= \frac{GM_2^2}{d(M_1 + M_2)}$$

$$v_2^2 = G\frac{M_1}{d^2}\frac{M_1 d}{M_1 + M_2}$$

$$= \frac{GM_1^2}{d(M_1 + M_2)}$$

The common period of rotation is therefore found from

$$T^2 = \left(\frac{2\pi R_1}{v_1}\right)^2$$

$$= \frac{4\pi^2 \frac{M_2^2 d^2}{(M_1+M_2)^2}}{\frac{GM_2^2}{d(M_1+M_2)}}$$

$$= \frac{4\pi^2 d^3}{G(M_1 + M_2)}$$

This shows that if one mass is much larger than the other, then the formula for T reduces to the familiar one from Kepler's third law.

The total energy of the binary star system is given by

$$E = \frac{1}{2}M_1 v_1^2 + \frac{1}{2}M_2 v_2^2 - G\frac{M_1 M_2}{d}$$

$$= \frac{1}{2}M_1 \frac{GM_2^2}{d(M_1 + M_2)}$$

$$+ \frac{1}{2}M_2 \frac{GM_1^2}{d(M_1 + M_2)} - G\frac{M_1 M_2}{d}$$

$$= \frac{1}{2}\frac{GM_1 M_2}{d}\left(\frac{M_2}{(M_1 + M_2)} + \frac{M_1}{(M_1 + M_2)} - 2\right)$$

that is

$$E = -\frac{1}{2}\frac{GM_1 M_2}{d}$$

If the binary star system loses energy, for example because of gravitational radiation, then the energy decreases and thus the separation of the two stars, d, decreases as well. This means that each star now moves faster and the rotational period decreases. This decrease in the rotational period of a binary star system has been observed and is indirect evidence for the existence of gravity waves.

Questions

1 What is the gravitational force between:
   (a) the earth and the moon;
   (b) the sun and Jupiter;
   (c) a proton and an electron separated by 10^{-10} m?
   (Use the data in Appendices 1 and 3.)

2 A mass m is placed at the centre of a thin, hollow, spherical shell of mass M and radius R (see Figure 10.15a).
   (a) What gravitational force does the mass m experience?
   (b) What gravitational force does m exert on M?

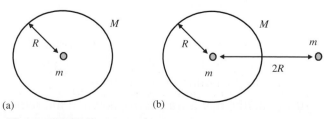

Figure 10.15 For question 2.

(c) A second mass m is now placed a distance of $2R$ from the centre of the shell (see Figure 10.15b). What gravitational force does the mass inside the shell experience?

(d) What is the gravitational force experienced by the mass outside the shell?

3 Stars A and B have the same mass and the radius of star A is 9 times larger than the radius of star B. Calculate the ratio of the gravitational field strength on star A to that on star B.

4 Planet A has a mass that is twice as large as the mass of planet B and a radius that is twice as large as the radius of planet B. Calculate the ratio of the gravitational field strength on planet A to that on planet B.

5 Stars A and B have the same density and star A is 27 times more massive than star B. Calculate the ratio of the gravitational field strength on star A to that on star B.

6 A star explodes and loses half its mass. Its radius becomes half as large. Find the new gravitational field strength on the surface of the star in terms of the original one.

7 Show by applying Newton's law of gravitation and the second law of mechanics that a satellite (or planet) in a circular orbit of radius R around the earth (or the sun) has a period (i.e. time to complete one revolution) given by

$$T^2 = \frac{4\pi^2 R^3}{GM}$$

where M is the mass of the attracting body (earth or sun). This is Kepler's third law.

8 Show that a satellite orbiting the earth (mass M) in a circular orbit of radius r and angular velocity ω satisfies

$$r^3 = \frac{GM}{\omega^2}$$

9 What is the speed of a satellite that orbits the earth at a height of 500 km? How long does it take to go around the earth once?

10 A satellite that *always* looks down at the same spot on the earth's surface is called a geosynchronous satellite. Find the distance of this satellite from the surface of the earth. Could the satellite be looking down at any point on the surface of the earth?

11 The mass of the moon is about 81 times less than that of the earth. At what fraction of the distance from the earth to the moon is the gravitational field strength zero? (Take into account the earth and the moon only.)

12 (a) What is the gravitational potential energy stored in the gravitational field between the earth and the moon?

(b) What is the earth's gravitational potential at the position of the moon?

(c) Find the speed with which the moon orbits the earth. (Use the data in Appendix 3.)

HL only

13 A spacecraft of mass 30 000 kg leaves the earth on its way to the moon. Plot the spacecraft's potential energy as a function of its distance from the earth's centre.

14 (a) What is the gravitational potential at a distance from the earth's centre equal to 5 earth radii?

(b) What is the gravitational potential energy of a 500 kg satellite placed at a distance from the earth's centre equal to 5 earth radii?

15 Point P is halfway between the centres of two equal spherical masses that are separated by a distance of 2×10^9 m (see Figure 10.16). What is the gravitational field strength at:
(a) point P;
(b) point Q?

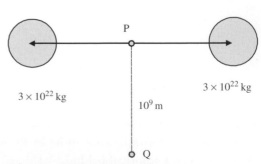

3×10^{22} kg 10^9 m 3×10^{22} kg

Figure 10.16 For question 15.

16 Consider two masses. There is a point somewhere on the line joining the masses where the gravitational field strength is zero, as shown in Figure 10.17. Therefore, if a third mass is placed at that point, the net force on the mass will be zero. If the mass is slightly displaced away from the equilibrium position to the left, will the net force on the mass be directed to the left or the right?

Figure 10.17 For question 16.

17 Figure 10.18 shows cross-sections of two satellite orbits around the earth. (To be in orbit means that only gravity is acting on the satellite.) Discuss whether either of these orbits is possible.

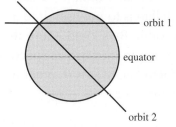

Figure 10.18 For question 17.

18 In the text it was calculated that the acceleration due to gravity at a height of 300 km above the earth's surface is far from negligible, yet astronauts orbiting in the space shuttle at such a height feel weightless. Explain why.

19 Earlier in the topic of mechanics we used the expression mgh for the gravitational potential energy of a mass m. This expression is only approximate. Show, by using $U = -\dfrac{GMm}{r}$, which is the correct expression, that the difference in gravitational potential energy of a mass on the surface of the earth and at a height h from the earth's surface is indeed mgh provided h is small compared with the radius of the earth. (Use the binomial expansion.)

20 Figure 10.19 shows the variation of the gravitational force with distance. What does the shaded area represent?

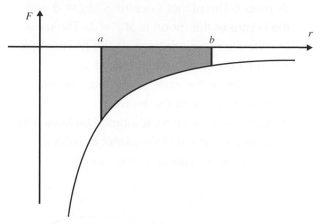

Figure 10.19 For question 20.

21 Figure 10.20 shows the variation with distance of the gravitational potential (in terajoules per kilogram) due to a planet whose radius is 2.0×10^5 m.
   (a) Calculate the mass of the planet.
   (b) Show that the escape speed from the surface of the planet is $v_{esc} = \sqrt{-2V}$, where V is the gravitational potential on the planet's surface.
   (c) Use the graph to determine the escape speed from this planet.
   (d) How much energy is required to move a rocket of mass 1500 kg from the surface of the planet to a distance of 1.0×10^6 m from the centre?
   (e) A probe is released from rest at a distance from the planet's centre of 0.50×10^6 m and allowed to crash onto the planet's surface. With what speed will the probe hit the surface?

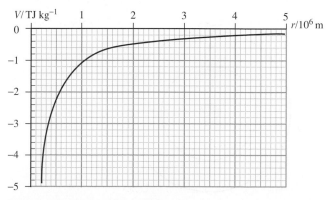

Figure 10.20 For question 21.

22 Figure 10.21 shows the variation with distance from the centre of the planet of the gravitational potential due to the planet and its moon. The planet's centre is at $r = 0$ and the centre of the moon is at $r = 1$. The units of separation are arbitrary. At the point where $r = 0.75$ the gravitational field is zero.
(a) Determine the ratio of the mass of the planet to that of the moon.
(b) With what speed must a probe be launched from the surface of the planet in order to arrive on the surface of the moon?

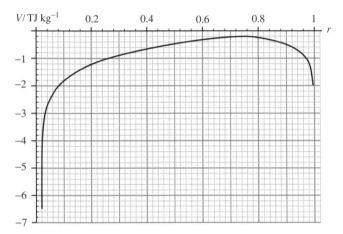

Figure 10.21 For question 22.

23 Prove that the total energy of the earth (mass m) as it orbits the sun (mass M) is $E = -\frac{1}{2}mv^2$ or $E = -\frac{GMm}{2r}$, where r is the radius of the earth's circular orbit. Calculate this energy numerically.

24 Figure 10.22 shows two identical satellites in circular orbits. Which satellite has the larger:
(a) kinetic energy;
(b) potential energy;
(c) total energy?

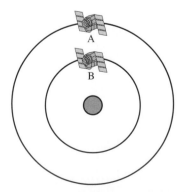

Figure 10.22 For question 24.

25 Show that the total energy of a satellite of mass m in orbit around the earth (mass M) at a distance from the Earth's centre of 5 earth radii is given by $E = -\frac{GMm}{10R}$.

26 The total energy of a satellite during launch from the earth's surface is $E = -\frac{GMm}{5R}$, where R is the radius of the earth. It eventually settles into a circular orbit; calculate the radius of that orbit.

HL only

27 What is the escape velocity from the earth if the launch takes place not on the surface of the earth but from a space station orbiting the earth at a height equal to R_e? You must find the velocity of launch as measured by an observer on the space station. The launch takes place in the direction of motion of the space station.

28 A satellite is in a circular orbit (A) around the earth. If the satellite is to put itself into a higher circular orbit (B), should it turn its engines on in order to increase its speed or should it run them backwards in order to slow down? (See Figure 10.23.)

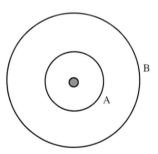

Figure 10.23 For question 28.

29 Figure 10.24 shows a planet orbiting the sun counter-clockwise, at two positions – A and B. Also shown is the gravitational force acting on the planet at each position. By decomposing the force into components normal and tangential to the path (dotted lines), explain why it is only the tangential component that does work. Hence explain why the planet will accelerate from A to P but will slow down from P to B.

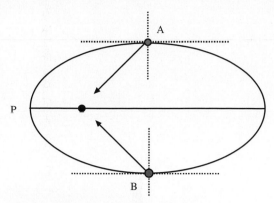

Figure 10.24 For question 29.

30 Figure 10.25 shows a planet orbiting the sun. Explain why at points A and P of the orbit the potential energy of the planet assumes its minimum and maximum values, and determine which is which. Hence determine at what point in the orbit the planet has the highest speed.

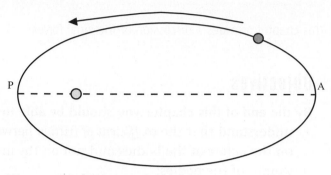

Figure 10.25 For question 30.

Friction

This chapter provides a discussion of frictional forces.

Objectives

By the end of this chapter you should be able to:

- understand that the *coefficient of friction* between two bodies depends on the *nature* of the bodies and not on the area of contact or the weight of the bodies;
- solve problems in which *frictional forces* are present, $F_{static} \leq \mu_s R$, $F_{kinetic} = \mu_k R$.
- understand that the presence of a frictional force *reduces the total energy* of a system by an amount equal to the *work done by the frictional force*.

Frictional forces

Friction arises whenever one body slides over another. In this case we speak of sliding or dynamic friction. Friction also arises whenever there is just a tendency for motion, not necessarily motion itself, such as when a block rests on an inclined plane or when a block on a level road is pulled by a small force that does not result in motion. In this case we speak of static friction. Frictional forces originate from the fact that surfaces that appear smooth are not smooth at a microscopic scale and so the ridges on one surface get caught on those of the other (see Figure 11.1).

The *maximum possible* frictional force that can exist between the two bodies in a static situation (no motion) is given by

$$f_{max} = \mu_s R$$

where R is the normal reaction force between the bodies, and μ_s is a constant determined by experiment and depends on the materials the bodies in contact are made of. It is called the

Figure 11.1 Surfaces that appear to be smooth are not smooth at a microscopic level. If one surface is pulled over the other, forces develop to oppose the motion.

static coefficient of friction. If there is motion between the two bodies, the frictional force between them will be given by

$$f = \mu_k R$$

μ_k being the *kinetic* or *dynamic* coefficient of friction, which is smaller than the static coefficient.

▶ The coefficients of friction between two bodies (static and kinetic) depend only on the kind of materials the two surfaces are made of. They do *not* depend on the area of contact between the two bodies or on how heavy the bodies are.

Thus, a brick placed on its long side on a wooden table will have the *same* coefficient when placed on the same table on its short side. Similarly, if a heavier brick is made out of the same material, it too will have the same coefficients on the same surface as the lighter brick. (See Figure 11.2.)

Figure 11.2 The coefficient of friction does not depend on the area of contact or on how massive the body is.

These 'laws of friction' are empirical relations that do not have a sound basis in microscopic physics.

Example questions

Q1

A brick of mass 5.00 kg rests on a horizontal surface. The static and dynamic coefficients of friction are 0.60 and 0.20, respectively. A horizontal force F is applied to the brick, its magnitude increasing slowly from zero. Find the acceleration with which the brick will begin to move.

Answer

The normal reaction force on the brick is 50.0 N. Thus, the maximum frictional force is 0.60 × 50.0 N = 30.0 N. This means that as long as F is less than 30.0 N, the frictional force equals F and the brick remains motionless. If F becomes slightly more than 30.0 N, the frictional force cannot match it and the brick will move. But as soon as the brick moves, the frictional force will drop to the dynamic value of 0.20 × 50.0 N = 10.0 N. So, when the brick begins to move, it is pushed forward by a force slightly larger than 30.0 N and is opposed by a frictional force of 10.0 N. The net force is thus 20.0 N and the acceleration is therefore 4.0 m s^{-2}.

Q2

In Figure 11.3, a block of mass M is connected to a smaller mass m by a string that goes over a pulley. Let the static coefficient of friction between the mass M and the table be μ_s. What is the largest mass m that can hang from the string without forcing M to move? Take $M = 8.0$ kg and $\mu_s = 0.50$.

Figure 11.3.

Answer

If there is no motion, $T = mg$ and also $T = f$, where f is the frictional force. The maximum f can become is

$$f = \mu_s R$$
$$= \mu_s Mg$$

and thus

$$mg = \mu_s Mg$$

So, finally

$$m = \mu_s M$$

Numerically

$$m = 0.50 \times 8.0 \,\text{kg} = 4.0 \,\text{kg}$$

Q3

Let the kinetic coefficient of friction between M and the table in example question 2 be 0.40. If $m = 4.000\,001$ kg, find the acceleration of each mass.

Answer

Since m is bigger than 4.0 kg, according to example question 2 the masses will move. The frictional force on M will then be

$$f = \mu_k Mg$$
$$= 0.40 \times 80.0$$
$$= 32.0 \,\text{N}$$

Thus

$$T - 32.0 = 8.0a$$
$$40.0 - T = 4.0a$$

This gives

$$a = \frac{8.0}{12.0}$$
$$= 0.67 \text{ m s}^{-2}$$

Note that it is not necessary to put in the value 4.000 001 kg for m. It is enough to know that m is big enough for motion to take place.

Mass on an inclined plane with friction

Consider now a block on an inclined plane again but this time imagine that there is friction between the block and the plane surface. Let μ_s be the static coefficient of friction. The forces on the block are as shown in Figure 11.4.

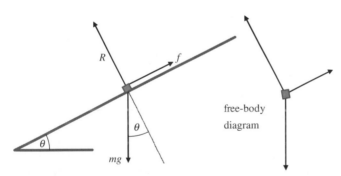

Figure 11.4 The three forces acting on a body on an inclined plane.

If the angle of the incline is slowly increased, there will come a moment when the block will stop being in equilibrium and will begin to slide down the plane. What is the angle at which the sliding begins? Just before equilibrium is ruined and the block begins to slide, the frictional force assumes its largest possible value, which is $f = \mu_s R$. Taking components along axes that are normal and parallel to the plane we find

$$R = mg \cos \theta$$
$$f = mg \sin \theta$$

and so

$$\frac{f}{R} = \frac{\sin \theta}{\cos \theta} = \tan \theta$$
$$\Rightarrow \mu_s = \tan \theta$$

This means that the tangent of the largest angle at which we can have equilibrium gives the static coefficient of friction between the block and the plane.

If the angle is now increased slightly further, the block will slide. The forces on the block along the plane are now the frictional force up the plane (now given by $\mu_k R$) and the component of the weight down the plane (given by $mg \sin \theta$). After the body begins to slide, Newton's second law gives

$$mg \sin \theta - \mu_k R = ma$$

for the acceleration of the block down the plane. But $R = mg \cos \theta$, so

$$a = g \sin \theta - \frac{\mu_k R}{m}$$
$$= g \sin \theta - \frac{\mu_k mg \cos \theta}{m}$$
$$= g(\sin \theta - \mu_k \cos \theta)$$

The following example question is a good application of both frictional forces and Newton's third law.

Example question

Q4 ▬▬▬▬▬▬▬

A block of mass 2.0 kg rests on top of another block of mass 10.0 kg, which in turn rests on a horizontal table. There is friction between the two blocks as well as between the bottom block and the table. Draw the forces on each block as an external force F acts horizontally on the bottom block making both blocks move as one body. The static coefficient of friction between the two blocks is 0.4 and the kinetic coefficient between the bottom block and the table is 0.2. What is the largest F that can be applied such that the two blocks move together? What is the acceleration of the blocks?

Answer

See Figure 11.5.

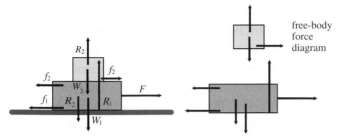

Figure 11.5.

The top block tends to slide to the left as the bottom block moves to the right, so the frictional force that opposes the motion of the top block (relative to the other block) is to the right. This force is f_2. By Newton's third law, an equal and opposite force acts on the bottom block. Friction from the table on the bottom block acts to the left, this is force f_1. In addition to the weights of the blocks, the other forces are: the reaction force from the floor onto the big block, R_1; the reaction from the bottom block onto the top, R_2 (and hence, by Newton's third law, an equal and opposite force acts on the bottom block directed vertically down). The external force F acts only on the bottom block. The force R_2 equals the weight of the top block: 20 N. Thus, the reaction force R_1 equals 120 N. The frictional force on the bottom block is thus $0.2 \times 120 = 24$ N, and that on the top block can become a maximum of $0.4 \times 20 = 8$ N. The net force in the horizontal direction on the top block is f_2, and so

$$f_2 = 8$$
$$= ma$$
$$= 2a$$
$$\Rightarrow a = 4 \, \text{m s}^{-2}$$

This is also the acceleration of the bottom block, since the two bodies move together. The net force on the bottom block is

$$F - f_1 - f_2 = F - 32$$
$$= Ma$$
$$= 10 \times 4$$
$$= 40$$
$$\Rightarrow F = 72 \, \text{N}$$

Non-conservative forces

When friction is present, the sum of kinetic and potential energies does not stay the same, since friction does work that is not included as a potential energy in the total energy E. Consider a steel ball of mass $m = 1$ kg that is dropped from rest into a long cylinder full of honey, as in Figure 11.6.

Figure 11.6 A ball falling through a viscous fluid at terminal velocity.

Suppose that after the ball has fallen a distance of $h = 0.45$ m, its speed is measured to be $v = 2$ m s^{-1}. The total energy of the ball initially is $E = 0$ (we take the gravitational potential energy of the ball to be zero at the initial position of the ball). After falling 0.45 m, the total energy is $E = \frac{1}{2}mv^2 - mgh = -2.5$ J. The total energy has been reduced by 2.5 J. This is the work done by the viscous force resisting the fall of the mass. This force (assumed to be constant) can be found from

$$W = \Delta E$$
$$fh \cos 180° = -2.5 - 0$$
$$\Rightarrow f = 5.55 \, \text{N}$$

Example questions

Q5 ▬▬▬▬▬▬▬▬▬▬▬▬▬▬▬▬

A mass of $m = 2.0$ kg slides from rest down an inclined plane of angle $\theta = 30°$ to the horizontal. After moving down the plane a distance of $d = 30$ cm, the speed of the mass is found to be $v = 1.0$ m s^{-1}. (See Figure 11.7.) What is the coefficient of friction between the mass and the inclined plane?

place! Consider a wheel, for example a car wheel, that is forced by the engine to rotate in the clockwise direction. If there is no friction between the wheel and the road, the wheel will simply rotate about its axle (i.e. spin) without moving forward, as happens when one tries to start a car on an icy road. If there is friction, the part of the wheel in contact with the road pushes the road to the left and so by Newton's third law the road exerts an equal and opposite force on the wheel, as illustrated in Figure 11.11. It is this force (i.e. friction) that then makes the wheel move forward. A similar argument shows that friction is necessary for walking. Can you supply the details?

push of tyre
on road

push of road
on tyre

Figure 11.11 As the wheel rotates, the part in contact with the road pushes the road to the left. A force to the right then acts on the wheel, pushing it forward.

Questions

1 A mass m is attached to two equal pieces of string each of length L, whose ends are attached to rings around a rod, as shown in Figure 11.12. If the static coefficient of friction between the rings and the rod is μ, find the largest distance d between the rings such that the mass is at equilibrium.

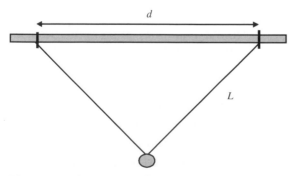

Figure 11.12 For question 1.

2 A mass of 10.0 kg rests on a horizontal table. The static coefficient of friction between the mass and the table is 0.45 and the kinetic coefficient of friction is 0.30. A force that is slowly increasing in magnitude is applied horizontally to the mass. (See Figure 11.13.)
(a) What is the magnitude of the force when the mass first begins to move?
(b) As soon as the mass starts to move, the force remains constant. What is the acceleration of the mass?

Figure 11.13 For question 2.

3 A mass M in the shape of a cube is accelerating forward with acceleration a. A smaller mass m is placed on the front face of the cube as shown in Figure 11.14. The coefficient of friction between m and the cube is μ. What must a be such that m does not slide down?

Figure 11.14 For question 3.

4 A stunt car moves along the inside surface of a vertical cone making horizontal circles as shown in Figure 11.15. The vertex angle of the

Figure 11.15 For question 4.

cone is a right angle and the coefficient of friction between the tyres and the road is 0.25. If the radius of the circle is 20 m, find the *range* of the possible values the velocity can have.

5 A 1400 kg car takes a circular flat turn of radius 130 m. The coefficient of static friction between the surface and the tyres is 0.65.
(a) Calculate the highest speed with which the car can negotiate the turn without skidding.
(b) The road is now elevated 5.0° to the horizontal. What would be the highest speed in that case?
(c) Why are we using the static coefficient even though the car is moving?

6 A block of mass m rests on a cart. The coefficient of static friction between the block and the cart is μ.
(a) Show that, if the cart accelerates forward with acceleration a, the block will not slip provided $a = \mu g$.
(b) The cart now takes a turn of radius 5.0 m and it is observed that the highest speed at which this can happen without the block slipping is 3.0 m s^{-1}. What is the coefficient of static friction between the block and the cart?

7 A block of mass 2.0 kg rests on top of another block of mass 10.0 kg, which in turn rests on a horizontal table. There is friction between the two blocks as well as between the bottom block and the table. Draw the forces on each block as an external force F acts horizontally on the bottom block. The static coefficient of friction between the two blocks is 0.400 and the kinetic coefficient between the bottom block and the table is 0.200. The kinetic coefficient of friction between the two blocks is 0.300. What is the acceleration of each block if:
(a) $F = 60.0$ N;
(b) $F = 80.0$ N?

8 A mass of 12 kg rests on an inclined plane that makes an angle of 30° to the horizontal. A force F is acting on the body as shown in Figure 11.16. The static coefficient of friction

is 0.40 and the kinetic coefficient of friction is 0.20.
(a) Find the minimum force F that is required to keep the body at rest on the plane.
(b) The force F is now increased so that the body moves up the plane with constant speed. Calculate the magnitude of the pulling force.

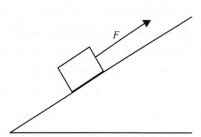

Figure 11.16 For question 8.

9 In an amusement park, a hollow cylinder of radius r rotates about a vertical axis through its centre. A person of mass m is standing inside the cylinder with his back on the wall, as shown in Figure 11.17. As the cylinder picks up speed, the floor is lowered leaving the person glued to the wall.
(a) Draw a free-body diagram of the forces on the person.
(b) Determine the minimum number of revolutions per second, N, necessary to make sure the person does not slide down the cylinder wall. Take the static coefficient of friction to be μ.

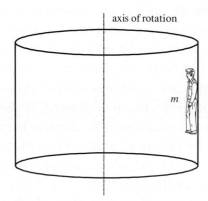

Figure 11.17 For question 9.

Statics

The problems of mechanics we have studied so far have been confined to point masses. Even though we did not always specify this explicitly, it was always assumed. In those problems in which the masses were clearly not point masses, we again assumed that it was a good approximation to treat them as such. The relevant difference between a point mass and an extended body is that under the action of a net force the two respond differently. A point mass will just accelerate in the direction of the net force (this is called translational motion). An extended body, however, will not only accelerate in the direction of the net force but will also rotate (there is rotational as well as translational motion). If the body is to be in equilibrium, the net force on it must be zero, but in addition there should be no net rotational effect from the individual forces on the body. This chapter discusses the equilibrium conditions of an extended body.

Objectives

By the end of this chapter you should be able to:
- appreciate that the equilibrium of an extended body requires that the *net force* as well as the *net torque* must be zero;
- appreciate that the weight of a body acts at its *centre of mass*;
- state the definition of *torque*: $\tau = Fd \sin \theta$;
- solve problems of *rotational equilibrium*.

Centre of mass

Given a body of finite size we can define a point called the centre of mass of the body. This is a point where all of the mass, M, of the body can be *assumed* to be concentrated. If the body is uniform in density, the centre of mass is the geometrical centre of the body. The weight of the body, Mg, is then assumed to be acting at the centre of mass (which, therefore, is also called the centre of gravity). If the body is irregular in shape or if its density is non-uniform, the centre of mass can be found by more advanced methods using calculus. The importance of the centre of mass is that, as far as the translational motion of the body is concerned, the body behaves as a point particle situated at the centre of mass. Thus,

the body will accelerate, with an acceleration given by

$$a = \frac{F}{M}$$

where F is the net force on the body and M its mass. The centre of mass will move in the direction of the net force. If the net force on an extended body is zero, the centre of mass will not accelerate. It will either remain at rest or continue to move along a straight line with constant speed, in agreement with Newton's first law.

Consider a rigid, uniform rod of length L that rests vertically on a horizontal table. If we give it a slight push, the rod will tilt and will fall over on the table. Assume that there is no friction between the table and the bottom of the rod. Then the only forces on the rod are its weight acting at its geometrical centre, a point $L/2$ from one end of the rod, and the normal reaction force. Both of these forces are in the vertical direction and so the centre of mass of the rod will move in a vertical straight line as the rod falls on the table, as shown in Figure 12.1. It cannot accelerate sideways as no force acts in the horizontal direction.

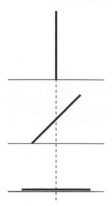

Figure 12.1 The centre of mass falls along a vertical line.

Torque

The difference in how a point mass and an extended body react to forces acting on them brings in the concept of the turning effect or *torque* of a force. Consider a plate with an axle through its top left corner so that the plate can rotate about that axle. Let a force F act on the body at the point shown (Figure 12.2).

▶ The torque of a force about an axis is defined as the product of the force times the *perpendicular distance* between the axis and the line along which the force acts (the *line of force*),

$$\tau = Fd$$

Its unit is newton times metre, N m.

The force shown in Figure 12.2a will rotate the body in the counter-clockwise direction.

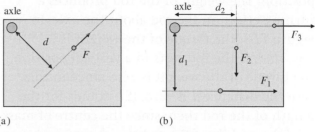

(a)   (b)

Figure 12.2 The force in diagram (a) has a counter-clockwise torque about the axis shown. The axis is perpendicular to the plane of the paper.

If more than one force acts on the body (Figure 12.2b), the torque of each can be found as

$$\tau_1 = F_1 d_1, \quad \tau_2 = F_2 d_2 \quad \text{and} \quad \tau_3 = 0$$

Force F_3 has zero torque about the axis shown. This is because the force is directed through the axis and thus the perpendicular distance between the axis and the line of action of the force is zero. The force F_1 rotates the body in a counter-clockwise direction whereas F_2 rotates it in a clockwise direction.

▶ Forces that are directed toward the axis have zero torque about that axis.

Consider a rod that hangs vertically through a horizontal axle at the top of the rod, as shown in Figure 12.3. The rod is free to rotate about this axle.

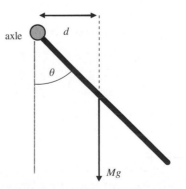

Figure 12.3 The weight of the rod has a torque about an axis through the axle.

If the rod is displaced by an angle θ with respect to the vertical and then released, the rod will begin to oscillate about the vertical position. The weight of the rod produces a turning effect on the rod about the axle. In Figure 12.3, the torque of the weight is $\tau = Mgd$. If the rod rests in a vertical position, the torque of the weight is zero since in this case the distance d is zero. If L stands for the length of the rod then, since the centre of mass is at the middle of the rod, $d = \frac{L}{2} \sin\theta$ and so the torque is also given by

$$\tau = Mg\frac{L}{2}\sin\theta$$

Torque is a vector and its proper definition takes its vector nature into account through the vector product

$$\vec{\tau} = \vec{r} \times \vec{F}$$

(given here only for the benefit of those taking mathematics at higher level), where $\vec{r}$ is the vector from the axis to the point of application of the force $\vec{F}$. This shows clearly that if the force is directed through the axis, then the torque is zero, since in that case the vectors $\vec{r}$ and $\vec{F}$ are parallel (or anti-parallel) and the vector product is then zero.

If the angle between the vectors $\vec{r}$ and $\vec{F}$ is θ, as in Figure 12.4, then the magnitude of the vector $\vec{\tau}$ is $\tau = rF\sin\theta = Fd$, as stated earlier – that is, the product of the force times the perpendicular distance to the axis.

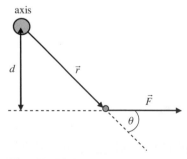

Figure 12.4.

Static equilibrium

A point particle is said to be in equilibrium if the net force on it is zero. The same condition is necessary for an extended body as well. But it is not sufficient, as the following example shows. Figure 12.5 shows a disc (assumed to be far from the earth so there is no gravity) on which two equal and opposite forces act. The net force is thus zero but the body is not in equilibrium. The two forces have a turning effect on the disc: a torque that will rotate the body with increasing angular speed.

> ▶ For a body to be in equilibrium:
> the net force on it must be zero, $F_{net} = 0$;
> the net torque on it must be zero, $\tau_{net} = 0$.

Figure 12.5 The net force on the disc is zero but the body is not in equilibrium. The forces have torques that accelerate the body by rotating it faster and faster.

If the net torque about some axis is zero and the net force on the body is zero, then it can be shown that the torque about any other axis is also zero. Thus, in problems of static equilibrium we may calculate torques about any convenient axis.

Let the radius of the disc be 5.0 m and $F = 20$ N. Each force has a torque of 100 N m, giving a *net torque* of 200 N m on the disc, which rotates the body in a clockwise sense. (Can you restore equilibrium with a single force?)

Consider now a rod of length 5.0 m and mass 12 kg (assumed to be of uniform density). The rod is balanced on a support at a distance of 1.0 m from the left end. A force F acting vertically downward is exerted on the left end

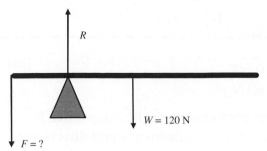

Figure 12.6 A rod on a support with a downward force acting at its left end.

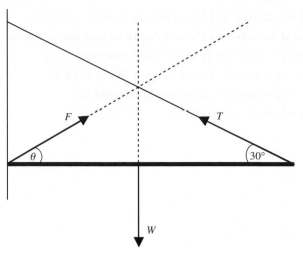

Figure 12.7 The three forces acting on a suspended rod.

of the rod. Figure 12.6 shows the forces on the rod. In addition to F and the weight W (acting at the middle of the rod) we also have the reaction force R at the support. We would like to find F. Applying the condition that the net force is zero gives

$$R = F + W = F + 120$$

and so F cannot be found since R is not known. To find F we must use the second condition for equilibrium, namely that the net torque is zero. Taking torques about an axis through the point of support we see that F has a torque of $F \times 1.0$ and W has a torque of $120 \times 1.5 = 180$ N m. R has zero torque about this axis (which is the reason why we chose it in the first place). F and W have opposite torques and so demanding that

$$F \times 1.0 = 180 \text{ N m}$$

gives $F = 180$ N. We can now find R to be 300 N.

A special case: three non-parallel forces in equilibrium

Consider now a rod of length 5.0 m and weight 120 N that rests horizontally with its left end attached to a vertical wall through a hinge and its right end suspended by a string making an angle of 30° to the horizontal as shown in Figure 12.7.

There are three forces on the rod – its weight, acting vertically downward at the rod's centre, the tension in the string, acting along the string, and the hinge force. This is a case where just three forces are acting on the body. If we are to have equilibrium, the three forces must pass through a common point, as shown in Figure 12.7. This, then, dictates the direction of the hinge force. To see why this is so, take torques about the common point of the lines of action of the forces due to the weight and the tension. The torque of the weight and the tension is zero, since the forces pass through this point. To have equilibrium means that the net torque must be zero. But only the hinge force is left, so its torque must be zero. This implies that the direction of the hinge force is through the point common to the other two lines, so the three forces have a common point as claimed.

It is then obvious by symmetry that $F = T$ and that $\theta = 30°$, and also

$$\begin{aligned} F \sin 30° + T \sin 30° &= W \\ \Rightarrow 2T \sin 30° &= W \\ \Rightarrow T &= W \\ &= 120 \text{ N} \end{aligned}$$

If you do not see the symmetry of the problem, you can still solve it in the conventional way as follows. The diagram of forces is shown again

(Figure 12.8) but this time the hinge force has been decomposed into its vertical and horizontal components. We have also decomposed the tension force T. (It is always a good idea to decompose forces into components in equilibrium problems.)

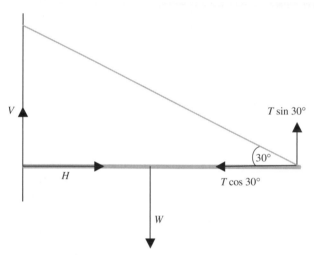

Figure 12.8 Diagram of forces with the hinge force decomposed into vertical and horizontal components.

Equilibrium of forces demands that

$$H = T \cos 30° \qquad (1)$$
$$V + T \sin 30° = W \qquad (2)$$

and taking torques about the hinge gives

$$W \frac{L}{2} = (T \sin 30°)L$$
$$\Rightarrow T = W$$
$$= 120 \text{ N}$$

(Note that the horizontal component of the tension force has no torque about the axis chosen – only the vertical component has a torque.) Putting this result in equations (1) and (2) gives

$$H = W \cos 30°$$
$$= 0.866W \qquad (1a)$$
$$= 103.9 \text{ N}$$

and

$$V = \frac{W}{2}$$
$$= 0.5W \qquad (2a)$$
$$= 60 \text{ N}$$

Having the components of the hinge force F allows us to find its magnitude and direction

$$F = \sqrt{(103.9)^2 + (60)^2}$$
$$= 120 \text{ N}$$

and

$$\theta = \arctan \frac{V}{H}$$
$$= \arctan \frac{60}{103.9}$$
$$= 30°$$

just as we found before.

Consider now a rod of length 6.0 m and weight 200 N resting against a smooth vertical wall and a rough horizontal floor. The rod makes an angle of 60° with respect to the horizontal. The forces on the rod are as shown in Figure 12.9a. Clearly, friction must be present, otherwise the rod could not remain in equilibrium.

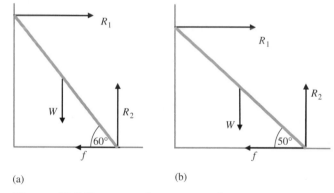

(a) (b)

Figure 12.9 Forces acting on a rod.

We would like to find the values of the forces on the rod. By demanding that the net force be zero we get the equations

$$R_1 = f \quad \text{and} \quad R_2 = W \qquad (3)$$

Thus, we find that $R_2 = 200$ N. We must now apply the condition that the net torque about any axis is zero. We may choose an axis through the point where the rod touches the floor. Then the torques of f and R_2 are zero. We are left with the torques of W and R_1. These torques tend to rotate the rod in the opposite sense, so they are opposing torques. To have zero net torque these two must be equal. Thus

$$R_1 \times 6\sin 60° = 200 \times 3\cos 60°$$
$$\Rightarrow R_1 = 57.7\,\mathrm{N}$$

Hence from (3) the frictional force is also 57.7 N.

Suppose now that we are told that the *smallest* angle with the horizontal the rod can make and still be in equilibrium is 50° (Figure 12.9b). What is the static coefficient of friction between the rod and the floor? In this situation, we again have

$$R_1 = f \quad \text{and} \quad R_2 = W$$

(thus $R_2 = 200$ N again)

but now

$$R_1 \times 6\sin 50° = 200 \times 3\cos 50°$$
$$\Rightarrow R_1 = 83.9\,\mathrm{N}$$

Thus, the frictional force is $f = 83.9$ N too, and since 50° is the smallest angle for equilibrium, it means that the frictional force assumes its largest possible value (i.e. $f = \mu R_2$), so the coefficient of static friction is $\mu = 0.42$.

Example questions

Q1 ▬▬▬▬▬▬▬▬▬▬▬▬
A uniform rod of length 10 m and mass 50 kg is suspended from two vertical ropes attached to its ends, as shown in Figure 12.10.

Figure 12.10.

(a) A woman of mass 70 kg stands at the middle of the rod. What is the tension in each rope?
(b) The ropes break if the tension in them exceeds 750 N. Can the woman walk to the end of the rod?

Answer

(a) This part can be solved without using torques. The two tensions are the same by symmetry, $T_1 = T_2 = T$. The net force on the rod is zero, so

$$2T = 1200\,\mathrm{N}$$

and therefore

$$T = 600\,\mathrm{N}$$

(b) If the woman walks to the end of the rod (the right say) then equilibrium of forces demands

$$T_1 + T_2 = 1200\,\mathrm{N}$$

and equilibrium of torques (about an axis through the right end) demands

$$T_1 \times 10 = 500 \times 5$$
$$\Rightarrow T_1 = 250\,\mathrm{N}$$

This implies that $T_2 = 950$ N, so the right rope will break before the woman gets to the right end.

Q2 ▬▬▬▬▬▬▬▬▬▬▬▬
How far to the right can the woman walk before the rope in example question 1 breaks?

Answer

See Figure 12.11.

Figure 12.11.

Let the distance be x from the right end. Equilibrium of forces gives

$T_1 + T_2 = 1200$ N

as before. The tension in the right rope will be taken as 750 N, since this is when the rope will just break. Then, $T_1 = 450$ N. Taking torques about the right end again gives

$450 \times 10 = 500 \times 5 + 700 \times x$
$\Rightarrow x = 2.86$ m

She can walk $5 - 2.86 = 2.14$ m to the right.

Q3

An 800 N rod of length 12.0 m is suspended by two ropes as shown in Figure 12.12. One is vertical and the other makes an angle of 60° with the horizontal. A horizontal force F acts at the left end of the rod as shown. Find the tension in each rope and the value of F if the rod is in equilibrium.

Figure 12.12.

Answer

Equilibrium of forces vertically and horizontally gives

$T_1 + T_2 \sin 60° = 800$ N (4)
$F = T_2 \cos 60°$ (5)

Taking torques about the right end gives

$T_1 \times 12 = 800 \times 6$
$\Rightarrow T_1 = 400$ N

Thus (4) implies

$400 + T_2 \sin 60° = 800$
$\Rightarrow T_2 = 462$ N

Finally, from (5)

$F = 231$ N

Questions

1 A constant force of 100 N is applied on the pedal of a bicycle wheel as shown in Figure 12.13. In each case find the torque applied about the centre of the axle. The distance between the axle and the pedal is 30 cm.

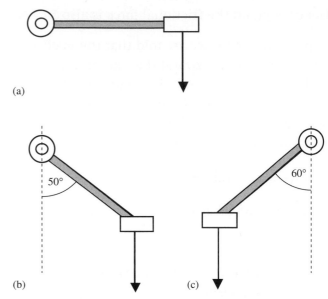

Figure 12.13 For question 1.

2 Find the torque of each of the forces in Figure 12.14 about an axis through the left end of the rod and into the page. The length of the rod is 1.5 m and each force has a magnitude of 100 N.

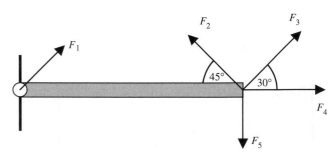

Figure 12.14 For question 2.

3 In Figure 12.15, find the torque of the tension force about the hinge:
(a) using the force directly;
(b) using the components of T.

Check that the answer in both cases is the same. Take the length of the rod to be L.

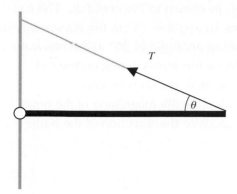

Figure 12.15 For question 3.

4 A rod of negligible mass is supported by a string, making an angle of 30° with the horizontal. The rod is in contact with a vertical wall. A body of mass 50 kg hangs from the right end of the rod, as shown in Figure 12.16. What is:
 (a) the tension in the string;
 (b) the reaction from the wall?

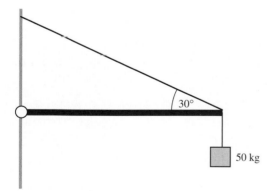

Figure 12.16 For question 4.

5 The mass of the rod in Figure 12.16 is now not neglected and equals 20 kg. Using the data of question 4 above, find:
 (a) the tension in the string;
 (b) the magnitude and direction of the hinge force.

6 Two identical books are stacked one on top of the other near the edge of a table, as shown in Figure 12.17. For this to be possible, the centre of mass of the top book must be over the first book and the combined centre of mass of the two books must be over the table.
 (a) What is the largest value of x for two books? (Give the answer in terms of L, the length of one book.)
 (b How many books must be stacked so that the top book is not directly over the table?

Figure 12.17 For question 6.

7 A wheel of radius 50 cm is to be lifted over the kerb of a pavement of height 20 cm, as shown in Figure 12.18. A force of 60 N must be applied horizontally at the centre of the wheel to do this.
 (a) What is the weight of the wheel?
 (b) What is the minimum force applied at the centre of the wheel that is needed to lift the wheel?

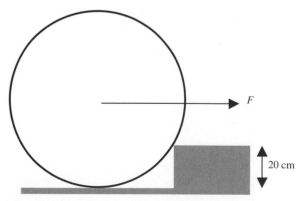

Figure 12.18 For question 7.

8 A ladder of length L and weight W rests against a frictionless vertical wall. The coefficient of friction with the floor is 0.6. What is the smallest angle the ladder can make with the horizontal and still be in equilibrium?

9 A ladder of length 5.0 m and weight 100 N rests against a smooth vertical wall and a rough horizontal floor. The top of the ladder is 4.0 m from the floor. Calculate the forces exerted on the ladder.

10 The ladder in question 9 has a person of mass 65 kg on it (see Figure 12.19). What is the coefficient of friction between the ladder and the floor if the furthest the person can climb without the ladder slipping is 3.0 m?

11 A rod of weight 150 N and length 4.0 m is connected to a vertical wall through a hinge and is supported from the right end with a string, as shown in Figure 12.20. The rod makes an angle of 15° to the horizontal and the string an angle of 20° to the horizontal.
  (a) Draw the forces acting on the rod.
  (b) Calculate the tension force.
  (c) Calculate the magnitude of the hinge force.
  (d) Calculate the direction of the hinge force.

Figure 12.19 For question 10.

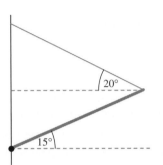

Figure 12.20 For question 11.

Thermal concepts

This chapter is an introduction to thermal physics. It introduces the concepts of temperature, heat, internal energy and thermal equilibrium. The mechanisms by which heat can be transferred from one body to another (conduction, convection and radiation) are also discussed. The first two of these require the presence of a medium through which heat will flow. Radiation does not: it can transfer heat through a vacuum.

Objectives

By the end of this chapter you should be able to:
- understand how a *temperature scale* is constructed;
- appreciate that heat is *energy* that is exchanged between systems at *different* temperatures;
- appreciate that *internal energy* is the total kinetic energy of the molecules of a system plus the potential energy associated with the intermolecular forces;
- understand that the absolute temperature of a gas is a measure of the *average kinetic energy* of its molecules;
- state the meaning of the *mole* and the *Avogadro constant* and do calculations using them;
- describe the mechanisms (*conduction*, *convection* and *radiation*) by which thermal energy can be transferred from one body to another.

Temperature

Temperature is the intuitive concept of 'hotness' or 'coldness' of a substance. To measure the temperature of a body we need to find *a property of the body that changes as the 'hotness' changes*. Consider a thin tube filled with mercury – as it becomes hotter, the *length* of mercury increases (see Figure 1.1). The length of the mercury column then becomes a measure of the temperature of the mercury in the tube. (Other properties such as electrical resistance, voltage and pressure may be used, depending on the kind of thermometer to be constructed.)

In 1742, Andreas Celsius created the temperature scale that is commonly used today and is known by his name. In the Celsius scale a value of zero degrees is assigned to the freezing point of water and a value of one hundred degrees is assigned to the boiling point of water. A *thermometer* employing the Celsius scale can be made by first placing a glass tube containing mercury in a mixture of ice and water and labelling the length of the mercury as 0, then placing it in boiling water and labelling the new length as 100. Finally, the range from zero to one hundred degrees is subdivided into equal

Figure 1.1 As the mercury column gets hotter, its length increases. This can be used to define a temperature scale on a thermometer.

intervals. The degree of the Celsius scale is denoted by °C. (It is a curious historical note that Celsius himself actually assigned 0 °C to the boiling point of water and 100 °C to the freezing point.)

A thermometer like the one just described actually measures the temperature of the mercury it contains. To measure the temperature of another body we must bring the thermometer into *thermal contact* with the body of interest. If a thermometer originally at room temperature is placed in a hot cup of coffee, the length of the mercury column (i.e. the reading of the thermometer) will go up and eventually will settle to a constant value. Similarly, if the thermometer is placed in a cup containing ice water, the reading will start going down until, eventually, a constant reading is obtained. While the thermometer reading is changing, there is a *thermal interaction* between the two bodies (the thermometer and the coffee, say). When the reading settles at a constant value, the two bodies (thermometer and coffee) are in *thermal equilibrium*. When thermal equilibrium is reached, the temperature of the two bodies is the same. Thus, the reading on the thermometer is also the temperature of the body.

Thermal equilibrium can exist between more than two bodies. Consider three bodies, A, B and C. Suppose that C is in thermal equilibrium with both A and B. This implies that A and B have the same temperature as C. They therefore also have the *same* temperature as one another and hence are in thermal equilibrium with one another (see Figure 1.2).

The **absolute temperature** scale (to be discussed in more detail in later chapters) is defined in terms of the conventional Celsius scale through

$$T \text{ (in kelvin)} = T \text{ (in degrees Celsius)} + 273$$

The lowest possible temperature on the absolute scale is zero kelvin, 0 K. It is not possible to achieve a lower temperature. On the Celsius scale the lowest possible temperature is, therefore, $-273\,°C$.

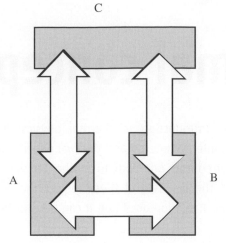

Figure 1.2 Body A and body B are each in thermal equilibrium with body C. Therefore they are in thermal equilibrium with each other and hence have the same temperature.

Heat and internal energy

It was not until the nineteenth century that 'heat' was recognized as a form of energy. Up to then it was regarded as a kind of fluid that moved from place to place. A historic experiment by Joule demonstrated the equivalence of heat and energy. This is described in Option E on The History and Development of Physics.

In the previous section, we mentioned that two bodies that are in thermal contact and have different temperatures will have a thermal interaction. This interaction involves *heat*.

▶ Heat is energy that is transferred from one body and into another as a result of a difference in temperature.

Thus, when a hot object is brought in contact with a colder body, heat will be transferred to the colder body and increase its temperature. We say that the colder body has been 'heated'.

Now, all substances consist of molecules and, whether in the solid, liquid or gas phase, the molecules are in constant motion. They therefore have kinetic energy. In a gas the molecules move randomly throughout the entire volume of the gas. In a solid the motion of the molecules is on a very much smaller scale – the molecules simply vibrate about their equilibrium positions. This requires kinetic energy as well. In addition, there are forces between molecules (intermolecular forces, which are electrical in nature). For gases these forces are very small (under reasonable conditions they are almost negligible). But they are substantial for solids. Increasing the average separation of two molecules of a solid requires work to be done. This work goes into potential energy associated with intermolecular forces. (The case of liquids is intermediate between gases and solids.)

We thus define the **internal energy** of a substance as follows:

> ▶ Internal energy is the total kinetic energy of the molecules of a substance, plus any potential energy associated with forces between the molecules.

Thus, the heat that is transferred from a hot to a cold body increases the internal energy of the cold body (and decreases the internal energy of the hot body by the same amount). So the term 'heat' refers to energy associated with the thermal interaction of two or more systems due to a difference of temperature.

Similarly, if we place a large number of lead pellets in a box and shake the box vigorously, the temperature of the lead pellets will go up. The lead pellets will be 'heated' and their internal energy increases. But there is no heat exchanged here. The internal energy of the pellets increases because of the *work* that we perform in shaking the box.

So the internal energy of a system can change as a result of heat added or taken out and as a result of work performed. Internal energy, heat and work are thus three different concepts. What they have in common is that they are all measured in joules. Temperature is yet another different concept. One of the big discoveries of nineteenth-century physics was the relation between temperature and kinetic energy of molecules.

> ▶ The absolute temperature is a measure of the average kinetic energy of the molecules of a substance. The average kinetic energy of the molecules is directly proportional to the absolute temperature in kelvin.

We therefore have a relationship between a *microscopic* concept (the average kinetic energy of molecules) and a *macroscopic* concept (temperature).

Note that sometimes the term 'thermal energy' is also used. Some books use thermal energy to mean heat as we defined it and others to mean internal energy. The term thermal energy will mostly be avoided in this book but when it is used it will mean *internal energy*.

The atomic model of matter

Ordinary matter can be found in three forms or phases: solid, liquid and gaseous. The solid phase is characterized by high density and the molecules are at fixed positions. In the liquid phase, the density is lower and the molecules are further apart. Unlike the solid phase, molecules are free to move about, thus the distance between them is not fixed. In the gas phase, the molecules experience little resistance to motion and move freely about – the average distance between molecules is large. This is illustrated in Figure 1.3.

(a) solid   (b) liquid   (c) gas

Figure 1.3 Typical arrangements of molecules in a solid, a liquid and a gas.

In all three cases there are forces acting between the molecules of the substance. These intermolecular forces are strongest in the solid phase and weakest (almost negligible) in the gas phase. In the solid phase they are responsible for keeping the molecules in their fixed positions (solids have fixed shapes) and are the reason why large forces are needed to compress or stretch solids.

If we consider a solid at low temperature, the kinetic energy of each molecule is quite small compared with the energy required to move any two molecules a large distance apart. The average distance between molecules does not change and so the solid stays a solid. As the temperature is increased, the average kinetic energy of the molecules increases and becomes comparable to the energy required for separation. When this happens, the molecules abandon their fixed positions and move apart. The solid begins to melt – it turns into a liquid. This phenomenon is called a *phase transition*. If the temperature is increased further, the molecules may have enough energy to move so far apart from each other that the intermolecular forces are no longer significant. The liquid turns into a gas.

Avogadro constant

One mole of any substance is that quantity of the substance whose mass in grams is numerically equal to the substance's molar mass, μ. The mole is the SI unit for quantity. The molar mass of hydrogen gas (H_2) is 2 g mol^{-1} and so one mole of hydrogen has a mass of 2 g; one mole of oxygen (O_2, molar mass 32 g mol^{-1}) has a mass of 32 g, and so on.

▶ One mole of any substance contains the same number of molecules as in 12 grams of carbon-12. This number is known as the Avogadro constant and its numerical value is

$$N_A = 6.02 \times 10^{23} \text{ molecules mol}^{-1}$$

It follows, therefore, that the number of moles of a substance can be found by dividing the total number of molecules in the substance by the Avogadro constant

$$n = \frac{N}{N_A}$$

Equivalently, the mass m, in grams, of a substance can be expressed in terms of the number of moles n, as

$$m = n\mu$$

Example question

Q1 ▬▬▬▬▬▬▬▬▬▬▬

How many grams are there in a quantity of oxygen gas containing 1.20×10^{25} molecules?

Answer

The number of moles is

$$\frac{1.20 \times 10^{25}}{6.02 \times 10^{23}} = 19.93 \text{ mol}$$

Since the molar mass is 32 g mol^{-1} the mass is

$$19.93 \times 32 = 638 \text{ g} = 0.638 \text{ kg}$$

Transfer of heat

Conduction

The handle of a metal spoon that is standing in a pan of hot soup (see Figure 1.4) will feel hot when you touch it. Heat has 'flowed' from the hot liquid through the spoon, increasing the temperature of the handle.

Figure 1.4 The typical example of conduction: heat flows from the hot soup to the other end of the spoon.

This is an example of conduction. Most of the heat is transferred by *free electrons* (electrons that are only loosely bound to particular atoms and are thus free to move throughout the metal). The free electrons collide with molecules in their path, transferring energy to them and forcing these molecules to vibrate more about their equilibrium positions. It is thus expected that good conductors of heat are also good conductors of electricity, and this is the case. Some of the heat is also transferred by molecules in *lattice vibrations*. Molecules of the spoon in contact with the hot liquid vibrate more violently and collide with their neighbours, giving them energy. These, in turn, collide with their neighbours, so that eventually the molecules at the end of the spoon's handle receive energy as well; that is, the temperature at the end of the handle increases. No molecules have actually moved from one end of the spoon to the other.

Although not required for examination purposes it is good to know that the flow of heat by conduction can be made quantitative through the concept of the heat current.

▶ The heat current is defined as the amount of heat per second, $\frac{\Delta Q}{\Delta t}$, that flows past a given point in a body. The heat current is:

- proportional to the cross-sectional area of the body it flows through;
- proportional to the difference in temperature at the ends of the body;
- inversely proportional to the length of the body.

In equation form

$$\frac{\Delta Q}{\Delta t} = kA\frac{\Delta T}{\Delta x}$$

The quantity $\frac{\Delta T}{\Delta x}$ is called the temperature gradient and k is the thermal conductivity. Some materials are better conductors of heat than others; in other words, different materials have different *thermal conductivities*. Good conductors have high thermal conductivity.

Figure 1.5 shows a rod with high thermal conductivity covered in a material with low

thermal conductivity (an insulator). A heat current is flowing uniformly in the rod.

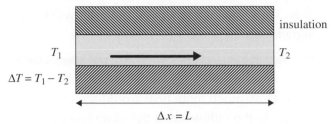

Figure 1.5 An insulated rod with a heat current flowing uniformly in it.

The temperature along the length of the (insulated) rod falls uniformly, as shown in Figure 1.6.

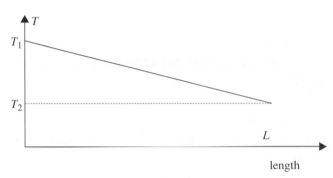

Figure 1.6 The temperature falls uniformly along the length of an insulated rod.

(How would you expect the temperature to fall if the rod was *not* insulated?)

Example questions

Q2 ▬▬▬▬▬▬

Two rods of the same length and cross-sectional area are joined together. The left rod is a better conductor of heat than the rod at right. The ends of the rod are kept at fixed temperatures as shown in Figure 1.7. In which rod is the rate of heat transfer the largest? Is the temperature at the joining point lower or higher than 50 °C?

100 °C   0 °C

Figure 1.7.

Answer

Let us imagine a vertical line through any part of the rods. The heat entering the line must equal the heat leaving it, since no heat can be lost or created at the line (law of conservation of energy).

Hence, the rate of heat transfer is the same everywhere. A much larger temperature difference can be maintained across a bad conductor of heat. Thus, the temperature at the joint will be higher than 50 °C.

Q3

A rod of radius R is placed in contact with a hot body. How much more heat would a second rod of double the radius but of the same length and material carry away in the same time?

Answer

The cross-sectional area of the second rod is four times as large, hence the amount of heat carried away will be four times as much.

Convection

This mechanism applies to fluids (liquids and gases). When a source of heat is placed in a fluid (e.g. a radiator in a room or a flame next to a pipe carrying a liquid) heat will flow to other parts of the fluid. Consider a radiator in a room (Figure 1.8).

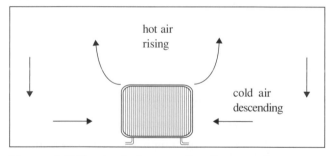

Figure 1.8 The typical example of convection. Warm air currents are set up by the radiator.

The air close to the radiator becomes hot (by conduction) and so its density decreases. It rises high in the room, raising the temperature there. This is large-scale motion of air molecules giving rise to a convection current. The space left by the rising air is now taken by colder air, which in turn will warm up, continuing the cycle.

Radiation

This mechanism is very different from the other two methods of heat transfer as it requires no medium for the propagation of

heat. The sun heats up the earth by radiation through the vacuum of space. Every body at some *absolute* temperature T radiates away energy in the form of electromagnetic waves.

> ► The amount of energy per second (i.e. the power) radiated by a body depends on its surface area, A, and absolute temperature, T.
>
> In equation form (not required for examination purposes)
>
> $$P \propto AT^4$$
>
> This is known as the Stefan–Boltzmann law.

The radiation emitted also depends on the nature of the surface of the body. A body that is black and dull on its surface is a better emitter of radiation than a body that is polished and shiny. For example, a piece of charcoal is a good emitter of radiation. At low temperatures the amount of radiation it emits is very small but when it is heated to a high temperature, the charcoal will glow as it emits radiation as visible light. The opening of a can of soft drink looks black because most of the light that enters it cannot escape. However, when the can is heated, the opening acts as a good emitter of radiation and at high temperatures the opening would glow much like a piece of charcoal at the same temperature.

Surfaces that are black and dull, as opposed to polished and shiny, are also good *absorbers* of radiation. Thus, we wear dark clothes in the winter to absorb the radiation from the sun. Light-coloured surfaces are good *reflectors* of radiation, which is why we wear light-coloured clothes in the summer.

The energy radiated by a body is electromagnetic radiation and is distributed over an infinite range of wavelengths. However, most of the energy is radiated at a specific wavelength that is determined by the temperature of the body. The higher the temperature, the smaller the wavelength. For a body at ordinary room temperature (293 K), the wavelength at which most of the energy is radiated is an infrared wavelength. This is why we associate infrared radiation with 'heat'.

Questions

1 Give definitions of:
   (a) temperature;
   (b) heat;
   (c) internal energy.

2 A hot body is brought into contact with a colder body until their temperatures are the same. Assume that no other bodies are around. Is the heat lost by one body equal to the heat gained by the other? Is the temperature drop of one body equal to the temperature increase of the other?

3 A body at a given uniform temperature of 300 K and internal energy 8×10^6 J is split into two equal halves.
   (a) Has any heat been exchanged?
   (b) What is the temperature of each half?
   (c) What is the internal energy of each half?

4 The volume of 1 mol of hydrogen gas (molar mass 2 g mol^{-1}) at stp (standard temperature and pressure) is 22.4 L.
   (a) Find out how much volume corresponds to each molecule of hydrogen.
   (b) Consider now 1 mol of lead (molar mass 207 g mol^{-1}, density 11.3×10^3 kg m^{-3}). How much volume corresponds to each molecule of lead?
   (c) Find the ratio of these volumes (hydrogen to lead).

5 The density of aluminium is 2.7 g cm^{-3} and its molar mass is 27 g mol^{-1}.
   (a) Find the mass of an atom of aluminium.
   (b) Find the number of aluminium atoms per cubic metre.

6 The density of copper is 8.96 g cm^{-3} and its molar mass is 64 g mol^{-1}.
   (a) Find the mass of an atom of copper.
   (b) Find the number of copper atoms per cubic metre.

7 Explain the design of a vacuum flask using what you have learned about heat transfer (see Figure 1.9).

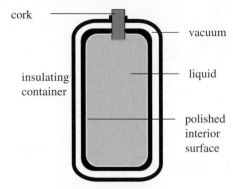

Figure 1.9 A vacuum flask. For question 7.

8 Can you think of any reason why one would want to use a ceiling fan in the winter?

9 Dark clothes absorb heat and so are not usually worn in the summer. But dark clothes are also good radiators, so why don't they radiate away the heat they absorb, causing no discomfort?

10 Figure 1.10 shows the variation of the temperature in a glass window with thickness. The glass separates a room, which has a constant temperature of 20 °C, from the outside, which has a constant temperature of 5 °C.
   (a) What would be a more realistic graph?
   (b) The window is replaced by a double window where the two glass planes have a layer of air in between them. The total thickness of the double window is the same as the one below. Draw the graph you would expect for the variation of temperature with distance.

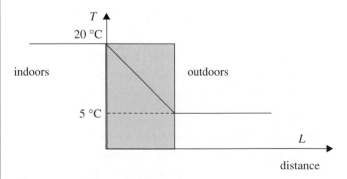

Figure 1.10 For question 10.

11 Heat flows at the same rate through two rods of equal cross-sectional area whose ends are kept at fixed temperatures. Which graph in

Figure 1.11 shows the rod that is the better conductor?

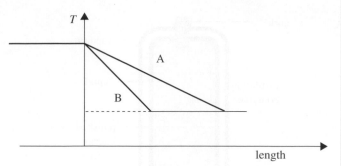

Figure 1.11 For question 11.

12 If you put your hand a certain distance above a candle flame it will burn. It will not feel hot though if you put it the same distance to the side of the candle. What *two* facts are responsible for this?

13 If you touch a metal rod and a plastic ruler lying on your desk, the metal rod will feel cooler even though both objects are at the same temperature. Why?

14 Consider a lit fireplace in a living room. What is the dominant method of heat transfer by which the fire heats the room?

15 Hot water is placed in three plastic pots that differ only in their outside colour. The first is painted a dull black, the second a shiny black and the third a shiny silver. Order the pots according to how fast they will cool down.

16 Homeless people often cover themselves with newspapers in order to keep warm at night. Why does this help?

17 Why does it get colder on a clear, cloudless night?

18 A room is kept at constant temperature by an electric heater with a power output of 1500 W. At what rate is the room losing heat to the outside?

19 Figure 1.12 shows how the temperature varies across a rod of constant cross-sectional area. The rod connects two reservoirs that are at constant temperatures of 100 °C and 30 °C.
   (a) What is the temperature gradient at the ends of the rod?
   (b) Explain how you can deduce that the rod is not insulated.

Figure 1.12 For question 19.

20 A layer of aluminium and a layer of wood of equal thickness are put together as shown in Figure 1.13. The temperature on the aluminium side is kept constant at 20 °C and that on the wood side at 0 °C.
   (a) Compare the rate of heat flow in aluminium and wood.
   (b) Compare the temperature gradients for aluminium and wood.

Figure 1.13 For question 20.

21 By what factor does the rate of radiation from a body increase when the temperature is increased from 100 °C to 200 °C?

22 If the distance between the sun and the earth, d, decreases, the average earth temperature, T, will go up. The fraction of the power radiated by the sun that is received on earth is proportional to $\frac{1}{d^2}$; the power radiated by the earth is proportional to T^4.
   (a) Deduce the dependence of the temperature of the earth, T, on d.
   (b) Hence estimate the expected rise in temperature if the distance decreases by 1.0%.
   Take the average temperature of the earth to be 287 K.

Thermal properties

This chapter is an introduction to the basic principles of calorimetry and to experimental methods used in measuring specific heat capacities and latent heats.

Objectives

By the end of this chapter you should be able to:

- state the basic definitions of calorimetry, such as *specific heat capacity* and *specific latent heats of fusion* and *vaporization*;
- understand why temperature stays constant during a phase change;
- outline methods for determining specific and latent heats experimentally;
- solve *calorimetry problems* using $Q = mc\Delta T$ and $Q = mL$;
- state the factors that affect the rate of *evaporation* and distinguish evaporation from boiling.

Specific heat capacity

When heat is provided to a body, the temperature of the body will, in general, increase.

▶ The amount of heat needed to raise the temperature of a mass of one kilogram of a substance by one kelvin is called the specific heat capacity, c, of the material. To raise the temperature of a mass m by ΔT degrees, the amount of heat required is therefore

$Q = mc\Delta T$

(assuming that c is temperature independent). The units of specific heat capacity are $J\ kg^{-1}\ K^{-1}$.

As Table 2.1 shows, different substances have different values of **specific heat capacity**.

Consider, for example, iron and silver. The heat required to raise the temperature of 1 kg of iron by 1 K is 470 J, whereas the energy required to raise the temperature of 1 kg of silver by 1 K is only 234 J, which is about half. On the other

hand, it is known that the heat required to raise the temperature of 1 mol of iron and 1 mol of silver by 1 K is about the same. This can be understood in terms of the molecular picture of matter as follows.

A given amount of heat provided to 1 mol of any substance will be divided among the same number of molecules (since 1 mol has Avogadro's

Substance	$c/J\ kg^{-1}\ K^{-1}$
Aluminium	910
Lead	130
Iron	470
Copper	390
Silver	234
Water	4190
Ethanol	2428
Ice	2218
Marble	879

Table 2.1 Specific heat capacities.

number of molecules) and so, on average, the kinetic energy of each molecule will increase by the same amount. This shows up macroscopically as the same increase in temperature. The reason that different materials show different temperature increases when the same amount of heat is provided to 1 kg of each material (i.e. they have different specific heat capacities) is that 1 kg of each material contains a different number of molecules.

The product of mass times specific heat capacity defines the heat capacity of a body, C:

$$C = mc$$

The concept of heat capacity is useful when a body consists of a number of parts of different specific heat capacities, such as, for example, a metal tank containing water. If the tank has mass M and specific heat capacity c and the water has mass m and specific heat capacity c', then the heat capacity of the water tank is

$$C = Mc + mc'$$

Knowing the heat capacity of the water tank allows us to say that, if a quantity of heat Q is given to the water tank, then the rise in temperature ΔT will be found from

$$Q = C\Delta T$$

Unlike specific heat capacity, which depends on the substance, heat capacity only depends on the particular body in question.

Example question

Q1 ▬▬▬▬▬▬▬

When a car brakes, an amount of heat equal to 112 500 J is generated in the brake drums. If the mass of the brake drums is 28 kg and their specific heat capacity is 460.5 J kg^{-1} K^{-1}, what is the change in their temperature?

Answer

From $Q = mc\Delta T$ we find

$$\Delta T = \frac{Q}{mc}$$

$$= \frac{112500}{28 \times 460.5}$$

$$= 8.7\,^\circ\text{C}$$

Thermal equilibrium

It is everyday experience that heat flows from hot bodies into cold bodies (see Figure 2.1). When a cold and a hot body are placed in contact, heat will flow until the temperature of both bodies is the same. (In fact, temperature can be defined as that property which is common to the two bodies in this case.) This state of affairs is called thermal equilibrium. The amount of heat lost by the hot body is equal to the amount of heat gained by the cold body.

Figure 2.1 In an isolated system heat always flows from the hotter body to the colder.

Example question

Q2 ▬▬▬▬▬▬▬

A piece of iron of mass 200 g and temperature 300 °C is dropped into 1.00 kg of water of temperature 20 °C. What will be the eventual temperature of the water? (Take c for iron as 470 J kg^{-1} K^{-1} and for water as 4200 J kg^{-1} K^{-1}.)

Answer

Let T be the final unknown temperature. The iron will also be at this temperature, so

amount of heat lost by the iron
$$= m_{\text{iron}} c_{\text{iron}} (300 - T)$$

and

amount of heat gained by water
$$= m_{\text{water}} c_{\text{water}} (T - 20)$$

Conservation of energy demands that heat lost = heat gained, so

$$m_{\text{iron}} c_{\text{iron}} (300 - T) = m_{\text{water}} c_{\text{water}} (T - 20)$$
$$\Rightarrow T = 26.1\,^\circ\text{C}$$

Note how the large specific heat capacity of water results in a small increase in the temperature of water compared with the huge drop in the temperature of the iron.

Change of state

Ordinary matter can exist as a solid, a liquid or a gas. These three are called states of matter. Heating can turn ice into water and water into steam. Ice will turn into water if the temperature of the ice is its melting temperature: 0 °C. Similarly, to turn water into steam the temperature must be 100 °C. This means that if we are given a piece of ice at a temperature of, say, −10 °C, to melt it we must first raise its temperature from −10 °C to zero.

▶ Once at the melting point, any additional heat supplied does not increase the temperature. Rather, this heat is used to overcome the forces between the water molecules in the ice: that is, to provide the work necessary to separate the molecules and bring the solid to the liquid phase at the same temperature.

After all of the ice has turned into water, we have water at a temperature of 0 °C. Any additional heat supplied will increase the temperature of the water. When the temperature reaches 100 °C, any additional heat supplied is used to turn water into steam at the same temperature of 100 °C. That is, the heat is used to do the work necessary to move the molecules further apart. After all of the water has turned into steam, the temperature begins to increase again. We thus see that when the state of matter is changing, the temperature does not change.

▶ The heat required to melt a unit mass of material at its melting point is called the *specific latent heat of fusion*, L_f, and the heat required to vaporize a unit mass at its boiling point is called the *specific latent heat of vaporization*, L_v. Thus to melt or vaporize a quantity of mass m, we require a quantity of heat

$$Q = mL_f \quad \text{and} \quad Q = mL_v$$

respectively. The specific latent heats have units of J kg^{-1}.

Table 2.2 shows values of the **specific latent heats** of fusion and vaporization for various substances.

The term latent heat (without the 'specific' in front) is used to denote the heat necessary to change the phase of a substance irrespective of mass.

Figure 2.2 shows how the temperature of 0.5 kg of a hypothetical substance changes as heat is provided to it.

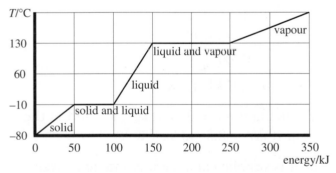

Figure 2.2 When heat is provided to a solid substance, the temperature increases, except when the phase is changing.

Substance	Specific latent heat of fusion/kJ kg^{-1}	Melting temperature/°C	Specific latent heat of vaporization/kJ kg^{-1}	Boiling temperature/°C
Water	334.4	0	2257	100
Ethanol	108.9	−114	840	78.3
Aluminium	395	660	10548	2467
Lead	23	327	849.7	1740
Copper	205	1078	2567	5190
Iron	275	1540	6285	2800

Table 2.2 Latent heats of fusion and vaporization together with the melting and boiling temperatures.

We may deduce the following from Figure 2.2. First, that the melting and boiling points are, respectively, −10 °C and 130 °C. The specific latent heat of fusion is found from

$$Q = mL_f$$

$$\Rightarrow L_f = \frac{Q}{m}$$

$$= \frac{50\,kJ}{0.5\,kg}$$

$$= 100\,kJ\,kg^{-1}$$

and the specific latent heat of vaporization is found from

$$Q = mL_v$$

$$\Rightarrow L_v = \frac{Q}{m}$$

$$= \frac{100\,kJ}{0.5\,kg}$$

$$= 200\,kJ\,kg^{-1}$$

The specific heat capacity in the solid phase is

$$Q = mc\,\Delta T$$

$$\Rightarrow c = \frac{Q}{m\Delta T}$$

$$= \frac{50\,kJ}{0.5\,kg \times 70\,K}$$

$$= 1.43\,kJ\,kg^{-1}\,K^{-1}$$

In the liquid it is $c = 0.71$ kJ kg^{-1} K^{-1} and in the vapour it is $c = 2.86$ kJ kg^{-1} K^{-1}.

If heat is supplied at a *constant* rate to a given mass of a solid, then its temperature as a function of time might be as shown in Figure 2.3.

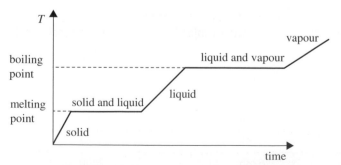

Figure 2.3 Graph of temperature as a function of time when a substance is heated at a constant rate.

The temperatures corresponding to the horizontal parts are the melting and boiling temperatures.

Knowledge of the rate of heat supply and the actual time over which melting and boiling take place enables us to determine the specific latent heats. (See example questions 4 and 5 below.)

Example questions

Q3

An ice cube of mass 25.0 g and temperature −10.0 °C is dropped into a glass of water of mass 300.0 g and temperature 20.0 °C. What is the temperature eventually? (Specific heat capacity of ice = 2218 J kg^{-1} K^{-1}; latent heat of fusion of ice = 334 kJ kg^{-1}.)

Answer

Let this final temperature be T. Ignoring heat lost by the glass itself, water will cool down by losing heat. This heat will be taken up by the ice to:
(a) increase its temperature from −10 °C to 0 °C, the heat required being $25 \times 10^{-3} \times 2218 \times 10$;
(b) melt the ice cube into water at 0 °C, the heat required being $25 \times 10^{-3} \times 334 \times 10^3$;
(c) increase the temperature of the former ice cube from 0 °C to the final temperature T.

Thus

$$0.3 \times 4190 \times (20 - T) = (25 \times 10^{-3} \times 2218 \times 10)$$
$$+ (25 \times 10^{-3} \times 334 \times 10^3)$$
$$+ (25 \times 10^{-3} \times 4190) \times T$$

Solving for T gives $T = 11.9$ °C.

Q4

Heat is provided at a constant rate of 833 J s^{-1} to 1 kg of copper at the melting temperature. If it takes 4 minutes to completely melt the copper, find the latent heat of fusion of copper.

Answer

The heat needed to melt 1 kg of copper is L, the specific latent heat of fusion. In 4 minutes the heat supplied is $833 \times 60 \times 4 = 200$ kJ, so $L_f = 200$ kJ kg^{-1}.

Q5

Look back at Figure 2.3 and determine the relative sizes of the specific latent heats and specific heat capacities. Recall that heat is provided at a constant rate.

Answer

To compare the specific heats in the solid, liquid and vapour phase remember that $\Delta Q = mc\,\Delta T$ and so

$$\frac{\Delta Q}{\Delta t} = mc\frac{\Delta T}{\Delta t}$$

$$\Rightarrow c = \frac{(\Delta Q/\Delta t)}{m(\Delta T/\Delta t)}$$

Since the rate of heat supplied is constant, it follows that the phase in which the rate of increase of temperature is the largest has the *smallest* specific heat capacity. Clearly, the transition that lasts the longer also has the largest specific latent heat.

Measuring specific heats

The *specific heat capacity* of a solid or liquid can be measured using an electrical method that directly measures the amount of heat flow into a body. The liquid or solid is placed inside a calorimeter of known heat capacity, C, and its mass and initial temperature recorded. The calorimeter is insulated and an electrical heating element is inserted through a small opening at the top into the liquid or into a hole drilled in the solid (see Figure 2.4). The heating element is connected to a source of potential difference and the voltage across it is recorded, as is the current through the element. A thermometer is also inserted into a hole drilled in the solid. If the material to be measured is liquid, then a similar arrangement can be used,

Figure 2.4 Apparatus for measuring the specific heat capacity of a solid (left) and a liquid (right).

stirring the liquid every time a temperature measurement is made.

The current is switched on at $t = 0$ and allowed to run until the temperature is increased by 40 to 50 °C. The temperature is recorded at regular intervals of about a minute. If the maximum temperature reached after time t is T_{max}, then the energy supplied by the battery to the liquid is

$$\text{heat supplied} = VIt$$

where I is the current in the heater and V the voltage across it. The heat absorbed by the liquid and the calorimeter is

$$\text{heat absorbed} = mc(T_{max} - T) + C(T_{max} - T)$$

Equating the two quantities of heat allows us to determine c.

Another method, the method of mixtures, measures the specific heat capacity as follows. A hot solid of known initial temperature is put in an insulated calorimeter, of known heat capacity and initial temperature, which contains a liquid such as water. The final temperature of the water is recorded after thermal equilibrium has been reached. Thus, consider a mass of 0.400 kg of a solid at 80 °C that is put in a 100 g copper calorimeter containing 800 g of water at 20 °C. The final temperature of the water is measured to be 22 °C. From these values, we may deduce the specific heat capacity of the solid as follows.

Amount of heat lost by the solid:

$$0.400 \times c \times (80 - 22) = 23.2c \text{ J}$$

Amount of heat gained by the calorimeter and the water:

$$0.100 \times 390 \times (22 - 20)$$
$$+ 0.800 \times 4200 \times (22 - 20) = 6798 \text{ J}$$

Equating the two we find

$$c = 293 \text{ J kg}^{-1}\text{K}^{-1}$$

Measuring specific latent heats

To measure the specific latent heat of fusion of ice, a simple method (the method of mixtures) is to put a quantity of ice at 0 °C (the ice is in a mixture with water at 0 °C) into a calorimeter containing water at a few degrees above room temperature. (The ice is blotted dry before being thrown into the calorimeter. Its mass can be determined by weighing the calorimeter at the end of the experiment.) Thus, suppose that 25 g of ice at 0 °C is placed in an aluminium calorimeter of mass 250 g containing 300 g of water at 24 °C. The temperature of the water is measured at regular intervals of time until the temperature reaches a minimum value. Suppose that this temperature is 17 °C. The calorimeter and water lost heat, which the ice received.

Heat lost by calorimeter and water:

$$0.250 \times 910 \times (24 - 17)$$
$$+ 0.300 \times 4198 \times (24 - 17) = 10408 \, \text{J}$$

Heat received by ice:

$$0.025 \times L + 0.025 \times 4198 \times 17$$
$$= 0.025 \times L + 1784$$

Equating the two gives

$$1784 + 0.025 \times L = 10408$$
$$\Rightarrow L = 335 \, \text{kJ} \, \text{kg}^{-1}$$

To measure the specific latent heat of vaporization of water we can use an electrical method. Water is heated in a double container (as shown in Figure 2.5) with an electric heater.

Figure 2.5 Steam condenses in the outer container and the water is collected in a beaker.

Steam can leave the inner container through a small hole and collects in the outer container, where it condenses into water. This water can be allowed to drip into a beaker, which can then be weighed to determine the mass of water that has been boiled away. If the experiment lasted for time t and the voltage and current in the heater were measured as V and I, respectively, the energy supplied was VIt. If m is the mass of water that boiled away, the energy it received was mL_v. Equating the two expressions allows us to determine the specific latent heat of vaporization.

Evaporation

The molecules of a gas move about with a distribution of speeds. The same is true for the molecules of a liquid. The *faster* molecules are the *most energetic* and if they find themselves at the surface of the liquid they may escape from the liquid. This phenomenon is known as *evaporation*. Note that unlike boiling (where molecules from anywhere within the volume occupied by the liquid can escape) only surface molecules participate in evaporation. This means that the average kinetic energy of the molecules that stay behind is *reduced*, which in turn means that the temperature of the liquid is *reduced*, since temperature is a measure of the average kinetic energy of the molecules of the substance.

The rate of evaporation (that is, the number of molecules escaping the liquid per second) increases as the surface area and temperature of the liquid are increased. If the liquid is placed in an enclosed volume, then the molecules that escape collect over the liquid and their pressure is called vapour pressure. The vapour pressure increases as more molecules escape and equilibrium is reached when as many molecules escape as fall back into the liquid. Thus, if a stream of air is directed at the vapour over the liquid, hence pushing away the evaporated molecules, the rate of evaporation will increase.

Questions

1 Define what is meant by specific heat capacity of a substance. Consider two metals that have different specific heat capacities. The heat required to increase the temperature of 1 mol of aluminium and 1 mol of copper by the same amount are about the same. Yet the specific heat capacities of the two metals are very different. Suggest a reason for this.

2 A body of mass 0.150 kg has its temperature increased by 5.00 °C when a quantity of heat 385 J is provided to it. What is the body's specific heat capacity?

3 A radiator made out of iron has a mass of 45.0 kg and is filled with 23.0 kg of water.
   (a) What is the heat capacity of the water-filled radiator?
   (b) If heat is provided to the radiator at the rate of 450 W, how long will it take for the temperature to increase by 20.0 °C?

4 A car of mass 1360 kg descends from a hill of height 86 m at a constant speed of 20 km h^{-1}. Assuming that all the potential energy of the car goes into heat in the brakes, find the rise in the temperature of the brakes (take the heat capacity of the brakes to be 16 kJ K^{-1} and ignore any heat losses to the surroundings.)

5 The water in an iron pipe has frozen to ice at −4.8 °C. The heat capacity of the pipe is 7.1 kJ K^{-1}. The volume of ice in the pipe is 12.3 L. What is the combined heat capacity of the pipe and ice? To melt the ice, a heater of power output 4.99 kW is connected to the pipe. How long will it take for the ice to melt? (Density of ice = 0.929 kg L^{-1}; specific heat capacity of ice = 2.20 kJ kg^{-1} K^{-1}; latent heat of fusion of ice = 334 kJ kg^{-1}.)

6 How much ice at −10 °C must be dropped into a cup containing 300 g of water at 20 °C in order for the temperature of the water to be reduced to 10 °C? The cup itself has a mass of 150 g and is made out of aluminium. Assume that no heat is lost to the surroundings.

7 The surface of a pond of area 20 m^2 is covered by ice of uniform thickness 6 cm. The temperature of the ice is −5 °C. How much heat is required to melt this amount of ice into water at 0 °C? (Take the density of ice to be 900 kg m^{-3}.)

8 A frozen pond, of surface area 50.0 m^2, is covered by a sheet of ice of thickness 15 cm. If the pond receives solar radiation of intensity 342 W m^{-2}, find out what fraction of the ice will be turned into water in 6.0 h. (Take the ice temperature to be 0.0 °C and the latent heat of fusion of ice as 334 kJ kg^{-1}. Take the density of ice to be 900 kg m^{-3}.)

9 Radiation from the sun falls on the frozen surface of a pond at a rate of 600 W m^{-2}. If the ice temperature is 0 °C, find how long it will take to melt a 1.0 cm thick layer of ice. (Take the density of ice to be 900 kg m^{-3}.) What assumption have you made in reaching your answer?

10 (a) How much heat is required to warm 1.0 kg ice initially at −10 °C to ice at 0 °C?
   (b) How much heat is required to melt the ice at 0 °C.
   (c) How much heat is required to further increase the temperature of the water from 0 °C to 10 °C.
   (d) In which stage (warming the ice, melting the ice, warming the water) is the heat requirement largest?

11 Ice at 0 °C is added to 1 L of water at 20 °C, cooling it down to 10 °C. How much ice was added?

12 A quantity of 100 g of ice at 0 °C and 50 g steam at 100 °C are added to a container that has 150 g water at 30 °C. What is the final temperature in the container? Ignore the container itself in your calculations.

13 A calorimeter of mass 90 g and specific heat capacity 400.0 J kg^{-1} K^{-1} contains 300.0 g of a liquid at 15.0 °C. An electric heater rated at 20.0 W warms the liquid to 19.0 °C in 3.0 min. Assuming there are no heat losses to the surroundings, find the specific heat capacity of the liquid.

14 A calorimeter of heat capacity 25 J K^{-1} contains 140 g of a liquid; an immersion heater is used to provide heat at a rate of 40 W for a total time of 4 min. The temperature of the liquid is measured every minute and the results are shown in Table 2.3. Calculate the specific heat capacity of the liquid.

$T/°C$	18.0	22.2	25.8	30.0
Time/min	0	1	2	3
$T/°C$	33.8	32.6	31.1	30.3
Time/min	4	5	6	7

Table 2.3 For question 14.

15 A hair dryer consists of a coil that warms air and a fan that blows the warm air out. The coil generates heat at a rate of 600 W. Take the density of air to be 1.25 kg m^{-3} and its specific heat capacity to be 990 J kg^{-1} K^{-1}. The dryer takes air from a room at 20 °C and delivers it at a temperature of 60 °C.

(a) What mass of air flows through the dryer per second?

(b) What volume of air flows per second?

16 An auditorium of size 40 m × 20 m × 8 m has 600 people in it. The temperature of the air is initially 27 °C. It takes 29 J of heat to raise the temperature of 1 mol of air by 1 K and the molar mass of air is about 29 g mol^{-1}. Take the density of air to be constant at 1.25 kg m^{-3}.

(a) How many moles of air are there in the auditorium?

(b) Assuming that each person gives off heat at a rate of 80 W, calculate how fast the temperature in the auditorium is rising. Assume that the auditorium is closed so that cooler air does not enter.

17 (a) Discuss the factors that affect the evaporation rate of a liquid.

(b) Explain, in terms of molecular behaviour, why cooling takes place as a result of evaporation.

(c) Give one practical application of the cooling effect of evaporation.

Ideal gases

A gas is a collection of a very large number of molecules. We call the gas ideal if the molecules do not exert any forces on each other. Many real gases show behaviour that is a very close approximation of ideal gas behaviour. As a result of collisions between the molecules and the walls of the container of the gas, pressure develops. The pressure, volume, temperature and the number of moles in the gas are related through the ideal gas law. Application of the laws of mechanics to the motion of the molecules leads to the connection between the average kinetic energy of molecules and the absolute temperature of the gas.

Objectives

By the end of this chapter you should be able to:

- state the definition of *pressure*: $P = \frac{F}{A}$;
- understand that an ideal gas is a gas in which the molecules *do not exert forces on each other* except when colliding; an ideal gas obeys the law $PV = nRT$ at *all* pressures, temperatures and volumes;
- understand the *ideal gas law* and solve problems using it: $\frac{P_1 V_1}{n_1 T_1} = \frac{P_2 V_2}{n_2 T_2}$;
- appreciate that pressure in a gas develops as a result of *collisions* between the molecules and the walls of the container in which the *momentum* of molecules changes;
- appreciate the fundamental relationship between the absolute temperature and the average kinetic energy of the molecules.

Pressure

Pressure is defined as the normal force to an area per unit area. The pressure on the small circular area A in Figure 3.1 is thus given by the expression

$$P = \frac{F \cos \theta}{A}$$

The unit of pressure is newton per square metre, N m^{-2}, also known as pascal, Pa. Another commonly used non-SI unit is the atmosphere, atm, which equals 1.013×10^5 Pa.

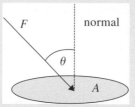

Figure 3.1 Pressure is the force normal to an area divided by that area.

Example question

Q1

Two hollow cubes of side 0.25 cm with one face missing are placed together at the missing face (see Figure 3.2). The air inside the solid formed is pumped out. What force is necessary to separate the cubes?

Figure 3.2 What force is necessary to separate the cubes?

Answer

The pressure inside the solid is zero and outside it equals atmospheric pressure, 1.013×10^5 Pa. Thus, the force is

$F = PA$

$= 1.013 \times 10^5 \times (0.25)^2$

$= 6.33 \times 10^3$ N

Gases

It is convenient to use the number of moles, n, of the gas rather than the mass itself to specify the quantity of a gas. Recall that 1 mol of any substance contains the same number of molecules, the Avogadro constant

$$N_A = 6.02 \times 10^{23} \text{ molecules mol}^{-1}$$

and that the number of moles of a gas can be found by dividing the total number of molecules by the Avogadro constant

$$n = \frac{N}{N_A}$$

The size of molecules varies from substance to substance, but the typical order of magnitude of molecular size is in the range from 10^{-8} m to 10^{-10} m.

The parameters P, V, T and n are related to each other. The equation relating them is called the equation of state. Our objective is to discover the equation of state for a gas. To do this a number of simple experiments can be performed as described in the following sections.

Example questions

Q2

How many molecules are there in 6 g of hydrogen gas?

Answer

A quantity of 6 g of hydrogen gas corresponds to 3 mol, since the molar mass of hydrogen gas is 2 g mol^{-1}. Thus, there are $3 \times N_A$ molecules or 1.81×10^{24}.

Q3

Make a rough estimate of the number of water molecules in an ordinary glass of water.

Answer

A glass contains about 0.3 L of water, which has a mass of about 300 g. Since the molar mass of water is 18 g mol^{-1}, it follows that the glass contains

$$\frac{300}{18} \approx 17 \text{ mol}$$

or 10^{25} molecules.

The Boyle–Mariotte law

The equipment shown in Figure 3.3 can be used to investigate the relationship between pressure and volume of a fixed quantity of gas that is kept at constant temperature.

Figure 3.3 Apparatus for verifying the Boyle–Mariotte law.

It consists of a syringe inside which a quantity of air is trapped. The pressure inside the syringe (i.e. the pressure of the air) can be increased by adding weights to the piston as shown. By varying the weights on the piston and recording the changes in the volume of the gas, the pressure–volume relationship can be established.

The results of a typical experiment are shown in Figure 3.4.

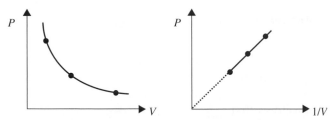

Figure 3.4 The relationship between pressure and volume at constant temperature. The points on the curves have the same temperature.

▶ We can deduce that at constant temperature and with a constant quantity of gas, pressure is inversely proportional to volume, that is

$PV = \text{constant}$

as illustrated in Figure 3.5. This is called the Boyle–Mariotte law. (The plot of pressure versus volume is a hyperbola, as in Figure 3.4.)

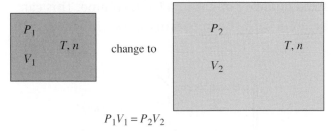

$$P_1V_1 = P_2V_2$$

Figure 3.5 The Boyle–Mariotte law.

The hyperbola in the pressure–volume diagram is also known as an isothermal curve or isotherm: the temperature at any point on the curve is constant.

Example question

Q4

The pressure of a gas is 2 atm and its volume 0.9 L. If the pressure is increased to 6 atm at constant temperature, what is the new volume?

Answer

From $P_1V_1 = P_2V_2$ we have $2 \times 0.9 = 6 \times V$ from which $V = 0.3$ L.

The volume–temperature law

The dependence of volume on temperature of a fixed quantity of gas kept at constant pressure can be investigated with the apparatus shown in Figure 3.6. This was how it was first done by Charles and Gay-Lussac. The gas is surrounded by water that is heated from below. As it expands, the pressure is kept constant by adjusting the amount of mercury in the tube so that h stays the same. The constant gas pressure is thus the sum of atmospheric pressure plus the amount $\rho g h$.

Figure 3.6 Apparatus for verifying the volume–temperature law.

It is found that the volume increases uniformly with temperature. If this same experiment is repeated with a different quantity of gas, or a gas at a different constant pressure, the result is the same. In each case, the straight-line graph of volume versus temperature is different. But the striking fact is that when each straight line is extended backwards it always crosses the temperature axis at $-273.15\ ^{\circ}\text{C}$, as in Figure 3.7.

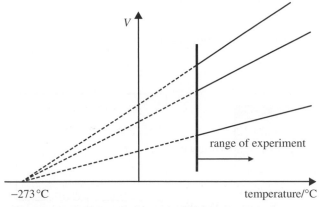

Figure 3.7 When the graph of volume versus temperature is extended backwards, all the lines intersect the temperature axis at the same point.

This suggests that there exists a minimum possible temperature, namely $-273.15\,°C$. Thus, we can devise a new temperature scale, in which the minimum possible temperature occurs at zero. This scale is called the Kelvin scale, and the relationship between the Celsius and Kelvin scales is

T (in kelvin) $= T$ (in degrees Celsius) $+ 273.15$

(We usually approximate 273.15 to 273.)

> ▶ When the temperature is expressed in kelvin, this experiment implies that at constant pressure
>
> $$\frac{V}{T} = \text{constant}$$

When the temperature in a graph of volume versus temperature is expressed in kelvin, the straight line passes through the origin, as in Figure 3.8.

V

T/K

Figure 3.8 If temperature is expressed in kelvin, the graph goes through the origin.

The volume–temperature law is illustrated in Figure 3.9.

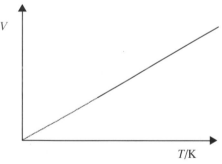

$$\frac{V_1}{T_1} = \frac{V_2}{T_2}$$

Figure 3.9 The volume–temperature law.

Example question

Q5

A gas expands at constant pressure from an original volume of 2 L at 22 °C to a volume of 4 L. What is the new temperature?

Answer

From

$$\frac{V}{T} = \text{constant}$$

it follows that

$$\frac{2}{295} = \frac{4}{T}$$

and so

$T = 590\,K$ or $317\,°C$

Note that we converted the original temperature into kelvin.

The pressure–temperature law

What remains now is to investigate the dependence of pressure on temperature of a fixed quantity of gas in a fixed volume. This can be done with the apparatus shown in Figure 3.10.

Figure 3.10 Apparatus for verifying the relationship between pressure and temperature.

The gas container is surrounded by water whose temperature can be changed and a pressure gauge measures the pressure of the gas. We find that pressure increases uniformly with increasing temperature. The graph of pressure versus temperature is a straight line that, when extended backwards, again intersects the temperature axis at −273.15 °C, as in Figure 3.11.

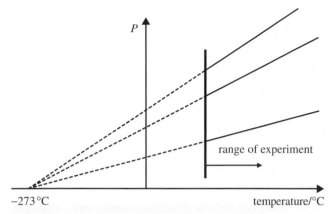

Figure 3.11 The graphs of pressure versus temperature when extended backwards intersect the temperature axis at the same point.

When the temperature in a graph of pressure versus temperature is expressed in kelvin, the straight line passes through the origin, as in Figure 3.12.

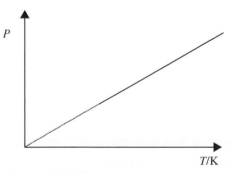

Figure 3.12 If temperature is expressed in kelvin, the graph goes through the origin.

This is more evidence in favour of the existence of an absolute temperature scale.

▶ This experiment implies that at constant volume

$$\frac{P}{T} = \text{constant}$$

The pressure–temperature law is illustrated in Figure 3.13.

$$\frac{P_1}{T_1} = \frac{P_2}{T_2}$$

Figure 3.13 The pressure–temperature law.

Example question

Q6

A gas in a container of fixed volume is heated from a temperature of 20 °C and pressure 3 atm to a temperature of 85 °C. What is the new pressure?

Answer

From

$$\frac{P}{T} = \text{constant}$$

we have

$$\frac{3}{293} = \frac{P}{358}$$

and so

$$P = 3.67 \text{ atm}$$

The equation of state

If we combine the results of the three preceding experiments, we see that what we have discovered is that

$$\frac{PV}{T} = \text{constant}$$

What is the value of the constant? To determine that, we repeat all of the preceding experiments, this time using different quantities of the gas. We discover that the constant in the last equation is proportional to the number of moles n of the gas in question:

$$\frac{PV}{T} = n \times \text{constant}$$

We can now measure the pressure, temperature, volume and number of moles for a large number of *different* gases and calculate the value of $\frac{PV}{nT}$. We find that this constant has the same value for all gases – it is a universal constant. We call this the gas constant R. It has the numerical value

$$R = 8.31 \text{ J K}^{-1} \text{mol}^{-1}$$

▶ Thus, finally, the equation of state is

$$PV = RnT$$

(Remember that temperature must always be in kelvin.)

A gas that obeys this law at all temperatures, pressures and volumes is said to be an **ideal gas**. Real gases obey this law only for a range of temperatures, pressures and volumes. The equation of state can be illustrated as in Figure 3.14.

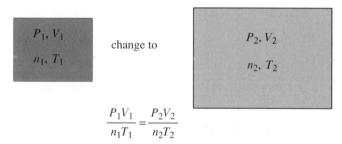

$$\frac{P_1 V_1}{n_1 T_1} = \frac{P_2 V_2}{n_2 T_2}$$

Figure 3.14 The equation of state.

Example questions

Q7 ▬▬▬▬▬▬▬▬▬▬

How many moles of gas are there in a gas of temperature 300 K, volume 0.02 m³ and pressure 2×10^5 Pa?

Answer

$$n = \frac{PV}{RT}$$
$$= \frac{2 \times 10^5 \times 0.02}{8.31 \times 300}$$
$$= 1.60 \text{ mol}$$

Q8 ▬▬▬▬▬▬▬▬▬▬

A container of hydrogen of volume 0.1 m³ and temperature 25 °C contains 3.20×10^{23} molecules. What is the pressure in the container?

Answer

The number of moles present is

$$n = \frac{3.20 \times 10^{23}}{6.02 \times 10^{23}}$$
$$= 0.53$$

So

$$P = \frac{RnT}{V}$$
$$= \frac{8.31 \times 0.53 \times 298}{0.1}$$
$$= 1.3 \times 10^4 \text{ N m}^{-2}$$

Q9 ▬▬▬▬▬▬▬▬▬▬

A gas of volume 2 L, pressure 3 atm and temperature 300 K expands to a volume of 3 L and a pressure of 4 atm. What is the new temperature of the gas?

Answer

$$\frac{PV}{T} = \text{constant}$$

so

$$\frac{3 \times 2}{300} = 4 \times \frac{3}{T}$$

giving

$$T = 600 \text{ K}$$

Q10 ▬▬▬▬▬▬▬▬▬▬

Figure 3.15 shows two isothermal curves for the same quantity of gas. Which is at the higher temperature?

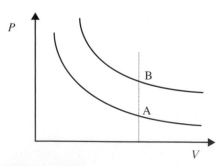

Figure 3.15.

Answer

Draw a vertical line that intersects the two isotherms at points A and B. Since B is at higher pressure than A and both have the same volume, it follows from $\frac{P}{T} = $ constant that B is at the higher temperature.

Q11

Figure 3.16 shows two curves obtained in an experiment to investigate the dependence of pressure on temperature at constant volume. Which straight line corresponds to the larger volume? (Both curves correspond to the same number of moles.)

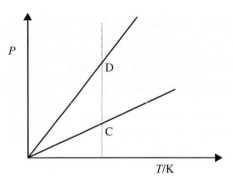

Figure 3.16.

Answer

Draw a vertical line which intersects the two straight lines at points C and D. Since D has higher pressure than C and both have the same temperature, it follows from $PV = $ constant that C is at higher volume.

Q12

Figure 3.17 shows how the pressure of a fixed quantity of gas depends on temperature in kelvin. As the temperature increases, is the volume of the gas changing?

Answer

If the volume is kept constant, a graph of pressure versus temperature will give a straight line *going through the origin*. Hence, in this problem, the volume must be changing.

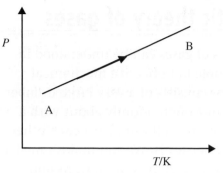

Figure 3.17.

Q13

Is the volume increasing or decreasing in example question 12?

Answer

Draw the dotted lines through the origin and going through points A and B, as shown in Figure 3.18. These are isochoric lines, which means the volume is constant along each one. Also, draw a horizontal line from A to C as shown. Points A and C have the same pressure. Since C is at higher temperature, it must also be at higher volume. Hence point B also has a higher volume than A. The gas is therefore expanding.

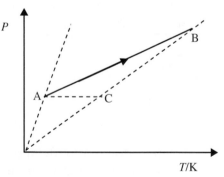

Figure 3.18.

Q14

If the temperature of a gas is increased by a factor of 4 and the density remains the same, what is the new pressure of the gas?

Answer

Since the density stays the same, the volume stays the same. Using $\frac{P}{T} = $ constant we deduce that the pressure must increase by a factor of 4.

The kinetic theory of gases

The properties of gases can be understood in terms of a simple but effective mechanical model. The gas consists of a very large number of molecules moving randomly about with a range of speeds and colliding with each other and the container walls. We can make a model of this by making certain assumptions and seeing what these lead to. The basic assumptions of the kinetic theory of gases are:

1 A gas consists of a large number of molecules.

2 Molecules move with a range of speeds.

3 The volume of the molecules is negligible compared with the volume of the gas itself.

4 The collisions of the molecules with each other and the container walls are elastic.

5 Molecules exert no forces on each other or the container except when in contact.

6 The duration of collisions is very small compared with the time between collisions.

7 The molecules obey Newton's laws of mechanics.

Some of these assumptions are illustrated in Figure 3.19.

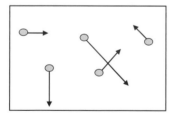

Figure 3.19 The molecules move randomly in the volume of the container with a range of speeds.

Using these assumptions together with the laws of mechanics and the equation of state allows the derivation of one of the most important formulae in physics, namely

$$\tfrac{1}{2}mv^2 = \tfrac{3}{2}kT$$

Here the speed v is defined by

$$v^2 = \frac{\left(v_1^2 + v_2^2 + \cdots + v_N^2\right)}{N}$$

So v is the square root of the *average of the squares of the speeds of the molecules of the gas* (the average of the velocity vectors of all the molecules is zero since they move randomly in all directions). We call v the root mean square speed or rms speed. (It must be realized that v is not the average speed of the molecules – but it is numerically close to the average, so we are usually excused for calling v the average molecular speed even if it is not technically correct.)

Appearing in this equation is a new constant of physics, the Boltzmann constant k, the value of which is $k = 1.38 \times 10^{-23}$ J K^{-1} (it is the ratio of the gas constant R to the Avogadro constant).

▶ The meaning of this important relation is that

average kinetic energy of molecules
$\propto$ absolute temperature

that is, the absolute temperature is a measure of the average kinetic energy of the molecules of a substance.

Example questions

Q15

Four molecules have speeds of 300 m s^{-1}, 350 m s^{-1}, 380 m s^{-1} and 500 m s^{-1}. Find the average speed and the root mean square speed.

Answer

$$\text{average speed} = \frac{300 + 350 + 380 + 500}{4} \text{ m s}^{-1}$$
$$= 382.5 \text{ m s}^{-1}$$

$$v = \sqrt{\frac{300^2 + 350^2 + 380^2 + 500^2}{4}} \text{ m s}^{-1}$$
$$= 389.5 \text{ m s}^{-1}$$

Q16

If v is doubled, what is the new temperature?

Answer

From the Boltzmann equation it follows at once that the temperature is four times as big.

Molecular explanation of pressure

The pressure of a gas originates from the collisions of the molecules with the walls of its container. At every collision, each molecule has its momentum changed and so a force acts from the wall onto the molecule. By Newton's third law, the molecule exerts an equal and opposite force on the wall. The total force due to all the colliding molecules divided by the area over which the force acts gives the pressure of the gas.

▶ The pressure in a gas results from the collisions of the gas molecules with the walls of its container (and *not* from collisions between molecules).

From the molecular point of view, we may identify two factors that affect the pressure of the gas. The first is the average molecular speed (the higher the speed, the larger the change in momentum of the molecules and so the higher the force – see Figure 3.20).

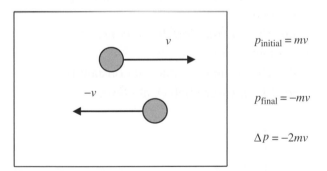

$p_{initial} = mv$

$p_{final} = -mv$

$\Delta p = -2mv$

Figure 3.20 A molecule exerts a force on the container wall because its momentum p changes with every collision.

The second factor is the frequency of collisions. The more frequent the collisions, the higher the pressure. Thus, in providing molecular explanations for pressure it is sufficient to remember that roughly

$P \propto$ speed × frequency of collisions

As an application of this, consider a gas that has been heated under constant volume. The molecules are moving faster on average (increased temperature) and the frequency with which the collisions take place also increases (the time between collisions is reduced since molecules are moving faster). For *both* reasons (speed and frequency) the pressure then goes up.

By contrast, if a gas is compressed isothermally, the average speed stays the same. But the distance molecules have to travel between collisions with the walls is reduced (since the volume is reduced) and so the frequency of collisions increases. Hence the pressure increases (because of frequency only).

Example questions

Q17
A gas is compressed *slowly* by a piston. Explain why the temperature of the gas will stay the same.

Answer

If a gas is compressed slowly, the speed with which the molecules rebound off the piston is the same as that before the collision with the piston. Hence, the average kinetic energy of the molecules stays the same. Since the average kinetic energy is proportional to the absolute temperature of the gas, the temperature will stay the same.

Q18
A gas is compressed *rapidly* by a piston (see Figure 3.21). Explain why the temperature of the gas will increase.

fast

Figure 3.21.

Answer

The rapid movement of the piston means that molecules will rebound off the piston with an *increased* speed. Hence the average kinetic energy of the molecules will increase, and since the average kinetic energy is proportional to the absolute temperature of the gas, the temperature will increase as well.

Q19

A gas expands isothermally. Explain from a molecular point of view why the pressure decreases.

Answer

The volume of the gas expands, which means that, on average, molecules have a larger distance to travel between successive collisions with the walls. Thus, the collisions are less frequent than before and so the pressure decreases.

Q20

A gas is heated at constant pressure. Explain why the volume must increase as well.

Answer

The temperature increases and so the molecules move faster, on average. From $P \propto$ speed $\times$ frequency, we deduce that the frequency of collisions must decrease if the pressure is to stay the same. This can happen if the volume of the gas increases so that molecules have a longer distance to travel in between collisions.

Questions

1 A volume of 2.00 L of a gas is heated from 20.0 °C to 80.0 °C at constant pressure. What is the new volume?

2 A sealed bottle contains air at 22.0 °C and a pressure of 12.0 atm. If the temperature is raised to 120.0 °C, what will the new pressure be?

3 A gas is kept at a pressure of 4.00 atm and a temperature of 30.0 °C. When the pressure is reduced to 3.00 atm and the temperature raised to 40.0 °C, the volume is measured to be 0.45 L. What was the original volume of the gas?

4 An air bubble exhaled by a diver doubles in radius by the time it gets to the surface of the water. Assuming that the air in the bubble stays constant in temperature, find by what factor the pressure of the bubble is reduced.

5 12.0 kg of helium is required to fill a bottle of volume 5.00 L at a temperature of 20.0 °C? What pressure will the helium have?

6 What mass of carbon dioxide is required to fill a tank of volume 12.0 L at a temperature of 20.0 °C and a pressure of 4.00 atm?

7 A flask of volume 300.0 mL contains air at a pressure of 5.00×10^5 Pa, and a temperature of 27.0 °C. If the flask loses molecules at a rate of 3.00×10^{19} per second, after how much time will the pressure in the flask be reduced to half its original value? (Assume that the temperature of the air remains constant during this time.)

8 The point in Figure 3.22 represents the state of a *fixed quantity* of ideal gas in a container with a movable piston. The temperature of the gas in the state shown is 600 K. Indicate on the diagram the point representing the new state of the gas after the following separate changes.
   (a) The volume doubles at constant temperature.
   (b) The volume doubles at constant pressure.
   (c) The pressure halves at constant volume.

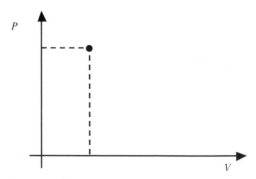

Figure 3.22 For question 8.

9 The point in Figure 3.23 shows the state of a fixed quantity of ideal gas kept at a temperature of 300 K. The state of the gas

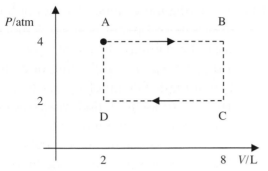

Figure 3.23 For question 9.

Figure 3.25 For question 11.

changes and is represented by the dotted route in the pressure–volume diagram. The gas is eventually returned to its original state.

(a) Find the temperature of the gas at the corners of the rectangle on the pressure–volume diagram.

(b) At what point on the dotted path is the internal energy of the gas greatest?

(a) What is the pressure of the gas?

(b) How many molecules are there in the gas?

(c) If the temperature is increased to 152.0 °C, what is the new volume of the gas?

12 The molar mass of a gas is 28 g mol^{-1}. A container has 2.00 mol of this gas at 0.00 °C and a pressure of 1.00 atm. What are the mass and volume of the gas?

HL only

10 Two ideal gases are kept at the same temperature in two containers separated by a valve as shown in Figure 3.24. What will the pressure be when the valve is opened? (The temperature stays the same.)

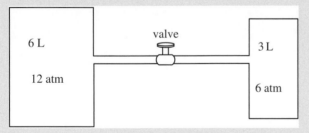

Figure 3.24 For question 10.

11 Figure 3.25 shows a cylinder in a vacuum, which has a movable, frictionless piston at the top. An ideal gas is kept in the cylinder. The piston is at a distance of 0.500 m from the bottom of the cylinder and the volume of the cylinder is 0.050 m^3. The weight on top of the cylinder has a mass of 10.0 kg. The temperature of the gas is 19.0 °C.

HL only

13 A container with a volume of 1.25 m^3 is filled with hydrogen gas at pressure 2.35 atm and temperature 25.0 °C.

(a) How many molecules are there?

The container has a safety valve that opens releasing hydrogen whenever the pressure exceeds 2.50 atm. The container is now heated and then cooled down again. When the temperature has fallen to 21.0 °C the pressure is 2.05 atm.

(b) How many molecules escaped?

(c) What was the highest temperature the hydrogen achieved during heating?

14 A container with a volume of 1.07 m^3 is filled with a monatomic gas. The temperature is 140 °C and the pressure 1.47 atm.

(a) What will the pressure be if the temperature becomes 215 °C?

(b) If the temperature of the gas falls below 140 °C, a number of the atoms in the gas will join together to form diatomic molecules. When the temperature falls to 46.0 °C, the pressure is measured to be only 0.760 atm. How many moles of the diatomic molecules are there at 46.0 °C?

15 A balloon has a volume of 404 m^3 and is filled with helium of mass 70.0 kg. If the temperature inside the balloon is 17.0 °C, find the pressure inside the balloon.

16 A flask has a volume of 5.0×10^{-4} m^3 and contains air at a temperature of 300 K and a pressure of 150 kPa.
   (a) Find the number of moles of air in the flask.
   (b) Find the number of molecules in the flask.
   (c) Find the mass of air in the flask. You may take the molar mass of air to be 29 g mol^{-1}.

17 A container of fixed volume is filled with an ideal gas at 0.00 °C. The total kinetic energy of the molecules in the container is E. An identical container has twice the mass of gas in it and the total kinetic energy of those molecules is $2E$. Find the temperature of the second container.

18 The molar mass of helium is 4.00 g mol^{-1}.
   (a) Calculate the volume of 1 mol of helium at stp ($T = 273$ K, $P = 1$ atm).
   (b) What is the density of helium at stp?
   (c) What is the density of oxygen gas at stp (the molar mass is 32 g mol^{-1})?

19 (a) By finding the volume of 1 mol of helium (molar mass 4 g mol^{-1}) at stp, 1 mol of water (molar mass 18 g mol^{-1}, density 1.0×10^3 kg m^{-3}) and 1 mol of uranium (molar mass 238 g mol^{-1}, density 18.7×10^3 kg m^{-3}), find what volume corresponds to each molecule.
   (b) Assuming this volume to be a cube, find the size of the side of this cube for each of the three cases.
   (c) How does this size compare with the actual size of each molecule?

20 The density of an ideal gas is 1.35 kg m^{-3}. If the temperature in kelvin and the pressure are both doubled, find the new density of the gas.

21 A container is filled with a mixture of nitrogen and oxygen. What is the ratio of the rms speed of oxygen molecules to that of nitrogen molecules? (Molar mass of oxygen = 32 g mol^{-1}; molar mass of nitrogen = 28 g mol^{-1}.)

22 By what factor does the rms speed of neon molecules increase if their temperature increases by a factor of 4?

Thermodynamics

Thermodynamics deals with the conditions under which heat can be transformed into mechanical work. The first law of thermodynamics states that the amount of heat given to a system is used to increase that system's internal energy and to do work. The second law invokes limitations to how much heat can actually be transformed into mechanical work.

Objectives

By the end of this chapter you should be able to:

- understand the meaning of *internal energy*;
- calculate *work* when a gas expands or compresses using $\delta W = P\,\delta V$;
- state the relationship between changes in the internal energy, the work done and the heat supplied through the *first law of thermodynamics*, $\Delta U = Q - W$;
- define the terms *adiabatic*, *isothermal*, *isobaric* and *isochoric* and show these on a pressure–volume diagram;
- understand what is meant by *irreversibility* and *disorder*;
- understand that entropy is a measure of disorder;
- state the second law of thermodynamics;
- solve problems with *heat engine efficiency*, $\eta = \frac{W}{Q_h} = \frac{Q_h - Q_c}{Q_h}$;
- appreciate the significance of the *Carnot engine*, $\frac{Q_h}{Q_c} = \frac{T_h}{T_c}$, and *Carnot efficiency*, $\eta = \frac{T_h - T_c}{T_h}$;
- understand the meaning of *energy degradation*.

Internal energy

In Chapter 3.1 we defined the internal energy of a gas as the total kinetic energy of the molecules of the gas plus the potential energy associated with the intermolecular forces. If the gas is ideal, the intermolecular forces are assumed to be strictly zero, and if the gas is also monatomic, all the internal energy of the gas comes from the random kinetic energy of the atoms of the gas (a non-monatomic gas would also have energy due to the rotation and vibration of the atoms within the molecule). The average kinetic energy of the molecules is given by

$$\bar{E}_k = \tfrac{1}{2}mc^2 = \tfrac{3}{2}kT$$

▶ It follows that the internal energy U of an ideal monatomic gas with N atoms is given by $N\bar{E}_k$, that is

$$U = \tfrac{3}{2}NkT$$

or, equivalently,

$$U = \tfrac{3}{2}nRT = \tfrac{3}{2}PV$$

where n is the number of moles. The change in internal energy due to a change in temperature is thus given by

$$\Delta U = \tfrac{3}{2}nR\,\Delta T$$

We can use any version of this formula that is convenient for a particular problem. As is seen from this formula, the internal energy of a fixed number of moles of an ideal gas depends only on temperature and not on the nature of the gas, its volume or other variables. In a classic experiment, Joule allowed a gas to expand freely from container A into container B as shown in Figure 4.1.

Figure 4.1 Joule's experiment in which internal energy is shown to depend only on temperature.

When the valve separating the two containers is opened, the gas fills the entire volume available to it. The containers are well insulated so no heat enters or leaves the system. Joule tried to observe a temperature difference as the gas expanded and found none. Despite its increased volume and reduced pressure, the internal energy stayed the same. Actually, in a real gas a small drop in temperature is expected, since the molecules must do a certain amount of work against the attracting intermolecular forces which, although very small, are not exactly zero. With more accurate measurements than those available to Joule, this temperature drop can be detected.

(In the case of polyatomic molecules, the internal energy includes additional contributions. A polyatomic molecule can rotate as well as vibrate and these motions require energy. The energy associated with these motions must be included in the internal energy of the gas.)

Example question

Q1

A flask contains a gas at a temperature of 300 K. If the flask is taken aboard a fast-moving aeroplane, will the temperature of the gas increase as a result of the molecules moving faster?

Answer

No. The temperature of the gas depends on the random motion of the molecules and not on any additional uniform motion imposed on the gas as a result of the motion of the container.

Systems

In thermodynamics we often deal with *systems*, which simply means the complete set of objects under consideration. Thus, a gas in a container is a system, as is a certain mass of ice in a glass. A system can be large – for example, it can be the entire earth. Perhaps we may even consider the entire universe as a system. A system can be *open* or *closed*: mass can enter and leave an open system but not a closed system. An *isolated* system is one in which no energy in any form enters or leaves. If all the parameters defining the system are given, we speak of the system being in a particular *state*. For example, an ideal gas is specified if its pressure, volume and temperature are specified. Any processes that change the state of a system are called *thermodynamic processes*. Thus, heating a gas may result in changed pressure, temperature or volume and is thus a thermodynamic process. Doing work on the gas by compressing it is also a thermodynamic process.

It is important to realize that internal energy is a property of the particular state of the system under consideration, and for this reason internal energy is called a state function. Thus, if two gases originally in different states are brought to the same state (i.e. same pressure, volume and temperature), they will have the same internal energy irrespective of what the original state was and how the gas was brought to that final state. By contrast, heat and work are not state functions. We cannot speak of the heat content of a system or of its work content. Heat and work are related to *changes* in the state of the system not to the state itself.

Work done on or by a gas

Imagine that we are given a quantity of a gas in a container with a frictionless, movable piston and that the gas is compressed slightly by exerting a force on the piston from the outside, as in Figure 4.2.

during the compression the pressure of the gas can be considered constant

Figure 4.2 When the piston is pushed in by a small amount, work is being done *on* the gas.

If the pressure in the gas initially is P, and the cross-sectional area of the piston is A, then the force with which one must push is PA. If the piston moves an infinitesimal distance δs, the work done is

$$\delta W = F\delta s$$
$$= PA\delta s$$

But $A\delta s$ is the amount by which the volume of the gas has been reduced, δV.

▶ Hence the (small) work done is

$$\delta W = P\,\delta V$$

Note that, as soon as the piston is moved, the pressure in the gas will, in general, change. This is why it is necessary to give the expression for work done in the form of infinitesimal quantities, as above. To find the work done under a large change of volume one must use calculus to integrate the expression given above; the pressure, and hence the force that must be exerted, is not constant. We will not be concerned with this here. There is, however, one

rather simple case where work done can be easily calculated. This is the expansion or compression of a gas at constant pressure. In this case, the work done is

$$W = P(V_2 - V_1)$$

where $(V_2 - V_1)$ is the total change in volume and need not be small.

Example question

Q2 ▬▬▬▬▬▬▬▬▬▬▬▬▬▬▬▬▬

A gas is compressed at constant pressure $2.00 \times 10^5\,\text{Pa}$ from a volume of $2.00\,\text{m}^3$ to a volume of $0.500\,\text{m}^3$. What is the work done? If the temperature initially was 40 °C what is the final temperature of the gas?

Answer

Since the compression takes place under constant pressure, the work done is

$$P \times \text{change in volume} = 2.00 \times 10^5\,\text{Pa} \times 1.50\,\text{m}^3$$
$$= 3.00 \times 10^5\,\text{J}$$

The final temperature is found from

$$\frac{V}{T} = \text{constant}$$

that is

$$\frac{2}{313} = \frac{0.5}{T}$$

giving

$$T = 78.25\,\text{K} = -195\,°\text{C}.$$

The work done has a simple interpretation on a pressure–volume diagram: in Figure 4.3, the volume of a gas changes by an infinitesimal amount δV, and the work done is thus $P\,\delta V$. This is approximately equal to the area of the strip whose width is δV and height P_0, where P_0 is the pressure of the gas as given by the graph during the change. Even though P changes as well during the change of volume, we can consider it to have the constant value given by P_0 on the graph.

▶ The *total* work done when the gas expands by an arbitrary amount is then the area under the graph in the pressure–volume diagram.

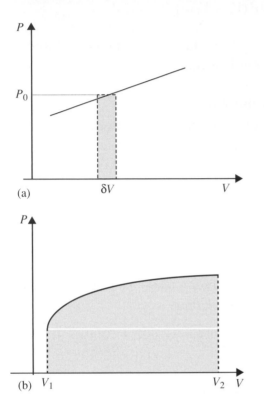

(a)

(b) V_1 V_2 V

Figure 4.3 (a) Even though the pressure is not constant, the work done can be calculated for an infinitesimal volume change by considering that for such a small change the pressure is constant. (b) For a change in volume that is not small, the work done is found from the area under the curve in the pressure–volume diagram.

The pressure–volume diagrams in Figure 4.4 show an arbitrary series of changes on an ideal gas that begin and end in the state A (diagram (c)). The gas expands from A to B and thus the work done by the gas is the area between the curve and the V axis from A to B (diagram (a)). From B to A, the gas is being compressed so the work is being done by an outside agent. That work equals the area between the curve and the V axis (diagram (b)).

▶ The net work done is the work done by the gas minus the work done on the gas. It equals the area enclosed by the closed loop.

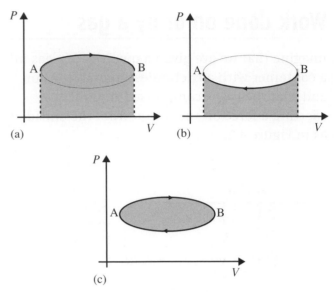

(a)   (b)

(c)

Figure 4.4 For a closed loop in a pressure–volume diagram, the work done is the area of the loop.

A number of interesting processes can be identified on a pressure–volume diagram. A process in which the gas expands or contracts at constant pressure is called an *isobaric* process. On a pressure–volume diagram it is represented by a horizontal straight line (Figure 4.5a). A process in which the volume of the gas stays fixed is called *isochoric* and is represented by a vertical line (Figure 4.5b).

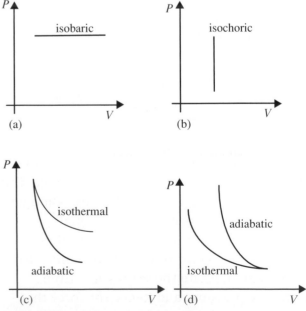

(a)   (b)

(c)   (d)

Figure 4.5 Isobaric, isochoric, isothermal and adiabatic processes.

Since pressure is fixed in an isobaric process, the work done is easy to calculate, $W = P\Delta V$. Note that in an isochoric process no work is done on or by the gas.

Apart from *isothermal* processes, which we met earlier, the last process of interest is called *adiabatic* and is a process during which the gas does not absorb or give out any heat, so $Q = 0$ (Figure 4.5c, d). We have also drawn an isotherm to show that the adiabatic curve is steeper than an isotherm going through the same point. In general, an isothermal process takes place slowly and the system must be in thermal equilibrium with its surroundings; an adiabatic process takes place very fast and the system is not in thermal equilibrium with its surroundings (see Figure 4.6). To help understand the difference between adiabatic and isothermal processes better, we will introduce the first law of thermodynamics here.

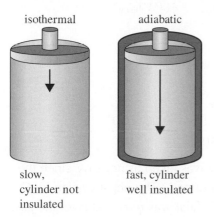

isothermal   adiabatic

slow, cylinder not insulated   fast, cylinder well insulated

Figure 4.6 Isothermal and adiabatic systems.

The first law of thermodynamics

▶ When a small amount of heat δQ is given to a gas, the gas will absorb that energy and use it to increase its internal energy and/or to do work by expanding. Conservation of energy demands that

$$\delta U = \delta Q - \delta W$$

where δU is the small change in internal energy and δW is the small amount of work done. In this formula, the convention is that a positive δQ denotes heat absorbed by the gas while a negative δQ stands for heat lost by the gas. Similarly, a positive δW stands for work done by the gas (the gas is expanding) and negative δW work done on the gas (the gas is being compressed). A positive δU thus represents an increase in the temperature and a negative δU represents a decrease in the temperature.

If the amounts of heat and work are not small, then

$$\Delta U = Q - W$$

where Q is the heat and W the work done.

This formula is known as the first law of thermodynamics and is a consequence of the law of conservation of energy. This law also incorporates what we stated earlier: namely that internal energy is a state function whereas heat and work are not.

Example questions

Q3

A gas in a container with a piston expands isothermally (i.e. the temperature stays constant). If heat $Q = 10^5$ J is given to the gas, what is the work done by the gas?

Answer

The pressure is not kept constant during the expansion, so we cannot use the formula we derived for work done. But since $T = $ constant, it follows that $\Delta U = 0$ and since

$$\Delta U = Q - W$$

we must have

$$W = Q$$

So, the work done by the gas in this case is equal to the heat supplied to it: 10^5 J.

Q4

A gas expands adiabatically (i.e. it does not receive or lose heat). Will its temperature increase or decrease?

Answer

Again using the first law with $\delta Q = 0$ we find

$$\delta U = -\delta W$$

The gas expands and so it is the gas that does the work, that is

$$\delta W > 0$$

Therefore

$$\delta U < 0$$

That is, the internal energy and thus temperature decrease. Similarly, if the gas is compressed adiabatically, the temperature will increase.

This explains why the adiabatic curve starting from a point on the pressure–volume diagram is steeper than the isothermal curve starting from that same point (see Figure 4.7). Consider an adiabatic and an isothermal process, both starting from the same point and bringing the gas to the same (expanded) final volume. Since the adiabatic process will reduce the temperature and the isothermal process will not, it follows that the pressure of the final state after the adiabatic expansion will be lower than the pressure of the state reached by the isothermal expansion. Hence, the adiabatic is steeper.

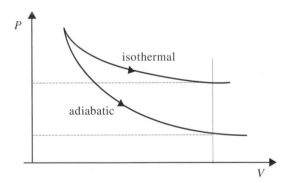

Figure 4.7.

Q5

A monatomic gas is kept at constant pressure 3.00×10^6 Pa, initial volume 0.100 m^3 and temperature 300 K. If the gas is compressed at constant pressure down to a volume of 0.080 m^3, find:

(a) the work done on the gas;

(b) the heat taken out of the gas.

Answer

(a) The work done is

$$3.00 \times 10^6 \times 0.020 = 6.00 \times 10^4 \text{ J}$$

When put in the first law, this must be taken as negative since this is work done on the gas

$$\Delta W = -6.00 \times 10^4 \text{ J}$$

(b) From the first law

$$Q = \Delta U + W$$

so to find the heat taken out we must first find the change in the internal energy of the gas. Since

$$U = \tfrac{3}{2} NkT \quad \text{or} \quad U = \tfrac{3}{2} PV$$

it follows that

$$\Delta U = \tfrac{3}{2} Nk\Delta T$$

or (which is more convenient here)

$$\Delta U = \tfrac{3}{2}(PV)_{\text{final}} - \tfrac{3}{2}(PV)_{\text{initial}}$$

Thus

$$\Delta U = -9.00 \times 10^4 \text{ J}$$

Finally

$$Q = -9.00 \times 10^4 - 6.00 \times 10^4$$
$$= -1.5 \times 10^5 \text{ J}$$

(Note that ΔU was taken as negative since the temperature dropped.) The negative sign in Q means that this heat was removed from the gas.

The second law of thermodynamics

There are many processes in thermodynamics that are consistent with the first law but are nonetheless impossible. A few of these processes involve:

- the spontaneous (i.e. without the action of another agent) transfer of heat from a cold body to a hotter body;

- the air in a room suddenly occupying just one half of the room and leaving the other half empty;

• a glass of water at room temperature suddenly freezing, causing the temperature of the room to rise.

These processes do not happen because they are forbidden by a very special law of physics – the second law of thermodynamics.

Order and disorder

To begin our discussion of this law, consider a 1 kg mass moving at 10 m s^{-1}. Friction brings it to rest and so the initial kinetic energy of 50 J has been lost. Suppose that all of this energy went into the internal energy of the body. This means that the molecules now vibrate about their equilibrium positions faster than before. The original kinetic energy of the ball was associated with the *ordered* motion of the body as a whole. Every molecule of the body moved forward with the same component of velocity in addition to the random or disordered motion associated with the vibrations of the atoms. (See Figure 4.8.)

Figure 4.8 The ordered mechanical energy of the ball has been converted into disordered internal energy.

The mechanical (i.e. kinetic) energy of the ball was totally converted into *disordered* energy as a result of friction. There is an irreversibility in this conversion of energy. The ball that has been brought to rest by friction is not expected to convert part of this disordered motion into ordered motion and start accelerating back towards the direction it came from. The original kinetic energy cannot be *recovered* from the internal energy of the ball. Because this energy cannot be *recovered*, we say that it has been degraded. Nothing in the laws of physics we have seen so far actually prevents the ball from

accelerating backwards. Wh[...]
the second law of thermod[...]

▶ The second law of therm[...]
with the limitations imp[...]
engines: that is, on devi[...]
to convert heat (disorde[...]
mechanical energy (ordered energy).

Reversibility

Before discussing heat engines, let us continue with a discussion on reversibility and irreversibility, concepts that, as we will soon see, are intimately related to the second law of thermodynamics. All natural processes are irreversible – they lead towards states of increased disorder. An irreversible process captured on film would look absurd if the film were to be run backwards. A glass of water looks ordered just before it slips from your hand and falls to the floor, breaking into many pieces. Capturing this on film and then running it in reverse would show the pieces of glass and drops of water assembling themselves into an unbroken glass full of water. It looks like thermodynamics is related to the arrow of time – the direction in which natural processes take place. A reversible process for a system consisting of a large number of molecules is reversible only as an idealized approximation. We may formally define a process as irreversible if it is impossible to reverse the process by an infinitesimal change in the conditions under which the change takes place. Thus, a hot body at 50 °C placed in contact with a colder body at 20 °C results in heat flowing from the hot to the cold body. This process is irreversible since it is not possible to reverse the flow of heat by small changes in the temperatures of the two bodies. On the other hand, if the two bodies have temperatures that differ by an infinitesimal amount, then a small change in the temperature of one body would reverse the flow of heat. Similarly, consider a gas expanding isothermally. The piston is moving out at infinitesimal constant speed and at all times we have thermal and mechanical um. The temperature of the gas is the as that of its surroundings and the ssure exerted on the piston by the gas is matched by an equal pressure from the outside. An infinitesimal change in these conditions might involve slightly increasing the outside pressure so that the gas will now start compressing. The outside pressure will, of course, increase only momentarily so that the expansion is reversed and when that happens the two pressures will again be made the same. The process just described is a reversible process.

Irreversibility can be quantified. There exists a quantity called *entropy* which, like internal energy, is a *state function*: that is, once the state of the system is specified, so is its entropy. Entropy depends only on the state of the system and not on how it got there.

▶ The definition of *change* in entropy is

$$\delta S = \frac{\delta Q}{T}$$

This gives the *small* change in the entropy of a system when a *small* quantity of heat is given to or removed from the system at a temperature T (in kelvin). The unit of entropy is $J\,K^{-1}$.

If heat is given to the system, $\delta Q > 0$ and entropy increases. If heat is removed, $\delta Q < 0$ and entropy decreases. For a reversible process that returns the system to its original state, $\delta S = 0$. One such example is the isothermal expansion of a gas and the subsequent isothermal compression back to the initial state. Since the expansion and compression are isothermal, leaving the temperature constant, we may write

$$\delta S_1 = \frac{|\delta Q|}{T}$$

during expansion and

$$\delta S_2 = -\frac{|\delta Q|}{T}$$

during compression. (The gas receives heat upon expanding and discards heat upon compressing – use the first law of thermodynamics.) The net entropy change is thus zero. Since natural processes are irreversible, we may claim that these processes increase the entropy of the system under consideration and those theoretical processes that are reversible leave the entropy of the system unchanged. (In general, we need calculus to evaluate the entropy changes in a system since the formula above is valid for small amounts, δQ, that do not change the temperature. Care must also be taken to evaluate the change in entropy along reversible paths connecting the initial and final states of the system – we will not spend any time on these technical problems here.)

Let us apply the expression for δS given above to the case of heat flow between a hot body A and a cold body B. If a very small quantity of heat δQ flows from the hot to the cold body, the total entropy change of the two bodies is

$$\delta S = -\frac{\delta Q}{T_h} + \frac{\delta Q}{T_c}$$

$$= \delta Q \left(\frac{1}{T_c} - \frac{1}{T_h} \right)$$

$$\Rightarrow \delta S > 0$$

(the temperature of each body is assumed unchanged during this infinitesimal exchange of heat) and in fact heat will flow from the hot body into the cold one (Figure 4.9a). The opposite (Figure 4.9b) does not happen because

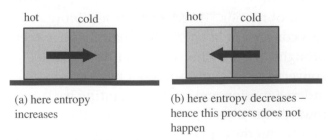

(a) here entropy increases

(b) here entropy decreases – hence this process does not happen

Figure 4.9 (a) When heats flows from a hot to a cold body, the entropy of the universe increases. (b) If the reverse were to happen without any performance of work, the entropy would decrease, violating the second law.

it corresponds to a decrease in the entropy of the system:

$$\delta S = \frac{\delta Q}{T_h} - \frac{\delta Q}{T_c}$$

$$= \delta Q \left(\frac{1}{T_h} - \frac{1}{T_c} \right)$$

$$\Rightarrow \delta S < 0$$

Similarly, when heat is given to a solid at its melting temperature, the solid will use that heat to turn into a liquid at the same temperature. The entropy formula again shows that the entropy increases as the solid absorbs the latent heat of fusion. The same is also true for vaporization.

This allows us to state the second law of thermodynamics in its general form:

▶ The entropy of an isolated system never decreases.

A number of equivalent statements of the second law also exist. If one of these statements is accepted, the others can be proved from it. The statement due to Clausius is:

▶ It is impossible for heat to (spontaneously) flow from a cold to a hot object.

The statement of the second law from Kelvin and Planck is that:

▶ It is impossible for a heat engine working *in a cycle* to absorb heat and perform an equal amount of work.

Finally, the statement due to Carnot is:

▶ The most efficient heat engine operating between two given temperatures is the Carnot engine.

Heat engines

A device that converts heat into mechanical work (energy) is called a heat engine (see Figure 4.10). By heat engine, we mean any such device irrespective of whether the device can

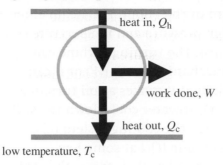

Figure 4.10 A schematic diagram of a heat engine.

actually be constructed in practice or not. The typical operation of a heat engine consists of the following steps. First, heat is taken into the engine. There must therefore be a source for this heat. We call this source the hot reservoir and assume that this reservoir is kept at some fixed temperature T_h. The quantity of heat that enters the engine is Q_h. A part of this heat is converted into mechanical work W. What is left (i.e. $Q_h - W$) is heat that the engine rejects, Q_c, into a reservoir at a temperature lower than T_h called T_c. Ideally, we would, of course, like to reject no heat at all, as this is wasted energy. It is a consequence of the second law (recall the Kelvin–Planck statement), however, that it is impossible to have a heat engine that converts a given amount of heat into mechanical work with 100% efficiency.

A more realistic heat engine (a steam engine) might look like Figure 4.11.

Figure 4.11 A schematic diagram of a steam engine. Heat boils water in the boiler (heat in); the steam produced at high pressure forces a turbine to turn, producing mechanical work. The steam is then condensed (heat out) and pumped back into the boiler.

Here, heat (Q_h) is provided to water, which turns into steam in the boiler. The steam enters a turbine at high pressure and temperature (T_h) and makes it turn. The turning turbine can thus perform mechanical work (W) or it can produce electricity if it makes a coil turn in a magnetic field. Cold water cools down the still hot steam and thus the cooling system takes heat out of the engine (Q_c) at some low temperature (T_c). A pump then forces the cold water back into the boiler to be heated again and the cycle is repeated. It is important to realize that the second, lower, temperature T_c is needed in this, and all other, heat engines. For if the temperature were the same throughout, the pressure on either side of the turbine blades would be the same, and hence the turbine would not turn. If a heat sink were not required, a ship sailing in the ocean could extract heat from the enormous internal energy content of the ocean water and perform work. It cannot do that because in such a case there would be no heat sink at a lower temperature (than the ocean).

We can define the efficiency of the engine by

$$\eta = \frac{W}{Q_h}$$

$$= \frac{Q_h - Q_c}{Q_h}$$

This is reasonable as Q_h represents what we pay for and W what we get out of the engine.

Example question

Q6

A heat engine takes 500 J of heat and performs 200 J of work. What is the efficiency of the engine?

Answer

From the definition

$$\eta = \frac{W}{Q_h}$$

$$= \frac{200}{500}$$

$$= 0.4$$

Equivalence of the different statements of the second law

Consider an engine working between a hot and a cold reservoir, as shown in Figure 4.12. The engine is enclosed in the dotted line and in fact consists of two heat engines. The first engine (left) converts all the heat extracted from the hot reservoir into work without rejecting any heat into the colder reservoir. This engine thus violates the second law of thermodynamics in its Kelvin–Planck form. If this work is then fed into the second heat engine, we see that the net result of the combined engine (in the dotted line) is to transfer heat from a cold to a hotter reservoir without the performance of work. And this violates the Clausius formulation of the law. By arguing in this way it can be shown that all the formulations of the second law are equivalent to each other.

Figure 4.12 A heat engine that transfers heat from a cold to a warmer reservoir without the performance of work is impossible.

An example of a heat engine

Consider now a heat engine whose working substance is an ideal, monatomic gas and is represented on a pressure–volume diagram by the cycle shown in Figure 4.13.

We are given that the pressure at A (the starting point of the cycle) is 4.0 atm, the volume is 0.10 m^3 and the temperature is 800 K. The volume at B is 0.40 m^3 and the pressure at C is 2.0 atm. We are asked to find the temperatures at points B, C and D, the amount of heat given to and taken from the gas, the internal energy

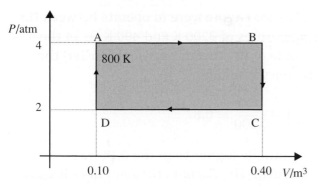

Figure 4.13 A cycle on a pressure–volume diagram, consisting of two isobaric and two isochoric processes.

changes and work done along each leg of the cycle. Finally, we want to calculate the efficiency of this engine.

The temperatures are easily found by use of the gas law, $PV = RnT$. Comparing A and B we see that (use the ideal gas law) since the volume increases by a factor of 4 at constant pressure, the temperature at B must be 4×800 K $= 3200$ K. Comparing B with C we find the temperature at C to be $3200 \times \frac{1}{2}$ K $= 1600$ K. That at D is half of that at A, namely 400 K.

From the data at point A we can find the number of moles of the gas, namely

$$n = \frac{PV}{RT}$$
$$= \frac{4 \times 10^5 \times 0.10}{8.31 \times 800}$$
$$= 6.0 \text{ mol}$$

(note that we converted atmospheres to pascal).

This can be used to find the internal energy changes:

$$\text{along AB,} \quad \Delta U = \tfrac{3}{2} Rn\Delta T = 180 \text{ kJ}$$
$$\text{along BC,} \quad \Delta U = -120 \text{ kJ}$$
$$\text{along CD,} \quad \Delta U = -90 \text{ kJ}$$
$$\text{along DA,} \quad \Delta U = 30 \text{ kJ}$$

There is no work done along CB or DA, since the volume stays the same along these legs.

Along AB the gas does work

$$W_{AB} = P\Delta V = 4.0 \times 10^5 \times 0.3 \text{ J} = 120 \text{ kJ}$$

Along CD the work is done on the gas

$$W_{CD} = -2 \times 10^5 \times 0.30 \text{ J} = -60 \text{ kJ}$$

To find the heat taken in or out we will use the first law, $Q = \Delta U + W$, along each leg:

$$\text{along AB,} \quad Q = 180 \text{ kJ} + 120 \text{ kJ} = 300 \text{ kJ}$$
$$\text{along BC,} \quad Q = -120 \text{ kJ}$$
$$\text{along CD,} \quad Q = -90 \text{ kJ} - 60 \text{ kJ} = -150 \text{ kJ}$$
$$\text{along DA,} \quad Q = 30 \text{ kJ}$$

(Positive Q means heat is given to the gas, negative Q implies heat taken out of the gas.)

The net heat given to the gas is

$$300 \text{ kJ} - 120 \text{ kJ} - 150 \text{ kJ} + 30 \text{ kJ} = 60 \text{ kJ}$$

The net work done by the gas is

$$120 \text{ kJ} - 60 \text{ kJ} = 60 \text{ kJ}$$

as it should be: the net work done is equal to the net heat into the gas. It also equals the area of the loop, as you can check. The efficiency of this engine is the ratio of the net work done to the amount of heat into the engine, that is

$$\frac{60 \text{ kJ}}{330 \text{ kJ}} = 0.18$$

(The highest and lowest temperatures achieved during this cycle are 3200 K and 400 K.)

The Carnot engine

In 1824, the French engineer Sadi Carnot realized that reversibility was the key to constructing an efficient heat engine. Since the difficulty in converting of degraded, disordered heat into mechanical work was related to the irreversibility of the conversion of mechanical work to heat, Carnot concluded that an efficient heat engine should avoid irreversible processes and transfers of heat across different temperatures. The theoretical engine Carnot constructed thus involved heat flowing into a system consisting of an ideal gas at constant temperature. Heat would also leave the system at a constant (lower) temperature. The connection between the two different temperatures should then involve no heat transfer; in other words it would have to be adiabatic.

The Carnot cycle operates along two adiabatic and two isothermal paths and the loop is thus reversible (see Figure 4.14); the total entropy change along the loop is zero (not because we go around a loop, but because we go around a loop along reversible paths).

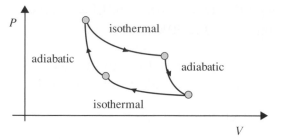

Figure 4.14 The pressure–volume diagram of a Carnot engine.

The entropy change along the two adiabatic paths is zero since $Q = 0$. Along the isotherm at temperature T_h, the entropy change is an increase of

$$\Delta S_1 = \frac{Q_h}{T_h}$$

and along the second isotherm it is a decrease of

$$\Delta S_2 = -\frac{Q_c}{T_c}$$

Thus

$$\Delta S = \Delta S_1 + \Delta S_2 = 0 = \frac{Q_h}{T_h} - \frac{Q_c}{T_c}$$

$$\Rightarrow \frac{Q_c}{Q_h} = \frac{T_c}{T_h}$$

▶ The efficiency of the Carnot engine is thus

$$\eta = \frac{W}{Q_h}$$

$$= \frac{Q_h - Q_c}{Q_h}$$

$$= 1 - \frac{Q_c}{Q_h}$$

$$= 1 - \frac{T_c}{T_h}$$

$$= \frac{T_h - T_c}{T_h}$$

If a Carnot engine were to operate between the temperatures of 3200 K and 400 K (as in the example of the rectangular loop earlier) the efficiency would be

$$1 - \frac{400}{3200} = 0.87$$

substantially higher than the 0.18 we calculated. (The Carnot efficiency does become 1 if the cold temperature is taken to be absolute zero. However, the *third* law of thermodynamics states that it is impossible to reach absolute zero.)

The formula for the efficiency shows that efficiency increases as the cold temperature decreases. Thus, in principle, a heat engine using the water of a river or just the air as the cold reservoir would be a bit more efficient in winter than in summer.

We can now appreciate that it is impossible (refer to the Kelvin–Planck statement of the second law) to have a heat engine (working in a cycle) in which *all* the heat supplied to the engine is converted into mechanical work.

The heat pump

A heat pump takes heat from a source at low temperature and delivers it at a higher temperature together with the work done on the heat pump. (Note that thermal energy will not by itself flow from a reservoir of low temperature into one at higher temperature. This is why work must be done on the pump.) This is shown schematically in Figure 4.15.

A heat pump can thus be used to heat a house in the following way: The source at low temperature from which heat is extracted can be the cold air outside the house or the earth (i.e. the ground) itself. If one inserts pipes down into the earth, the temperature there is more or less constant throughout the year, typically at 6 °C. A vapour circulating in the exterior coils of the heat pump absorbs heat from the outside. This vapour is then compressed, which increases its temperature; when it circulates in

(a) cold outdoors – winter heat pump

(b) warm outdoors – summer air-conditioner

Figure 4.15 Schematic diagram of a heat pump used as (a) a heating system in the winter and (b) a cooling unit in the summer.

the interior coils (as a condensed liquid now) of the heat pump, it will release heat. If the heat extracted from the cold reservoir is Q_c and the work done on the pump is W, then by the first law of thermodynamics (conservation of energy) the heat delivered to the house, Q_h, is

$$Q_h = Q_c + W$$

We define the coefficient of performance (or efficiency) of the heat pump (used as a heater) by

$$\zeta = \frac{\text{heat delivered}}{\text{work done}} = \frac{Q_h}{W}$$

Assuming ideal conditions, it is true that

$$\frac{Q_c}{Q_h} = \frac{T_c}{T_h}$$

so the coefficient of performance of the heat pump is

$$\zeta = \frac{T_h}{T_h - T_c}$$

Thus, for outside temperature of 6 °C and room temperature of 20 °C, the ideal coefficient of performance is

$$\zeta = \frac{T_h}{T_h - T_c}$$
$$= \frac{293}{293 - 279}$$
$$\approx 21$$

Real heat pumps have coefficients of performance considerably lower, about 4.

The heat pump run in reverse acts as a cooling system and resembles a refrigerator. Heat is extracted from the lower temperature house and ejected into the warmer surroundings. The coefficient of performance of a refrigerator or a heat pump that is used for cooling is defined as the heat extracted from the cold reservoir divided by the work done

$$\zeta = \frac{\text{heat extracted}}{\text{work done}} = \frac{Q_c}{W}$$

(Note this is different from the coefficient of performance when the heat pump is used as a heater.)

Example questions

Q7

A refrigerator with a coefficient of performance equal to 5.0 is to cool 1.0 kg of water at 20 °C into ice at −10 °C in 1 h. How much heat must be extracted from the water? How much electrical power is needed?

Answer

The heat extracted is the heat that must be removed from water at 20 °C to turn it into ice at −10 °C. This heat is

$$1.0 \times 4200 \times 20 + 1.0 \times 334 \times 10^3$$
$$+ 1.0 \times 2200 \times 10 = 4.4 \times 10^5 \text{ J}$$

The work performed on the refrigerator is thus

$$W = \frac{Q_c}{\zeta}$$
$$= \frac{4.4 \times 10^5}{5}$$
$$= 8.8 \times 10^4 \text{ J}$$

The power needed is

$$P = \frac{E}{t}$$

$$= \frac{8.8 \times 10^4}{3600} \text{W}$$

$$= 24 \text{ W}$$

Q8

Assuming an ideal (Carnot) refrigerator, find an expression for the coefficient of performance in terms of the operating temperatures.

Answer

The coefficient of performance is given by

$$\zeta = \frac{Q_c}{W}$$

$$= \frac{Q_c}{Q_h - Q_c}$$

$$= \frac{1}{\left(\frac{Q_h}{Q_c} - 1\right)}$$

$$= \frac{1}{\left(\frac{T_h}{T_c} - 1\right)}$$

$$= \frac{T_c}{T_h - T_c}$$

More on the second law

The second law of thermodynamics leads, as we have seen, to an increase in the entropy in the universe, a state of increased disorder. Many processes that are possible under the first law (i.e. the law of energy conservation) do not happen because they would violate the second law. For example, a glass of water at 0 °C has never been observed to freeze into ice by giving heat into the warm surroundings, making them even warmer. To say that this violates the second law does not imply that such a process is impossible – only very unlikely. The probability of this happening is

$$p \approx e^{\frac{\Delta S}{k}}$$

$$= e^{-\frac{\Delta Q}{kT}}$$

$$= e^{-\frac{mL}{kT}}$$

For 1 kg of water this is about $e^{-10^{26}}$ – an infinitesimal number.

Life has evolved from less ordered to more ordered species. This does not violate the second law. Although the entropy of any one particular species has decreased, the metabolic processes that have led to the growth of that species involve a larger entropy increase, so the overall entropy has increased.

Degradation of energy

Heat flows, as we have seen, from hot to cold bodies. The difference in temperature between the two bodies initially offers us the opportunity to run a heat engine between those two temperatures, extracting useful mechanical work in the process. With time, the two bodies will approach the same temperature and the opportunity for using those two bodies to do work will be lost. Thus, the flow of heat from the hotter to the colder body tends to equalize the two temperatures and deprives us of the opportunity to do work.

> ▶ It is a consequence of the second law that energy, while always being conserved, becomes less useful – this is called energy degradation.

The energy of the universe tends to move from highly ordered, useful forms to disordered, useless forms. If the second law is applied to the universe as a whole, then since it has nowhere to receive heat from or give heat away to, its expansion is adiabatic. Despite the small-scale non-uniformity of the universe (planets, solar systems, stars, galaxies, clusters of galaxies) we can still think of it on a very large scale as an expanding gas. If so, then by the first law of thermodynamics

$$\Delta U = 0 - W < 0$$

and so the temperature of the universe is decreasing. The universe is filled with electromagnetic radiation, produced during the original explosion (the Big Bang) that created the universe some 14 billion years ago. The spectrum of this radiation (i.e. how much energy is stored per interval of wavelength) is a direct function of the ambient temperature

owed to expand at constant
volume doubles.

w temperature of the gas?

f efficiency 0.4 is connected
ot engine of efficiency 0.6,
cted heat from the first
t heat in the second. What is
ciency of the two engines?

a Carnot engine can be
easing the hot reservoir
by decreasing the cold
ature.

in a larger efficiency:
temperatures by the same
.e. $\frac{\Delta T_h}{T_h} = -\frac{\Delta T_c}{T_c}$), or by the
t of kelvin (i.e. $\Delta T_h = -\Delta T_c$)?
u had to change the
of only one of the two reservoirs
ture of x kelvin, should you
hot temperature by x kelvin or
cold one by x kelvin?

cy of a heat engine (assumed
e the temperature of the hot
ng heat to the engine is 550 °C
ature of the cooler reservoir is

as an efficiency of 0.70. If
y is provided to this engine,
t is lost?

e operates between the
800 K and 400 K. Its working
mol of an ideal monatomic gas.
eat of 1000 J is provided to this

one in one cycle;
in the internal energy of the
he adiabatic expansion.

container with a movable piston at a p...
of 5.0 × 10^5 Pa and a temperature of
300.0 K. The gas is heated so that the
temperature is increased to 400.0 K without
changing the volume. Find:
(a) the heat that must be provided to the gas;
(b) the new pressure of the gas;
(c) the change in the internal energy of the
gas.

11 Prove, using calculus, that the work done by
a gas at temperature T during an isothermal
expansion from a volume V_1 to a volume V_2 is

$$W = RnT \ln\left(\frac{V_2}{V_1}\right)$$

(where n is the number of moles in the gas).

Message

Lee, Cliff

From: Dr. Catherine Coyle Lee [clee@cse.edu]
Sent: Tuesday, August 22, 2006 11:00 AM
To: Lee, Cliff
Subject: FW: Opera In The Park

Cliff,
The response was so great for the reunion that they moved it to a concert in Brooklyn instead......no only kidding.
Love you. Stretch

From: Arcilla, Sonny (Process Efficiency) [mailto:Sonny_Arcilla@ml.com]
Sent: Tue 8/22/2006 8:49 AM
To: Dr. Catherine Coyle Lee
Subject: FW: Opera In The Park

-----Original Message-----
From: Arcilla, Sonny (Process Efficiency)
Sent: Monday, August 21, 2006 12:16 AM
To: Sonny Arcilla
Subject:

Hello Everyone!

12 A refrigerator has a freezer temperature of $-20\,°C$ and the heat is rejected to a room at a temperature of $20\,°C$.
  (a) What is its coefficient of performance, assuming ideal conditions?
  (b) If work is performed on the refrigerator at a rate of 35 W, at what rate is heat extracted from the freezer?
  (c) How long would it take this refrigerator to cool 2 L of water initially at $20\,°C$ down to $8\,°C$?

13 A heat pump used to heat a house has a coefficient of performance of 4 and work is being done on it at a rate of 1200 W.
  (a) At what rate is heat being supplied to the house?
  (b) At what rate is heat being extracted from the outside?
  (c) If this heat pump were to operate as an air conditioner, what would its coefficient of performance be?

14 In an experiment in which a number of coins are tossed, the entropy of a given outcome may be defined by $k \ln N$, where N is the number of ways a particular outcome may be realized. Ten coins are thrown and the outcome is 5 heads and 5 tails. In a second throwing the outcome is 3 heads and 7 tails.
  (a) What is the change in entropy?
  (b) Does this violate the second law of thermodynamics? Explain.

15 Find the change in entropy of 10.0 g of water that boils into steam at $100\,°C$. (Latent heat of vaporization of water = $2257\,kJ\,kg^{-1}$.)

16 Find the change in entropy of 10.0 g of water that freezes into ice at $0.0\,°C$. (Latent heat of fusion of ice = $334.4\,kJ\,kg^{-1}$.)

17 A gas is suddenly heated from A to B from a pressure of 2.0 atm and temperature 300 K to a pressure of 5.0 atm. The volume stays constant at 2.0 L. From B the gas expands isothermally to a volume of 5.0 L at C. The gas then returns to its original state at A by an isobaric compression at a pressure of 2.0 atm.
  (a) Sketch these changes on a pressure–volume diagram.
  (b) Find the temperature of the gas at B.
  (c) Find the internal energy change and the heat given to or taken from the gas from A to B.
  (d) For the leg from C to A find (i) the work done, (ii) the change in internal energy and (iii) the heat given to or taken from the gas.

18 Can you cool down your kitchen by leaving the refrigerator door open? Explain your answer.

19 In an isothermal expansion all the heat that is given to a gas is converted to work as the gas expands. Why does this not violate the second law?

20 Explain (in terms of entropy) why the following processes are irreversible:
  (a) the lid of a container of gas is opened and the gas leaks out;
  (b) two different liquids mix;
  (c) an ice cube melts in a warm room.

Travelling waves

This chapter introduces a new and special kind of motion: wave motion. There are two large classes of waves: mechanical and electromagnetic waves. Waves can be further classified into transverse and longitudinal waves.

Objectives

By the end of this chapter you should be able to:
- state what is meant by *wave motion*;
- distinguish between *longitudinal* and *transverse* waves;
- define *amplitude*, *wavelength*, *period* and *frequency* and state the relationship between them, $f = \frac{1}{T}$;
- state what is meant by *crest* and *trough* and identify these on a graph;
- find amplitude and period from a *displacement–time* graph;
- find amplitude and wavelength from a *displacement–position* graph;
- understand the meaning of the terms *wavefront* and *ray*;
- use $v = \lambda f$.

What is a wave?

Waves are a very special kind of motion that differs significantly from the motion we have studied in earlier chapters. To understand the difference, and to appreciate this new kind of motion, let us look at what we have learned in a somewhat different way. If a stone is thrown at a window and the window breaks, this is because the stone transferred its kinetic energy from the point at which it was thrown onto the window. The stone exerted a force on the window (transfer of momentum) and broke it. A wave is also a way of transferring energy and momentum from one place to another but *without the actual large-scale motion of a material body*. For example, light (a kind of wave) from the sun arrives on earth having travelled a large distance in a vacuum, and upon arrival warms up the earth. A soprano singing can break a crystal glass because energy and momentum have been transferred through air by a sound wave.

Light is an example of a wave that does not need a medium in which to travel. It can travel in a vacuum as well as in solids (e.g. glass) or liquids (e.g. water). Light is part of a large family of waves called *electromagnetic waves*. Sound, along with water waves, string waves, etc., belongs to a family called *mechanical waves*. These do require a medium for their propagation. Sound, for example, cannot travel in a vacuum. Sound can travel in solids and liquids as well as, of course, in gases. Similarly, water waves travel, not surprisingly, in water.

How do we describe a wave? A wave is always associated with a *disturbance* of some kind. A rope held tight is horizontal when no wave is travelling on it. By moving one end up and down, we create a disturbance and individual points on the rope are now higher or lower than their original undisturbed positions. In the case of sound, the density of air becomes successively higher or lower when a sound wave travels through the air compared with when there is no sound wave. (The case of light is a bit more complicated and we will not discuss it here.)

> ▶ A wave is a disturbance that travels in a medium (which can be a vacuum in the case of electromagnetic waves) transferring energy and momentum from one place to another. The direction of energy transfer is the direction of propagation of the wave.

Note that in all the examples we have talked about, there is no large-scale motion of the medium. Points on a rope oscillate up and down, and molecules in air move back and forth along the direction of a sound wave that is travelling through the air. This is local, small-scale motion; the material of the medium does not itself travel large distances.

Transverse and longitudinal waves

In addition to the division into mechanical and electromagnetic, waves can be further divided into two classes. The first class is called **transverse** and consists of those waves in which the disturbance is *at right angles* to the direction of propagation of the wave. A typical example is a wave on a string: the direction of propagation is along the string but the disturbance is at right angles to the string (see Figure 1.1). Electromagnetic waves are also transverse.

The second class is called **longitudinal** and consists of those waves in which the disturbance is *along* the direction of propagation of the wave. A typical example is sound: if we imagine that a sound wave is moving from left to right in a thin tube, the disturbance is the motion of air molecules back and forth along the tube. In Figure 1.2 the dots represent molecules of air. In the top picture the molecules are equally spaced, representing the gas in its equilibrium state. As the wave passes through the gas, the

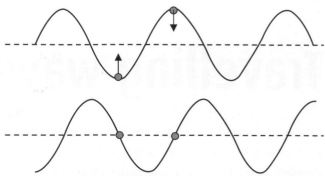

Figure 1.1 A transverse wave on a string travelling to the right. At the early time of the top picture, the parts of the string marked are at their maximum displacement above and below the equilibrium position of the string. Some time later the left part has moved up and the right part down – their motion is at right angles to the direction of motion of the wave.

Figure 1.2 In a longitudinal wave, molecules execute simple harmonic motion along the direction of propagation of the wave.

molecules move to the right or left. As they do so they create regions of higher than normal density (compressions) and regions of lower than normal density (rarefactions). For convenience we have marked one molecule grey to indicate that molecules execute simple harmonic oscillations about their equilibrium positions (dotted line for the grey molecule). Figure 1.3 shows the compressions and rarefactions that occur in the medium in which the wave moves.

▲ compressions ▲   ▲ rarefactions ▲

Figure 1.3 The motion of the molecules causes compressions and rarefactions in the medium in which the wave moves.

Wave pulses

To help us to understand waves we will start with a simple case, that of a wave pulse. If you tie one end of a rope to a wall and move the other end sharply up and then back down to its starting position, you will produce a wave pulse that will travel along the rope. It looks like Figure 1.4 (this is idealized to a triangular pulse – the real pulse would be curved):

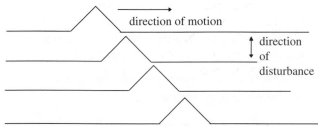

Figure 1.4 The pulse is moving to the right. The disturbance is normal to the direction of motion.

If your hand is first moved down below the rope then back up to the starting point, continues up above the rope and finally back down to the starting point, the pulse will look like Figure 1.5.

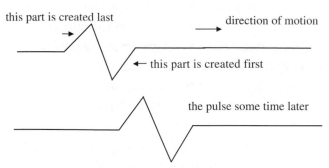

Figure 1.5 A full pulse travelling to the right.

It takes a certain time for this disturbance to move along the rope (i.e. for this wave pulse to reach another point in the rope). The wave pulse travels with a certain **speed** down the rope. In the case of the wave pulse on the rope, the speed of the pulse is determined not by the way in which the pulse was created (big or small pulse, wide or narrow) nor by how fast or slow your hand moved the rope; rather, it is determined by the tension T in the rope and the mass per unit length $\mu = \frac{m}{L}$ of the rope. Although not required for examination purposes, it is good to know the following:

> ▶ The speed of the pulse on the string is given by
>
> $$v = \sqrt{\frac{T}{\mu}}$$
>
> The speed of the wave is determined by the properties of the medium and not by how the wave is created.

The greater the tension in the medium, the greater the speed of the wave produced. You can convince yourself that the speed is greater when the tension is greater by creating pulses on a slinky, which can be kept at various tensions by having it stretched by different amounts. You will then also see that v is independent of the shape of the pulse you produce and of how fast you produced it.

The statement that the speed of the pulse is independent of the amplitude is true provided the amplitude is not too big. If the amplitude is big, then the string is more stretched and thus the tension is greater, implying a greater pulse speed. Not too big an amplitude means not big compared with the length of the string.

Travelling waves

In the previous section we saw how a single pulse can be produced on a stretched rope. We can create a *travelling wave* if we now produce one pulse after another. If, in addition, the agent forcing the rope up and down executes simple harmonic motion, then the wave will look like a sine wave (also called a harmonic wave) – see Figure 1.6 (top).

If the sequence of pulses produced are square pulses, then the wave generated is a travelling square wave – see Figure 1.6 (bottom).

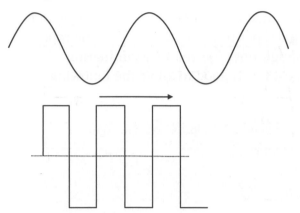

Figure 1.6 A periodic sine wave and a periodic square wave.

Harmonic waves are very important because any periodic disturbance can be expressed as a sum (superposition) of a number of harmonic waves. This is a general theorem in mathematics known as Fourier's theorem.

Harmonic waves

A simple way of producing harmonic waves is to attach one end of a rope to a tuning fork, as shown in Figure 1.7. If the tuning fork is then made to oscillate, one full wave will be produced on the rope after a time equal to the **period** of the tuning fork.

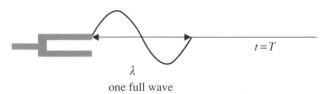

Figure 1.7 A full wave is produced in a time equal to one period.

▶ The length of a full wave is called the wavelength, λ, and the time needed to produce one full wave (or the duration of a full wave) is the period, T.

After a second full period, a second full wave will be produced (see Figure 1.8). The original full wave has moved forward a distance equal to the **wavelength**.

Figure 1.8 Two full waves are produced in sequence by the oscillating tuning fork.

▶ It thus follows that, since the wave moves forward a distance equal to a wavelength in a time equal to one period, the speed of the wave is given by

$$v = \frac{\lambda}{T}$$

Since one full wave is produced in a time of T s, it follows that the number of full waves produced in 1 s is $1/T$. This is the **frequency**.

▶ The number of full waves produced in 1 s is called the frequency of the wave, $f = \frac{1}{T}$. The unit of frequency is the inverse second, which is given the special name hertz (Hz). In terms of frequency the wave speed is thus

$$v = \lambda f$$

Waves can be represented graphically. This is a bit complicated because a wave depends on distance (where along the wave are we looking?) as well as time (at what time are we looking at the wave?). First we have to decide how we will quantify the 'disturbance' of the wave. For a wave on a string the obvious choice is to measure the height of a point on the string above or below the undisturbed position of the string. The disturbance here is thus the *displacement* of a point on the string and is measured in units of length. We normally denote this displacement by y, which will be a function of distance (*x*) and time (*t*).

In the case of sound, the disturbance may be associated with the density of the medium through which sound propagates. We may then define the difference $y = \rho - \rho_0$ as the *displacement* of density (ρ) relative to the equilibrium density of the medium when no sound is present in it (ρ_0). The displacement here has units of density and is also a function of position and time. In the case of sound, we could equally well define displacement as the difference $y = p - p_0$, which is the difference between the pressure of the medium when sound is present and the equilibrium pressure when no sound is present. Displacement would then have units of pressure.

This discussion can be generalized to all waves. All waves have a displacement that is the difference of some quantity and the equilibrium value of that quantity when no wave is present. The displacement of any wave is a function of position and time. We may therefore represent waves in graphs of displacement versus position (distance) and graphs of displacement versus time.

Let us consider a wave propagating along a string from left to right. The left end of the string is represented by $x = 0$ m and any other point on the string is specified by giving its corresponding x coordinate (see Figure 1.9).

Figure 1.9.

As the wave propagates along the string, we would like to know the displacement at each point on the string *at a specific point in time*. This is given by a graph of displacement versus position – Figure 1.10.

The first important piece of information from such a graph is the wavelength.

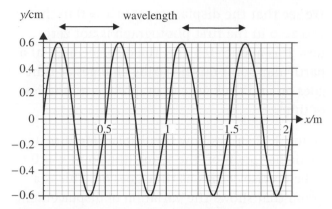

Figure 1.10 A graph of displacement versus position tells us the disturbance of any point on the string at a specific moment in time.

▶ Graphs showing the variation of displacement with position enable us to determine the wavelength of the wave as the distance from peak to next peak (or the length of a full wave).

This graph also tells us that at the point on the string that is 0.5 m from the string's left end the displacement is zero at some point in time. At that *same point in time* at a point 1.125 m from the left end the displacement is 0.6 cm, etc. Thus, a graph of displacement versus position is like a *photograph* of the string taken at a particular time. If we take a second photograph of the string some time later, the string will look different because the wave has moved in the meantime. It might look like Figure 1.11.

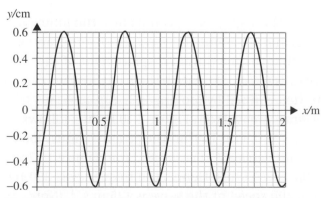

Figure 1.11 A graph of the disturbance of any point on the string at a later moment in time. Note that every point has a different disturbance from that shown in Figure 1.10.

We see that the displacement at $x = 0$ m that was zero in the first photograph is not zero now. It is about -0.5 cm. The displacement at a particular point on the string changes as time goes on and thus we can graph it as a function of time.

Figure 1.12 shows how the displacement of a particular point on the string (the point $x = 0$ m to be precise) varies as time goes on. This is a graph that shows the variation of displacement with time.

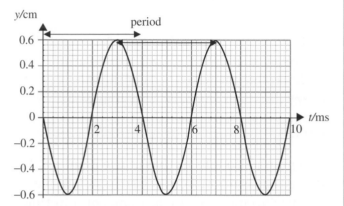

Figure 1.12 A graph of displacement versus time tells us the disturbance of a specific point on the string as time goes on.

> ▶ Graphs showing the variation of displacement with time enable us to determine the period of the wave as the time from peak to next peak (or the duration of a full wave).

From these graphs we can deduce the following information about the wave. From *any* graph we see that the maximum displacement of the wave is 0.6 cm. The *wavelength* of the wave can be determined by looking at a *displacement–position graph*. From Figure 1.10 it thus follows that $\lambda = 0.5$ m. To find the *period* we must look at a *displacement–time graph*. From Figure 1.12 we find $T = 4.0$ ms. Hence, the frequency is 250 Hz and the speed of the wave is 125 m s^{-1}. (Note that by comparing Figures 1.10 and 1.11 we see that the wave moved forward a distance of

0.1 m. Since the speed of the wave is 125 m s^{-1}, it follows that the photograph of Figure 1.11 was taken $0.1/125$ s $= 0.8$ ms later than that of Figure 1.10.)

Consider now the wave of Figure 1.13. We deduce that the disturbance is a pressure measured in kPa. However, in this graph the experimenter has not plotted the difference of pressure and the equilibrium value of the pressure. We may then deduce that the pressure in the medium when no wave travels through (the equilibrium pressure) is 4.0 kPa. We may also deduce that the maximum displacement (the amplitude) is 0.5 kPa. The wavelength is 4.0 m and in the absence of a displacement–time graph we can say nothing about the period or frequency, and hence speed, of this wave. On the other hand, if we are given the additional information that this is a sound wave of speed 340 m s^{-1}, then we deduce that the frequency is 85 Hz and so the period is 11.8 ms.

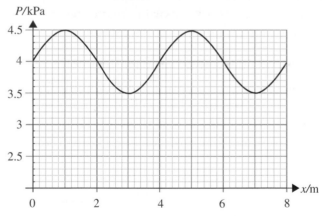

Figure 1.13 A wave in which the disturbance is about a non-zero value.

The wave of Figure 1.14 is an electromagnetic wave in which the displacement is the electric field measured in volts per metre. The amplitude is 0.2 V m^{-1} and the period is 3×10^{-15} s. The frequency is thus 3.33×10^{14} Hz. If we are told further that this wave moves in a vacuum then we know that the speed of such a wave

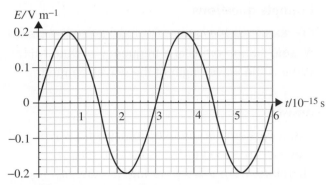

Figure 1.14 An electromagnetic wave as a function of time.

is 3×10^8 m s^{-1} and so the wavelength is 9.0×10^{-7} m.

> ▶ The wavelength (which we defined to be the length of one full wave) is also equal to the distance between successive crests or successive troughs in a displacement–position graph.
>
> The period (which we defined to be the duration of one full wave) is also equal to the time between successive crests or successive troughs in a displacement–time graph.

The wavelength and frequency are two of the characteristics of a wave. A third characteristic is **amplitude**.

> ▶ The amplitude of a wave is defined to be the maximum displacement of the wave away from the position when no wave is present.

The amplitude of a wave is a measure of the energy the wave carries. In general, the energy carried is proportional to the square of the amplitude, which means that (all other things being equal) a water wave of amplitude 2.0 m carries four times as much energy as a water wave of amplitude 1.0 m.

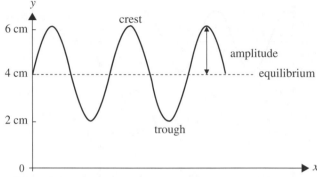

Figure 1.15 Diagrams showing the amplitude, crests and troughs of a travelling wave. In the second case, the equilibrium value is not at zero.

In the first diagram of Figure 1.15 the amplitude of the wave is 2.0 cm. In the second it is 2.0 cm as well. The dotted line at 4.0 cm shows the equilibrium position, when no wave is present. The 4.0 cm might represent the height of a bit of water in a container. When no waves are present on the surface of the water, all points on the surface are 4.0 cm from the bottom of the container. When a small water wave is established in the container, the distance of various points on the surface varies as shown in the diagram. As the amplitude is the maximum displacement away from the equilibrium position, it is thus 2.0 cm.

> ▶ Points on the wave with maximum displacement are called crests while those at minimum displacement are called troughs.

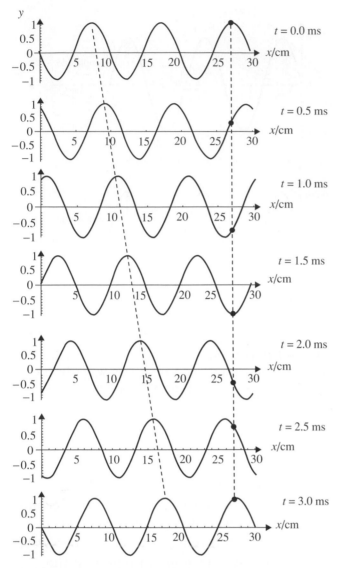

Figure 1.16 A sequence of pictures taken every 0.5 ms showing a travelling harmonic wave. Note how the peaks move forward. We have marked a point on the string to show that in a transverse wave points on the string move perpendicularly to the direction of the wave. After a full period ($T = 3.0$ **ms**) a picture of the rope looks like it did at the beginning ($t = 0$ **ms**), which is what allowed us to determine the period of the wave in the first place. The speed of the wave is 33.3 m s^{-1} (found by dividing the wavelength by the period) and the frequency is 333 Hz.

The diagrams in Figure 1.16 show the variation of displacement with position at various times. We see the meaning of the term travelling wave. The crests of the wave move forward.

Example questions

Q1

A radio station emits at a frequency of 90.8 MHz. What is the wavelength of the waves emitted?

Answer

The waves emitted are electromagnetic waves and move at the speed of light (3×10^8 m s^{-1}). Therefore, from $v = \lambda f$ we find $\lambda = 3.3$ m.

Q2

A sound wave of frequency 450 Hz is emitted from A and travels towards B, a distance of 150 m away. Take the speed of sound to be 341 m s^{-1}. How many wavelengths fit in the distance from A to B?

Answer

The wavelength is

$$\lambda = \frac{341}{450} \, \text{m}$$
$$= 0.758 \, \text{m}$$

Thus the number of wavelengths that fit in the distance 150 m is

$$N = \frac{150}{0.758}$$
$$= 198 \text{ wavelengths (approximately)}$$

Q3

The noise of thunder is heard 3 s after the flash of lightning. How far away is the place where lightning struck? (Take the speed of sound to be 340 m s^{-1}.)

Answer

Light travels so fast that we can assume that lightning struck exactly when we see the flash of light. If thunder is heard 3 s later, it means that it took 3 s for sound to cover the unknown distance, d. Thus

$$d = vt$$
$$= 340 \times 3 \, \text{m}$$
$$= 1020 \, \text{m}$$

Q4

Water wave crests in a lake are 5.0 m apart and pass by an anchored boat every 2.0 s. What is the speed of the water waves?

Answer

$$v = \frac{5.0}{2.0} \, \text{m s}^{-1}$$
$$= 2.5 \, \text{m s}^{-1}$$

Q5

A toothed wheel has 300 teeth on its circumference. It rotates at 30 rpm (revolutions per minute). A piece of cardboard is placed such that it is hit by the teeth of the wheel as the wheel rotates. What is the frequency of the sound produced?

Answer

In 1 min the cardboard will be hit by a tooth $30 \times 300 = 9000$ times, which is 150 times in 1 s. The frequency of the sound is thus 150 Hz.

Q6

A railing consists of thin vertical rods a distance of 2 cm apart. A boy runs past the railing at a speed of 3 m s^{-1} dragging a stick against the rods. What is the frequency of the sound produced?

Answer

In 1 s the boy moves a distance of 3 m, or past $300/2 = 150$ rods. The frequency of the sound is thus 150 Hz.

Wavefronts

Imagine a wave propagating in some direction, for example, water waves approaching the shore (see Figure 1.17).

The direction of the waves is horizontal, so if we imagine vertical planes going through the crests, the planes will be normal to the direction of the wave. These planes are called

Figure 1.17 A two-dimensional wave.

wavefronts; and lines at right angles to them are called **rays**.

▶ A *wavefront* is a surface through crests and normal to the direction of propagation of the wave. Lines in the direction of propagation of the wave (and hence normal to the wavefronts) are called *rays*. (See Figure 1.18.)

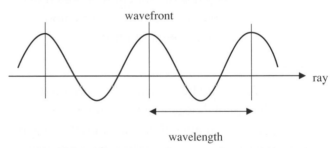

Figure 1.18 Surfaces through crests and normal to the direction of energy propagation of the wave are called wavefronts or wavecrests. Rays are mathematical lines perpendicular to the wavefronts in the direction of propagation of the wave.

(A wavefront is properly defined through the concept of *phase*. All points on a wavefront have the same phase. This will be discussed in Chapter 4.4.)

On the other hand, if we consider the surfaces going through crests of water waves caused by a stone dropped in the water, we would find that in this case the wavefronts are cylindrical surfaces (see Figure 1.19).

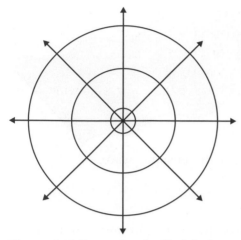

Figure 1.19 Example of cylindrical wavefronts. The cylinders go through the crests and are normal to the plane of the paper. The rays are radial lines.

Example question

Q7

A stone dropped in still water creates circular ripples that move away from the point of impact. The initial height of the ripple is about 2.4 cm and the wavelength is 0.5 m. Draw a sketch of the displacement of the ripples as a function of the distance from the point of impact.

Answer

The energy carried by the wave is distributed along the (circular) wavefronts. As the wave moves away from the point of impact, the length of the wavefront increases and so the energy per unit wavefront length decreases. Thus, the amplitude has to decrease as well. So we get the graph shown in Figure 1.20.

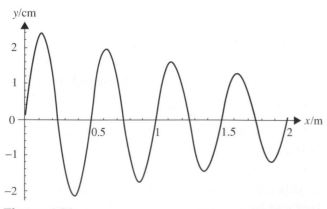

Figure 1.20.

The wavefronts of light waves leaving a point source (a very small lamp) would be spherical. We can thus speak of plane, cylindrical and spherical waves, according to the shape of the wavefronts. Note that cylindrical and spherical waves tend to become plane waves very far away from their source.

Questions

1 In football stadiums fans often create a 'wave' by standing up and sitting down again. What determines the speed of the 'wave'?

2 A number of dominoes are stood next to each other along a straight line. A small push is given to the first domino and one by one the dominoes fall over. How is this an example of wave motion? How can the speed of the wave pulse be increased? Design an experiment in which this problem can be investigated.

3 What is the wavelength that corresponds to a sound frequency of:
   (a) 256 Hz;
   (b) 25 kHz?
   Take the speed of sound to be 330 m s^{-1}.

4 By making suitably labelled diagrams explain the terms:
   (a) wavelength;
   (b) period;
   (c) amplitude;
   (d) crest;
   (e) trough.

5 The tension in a steel wire of length 0.800 m and mass 150.0 g is 120.0 N. What is the speed of transverse waves on this string? (Use $v = \sqrt{\frac{T}{\mu}}$.)

6 A string has a length of 20.0 m and is kept at a tension of 50.0 N. Its mass is 400.0 g. A transverse wave of frequency 15.0 Hz travels on this string.
   (a) What is its wavelength?
   (b) If the same wave is created on the same kind of string (same mass per unit length and same tension) but of double the length, what will the wavelength of the wave be? (Use $v = \sqrt{\frac{T}{\mu}}$.)

7 A stone is dropped on a still pond at $t = 0$. The wave reaches a leaf floating on the pond a distance of 3.00 m away. The leaf then begins to oscillate according to the graph shown in Figure 1.21.
   (a) Find the speed of the water waves.
   (b) Find the period and frequency of the wave.
   (c) Find the wavelength and amplitude of the wave.

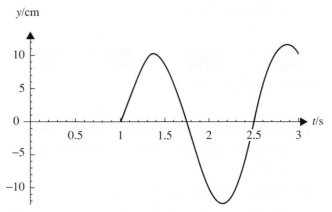

Figure 1.21 For question 7.

8 A sound wave of frequency 500 Hz travels from air into water. The speed of sound in air is 330 m s^{-1} and in water 1490 m s^{-1}. What is the wavelength of the wave in:
   (a) air;
   (b) water?

9 The speed of ocean waves approaching the shore is given by the formula $v = \sqrt{gh}$, where h is the depth of the water. It is assumed here that the wavelength of the waves is much larger than the depth (otherwise a different expression gives the wave speed). What is the speed of water waves near the shore where the depth is 1.0 m? Assuming that the depth of the water decreases uniformly, make a graph of the water wave speed as a function of depth from a depth of 1.0 m to a depth of 0.30 m.

10 (a) Explain, in the context of wave motion, what you understand by the term *displacement*.

(b) Using your answer in (a), explain the difference between longitudinal and transverse waves.
(c) A rock thrown onto the still surface of a pond creates circular ripples moving away from the point of impact. Why is more than one ripple created?
(d) Why does the amplitude decrease as the ripple moves away from the centre?

11 A ship sends a sonar pulse of frequency 30 kHz and duration 1.0 ms towards a submarine and receives a reflection of the pulse 3.2 s later. The speed of sound in water is 1500 m s^{-1}. Find the distance of the submarine from the ship, the wavelength of the pulse and the number of full waves emitted in the pulse.

12 Figure 1.22 shows three points on a string on which a transverse wave propagates to the right. Indicate how these three points will move in the next instant of time.

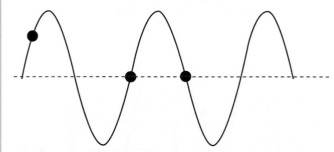

Figure 1.22 For question 12.

13 How would your answers change if the wave in question 12 were moving to the left?

14 Figure 1.23 shows a piece of cork floating on the surface of water when a wave travels through the water. On the same diagram draw the position of the cork half a wave period later.

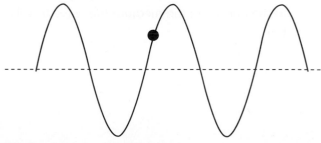

Figure 1.23 For question 14.

15 Figure 1.24 shows the same wave at two different times. The wave travels to the right and the bottom diagram represents the wave 0.2 s after the time illustrated in the top diagram. For this wave determine:

(a) the amplitude;

(b) the wavelength;

(c) the speed;

(d) the frequency.

(e) Can the graph be used to determine whether the wave is transverse or longitudinal?

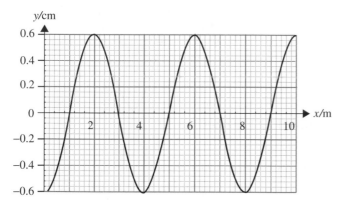

Figure 1.24 For question 15.

16 Figure 1.25 is a picture of a longitudinal wave travelling towards the right taken at a specific time. The density of the lines is proportional to the density in the medium the wave travels through.

(a) Draw this wave a very small interval of time later.

(b) Indicate on the diagram the wavelength of this wave.

Figure 1.25 For question 16.

17 Indicate on Figure 1.26 a crest, a trough and the wavelength. Draw the picture of this wave half a period later.

Figure 1.26 For question 17.

18 By drawing suitable diagrams, explain the difference between transverse and longitudinal waves.

19 In the context of wave motion explain, with the aid of a diagram, the terms:

(a) wavefront;

(b) ray.

20 An earthquake creates waves that travel in the earth's crust; these can be detected by seismic stations. Explain why three seismic stations must be used to determine the position of the earthquake. Describe *two* differences in the signals recorded by three seismic stations, assuming they are at different distances from the centre of the earthquake.

Wave phenomena I: reflection and refraction

This chapter introduces the principle of superposition, which allows us to find the wave disturbance when two or more waves arrive at the same point in space at the same time. Two basic wave phenomena, reflection and refraction, are discussed. We also introduce Huygens' principle, which determines the evolution of a wavefront and explains reflection and refraction.

Objectives

By the end of this chapter you should be able to:

- state the principle of *superposition* and apply it to pulses and waves;
- state the laws of *reflection* and *refraction* and solve problems involving these phenomena;
- give the definition of *index of refraction*, $n = \frac{c_{vacuum}}{c_{medium}}$;
- state *Snell's law* $\frac{\sin \theta_1}{c_1} = \frac{\sin \theta_2}{c_2}$ and $n_1 \sin \theta_1 = n_2 \sin \theta_2$ for light;
- understand *Huygens' principle* and use it to explain the laws of reflection and refraction.

The principle of superposition

Suppose that two pulses are produced in the same rope and are travelling towards each other from opposite ends. Something truly amazing happens when the two pulses meet. Figure 2.1 shows what happens in a sequence of pictures. For simplicity we have drawn idealized square pulses.

The disturbance gets bigger when the two pulses meet but subsequently the two pulses simply 'go through each other' as if nothing had happened. You should contrast this with what happens in the ordinary kind of motion: when two balls collide they *bounce off* each other.

What happens when two (or more) pulses meet at some point in space is described by the principle of **superposition**, which states that

the displacement at that point is the algebraic sum of the individual displacements. As we can see in Figure 2.1, when the two pulses meet, the displacement is quite large; it is, in fact, the sum of the displacements of the two pulses. Note the word 'algebraic'. This means that if one pulse is 'up' and the other is 'down', then the resulting displacement is the difference of the individual ones.

> ▶ Mathematically, the principle of superposition states that if y_1 and y_2 are the individual displacements, then at the point where the two meet the total displacement has the value
>
> $$y = y_1 + y_2$$

(a) The pulses are approaching each other.

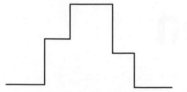

(b) The pulses are beginning to overlap.

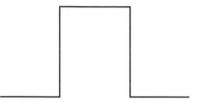

(c) The overlap is complete; the pulses are on top of each other.

(d) The pulses move through each other.

Figure 2.1 The superposition of two positive pulses.

Let us look at Figures 2.1b and c in detail. In Figure 2.1b the two pulses are partially overlapping – Figure 2.2 shows both of them separately (the pulse moving toward the right is drawn in black and the one moving to the left in grey). There are five regions to consider. In region a, both pulses are zero. In region b, the black pulse is non-zero and the grey is zero. In region c, both are non-zero. In region d, the black is zero and the grey is not. In region e, both are zero. The shape of the resulting pulse is simply the sum of the two pulses. Thus, in region a, we get zero. In region b, we get the height of just the black pulse. In region c, we get a pulse whose height is the sum of the heights of the black and grey pulses. In region d, the height equals the height of just the grey pulse. In region e, we get zero.

In Figure 2.1c we have three regions to consider (see Figure 2.3). In a and c, both pulses are zero,

Figure 2.2 The situation in Figure 2.1b analysed.

so the resulting pulse is also zero. In region b, both are non-zero and the resulting pulse is the sum of the individual pulse heights.

Figure 2.3 The situation in Figure 2.1c analysed.

If the two pulses are like the ones shown in the sequence in Figure 2.4, the resulting pulse when the two meet is momentarily zero. The situation in Figure 2.4b is analysed in Figure 2.5.

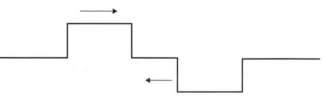

(a) Positive and negative pulses are approaching each other.

(b) The positive and negative pulses momentarily cancel each other out when they totally overlap.

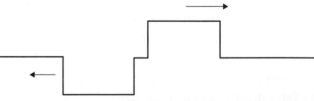

(c) The positive and negative pulses move through each other.

Figure 2.4 The superposition of a positive and a negative pulse.

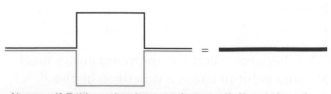

Figure 2.5 The situation in Figure 2.4b analysed.

At that instant when there is complete cancellation of the two pulses, the rope looks flat but it is moving as shown in Figure 2.6.

Figure 2.6 Parts of the rope are moving when the two pulses cancel each other out.

You should be able to convince yourself that when the rope looks like the first diagram in Figure 2.7 it is because the individual pulses are only partially overlapping, as in the second diagram.

Figure 2.7.

Reflection of pulses

What happens when a pulse created in a rope with one end fixed approaches that fixed end? Consider the pulse of Figure 2.8. The instant the pulse hits the fixed end, the rope attempts to move the fixed end upward: that is, it exerts an upward force on the fixed end. By Newton's third law, the wall will then exert an equal but opposite force on the rope. This means that a displacement will be created in the rope that will be negative and will start moving towards the left.

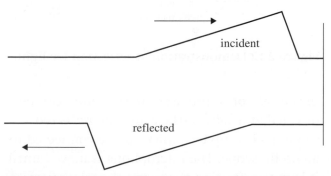

Figure 2.8 A pulse reflecting from a fixed end is inverted.

The pulse has been reflected by the wall and has been *inverted*. We can understand this in a different, more abstract, way as follows. The fixed end of the rope must remain fixed at all times. Imagine a pulse travelling along an imaginary rope that is an extension of the real rope into the wall. This imaginary pulse is moving from right to left. Using the principle of superposition, we ask: what is the shape of the imaginary pulse in order that when the real and imaginary pulses meet, the end of the rope (that tied to the wall) always stays fixed? The answer is a pulse that is identical to the real pulse but is inverted (see Figure 2.9). It is as if the real and imaginary pulses exchange places upon reflection.

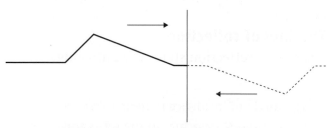

Figure 2.9 The real and imaginary pulses meet, keeping the end of the rope fixed.

If the end of the rope is not fixed but free to move (imagine that the end of the rope is now tied to a ring that can slide up and down a vertical pole), the situation is different (see Figure 2.10). Here the reflected pulse is the same as the original pulse. There is a change of direction but no inversion here. Can you see why?

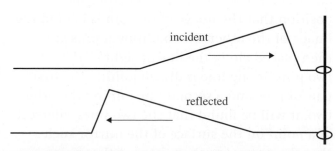

Figure 2.10 A pulse reflecting from a free end is not inverted.

Reflection and refraction of waves

This section deals with the wave phenomena of reflection and refraction as they apply to waves, especially light. The study of light has played a crucial role in the history of science. Newton discovered that ordinary white light is composed of different colours when he let sunlight go through a prism and saw the colours of the rainbow emerging from the other side. The wave nature of light was put forward by the Dutch physicist Christiaan Huygens in his book *A Treatise on Light* published in 1690. A bitter controversy between Huygens and Newton (Newton had postulated a particle theory of light) ended in Huygens' favour.

The law of reflection

The law of reflection states the following:

> ▶ The angle of incidence *i* (angle between the ray and the normal to the reflecting surface at the point of incidence) is equal to the angle of reflection *r* (angle between the normal and the reflected ray).
>
> The reflected and incident rays and the normal to the surface lie on the same plane, called the plane of incidence.
>
> (See Figure 2.11.)

Reflection can be demonstrated experimentally in a variety of ways. For light, this is most easily done by placing two pins in front of a mirror and then looking at the mirror from such a position that the image of one pin is behind the image of the other. Two additional pins are then placed along the line of sight of the first two pins. If one line is drawn joining the first pair of pins and a second line joining the other two, it will be found that the two lines intersect at a point on the surface of the mirror such that the normal to the mirror at that point bisects the angle between the original lines.

(a)

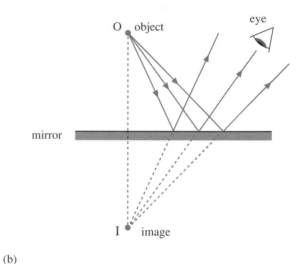

(b)

Figure 2.11 (a) Reflection at a plane (flat) surface. (b) The position of an image seen in a plane mirror.

This shows that the angle of incidence $\angle i$ is equal to the angle of reflection $\angle r$. This is illustrated in Figure 2.12.

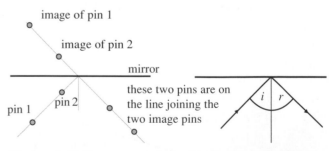

Figure 2.12 Demonstration of reflection for light.

In the case of sound, a source of sound can be directed at a solid surface and the reflected sound picked up by a microphone connected to an oscilloscope. The microphone is moved until it is in the position that gives the maximum reading on the oscilloscope. When this position is recorded, it is again found that the angle of incidence equals the angle of reflection. This is illustrated in Figure 2.13.

Figure 2.13 Demonstration of reflection for sound.

Reflection takes place when the reflecting surface is sufficiently smooth. This means that the wavelength of the incident wave has to be larger than the size of any irregularities of the surface.

Refraction

Light travels with a velocity of 3×10^8 m s^{-1} in a vacuum. In all other media, the velocity of light is smaller. The difference in the speed of propagation of light in different media is responsible for an effect called **refraction**. (In fact, any wave whose speed of propagation is different in different media will experience the same effect.) When a ray of light travelling in a given medium, say air, strikes an interface with another medium, say the surface of water in a pond, it will change direction as it enters the second medium.

Usually, when a ray of light strikes an interface between two media, there is both reflection and refraction (see Figure 2.14).

▶ Referring to Figure 2.14, it can be shown that

$$\frac{\sin \theta_1}{c_1} = \frac{\sin \theta_2}{c_2}$$

This is known as Snell's law (see also page 233). This law relates the sines of the angles of incidence and refraction to the speed of the wave in the two media.

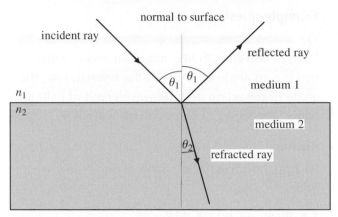

Figure 2.14 A ray of light incident on the interface of two media partly reflects and partly refracts.

In the case of *light only*, we usually define a quantity called the **index of refraction** of a given medium as

$$n = \frac{c}{c_m}$$

where c is the speed of light in vacuum and c_m is the speed of light in the medium in question.

▶ In terms of the index of refraction, Snell's law for *light* then reads

$$n_1 \sin \theta_1 = n_2 \sin \theta_2$$

(see Figure 2.14).

Since the speed of light is always largest in a vacuum, the index of refraction is always larger than one. By definition, the index of refraction of a vacuum (and approximately of air) is one. Thus, if we are given the index of refraction of a medium we can find the speed of light in that medium. For example, in a glass with $n = 1.5$, the speed of light is

$$c_g = \frac{c}{n_g} = \frac{3 \times 10^8}{1.5} \text{ m s}^{-1} = 2 \times 10^8 \text{ m s}^{-1}$$

The index of refraction depends slightly on wavelength, so rays with the same angle of incidence but of different wavelength are refracted by different angles. This phenomenon is called **dispersion**.

Example questions

Q1

Light of wavelength 680 nm in air enters water making an angle of 40° with the normal. Find the angle of refraction and the wavelength of light in water. The index of refraction of water is 1.33.

Answer

By straightforward application of Snell's law we find

$$1 \times \sin 40° = 1.33 \times \sin \theta$$
$$\Rightarrow \theta = 28.9°$$

The wavelength in air is 680 nm, so the frequency in air is

$$f = \frac{3.00 \times 10^8}{680 \times 10^{-9}}$$
$$= 4.41 \times 10^{14} \text{ Hz}$$

The frequency cannot change as the wave moves into the second medium. Imagine an observer right at the interface of the two media. The frequency can be found from the number of wavefronts that cross the interface per second. This number is the same for both media. Since the speed of light in water is

$$c_w = \frac{3.00 \times 10^8}{1.33}$$
$$= 2.26 \times 10^8 \text{ m s}^{-1}$$

it follows that the wavelength in water is

$$\lambda = \frac{2.26 \times 10^8}{4.41 \times 10^{14}}$$
$$= 512 \text{ nm}$$

Q2

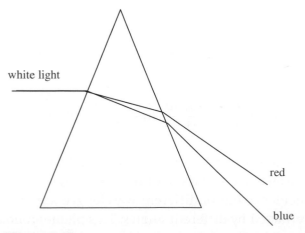

white light

red

blue

Figure 2.15.

The paths of rays of red and blue light passing through a glass prism are as shown in Figure 2.15. What can be deduced about the index of refraction of glass for red and blue light?

Answer

Considering the first refraction when the rays first enter the glass, we see that blue makes a smaller angle of refraction (draw the normal at the point of incidence to see that this is so). Hence its index of refraction must be larger.

Refraction for other waves

We have talked at length about refraction of light. Refraction, of course, is a phenomenon that applies to all waves. It happens whenever the wave changes its speed when going from one medium to another. For example, water waves will move more slowly when they enter a region of shallow water. Since the frequency is always unchanged, this means that the water waves will have a shorter wavelength in the shallow water (see Figure 2.16).

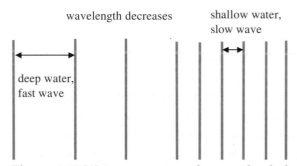

wavelength decreases   shallow water, slow wave

deep water, fast wave

Figure 2.16 Water waves travel more slowly in shallow water. Thus refraction takes place when a water wave travels in water of variable depth.

It is a common observation that water waves approach the shore almost always parallel to the shoreline, even though when they were first created their direction was arbitrary. This is because as the waves approach the shore they refract into a medium of lower wave speed (shallow water). Thus, the direction of motion of the wave bends toward the normal, so the waves tend to become parallel to the shore (see Figure 2.17).

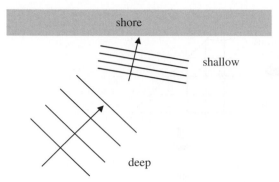

Figure 2.17 Wavefronts approaching the shore where the water is shallow slow down and so refract parallel to the shore.

A sound wave directed at a balloon filled with hydrogen will change its direction (i.e. refract) because the speed of sound in hydrogen is different from the speed of sound in air. The same is true when sound enters a liquid from, say, air. The speed of sound is greater in liquids than in gases, so sound entering a liquid will increase its wavelength. Finally, sound travels even faster in solids, metals, rock, etc. Typically, the speed of sound in a solid is a few thousand metres per second, compared with a few hundred metres per second in gases. The speed in liquids is in between. Table 2.1 gives the speed of sound in various media.

Medium	Speed/m s^{-1}
Air (0 °C)	331
Air (100 °C)	366
Helium (0 °C)	972
Oxygen (0 °C)	332
Water	1480
Sea water	1530
Mercury	1454
Aluminium	5100

Table 2.1 The speed of sound in various media.

Huygens' principle

How does a wavefront propagate in space? Huygens' idea was to consider every single point on the wavefront of the wave as itself a source of waves. This is now known as **Huygens' principle**.

> ▶ Every point on the wavefront emits a spherical wavelet or secondary wave, of the same velocity and wavelength as the original wave. The wavelet is assumed to be emitted in the forward direction only. The amplitude of the wavelet is maximum in the forward direction and decreases rapidly away from that direction. The new wavefront is then the surface that is tangent to all the wavelets.

We can easily see that a plane or circular wavefront moving undisturbed forward easily obeys this construction (see Figure 2.18). The same is true for a spherical wave.

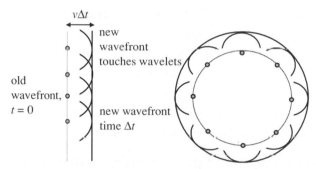

Figure 2.18 Each point on the old wavefronts acts as a source of spherical wavelets in the forward direction. The new wavefront touches all these wavelets.

The test comes when the wavefront encounters an obstacle of some kind or another. As we will soon see, the principle allows us to understand the phenomena of reflection and refraction.

Reflection

Huygens' principle allows us to theoretically understand the law of reflection in the following way. Consider a wave that is incident on a plane surface. Figure 2.19 shows two incident wavefronts, I_1 and I_2. The first wavefront to touch the surface is I_1 and it touches at point A. I_2 touches later, say a period T later, at B. We have drawn a wavelet centred

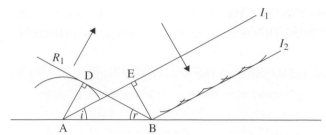

Figure 2.19 Huygens' construction applied to reflection.

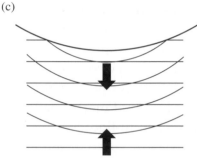

Figure 2.20 Waves in a ripple tank. (a) Waves reflected from a 45° barrier. Their wavelength stays the same. (b) Straight (plane) waves approach a concave barrier. The reflectred waves are focused to a point. (c) Plane waves approach a convex barrier. The reflected waves spread out.

at A. All points on this wavelet have been emitted one period after those on I_1 and the same is true for point B. Thus, there must be a wavefront that contains both point B and a point on the wavelet. This wavefront is found by drawing a tangent from B to the wavelet. We call this the reflected wavefront R_1.

It is then clear from simple geometry that the angle of incidence ($\angle i$) equals the angle of reflection ($\angle r$): lengths AD and EB are equal since they both represent a wavelength. Thus, triangles ADB and AEB are equal, being right angled and having two equal sides. Hence $\angle EAB$ ($= \angle i$) equals $\angle DBA$ ($= \angle r$); that is, the angle of reflection equals the angle of incidence.

Notice that the angle of incidence is defined as the angle between the normal to the surface and the incident ray. This angle is exactly the same as the angle between the *surface* and the incident *wavefront*. The same is true for the angle of reflection.

Figure 2.20 shows the effects of various barriers on waves in a ripple tank.

Refraction

The law of refraction is a consequence of Huygens' principle as follows. Figure 2.21 shows a wavefront (AB) that has hit the interface at A. A previous wavefront (CD) has already hit the interface at C at a time equal to one period earlier. (Since we are plotting wavefronts one wavelength apart it means that wavefront CD hit the interface a time equal to one wave period earlier.)

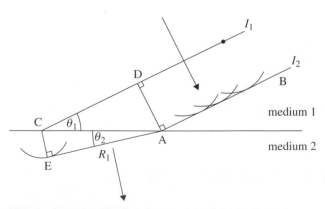

Figure 2.21 Huygens' construction applied to refraction.

Notice again that the angles of incidence and refraction are equal to the angles between the *surface* and the incident and refracted *wavefronts*, respectively.

At time $t = 0$, say, which is the time wavefront CD hits the interface, point C will emit a wavelet as shown. The radius of this wavelet is the wavelength in medium 2. Assuming that the wave is slower in medium 2, it follows that the wavelength will be smaller than the wavelength in medium 1. To find the new wavefront we must draw a tangent from A to this wavelet. Hence, the refracted wavefront is R_1 as shown in Figure 2.21. From trigonometry

$$\sin \theta_1 = \frac{DA}{AC}$$

$$\sin \theta_2 = \frac{CE}{AC}$$

But DA is the wavelength in medium 1 and CE the wavelength in medium 2, so it follows that

$$\frac{\sin \theta_1}{\sin \theta_2} = \frac{\lambda_1}{\lambda_2} = \frac{c_1}{c_2}$$

where the last equality holds since the frequency is the same in both media. This is Snell's law.

Figure 2.22 shows refraction of water waves in a ripple tank as the waves move from deep to shallower water. In shallower water the waves have a lower speed.

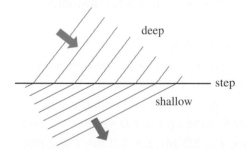

Figure 2.22 Refraction of water waves at a 'step'.

The fact that the law of refraction (Snell's law) is a consequence of a principle of wave motion (Huygens' principle) is strong evidence that light is indeed a kind of a wave.

Questions

1 Two pulses of equal width and height are travelling in opposite directions on the same string as shown in Figure 2.23. When the pulses completely overlap, what is the shape of the string?

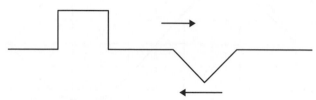

Figure 2.23 For question 1.

2 Two pulses of equal width and height are travelling in opposite directions on the same string as shown in Figure 2.24. When the pulses completely overlap, what is the shape of the string?

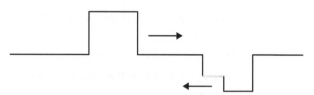

Figure 2.24 For question 2.

3 The wave pulses shown in Figure 2.25 travel at 1 cm s^{-1} and both have width 2 cm. The heights are indicated on the diagram. In each case, draw the shape of the resulting pulse according to the principle of superposition at times $t = 0.5$ s, $t = 1.0$ s and $t = 1.5$ s. Take $t = 0$ s to be the time when the pulses are about to meet each other.

height = 1 unit

height = 2 units

Figure 2.25 For question 3.

4 Two waves are simultaneously generated on a string as shown in Figure 2.26. Draw the actual shape of the string.

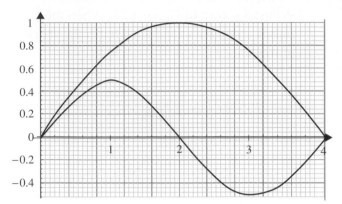

Figure 2.26 For question 4.

5 Red light of wavelength 6.8×10^{-7} m enters glass with an index of refraction of 1.583 from air, with an angle of incidence of 38°. Find:
(a) the angle of refraction;
(b) the speed of light in the glass;
(c) the wavelength of light in the glass.

6 Light of frequency 6.0×10^{14} Hz is emitted from point A and is directed toward point B a distance of 3.0 m away.
(a) How long will it take light to get to B?
(b) How many waves fit in the space between A and B?

7 A ray of light is incident on a rectangular block of glass of index of refraction 1.450 at an angle of 40°, as shown in Figure 2.27. If the thickness of the block is 4.00 cm, find the amount d by which the ray is deviated.

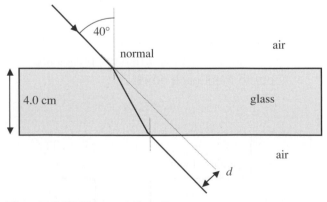

Figure 2.27 For question 7.

8 A ray of light enters glass from air at an angle of incidence equal to 45°, as shown in

Figure 2.28. Draw the path of this ray assuming that the glass has an index of refraction equal to 1.420 and the plastic has an index of refraction of 1.350.

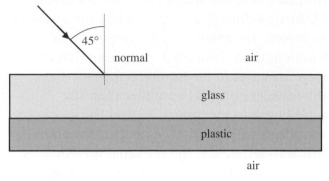

Figure 2.28 For question 8.

9 A ray of light moving in air parallel to the base of a glass prism of angles 45°, 45° and 90° enters the prism, as shown in Figure 2.29. Investigate the path of the ray as it enters the glass. The index of refraction of glass is 1.50.

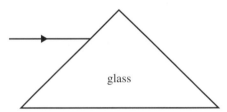

Figure 2.29 For question 9.

10 The speed of sound in air is 340 m s^{-1} and in water it is 1500 m s^{-1}. At what angle must a beam of sound waves hit the air–water interface so that no sound gets transmitted into the water?

11 A pulse with the shape shown in Figure 2.30 travels on a string at 40 m s^{-1} towards a fixed end. Taking $t = 0$ s to be when the front of the pulse first arrives at the fixed end, draw the shape of the string at: $t = 1.0$ ms; $t = 1.5$ ms; $t = 2.0$ ms; $t = 2.5$ ms; $t = 3.0$ ms; $t = 4$ ms.

Figure 2.30 For question 11.

Wave phenomena II: diffraction, interference and the Doppler effect

This chapter introduces two of the fundamental wave phenomena, diffraction and interference. These phenomena are so characteristic of wave behaviour that anything showing these phenomena can be defined to be a wave. We also discuss the Doppler effect, the change in frequency of a wave when there is relative motion between the source and the observer.

Objectives

By the end of this chapter you should be able to:
- understand that diffraction is the *spreading* of a wave through an opening or past an obstacle;
- appreciate that *significant diffraction* takes place only if the *wavelength is comparable to or bigger than the size of the opening*;
- decide if *diffraction* for a given wave will take place in a given situation;
- understand that, as a result of *superposition*, when two identical waves arrive at the same place they will experience *constructive interference* if the crest of one matches the crest of the other, or *destructive interference* if the crest of one matches the trough of the other;
- appreciate the significance of the *path difference* in the phenomenon of interference;
- understand the *Doppler effect in a qualitative way* and explain it by drawing appropriate diagrams for a moving source or a moving observer.

Diffraction

The spreading of a wave as it goes past an obstacle or through an aperture is called **diffraction**. Let us consider a plane wave of wavelength λ propagating towards an aperture of size a.

▶ What will the wavefronts look like after the wave has gone through the aperture? As we will see, the value of the wavelength in relation to the aperture size will be crucial in determining what answer we get.

Let us first assume that the wavelength is very small compared with *a* (see Figure 3.1).

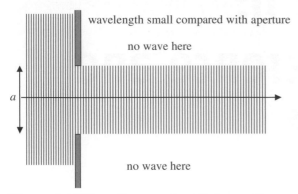

Figure 3.1 When the wavelength is small compared with the opening of the aperture, the amount of diffraction is negligible.

That part of the wave that is blocked by the screen does not propagate through and only the part which is free to go through does so. If the wave in question is light, this picture says that light goes through the opening, so that if we put a screen beyond the aperture we will see light on an area of the screen identical to the opening and darkness around it. Light travels in straight lines and does not bend as it goes through the aperture. There is no diffraction.

On the other hand, if the wavelength is comparable to or bigger than *a*, the new wavefronts are curved and the wave spreads around the edges of the opening (see Figure 3.2).

wavelength comparable to aperture

the wave is spreading

A

B

Figure 3.2 When the wavelength is comparable to the opening of the aperture, diffraction takes place.

If we put a screen some distance away from the aperture, we would see light in places where we would not expect any, such as at points A and B. This is the phenomenon of diffraction.

▶ Diffraction takes place whenever a wave whose wavelength is comparable to or bigger than the size of an aperture or an obstacle attempts to move through or past the aperture or obstacle.

(Note that here 'comparable to' can mean that the wavelength is a few times smaller than the aperture size.)

Application of Huygens' principle helps to understand the phenomenon of diffraction. If the aperture size is very small, it is as if only one point on the wavefront will act as a source of waves and these will be circular: that is, the wave will spread. If the aperture is large, then many points on the wavefront will act as sources of secondary waves and these will tend to be planar: that is, there will not be appreciable diffraction.

(It must be realized, though, that Huygens' principle works in the same way for small and large wavelengths, so the principle by itself would give the same answer in both cases. It is a refined and much more sophisticated principle, the Huygens–Fresnel principle, that gives the correct wavefronts past the aperture. This principle is, however, beyond the scope of this book.)

Diffraction explains why we can hear, but not see, around corners. For example, a person talking in the next room can be heard through the open door because sound diffracts around the opening of the door – the wavelength of sound for speech is roughly the same as the door size. On the other hand, light does not diffract around the door since its wavelength is much smaller than the door size.

Other examples of diffraction are shown in Figures 3.3 and 3.4. Figure 3.3 shows diffraction around an obstacle.

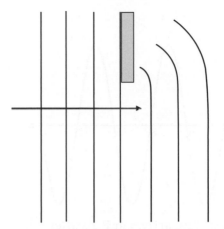

Figure 3.3 Diffraction also takes place when a wave moves past an obstacle.

If the wavelength is much smaller than the obstacle size, no diffraction takes place, as seen in Figure 3.4a. Diffraction does takes place if the wavelength is comparable to the obstacle size as seen in Figure 3.4b.

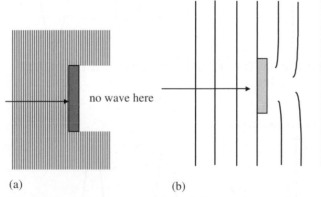

(a)   (b)

Figure 3.4 (a) If the wavelength is much smaller than the obstacle, no diffraction takes place and a shadow of the object is formed. (b) If the wavelength is comparable to the obstacle size, diffraction takes place and the wave appears far from the object in the region where the shadow was expected.

Interference

The most characteristic property of waves is their ability to interfere and diffract. The fact that light exhibits these phenomena is evidence that light is a wave. **Interference** is the result of superposition of two waves. We have met this principle in the previous chapter

where we applied it mainly to individual pulses. Interference for light was demonstrated in 1801 by Thomas Young, an English scholar who also came close to deciphering hieroglyphics.

Let us be specific by considering two sources S_1 and S_2. Waves from the two sources meet at some point, say P, some distance away (see Figure 3.5).

Figure 3.5 Interference from two sources. In the top diagram the waves arrive at P from the two sources and travel different distances in getting there. In the bottom diagram there is really only one source but the point P receives two waves. The first comes from the source S directly and the second wave is first reflected off the screen and then travels to P.

Suppose that at time $t = 0$ both sources emit identical waves (same amplitude A, wavelength λ and frequency f). The wave from S_1 will take a certain time to arrive at P. From Figure 3.6, we read off this time as 2 s. The wave from the second source will take longer. Suppose that it takes 4 s (see Figure 3.7).

We see that, even though the waves are identical at emission, when they arrive at the observation point P, the crest of one matches the trough of the other. Thus, when they are added, according to the principle of superposition the resulting wave will be zero. We have a case of *destructive interference*: the two waves have cancelled each other out. If the two waves are sound waves, it means that at point P we hear no sound at all.

Suppose that we now change the distances of the two sources from P and the two waves arrive at P as shown in Figures 3.8 and 3.9.

wave from S$_1$

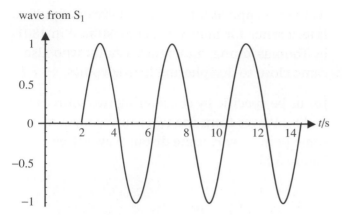

Figure 3.6 The first wave arrives at P 2 s after emission from the source.

wave from S$_2$

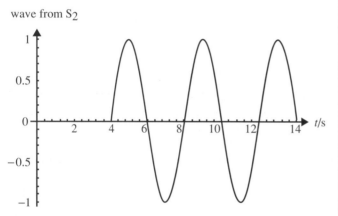

Figure 3.7 The second wave arrives at P 4 s after emission.

The arrival time from the first source is still 2 s but that from the second source is 6 s. Now the crests of one wave match the crests of the other. Thus, when we add them, we obtain a wave with double the amplitude of the individual waves (from 6 s on), as shown in Figure 3.10.

This is a case of *constructive interference*. If the waves are sound waves, we would hear a very loud sound at point P. (Since loudness is proportional to the energy carried by the wave, and energy is proportional to the *square* of the amplitude, the loudness would be *four* times as great as the loudness of one wave alone.)

Note that the period of the individual waves is 4 s. In the first case of destructive interference the difference in arrival times was 2 s. In the case of constructive interference the difference in arrival times was 4 s. You must be able to

wave from S$_1$

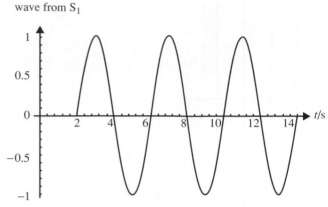

Figure 3.8 The first wave arrives at P 2 s after emission.

wave from S$_2$

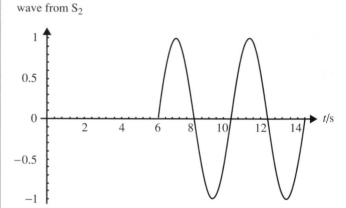

Figure 3.9 The second wave arrives at P 6 s after emission.

sum of two waves

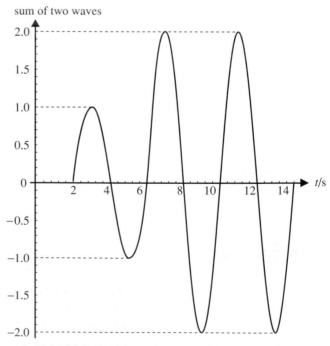

Figure 3.10 The sum of the waves from 6 s on (when both waves are present) has an amplitude that is double that of the individual waves.

convince yourself that, we would get destructive interference also when the difference in arrival times is 6 s, 10 s, 14 s, and so on (i.e. half-integral multiples of the period). Similarly, we would get constructive interference for differences in arrival times of 0 s, 4 s (as in the example), 8 s, 12 s, and so on (i.e. integral multiples of the period).

What is the general rule? If the distance from S_1 to P is d_1 and the distance from S_2 to P is d_2 (as shown in Figure 3.5), then the time of arrival of the first wave is d_1/v, where v is the wave velocity. Similarly, the wave from S_2 will arrive at P after a time d_2/v. The difference in arrival times is thus

$$\frac{d_1}{v} - \frac{d_2}{v}$$

There are two extreme cases: in case (i), the difference $\frac{d_1}{v} - \frac{d_2}{v}$ is an *integral multiple of the period T* of the wave. Then the crests of the wave from S_1 match the crests of the wave from S_2. The resultant wave has therefore the maximum possible amplitude, twice the amplitude of one of the waves. In case (ii), the difference $\frac{d_1}{v} - \frac{d_2}{v}$ is a *half-integral multiple of the period*. Then the maxima of one wave match the minima of the other. The two waves cancel each other out completely. The wave observed is zero. In case (i) we have constructive interference, and in case (ii) we have destructive interference.

▶ The condition for constructive interference is

$$\frac{d_1}{v} - \frac{d_2}{v} = nT$$
$$\Rightarrow d_1 - d_2 = nTv$$

but $Tv = \lambda$ so

$$d_1 - d_2 = n\lambda$$
$$n = 0, \pm 1, \pm 2, \pm 3, \ldots$$

that is, the *path difference* must be an integral multiple of the wavelength.

The condition for destructive interference is

$$d_1 - d_2 = (n + \tfrac{1}{2})\lambda$$
$$n = 0, \pm 1, \pm 2, \pm 3, \ldots$$

As we already mentioned, if the wave is a sound wave, points of constructive interference are points of high intensity of sound. Points of destructive interference are points of no sound at all. If the wave involved is light, and then constructive interference means bright light, and destructive interference means points of darkness.

▶ If the path difference is anything other than an integral or half-integral multiple of the wavelength, then the resultant amplitude of the wave at P will be some value between zero and $2A$, where A is the amplitude of one of the waves.

Example question

Q1 ▬▬▬▬▬▬▬▬▬▬▬▬▬▬▬
Waves leaving two sources arrive at point P. Point P is 12 m from the first source and 16.5 m from the second. The waves have a wavelength of 3 m. What is observed at P?

Answer

The path difference is 4.5 m. It equals $(1 + \frac{1}{2}) \times 3$ m: that is, it is a half-integral multiple of the wavelength. We thus have destructive interference.

The Doppler effect

Consider a source of waves and an observer who receives them.

▶ If there is relative motion between the observer and the source (i.e. the source or the observer, or both, move) then, in general, the observer will receive the wave at a frequency that is *different* from the emitted frequency.

This is a phenomenon of everyday life. For example, if an approaching car creates a high-pitched sound, as it goes past us and recedes the frequency of the sound becomes lower.

We can understand the Doppler effect in terms of wavefront diagrams. Consider first a stationary source of waves emitting circular wavefronts (Figure 3.11). Suppose for simplicity that the source emits a wave of frequency f. This means that f wavefronts are emitted per second. An observer who is also stationary will clearly receive f wavefronts every second as well, so there is no Doppler effect.

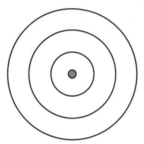

Figure 3.11 The wavefronts emitted by a stationary source are concentric. The common centre is the position of the source.

Consider, though, what happens when the source moves, say to the right: the source moves *towards* observer B and *away* from observer A in Figure 3.12. The wavefronts are piling up in front of the source and thus observer B will receive more than f wavefronts in one second. This means that observer B will measure a frequency larger than f for the wave. On the other hand, observer A will receive fewer than f wavefronts in one second, and so will measure a frequency smaller than f.

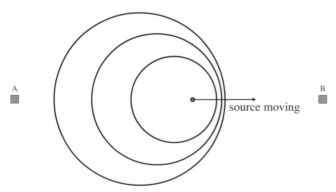

Figure 3.12 A source is approaching observer B and moves away from observer A. The centre of each wavefront was the position of the source at the time the wavefront was emitted.

▶ If the source approaches a stationary observer, the measured frequency is higher than that emitted. If the source moves away from a stationary observer, the measured frequency is lower. Similarly, an observer who moves toward a stationary source will measure a higher frequency than that emitted while an observer moving away from a stationary source will measure a lower frequency.

The Doppler effect also applies to light. Thus, if we observe light from a distant galaxy and find that the frequency is lower than the frequency at emission, we know that the galaxy is moving away from us.

Questions

1 Planar waves of wavelength 1.0 cm approach an aperture whose opening is also 1.0 cm. Draw the wavefronts of this wave as they emerge through the aperture.

2 Repeat question 1 for waves of wavelength 1 mm approaching an aperture of size 20 cm.

3 In the corridor shown in Figure 3.13 an observer at point P can hear someone at point Q but cannot see them. What physical phenomena may account for this? How could P *see* Q?

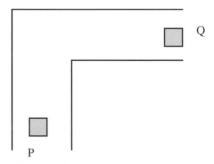

Figure 3.13 For question 3.

4 Two loudspeakers are connected to the same audio oscillator. An observer walks along the straight line joining the speakers (see Figure 3.14). At a point M halfway between the speakers he hears a loud sound. By the

time he gets to point P a distance of 2.00 m from M he hears no sound at all. Explain how this is possible. Find the largest possible wavelength of sound emitted by the loudspeakers.

Figure 3.14 For question 4.

5 A radio station, R, emits radio waves of wavelength 1600 m which reach a house, H, directly and after reflecting from a mountain, M, behind the house (see Figure 3.15). If the reception at the house is very poor, what is the shortest possible distance between the house and the mountain?

Figure 3.15 For question 5.

6 A car moves along a road that joins the twin antennas of a radio station that is broadcasting at a frequency of 90.0 MHz (see Figure 3.16). When in position A, the reception is good but it drops to almost zero at position B. What is the minimum distance AB?

Figure 3.16 For question 6.

7 Two sources emit identical sound waves with a frequency of 850 Hz.

(a) An observer is 8.2 m from the first source and 9.0 m from the second. Describe and explain what this observer hears.
(b) A second observer is 8.1 m from the first source and 8.7 m from the second. Describe and explain what this observer hears.
(Take the speed of sound to be 340 m s^{-1}.)

8 In the context of wave motion, state what you understand by the term superposition. Illustrate constructive and destructive interference by suitable diagrams.

9 Using a suitable diagram, explain why an observer who moves toward a source of sound will measure a frequency higher than that emitted.

10 A source of sound is directed at an approaching car. The sound is reflected by the car and is received back at the source. *Carefully* explain what changes in frequency the observer at the source will detect.

11 Light from a nearby galaxy is emitted at a wavelength of 657 nm and is observed on earth at a wavelength of 654 nm. What can we deduce about the motion of this galaxy?

12 The sun rotates about its axis as shown in Figure 3.17. Assume that the sun emits light of yellow wavelength only. What will we measure for the wavelength of light emitted from points A and B on the sun's surface.

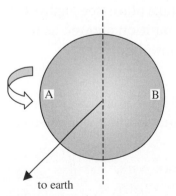

Figure 3.17 For question 12.

Two-source interference

This chapter is a detailed account of the phenomenon of interference from two coherent sources.

Objectives

By the end of this chapter you should be able to:
- appreciate the meaning of the terms *coherence* and *coherent sources*;
- give the meanings of the terms *phase difference* and *path difference*;
- describe *Young's two-slit experiment*;
- derive, understand and use the formula $d \sin \theta = n\lambda$ for *constructive interference*, and derive from this the formula

$$s = \frac{\lambda D}{d};$$

- describe one method to measure the *wavelength of light*;
- appreciate that under the right conditions, *interference takes place for all waves*.

Two-source interference

In Chapter 4.3 we saw that, when identical waves are emitted from two coherent sources and observed at the same point in space, interference will take place (see Figure 4.1). The principle of superposition allowed us to determine the following:

Figure 4.1 Interference from two coherent sources. The waves arriving at P from the two sources travel different distances in getting there and hence arrive with a path difference.

▶ If the path difference is an integral multiple of the wavelength, *constructive* interference takes place:

path difference $= n\lambda$,
$\quad n = 0, \pm 1, \pm 2, \pm 3 \ldots$

If the path difference is a half-integral multiple of the wavelength, *destructive* interference takes place:

path difference $= (n + \frac{1}{2})\lambda$,
$\quad n = 0, \pm 1, \pm 2, \pm 3 \ldots$

The two sources (black circles) in Figure 4.2 emit circular wavefronts (four are shown from each source). These represent crests. At points such as A, B and C crests of one source meet crests from the other and so constructive interference takes place. The path difference for each case is zero, since these are equidistant from the sources. Constructive interference also takes place for a point such as D, for which the path difference is three wavelengths (a distance

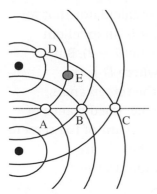

Figure 4.2 Interference between circular wavefronts.

of one wavelength from one source and four wavelengths from the other). On the other hand, for a point such as E, destructive interference takes place. This is because point E is a distance of two wavelengths from one source but three and a half from the other, resulting in a path difference of one and a half wavelengths.

Two-source interference for light, sound and water waves can be studied using the arrangements in Figure 4.3. In the case of light, monochromatic light (i.e. light of one specific wavelength) from a laser is allowed to fall on two very thin slits separated by a small distance (0.1 mm or less). Interference fringes are observed on a screen some distance away. Sound interference can be observed if sound from a signal generator is fed into two loudspeakers and an observer some distance away listens to

both speakers, or if a microphone picks up the sound and feeds it into an oscilloscope. At points of constructive interference the oscilloscope signal will be large and at points of destructive interference it will be almost zero. For water waves, two-source interference is observed if a signal generator drives two dippers in a ripple tank. Where destructive interference takes place, the water surface is almost flat.

If the wave is a sound wave, points of constructive interference are points of high intensity of sound. Points of destructive interference are points of no sound at all. If the wave involved is light, then constructive interference means bright light, and destructive interference means points of darkness.

If the path difference is anything other than an integral or half-integral multiple of the wavelength, then the resultant amplitude of the wave at P will be some value between zero and $2A$, where A is the amplitude of one of the waves.

Interference for light

In Figure 4.4, monochromatic laser light falls on two slits, which then act as the two sources of coherent light. The precise meaning of coherence and coherent light will be given later. Point Z is such that the distance S_1P equals the distance ZP. The path difference is thus S_2Z. We want to calculate this path difference in order to derive the conditions for constructive

Figure 4.3 Experimental arrangements to observe interference for light, sound and water waves.

interference at P. Note that, in practice, the distance between the slits, d, is only 0.1 mm and the distance to the screen is a few metres. This means that, approximately, the lines S_1P and ZP are parallel and the angles PS_1Z and PZS_1 are right angles. Thus, the angle S_2S_1Z equals θ, the angle defining point P (since these two angles have their sides mutually perpendicular).

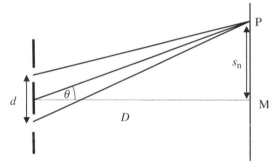

Figure 4.4 The geometry of the problem that enters in the calculation of the path difference. The nth maximum at P is a distance y_n from the centre of the screen.

The distance S_2Z (i.e. the path difference) is (by trigonometry) equal to $d \sin \theta$ and so:

> ▶ The condition for *constructive interference* at P becomes
>
> $$d \sin \theta = n\lambda$$

Here, d is the separation of the two slits. As implied above, the angle θ is quite small, so $\sin \theta$ is small, which means we can approximate

$\sin \theta$ by $\tan \theta$ (check on your calculator that for small angles θ, in radians, it is an excellent approximation that $\sin \theta \sim \tan \theta \sim \theta$). But $\tan \theta = \frac{s_n}{D}$ (see Figure 4.4) where D is the distance of the slits from the screen and s_n stands for the distance MP, i.e. the distance of the point P from the middle point of the screen. The suffix n in s_n signifies that we are considering the nth maximum in the interference pattern. Thus,

$$s_n = \frac{n\lambda D}{d}$$

> ▶ The linear separation, s, on a screen of *two consecutive maxima* is thus
>
> $$s = s_{n+1} - s_n = (n + 1)\frac{\lambda D}{d} - n\frac{\lambda D}{d}$$
>
> $$s = \frac{\lambda D}{d}$$
>
> Therefore, in an interference experiment, measurement of the separation s of two successive maxima, D and d, gives a value for the wavelength λ of the wave.

This last formula shows that the maxima of the interference pattern are equally separated. Additional work shows that these maxima are also equally bright.

Young's two-slit experiment

Modern versions of the two-slit interference experiment are performed with laser light. This makes sure that the two slits act as coherent sources of light. An early demonstration of the phenomenon of interference for light was performed by Thomas Young in 1801. Monochromatic light from a source S falls upon a small slit as shown in Figure 4.5. As a result of diffraction, the light spreads around the slit so that it is incident on two narrow, parallel slits separated by a very small distance. The light falling on the slits has come from the *same* source (S) and so the slits behave as coherent sources.

The interference pattern is observed on a screen placed some distance from the slits. A filter placed in front of the light source ensures the light hitting the slits is monochromatic. The lens between the source and the single slit is there to make sure that the wavefronts hitting the single slit are *planar* (this is a technicality known as Fraunhoffer diffraction and need not concern us further). The lens, filter and single slit are unnecessary if a laser is used.

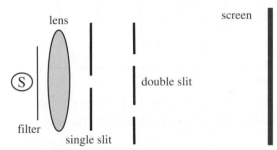

Figure 4.5 Young's two-slit experiment.

Example question

Q1

In a Young's two-slit experiment, a source of light of unknown wavelength is used to illuminate two very narrow slits a distance of 0.15 mm apart. On a screen at a distance of 1.30 m from the slits, bright spots are observed separated by a distance of 4.95 mm. What is the wavelength of light being used?

Answer

By straightforward application of the result $s = \frac{\lambda D}{d}$ we find a wavelength of 571 nm.

Why must the two sources be coherent?

We have postponed until the end a discussion of the very important fact that for interference to be observed the two sources must be **coherent**.

First, we introduce the concept of phase. The equation giving the displacement of a wave travelling toward the right with amplitude A, period T and wavelength λ is given by

$$y = A \sin\left(\frac{2\pi t}{T} - \frac{2\pi x}{\lambda} + \phi\right)$$

where the angle ϕ is known as the *phase* of the wave. Two waves given by the equations

$$y_1 = A \sin\left(\frac{2\pi t}{T} - \frac{2\pi x}{\lambda}\right)$$

and

$$y_2 = A \sin\left(\frac{2\pi t}{T} - \frac{2\pi x}{\lambda} + \frac{\pi}{4}\right)$$

are identical in that they have the same amplitude, frequency and wavelength but are said to have a *phase difference* between them of $\frac{\pi}{4}$.

> ▶ If the phase difference between the waves stays the same as time goes on, the sources are said to be coherent. Coherence means a constant phase difference between two sources.

Two loudspeakers connected to the same amplifier would produce sound waves with a constant phase difference between them (usually a zero phase difference); they would be coherent sources. Similarly, waves produced on two identical strings by two people shaking the ends of the strings in identical fashion without stopping would also produce coherent waves on the strings.

The case of light, however, is very different. Unlike a loudspeaker, which produces a continuous stream of sound waves, a source of light, such as a lamp, produces a non-continuous stream of light waves. Assume that the lamp is a point source of light, i.e. that just one point in the lamp filament produces the emitted light. If we could film that point while it is emitting light and then play the film in slow motion (slowed down by a factor of a few billion times) we would see the point being on for while, then off for a while, and so on. Consider now two such lamps. Even if the lamps are identical, the light emitted from one lamp will not be correlated with that from the other. Even if the on–off times coincide, there is no reason why the phase difference between the waves emitted will be the same as time goes on. The two lamps are incoherent sources of light.

The conditions derived earlier for two-slit interference hold for the case where the phase difference between the two sources initially is zero. If the sources are coherent but there is a phase difference ϕ between them, the relevant path difference now is $\frac{\phi}{2\pi}\lambda + (d_1 - d_2)$, where d_1 and d_2 are the distances from S_1 to P and from S_2 to P, respectively.

Working precisely as before, the condition for constructive interference is

$$d_1 - d_2 = n\lambda + \frac{\phi}{2\pi}\lambda$$
$$n = 0, 1, 2, 3, \ldots$$

and for destructive interference, we get

$$d_1 - d_2 = \left(n + \tfrac{1}{2}\right)\lambda + \frac{\phi}{2\pi}\lambda$$
$$n = 0, 1, 2, 3, \ldots$$

For $\phi = 0$, these conditions give the familiar ones derived earlier.

The conditions for arbitrary phase difference explain, finally, why the two sources must be coherent. Coherence between the two sources means that the phase difference between them, ϕ (whatever it is, not necessarily zero) stays the same as time goes on. If it does not remain constant (if ϕ is some function of time, $\phi(t)$), then at a particular point P the issue of whether we get a maximum or a minimum also depends on time. For example, if ϕ starts from zero, increases to 2π and then drops back to zero again periodically, with a period of, say, 10^{-9} s, then what is observed at P is a rapid succession of maxima and minima with a period of 10^{-9} s. The observer thus only sees an average of these effects – there is no interference pattern at all.

Intensity in two-slit interference

The fringes in a Young's two-slit experiment, *where the slit width is assumed negligible*, are equally bright.

The formula for intensity is a function of the angle θ, defined in Figure 4.4. This is graphed in Figure 4.6 for the case of $d = 2\lambda$. The horizontal variable is θ (in degrees). It is seen that the fringes are equally bright as mentioned earlier.

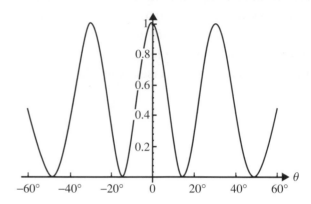

Figure 4.6 The intensity pattern for two slits of negligible width. The separation of the slits is $d = 2\lambda$.

For larger slit separations the maxima are closer to each other. Figure 4.7 shows the intensity for $d = 4\lambda$.

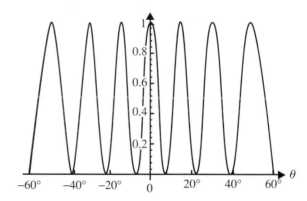

Figure 4.7 The intensity pattern for two slits of negligible width. The separation of the slits is $d = 4\lambda$.

▶ This shows that, for accurate measurement of the fringe separation, as small a slit separation as possible should be used.

Example question

Q2 ▬▬▬▬▬▬▬▬

Calculate the fringe separation for light of wavelength 680 nm that falls on two slits separated by 0.1 mm when the screen is placed 1.3 m from the slits.

Answer

$$s = \frac{\lambda D}{d}$$

$$= \frac{680 \times 10^{-9} \times 1.3}{0.1 \times 10^{-3}} \text{ m}$$

$$= 8.8 \text{ mm}$$

▶ The *width* of the slits has not entered in this discussion. This is because we are assuming that the two slits have a very small width compared with the wavelength of the wave. In this idealized case, the conclusions we stated are valid.

In a more realistic case, the width is also important and, because of diffraction at each slit, there is a *modulating effect* on the interference pattern (i.e. the fringes are no longer of equal intensity). In the thin-slit approximation, covering one of the slits would completely wipe out the interference pattern (no dark and bright fringes – just uniform illumination) – see Figure 4.8.

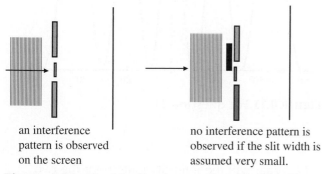

an interference pattern is observed on the screen

no interference pattern is observed if the slit width is assumed very small.

Figure 4.8 In the idealized case of negligible slit widths, covering one slit destroys the interference pattern.

In the realistic case, covering one slit would still result in a complicated diffraction pattern on the screen.

Two-slit experiments can also be performed with water waves in a ripple tank, sound waves (two speakers connected to a signal generator), microwaves, radio waves, etc. All waves show interference phenomena.

Questions

1 In a Young's two-slit experiment it is found that an *n*th-order maximum for a wavelength of 680.0 nm coincides with the (*n* + 1)th maximum of light of wavelength 510.0 nm. What is *n*?

2 Two loudspeakers are 1.00 m apart and are connected to the same audio oscillator. An observer walks along a straight line a distance of 12.0 m from the loudspeakers as shown in Figure 4.9. The observer hears a loud sound at M but almost no sound by the time she gets to point P a distance of 2.00 m from M. Explain how this is possible. Find the wavelength of sound emitted by the loudspeakers.

12 m

P

M

Figure 4.9 For question 2.

3 In a Young's two-slit experiment, a coherent source of light of wavelength 680 nm is used to illuminate two very narrow slits a distance of 0.12 mm apart. If a screen is placed at a distance of 1.50 m from the slits, find the separation of two successive bright spots.

4 Explain why two identical flashlights pointing light to the same spot on a screen will never produce an interference pattern.

5 Explain what will happen to the interference pattern in a Young's two-slit experiment if *one* of the slits is covered with transparent film that absorbs some of the light through it.

6 In a typical classroom demonstration, two loudspeakers are connected to the same audio signal generator and students are asked to stand at various positions in the room to listen to the sound produced. Depending on where they stand, the sound is sometimes loud and sometimes very soft. What wave phenomenon does this demonstrate? Give *three* reasons

why there are no spots where the intensity of sound is completely reduced to zero.

7 Discuss the effect on the bright spots in a Young's two-slit experiment of:
(a) decreasing the separation of the slits;
(b) increasing the wavelength of light;
(c) increasing the distance to the screen;
(d) increasing the distance of the source from the slits;
(e) using white light as the source.

8 Light of wavelength 644 nm (in air) is incident normally on two narrow parallel slits a distance of 1 mm apart. A screen is placed a distance of 1.2 m from the slits.
(a) Determine the distance on the screen between the central maximum and the fifth bright spot.
(b) If this experiment were repeated in water (index of refraction 1.33), how would your answer change?

9 A car moves along a road that is parallel to the twin antennas of a radio station broadcasting at a frequency of 95.0 MHz (see Figure 4.10). The antennas are 30.0 m apart and the distance of A from the mid-point of the antennas is 2.0 km. When in position A, the reception is good, but it drops to almost zero at position B. What is the distance AB?

Figure 4.10 For question 9.

10 Two radio transmitters are 80.0 m apart on a north–south line. They emit coherently at a wavelength of 1.5 m. A satellite in a north–south orbit travelling at 7.5 km s^{-1} receives a signal that alternates in intensity with a frequency of 3.5 Hz. Assuming that the signal received by the satellite is the superposition of the waves from the individual transmitters, find:
(a) the distance between two consecutive points where the satellite receives a strong signal;
(b) the height of the satellite from the earth's surface.

11 Figure 4.11 is the intensity pattern from a two-slit interference experiment. Determine the separation of the slits in terms of the wavelength of light used.

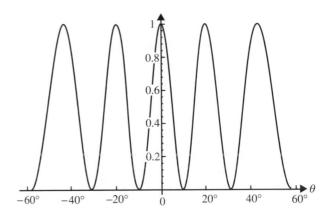

Figure 4.11 For question 11.

12 What will the intensity pattern for the two slits of question 11 be if the slit separation is halved?

The Doppler effect

The Doppler effect is a fundamental wave phenomenon with many applications. This chapter continues the earlier discussion of this phenomenon quantitatively. The phenomenon applies to all waves but sound waves only are considered here.

Objectives

By the end of this chapter you should be able to:
*   derive the *Doppler formula* for a moving source $f = f_0 \frac{c}{c - v_s}$ and a moving observer $f = f_0 \frac{c + v_r}{c}$, and use these in solving problems;
*   qualitatively *explain* the Doppler effect by suitable *wavefront diagrams*.

The Doppler effect

▶ The Doppler effect is the change in the frequency of a wave received by an observer, compared with the frequency with which it was emitted. The effect takes place whenever there is motion between the emitter and receiver.

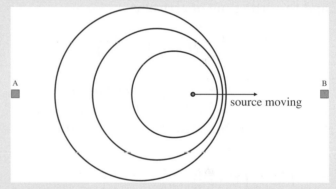

Figure 5.1 A source is approaching observer B and moves away from observer A.

We can explain the Doppler effect in diagrams as follows: The source moves towards observer B and away from observer A. The wavecrests are piling up in front of the source and thus the crests reach B at time intervals which are shorter than those on emission. Thus the received period is smaller and hence the frequency is larger. On the other hand, the crests reach A at longer time intervals and thus the measured frequency is smaller (Figure 5.1).

We can analyse this phenomenon in detail in the following way. Consider first the case when the observer is at rest and the emitter moves towards her. Suppose that at time $t = 0$ the emitter emits a wavecrest that reaches the receiver at a time of t s later. The second crest is emitted by the emitter at time T_0, where T_0 is the period of the wave (and therefore the emitted frequency is $f_0 = 1/T_0$). At what time does the receiver receive this second crest? Notice that during this interval of time T_0, the emitter has moved towards the receiver. The speed of the source is v_s and the wave speed is c. The wavecrest has therefore a shorter distance to travel (see Figure 5.2).

The time taken for the second wavecrest to travel the distance AB in the figure is

$$\frac{ct - v_s T_0}{c} = t - \frac{v_s}{c} T_0$$

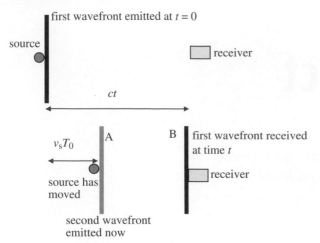

Figure 5.2 The first wavefront is emitted at $t = 0$ and is received a time of t s later. The second wavefront is emitted T s after the first. It will be received by the observer at a time less than T since the source is closer to the observer when it emits the second wavefront.

and thus the time of arrival is

$$T_0 + t - T_0 \frac{v_s}{c} = t + T_0 \left(1 - \frac{v_s}{c}\right)$$

That is to say, the second wavefront arrives a time of $T_0 \left(1 - \frac{v_s}{c}\right)$ after the first one. Hence the period of this wave as far as the observer is concerned is

$$T = T_0 \left(1 - \frac{v_s}{c}\right)$$

Thus, the frequency measured by the receiver is

$$f = \frac{1}{T}$$

$$= f_0 \frac{1}{1 - \frac{v_s}{c}}$$

$$= f_0 \frac{c}{c - v_s}$$

This shows that, as the emitter approaches the receiver, the receiver measures a higher frequency than was sent out. If the emitter is receding from the observer, the same formula applies but the velocity of the source must be taken as negative.

Consider now the case of a stationary emitter and a receiver moving with velocity v_r. We can get the answer from the previous formula by using the concept of relative velocity. The

receiver is free to call himself at rest, in which case the emitter is coming at him with velocity v_r. In addition, the wave appears to be moving with velocity $c + v_r$. Hence, the previous formula gives the following answer for the frequency received by the receiver:

$$f = f_0 \frac{(c + v_r)}{(c + v_r) - v_r}$$

$$= f_0 \frac{c + v_r}{c}$$

Again, if the receiver moves towards the emitter, the velocity is taken as a positive number; if the receiver moves away from the emitter, it is negative.

Note that, in the case of the *moving receiver*, the wavelength received is

$$\lambda = \frac{c + v_r}{f} \quad \text{(speed of wave over frequency)}$$

$$= \frac{c}{f_0}$$

$$= \lambda_0$$

that is, the same as that emitted.

A more complicated formula exists for the Doppler effect for light. Qualitatively, however, the phenomenon is the same for light as well. More details on the Doppler effect for light are provided in Option F on Astrophysics.

Example questions

Q1

A sound wave of frequency 300 Hz is emitted towards an approaching car. The wave is reflected from the car and is then received back at the emitter at a frequency of 315 Hz. What is the velocity of the car? (Take the speed of sound to be 340 m s⁻¹.)

Answer

The car is approaching the emitter so the frequency it receives is

$$f_1 = 300 \times \frac{340 + u}{340} \text{ Hz}$$

where u is the unknown car speed. The car now acts as an emitter of a wave of this frequency (f_1), and the original emitter will act as the new receiver. Thus, the frequency received (315 Hz) is (car is approaching)

$$315 = \left(300 \times \frac{340 + u}{340}\right) \times \frac{340}{340 - u}$$

from which we find $u = 8.29$ m s^{-1}.

Q2

A train with a 500 Hz siren on is moving at a constant speed of 8 m s^{-1} in a straight line. An observer is in front of the train and off its line of motion. What frequencies does the observer hear? (Take the speed of sound to be 340 m s^{-1}.)

Answer

What counts is the velocity of the train along the *line of sight* between the train and the observer. When the train is *very far away* (Figure 5.3) it essentially comes straight at the observer and so the frequency received is

$$f = f_0 \frac{c}{c - v_s}$$
$$= 500 \times \frac{340}{340 - 8}$$
$$= 512 \text{ Hz}$$

When the train is again *very far away* to the right, the frequency received will be

$$f = f_0 \frac{c}{c - v_s}$$
$$= 500 \times \frac{340}{340 - (-8)}$$
$$= 488.5 \text{ Hz}$$

As the train approaches, we take components of the train's velocity vector along a direction along the line of sight and a direction normal to it (see Figure 5.3).

As is seen from the diagram, the component along the line of sight is decreasing as the train gets closer to the observer. Thus, the observer will measure a *decreasing* frequency. It starts at 512 Hz and falls to 500 Hz when the train is at position P. As the train moves past P to the right, the observer will hear sound of *decreasing* frequency starting at 500 Hz and ending at 488.5 Hz.

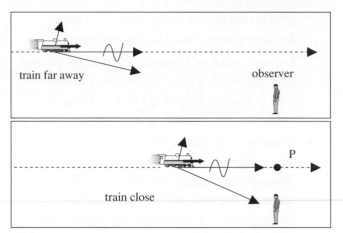

Figure 5.3.

Thus, the observer hears frequencies in the range of 512 Hz to 488.5 Hz, as shown in Figure 5.4.

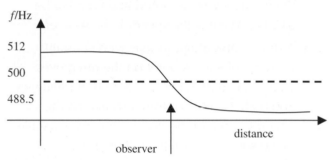

Figure 5.4.

Questions

Take the speed of sound to be 343 m s^{-1} in all the problems that follow.

1 Explain, with the help of diagrams, the Doppler effect. Show clearly the cases of a source that (a) moves towards and (b) goes away from a stationary observer as well the case of a moving observer.

2 A source approaches a stationary observer at 40 m s^{-1} emitting sound of frequency 500 Hz. What frequency does the observer measure?

3 A source is moving away from a stationary observer at 32 m s^{-1} emitting sound of frequency 480 Hz. What frequency does the observer measure?

4 A sound wave of frequency 512 Hz is emitted by a stationary source toward an observer

who is moving away at 12 m s^{-1}. What frequency does the observer measure?

5 A sound wave of frequency 628 Hz is emitted by a stationary source toward an observer who is approaching at 25 m s^{-1}. What frequency does the observer measure?

6 A sound wave of frequency 500 Hz is emitted by a stationary source toward a receding observer. The signal is reflected by the observer and received by the source, where the frequency is measured and found to be 480 Hz. What is the speed of the observer?

7 A sound wave of frequency 500 Hz is emitted by a moving source toward a stationary observer. The signal is reflected by the observer and received by the source, where the frequency is measured and found to be 512 Hz. What is the speed of the source?

8 A disc rotates about its axis with constant angular velocity. A point on the rim moves with a speed of 7.5 m s^{-1}. Sound of frequency 500.0 Hz is emitted from a source on the circumference of the disc in directions parallel to the source's velocity as shown in Figure 5.5, and is received by an observer very far away from the disc. What frequencies does the observer measure?

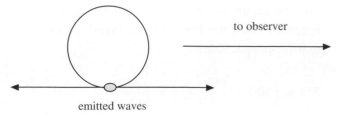

emitted waves

Figure 5.5 For question 8.

9 Consider the general case when both the source and the receiver move. Let v_s be the velocity of the source and v_r that of the receiver. In the frame of reference in which the receiver is at rest, the waves appear to move with velocity $c + v_r$ and the source appears to move with velocity $v_s + v_r$. Thus, show that the frequency received by the receiver is

$$f = f_0 \frac{c + v_r}{c - v_s}$$

10 Consider a source moving away from a stationary receiver with speed v. The source emits waves of speed c and wavelength λ_0. Explain why the receiver will measure a *longer* wavelength for the waves received and show that the *shift* in wavelength $\Delta\lambda = \lambda - \lambda_0$ obeys $\frac{\Delta\lambda}{\lambda_0} = \frac{v}{c}$.

Standing waves

A special wave is formed when two ordinary identical waves travelling in opposite directions meet. The result is a standing wave: a wave in which the crests do not move.

Objectives

By the end of this chapter you should be able to:

- state the differences between a *standing* wave and a *travelling* wave;
- describe how *a standing wave is formed*;
- draw the *various harmonics on strings and tubes* and find the *wavelength in terms of the string or tube length*;
- state the meaning of the terms *fundamental* and *harmonics*;
- state the meaning of the term *resonance*;
- solve problems with *standing waves*.

Standing waves on strings and tubes

> When two waves of the same speed and wavelength and equal or almost equal amplitudes travelling in opposite directions meet, a standing wave is formed. This interesting wave is the result of the superposition of the two waves travelling in opposite directions.

The main difference between a standing wave and a travelling wave is that in the former no energy or momentum is transferred. A standing wave is characterized by having a number of points at which the displacement is *always* zero. These are called nodes. (In a travelling wave, there are no points where the displacement is *always* zero.) The points at which the displacement is a maximum are called antinodes. (Note that the nodes always have zero displacement whereas the antinodes are at

maximum displacement for an instant of time only.) In Figure 6.1 a string of length L has been plucked in the middle and is about to be released.

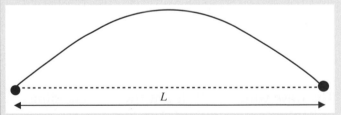

Figure 6.1 A standing wave on a string with both ends fixed. The string is held in this position and then released. A standing wave like this with a single antinode is known as a fundamental standing wave.

Successive pictures of the string will then look like Figure 6.2: the end points of the string remain fixed at all times (nodes) but the rest of the string oscillates. The middle point is the point on the string with the largest displacement (antinode). The string will return to its original position after a time equal to the period of the wave. In the absence of friction,

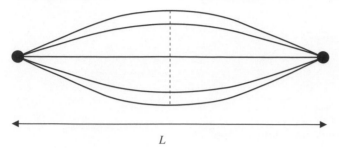

Figure 6.2 Positions of the string at various time intervals after being released. The dark circles show the positions of the nodes. The dotted line shows the position of the antinode.

this oscillation will continue forever. When the string is in its original position ($t = 0$) all the energy of the wave is in the form of potential energy of the stretched string. When the string assumes its undisturbed position, all the energy is in the form of kinetic energy. At all other positions the energy of the string consists of both potential and kinetic energy. Note that the crest of this wave (i.e. the antinode) does not move to the right or left as a crest does in a travelling wave.

The standing wave depicted above has a specific wavelength. Note that we have fitted half a full wave on the length of the string. This means that

$$\frac{\lambda}{2} = L$$
$$\Rightarrow \lambda = 2L$$

The wave with $\lambda = 2L$ is not the only standing wave that can exist on this string, however. Figure 6.3 shows the next standing wave. Note

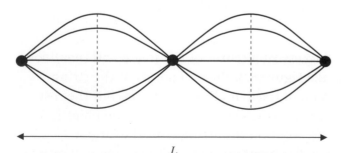

Figure 6.3 A standing wave with three nodes and two antinodes. A standing wave like this is known as the second harmonic.

that the only constraint we have is that the ends of the string are nodes. Here, we have fitted one full wave on the string. Thus, $\lambda = L$. This standing wave has three nodes and two antinodes.

An infinity of standing waves can thus exist on the string by 'fitting' waves with the constraint that the ends are nodes. The next standing wave is shown in Figure 6.4.

Figure 6.4 A standing wave with four nodes and three antinodes. A standing wave like this is known as the third harmonic.

For the third harmonic, we have fitted one and a half full waves on the string. Thus,

$$\frac{3}{2}\lambda = L$$
$$\Rightarrow \lambda = \frac{2L}{3}$$

In general, we find that the wavelengths satisfy

$$\lambda = \frac{2L}{n}, \quad n = 1, 2, 3, 4, \ldots$$

The wave with wavelength corresponding to $n = 1$ is called the fundamental mode of the string or the first harmonic. All other modes are called higher harmonics. So, for example, the mode with $n = 3$ is the third harmonic. The fundamental mode has the largest wavelength and thus the smallest frequency ($f = \frac{v}{\lambda}$, where v is the speed of the wave).

▶ If f_0 is the fundamental's frequency, then all other harmonics have frequencies that are integral multiples of f_0.

Note that the distance between two successive nodes is half a wavelength. The same is true for successive antinodes. The distance between a node and the next antinode is a quarter of a wavelength.

Figure 6.5 shows that particles between two consecutive nodes move in the same direction. Particles between the adjacent pair of nodes move in the opposite direction.

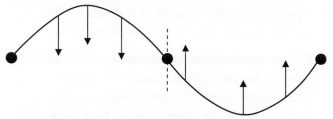

Figure 6.5 All points between two consecutive nodes are in phase: that is to say, they move in the same direction. They differ in phase by 180° with those between the next pair of nodes, which are moving in the opposite way.

If one end of the string is free and the other fixed, then the free end must be an antinode and the fixed end a node. The allowed wavelengths are then

$$\lambda = \frac{4L}{n}, \quad n = 1, 3, 5, \ldots$$

(Here n is an odd integer.) Examples of these standing waves are shown in Figures 6.6–6.8.

You must convince yourself that the wavelengths of these harmonics are indeed those given by the formula $\lambda = \frac{4L}{n}, n = 1, 3, 5, \ldots$

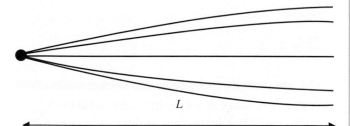

Figure 6.6 The fundamental standing wave on a string with one end fixed and the other free.

Figure 6.7 The second harmonic.

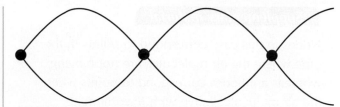

Figure 6.8 The third harmonic.

When both ends are free, the condition is

$$\lambda = \frac{2L}{n}, \quad n = 1, 2, 3, 4, \ldots$$

The situation here is entirely analogous to that with both ends fixed with the roles of node and antinode interchanged (see Figure 6.9).

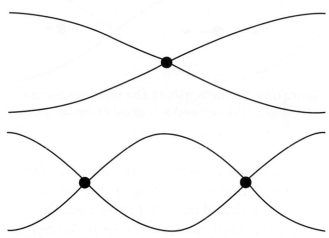

Figure 6.9 Standing waves on a string with both ends free are similar to those for both ends fixed except that nodes and antinodes are interchanged. The fundamental and second harmonic are shown here.

We have discussed standing waves exclusively in terms of waves on a string whose ends are fixed or free. Exactly the same results apply to sound standing waves formed in a pipe (such as a musical instrument) whose ends are open (corresponding to free string ends) or closed (corresponding to fixed string ends) – see Figure 6.10. Nodes exist at closed ends and antinodes at open ends.

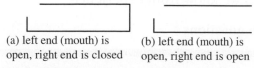

(a) left end (mouth) is open, right end is closed

(b) left end (mouth) is open, right end is open

Figure 6.10 (a) A pipe with one end closed and one open. (b) A pipe with both ends open.

Supplementary material

Nodes in this case correspond to points in the pipe where the air molecules are not moving whereas antinodes correspond to points where the air molecules move with maximum displacement (see Figure 6.11). These are called displacement nodes and antinodes. Note, however, that at a displacement node the pressure of the gas varies the most (i.e. we have a pressure antinode), and at a displacement antinode the pressure variation is zero (i.e. we have a pressure node).

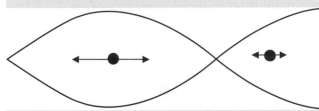

Figure 6.11 Air molecules in the pipe vibrate the most at antinodes and not at all at nodes.

You don't need to memorize the formulae for wavelength in terms of string or tube length. Rather, you should note that in all cases the distance between successive nodes or antinodes is half a wavelength and that the distance between a node and the next antinode is a quarter of a wavelength. This should allow you to figure out what kind of standing wave you can fit in the particular case you are examining. We see from these formulae that, as the length of the tube becomes smaller, the allowed wavelengths also get smaller, which means that the corresponding frequencies get larger. This is seen when you put a bottle under a tap and start to fill it with water. The falling water excites a standing wave in the bottle whose length of air column is getting smaller as the bottle fills. This means that the frequency of the sound emitted by the bottle becomes high pitched, as we know from experience.

Example questions

Q1
A standing wave is set up on a string kept under tension T. What must be done to the tension in order to double the fundamental frequency of the wave?

Answer

Since $f = \frac{v}{\lambda}$, and the wavelength is fixed in terms of the length of the string $\lambda = 2L$, we can double f by doubling the velocity of the wave. This means that the tension must increase by 4.

Q2
What is the ratio of the frequencies of the fundamental to the second harmonic for a standing wave set up on a string, both ends of which are kept fixed?

Answer

The frequencies are

$$f_0 = \frac{v}{2L} \quad \text{and} \quad f_1 = \frac{v}{L}$$

hence

$$\frac{f_0}{f_1} = \frac{1}{2}$$

Q3
A tube has one end open and the other closed. What is the ratio of the wavelengths of the fundamental to the second harmonic?

Answer

The fundamental and second harmonic have wavelengths

$$\lambda_0 = 4L \quad \text{and} \quad \lambda_1 = \frac{4L}{3}$$

hence

$$\frac{\lambda_0}{\lambda_1} = 3$$

Q4
A standing wave is set up in a tube with both ends open. The frequency of the fundamental is 300 Hz. What is the length of the tube? Take the speed of sound to be 340 m s^{-1}.

Answer

The wavelength is

$$\frac{340}{300} \, \text{m} = 1.13 \, \text{m}$$

The fundamental's wavelength is equal to $2L$ and so $L = 0.57$ m.

Resonance and the speed of sound

When a vibrating tuning fork is brought near to the end of a long tube partially filled with water, a buzzing sound may be heard from the tube. When that happens, addition of more water in the tube will ruin the effect. This is an example of resonance. The tuning fork will excite the air in the tube and force it to vibrate with a frequency equal to the tuning fork's frequency. The amplitude of this standing wave will be appreciable, though, only if the frequency of the standing wave that the tube can support is equal to the tuning fork's frequency. When these two frequencies are the same, we hear the buzzing sound from the tube. Pouring more water in the tube changes the frequency of the tube and so the amplitude is now very small – no sound is heard from the tube.

This actually provides a simple method for measuring the speed of sound in air. A set of tuning forks of known frequencies are each sounded over a column of air in a long tube partially filled with water. The height of the column of water is adjusted (by pouring water in or out) until resonance is obtained (i.e. the tube emits a sound). The corresponding height of the air column and the frequency are recorded and this is repeated with the other tuning forks. The standing wave inside the tube must have a wavelength such that $\lambda = 4L$, where L is the length of the air column. But $\lambda = \frac{v}{f}$, where f is the corresponding frequency, which equals the known frequency of the tuning fork. Thus, v, which is the speed of sound, can be determined by repeating this procedure for various different tuning forks and then plotting L versus $1/f$. One must get a straight line with slope $v/4$.

Supplementary material

This discussion ignores end corrections. End corrections are necessary in practice because the standing wave may have a wavelength that does not satisfy $\frac{\lambda}{4} = L$ but rather $\frac{\lambda}{4} = L + e$, where e is a constant depending on the diameter of the tube. In an experiment to measure the speed of sound by resonance the end correction *must* be included.

Resonance is a general phenomenon. It occurs whenever a system that is capable of oscillation or vibration is subjected to an external disturbance with a frequency equal to the natural frequency of the system itself. In that case, the system oscillates with a large amplitude. If the frequencies do not match, the system still vibrates but the amplitude is very small. Clearly, resonance can be a dangerous phenomenon. A system that is set into vibration by something external and develops large amplitudes may eventually break or fall apart. Aeroplane wings, engines, bridges, tall buildings, etc., must all be protected against resonance from external vibrations due to wind, other vibrating objects, etc. Soldiers always break their step when walking over a bridge, in case the force that they exert on the bridge starts uncontrollable oscillations of the bridge. An earthquake may set a building into oscillation if the frequency of the longitudinal wave created by the earthquake is equal to the natural frequency of vibration of the building. This frequency is $\frac{c}{2L}$, where c is the speed of sound in the structure of the building and L is its height. (See Figures 6.12–6.14.)

Figure 6.12 The Tacoma Narrows bridge collapsed in 1940, a victim of resonant failure.

wavelength of fundamental is 2L

Figure 6.13 A building will be made to oscillate in a standing wave mode if the frequency of the earthquake wave matches the natural frequency of oscillation of the building.

Figure 6.14 The severe earthquake that struck northern Turkey in August 1999 released vast amounts of energy. Hundreds of buildings toppled and tens of thousands of people were killed.

Questions

1 Describe what is meant by a standing wave. In what ways does a standing wave differ from a travelling wave?

2 How is a standing wave formed?

3 In the context of standing waves describe what is meant by:
   (a) node;
   (b) antinode.

4 Describe how you would arrange for a string that is kept under tension, with both ends fixed, to vibrate in its second harmonic mode. Draw the shape of the string when it is vibrating in its second harmonic mode.

5 Explain what is meant by resonance and give two examples where it occurs.

6 Car drivers occasionally experience a 'shaking steering wheel' when travelling at a particular speed. The shaking disappears at lower or higher speeds. Suggest a reason for this observation.

7 A string is held under tension, with both ends fixed, and has a fundamental frequency of 250 Hz. If the tension is doubled, what will the new frequency of the fundamental mode be?

8 A string has both ends fixed. What is the ratio of the frequencies of the first to the second harmonic?

9 The fundamental mode on a string with both ends fixed is 500 Hz. What will the frequency become if the tension in the string is increased by 20%?

10 The wave velocity of a transverse wave on a string of length 0.500 m is 225 m s^{-1}.
   (a) What is the fundamental frequency of a standing wave on this string if both ends are kept fixed?
   (b) While this string is vibrating in the fundamental harmonic, what is the wavelength of sound produced in air?
   (Take the speed of sound in air to be 330 m s^{-1}.)

11 Figure 6.15 shows a tube with one end open and the other closed. Draw the standing wave representing the third harmonic standing wave in this tube.

Figure 6.15 For question 11.

12 A glass tube is closed at one end. The air column it contains has a length that can be varied between 0.50 m and 1.50 m. If a tuning fork of frequency 306 Hz is sounded at the top of the tube, at which lengths of the air

column would resonance occur? (Take the speed of sound to be 330 m s^{-1}.)

13 A glass tube with one end open and the other closed is used in a resonance experiment to determine the speed of sound. A tuning fork of frequency 427 Hz is used and resonance is observed for air column lengths equal to 17.4 cm and 55.0 cm.
   (a) What speed of sound does this experiment give?
   (b) What is the end correction for this tube?

14 A tube with both ends open has two consecutive harmonics of frequency 300 Hz and 360 Hz.

(a) What is the length of the tube?
(b) What are the harmonics?
(Take the speed of sound to be 330 m s^{-1}.)

15 A string of length 0.50 m is kept under a tension of 90.0 N and vibrates in its fundamental mode. The mass of the string is 3.0 g.
   (a) What is the frequency of the sound emitted? (Take the speed of sound to be 330 m s^{-1}.)
   (b) The same string now vibrates in water. What is the wavelength of the sound emitted? (Take the speed of sound in water to be 1500 m s^{-1}.)

Beats

This chapter introduces the phenomenon known as beats, which arises when two waves of equal amplitude but slightly different frequency superpose.

Objectives

By the end of this chapter you should be able to:
- derive the *beat frequency* formula $f_B = |f_1 - f_2|$ and use it in problems;
- use the principle of superposition to add two waves of slightly different frequency and get the *beat envelope* of the resulting wave, the frequency of which is $\frac{f_1 + f_2}{2}$;
- describe one use of beats in *music*.

The phenomenon of beats

We have already mentioned that when two waves of individual disturbances y_1 and y_2 arrive together at the same point in space, then the principle of superposition states that the resulting disturbance is

$$y = y_1 + y_2$$

Something very special happens when we apply this principle to two travelling waves of equal amplitude but *slightly different* frequency (Figures 7.1–7.3). Figure 7.3 shows the result of adding together two waves of amplitude one unit each: the first has a frequency of 10 Hz (Figure 7.1) and the second a frequency of 11 Hz (Figure 7.2).

We see that the resulting wave has an amplitude that is not constant. It varies from a maximum of two units to zero. Note that in an interval of 1 s the amplitude assumes its maximum value once. If these are sound waves, it means that every second there is one loud sound. The number of loud sounds per second (one in this example) is the difference between the frequencies of the individual waves (10 Hz and 11 Hz). These periodic noises are called beats and the beat frequency (i.e. the number of loud sounds per second) is

$$f_B = |f_1 - f_2|.$$

Musicians use beats to tune their instruments: the first violin (usually) sounds a note and the other musicians listen for beats between the violin and their own instrument. As the frequency of their instrument approaches that of the first violin, the beat frequency approaches zero and the beats disappear. The instrument is then correctly tuned.

The frequency of the sound heard is the average of f_1 and f_2, i.e.

$$\frac{f_1 + f_2}{2}$$

Example questions

Q1 ▬▬▬▬▬▬▬

Two tuning forks have frequencies of 310 and 316 Hz. How many loud noises are heard per second when both forks are sounded together? What is the frequency of the sound heard?

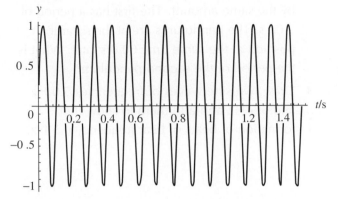

Figure 7.1 A harmonic wave of frequency 10 Hz.

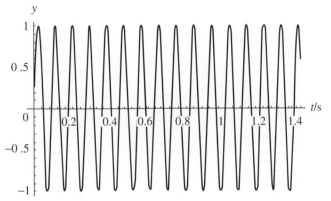

Figure 7.2 A harmonic wave of frequency 11 Hz.

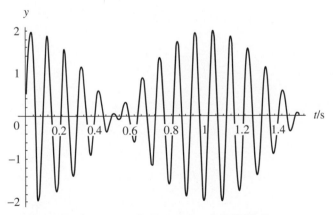

Figure 7.3 The sum of two waves of slightly different frequencies produces beats. In this example, it is the sum of the waves in Figures 7.1 and 7.2.

Answer

The beat frequency is 6 Hz, so there are six loud noises per second. The frequency of the sound is 313 Hz.

Q2

Two tuning forks are sounded together and an observer hears a sound with a frequency of 302 Hz whose intensity oscillates with a frequency of 4.0 Hz. What are the frequencies of the two tuning forks?

Answer

The beat frequency is 4.0 Hz, so

$$f_1 - f_2 = 4$$

and

$$\frac{f_1 + f_2}{2} = 302$$

Solving simultaneously we find $f_1 = 304$ Hz and $f_2 = 300$ Hz.

To derive the formula for the beat frequency we work as follows. Let T_1 be the period of the first wave and T_2 that of the second. Assume that $T_1 < T_2$. Suppose that at time zero the crest of one wave meets the crest of the other. After how much time will the *next* meeting of crests take place? Let this time be T. Then we must have that

$$T = (n + 1)T_1$$

and

$$T = nT_2$$

for *some integer n*. Solving the first equation for n and substituting in the second, we find

$$T = \left(\frac{T}{T_1} + 1\right) T_2$$

$$\Rightarrow T = \frac{T_1 T_2}{T_2 - T_1}$$

In this time interval, there has been one loud sound. This means the beat frequency is $1/T$ and so

$$f_B = \frac{1}{T}$$

$$= \frac{T_2 - T_1}{T_1 T_2}$$

$$= \frac{1}{T_1} - \frac{1}{T_2}$$

$$= f_1 - f_2$$

Questions

1 An observer hears a sound with a frequency of 450 Hz when two tuning forks are sounded together. The intensity of the sound oscillates with a frequency of 6.0 Hz. What are the frequencies of the two tuning forks?

2 Two pendulums of slightly different lengths are released from rest after having been displaced by the same amount. The first has a period of 2.00 s. The pendulums are at their starting position at the *same time* 60.0 s later. What is the period of the second pendulum?

3 Draw two sine waves of frequencies 5.0 Hz and 5.5 Hz and add them to show the formation of beats of beat frequency 0.5 Hz.

Electric charge

Electricity is the study of electric charge, of which there are two kinds: positive and negative. Electric charge is a quantity that is conserved; like total energy, electric charge cannot be created or destroyed. It is believed that the total charge of the universe is zero – there is exactly as much positive charge as there is negative. Another important property of electric charge is that it is quantized, which means the charge on a body is always an integral multiple of a basic unit. Basic investigations into the nature and interactions of electric charge were carried out in the 1780s by Charles Coulomb, who discovered the law for the force between electric charges. Ingenious experiments in electrostatic induction and many other aspects of electricity were performed by Michael Faraday in the nineteenth century.

Objectives

By the end of this chapter you should be able to:
- appreciate that there is *a force between electric charges* and that vector methods must be used to find the net force on a given charge;
- describe the methods of charging by *friction* and *electrostatic induction* and outline their differences;
- understand the use of the *electroscope*;
- understand that charge resides on the *outside* surface of a conductor – the net charge *inside* a conductor is *zero*;
- use the formula for the *electric force between point charges* (Coulomb's law)

$$F = \frac{1}{4\pi \varepsilon_0} \frac{Q_1 Q_2}{r^2} \quad \text{or} \quad F = k \frac{Q_1 Q_2}{r^2}$$

Properties of electric charge

Negative charge resides on particles called electrons (and on many others – but we will only deal with electrons here). Positive charge resides on protons (and others), which exist in the nuclei of atoms. Electrons are much lighter than nuclei and so it is much easier for electrons to move than nuclei. This means that in solid bodies the motion of electric charge is brought about by the motion of electrons, but in liquids and especially in gases positive ions can also transport charge. As we will see later, the electron carries the smallest unit of electric charge. (Quarks, particles found in protons and neutrons, carry charges that are 1/3 or 2/3 of the electron charge. These particles cannot be observed as free particles so the electron can still be thought of as the carrier of the smallest unit of charge.) Electric charge is measured in a unit called the coulomb (C), and the electron's charge is (negative) 1.6×10^{-19} C. Materials can be classified into two large classes. The first class is *conductors*, which are materials that contain many free electrons inside them (free electrons are those that do not belong to one particular atom). The second class is *insulators*, which do not have many such free electrons. This means that in an electric field (explained later) the free electrons of a conductor will begin to move parallel to the electric field whereas no motion takes place in an insulator. This distinction between conductors and insulators is not completely clear-cut. There also exist materials called *semiconductors*, which have intermediate properties.

> ▶ A very important property of electric charge is that it is conserved. The total charge of an isolated system cannot change.

Example question

Q1 ▬▬▬▬▬▬▬▬▬▬▬▬▬▬▬

Two separated, identical conducting spheres are charged with charges of $4\,\mu C$ and $-12\,\mu C$, respectively. If the spheres are allowed to touch and then separated again, what will be the charge on each sphere?

Answer

The net charge on the two spheres is $-8\,\mu C$. When the spheres are allowed to touch they will end up with the same charge since they are identical. When they separate, each will therefore have a charge of $-4\,\mu C$.

The electric force

Simple experiments allow us to deduce that there is a force between electric charges. This is the electric force. The details of this force were discovered by Coulomb and Henry Cavendish and are presented later in this chapter. For our purposes in this section it will be sufficient to know that the force is attractive between charges of opposite sign and repulsive for charges of similar sign.

Charging by friction

When a glass rod is rubbed with silk, it will develop a positive charge. This is because frictional forces between the silk and the glass remove electrons from the glass rod and deposit them on the silk. This method is called *charging by friction*.

Charging by induction

Suppose that a charged rod is brought near to, but does not touch, a conductor that rests on an insulating stand. Let us assume that the charge on the rod is negative. Then, electrons in the conductor nearest the charged rod will be repelled towards the other side of the conductor. This means that the side of the conductor nearest the rod will have a positive charge and the side furthest from it a negative charge. Note that since the conductor was originally electrically neutral, it remains so: the negative and positive charges on the sides of the conductor are equal. This is illustrated in Figure 1.1.

Figure 1.1 A negatively charged rod brought near to an insulated conductor forces electrons in the conductor to the side furthest from the rod.

Now imagine that, with the charged rod still nearby, you touch the conductor with your finger. What happens is that the electrons will flow to the earth through your body, leaving the conductor with a surplus of positive net charge (see Figure 1.2). If the charged rod is now removed, this positive charge will distribute itself on the surface of the conductor and we are left with a charged conductor. This method of charging is called *electrostatic induction*. We have *induced* charge on a body without actually touching that body with a charged object.

Figure 1.2 If the conductor is earthed, electrons from the conductor flow into the earth, leaving the conductor positively charged.

The induced charge in this case was positive, which is *opposite to the charge of the charging body*. This is always the case. Suppose, for example, that the external charge was positive. Then electrons would move towards this external charge, leaving a positive charge behind. By touching the conductor, we allow electrons from the earth to move *up to the conductor* and neutralize this positive charge, leaving the conductor with a net negative charge. You may wonder what determines which way the electrons will move. (In our example here, electrons moved toward the earth the first time, and on to the body from the earth the second

time). Electrons always move in a direction that will increase their potential. The concept of a potential is something we will meet later and, when we do, this point will be clarified.

Here is another example of electrostatic induction. A charged body is brought near to two touching conducting spheres, each resting on insulating stands, as shown on the left of Figure 1.3.

If the external charge is negative, then electrons in the left sphere will be pushed away, leaving a positive charge on the left sphere. If *we now separate* the two spheres, as on the right of Figure 1.3, we will find that the left sphere has a net positive charge while the right sphere has a net negative charge. Again, the amount of positive charge on one body equals the amount of negative charge on the other, as required by the law of conservation of charge.

The electroscope

The electroscope is a simple and useful device for investigating electrostatic properties. A metallic rod with a metallic sphere on the top end is inserted through a piece of plastic into a glass cage (the cage may also be conducting, in which case it is earthed). The lower end of the rod has a strip of aluminium foil attached to it so it can move (in the original instruments a gold leaf was used instead). Figure 1.4 illustrates how an electroscope is used.

When an electric charge is placed near to (but not touching) the ball, the foil diverges. Let us assume that the charge is

Figure 1.3 A negatively charged rod brought near two touching conductors will induce equal and opposite charges when the conductors are separated (in the presence of the rod).

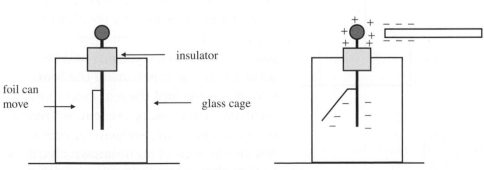

Figure 1.4 A negatively charged rod placed near the ball of the electroscope forces electrons from the ball down to the foil, causing it to diverge.

negative. This negative charge pushes electrons away from the ball. These electrons collect at the lower end of the rod and on the foil, and so the repulsive electric force between the similar charges causes the foil to diverge. (Note: If the cage had been made of a conducting material, a positive charge would be induced on the inside surface of the cage.)

The metal ball of the electroscope is thus left with a positive charge. Note that the net charge on the electroscope is still zero (conservation of charge). If we remove the external charge, the electrons will move back up to the ball, cancel the positive charge there and the foil will collapse completely.

If, when the foil is diverged, we keep the external charge nearby and then touch the ball of the electroscope, the foil will again collapse (Figure 1.5a). What happens is that the electrons from the foil and the lower end of the electroscope flow to the earth, leaving the electroscope with a net positive charge. *It is important to observe that even though the electroscope is now charged, the foil is collapsed.* Therefore, the electroscope *does not* measure the amount of charge on it. Rather, it measures its electric potential, relative to the zero potential of the earth. The concept of potential will be introduced in the next chapter. When the electroscope is connected to the earth, it has the earth's potential (i.e. zero) and so the foil is collapsed.

Why did the electrons move to the earth? This is because electrons always tend to move to a place of higher potential. The earth is at zero potential whereas the electrons on the lower end of the rod and the aluminium leaf are at some negative potential. Thus, by moving to the earth, the electrons increase their potential.

After earthing the electroscope, the rod can be moved away. The electroscope foil again diverges and stays raised (Figure 1.5b). This is because now there is a positive charge everywhere in the electroscope and so the foil is pushed away from the electroscope rod. Equivalently, the electroscope is now at a positive potential, higher than the potential of the earth. Note that the original external charge was negative. Charging the electroscope in this way always results in a charge opposite to the external one. It is another example of electrostatic induction.

Actually, we can test the sign of the charge of a charged electroscope in the following way. Suppose that we have charged our electroscope with an external negative charge as described above. Now bring the negative external charge close to the ball of the electroscope again. This negative charge will push electrons towards the lower end of the rod and the aluminium leaf. But these already have positive charge on them. The arrival of these extra electrons will reduce the amount of positive charge on the rod and leaf and will therefore cause the leaf to diverge less. On the other hand, if we bring a positive charge close to this positively charged electroscope, then electrons will be attracted to the top, leaving the lower end of the rod and the leaf even more positive, thus causing the leaf to diverge even further. Thus, the general rule for testing the sign of an unknown charge is to first charge the electroscope with a known charge. (You need that much to begin with.) Then bring the unknown

(a)   (b)

Figure 1.5 If the electroscope is earthed (a) and the rod then removed (b), the electroscope stays positively charged. A positively charged rod would result in a negatively charged electroscope.

charge near to the ball of the electroscope. If the leaf diverges more, the unknown charge is of the same sign as the charge on the electroscope (which, remember, is opposite to the external charge that charged it). If the leaf collapses, then the unknown charge is opposite to that of the electroscope. (See, however, the first question at the end of the chapter.)

Electrostatic experiments

In static electricity, the charge that is deposited on a conductor always stays on the *outside* surface of the conductor. The net charge inside any conductor is zero. This amazing result was deduced experimentally by Benjamin Franklin, and later by Michael Faraday, in the following simple but ingenious experiment (see Figure 1.6). A metal sphere, on which an amount of

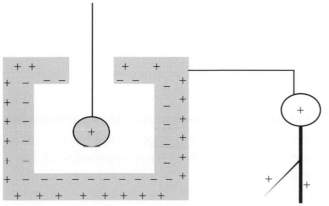

Figure 1.6 A positively charged sphere is lowered into a conducting bucket. Negative charge is induced in the interior of the bucket and an equal amount of positive charge is induced on the outside.

charge was placed, was lowered into an ordinary metal bucket. The outside of the bucket was connected to an electroscope. With the sphere inside the bucket, the electroscope leaf diverged.

The charge on the sphere (assumed positive) attracted electrons to the inside surface of the bucket, leaving the outside surface of the bucket (and hence also the electroscope) with a positive charge, which caused the leaf to diverge. The sphere was then allowed to move inside the bucket but the amount of divergence of the electroscope leaf never changed. The sphere was then allowed to touch the inside of the bucket (Figure 1.7a). It was then taken out (Figure 1.7b) and connected to a second electroscope (Figure 1.7c).

The second electroscope's leaf did not diverge, indicating that the sphere was not charged: the sphere's positive charge was cancelled by the negative charge of the inside of the bucket. But the charge on the outside of the bucket did not change, since the leaf of the first electroscope did not change its divergence. Thus, the amount of charge on the sphere must have been exactly equal and opposite to the charge on the inside of the bucket. *The amount of net charge inside the bucket was thus zero all along.*

▶ This is a general result: in static situations the net charge inside a conductor is zero.

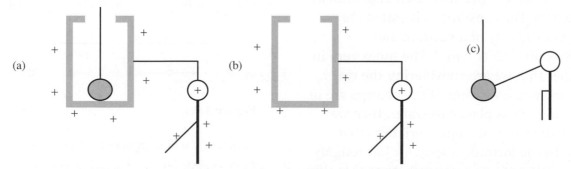

Figure 1.7 If the sphere is allowed to touch the interior of the bucket, its positive charge is completely cancelled by the negative charge in the bucket's interior. The sphere is completely neutral, as can be checked by connecting it to another electroscope.

Coulomb's law for the electric force

The electric force between two electric charges, Q_1 and Q_2, was investigated by Coulomb and, independently, by Cavendish. They discovered that this force is inversely proportional to the square of the separation of the charges and is proportional to the product of the two charges. It is attractive for opposite-sign charges and repulsive for similar-sign charges.

> ▶ In equation form, Coulomb's law states that the electric force between two point charges Q_1 and Q_2 is given by
>
> $$F = \frac{1}{4\pi\varepsilon_0}\frac{Q_1 Q_2}{r^2}$$
>
> where r is the separation of the two charges (see Figure 1.8). The two charges are assumed to be point charges.

Figure 1.8 The force between two point electric charges is given by Coulomb's law. Shown here is the case of opposite charges.

We may call the factor $\frac{1}{4\pi\varepsilon_0}$ simply k, so that Coulomb's law reads

$$F = k\frac{Q_1 Q_2}{r^2}$$

The numerical value of the factor $\frac{1}{4\pi\varepsilon_0}$ or k is 8.99×10^9 N m^2 C^{-2} (we will often approximate the 8.99 to 9). The constant ε_0 is called the electric permittivity of a vacuum and $\varepsilon_0 = 8.85 \times 10^{-12}$ C^2 N^{-1} m^{-2}. The index zero in ε_0 signifies that we are considering the two charges to be in a vacuum. If the charges are in a medium, such as plastic or water, then we must use the value of ε appropriate to that medium in the formula above. Air has roughly the same value of ε as a vacuum. Note that this law is very similar to Newton's law of gravitation. Both forces are proportional to

products of masses or charges and both are inversely proportional to the square of the separation. This means that many problems in electricity have the same solution as corresponding problems in gravitation; the big difference is, of course, that there are two kinds of electric charge but only one kind of mass. Also, the gravitational force is always attractive whereas the electrical force can be either attractive or repulsive.

Example questions

Q2

Two charges, $q_1 = 4\ \mu C$ and $q_2 = 6\ \mu C$, are placed along a straight line separated by a distance of 2 cm. Find the force exerted on each charge.

Answer

This is a straightforward application of the formula $F = \frac{1}{4\pi\varepsilon_0}\frac{Q_1 Q_2}{r^2}$. We find that

$$F = \frac{9 \times 10^9 \times 4 \times 6 \times 10^{-12}}{4 \times 10^{-4}}\text{N}$$
$$= 540\ \text{N}$$

This is the force that q_1 exerts on q_2 and vice-versa.

Q3

At what distance from q_1 of example question 2 would a third positive charge experience no net force?

Answer

Let that distance be x. A positive charge Q at that point would experience a force from q_1 equal to $F_1 = \frac{1}{4\pi\varepsilon_0}\frac{q_1 Q}{x^2}$ and a force in the opposite direction from q_2 equal to $F_2 = \frac{1}{4\pi\varepsilon_0}\frac{q_2 Q}{(d-x)^2}$, where $d = 2$ cm is the distance between q_1 and q_2 (see Figure 1.9).

Figure 1.9.

Charge Q will experience no *net* force when $F_1 = F_2$, so

$$\frac{1}{4\pi\varepsilon_0}\frac{q_1 Q}{x^2} = \frac{1}{4\pi\varepsilon_0}\frac{q_2 Q}{(d-x)^2}$$

that is (substituting $q_1 = 4$ and $q_2 = 6$)

$$4(d-x)^2 = 6x^2$$
$$\Rightarrow x^2 + 4dx - 2d^2 = 0$$
$$\Rightarrow x = -2d \pm \sqrt{4d^2 + 2d^2}$$
$$= -2d \pm d\sqrt{6}$$

The two values of x are $x = 0.90$ cm and $x = -8.90$ cm. The second value is meaningless, so $x = 0.90$ cm.

Q4

Three charges $q_1 = 2\ \mu C$, $q_2 = 2\ \mu C$ and $q_3 = -3\ \mu C$ are at the vertices of an equilateral triangle, of side 3 cm. Find the net force on q_1.

Answer

q_1 experiences a force F_2 from q_2 and a force F_3 from q_3. Finding the magnitudes of F_2 and F_3 is easy: $F_2 = 40$ N and $F_3 = 60$ N. To find the net force (see Figure 1.10) we take horizontal and vertical components of the forces.

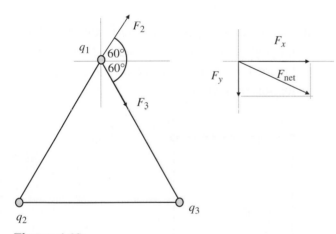

Figure 1.10.

Then

$$F_{2x} = F_2 \cos 60°$$
$$= 20 \text{ N}$$

$$F_{2y} = F_2 \sin 60°$$
$$= 34.64 \text{ N}$$

$$F_{3x} = F_3 \cos 60°$$
$$= 30 \text{ N}$$

$$F_{3y} = F_3 \sin 60°$$
$$= 51.96 \text{ N}$$

Thus, the net force in the x-direction is 50 N and that in the y-direction 17.32 N down. The

magnitude of the net force is therefore 52.9 N making an angle of 19.1° with the horizontal, as shown on the right of Figure 1.10.

Q5

Two equal charges q are suspended from strings as shown in Figure 1.11. Show that $\tan \theta = \frac{kq^2}{mgr^2}$.

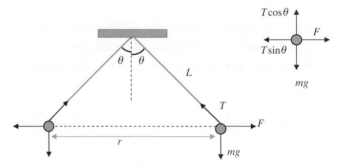

Figure 1.11.

Answer

Equilibrium demands that

$$T \cos \theta = mg$$
$$\Rightarrow T = \frac{mg}{\cos \theta}$$

and that

$$T \sin \theta = F$$
$$\Rightarrow F = \frac{mg}{\cos \theta} \sin \theta$$
$$= mg \tan \theta$$
$$\Rightarrow \tan \theta = \frac{F}{mg}$$

The electric force F is given by Coulomb's law as

$$F = k\frac{q^2}{r^2}$$

and so

$$\tan \theta = \frac{kq^2}{mgr^2}$$

Q6

Two identical conducting spheres are kept a certain distance r apart. One sphere has a positive charge Q on its surface and the other is neutral. The spheres are allowed to touch and are then separated. Write down an expression for the electric force between the spheres. One of the spheres is discharged. The spheres are then allowed to touch and then are separated again. Write down an expression for the electric force between the spheres now.

Answer

After touching each sphere has a charge $Q/2$ and so the force is

$$F = k\frac{(Q/2)(Q/2)}{r^2}$$

$$= k\frac{Q^2}{4r^2}$$

After discharging one of the spheres and then allowing the spheres to touch again, the charge on each sphere will be $Q/4$. The force is then

$$F = k\frac{(Q/4)(Q/4)}{r^2}$$

$$= k\frac{Q^2}{16r^2}$$

that is, one-quarter of the original force.

Questions

1 A positively charged electroscope is found to diverge even further when a body of unknown charge is brought near to (but does not touch) the electroscope. What sign does this charge have? A second body brought into the vicinity of the electroscope makes the electroscope leaf diverge less. If this body is known to be charged, what is the sign of the charge? How would the leaf of the positively charged electroscope react if the body were neutral?

2 When a flame is brought near a charged electroscope, the foil collapses. How is this explained?

3 Three identical conducting spheres have charges of $+3\,C$, $-2\,C$ and $-7\,C$. If all three are allowed to touch and are then separated, what will be the charge on each sphere?

4 (a) What is the force between two charges of $2.0\,\mu C$ and $4.0\,\mu C$ separated by 5.0 cm?
   (b) What does the force become if the separation is doubled?

5 Three charges are placed on a straight line as shown in Figure 1.12. Find the net force on the middle charge.

Figure 1.12 For question 5.

6 (a) In the previous question, where should the middle charge be placed so that it is in equilibrium?
   (b) Is this a position of stable or unstable equilibrium?

7 Find the force (magnitude and direction) on the charge Q in Figure 1.13 where $Q = 3\,\mu C$.

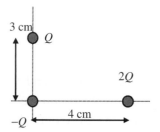

Figure 1.13 For question 7.

8 Four equal charges $Q = -5\,\mu C$ are placed at the vertices of a square of side 12 cm, as in Figure 1.14. Find the force on the charge at the top right vertex.

Figure 1.14 For question 8.

9 Two plastic spheres each of mass 100.0 mg are suspended from very fine insulating strings of length 85 cm. When equal charges are placed on the spheres, the spheres repel and are in equilibrium when 10 cm apart.
   (a) What is the charge on each sphere?
   (b) How many electron charges does this correspond to?

10 A small plastic sphere is suspended from a fine insulating thread near, but not touching, the sphere of a Van de Graaff generator that is

being charged. It is observed that the plastic sphere is slowly attracted toward the Van de Graaff sphere and eventually touches it, at which point it is violently repelled. Carefully explain these observations.

11 Consider two people, each of mass 60 kg, a distance of 10 m apart.
  (a) Assuming that all the mass in each person is made out of water, estimate how many electrons there are in each person.
  (b) Hence, *estimate* the electrostatic force of repulsion between the two people due to the electrons.
  (c) What other simplifying assumptions have you made to make your estimate possible?
  (d) No such force is observed in practice. Give one reason why this is so.

12 A negatively charged rod is allowed to touch the sphere of an electroscope that is initially uncharged. The rod is then removed. Draw the charge distribution of the electroscope and explain your drawing.

13 A positively charged rod is allowed to come close to, but not touch, the sphere of an electroscope that is initially uncharged.
  (a) Draw the charge distribution of the electroscope and explain your drawing.
  (b) The electroscope sphere is earthed while the rod is still nearby. Draw the charge distribution of the electroscope and explain your drawing.
  (c) The rod is now removed. Draw the charge distribution of the electroscope and explain your drawing.

14 Repeat the previous question but now assume that the cage of the electroscope is conducting and earthed.

15 A negatively charged sphere is lowered inside a hollow metallic container and is allowed to touch the inside of the container. The sphere is then removed. What is the charge on the sphere? How is the law of conservation of charge satisfied in this experiment?

Electric field and potential

Electric charges create electric fields in space. The notion of electric field and the related concept of electric potential are introduced in this chapter.

Objectives

By the end of this chapter you should be able to:

- appreciate that a charge q in an *electric field of magnitude E* will experience a force of magnitude $F = qE$;
- understand that the electric field of a point or spherical charge Q a distance r away has a magnitude given by $E_P = k\frac{Q}{r^2}$ and is radial in direction – the *field is zero inside* a charged conductor;
- understand that the *electric field inside parallel plates is uniform* and its magnitude is given by $E = \frac{V}{d}$;
- understand that the work done in moving a charge q across a *potential difference* ΔV is $W = q\,\Delta V$;
- understand that a charge q that is at a point where there is potential V will have an *electric potential energy* of $U = qV$;
- understand that a charge moving in an electric potential satisfies the *law of conservation of energy*: $\frac{1}{2}mv_A^2 + qV_A = \frac{1}{2}mv_B^2 + qV_B$.

Electric field

The space around a charge or an arrangement of charges is different from space in which no charges are present. We say that it contains an **electric field**. We can test whether a space has an electric field by bringing a small positive charge q into the space. If this small charge q experiences a force, then there exists an electric field there. If no force is experienced, then there is no electric field (the electric field is zero). This small charge is called a test charge, because it tests for the existence of electric fields. It has to be small so that its presence does not disturb other charges in its vicinity.

▶ We define the electric field as the force per unit charge experienced by a small positive test charge q:

$$\vec{E} = \frac{\vec{F}}{q}$$

Note that the electric field is a vector, its direction being the same as that of the force a positive charge would experience at the given point. It follows that the unit of electric field is $N\,C^{-1}$.

The concept of electric field allows us to understand how a force is transmitted from one charge to another. A charge q placed at a point where the electric field is $\vec{E}$ will experience a force given by $\vec{F} = q\vec{E}$.

> ▶ The electric field from a single point charge Q at a point a distance r away is
>
> $$E_P = k\frac{Q}{r^2}$$

This is because the force experienced by a test charge q placed at point P a distance r from Q is (by Coulomb's law)

$$F = k\frac{Qq}{r^2}$$

and so the electric field is

$$
\begin{aligned}
E_P &= \frac{F}{q} \\
&= \frac{k\left(Qq/r^2\right)}{q} \\
&= k\frac{Q}{r^2}
\end{aligned}
$$

(see Figure 2.1).

Figure 2.1.

Similarly, at a distance r from the centre of a sphere on which a charge Q has been placed, the electric field is given by the same formula as above. On the *surface* of the sphere of radius R the electric field is

$$E_P = k\frac{Q}{R^2}$$

but inside the sphere the electric field is zero.

> ▶ In electrostatics, the electric field is zero inside any conducting body (see Figure 2.2). This is because electrostatics deals with situations in which electric charge does not move. If an electric field existed inside a conductor it would force charges to move.

Figure 2.2 The electric field inside a conductor is zero.

Electric field lines

A very useful concept in dealing with electric fields is that of electric field lines. These are imaginary lines (curved or straight) with the property that the tangent to a field line at some point P gives the direction of the electric field at P. A single positive charge creates an electric field that is directed radially out of the charge. Thus the electric field lines in this case are straight lines coming radially out of the charge. In the case of a negative charge, the lines are directed into the charge. Figures 2.3–2.6 show the field lines for various arrangements of charges.

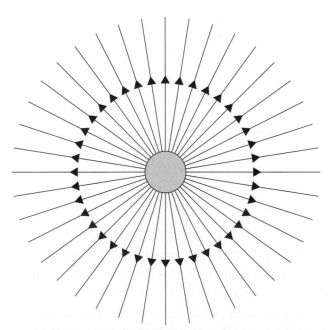

Figure 2.3 The electric field of a point or spherical charge is radial. The field of a negative charge would be directed inward.

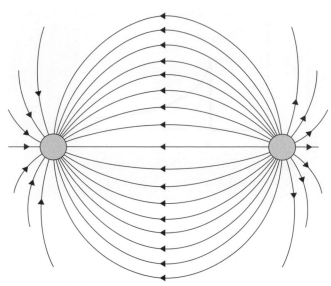

Figure 2.4 Electric field lines for two equal and opposite charges.

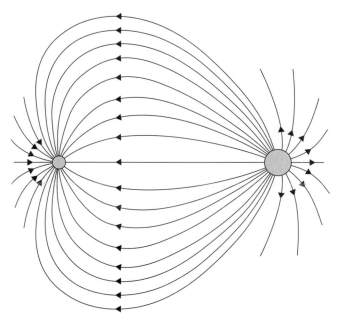

Figure 2.5 The electric field of two opposite and unequal charges. The charge to the right is three times larger than the left charge.

Electric field lines are usually drawn with the convention that the more lines starting from a charge, the larger the charge. The density of lines at a given point (i.e. the number of lines crossing a small area centred at the point) is proportional to the magnitude of the electric field at that point.

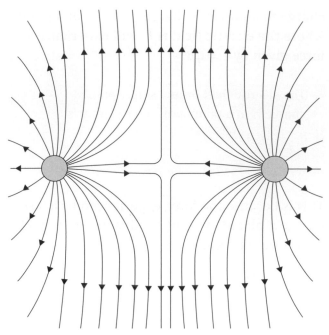

Figure 2.6 The electric field of two equal positive charges. The mid-point of the line joining the charges has zero electric field.

A *uniform* electric field is one that has constant magnitude and direction. Such a field is generated between two oppositely charged parallel plates (see Figure 2.7). Near the edges of the plates the field lines are curved, indicating that the field is no longer uniform there. This *edge effect* is minimized when the length of the plates is long compared with their separation.

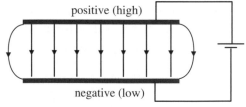

positive (high)

negative (low)

Figure 2.7 The electric field lines for two long, parallel charged plates.

Example question

Q1

The electric field between two parallel plates is 100.0 N C^{-1}. What acceleration would a charge of 2.0 μC and mass 10^{-3} kg experience if placed in this field? (Ignore its weight.)

Answer

The force is found from $F = Eq$ to be
$F = 2.0 \times 10^{-4}$ N. Now, using $F = ma$, we find
$a = 0.2 \text{ m s}^{-2}$.

Electric potential

An electric charge creates an electric field in
the space around it. It also creates a related
quantity, an **electric potential**. Consider a
positive charge Q and a positive test charge q.
If the charge q is moved closer to Q, work must
be done on q. This is because the two charges
repel and so a force must be applied to q to
make it move closer to Q.

▶ If the work done in moving the positive
test charge q from very far away to some
position P near Q is W, then the quantity

$$V = \frac{W}{q}$$

defines the potential at P. In other words,
the potential at a point is the *work per unit
charge* that must be done to bring the
positive test charge from far away to the
point of interest. The unit of potential is
the volt, and $1 \text{ V} = 1 \text{ J C}^{-1}$. (See Figure 2.8.)

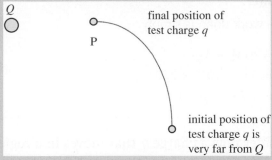

Figure 2.8 The work performed to bring the
small positive charge from far away to a
point near the charge Q goes into electric
potential energy.

Example question

Q2 ▬▬▬▬▬▬▬▬

The work done in moving a test charge of 2.0 μC
from very far away to a point P is 150×10^{-6} J.
What is the potential at P?

Answer

From the definition, the electric potential at P is

$$V = \frac{W}{q}$$
$$= \frac{150 \times 10^{-6}}{2 \times 10^{-6}}$$
$$= 75 \text{ V}$$

The route taken by a charge q to get to P does
not affect the amount of work that has to be
done on the charge (see Figure 2.9).

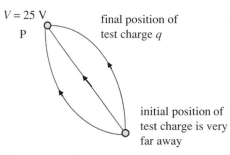

Figure 2.9 The work done in moving a charge q
from far away to P is the same no matter what
path is followed. If $q = 2$ C the work done is 50 J
for all three paths.

The work that is done in moving the test charge
q from far away to point P goes into electric
potential energy of the charge q. Thus, if the
potential at some point in space is V volts and a
charge q is placed at that point, the electric
potential energy of the charge is

$$U = qV$$

Example question

Q3 ▬▬▬▬▬▬▬▬

The potential at a point P is 12 V and a charge of
3 C is placed there. What is the electric potential
energy of the charge? What is the electric
potential energy if, instead, a charge of −2 C is
placed at P?

Answer

The electric potential energy of the charge is

$$U = qV$$
$$= 3 \times 12$$
$$= 36 \text{ J}$$

If a negative charge is placed at P, the electric potential energy is

$$U = qV$$
$$= (-2) \times 12$$
$$= -24 \text{ J}$$

Potential difference

Consider now an arrangement of charges that creates an electric potential in the space around it. What happens when a charge q is moved from one point to another? In Figure 2.10 the electric potential at point A is 15 V and at point B it is 28 V. A charge of 2 C initially at A is to be moved to B. What work must be done on the charge?

Figure 2.10 A charge moving across a potential difference.

The electric potential energy of the charge in position A is

$$U_A = qV_A$$
$$= 2 \times 15$$
$$= 30 \text{ J}$$

The electric potential energy at position B is

$$U_B = qV_B$$
$$= 2 \times 28$$
$$= 56 \text{ J}$$

The change in the potential energy is thus

$$\Delta U = U_B - U_A$$
$$= 56 - 30$$
$$= 26 \text{ J}$$

This is the work that must be done.

▶ In general, the work that must be done *on* a charge q to move it from point A, where the potential is V_A, to point B, where the potential is V_B, is given by

$$W = \Delta U$$
$$= U_B - U_A$$
$$= qV_B - qV_A$$
$$= q(V_B - V_A)$$

that is, it is the product of the charge times the potential difference between the two points.

Example question

Q4

What work must be performed in order to move a charge of 5.0 μC from the negative to the positive plate if a potential difference of 250 V is established between the plates? (See Figure 2.11.)

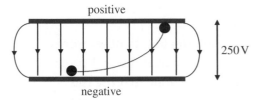

Figure 2.11.

Answer

The work done is simply

$$W = q(V_B - V_A)$$
$$= 5.0 \times 10^{-6} \times 250$$
$$= 1.25 \times 10^{-3} \text{ J}$$

Consider now a charge q that moves in a region of electric potential. Let the speed of the charge be v_A at position A and v_B at position B. The electric potential at point A is V_A and at point B it is V_B (see Figure 2.12). The mass of the charge is m.

The work done *by* the electric force acting on the charge is opposite to the work done *on* the charge and so

$$W_{\text{electric}} = -q(V_B - V_A)$$

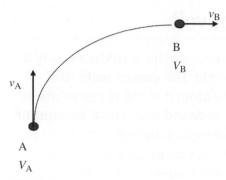

Figure 2.12.

but from mechanics we know that the work done by the net force on a body equals the change in the kinetic energy of the body. Thus

$$W_{electric} = -q(V_B - V_A) = \tfrac{1}{2}mv_B^2 - \tfrac{1}{2}mv_A^2$$

which simplifies to

$$\tfrac{1}{2}mv_A^2 + qV_A = \tfrac{1}{2}mv_B^2 + qV_B$$

We can easily interpret this equation: it simply says that, as the charge moves, the sum of the kinetic and electric potential energies stays the same (i.e. the total energy is conserved).

Example questions

Q5

A charge of 5 μC and mass 2×10^{-6} kg is shot with speed 3×10^2 m s^{-1} between two parallel plates kept at a potential of 200 V and 500 V, respectively, as shown in Figure 2.13. What will the speed be when the charge gets to the right plate?

200 V   500 V

Figure 2.13.

Answer

We apply conservation of energy and so

$$\tfrac{1}{2}\left[2 \times 10^{-6} \times (3 \times 10^2)^2\right] + (5 \times 10^{-6} \times 200)$$
$$= \tfrac{1}{2}(2 \times 10^{-6} \times v_B^2) + (5 \times 10^{-6} \times 500)$$
$$\Rightarrow v_B = 86.6 \text{ m s}^{-1}$$

Q6

What must the initial velocity of an electron be if it is to reach the right plate of Figure 2.14 and momentarily stop there? (Charge of electron $= -1.6 \times 10^{-19}$ C; mass of electron $= 9.1 \times 10^{-31}$ kg.)

2 V   0 V

Figure 2.14.

Answer

We use conservation of energy again to find

$$\tfrac{1}{2}(9.1 \times 10^{-31} \times v^2) + (-1.6 \times 10^{-19}) \times 2 = 0$$
$$\Rightarrow v = 8.4 \times 10^5 \text{ m s}^{-1}.$$

The electric field between parallel plates

So far we only have a formula for the electric field of a point or spherical charge. In the case of parallel plates, the expression for the electric field is

$$E = \frac{V}{d}$$

where V is the potential difference between the plates and d is their separation. The electric field has this value at all points in between the plates. Its direction is from high to low potential (see Figure 2.15).

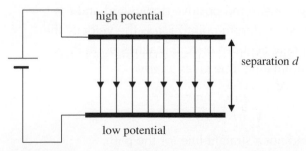

Figure 2.15.

Example question

Q7

Figure 2.16 shows two long, parallel, oppositely charged, vertical plates. Draw and explain the path followed by a positively charged sphere of charge q and mass m when:

(a) the sphere is released from rest at point P;

HL only

(b) the sphere is released from rest outside the plates at point Q above P.

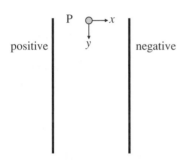

Figure 2.16.

Answer

The sphere is acted upon by two forces: the weight mg and the electrical force qE, where E is the horizontal electric field between the plates. Thus, the sphere has a vertical component of acceleration equal to g and a horizontal component of qE/m to the right.

(a) There is no initial velocity here and so the charge will follow a straight-line path along the direction of the resultant force.

(b) Between the two plates, the horizontal and vertical components of displacement are

$$x = \frac{1}{2}\frac{qE}{m}t^2 \qquad y = ut + \frac{1}{2}gt^2$$

(y is measured positive downward and t is measured from point P). u is the velocity the sphere acquires once it reaches point P. Eliminating time gives a curve

$$y = u\sqrt{\frac{2mx}{qE}} + \frac{mg}{qE}x$$

and not a straight line for the path.

The electronvolt

The study of atomic physics introduces us to a world of small scale. The energy scale that characterizes the atomic world is one of about 10^{-18} J. This is a tremendously small amount of energy by macroscopic standards; the joule is not the appropriate energy unit for atomic physics. A more convenient unit is the electronvolt, eV. When a charge q is moved from a point A to a point B between which a potential difference ΔV exists, then the work done is $W = q\Delta V$.

▶ This relationship allows us to define the electronvolt as the work done when a charge equal to one electron charge is taken across a potential difference of one volt. Thus

$$1\,\text{eV} = 1.6 \times 10^{-19}\,\text{C} \times 1\,\text{V}$$
$$= 1.6 \times 10^{-19}\,\text{J}$$

If a charge equal to two electron charges is taken across a potential difference of 1 V, the work done is 2 eV; a charge of three electron charges across a potential difference of 5 V results in work of 15 eV and so on.

Example question

Q8

What is the speed of a mass $m = 1.6 \times 10^{-27}$ kg whose kinetic energy is 5000 eV?

Answer

From

$$E_k = \tfrac{1}{2}mv^2$$

$$\Rightarrow v = \sqrt{\frac{2E_k}{m}}$$

$$= \sqrt{\frac{2 \times 5000 \times 1.6 \times 10^{-19}}{1.6 \times 10^{-27}}}\ \text{m s}^{-1}$$

$$= 10^6\ \text{m s}^{-1}$$

The point being made here is that in calculations electronvolts must be changed to joules, the SI unit of energy.

Questions

1 Draw the field lines for:
  (a) two equal charges;
  (b) two equal and opposite charges;
  (c) two charges of the same sign, one double the other;
  (d) two charges of opposite sign, one double the other.

2 Why must field lines be normal to conducting surfaces in electrostatics?

3 Draw the electric field at the points indicated in Figure 2.17 showing their relative size. The charges on the spheres are equal in magnitude.

Figure 2.17 For question 3.

4 Two parallel plates are separated by 10.0 cm and a potential difference of 500.0 V is maintained between them. What is the force on an electron placed:
  (a) 2.0 cm from the bottom plate;
  (b) 4.0 cm from the bottom plate;
  (c) 6.0 cm from the bottom plate?
  (d) How much work is required to move an electron from a position 2.0 cm from the bottom plate to a position 2.0 cm from the top plate?

5 The electric field at a point in space has magnitude 100 N C^{-1} and is directed to the right. If an electron is placed at that point, what force and acceleration would it experience?

6 If a charge of magnitude +5.0 μC experiences an electric force of magnitude 3.0×10^{-5} N when placed at a point in space, find the electric field at that point.

7 The electric field is a vector and so two electric fields at the same point in space must be added according to the laws of vector addition. Consider two equal positive charges, each 2.00 μC, separated by $a = 10.0$ cm and a point P a distance of $d = 30.0$ cm as shown in Figure 2.18. The diagram shows the directions of the electric fields produced at P by each charge. Find the magnitude and direction of the net electric field at P.

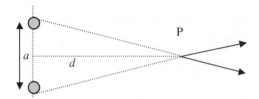

Figure 2.18 For question 7.

8 Repeat the calculation of question 7 for two charges that are unequal. Take the top charge to be 4.00 μC and the other 2.00 μC.

9 Figure 2.19 shows lines along which the electric potential is constant and has the value given.
  (a) Find the work that is required if a charge of 5.0 C is to be moved from the 100.0 V line to the 200.0 V line along path I.
  (b) How much work would be required if the same charge were moved along path II?
  (c) If the 5.0 C charge were first to move to the 300.0 V line along path II and then to the 200.0 V line along path III, how much work would be required then? Compare your answer to that in part (a).

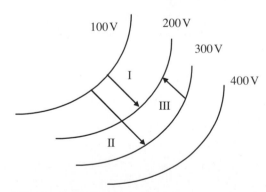

Figure 2.19 For question 9.

10 (a) An electron placed on the 100.0 V surface described in question 9 and released from rest would accelerate toward higher potential. What speed would it acquire by the time it reached the 200.0 V surface?

(b) If a proton were released from the 200.0 V surface, it would accelerate toward lower potential. What speed would it have when it reached the 100.0 V surface?

11 Two uniform electric fields of magnitude $E_1 = 115 \text{ N C}^{-1}$ and $E_2 = 125 \text{ N C}^{-1}$ are produced by two pairs of parallel plates as shown in Figure 2.20. Find the magnitude and direction of the net electric field at the points indicated.

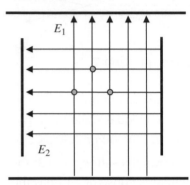

Figure 2.20 For question 11.

12 A conducting sphere of radius 15.0 cm has a positive charge of 4.0 μC deposited on its surface. Find the magnitude of the electric field produced by the charge at distances from the centre of the sphere of:

(a) 0.0 cm;

(b) 5.0 cm;

(c) 15.0 cm;

(d) 20.0 cm.

Electric field and potential

This chapter deals with more involved examples of electric fields and potentials and discusses the connection between electric field and electric potential. The concept of electric potential energy is introduced and discussed in simple situations.

Objectives

By the end of this chapter you should be able to:

* define the terms *electric field*, *electric potential* and *electric potential energy* ($U_{el} = qV_P$) and calculate these quantities in simple situations;
* define *equipotential surfaces* and *field lines* and state the *relationship between them*;
* understand that *electric fields* and *electric potentials* are *related* by
$E = \frac{\Delta V}{\Delta r}$ or $E = -\frac{dV}{dr}$;
* understand that the *potential is constant inside a conductor* and the *electric field is zero*;
* understand that *work is done when a charge moves across a potential difference* $W_{B \to A} = q(V_A - V_B)$;
* state the similarities and differences between *gravitation* and *electricity*.

Electric fields

As we saw in Chapter 5.2, if a positive test charge q experiences an electric force $\vec{F}$, the electric field at the position of the test charge is defined as the ratio of the force to the charge:

$$\vec{E} = \frac{\vec{F}}{q}$$

The direction of the electric field is the same as the direction of the force (on the *positive* test charge q). At a point a distance r away from a charge Q, the magnitude of the electric field is

$$E_P = k\frac{Q}{r^2}$$

Vector methods can then be used to find the electric field due to an arrangement of point charges. An example is that of the dipole, which has two equal and opposite charges separated by a distance a (see Figure 3.1).

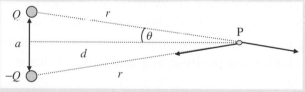

Figure 3.1 Two equal and opposite charges separated by a given distance form an electric dipole. The diagram shows the electric fields that must be added as vectors to get the net electric field at P.

We would like to find the electric field created by a dipole. It is easiest to find this field on the perpendicular bisector of the line joining the charges. At other points, the answer is more involved. Thus, consider a point a distance d from the midpoint of the line joining the charges. The electric field at P has a contribution of $E_P = \frac{1}{4\pi\varepsilon}\frac{Q}{r^2}$ from each charge, directed as shown. The horizontal components will cancel each other out but the vertical components add up. The vertical component of E_P is $E_P \sin\theta$ and since $\sin\theta = a/2r$ we find (recall $r^2 = d^2 + \frac{a^2}{4}$)

$$E = \frac{1}{4\pi\varepsilon_0} \frac{Qa}{\left(d^2 + \frac{a^2}{4}\right)^{\frac{3}{2}}}$$

This is directed vertically downwards, in the direction of the vector from Q to $-Q$. The quantity Qa is called the *dipole moment*.

If both charges were positive, the corresponding electric field would be given by

$$E = \frac{1}{4\pi\varepsilon_0} \frac{2Qd}{\left(d^2 + \frac{a^2}{4}\right)^{\frac{3}{2}}}$$

and would be horizontal (along the perpendicular bisector to the line joining the charges).

Electric potential and energy

Suppose that at some point in space we place a charge Q. Assume for concreteness that it is a positive charge. If we place another positive charge q nearby and try to move it even closer to the large charge Q, we will have to exert a force on q, since it is being repelled by Q (see Figure 3.2). That is, we have to do work in order to change the position of q and bring it closer to Q.

Q

q brought near Q ⟵ q at infinity

Figure 3.2.

▶ We have already defined (in the previous chapter) the electric potential at a point P as the amount of work done per unit charge as a small positive test charge q is moved from infinity to the point P, that is

$$V_P = \frac{W}{q}$$

The unit of potential is the volt (V), and $1\,\text{V} = 1\,\text{J}\,\text{C}^{-1}$.

The work done in moving a charge q from infinity to point P goes into *electric potential energy*. Thus

▶ If the potential at some point P is V_P, and we place a charge q at P, the quantity

$$U_{\text{el}} = qV_P$$

is the electric potential energy of the charge q.

Electric potential and electric potential energy are scalar quantities. Note the definition of potential, which involves taking a charge from infinity to some point P. This definition does not specify along which path the charge must be moved from infinity to point P. In fact, the properties of electric potential are such that the amount of work done would be the same irrespective of which path is taken. This is reminiscent of gravity: the change in gravitational potential energy when a mass m is moved from a position A to a position B is always mgh where h is the vertical separation of the two points A and B. The actual path followed by the mass is irrelevant. The gravitational and electric forces are called *conservative* for this reason. Friction is an example of a force where the amount of work done does depend on the path followed: it is obviously harder to push a heavy suitcase a long distance as opposed to a short distance. Such forces are called *dissipative*. An immediate property of conservative forces is that, if a body is moved along a closed path, the amount of work done is zero. This also means that, if the potential at point P is V volts, the amount of work done when a charge q is taken from P to infinity is $-qV$.

Consider now two points, A and B, in the vicinity of a charge Q (see Figure 3.3). The electric charge creates an electric potential everywhere in space, and at points A and B the potential is V_A and V_B, respectively. If we place a charge q at point B and move it from B to A, what is the work done? Since the amount of work done is independent of the path followed, we can calculate this work along paths for which we know the answer. We first take the charge from B to infinity and then from infinity to A.

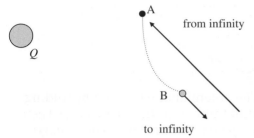

Figure 3.3 Work must be done in order to move a charge from one point to another where the potential is different.

On the first leg, the work done is $-qV_B$ and on the second leg it is qV_A. Thus, the total work done is

$$W_{B \to A} = q(V_A - V_B)$$

The quantity $V_A - V_B$ is the potential difference between A and B. Points at infinity are considered to be at zero potential. We have talked at some length about the electric potential that a charge Q creates in space. But how do we calculate this potential? To do this we need calculus, so what follows may be omitted and only the result may be noted.

Supplementary material

When the positive charge q is at some distance r from Q, it experiences a repulsive force

$$F = \frac{1}{4\pi\varepsilon_0}\frac{Qq}{r^2}$$

Thus, the force with which we must push the charge q to move it closer to Q is directed as shown in Figure 3.4. If we push a small distance dr, the work done is dW and

$$dW = -Fdr$$

$$= -\frac{1}{4\pi\varepsilon_0}\frac{Qq}{r^2}dr$$

Figure 3.4 Diagram for calculating the work done in moving a positive charge from infinity to a point near another charge.

(The minus sign in dW is there because the force pushes the charge towards Q but dr is positive when directed away from Q.) The total work done is therefore

$$W = -\int_{\infty}^{R}\frac{1}{4\pi\varepsilon_0}\frac{Qq}{r^2}dr$$

$$= \frac{1}{4\pi\varepsilon_0}\frac{Qq}{r}\Big|_{\infty}^{R}$$

$$= \frac{1}{4\pi\varepsilon_0}\frac{Qq}{R}$$

But, by definition, $W = qV_P$, so

$$V_P = \frac{1}{4\pi\varepsilon_0}\frac{Q}{R}$$

Thus, the electric energy of a charge q a distance r from another charge Q is

$$U = \frac{1}{4\pi\varepsilon_0}\frac{Qq}{r}$$

In all these formulae, the charges must be entered with their correct sign.

Example questions

Q1
Find the electric potential energy between the proton in a hydrogen atom and an electron orbiting the proton at a radius 0.5×10^{-10} m. The proton has a charge 1.6×10^{-19} C, equal and opposite to that of the electron.

Answer
From the formula

$$U = \frac{1}{4\pi\varepsilon_0}\frac{Qq}{r}$$

$$= 9 \times 10^9 \times \frac{1.6 \times 10^{-19} \times (-1.6 \times 10^{-19})}{0.5 \times 10^{-10}}$$

$$= -46 \times 10^{-19} \text{ J}$$

Q2

Find the electric potential a distance of 0.50×10^{-10} m from the proton of the hydrogen atom.

Answer

$$V_0 = \frac{1}{4\pi\varepsilon_0}\frac{Q}{r}$$

and so

$$V_P = 9 \times 10^9 \times \frac{1.60 \times 10^{-19}}{0.50 \times 10^{-10}}$$

$$= 29 \text{ V}$$

Q3

Find the electric potential energy for four charges of 2 μC each placed at the vertices of a square of side 10 cm.

Answer

Naming the charges as 1, 2, 3 and 4 (see Figure 3.5) we see that there are six pairs of charges: (1, 2), (1, 3), (1, 4), (2, 3), (2, 4) and (3, 4)

Figure 3.5.

Therefore

$$U = 9 \times 10^9 \times 4 \times 10^{-12}$$

$$\times \left[\frac{1}{10} + \frac{1}{10} + \frac{1}{10} + \frac{1}{10} + \frac{1}{10\sqrt{2}} + \frac{1}{10\sqrt{2}} \right]$$

$$\times 10^2 \text{ J}$$

Thus

$$U = 1.9 \text{ J}$$

Electric potential is a scalar quantity. So if we have not one but two charges, Q_1 and Q_2, the electric potential at a point P that is a distance r_1 from Q_1 and a distance r_2 from Q_2 is just

$$V_P = \frac{1}{4\pi\varepsilon_0}\frac{Q_1}{r_1} + \frac{1}{4\pi\varepsilon_0}\frac{Q_2}{r_2}$$

that is, we first find the potential at P from Q_1 alone then from Q_2 alone and add up the two (see Figure 3.6).

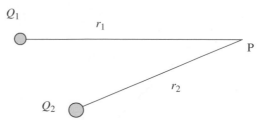

Figure 3.6 The potential at P is found by finding the potential there from the first charge, then finding the potential from the second charge, and finally adding the two.

Figure 3.7 shows the electric potential from one positive and one negative charge. In the absence of charges, the surface would be flat. The potential is represented by the height from the flat surface.

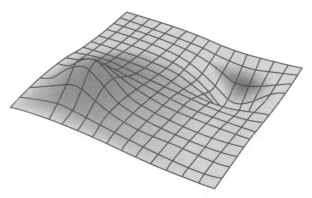

Figure 3.7 The electric potential due to two equal and opposite charges. The potential is proportional to the height of the surface.

The same procedure is followed for more than two charges. This simple formula for electric potential works in the case of point charges: that is, the objects on which the charges Q_i are placed are mathematical points or close to it. It also works in another special case. It works if the object on which the charge Q is placed is a sphere. But this is somewhat more delicate. If the point P is outside the sphere and at a distance r from the centre of the sphere, then

the potential at P is indeed

$$V_P = \frac{1}{4\pi\varepsilon_0}\frac{Q}{r}$$

On the surface of the sphere the potential is

$$V_P = \frac{1}{4\pi\varepsilon_0}\frac{Q}{R}$$

where R is the radius of the sphere. But at any point inside the sphere the electric potential is constant and has the same value as the potential at the surface. (See Figure 3.8.)

(a)

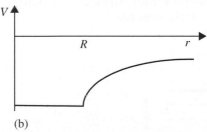

(b)

Figure 3.8 The electric potential is constant inside the sphere and falls off as $1/r$ outside. Shown here are (a) a positively charged sphere and (b) a negatively charged sphere.

Example questions

Q4

Two spheres of radii r and $R = 10r$ are connected by a long conducting wire. Before connecting, the big sphere had an amount of charge Q on it. How much charge is there on each sphere now?

Answer

See Figure 3.9.

The potential on the big sphere is $V_1 = \frac{Q_1}{4\pi\varepsilon_0 R}$ and on the small sphere $V_2 = \frac{Q_2}{4\pi\varepsilon_0 r}$. Here $Q_1 + Q_2 = Q$, by conservation of electric charge. When connected by the wire the two surfaces

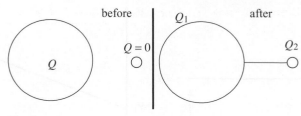

Figure 3.9.

must be at the same potential, $V_1 = V_2$, and so

$$\frac{1}{4\pi\varepsilon_0}\frac{Q_1}{R} = \frac{1}{4\pi\varepsilon_0}\frac{Q_2}{r}$$

$$\Rightarrow \frac{Q_1}{R} = \frac{Q_2}{r}$$

Using $R = 10r$ we find $Q_1 = \frac{10}{11}Q$ and $Q_2 = \frac{1}{11}Q$. It can be seen that the big sphere has more charge than the small one even though they are both at the same potential.

Q5

Find the ratio of the electric field on the surface of the small sphere to that on the surface of the big sphere in example question 4.

Answer

$$E_1 = \frac{Q_1}{4\pi\varepsilon_0 R^2}$$

$$= \frac{10\,Q/11}{4\pi\varepsilon_0(10r)^2}$$

$$= \frac{10\,Q/11}{4\pi\varepsilon_0 100r^2}$$

$$= \frac{Q}{4\pi\varepsilon_0 r^2} \times \frac{1}{10 \times 11}$$

$$E_2 = \frac{Q_2}{4\pi\varepsilon_0 r^2}$$

$$= \frac{Q/11}{4\pi\varepsilon_0 r^2}$$

$$= \frac{Q}{4\pi\varepsilon_0 r^2} \times \frac{1}{11}$$

and so

$$\frac{E_2}{E_1} = 10$$

that is, the small sphere has a bigger electric field on its surface. The small sphere is more curved than the big one and electric fields are largest near sharp objects.

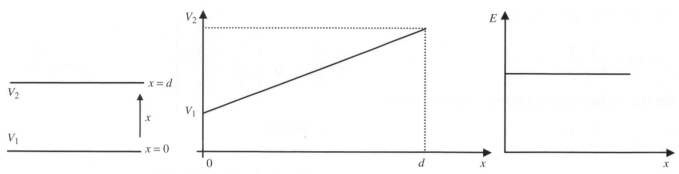

Figure 3.10 The potential increases uniformly as we move from the lower to the upper plate.

Parallel plates

There is one other case that is straightforward enough to allow us to write down a simple formula for the electric potential. This is the case of two long parallel plates separated by a distance d (see Figure 3.10).

If, for the sake of convenience, we take the top plate to have the higher potential, V_2, and the lower plate to have potential V_1, then the potential at any point with vertical distance x from the lower plate is

$$V(x) = V_1 + (V_2 - V_1)\frac{x}{d}$$

You can check that this formula gives the correct answers when $x = 0$ (lower plate) and $x = d$ (top plate). Halfway between the plates $x = \frac{d}{2}$ and $V = \frac{V_1 + V_2}{2}$. The potential increases uniformly from the lower plate to the top. The electric field between the plates is uniform, as we already know.

Equipotential surfaces

Points in space that have the same potential are said to define equipotential surfaces. For example, for a single charge Q, the equipotential surfaces are concentric spheres centred at the charge, as shown in Figure 3.11.

All the points on a given sphere are at the same distance from the charge and hence at the same potential. For the two parallel plates, the

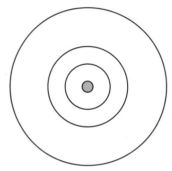

Figure 3.11 The equipotential surfaces of a point charge are concentric spheres.

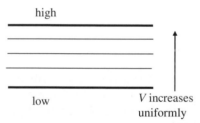

Figure 3.12 The equipotential surfaces for two parallel charged plates are planar.

equipotential surfaces are planes parallel to the plates (see Figure 3.12).

Figure 3.13 shows the equipotential lines for two charges: a positive charge of 4 C at point (−0.3, −0.3) and a negative one of −1 C at point (0.7, 0.7).

When a charge moves from one point of an equipotential surface to another point on the same equipotential surface, the work done is zero, since the potential difference between the two points is zero.

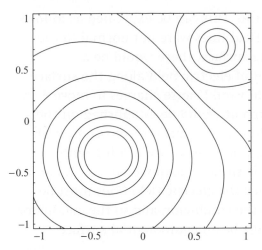

Figure 3.13 The equipotential surfaces of two opposite, unequal charges.

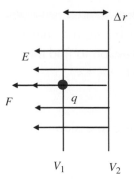

Figure 3.14 The electric field lines are directed to the left and so is the force on the positive charge q. If the charge is moved to the right, work must be performed.

The connection between electric potential and electric field

There is a deep connection between electric potential and electric field.

▶ If the electric potential at a point in space is V and the electric field at that same point has a magnitude E then

$$E = \frac{\Delta V}{\Delta r} \quad \left(\text{in calculus } E = -\frac{dV}{dr} \right)$$

(the minus sign is needed if we use calculus methods but not otherwise). This says that the electric field is the gradient of the electric potential. Thus, in a graph of electric potential versus distance, the slope is the electric field.

We can show this as follows (see Figure 3.14). Let a small positive charge q be placed at a point where the potential is V_1. We want to move it a distance Δr away to a position where the potential is at a higher value V_2. The force on the charge is $F = qE$ and so the work done is $W = F\,\Delta r = qE\,\Delta r$. But the work can also be found from $W = q\,\Delta V$, and so

$$qE\,\Delta r = q\,\Delta V$$
$$\Rightarrow E = \frac{\Delta V}{\Delta r}$$

This says, in particular, that if the electric potential is constant in some region of space, then the electric field is zero there. (Recall that the electric potential is constant inside a conducting sphere; the result above says therefore that the electric field is zero inside the sphere as we stated earlier.) This relationship also states that if the potential difference between two parallel plates is V and the separation between the plates is d then $E = \frac{V}{d}$ and is the same at all points inside the plates. It is perpendicular to the plates and is directed from high to low potential.

Example questions

Q6

A wire of length L has a potential difference V across its ends. Find the electric field inside the wire. Hence find the work done when a charge q is moved from one end of the wire to the other.

Answer

From $E = \frac{\Delta V}{\Delta r}$ it follows that $E = \frac{V}{L}$. The work done can be found in two ways. Either by using

$$W = q\Delta V = qV$$

or by

$$W = Fd = qEL = q\frac{V}{L}L = qV$$

as before.

Q7

The electric potential a distance r from a charge Q is $V = \frac{1}{4\pi\varepsilon_0}\frac{Q}{r}$. Use this expression to find the electric field at the same point.

Answer

Here we must use the calculus expression

$$E = -\frac{dV}{dr}$$
$$= -\frac{d}{dr}\left(\frac{1}{4\pi\varepsilon_0}\frac{Q}{r}\right)$$
$$= \frac{1}{4\pi\varepsilon_0}\frac{Q}{r^2}$$

as we expect.

The connection between electric potential and electric field extends to equipotential surfaces and electric field lines. It can be shown that electric field lines are always normal to equipotential surfaces. Figure 3.15 illustrates the equipotential surfaces due to a positive point charge and superimposed on these surfaces are arrows representing the electric field lines of the charge.

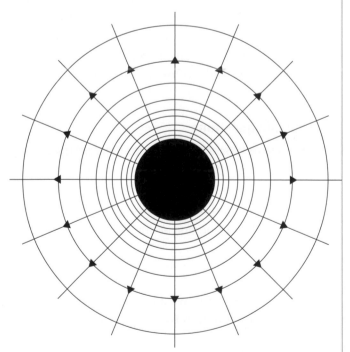

Figure 3.15 The electric field is normal to the equipotential surfaces.

The surfaces of conductors are equipotential surfaces, so electric field lines in the presence of conducting surfaces are normal to them, as

in Figure 3.16. This can be explained as follows. If electric field lines were not normal to the conducting surface, there would be a component of electric field along the surface. Such a field would cause charges to move – an electric current would be established on the surface. This, however, is not consistent with the assumption that we are dealing with electrostatic situations, in which charges do not move. Hence the electric field lines must be normal to the conductor, and so the conductor surface must be an equipotential surface.

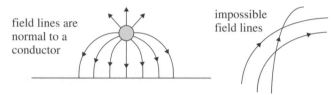

field lines are normal to a conductor

impossible field lines

Figure 3.16 Properties of field lines. Field lines are normal to conducting surfaces. Field lines cannot cross.

Electricity and gravitation

As is clear from a comparison between Newton's law of gravitation and Coulomb's law, there are many similarities between electricity and gravitation. Table 3.1 shows a few of the

	Gravitation	**Electricity**
Acts on	Mass (positive only)	Charge (positive or negative)
Force	$F = G\frac{M_1 M_2}{r^2}$ Attractive only Infinite range	$F = \frac{1}{4\pi\varepsilon_0}\frac{Q_1 Q_2}{r}$ Attractive or repulsive Infinite range
Relative strength	1	10^{42}
Field	$g = G\frac{M}{r^2}$	$E = \frac{1}{4\pi\varepsilon_0}\frac{Q}{r^2}$
Potential	$V = -G\frac{M}{r}$	$V = \frac{1}{4\pi\varepsilon_0}\frac{Q}{r}$
Work done	Independent of path	Independent of path
Potential energy	$U = -G\frac{Mm}{r}$	$U = \frac{1}{4\pi\varepsilon_0}\frac{Qq}{r}$

Table 3.1 A comparison of gravitation and electricity.

similarities and differences between the two. The biggest difference is, of course, the existence of two kinds of electric charge, which implies that the electric force can be attractive or repulsive. The one kind of mass leads to only attractive forces.

Supplementary material

In some innovative work during the early part of the twentieth century, T. Kaluza and O. Klein considered that the universe has four space and one time dimensions instead of the usual three plus one. The extra dimension, they claimed, is curled up as a tiny circle and is essentially unobservable. They then showed that if gravitation is the only force in this five-dimensional universe and we now insist on looking at only its four-dimensional part, electricity arises naturally from gravitation in this reduction from five to four dimensions!

Questions

1 A charged rod is brought near three conducting spheres resting on insulated stands, as shown in Figure 3.17. The spheres are originally touching. If they are now separated with the rod still nearby, what will be the sign of the charge on each sphere after the rod is taken away?

Figure 3.17 For question 1.

2 Four equal charges of 5 μC are placed at the vertices of a square of side 10 cm.
   (a) What is the value of the electric potential at the centre of the square?
   (b) What is the electric field there?
   (c) How do you reconcile your answer with the fact that the electric field is the derivative of the potential?

3 (a) What is the electric potential at the mid-point of the line joining two equal positive charges Q? Take their separation to be d.
   (b) What is the electric potential at the mid-point of the line joining two equal but opposite charges?

4 Two charges, $Q_1 = 2\,\mu C$ and $Q_2 = -4\,\mu C$, are 0.3 m apart. Find the electric potential at a point P which is 0.4 m from Q_1 and 0.6 m from Q_2.

5 A charge Q of 10.0 C is placed somewhere in space. What is the work required to bring a charge of 1.0 mC from a point X, 10.0 m from Q, to a point Y, 2.0 m from Q? Does the answer depend on which path the charge follows?

6 An electron is brought from infinity to a distance of 10.0 cm from a charge of −10.0 C. How much work was done on the electron?

7 An electron moves from a point in space where the potential is 100.0 V to another point where the potential is 200.0 V. If it started from rest, what is its speed at the end of the trip?

8 Four charges are placed at the vertices of a square of side 5.00 cm, as shown in Figure 3.18.
   (a) On the diagram, show the forces acting on the 2 μC charge. Find the magnitude and direction of the net force on the 2 μC charge.
   (b) Calculate the value of the electric potential at the centre of the square.
   (c) How much work must be done in order to move a charge of 1 nC initially at infinity to the centre of the square?

Figure 3.18 For question 8.

9 The electric dipole moment of a molecule is 6.2×10^{-30} cm and the charges are assumed to be $\pm 1.6 \times 10^{-19}$ C. The molecule finds itself in a uniform electric field of value 2.00×10^6 V m^{-1} that is directed along the plane of the page (see Figure 3.19). The dipole also lies on the page.

(a) What is the separation of the charges?

(b) What is the net force on the dipole?

(c) What is the largest torque on the molecule about an axis through its middle and normal to the plane?

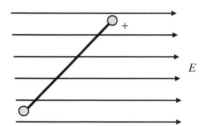

Figure 3.19 For question 9.

10 Two conducting spheres are separated by a distance that is large compared with their radii. The first sphere has a radius of 10.0 cm and has a charge of 2.00 μC on its surface. The second sphere has a radius of 15.0 cm and is neutral. The spheres are then connected by a long conducting wire.

(a) Find the charge on each sphere.

(b) Calculate the charge density on each sphere (charge density is the total charge on the sphere divided by the surface area of the sphere).

(c) Calculate the electric field on the surface of each sphere.

(d) Comment on your result in the light of your answer to part (b). Why is it stated that the wire is long?

11 Figure 3.20 shows the equipotential lines for two equal and opposite charges. Draw the electric field lines for these two charges.

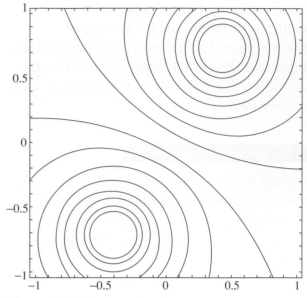

Figure 3.20 For question 11.

12 Two long parallel plates are separated by a distance of 15.0 cm. The bottom plate is kept at a potential of -250 V and the top at $+250$ V. A charge of -2.00 μC is placed at a point 3.00 cm from the bottom plate.

(a) Find the electric potential energy of the charge.

The charge is then moved vertically up to a point 3.00 cm from the top plate.

(b) What is the electrical potential energy of the charge now?

(c) How much work was done on the charge?

13 An electron is shot with a speed equal to 1.59×10^6 m s^{-1} from a point where the electric potential is zero toward an immovable negative charge Q (see Figure 3.21).

(a) What should the potential at P be so that the electron stops momentarily at P and then turns back?

(b) What is the magnitude of Q?

Figure 3.21 For question 13.

14 Two equal and opposite charges are placed at points with coordinates $x = 0$, $y = a$ and $x = 0$, $y = -a$, as shown in Figure 3.22.
  (a) Find the electric field at the point with coordinates $x = d$, $y = 0$.
  (b) Repeat for two equal negative charges $-q$ on the y-axis.
  (c) Plot these fields as functions of d.

Figure 3.22 For question 14.

15 A charge Q is placed a distance d from a very large conducting plane. What is the electric field at a point P a distance $2d$ from the plane? (See Figure 3.23.)

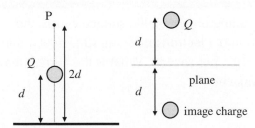

Figure 3.23 For question 15.

[*Hint*: Answer this as follows (the method of images). Draw field lines to convince yourself that the same lines would be obtained if, instead of the plane, an equal and opposite charge were placed at a position that is the mirror image of the charge in the plane. Thus, the electric field in the presence of the plane would be the same as the electric field of two equal and opposite charges without the plane. Thus, find this field at point P.]

16 A charge q whose mass is m moves in a circle of radius r around another stationary charge q located at the centre of the circle, as shown in Figure 3.24.
  (a) Draw the force on the moving charge.
  (b) Show that the velocity of the charge is given by $v^2 = \frac{1}{4\pi\varepsilon_0}\frac{q^2}{mr}$.
  (c) Show that the total energy of the charge is given by $E = -\frac{1}{8\pi\varepsilon_0}\frac{q^2}{r}$.
  (d) Hence find out how much energy must be given to the charge if it is to orbit around the stationary charge at a radius equal to $2r$.

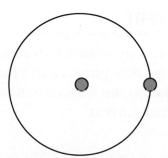

Figure 3.24 For question 16.

Electric current and resistance

The motion of electric charges creates electric currents. This chapter discusses the definition of electric current and electric resistance.

Objectives

By the end of this chapter you should be able to:
- state the definition of *electric current*, $I = \frac{\Delta Q}{\Delta t}$;
- state the definition of *electric resistance*, $R = \frac{V}{I}$;
- appreciate that metallic conductors at constant temperature satisfy *Ohm's law*, $I \propto V$;
- appreciate that the *potential* drops as one moves across a resistor in the direction of the current;
- understand that a resistor dissipates *power*, $P = VI$.

Electric current

Our study of electricity so far has dealt with stationary charges. New phenomena take place when electric charges are allowed to move, one of which is **electric current**.

▶ A moving charge creates an electric current. Electric current is the amount of charge that moves through the cross-sectional area of a wire per unit interval of time:

$$I = \frac{\Delta Q}{\Delta t}$$

The unit of electric current is the ampere, one of the fundamental units of the SI system, and $1 \text{ A} = 1 \text{ C s}^{-1}$. (The *definition* of the ampere is in terms of the magnetic force between two parallel conductors; this will be given in Chapter 5.6.)

Example question

Q1 ▬▬▬▬▬▬▬▬▬▬▬▬

Light falling on a metallic surface causes the emission of electrons from the surface at a rate of 2.2×10^{15} per second. What is the current leaving the surface?

Answer

The current is

$$2.2 \times 10^{15} \times 1.6 \times 10^{-19} \text{ C s}^{-1} = 3.5 \times 10^{-4} \text{ A}$$

In a conductor the 'free' electrons move randomly, much like gas molecules in a container. They do so with high speeds, of the order of 10^5 m s^{-1}. This random motion, however, does not result in electric current – as many electrons move to the right as to the left (see Figure 4.1).

Figure 4.1 The random motion of the electrons inside a conductor takes place at high speeds but does not result in electric current. Current is the amount of charge that goes past a given point per unit interval of time.

▶ The presence of an electric field inside the conductor forces the electrons to accelerate in a direction opposite to the electric field (remember, the charge of the electron is negative) and this orderly motion of the electrons in the same direction is what makes electric current.

The electrons increase their kinetic energy as they move through the metal but soon they will suffer inelastic collisions with the atoms of the material, which means they will lose energy to the atoms. The electric field will again accelerate the electrons until the next collision and this process repeats. Thus, the electrons lose energy constantly, which the atoms of the material pick up. This means that these atoms will vibrate about their equilibrium positions more and this will show up *macroscopically* as increased temperature of the material. We can make a mechanical analogy of this (see Figure 4.2). Imagine a ball rolling down an inclined plane on which a number of pegs have been placed.

Figure 4.2 A mechanical model of the electron's motion inside a metal. The speed of the electron is increasing while the electric field is accelerating it, in between collisions. After a collision, the speed is reduced to zero and the electron begins to accelerate again. The electron's kinetic energy has been transferred to the atoms of the metal. The dotted line represents the drift velocity of the electron.

Gravity accelerates the ball down but as soon as a collision with a peg takes place, energy is lost and the ball will accelerate again from a reduced speed.

HL only

We can estimate the magnitude of the drift velocity as follows. Suppose that the conductor is a wire of cross-sectional area A and that there are n free electrons per unit volume in the material. If the electrons move with speed v, then in time Δt the number of electrons that have gone through the cross-section of the wire is simply the number of electrons inside the volume of a cylinder of cross-sectional area A and height $v\Delta t$. The number of electrons in this volume is $nAv\Delta t$, and hence the amount of charge that they carry is $enAv\Delta t$. This is the amount of charge that went past the wire in time Δt, and thus the current is

$$I = enAv$$

For a typical metal, $n = 10^{28}$ m^{-3}; if the current is $I = 1$ A in a wire of cross-sectional area 10^{-6} m^2 (a typical wire), we find $v = 6 \times 10^{-4}$ m s^{-1}. This is quite a low speed, perhaps surprisingly so. If we turn on the switch for the lights in the classroom (which are about 5 m from the switch), we certainly do not have to wait for $\frac{5}{(6 \times 10^{-4})}$ s $= 139$ min for the lights to come on! This is because, when the switch is turned on, an electric field is established within the wire. This happens at a speed close to the speed of light. As soon as the field is established, every free electron in the wire starts moving at the drift velocity, so the electric current is established in the conductor much faster than the velocity of the electrons making up the current.

It is a convention that the direction of electric current is taken to be opposite to the motion of the electrons, as shown in Figure 4.3. (See Option E4 for the reason for the convention.)

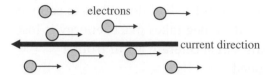

Figure 4.3 The direction of the current is taken to be opposite to the actual electron motion.

An electric current is also produced when a wire is heated so that it begins to emit electrons in a phenomenon known as thermionic emission. If the wire emits N electrons per second, the current leaving the hot wire is $I = eN$. Similarly, in the photoelectric effect, light or other electromagnetic radiation causes the emission of electrons from a metallic surface on which it falls. The emission of electrons is electric current that leaves the surface. Whereas in solid materials electric current consists exclusively of moving electrons, in liquids and especially gases positive ions may also be accelerated by electric fields, resulting in currents due to positive charges. In gases, even small electric fields can produce currents due to positive ions. This is because at low pressure electrons have a long mean free path, so they can be accelerated to high speeds by the electric field before colliding with gas molecules. These high-velocity electrons can then ionize atoms of the gas by knocking electrons out of the atoms, leaving behind positive ions, which also move under the influence of the electric field.

As a consequence of the law of conservation of charge, it follows that two devices connected in series will take the same current. When a wire comes to a junction, the current splits (not necessarily equally) so that the current entering the junction equals the total current leaving it. (See Figure 4.4.)

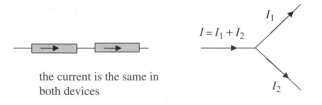

the current is the same in both devices

Figure 4.4 The current entering a junction equals the total current leaving it.

Electric resistance

Now we look at **electric resistance** and **Ohm's law**.

▶ The electric resistance of a conductor (for example, a wire of given length) is defined as the potential difference *across its ends* divided by the current flowing *through* it:
$$R = \frac{V}{I}$$
The unit of electric resistance is the volt per ampere and this is defined to be the ohm, symbol Ω. The equation above is the definition of resistance.

In 1826, Georg Ohm discovered that, when the temperature of a metallic conductor is kept constant, the current through the conductor is proportional to the potential difference across it
$$I \propto V$$
This statement is known as Ohm's law. Materials obeying Ohm's law thus have a constant resistance at constant temperature. A graph of I versus V gives a straight line if the material obeys Ohm's law.

Most materials obey Ohm's law at low temperatures, but as temperature increases, deviations from this law are seen. For example, an ordinary light bulb will obey Ohm's law as long as the current through it is small. As the current is increased, the temperature of the bulb increases and so does the resistance. Other devices, such as the diode, also deviate from Ohm's law. These are illustrated in Figure 4.5.

A conductor with zero electric resistance is known as a perfect conductor. In a perfect

conductor, electric current can flow without a potential difference established at its ends. A class of materials known as *superconductors* have zero resistance below a certain temperature (known as the critical temperature) and are thus perfect conductors.

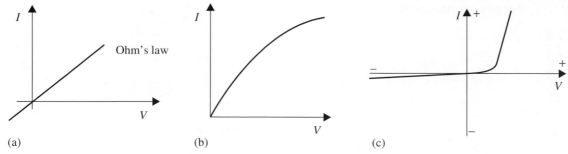

Figure 4.5 Graph (a) shows the current–voltage graph for a material obeying Ohm's law. A lamp filament (b) and a diode (c) do not obey this law.

Factors affecting the resistance of a wire

Three factors affect the resistance of a wire *kept at constant temperature*. They are the nature of the material, the length of the wire and the cross-sectional area of the wire. For metallic materials, an increase in the temperature results in an increase in the resistance.

▶ It is found from experiment that the electric resistance of a wire (at fixed temperature) is proportional to its length L and inversely proportional to the cross-sectional area A:

$$R \propto \frac{L}{A}$$

(see Figure 4.6).

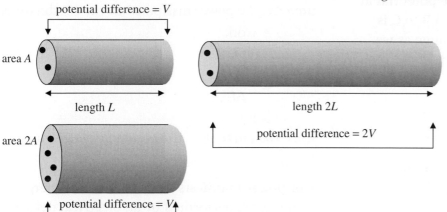

Figure 4.6 If we double the cross-sectional area A, the current that can flow through the metal for the same potential difference is doubled as well. Hence, the resistance R halves. If we double the length L, the potential difference at the ends of the wire will double while the current stays the same. Hence, the resistance R doubles.

Supplementary material

The dependence of resistance on length and cross-sectional area can also be understood as follows. If we combine the definition of resistance with $I = enAv$ and the fact that the potential difference across a length L of a wire is related to the electric field E in the wire through $V = EL$, we find that

$$R = \frac{L}{enAv}E$$

which explains the dependence on L and A.

Example question

Q2

A wire is subjected to a tension so that its length increases by 10% while the volume of the wire stays the same. How does the resistance of the wire change?

Answer

Let L and A be the original length and cross-sectional area of the wire. The new length is $1.1L$ and since the volume stays the same, the new cross-sectional area A' must satisfy

$$A'(1.1L) = AL$$

$$\Rightarrow A' = \frac{A}{1.1}$$

Since $R \propto \frac{L}{A}$, the new resistance is

$$R' = \frac{L'/A'}{L/A}$$

$$= \frac{L'}{L}\frac{A}{A'}$$

$$= 1.1 \times 1.1$$

$$= 1.21$$

$$\Rightarrow R' = 1.21\,R$$

that is, it increases by 21%.

Potential drop

The defining equation for resistance, $R = \frac{V}{I}$, can be looked at in the following way. Solving for the potential difference V we find

$$V = IR$$

which says that if a current flows through a resistor, then there must be a potential difference across the ends of that resistor given by the formula above. A resistor is thus said to drop the potential. (In an electric circuit we will often indicate a resistor by a box. The conducting wires also have resistance, but typically this is very small so we neglect it. The words potential and voltage will mean the same thing.) Suppose that in Figure 4.7, the potential at point A is 100 V, the current is 5 A and the resistance is 15 Ω. Then the *potential difference* at the ends of the resistor is $V = IR = 5 \times 15 = 75$ V. Thus, the potential at point B is 25 V. The resistance from B to C is zero, so the potential does not change as we move from B to C. The potential at all points from B to C is 25 V.

Figure 4.7 There is a potential difference across points A and B but not between B and C.

Example question

Q3 ▬▬▬▬▬▬▬▬▬▬▬▬▬▬▬▬▬▬

In Figure 4.8, two resistors are joined as shown. The top resistor receives a current of 3 A. What is the current in the other resistor? What is the current that enters at junction A?

Figure 4.8.

Answer

Both resistors have the same potential difference across them (why?). The potential difference across the top resistor is

$$V = IR$$

$$= 3 \times 10$$

$$= 30\text{ V}$$

and so for the lower resistor we have

$$30 = I \times 30$$

$$\Rightarrow I = 1\text{ A}$$

The current entering at A is 4 A.

Electric power

We saw earlier that whenever an electric charge ΔQ moves from a point A to a point B such that there exists a potential difference V between these points, work is being done. This work is $W = (\Delta Q)V$. Consider a conductor with a potential difference across its ends of V. In moving a charge ΔQ across the conductor in time Δt, the power dissipated in the conductor is

$$P = \frac{\text{work}}{\text{time}}$$

$$= \frac{V\Delta Q}{\Delta t}$$

$$= VI$$

since the current in the conductor is given by $I = \frac{\Delta Q}{\Delta t}$.

This power manifests itself in thermal energy and/or work performed by an electrical device (see Figure 4.9). In devices obeying Ohm's law (i.e. when the resistance is constant), we can use $R = \frac{V}{I}$ to rewrite the formula for power in equivalent ways:

$$P = RI^2 = \frac{V^2}{R}$$

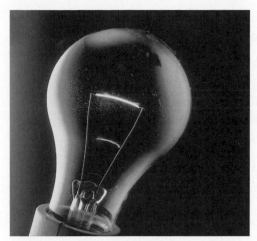

Figure 4.9 The metal filament in a light bulb glows as the current passes through it. It also feels warm. This shows that the bulb produces both heat and light.

Example question

Q4

A resistor of resistance 12 Ω has a current of 2.0 A flowing through it. How much energy is generated in the resistor in one minute?

Answer

The power generated in the resistor is

$P = RI^2$

$= 12 \times 4$ W

$= 48$ W

Thus, in one minute (60 s) the energy generated is

48×60 J $= 2.9 \times 10^3$ J

Electrical devices are usually rated according to the power they use. A light bulb rated as 60 W at 220 V means that it will dissipate 60 W *when a potential difference of 220 V is applied across its ends*. If the potential difference across its ends is anything other than 220 V, the power dissipated will be different from 60 W.

Example questions

Q5

A light bulb rated as 60 W at 220 V has a potential difference of 110 V across its ends. Find the power dissipated in this light bulb.

Answer

Let R be the resistance of the light bulb and P the power we want to find. Assuming R stays constant

(so that it is the same when 220 V and 110 V are applied to its ends) we have

$$P = \frac{110^2}{R} \quad \text{and} \quad 60 = \frac{220^2}{R}$$

Dividing these equations side by side we find

$$\frac{P}{60} = \frac{110^2 / R}{220^2 / R}$$

$$= \frac{110^2}{220^2}$$

$$= \frac{1}{4}$$

$$\Rightarrow P = 60 \times \frac{1}{4}$$

$$= 15 \text{ W}$$

Q6

Figure 4.10 shows the variation of voltage across a conductor with the current through the conductor. Does it obey Ohm's law? What is the resistance of the conductor when the current through it is 0.6 A? What is the power dissipated in the conductor when the voltage across it is 1.5 V?

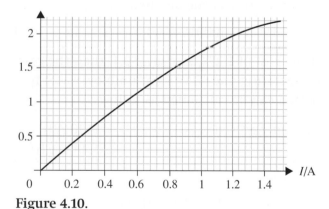

Figure 4.10.

Answer

The graph is straight only for small currents (less than about 0.5 A) and so the conductor obeys Ohm's law only for these small currents.

The resistance at 0.60 A is

$$R = \frac{V}{I}$$

$$\approx \frac{1.2}{0.60}$$

$$= 2.0 \text{ Ω}$$

When the voltage is 1.5 V, the current is about 0.82 A, so

$$P = VI$$
$$\approx 1.5 \times 0.82$$
$$= 1.2 \text{ W}$$

The cost of electricity

Electricity companies charge for electricity according to the amount of energy used by the consumer. A device that is rated at a power value of 60 W, for example an ordinary light bulb, uses 60 J of energy every second (when connected to the appropriate source of voltage). The energy used by the light bulb over a time of t s is thus $E = 60t$ J. In general, for a device of power rating P the energy used in t s is

$$E = Pt$$
$$= VIt$$

Electricity companies find it more convenient to use a different energy unit by which to charge consumers. They use the kilowatt-hour (kW h) as their energy unit, which is defined as the energy used by a device of power rating 1 kW in 1 h. This means that

$$1 \text{ kW h} = 1000 \text{ W} \times 60 \times 60 \text{ s} = 3.6 \times 10^6 \text{ J}$$

If the cost of 1 kW h is, say, \$0.1, then the cost of operating one 60 W light bulb over a 24 h period can be calculated as follows:

$$\text{energy used} = 60 \text{ W} \times 24 \text{ h} = 1440 \text{ W h}$$
$$= 1.44 \text{ kW h}$$

Hence

$$\text{cost} = 1.44 \times \$0.1 = \$0.144$$

Questions

1 Outline the mechanism by which electric current heats up the material through which it flows.

2 Explain why a light bulb is most likely to burn out when it is first turned on rather than later.

3 State the factors that affect the resistance of a metal wire.

4 Explain why doubling the length of a wire will double its resistance.

5 By what factor does the resistance of a wire change if its radius is doubled?

6 Give an estimate for the number of free electrons per unit volume for gold (density 19 390 kg m^{-3}; molar mass 197 g mol^{-1}). Assume that each atom contributes just one electron to the set of free electrons.

7 Silver has 5.8×10^{28} free electrons per m^3. If the current in a 2 mm radius silver wire is 5.0 A, find the velocity with which the electrons drift in the wire.

8 (a) If a current of 10.0 A flows through a heater, how much charge passes through the heater in 1 h?
   (b) How many electrons does this charge correspond to?

9 The graphs in Figure 4.11 show the current as a function of voltage across the same piece of metal wire which is kept at two different temperatures.
   (a) Does the wire obey Ohm's law?
   (b) Which of the two graphs corresponds to the higher temperature?

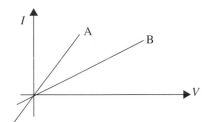

Figure 4.11 For question 9.

10 The current in a device obeying Ohm's law is 1.5 A when connected to a source of potential difference 6.0 V. What will the potential difference across the same device be when a current of 3.5 A flows in it?

11 In an experiment the current through and potential difference across a device were recorded as shown in Table 4.1. Does the device obey Ohm's law?

I/mA	5.0	9.8	12.4	16.8	21.5	24.6
V/mV	100	200	300	400	500	600

Table 4.1 For question 11.

12 A resistor obeying Ohm's law is measured to have a resistance of 12 Ω when a current of 3 A flows in it. What is the resistance when the current is 4 A?

13 The heating element of an electric kettle has a current of 15 A when connected to a source of potential difference 220V. What is its resistance?

14 The resistance of a fixed length of wire of circular cross-section is 10.0 Ω. What will be the resistance of a wire of the same length made of the same material but with only half the radius?

15 Look at Figure 4.12. The potential at point A is 24 V and a current of 2 A flows in the wire.
(a) What is the potential difference across each resistor?
(b) Find the potential at points B, C and D.

Figure 4.12 For question 15.

16 Look at Figure 4.13.
(a) Find the current in, and potential difference across, each resistor. The potential at A is 12 V.
(b) What is the potential difference between A and B?

Figure 4.13 For question 16.

17 A light bulb is rated as 60 W at 220 V.
(a) How much current flows in the light bulb if it is connected to a 220 V source of voltage?
(b) If the light bulb is connected to a 110 V source of voltage, what current flows in it? (Assume the resistance stays the same.)
(c) What is the power output of the light bulb when it is connected to the 110 V source?

18 The resistance of a wire of length L and cross-sectional area A is given by $R = \rho\frac{L}{A}$, where ρ is a constant called the resistivity. The filament of an ordinary 120 W light bulb has a resistivity of 2.0×10^{-6} Ω m.
(a) What is its resistance when it is connected to a source of 220 V?
(b) If the radius of the filament is 0.03 mm, find its length.

19 Find the energy used when a 1500 W kettle is used for 4 minutes:
(a) in kW h;
(b) in joules.

20 In the USA the voltage supplied by the electricity companies is 110 V and in Europe it is 230 V. Consider a light bulb rated as 60 W at 110 V in the USA and a light bulb rated as 60 W at 230 V in Europe. Take the cost of electricity per kW h to be the same. Where does it cost more to operate a light bulb for 1 hour?

Electric circuits

This chapter explains how simple electric circuits can be solved: that is, how the current through and potential difference across resistors can be determined. The chapter begins with the concept of emf (which stands for electromotive force). The name is unfortunate, as emf is a potential difference and not a force. Hence, we always use the initials emf and never the full name.

Objectives

By the end of this chapter you should be able to:
- define *emf* and explain the role of *internal resistance* – the potential difference across a battery is $V = \mathcal{E} - Ir$;
- find the total resistance in *series* and *parallel* connections using $R_{total} = R_1 + R_2 + \cdots$ and $\frac{1}{R_{total}} = \frac{1}{R_1} + \frac{1}{R_2} + \cdots$;
- find the current through, and potential difference across, resistors in simple circuits;
- find the *power dissipated* by a resistor in a circuit using $P = VI$.

Emf

Charges will not drift in the same direction inside a conductor unless a potential difference is established at the ends of the conductor. There are many ways of providing *a source of potential difference* to the circuit. The most common is the connection of a *battery* in the circuit. Others include a *generator*, a *thermocouple* and a *photosurface*. To understand the function of the battery, we can use the standard analogy in which the battery is likened to a pump that forces water through pipes up to a certain height and down again (see Figure 5.1). The gravitational force does work equal to $-mgh$ in lifting a mass m of water up to the height h, and work equal to $+mgh$ on the way down. The net work done by the gravitational force is thus zero. Because frictional forces are present, work must be done by the pump to compensate for the work done by these forces.

In the absence of the pump, the water flow would stop.

If, in addition, the water drives a machine to perform useful work (for example, by turning a paddle wheel), then the pump would have to do work to allow for that as well.

Figure 5.1 In the absence of the pump, the water flow would stop. The work done by the pump equals the work done to overcome frictional forces plus work done to operate devices, such as, for example, a paddle wheel.

In an electric circuit a battery performs a role similar to the pump's. A battery converts the energy it stores (chemical energy) into electrical energy. The work done by the electrical forces on a charge that moves in the circuit is zero, just as the net work done by gravitational force in the pump and water system described above is zero. Similarly, if a generator is used, the energy that gets converted into electrical energy is the mechanical energy that turns the coils of the generator. In the case of the thermocouple, it is thermal energy. In the case of the photosurface, it is solar energy.

In a battery, the electrons must be pushed from the positive to the negative terminal, which means work must be done *on the electrons* (see Figure 5.2).

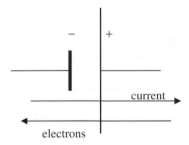

Figure 5.2.

This is what we mean by **emf**:

▶ In the case of the battery, the ratio of work done by non-electrical forces, W, to a quantity of charge q that moves from one terminal of the battery to the other is called the emf of the battery. Emf thus has units of electric potential, i.e. volts:

$$\mathcal{E} = \text{emf} = \frac{W}{q}$$

Suppose we connect a voltmeter to the ends of a battery. We may assign the value of 0 V to the negative terminal of the battery. Then the positive terminal has a potential equal to the emf, $\mathcal{E}$. The chemicals inside the battery create a small resistance r, called the internal resistance of the cell. We cannot isolate this resistance – it is inside the battery and we may assume that it is connected in series to the cell. If the current

that leaves the battery is I, then the potential difference across the internal resistance is Ir. In other words, the internal resistance reduces the voltage from a value of $\mathcal{E}$ on its left side to the value $\mathcal{E} - Ir$ on the right side. The potential difference across the battery is therefore

$$V = \mathcal{E} - Ir$$

We see that $V = \mathcal{E}$ when $I = 0$. This gives an alternative and less precise definition of the emf: the emf is the potential difference across the battery when the battery sends out zero current. (See Figure 5.3.)

potential drops by Ir

voltage across battery

Figure 5.3 The potential difference across the battery terminals is less than the emf of the battery.

Example question

Q1

A battery of emf 12 V and internal resistance $r = 1.5\ \Omega$ produces a current of 3.0 A. What is the potential difference across the battery terminals?

Answer

We find

$$V = \mathcal{E} - Ir$$
$$= 12 - 3 \times 1.5$$
$$= 7.5\ \text{V}$$

In Figure 5.4, a battery forces a current I into a circuit that contains a resistor of resistance R. The connecting wires are assumed to have zero resistance.

If the emf of the battery in the circuit is 3.0 V (neglecting its internal resistance) and the resistance of the circuit is 1.5 Ω, the current can easily be determined. The positive terminal of the battery may be taken to be 3.0 V and so the negative terminal must be taken to be at 0 V

Figure 5.4 A battery connected to a circuit. The current flows into the circuit away from the positive terminal. This is the conventional definition of current. The electrons actually move in the opposite way.

(to give an emf of 3 V). Thus, the right end of the resistor is also at 3.0 V. The left end of the resistor is at 0.0 V and so the potential difference across the resistor is 3.0 V. Hence, the current is 2.0 A.

Simple electric circuits

A simple circuit will consist of a single battery and a number of resistors. When we talk about solving a circuit, we mean finding the current through and voltage across every resistor in the circuit. Here we will develop the methods to do just that. Table 5.1 shows the circuit symbols that you need.

Series circuits

First, let us consider a part of a circuit consisting of a number of resistors connected in *series*. This means that the resistors have the same current through them. An example with three resistors is shown in Figure 5.5. Let I be the common current in the three resistors.

Figure 5.5 Three resistors in series.

The potential difference across the resistors is

$$V_1 = IR_1, \quad V_2 = IR_2 \quad \text{and} \quad V_3 = IR_3$$

The sum of the potential differences is thus

$$V = IR_1 + IR_2 + IR_3 = I(R_1 + R_2 + R_3)$$

Symbols	Component name
	connection lead
	cell
	battery of cells
	resistor
	power supply
	junction of conductors
	crossing conductors (no connection)
	filament lamp
	voltmeter
	ammeter
	switch
	ac supply
	galvanometer
	potentiometer
	heating element

Table 5.1 Names of electrical components and their circuit symbols.

If we were to replace the three resistors by a *single* resistor of value $R_1 + R_2 + R_3$ (in other words, if we were to replace the contents of the dotted box in Figure 5.5 with a single resistor, as in the circuit shown in Figure 5.6), we would not be able to tell the difference. The *same current* flows into the dotted box and the *same potential difference* exists across its ends. We thus define the equivalent or total resistance of the three resistors of Figure 5.5 by

$$R_{\text{total}} = R_1 + R_2 + R_3$$

(If more than three were present, we would simply add all of them. The formula shows that the total resistance is larger than the individual ones being added.)

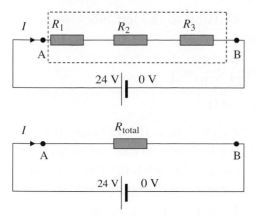

Figure 5.6 The top circuit is replaced by the equivalent circuit containing just one resistor.

In a circuit, the combination of resistors of Figure 5.5 is equivalent to the single total or equivalent resistor. Suppose we now connect the three resistors to a battery of negligible internal resistance and emf equal to 24 V. Suppose that $R_1 = 2\,\Omega$, $R_2 = 6\,\Omega$ and $R_3 = 4\,\Omega$. The circuit is shown in the top diagram of Figure 5.6. Note that we know that the potential at point A is 24 V and at point B it is 0 V. (We *do not* know the potential difference across any of the three resistors individually.) In the bottom diagram, we have replaced the three resistors by the equivalent resistor of $R_{\text{total}} = 2 + 6 + 4 = 12\,\Omega$. We now observe that the potential difference across the equivalent resistor is known. It is simply 24 V and hence the current through the equivalent resistor is found as follows:

$$R = \frac{V}{I}$$

$$\Rightarrow I = \frac{V}{R} = \frac{24}{12} = 2\,\text{A}$$

This current, therefore, is also the current that enters the dotted box: that is, it is the current in each of the three resistors of the original circuit. We may thus deduce that the potential differences across the three resistors are

$$V_1 = IR_1 = 4\,\text{V}$$

$$V_2 = IR_2 = 12\,\text{V}$$

$$V_3 = IR_3 = 8\,\text{V}$$

Suppose now that we cannot neglect the internal resistance of the battery. The internal resistance is connected in series to the other resistances and so, if its value is $r = 1.0\,\Omega$, the total circuit resistance is $1 + 2 + 6 + 4 = 13\,\Omega$. The current leaving the battery is thus $\frac{24}{13} = 1.85\,\text{A}$. The potential difference across the battery terminals is

$$V = \mathcal{E} - Ir$$
$$= 24 - 1.85 \times 1$$
$$= 22.15\,\text{V}$$

which is less than the emf, as we expected.

Parallel circuits

Consider now part of another circuit, in which the current splits into three other currents that flow in three resistors, as shown in Figure 5.7. The current that enters the junction at A must equal the current that leaves the junction, by the law of conservation of charge. Furthermore, we note that the left ends of the three resistors are at the same potential (the potential at A) and the right ends are all at the potential of B. Hence, the three resistors have the same potential difference across them. This is called a *parallel* connection.

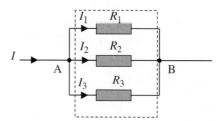

Figure 5.7 Three resistors connected in parallel.

We must then have that

$$I = I_1 + I_2 + I_3$$

Let V be the common potential difference across the resistors. Then

$$I_1 = \frac{V}{R_1}, \quad I_2 = \frac{V}{R_2} \quad \text{and} \quad I_3 = \frac{V}{R_3}$$

and so

$$I = \frac{V}{R_1} + \frac{V}{R_2} + \frac{V}{R_3}$$
$$= V\left(\frac{1}{R_1} + \frac{1}{R_2} + \frac{1}{R_3}\right)$$

If we replace the three resistors in the dotted box with a single resistor, the potential difference across it would be V and the current through it would be I. Thus

$$I = \frac{V}{R_{\text{total}}}$$

Comparing with the last equation, we find

$$\frac{1}{R_{\text{total}}} = \frac{1}{R_1} + \frac{1}{R_2} + \frac{1}{R_3}$$

The formula shows that the total resistance is *smaller* than any of the individual resistances being added.

> ▶ We have thus learned how to replace resistors that are connected in series (same current) or parallel (same potential difference across) by a single resistor in each case, thus greatly simplifying the circuit.

A typical circuit will contain both series and parallel connections. In Figure 5.8, the two top resistors are in series. They are equivalent to a single resistor of 12 Ω. This resistor and the 6 Ω resistor are in parallel, so together they are equivalent to a single resistor of

$$\frac{1}{R_{\text{total}}} = \frac{1}{12} + \frac{1}{6} = \frac{1}{4}$$

$$\Rightarrow R_{\text{total}} = 4\,\Omega$$

Figure 5.8 Part of a circuit with both series and parallel connections.

Consider now Figure 5.9. The two top 6 Ω resistors are in series, so they are equivalent to a 12 Ω resistor. This, in turn, is in parallel with

the other 6 Ω resistor, so the left block is equivalent to

$$\frac{1}{R_{\text{total}}} = \frac{1}{12} + \frac{1}{6} = \frac{1}{4}$$

$$\Rightarrow R_{\text{total}} = 4\,\Omega$$

Let us go to the right block. The 12 Ω and the 24 Ω resistors are in series, so they are equivalent to 36 Ω. This is in parallel with the top 12 Ω, so the equivalent resistor of the right block is

$$\frac{1}{R_{\text{total}}} = \frac{1}{36} + \frac{1}{12} = \frac{1}{9}$$

$$\Rightarrow R_{\text{total}} = 9\,\Omega$$

The overall resistance is thus

$$4 + 9 = 13\,\Omega$$

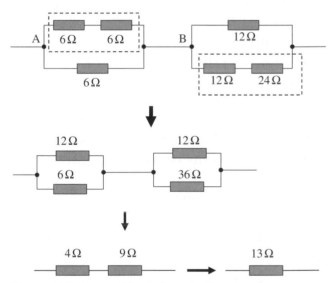

Figure 5.9 A complicated part of a circuit containing many parallel and series connections.

Suppose now that this part of the circuit is connected to a source of emf 156 V (and negligible internal resistance). The current that leaves the source is $I = \frac{156}{13} = 12$ A. When it arrives at point A, it will split into two parts. Let the current in the top part be I_1 and that in the bottom part I_2. We have $I_1 + I_2 = 12$ A. We also have that $12I_1 = 6I_2$, since the top and bottom resistors of the block beginning at point A are in parallel and so have the same potential difference across them. Thus, $I_1 = 4$ A and $I_2 = 8$ A. Similarly, in the block beginning at point B the top current is 9 A and the bottom current is 3 A.

Example questions

Q2

Find the total resistance in each of the circuits shown in Figure 5.10.

(a)

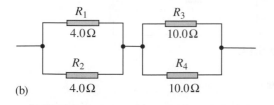

(b)

Figure 5.10.

Answer

(a) R_1 and R_2 are in parallel, so together they are equivalent to a resistor R where

$$\frac{1}{R} = \frac{1}{2.0} + \frac{1}{3.0}$$

$$= \frac{5.0}{6.0}$$

$$\Rightarrow R = \frac{6.0}{5.0}$$

$$= 1.2\,\Omega$$

Now, this R is in series with R_3, so together they are equivalent to

$$R_{\text{total}} = (1.2 + 1.8)\,\Omega$$

$$= 3.0\,\Omega$$

(b) R_1 and R_2 are in parallel, so together they are equivalent to a resistor R where

$$\frac{1}{R} = \frac{1}{4.0} + \frac{1}{4.0}$$

$$= \frac{1.0}{2.0}$$

$$\Rightarrow R = \frac{2.0}{1.0}$$

$$= 2.0\,\Omega$$

Similarly, R_3 and R_4 are in parallel so they are equivalent to a resistor of $5.0\,\Omega$. The $2.0\,\Omega$ and $5.0\,\Omega$ are in series, so the overall total is $7.0\,\Omega$.

Q3

What is the total current in the circuit in Figure 5.11?

Figure 5.11.

Answer

The emf of the battery is 12 V. The total resistance of the circuit is $2.0 + 4.0 = 6.0\,\Omega$. Thus, the total current is

$$I = \frac{12.0}{6.0}\text{A}$$

$$= 2.0\ \text{A}$$

Q4

What is the potential difference across each resistor in example question 3?

Answer

The current through the $2.0\,\Omega$ resistor is 2.0 A, so the potential difference across it is $RI = 4.0$ V. Across the other resistor it is $RI = 4.0 \times 2.0\ \text{V} = 8.0$ V. Note that the sum of the potential differences across each resistor adds up to the emf of the battery.

Q5

Find the current in each of the resistors in the circuit shown in Figure 5.12.

Figure 5.12.

Answer

The resistors of $2.0\,\Omega$ and $3.0\,\Omega$ are connected in parallel and are equivalent to a single resistor of resistance R found from

$$\frac{1}{R} = \frac{1}{2} + \frac{1}{3}$$

$$= \frac{5}{6}$$

$$\Rightarrow R = \frac{6}{5}$$

$$= 1.2\,\Omega$$

In turn, this is in series with the resistance of $1.8\,\Omega$, so the total equivalent circuit resistance is $1.8 + 1.2 = 3.0\,\Omega$. The current that leaves the battery is thus

$$I = \frac{6.0}{3.0}$$

$$= 2.0\text{ A}$$

The potential difference across the $1.8\,\Omega$ resistor is thus $V = 1.8 \times 2.0 = 3.6$ V, leading to a potential difference across the two parallel resistors of $V = 6.0 - 3.6 = 2.4$ V. Thus the current in the $2\,\Omega$ resistor is

$$I = \frac{2.4}{2.0}$$

$$= 1.2\text{ A}$$

and in the $3\,\Omega$ resistor is

$$I = \frac{2.4}{3.0}$$

$$= 0.80\text{ A}$$

As a check, we see that $1.2 + 0.80 = 2.0$ A, as it should be.

Q6

Find the current in each resistor in the circuit in Figure 5.13.

Figure 5.13.

Answer

The voltage across the $4.0\,\Omega$ resistor is 24.0 V and thus the current is 6.0 A. The voltage is 24.0 V across the other resistor as well, and so the current through it is 4.0 A. The current leaving the battery is 10.0 A.

Q7

Look at Figure 5.14. What is the potential difference between A and B? What is the current leaving the battery?

Figure 5.14.

Answer

The potential difference is 24 V for all resistors. The currents in the resistors are 8 A, 6 A and 4 A, respectively. The total current is thus 18 A.

Q8

Look at Figure 5.15. What is the current in the $2.0\,\Omega$ resistor when the switch is open and when the switch is closed? What is the potential difference across the two marked points, A and B, when the switch is open and when the switch is closed?

Figure 5.15.

Answer

When the switch is open, the total resistance is $4.0\,\Omega$ and thus the total current is 3.0 A. This is the current through the $2.0\,\Omega$ resistor. The potential at A is 12 V. The potential difference across the $2.0\,\Omega$ resistor is $2 \times 3 = 6$ V and so the potential at its right end, and hence at B, is 6 V. The potential difference across points A and B is thus 6 V.

When the switch is closed, no current flows through the $2.0\,\Omega$ resistor, since all the current takes the path through the switch, which offers no resistance. (The $2.0\,\Omega$ resistor has been *shorted out*.) The resistance of the circuit is then $2.0\,\Omega$ and the current leaving the battery is 6 A. The potential difference across points A and B is now zero. There is current flowing from A to B, but the resistance from A to B is zero. Hence the potential difference is $6 \times 0 = 0\,\text{V}$.

Q9

Four light bulbs each of constant resistance $60\,\Omega$ are connected as shown in Figure 5.16. Find the power in each light bulb. If light bulb A burns out, find the power in each light bulb and the potential difference across the burned-out light bulb.

Figure 5.16.

Answer

A and B are connected in series so they are equivalent to one resistor of value $R = 60 + 60 = 120\,\Omega$. This is connected in parallel to C, giving a total resistance of

$$\frac{1}{R} = \frac{1}{120} + \frac{1}{60}$$
$$= \frac{1}{40}$$

$$\Rightarrow R = 40\,\Omega$$

Finally, this is in series with D, giving a total circuit resistance of $R = 40 + 60 = 100\,\Omega$. The current leaving the battery is thus $I = \frac{30}{100} = 0.3\,\text{A}$. The current through A and B is 0.1 A and that through C is 0.2 A. The current through D is 0.3 A. Hence the power in each light bulb is

$$P_A = P_B$$
$$= 60 \times (0.1)^2$$
$$= 0.6\,\text{W}$$
$$P_C = 60 \times (0.2)^2$$
$$= 2.4\,\text{W}$$

$$P_D = 60 \times (0.3)^2$$
$$= 5.4\,\text{W}$$

With light bulb A burnt out, the circuit is as shown in Figure 5.17.

Figure 5.17.

Light bulb B gets no current, so we are left with only C and D connected in series, giving a total resistance of $R = 60 + 60 = 120\,\Omega$. The current is thus $I = 0.25\,\text{A}$. The power in C and D is thus

$$P_C = P_D$$
$$= 60 \times (0.25)^2$$
$$= 3.75\,\text{W}$$

We see that D becomes dimmer and C brighter. The potential at point a is 30 V. The potential difference across light bulb C is

$$V = IR$$
$$= 0.25 \times 60$$
$$= 15\,\text{V}$$

and so the potential at the right end of C is 15 V. Light bulb B takes no current, so the potential difference across it is zero. Thus, the potential at point b is also 15 V. The potential difference across points a and b is therefore 15 V.

Ammeters and voltmeters

The current through a resistor is measured by an instrument called an ammeter, which is connected in series to the resistor as shown in Figure 5.18.

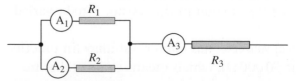

Figure 5.18 An ammeter measures the current in the resistor connected in series to it.

The ammeter itself has a small electric resistance. However, an *ideal ammeter has zero resistance* and throughout this book we are assuming that we are dealing with ideal ammeters.

Example question

Q10

How are the readings of the ammeters of Figure 5.18 related?

Answer

$I_3 = I_1 + I_2$

The potential difference across the ends of a resistor is measured by a voltmeter, which is connected in parallel to the resistor, as shown in Figure 5.19.

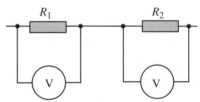

Figure 5.19 A voltmeter measures the potential difference across a resistor it is connected in parallel to.

Thus, to measure the potential difference across and current through a resistor, the arrangement shown in Figure 5.20 is used.

Figure 5.20 The correct arrangement for measuring the current through and potential difference across a resistor. The variable resistor allows the current in the resistor R to be varied.

An ideal voltmeter has infinite resistance (in practice about 50 000 Ω), which means that it takes no current when it is connected to a resistor. Voltmeters and ammeters are essentially the

same instrument as a galvanometer. An ammeter has a small resistance connected in parallel to the galvanometer and a voltmeter is a galvanometer connected to a large resistance in series.

Example question

Q11

In the circuit in Figure 5.21, the emf of the battery is 9.00 V and the internal resistance is assumed negligible. A voltmeter whose resistance is 500 Ω is connected in parallel to a resistor of 500 Ω. What is the reading of the ammeter? If we assume that the current registered by the ammeter actually flows into the resistor, what value of the resistance would we measure? Repeat this calculation, this time assuming that the voltmeter's resistance is 5000 Ω.

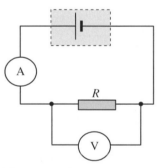

Figure 5.21.

Answer

The total resistance of the circuit is 250 Ω and so the current that leaves the battery is 36.0 mA. If this current is assumed to flow in the resistor, the resistance would be measured as $\frac{9.0\,\text{V}}{36\,\text{mA}} = 250\,\Omega$. With the higher voltmeter resistance, the total circuit resistance is 454.5 Ω. The current flowing is then $\frac{9.0\,\text{V}}{454.5\,\Omega} = 19.8\,\text{mA}$. If we assume all of this current goes into the resistance, the resistance would be measured as 454.5 Ω. In other words, what the experimental arrangement actually measures is not the resistance of the resistor R but the total resistance of R and the voltmeter's resistance. The higher the voltmeter resistance, the closer the total is to R.

The potential divider

Figure 5.22 shows a circuit containing a potential divider. It can be used to investigate, for example, the current–voltage characteristic of some device represented by resistor R. The current that leaves the battery splits at point A. Part of the current goes from A to C and the rest goes into the device R. The right end of the resistance can be connected to a point C on wire AB. By varying the point C where we connect, different potential differences and currents are obtained for device R. AB can be a wire of uniform diameter. One advantage of the potential divider over the conventional circuit arrangement (Figure 5.20) is that now the potential difference across the resistor can be varied from a minimum of 0 V (the connection point C is placed at A) to a maximum of $\mathcal{E}$, the emf of the battery (assuming zero internal resistance) (by connecting point C to point B). In the conventional arrangement of Figure 5.20, the voltage can be varied from some *non-zero* value to a maximum equal to the emf of the battery. This is because the maximum value of the variable resistor cannot be infinite.

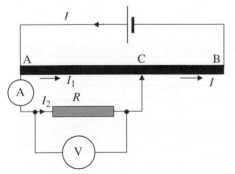

Figure 5.22 This circuit uses a potential divider. The voltage and current in the resistor R can be varied by varying point C.

Questions

1 Find the total resistance for each of the circuit parts in Figure 5.23.

Figure 5.23 For question 1.

2 What is the resistance between A and B in Figure 5.24?

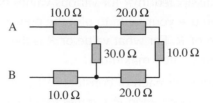

Figure 5.24 For question 2.

3 Each resistor in Figure 5.25 has a value of $6.0\,\Omega$. Calculate the resistance of the combination.

Figure 5.25 For question 3.

4 You are given one hundred $1\,\Omega$ resistors. What is the smallest and largest resistance you can make in a circuit using these?

5 A wire that has resistance R is cut into two equal pieces. The two parts are joined in parallel. What is the resistance of the combination?

6 Find the current in, and potential difference across, each resistor in the circuits shown in Figure 5.26.

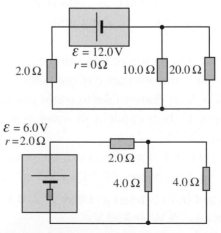

Figure 5.26 For question 6.

7 A battery has emf = 10.0 V and internal resistance 2.0 Ω. The battery is connected in series to a resistance R. Make a table of the power dissipated in R for various values of R and then use your table to plot the power as a function of R. For what value of R is the power dissipated maximum?

8 Six light bulbs, each of constant resistance 3.0 Ω, are connected in parallel to a battery of emf = 9.0 V and negligible internal resistance. The brightness of a light bulb is proportional to the power dissipated in it. Compare the brightness of one light bulb when all six are on, to that when only five are on, the sixth having burned out.

9 A toaster is rated as 1200 W and a mixer as 500 W, both at 220 V.
   (a) If both appliances are connected (in parallel) to a 220 V source, what current does each appliance draw?
   (b) How much energy do these appliances use if both work for one hour?

10 Find the current in each of the resistors in the circuit shown in Figure 5.27. What is the total power dissipated in the circuit?

Figure 5.27 For question 10.

11 An electric kettle rated as 2000 W at 220 V is used to warm 2.0 L of water from 15 °C to 90 °C.
   (a) How much current flows in the kettle?
   (b) What is the resistance of the kettle?
   (c) How long does it take to warm the water? (Specific heat capacity of water = 4200 J kg^{-1} K^{-1}.)
   (d) How much does this cost if the power company charges $0.10 per kW h?

12 One light bulb is rated as 60 W at 220 V and another as 75 W at 220 V.
   (a) If both of these are connected in parallel to a 110 V source, find the current in each

light bulb. (Assume that the resistances of the light bulbs are constant.)
   (b) Would it cost more or less (and by how much) to run these two light bulbs connected in parallel to a 110 V or a 220 V source?

13 Three appliances are connected (in parallel) to the same outlet, which provides a voltage of 220 V. A fuse connected to the outlet will blow if the current drawn from the outlet exceeds 10 A. If the three appliances are rated as 60 W, 500 W and 1200 W at 220 V, will the fuse blow?

14 An electric kettle rated as 1200 W at 220 V and a toaster rated at 1000 W at 220 V are both connected in parallel to a source of 220 V. If the fuse connected to the source blows when the current exceeds 9.0 A, can both appliances be used at the same time?

HL only

15 The graph in Figure 5.28a shows the temperature dependence of a special resistor R. The resistance drops with increasing temperature.

(a)

(b)

Figure 5.28 For question 15.

(a) Estimate the resistance of this resistor at 20 °C.

(b) If this resistor is connected in a circuit as shown in Figure 5.28b, find the current in the resistor when the temperature is 20 °C.

16 The temperature-dependent resistor of question 15 is connected in a circuit to a lamp as shown in Figure 5.29. What will happen to the brightness of the lamp if the temperature of the room increases from 20 °C to 30 °C?

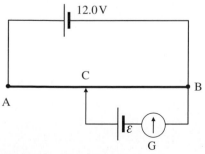

Figure 5.29 For question 16.

17 A clothes dryer operates at 220 V and draws a current of 20.0 A.
(a) What is the power of the machine?
(b) If the dryer is filled with wet clothes that contain 2.0 kg of water at 40 °C, how long will it take to dry them? (The specific heat capacity of water is 4200 J kg^{-1} K^{-1} and the specific latent heat of vaporization of water is 2257 kJ kg^{-1}.) Ignore any heat absorbed by the clothes themselves.

18 In the *potentiometer* in Figure 5.30 wire AB is uniform and has a length of 1.00 m. When contact is made at C with BC = 54.0 cm, the galvanometer G shows zero current. What is the emf of the second cell?

Figure 5.30 For question 18.

19 Two light bulbs are rated as 60 W and 75 W at 220 V. If these are connected in series to a source of 220 V, what will the power in each be? Assume a constant resistance for the light bulbs.

20 At a given time a home is supplied with 100.0 A at 220 V. How many 75 W (rated at 220 V) light bulbs could be on in the house at that time, assuming they are all connected in parallel?

21 (a) What is the reading of the voltmeter in the circuit shown in Figure 5.31 if both resistances are 200 Ω and the voltmeter also has a resistance of 200 Ω?
(b) What is the reading of the ammeter?
(c) If the voltmeter was ideal, what would the readings of the voltmeter and ammeter be?

Figure 5.31 For question 21.

22 For the circuit shown in Figure 5.32, find the current taken from the supply.

Figure 5.32 For question 22.

23 A direct current supply of constant emf 12.0 V and internal resistance 0.50 Ω is connected to a load of constant resistance 8.0 Ω. Find (a) the power dissipated in the load resistance and (b) the energy lost in the internal resistance in 10 min.

24 Consider the circuit in Figure 5.33, where A, B and C are three identical light bulbs of constant resistance. The battery has negligible internal resistance.

(a) Order the light bulbs in order of increasing brightness.

(b) If C burns out, what will be the brightness of A now compared with before?

(c) If B burns out instead, what will be the brightness of A and C compared with before?

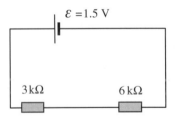

Figure 5.33 For question 24.

25 (a) Determine the potential difference across each resistor in the circuit in Figure 5.34.

(b) A voltmeter of resistance 2 kΩ is connected in parallel across the 3 kΩ resistor. What is the reading of the voltmeter?

Figure 5.34 For question 25.

26 A battery of emf $\mathcal{E}$ and internal resistance r sends a current I into a circuit.

(a) Sketch the potential difference across the battery as a function of the current.

(b) What is the significance of (i) the slope and (ii) the vertical intercept of the graph?

27 Each resistor in the circuit shown in Figure 5.35 has value R and the circuit extends to the right forever. Find the total resistance between A and B.

Figure 5.35 For question 27.

28 Twelve 1.0 Ω resistors are placed on the edges of a cube and connected to a 5.0 V battery, as shown in Figure 5.36. What is the current leaving the battery?

Figure 5.36 For question 28.

Magnetic fields

We have all observed with fascination how magnets attract or repel each other and we are familiar with compasses, which align with the magnetic field of the earth (a fact that has been used for navigation for hundreds of years). But it was only in 1820 that scientists began to understand the cause of magnetism, when the Danish scientist H. C. Ørsted discovered that a wire in which electric current was flowing influenced a magnetic needle placed near the wire. It was thus discovered that the origin of magnetism is electrical. The magnetic field of the earth is presumably caused by moving charges in the interior of the earth and the magnetic field of an iron bar magnet is caused by the motion of electrons in the atoms of the iron. Thus, electric currents cause forces on magnets and, as we will see in this chapter, magnets cause forces on electric currents as well – a result that we might expect from Newton's third law.

Objectives

By the end of this chapter you should be able to:

- understand the meaning of *magnetic field* and find its magnitude and direction in simple situations involving *straight-line conductors* ($B = \frac{\mu_0}{2\pi} \frac{I}{r}$) and *solenoids* ($B = \mu_0 \frac{NI}{L}$) using the right-hand rule where appropriate;
- find the *force on moving charges* ($F = qvB \sin \theta$) and *currents* ($F = BIL \sin \theta$) in magnetic fields and appreciate the definition of the *ampere* as a fundamental SI unit, using the right-hand rule for forces where appropriate;
- explain the operation and importance of the *DC motor*;
- explain the significance of the *split-ring commutator*.

The concept of magnetic field

In the chapters on electricity, it was useful to introduce the concept of an electric field. A charge creates an electric field around itself and any other charge that enters this electric field will experience, as a result, an electric force. The same idea can be extended to magnetism. Both magnets and electric currents create magnetic fields around themselves and when another magnet or electric current (or moving charge in general) enters this magnetic field it will experience a *magnetic* force. The magnetic field is a vector quantity just like the electric field – it has magnitude and direction.

The direction of the magnetic field

The magnetic field direction is determined by the effect it has on a compass needle (i.e. a small bar magnet), as shown in Figure 6.1. A magnetic needle aligns itself in the direction of the magnetic field vector.

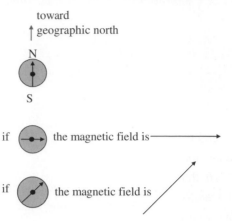

if the magnetic field is ───────→

if the magnetic field is ⟋

Figure 6.1 A magnetic needle is a small bar magnet whose north pole points in the direction of the geographic north pole of the earth. In the presence of another strong magnet, the needle will align itself with the magnetic field.

Magnetic field lines

Just like electric field lines, magnetic field lines are defined as imaginary lines around magnets and currents, tangents to which give the direction of the magnetic field. The magnetic field lines of permanent magnets and the field created by a solenoid (a coil of wire in which electric current flows) are shown in Figures 6.2 and 6.3.

In Figure 6.3, current is flowing in a solenoid and a magnetic field is created inside and outside the solenoid. The current is flowing in the clockwise direction if we look along the axis of the solenoid from right to left.

The magnetic field of a single loop of wire in which current flows is somewhat more complicated and is shown in Figure 6.4. In the right-hand diagram, we are looking at the loop 'from above'; the crosses indicate that the magnetic field is directed into the page while the dots indicate a magnetic field coming out of the page.

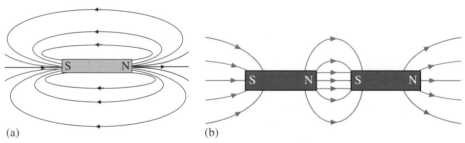

(a)　　　　　　　　　(b)

Figure 6.2 (a) The magnetic field lines of a bar magnet. The field is strongest near the poles of the magnet where the lines crowd together. (b) A uniform magnetic field is obtained if two opposite poles are placed near each other.

Figure 6.5 shows the magnetic field lines of a long straight wire. In Figure 6.5a, the current is coming out of the page. The magnetic field lines are circles centred at the wire. In Figure 6.5b, the current goes into the page. Remember that the magnetic field direction is tangent to the magnetic field lines and the arrows on the lines tell us which tangent to take.

The magnetic field of the earth resembles that of a bar magnet except that the bar magnet does not coincide with the line through the geographic north and south poles of the earth.

The direction of the magnetic field caused by a given current (a few examples of which we have seen in this section) is given by a right-hand rule, which we will describe later.

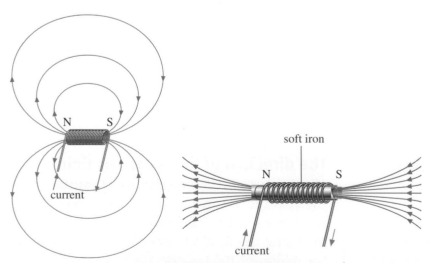

Figure 6.3 The magnetic field lines of a solenoid. The field is fairly uniform in the interior of the coil. Outside it resembles that of a bar magnet.

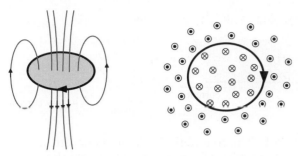

Figure 6.4 The magnetic field lines of a single turn of wire. In the plane of the loop the magnetic field is going into the page inside the loop and out of the page outside the loop. The current in the loop is flowing in the clockwise direction.

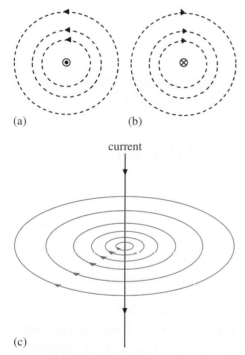

(a) (b)

current

(c)

Figure 6.5 Magnetic field lines for straight current wires. The magnetic field magnitude is largest near the wire.

Example question

Q1 ▰▰▰▰▰▰▰

A magnetic monopole is a particle that is a pure north or pure south magnetic pole. (These are predicted to exist by modern theories of elementary particle physics but none have been found.) Suppose that a *south* magnetic monopole is placed at various positions in the vicinity of a bar magnet, as shown in Figure 6.6. Draw the force experienced by the monopole at the positions shown.

Figure 6.6.

Answer

The force on a north monopole would be in the same direction as the magnetic field direction at the position of the monopole. The force on a south monopole would be opposite to the direction of the magnetic field. Thus, the forces on the south monopole are as shown in Figure 6.7.

Figure 6.7.

The magnetic force on a current

If a current is placed in a region of magnetic field, it will experience a magnetic force. In Figure 6.8 a magnetic field is established out of the page and a wire carries a current from left to right, perpendicular to the magnetic field. The magnitude of the force is proportional to the current I, the magnetic field magnitude B and the length L of the wire that is in the magnetic field.

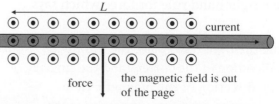

Figure 6.8 A current in a magnetic field experiences a magnetic force. The force is on that part of the wire that is in the magnetic field.

Mathematically

$$F \propto BIL$$
$$\Rightarrow F = kBIL$$

where k is a constant of proportionality. This constant can be made to equal one by proper choice of the unit of magnetic field. We can make $k = 1$ by saying that when the force on 1 m of wire carrying a current of 1 A is 1 N, then the magnitude of the magnetic field is defined to be 1 tesla (so $1\ T = 1\ N\ A^{-1}\ m^{-1}$). So the force on the current-carrying wire is

$$F = BIL$$

Remember, though, that the magnetic field was at right angles to the wire. If there is an angle between them then:

▶ The force on a length L of the wire is given by

$$F = BIL \sin \theta$$

where θ is the angle between the current and the direction of the magnetic field

Figure 6.9 The force on a current-carrying wire in a magnetic field is normal to the plane containing the field and the current. If the ends of the wire are kept fixed, the wire will bend.

The formula above gives the magnitude of the force on the wire. The direction of the magnetic force is always normal to both the current and the magnetic field: that is, it is normal to the plane containing the current and the magnetic field vectors (see Figure 6.9). To find this direction we use a right-hand rule for force which says:

▶ Using the right hand place the thumb in the direction of the current and the fingers in the direction of the magnetic field. The direction *away* from the palm is the direction of the magnetic force. (See Figure 6.10.)

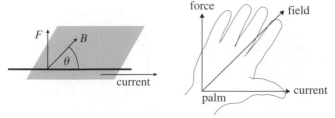

Figure 6.10 The magnetic force on a current is normal to both the magnetic field and the current direction. Its direction is given by a right-hand rule for force.

Supplementary material

Those familiar with the vector product of two vectors may recognize that the equation for the magnetic force is

$$\vec{F} = I\vec{L} \times \vec{B}$$

This equation correctly gives the magnitude as well as the direction of the force.

The magnetic force on a moving charge

An electric current that is in a magnetic field will experience a force as we just saw. But an electric current is just moving charges, so a moving charge will experience a magnetic force as well.

Consider a positive charge q that moves with speed v to the right. In time Δt the charge will move a distance $L = v\Delta t$. The current created by this charge is $I = \frac{q}{\Delta t}$, so the force on this current is

$$F = BIL \sin \theta$$
$$= B \frac{q}{\Delta t} v \Delta t \sin \theta$$
$$= qvB \sin \theta$$

▶ A charge q moving with speed v in a magnetic field of magnitude B will experience a force F given by

$$F = qvB \sin \theta$$

where θ is the angle between the direction of the velocity and the magnetic field. (See Figure 6.11.)

Figure 6.11 An electric charge moving in a magnetic field experiences a magnetic force. The charge shown is positive. The right hand is placed palm up on the page with the thumb pointing in the direction of the velocity and the fingers pointing in the direction of the magnetic field. The direction away from the palm (i.e. out of the page) is the direction of the force on a positive charge.

This implies that the magnetic force is zero if the charge moves parallel or antiparallel to the magnetic field. There is also no magnetic force if the charge is not moving. This is to be contrasted with the electric force on a charge, which is always non-zero irrespective of whether the charge moves or not. The magnetic force on particles that are electrically neutral ($q = 0$) is, of course, zero.

Supplementary material

Those familiar with the vector product of two vectors may recognize that the equation for the magnetic force is

$$\vec{F} = q\vec{v} \times \vec{B}$$

This equation correctly gives the magnitude as well as the direction of the force.

Example question

Q2

An electron approaches a bar magnet as shown in Figure 6.12. What is the direction of the force on the electron?

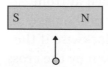

Figure 6.12.

Answer

The magnetic field at the position of the electron is to the left. Placing the right hand such that the thumb points up the page (velocity direction) and the fingers to the left (field direction), the palm is pointing out of the page. But the charge is negative and so the force is into the page.

Motion of charges in magnetic fields

The fact that the magnetic force on a charge is always normal to the velocity means that the path of a charge in a magnetic field must be a circle, as shown in Figure 6.13 (the path can also be helical – see question 21 at the end of the chapter).

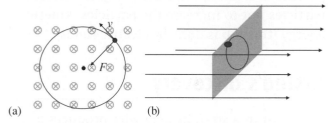

Figure 6.13 A charge in a magnetic field moves in a circle, as shown in (a). The plane of the circle is normal to the magnetic field, as shown in (b). (The charge here is positive.) The magnetic field is into the page in (a).

Consider a charge q moving with speed v in a magnetic field B. Assume that the charge's velocity is normal to the magnetic field, then the force on the charge is $F = qvB$ and so by Newton's second law

$$qvB = m\frac{v^2}{R}$$

where R is the radius of the circle the charge will move on. Therefore

$$R = \frac{mv}{qB}$$

Very massive or very fast charges will move on large circles; large charges and large magnetic fields will result in small circles. The time to make one full revolution in a magnetic field is found from

$$T = \frac{2\pi R}{v}$$
$$= \frac{2\pi}{v} \frac{mv}{qB}$$
$$= \frac{2\pi m}{qB}$$

and is thus independent of the speed. This is an important result in experimental particle physics and forms the basis for an accelerator called the cyclotron.

Work done and magnetic forces

Since the magnetic force is always normal to the velocity of the charge, it follows that it cannot do any work. The big magnets in particle accelerators are used only to deflect particles not to increase the particles' kinetic energy (this job is done by electric fields).

Ørsted's discovery

A current in a straight long wire produces a magnetic field around it. The Danish scientist H. C. Ørsted found that:

> ▶ The magnitude of the magnetic field B created by the current in a wire varies linearly with the current in the wire and inversely with the perpendicular distance from the wire (see Figure 6.14). In equation form
>
> $$B = \frac{\mu_0}{2\pi} \frac{I}{r}$$

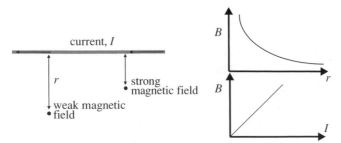

Figure 6.14 The magnitude of the magnetic field vector is inversely proportional to the distance from the wire. The magnetic field is directly proportional to the current.

The constant of proportionality involves the new physical constant μ_0, which is called the *magnetic permeability of vacuum*. If the wire is surrounded by something other than a vacuum, the appropriate permeability of that medium must be used in the formula above. The value of the magnetic permeability of the vacuum is (exactly)

$$\mu_0 = 4\pi \times 10^{-7} \, \mathrm{N\,A^{-2}}$$

It is the analogue in magnetism of the electric permittivity ε in electricity. The unit of the magnetic field is the tesla (T). The tesla is a big unit. The magnetic field of the earth is about 10^{-4} T on the earth's surface. A wire carrying a current of about 2000 A (as in some high-voltage transmission lines) produces a magnetic field of 8×10^{-5} T at a distance of 5 m from the wire.

Whereas the magnitude of the magnetic field is straightforward to investigate, its direction is less so. Let us consider a wire that carries a current normal to the page. The direction of the magnetic field at a given point in space is found by placing magnetic needles around the wire and seeing how they align themselves. Figure 6.15 shows the result of this simple experiment for various points around the wire.

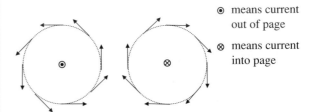

⊙ means current out of page

⊗ means current into page

Figure 6.15 The direction of the magnetic field at various points around straight wires carrying current out of the page (left) and into the page (right).

The structure of the magnetic field direction is thus vectors that are tangent to a circle centred on the wire and 'flow' around the circle in the counter-clockwise sense (as looked at from above) if the current comes out of the page (shown by the full circle) and clockwise if the current goes into the page (shown by the cross in the circle).

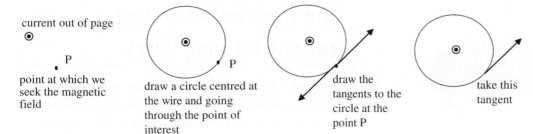

Figure 6.16 To find the magnetic field at a point near a straight wire, draw the imaginary circle centred at the wire, and going through the point of interest. Grip the wire with the fingers of the right hand with the thumb pointing in the direction of the current. Draw the tangent to the circle at the point of interest so that the vector drawn follows the curl of the fingers.

We can formalize this finding into a 'right-hand rule'.

▶ Grip the wire with the fingers of the right hand in such a way that the thumb points in the direction of the current. Then the direction in which the fingers curl is the direction of the 'flow' of the magnetic field vectors. (See Figures 6.16–6.18.)

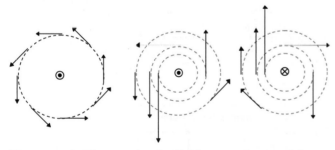

Figure 6.17 The magnetic field around a straight wire at various distances from the wire. Note that as the distance gets bigger the length of the arrow representing the magnetic field gets smaller.

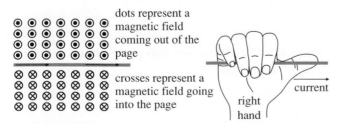

Figure 6.18 The magnetic field of a straight current-carrying wire looked at from a different point of view.

Example question

Q3 ▄▄▄▄▄▄▄▄▄▄▄▄▄▄▄▄▄▄▄▄▄▄▄▄

Find the magnetic field at point P in Figure 6.19.

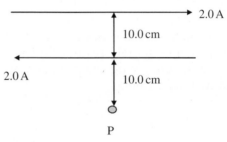

Figure 6.19.

Answer

The top wire produces a magnetic field into the page of magnitude

$$B_1 = 4\pi \times 10^{-7} \frac{2.00}{2\pi \times 0.200} \text{ T}$$
$$= 2.00 \times 10^{-6} \text{ T}$$

and the second wire produces a magnetic field out of the page of magnitude

$$B_2 = 4\pi \times 10^{-7} \frac{2.00}{2\pi \times 0.100} \text{ T}$$
$$= 4.00 \times 10^{-6} \text{ T}$$

resulting in a net magnetic field of 2.00×10^{-6} T out of the page.

The solenoid

In various applications it is necessary to have a uniform magnetic field – one that has the same magnitude and direction in a region of space. A way of achieving such a field is through a solenoid, which is a wire wound tightly many times around an axis (see Figure 6.20a).

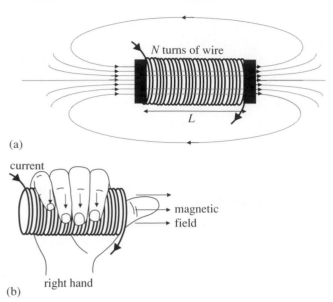

(a)

(b)

Figure 6.20 (a) A solenoid. If it has an iron core, a much stronger magnetic field results. (b) The second right-hand rule giving the direction of the solenoid magnetic field.

> In the *interior* of the solenoid the magnetic field is uniform in magnitude and direction and is given by
>
> $$B = \mu_0 \frac{NI}{L}$$
>
> where N is the number of turns, L the length of the solenoid and I the current through it.

A much stronger magnetic field can be obtained if the solenoid has an iron core.

The direction of the magnetic field of a solenoid is found by a second right-hand rule (see Figure 6.20b).

> Hold the solenoid with the right hand so that the fingers curl in the direction of the current in the coils of the solenoid. Then the thumb points in the direction of the magnetic field.

The solenoid magnetic field outside the solenoid resembles that of a bar magnet.

The force between two current-carrying wires

Consider now two long, straight, parallel wires each carrying current, say I_1 and I_2. The first wire (wire 1) creates a magnetic field in space, and in particular at the position of the second wire (wire 2). Thus, wire 2 will experience a magnetic force. Similarly, wire 2 will produce a magnetic field at the position of wire 1, so that wire 1 will also experience a magnetic force. By Newton's third law, the forces experienced by the two wires are equal and opposite (see Figure 6.21). If the currents are parallel, the forces are attractive and if they are antiparallel, the forces are repulsive.

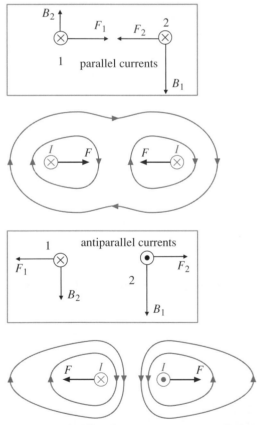

Figure 6.21 The forces on two parallel currents are equal and opposite.

Let us look at the problem of the forces between the two wires in more detail. Consider two long, straight, parallel wires each carrying electric current, say I_1 and I_2. The first wire (wire 1) creates a magnetic field B_1 and the second wire a magnetic field B_2. This means that wire 2 is in the magnetic field of wire 1 (B_1), and so will experience a force. Similarly, wire 1 is in the magnetic field of wire 2 (B_2), and so it too will experience a force. If the two parallel wires are separated by a distance r, then

$$B_1 = \mu_0 \frac{I_1}{2\pi r}$$

$$B_2 = \mu_0 \frac{I_2}{2\pi r}$$

Note that since the currents are different, the magnetic fields are different too. Now, the force on a length L of wire 2 is

$$F_2 = B_1 I_2 L$$

$$\Rightarrow F_2 = \mu_0 \frac{I_1}{2\pi r} I_2 L$$

and similarly the force on an equal length of wire 1 is

$$F_1 = B_2 I_1 L$$

$$\Rightarrow F_1 = \mu_0 \frac{I_2}{2\pi r} I_1 L$$

so, the two forces are equal in magnitude even though the magnetic fields are different. The equality of the forces is expected. The force that wire 1 exerts on wire 2 must be accompanied (Newton's third law) by an equal and opposite force. Let us now use the right-hand rule to find the directions of these forces. Assume first that the currents are flowing into the page. Then the magnetic fields are as shown and the forces are therefore attractive. If wire 1 carries current into the page and wire 2 carries current out of the page, the forces are repulsive. In both cases, we are consistent with Newton's third law. This is how it should be.

This fact is used to define the ampere, the unit of electric current. The ampere *equals* a coulomb divided by a second but it is no longer defined this way.

▶ The ampere is defined through the magnetic force between two parallel wires. If the force on a 1 m length of two wires that are 1 m apart and carrying equal currents is 2×10^{-7} N, then the current in each wire is defined to be 1 A.

The coulomb is defined in terms of the ampere as the amount of charge that flows past a certain point in a wire when a current of 1 A flows for 1 s.

The DC motor

Consider now a coil, taken to be rectangular in shape for simplicity, carrying a current I in a uniform magnetic field B as shown in Figure 6.22.

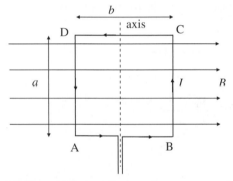

Figure 6.22 A coil-carrying current in a magnetic field will experience a torque.

There are magnetic forces on each of the sides of the coil. On side AB the force is zero, since the current is parallel to the magnetic field. The same is true for side CD – the current there being antiparallel to B. On BC the magnetic force is, by the right-hand rule, directed into the page and on DA it is directed out of the page. Note that the two forces are equal in magnitude, $F = BIa$, where a is the length of sides BC and DA. Since the coil is free to rotate about the vertical axis shown, the effect of the magnetic forces is to make the coil turn.

Supplementary material

The torque exerted by the magnetic forces on the coil is

$$\tau = F\frac{b}{2} + F\frac{b}{2}$$
$$= Fb$$
$$= BIab$$
$$= BIA$$

where $A = ab$ is the area of the coil. Note that we have calculated the torque in the special case in which the plane of the coil is parallel to the magnetic field. After the coil has turned a bit so that there is an angle θ between the direction of the magnetic field and the normal to the plane of the coil, the torque is

$$\tau = 2Fd$$
$$= 2F\frac{b\sin\theta}{2}$$
$$= Fb\sin\theta$$
$$= (BIa)\,b\sin\theta$$
$$= BIA\sin\theta$$

This follows from the diagram in Figure 6.23.

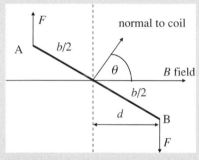

Figure 6.23 The torque on the coil depends on the area of the coil, the magnetic field, the current and the orientation of the magnetic field relative to the coil.

A current-carrying coil in a magnetic field will tend to align itself in such a way that the torque on it is zero, i.e. $\theta = 0°$.

The turning effect of the magnetic force is used in an important device known as the electric motor. Figure 6.24 shows a coil in the form of a rectangle in a magnetic field. The coil is attached in such a way that it is free to rotate about the axis and a current I enters the coil as

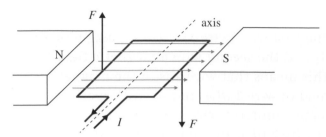

Figure 6.24 A current-carrying coil in a magnetic field experiences a turning effect.

shown. The magnetic field is directed from left to right.

Figure 6.25 shows a sequence of positions of the coil in cross-section. Diagram (a) has the coil as in Figure 6.24. The circled dot indicates that the current is coming out of the page. In (b) the coil

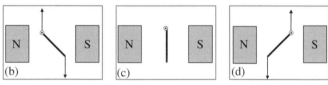

Figure 6.25 Sequence of pictures of the coil in the magnetic field showing the effect of the forces on its rotation. In (d) the rotation would be reversed.

begins to turn in a clockwise direction and continues to do so until (c). At position (c) there is no torque to turn the coil but since it is already moving it will rotate further. As soon as position (c) is left behind, however, the forces on the coil change direction and the coil will now be forced to rotate in the opposite direction.

To avoid this we must change the direction of the current into the coil at position (c). This can be achieved by connecting the coil to the outside circuit that provides the current to it using a *split-ring commutator*. Figure 6.26 shows a split ring that is attached to the two wires leading into the coil and so rotates along with the coil. The ring touches two stationary *brushes*, which are part of the external circuit. The current enters the coil from the right brush and exits from the left. Looked at from above, the current in the coil flows in a counter-clockwise direction, resulting in a rotation of the coil as in Figure 6.24. This is so during half

Figure 6.26 The split-ring commutator ensures that every half a revolution the current in the coil changes direction.

of a revolution. In the next half of a revolution, the split rings switch brushes they are in contact with. This means that the current in the coil has changed direction, which is what we wanted.

Questions

1 Draw the magnetic field lines for two parallel wires carrying equal currents into the page. Repeat for antiparallel currents.

2 Find the direction of the missing quantity from B, v and F in each of the cases shown in Figure 6.27. The circle represents a positive charge.

Figure 6.27 For question 2.

3 Two long, straight wires lie on the page and carry currents of 3.0 A and 4.0 A as shown in Figure 6.28. Find the magnetic field at point P.

Figure 6.28 For question 3.

4 Find the magnetic field at points P, Q and R in Figure 6.29. The currents are parallel and each carry 5.00 A. Point Q is equidistant from the wires. (The three points lie on the same plane as the wires.)

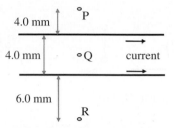

Figure 6.29 For question 4.

5 Draw the magnetic field lines that result when the magnetic field of a long straight wire carrying current into the page is superimposed on a uniform magnetic field pointing to the right that lies on the page. (See Figure 6.30.)

Figure 6.30 For question 5.

6 A long straight wire carries current as shown in Figure 6.31. Two electrons move with velocities that are parallel and perpendicular to the current. Find the direction of the magnetic force experienced by each electron.

Figure 6.31 For question 6.

7 A proton moves past a bar magnet as shown in Figure 6.32. Find the direction of the force it experiences in each case.

Figure 6.32 For question 7.

8 An electron is shot along the axis of a solenoid that carries current. Will it experience a magnetic force?

9 What is the direction of a magnetic field in each of the four cases in Figure 6.33 that results in a force on the current as shown?

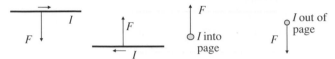

Figure 6.33 For question 9.

10 A rectangular loop of wire of size 5 cm × 15 cm is placed near a long straight wire with side CD at a distance of 5 cm from it, as shown in Figure 6.34. What is the net force exerted on the loop (magnitude and direction)? How does your answer change if the current in the loop is reversed?

Figure 6.34 For question 10.

11 A rectangular coil of size 20 cm × 10 cm is placed in a horizontal uniform magnetic field of magnitude 0.050 T, as shown in Figure 6.35. A current of 2.0 A flows in the coil in a counter-clockwise direction as shown.
  (a) Find the force on sections AB, BC, CD and DA.
  (b) What is the net force on the coil?

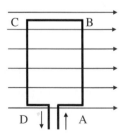

Figure 6.35 For question 11.

12 A tightly wound solenoid of length 30 cm is to produce a magnetic field of 2.26×10^{-3} T along its axis when a current of 15.0 A flows in it. If the radius of the solenoid is 12.0 cm, what length of wire is required to make the solenoid?

13 What is the direction of the magnetic field at points P and Q in the plane of a circular loop carrying a counter-clockwise current, as shown in Figure 6.36?

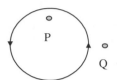

Figure 6.36 For question 13.

14 Two parallel wires a distance of 20.0 cm apart carry currents of 2.0 A and 3.0 A as shown in Figure 6.37.
  (a) At which points is the magnetic field zero?
  (b) How would your answer change if the direction of the 3.0 A current were reversed?

Figure 6.37 For question 14.

15 Figure 6.38 shows two parallel plates with a potential difference of 120 V a distance 5.0 cm apart. The top plate is at the higher potential and the shaded region is a region of magnetic field normal to the page.
  (a) What should the magnetic field magnitude and direction be such that an electron experiences zero net force when shot through the plates with a speed of 2×10^5 m s^{-1}.
  (b) Would a proton shot with the same speed through the plates experience zero net force?
  (c) If the electron's speed were doubled, would it still be undeflected if the magnetic field took the value you found in (a)?

Figure 6.38 For question 15.

16 A bar magnet is placed in a uniform magnetic field as shown in Figure 6.39.
   (a) Is there a net force on the bar magnet?
   (b) Will it move? If so, how?

Figure 6.39 For question 16.

17 A high-tension electricity wire running along a north–south line carries a current of 3000.0 A. If the magnetic field of the earth at the position of the wire has a magnitude of 5.00×10^{-5} T and makes an angle of 30° below the horizontal, what is the force experienced by a length of 30.0 m of the wire?

HL only

18 Two circular loops of wire have their planes parallel and one is directly below the other, as shown in Figure 6.40. Current flows in a counter-clockwise direction (when looked at from above the loops) in both loops. Will there be a force between the loops? If yes, what will its direction be. If not, why is the force zero?

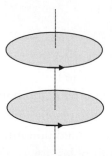

Figure 6.40 For question 18.

19 Figure 6.41 shows two parallel conductors carrying current out of the page. Conductor 1 carries double the current of conductor 2. Draw to scale the magnetic fields created by each conductor at the position of the other and the forces on each conductor.

Figure 6.41 For question 19.

20 An electron of speed v enters a region of magnetic field B directed normally to its velocity and is deflected into a circular path. Find an expression for the number of revolutions per second the electron will make. If the electron is replaced by a proton, how does your answer change?

HL only

21 A proton of velocity 1.5×10^6 m s^{-1} enters a region of uniform magnetic field $B = 0.50$ T. The magnetic field is directed vertically up (along the positive z direction) and the proton's velocity is initially on the z–x plane making an angle of 30° with the positive x axis. (See Figure 6.42.)
   (a) Show that the proton will follow a helical path around the magnetic field lines.
   (b) What is the radius of the helix?
   (c) How many revolutions per second does the proton make?
   (d) How fast is the proton moving along the field lines?
   (e) What is the vertical separation of the coils of the helix?

Figure 6.42 For question 21.

22 An electron enters a region of uniform magnetic field $B = 0.50$ T, its velocity being normal to the magnetic field direction. The electron is deflected into a circular path and leaves the region of magnetic field after being deflected by an angle of 30° with respect to

its original direction. How long was the electron in the region of magnetic field?

23 Find the magnetic field at point P due to three currents as shown in Figure 6.43.

Figure 6.43 For question 23.

24 Find the magnetic field at point P due to the currents shown in Figure 6.44.

Figure 6.44 For question 24.

25 Three parallel wires carry currents as shown in Figure 6.45. Find the force per unit length that wires 1 and 3 exert on wire 2.

Figure 6.45 For question 25.

26 The magnetic field at the centre of a circular loop of wire of radius r carrying current I is given by the formula

$$B = \mu_0 \frac{I}{2r}$$

Use this expression to find the magnetic field created by an electron as it rotates with speed v in a circular orbit of radius r around a nucleus.

27 A tightly wound solenoid is to be made with wire from a fixed quantity (mass) of copper. It will then be connected to a source of *fixed* potential difference. How should the solenoid be made in order to produce the largest magnetic field?

28 Two parallel wires separated by a distance d carry the same current I, as shown in Figure 6.46.
   (a) Calculate the magnitude of the magnetic field at a point on the plane of the wires a distance r from the middle of the wires.
   (b) By using the binomial expansion when r is much larger than d, show that the leading term in the expansion is $B = \mu_0 \frac{2I}{2\pi r}$. Why is this so?
   (c) Repeat for the case where the currents are antiparallel. This time show that the leading term is $B = \mu_0 \frac{Id}{2\pi r^2}$. Why are the two expansions so different?

Figure 6.46 For question 28.

29 In a particle accelerator called the cyclotron, a charged particle is accelerated by an electric field and bent into a circular path by a magnetic field. The magnetic field is assumed uniform and the north and south poles are separated by a small gap. The particles to be accelerated originate from a source at the centre of the bottom magnet pole (the south pole in Figure 6.47) and begin to move outward in a circular path. The bottom magnet pole is split into two pieces called dees. An alternating

Figure 6.47 For question 29.

potential difference is set up between the two dees so that every time the particle crosses from one dee to the other it increases its kinetic energy and thus moves on a circle of larger radius.

(a) Explain why the particle follows a spiral path.

(b) Show that the operation of the cyclotron depends on the frequency of the alternating voltage source, being equal to the frequency of revolution of the particle to be accelerated.

(c) If the mass and charge of the particle are m and q, respectively, show that the period of revolution is

$$T = \frac{2\pi m}{qB}$$

where B is the magnetic field, and is thus independent of the speed of the particle.

(d) Find the frequency (i.e. the number of revolutions per second) of an electron assuming that the magnetic field has a value of 0.50 T.

(e) If the potential difference between the dees at the instant the electrons cross is 120 kV, what would the kinetic energy of the electrons be after 100 revolutions?

30 A uniform magnetic field is established in the plane of the paper and has magnitude 0.3 mT. Two parallel wires separated by 5.0 cm carry currents of 200 A and 100 A into the plane of the paper as shown in Figure 6.48. Find the magnetic force per unit length on the 100 A wire.

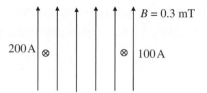

Figure 6.48 For question 30.

31 A uniform magnetic field is established in the plane of the paper as shown in Figure 6.49. Two wires carry *parallel* currents of equal magnitudes normally to the plane of the paper at P and Q. Point R is on the line joining P to Q and closer to Q. The magnetic field at position R is zero.

(a) Are the currents going into the paper or out of the paper?

(b) If the current is increased slightly, will the point where the magnetic field is zero move to the right or to the left of R?

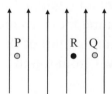

Figure 6.49 For question 31.

Electromagnetic induction

This chapter deals with Faraday's law, which dictates how a changing magnetic flux through a loop induces an emf in the loop. A related law, Lenz's law, determines the direction of this emf. The principles of electromagnetic induction are the result of ingenious experimenting by the English physicist Michael Faraday.

Objectives

By the end of this chapter you should be able to:
- calculate *flux* or *flux linkage* using $\Phi = BA \cos \theta$ or $\Phi = NBA \cos \theta$;
- identify situations in which an emf is *induced* and determine the magnitude of the emf by using *Faraday's law*, $\mathcal{E} = \frac{\Delta \Phi}{\Delta t}$ or $\mathcal{E} = -\frac{d\Phi}{dt}$; included are cases of a *changing area*, a *changing magnetic field* or a *changing angle between magnetic field and normal to loop*;
- find the direction of the induced current using *Lenz's law*.

A wire moving in a magnetic field

Let us imagine that a wire of length L is moved with velocity v in a region of a magnetic field of constant magnitude B. Assume for convenience that the magnetic field is coming out of the page and that the wire moves from top to bottom (see Figure 7.1).

The wire is conducting: that is, it has many 'free' electrons. As the wire moves, the electrons also move from top to bottom. Thus, the magnetic field will exert a force on these moving electrons. (We are talking here about the force on a moving charge, not the force on a current in the wire. There is no current in the wire since the wire is not part of any closed circuit.) The force on the electrons is directed from left to right and therefore the electrons are pushed to the right. This means that the left end of the wire has a net positive charge and the right end has an equal net negative charge accumulated

Figure 7.1 The wire is made to move normally to the magnetic field at constant speed. An emf develops between the ends of the wire.

there. (The net charge of the wire is zero.) The flow of electrons towards the right end of the wire will stop when the electrons already there are numerous enough to push any new electrons back by electrostatic repulsion. There is, in other words, an electric field established in the wire whose direction is from left to right. The value of this electric field is

$$E = \frac{\Delta V}{\Delta x} = \frac{V}{L}$$

where V is the potential difference between the ends of the wire that is established because of the accumulation of electric charge at its ends. The flow of electrons will thus stop when the electric force eE pushing the electrons back equals the magnetic force evB pushing them towards the right end. Thus

$$eE = evB$$

and so (substituting for the electric field)

$$V = vBL$$

We have found the extraordinary result that a conducting wire of length L moving with speed v normally to a magnetic field B will have a potential difference vBL across its ends. This is called a *motional emf*: it has been induced as a result of the motion of the conductor in the magnetic field. It is instructive to check that the quantity vBL really has the units of potential difference, namely volts:

$$[vBL] = \mathrm{m\,s^{-1}\,T\,m} = \mathrm{m\,s^{-1}}\frac{N}{A\,m}m$$

$$= \mathrm{s^{-1}}\frac{J}{C\,s^{-1}} = \frac{J}{C} = V$$

It is worthwhile pointing out that, whereas in electrostatics the electric field inside a conductor is zero, this is no longer the case when charges are allowed to move. Instead, the condition of zero electric field is replaced by a more general condition, namely that $eE = evB$ on a moving charge e.

Also part of Option E4

Faraday's law

As we saw earlier, an electric current creates a magnetic field. In the previous section we saw that a wire that moves in a magnetic field has an induced emf at its ends. Actually producing a current by a magnetic field was a difficult problem in nineteenth-century physics.

Consider the following experiment. A magnet is moved towards a loop of wire whose ends are connected to a sensitive galvanometer and in a direction normal to the plane of the loop, as shown in Figure 7.2. The galvanometer registers a current.

Figure 7.2 A bar magnet moving through a loop of wire connected to a galvanometer. An emf is induced in the loop and the galvanometer registers a current.

If the magnet is simply placed near the coil but does not move relative to it, nothing happens. The current has been created as a result of the motion of the magnet relative to the loop of wire. If we now move the magnet toward the coil faster, the reading on the galvanometer is greater. If we move the coil toward the magnet, we again find a reading. This indicates that it is the relative motion of the coil and magnet that is responsible for the effect. If a magnet of greater strength is used, the current produced is greater. If we try a different loop of wire, one with the same area but a larger number of turns of wire we find a greater current when a magnet is moved toward the wire. We also observe that if the area of the loop is increased, the current also increases. If the magnet is moved at an angle to the plane of the loop other than a right angle, the current decreases. Our problem is now to find the common thread in all these observations. To summarize, the observations are that the current registered by the galvanometer increases when:

- the relative speed of the magnet with respect to the coil increases;

- the strength of the magnet increases;

- the number of turns increases;

- the area of the loop increases;

- the magnet moves at right angles to the plane of the loop.

Faraday found that the common thread behind all these observations is the concept of *magnetic flux*. Imagine a loop of wire, which for simplicity we take to be planar (i.e. the entire loop lies on one plane). If this loop is in a region of magnetic field whose magnitude and direction is constant, then we define magnetic flux as follows.

▶ The *magnetic flux* Φ through the loop is

$$\Phi = BA \cos \theta$$

where A is the area of the loop and θ is the angle between the magnetic field direction and the direction *normal to the loop area*. (See Figure 7.3.) If the loop has N turns of wire around it, the flux is given by

$$\Phi = NBA \cos \theta$$

in which case we speak of *flux linkage*. The unit of magnetic flux is the Weber (Wb): $1\ \text{Wb} = 1\ \text{T m}^2$.

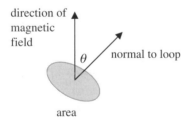

Figure 7.3.

This means that if the magnetic field is along the plane of the loop, then $\theta = 90°$ and hence $\Phi = 0$ (see Figure 7.4a). The maximum flux through the loop occurs when $\theta = 0°$, when the magnetic field is normal to the loop area and its value is then BA (see Figure 7.4b).

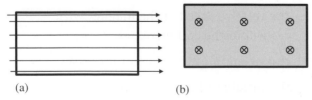

(a)   (b)

Figure 7.4 (a) The loop is not pierced by any magnetic field lines, so the flux through it is zero. (b) The magnetic field is normal to the loop, so the flux through it is the largest possible.

The intuitive picture of magnetic flux is the number of magnetic field lines that cross or pierce the loop area. Note that if the magnetic field went through only half the loop area, the other half being in a region of no magnetic field, then the flux in that case would be $\Phi = \frac{BA}{2}$. In other words, what counts is the part of the loop area that is pierced by magnetic field lines. Thus, to increase the magnetic flux of a loop of wire we must

• increase the loop area that is exposed to the magnetic field;

• increase the value of the magnetic field;

• have the loop normal to the magnetic field.

The loop area has two sides (excluding Möbius strips!). Which of the two sides do we choose in order to define the normal direction to the loop? There are clearly two vectors normal to the loop and they point in opposite directions (see Figure 7.5). The answer is that it does not matter: the choice is a question of convention. But once the choice has been made, we must stick with it.

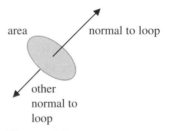

Figure 7.5.

Example question

Q1 ▬▬▬▬▬▬▬▬

A loop of area 2 cm² is in a constant magnetic field of $B = 0.10$ T. What is the magnetic flux through the loop when:

(a) the loop is perpendicular to the field;

(b) the loop is parallel to the field;

(c) the normal to the loop and the field have an angle of 60° between them?

Answer

(a) In this case $\theta = 0°$ and $\cos 0° = 1$, so

$$\text{flux} = 0.10\ \text{T} \times 2 \times 10^{-4}\ \text{m}^2$$
$$= 2 \times 10^{-5}\ \text{Wb}$$

(b) In this case $\theta = 90°$ and $\cos 90° = 0$, so

flux $= 0$

(c) In this case $\theta = 60°$, so

flux $= 0.10 \text{ T} \times 2 \times 10^{-4} \text{ m}^2 \times 0.5$

$= 10^{-5} \text{ Wb}$

What does magnetic flux have to do with the problem of how a magnetic field can create an electric field? The answer lies in a *changing magnetic flux*. In all the cases we described when looking at Figure 7.2 we had a magnetic flux through the loop, which was changing with time. As a magnet is brought closer to the loop area, the value of the magnetic field at the loop position is increasing and so is flux. If the magnet is held stationary near the loop, there is flux through the loop but it is not changing – so nothing happened. If the number of turns is increased, so is the flux linkage. Thus, there seems to be a connection between the amount of current induced and the rate of change of magnetic flux through the loop. This is known as **Faraday's law**.

> ▶ Faraday found that the induced emf is equal to the (negative) rate of change of magnetic flux, that is
>
> $$\mathcal{E} = -\frac{\Delta \Phi}{\Delta t}$$

The minus sign need not concern us, as we will be finding the *magnitude* of the induced emf. However, if we use calculus (i.e. $\mathcal{E} = -\frac{d\Phi}{dt}$), then the minus sign must be included. We will use calculus only in the next chapter.

Example questions

Q2

The magnetic field through a single loop of area 0.2 m^2 is changing at a rate of 4 T s^{-1}. What is the induced emf?

Answer

The magnetic flux through the loop is changing because of the changing magnetic field, hence

$\Phi = BA$

$\Rightarrow \mathcal{E} = \frac{\Delta \Phi}{\Delta t}$

$= \frac{\Delta B}{\Delta t} A$

$= 4 \times 0.2$

$= 0.8 \text{ V}$

Q3

A uniform magnetic field $B = 0.40 \text{ T}$ is established into the page, as shown in Figure 7.6. A rod of length $L = 0.20 \text{ m}$ is placed on a railing and pushed to the right at constant speed $v = 0.60 \text{ m s}^{-1}$. What is the induced emf in the loop?

magnetic field into page

Figure 7.6.

Answer

The flux in the loop is clearly changing since the area of the loop decreases. Thus, there will be an emf induced. In a time interval Δt the rod will move to the right a distance $v\Delta t$ and so the area will decrease by $\Delta A = Lv\Delta t$, thus

$\Phi = BA$

$\Rightarrow \mathcal{E} = \frac{\Delta \Phi}{\Delta t}$

$= B\frac{\Delta A}{\Delta t}$

$= B\frac{Lv\Delta t}{\Delta t}$

$= BLv$

$= 0.40 \times 0.20 \times 0.60$

$= 48 \text{ mV}$

We began this chapter with a discussion of a wire that is dragged in a region of magnetic field. We saw, by considering the forces acting on the electrons of the wire, that a potential difference was induced at its ends that is given by

$\mathcal{E} = BLv$

We may re-derive this result by making use of the concept of changing flux and Faraday's law. The wire cuts magnetic field lines as it moves in the magnetic field. In time Δt it will move a distance of $v\,\Delta t$ and so the flux through *the area swept by the wire* is

$$\Delta\Phi = BLv\Delta t$$
$$\Rightarrow \mathcal{E} = \frac{\Delta\Phi}{\Delta t}$$
$$= BLv$$

(see Figure 7.7).

Figure 7.7 The wire sweeps out an area pierced by magnetic field lines as it moves.

Lenz's law

Having seen that a changing magnetic flux will produce an emf and therefore a current in a conducting loop of wire, we now move to the interesting problem of determining the direction of this induced current. We can guess the answer on the following intuitive grounds. Let us look again at example question 3. Which will be the direction of the induced current? There are two possibilities, the current will either flow in a clockwise or a counter-clockwise fashion in the loop. In either case, there will be a force on the rod because it is a current-carrying wire in a magnetic field.

If the current flows in the counter-clockwise direction:

By the right-hand rule, the force is directed towards the right – in the direction of motion of the rod.

If the current flows in the clockwise direction:

By the right-hand rule, the force is directed towards the left – in the direction opposite to the motion of the rod.

Which choice makes physical sense? If we decide that the current flows in the counter-clockwise direction, the magnetic force will accelerate the rod to the right, thereby increasing its speed. An increased speed leads to an increased emf (recall that $\mathcal{E} = BLv$) and thus increased current. This in turn means that the force on the rod will also get bigger and thus the acceleration will get bigger. And we go on forever. The rod accelerates forever without anyone providing the necessary energy. This choice is absurd. It violates the law of conservation of energy.

The current *must* flow in the clockwise direction. The force now is to the left and it opposes the motion of the rod. If we want the rod to move at constant speed, then we must apply on the rod a force equal and opposite to the magnetic force on the rod. If we do not apply any force on the rod, then the magnetic force will bring it to rest.

The reasoning applied above involves analysing forces. It can be used in almost any situation involving Faraday's law to find the direction of the induced current, but it would be good if we had a very general principle that would give us the answer. Such a general statement has been given by the Russian physicist Emil Lenz, and is called **Lenz's law**.

> ▶ Lenz's law states that the induced current will be in such a direction as to *oppose the change in the magnetic flux* that created the current.

This is a rather subtle and tricky formulation. Let us apply it to example question 3. The change in the magnetic flux has been a *decrease* in magnetic flux (area gets smaller). Lenz's law states that the induced current will be in a direction so as to oppose this *decrease*. The induced current will create *its own magnetic field*, as we learned from Ørsted's discovery. (This magnetic field has nothing to do with the magnetic field whose changing flux created the current.) But the magnetic field created by the induced current will also have a magnetic flux through the same loop. If the created magnetic field is in the same direction as the original magnetic field, its flux will add to the original flux (which, remember, is decreasing) and will thus prevent it from decreasing as fast. In this case the induced current is opposing the decrease in flux and this is what Lenz's law demands. If the induced magnetic field is to be in the same direction as the external magnetic field, the current must flow in a clockwise direction, as we found earlier. (It is assumed that you can find the direction of the current given the direction of the magnetic field it produces – the right-hand rule that allows us to do this is discussed in the previous chapter.)

Let us make sure that we understand what is going on by looking at another example.

Example question

Q4

A loop of wire has its plane horizontal and a bar magnet is dropped from above so that it falls through the loop with (a) the north pole first and (b) the south pole first, as shown in Figure 7.8. Find the direction of the current induced in the loop in each case.

view from above   side view

Figure 7.8.

Answer

(a) In this case, the north pole of the magnet enters first. The flux in the loop is *increasing* because the magnetic field at the loop is getting bigger as the magnet approaches. (We are taking the normal to the loop to be in the vertically down direction. This means that the flux is getting more and more positive.) The induced current must then oppose the *increase* in the flux. This can be done if the induced current produces a magnetic field in the *opposite* direction to that of the bar magnet. Thus, the current will flow in

a counter-clockwise direction when looked at from above.

(b) In this case, the south pole of the magnet enters first. This time let us take the normal to the loop plane to be vertically up. Then the flux in the loop is again increasing and so the current will again produce a magnetic field opposite to the field of the bar magnet. This means that the induced magnetic field will be vertically down, thus the induced current is clockwise.

It is left as an exercise for you to show that the current (in both cases) flows in the opposite direction when the magnet is on its way out of the loop. You should also show that these conclusions are *independent* of the choice of the normal to the loop.

A good example that illustrates many of the principles of electromagnetic induction follows. Consider the motion of a rectangular loop of conducting wire of size $L \times L$ that moves with velocity v and enters a region of magnetic field of constant value B. The plane of the loop is normal to the magnetic field. This is illustrated in Figure 7.9.

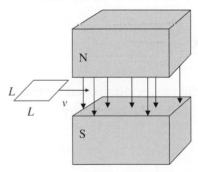

Figure 7.9 A horizontal loop entering a vertical magnetic field at constant speed.

As the loop begins to enter the region of magnetic field, the magnetic flux through the loop is increasing and so an emf will be induced in the loop. The flux equals $\Phi = BLx$ where x is the length of the loop that has entered the magnetic field region and so the rate of change of magnetic flux (and hence the emf) is BLv. A current then flows in the loop of value

$$I = \frac{\varepsilon}{R} = \frac{BLv}{R}$$

where R is the loop's resistance. By Lenz's law, the direction of the current is counter-clockwise (looked at from above). Therefore, there is a force acting on the part of the loop of length L that is inside the magnetic field. (The rear part of the loop is not inside the magnetic field and so experiences zero force.) The magnitude of the force is

$$F = BIL = \frac{B^2L^2v}{R}$$

and is directed against the velocity of the loop. Thus, if the loop is to maintain a constant velocity, a force pushing it to the right and equal to F must be applied to the loop. This means that this force does work. The rate at which work is being done (power dissipated) is

$$P = Fv = \frac{B^2L^2v^2}{R}$$

Where does this work go? It does *not* go into changing the kinetic energy of the loop since the loop is made to move at constant speed. The work goes into heating the wire. The wire has resistance and current flows in it. The power dissipated in the loop as a result of the current in it is

$$P = \mathcal{E}I = \frac{B^2L^2v^2}{R}$$

and is identical to the power dissipated by the external force, as it should be by energy conservation.

Faraday's disc

An interesting example of induced emf is provided by *Faraday's disc*. Like the example of the rod moving in a magnetic field, an emf is induced even though no magnetic flux is changing. This is a motional emf. A conducting disc of radius R rotates about an axis normal to its plane and going through its centre (see Figure 7.10). A magnetic field of constant value is established everywhere in space and is directed along the axis of rotation, which means it is also normal to the plane of the disc.

There is magnetic flux though the disc but it is constant in time. Imagine that the disc rotates with constant angular velocity in a counter-clockwise direction.

magnetic field into page

Figure 7.10 The disc is rotating at right angles to the magnetic field. A potential difference develops between the centre and the circumference.

This means that electrons in the disc experience a magnetic force that pushes them towards the circumference of the disc. The accumulation of electrons on the rim means that there is potential difference between the circumference and the centre of the disc. The flow of electrons will stop when the electric force on electrons trying to move to the circumference equals the magnetic force. The magnetic force on an electron at a distance r from the centre is

$$F = evB = e\omega rB$$

The magnitude of the electric field is $\frac{dV}{dr}$ and so

$$e\frac{dV}{dr} = e\omega rB$$

which can be integrated to give

$$\Delta V = \tfrac{1}{2}\omega R^2 B$$

for the potential difference between the centre and the circumference.

As with the case of the wire that moved in a magnetic field, the potential difference above can also be obtained through the concept of *flux through a swept area*. Thus, consider a radius of the disc. As the disc rotates, the radius can be thought to rotate too, and thus sweeps out an area given by

$$\Delta A = \tfrac{1}{2}R^2\Delta\theta$$

where $\Delta\theta$ is the angle the radius rotates by in a time equal to Δt. This is just the formula for the area of a sector of a circle of radius R and angle $\Delta\theta$. (See Figure 7.11.)

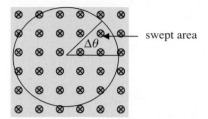

Figure 7.11 As a disc rotates, the radius can be thought to rotate too, sweeping out an area.

If the angular velocity of rotation is ω, then $\Delta\theta = \omega\Delta t$ and the flux through the swept area is $\Delta\Phi = B\frac{1}{2}R^2\omega\Delta t$. This means that the potential difference at the ends of the radius is

$$\mathcal{E} = \frac{\Delta\Phi}{\Delta t}$$

$$= \frac{B\frac{1}{2}R^2\omega\Delta t}{\Delta t}$$

$$= \frac{1}{2}BR^2\omega$$

as we found previously.

Questions

1 The flux through a loop as a function of time is given by the graph in Figure 7.12. Make a sketch of the emf induced in the loop as a function of time.

flux/Wb

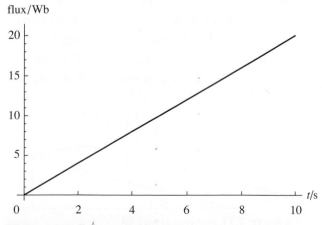

Figure 7.12 For question 1.

2 The flux through a loop as a function of time is given by the graph shown in Figure 7.13. Make a sketch of the emf induced in the loop as a function of time.

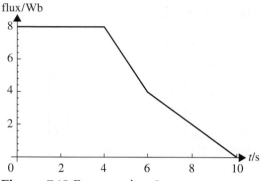

Figure 7.13 For question 2.

3 Figure 7.14 shows the emf induced in a loop as a result of a changing flux in the loop.
   (a) What is a *possible* flux versus time graph that would give rise to such an emf?
   (b) Why isn't there a unique answer?

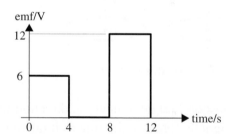

Figure 7.14 For question 3.

4 Figure 7.15 shows a top view of two solenoids with their axes parallel, one with a smaller diameter so that it fits inside the other. If the bigger solenoid has a current flowing in the clockwise direction (looked at from above) and the current is increasing in magnitude, find the direction of the induced current in the smaller solenoid.

Figure 7.15 For question 4.

5 A metallic ring is dropped from a height above a bar magnet as shown in Figure 7.16. Determine the direction of the induced current in the ring as the ring falls over the magnet in each case, giving full explanations for your choices.

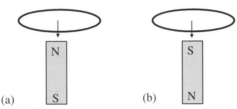

(a)   (b)

Figure 7.16 For question 5.

6 A magnet is dropped from above into a metallic ring as shown in Figure 7.17. Determine the direction of the current induced in the ring in each case.

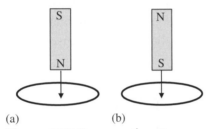

(a)   (b)

Figure 7.17 For question 6.

7 For question 5(a) determine the direction of the magnetic force on the ring as it (a) enters and (b) leaves the magnetic field.

8 A metallic rod of length L is dragged with constant velocity v in a region of magnetic field directed into the page (shaded region), as shown in Figure 7.18. By considering the force on electrons inside the rod, show that the ends of the rod will become oppositely charged. Which end is positively charged?

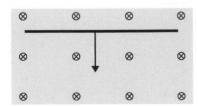

Figure 7.18 For question 8.

9 Find the direction of the current in the loop shown in Figure 7.19 as the current in the

straight wire:
(a) increases;
(b) decreases.

Figure 7.19 For question 9.

10 A coil of 1000 turns and length 20.0 cm has a smaller coil of diameter 2.0 cm and 200 turns inserted inside it. If the current in the big coil is changing at 150 A s^{-1}, find the emf induced in the smaller coil.

11 How can the Faraday disc be connected to an outside circuit to provide it with electric current? Is the current provided AC or DC?

12 Look at Figure 7.20, which we used earlier in the text. If the magnetic field is increasing, what will happen to the rod AB?

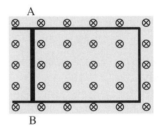

Figure 7.20 For question 12.

HL Mathematics only

13 The problem of the rod sliding over a wire in the shape of a Π that we met in example question 3 and question 12 will now be re-examined for the case in which the railing is no longer horizontal but is inclined by an angle θ, as shown in Figure 7.21. The rod has mass m, length L, resistance R and the

Figure 7.21 For question 13.

magnetic field B is uniform and directed vertically upward. The rod starts from rest; find the terminal velocity reached by the rod.

Hint: Do this in steps as follows.

Part A: (a) Find the flux of the magnetic field through the loop. (b) Find the rate of change of this flux and hence the induced emf. (c) What is the direction of the induced current? (d) Find the magnitude and direction of the magnetic force on the rod. (e) Assume terminal velocity is reached and find an expression for it.

Part B: To find the precise dependence of the velocity on time, write down an expression for the acceleration of the rod down the plane by applying Newton's second law. Realize that the acceleration is the time derivative of velocity and hence solve the differential equation to find the velocity as a function of time. Verify that the rod reaches the terminal velocity you found in (e).

14 A square conducting loop of wire of side a, mass m and resistance R falls under gravity normally to a uniform, horizontal magnetic field B, as shown in Figure 7.22. The area of the loop is small enough so that it can be contained totally within the region of the field.

(a) While the loop is entering the magnetic field, find the magnitude and direction of the induced current.

(b) Write down an expression for the acceleration of the loop as it is entering the field.

(c) Write the acceleration as the time derivative of the velocity and hence show that after time t the velocity of the loop is

$$v = \frac{gmR}{B^2 a^2}\left[1 - \exp\left(\frac{B^2 a^2}{mR}t\right)\right]$$

where we have assumed for simplicity that the loop is dropped from rest from a position where the bottom leg is just

about to enter the region of magnetic field.

(d) Show that the quantity $\frac{gmR}{B^2 a^2}$ has units of velocity and $\frac{mR}{B^2 a^2}$ units of time.

Figure 7.22 For question 14.

15 It was shown in the text that the potential difference between the centre and a point on the circumference of a metallic disc of radius r that rotates with constant angular velocity ω normally to a magnetic field B is $\Delta V = \frac{1}{2}\omega r^2 B$.

Assume the disc shown in Figure 7.23 is rotating in a clockwise sense and that the magnetic field is directed into the page.

(a) Which point is at the higher potential, the centre or a point on the circumference?

(b) If an external circuit of resistance R is connected between the centre and a point on the circumference, show that the current that will flow is $I = \frac{\omega r^2 B}{2R}$.

(c) What will be the direction of the current?

(d) Show that the power dissipated in the resistor is $P = \frac{\omega^2 r^4 B^2}{4R}$.

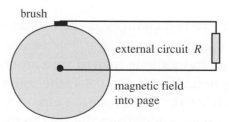

Figure 7.23 For question 15.

Alternating current

This chapter discusses the production of alternating current by the AC generator and the properties of alternating current. We prove the transformer equation and discuss the use of transformers in power transmission.

Objectives

By the end of this chapter you should be able to:
- appreciate that the induced emf in a uniformly rotating coil is sinusoidal;
- explain the operation and importance of the *AC generator*;
- understand the operation of the *transformer*;
- apply the *transformer equation*, $\frac{V_p}{V_s} = \frac{N_p}{N_s}$, and explain the use of transformers in power transmission;
- understand the terms *rms* and *peak current* ($I_{rms} = \frac{I_0}{\sqrt{2}}$) and *voltage* ($\mathcal{E}_{rms} = \frac{\mathcal{E}_0}{\sqrt{2}}$) and calculate the average power in simple AC circuits ($\langle P \rangle = \frac{\mathcal{E}_0 I_0}{2} = \mathcal{E}_{rms} I_{rms}$).

The AC generator

One very important application of electromagnetic induction is the AC (alternating current) generator – the method used universally to produce electricity (see Figure 8.1). The generator is in some sense a motor in reverse. A coil is made to rotate in a region of magnetic field. This can be accomplished in a variety of ways: by a diesel engine burning oil, by falling water in a hydroelectric power station, by wind power, etc.

The flux in the coil changes as the coil rotates and so an emf is produced in it. We assume that the coil has a single turn of wire around it, the magnetic field is $B = 0.4$ T, the coil has an area of 0.318 m^2 and a rotation rate of 50 revolutions per second. Then the flux in the coil changes as time goes on according to a cosine function as shown in Figure 8.2. (Time zero is taken to correspond to the coil in the

Figure 8.1 A coil that is forced to turn in a region of magnetic field will produce an emf.

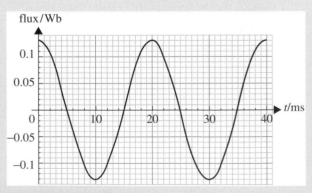

Figure 8.2 The flux in the coil is changing with time.

position of Figure 8.1 so that the flux is a maximum.)

The equation of the flux (linkage) is, in general,

$$\Phi = NBA \cos\theta$$

where θ is the angle between the magnetic field and the normal to the coil and N is the number of turns in the coil. Assuming that the coil rotates at a constant angular velocity ω, it follows that $\theta = \omega t$ and so the flux becomes

$$\Phi = NBA \cos(\omega t)$$

> By Faraday's law, the emf induced in the coil is (minus) the rate of change of the flux linkage and thus is given by
>
> $$\mathcal{E} = -\frac{d\Phi}{dt}$$
> $$\Rightarrow \mathcal{E} = \omega NBA \sin(\omega t)$$

The quantity $\mathcal{E}_0 = \omega NBA$ is the peak voltage produced by the generator. For the same numerical values as in the previous example, the emf induced is given by the graph shown in Figure 8.3 ($\omega = 2\pi f = 314.6 \text{ s}^{-1}$).

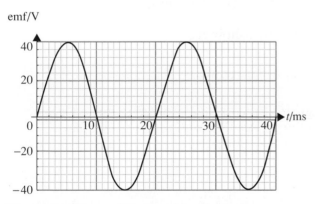

Figure 8.3 The emf induced in the loop as a function of time. The peak voltage is 40 V.

Note that the emf induced is zero whenever the flux assumes its maximum or minimum values and, conversely, it is a maximum or minimum whenever the flux is zero. The noteworthy thing here is that the voltage can be negative as well as positive. This is what is called

alternating voltage and the current that flows in the coil is alternating current (AC). This means that, unlike the ordinary direct current (DC) that flows in a circuit connected to a battery, the electrons do not drift in the same direction but oscillate back and forth with the same frequency as that of the voltage.

The current that will flow in a circuit of resistance R can be found from

$$I = \frac{\mathcal{E}}{R}$$
$$= \frac{\mathcal{E}_0 \sin(\omega t)}{R}$$
$$= I_0 \sin(\omega t)$$

where $I_0 = \frac{\mathcal{E}_0}{R}$ is the peak current. For the emf of Figure 8.3 and a resistance of 16 Ω the current is shown in Figure 8.4.

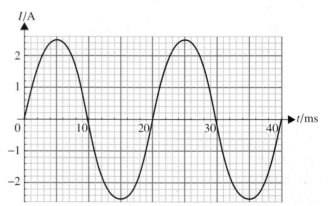

Figure 8.4 The induced current in the rotating loop. Note that the current is in phase with the emf. The peak current is found from peak voltage divided by resistance, i.e. $40/16 = 2.5$ A.

Power in AC circuits

The power generated in an AC circuit is

$$P = \mathcal{E}I$$
$$= \mathcal{E}_0 I_0 \sin^2(\omega t)$$

and, just like the current and the voltage, is not constant in time. It has a peak value given by the product of the peak voltage and peak current (i.e. $40 \times 2.5 = 100$ W, for the previous example). The power as a function of time is shown in Figure 8.5.

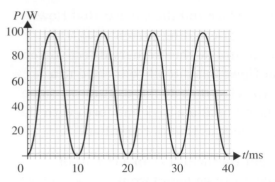

Figure 8.5 The power dissipated in a resistor as a function of time. Note that the period of one rotation of the coil is 20 ms. The power becomes zero every half rotation of the coil. The peak power is 100 W. The horizontal line indicates the average power of 50 W.

▶ It is instructive to write the expression for power in terms of the parameters of the rotating coil:

$$P = \mathcal{E}I$$

$$= \omega NBA \sin(\omega t) \times \frac{\omega NBA \sin(\omega t)}{R}$$

$$= \frac{(\omega NBA)^2}{R} \sin^2(\omega t)$$

This shows, for example, that if the speed of rotation of the coil is doubled, the power is increased by a factor of 4.

Root mean square (rms) quantities

It would be convenient to define an average voltage, average current and average power. For power this is not difficult, as power is always positive. Trying to find the average of the current or voltage, though, would give zero. In any one cycle, the voltage and current are as much positive as they are negative and so average to zero. To get around this problem we use the following trick. First, we square the current, getting a quantity that is always positive during the entire cycle. Then we find the average of this positive quantity. Finally, we take its square root. The result is called the rms value of the current (from root mean square).

How do we evaluate an rms quantity? Squaring the current gives

$$I^2 = I_0^2 \sin^2(\omega t)$$

$$= \frac{I_0^2}{2}[1 - \cos(2\omega t)]$$

where in the last step we used the identity

$$\sin^2 \theta = \frac{1 - \cos 2\theta}{2}.$$

Over one cycle, the cosine term averages to zero and so the average of the square of the current is

$$\langle I^2 \rangle = \frac{I_0^2}{2}$$

(angular brackets denote an average). Thus

$$I_{rms} = \frac{I_0}{\sqrt{2}}$$

Doing exactly the same thing for the voltage results in an rms voltage of

$$\mathcal{E}_{rms} = \frac{\mathcal{E}_0}{\sqrt{2}}$$

Since

$$P = \mathcal{E}_0 I_0 \sin^2(\omega t)$$

$$= \frac{\mathcal{E}_0 I_0}{2}[1 - \cos(2\omega t)]$$

we get the following:

▶ The *average* power is

$$\langle P \rangle = \left\langle \frac{\mathcal{E}_0 I_0}{2}[1 - \cos(2\omega t)] \right\rangle$$

$$= \frac{\mathcal{E}_0 I_0}{2}$$

$$= \frac{\mathcal{E}_0}{\sqrt{2}} \frac{I_0}{\sqrt{2}}$$

$$= \mathcal{E}_{rms} I_{rms}$$

(again the term with the cosine averages to zero over one period).

On a very non-rigorous level, we might say that dealing with rms quantities turns AC circuits into DC circuits. The product of the rms current times the rms voltage gives the *average* power in the circuit.

> We may also use the alternative formulae for average power
>
> $$\langle P \rangle = R I_{rms}^2$$
> $$= \frac{\mathcal{E}_{rms}^2}{R}$$

Example question

Q1

Find the rms quantities corresponding to the current and voltage of Figures 8.3 and 8.4.

Answer

The peak voltage is 40 V giving

$$\mathcal{E}_{rms} = \frac{40}{\sqrt{2}}$$
$$\approx 28 \text{ V}$$

Similarly, the peak current is 2.5 A, giving

$$I_{rms} = \frac{2.5}{\sqrt{2}}$$
$$\approx 1.8 \text{ A}$$

From Figure 8.5, the peak power is 100 W and the average power is 50 W. The product of the rms current times the rms voltage is indeed

$$1.8 \times 28 = 50 \text{ W}$$

The slip-ring commutator

The current must now be fed from the rotating coil into an external circuit where it can be put to use. The rotating coil is connected to the outside circuit, to which it provides current, through *slip rings*, as shown in Figure 8.6. Each of the wires leading into the coil is firmly

Figure 8.6 The slip-ring connection of the rotating coil to the outside circuit.

connected to its own ring S. As the coil rotates, the ring rotates along with it, but each ring is always in contact with the same brush (B) that connects to the outside circuit. This means that since AC current is produced in the coil, AC current will be fed to the external circuit as well.

(What current would flow in an external circuit if the generator were connected to it via a *split ring*?)

The great advantage of AC voltage and current is that they allow the use of the transformer (see later).

Back-emf in the DC motor

In an earlier chapter we discussed the DC motor in which current fed into a loop that is in a magnetic field makes the coil turn as a result of the forces that develop on the sides of the loop. Because of Faraday's law an emf (the back-emf) will be induced in the loop as it begins to rotate, since there is a changing magnetic flux in the loop. By Lenz's law, this emf will oppose the change in the flux that created it. This means that a current will flow in the loop that is opposite to the current that the external battery feeds into the loop. The current in the loop will thus be less when the coil is rotating than initially, when the rotation had not yet started. The back-emf is the reason that lights sometimes dim when the motor of the refrigerator turns on. Initially the current drawn by the motor is large and only after the coil of the motor achieves a constant speed of rotation does the current drop to lower values.

The transformer

Consider two coils placed near each other as shown in Figure 8.7. The turns of both coils are wrapped around an iron core.

The first coil (the primary) has N_p turns of wire and the second (the secondary) N_s turns. If the

Figure 8.7 The changing flux in the secondary coil produces an emf in that coil.

primary coil is connected to an AC source of voltage, an alternating current will pass through this coil. The magnetic field this current will create will be changing in both magnitude and direction, since the current is. As the two coils are near each other, the magnetic field of the first coil enters the second coil and thus there is magnetic flux in this second coil. The purpose of the iron core is to ensure that as much of the flux produced in the primary coil as possible enters the secondary coil. Iron has the property that it confines magnetic flux and so no magnetic field lines spread out into the region outside the core. Since the magnetic field is changing, the flux is also changing and thus, by Faraday's law, there will be an *induced* emf in the secondary coil.

If the flux is changing at a rate $\frac{\Delta\Phi}{\Delta t}$ through one turn of wire, then the rate of change of flux linkage in the second coil is $N_s\frac{\Delta\Phi}{\Delta t}$, and that, therefore, is the emf induced in the secondary coil, $V_s = N_s\frac{\Delta\Phi}{\Delta t}$. Similarly, the emf, V_p, in the first coil is $V_p = N_p\frac{\Delta\Phi}{\Delta t}$. Hence

$$\frac{V_p}{V_s} = \frac{N_p}{N_s}$$

The arrangement just described is called a *transformer*. What we have achieved is to make a device that takes in AC voltage (V_p) in the primary coil and delivers in the secondary coil a *different* AC voltage (V_s). If the secondary coil has more turns than the primary, the secondary voltage is bigger than the primary voltage (if the secondary coil has fewer turns, the secondary voltage is smaller). *Note that the transformer works only when the voltage in the*

primary coil is changing. Direct (i.e. constant) voltage fed into the primary coil would result in zero voltage in the secondary (except for the short interval of time it takes the current in the primary coil to reach its final steady value). In the case of standard AC voltage, there is a sine dependence on time with a frequency of 50 or 60 Hz. The frequency of the voltage in the secondary coil stays the same – the transformer cannot change the frequency of the voltage.

If the primary coil has a current I_p in it, then the power dissipated in the primary coil is $V_p I_p$. Assuming no power losses, the power dissipated in the secondary coil is the same as that in the primary and thus

$$V_p I_p = V_s I_s$$

Therefore, using $\frac{V_p}{V_s} = \frac{N_p}{N_s}$ the relationship between the currents is

$$\frac{I_p}{I_s} = \frac{N_s}{N_p}$$

(Power losses are reduced by having a laminated core rather than a single block for the core – this reduces power losses by eliminating eddy currents. Eddy currents are created in the core because the free electrons of the core move in the presence of a magnetic field. Thus these electrons are deflected into circular paths and they create small currents in the core. See Figure 8.8.)

a solid core will have eddy currents

a laminated core with insulation between layers reduces eddies

Figure 8.8 Free electrons move in circular paths creating eddy currents in the magnetic field that is established in the core. Nearly all of these currents are eliminated if the core is laminated.

Transformers and power transmission

Transformers are used in the transport of electricity from power stations, where electricity is produced, to the consumer. At any given time, a city will have a power demand, P, which is quite large (many megawatts for a large city). If the power station sends out electricity at a voltage V and a current I flows in the cables from the power station to the city and back, then

$$P = VI$$

The cables have resistance, however, and thus there is power loss $P_{loss} = RI^2$ where R stands for the total resistance of the cables. To minimize this loss it is necessary to minimize the current (there is not much that can be done about minimizing R). However, small I (I is still a few thousand amperes) means large V (recall, $P = VI$), which is why power companies supply electricity at large voltages. Transformers are then used to reduce the high voltage down to that required for normal household appliances (220 V or 110 V). (See Figure 8.9.)

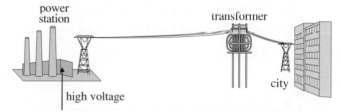

power station — transformer — city — high voltage

Figure 8.9 The voltage produced in the power station is high in order to reduce losses during transmission. Transformers are used to step down the voltage to what the consumer requires.

Example question

Q2

A power company produces 500 MW of electricity at a voltage of 1.2×10^5 V. The total resistance of the cables leading to and from a town is 4 Ω. How much current flows from the power station? What is the percentage loss of power in the cables? If the electricity were transmitted at the lower voltage of 0.8×10^5 V, what would the power loss be?

Answer

From $P = VI$ the current is

$$I = \frac{500 \times 10^6}{1.2 \times 10^5}$$
$$= 4.2 \times 10^3 \, A$$

The power loss in the cables is

$$P_{loss} = RI^2$$
$$= 4.0 \times (4.2 \times 10^3)^2$$
$$= 7.1 \times 10^7 \, W$$
$$= 71 \, MW$$

This corresponds to a power loss of $71/500 \times 100\% = 14\%$ of the produced power. With the lower voltage the current is

$$I = \frac{500 \times 10^6}{0.8 \times 10^5}$$
$$= 6.2 \times 10^3 \, A$$

The power lost is then

$$P = RI^2$$
$$= 4.0 \times (6.2 \times 10^3)^2$$
$$= 1.5 \times 10^8 \, W$$
$$= 150 \, MW$$

The percentage of power lost is now $150/500 \times 100\% = 30\%$.

Questions

1 A transformer has 500 turns in its primary coil and 200 in the secondary coil.
   (a) If an AC voltage of 220 V and frequency 50 Hz is established in the primary coil, find the voltage and frequency induced in the secondary coil.
   (b) If the primary current is 6.0 A, find the current in the secondary coil assuming an efficiency of 70%.

2 A 300 MW power station produces electricity at 80 kV, which is then supplied to consumers along cables of total resistance 5.0 Ω.
   (a) What percentage of the produced power is lost in the cables?
   (b) What does the percentage become if the electricity is produced at 100 kV?

3 The rms power output of a generator is 220 V. The coil is a square of side 20.0 cm, has 300 turns of wire and rotates at 50 revolutions per second. What is the magnetic field?

4 Figure 8.10 shows the variation, with time, of the magnetic flux linkage through a loop. What is the rms value of the emf produced in the loop?

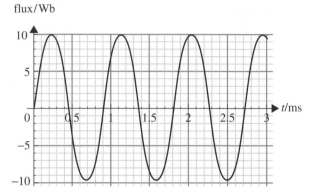

Figure 8.10 For question 4.

5 A power station produces 150 kW of power, which is transmitted along cables of total resistance 2.0 Ω. What fraction of the power is lost if it is transmitted at:
 (a) 1000 V;
 (b) 5000 V?

6 If the connection of a rotating generator coil to the outside circuit were made through a split ring (as discussed in the case of the DC motor), what sort of current would flow in the external circuit?

7 Figure 8.11 shows the variation with time of the power dissipated in a resistor when an alternating voltage from a generator is established at its ends. Assume that the resistance is constant at 2.5 Ω.
 (a) Find the rms value of the current.
 (b) Find the rms value of the voltage.

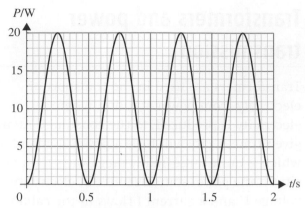

Figure 8.11 For question 7.

 (c) Find the period of rotation of the coil.
 (d) The coil is now rotated at double the speed. Draw a graph to show the variation with time of the power dissipated in the resistor.

8 Figure 8.12 shows the variation of the flux in a coil as it rotates in a magnetic field with the angle between the magnetic field and the normal to the coil.
 (a) Draw a graph to show the variation of the induced emf with angle.
 The same coil is now rotated at double the speed in the same magnetic field. Draw graphs to show:
 (b) the variation of the flux with angle;
 (c) the variation of the induced emf with angle.

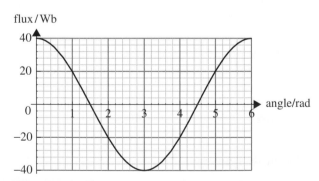

Figure 8.12 For question 8

The atom and its nucleus

In ancient times, the Greek philosopher Demokritos asserted that all matter is made out of indivisible units. This chapter introduces the basic ideas and models that have given rise to our present understanding of the atom and its nucleus. We begin with Rutherford's experiment that provided the evidence for the existence of a small, massive and positively charged atomic nucleus and close with a discussion of the fundamental forces that operate within the nucleus.

Objectives

By the end of this chapter you should be able to:
- appreciate that *atomic spectra* provide evidence for an atom that can only take *discrete values in energy*;
- explain what *isotopes* are and how their existence implies that neutrons are present inside the nucleus;
- state the meaning of the terms *nuclide*, *nucleon*, *mass number* and *atomic number* (proton number);
- outline the properties of the *forces* that operate within the nucleus.

The discovery of the nuclear atom

In 1909, Geiger and Marsden, working under Rutherford's direction, performed a series of experiments in which they studied the scattering of alpha particles shot at a thin gold foil. Alpha particles have a mass approximately four times that of the hydrogen atom and a positive electric charge of two units ($2e$). Alpha particles are emitted when unstable elements decay; we will study them in more detail later.

Geiger and Marsden used radon as their source of alpha particles, which they directed in a fine beam toward the thin gold foil. The scattered alpha particles were detected (through a microscope) by the glow they caused on a fluorescent screen at the point of impact. As

expected, most of the alpha particles were detected at very small scattering angles, such as at positions A, B and C in Figure 1.1.

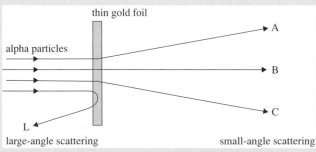

Figure 1.1 The majority of alpha particles are slightly deflected by the gold foil. Very occasionally, large-angle scatterings take place. The small deflections could be understood in terms of alpha particles approaching the nucleus at large distances. The large deflections were due to alpha particles approaching very close to the nucleus.

These small deflections could be understood in terms of the electrostatic force of repulsion between the positive charge of the gold atoms and the positive charge of the alpha particles. (Note that an alpha is about 8000 times more massive than the electron and so the effect of the electrons of the gold atoms on the path of the alphas is negligible.)

▶ To their great surprise, Rutherford, Geiger and Marsden found that, occasionally, alpha particles were detected at *very large scattering angles*, as can be seen in Figure 1.1. These large-angle scattering events could not be understood in terms of the prevailing model of the time – Thomson's model of the atom.

Consequences of the Geiger–Marsden–Rutherford experiment

The very large deflection was indicative of an enormous force of repulsion between the alpha particle and the carrier of the positive charge of the atom. Such a large force could not be produced if the positive charge was distributed over the entire atomic volume, as Thomson had suggested earlier (see Figure 1.2). Rather, it suggested that the positive charge resided on a tiny object (thus the alpha particle could come very close to it) but massive (because there is no recoil of the gold atoms) (see Figure 1.3). In this way, the alpha particle could approach the positive charge at a very small distance, and

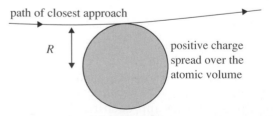

Figure 1.2 In Thomson's model, the closest an alpha particle can come to the atom's centre is a distance equal to the atomic radius.

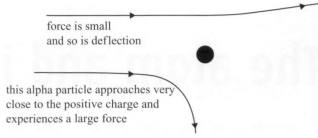

force is small and so is deflection

this alpha particle approaches very close to the positive charge and experiences a large force

Figure 1.3 In Rutherford's model, the alpha particle can approach much closer if the nucleus is very small.

the Coulomb force of repulsion, being proportional to the inverse of the square of the separation, would then be enormous. This force causes the large deflection in the alpha particle's path.

Rutherford calculated theoretically the number of alpha particles expected at particular scattering angles based on Coulomb's force law. He found agreement with his experiments if the positive atomic charge was confined to a region of linear size approximately equal to 10^{-15} m. This and subsequent experiments confirmed the existence of a nucleus inside the atom – a small, massive object carrying the positive charge of the atom.

Example question

Q1

Calculate the electric field at the surface of a nucleus of one unit of positive charge and radius 10^{-15} m. Compare this with the value of the electric field of the same charge that is now spread over a sphere of radius 10^{-10} m.

Answer

Applying the formula for the electric field $E = k\frac{Q}{r^2}$ we find

$$E = 9 \times 10^9 \times \frac{1.6 \times 10^{-19}}{(10^{-15})^2}$$
$$= 1.4 \times 10^{21} \, \text{N C}^{-1}$$

Near the larger sphere, the electric field is $E = 1.4 \times 10^{11} \, \text{N C}^{-1}$, which is a factor of 10^{10} smaller. This is why the deflecting forces in *Rutherford's model* are so large compared with what one might expect from *Thomson's model*.

(See Chapter E5 for historical information about Thomson's model.)

The Rutherford model of the atom

These discoveries led to a new picture of the atom. A massive, positively charged nucleus occupied the centre of the atom and electrons orbited this nucleus in much the same way that planets orbit the sun: this was the Rutherford model (see Figure 1.4). The force keeping the electrons in orbit was the electrical force between the negative electron charge and the positive nuclear charge.

Figure 1.4 Rutherford's atomic model has the electrons orbiting the nucleus like planets orbiting the sun.

Immediately after these discoveries, difficulties arose with the Rutherford model.

▶ The main difficulty was that, according to the theory of electromagnetism, an accelerated charge should radiate electromagnetic waves and thus lose energy. The electrons in Rutherford's atom move in circular paths around the nucleus and so suffer centripetal acceleration. If they radiate and lose energy, it can be shown that this would lead to electron orbits that would spiral into the nucleus. The time required for the electron to fall into the nucleus is of the order of nanoseconds. Thus, the Rutherford model cannot explain why matter is stable, i.e. why atoms exist.

The Bohr model

The first attempt to solve this problem came from the Danish physicist Niels Bohr in 1911. These are the **Bohr postulates**. (There is more on the Bohr model in Chapter 6.5.)

▶ Bohr examined the simplest atom, that of hydrogen, and realized that the electron could exist in certain specific states of definite energy, without radiating away energy, if a certain condition was met by the orbit radius. The electron energy is thus *discrete* as opposed to continuous. The electron can only lose energy when it makes a transition from one state to another of lower energy. The emitted energy is then the difference in energy between the initial and final states. (See Figure 1.5.) The strongest piece of evidence in support of Bohr's idea is the existence of *emission* and *absorption spectra*.

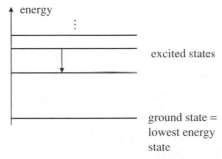

Figure 1.5 In the Bohr model the electron occupies one of a number of specific states each with a well-defined energy. While it is in one of these states, the electron does not radiate away energy.

Spectra

Consider hydrogen as an example. Under normal conditions (i.e. normal temperature, pressure, etc.) the electron in each hydrogen atom occupies the lowest energy state or **energy level** (the ground state). If the atoms are somehow excited (by increasing their temperature, for example) the electrons leave the ground state and occupy one of the higher energy, excited states. As soon as they do so, however, they make a transition back down to lower energy states, radiating energy in the process. The energy of the light emitted is very well defined since it corresponds to the difference in energy between the states involved in the transition. Knowing this energy difference allows us to calculate the wavelength of the emitted light, and so the wavelength, too, is well defined since the energy is. In this way it is found, for example, that hydrogen emits light of wavelengths 656 nm, 486 nm and 410 nm. Only hydrogen emits light of these wavelengths since only hydrogen has states whose energy differences lead to these wavelengths. Helium, for example, has energy states of different energy, so the wavelengths of light emitted when helium atoms are heated are different from those of hydrogen.

> The set of wavelengths of light emitted by the atoms of an element is called the *emission spectrum* of the element.

Conversely, consider atoms of hydrogen that are in their ground states and imagine sending light of a specific wavelength through a given quantity of hydrogen. If the wavelength of light does not correspond to any of the wavelengths in the emission **spectrum** of hydrogen, the light is transmitted through the atoms of hydrogen without any absorption. If, however, it matches one of the emission spectrum wavelengths, then this light is absorbed.

> The electrons simply take this energy and use it in order to make a transition to a higher energy state. The wavelengths that are so absorbed make up the *absorption spectrum* of the element and (as indicated above) they are the same wavelengths as those in the emission spectrum.

Thus, if white light (i.e. light containing all wavelengths) is sent through the gas and the transmitted light is analysed through a spectrometer, dark lines will be found at the position of the absorbed wavelengths.

Nuclear structure

Nuclei are made up of smaller particles, called protons and neutrons. The word *nucleon* is used to denote a proton or a neutron.

> - The number of protons in a nucleus is denoted by Z, and is called the atomic (or proton or baryon) number.
> - The total number of nucleons (protons + neutrons) is called the mass (or nucleon) number, and is denoted by A.

Then the electric charge of the nucleus is $Z|e|$. The number of neutrons in the nucleus (the neutron number N) is thus $N = A - Z$. We will use the atomic and mass numbers to denote a nucleus in the following way: the symbol $^{A}_{Z}X$ stands for the nucleus of element X, whose atomic number is Z and mass number is A. Thus $^{1}_{1}H$, $^{4}_{2}He$, $^{40}_{20}Ca$, $^{210}_{82}Pb$ and $^{238}_{92}U$ are, respectively, the nuclei of hydrogen, helium, calcium, lead and uranium, with one, two, twenty, eighty-two and ninety-two protons. A nucleus with a specific number of protons and neutrons is also called a *nuclide*.

We can apply this notation to the nucleons themselves. For example, the proton (symbol p) can be written as $^{1}_{1}p$ and the neutron (symbol n) as $^{1}_{0}n$. We can even extend this notation to the electron, even though the electron has nothing to do with the nucleus and nucleons. We note that the atomic number is not only the number of protons in the nucleus but also its electric charge in units of $|e|$. In terms of this unit, the charge of the electron is -1 and so we represent the electron by $^{0}_{-1}e$. The mass number of the electron is zero – it is so light with respect to the protons and neutrons that it is, effectively, massless. The photon (the particle of light) can also be represented in this way: the photon has the Greek letter gamma as its symbol, and since it has zero electric charge and (strictly) zero mass it is represented by $^{0}_{0}\gamma$. Table 1.1 gives a summary of these particles and their symbols.

Particle	Symbol
Proton	^1_1p
Neutron	^1_0n
Electron	$^0_{-1}\text{e}$
Photon	$^0_0\gamma$
Alpha particle	^4_2He or $^4_2\alpha$

Table 1.1

Isotopes

Nuclei that have the same number of protons (and therefore the same atomic number Z) but different number of neutrons (i.e. different N and mass number A) are called *isotopes* of each other. Since isotopes have the same number of protons, their atoms have the same number of electrons as well. This means that isotopes have identical chemical but different physical properties. The existence of isotopes can be demonstrated with an instrument called the mass spectrometer (this is discussed further in Chapter 6.6). The existence of isotopes is evidence for the existence of neutrons inside atomic nuclei.

The forces within the nucleus

The nucleons (i.e. protons and neutrons) are bound together in the nucleus by a force we have not yet met – *the strong nuclear force*. It is necessary to have a new force inside the nucleus, because otherwise the electrical repulsion between the positively charged protons would break the nucleus apart (see Figure 1.6).

▶ The strong nuclear force is an attractive force and much stronger than the electrical force if the separation between two nucleons is very small (i.e. about $r = 10^{-15}$ m or less). For larger separations, the nuclear force becomes so small as to be negligible – we say that the nuclear force has a *short range*.

The experimental evidence for the properties of the nuclear force comes from scattering

In a helium-4 nucleus, Coulomb forces push the protons apart.

There must be forces between nucleons pulling them together. Gravitational forces are far too small.

Figure 1.6 There is an attractive force between nucleons that keeps them bound inside the nucleus.

experiments in which electrons of energy equal to about 200 MeV (in later experiments neutrons were also used) are allowed to hit nuclei and their scattering is studied. If we make the assumption of short-range forces, we obtain agreement with the data. A result of these experiments is that the nuclear radius R is given by

$$R = 1.2 \times A^{1/3} \times 10^{-15} \text{ m}$$

where A is the total number of protons and neutrons in the nucleus (the mass number). This implies that the nuclear density is the same for all nuclei (you will look at this further in the questions at the end of this chapter). The short range of the force implies that a given nucleon can only interact with a few of its immediate neighbours and not with all of the nucleons in the nucleus (see Figure 1.7).

Figure 1.7 Irrespective of the size of the nucleus, any one nucleon is surrounded by the same number of neighbours, and only those act on it with the nuclear force.

Force	Electromagnetic	Strong nuclear	Weak nuclear
Acts on	Protons only	Protons and neutrons	Protons and neutrons
Nature	Repulsive	Attractive (mainly)	Attractive/repulsive
Range	Infinite	Short (10^{-15} m)	Short (10^{-17} m)
Relative strength	1/137	1	10^{-9}

Table 1.2 Forces operating in the nucleus.

There is one other force acting in the nucleus apart from the electrical and strong nuclear forces. This is the weak nuclear force, a force that is responsible for the decay of a neutron into a proton. The details of this decay (beta decay) will be examined in the next chapter. The forces acting in the nucleus are summarized in Table 1.2.

(Since the masses of subatomic particles are so small, the gravitational force is irrelevantly small compared with the other three forces.)

Questions

1 The radius of an atomic nucleus is given by the expression

$$R = 1.2 \times A^{1/3} \times 10^{-15} \, \text{m}$$

where A is the mass number of the nucleus.
(a) Use this expression to find the density of a nucleus of iron ($^{56}_{26}$Fe) in kg m^{-3}.
(b) How does this density compare with the normal density of iron?
(c) If a star with a mass equal to 1.4 times the mass of our sun (solar mass = 2.0×10^{30} kg) were to have this density, what should its radius be? (Such stars are formed in the end stage of the evolution of normal stars and are called neutron stars.)

2 Use the expression for the radius of a nucleus to show that all nuclei have the same density.

3 Describe carefully how the Geiger–Marsden–Rutherford experiment gave rise to the Rutherford model of the atom. Why is the experiment you just described inconsistent with Thomson's model of the atom? (You can read about Thomson's model in Chapter E5.)

4 Explain why the dark lines of an absorption spectrum have the same wavelengths as the bright lines of an emission spectrum for the same element.

5 What is an isotope? How do we know that isotopes exist?

6 Find the number of neutrons in these nuclei: $^{1}_{1}$H; $^{4}_{2}$He; $^{40}_{20}$Ca; $^{210}_{82}$Pb.

7 What is the electric charge of the nucleus $^{3}_{2}$He?

8 What is meant by the statement that the energy of atoms is discrete? What evidence is there for this discreteness?

9 What do you understand by the statement that the strong nuclear force has a short range?

10 What is the dominant force between two protons separated by a distance of:
(a) 1.0×10^{-15} m;
(b) 1.0×10^{-14} m?

11 Explain why a nucleon feels the strong force from roughly the *same number* of other nucleons, irrespective of the size of the nucleus.

HL only

12 Compare the gravitational force between two electrons a distance of 10^{-10} m apart with the electrical force between them when at the same separation.

Radioactivity

At the end of the nineteenth century and in the early part of the twentieth, it was discovered, mainly due to the work of Henri Becquerel and Marie and Pierre Curie, that some nuclei are unstable. That is to say, nuclei spontaneously emit a particle or particles, they decay, and become different nuclei. This phenomenon is called radioactivity. It was soon realized that three distinct emissions take place, called alpha, beta and gamma radiations.

Objectives

By the end of this chapter you should be able to:
- describe the properties of *alpha*, *beta* and *gamma* radiations;
- explain why some nuclei are *unstable* in terms of the relative number of neutrons to protons;
- define *half-life* and find it from a graph;
- solve problems of *radioactive decay*.

The nature of alpha, beta and gamma particles

Early experiments with radioactive sources confirmed that three separate kinds of emissions took place. Called alpha, beta and gamma radiations, or particles, these emissions could be distinguished on the basis of their different ionizing and penetrating power.

Ionization

Alpha, beta and gamma particles ionize air as they pass through it; this means they knock electrons out of the atoms of the gases in the air. An alpha particle of energy 2 MeV will produce about 10 000 ion pairs per mm along its path in air. A beta particle of the same energy will only produce about 100 ion pairs per mm in air. Gamma rays will produce about one ion pair per mm.

By letting these **ionizing radiations** pass through regions of magnetic (or electric) fields,

Figure 2.1 The existence of three distinct emissions is confirmed by letting these pass through a magnetic field and observing the three separate beams.

it was seen that two of the emissions were oppositely charged and the third electrically neutral (see Figure 2.1).

Alpha particles

The positive emissions were called alpha particles and were soon identified as nuclei of helium in an experiment by Rutherford and Rhoyd. By collecting the gas that the alpha particles produced when they came in contact with electrons and analysing its spectrum, its properties were found to be identical to those of helium gas. Thus, the alpha particles have a mass that is about four times the mass of the hydrogen atom and an electric charge equal to $+2e$.

Beta particles

The negative emissions (beta particles) were identified as electrons (charge $-e$) by experiments similar to Thomson's e/m experiment (see Chapter E5), which measured the charge-to-mass ratio. (Actually, the measured charge-to-mass ratio for the beta particles decreased slightly from the standard value as the speed of the betas increased. This is consistent with the theory of special relativity, which states that the mass of an object increases as the speed becomes comparable to the speed of light. This was an early test of the theory of relativity.)

Gamma rays

The electrically neutral emissions are called gamma rays and are photons (just like the photons of ordinary electromagnetic radiation) with very small wavelengths. Typically these wavelengths are smaller that 10^{-12} m, which is smaller than X-ray wavelengths. This identification was made possible through diffraction experiments in which gamma rays from decaying nuclei were directed at crystals and a diffraction pattern was observed on a photographic plate placed on the other side of the crystal.

Absorption

Alpha particles are the easiest to absorb. A few centimetres of air will stop most alpha particles (see Figure 2.2). Beta particles will be stopped by a few centimetres of paper or a thin sheet of metal (a few millimetres in thickness)

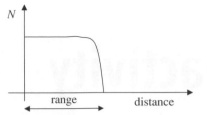

Figure 2.2 The penetration of matter by alpha particles of a fixed energy. The number of particles transmitted falls sharply to zero after a distance called the range. Particles of higher energy will have a larger range.

while gamma particles will easily penetrate metallic foils; if they are energetic enough they will be stopped only by many centimetres of lead.

Further studies show that alpha particles have specific energies, whereas beta particles have a continuous range of energies. Gamma rays from a particular nucleus also have a few discrete values with maximum energies of about 1 MeV or so. Alphas are rather slow (about 6% of the speed of light) whereas betas are very fast (about 98% of the speed of light). Gammas, being photons, travel at the speed of light. These findings are summarized in Table 2.1.

Characteristic	Alpha particle	Beta particle	Gamma ray
Nature	Helium nucleus	(Fast) electron	Photon
Charge	$+2e$	$-e$	0
Mass	6.64×10^{-27} kg	9.1×10^{-31} kg	0
Penetrative power	A few cm of air	A few mm of metal	Many cm of lead
Ions per mm of air for 2 MeV particles	10 000	100	1
Detection	Causes strong fluorescence	Causes fluorescence	Causes weak fluorescence
	Affects photographic film	Affects photographic film	Affects photographic film
	Is affected by electric and magnetic fields	Is affected by electric and magnetic fields	Is not affected by electric and magnetic fields

Table 2.1 Properties of alpha, beta and gamma radiations.

Detecting radiation

One way to detect radiation is to take advantage of their ionizing effect. In the Geiger–Müller (GM) tube (Figure 2.3), radiation enters a chamber through a thin window. The chamber is filled with a gas, which is ionized by the incoming radiation. The positive ions accelerate toward the earthed casing and the electrons toward the positive electrode (kept at a few hundred volts) and so more ions are created as a result of collisions with the gas molecules. This registers as a current in the counter connected to the GM tube. The counter can also turn the current into an audible sound, giving a 'click' whenever an ionizing particle enters the tube.

Figure 2.3 A Geiger–Müller tube for detecting ionizing radiation.

Segre plots

There are about 2500 nuclides (nuclei with a specific number of protons and neutrons), but only about 300 of them are stable; the rest are unstable (i.e. radioactive). Figure 2.4 is a plot of neutron number versus proton number (called a Segre plot) for the stable nuclei. The straight line corresponds to nuclei that have the same number of protons and neutrons. The plot shows that stable nuclei have, in general, more neutrons than protons. As the number of protons in the nucleus increases, the electrostatic repulsion between them grows as well, but the strong nuclear force does not grow proportionately since it is a short-range force. Thus, *extra* neutrons must be put in the nucleus in order to ensure stability through an increased nuclear force without participating in the repulsive electric force. (On the other hand, *too many* neutrons will also make the nucleus unstable by energetically favouring decays of neutrons into protons – hence there is a limit as to how large a nucleus can get).

A similar principle is also used in the *ionization chamber*. Gas contained in the chamber is ionized by incoming radiation and the current so produced is a measure of the amount of radiation entering the chamber.

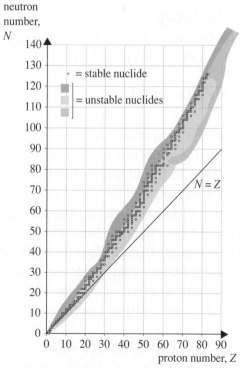

Figure 2.4 A Segre plot of stable nuclides.

Radioactive decay equations

Alpha decay

An example of alpha decay is that of uranium decaying into thorium:

$$^{238}_{92}\text{U} \rightarrow {}^{234}_{90}\text{Th} + {}^{4}_{2}\alpha$$

We say that the nucleus of uranium, being unstable, decayed into a nucleus of thorium and a nucleus of helium. Helium nuclei, being much lighter than thorium, actually move away from the uranium nucleus with a certain amount of kinetic energy. The energy of the alpha particle emitted can be either one specific value or a series of specific energy values (a discrete spectrum of energies). Note that in the reaction representing this decay, the total atomic number on the right-hand side of the arrow matches the atomic number to the left of the arrow. The same holds also for the mass number. This is true of all nuclear decays. Other examples are

$$^{224}_{88}\text{Ra} \rightarrow {}^{220}_{86}\text{Rn} + {}^{4}_{2}\alpha$$

$$^{212}_{84}\text{Po} \rightarrow {}^{208}_{82}\text{Pb} + {}^{4}_{2}\alpha$$

Beta decay

The second example of a radioactive decay is that of beta decay, such as

$$^{234}_{90}\text{Th} \rightarrow {}^{234}_{91}\text{Pa} + {}^{0}_{-1}\text{e} + {}^{0}_{0}\bar{\nu}_e$$

Note the appearance of the electron (the beta particle) in this decay. The last particle (the electron antineutrino) is included for completeness and need not concern us further here. Unlike alpha decay, the energy of the emitted beta particle has a continuous range of energy, a continuous spectrum. Note again how the atomic and mass numbers match. This is a decay of a nucleus of thorium into a nucleus of protactinium. Other examples are

$$^{214}_{82}\text{Pb} \rightarrow {}^{214}_{83}\text{Bi} + {}^{0}_{-1}\text{e} + {}^{0}_{0}\bar{\nu}_e$$

$$^{14}_{6}\text{C} \rightarrow {}^{14}_{7}\text{N} + {}^{0}_{-1}\text{e} + {}^{0}_{0}\bar{\nu}_e$$

Gamma decay

The third example of a decay involves the emission of a photon:

$$^{238}_{92}\text{U}^* \rightarrow {}^{238}_{92}\text{U} + {}^{0}_{0}\gamma$$

The star on the uranium nucleus on the left side of the arrow (the decaying nucleus) means that the nucleus is in an excited state, very much like a hydrogen atom in an energy state above the ground state. Nuclei, like atoms, can only exist in specific energy states. There exists a lowest energy state, the ground state, and excited states with energies larger than that of the ground state. Whenever a nucleus makes a transition from a high to a lower energy state, it emits a photon whose energy equals the energy difference between the initial and final energy states of the nucleus. The typical energies of nuclear states are a few million electronvolts (MeV). This means that the emitted photon in a nuclear transition will have an energy of the order of a few million electronvolts and will thus have a wavelength of

$$\lambda = \frac{hc}{\Delta E}$$

where ΔE is the photon's energy, h is Planck's constant (6.63×10^{-34} J s) and c is the speed of light. Substituting, say, 1 MeV for this energy, we find $\lambda = 1.2 \times 10^{-12}$ m. In contrast to the photons in atomic transitions, which can correspond to optical light, these photons have very small wavelengths. They are called gamma rays.

The changes in the atomic and mass numbers of a nucleus when it undergoes radioactive decay can be represented in a diagram of mass number against atomic number. A radioactive nucleus such as thorium ($Z = 90$) decays first by alpha decay into the nucleus of radium ($Z = 88$). Radium, which is also radioactive, decays into actinium ($Z = 89$) by beta decay. Further decays take place until the resulting nucleus is stable. The set of decays that takes place until a given nucleus

beta decay

alpha decay

Figure 2.5 The decay series of thorium ($Z = 90$, $A = 232$). One alpha decay reduces the mass number by 4 and the atomic number by 2. One beta decay increases the atomic number by one and leaves the mass number unchanged. The end result is the nucleus of lead ($Z = 82$, $A = 208$).

ends up as a stable nucleus is called the *decay series* of the nucleus. Figure 2.5 shows the decay series for thorium. Successive decays starting with thorium end with the stable nucleus of lead.

Example question

Q1

A nucleus $^A_Z X$ decays by alpha decay followed by two successive beta decays. Find the atomic and mass numbers of the resulting nucleus.

Answer

The decay equation is

$$^A_Z X \rightarrow {}^{A-4}_{Z} Y + {}^4_2 \alpha + 2 {}^{\ 0}_{-1} e$$

so the atomic number is Z and the mass number is $A - 4$.

The law of radioactive decay

We now come to the details of a decay. Suppose we concentrate on the particular decay $^{238}_{92} U \rightarrow {}^{234}_{90} Th + {}^4_2 \alpha$, and that we are given a container with a specific number of atoms of uranium.

▶ The law of radioactive decay states that the number of nuclei that will decay per second (i.e. the rate of decay) is proportional to the number of atoms present that have not yet decayed.

This is a form of a physical law implying a *statistical* or *random* nature. This means that we cannot predict exactly when a *particular* nucleus will decay. But, given a large number of nuclei, the radioactive decay law can be used to predict the number of atoms that will have decayed after a given interval of time. The radioactive decay law leads to an exponential decrease of the number of decaying nuclei. Figure 2.6 shows an example of a radioactive decay in which the initial number of nuclei present is 200×10^{26}. As time passes, the number of undecayed nuclei is decreased. After a certain interval of time (5 s in this example), the number of undecayed nuclei left behind is half of the original number. If another 5 s goes by, the number of undecayed nuclei is reduced by another factor of 2, which is a factor of 4 relative to the original number at $t = 0$. This **half-life** is a general property of the decay law.

▶ There exists a certain interval of time, called the half-life, such that after each half-life the number of nuclei that have not yet decayed is reduced by a factor of 2.

Thus, consider a decay in which nuclei X decay into nuclei Y (the daughter nuclei) by, say, alpha emission. Assume that nuclei Y are stable. Then as time goes by, the number of X nuclei is reduced (Figure 2.6a). The number of Y nuclei is increasing with time, as shown in Figure 2.6b.

The half-life can be found from the graph as follows. The initial value is 200×10^{26} nuclei. We find half of this value, i.e. 100×10^{26}, and see that 100×10^{26} corresponds to a time of 5 s. This is the half-life.

We may also define a concept useful in experimental work: that of decay rate or

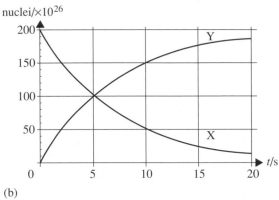

(b)

Figure 2.6 (a) The number of nuclei X that have not yet decayed as a function of time. This is an exponential decay curve. (b) The number of the daughter nuclei Y is increasing.

activity A – the number of nuclei decaying per second. It can be shown that activity obeys the same decay law as the number of nuclei, so in a period equal to a half-life the initial activity is reduced by a factor of 2. The unit of activity is the becquerel (Bq): 1 Bq is equal to one decay per second.

Example questions

Q2
An isotope has a half-life of 20 min. If initially there is 1024 g of this isotope, how much time must go by for there to be 128 g left?

Answer

The nuclei have been reduced by a factor of 8. Thus, 3 half-lives or 60 min must have gone by.

Q3
The activity of a sample is initially 80 decays per minute. It becomes 5 decays per minute after 4 h. What is the half-life?

Answer

The activity is reduced from 80 to 5 decays in 4 half-lives. The half-life is 1 h.

Q4
The activity of a sample is 15 decays per minute. The half-life is 30 min. When was the activity 60 decays per minute?

Answer

One half-life before the sample was given to us the activity was 30 decays per minute and one half-life before that it was 60 decays per minute, that is 60 minutes before.

The meaning of a half-life can also be understood in the following sense. Any given nucleus has a 50% chance of decaying within a time interval equal to the half-life. If a half-life goes by and the nucleus has not decayed, the chance of a decay in the next half-life is still 50%. Thus, the probability that a nucleus will have decayed by the second half-life is (see the tree diagram in Figure 2.7) $\frac{1}{2} + \frac{1}{2} \times \frac{1}{2} = \frac{3}{4} = 0.75$ or 75%.

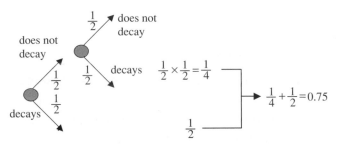

Figure 2.7 Tree diagram for nuclear decay.

(There is more on radioactive decay in Chapter 6.6.)

Questions

1 In a study of the intensity of gamma rays from a radioactive source it is suspected that the counter rate C at a distance d from the source should behave as

$$C \propto \left(\frac{1}{d + d_0} \right)^2$$

where d_0 is an unknown constant. If a set of data for C and d is given, how should these be plotted in order to get a straight line?

2 The intensity of gamma rays of a specific energy (monochromatic rays) falls off exponentially with the thickness x of the absorbing material

$$I = I_0 \, e^{-\mu x}$$

where I_0 is the intensity at the face of the absorber and μ a constant depending on the material. (See Figure 2.8.)

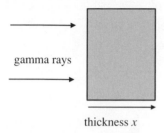

gamma rays

thickness x

Figure 2.8 For question 2.

How should intensity I and thickness x be plotted in order to allow an accurate determination of the constant μ?

3 A radioactive source has a half-life of 3.00 min. At the start of an experiment there was 32.0 mg of the radioactive material present. How much will there be after 18.0 min?

4 The initial activity of a radioactive sample is 120 Bq. If after 24 h the activity is measured to be 15 Bq, find the half-life of the sample.

5 Beryllium-8 ($^8_4$Be) decays into two identical particles. What are they?

6 The only stable nuclei with more protons than neutrons are those of hydrogen and helium-3 ($^3_2$He). Why do you think there are so few?

7 An alpha particle and an electron with the same velocity enter a region of a uniform magnetic field at right angles to the velocity. Explain why they are deflected in opposite directions. Find the ratio of the radii of the circular paths the particles are deflected into.

8 Tritium ($^3_1$H) is a radioactive isotope of hydrogen and decays by beta decay. Write

down the equation for the reaction and name the products of the decay.

9 Nitrogen ($^{14}_7$N) is produced in the beta decay of a radioactive isotope. Write down the reaction and name the particles in the reaction.

10 Bismuth ($^{210}_{83}$Bi) decays by beta and gamma emission. Write down the reaction and name the nucleus bismuth decays into.

11 Plutonium ($^{239}_{94}$Pu) decays by alpha decay. Write down the reaction and name the element produced in the decay.

12 A nucleus (^A_ZX) decays by emitting two electrons and one alpha particle. Find the atomic and mass numbers of the produced nucleus.

13 Name the two missing particles in the reaction $^{22}_{11}$Na $\rightarrow$ $^{22}_{10}$Ne $+ ? + ?$.

14 Discuss how one could confirm that a particular element emits:
(a) alpha particles;
(b) beta particles;
(c) gamma rays.

15 The track of an alpha particle in a cloud chamber was measured to be 30 mm. The energy required to produce an ion pair is about 32 eV, on average. Assuming that alpha particles create 6000 ions per mm along their path, estimate the energy of the alpha particle.

16 Many of the most stable nuclei have an even number of protons and an even number of neutrons. Can you suggest a reason why this might be so?

17 Explain why the heavy stable nuclei tend to have many more neutrons than protons.

18 Referring to the Segre plot in the text (Figure 2.4), what would be a likely decay for an unstable nucleus that has a large neutron-to-proton ratio? Where on the plot would such a nucleus be? What would be the likely decay for an unstable nucleus that has a small neutron-to-proton ratio? Where on the plot would this nucleus be?

Nuclear reactions, fission and fusion

This chapter is an introduction to the physics of atomic nuclei. We will see that the sum of the masses of the constituents of a nucleus is not the same as the mass of the nucleus itself, which implies that the nucleus has enormous amounts of energy stored in it. Methods used to calculate energy released in nuclear reactions are presented.

Objectives

By the end of this chapter you should be able to:
- define the *unified mass unit*;
- state the meaning of the terms *mass defect* and *binding energy* and solve related problems;
- write *nuclear reaction equations* and balance the atomic and mass numbers;
- understand the meaning of the graph of *binding energy per nucleon* versus *mass number*;
- state the meaning of and difference between *fission* and *fusion*;
- understand that nuclear fusion takes place in the *core of the stars*;
- solve problems of *fission* and *fusion reactions*.

The unified mass unit

In nuclear physics, it is convenient to use a smaller unit of mass than the kilogram. We define a new unit called the *unified atomic mass unit*, u for short. It is defined to be $\frac{1}{12}$ of the mass of an atom of carbon-12, $^{12}_{6}\text{C}$. A mole of carbon $^{12}_{6}\text{C}$ is 12 g and the number of molecules is the Avogadro constant, therefore the carbon-12 atom has a mass M given by

$$6.0221367 \times 10^{23} \times M = 12\,\text{g}$$

$$M = \frac{12}{6.0221367 \times 10^{23}} \times 10^{-3}\,\text{kg}$$

$$= 1.992648 \times 10^{-26}\,\text{kg}$$

Hence

$$1\,\text{u} = \frac{1}{12}\left(1.992648 \times 10^{-26}\,\text{kg}\right)$$

$$= 1.6605402 \times 10^{-27}\,\text{kg}$$

Example question

Q1

Find in units of u the masses of the proton, neutron and electron (use Table 3.1).

Unified mass unit	$1.6605402 \times 10^{-27}$ kg
Electron	$9.1093897 \times 10^{-31}$ kg
Proton	$1.6726231 \times 10^{-27}$ kg
Neutron	$1.6749286 \times 10^{-27}$ kg

Table 3.1.

Answer

From the table of the masses in kilograms (Table 3.1) we find

$m_p = 1.007276$ u
$m_n = 1.008665$ u
$m_e = 0.0005486$ u

The mass defect and binding energy

To find the mass of a particular nucleus we have to subtract the mass of the electrons in the atom from the mass of the atom. If there are Z electrons in the atom, then

$$M_{nucleus} = M_{atom} - Zm_e$$

The mass of the atom is obtained from the periodic table and m_e is given above. We can find, for example, that the mass of the nucleus of helium is

$$M_{nucleus} = 4.0026 - 2 \times 0.0005486$$
$$= 4.00156 \, u$$

We now recall that the helium nucleus is made up of two protons and two neutrons. If we add up their masses we find

$$2m_p + 2m_n = 4.0320 \, u$$

which is *larger* than the mass of the nucleus by 0.0304 u. This leads to the concept of **mass defect**.

▶ We can see by examining each nucleus that this is generally true: the mass of the protons plus the mass of the neutrons is larger than the mass of the nucleus. We define their difference as the mass defect δ:

$\delta =$ total mass of nucleons
$\quad -$ mass of nucleus

or

$$\delta = Zm_p + (A - Z)m_n - M_{nucleus}$$

(remember that $A - Z$ is the number of neutrons in the nucleus). This formula allows us to calculate the mass defect for any nucleus.

Example question

Q2 ▬▬▬▬▬▬▬▬▬▬▬▬▬▬▬▬▬▬▬▬

Find the mass defect of the nucleus of gold, $^{197}_{79}$Au.

Answer

From the periodic table, the mass of the *atom* of gold is 196.967 u, and since it has 79 electrons the *nuclear* mass is

196.967 u $-$ 79 $\times$ 0.0005486 u = 196.924 u.

The nucleus has 79 protons and 118 neutrons, so

$\delta = (79 \times 1.007276 + 118 \times 1.008665 - 196.924)$ u
$\quad = 1.67 \, u$

Einstein's mass–energy formula

Where is the missing mass? The answer is given by Einstein's theory of special relativity, which states that mass and energy are equivalent and can be converted into each other. Einstein's famous formula from 1905 reads

$$E = mc^2$$

where c stands for the speed of light. The mass defect of a nucleus has been converted into energy and is stored in the nucleus. This energy is called the **binding energy** of the nucleus, and is denoted by E_b. Thus:

▶ $E_b = \delta c^2$

The binding energy of the nucleus is the work (energy) required to completely separate the nucleons of a nucleus.

The work required to remove one nucleon from the nucleus is *very roughly* the binding energy divided by the total number of nucleons.

According to the periodic table:

$$\text{mass of radium} = 226.0254 \text{ u}$$

$$
\begin{aligned}
\text{mass of radon} &= 222.0176 \text{ u} \\
+ \quad \text{mass of helium} &= 4.0026 \text{ u} \\
\hline
\text{sum} &= 226.0202 \text{ u}
\end{aligned}
$$

We see that the mass of radium exceeds that of radon plus helium by 0.0052 u. Thus, there is an amount of energy released in the form of kinetic energy of radon and helium of 0.0052×931.5 MeV = 4.84 MeV. If 50 g of radium were to decay in this way, the total energy released would be $N \times 4.84$ MeV where N is the total number of nuclei in the 50 g of radium. In 50 g of radium there are $\frac{50}{226} = 0.22$ mol and so

$$N = 0.22 \times 6 \times 10^{23} = 1.3 \times 10^{23}$$

Hence the total energy released is

$$
\begin{aligned}
E &= 1.3 \times 10^{23} \times 4.84 \text{ MeV} \\
&= 6.3 \times 10^{23} \text{ MeV} \\
&\approx 10^{11} \text{ J}
\end{aligned}
$$

The momenta of radon and helium are opposite in direction and equal in magnitude by the law of conservation of momentum. (We assume that the decaying radium nucleus is at rest, so its momentum is zero.) Thus

$$M_{\text{radon}} v_{\text{radon}} = M_{\text{helium}} v_{\text{helium}}$$

Therefore

$$
\begin{aligned}
\frac{v_{\text{helium}}}{v_{\text{radon}}} &= \frac{M_{\text{radon}}}{M_{\text{helium}}} \\
&\approx \frac{222}{4} \\
&\approx 55
\end{aligned}
$$

the velocity of radon is smaller than the velocity of helium by the ratio of the masses: approximately 55. (As an exercise you can show that the ratio of kinetic energies of the helium to the radon nuclei is also 55.)

Let us now re-examine these findings in terms of the binding energy curve. For the decay to take place, the mass of the decaying nucleus has to be greater than the combined masses of the products. This means that the binding energy of the decaying nucleus must be less than the binding energies of the product nuclei. This is why radioactive decay is possible for heavy elements lying to the right of nickel in the binding energy curve.

Nuclear reactions

If a nucleus cannot decay by itself, it can still do so if energy is supplied to it. This energy can be transferred to the nucleus by a fast-moving particle that collides with it. For example, an alpha particle colliding with nitrogen produces oxygen and hydrogen (i.e. a proton):

$$^{14}_{7}\text{N} + {}^{4}_{2}\alpha \rightarrow {}^{17}_{8}\text{O} + {}^{1}_{1}\text{p}$$

(see Figure 3.3). This is an example of a nuclear reaction. Note how the atomic and mass numbers match as they did in nuclear decays. This is a famous reaction called the transmutation of nitrogen; it was studied by Rutherford in 1909. Note that if we add up the masses to the left of the arrow we find 18.0057 u, whereas the masses to the right are 18.0070 u (i.e. larger). Thus, this reaction will only take place if the alpha particle has enough kinetic energy to make up for the imbalance in mass between the two sides.

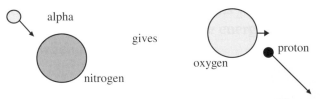

Figure 3.3 An alpha particle colliding with nitrogen produces oxygen and a proton

(Actually, the required minimum kinetic energy of the alpha particle has to be bigger than the energy equivalent of the mass difference between the two sides of the reaction. This is because the products of the reaction themselves will have kinetic energy.)

In a reaction in which four particles participate

$$A + B \rightarrow C + D$$

energy will be released if the quantity Δm given by

$$\Delta m \rightarrow (m_A + m_B) - (m_C + m_D)$$

is positive (i.e. if the total mass on the left is larger than the total mass on the right). The amount of energy released is then equal to

$$\Delta E = (\Delta m)c^2$$

There are two kinds of energy-producing nuclear reactions and we consider them separately in the following sections.

Nuclear fission

Nuclear fission is the process in which a heavy nucleus splits up into lighter nuclei. When a neutron is absorbed by a nucleus of uranium-235, uranium momentarily turns into uranium-236 according to the reaction

$$^{1}_{0}n + ^{235}_{92}U \rightarrow ^{236}_{92}U$$

Uranium-236 then splits into lighter nuclei. This is the fission reaction. A number of possibilities exist as to what these nuclei are. One possibility is

$$^{144}_{56}Ba + ^{89}_{36}Kr + 3^{1}_{0}n$$

The production of neutrons is a feature of fission reactions. The produced neutrons can be used to collide with other nuclei of uranium-235 in the reactor, producing more fission, energy and neutrons. The reaction is thus self-sustaining – it is called a *chain reaction*. For the chain reaction to get going a certain minimum mass of uranium-235 must be present, otherwise the neutrons escape without causing further reactions – this is called the *critical mass*.

The energy released can be calculated as shown in Table 3.2.

mass of uranium plus neutron	= 236.0526 u
mass of products	
= 143.92292 u + 88.91781 u + 3 × 1.008665 u	= 235.8667250 u
mass difference	= 0.185875 u
energy released	= 0.185875 × 931.5 MeV
	= 173.14 MeV

Table 3.2

This energy appears as kinetic energy of the products.

Thus, an energy of about 173 MeV per fissioning nucleus of uranium is released. This is a lot of energy! A mass of 1 kg of uranium-235 undergoing fission would produce an amount of energy that can be found as follows: 1 kg is $1000/235$ mol of uranium and thus contains $(1000/235) \times 6 \times 10^{23}$ nuclei. Each nucleus produces about 173 MeV of energy and thus the total is $(1000/235) \times 6 \times 10^{23} \times 173$ MeV or about 7×10^{13} J. This energy is harnessed in nuclear reactors as explained in Option C, Energy. In a nuclear reactor, the release of energy is done in a controlled way. If the rate of neutron production is too high, too much energy is produced in a very short time. This is what happens in a nuclear bomb.

Note that the fission process begins when a neutron collides with a nucleus of uranium-235. An alpha particle cannot be used to start this process because its positive charge would be repelled by the positive charge of the uranium nucleus and so would not lead to the capture of the alpha. An electron, on the other hand, would easily be captured but its small mass would not perturb the heavy nucleus sufficiently for fission to start.

Nuclear fusion

Nuclear fusion is the joining of two light nuclei into a heavier one with the associated production of energy. An example of this reaction is:

$$^{2}_{1}H + ^{2}_{1}H \rightarrow ^{3}_{2}He + ^{1}_{0}n$$

where two deuterium nuclei (isotopes of hydrogen) produce helium-3 (an isotope of helium) and a neutron. Computing masses to the left and right of the reaction arrow as in Table 3.3 we can find the energy released.

2 × mass of deuterium	= 4.0282 u
mass of helium + neutron	= 4.0247 u
mass difference	= 0.0035 u
energy released	= 0.0035 × 931.5 MeV = 3.26 MeV

Table 3.3

A kilogram of deuterium would thus release energy of about 10^{13} J, which is comparable to the energy produced by a kilogram of uranium in the fission process.

Example question

Q5

Another fusion reaction is $4\,^1_1\text{H} \rightarrow \,^4_2\text{He} + 2\,^0_1\text{e} + 2\nu_e + \,^0_0\gamma$, where four hydrogen nuclei fuse into a helium nucleus plus two positrons (the antiparticle of the electron – same mass, opposite charge), two electron neutrinos and a photon. Calculate the energy released in this reaction.

Answer

We must find the masses before and after the reaction.

Mass of 4 protons (hydrogen nuclei)
= 4 × 1.007276 u = 4.029104 u

Mass on right-hand side
= (4.0026 − 2 × 0.0005486) u
+ 2 × 0.0005486 u = 4.002600 u

Mass difference = 0.026504 u

This gives an energy of 24.7 MeV. The two positrons annihilate into energy by colliding with two electrons giving an additional 2 MeV (= 4 × 0.511 MeV), for a total of 26.7 MeV.

For the light nuclei to fuse, very large temperatures are required. This is so that the electrostatic repulsion between the two nuclei that fuse is overcome. The enormous temperature (recall the kinetic theory of gases) causes the nuclei to move fast enough so as to approach each other sufficiently for fusion to take place. The very hot material (over ten million kelvin) undergoing fusion is in a state called plasma (ionized atoms). Plasma, being very hot, cannot come into contact with anything else (either because it causes it to melt or because it will result in heat losses) and therefore has to be contained by unusual methods such as magnetic fields in big machines called tokamaks. There are serious unsolved problems with the prolonged confinement of plasmas and this is one reason why nuclear fusion, still, is not a commercially viable source of energy. Commercial energy from the nucleus comes now only from the fission process, which unlike fusion, however, is environmentally suspect.

Fusion in stars

The high temperatures and pressures in the interior of stars make stars ideal places for nuclear fusion. As we saw in the previous section, high temperatures are required so that the nuclei have sufficiently large kinetic energy to approach each other, overcoming the electrostatic repulsion due to their positive charges. The high pressure ensures that sufficient numbers of nuclei are found close to each other, thus increasing the probability of them coming together and fusion taking place.

The reaction $4\,^1_1\text{H} \rightarrow \,^4_2\text{He} + 2\,^0_1\text{e} + 2\nu_e + \,^0_0\gamma$ is a typical reaction that takes place in stellar cores. Nuclear fusion is the source of energy for a star; it prevents the star from collapsing under its own weight and provides the energy the star sends out in the form of light and heat, for example. Stars are, in fact, element factories, producing, for example, all the elements that our bodies are made of. More details on this can be found in Option F on Astrophysics.

Fusion and fission processes are summarized in Figure 3.4.

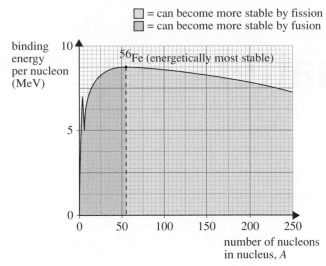

Figure 3.4 When a heavy nucleus splits up, energy is released because the produced nuclei have a higher binding energy than the original nucleus. When two light nuclei fuse, energy is produced because the products again have a higher binding energy.

Questions

1 Find the binding energy and binding energy per nucleon of the nucleus $^{62}_{28}$Ni. The atomic mass of nickel is 61.928348 u.

2 How much energy is required to remove one proton from the nucleus of $^{16}_{8}$O? A rough answer to this question is obtained by giving the binding energy per nucleon. A better answer is obtained when we write a reaction that removes a proton from the nucleus. In this case $^{16}_{8}$O $\rightarrow$ $^{1}_{1}$p + $^{15}_{7}$N. Find the energy required for this reaction to take place. This is the proton separation energy. Get both values and compare them. (The atomic mass of oxygen is 15.994 u; that of nitrogen is 15.000 u.)

3 What is the energy released in the beta decay of a neutron?

4 The first excited state of the nucleus of uranium-235 is 0.051 MeV above the ground state.
  (a) What is the wavelength of the photon emitted when the nucleus makes a transition to the ground state?
  (b) What part of the spectrum does this photon belong to?

5 Calculate the energy released in the alpha decay $^{234}_{90}$Th $\rightarrow$ $^{230}_{88}$Ra + $^{4}_{2}$He. (The atomic mass

of thorium is 234.043596 u; that of radium is 230.03708 u.)

6 Assume uranium-236 splits into two nuclei of palladium-117 (Pd). (The atomic mass of uranium is 236.0455561 u; that of palladium is 116.9178 u.)
  (a) Write down the reaction.
  (b) What other particles must be produced?
  (c) What is the energy released?

7 One possible outcome in the fission of a uranium nucleus is the reaction
$$^{235}_{92}U + {}^{1}_{0}n \rightarrow {}^{95}_{42}Mo + {}^{139}_{57}La + 2{}^{1}_{0}n + ?$$
  (a) What is missing in this reaction?
  (b) How much energy is released?
     (Atomic masses: U = 235.043922 u; Mo = 94.905841 u; La = 138.906349 u.)

8 Another fission reaction involving uranium is
$$^{235}_{92}U + {}^{1}_{0}n \rightarrow {}^{98}_{40}Zr + {}^{135}_{52}Te + 3{}^{1}_{0}n$$
Calculate the energy released. (Atomic masses: U = 235.043922 u; Zr = 97.91276 u; Te = 134.9165 u.)

9 Calculate the energy released in the fusion reaction $^{2}_{1}$H + $^{3}_{1}$H $\rightarrow$ $^{4}_{2}$He + $^{1}_{0}$n. (Atomic masses: $^{2}_{1}$H = 2.014102 u; $^{3}_{1}$H = 3.016049 u; $^{4}_{2}$He = 4.002603 u.)

10 In the text, it was stated that the reaction $4{}^{1}_{1}$H $\rightarrow$ $^{4}_{2}$He + $2{}^{0}_{1}$e + $2\nu_e$ + $^{0}_{0}\gamma$ is the mechanism by which hydrogen in stars is converted into helium and that the reaction releases about 26.7 MeV of energy. The sun radiates energy at the rate of 3.9×10^{26} W and has a mass of about 1.99×10^{30} kg, of which 75% is hydrogen. Find out how long it will take the sun to convert 12% of its hydrogen into helium.

11 In the first nuclear reaction in a particle accelerator, hydrogen nuclei were accelerated and then allowed to hit nuclei of lithium according to the reaction $^{1}_{1}$H + $^{7}_{3}$Li $\rightarrow$ $^{4}_{2}$He + $^{4}_{2}$He. Find the energy released. (The atomic mass of lithium is 7.016 u.)

12 Outline the role in nuclear fusion reactions of:
  (a) temperature; (b) pressure.

13 Show that an alternative formula for the mass defect is $\delta = ZM_H + (A - Z)m_n - M_{atom}$ where M_H is the mass of a hydrogen atom and m_n is the mass of a neutron.

Interactions of matter with energy

The photoelectric effect was one of the first signs that classical physics was inadequate when applied to the microscopic world. This chapter discusses the photoelectric effect and other aspects of the interaction of matter with energy, leading to the duality of matter and energy.

Objectives

By the end of this chapter you should be able to:
* describe the *photoelectric effect*;
* describe which aspects of this effect cannot be explained by classical physics and how the *new physics* introduced by Einstein provides explanations for them;
* understand the meaning of the terms *stopping voltage*, *threshold frequency* and *work function*;
* state the meaning of the term *photon* and use the equation for its energy, $E = hf$;
* solve problems on the photoelectric effect, $eV_s = hf - \phi$;
* state the meaning of the term *wave–particle duality*;
* state *de Broglie's* formula, $\lambda = \frac{h}{p}$, and use it in problems;
* describe the *Davisson–Germer experiment* and understand its significance.

The photoelectric effect

When light (or other electromagnetic radiation) falls on a metallic surface, electrons may be emitted from that surface in a phenomenon known as the **photoelectric effect**. An electroscope connected to the surface becomes positively charged when light falls on the metal (see Figure 4.1).

It is not difficult to imagine that electrons will be emitted, because electromagnetic radiation contains energy that can be transferred to electrons of the atoms of the photosurface, thus enabling them to pull themselves away from

the attraction of the nuclei and leave the surface altogether. An apparatus to investigate this effect (first used by R. Millikan) is shown in Figure 4.2.

It consists of an evacuated tube, inside which is the photosurface and across from that a collecting plate where the emitted electrons arrive. The photosurface and the collecting plate are part of a circuit as shown. Light passes through an opening in the tube and falls on the photosurface, and the emitted electrons move toward the right, completing the circuit; thus, an electric current flows. The magnitude of the current can be detected

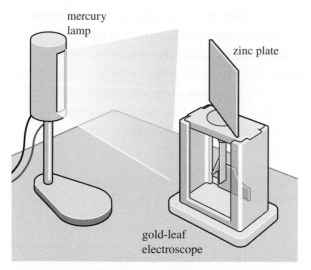

Figure 4.1 A photosurface becomes positively charged when light falls on it.

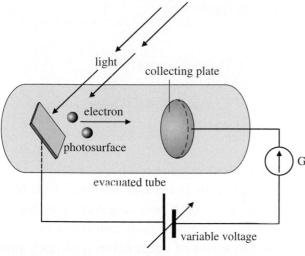

Figure 4.2 Apparatus for investigating the photoelectric effect. The variable voltage decelerates the emitted electrons and eventually stops them.

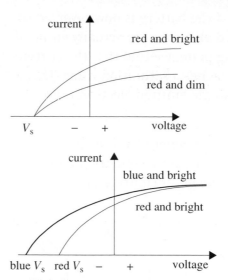

Figure 4.3 The photocurrent is larger for larger intensity light source. The stopping voltage depends on the frequency not the intensity.

by the galvanometer G. It is readily found that, as the intensity of the light source increases, the current also increases. In fact, current and intensity are directly proportional to each other. A larger current can be due to either a larger number of electrons being emitted per second or electrons with higher speed (or both). To distinguish between the two cases we need a method to measure the energy (and hence speed) of the emitted electrons. This can be done by connecting a battery between the photosurface and the collecting plate as shown in Figure 4.3 (*note*: pay attention to where the negative terminal of the battery

goes). By increasing the voltage of the battery we can make the current in the circuit zero. This is called the stopping voltage, V_s. It follows that the maximum kinetic energy of the emitted electrons must be eV_s. We see this as follows: Let the maximum kinetic energy of the electrons be E_k; then the work done in moving an electron from the cathode to the collecting plate is eV_s, and from mechanics we know that the work done is the change in the kinetic energy of the electron. So

$$eV_s = E_k$$

▶ We find that the stopping voltage stays the same no matter what the intensity of the light source is. Thus, the increase in the current is due to more electrons being emitted. The intensity of light has no effect on the maximum energy of the electrons (see Figure 4.3).

This is a very surprising result and we shall return to it soon. Another surprise awaits us if we allow monochromatic light (light of one specific frequency) to fall on the photosurface. We find that the stopping voltage depends on the frequency of the light source. The larger the frequency, the larger the stopping voltage (i.e. the larger the energy of the emitted electrons).

If the polarity of the battery is now reversed so that the emitted electrons are actually *attracted* to the collecting plate, we find that the current increases but reaches a saturation value. This is because every single emitted electron is now collected.

If we plot the kinetic energy of the electrons (which equals eV_s) versus frequency, we find a straight line as shown in Figure 4.4a.

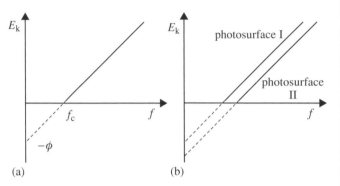

(a)   (b)

Figure 4.4 (a) The graph of kinetic energy versus frequency is a straight line. The horizontal intercept is the critical frequency. (b) When another photosurface is used, a line parallel to the first is obtained.

The puzzling feature of this graph is that there exists a frequency, called the critical (or threshold) frequency f_c, such that no electrons at all are emitted if the frequency of the light source is less than f_c, even if very intense light is allowed to fall on the photosurface. If the photoelectric experiment is repeated with a different photosurface and the kinetic energy of the electrons is plotted versus frequency, a line parallel to the first is obtained, as shown in Figure 4.4b.

▶ We now have two surprising observations:
 1 The intensity of light plays no role in the energy of the emitted electrons.
 2 The electron energy depends on the frequency of the light source, and there exists a certain minimum frequency below which no electrons are emitted.

Both observations are in violation of the standard laws of physics. According to the laws of classical electromagnetism, a more intense beam of light contains more energy and therefore should cause the emission of more energetic electrons. Classical electromagnetism offers no explanation as to why the frequency of light should affect the electron energy, nor does it explain why there should exist a critical frequency.

The explanation of all these strange observations was provided by Albert Einstein in 1905.

▶ Einstein suggested that light (like any other form of electromagnetic radiation) consists of quanta, which are *packets of energy and momentum*. The energy of one such quantum is given by the formula

$$E = hf$$

where f is the frequency of the electromagnetic radiation and $h = 6.63 \times 10^{-34}$ J s is a constant, known as Planck's constant.

(Max Planck had introduced h a few years earlier in his investigation of the spectrum of a black body. It is worth pointing out here that the spectrum of a black body could not be explained in terms of conventional physics, just as the photoelectric experiment could not.)

This suggestion implies, therefore, that light behaves in some cases as particles do, but in addition the energy of one of the particles making up light depends only on the frequency and not on the intensity. Thus, if a photon of frequency f is absorbed by an electron in the photosurface, the electron's energy will increase by hf. Now, it takes a certain amount of energy, let us say ϕ, to free the electron from the pull of the nuclei of the atoms of the photosurface. The electron will be emitted (become free) if hf is bigger than ϕ; the difference $hf - \phi$ will simply be the kinetic energy of the (now) free electron (see Figure 4.5). That is

$$E_k = hf - \phi$$

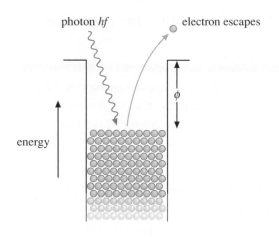

photon *hf*   electron escapes

energy ϕ

photon *hf*

electron just
escapes

energy ϕ

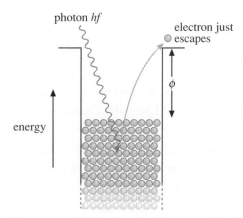

Figure 4.5 (a) A single photon of light may release
a single electron from a metal. (b) A more
tightly bound electron needs more energy to
release it from the metal.

But this is exactly what our discussion of the
photoelectric experiment gave. The value of ϕ
(called the work function) is read off the graph,
from the intercept of the straight line with the
vertical axis. Note that the work function and
the critical frequency are related by

$$hf_c = \phi$$

since $E_k = 0$ in that case.

Recalling that the kinetic energy of the
electrons is measured in the photoelectric
effect apparatus to be $eV_s = E_k$, it follows that:

▶ $eV_s = hf - \phi$

$$\Rightarrow V_s = \frac{h}{e}f - \frac{\phi}{e}$$

that is, in a graph of stopping voltage
versus frequency, one obtains a straight
line with slope h/e.

Example questions

Q1

A photosurface has a work function of 1.50 eV.
Find the critical frequency. If light of frequency
6.1×10^{14} Hz falls on this surface, what is the
energy and speed of the emitted electrons?

Answer

The critical frequency f_c is given in terms of the
work function by $hf_c = \phi$ and thus

$$f_c = \frac{\phi}{h} = \frac{1.5 \times 1.6 \times 10^{-19}}{6.63 \times 10^{-34}} \text{ Hz}$$

$$= 3.62 \times 10^{14} \text{ Hz}$$

The kinetic energy of the electron is given by
$E_k = hf - \phi$, that is

$$E_k = 1.64 \times 10^{-19} \text{ J} = 1.03 \text{ eV}$$

From $E_k = \frac{1}{2}mv^2$ we find $v = 6.0 \times 10^5$ m s^{-1}.
(*Note*: use joules for E_k to find v.)

Q2

Monochromatic light of intensity 4 W and
wavelength 4×10^{-7} m falling on a photosurface
whose critical frequency is 6×10^{14} Hz releases
10^{10} electrons per second. What is the current
collected in the anode? If the intensity of the light
is increased to 8 W, what will the current be? If
light of intensity 8 W and wavelength 6×10^{-7} m
falls on this photosurface, what will the current be
in that case?

Answer

From $I = \frac{\Delta Q}{\Delta t}$, the definition of electric current, we
find

$$I = e \times 10^{10}$$

that is

$$I = 1.6 \times 10^{-9} \text{ A}$$

If the intensity doubles, so will the current, giving

$$I = 3.2 \times 10^{-9} \text{ A}$$

We note that the critical wavelength is

$$\frac{3 \times 10^8}{6 \times 10^{14}} \text{ m} = 5 \times 10^{-7} \text{ m}$$

and so if the wavelength becomes 6×10^{-7} m, no
electrons will be emitted at all, hence $I = 0$ then.

Q3

Light of wavelength 5×10^{-7} m falls on a spherical photosurface whose critical frequency is 5×10^{14} Hz. The photosurface is in an insulated enclosure. What is the electric potential that the sphere will develop?

Answer

The kinetic energy of the emitted electrons will be

$$E_k = hf - \phi$$
$$= \frac{hc}{\lambda} - hf_c$$
$$= 6.63 \times 10^{-20} \text{ J}$$
$$= 0.4 \text{ eV}$$

Hence electrons will be emitted until the electric potential on the sphere becomes 0.4 V, in which case the attraction of the electrons to the sphere will be strong enough to prevent further electrons from escaping.

More on the photon

The energy of the photon is given by the equation $E = hf$, which is a relation that is being directly tested in the photoelectric effect. The photon also carries momentum, given by

$$p = \frac{E}{c} = \frac{hf}{c} = \frac{h}{\lambda}$$

The existence of a photon momentum is supported by the Compton effect: the scattering of photons off electrons or protons. The photon, although a 'particle' with energy and momentum, has no mass (it also has zero electric charge). This implies (because of the theory of relativity – see Option G) that it always travels at the speed of light. For such particles (they are called relativistic), a more general definition of momentum allows zero-mass particles to have momentum.

Example questions

Q4

How many photons of wavelength 5×10^{-7} m are emitted per second by a 75 W lamp, assuming that 1% of the energy of the lamp goes into photons of this wavelength?

Answer

Let there be N photons per second emitted. Then the energy is $N\frac{hc}{\lambda}$ and this has to be 1% of 75 J,

that is 0.75 J. So, $N = 0.19 \times 10^{19}$ photons per second.

Q5

If all the photons from example question 4 hit a mirror and are reflected by it, what pressure do these photons exert on the mirror? Take the area of the mirror to be 0.5 m^2.

Answer

Each photon has a momentum of $\frac{E}{c}$ or $\frac{h}{\lambda}$. The momentum change upon reflection is $2\frac{h}{\lambda}$. Since there are N such reflections per second, the force F on the mirror is $2N\frac{h}{\lambda}$, which is 0.5×10^{-8} N. The pressure is thus

$$\frac{F}{A} = 1.0 \times 10^{-8} \text{ N m}^{-2}$$

(Note that if the photons were absorbed rather than reflected the pressure would be half of what we got.)

We close this section with an observation made by G. I. Taylor in 1924. Imagine that light (i.e. a stream of photons) is directed at two slits in a Young-type experiment. Interference at a screen some distance away gives the familiar fringes of high and low intensity. Taylor now argues that if the intensity of light is reduced sufficiently, a stage will be reached when only one photon at a time arrives at the slits. We are now faced with the problem that a single photon, *which will go through either one slit or the other*, somehow produces the interference pattern on the screen. Taylor's observation is a sign that even when we treat light as photons, its wave nature is not completely forgotten.

Also for Option E6

De Broglie's wavelength

In 1923, Louis de Broglie suggested that to a particle of momentum p there corresponds a wave of wavelength given by the formula

$$\lambda = \frac{h}{p}$$

The de Broglie hypothesis, as this is known, thus assigns wave-like properties to something that is normally thought to be a particle. This state of affairs is called the duality of matter.

Example question

Q6

Find the de Broglie wavelength of a proton that has been accelerated from rest by a potential difference of 500 V.

Answer

The kinetic energy of the proton is given by

$$E_k = \frac{p^2}{2m}$$

The work done in accelerating the proton through a potential difference V is qV and this work goes into kinetic energy. Thus

$$\frac{p^2}{2m} = qV$$

$$\Rightarrow \quad p = \sqrt{2mqV}$$

Hence

$$\lambda = \frac{h}{\sqrt{2mqV}}$$

$$= \frac{6.63 \times 10^{-34}}{\sqrt{2 \times 1.67 \times 10^{-27} \times 1.60 \times 10^{-19} \times 500}} \text{ m}$$

$$= 1.3 \times 10^{-12} \text{ m}$$

The electron as a wave

The question is, given an electron, when do we treat it as a particle and when as a wave? Remember that if we call something a wave then it must show wave-like properties – in particular, diffraction. A wave of wavelength λ will diffract around an obstacle of size d if and only if λ is comparable to or bigger than d. To find a typical electron wavelength, consider an electron moving at a speed of 10^5 m^{-1}. It has a momentum $p = 9.1 \times 10^{-26}$ kg m^{-1} and therefore $\lambda = 7.2 \times 10^{-9}$ m. This is quite small. To see the wave-like nature of this electron we would need an 'obstacle' or an 'opening' of about this size. This is provided in nature by crystals. In a crystal, the atoms are regularly placed and the distance between them is typically of the order of 10^{-8} m. The spacing between the atoms is the 'opening' we are looking for. The reason the electron microscope can resolve small distances (down to 10^{-8} m) is

precisely because these distances are of the same order of magnitude as the de Broglie wavelength of the electrons used.

A beam of electrons directed at such a crystal would scatter off the crystal in much the same way that X-rays do. The scattering of X-rays off the periodic arrangement of atoms in a crystal had been shown earlier (by Sir William Henry Bragg) to be the result of diffraction. Bragg derived a relation (the Bragg formula) between the spacing of the atoms in the crystal and the wavelength of the X-rays, so knowing one quantity made the calculation of the other possible. (See Figure 4.6.)

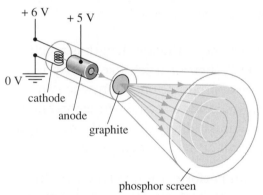

Figure 4.6 Electrons are accelerated from the cathode to the anode: they form a beam, which is diffracted as it passes through the graphite.

▶ Experiments showing the wave nature of the electron were carried out in 1927 by Clinton J. Davisson and Lester H. Germer, and also by George Thomson, son of J. J. Thomson, the discoverer of the electron. In the Davisson–Germer experiment, electrons of kinetic energy 54 eV were directed at a surface of nickel where a single crystal had been grown and were scattered by it (see Figure 4.7). Using the Bragg formula and the known separation of the crystal atoms allowed the determination of the wavelength, which was then seen to agree with the de Broglie formula.

Figure 4.7 The apparatus of Davisson and Germer. Electrons emitted from the hot filament of the electron gun are accelerated through a known potential difference V and are then allowed to fall on a crystal. The positions of the scattered electrons are recorded by a detector.

On the other hand, if the wavelength is much smaller than d, then a particle-like description would be the appropriate one. Only when an electron moves inside a crystal whose interatomic spacing has similar dimensions as the de Broglie wavelength will diffraction take place.

Thus, one can perform a Young-type two-slit experiment with both photons and electrons. What is quite extraordinary about these experiments is that an interference pattern is observed beyond the two slits even if the intensity of light or the electrons is so low that only one photon or electron goes through the slits at a time. The photon or electron 'knows' of the existence of both slits.

Example question

Q7 ▬▬▬▬▬▬▬▬▬▬▬▬▬▬▬▬▬▬

In a neutron diffraction experiment, a beam of neutrons of energy 85 MeV are incident on a foil made out of lead and diffracted. The first diffraction minimum is observed at an angle of 16° relative to the central position where most of the neutrons are observed. From this information, determine the size of the lead nucleus.

Answer

The neutrons are diffracted from the lead nuclei, which act as 'obstacles' of size b. From our knowledge of diffraction, the first minimum is given by $\sin \theta = \frac{\lambda}{b}$, where λ is the de Broglie wavelength of the neutron. The mass of a neutron is $m = 1.67 \times 10^{-27}$ kg and, since its kinetic energy is 85 MeV, the wavelength is $\lambda = \frac{h}{p}$ where

$$p = \sqrt{2 E_k m}$$
$$= \sqrt{2 \times 85 \times 10^6 \times 1.6 \times 10^{-19} \times 1.67 \times 10^{-27}}$$
$$= 21.3 \times 10^{-20} \text{ kg m s}^{-1}$$

Hence

$$\lambda = \frac{6.6 \times 10^{-34}}{21.3 \times 10^{-20}} \text{ m}$$
$$= 0.31 \times 10^{-14} \text{ m}$$

Therefore the size of the nucleus is given by

$$b = \frac{0.31 \times 10^{-34}}{\sin 16°} \text{ m}$$
$$= 1.12 \times 10^{-14} \text{ m}$$

A wave of what?

When we say that a sound wave has a wavelength of 2.2 m, we mean that the distance between successive maxima in the density of air is 2.2 m. When we say that the wavelength of light is 500 nm, we mean that the electric field that is part of the electromagnetic wave making up light is such that the distance between two successive peaks in the value of the electric field is 500 nm. This is the ordinary definition of a wavelength that we understand and have used many times so far. But what do we mean when we say that the wavelength of an electron is 10^{-8} m? What is the wave here? The answer is rather abstract. Imagine a mathematical function Ψ, called the *wavefunction*, which is a function of position x and time t such that its absolute value squared, $|\Psi|^2$, gives the probability that a particle, say an electron, will be found in the immediate neighbourhood of a given point in space and time. Consider, for example, the function $|\Psi|^2$ whose graph is given in Figure 4.8.

The function is practically zero for all x except near $x = 0$. This means that the probability of finding the electron anywhere except near

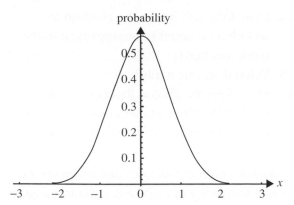

Figure 4.8 The wavefunction gives the probability of finding the electron at a particular place.

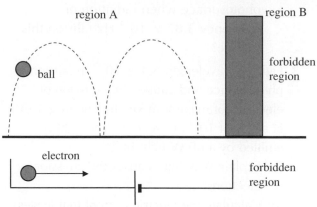

Figure 4.9 A high barrier makes region B forbidden for the bouncing particle in region A.

$x = 0$ is negligible. The electron is localized near $x = 0$, but note that we cannot with absolute certainty say that it is at exactly $x = 0$. A particle has associated with it one such function Ψ, called the wavefunction, which is the solution of a complicated equation called the Schrödinger wave equation. This mathematical probability function is the wave we are looking for. This wave travels at the speed of the particle it describes. The wavelength of this wave is precisely what the de Broglie wavelength is and the wave in question is thus a wave of probability. In the case of a charged particle, the absolute value squared of the wavefunction times the electric charge of the particle gives the distribution of electric charge around the particle. (Note that this implies that the electric charge is spread out all over space and not sitting firmly on the particle itself.)

Probability waves have rather curious properties. One of them is described here: a ball bouncing back and forth in region A in Figure 4.9 cannot jump over the barrier and move in region B if the ball's kinetic energy, E_k, is less than mgh, where h is the height of the barrier.

In atomic physics the analogue of this problem would be an electron confined to region A by a repelling voltage. If the kinetic energy of the electron, E_k, is less than eV, where V is the voltage, then the electron would never appear

in region B. The probability wave of the electron, however, does not become zero exactly where region B begins but rather 'leaks' into region B. As a result, there is a very small but finite probability that the electron makes it into a region that is classically forbidden to it (see Figure 4.10). This is called 'tunnelling', and is the operating principle of the tunnelling electron microscope.

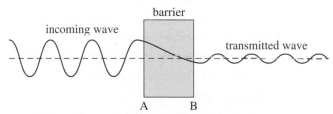

Figure 4.10 An electron tunnels through the barrier; the wavefunction 'leaks' in the forbidden region B. The amplitude of the transmitted wave has been reduced exponentially by the barrier. The greater the width of the barrier, the more the suppression.

Questions

1 (a) Explain what is meant by the photoelectric effect.
  (b) A photosurface has a work function of 3.00 eV. What is the critical frequency?

2 (a) What evidence is there for the existence of photons?
  (b) A photosurface has a critical frequency of 2.25×10^{14} Hz. What is the voltage required to stop electrons emitted from a

photosurface when radiation of frequency 3.87×10^{14} Hz falls on this surface?

3 Light of wavelength 5.4×10^{-7} m falls on a photosurface and causes the emission of electrons of maximum kinetic energy 2.1 eV at a rate of 10^{15} per second. The light is emitted by a 60 W light bulb.
   (a) Explain why light causes the emission of electrons.
   (b) Calculate the electric current that leaves the photosurface.
   (c) Find the work function of the surface.
   (d) Find the maximum kinetic energy of the electrons if the intensity of the light becomes 120 W.
   (e) Find the current from the photosurface when the intensity is 120 W.

4 (a) State three aspects of the photoelectric effect that cannot be explained by the wave theory of light. For each, outline how the photon theory provides an explanation.
   (b) When light of wavelength 2.08×10^{-7} m falls on a photosurface, a voltage of 1.40 V is required to stop the emitted electrons from reaching the anode. What is the largest wavelength of light that will result in emission of electrons from this photosurface?

5 (a) What is the effect of the intensity of light in the photoelectric experiment?
   (b) To determine the work function of a given photosurface, light of wavelength 2.3×10^{-7} m is directed at the surface and the stopping voltage, V_s, recorded. When light of wavelength 1.8×10^{-7} m is used, the stopping voltage is twice as large as the previous one. Find the work function.

6 Light falling on a metallic surface of work function 3.0 eV gives energy to the surface at a rate of 5×10^{-4} W per square metre of the metal's surface. Assume that an electron on the metal surface can absorb energy from an area of about 1.0×10^{-18} m^2.

(a) How long will it take the electron to absorb an amount of energy equal to the work function?
(b) What does this imply?
(c) How does the photon theory of light explain the fact that electrons are emitted almost instantaneously with the incoming photons?

7 From the graph of electron kinetic energy E_k versus frequency of incoming radiation (Figure 4.11), deduce:
   (a) the critical frequency of the photosurface;
   (b) the work function.
   (c) What is the kinetic energy of an electron ejected when light of frequency $f = 8.0 \times 10^{14}$ Hz falls on the surface?
   (d) Another photosurface has a critical frequency of 6.0×10^{14} Hz. Sketch on Figure 4.11 the variation with frequency of the emitted electrons' kinetic energy.

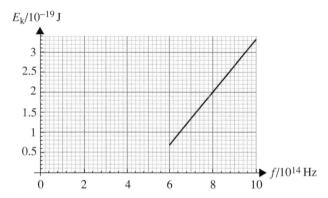

Figure 4.11 For question 7.

8 Consider a brick of mass 0.250 kg moving at 10 m s^{-1}.
   (a) What is its de Broglie wavelength?
   (b) Does it make sense to treat the brick as a wave? Explain.

9 (a) Describe an experiment in which the de Broglie wavelength of an electron can be measured directly.
   (b) What is the speed of an electron whose de Broglie wavelength is equal to that of red light (680 nm)?

10 Consider an electron that is confined to move along a straight line of length L. The electron's probability wave must vanish at the end points of this straight line and so resembles a standing wave on a string. Working by analogy, demand that L must be an integral multiple of a half-wavelength

$$L = n\frac{\lambda}{2}, \quad n = 1, 2, 3, \cdots$$

Thus, find the momentum of the electron and from $E_k = \frac{p^2}{2m}$ find an expression for its kinetic energy in terms of n. What is the lowest possible energy this electron can have?

The Bohr model

This chapter introduces the discrete atomic world. We will see that, contrary to what occurs in the macroscopic world, the energy of an atom cannot be arbitrary but rather assumes values from a discrete set. The limitations of the Bohr model are discussed and an elementary introduction to the Schrödinger theory is given. The nature and mechanisms of X-ray production are also discussed.

Objectives

By the end of this chapter you should be able to:
- describe *emission* and *absorption spectra* and understand their significance for atomic structure;
- describe *Bohr's postulates* and the conclusions they lead to;
- describe the hydrogen atom according to Bohr;
- do calculations on the *Bohr model*, especially calculations of the frequency of the photon emitted in a transition through $hf = \Delta E$;
- appreciate the *limitations* of the Bohr model;
- describe the *Schrödinger theory* and say how it differs from Bohr's model;
- describe the mechanisms for the *production of X-rays*;
- predict the effect on the *X-ray spectrum* of changes in the *accelerating voltage* and the nature of the *target material*.

Also part of Option E6

Atomic spectra

When a gas is heated to a very high temperature, it begins to glow. If we look at the light from this hot gas through a spectrometer, we find something very interesting. We see a series of sharp bright lines of different colours (i.e. different wavelengths) separated by darkness; this is an *emission line* spectrum (see Figure 5.1 top). Late in the nineteenth century, physicists investigated the appearance of these lines in the spectra of gases and found that different gases exhibited these lines at different wavelengths. The pattern of lines was unique to particular elements, so that a picture of the emission spectrum of a gas was sufficient to identify the gas. Similarly, we can send light through a cold gas and then use a spectrometer to examine the light that emerges. We see something similar. This time, there are sharp dark lines at wavelengths precisely where there were bright lines before, separated by a continuous spread of bright colours. This kind of spectrum is called an *absorption line* spectrum (see Figure 5.1 bottom).

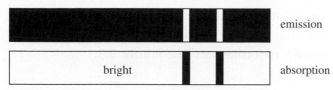

emission

bright | absorption

Figure 5.1 Emission and absorption spectra.

Our task is to try to understand why atoms glow when hot, why they absorb light when cold, and why this takes place at specific wavelengths. This was a formidable problem at the end of the nineteenth century and the beginning of the twentieth. To solve it, new ideas had to be introduced and new laws of physics discovered.

Also part of Option E6

The Bohr model

At the beginning of the twentieth century, the prominent model of the atom was due to Rutherford. He viewed the atom much like a solar system, with electrons orbiting the nucleus like planets orbiting a sun. An immediate problem with this model is that the electrons are experiencing centripetal acceleration and the theories of the time predicted that in such a case an electron would have to be constantly losing energy by radiating. This, and other problems, led the young Danish physicist Niels Bohr to a radically different approach in 1913. Bohr realized that the secret of atomic structure lay in its discreteness as revealed by studies of atomic spectra. He therefore proceeded to calculate the energy of a hydrogen atom (the simplest atom), hoping to introduce in this calculation some kind of discreteness.

The mathematical details that follow are not required for examination purposes.

The total energy of a hydrogen atom, consisting of an electron and a proton, is made up of the kinetic energy of the electron, the kinetic energy of the proton, and the electric potential energy

of the electron and proton. The proton, being very much heavier than the electron, is assumed not to move and thus its kinetic energy is taken to be zero. The kinetic energy of the electron is $\frac{1}{2}mv^2$ and the potential energy is $-\frac{e^2}{4\pi\varepsilon_0 r}$, where r is the radius of the electron's orbit, assumed circular. Thus

$$E = \frac{1}{2}mv^2 - \frac{e^2}{4\pi\varepsilon_0 r}$$

Figure 5.2 The electron is acted upon by the Coulomb force of the attracting proton.

Noting that the electron is acted upon by the Coulomb force of the attracting proton (see Figure 5.2), and applying Newton's second law, we see that

$$\frac{e^2}{4\pi\varepsilon_0 r^2} = \frac{mv^2}{r}$$

Cancelling one power of r in the last equation we find

$$mv^2 = \frac{e^2}{4\pi\varepsilon_0 r}$$

We can now substitute this last result into the formula for the total energy to find

$$E = -\frac{e^2}{8\pi\varepsilon_0 r}$$

or, if you prefer to express E in terms of the electron's speed,

$$E = -\frac{1}{2}mv^2$$

Note that the total energy is negative; that is simply an indication of the fact that the electron is bound to the proton and cannot simply move far away from it. (This is just like the case for a planet orbiting the sun. Its total energy is also negative.) There is nothing in this formula yet suggesting the existence of discrete spectral lines. E appears to have arbitrary values.

▶ At this stage Bohr made the revolutionary suggestion that the electron's angular momentum is an integral multiple of the unit $\frac{h}{2\pi}$, so that

$$mvr = n\frac{h}{2\pi}$$

where n is a positive integer. This is known as the first Bohr condition. Electrons obeying this condition are said to be in a *stationary state*.

Squaring both sides of $mvr = n\frac{h}{2\pi}$ and combining with $mv^2 = \frac{e^2}{4\pi\varepsilon_0 r}$ gives

$$r = \frac{\varepsilon_0 h^2}{\pi m e^2}n^2$$

This formula involves a lot of physical constants. It is a good exercise to put the numbers in, to find

$$r = a_0 n^2$$

where

$$a_0 = 0.53 \times 10^{-10} \text{ m}$$

This says that the orbit of the electron exists at specific radii. (The constant a_0 is known as the Bohr radius.) The diameter of the $n = 1$ orbit is taken as the typical size of the hydrogen atom. This is a very useful formula: knowing n determines r, which through $mvr = n\frac{h}{2\pi}$ gives the speed v. If now we substitute this value of r in the formula for the total energy we find

$$E = -\frac{me^4}{8\varepsilon_0^2 h^2}\frac{1}{n^2}$$

or numerically

$$E = -\frac{13.6}{n^2} \text{ eV}$$

This is extraordinary again. It shows that the total energy of the hydrogen atom cannot have arbitrary values! It is quantized. If $n = 1$ then $E = -13.6 \text{ eV}$; if $n = 2$, $E = -3.4 \text{ eV}$, and so on. The energy cannot be -8 eV, for example. The significance of the integer n is, therefore, that it specifies the energy of the atom. We say that

the atom can exist in a number of states, $n = 1$, $n = 2$, $n = 3$, and so on. These states are usually shown in a diagram like Figure 5.3.

Figure 5.3 The energy level diagram for hydrogen according to the Bohr model.

This is the discreteness that Bohr was looking for. The assumption about the electron's angular momentum gave the required result.

Each line represents a state or an energy level. Note that, as n becomes larger and larger, the energy levels come closer and closer together. Eventually as n becomes infinite, $E = 0$. As the energy approaches zero, the electron is less and less tightly bound to the nucleus. At $E = 0$, the electron is free to move away from the nucleus – the atom is ionized. The state with $n = 1$ has the lowest energy. It is called the *ground state* of the hydrogen atom. An electron in the ground state cannot lose any energy since there is nothing lower to which it can go. It is a stable state. All other states are called *excited states*. An electron in one of these excited states can lose energy and end up in a lower state (see the next section).

Example questions

Q1 ▆▆▆▆▆▆▆▆▆▆▆▆▆▆▆

Find the radius of the first three states of hydrogen.

Answer

We proved that the radius of the nth state is given by $r = 0.53 \times 10^{-10} \text{ m} \times n^2$ so

$$r_1 = 0.53 \times 10^{-10} \text{ m}$$

$$r_2 = 2.12 \times 10^{-10} \text{ m}$$

$$r_3 = 4.77 \times 10^{-10} \text{ m}$$

Q2

What is the speed of the electron in the state $n = 3$?

Answer

From $E = -\frac{1}{2}mv^2$ and $E = -\frac{13.6}{9}$ eV we find

$v = 7.3 \times 10^5$ m s^{-1}

Also we could use the radius for $n = 3$ we just found in the previous example and then find v from $mvr = n\frac{h}{2\pi}$.

In view of de Broglie's hypothesis, the first Bohr condition can be rewritten if we make use of the wavelength of the electron

$$(mv)r = n\frac{h}{2\pi}$$

$$pr = n\frac{h}{2\pi}$$

or

$$2\pi r = n\lambda$$

where n is any positive integer. This says that an integral number of electron de Broglie wavelengths fit on the circumference of the orbit. Figure 5.4 shows the case with $n = 8$.

Thus, the electron wave is like a standing wave on the circumference. Like all standing waves it does not involve energy transfer, which is an imprecise way of explaining why the electron does not radiate when in such a state (hence 'solving' the problem with Rutherford's model).

The Bohr model as presented here can only be applied to atoms with a single electron: namely, the hydrogen atom. However, more complicated atoms can also be treated in this way provided they are ionized so that only one electron remains behind. The energy of the various levels is found by repeating our derivation for hydrogen and noting that the force and the potential energy between the nucleus and the single electron have to be increased by a factor of Z, where Z is the number of protons inside the nucleus. This results in the formula for the nth level

$$E = -\frac{Z^2}{n^2} \times 13.6 \text{ eV}$$

Also part of Option E6

Atomic transitions

If a hydrogen atom is in an excited state, it can make a transition to a lower state. Thus, a hydrogen atom in the state $n = 2$ can go to $n = 1$. (That is to say, initially the electron is at an orbit radius corresponding to $n = 2$ but after the transition the electron is at the first orbit radius.) An atom in $n = 3$ can either go to $n = 1$ directly or it can first make a transition down to $n = 2$ and from there to $n = 1$ (see Figure 5.5).

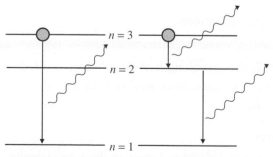

Figure 5.5 An electron in the state $n = 3$ can return to the ground state through three transitions.

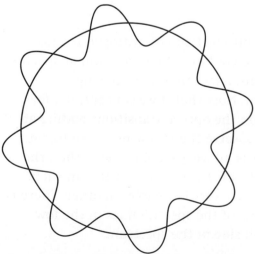

Figure 5.4 The electron wave is a standing wave on the circumference of the classical orbit.

Every time an atom makes such a transition, a single photon is being emitted. Suppose that initially the atom is in the state $n = n_{init}$ and makes a transition to a state $n = n_{fin}$. If the energy difference between these states is ΔE, then the emitted photon will have a frequency and wavelength given by

$$hf = \Delta E$$

or

$$\frac{hc}{\lambda} = \Delta E$$

In the case of the hydrogen atom, since $E = -\frac{me^4}{8\varepsilon_0^2 h^2}\frac{1}{n^2}$, the wavelength of the photon in the transition from state n_2 to state n_1 is given by

$$\frac{1}{\lambda} = \frac{me^4}{8\varepsilon_0^2 ch^3}\left(\frac{1}{n_1^2} - \frac{1}{n_2^2}\right)$$

$$= R_H\left(\frac{1}{n_1^2} - \frac{1}{n_2^2}\right)$$

where $R_H = \frac{me^4}{8\varepsilon_0^2 ch^3}$ is known as the Rydberg constant.

▶ We see, therefore, that since the atom exists in specific energy states, the emitted photons during atomic transitions have very specific frequencies (wavelengths), which is of course the striking and mysterious feature of emission spectra. Thus, an atom can only emit light (energy) when making a transition from a high to a low n state; in a stationary state the electron does not radiate. This is known as the second Bohr condition.

Example questions

Q3

What is the wavelength of the photon emitted when a hydrogen atom makes a transition from $n = 3$ to $n = 1$?

Answer

The energy difference between the two states is

$$13.6 - \frac{13.6}{9} \text{ eV} = 12.09 \text{ eV}$$

Thus $\frac{hc}{\lambda} = 12.09$ eV and so (remember the conversion of eV into joules)

$$\lambda = \frac{6.6 \times 10^{-34} \times 3 \times 10^8}{12.09 \times 1.6 \times 10^{-19}} \text{ m}$$

$$= 1.02 \times 10^{-7} \text{ m}$$

This is a UV (ultraviolet) wavelength.

Q4

Which transition corresponds to photons of larger wavelength, $n = 5$ to $n = 3$ or $n = 6$ to $n = 4$?

Answer

Largest wavelength photons correspond to the smallest energy difference. This is between states 6 and 4.

In the case of hydrogen, transitions down to the $n = 1$ state result in UV (ultraviolet) wavelengths (the Lyman series). Transitions to $n = 2$ give optical wavelengths (the Balmer series) and those to $n = 3$ give IR (infrared) wavelengths (the Paschen series). (See Figure 5.6.)

Figure 5.6 Transitions in hydrogen. Many of those ending at $n = 2$ are optical.

The emission spectrum of hydrogen is thus predicted to contain a line spectrum at specific wavelengths: a fact that is verified by experiment. Note that if we concentrate, for example, on the optical transitions ending at $n = 2$, we observe the following. Since higher energy levels are very close to each other, the wavelengths of the photons emitted in such transitions are very close to each other. There is a 'crowding' of the spectral lines in the low wavelength side of the spectrum.

An atom can also make a transition from a low to a high state (i.e. from a state of low n to a state of high n). This means that energy has to be provided to the atom. Energy can be provided to the atom in a variety of ways:

- by heating to a high temperature;
- by bombarding it with electrons;
- by having photons fall on the atom.

If electrons of kinetic energy E_k collide with the atom, then energy may be transferred to the atom. If the electron's kinetic energy is less than the energy required to make the atom move to a higher state, the energy will not be accepted. The electron will simply suffer an elastic collision with the atom. The electron will transfer energy to the atom only if E_k is at least equal to the energy needed to excite the atom. The collision will then be inelastic, with the electron rebounding off the atom with a kinetic energy equal to E_k minus whatever energy the atom used to go to a higher state.

Example question

Q5 ▰▰▰▰▰▰▰▰▰

Electrons of kinetic energy equal to 10.15 eV, 12.84 eV and 13.26 eV collide with hydrogen atoms in their ground state. In each case, find the largest n number of the state the atoms can be excited to.

Answer

With 10.15 eV there is not enough energy to jump to a higher state. With 12.84 eV the atom can jump up to $n = 4$ and with 13.26 eV it can jump up to $n = 6$.

The case of photons falling on the atom is similar to that of electrons, with one important difference. The photon will be absorbed by the atom if the photon's energy corresponds exactly to the energy difference between the state the atom finds itself in and another, higher, state. The photon, unlike the electron, cannot give part of its energy to the atom and rebound off the atom with whatever energy is left over. The photon will either give all of its energy to the atom, which then makes a transition, or will

just scatter off the atom without any loss of energy, leaving the atom in the same energy level as before.

Here are some examples.

- If a hydrogen atom is in $n = 1$ and a photon of energy 12.20 eV falls on the atom, this energy would not be accepted, since the energy difference between the ground state of hydrogen and any other state is not 12.20 eV. The photon would bounce off the atom with energy 12.20 eV.
- If an electron of kinetic energy 12.20 eV collides with the atom, a number of possibilities arise. The electron may give away an amount of energy equal to 10.20 eV, which is the energy difference between $n = 1$ and $n = 2$ and the atom will then jump up to $n = 2$. The energy left over is 1.80 eV, which is the kinetic energy the electron would have after bouncing off the atom. The electron could, however, also give away to the atom an energy of 12.09 eV (the energy difference between $n = 1$ and $n = 3$), raise the atom to the state $n = 3$ and bounce off with a kinetic energy of 0.11 eV.
- If the atom is in some state with energy $-E$ and we give this atom an energy bigger than E, then the atom will accept this energy; the electron will use an amount E to free itself from the pull of the nucleus and the amount left over would be its kinetic energy.

Example question

Q6 ▰▰▰▰▰▰▰▰▰

A hydrogen atom is in the state $n = 2$. An energy of 10 eV is provided to this atom. What is the energy and speed of the electron after it leaves the atom?

Answer

The atom in the state $n = 2$ has energy

$$E = -\frac{13.6}{4} \text{ eV}$$
$$= -3.4 \text{ eV}$$

Thus, this electron will use 3.4 eV of the given 10 eV to escape the pull of the atom and will be left with $10 - 3.4 = 6.6$ eV of kinetic energy. Using $E_k = \frac{1}{2}mv^2$, its speed is

$$v = 1.52 \times 10^6 \, \text{m s}^{-1}$$

What determines the state the atom is in is a more complicated question. If the temperature is low enough, the probability is high for finding the atom in its ground state. If the temperature is increased, the probability for finding it in an excited state increases. The Bohr model does not predict in which state an atom will be. In fact, it makes the erroneous prediction that all states are equally likely to be occupied. The full quantum theory that replaces the Bohr model predicts the probabilities for an atom in a specific energy state. In general, higher n states are less and less likely to be occupied.

Limitations of the Bohr model

Although the Bohr model is successful in describing the general behaviour of the hydrogen atom, it has a number of difficulties:

- it can only treat one-electron atoms (i.e. just the hydrogen atom or ions);
- it treats circular orbits only;
- it does not predict the intensities of different spectral lines;
- it is inconsistent with the uncertainty principle;
- it does not predict the splittings of energy levels due to the interaction of the magnetic field of the proton and the electron's angular momentum and spin.

Thus, a new theory is needed to account for all the complexities of big atoms. This theory is the full modern quantum theory of atoms and molecules, which correctly accounts for all observed atomic phenomena. The beginnings of this theory are presented in the next section.

Also part of Option E6
The Schrödinger theory

The Bohr model marked the beginning of a very active period in the history of physics: the birth and development of quantum mechanics. The Bohr model was a very important step away from the difficulties of the classical Rutherford model of the atom and in the right direction, but as we have seen, it was a model with serious difficulties of its own.

The many problems of the Bohr model were corrected by Erwin Schrödinger, an Austrian physicist, who developed the first true quantum theory of the atom. Schrödinger introduced the *wavefunction* – a function of position and time whose absolute value squared is related to the *probability* of finding the electron near a specific point in space and time. In this theory, the electron cannot be thought of as having a specific position at a specific time. Rather, it is spread out over a large volume and there are places where it is more likely to be found than others. Thus, the electron does not orbit the nucleus in well-defined orbits as Bohr asserted but rather exists around the nucleus as an *electron cloud*: spread out negative charge around the positive nucleus. The theory retains Bohr's idea of energy states, however. In Schrödinger's theory, too, the electron has well-defined energy. For the ground state of hydrogen, the square of the wavefunction $|\Psi|^2$ as a function of distance from the nucleus is shown in Figure 5.7. The average distance of the electron from the nucleus according to Schrödinger's theory is approximately equal to the orbit radius according to the Bohr model.

The wavefunction satisfies a differential equation known as Schrödinger's equation, and we present it here because it is an elegant equation. If the electron is constrained to move along a straight line, E stands for its total energy and V for the potential in which it finds itself, the equation is

$$\frac{d^2\Psi}{dx^2} = -\frac{8\pi^2 m}{h^2}(E - V)\Psi$$

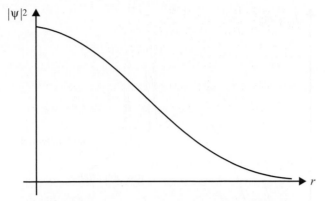

Figure 5.7 The square of the wavefunction for the ground state of hydrogen as a function of distance from the nucleus. The function decreases away from the nucleus, showing a small probability for finding the electron far away. The average distance of the electron from the nucleus is approximately equal to the first Bohr orbit radius.

Suppose that the electron is free to bounce back and forth between two walls at $x = 0$ and $x = L$ but is not otherwise subject to any forces (see Figure 5.8).

here $V = 0$

$x = 0$ $x = L$

Figure 5.8.

Then between the walls $V = 0$ and the equation gives

$$\frac{d^2\Psi}{dx^2} + \frac{8\pi^2 m}{h^2} E\, \Psi = 0$$

$$\Rightarrow \Psi = A \sin\left(x\sqrt{\frac{8\pi^2 m}{h^2}E}\right)$$

$$+ B \cos\left(x\sqrt{\frac{8\pi^2 m}{h^2}E}\right)$$

where A and B are constants. When $x = 0$, the wavefunction must vanish and so

$$0 = A \times 0 + B \times 1$$
$$\Rightarrow B = 0.$$

It must also vanish when $x = L$ and so

$$0 = A \sin\left(L\sqrt{\frac{8\pi^2 m}{h^2}E}\right)$$

$$\Rightarrow L\sqrt{\frac{8\pi^2 m}{h^2}E} = n\pi, \quad n = 1, 2, 3, \ldots$$

$$L^2 \frac{8\pi^2 m}{h^2} E = n^2 \pi^2$$

$$\Rightarrow E = \frac{\pi^2 h^2}{8\pi^2 m L^2} n^2$$

This gives the energy the electron is allowed to have. The wavefunction is then

$$\Psi = A \sin\left(x\sqrt{\frac{8\pi^2 m}{h^2}E}\right)$$

$$= A \sin\left(x\sqrt{\frac{8\pi^2 m}{h^2}\frac{\pi^2 h^2}{8\pi^2 m L^2} n^2}\right)$$

$$= A \sin\left(\frac{\pi n x}{L}\right)$$

where A is a constant. Those of you taking Higher Level Mathematics will appreciate that the square of the wavefunction is a *probability distribution density*. This means that to find the probability that the electron is somewhere between say, $x = 0.2$ and $x = 0.4$, we must find

$$\text{prob}(0.2 \leq x \leq 0.4) = \int_{0.2}^{0.4} |\Psi|^2 \, dx$$

The probability of finding the electron somewhere between $x = 0$ and $x = L$ must be one and so

$$\int_0^L |\Psi|^2 \, dx = 1$$

$$\Rightarrow 1 = \int_0^L \left| A \sin\left(\frac{\pi n x}{L}\right) \right|^2 dx$$

$$= A^2 \int_0^L \sin^2\left(\frac{\pi n x}{L}\right) dx$$

$$= A^2 \frac{L}{2}$$

$$\Rightarrow A = \sqrt{\frac{2}{L}}$$

We have been able to determine the constant A as well. The nth energy state thus has wavefunction

$$\Psi = \sqrt{\frac{2}{L}} \sin\left(\frac{\pi n x}{L}\right)$$

and energy

$$E = \frac{\pi^2 h^2}{8\pi^2 m L^2} n^2$$

> ▶ Imposing the appropriate boundary conditions on the solution to the Schrödinger equation has given both the wavefunction and the energy.

X-rays

Suppose that electrons emitted from a hot wire (as in a cathode-ray tube) are accelerated through a very high potential difference, say 30 kV. We then let these electrons hit a piece of material (e.g. tungsten) called the 'target'. (See Figure 5.9.)

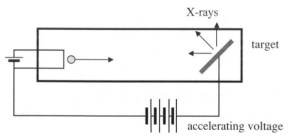

Figure 5.9 Apparatus for producing X-rays. The emitted electrons are accelerated toward the target by a high potential difference.

As we saw earlier, when charges accelerate, they emit electromagnetic radiation. Here the electrons are rapidly brought to rest by the collisions with the atoms of the target and thus radiate electromagnetic radiation. The radiation emitted will have a whole range of wavelengths. Figure 5.10 gives the intensity of the radiation (i.e. the number of photons emitted for a given wavelength times the energy of one of those photons) as a function of the wavelength.

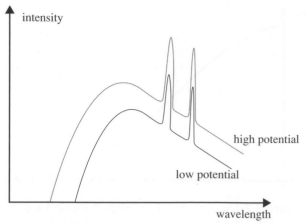

Figure 5.10 The spectrum of X-rays. Increasing the accelerating potential decreases the minimum wavelength.

The striking feature is the existence of a minimum wavelength below which no radiation is emitted. How is this explained? Let us imagine that the electrons have been accelerated through a potential difference of V volts. Then, just before hitting the target, the electrons have kinetic energy $E_k = eV$. When an electron converts all of this energy into a single photon, we must have, by conservation of energy, $\frac{hc}{\lambda} = eV$, and thus we obtain a minimum wavelength

$$\lambda = \frac{hc}{eV}$$

This shows that an increased accelerating voltage results in a smaller minimum wavelength. If the electron converts part of its kinetic energy to one photon and the rest to another, this results in photons of wavelengths larger than the minimum one we just found (see Figure 5.11).

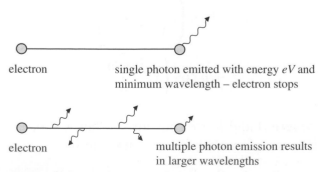

Figure 5.11 Ways in which an electron can give its energy to photons.

Of the total energy supplied to the electrons by the accelerating voltage, only a small part (a fraction of 1%) is radiated as energy of X-rays. The rest heats up the target, which means that it must be cooled if it is not to melt.

The spectrum of X-rays indicated in Figure 5.10 has two parts, the continuous spectrum whose origin we just discussed and the discrete spectrum, which is the set of spikes on top of the continuous spectrum, at specific wavelengths. If we increase the accelerating voltage, the positions of these wavelengths remain unchanged. This suggests that the spikes have to do only with the target material. What happens is that the incoming electrons knock electrons out of their ground state in the target atoms. Electrons in the atom in higher states then make the transition to occupy the now empty ground state, thus radiating photons (see Figure 5.12).

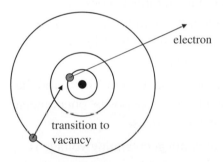

Figure 5.12 An inner-shell electron is ejected from the atom by the incoming electron. Its place is then taken by a higher-shell electron, which emits a photon in the transition.

These photons have wavelengths in the X-ray region. (In a big atom, the energy of the ground state can be many keV. Tungsten's ground state energy is -67 keV. This is why the emitted photons are in the X-ray region.) As we already know, these photons will have specific wavelengths corresponding to the energy difference between the ground state energy and the energy of the state they came from. This energy difference is, of course, characteristic of the atoms of the target and thus does not depend on the accelerating voltage V. If we change the target, we will find spikes at different wavelengths.

Example question

Q7 ▄▄▄▄▄▄▄▄▄▄▄

What is the minimum wavelength of X-rays emitted in a 50 kV tube?

Answer

The minimum wavelength is
$$\lambda = \frac{hc}{eV}$$
$$= 2.49 \times 10^{-11} \text{ m.}$$

Questions

1 State what you understand by the terms:
   (a) energy level;
   (b) atomic transition;
   (c) spectrum of an element.

2 An absorption spectrum is formed when photons of specific wavelengths are absorbed by the electrons of an atom, which then make transitions to higher energy levels. But as soon as the electrons reach the higher energy level they will fall back to the state they came from, re-radiating photons of precisely the same wavelength as those they absorbed. So there should not be any dark lines. What do you say?

3 An electron of kinetic energy 11.5 eV collides with a hydrogen atom in its ground state. With what possible kinetic energy can this electron rebound off the atom?

4 (a) What is the evidence for the existence of energy levels in atoms?
   (b) Electrons of kinetic energy (i) 10.10 eV, (ii) 12.80 eV and (iii) 13.25 eV collide with hydrogen atoms and can excite these to higher states. In each case, find the largest n corresponding to the state the atom can be excited to. Assume that the hydrogen atoms are in their ground state initially.

5 (a) What do you understand by the term energy levels?
   (b) What is the speed of an electron in the state $n = 5$ of hydrogen?

6 (a) What are the two Bohr postulates?
   (b) What is the wavelength of light emitted when a hydrogen atom makes a transition from $n = 4$ to $n = 2$?

7 How many revolutions per second does an electron in the hydrogen atom make when in the state $n = 2$ according to the Bohr model?

8 (a) What do you understand by the term ionization energy?

 (b) What is the ionization energy for a hydrogen atom in the state $n = 3$?

9 (a) The Bohr model can be applied to a helium atom that is ionized but not to the neutral atom of helium. Why?

 (b) The spectrum of doubly ionized atoms of lithium (Li^{2+}) contains the wavelength 2.08×10^{-7} m. If this is a transition down to $n = 3$, from which state did the atom make the transition?

10 (a) Find the smallest wavelength that can be emitted in a transition in atomic hydrogen.

 (b) What is the minimum speed an electron must have so that it can ionize an atom of hydrogen in its ground state?

11 In view of what you have learned about the atomic structure of hydrogen, discuss the validity of one of the assumptions of the kinetic theory of gases: namely, that the collisions between molecules are elastic.

12 Using the result that a molecule of a gas has an average kinetic energy of $\frac{3}{2}kT$ when the gas is kept at a temperature T, estimate the temperature at which hydrogen is ionized. Is your answer realistic?

13 The electron of a hydrogen atom is in the state $n = 3$.

 (a) With the help of a diagram, show what this means in terms of the de Broglie wavelength of the electron.

 (b) Find the speed of the electron.

 (c) The electron makes a transition down to the state $n = 2$. Find the wavelength of the radiation emitted.

 (d) To which part of the electromagnetic spectrum does this radiation belong?

14 (a) Find the de Broglie wavelength of a proton (mass 1.67×10^{-27} kg) whose kinetic energy is 200.0 MeV.

 (b) What is the de Broglie wavelength of an electron in the $n = 2$ state of hydrogen?

15 (a) Describe how X-rays are produced.

 (b) What is the minimum wavelength of X-rays emitted in a 67.0 kV machine?

16 (a) Describe what happens to the maximum frequency of the X-rays produced in an X-ray tube when the accelerating voltage is increased.

 (b) In a television screen, electrons are accelerated by a potential difference of 30 kV. How fast are the electrons moving just before they hit the screen?

 (c) What is the maximum frequency of the X-rays produced when the electrons in (b) are brought to rest?

17 It is said that the production of X-rays and the photoelectric effect are 'opposite' phenomena. Make this statement precise.

18 In an X-ray tube, the accelerating voltage is 40.0 kV and the current between the cathode and the anode is 20.0 mA.

 (a) What is the smallest wavelength of X-rays produced in this tube.

 (b) If only 0.50% of the total energy supplied is converted into X-rays, the rest going to heat up the anode, find the rate at which heat must be removed from the anode in order to keep it at a constant temperature.

Nuclear physics

This chapter provides a more detailed discussion of the radioactive decay law and scattering experiments in which nuclear sizes may be determined. The mass spectrometer is discussed as well as the existence of isotopes. The prediction of the neutrino in beta decays on the basis of energy and momentum conservation is also discussed.

Objectives

By the end of this chapter you should be able to:

- solve problems of *closest approach* using the law of conservation of energy and appreciate that nuclei have well-defined radii;
- describe a *mass spectrometer* and its implications for *isotope* existence;
- state the theoretical arguments that have been used to postulate the existence of the *neutrino*;
- state the *radioactive decay law*, $N = N_0 \, e^{-\lambda t}$, $A = -\frac{dN}{dt} = (N_0 \lambda) \, e^{-\lambda t}$;
- state the meaning of *half-life* and *decay constant* and derive the relationship between them;
- appreciate that the decay constant is the *probability of decay per unit time*;
- understand that the *initial activity* of a sample is $A_0 = N_0 \lambda$;
- obtain *short* and *long* half-lives from experimental data;
- solve problems with *activities* and the *radioactive decay law*.

Scattering experiments and distance of closest approach

In scattering experiments such as Rutherford's, simple energy considerations can be used to calculate the distance of closest approach of the incoming particle to the target. Thus, consider, as an example, an alpha particle (of charge $q = 2e$) that is shot head-on toward a stationary nucleus of charge $Q = Ze$ (see Figure 6.1). Initially the system has a total energy consisting of the alpha particle's kinetic energy $E = E_k$. We take the separation of the alpha and the nucleus to be large so no potential energy exists. At the point of closest

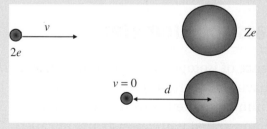

Figure 6.1 The closest approach of an alpha particle happens in a head-on collision.

approach, a distance d from the centre of the nucleus, the alpha particle stops and is about to turn back. Thus, the total energy now is the electric potential energy of the alpha and the nucleus, given by

$$E = k\frac{Qq}{d}$$
$$= k\frac{(2e)(Ze)}{d}$$
$$= k\frac{2Ze^2}{d}$$

(We are assuming that the nucleus does not recoil so its kinetic energy is ignored.)

Then, by conservation of energy

$$E_k = k\frac{2Ze^2}{d}$$
$$\Rightarrow d = k\frac{2Ze^2}{E_k}$$

Assuming a kinetic energy for the alpha particle equal to 2.0 MeV directed at a gold nucleus ($Z = 79$) gives $d = 1.1 \times 10^{-13}$ m. This is outside the range of the nuclear force, so the alpha particle is simply repelled by the electrical force.

As the energy of the incoming particle is increased, the distance of closest approach decreases. The smallest it can get is, however, of the same order as the radius of the nucleus. Thus, experiments of this kind have been used to estimate the nuclear radii. A result of these experiments is that the nuclear radius R depends on mass number A through

$$R = 1.2 \times A^{1/3} \times 10^{-15} \text{ m}$$

The mass spectrometer

The existence of isotopes (i.e. atoms of the same element having slightly different masses due to differing number of neutrons in the nucleus) can be demonstrated with an instrument called a mass spectrometer. Imagine that singly ionized ions of an element are emitted from the black box in Figure 6.2. Singly ionized means that each atom has lost a single electron and thus has a net positive charge of e. The ions move through a pair of slits (S_1), which collimates the beam. They then enter a region of electric and magnetic fields at right angles to each other. The magnetic field is directed into the page in the region shaded grey. The positive

Figure 6.2 A mass spectrometer. Ions enter through the collimating slits S_1. They then enter a region of magnetic and electric fields and approach a second slit, which only allows ions of a given velocity to pass. A second magnetic field bends these ions into circular paths according to their mass.

ions are deflected to the left by the electric field and to the right by the magnetic field. By choosing a suitable value for the magnetic field, the ions can continue through undeflected if the magnetic and electric forces are equal. This means that $eE = evB$ or simply that

$$v = \frac{E}{B}$$

Thus, only ions with this specific velocity can pass through the second slit S_2. Ions with other velocities will be deflected and so will be prevented from going through this second slit. This arrangement acts as a velocity selector for the ions. The selected ions then enter a second region of magnetic field (also directed into the page) and are thus deflected into a circular path, hitting a photographic plate where they are recorded.

▶ The radius of the circular path is given by

$$R = \frac{mv}{eB}$$

If the beam contains atoms of equal mass, all atoms will hit the plate at the same point. If, however, isotopes are present, the heavier atoms will follow a longer radius circle and will hit the plate further to the right. Measurement of the radius of each isotope's path thus allows for the determination of its mass.

Beta decay and the neutrino

The process of beta decay described earlier originates from a decay of a neutron inside an atomic nucleus:

$$_0^1n \rightarrow \,_1^1p + \,_{-1}^0e + \,_0^0\bar{\nu}_e$$

The neutron decays into a proton (thus increasing the atomic number of the nucleus by 1), an electron and an antineutrino. A free neutron (i.e. one not inside a nucleus) decays into a proton according to the reaction equation above, with a half-life of about 11 min. A related decay is that of *positron emission*, in which a proton inside a nucleus turns itself into a neutron accompanied by the emission of a positron (the antiparticle of the electron) and a neutrino:

$$_1^1p \rightarrow \,_0^1n + \,_{+1}^0e + \,_0^0\nu_e$$

Unlike a free neutron, a free proton cannot decay into a neutron since the rest energy of a neutron is larger than that of a proton. Inside a nucleus the reaction is, however, possible (because binding energy is used to make up for the difference). These reactions must be understood as the disappearance of one particle and the appearance or creation of the three particles on the right-hand side of the decay equation. We must *not* think that the decaying particle actually consists of the three particles into which it somehow splits in the decay.

There is an unfamiliar particle in beta decay, the electron antineutrino, $\bar{\nu}_e$, a particle that went undetected until 1953. Its presence in beta decay was predicted on theoretical grounds as follows. Consider the decay $_0^1n \rightarrow \,_1^1p + \,_{-1}^0e + \,_0^0\bar{\nu}_e$. The mass of the neutron is larger than that of the proton and electron together by

$$1.008665 \text{ u} - (1.007276 + 0.0005486) \text{ u}$$
$$= 0.00084 \text{ u}$$

corresponding to an energy of

$$0.00084 \times 931.5 \text{ MeV} = 0.783 \text{ MeV}$$

This is the available energy in the decay, which will show up as kinetic energy of the products. If only the electron and the proton are produced, then the electron being the lighter of the two will carry most of this energy away as kinetic energy. Thus, we should observe electrons with kinetic energies of about 0.783 MeV. In experiments, however, the electron has a *range* of energies from zero up to 0.783 MeV. The question is then, where is the missing energy?

Figure 6.3 shows two ways in which a neutron may decay.

▶ Wolfgang Pauli and Enrico Fermi hypothesized the existence of a third particle in the products of a beta decay in 1933. Since the energy of the electron in beta decay has a *range* of possible values, it means that a third very light particle must also be produced so that it carries the remainder of the available energy. Enrico Fermi coined the word neutrino for the 'little neutral one'.

(a)

(b)

Figure 6.3 (a) A neutron at rest decaying into just two particles. The two particles must have equal and opposite momentum so they move in opposite directions. (b) A neutron at rest decaying into three particles. There are now many possibilities as to how the three particles move.

Electron capture

A process related to beta decay is electron capture, in which a proton inside a nucleus captures an electron and turns into a neutron and a neutrino:

$$_1^1p + \,_{-1}^0e \rightarrow \,_0^1n + \,_0^0\nu_e$$

The creation of a neutron star rests on this process, in which the huge pressure inside the star drives electrons into protons in the nuclei of the star, turning them into neutrons.

Table 6.1 gives some examples of beta decays.

Decay	Half-life	Maximum energy
$^3_1\text{H} \rightarrow {}^3_2\text{He} + {}^{\ 0}_{-1}\text{e} + {}^0_0\bar{\nu}_e$	12.3 yr	0.0186 MeV
$^{14}_6\text{C} \rightarrow {}^{14}_7\text{N} + {}^{\ 0}_{-1}\text{e} + {}^0_0\bar{\nu}_e$	5730 yr	0.156 MeV
$^{22}_{11}\text{Na} \rightarrow {}^{22}_{10}\text{Ne} + {}^{\ 0}_{+1}\text{e} + {}^0_0\nu_e$	2.60 yr	0.546 MeV
$^{13}_7\text{N} \rightarrow {}^{13}_6\text{C} + {}^{\ 0}_{+1}\text{e} + {}^0_0\nu_e$	9.99 min	1.19 MeV

Table 6.1 Examples of beta decay.

Nuclear energy levels

Unlike beta decay, in which the emitted electron has a range of energies, alpha and gamma decays result in emissions of alpha particles and photons of specific energies. This is evidence that the nucleus, like the atom, exists in well-defined energy levels with specific energy. An alpha particle or a photon emitted in the decay of a nucleus then has an energy that is equivalent to the difference between the energy levels involved in the transition of the nuclei.

As an example, consider the alpha decay of plutonium into uranium. A plutonium nucleus in a state of energy 51.57 MeV can decay by alpha decay into uranium at one of three possible energy levels, as shown in Figure 6.4. (Which of the three is determined by probabilistic laws.) The state denoted by 0.00 MeV is the ground state of uranium-235. If the alpha decay of plutonium takes us to the ground state, an alpha particle of energy 51.57 MeV is emitted. If instead we end up in the second excited state of uranium, the alpha particle will have an energy of $51.57 - 0.051 = 51.52$ MeV. The uranium nucleus is now in an excited state and can decay further by gamma emission into the ground state. The photon emitted will have an energy of 0.051 MeV. (From the second excited state, the uranium nucleus

could actually decay to the first excited state emitting a photon of energy $0.051 - 0.013 = 0.038$ MeV and *then* to the ground state emitting a second photon of energy 0.013 MeV.)

Figure 6.4 Energy-level diagram for alpha decay of plutonium into uranium.

The radioactive decay law

> The law of radioactive decay states that the number of nuclei that will decay per second is proportional to the number of atoms present that have not yet decayed,
>
> $$\frac{dN}{dt} = -\lambda N$$
>
> Here λ is a constant, known as the decay constant. Its physical meaning is that it represents the probability of decay per unit time (see later for an explanation of this statement).

If the number of nuclei originally present (at $t = 0$) is N_0, by integrating the previous equation it can be seen that the number of nuclei of the decaying element present at time t is

$$N = N_0\, e^{-\lambda t}$$

As expected, the number of nuclei of the decaying element is decreasing exponentially as time goes on (see Figure 6.5). This form of the decay law can be shown to be equivalent to the simpler version described earlier. After one half-life, $T_{1/2}$, half of the nuclei present have decayed, so

$$\frac{N_0}{2} = N_0 \exp\left(-\lambda T_{1/2}\right)$$

On taking logarithms we find

$$\lambda T_{1/2} = \ln 2$$
$$= 0.693$$

This is the relationship between the decay constant and the half-life.

(This means that an equivalent and more convenient formula for the decay equation is $N = N_0 \left(\frac{1}{2}\right)^{t/T_{1/2}}$. Can you see how?)

undecayed nuclei/$\times 10^{26}$

Figure 6.5 The decay of radioactive nuclei obeys an exponential law.

The number of decays per second is called activity. It follows from the exponential decay law that activity also satisfies an exponential law:

$$N = N_0 e^{-\lambda t}$$
$$A = -\frac{dN}{dt}$$
$$= (N_0 \lambda) e^{-\lambda t}$$

Thus, the initial activity of a sample is given by the product of the decay constant and the number of atoms initially present, $A_0 = N_0 \lambda$.

Example question

Q1

Carbon-14 has a half-life of 5730 yr and in living organisms it has a decay rate of 0.25 Bq g^{-1}. A quantity of 20 g of carbon-14 was extracted from an ancient bone and its activity was found to be 1.81 Bq. What is the age of the bone?

Answer

The decay constant is

$$\lambda = \frac{\ln 2}{5730} \text{ yr}^{-1}$$
$$= 1.21 \times 10^{-4} \text{ yr}^{-1}$$

When the bone was part of the living body the 20 g would have had an activity of 5 Bq. If the activity now is 1.81 Bq, then

$$A = A_0 e^{-\lambda t}$$
$$\Rightarrow 1.81 = 5e^{-1.21 \times 10^{-4}t}$$
$$\Rightarrow -1.21 \times 10^{-4}t + \ln 5 = \ln 1.81$$
$$\Rightarrow -1.21 \times 10^{-4}t = -1.016$$
$$\Rightarrow t = \frac{1.016}{1.21 \times 10^{-4}}$$
$$\approx 8400 \text{ yr}$$

Why the decay constant is the probability per unit time

Since $\frac{dN}{dt} = -\lambda N$, we know that in a short time interval dt the number of nuclei that will decay is d$N = \lambda N$dt (we ignore the minus sign by considering dN to be positive). The probability that any one nucleus will decay within the time interval dt is thus

$$\text{probability} = \frac{dN}{N} = \lambda dt$$

and so the probability of decay per unit time is equal to the **decay constant**:

$$\frac{\text{probability}}{dt} = \lambda$$

Questions

1 With what velocity should an alpha particle be fired head-on at a stationary gold nucleus so that the distance of closest approach is 2.5×10^{-15} m? (Take the alpha mass to be 6.64×10^{-27} kg.)

2 A particle of mass m and charge $+e$ is directed from very far away toward a massive ($M \gg m$) object of charge $+Ze$ with a velocity v, as shown in Figure 6.6. The distance of closest approach is d. Sketch (on the same axes) a graph to show the variation with separation of:
   (a) the particle's kinetic energy;
   (b) the particle's electric potential energy.

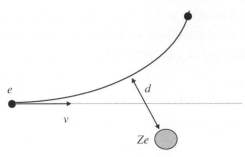

Figure 6.6 For question 2.

3 Singly ionized atoms of neon-20 of velocity 2.0×10^5 m s^{-1} enter the velocity selector of a mass spectrometer, where the magnetic field has the value 0.15 T.

(a) What electric field is established in the velocity selector?

(b) The ions then enter the region where a second magnetic field of value 0.50 T deflects them into circular paths. What is the radius of the circular path?

(c) If the beam of ions also contains traces of neon-22, what would the detection radius for this isotope be?

(Molar masses: neon-20 = 19.992 g mol^{-1}; neon-22 = 21.99 g mol^{-1}.)

4 What might be a reason for the high penetrating power of neutrons?

5 Show that in an elastic collision between a neutron of mass m and a nucleus of mass M (with the nucleus initially at rest), M will recoil with a velocity given by

$$w = \frac{2m}{m + M} v$$

where v is the initial velocity of the incoming neutron.

6 (a) Find the decay constant for krypton-92, whose half-life is 3.00 s.

(b) Suppose that you start with 1/100 mol of krypton. How many undecayed atoms of krypton are there after (i) 1 s, (ii) 2 s, (iii) 3 s?

7 (a) What is the probability that a radioactive nucleus will decay during a time interval equal to a half-life?

(b) What is the probability that it will have decayed after the passage of three half-lives?

(c) A nucleus has remained undecayed after the passage of four half-lives. What is the probability it will decay during the next half-life?

8 What is the activity of 1.0 g of radium-226 (molar mass = 226.025 g mol^{-1}). The half-life of radium-226 is 1600 yr.

9 The half-life of an unstable element is 12 days. Find the activity of a given sample of this element after 20 days if the initial activity was 3.5 MBq.

10 A radioactive isotope of half-life 6.0 days used in medicine is prepared 24 h prior to being administered to a patient. If the activity must be 0.50 MBq when the patient receives the isotope, what number of atoms of the isotope should have been prepared?

11 The age of very old rocks can be found from uranium dating. Uranium is suitable because of its very long half-life: 4.5×10^9 yr. The final stable product in the decay series of uranium-238 is lead-206. Find the age of rocks that are measured to have a ratio of lead to uranium atoms of 0.80. You must assume that no lead was present in the rocks other than that due to uranium decaying.

12 The isotope $^{40}_{19}$K of potassium is unstable, with a half-life of 1.37×10^9 yr. It decays into the stable isotope $^{40}_{18}$Ar. Moon rocks were found to contain a ratio of potassium to argon atoms of 1:7. Find the age of the moon rocks.

13 (a) In an experiment to measure the half-life of an isotope it is found that the readings of the counter never become zero no matter how long one waits, as shown in Figure 6.7. Why?

Figure 6.7 For question 13(a).

(b) The experimenter then 'corrects' the data and obtains the graph shown in Figure 6.8. What has he done and what half-life does he obtain for this isotope?

Figure 6.8 For question 13(b).

14 Two unstable isotopes are present in equal numbers (initially). Isotope A has a half-life of 4 min and isotope B has a half-life of 3 min. What is the ratio of the activity of A to that of B after:
(a) 0 min;
(b) 4 min;
(c) 12 min?

15 A sample contains two unstable isotopes and a counter placed near it is used to record the decays. How would you determine each of the half-lives of the isotopes from the data?

16 The half-life of an isotope with a very long half-life cannot be measured by observing its activity as a function of time, since the variation in activity over any reasonable time interval would be too small to be observed. Let m be the mass in grams of a given isotope of long half-life.
(a) Show that the number of nuclei present in this quantity is $N_0 = \frac{m}{\mu} N_A$ where μ is the molar mass of the isotope in g mol^{-1} and N_A is the Avogadro constant.
(b) From $A = -\frac{dN}{dt} = (N_0 \lambda) e^{-\lambda t}$ show that the initial activity is $A_0 = \frac{m N_A}{\mu} \lambda$ and hence that the half-life can be determined by

measuring the initial activity (in Bq) and the mass of the sample (in grams).

17 Show that the nuclear density is the same for all nuclei. (Take the masses of the proton and neutron to be the same.)

18 Figure 6.9 shows the nuclear force between two protons as a function of their separation.
(a) What is the range of the nuclear force that can be deduced from this graph?
(b) What would the nuclear force between two protons be when they are separated by a distance of 10^{-15} m?
(c) What is the electrical force between these two particles at this separation?
(d) What is the gravitational force between two protons at this separation?
(e) What is the ratio of the electrical to the gravitational force between the two protons?

Figure 6.9 For question 18.

19 In electron capture, ${}^1_1p + {}^{\,0}_{-1}e \rightarrow {}^1_0n + {}^0_0\nu$, the only emitted particle is the neutrino, which, being extremely weakly interacting, cannot be observed. So how do we know when electron capture takes place?

20 Radium's first excited nuclear level is 0.0678 MeV above the ground state.
(a) Write down the reaction that takes place when radium decays from the first excited state to the ground state.
(b) What is the wavelength of the photon emitted?

Particle physics

Particle physics is the branch of physics dealing with the properties of elementary particles. A particle is said to be elementary if it does not itself consist of other, smaller, particles. The property of being elementary may be temporary. Particles that only recently were thought to be elementary were subsequently discovered to consist of smaller entities. The aim of particle physics is to probe the structure of particles deeper and deeper in order to find the ultimate building blocks of matter, if these exist, and the interactions between them. The particles we have met so far in this book are the electron, the proton, the neutron and the photon, the quantum or particle of light. We know that the proton and neutron are composed of other particles called quarks, whereas the electron and photon are elementary.

Objectives

By the end of this chapter you should be able to:
- state the meaning of the term *antiparticle*;
- name the *fundamental particles* of physics and describe their interactions;
- state the meaning of the term *gauge boson*;
- state the meaning of the terms *lepton*, *hadron*, *baryon* and *meson*;
- outline how quarks build *hadrons*;
- describe how interactions are mediated by *exchange* particles;
- state the conservation laws of *baryon number*, *lepton number*, energy and electric charge.

Particles and antiparticles

The development of quantum mechanics in the first quarter of the twentieth century, through the work of Bohr, Schrödinger, Heisenberg, Pauli and Born, gave rise to a satisfactory treatment of the properties of atoms and molecules. However, this theory was inconsistent with Einstein's theory of special relativity. In 1928, Paul Dirac managed to construct a relativistic version of quantum mechanics. This theory reduced to the old quantum theory when the speeds of the particles involved were small compared with the speed of light, but at the same time it made new and unexpected predictions. The first was that the electron had spin (i.e. angular momentum). The spin of the electron was predicted to be $\frac{\hbar}{2}$, where $\hbar = \frac{h}{2\pi}$ and h is Planck's constant. This prediction was verified experimentally, lending support to the new theory. The spin of particles is measured in units of $\hbar$ and can be an integral number times this unit (such particles are called *bosons*) or a half-integral number times this unit (*fermions*).

▶ Particles are called *bosons* if they have an integral spin, and are called *fermions* if they have a half-integral spin.

Electrons, protons and neutrons are fermions, while the photon is a boson.

The second prediction of the Dirac theory was the existence of a particle of *equal mass to that of the electron but of opposite electric charge*. This is the positron, the *antiparticle* of the electron. The positron was discovered in 1932 by Carl Anderson. Its existence was inferred from a cloud chamber picture (see Figure 7.1), in which momentum measurements (from the path's curvature) and direction of motion indicated a small, light, positively charged, hitherto unknown particle.

Figure 7.1 Positron traces in a cloud chamber.

Dirac's reasoning in reaching the conclusion on antiparticles was as follows. His solutions to the equations of the new theory were peculiar in that they allowed for possible electron energies that were negative as well as positive. In fact, the situation was similar to that of the hydrogen atom with its energy levels. There, the negative energy was a simple and understood consequence of the fact that the

electron was bound to the atom. In the case of the electron here, however, there were negative and positive energy levels even though the electron was free and not bound to a nucleus (see Figure 7.2).

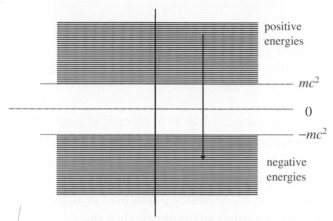

Figure 7.2 Energy levels of an electron, including the negative energy states. An electron would not be stable in this model as it could make transitions to lower energy states.

In addition, the negative energy levels available to the electron extended to very large negative energies (infinite in fact), which posed a stability problem for the electron. An electron of positive energy would make transitions to ever more negative energy states (lower energy), radiating away energy in the process.

The electron simply could not exist as a free particle. To get out of this difficulty, Dirac suggested that the negative energy states were filled, and thus the electron could not make the transition to any one of them. Immediately, Dirac's suggestion implies that a vacuum, which we are used to thinking of as 'empty', is in fact filled with electrons – the Dirac 'sea'. But what would happen if a photon with sufficient energy collided with one of these negative energy electrons in the Dirac sea? The electron would absorb enough energy to appear as an ordinary, positive energy, free electron (the Dirac sea would be 'ionized'), leaving behind a 'hole' in the Dirac sea (see Figure 7.3).

Figure 7.3 An electron jumping away from a negative energy state results in a hole in the negative energy states.

Since the vacuum has zero electric charge when all negative energy states are filled, the hole created by the departed electron would thus appear as a positive charge. Dirac interpreted this hole as an ordinary particle of positive charge, but otherwise identical to the electron – the positron.

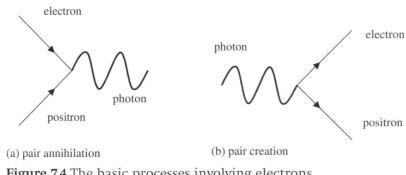

(a) pair annihilation

(b) pair creation

Figure 7.4 The basic processes involving electrons, positrons and photons.

▶ Looked at in a different way, we can say that the photon has created out of the vacuum an electron–positron pair (pair creation) (see Figure 7.4b). The reverse process, the collision of an electron and a positron and the formation of a photon, is called pair annihilation (see Figure 7.4a).

These processes are used in particle accelerators where a particle and its antiparticle are accelerated to very high speeds (close to that of light) and are then allowed to collide. First pair annihilation takes place and a photon appears; it then materializes into another particle–antiparticle pair by the process of pair creation. This new pair may be another electron–positron pair or a pair of new, previously unknown, particles. This process is shown in Figure 7.5(a).

As a result of the collision, the energy can be converted into matter by Einstein's relation $E = mc^2$, and thus new particles may be produced. This is most apparent in *synchrotrons*, accelerators in which particles (say electrons) are accelerated in a circular ring while their

(a)

(b)

Figure 7.5 (a) Very energetic electrons and positrons collide producing new particle–antiparticle pairs. (b) Aerial photograph of the particle accelerator at CERN in Geneva, with the ring outlined.

corresponding antiparticles (positrons) are accelerated in the opposite direction. The beams of electrons and positrons are allowed to collide with each other at specific points and will annihilate each other into photons. The photons will then materialize into pairs of particles and antiparticles by converting their energy into mass (and kinetic energy).

Particle physics

Our current understanding of the interactions among elementary particles has resulted in the following picture of particle physics.

▶ There are three classes of *fundamental* particles. These are quarks, leptons and gauge bosons (or exchange particles). Quarks and leptons are arranged in three *families* or *generations*. Fundamental particles do not have smaller constituents.
  - Quarks make up particles such as the proton and the neutron (and others).
  - Leptons are particles such as the electron and the neutrino (and others).
  - Gauge bosons are intimately involved with the fundamental forces or interactions of physics. We will discuss these separately in the next section.

The generation structure is shown in Table 7.1. The charges are given in terms of the proton charge; rest energy means the product of the particle's mass times the square of the speed of light.

The muon family appears to be just a heavier version of the electron family and the tau family an even heavier version. We see that there exist six kinds (or *flavours*) of quarks (u, d, s, c, b and t) and six leptons (the electron, muon and tau and their corresponding neutrinos). To these we must add the antiparticles of all of them.

Name and symbol	Rest energy	Electric charge
Electron generation		
Electron, e^-	0.511 MeV	-1
Electron neutrino, ν_e	<5.1 eV	0
Up quark, u	350 MeV	2/3
Down quark, d	350 MeV	$-1/3$
Muon generation		
Muon, μ^-	105.7 MeV	-1
Muon neutrino, ν_μ	<0.27 MeV	0
Strange quark, s	540 MeV	$-1/3$
Charm quark, c	1.5 GeV	2/3
Tau generation		
Tau, τ^-	1780 MeV	-1
Tau neutrino, ν_τ	<31 MeV	0
Bottom quark, b	5 GeV	$-1/3$
Top quark, t	170 GeV	2/3

Table 7.1 The quarks and leptons of the standard model arranged in three generations.

The standard model, as this theory is called, also seems to need the existence of one additional particle. This is called the Higgs boson (H), a particle that has not yet been discovered (even though at the time of writing people have claimed to have seen evidence of it). The Higgs particle is crucial in making sure that the theory is consistent.

▶ As we will soon see, *it is not possible to observe isolated quarks*. Thus, the classes of *observed* particles (as opposed to fundamental particles) are *hadrons*, leptons and gauge bosons.

The new class here is the class of hadrons. All hadrons are made out of quarks.

The idea of the quark came about as follows. By the 1960s, scores of particles (now known to be hadrons, i.e. made out of quarks) had been discovered, filling long tables with their various properties. In 1964, Murray Gell-Mann and George Zweig proposed, on *purely mathematical* grounds, that the hadrons and their properties could be understood quite simply, if one made the assumption that these particles had smaller constituents. It was proposed that three kinds (*flavours*) of a new particle should exist and these were named *quarks* by Gell-Mann (who found the word in a passage in James Joyce's *Finnegan's Wake*). They were given the names *up* (or u quark), *down* (or d quark) and *strange* (or s quark). The u quark was the lightest of the three and was assigned an electric charge of $\frac{2}{3}$ that of the proton (i.e. $\frac{2}{3}|e|$). This was a radical step, since every known particle up to that time had a charge that was an integral multiple of the electron charge. The d and s quarks were assigned a charge of $-\frac{1}{3}|e|$.

▶ The Gell-Mann–Zweig hypothesis then stated that hadrons could be made out of quarks in two ways:
- by combining three quarks giving a *baryon*;
- by combining a quark with an antiquark, giving a *meson*.

Note that it is only hadrons that are made out of quarks. Leptons (for example, electrons and neutrinos) or gauge bosons (for example, photons) are not made out of quarks (or out of anything else).

Consider two well-known baryons, the proton and the neutron. The proton consists of two u and one d quarks:

$$p = (uud)$$

and the neutron of one u and two d quarks:

$$n = (udd)$$

The electric charge of the proton is thus predicted to be

$$Q_p = \frac{2}{3}|e| + \frac{2}{3}|e| - \frac{1}{3}|e|$$
$$= |e|$$

and that of the neutron

$$Q_n = -\frac{1}{3}|e| - \frac{1}{3}|e| + \frac{2}{3}|e|$$
$$= 0$$

which are, of course, the correct values.

Pions are examples of mesons. The positively charged pion is made out of

$$\pi^+ = (u\bar{d})$$

where the bar on a quark denotes an antiparticle. Thus, the positive pion is made out of a u quark and the antiparticle of the d quark or just an anti-d quark. The negative pion is

$$\pi^- = (d\bar{u}).$$

Example question

Q1
What is the antiparticle of the π^+ meson?

Answer
Replace every particle in π^+ by its antiparticle to get $\bar{u}d$, which is the π^-.

We have so far seen the use of the up and down quarks in making up protons and neutrons. What about the strange quark? This quark does not participate in making up ordinary matter. However, particles known as kaons were discovered in cosmic-ray experiments and the strange quark is one of their ingredients. Gell-Mann predicted the existence of a particle made out of three strange quarks and could in fact predict its rest energy as well at 1672 MeV. The $\Omega^-(= sss)$ a 'strangeness minus three' particle was discovered soon afterwards (1964) at Brookhaven, lending further support to the whole quark idea.

Since Gell-Mann and Zweig's original work in the 1960s, three new flavours of quarks have been needed, the charm (c), bottom (b) and top (t) quarks. These and the original three (u, d and s) account for all the hadrons known today.

The quark idea introduced order, in the sense that the properties of many particles could now be understood in terms of the properties of quarks. The only problem was that, despite much effort, no quarks were found. However, the quark idea persisted, at least as a mathematical method of classifying hadrons. Soon afterwards, experimental results were obtained that indicated that quarks were not just convenient mathematical tools for classifying particles but real particles with definite mass, electric charge and other properties.

Confinement

The evidence in favour of the existence of quarks is solid and indisputable but it is also indirect, in the sense that no single isolated quark has ever been observed. There is no analogue, for example, of an electron gun that shoots quarks. The force between quarks in a nucleon is rather peculiar. (This force is called the *colour* force – see the next section.) Suppose one attempts to remove a quark from inside a proton. The force between a quark and the other two is *constant no matter what the separation of the quarks is*. Therefore, the energy needed to separate the quark from the other two gets larger and larger as the separation increases. To free the one quark completely would require an infinite amount of energy and so is impossible. If one insisted on providing more and more energy in the hope of isolating a quark, all that would happen would be the production of a meson–antimeson pair and not free quarks. (Does this remind you of trying to break a bar magnet in two hoping to isolate a north or south magnetic pole only to find that you just created two smaller bar magnets?)

> ▶ A property called *quark confinement* states that it is impossible to observe a free quark in isolation.

This situation is in sharp contrast to the electric force between two opposite electric charges, which decreases as the separation between the charges increases (see Figure 7.6).

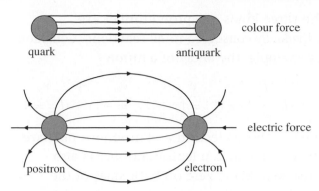

Figure 7.6 The lines of force between two quarks are very different from those of a positive and a negative electric charge; this leads to quark confinement.

Properties of particles and antiparticles

Mass and electric charge are the first obvious properties of particles and antiparticles. The components of a particle–antiparticle pair have the same mass but opposite electric charge, as we have already seen. If the particle is electrically neutral, then the antiparticle is also neutral. In this case, the antiparticle *may* be indistinguishable from the particle. This happens in the case of the photon. The antiphoton is in no way different from the photon, so we do not bother to talk of an antiphoton. However, a particle has additional characteristics or properties. For example, leptons are assigned a property called *lepton number* (*only* leptons are assigned this number). Lepton numbers are shown in Table 7.2.

	L_e	L_μ	L_τ
Electron, e^-	+1	0	0
Electron neutrino, ν_e	+1	0	0
Muon, μ^-	0	+1	0
Muon neutrino, ν_μ	0	+1	0
Tau, τ^-	0	0	+1
Tau neutrino, ν_τ	0	0	+1

Table 7.2 Lepton number assignments.

The antiparticles of these leptons are assigned the opposite lepton number. Thus, the electron neutrino differs from the electron antineutrino (even though they are both electrically neutral) because they have opposite lepton numbers.

The three kinds of lepton number are *individually* conserved in *all* reactions. Consider, for example, the decay of a muon

$$\mu^- \rightarrow e^- + \bar{\nu}_e + \nu_\mu$$
$$(L_\mu = 1) = (L_e = 1) + (L_{\bar{\nu}_e} = -1) + (L_\mu = 1)$$

in which both electron and muon number are conserved. (The tau lepton number is also conserved, being zero on both sides of the reaction.)

Baryons are assigned a number called *baryon number*. (*Only* baryons are assigned such a number.) The proton and neutron have baryon number $+1$ and their antiparticles have baryon number -1. Again, the neutron and the antineutron differs in that they have opposite baryon number. Hence, they are different particles. Baryon number is also conserved in *all* reactions.

For example, consider the reaction (which does take place)

$$n + p \rightarrow n + p + p + \bar{p}$$
$$(B=1)+(B=1)=(B=1)+(B=1)+(B=1)+(B=-1)$$

(In this reaction, the mass on the right-hand side is larger than that on the left. Thus, for the reaction to take place, the proton or neutron on the left-hand side must have sufficient kinetic energy.)

▶ We can summarize by saying that in all reactions the following quantities are always conserved:
  • energy;
  • momentum;
  • electric charge;
  • lepton number;
  • baryon number.

Fundamental interactions and gauge bosons

In elementary physics we say that two electrons repel each other with a force given by Coulomb's law or that two masses attract each with a force given by Newton's law of gravitation. In particle physics we say instead that two electrons *interact* via the electromagnetic interaction or that two masses *interact* via the gravitational interaction. This interaction of two particles is understood as *an exchange of a particle*. In the case of the electromagnetic interaction the particle exchanged is the photon (see Figure 7.7). The photon is thus the *mediator* of the electromagnetic interaction. An electron emits a photon and so changes its momentum: that is, it experiences a force. The other electron absorbs the photon, so it too changes its momentum and experiences a force.

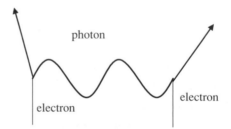

Figure 7.7 The Coulomb force between two electrons is understood as an exchange of a photon.

Similarly, the gravitational force between two masses is understood as the exchange of a *graviton* between the two masses. The graviton is the mediator of the gravitational interaction.

Thus, for every interaction there is one (or more) exchange particle. For the weak interaction, the exchange particles are the W and Z bosons ($W^\pm$, W^0 and Z^0). (The weak nuclear force and the electromagnetic force are actually two faces of the same force, the *electroweak* interaction.)

The case of the strong nuclear force is a bit confusing. The relevant *fundamental* interaction involves the exchange of *gluons* between *quarks*, in much the same way as photons are exchanged between electrons, except that there are eight gluons but only one photon. However, as we saw earlier, quarks are confined and cannot be observed directly as free particles. Instead we observe the forces between protons and neutrons that bind them in nuclei. The strong nuclear force was observed before we had any understanding of quarks and gluons. It was explained by the Japanese physicist Hideki Yukawa in the 1930s as an exchange of *pions* between protons and neutrons. In reality, this force is what the exchange of gluons between quarks *appears* to be to an observer who cannot see individual quarks. (In fact, other mesons such as the ω and ρ also mediate the strong nuclear force between protons and neutrons.)

What, then, is the answer to the question of what particle is exchanged during the strong interaction? The correct answer is gluons, if we are talking at a fundamental level, and (less correctly) pions and other mesons, if instead we are talking at a level of observed particles. One could thus say, a bit vaguely, that in alpha decay (a strong interaction process) the exchanged particle is a meson. The fundamental interactions and gauge bosons are summarized in Tables 7.3 and 7.4.

The evidence for quarks

The experimental evidence for quarks comes from what are called *deep inelastic scattering* experiments (modern versions of Rutherford's experiment) in which very energetic electrons are directed toward protons and their scattering studied. It is found that the scattering pattern (scattering angles and energies) is consistent with the existence of small, hard objects inside the proton (see Figure 7.8). The electrons have to be energetic in order to penetrate the proton volume and 'see' the individual quarks. If the

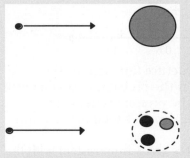

Figure 7.8 Shooting a high-energy electron at a solid proton would give different results from shooting it at a proton with three smaller particles inside it.

Name and symbol (and number that exist)	Rest energy	Electric charge	Interaction
Photon, γ (one)	0	0	Electromagnetic (electroweak)
Z^0 (one)	91.87 GeV	0	Weak (electroweak)
$W^\pm$, W^0 (three)	80.22 GeV	$\pm 1, 0$	Weak (electroweak)
Gluons (eight)	0	0	Colour or strong interaction
Graviton (one)	0	0	Gravitational

Table 7.3 The gauge bosons mediating the four fundamental interactions.

	Interaction			
	Electromagnetic	Colour	Weak	Gravitational
Acts on	All charges	Quarks	Quarks and leptons	All masses
Relative strength	1/137	1	10^{-9}	10^{-38}

Table 7.4 The fundamental interactions of physics.

energy of the electrons is not high enough, they scatter off the proton volume as a whole without 'feeling' what is inside the proton.

These experiments can also measure the probability that a given constituent of the proton can carry a given fraction x of the proton's momentum. This probability is known as the structure function of the proton and is denoted by $F_2(x)$. Figure 7.9 shows this function for the proton as the proton is being probed by very energetic electrons.

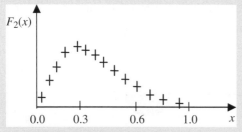

Figure 7.9 The structure function for the proton measures the probability that a given constituent of the proton carries a given fraction x of the proton's total momentum.

The peak at about $x = 0.3$ is consistent with the expectation that with three quarks inside the proton each would, on average, carry a third of the momentum of the proton.

Other experiments include shooting high-energy photons at protons (Compton scattering type experiments). The way the photon scatters off the proton is consistent with the proton being made up of three individual, charged objects (see Figure 7.10).

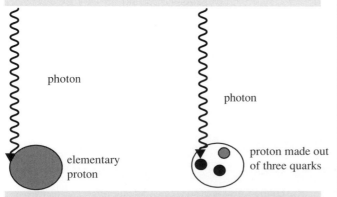

Figure 7.10 The scattering of a photon off a proton is different if the proton has constituents as opposed to being elementary.

The power of a pattern: Gell-Mann's prediction of the omega minus

Here is an example of how the assumption of quark constituents helps in understanding the properties of hadrons. Since each quark has spin of $\frac{1}{2}$, putting three of them together in a baryon can result in a total spin of $\frac{3}{2}$ (all three have spin 'up'; another possibility also exists, namely spin $\frac{1}{2}$, when two have spin 'up' and one spin 'down'). This explains the existence of spin $\frac{3}{2}$ baryons. Spin $\frac{3}{2}$ baryons vary in charge from -1 to $+2$ units and their strangeness varies from -3 to 0. The strangeness of a baryon is a new quantum number that is obtained by looking at how many strange quarks there are in the baryon. For each strange quark, the baryon gets -1 units of strangeness. The known spin $\frac{3}{2}$ baryons could thus be grouped in the pattern shown in Figure 7.11 according to charge and strangeness.

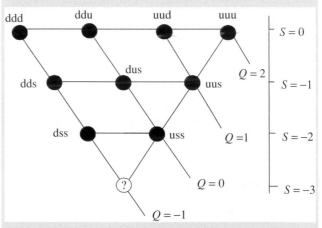

Figure 7.11 Spin $\frac{3}{2}$ baryons grouped according to charge and strangeness.

Gell-Mann could then predict the existence of a negatively charged strangeness -3 spin $\frac{3}{2}$ baryon consisting of three strange quarks. Based on the pattern of the masses in this diagram, Gell-Mann could also predict the mass of the new particle. The omega minus was discovered shortly afterwards.

Questions

1 An electron and a positron moving in opposite directions with equal kinetic energies collide and produce two photons, each of energy 1.2 MeV.
   (a) What is the wavelength of each photon?
   (b) What is the kinetic energy of the electron and the positron?

2 A proton and an antiproton with equal kinetic energies collide, annihilating themselves into a pair of photons, each of wavelength 4.7×10^{-16} m. What was the kinetic energy of the proton?

3 Write down the quark structure of the antineutron.

4 Describe what is meant by a hadron? How many kinds of hadrons are there?

5 Write down the quark structure of the antiparticle of the meson $K^1 = (u\bar{s})$.

6 The neutral K meson is given by $K^0 = (d\bar{s})$. Is it its own antiparticle?

7 A charmed D meson is made out of $D = (c\bar{d})$. What is its charge?

8 What is the charge of the baryon $\Lambda = (uds)$?

9 The decay $K^+ \rightarrow \mu^- + \bar{v}_\mu + e^+ + e^+$ is impossible because it violates which conservation law?

10 The decay $\mu^- \rightarrow e^- + \gamma$ is impossible because it violates which conservation law?

11 The decay $\tau^+ \rightarrow \gamma + \bar{v}_\tau$ is impossible because it violates which conservation law?

12 The decay $p + n \rightarrow p + \pi^0$ is impossible because it violates which conservation law?

13 The decay $e^+ \rightarrow \mu^+ + v_\mu + \bar{v}_e$ is impossible because it violates which conservation law?

14 The decay $p \rightarrow \pi^+ + \pi^-$ is impossible because it violates which conservation law?

15 In the decay $p + p \rightarrow p + p + X$, which *baryon* could X stand for?

16 Can one ask for the baryon number of the quark combination $u\bar{b}$?

17 What is the baryon number of the quark combination $\bar{c}\bar{c}\bar{c}$?

18 When two quarks are interacting electromagnetically, which particle are they exchanging?

19 A neutron can decay into a proton via the weak interaction. Describe this decay in terms of quarks.

20 What do you understand by the term quark confinement?

21 The idea of a particle exchanged in an interaction is sometimes explained in terms of the following description. You stand on ice (no friction) and throw a ball to a friend. Throwing the ball makes you move away. When your friend catches the ball, she moves away. This explains a repulsive force. How would you change the description to explain an attractive force?

22 Does the weak force act on:
   (a) mesons;
   (b) baryons?

23 Does the electric force act on:
   (a) quarks;
   (b) neutrinos?

24 The neutron is electrically neutral. Could it possibly have electromagnetic interactions?

25 Neutrinos are electrically neutral. How do we distinguish neutrinos from antineutrinos?

Part 2

Options

Energy

This option discusses electricity production and fossil fuels, and alternative sources such as nuclear power, solar energy, hydropower and wind energy. This option requires study of Chapter 3.4 on Thermodynamics in addition to the material presented here.

Objectives

By the end of this chapter you should be able to:
- state the difference between *renewable* and *non-renewable* forms of energy;
- describe how *electricity* is produced;
- describe how energy is produced by *nuclear fuels*;
- outline the basics of *solar energy*, *wind energy* and *hydropower*;
- state the meaning of the term *solar constant*.

Energy sources

The development of civilization has gone hand in hand with an increase in the use of energy. Whereas ancient people had food and sunlight as their only sources of energy, consuming no more than about 8 MJ of energy per day, modern people depend on energy for our food, shelter, transportation, communication, manufacture of goods, services and entertainment. The average world use of energy per person now amounts to about 300 MJ per day in the more developed countries, giving a power consumption per person of about $300 \times 10^6/(24 \times 60 \times 60) = 3.5$ kW. In the USA, the power consumption per person is at a high of 10 kW whereas in parts of Africa it is below 0.1 kW. The world average is about 0.8 kW per person. Taking 2 kW as a conservative estimate for living in comfortable conditions and a world population of around 6 billion results in a total energy demand for one year of close to 4×10^{20} J. Taking into account that the world's population is increasing (doubling in as little as 30 years at present growth rates), it is obvious that we are faced with an extremely serious problem.

► We may classify energy sources into two large classes, *renewable* and *non-renewable*.

Non-renewable sources of energy are finite sources, which are being depleted and will run out. They include fossil fuels (oil, natural gas and coal) and nuclear fuels (uranium). The energy stored in these sources is, in general, a form of potential energy, which can be released by human action.

Renewable sources include solar energy (and the other forms indirectly dependent on solar energy, such as wind energy, ocean thermal energy and wave energy) and tidal energy. They also include fuels from plant materials, such as wood and ethanol.

Electricity production

We are heavily dependent on electricity and many of the energy sources that are available to us today are used to produce electricity. The production of electricity (almost universally) takes place in *electric generators*, such as the one described in Chapter 5.8. The main idea is to *rotate* a coil in a magnetic field so that the magnetic flux in the coil will constantly be changing. According to Faraday's law, a voltage will be created in the coil, which can then be delivered to consumers. A generator thus converts mechanical energy (the rotational energy of the coil) into electrical energy. The various other forms of energy available to us can be used to provide the mechanical energy of the rotating coil (see Figure C1.1).

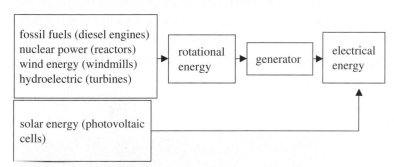

Figure C1.1 Various forms of energy are available to provide electrical energy.

Nuclear power

Nuclear fission is the process in which a heavy nucleus splits into lighter nuclei. The details of the process and the methods used to calculate the energy produced have been presented in detail in Chapter 6.3, which you should review.

Nuclear reactors

A nuclear reactor is a machine in which nuclear reactions take place, producing energy. The *fuel* of a nuclear reactor is uranium-235. The isotope of uranium that is most abundant in nature is uranium-238, which contains about 1% of uranium-235. When a nucleus of uranium-235 captures a neutron, it turns itself into uranium-236, which then splits, releasing energy and more neutrons. The neutrons produced can be used to collide with other nuclei of uranium-235 in the reactor, producing more fission, energy and neutrons. The

reaction is thus self-sustaining; it is called a *chain reaction*. For the chain reaction to get going, a certain minimum mass of uranium-235 must be present, otherwise the neutrons escape without causing further reactions – this is called the *critical mass*. Uranium-235 will only capture neutrons if they are not too fast. The neutrons produced in the chain reaction are too fast to be captured by uranium-235 (they have typical kinetic energies of about 2 MeV) and must therefore be slowed down to the appropriate speed. This is achieved by using a *moderator*, which is a material surrounding the fuel rods (tubes containing uranium-235) and can be graphite or water. The rate of the reaction is determined by the number of neutrons available to be captured by uranium-235. Too few neutrons would result in the reaction stopping, while too many neutrons would lead to an uncontrollably large release of energy. Thus, *control rods* are introduced into the moderator, to absorb excess neutrons whenever this is necessary. The control rods can be removed when not needed and reinserted when necessary again. Figure C1.2 is schematic diagram of the core of a nuclear reactor.

Figure C1.2 A schematic diagram of a pressurized water reactor (PWR).

The energy released in the reaction is in the form of kinetic energy of the produced neutrons. This kinetic energy is converted into heat (in the moderator) as the neutrons are slowed down by the moderator. A coolant (such as water) passing through the moderator can then extract this energy by, for example, turning the water in the coolant into steam at high temperature and pressure. The steam can then be used to turn the turbines of a power station, finally producing electricity.

Problems with nuclear reactors

The spent fuel in a nuclear reactor and the products of the reactions are all highly radioactive with long half-lives. Disposing of this material safely is a serious disadvantage of the fission process in commercial energy production. At present, this material is buried deep into the ground in containers that are supposed to prevent leakage to the outside. The possibility of an accident (such as uncontrolled heating of the moderator) in which radioactive material leaks from the sealed core of a reactor or even the meltdown of the entire core resulting in an explosion that might disperse radioactive material in the environment has created serious second thoughts about the use of nuclear fission reactors for energy production.

Advantages of nuclear energy

- High power output.
- Large reserves of nuclear fuels.

Disadvantages of nuclear energy

- Radioactive waste products difficult to dispose of.
- Major public health hazard should 'something go wrong'.

Fossil fuels

Fossil fuels – oil, coal and natural gas – have been created over millions of years when buried animal and plant matter decomposed under the combined action of the high pressure due to the material above it and bacteria.

Coal and oil have been the traditional fuels used in electricity production. They are burnt and the heat released in the combustion process is used to power steam engines, which in turn power generators. Gasoline (petrol) has been powering cars in internal combustion engines for a century. Although generally efficient (30–40%), these engines are primarily responsible for atmospheric pollution. Gas will be the first fossil fuel to run out, some time in the twenty-first century. Oil will follow, perhaps 30–50 years later, while there are still plentiful supplies of coal, the most polluting of the three fuels. At present, fossil fuels provide almost 90% of the world's energy requirements. Table C1.1 shows the heat of combustion of various fossil fuels.

Substance	Heat of combustion/MJ kg^{-1}
Coal	32.6
Wood	18.8
Diesel oil	44.8
Gasoline	47.3
Kerosene	46.0
Natural gas	33–70 MJ/m^3 (at stp)

Table C1.1 Heat of combustion of fossil fuels.

Example question

Q1

A power plant produces electricity by burning coal, using the heat produced as input to a steam engine, which in turn makes a turbine turn, producing electricity. The plant has a power output of 400 MW and operates at an efficiency of 35%.

(a) Find the rate at which heat is provided by the burning coal and hence find the rate at which coal is being burned.

(b) The heat discarded by the power plant is removed by water that flows into a nearby river (see Figure C1.3). At what rate must water flow so that the water's increase in temperature does not exceed 5 °C?

Figure C1.3.

Answer

(a) The efficiency is the ratio of power output to power input and so heat must be provided at a rate of

$$\frac{400\ \text{MW}}{0.35} = 1143\ \text{MW}$$

The mass of coal that must be burned per second is found (using the table of heats of combustion – Table C1.1) from

$$\frac{\Delta m}{\Delta t} \times 32.6 \times 10^6 = 1143 \times 10^6$$

$$\Rightarrow \frac{\Delta m}{\Delta t} = 35.1\ \text{kg s}^{-1}$$

or 1.1×10^9 kg per year.

(b) The heat discarded enters the water at a rate of

$$\frac{\Delta Q}{\Delta t} = 1143 - 400$$

$$= 743\ \text{MW}$$

This heat warms up water according to $\Delta Q = (\Delta m)c\Delta T$, where Δm is the mass of water the heat goes into, c the specific heat capacity of water and ΔT the temperature increase of the water. The rate at which heat enters the water is

$$\frac{\Delta Q}{\Delta t} = \frac{\Delta m}{\Delta t}c\Delta T$$

$$= \text{rate of heat input}$$

$$= 743\ \text{MW}$$

Thus, we can find

$$\frac{\Delta m}{\Delta t} = \frac{743 \times 10^6}{4200 \times 5}\ \text{kg s}^{-1}$$

$$= 35400\ \text{kg s}^{-1}$$

Advantages of fossil fuels

- Relatively cheap.

- High power output.

- A great variety of engines and devices use them directly and easily.

Disadvantages of fossil fuels

- Will run out.

- Pollute the environment.

- Contribute to the greenhouse effect.

Hydropower

Hydropower, the power derived from moving water masses, is the oldest and most established of all renewable energy sources. This highly site-dependent energy source is capable of producing very cheap electricity; its use has expanded very rapidly, with the power output from hydroplants doubling every 15 years. Turbines driven by falling or moving water have a long working life without major maintenance costs and, despite the high costs of the initial construction of hydroplants, hydropower is very promising for many parts of Africa and South America. It is widely used in Norway. Hydropower stations are, however, associated with massive changes in the ecology of the area surrounding the plants.

The principle behind hydropower is simple: consider a mass m of water that falls down a vertical height h, as shown in Figure C1.4.

Figure C1.4 Water falling from a vertical height h has its potential energy converted into kinetic energy, which can be used to drive turbines.

▶ The potential energy of the mass is mgh and this gets converted into kinetic energy when the mass descends the vertical distance h. The mass is given by $\rho \Delta V$, where ρ is the density of water and ΔV the volume it occupies. The rate of change of this potential energy (i.e. the power) is

$$P = \rho \frac{\Delta V}{\Delta t} gh$$

The quantity $Q = \frac{\Delta V}{\Delta t}$ is known as the flow rate (volume per second) and so (see Figure C1.5)

$$P = \rho Q g h$$

Figure C1.5 Within a time of Δt the mass of water that will flow through the tube is $\rho Q \Delta t$.

This is the power available for generating electricity (or to convert into some other mechanical form) and it is thus clear that hydropower requires large volume flow rates, Q, and large heights h.

Example question

Q2

Find the power developed when water in a stream with a flow rate 50 L s^{-1} falls from a height of 15 m.

Answer

Applying the power formula we find

$P = \rho Q g h$

$\quad = 1000 \times (50 \times 10^{-3}) \times 10 \times 15$ W

$\quad = 7.5$ kW

Advantages of hydroelectric energy

• 'Free'.

• Inexhaustible.

• Clean.

Disadvantages of hydroelectric energy

• Very location-dependent.

• Requires drastic changes to the environment.

• Initial costs high.

Solar energy

The nuclear fusion reactions in the sun send out an incredible, and practically inexhaustible, energy, at a rate of about 3.9×10^{26} W. This means that the earth receives, on average, an amount of about 1379 W per square metre of the surface of the outer atmosphere. Some of this radiation is reflected back into space, some is trapped by the atmosphere's gases and about 1000 W m^{-2} is received on the surface of the earth. This amount assumes direct sunlight on a clear day and thus is the maximum that can be received at any one time. Averaged over a 24 h time period, the intensity of sunlight is about 340 W m^{-2}. This high-quality, free and inexhaustible energy can be put to various uses.

Active solar devices

An early application of solar energy has been in what are called active solar devices, whereby sunlight is used directly to heat water or air to heat a house, for example (see Figure C1.6). The collecting surface is usually flat and covered by glass for protection; the glass should be coated to reduce reflection. A blackened surface underneath collects sunlight, and water circulating in pipes underneath is heated; this heat can then be used for household purposes such as in bathrooms (the heated water is kept in well-insulated containers) or, with the help of a pump, it can circulate through a house to provide central heating.

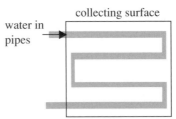

Figure C1.6 A device for collecting sunlight. The water in the pipes is heated and can be put to use.

Such a collector works not only with direct sunlight but also with diffuse light on cloudy days.

These simple collectors are cheap and are usually put on the roof of a house. Their disadvantage is that they tend to be bulky and cover too much space.

More sophisticated collectors include a concentrator system in which the incoming solar radiation is focused, for example by a parabolic mirror, before it falls on the collecting surface. Such systems can heat water to much higher temperatures (500–2000 °C) than a simple flat collector. These high temperatures can be used to turn water into steam, which can drive a turbine to produce electricity. Such as system is illustrated in Figure C1.7. Obviously, back-up systems must be available in case of cloudy days, etc.

Figure C1.7 Energy-flow diagram for electricity production by solar collectors.

Solar ponds

A very ingenious method for heating and storing water by sunlight is the solar pond (see Figure C1.8). A pond with a large surface area and about 1.5 m deep is carefully layered with salt so that the deeper layers of water are more salty than layers above. Skill is required in layering the pond with different concentrations of salt at different depths and this normally requires considerable time. Radiation from the sun is absorbed by the bottom of the pond, heating up the water above. In an ordinary pond the warm water would rise and thus heat

Figure C1.8 A solar pond. Heat absorbed at the bottom of the pond does not rise to the top because of the high salinity of the bottom layers.

would be moved by convection to the surface from which it would be lost into the surrounding air. However, with the saltiest layer at the bottom, the density there remains high even after the water heats up. This means that the water doesn't rise even though it is warmer than the water above it. So the hot water is trapped at the bottom of the pond, eliminating convection losses. The warmest layer at the bottom of the pond is about 20 cm deep and there temperatures in excess of 80 °C can be reached. The costs of creating and maintaining such a pond are quite small, about US$15 per square metre of pond.

A 7400 m^2 solar pond at Ein Borek in Israel produces 150 kW of electricity at a cost of US$0.10 per kWh, which is comparable to the cost of conventionally produced electricity.

Photovoltaic cells

A promising method for producing electricity from sunlight is provided by photovoltaic cells. The photovoltaic cell was developed in 1954 at Bell Laboratories and was used extensively in the space programme. The cell converts sunlight into DC current at an efficiency of about 30% at present. The major cost of photovoltaic systems has been the cost of manufacturing the actual cell, but this cost is decreasing. From a cost of about US$100 per watt of power produced per cell the price is now less than US$4. Adding on the price of related equipment estimated at $2 per watt and used at a site with medium sunshine, 400 W m^{-2}, and taking into account a lifetime of the cell of about 20 years, this works out to a cost per kW h only slightly higher than that produced by diesel-powered generators.

The actual workings of the photovoltaic cell depend on the physics of semiconductors and will not concern us here. It must, however, be understood that the photovoltaic principle of electricity generation from sunlight is not the same as the photoelectric effect in which sunlight falling on certain surfaces also produces electric current. In the photoelectric effect, the electrons are actually ejected from the metal, whereas in the photovoltaic phenomenon, electrons, having absorbed photons of the right energy, make a transition from the valence band energy levels across the gap and into the conduction energy levels (see Figure C1.9).

Figure C1.9 Energy-level diagram for a silicon semiconductor.

As the price of photovoltaic systems drops, they are bound to become more dominant in electricity production around the world. Already, in places far from major power grids, their use is more economical than grid expansion and these systems can usefully be used to power small remote villages, pump water in agriculture, power warning lights, etc. Their negative environmental effects are practically zero, with the exception of chemical pollution at the place of their manufacture.

Advantages of solar energy

*   'Free'.
*   Inexhaustible.
*   Clean.

Disadvantages of solar energy

*   Works during the day only.
*   Affected by cloudy weather.
*   Low power output.
*   Requires large areas.
*   Initial costs high.

The solar constant

The sun's total power output is $P = 3.9 \times 10^{26}$ W (this is also known as the sun's luminosity). On earth, we receive only a small fraction of this total power output. The average distance between the sun and the earth is 1.50×10^{11} m. The sun's power is distributed uniformly over the surface of an imaginary sphere of radius $r = 1.50 \times 10^{11}$ m (see Figure C1.10).

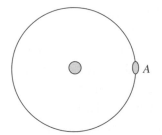

Figure C1.10 Area A receives only a small fraction of the total power.

The power that is collected by area A is the fraction $\frac{A}{4\pi r^2}$ of the total power P. (Note that $4\pi r^2$ is the surface area of the big sphere.) The power through the area is simply

$$P \frac{A}{4\pi r^2}$$

▶ The *power per unit area* received a distance r from the sun is called the intensity, I, and so

$$I = \frac{P}{4\pi r^2}$$

This amounts to 1379 W m^{-2}, and is known as the *solar constant*. It is the power received by one square metre placed normally to the path of the incoming rays a distance of 1.50×10^{11} m from the sun.

This actual amount received varies somewhat due to the fact that the power output of the sun is not entirely constant. This gives variations of $\pm 1.5\%$. In addition, the distance between the earth and the sun is not constant (earth's orbit is slightly elliptical) and this gives additional variations of $\pm 4\%$. To find the radiation received on the earth's *surface* we must take into account reflection of the radiation from the atmosphere and from the earth's surface, latitude, angle of incidence and average between day and night.

It is useful to define the total amount of energy received by one square metre of earth's surface in the course of one day. This is called the *daily insolation*. Figure C1.11 shows the daily insolation at two different latitudes as a function of time. Month 6 represents December, month 7 is January, and so on. The curve with the big dip corresponds to a latitude of 60°. The other is for a latitude of 36°. At zero latitude (the equator), the insolation is almost constant at about 25 MJ m^{-2} day^{-1}.

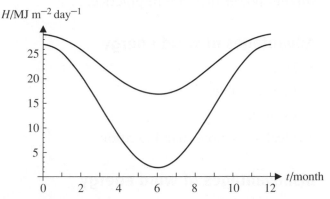

Figure C1.11 The daily insolation at two latitudes. The curve with the big dip corresponds to a latitude of 60°. The other is for a latitude of 36°.

The reduction of the daily insolation in the winter for high latitudes is explained by the shorter length of daylight and the oblique incidence of light.

Wind energy

The ancient practice of extracting energy from wind is particularly useful for agricultural purposes and for isolated houses, where small windmills extracting 3 kW of power from the wind can provide all the energy needed for simple living conditions. Small windmills have vanes no larger than about 1 m. Modern windmills are capable of producing up to a few megawatts of power and, of course, they tend to be big, with vanes larger than 50 m. Wind power devices have no adverse effects on the environment, but a very large number of them in a windmill park is not an attractive sight to most people and there is a noise problem. The cost of wind energy conversion systems varies from about \$500 to \$5000 per kW of produced power. The blades are

susceptible to stresses in high winds and damage due to metal fatigue frequently occurs. The design must also take into account gale force winds, which may be very rare for a particular site, but would certainly result in very serious damage to an inadequately designed system. Wind speed is the crucial factor for these systems, the power extracted being proportional to the cube of the wind speed; wind speeds of up to about 4 m s^{-1} are not particularly useful for energy extraction. Serious power production from wind occurs at speeds from 6 m s^{-1} to 14 m s^{-1}. Generally, about a quarter of the power extracted from the wind can be converted into electricity. Figure C1.12 is an energy-flow diagram for wind energy extraction

Figure C1.12 Energy-flow diagram for wind energy extraction.

Figure C1.13 shows a typical wind generator with two blades.

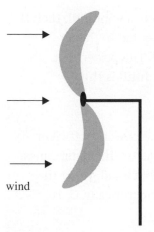

Figure C1.13 A horizontal axis machine with two blades.

The dependence of the power on the area of the blades and cube of the wind speed can be understood as follows.

Let us consider the amount of mass that can pass through a tube of cross-sectional area A with velocity v. Let ρ be the density of air. Then the mass enclosed in a tube of length $v\,\Delta t$ is $\rho A v\,\Delta t$. This is the mass that will exit from the right end of the tube *within* a time interval of Δt (see Figure C1.14). The kinetic energy of this mass of air is thus

$$\tfrac{1}{2}(\rho A v\,\Delta t)v^2 = \tfrac{1}{2}\rho A\,\Delta t\,v^3$$

▶ The kinetic energy per unit time is the power and so dividing by Δt we find

$$P = \tfrac{1}{2}\rho A v^3$$

which shows that the power carried by the wind is proportional to the cube of the wind speed and proportional to the area spanned by the blades.

$v\Delta t$

Figure C1.14 The mass of air within this cylinder will exit from the right side within a time of Δt.

▶ If this stream of air meets a windmill, then A stands for the area presented to the air stream by the windmill. The power that can be extracted by the windmill is thus

$$P = C_p\tfrac{1}{2}\rho A v^3$$

where C_p is known as the power coefficient. It is simply an efficiency factor that determines how much of the available wind power the windmill can extract. Theoretically, C_p is between 0.35 and 0.45.

Assuming a wind speed of 12 m s^{-1}, an air density of 1.2 kg m^{-3} and an efficiency coefficient of 0.40 we find

$$\frac{P}{A} = C_p\frac{1}{2}\rho v^3$$
$$= 0.40 \times \tfrac{1}{2} \times 1.2 \times 12^3 \ \mathrm{W\,m^{-2}}$$
$$\approx 415 \ \mathrm{W\,m^{-2}}$$

as the theoretical power extracted per unit windmill area. A 2 m^2 windmill area thus extracts about 830 W of power from the wind.

Doubling the windmill area doubles the power extracted but doubling the wind speed increases the power (in theory) by a factor of eight. Frictional and other losses result in a smaller power increase in practice.

Advantages of wind energy

- Free.
- Inexhaustible.
- Clean.
- Ideal for remote island locations.

Disadvantages of wind energy

- Works only if there is wind – it is not dependable.
- Low power output.
- Aesthetically unpleasant (and noisy).
- Best locations are far from large cities.
- Maintenance costs are high.

Questions

1 A power plant produces 500 MW of power. How much energy is produced in 1 s? Express the answer in
   (a) joule;
   (b) kW h;
   (c) MW h.
   How much energy is produced in 1 yr. Express the answer in:
   (e) joule;
   (f) kW h;
   (g) MW h.

2 A power plant operates in four stages. The efficiency in each stage is 80%, 40%, 12% and 65%. What is the overall efficiency of the plant?

3 Sunlight of intensity 700 W m^{-2} is captured with a 50% efficiency by a radiator, which

then sends the captured energy into a house with 70% efficiency. If the house loses heat because of bad insulation at a rate of 3 kW, find the area of the radiator needed in order to keep the temperature of the house constant.

4 A solar heater is to heat 300 L of water initially at 15 °C to a temperature of 50 °C in a time of 12 h. The amount of solar radiation falling on the collecting surface of the solar panel is 240 W m^{-2} and is collected at an efficiency of 65%. What is the area of the collecting panel that is required?

5 A coal-burning power plant produces 1.0 GW of electricity. The efficiency of the power plant is 40%. Taking the heat of combustion of coal to be 32.6 MJ kg^{-1}, calculate the amount of coal that must be burned in one day.

6 A coal power plant with 40% efficiency burns 10 000 000 kg of coal a day (take the heat of combustion of coal to be 20 MJ kg^{-1}).
   (a) What is the power output of the plant?
   (b) At what rate is heat discarded by this plant?
   (c) If the discarded heat is carried away by water whose temperature is not allowed to increase by more than 5 °C, find the rate at which water must flow away from the plant.

7 Consult a map for your country.
   (a) Estimate the area that is at an altitude higher than 500 m.
   (b) Find out what the average rainfall is and thus estimate the mass of water that would accumulate over the area you found in part (a) in 1 yr.
   (c) Calculate the power that would be developed if all the potential energy of this water could be used. If a hydropower station is established in your area, find out its power output and compare this with your answer.

8 Figure C1.15 shows the power curve of a windmill as a function of the wind speed. If the wind speed is 10 m s^{-1}, calculate the energy produced in the course of 1 yr,

assuming that the wind blows at this speed for 1000 h in the year.

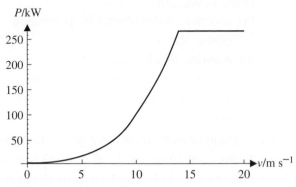

Figure C1.15 For question 8.

9 Find the power developed when water in a waterfall with a flow rate 500 L s^{-1} falls from a height of 40 m.

10 (a) Calculate the energy released in the fission reaction

$$^{235}_{92}U + {}^{1}_{0}n \rightarrow {}^{88}_{38}Sr + {}^{136}_{54}Xe + 12{}^{1}_{0}n$$

   (b) How much coal (heat of combustion 30 MJ kg^{-1}) must be burned in order to give the same energy as that released in this reaction with 1 kg of uranium-235 available? (The atomic masses are: U = 235.04392 u; Sr = 87.905617 u; Xe = 135.90722 u.

11 (a) Assuming that the efficiency of a 500 MW nuclear power plant converting the energy released in nuclear reactions into electrical energy is 40%, find out how many splittings of uranium-235 are required per second. Take the energy released per reaction to be 208 MeV.
   (b) What quantity of uranium-235 is required to react per second?

12 Make a schematic diagram of a fission reactor explaining the role of:
   (a) fuel rods;
   (b) control rods;
   (c) moderator.
   In what form is the energy released in a fission reactor?

13 By looking up sources in your library, write an essay about the problem of radioactive waste disposal.

14 Make an annotated energy-flow diagram showing the energy changes that are taking place in each of:
  (a) a conventional electricity-producing power station;
  (b) a hydroelectric power plant;
  (c) an electricity-producing windmill;
  (d) an electricity-producing nuclear power station.

15 Sunlight of intensity 800 W m^{-2} is captured by a tank containing 100.0 kg of water with an efficiency of 80%. The tank is rectangular in shape and has dimensions $1.0 \times 1.0 \times 0.10$ m. It has walls of thickness 5.0 mm. The surrounding air has a temperature of 20 °C. Assume that the tank is well insulated from all sides except the top surface (of area 1.0 m^2). The material of the tank has a thermal conductivity of 0.3 W K^{-1} m^{-1}, its density is 1200 kg m^{-3} and its specific heat capacity is 450 J kg^{-1} K^{-1}.
  (a) Calculate the mass of the tank.
  (b) By equating the heat received from the sunlight to the heat lost by conduction to the surrounding air, estimate the final temperature of the water.
  (c) Find the heat capacity of the tank–water system.
  (d) Show that the temperature of the water is increasing at a rate that can be found from the equation

$$C \frac{\Delta T}{\Delta t} = A P_{\text{in}} - kA \frac{T - 20°}{x}$$

  where P_{in} is the power received from the sunlight, C is the heat capacity of the system, k is the thermal conductivity of the tank, A is the area of the top surface of the tank and x is the thickness of the tank wall.
  (e) Evaluate the rate of temperature increase when the temperature is the average of the initial temperature of 20 °C and the final temperature you found in part (b).
  (f) Assuming temperature is increasing at this rate, calculate how long it will take the water to reach its final temperature.

The physics of scaling

Scaling is an important physical principle that allows the approximate solution of many apparently difficult problems. This chapter introduces this concept with applications mainly in mechanics.

Objectives

By the end of this chapter you should be able to:
- describe how basic quantities such as *area*, *volume* and *mass* scale with a linear dimension of the body;
- perform simple calculations in order to show how physical quantities *scale with the linear dimension* of a system;
- appreciate that change of scale may imply *change of form and function*.

Scaling

What would you rather do: peel 2 kg of large potatoes or 2 kg of potatoes half the size? The answer can be given by a simple but powerful argument called scaling. If L stands for the typical size of a small potato, then $2L$ is the typical size of a large potato in our problem. As was known in ancient times, given two *similar* bodies, the ratio of volumes is given by the third power of the ratio of typical linear sizes while the ratio of surface areas is given by the square of this ratio. This means that the number of large potatoes making the 2 kg is less than the number of small ones by a factor of 8.

$$\frac{N_{\text{large}}}{N_{\text{small}}} = \frac{V_{\text{small}}}{V_{\text{large}}} = \left[\frac{L}{2L}\right]^3 = \frac{1}{8}$$

On the other hand, the area of a large potato is 4 times larger than that of a small one:

$$\frac{A_{\text{large}}}{A_{\text{small}}} = \left[\frac{2L}{L}\right]^2 = 4$$

This means that the job of peeling large potatoes will finish twice as fast, since although

one large potato will take 4 times as long to peel, there are 8 times fewer of them.

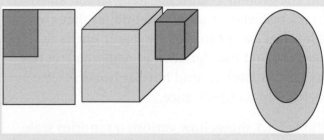

Figure D1.1 The darker shapes have half the linear dimension of the corresponding larger body.

In Figure D1.1 the dark shapes have half the linear size of the larger shapes. Thus, the small rectangle has an area that is $2^2 = 4$ times as small, the cube has a volume that is $2^3 = 8$ times as small and the smaller ellipse has an area $2^2 = 4$ times as small. Note that we can get these results without ever using the detailed formula for area or volume of the particular shape involved.

The shapes do not have to be regular for this result to hold. In Figure D1.2 every linear dimension of the small object is half the

Figure D1.2 Two similar solid shapes. Every linear dimension of the small object is half that of the corresponding dimension of the larger object.

corresponding dimension of the larger object. Thus, the *surface area* of the large object is $2^2 = 4$ times as large and the *volume* is $2^3 = 8$ times as large.

As we will see in this chapter, the scale of a system (i.e. its typical linear size) determines many of the properties of the system. It determines, for example: that giants 10 times our size cannot exist; that watermelons grow on the ground and do not hang in the air from thick branches; that of two bridges that are identical except in size the larger one is the weaker; and that horses and dogs can run just as fast on level ground but the horse is left behind in an uphill race.

Table D1.1 shows how various quantities scale with a typical linear length of a body.

Quantity	Scales as
Volume	L^3
Mass	L^3
Area	L^2
Rate of heat loss	L^2
Power developed by muscles	L^2
Pressure on feet	L

Table D1.1 Typical scaling dependence of standard quantities with a typical linear length of a body.

To say that mass scales as L^3 (i.e. $M \propto L^3$) means that doubling the linear length makes the mass

8 times bigger. Since $M \propto L^3$ and rate of heat loss $\propto L^2$ it follows, for example, that

$$\frac{\text{rate of heat loss}}{\text{mass}} \propto \frac{L^2}{L^3} \propto \frac{1}{L}$$

Size and strength

To begin the discussion of the role of scale, imagine a class of people who are in every way identical to us but larger in height (and thus also in width and depth) by a factor of 10 (see Figure D1.3). Identical to us means that they have the same density and proportions as us. Since their volume is $10^3 = 1000$ times larger than our volume, their mass is also 1000 times larger. The strength of human beings is proportional to the cross-sectional area of our bones.

Figure D1.3 The giant is 10 times taller than the normal person. The giant's mass is 1000 times larger.

The giant will thus have 100 times the strength of the average normal human. Since, however, its mass and hence its weight are 1000 times larger, the pressure exerted on its bones would be 10 times the pressure felt by the average human.

Mathematically, since

$$M \propto L^3$$

and

$$\text{pressure} = \frac{\text{weight}}{\text{area}} \propto \frac{L^3}{L^2} \propto L$$

it follows that

$$\frac{(\text{pressure})_{\text{giant}}}{(\text{pressure})_{\text{normal}}} = \frac{L_{\text{giant}}}{L_{\text{normal}}} = 10$$

Walking would be as difficult for this giant as for an ordinary human forced to carry nine of her friends on her back.

The point of this example is that we cannot blindly extrapolate to larger scales from what we know at scales familiar to us. An ordinary human may walk and function well, but a similar being that is much larger cannot function the same way. Thus, if we know that a heavy sphere of radius R can be safely suspended by a rope of diameter D we have to be careful in claiming that a sphere of radius, say, $5R$ can be suspended from a rope of diameter $5D$. For the larger sphere will have a mass that is $5 \times 5 \times 5 = 125$ times larger than the small one, whereas the strength of the thicker rope will be only $5 \times 5 = 25$ times larger than the thin rope.

These considerations imply that animals that are substantially larger in size than others, for example elephants or rhinoceroses in relation to cats, have disproportionately thicker bones.

On the other hand, a second class of imaginary beings with a size 10 times smaller than us would be quite an agile class of beings. The stress experienced by their bones would be 10 times less than the stress on our bones. But these creatures would suffer from another problem. The amount of energy lost by a human body is proportional to its surface area (energy lost as heat from an unprotected body) and thus the amount of energy that must be re-supplied in the form of food must also be proportional to the surface area. The small creature has 100 times less surface area than us

and so it would seem that its food supply problem is less severe than ours. Let us imagine that one loaf of bread is all that is required to provide the energy we need for a day. The smaller creature needs only 1/100 of that amount. But the mass of one loaf of our bread corresponds to the mass of 1000 loaves of bread in the world of the small creature and thus it has to consume 10 of its loaves per day to make up for the energy it loses. The small creature would have a serious problem of food supply in its world. In fact, it is known that small animals such as mice are quite agile and eat a lot. A mouse may consume a quantity of food equal to its own mass in one day, whereas we may consume as little as 1/50 of our mass in one day. This explains why in polar regions the most successful animals are big animals such as bears. Few mammals are found there since their disproportionately high loss of energy would result in disproportionately high demands for food. The link between heat loss and surface area is also important in non-biological systems – see Figure D1.4.

Figure D1.4 The rate of heat loss is proportional to area. Can you see why old-fashioned wood ovens have a spherical dome?

Small size creates other serious problems as well. If a human walks out of a swimming pool he or she will carry a layer of water from the pool. This increases their mass by a tiny amount, less than half a kilogram – the mass of the water they carry away is a small fraction of their own mass. Let L be the typical linear size of a person and M their mass. Let m be the mass of the water carried away by such a person. Assuming that the thickness of the water layer is t we have

$$m \propto L^2 t \quad \text{and} \quad M \propto L^3$$

Thus

$$\frac{m}{M} \propto \frac{L^2 t}{L^3} \propto \frac{t}{L}$$

The smaller creature who also decides to take a swim in its pool will also walk away with a layer of water on its body. Assuming that the thickness of water is the same

$$\left(\frac{m}{M}\right)_{\text{small creature}} \propto \frac{t}{L_{\text{small creature}}}$$

Hence

$$\frac{(m/M)_{\text{small creature}}}{(m/M)_{\text{normal}}} \propto \frac{(t/L_{\text{small creature}})}{(t/L_{\text{normal}})}$$

$$= \frac{L_{\text{normal}}}{L_{\text{small creature}}} = 10$$

In other words, the small creature walks away with 100 times less water than the average human since the small creature's surface area is 100 times less. Its mass, though, is 1000 times less and thus the mass of water carried away relative to its mass is 10 times more. The small creature may find it impossible to walk away from the pool. This is seen commonly with insects, which carefully sip water well away from drops of water. If they fall in the drops and get wet they will surely drown. Various small animals survive the danger of water by having skins or coats that allow the water to run off without clinging to them.

Size and motion

The pace at which an animal walks or runs can be estimated in the following way. Imagine that the legs of an animal have length L. This is the length from the hip to the foot. As an approximation to walking, we may consider that the leg behaves like a pendulum that swings from an extreme backward position to an extreme forward position. The period of a pendulum is $T = 2\pi\sqrt{\frac{L}{g}}$, and so if the animal takes a step whose length is d, the time taken is half the pendulum period. The speed of walking is thus $v = \frac{d}{\pi}\sqrt{\frac{g}{L}}$. This says that the walking

pace is inversely proportional to the square root of the size of the animal. If we now assume that the length of the step is also proportional to linear size, then the speed scales as

$$v \approx \sqrt{L}$$

This says the obvious fact that taller people walk faster than short people. (This does not mean, however, that tall people win walking races. In fact, the opposite is true. This is because tall people have to use more energy in walking than shorter people and thus get tired sooner.)

When running at top speed, other considerations enter the problem of the relation of size and motion. Whether for a land animal, a bird or a fish, the top speed is mainly determined by the forces of resistance to its motion. The introduction of resistance forces alters the scaling law just derived. In motion through air, it is a good approximation that the force of air resistance is proportional to the square of the speed (at least if the speed is not too small). The constant of proportionality is in turn proportional to the surface area that the animal presents to air as it moves. It is here that size enters the picture. A large animal presents a larger surface area and hence a larger force of air resistance acts on it. Consider, therefore, an animal of linear size L which has a top speed v on level ground. How does this top speed relate to its size L?

The power developed by the animal is $P = Fv$, where F is the force pushing the animal forward and equals the wind resistance when the animal moves at constant speed. The wind resistance force is

$$F = kv^2$$

where the constant k is proportional to the surface area of the animal, L^2. Thus, it follows that $P \propto L^2 v^3$. How does the power developed by the animal depend on its size? The amount of power generated in the muscles is about 25% of the total power produced in the animal by chemical means (burning of food). Since this chemical energy is transformed into heat and the amount of heat loss is proportional to the animal's surface area, it is more reasonable to assume that the main dependence of P on L comes solely from the surface, so that

$$P \propto L^2$$

In this case, it follows that $L^2 \propto L^2 v^3$. Hence the top speed v is independent of the size of the animal. A rabbit, a dog and a horse have no appreciable differences in their top speed as long as they run on level ground. Note that the scaling law $P \propto L^2$ implies that the power developed per unit mass of muscle is

$$\frac{P}{M} \propto \frac{L^2}{L^3} \propto \frac{1}{L}$$

Example questions

Q1

How does the top speed of an animal depend on its size when it runs uphill?

Answer

The power necessary to run with constant speed v up an incline of angle θ to the horizontal is

$$P = mg \sin \theta \, v \propto mgv$$

(we take the angle to be an irrelevant constant). This is because the force necessary to keep the mass moving up the hill is equal and opposite to the component of the weight of the animal along the plane, $mg \sin \theta$. Since $mg \propto L^3$, the power is proportional to $P \propto L^3 v$. But the power generated by the animal is proportional to L^2. Hence $L^2 \propto L^3 v$, from which it follows that $v \propto L^{-1}$. This means that the longer the animal, the slower it runs up a hill. A rabbit can easily outrun a horse uphill.

Q2

How does the height an animal can jump depend on its size?

Answer

To jump to a height h means an increase in gravitational potential energy mgh. Since $mg \propto L^3$, this energy is $E \propto L^3 h$. This energy must come from the work done by the tension in the muscles as they decompress upon jumping up. This work is Fx, where x is the amount the muscles were compressed by. It is reasonable to assume that the amount of compression is proportional to the animal's linear size L; since the force that can develop in the muscles is proportional to the cross-sectional area of the bones (i.e. L^2), it follows that $L^2 L \propto L^3 h$, which means the height is independent of the animal's size.

Q3

How does the time a desert animal can go without water depend on the animal's linear size L?

Answer

The amount of water stored is proportional to the animal's volume, L^3. The rate of evaporation (water loss) is proportional to the area of the animal, L^2. The time T in which the animal's stores of water will run out is thus given by $L^2 T \propto L^3$, i.e. $T \propto L$.

This means that the time an animal can go without water is dependent on its length. So, if a particular animal must drink water once a week, an animal half the linear size (length) must drink water every 3.5 days.

Consider now an animal that lands on a hard surface after falling from a height h. As is well known, a small animal can survive a fall from a height many times its size, whereas bigger animals could suffer death from a fall only a few times their size. The speed with which the animal lands after falling from a height h is $v = \sqrt{2gh}$ and is independent of its mass. The force experienced by the animal is thus $F = \frac{mv}{\Delta t}$, where Δt is the time taken for the speed to be reduced to zero. From the theory of elasticity, it is known that $F = \sigma A$, where the constant σ is the strain on the bones of the landing animal and A is the cross-section of the bone. Thus, $\sigma A = mv$. Putting the dependence on size into this equation, we have $A \propto L^2$ and $m \propto L^3$ so that $\sigma L^2 \propto L^3$ giving

$$\sigma \propto L$$

The strain on the landing animal's bones increases with the size of the animal, as we expected.

Scaling can also be used to explain why small animals, for example bats or mice, tend to produce sounds of high frequency. Recall that the frequency of a standing wave on a string of length l is given by $f = \frac{c}{\lambda}$, where λ is the wave's wavelength and c the speed of the wave on the string. The wavelength is proportional to the length of the string, $\lambda \propto l$, and the speed of the wave depends on the tension of the string and its mass per unit length: $c = \sqrt{\frac{Tl}{m}}$. If a stands for the diameter of the string, $m = \rho al$, and so $f \propto \frac{1}{l}\sqrt{\frac{T}{\rho a}}$. Considering now animals of different sizes, it is reasonable to assume that $l \propto L$ and $a \propto L^2$, where L is the animal's typical linear size. Thus (assuming constant tension and density)

$$f \propto \frac{1}{L^2}$$

Thus, if an animal produces a sound of frequency 500 Hz, an animal whose typical size is 2 times smaller would be expected to produce a sound of frequency

$$\frac{f_{small}}{f_{large}} = \frac{\left(\frac{1}{(L/2)^2}\right)}{\left(\frac{1}{L^2}\right)}$$
$$= 4$$
$$\Rightarrow f_{small} = 4 \times f_{large}$$
$$= 2000 \text{ Hz}$$

Questions

1 A sports car has a mass of 1200 kg. If a small *exact* copy were to be made with a linear scale of 1:24, what would the mass of the model be?

2 Assume that the amount of water you drink is proportional to your surface area. How much more water do you consume than a small child whose height (and every other linear dimension) is 0.7 of yours?

3 Assume that your height is 1.5 times larger than the height of a child.
   (a) How many times larger is your mass?
   (b) How many times larger is your surface area?
   (c) How many times larger is the pressure on your feet while you stand?

4 Explain why children are more sensitive to exposure to cold than adults. Make this more

quantitative by finding the scaling law for the rate of heat loss per unit mass for a person of linear size L.

5 Show that the maximum speed with which an animal jumps vertically is independent of its size.

6 The maximum length of a column that can support its own weight without buckling is given by the scaling law $L \propto R^{2/3}$. If it is desired to double this maximum length, by what factor should the radius be changed?

7 In the text it was stated that the power output of a person of linear size L scales as $P \propto L^2$. If power is also proportional to the rate at which oxygen is absorbed by the tissue of a person, what does this imply about the dependence of the heartbeat rate on size?

8 Show that the maximum time an animal of linear size L can stay under water scales as L. List carefully any assumptions you make.

9 If the power developed per unit mass of muscle is constant for all animals – that is, if the scaling law for power is

$$P \propto L^3$$

show that:
   (a) the maximum height an animal of size L can jump to scales as $L^{2/3}$;
   (b) the maximum speed the animal can run uphill is independent of L.

10 Find the scaling law for the maximum time a bird of size L can fly before resting.

11 The scaling law used in the text for the power produced by a body of size L is $P \propto L^2$. Assuming this law to be true, show that the speed with which muscle contracts is independent of the size of the body.

12 Show that the force developed by a muscle per unit cross-sectional area of bone is independent of size.

13 You wake up one morning not knowing that while you slept every length in the universe was reduced by a factor of 2. This includes your own height, width and depth, the length of all rulers, etc. Would you know the difference? Explain.

Sound and hearing

This chapter introduces the basic ideas behind the functioning of the human ear and the related physics questions on sound perception, intensity, frequency response and frequency discrimination. Hearing defects are also briefly discussed.

Objectives

By the end of this chapter you should be able to:
- describe the basic components of the *human ear*;
- define *sound intensity* and the *sound intensity scale* based on the decibel;
- perform calculations with intensity and the *decibel scale*;
- understand how the ear functions;
- describe how the ear separates sound according to frequency in the *cochlea*;
- state the meaning of the terms *threshold of hearing* and *audiogram*;
- understand basic *hearing defects* and say how they might be corrected.

The ear

The human ear is an exceptionally efficient and sensitive instrument that detects and analyses sound, and converts the mechanical energy carried by a sound wave into electrical energy that is fed into the brain. The ear is sensitive to sounds of frequency ranging from 20 Hz to 20 kHz. At 1000 Hz, the ear responds to sound that displaces the eardrum by only one-tenth of the diameter of the hydrogen atom! The ear can be divided into three main parts: the outer, middle and inner ear (see Figure D2.1).

Sound waves reaching the ear are fed into the *auditory canal* and fall on the *eardrum*, a membrane that begins to vibrate as a result. The eardrum forms the entrance to the middle ear, an air cavity of 2 cm³ in volume that contains the *ossicles* (three small bones), the *malleus* (hammer), *incus* (anvil) and *stapes* (stirrup). This cavity is connected to the throat by the *Eustachian tube*, which is normally closed but can be opened by swallowing or yawning to equalize the pressure on each side of the eardrum. The ossicles act as a lever system, which transmits the energy falling on the eardrum onto the *oval window*, an opening marking the beginning of the inner ear. The tension in the muscles attached to the ossicles increases in the presence of a very loud sound, thus limiting the motion of the stapes and hence the energy transferred to the oval window and protecting the delicate inner ear from damage. This is known as the *acoustic reflex*; this takes about 10 ms to become effective, so it offers no protection in the case of sudden very loud sounds, such as gunfire.

The purpose of the lever system is to amplify the amplitude of the incoming sound wave. As seen in the example that follows, the lever system amplifies by a factor of 1.5. However, as a result of the difference in the areas of the oval window and the eardrum, the

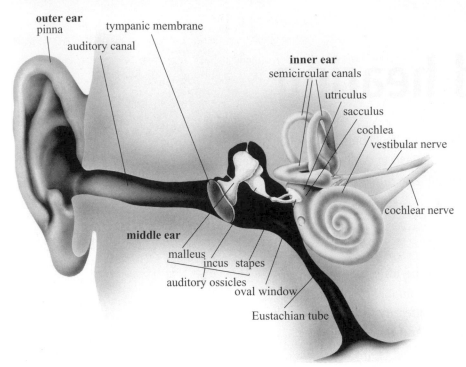

Figure D2.1 A diagram of the ear showing its division into outer, middle and inner ear. The cochlea is responsible for the resolution of the incoming sound into its various components. © 1995 Dorling Kindersley Multimedia.

amplification is increased further by a factor of about 13, resulting in a total amplification of about 20.

The inner ear has three main parts: the *vestibule* (the entrance cavity), the *semicircular canals* and the *cochlea*. The vestibule is surrounded by bone except for the opening to the middle ear (the oval window); this opening is sealed by the stapes and the round window, which is covered by a membrane. This cavity is filled with a liquid. The semicircular canals play no role in hearing – their function is to provide us with a sense of balance. The cochlea is a tube, coiled like a snail (making 2.5 turns) and has a length of about 3.5 cm.

The sound wave entering the oval window travels in the liquid-filled canals of the cochlea. First in the *vestibular*, then through the *helicotrema* and into the *tympanic canal*. It ends at the round window membrane, which acts as a pressure release point (a total length of about

2 cm). Between these two canals is a third, the *scala media* or cochlean duct. The *basilar membrane* separates the cochlean duct from the tympanic canal and this membrane contains a large number of nerve endings, whose purpose is to transmit the electrical signals to the brain. These signals are generated when vibrations in the basilar membrane are fed into the *organ of Corti*, which is attached to the membrane. Different parts of the basilar membrane are sensitive to different frequency ranges of the incoming sound wave.

The three parts of the ear are illustrated schematically in Figure D2.2, and Figure D2.3 is a schematic cross-section through the cochlea.

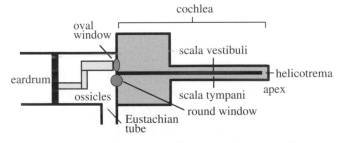

Figure D2.2 A schematic diagram showing the three parts of the ear. Here the cochlea is shown as a straight uncoiled tube. The cochlea is separated into three canals or scalae. The top, scala vestibuli, and the bottom, scala tympani, which communicate through an opening at the apex of the cochlea called the helicotrema. The scala vestibuli starts at the oval window while the scala tympani starts at the round window. The middle canal is known as scala media or cochlean duct.

The auditory pathways from the cochlea into the brain are highly complex and not yet fully understood. There is, however, a considerable amount of processing of the information along the pathway in processing centres, with

Figure D2.3 A schematic cross-section through the cochlea. The scala media is separated from the scala vestibuli by Reissner's membrane and from the scala tympani by the basilar membrane.

connections between the left ear and the right ear's main pathway and vice versa.

Mismatch of impedances

When a wave enters a new medium, only part of it will be transmitted into the new medium; part will be reflected back into the old medium. The fraction of the transmitted intensity depends on the *impedances* of the two media. The least amount of reflection takes place when the impedances of the two media are as close to each other as possible. For exactly equal impedances no reflection takes place at all.

▶ For sound transmission, the acoustic impedance of a medium is defined as the product of the speed of sound in the medium times the medium's density

$$Z = \rho c$$

The region up to the oval window is filled with air and its impedance is thus about 450 kg m^{-2} s^{-1}. The region behind the oval window is filled with the cochlear liquid and its impedance is about 1.5×10^6 kg m^{-2} s^{-1}. This large mismatch of impedances means that it is necessary to amplify the sound wave arriving at the oval window so that a substantial fraction of it can be transmitted.

Example question

Q1

The area of the eardrum is $A = 43$ mm^2 and that of the oval window $a = 3.2$ mm^2. Using Figure D2.4 as a model for the action of the ossicles, find the pressure amplification at the oval window.

Figure D2.4.

Answer

Taking torques about an axis through the pivot we find

$$F_1 x = F_2 \frac{2x}{3}$$

$$\Rightarrow F_2 = \frac{3}{2} F_1$$

therefore, the pressure on the oval window is

$$
\begin{aligned}
P_2 &= \frac{F_2}{a} \\
&= \frac{3}{2} \frac{F_1}{a} \\
&= \frac{3}{2} \frac{P_1 A}{a} \\
&= \frac{3}{2} \frac{A}{a} P_1 \\
&= 20.2 P_1
\end{aligned}
$$

that is, an amplification of about 20.

Complex sounds

Few sounds are as simple and pure as the single-frequency harmonic waves we discussed in Chapters 4.1–4.7 on waves. When a human voice is fed into an oscilloscope through a microphone, the trace that appears on the oscilloscope screen will not be a sine wave.

> ► Harmonic waves (i.e. waves of one specific frequency) are important, however, because of a powerful mathematical technique, called Fourier analysis, that is used to analyse complex sounds. It can be shown that any complex sound is a superposition of many (perhaps infinite) simple sine or cosine waves.

To illustrate this point, consider an extreme example, the graph of the function $y = t^2$ from $-\pi$ to $+\pi$ (see Figure D2.5).

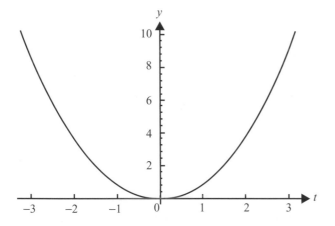

Figure D2.5 The graph of the function $y = t^2$.

This function can be well approximated by a sum of harmonic functions:

$$\frac{\pi^2}{3} + 4 \sum_{n=1} (-1)^n \frac{\cos(nt)}{n^2}$$

Figure D2.6 is the graph of this function for only the first five terms in the sum.

The approximation is quite good. It can be made even better by keeping more terms in the sum. The point here is that any periodic function can be written as a sum of harmonic functions. Thus, complex sounds entering the ear can be decomposed into the component frequencies of the harmonic functions making

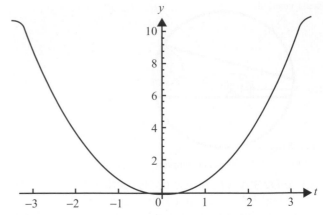

Figure D2.6 Complex sounds can be expressed as combinations of Fourier components (i.e. harmonic waves).

up the complex sound. This happens in the cochlea and is explained in a later section.

Intensity of sound

Consider a source of sound S. The power of the source is the energy per second emitted by the source.

The energy emitted by the source can be thought of as being spread uniformly on the surface of an imaginary sphere of radius r centred on the source (see Figure D2.7). Thus, at a distance r from the source the energy received per second by an instrument of area A is

$$P\, \frac{A}{4\pi r^2}$$

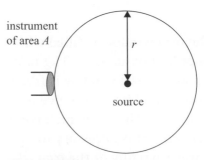

Figure D2.7 The energy emitted by the source goes through an imaginary sphere around the source.

▶ The energy per second per unit instrument area, that is

$$I = \frac{P}{4\pi r^2}$$

is known as the intensity of the sound wave at a distance r from the point source. The unit of intensity is thus W m^{-2}. The lowest intensity the human ear can perceive is called the threshold of hearing and is $I_0 = 1.0 \times 10^{-12} \text{ W m}^{-2}$. The intensity is proportional to the square of the amplitude of the wave.

It is known that the 'sensation of hearing' (let us call this quantity β) does not increase linearly with intensity I. Rather, the ear has a logarithmic response to intensity: the increase in the hearing sensation is proportional to the *fractional* increase in intensity (the Weber–Fechner law). Mathematically this means that

$$\Delta\beta \propto \frac{\Delta I}{I}$$

We can exploit this law to define a scale of sound intensity level as follows. On this scale (the decibel scale) an increase of 10 units

Source of sound	Intensity level/dB	Pressure amplitude/Pa
Threshold of hearing	0	0.00002
Falling leaves	10	0.00006
Radio studio	20	0.0002
Whisper	30	0.0006
Library	40	0.002
Office space	50	0.006
Conversation	60	0.02
Room with TV on	70	0.06
Noisy street	80	0.2
Rock concert	110	6
Pain setting in	120	20
Pneumatic hammer	130	60
Jet plane 3 m away	140	200

Table D2.1 Typical decibel values and the corresponding amplitude of the sound wave in pascal.

implies an increase of intensity by a *factor* of 10. The zero on this scale corresponds to the threshold of hearing. This implies that

$$\beta\,(\text{in decibels}) = 10\log\left(\frac{I}{I_0}\right)$$

Table D2.1 shows some typical intensity levels of common sounds along with their pressure amplitudes.

Example questions

Q2 ▬▬▬▬▬▬▬▬▬▬▬▬▬▬▬▬
The intensity of a sound increases from $10^{-10} \text{ W m}^{-2}$ to 10^{-8} W m^{-2}. By how much does the sound intensity level change?

Answer

The original level was

$$\beta_1 = 10\log\left(\frac{10^{-10}}{10^{-12}}\right)$$
$$= 10\log 10^2$$
$$= 20\,\text{dB}$$

The new sound intensity level is

$$\beta_2 = 10\log\left(\frac{10^{-8}}{10^{-12}}\right)$$
$$= 10\log 10^4$$
$$= 40\,\text{dB}$$

The increase is thus 20 dB.

Note: Since the increase in the intensity level is proportional to the fractional increase in intensity, we could have written directly

$$\Delta\beta = 10\log\left(\frac{10^{-8}}{10^{-10}}\right) = 10\log 10^2 = 20\,\text{dB}$$

Q3 ▬▬▬▬▬▬▬▬▬▬▬▬▬▬▬▬
One sound has intensity $2 \times 10^{-6} \text{ W m}^{-2}$ and another has intensity $4 \times 10^{-8} \text{ W m}^{-2}$. What is the difference of the sound intensity levels?

Answer

The first sound has intensity level

$$\beta_1 = 10\log\left(\frac{2 \times 10^{-6}}{10^{-12}}\right)$$
$$= 10\log\left(2 \times 10^6\right)$$
$$= 63\,\text{dB}$$

The second sound has intensity level

$$\beta_2 = 10 \log \left(\frac{4 \times 10^{-8}}{10^{-12}} \right)$$
$$= 10 \log \left(4 \times 10^4 \right)$$
$$= 46 \, \text{dB}$$

Their difference is thus 17 dB.

Q4

The sound intensity level in a room is 70.0 dB. A radio produces sound of intensity level 72.0 dB. What is the sound intensity level in the room now?

Answer

The intensity in the room is found from

$$70 \, \text{dB} = 10 \log \left(\frac{I}{10^{-12}} \right)$$
$$\Rightarrow \frac{I}{10^{-12}} = 10^7$$
$$\Rightarrow I = 10^{-5} \, \text{W m}^{-2}$$

Similarly, the intensity due to the radio is

$$72 \, \text{dB} = 10 \log \left(\frac{I}{10^{-12}} \right)$$
$$\Rightarrow \frac{I}{10^{-12}} = 10^{7.2}$$
$$\Rightarrow I = 10^{-4.8} \, \text{W m}^{-2}$$

The combined intensity is

$$I_{\text{total}} = (10^{-5} + 10^{-4.8}) \, \text{W m}^{-2}$$

Thus, the new sound intensity level is

$$10 \log \left(\frac{10^{-5} + 10^{-4.8}}{10^{-12}} \right) = 74.1 \, \text{dB}$$

Note: It is important to realize that it is intensities that must be added not the sound intensity levels in decibels.

Q5

A shouting voice has a power output of about 10^{-3} W. At what distance from the source is the sound intensity level 80 dB?

Answer

Using

$$\beta = 10 \log \left(\frac{I}{10^{-12}} \right)$$

$$= 80$$
$$\Rightarrow \log \left(\frac{I}{10^{-12}} \right) = 8$$
$$\Rightarrow I = 10^{-4} \, \text{W m}^{-2}$$

Now using the definition of intensity

$$I = \frac{P}{4\pi r^2}$$

it follows that

$$10^{-4} = \frac{10^{-3}}{4\pi r^2}$$
$$\Rightarrow r = \sqrt{\frac{10}{4\pi}}$$
$$= 0.89 \, \text{m}$$

Q6

Assume that in a football stadium 40 000 fans cheer their teams, each producing a power output of 10^{-3} W. If the average distance of the fans from the centre of the stadium is 150 m, find the sound intensity level there.

Answer

The combined power output is
$40\,000 \times 10^{-3} \, \text{W} = 40 \, \text{W}$. The intensity at the centre of the stadium is thus

$$I = \frac{P}{4\pi r^2}$$
$$= \frac{40}{4\pi (150)^2}$$
$$= 1.41 \times 10^{-4} \, \text{W m}^{-2}$$

The sound intensity level is

$$\beta = 10 \log \left(\frac{1.41 \times 10^{-4}}{10^{-12}} \right)$$
$$= 81.5 \, \text{dB}$$

Frequency response and loudness

The human ear has a threshold when it comes to the frequency of the sound wave. The lowest frequency that can be heard is about 20 Hz and the largest about 20 kHz. With age, the upper frequency threshold is reduced.

▶ The ear is not equally sensitive at all frequencies. This means that the ear responds differently to a sound of given intensity depending on the frequency of the sound.

Thus, the statement made earlier that the normal human ear has a threshold of hearing of 1.0×10^{-12} W m^{-2} is correct provided the sound has a frequency of 1000 Hz. Sounds of larger or smaller intensity than this may be heard or are barely audible depending on the frequency of the sound. The graph in Figure D2.8 shows the intensity level of barely audible sounds (the threshold of hearing) as a function of frequency. Thus, a sound at 100 Hz must have an intensity level of 35 dB to be barely audible, and a sound at 20 Hz must have an intensity level of 72 dB. All points on this curve are perceived by the ear to have the same loudness, even though they have different intensities. These points define the 'zero phon loudness curve'. The 'N phon loudness curve' consists of those sounds that the ear perceives to be equally loud as a sound of N dB at 1000 Hz.

Figure D2.8 The threshold of hearing curve as a function of frequency. A sound of frequency 3 kHz is just audible even at -8 dB.

▶ The ear is most sensitive for frequencies around 3 kHz and least sensitive for frequencies less than (about) 50 Hz and higher than (about) 10 kHz.

The sensitivity of the human ear for frequencies around 3 kHz can be understood in terms of resonance in the ear canal. The canal can be thought of as a tube with one open and one closed end, so standing waves in this tube have a wavelength in the fundamental mode equal to $4L$, where L is the length of the canal – about 2.8 cm (see Figure D2.9).

2.8 cm

Figure D2.9 Schematic diagram of standing waves in the ear canal.

This means that the frequency corresponding to this wavelength is

$$f = \frac{340}{0.112} = 3036 \text{ Hz}$$

which is in good agreement with the most sensitive frequency.

Pitch

'Pitch' is a subjective characteristic of sound. It measures how high or low a sound is. It is determined *primarily by frequency* (which is why pitch is often taken to mean the same thing as frequency) *but also by intensity*. Imagine a pure tone of frequency 100 Hz that is sounded first at low intensity and then at high intensity. The louder sound will 'feel' lower in pitch than the soft sound.

Frequency separation in the cochlea

As mentioned earlier, a complex sound can, in general, be decomposed into its component harmonic waves.

▶ The ear analyses the different frequencies of a sound wave reaching it in the cochlea.

A wave entering the oval window travels along the basilar membrane, which separates the tympanic canal from the cochlean duct. The basilar membrane decreases in stiffness along its length (of about 35 mm). The velocity of the sound wave is thus high at the beginning of the membrane and drops along its length. In general, the response of a given point on the basilar membrane is small unless that part of the membrane is in resonance with the sound wave.

> ▶ From the pioneering work of Georg von Bekesy in the 1950s, we have learned that the beginning of the basilar membrane is in resonance with high frequencies and the end with low frequencies. The brain thus perceives frequency by locating the part of the basilar membrane that is vibrating.

This is done through the organ of Corti, which lies on the basilar membrane, and its hair cell receptors, which feed the information into the nerves that end at the base of the receptor cells. A wave of frequency 8 kHz will be in resonance at a point at about 2.5 mm from the beginning of the basilar membrane, a frequency of 1 kHz will be in resonance at a distance of about 22 mm and a frequency of 100 Hz will be in resonance a full 32 mm along the basilar membrane (see Figure D2.10).

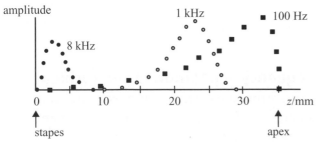

Figure D2.10 The amplitude of vibration of the basilar membrane for three different frequencies as a function of distance from the stapes. The point of largest amplitude shifts toward the apex of the basilar membrane as the frequency decreases.

Hearing defects

Two hearing losses may be distinguished.

- *Sensory nerve deafness,* which involves damage to the hair cells and neural pathways (e.g. due to tumours of the acoustic nerve or meningitis).

- *Conduction deafness,* in which damage to the middle ear prevents the transmission of sound into the cochlea. (This may be due to the plugging of the auditory canal by foreign bodies, such as wax, thickening of the ear drum because of repeated infections, destruction of the ossicles, or too rigid an attachment of the stapes to the oval window.)

Hearing can be monitored with an audiogram: the patient is supplied with very faint sounds of a specific frequency through earphones and their intensity is increased until they are just audible to the patient. A typical example is the audiogram of Figure D2.11 (consider first the data points represented by circles). At a frequency of 1000 Hz a sound must increase in intensity by 45 dB and at 4000 Hz by 70 dB if these sounds are to be audible to the patient. This defines what is called a *hearing loss* in dB. At 1000 Hz, therefore, the intensity of sound must be increased (for example, by a hearing aid) by a factor of

$$\Delta\beta = 45 \text{ dB}$$

$$= 10 \log \frac{I}{I_0}$$

$$\Rightarrow I = I_0 \times 10^{4.5}$$

where I_0 is the intensity prior to amplification. This audiogram shows a substantial loss of hearing, especially in the higher frequencies. The damage was possibly caused by excessive exposure to loud sounds over very long periods of time. Ageing, which also results in hearing loss, would show in a more gently varying curve in the audiogram and with smaller loss in decibels.

Sound can reach the cochlea through the bones of the head and thus the audiogram is performed not only with earphones but also

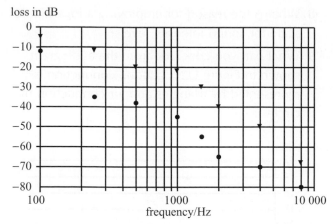

Figure D2.11 Audiogram for air (circles) and bone (triangles) conduction.

with an oscillator (placed at the bottom of the skull) that transmits the sound into the bones. The data points represented by triangles in the audiogram in Figure D2.11 are the results of bone transmission.

There is a *gap* between the two sets of data points of about 25 dB (at 1000 Hz). This is most likely an indication of a *conduction* hearing problem, the origin of which is in the middle or outer ear. Audiograms in which the data points for air and bone conduction *almost coincide* indicate *cochlea/nerve* problems in the inner ear.

In conductive hearing loss (where the sound *does* reach the inner ear) use of a hearing aid that amplifies the sound may help a patient. A hearing aid responds to and amplifies sound within a limited range of frequencies (the frequency range of human speech) but does not work well outside this range. For sensory nerve hearing loss, where the damage is to the hair cells, a *cochlear implant* may be useful. This is a device that consists of a microphone to pick up the sound, a signal processor to convert the sound into an electrical signal and a transmission system to transmit the electrical signal to electrodes. The electrodes are then surgically implanted in the cochlea. Different electrodes are stimulated according to the frequency of the sound so, in effect, the cochlear implant mimics the function of the cochlea. Assuming that enough healthy nerves

are left near the electrodes, stimulation of the electrodes induces stimulation of the neighbouring nerves and the signal can be carried to the brain.

Speech recognition

All the information in speech is contained within the frequency interval from 200 Hz to 6 kHz. Noise and loss of frequency discrimination affect speech intelligibility. Generally, the meaning of a sentence can still be extracted from context but the intelligibility of isolated words is more strongly affected. The shorter the word, the bigger the loss of intelligibility. It has been found that, in cases of hearing loss at high frequencies (>3000 Hz), amplifying the sound does not help the patient to identify spoken syllables. Similarly, the inability of the cochlea to correctly identify frequencies also leads to errors in the identification of syllables.

Questions

1 A point sound source emitting uniformly in all directions is observed to have a sound intensity level of 70 dB at a distance of 5 m. What is the power of the source?

2 The sound level intensity of a screaming child in a room is 75 dB. What is the sound level intensity when three screaming children are put together in the same room?

3 The sound intensity level a certain distance from a source is 68 dB. If the distance to the source is halved, what is the new sound intensity level?

4 The sound level intensity of a given sound wave is 15 dB higher than that of another sound wave. What is the ratio of the intensities of the two waves?

5 If a radio creates sound of intensity level 70 dB, how many radios are required to create sound of intensity level 80 dB?

6 The audiogram of Figure D2.11 shows that the loss in dB for a person at 4000 Hz is 70 dB. What is the least intensity of sound this person

can hear at 4000 Hz? (Use the diagram of Figure D2.8 to find the threshold of hearing at 4000 Hz.)

7 Figure D2.12 shows the threshold of hearing curve for a patient. Explain what this means. What is the frequency at which this patient is most sensitive? What is the intensity of sound this patient receives at 200 Hz?

8 What is the reason for employing a logarithmic scale for sound intensity levels?

9 What can you conclude from the audiogram shown in Figure D2.13? Bone conduction is represented by triangles and air conduction by circles.

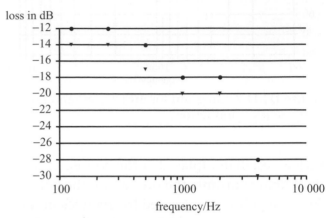

Figure D2.13 For question 9.

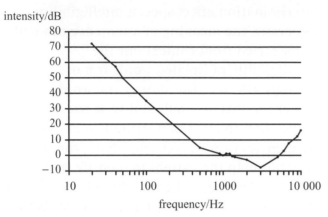

Figure D2.12 For question 7.

Medical imaging

This chapter introduces the use of X-rays and ultrasound in medical imaging. Other imaging techniques such as PET scans and the method based on nuclear magnetic resonance are also discussed. The chapter closes with a short account of the diagnostic use of radioactive tracers.

Objectives

By the end of this chapter you should be able to:
- state the *properties of ionizing radiations*;
- state the meaning of the terms *quality of X-rays*, *half-value thickness* (HVT) and *linear attenuation coefficient*;
- perform *calculations* with X-ray intensity and HVT, $I = I_0\,e^{-\mu x}$, HVT $= \frac{0.693}{\mu}$;
- describe the *main mechanisms by which X-rays lose energy* in a medium;
- state the meaning of *fluoroscopy* and *moving-film techniques*;
- describe the basics of *CT and PET scans*;
- describe the *principle of MRI*;
- state the uses of *ultrasound* in imaging;
- state the main uses of *radioactive sources in diagnostic medicine*.

Properties of radiation

The uses of radiation in medicine fall into two classes: first in diagnostic imaging (described in this chapter) and second in radiation therapy (discussed in Chapter D5). The first radiation to be used in medicine was X-rays – short-wavelength electromagnetic radiation (photons) discovered by W. Röntgen in 1895. Other ionizing radiations, such as alpha particles (helium nuclei), beta particles (fast electrons), gamma rays and radioactive isotopes have uses in medicine or have an effect on living organisms.

Table D3.1 gives a summary of the main properties of these radiations.

If we consider a point source of X- or gamma rays radiating uniformly in all directions, the *intensity* at a distance r from the source falls off according to an inverse square law. We have

	α	β	γ
Nature	Helium nucleus	Electron	Photon
Mass (in units of the proton mass)	4	1/1840	0
Charge	$+2e$	$-e$	0
Ions produced per mm of path	10 000	1000	1
Stopped by	A few cm of air	A few mm of Al	10 cm of Pb

Table D3.1 The main properties of different forms of radiation.

seen the argument leading to this result before in this book.

> Let P be the energy per unit time (the power) radiated by the source. The energy radiated can be thought to pass through the area of a sphere of radius r and so the energy per unit area of the sphere is
>
> $$I = \frac{P}{4\pi r^2}$$
>
> This is the intensity of the source at a distance r from it.

Example questions

Q1 ▬▬▬▬▬▬▬▬▬▬▬

A radioactive gamma ray source has an activity of 50 kBq. Each gamma ray radiated has an energy of 0.2 MeV. What is the intensity of the source at a distance of 25 cm?

Answer

The power radiated by the source is

$$P = \frac{\Delta E}{\Delta t}$$
$$= 50 \times 10^3 \times 0.2 \text{ MeV s}^{-1}$$
$$= 1.6 \times 10^{-9} \text{ W}$$

and so the intensity 25 cm away is

$$I = \frac{P}{4\pi r^2}$$
$$= \frac{1.6 \times 10^{-9}}{4\pi \times (0.25)^2} \text{ W m}^{-2}$$
$$= 2.04 \times 10^{-9} \text{ W m}^{-2}$$

Q2 ▬▬▬▬▬▬▬▬▬▬▬

By what factor is the intensity reduced when a worker doubles his distance from a source of X-rays?

Answer

Since we have an inverse square law, the intensity will be reduced by a factor of 4.

Attenuation

If, however, monochromatic radiation is directed into a medium that can absorb

radiation, the fall in intensity is exponential. The degree to which X-rays can penetrate matter is called the *quality* of the radiation.

> It can be shown that the transmitted intensity decreases as
>
> $$I = I_0\, e^{-\mu x}$$
>
> Here μ is a constant called the *linear attenuation coefficient*. This coefficient can be determined from the slope of a plot of the logarithm of the intensity versus distance. It depends both on the *material through which the radiation passes* and on the *energy of the photons*. (See Figure D3.1.)

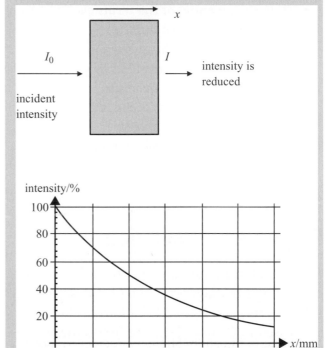

Figure D3.1 Attenuation of radiation through an absorbing medium. The graph gives the percentage of the intensity transmitted after going through a thickness x of the material.

This law is similar to the radioactive decay law and we define by analogy the *half-value thickness* (HVT), which is the length that must be travelled through in order to reduce the intensity by a factor of 2. Then

$$\text{HVT} = \frac{0.693}{\mu}$$

Figure D3.2 shows the dependence on energy of the HVT for X-rays and gamma rays in water.

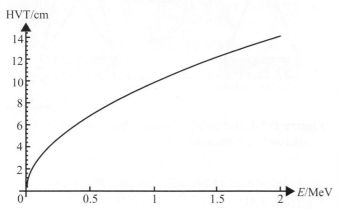

HVT/cm

Figure D3.2 The half-value thickness as a function of photon energy. The curve is the same for both X-rays and gamma rays.

Example questions

Q3

A metal sheet of thickness 4 mm and half-value thickness 3 mm is placed in the path of radiation from a radioactive source. What fraction of the source's incident intensity gets transmitted through the sheet?

Answer

$I = I_0 \, e^{-\mu x}$

$= I_0 \exp\left(-\dfrac{0.693 \times 4}{3}\right)$

$= 0.397 I_0$

that is, about 40% goes through.

Q4

A worker used to work at a distance of 2 m from a source of radiation. She now decides to move away to a distance of 3 m and to work behind a 3 mm screen with HVT equal to 2 mm. By what factor is the radiation she receives reduced?

Answer

Let P be the power of the source. At a distance of 2 m the worker received an intensity of

$I = \dfrac{P}{4\pi r^2}$

$= \dfrac{P}{4\pi 2^2}$

$= \dfrac{P}{16\pi}$

$= 0.0199\, P$

At the increased distance of 3 m the received intensity is

$I = \dfrac{P}{4\pi 3^2}$

$= \dfrac{P}{36\pi}$

After going through the screen, the intensity is further reduced to

$I = I_0 \, e^{-\mu x}$

$= \dfrac{P}{36\pi} \exp\left(-\dfrac{0.693 \times 3}{2}\right)$

$= 0.354 \dfrac{P}{36\pi}$

$= 0.0031\, P$

The overall reduction is thus a factor of about 6.4.

> ▶ The main methods by which X-rays are absorbed are the photoelectric and Compton effects.

In the photoelectric effect, the X-ray photon is absorbed by an electron, which is then emitted from its atom or molecule. In the Compton effect, the photon gives part of its energy to a *free* electron and scatters off it with a reduced energy and so increased wavelength. The energy given to the electron appears as kinetic energy for the electron. The importance of the photoelectric effect is mostly for low-energy photons and increases sharply with increasing atomic number of the specimen upon which the photons fall. The Compton effect, on the other hand, does not vary much with energy and increases linearly with atomic number. In both cases the electrons can ionize matter along their paths.

X-ray imaging

As mentioned at the beginning, X-rays were the first radiation to be used for medical imaging. X-ray machines used for taking an ordinary 'X-ray picture' operate at voltages of around 15–30 kV for a mammogram and at about 50–150 kV for a chest X-ray (see Figure D3.3).

Figure D3.3 Schematic diagram of an X-ray tube.

> ▶ At these voltages the dominant
> mechanism for energy loss by the X-rays is
> the photoelectric effect. Since this effect is
> strongly dependent on atomic number and
> there is a substantial difference between
> the atomic numbers of the elements
> present in bone ($Z = 14$) and soft tissue
> ($Z = 7$), it follows that bone will absorb
> X-rays much more strongly than soft tissue.
> Hence, the X-ray picture will show a
> contrast between bone and soft tissue.

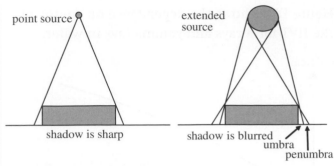

Figure D3.4 The shadow cast is blurred when the
source is extended.

must be made as *point-like* as possible (see
Figure D3.4).

The quality of the image is thus improved if the
film is as close to the patient as possible, or if
the distance from the source to the patient is
large. (In the latter case, the intensity of X-rays
reaching the patient is diminished, which in
turn implies a longer exposure time.) The image
is also improved if as many scattered rays as
possible are prevented from reaching the film.
(See Figure D3.5.)

The X-rays that are directed
through a patient's body will
penetrate the body and those
that make it through to the
other side fall on *photographic
film*, which they expose. In
those cases where there is no
substantial difference
between the Z number of the
area to be imaged and the
surrounding area, the image
can be improved by giving
the patient a *contrast medium*. Usually this
consists of what is called a *barium meal*, barium
sulphate, which the patient swallows. When
this moves into the intestinal tract and an X-ray
is taken, the barium will absorb X-rays more
strongly than the surrounding tissue, resulting
in a sharper image. The image created by the
X-ray on the film is actually a shadow of the
high-Z material in the body (e.g. bones) against
the surrounding low-Z tissue. To increase the
sharpness of the shadow the source of X-rays

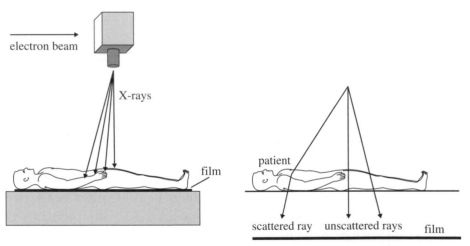

Figure D3.5 A beam of X-rays entering a patient.
Scattered rays blur the image.

This can be achieved with the use of a grid of
lead (i.e. X-ray opaque) strips, which are placed
between the patient and the film, as shown in
Figure D3.6. The strips are oriented along the
direction of the incoming X-rays, and so
scattered rays are blocked and do not make it to
the film. The strips are about 0.5 mm apart.
This creates unwanted images of the lead strips
on the film, however. These can be eliminated

to some extent by moving the grid sideways back and forth during exposure so that the strip images are blurred.

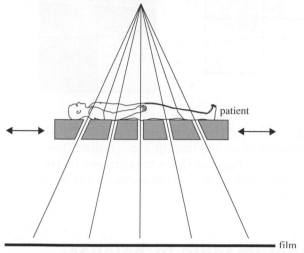

Figure D3.6 The use of a grid with lead strips blocks scattered rays, improving the image.

Low-energy X-rays will simply be absorbed by the skin of the patient and cannot therefore penetrate the body. Such X-rays are usually removed from the X-ray beam in a process called *filtering*.

Because photographic film is much more sensitive to ordinary visible light than to X-rays, the time of exposure in making an X-ray image needs to be longer. However, it can be significantly reduced by using intensifying screens. An intensifying screen is a piece of plastic containing fluorescent crystals in the top and bottom surfaces and a double-sided photographic film in between. X-rays that have gone through the patient enter this screen and transfer some of their energy to the crystals. The energy absorbed by the crystals is then emitted as visible light that exposes the film. (See Figure D3.7.)

Figure D3.7 The use of intensifying screens increases the brightness of the image.

In another X-ray technique called *fluoroscopy*, a *real-time* dynamic image is created on a TV monitor. X-rays that have passed through the patient fall on a fluorescent screen and visible light is emitted. The photons cause the emission of electrons from a photosurface, which are then accelerated by a potential difference so that they fall on a second fluorescent screen from which they cause emission of light that is fed into the TV monitor.

The advantage of the real-time image is, however, outweighed by the unusually high doses of radiation the patient receives in the process.

Computed tomography (CT scan)

One of the biggest advances in the medical use of X-rays has been the discovery (in 1973), through work of G.N. Hounsfield and A. Cormack, of a technique known as computed (axial) tomography (CT) or computer-assisted tomography (CAT). This diagnostic method has made possible much more accurate diagnosis with much less invasive action on the patient. It does use X-rays, however, and so its use does present dangers to the patient. A complete brain CAT scan lasts about 2 s and a whole-body scan lasts about 6 s.

Imagine a patient standing up with a beam of X-rays directed horizontally, at right angles to the long vertical axis of the patient. The CT scan creates an image of a horizontal slice through the patient. In Figure D3.8 we look at a patient (represented by the grey circle) from above. A movable source of X-rays emits a beam that is confined to a horizontal plane and travels through the patient's body so that it is received by detectors on the other side. The source then is rotated so that the beam enters the body from a different angle.

The use of many detectors as opposed to just one cuts down the time required for the scan and the amount of radiation deposited in the patient. The detectors record the intensity of the X-rays reaching them and the information

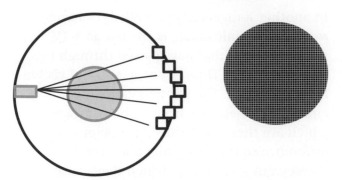

Figure D3.8 In a CT scan, an array of detectors records the X-rays passing through the patient in a given direction and the amount of absorption in each pixel is computed.

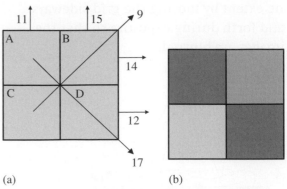

(a)   (b)

Figure D3.9 (a) The detectors measure the total amount of absorption in a given direction. (b) On the basis of these measurements the computer then assigns absorption values to each pixel.

is then sent to a computer, which analyses the data and constructs the image.

The image is constructed as follows. Imagine for convenience that the horizontal slice to be imaged is broken down into a square grid of a suitably small size so as to get acceptable resolution. Typically the size of the grid is about 2 mm or smaller. The objective is to get information about the amount of X-rays that has been absorbed by each grid element (also called a pixel). A detector, of course, only measures the total amount of X-rays absorbed along a straight line joining the source of X-rays to the detector. A method is needed to find the amount absorbed by each pixel. This is done by a computer using sophisticated mathematical techniques. To illustrate the point, consider an oversimplified example in which the area to be imaged has just 4 pixels (see Figure D3.9a). The numbers next to the arrows indicate the total amount of absorption along the direction of the arrow in arbitrary units. If the amount of absorption in each pixel is A, B, C and D, we have, for example, that $A + B = 14$. In a real situation, there would be tens of thousands of pixels and fast computer techniques must be used to determine the individual amounts of absorption in each pixel. Once the numbers for each pixel are found, a colour code can be applied to each pixel to represent its absorption. Here we use shades of grey – darker shades meaning higher absorption – to get Figure D3.9b using the values $A = 8$, $B = 6$, $C = 3$, $D = 9$.

Other imaging techniques

Magnetic resonance imaging (MRI)

Magnetic resonance imaging is based on a nuclear physics phenomenon known as *nuclear magnetic resonance* and is a superior method to the CT scan. Unlike the CT scan, the image is constructed without dangerous radiation (despite the word *nuclear*) but it is significantly more expensive.

Electrons and protons have a property called spin (see Chapter 6.7 on Particle physics). Particles with electric charge and spin behave as tiny microscopic magnets – the technical term is magnetic moment. In the presence of an external magnetic field, the magnetic moment will align itself either parallel ('spin-up') or antiparallel ('spin-down') to the direction of the magnetic field.

Protons inside nuclei belong to energy levels of specific energy. If the protons are put in a region of external magnetic field, the energy of the level will change depending on how the proton magnetic moment aligns itself with respect to the magnetic field (see Figure D3.10). The difference in energy between the split levels is proportional to the external magnetic field.

As seen from Figure D3.10, the state with spin-up has the lower energy. If a radio-frequency

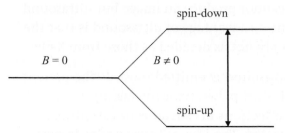

Figure D3.10 A normal energy level splits into two in a magnetic field. The state with spin-up has a lower energy than the state with spin-down.

(RF) source (i.e. electromagnetic radiation) provides energy to a sample of hydrogen nuclei in a magnetic field, the protons in the lower energy spin-up state may absorb photons and make a transition to the higher spin-down state. This will happen if the frequency of the electromagnetic radiation corresponds to the energy difference between the spin-up and spin-down states (an example of resonance). Once the transition to the higher energy state is made, it will be followed by a transition down again with the accompanying emission of a photon of the same frequency. Detectors can record these photons and techniques similar to CT scanning are used to create the magnetic resonance image so that the photons detected can be correlated with specific points of emission. Of great interest in MRI is the rate at which the transitions take place, since the rate is related to the type of tissue in which the transition occurs. Thus, measuring the rate gives information about the type of tissue.

The point of emission of the emitted photons can be located by placing the patient in an additional magnetic field that destroys the high degree of uniformity of the original magnets. Suppose that the magnetic field now varies across the patient (shown in cross-section in Figure D3.11), so that it becomes stronger as we move upwards. Imagine that the variation of the magnetic field is the same along horizontal planes through the patient.

The frequency that can be absorbed by the hydrogen nuclei depends on the external magnetic field, so for a fixed RF frequency only one plane within the body will have the correct value of magnetic field for absorption to take place. To measure absorption in other planes through the body, the frequency of the RF source can be varied. The image so created shows the density of hydrogen nuclei since it is hydrogen that is primarily responsible for absorption. More sophisticated techniques measure the rate at which excited nuclei return to their ground state (the relaxation times) and these produce images of especially high resolution. Different kinds of tissue show different relaxation times, thus allowing the identification of tissue type.

Positron emission tomography (PET scan)

This technique is similar to the CT scan and involves the annihilation of an electron and a positron (the antiparticle of the electron) and

Figure D3.11 In MRI the patient is surrounded by powerful magnets that produce very uniform fields, and RF coils. The magnetic field is given a gradient – it is made stronger at some places. Here the field increases as we move upwards.

the detection of the two photons so produced. The patient is injected with a solution of radioactive material containing isotopes that decay by positron emission. As soon as the positron is emitted, it will collide with an electron in the tissue of the patient. The electron–positron pair will annihilate into two photons each of energy 0.511 MeV

$$e^- + e^+ \to 2\gamma$$

The electron–positron total momentum is, essentially, zero, which means that the two photons must move in opposite directions with the same energy (in order to conserve momentum). The detectors surrounding the patient (see Figure D3.12) can therefore determine the line along which the emissions took place and eventually locate the point of emission. PET scans have a resolution of about 1 mm. They are used mainly for biochemical and metabolism-related studies. They produce superior brain images.

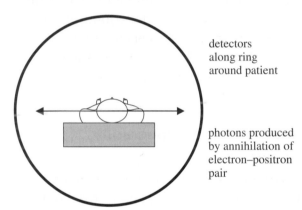

Figure D3.12 The patient is surrounded by a ring of detectors which record the line along which the two photons are emitted.

Ultrasound

A major tool in diagnostic medicine is ultrasound. Ultrasound is sound that is not audible to the human ear – its frequency is higher than about 20 kHz. The ultrasound used in diagnostic medicine is in the range of about 1 to 10 MHz. Ultrasound has the advantage over X-rays in that it does not deposit radiation in the body and no adverse side effects of its use are known. For certain organs, for example the lungs,

X-rays cannot produce an image but ultrasound can. One disadvantage of ultrasound is that the images are not as detailed as those from X-rays.

The ultrasound is emitted towards the patient's body in *short pulses*, typically lasting 1 μs, and their reflections off surfaces of various organs are detected. The idea is thus similar to *sonar*. The speed of sound in soft tissue is 1540 m s^{-1}, similar to that in water. This means that the wavelengths involved are 1.54 mm for 1 MHz waves and 0.154 mm for 10 MHz waves. Thus, if we use 1 MHz waves, the length of the pulse is 1.54 mm and so contains just one full wave. For 10 MHz waves, the wavetrain contains 10 full waves. In general, diffraction considerations place a limit on the size, d, that can be resolved by a wave of wavelength λ. The constraint is that

$$\lambda < d$$

If a resolution of a couple of millimetres is required, the wavelength used must therefore be less than a few millimetres. In view of the frequencies used, this is not a problem. As we saw, a 10 MHz ultrasound has a wavelength of about 0.15 mm and so, in principle, such an ultrasound can 'see' objects of linear size of about 0.15 mm.

On the other hand, in practice, the pulse used must contain at least a few full waves for resolution to be possible.

▶ Thus, in the case of the ultrasound frequencies used in medicine, it is the pulse duration, and not diffraction, that sets the limit on resolution.

The frequency used is usually determined by the organ to be studied and the resolution desired. A rough rule is to use a frequency given by

$$f = 200 \frac{c}{d}$$

where c is the speed of sound in tissue and d is the depth of the organ below the body surface. (In other words, the organ should be at a depth of about 200 wavelengths.)

Example question

Q5

The stomach is about 10 cm from the body's surface. What frequency should be used to get a scan of the stomach?

Answer

Applying the formula gives

$$f = 200\frac{c}{d}$$

$$= 200 \times \frac{1548}{0.10} \text{ Hz}$$

$$\approx 3 \text{ MHz}$$

The source of ultrasound is a transducer that converts electrical energy into sound energy. This is based on a phenomenon called piezoelectricity. An alternating voltage applied to opposite faces of a crystal such as strontium titanate or quartz will force the crystal to vibrate, emitting ultrasound (see Figure D3.13). Similarly, ultrasound falling on such a crystal will produce an alternating voltage at the faces of the crystal. This means that the source of ultrasound can also act as a receiver.

Figure D3.13 A piezoelectric crystal vibrates when an AC source is applied to it.

The sound energy must then be directed into the patient's body. In general, when a wave encounters an interface between two different media, part of the wave will be reflected and part will be transmitted into the other medium. The amount of transmission depends on the impedances of the two media. Acoustic impedance is defined as

$$Z = \rho v$$

where ρ is the density of the medium and v is the speed of sound in that medium. The units of impedance are $kg \, m^{-2} \, s^{-1}$. If I_0 is the

incident, I_t the transmitted and I_r the reflected intensity then

$$\frac{I_t}{I_0} = \frac{4Z_1Z_2}{(Z_1 + Z_2)^2}$$

$$\frac{I_r}{I_0} = \frac{(Z_1 - Z_2)^2}{(Z_1 + Z_2)^2}$$

This shows that for most of the energy to be transmitted, the impedances of the two media must be as close to each other as possible (impedance matching). The impedance of soft tissue differs from that of air by a factor of about 10^4, so most of the sound would be reflected by the body. This is why the area between the body and the transducer is filled with a gel-like substance whose impedance matches that of the body.

In a type of ultrasound scan called the A scan, the ultrasound pulse is directed into the body and the reflected pulse from various interfaces in the body is recorded by the transducer. This time it converts the sound energy into electrical energy. The reflected signal is then displayed on a cathode-ray oscilloscope. The CRO signal is, in fact, a graph of signal strength versus time of travel from the transducer to the reflecting surface and back. An example of such a trace is shown in Figure D3.14.

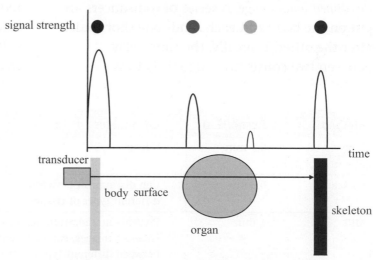

Figure D3.14 A short beam of ultrasound is directed into the patient. The beam is partially reflected from various organs in the body and the reflected signal is recorded. The dots at the top of the figure represent the strength of the reflected signal.

The dots in the graph show another way of representing the results. The dot brightness is proportional to the signal strength (darker colours representing stronger signal).

The A scan provides a one-dimensional image. Imagine a whole series of A scans performed by sending parallel beams of ultrasound into the patient by a transducer that moves up along the surface of the body or by a series of transducers, as shown in Figure D3.15.

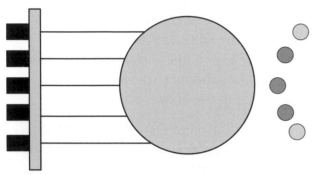

Figure D3.15 As the source of ultrasound is moved along the body, a series of dots whose brightness represents the strength of the reflected signal is formed. These dots build up the ultrasound image.

If the A scans *are put together*, the result is the dots on the right of the diagram, which begin to form an outline of the surface of the organ in a *two-dimensional image*. A series of transducers are put on the body and each sends one short pulse after the other. Typically, the time delay between two consecutive signals is 1 ms.

▶ When the results are displayed on the CRO screen, the image is a *real-time, two-dimensional representation of the object which is viewed as a movie*. This is called a B scan.

Ultrasound can also be put to other uses. One is to measure blood-flow velocities and foetal heart movement. Ultrasound is directed at the heart, say, and the reflected signal detected. Because the heart moves, the reflected signal will have a slightly different frequency because of the Doppler effect. Comparison of the emitted and received frequencies gives the speed of the reflecting surface.

The various imaging techniques described are summarised in Table D3.2.

Diagnostic uses of radioactive sources

Radioisotopes are used for diagnosis and to monitor specific body organs and their functions. Uses include the monitoring of the thyroid gland using radioactive iodine, measurement of body fluids, studies of how food is digested, vitamin absorption, how amino acids are synthesized, how ions can penetrate cell walls, etc. Most commonly used is the radioisotope technetium-99 ($^{99m}_{43}$Tc), a

Method	Resolution	Advantages	Disadvantages
X-rays	0.5 mm	Cheap	Presents radiation danger; some organs are not accessible; some images are obscured
CT scans	0.5 mm	Can distinguish between different types of tissue	Presents radiation danger
MRI	1 mm	Presents no radiation dangers; superior images; can distinguish between different types of tissue	Expensive; difficult for patients who are claustrophobic
Ultrasound	2 mm	Presents no radiation dangers	Some organs are not accessible
PET scans	1 mm	Organ function studies; superior brain images	Some organs are not accessible

Table D3.2 Advantages and disadvantages of different imaging techniques.

metastable (i.e. long-lived) excited state of technetium-99. It is produced in the decay of molybdenum-99:

$$^{99}_{42}\text{Mo} \rightarrow \,^{99\text{m}}_{43}\text{Tc} + \,^{0}_{-1}\text{e} + \,^{0}_{0}\bar{\nu}_\text{e} + \,^{0}_{0}\gamma$$

The produced technetium then decays by gamma emission

$$^{99\text{m}}_{43}\text{Tc} \rightarrow \,^{99}_{43}\text{Tc} + \,^{0}_{0}\gamma$$

The photon energies are about 140 keV. This is an advantage since any alpha or beta particles emitted would be absorbed within the body and would not reach an outside detector; also, photons of these energies are easily detectable. Technetium has a half-life of about 6 h, which is conveniently short, and can combine into a large number of compounds.

Technetium is useful in diagnostic studies of most body organs, such as the heart, the lungs and the liver. In investigations of calcium absorption by bones, technetium and calcium-45 or calcium-47 are used. Iodine-131 is another commonly used radioisotope. It is used in blood volume measurements and in studies of the thyroid gland. Thallium-201 is used in studies of muscle function and disease.

The compound to be tagged with technetium is chosen according to what part or organ of the body needs to be imaged – different compounds will accumulate in different parts of the body. The radioactive compound so formed is called a *radiopharmaceutical*. This is given to the patient (orally or by injection) and the radiation emitted by technetium can then be recorded by a detector placed over the relevant part of the patient's body. The amount of radiation compared with the amount expected from a healthy body then provides information about the function of the particular body organ.

The example question that follows shows the theory of a method used to determine the amount of blood in a patient (who might have been involved in an accident resulting in massive blood loss).

Example question

Q6 ▮▮▮▮▮▮▮▮▮▮▮▮▮▮▮▮

A patient is injected with 5 cm³ of albumen labelled with iodine-131 (albumen is part of the blood plasma). A 5 cm³ sample drawn from the patient's blood has an activity of 100 Bq. Another 5 cm³ of iodine-131 is mixed with 3000 cm³ of water. The activity of a 5 cm³ sample is found to be 170 Bq. Determine the volume of blood of the patient.

Answer

Let A be the activity of the 5 cm³ of iodine-131. Then the activity of 5 cm³ drawn from the entire blood volume V is

$$100 = \frac{5}{V} A$$

The activity of the 5 cm³ drawn from the diluted sample is

$$170 = \frac{5}{3000} A$$

and so dividing these two equations side by side we find $V = 5100$ cm³.

Questions

1 Figure D3.16 shows the fraction of X-rays of two specific energies transmitted through a thickness x of a sheet of metal.
   (a) For each energy, determine the HVT for these X-rays in the metal.
   (b) Which graph corresponds to X-rays of higher energy?

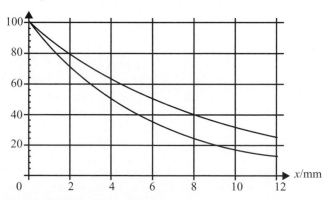

Figure D3.16 For question 1.

2 Figure D3.17 shows the fraction of X-rays of a specific energy transmitted through a thickness x of a sheet of metal.
  (a) Determine the value of the linear attenuation coefficient for these X-rays in this metal.
  (b) What thickness of metal is required to reduce the transmitted intensity by 80%?

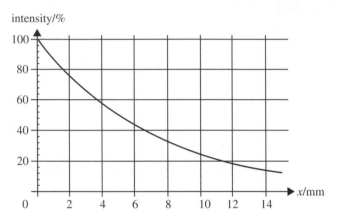

Figure D3.17 For question 2.

3 A piece of metal 4 mm thick reduces the intensity of X-rays passing through it by 40%. What thickness of the same metal is required to reduce the intensity by 80%?

4 The HVT for a beam of X-rays is 3 mm. What fraction of the X-ray intensity is transmitted through 1 mm of this metal?

5 The X-rays used in medicine are usually not monoenergetic (i.e. of a single energy). It is said that these beams become 'harder' as they are allowed to pass through material. What is meant by this statement and why is it true? The HVT of a certain absorber for X-rays of energy 20 keV is 2.2 mm and that for 25 keV X-rays is 2.8 mm. A beam containing equal quantities of X-rays of these two energies is incident on 5.0 mm of the absorber. What is the ratio of 25 keV to 20 keV photons that are transmitted?

6 The intensity of a beam of monoenergetic X-rays is 0.28 kW m^{-2} at a distance of 20 cm from the X-ray source.
  (a) What is the intensity at a distance of 10 cm from the source (assume no absorption between the point of interest and the source)?
  (b) If an aluminium foil of thickness 3 mm and HVT 2 mm is wrapped around the source, what will the intensity be 10 cm away?

7 A radioactive isotope with a half-life of 14 h and activity of 3.6 kBq is injected into a patient's blood. A 10 cm^3 sample is taken from the patient 6 h later and its activity is measured to be 5.0 Bq. Estimate the volume of the patient's blood.

8 What resolution can be achieved with ultrasound of frequency 5 MHz? (Take the speed of sound in soft tissue to be 1540 m s^{-1}.)

Biomechanics

This chapter is an application of the conditions of mechanical equilibrium (zero net force and zero net torque) to the human body. The conditions for static equilibrium were discussed in Chapter 2.12 and you should be familiar with that chapter before proceeding with this one. Energy considerations in the human body such as the metabolic rate and temperature regulation are also discussed.

Objectives

By the end of this chapter you should be able to:

*   apply the laws of *translational and rotational equilibrium* to problems involving the *human body*;
*   state the meaning of the terms *basal metabolic rate* and *metabolic rate*;
*   solve problems involving the *metabolic rate*;
*   understand the *main mechanisms with which the human body controls its temperature*.

Torque and equilibrium

We begin with a reminder of the main result of Chapter 2.12, namely that an extended body is in equilibrium if the net force and net torque on the body are both zero. As a warm-up consider the following example.

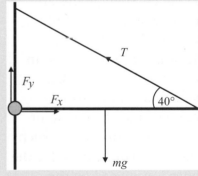

Figure D4.1.

Example question

Q1

A uniform rod of length 4.20 m and mass $m = 40.0$ kg is mounted on a hinge at a wall as shown in Figure D4.1. The rod is kept horizontal by a rope attached to the other end of the rod such that the rope makes an angle of 40° with the horizontal. Find the force at the hinge and the tension in the rope.

Answer

It is easiest to deal with the components F_x and F_y of the hinge force separately. Equilibrium of

forces means that

$$F_x = T \cos 40°$$
$$F_y + T \sin 40° = mg$$

These are two equations with three unknown quantities (F_x, F_y and T), so we need one more equation. This is obtained from the condition that torques are also in balance. Taking torques about the hinge we find (here $L =$ length of rod)

$$mg \frac{L}{2} = T L \sin 40°$$

$$\Rightarrow T = \frac{mg}{2 \sin 40°} \approx 311 \, \text{N}$$

Putting this value in the first two equations gives

$$F_x = T \cos 40°$$
$$= 238.4 \, \text{N}$$
$$F_y = mg - T \sin 40°$$
$$= 200 \, \text{N}$$

It follows that the hinge force has magnitude

$$\sqrt{200^2 + 238.4^2} \, \text{N} = 311 \, \text{N}$$

It makes an angle of

$$\arctan \frac{200}{238.4} = 40°$$

with the horizontal.

Skeleton, muscle and movement

The human body is supported by a skeleton, a structure of over 200 bones. Some bones are fused together, as in the bones of the skull, which means there is no relative motion between them, while others are connected in joints that do allow relative motion. These joints are called *synovial* and can be simple hinge-like connections, such as the elbow, or more complex ball-in-socket connections, such as the hip and the shoulder. Lubrication for the movement of the bones is provided by the *synovial fluid* that fills the *synovial cavity* of the joint. Bones in synovial joints are connected to each other by ligaments. Tendons attach bones and muscles together and muscle contractions and relaxations make bones move. Bones make up about 17% of our body mass and muscles about 40%. The rest of our mass is in the tissues of the organs and the fluids of the body.

Centre of mass of the body

Table D4.1 shows the approximate mass of various parts of an adult's body as a percentage of the total mass, as well as the height of the

centre of mass (CM) of the body part from the floor as a percentage of the total height of the person. The person is assumed to be standing up straight with arms hanging vertically.

Body part	Distance of CM from floor as % of height	Mass of body part as a % of total mass
Head	94	7
Upper body and neck	70	46
Upper arms	71	7
Lower arms	55	4
Hands	43	2
Upper legs	41	21
Lower legs	19	10
Feet	2	3

Table D4.1 Mass and centre of mass of parts of the body.

Example question

Q2

Using Table D4.1, find the position of the CM of the entire body.

Answer

The height of the CM from the floor is given by

$$y = 0.94 \times 0.07 + 0.70 \times 0.46 + 0.71 \times 0.07$$
$$+ 0.55 \times 0.04 + 0.43 \times 0.02 + 0.41 \times 0.21$$
$$+ 0.19 \times 0.10 + 0.02 \times 0.03$$
$$= 0.57$$

that is, a distance of 57% of the total height from the floor.

Levers

When the arm lifts a weight, it acts as a simple lever, as shown in Figure D4.2. The muscles of the arm provide the upward force E (effort). The weight of the arm and that of the weight are the loads, L, that the effort is working against. The arm can rotate at the elbow, which thus acts as the fulcrum of the lever. This type of lever is called a *third-class lever*, which means the effort force is positioned between the fulcrum and loads.

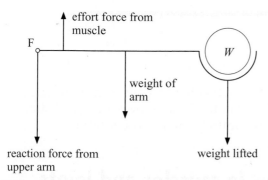

Figure D4.2 The force from the upper arm muscle holding the forearm and a weight in equilibrium acting between the load and the fulcrum F is a third-class lever.

The human body has a large number of lever systems. A *first-class lever* is one in which the fulcrum is in the middle. An example of this in the human body is provided by the lever system that supports the head at the top of the spine (the position of the fulcrum). The neck muscles provide the effort force pulling down at the back of the head while the load (the weight of the head) acts downward, as shown in Figure D4.3.

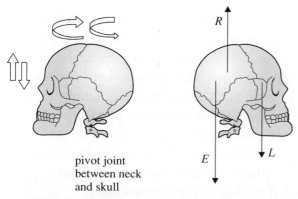

Figure D4.3 A first-class lever holding the head in equilibrium. The fulcrum is between the load and effort forces.

A *second-class lever* has the load in the middle; an example of this is provided by the leg–foot system that allows a person to reach high for something. The fulcrum is just before the toes of the foot, the load is the weight of the leg and foot and the effort is provided by the muscles at the back of the lower leg, as shown in Figure D4.4.

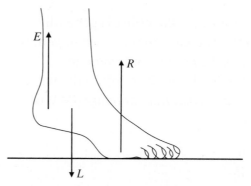

Figure D4.4 The load is acting between the effort and the fulcrum in this second-class lever.

In any lever system, we define the mechanical advantage (MA) of the lever by the ratio of load to effort:

$$\text{MA} = \frac{\text{load}}{\text{effort}} = \frac{L}{E}$$

Consider the simplified diagram in Figure D4.5, in which a weight of 50 N is lifted by the arm (we neglect the weight of the arm). Taking

Figure D4.5 The muscles of the upper arm supporting a weight while the forearm is resting horizontally.

torques about the fulcrum (thus, the force acting at the fulcrum has zero torque) and demanding equilibrium results in

$$E \times 0.04 = 50 \times 0.35$$

that is, the effort force is $E = 438\,\text{N}$. The mechanical advantage is thus

$$\text{MA} = \frac{L}{E} = \frac{50}{438} = 0.11$$

In a real lever system, the effort is generally higher than in an ideal system, since in general frictional forces have to be overcome in addition to the load. We thus define the *velocity ratio* or the *ideal mechanical advantage* (IMA) of the lever by

$$\text{IMA} = \frac{d_e}{d_l}$$

where the distances refer to the distances moved by the effort and load. The work done by the effort is $E \times d_e$ and that by the load is $L \times d_l$. The efficiency of the lever system is defined as

$$
\begin{aligned}
\eta &= \frac{\text{work by load}}{\text{work by effort}} \\
&= \frac{L \times d_l}{E \times d_e} \\
&= \frac{L/E}{d_e/d_l} \\
&= \frac{\text{MA}}{\text{IMA}}
\end{aligned}
$$

Clearly, the efficiency is 1 (or 100%) when the velocity ratio (i.e. ideal mechanical advantage) is the same as the actual mechanical advantage.

> ▶ A mechanical advantage that is larger than one means that a load can be moved with less effort at the price of the effort having to move a larger distance than the load. The reverse is true for mechanical advantages less than one (see Figure D4.6). In the human body, most lever systems

have mechanical advantages less than one. This means sensitivity in motion: a small muscle movement results in a large body part movement.

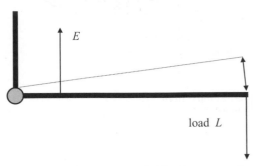

Figure D4.6 A mechanical advantage less than one implies that the hand moves a larger distance than the muscle forcing the motion.

Forces in muscles and joints

Let us begin our discussion of the forces developed by muscles and at the joints with a simple example. Figure D4.7 shows the foot of a ballerina when she is in the 'arabesque' position. She balances her entire weight on the tip of *one foot*. We will consider the forces on just a part of her body, namely the foot. These forces are:

- the reaction from the floor, R;
- the force due to the Achilles tendon, A, acting in the direction shown;
- the reaction force at the joint of the foot to the lower leg, J.

We also have the weight of the foot itself but, since this is small, we will neglect it in this discussion. The dotted line is a vertical line through the joint. The distance between the line of action of the reaction force and the dotted line is about 2 cm. The perpendicular distance between the line of action of the Achilles tendon force A and the joint is about 2.8 cm. (These numbers are known from detailed studies of the human body.)

Suppose that the weight of the ballerina is 500 N. Equilibrium *of her entire body* demands that

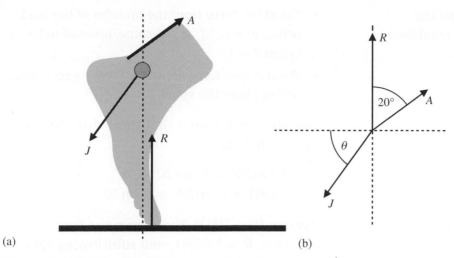

(a)   (b)

Figure D4.7 (a) Free-body diagram of the forces on the foot of a ballerina in the 'arabesque' position. (b) Diagram used to find components of forces. (Not to scale.)

$R = W$, that is $R = 500$ N. Equilibrium *of her foot* demands that the net force and net torque *on the foot are zero*. Let us first apply the condition of zero net torque. Taking torques about the joint means that the torque of force J is zero. The torques of R and A are opposite and so must be set equal to each other. This means that

$$A \times 2.8 = R \times 2$$
$$\Rightarrow A = \frac{500 \times 2}{2.8}$$
$$= 357\,\text{N}$$

We have found the force exerted by the Achilles tendon.

To find the joint force requires additional information. Assume that the Achilles tendon force makes an angle of $20°$ with the vertical. We now apply the other condition for equilibrium, namely that the net force be zero. We must first take components of forces. We have

$$A_x = 357\sin 20° = 122.1$$
$$A_y = 357\cos 20° = 335.5$$
$$J_x = J\cos\theta$$
$$J_y = J\sin\theta$$

Thus, we have

$$J_y = 500 + 335.5 = 835.5\,\text{N}$$
$$J_x = 122.1\,\text{N}$$

Dividing side by side gives

$$\tan\theta = \frac{835.5}{122.1} = 6.842$$
$$\Rightarrow \theta = 81.7°$$

The magnitude of J is

$$\sqrt{122.1^2 + 835.5^2} = 844\,\text{N}$$

Let us consider as another example a man doing 'curl-ups'. He is lying face down on a bench with his upper body (from the waist up) hanging over the bench. To strengthen his back muscles he pulls his upper body up. Figure D4.8 shows the situation when the upper body makes an angle of $30°$ with the horizontal. We would like to find the muscle force. The figure also shows the three forces acting on the *upper body*. These are:

- the weight of the upper body, W;
- the joint force, J;
- the muscle force, M.

We will take an upper body weight of 400 N, acting at a point 42 cm from the joint. The muscle force is at a perpendicular distance of 4 cm from the joint.

Applying the condition that the net torque be zero (we will take torques about the joint) we find that

$$400 \times 42 \times \cos 30° = M \times 4$$
$$\Rightarrow M = 3637\,\text{N}$$

which is a substantial force.

Figure D4.8 Forces on the upper body of a person doing 'curl-ups'.

To find the joint force we must use the condition for zero net force. This condition amounts to

$$M \cos 30° = J \cos \theta$$
$$\Rightarrow J \cos \theta = 3149.7 \text{ N}$$
$$M \sin 30° + J \sin \theta = W$$
$$\Rightarrow J \sin \theta = -1418.5 \text{ N}$$

Thus

$$\tan \theta = -\frac{1418.5}{3149.7} = -0.45$$
$$\Rightarrow \theta = 24.2°$$

below the horizontal. (The diagram we used showed the force above the horizontal.) We can now find the magnitude of the joint force to be $\sqrt{3149.7^2 + 1418.5^2} = 3454 \text{ N}$.

Lifting heavy objects

Figure D4.9 shows a woman bending such that her spine (assumed straight) makes an angle of 60° to the vertical.

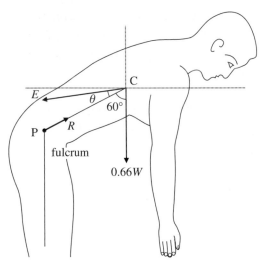

Figure D4.9 A person supporting herself in a bent position has a force acting on her from the back muscles ensuring equilibrium.

The forces acting on the person are:

- the weight of the upper part of her body (take this to be about 66% of the total weight) acting at point C, the centre of mass of the upper body about 2/3 of the distance from the lumbrosacral disc to the shoulder joint;

- the effort force from the muscles of her back acting at $\theta = 10°$ to the spine, *assumed* to be centred at C;

- the reaction force, R, at the lumbrosacral disc, acting along the spine.

Equilibrium demands that these three forces balance out, so

$$R \cos 30° = E \cos 20°$$
$$0.66W + E \sin 20° = R \sin 30°$$

Assume $W = 700 \text{ N}$. Then, from the first equation, $R = 1.0851E$ and substituting this value in the second equation we find $E = 2304 \text{ N}$, which is a considerable force. This means that $R = 2500 \text{ N}$.

If the person now attempts to lift a weight, $F = 200 \text{ N}$, an additional force acting vertically down at the height of her shoulders and equal to F is acting on her body (see Figure D4.10).

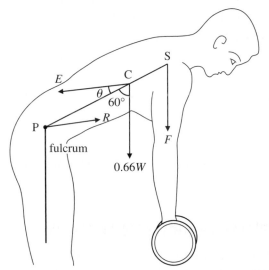

Figure D4.10 If the person attempts to lift a weight, the forces from the back muscles and the reaction at the lumbrosacral disc may get dangerously high.

Let d stand for the distance PS, then, approximately, PC = $(2/3)d$. Note that the reaction force R can no longer act along the spine. Taking torques about point P eliminates the torque of the reaction force R and gives

$$F d \sin 60° + 0.66W \frac{2d}{3} \sin 60° = E \frac{2d}{3} \sin 10°$$

resulting in $E = 3800$ N. This shows how dangerous it is to lift heavy objects from such a position. The reaction force can be found by considering components of forces: assume that R makes an angle ϕ with the horizontal. Then, balancing forces in the horizontal and vertical directions results in

$$R \cos \phi = E \cos 20° = 3571 \text{ N}$$
$$R \sin \phi = F + 0.66W + E \sin 20° = 1962 \text{ N}$$

from which

$$\tan \phi = \frac{1962}{3571} = 0.549$$
$$\Rightarrow \phi = 28.8°$$

and hence $R = 4074$ N, which is another large and potentially dangerous force.

Energy conversions in the body

The body needs energy in order to function. Part of the energy needed is used to maintain the basic functions of the body, such as brain activity, the beating of the heart, breathing, digestion and growth.

> The rate of energy supplied for these *involuntary functions* for a resting, awake, person is called the *basal metabolic rate* (BMR).
>
> The total energy needed by the body for its involuntary functions plus any work the body is performing (such as walking, running, exercising, etc.) is called the *metabolic rate* (MR).

The BMR depends on age. Children have the highest BMR because of the energy needed for growth. Men have slightly higher BMR than women because of the smaller amounts of fat in the male body. The BMR decreases sharply from age zero to about 20 years. It then reaches a plateau, where it remains until about age 60, and then gently falls.

Suppose that a person does an amount of work δW in a time interval of δt. This work may involve running up the stairs, swimming, bicycling, etc. An amount of heat δQ will leave the body during this time interval and hence by the first law of thermodynamics we know that

$$\delta Q = \delta U + \delta W$$
$$\Rightarrow \delta U = \delta Q - \delta W$$

where δU is the change in the *internal energy* of the body.

Dividing by δt converts the last equation into one relating rates of change of energy, that is power:

$$\frac{\delta U}{\delta t} = \frac{\delta Q}{\delta t} - \frac{\delta W}{\delta t}$$

> The quantity $\frac{\delta U}{\delta t}$ is the rate at which energy is being converted in the body: it is the *metabolic rate*. This conversion takes place when oxygen combines with food to produce carbon dioxide, water and energy. On average, 20.2 kJ of energy is released for every litre of oxygen used.

As an example, consider a person who is consuming oxygen at a rate of 50 L h^{-1}. The energy is produced at a rate of

$$\frac{\delta U}{\delta t} = 50 \text{ L h}^{-1} \times 20.2 \text{ kJ L}^{-1}$$
$$= 1010 \text{ kJ h}^{-1}$$
$$= 1010 \frac{1000 \text{ J}}{3600 \text{ s}}$$
$$\approx 281 \text{ W}$$

The rate at which energy is produced for various activities is shown in Table D4.2. We show the power per unit mass of the person. The person is assumed to be a 20-year-old male. These numbers change with age.

Thus, a 60 kg person would be using energy at a rate of 60 kg $\times$ 8 W kg^{-1} = 480 W when bicycling. This implies that the cyclist is

Activity	Metabolic rate per mass $\left(\dfrac{1}{m}\dfrac{\delta U}{\delta t}\right)$ / W kg^{-1}
Sleeping	1.1
Walking	4.5
Bicycling	8.0
Climbing stairs	10.0
Swimming	11.0
Running	18.0

Table D4.2 Metabolic rate per unit mass for a 20-year-old male performing various activities.

Food	Energy released per unit mass of food/MJ kg^{-1}
Carbohydrates	16.5
Fat	37.5
Protein	16.5

Table D4.3 The energy content of various foods.

consuming oxygen at a rate of

$$480\,\text{W} = 20.2\,\text{kJ}\,\text{L}^{-1} \times \text{rate}$$
$$\Rightarrow \text{rate} = \frac{480\,\text{W}}{20.2\,\text{kJ}\,\text{L}^{-1}}$$
$$= \frac{480\,\text{J}\,\text{s}^{-1}}{20.2 \times 10^3\,\text{J}\,\text{L}^{-1}}$$
$$= 2.38 \times 10^{-2}\,\text{L}\,\text{s}^{-1}$$
$$= 85.5\,\text{L}\,\text{h}^{-1}$$

Increasing the rate of oxygen consumption increases the rate of energy production in the body. Suppose now that the person has been cycling for 2 h. The total energy required is

$$P = \frac{E}{t}$$
$$\Rightarrow E = Pt$$
$$= 480\,\text{W} \times 2 \times 3600\,\text{s}$$
$$= 3.46 \times 10^6\,\text{J}$$

How much food must be used to produce this energy? This depends on the food used. Table D4.3 gives the energy content for various types of food. If carbohydrates are used, the mass required is

$$m \times 16.5\,\text{MJ}\,\text{kg}^{-1} = 3.46 \times 10^6\,\text{J}$$
$$\Rightarrow m = \frac{3.46 \times 10^6\,\text{J}}{16.5\,\text{MJ}\,\text{kg}^{-1}}$$
$$= 0.209\,\text{kg}$$

Almost half of the energy produced by food is in the form of heat; the rest is what is used to maintain the function of basic body organs and to do work.

To find the efficiency of how internal energy is being used to do work, we realize that if the metabolic rate is $\frac{\delta U}{\delta t}$ and the basal metabolic rate is $\frac{\delta U}{\delta t}\big|_{\text{basal}}$, then the amount of internally produced power that can in principle be used to do work is $\frac{\delta U}{\delta t} - \frac{\delta U}{\delta t}\big|_{\text{basal}}$. If the work is being done at a rate of $\frac{\delta W}{\delta t}$, the efficiency is defined by

$$\text{efficiency} = \frac{\frac{\delta W}{\delta t}}{\frac{\delta U}{\delta t} - \frac{\delta U}{\delta t}\big|_{\text{basal}}} \times 100\%$$

Example question

Q3

The metabolic rate of a 60 kg, 20-year-old man climbing a hill is 8 W kg^{-1}. His basal metabolic rate is 1.2 W kg^{-1}. The hill is 300 m high and the man gets to the top in half an hour. How much work is performed in climbing the hill? How much power did the person develop in climbing? What is the efficiency of the man in climbing the hill?

Answer

The work done is equal to the change in the person's gravitational potential energy, that is

$$\Delta W = mgh$$
$$= 60 \times 10 \times 300$$
$$= 1.8 \times 10^5\,\text{J}$$

The average power used was

$$P = \frac{\Delta W}{\Delta t}$$
$$= \frac{1.8 \times 10^5\,\text{J}}{30 \times 60\,\text{s}}$$
$$= 100\,\text{W}$$

The man is producing internal energy at a metabolic rate of 8 W kg^{-1}, that is

$$\frac{\Delta U}{\Delta t} = 8 \times 60$$
$$= 480 \text{ W}$$

His basal metabolic rate is 1.2 W kg^{-1}, which means only

$$(480 - 1.2 \times 60) \text{ W} = 408 \text{ W}$$

is available to do work. His efficiency is thus

$$\frac{100}{408} \times 100\% = 24.5\%$$

Temperature regulation

The various organs of the body are kept at a constant temperature of about 37 °C. If this temperature exceeds 41 °C, serious damage may take place; death occurs for temperatures above 43 °C and below 28 °C. The temperature of the skin is lower than the organ temperature by about 4 °C. The skin temperature is highly dependent on the ambient conditions and the amount of clothing worn.

▶ The body controls its temperature by radiation and convection from the skin, evaporation from the skin and expiration from the lungs. The skin is a very bad conductor of heat and so the role of conduction in body temperature regulation is minimal in most cases.

Radiation

The adult human body has a surface area of about 1.5 m^2 and radiates energy (electromagnetic waves in the infrared region) from this area to the colder surroundings. (If the surroundings are warmer than the skin temperature, then the human body absorbs energy.) The rate of heat loss is proportional to the *area* of the body and to the *difference in temperature* between the skin and the surroundings (provided the difference is not too large).

Convection

When cool air comes in contact with the skin, it is warmed, it expands and its density is lowered, and so it rises, giving its place to additional cool air. In this way, heat is being removed from the body. The lower the air temperature, the more heat the body loses. The presence of wind increases the efficiency of cooling by convection.

Evaporation

The human body constantly evaporates water from the skin, even if the person is not visibly perspiring. The higher the temperature of the surroundings, the higher the rate of heat loss by evaporation. If there is a wind, the rate of evaporation is increased. Humidity in the air reduces evaporation. On a day with a humidity of 100% no evaporation would take place. Heat is required to evaporate water and thus heat is removed from the body whenever evaporation takes place, cooling the body. On a very hot day as much as one kilogram of sweat per hour can be evaporated. This implies that on hot days the body must be replenished with water and other fluids. Evaporation is the dominant mechanism of heat loss from the body when the ambient temperature is high.

Expiration

Heat is lost by the body when warm air is exhaled. Moisture in the lungs evaporates (extracting the latent heat of vaporization) and heat loss results when the air containing this water vapour is exhaled.

Conduction

As mentioned earlier, this is not a significant heat-loss mechanism because of the very low thermal conductivity of the human body surface and because the body is often covered by clothing. When swimming in very cold water, heat loss by conduction does take place.

Questions

1 A person holds her arm outstretched in a horizontal position, as shown in Figure D4.11.

The arm is held in equilibrium by the deltoid muscle in the upper arm, which we assume is acting at 12° to the horizontal a distance of 8 cm from the shoulder. Take the weight of the arm to be 33 N, acting at a distance of 30 cm from the shoulder. Find:

(a) the deltoid muscle force;

(b) the reaction force (magnitude and direction) from the shoulder.

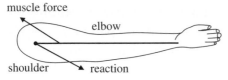

Figure D4.11 For question 1.

2 A person holds his forearm horizontal with a weight of 12 N in his hand, as shown in Figure D4.12. Assume that the biceps muscle exerts a force at 15° to the horizontal on the forearm at a distance of 8 cm from the elbow. The weight in the hand is at a distance of 35 cm from the elbow. Find the force exerted by the muscle. Assume that the forearm plus hand have a weight of 13 N acting at the centre of mass of the forearm, which you may take to be at a distance of 15 cm from the elbow.

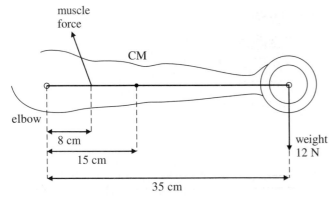

Figure D4.12 For question 2.

3 A person's lower leg is kept at an angle of 45° to the vertical by the quadriceps muscle of the upper leg acting at a distance of 6 cm from the knee at 20° to the vertical (see Figure D4.13). Assume that the combined weight of lower leg and foot of 41 N is acting at a distance of 20 cm from the knee. Find the force the muscle exerts on the leg.

Figure D4.13 For question 3.

4 A person of weight 600 N has her feet horizontal but her heels are slightly off the ground so that her weight is supported by the reaction force from the floor on each foot (see Figure D4.14). Two other forces are assumed to be acting on the foot: a reaction force from the tibia (the lower leg bone) on the foot and the force due to the Achilles tendon. The person's weight is assumed to be evenly distributed on the two feet. Find the magnitudes of the forces acting on the foot.

Figure D4.14 For question 4.

5 A person bends in order to lift an object from the floor in such a way that the spine is horizontal (see Figure D4.15). Assume that the weight W of the upper body and head is 450 N and is acting at a distance of 30 cm from the lumbrosacral disc and that the muscle force is acting at 12° to the horizontal at the same point as W. Find the magnitudes of:

(a) muscle force;

(b) reaction force.

Figure D4.15 For question 5.

6 A 700 N, 1.70 m tall person rests horizontally on two scales as shown in Figure D4.16. Assuming the centre of mass of the person is at a distance of 96 cm from the feet and that the distance between the scales is 1.60 m, find the reading of each scale.

Figure D4.16 For question 6.

7 A simplified mechanical model of the legs is shown in Figure D4.17. The body rests vertically on both legs. Take the body weight to be 700 N and equally distributed on the two legs. The weight of each leg may be taken as 85 N. If the muscle forces are acting at 70° to the horizontal and the joint forces at 80°

Figure D4.17 For question 7.

below the horizontal, find their magnitude. (You do not have to consider torques – just apply equilibrium of forces.)

8 We will now reconsider question 7. Take the weight of the person to be 700 N and the weight of one leg to be about 110 N (roughly one-sixth of the total weight). The muscle force is assumed to act at 70° to the horizontal. Various distances are indicated in Figure D4.18. Evaluate:
(a) the muscle force;
(b) the magnitude of the joint reaction force;
(c) the direction of the joint reaction force.

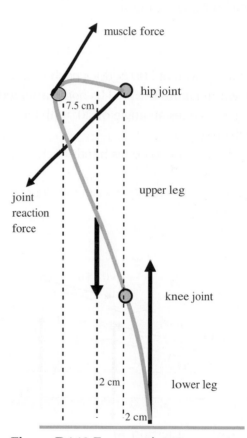

Figure D4.18 For question 8.

9 Refer to Figure D4.19, which shows a person bending to lift an object. The object has a weight of 300 N, the spine makes an angle of 70° to the vertical and the muscle force makes an angle of 10° with the spine. The weight of the upper body is 460 N acting at C such that PC = (2/3)PS. Find:
(a) the muscle force E;
(b) the reaction force R;
(c) the angle the force R makes with the spine.

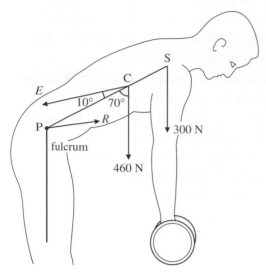

Figure D4.19 For question 9.

10 A man of weight 700 N does push-ups, as shown in Figure D4.20. His body, assumed straight, makes an angle of 20° with the horizontal.
   (a) What is the force his hands exert on the floor?
   (b) What is the reaction from the floor on his feet?

Figure D4.20 For question 10.

11 What is the rate of oxygen consumption by a 50 kg person with a metabolic rate per mass of 4 W kg^{-1}.

12 Your mass is 80 kg. For how long must you exercise if your metabolic rate per mass is 9 W kg^{-1} and you want to burn 1 kg of fat?

13 The basal metabolic rate decreases with age. Will an older person get cold faster than a young adult (of the same size and mass)?

14 A 50 kg person with a basal metabolic rate per mass of 1.2 W kg^{-1} and a metabolic rate per mass of 9 W kg^{-1} is walking up an incline at an angle of 5° to the horizontal, with a constant speed of 2.0 m s^{-1}.
   (a) At what rate is the person's potential energy increasing?
   (b) At what rate is energy being produced internally in the person?
   (c) With what efficiency is the person walking uphill?
   (d) Why is the person likely to sweat during the climb?

15 Explain why an overweight person is likely to sweat much more than a person of the same age but of normal weight after the same amount of identical exercise.

16 A person of mass 75 kg runs up a staircase of total vertical height 14 m in 5.0 s.
   (a) What is the rate of increase of his gravitational potential energy?
   (b) If the efficiency of the run is 20% and his basal metabolic rate is 1.1 W kg^{-1}, find his metabolic rate.
   (c) *Estimate* the mass of sweat that must be excreted? (The latent heat of vaporization of water at 100 °C is 2257 J g^{-1}.) Name *two* assumptions you have made in getting the answer for the mass.

17 People who, as a result of an accident perhaps, are forced to endure a long exposure to cold are found curled up. Why do they curl up?

18 Why do wet clothes provide less protection from heat loss than dry clothes?

19 What would be the dominant mechanisms for heat loss when:
   (a) walking briskly on a hot sunny day at 35 °C;
   (b) walking briskly on a very cold day at −10 °C?

Radiation in medicine

This chapter introduces the main effects of radiation on living things and the methods used to measure the radiation absorbed.

Objectives

By the end of this chapter you should be able to:
* outline the *effects of ionizing radiations on living things*;
* describe *how radiation is measured*;
* solve problems involving *absorbed dose*, $D = \frac{E}{m}$, *dose equivalent*, $H = QD$, and *exposure*, $X = \frac{Q}{m}$;
* state the meaning of *half-life*, *biological half-life* and *effective half-life* and solve problems using $\frac{1}{T_E} = \frac{1}{T_P} + \frac{1}{T_B}$.

Biological effects of radiation and dosimetry

We are all exposed to radiation in our daily lives from either natural or artificial sources, or because of special conditions in the workplace. Natural sources include radon, gamma rays from the earth, unstable isotopes found in food and cosmic rays. Artificial sources include the exposure to radiation for medical reasons, radiations from building materials, radiation from nuclear weapons testing, and accidents in nuclear power plants. Workers in research labs and radiology personnel in hospitals are exposed to radiation as a result of their work.

The starting point of any discussion on the effects of radiation on living matter might be to realize that the energy that is required to break a molecular bond is of the order of 1 eV. Radiations that deposit energies of this order, or more, are therefore bound to alter the molecular structure of the matter they travel through. It is now generally accepted that any amount of radiation, no matter how small, is harmful, and that in dealing with radiation the following general rules must be followed:

> * Keep as far as possible from the source.
> * Keep the exposure as short as possible.
> * Use shielding whenever possible.

The absorption of even a single photon of energy by a single molecule of a living organism may not be harmless. The absorbed photon may have the effect of ejecting an electron from its molecule and this may imply that the structure of the molecule changes. For example, if the ejected electron was crucial in the chemical bonds holding the molecule together, then the molecule may break apart. Enzymes may not operate correctly if the molecule is altered in any way. It is also known that irradiation of water produces very reactive free radicals (see the reactions below). As most living organisms contain water, the production of these free radicals induces changes in the chemical structures of the surrounding molecules with biological implications. Such reactions include

$$H_2O \xrightarrow{radiation} H_2O^+ + e^-$$
$$H_2O^+ + H_2O \rightarrow H_3O^+ + HO^\bullet$$
$$e^- + H_2O \rightarrow OH^- + H^\bullet$$

The damage of a few molecules from radiation will not, in general, result in loss of function for the cell, but if the amount of radiation received is large, then the cell may not be able to recover its function. By contrast, damage to a gene will, in general, affect the function of the cell. Radiation is particularly damaging to the bone marrow, which is responsible for producing blood cells, and seriously impairs the human immune system. Thus, leukaemia and other forms of cancer are common results of exposure to radiation.

To understand the effect of radiation on living matter we must first define appropriate quantities that measure the amount of radiation received.

▶ *Absorbed dose* is defined as the amount of energy E absorbed by a unit mass of the irradiated material, that is

$$D = \frac{E}{m}$$

where E is the energy absorbed by a mass m. Its unit is joule per kilogram ($J\,kg^{-1}$) and this is defined as the gray (Gy).

An older unit still in use is the rad:

$$1\,Gy = 1\,J\,kg^{-1} = 100\,rad$$

▶ The *damage* produced by radiation is not only proportional to the absorbed dose but also depends on the *type of radiation* used. Thus, we define the *dose equivalent* to be

$$H = QD$$

where Q is a dimensionless number that characterizes various different radiations. It

is called the *quality factor* of the radiation. The unit of H is the same as that for absorbed dose (i.e. joule per kilogram) but to distinguish the two quantities we use the sievert (Sv) for the dose equivalent.

Another unit still in use is the rem (standing for radiation equivalent man)

$$1\,Sv = 1\,J\,kg^{-1} = 100\,rem$$

Table D5.1 gives the quality factor values of some different types of radiation.

Type of radiation	Q
β, γ and X-rays	1
Fast protons	1
Slow neutrons	3
Fast neutrons	10
α particles	20

Table D5.1 Quality factor values of different types of radiation.

The quality factor is related to the relative biological equivalent, which is defined as

$$RBE = \frac{\text{absorbed dose to produce an effect with 250 keV X-rays}}{\text{absorbed dose to produce same effect with radiation used}}$$

For our purposes here we will take Q and RBE to be the same.

Example questions

Q1

A person of mass 60 kg receives 0.8 J of energy from radiation of quality 5 to her whole body. What is the absorbed dose? What is the dose equivalent she receives?

Answer

The absorbed dose is

$$D = \frac{E}{m}$$
$$= \frac{0.8\,J}{60\,kg}$$
$$= 13.3\,mGy$$

The dose equivalent is

$H = QD$

$= 5 \times 13.3 \, \text{mSv}$

$= 66.7 \, \text{mSv}$

Q2

A person of mass 70 kg receives a whole-body dose equivalent of 30 mSv. Half of this amount is of quality 1 and the other half of quality 10. How much energy did the person receive?

Answer

The dose equivalent is

$H = QD$

and so

$15 = 1 \times D_1$

$\Rightarrow D_1 = 15 \, \text{mGy}$

$\Rightarrow E_1 = 70 \, \text{kg} \times 15 \times 10^{-3} \, \text{J kg}^{-1}$

$\quad = 1.05 \, \text{J}$

and

$15 = 10 \times D_2$

$\Rightarrow D_2 = 1.5 \, \text{mGy}$

$\Rightarrow E_2 = 70 \, \text{kg} \times 1.5 \times 10^{-3} \, \text{J kg}^{-1}$

$\quad = 0.10 \, \text{J}$

giving a total energy of 1.15 J.

To get an idea of the meaning of the sievert, note that a dose equivalent of more than 100 Sv results in death in a few days due to massive damage to large numbers of cells. With an amount of about 10 Sv symptoms of *radiation sickness* (nausea, diarrhoea, vomiting) begin to appear a few hours after exposure and death follows in a few weeks. In radiation therapy, amounts up to 3 Sv are administered but patients have survived much larger amounts. A typical chest X-ray examination gives 0.1 mSv and a flight at a height of 8 km gives 2 μSv per hour. Generally, the danger increases with the amount of dose equivalent and the probability of cancer increases by 1% for every sievert of radiation received.

The International Commission on Radiological Protection recommends that on a yearly basis:

- a person working with radioactive materials should not be exposed to more than 50 mSv;
- other adults should not be exposed to more than 5 mSv;
- children should not be exposed to more than 0.5 mSv.

The ICRP's recommendations for protection also include short-term limits of exposure of:

- no more than 10 μSv per hour for γ rays at a distance of 10 cm;
- no more than 50 μSv per hour for β particles, also at a distance of 10 cm from the source;
- particle sources with activity larger than 40 kBq should be avoided.

(Recall that the becquerel (Bq) is a unit of activity and equals one decay per second.)

The amounts of dose equivalent from various sources in everyday life depend on the location and elevation above sea level. Table D5.2 summarizes the average amounts of radiation a person receives in a year. The total is 3.37 mSv per person per year. Radon contributes 59% of this radiation.

Source	Equivalent dose/mSv	Percentage
Radon	2.0	59
Cosmic rays	0.27	8
Building materials	0.30	9
Isotopes in body from food	0.20	6
Isotopes in the earth	0.20	6
Medical procedures	0.40	12
TOTAL	3.37 mSv	100%

Table D5.2 Amounts of radiation received per year by an average person living in a modern city at sea level.

(The amount from cosmic rays increases by about 0.2 mSv for every 1 km of elevation.)

> ▶ A related quantity is *exposure*, X, which is defined as the total amount of produced charge q due to ionization in a mass m of air:
>
> $$X = \frac{q}{m}$$

Ionization means that positive and negative charges are produced. In defining exposure we measure only the positive charges. The unit for exposure is coulomb per kilogram ($C\ kg^{-1}$). Thus, ionization of exposure $50\ C\ kg^{-1}$ means that in 1 kg of air 50 C of positive or negative charge is produced as a result of ionization by a particular radiation. The *exposure rate* is defined as the exposure per unit time, which is the amount of charge produced in 1 kg of air per second.

There is a connection between exposure and absorbed dose. This is because in order to produce one ion in air an energy of approximately 34 eV is needed. Thus, let the exposure of a given radiation be E (in units of $C\ kg^{-1}$). This radiation produces

$$E\ \frac{C}{kg} = E \times \frac{1}{1.6 \times 10^{-19}}\ \frac{electrons}{kg}$$

Each electron requires an energy of 34 eV and thus the energy absorbed (absorbed dose) is

$$D \text{ (in Gy)} = E \times \frac{1}{1.6 \times 10^{-19}}\ \frac{34\ eV}{kg}$$
$$= E \times 34\ \frac{J}{kg}$$
$$= 34E\ (\text{in J kg}^{-1})$$

This is the connection between absorbed dose *in air* and exposure. For materials other than air, we must take into account the fact that it takes different energies to produce an ion. Thus, the relationship between exposure and absorbed dose is

$$D \text{ (in Gy)} = fE \text{ (in J kg}^{-1})$$

where f is a factor that depends on the material and the photon energy. For muscle, f is approximately 40, independent of the photon energy. For bone, f drops from 150 at very low photon energies to about 40 for energies up to 0.1 MeV. For higher energies, f stays at about 40.

Example question

Q3 ▬▬▬▬▬▬

Potassium-40 (^{40}K) is a natural radioactive isotope of ordinary potassium with a half-life of 1.27×10^9 yr. The abundance by mass of ^{40}K is 0.0118%. ^{40}K decays by beta emission. The electrons in this decay have an average energy of 0.44 MeV. Calculate the yearly dose equivalent due to ^{40}K in a 70 kg body. The K content by mass of an average human body is 0.18%.

Answer

The amount of potassium-40 in the body of a 70 kg person is

$$70 \times 0.0018 \times 0.000118\ kg = 1.5 \times 10^{-2}\ g$$

The activity of this amount of ^{40}K is $A = \lambda N_0$, where the decay constant can be found from

$$\lambda = \frac{0.693}{T_{1/2}}$$
$$= 1.73 \times 10^{-17}\ s^{-1}$$

and the number of ^{40}K nuclei present is

$$N_0 = \frac{1.5 \times 10^{-2}}{40} \times 6.02 \times 10^{23}$$
$$= 2.3 \times 10^{20}$$

Thus, the activity is

$$A = \lambda N_0$$
$$= 1.7 \times 10^{-17} \times 2.3 \times 10^{20}$$
$$= 3.9 \times 10^3\ Bq$$

The number of nuclei that decay in one year is thus (approximately)

$$3.9 \times 10^3 \times 365 \times 24 \times 60 \times 60 = 1.2 \times 10^{11}$$

Each deposits an average energy of 0.44 MeV and hence the total energy in a year is

$$1.2 \times 10^{11} \times 0.44 = 0.53 \times 10^{11}\ MeV$$
$$= 8.4 \times 10^{-3}\ J$$

The absorbed (whole-body) dose is thus

$$D = \frac{8.4 \times 10^{-3}}{70}\ Gy$$
$$= 0.12\ mGy$$

Since the Q factor for electrons is 1, the dose equivalent is $H = 0.12$ mSv.

Radiation therapy

Radiation is harmful to healthy cells, but it can also be harmful to malignant, cancerous cells. Radiation can thus be used to destroy such cells. In radiation therapy, X-rays or gamma rays can be directed in *very narrow beams* at the collection of cancerous cells to destroy them. In order to minimize the damage to the surrounding normal cells, tissue and bone, it is necessary to direct the beam at the tumour from a number of different angles. This assumes that the tumour is well localized and it is only in this case that radiation therapy can be effective. The energies of X-rays and gamma rays used in cancer treatment vary from 200 keV to 5 MeV.

The tumour may also be *injected* or *implanted* with radioactive material whose radiation is released *within* the tumour, thus destroying it. Radium, which is an alpha particle emitter, is commonly used in this way. A related technique is to give the patient a quantity of a radioactive isotope of iodine, $^{131}_{53}$I, which, once in the blood stream, will accumulate in the thyroid gland. Its radiation can then kill cancerous cells in that gland. An isotope of gold, ^{198}Au, collects in the lungs, destroying cancerous cells in the fluids that line the lungs.

Physical and biological half-life

A radioactive isotope decays, as we have seen in nuclear physics, according to an exponential decay law, so that the number of nuclei that are undecayed after time t is given by

$$N = N_0 e^{-\lambda t}$$

or equivalently

$$N = N_0 \left(\frac{1}{2}\right)^{t/T_{1/2}}$$

where the *physical decay constant* λ_P is related to the *physical half-life* through

$$T_{1/2} = \frac{0.693}{\lambda_P}$$

Note that by differentiating this equation we obtain

$$\Delta N = -\lambda_P N \Delta t$$

The activity of the isotope (i.e. the number of decays per second) obeys a similar exponential decay law:

$$A = A_0 e^{-\lambda_P t}$$

where the initial activity is given by $\lambda_P N_0$. Here, and in the decay formula above, N_0 stands for the number of radioactive nuclei initially present. When a radioactive isotope is taken in by a patient, however, its activity falls off faster than the law above implies. This is because the number of isotope nuclei in the body decreases not only by radioactive decay (*physical decay*) but also because some of the radioactive material is removed from the body as waste (sweat, urine, etc.), in other words, by *biological decay*. If we assume that the biological removal of the isotope obeys an exponential law as well, with a decay constant λ, then in a time Δt the number of nuclei removed is

$$\Delta N = -\lambda_P N \Delta t - \lambda_B N \Delta t$$
$$= -\lambda_E N \Delta t$$
$$\lambda_E = \lambda_P + \lambda_B$$

where λ_E is the effective decay constant, which represents both physical decay and biological decrease of nuclei in the body. Thus, we may define effective, physical and biological half-lives from these constants and hence (recall the definition of a decay constant)

$$\frac{1}{T_E} = \frac{1}{T_P} + \frac{1}{T_B}$$

▶ In other words, *physical* half-life is the time for half of the radioactive nuclei to *decay* away and *biological* half-life is the time for half of the radioactive nuclei to be *removed* from the body by biological processes. The effective half-life is the time for half of the radioactive nuclei to be removed by both decay and biological removal.

Example question

Q4

A radioactive isotope has a physical half-life of 24 days and a biological half-life of 12 days. If 4 g of this isotope are injected into a patient, how much is left after 24 days?

Answer

The effective half-life is

$$\frac{1}{T} = \frac{1}{24} + \frac{1}{12}$$
$$\Rightarrow T = 8 \text{ days}$$

After 24 days (i.e. three effective half-lives) the amount that is left is

$$4\left(\frac{1}{2}\right)^3 = 0.5 \text{ g}$$

Questions

1 How much energy is deposited in a 70 kg person who receives an absorbed dose of radiation of 0.2 Gy?

2 How much energy is deposited in a 70 kg person who receives a dose equivalent of 0.2 Sv of slow neutrons?

3 (a) Which does more damage, 10 Gy of alpha particles or 10 Gy of gamma rays?
   (b) Which does more damage, 10 Sv of alpha particles or 10 Sv of gamma rays?

4 If a person receives 2 μSv per hour during a flight at an altitude of 8 km, how many trips can a person take in a year if their dose equivalent is not to exceed 1 mSv. (Take each trip to be 3 h long.)

5 A student with a broken leg receives X-rays from a 50 keV machine. If the broken bone has a mass of 0.75 kg and the equivalent dose

is 0.40 mSv, find:
(a) the absorbed dose;
(b) the energy deposited in the bone;
(c) the number of photons absorbed by the bone.

6 A beta ray source of activity 8.0×10^4 Bq and a half-life of 6 h is injected into a spherical tumour of radius 1.0 cm and density 1.3×10^3 kg m^{-3}. The energy of the electrons emitted is 3.5 MeV. Calculate the dose equivalent in the tumour 30 min after injection. Mention any assumptions you make in your calculations. How would the result of your calculation change if the source had been a gamma ray source.

7 A patient is exposed for 5.0 s to a radioactive source that emits gamma rays of energy 2.7 MeV. The activity of the source was 3.0×10^{12} Bq, and about 3% of the gamma rays reach the patient. If his mass is 70 kg, find the dose equivalent he receives.

8 A 70 kg person stands at a distance of 5 m from a source of gamma rays of activity 1.5×10^9 Bq, exposing a body surface area of 0.09 m^2 to the source. Each gamma ray has an energy of 1.4 MeV. Assume that 1/4 of the emitted gamma rays are absorbed by the person.
(a) What is the intensity of the gamma rays at the position of the person?
(b) How much energy does the person receive in 1 s?
If the person works for 2 h near this source find:
(c) the whole-body absorbed dose;
(d) the effective dose she receives.

9 The radioisotopes used in therapy generally have very much longer half-lives than those used in diagnosis. Why is such a difference desirable?

Models of the universe

The earliest astronomers were fascinated by their observations of the motion of the celestial bodies such as the moon, the sun, the planets and the stars. This chapter is a very brief introduction to these motions and the attempts of the ancient astronomers to come to an understanding of them by constructing models of the universe. The early models of Ptolemy were geocentric, in that the earth was considered to be at the centre of a huge celestial sphere. All other bodies were firmly embedded on this sphere, which rotated around the earth. This model was to survive for almost 2000 years until Copernicus showed that things were otherwise.

Objectives

By the end of this chapter you should be able to:

- state the main astronomical observations about the *motion of the stars, the sun, the moon and the planets*;
- describe the attempts by the ancients to *understand these observations*;
- state the main facts about the *geocentric Ptolemaic system*;
- state the main facts about the *heliocentric Copernican system*;
- appreciate the *contributions made by Brahe and Kepler* to our understanding of planetary motion;
- appreciate the understanding of planetary motion that was provided to us by *Newton's theories of mechanics and gravitation*.

Astronomical observations

The observation of the motion of the stars is greatly complicated by the fact that the earth is itself moving. In the course of a night, stars and constellations appear to move across the sky from east to west. The ancient astronomers noticed, however, that the *relative* positions of the stars and constellations remained unchanged. That gave rise to the notion of the *celestial sphere*, a huge sphere surrounding and rotating around the earth, on whose surface the stars and constellations were firmly embedded (see Figure E1.1). We know now that the rotation of the stars and constellations is a consequence of the rotation of the earth about its axis. The axis of rotation of the earth, when extended, intersects the celestial sphere at the north and south celestial poles. The star Polaris (the North Star) is almost exactly on the celestial north pole and so appears not to move at all. The rest of the stars and constellations appear to rotate about it.

For an observer at an arbitrary point on the surface of the earth, a vertical straight line extended upwards will intersect the celestial sphere at a point called the *zenith*. If the observer is at the north pole of the earth, the zenith and the celestial north pole coincide. At the south pole of the earth, the zenith coincides with the celestial south pole.

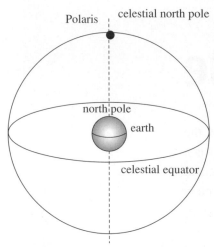

Figure E1.1 The celestial sphere on which the stars seem to be fixed. The star Polaris is almost right on the celestial north pole.

The motion of the stars

Consider first an observer at the north pole of the earth (see Figure E1.2). The stars appear to move in circles in the course of one day. The plane of each circle is parallel to the plane of the equator of the earth. All the stars in the north celestial hemisphere are visible and *none* rises or sets; the stars in the south celestial hemisphere never come into view. For this observer, the sun, the moon and the planets rise and set every time their orbit crosses the celestial equator. The sun rises on 21 March (the *vernal equinox*) and sets on 21 September (the *autumnal equinox*).

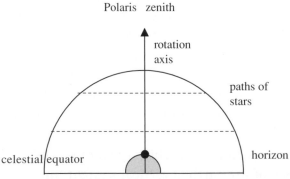

Figure E1.2 Paths of stars for an observer at the north pole of the earth. No stars rise or set since none crosses the horizon.

For an observer at the equator of the earth, *all* stars rise and set as they cross the horizon (see Figure E1.3). The paths of stars (including the sun) are at right angles to the horizon and each

star spends half the day (i.e. 12 hours) above the horizon and the other half below the horizon. The amount of sunshine is therefore 12 hours per day at the equator.

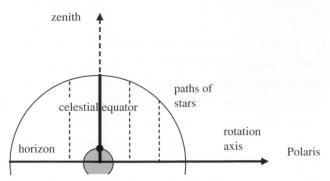

Figure E1.3 Paths of stars for an observer on earth's equator. All stars rise and set as they cross the horizon. All parts of the sky become visible.

Let us consider, finally, another observer at an arbitrary latitude (see Figure E1.4). Here we see that some stars never rise or set since their paths never cross the horizon, while others do. The paths of the stars are at an angle to the horizon.

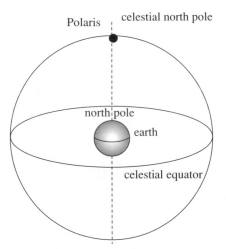

Figure E1.4 The motion of the stars, according to an observer at an arbitrary latitude. Those stars that cross the horizon rise and set. Some stars never cross the horizon and so never rise or set.

Example question

Q1

Show in a diagram based on Figure E1.4 those stars that never rise for an observer at an arbitrary latitude.

Answer

See Figure E1.5.

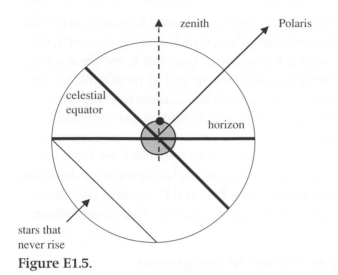

Figure E1.5.

A photograph taken of the night sky with a long time exposure would show arcs traced by stars as the 'celestial sphere rotates' (i.e. as the earth rotates about its axis). Such a photograph of star trails is shown in Figure E1.6.

The motion of the sun

The sun appears to trace a path on the celestial sphere known as the ecliptic. The plane of the ecliptic makes an angle of about 23° with the plane of the celestial equator (see Figure E1.7a). The point on the ecliptic when the sun is at its highest point above the equatorial plane is known as the *summer solstice* (see Figure E1.7b). It takes place on 21 June; it is the longest day of the year in the northern hemisphere and the shortest in the south. It corresponds to the earth's north pole pointing almost directly at the sun. Six months later, on 21 December, the sun is at the lowest point below the equatorial plane, marking the *winter solstice* (see Figure E1.7c). This day is the longest in the southern hemisphere and the shortest in the north. During the northern hemisphere summer, the sun stays high in the sky and as one moves north and past a latitude of about 67°, the sun actually does not set, creating the effect of the 'midnight sun'. Conversely, during the northern hemisphere winter, the sun stays low in the sky and as we move north of points with latitude 67°, the sun does not rise.

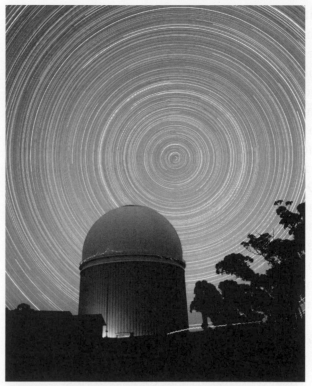

Figure E1.6 Photograph of the night sky over a long period of time showing stars moving along arcs. Copyright: Anglo-Australian Observatory. Photograph by David Malin.

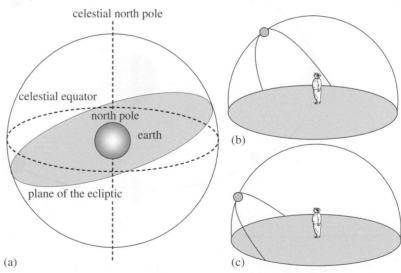

Figure E1.7 The sun appears to trace a path on the celestial sphere known as the ecliptic. The plane of the ecliptic makes an angle of about 23° with the plane of the celestial equator. In the summer, the sun rises high in the sky. In the winter, the sun stays closer to the horizon. Shown are views from a point with a latitude of about 40°.

The motion of the moon

The earth's satellite, the moon, fascinated early people. We know from Aristotle's writings that the ancients knew and understood many of the facts about the moon, such as its phases, eclipses and its distance from earth relative to the earth–sun distance. When the moon is between the earth and the sun, on the line joining them, it is hardly visible. This is the beginning of a 29-day cycle (the time it takes the moon to orbit the earth) in which we see it in different shapes – these are the *phases* of the moon. The Babylonians defined the interval of 29 days to be the length of a *month*. The root of the words 'moon' and 'month' is common in many Indo-European languages. For example, it is 'μην' in Greek.

> ▶ Contrary to what is commonly believed, the phases of the moon are not caused by the shadow of the earth on the moon. Since the moon only reflects light, the shape we observe depends on what fraction of the moon's illuminated side we are able to see.

Thus, in position A of Figure E1.8, no part of the illuminated side is visible and we have what is called a *new moon*. In position B, we see a *waxing* (or increasing) *crescent* and in position C we are able to see half of the illuminated side. This moon is in a phase called the *quarter moon*. In position D, the lit moon has grown even more (*waxing gibbous*) and in position E we have a *full moon*. The moon now begins to wane (or decrease) and in positions F, G and H we have the moon in its *waning gibbous*, *quarter* and *crescent phases*.

The motion of the planets

The word 'planet' comes from the Greek word *planetes*, meaning wanderer. The early astronomers observed that the motion of the planets on the celestial sphere was circular, but it soon became evident from more careful observations that planets appeared to show *retrograde* motion, which means they sometimes turned back on their path before turning again and continuing on the original path – the planets wandered (see Figure E1.9).

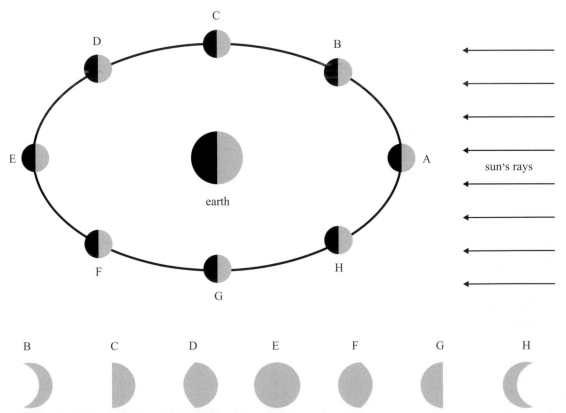

Figure E1.8 The phases of the moon. The shape we observe depends on what fraction of the moon's illuminated surface we can see. Note that the moon always has the same hemisphere turned to us.

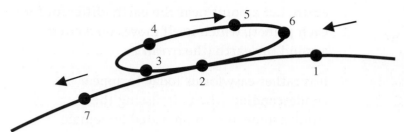

Figure E1.9 The retrograde motion of a planet is the apparent turning back on its orbit. This is the observed motion of the planet relative to the distant stars. The diagram shows seven successive positions of a planet.

This is motion that we observe on earth as we look at a planet with respect to a background of very distant stars.

Models of the universe

The earliest written astronomical records date back to the Babylonians, who were especially interested in the motion of the moon, as it fixed their calendar. Somewhat later, the Egyptians paid particular attention to the motion of the star Sirius, which was considered to determine the flooding of the Nile. (Interestingly, on a different continent and a vastly different time period, the Mayas of Central America confined their attention to the planet Venus and used its motion as an aid in fixing their calendar.)

It was, however, the ancient Greeks who organized the existing astronomical knowledge and vastly expanded it.

Aristotle and Ptolemy

One of the first models to be built to explain the motion of the celestial bodies is due to Thales of Miletus (c.636–c.546 BC). Thales considered the earth to be at the centre of the universe. The rest of the heavens rotated around the earth and the earth was flat and motionless. The stars and the planets were assumed to rest on spheres that rotated around the earth. The ancient Greeks knew well the difference between planets and stars. Stars were holes in the fabric of the heavens giving a glimpse of the residence of the gods beyond the heavens. Planets moved (or wandered) on this fabric, i.e. they moved with respect to the stars, sometimes briefly reversing direction to trace back their path only to reverse again and continue in the original direction. The circle being a perfect shape was the ancients' natural choice for the path of the celestial bodies and the sphere the natural candidate for their shape. The idea of the earth at the centre of the universe was developed further by the mathematician Eudoxus of Cnidus (c.400–c.353 BC). The geocentric view of the universe was made part of the established knowledge of the times by Aristotle (384–322 BC).

> ▶ It soon became evident that the observed motion of the planets was not exactly circular. As indicated above, planets appeared to move in a very complicated way, sometimes turning back on their path before turning again and continuing on the original path (*retrograde motion*). Their brightness and speed were also not constant as they moved through space.

These phenomena had to be explained. The preoccupation with the circle led the early astronomers to hypothesize that planets, in addition to the circular path around the earth, moved, at the same time, along smaller circles, *epicycles*, around the circular orbit. This required that the older ideas of Aristotle and Eudoxus had to be modified. It was Hipparchos (fl.160–125 BC) who made the crucial modification by introducing epicycles (c.130 BC).

> ▶ These smaller circles were called *epicycles*. In other words, the centre of the epicycle moves on a circle around the earth and *at the same time* the planet moves along the epicycle – see Figure E1.10.

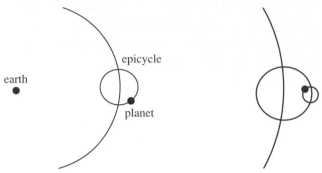

Figure E1.10 A model of a planet orbiting the earth with one and two epicycles.

It is clear that by choosing an appropriate epicycle centre speed and a planet speed along the epicycle, an arbitrary path may be constructed.

Using one epicycle for each planet was not enough, however. Ptolemy (AD *c*.90–168), who had perfected the geocentric model around AD 140, was forced to introduce over 50 epicycles in order to reach agreement with observations (see Figure E1.11). Figure E1.12 shows how epicycles help solve the problem of retrograde motion. In addition to epicycles Ptolemy also assumed that the centre of each planet's orbit was not the

earth, but a point near the earth (different for each planet), which itself moves on a circle around the earth (the *eccentric*).

It is rather easy for us today to appear condescending when discussing the cumbersome and complicated Ptolemaic system. It must be remembered, though, that his model could explain practically every observation available to him. Ptolemy knew that the speed of the moon around the earth was not constant and could explain it by giving the moon an epicycle whose period was almost (but not quite) equal to the orbit period. The motion of Mercury and Venus could similarly be explained, in particular why sometimes one planet and then the other appear as 'morning stars'. In addition, the combination of epicycles and eccentrics allowed him to account for the eccentricity of the orbit of Mars while maintaining at all times motion on circles at constant speed! Ptolemy's great work *The Almagest*, known by its Arabic translation, was the basis of western astronomy from ancient times until the end of the Middle Ages.

To see how an epicycle helps explain the puzzling retrograde motion, consider Figure E1.12.

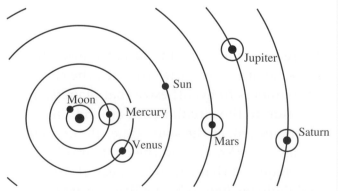

Figure E1.11 The Ptolemaic geocentric system with one epicycle per planet. Ptolemy was forced to consider more than 50 epicycles to account for the observed motion of the planets.

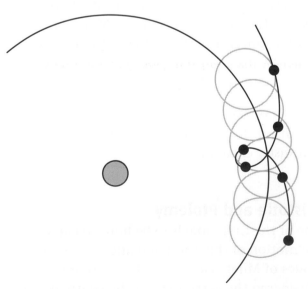

Figure E1.12 The centre of the epicycle moves along the circular orbit. The planet moves along the epicycle. Observed from the earth this gives retrograde motion.

Aristarchos

Hipparchos and Aristarchos of Samos (310–230 BC) were the two greatest astronomers of the ancient world. Less than a century after Aristotle's death, Aristarchos put forth the view that the sun, and not the earth, was at the centre of rotation of the celestial bodies. His argument followed an earlier one by Herakleides of Pontos (390–310 BC).

> ▶ Both men observed that nothing in the way the heavens looked would change if one assumed that it was the sun that was at rest and the earth moving. Furthermore, the daily rotation of the stars could be explained by the rotation of the earth and not necessarily by the rotation of the heavenly sphere.

However, his model went largely unnoticed, one reason being the total respect that was afforded to Aristotle's ideas. Aristarchos was closer to what we might call scientific thinking than many of his predecessors. One of his many ingenious discoveries was the measurement of the distance between the earth and the sun in terms of the distance between the earth and the moon. He knew that at quarter moon (i.e. when half of the side of the moon facing the earth is illuminated) the line from the earth to the moon and that from the sun to the moon made a right angle. He measured the angle θ in Figure E1.13 to be 87° and, using trigonometry, he deduced that

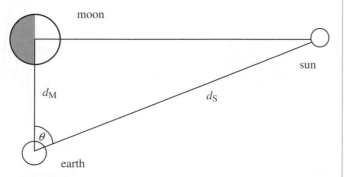

Figure E1.13 At quarter moon the line from the earth to the moon and that from the sun to the moon meet at a right angle.

$$\cos 87° = \frac{d_M}{d_S}$$

$$\Rightarrow d_S = \frac{d_M}{\cos 87°} = 19.1 \times d_M$$

It is not easy to decide when exactly the moon is at quarter moon and so the measurement of the angle is difficult. The correct angle is only slightly larger (but the answer depends on the cosine of the angle and a small change in the angle results in a big change in the cosine), giving the correct distance of $d_S = 390 \times d_M$.

Supplementary material

Eratosthenes

It is not possible to leave the ancients behind without mentioning Eratosthenes (c.276–194 BC), who knew not only that the earth is round (Aristotle knew that also), but actually measured its radius with extraordinary accuracy. His method is a true jewel of scientific thinking and we include it even though it is not part of the IB syllabus!

Eratosthenes observed that at noon on the summer solstice the sun reflected in the water of a well in the city of Syene (today, Aswan), indicating that the rays of light were coming straight down into the well. At the same time, in Alexandria, a distance of 5000 *stadia* away in the north (1 *stadium* = 158 m), a tower of known height cast a shadow on the ground whose length could be measured. This is illustrated in Figure E1.14. From these measurements, Eratosthenes could deduce that the angle the rays of light made with the vertical at Alexandria (the direction of the tower) was 7.2°. The distance between Alexandria and Syene is given by $s = R\theta$, where R is the earth's radius and the angle θ is expressed in radians. Thus

$$R = \frac{s}{\theta}$$
$$= \frac{5000 \times 158}{7.2° \times (\pi/180°)} \text{ m}$$
$$= 6287 \text{ km}$$

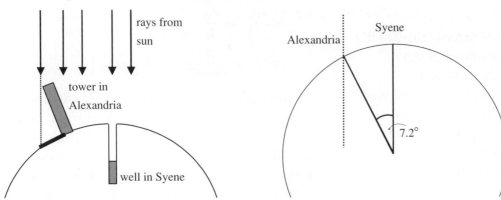

Figure E1.14 The angle between the rays of the sun and the tower is the same as the angle subtended at the earth's centre by the radii to Alexandria and Syene.

Copernicus and Galileo

We come finally to Nicolas Copernicus (1473–1543), who was the first after Aristarchos to propose a *heliocentric* model of the solar system (Figure E1.15a). The sun was at the centre and the planets rotated around it. The earth rotated about its axis, which could explain the (apparent) motion of the sun in the sky in the course of a day from sunrise to sunset, as well as the seasons. To explain observations in detail, however, he was forced to introduce epicycles, just as Ptolemy did, as well as eccentric circles; very soon his model was just as complicated as Ptolemy's, without being any more precise. He did, however, explain retrograde motion in a simple way. It was the *difference in speed* with which the earth and another planet orbit the sun that gave the illusion of retrograde motion as the planet was observed from earth at different angles relative to the background of the distant stars (see Figure E1.15b).

The model was attacked by the church as it was considered to deviate from the Holy Scriptures. One of the most ardent supporters of the Copernican theory, Giordano Bruno (1548–1600), paid with his life for his beliefs.

Galileo Galilei (1564–1642) (about whom we will say more in Chapter E2) also knew that the Ptolemaic system was wrong. His own observations clearly showed that there were features on the moon, which thus was not the perfect sphere the ancients believed it to be. He could also observe the phases of Venus, for which the Ptolemaic system could offer no explanation. For his belief in a heliocentric system, Galileo was also to have his confrontation with the church. He escaped Bruno's fate by recanting his views.

(a)

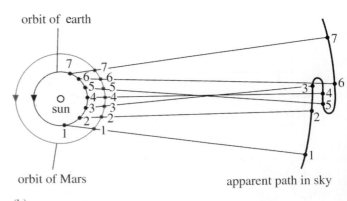

(b)

Figure E1.15 (a) Copernicus's sun-centred model of the universe. (b) Explanation of retrograde motion in a heliocentric model.

▶ Using his telescope, Galileo observed that Jupiter had moons orbiting it. Here was more evidence that celestial bodies orbited centres other than the earth. He also observed the phases of Venus and knew that the old Ptolemaic system could not account for them. So, he too put forth the view that the earth revolved around the sun.

In 1616, Pope Paul V ordered Galileo to stop his 'heretical' statements. Under the more liberal Pope Urban VIII, Galileo was able to publish his *Discorsi* (Dialogues) in 1638. We will mention this book again in Chapter E2. One of the three characters in the book, Simplicio, is a defender of the old scholastic tradition and the Ptolemaic system, and is not a particularly intelligent character. It is said that the Pope recognized himself in Simplicio and, as a result, Galileo was forced to retract all his 'heretical' statements and spend the last years of his life under house arrest.

Kepler's laws

In the years between 1576 and 1596, Tycho Brahe (1546–1601), a Danish astronomer, made a precise catalogue of over 1000 stars based on very many and accurate observations. At the same time, he undertook very precise measurements of the motion of the planets – and all this before the invention of the telescope! One of Tycho Brahe's great discoveries was the observation in 1572 of a supernova in the constellation of Cassiopeia. This showed clearly that the 'heavens' were not a static, unchanging pattern but a dynamic arena of physical phenomena. Brahe's observations, made almost half a millennium ago, were so accurate that many present measurements do not deviate from his measurements by more than one arcminute (1/60 of a degree). It was the precision of these measurements that would allow new theories to come forth. Brahe himself saw the problems of the Ptolemaic system but did not totally embrace Copernicus's ideas.

Instead, he developed a model of his own in which the planets did move around the sun, but the sun revolved around the earth. Brahe reasoned (correctly) that if the earth moved, then the stars would appear in different positions when viewed from different places along the earth's orbit (an early use of parallax). His observations, however, did not show such differences. Now we know that stars are so very far away that their parallaxes are too small for Brahe to have been able to measure. On the other hand, Brahe could not dare imagine that the universe was so big for the stars to be so far away.

In 1600, Brahe's observations on the motion of the planet Mars were handed to his mathematically (and mystically) minded assistant, Johannes Kepler (1571–1630), with the task of making sense out of them. Kepler struggled with Brahe's data for nine years, calculating and recalculating possible orbits, toying with old ideas of epicycles and circular orbits until, finally, he came up with two laws that were consistent with Brahe's observations:

1 Planets move in ellipses around the sun, the sun being at one of the foci of each ellipse.

2 The line from the sun to the planet sweeps out equal areas in equal times (see Figure E1.16).

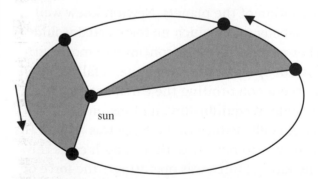

Figure E1.16 An illustration of Kepler's second law.

After another nine years' work, in 1618 he figured out his third law:

3 The time taken to complete one full revolution is proportional to the 3/2 power of the mean distance from the sun.

Example question

Q2 ▬▬▬▬▬▬

Jupiter orbits the sun at a distance that is 5.2 times larger that the earth–sun distance. Determine the length of a year on Jupiter.

Answer

From Kepler's third law

$$\frac{T_J}{T_E} = \frac{R_J^{3/2}}{R_E^{3/2}}$$

$$\Rightarrow \frac{T_J}{T_E} = 5.2^{3/2}$$

$$= 11.86$$

Thus, the year on Jupiter is 11.86 earth years.

Kepler's laws represented an enormous advance in the knowledge about the motion of the planets but they lacked a theoretical basis, a reason why they were true other than the fact that they agreed with observations. Kepler, in other words, had no *theory* as to *why* the planets behaved the way they did. The answer to this question was to be given by Isaac Newton.

Newton's synthesis

Isaac Newton (1642–1727) was aware of the conclusions reached by Johannes Kepler about the motion of the planets. Newton knew well that a body upon which no force acted would either remain at rest or continue to move with constant speed in a straight line. A falling apple and the moon orbiting the earth both violated this state of equilibrium and Newton could immediately deduce that a force was at play. His genius was to recognize that in both cases the same kind of force was operating – the force of gravitation. In the case of the falling apple, it is the force of attraction between the earth and the apple. In the case of the moon, it is the force of attraction between the moon and the earth. The apple, having no initial velocity, falls vertically down. The moon, having an initial velocity at an angle to the force, avoids falling into the earth but orbits it instead.

Newton's law of gravitation is a *universal* law: it applies to objects on earth as well as to objects at any other place in the universe. This idea was later to pervade all of physics. The laws of physics that have been discovered on earth apply everywhere else in the universe.

Newton hypothesized that any two *point* masses attract each other with a force that is given by

$$F = G\frac{M_1 M_2}{r^2}$$

This was not a lucky guess. By considering a planet in a circular orbit around the sun he could deduce that

$$G\frac{Mm}{r^2} = m\frac{v^2}{r}$$

$$\Rightarrow v^2 = \frac{GM}{r}$$

But

$$v = \frac{2\pi r}{T}$$

$$\Rightarrow \frac{GM}{r} = \frac{4\pi^2 r^2}{T^2}$$

$$T^2 = \frac{4\pi^2 r^3}{GM}$$

which is simply Kepler's third law. Newton's law of gravitation leads to Kepler's law; thus, Newton knew he was on the right track. Moreover, Newton also knew that a force behaving like an inverse square law leads to *closed elliptical* orbits for the planets, and this was additional evidence in favour of his law. In fact, using mathematics along with Newton's law of gravitation and Newton's second law of mechanics is enough to *derive* all three of Kepler's laws.

Of course, Newton's law of gravitation applied to point masses. When he tried to apply the law to spherical bodies, he was forced to develop a brand new type of mathematics – calculus – and with its help he was able to show that the same law applies to spherical bodies as well.

Questions

1 Aristotle knew that the brightnesses of Mercury and Venus change. Why is this a problem for the Aristotelian model of the universe?

2 One of the ancient (and not so ancient) objections to a spinning earth was that objects on the earth's surface would fly away. What is the modern answer to this objection?

3 Aristarchos knew that if the earth revolved around the sun, then the position of near stars would shift relative to a background of much more distant stars (the idea of parallax). Yet, Aristarchos could not detect any such shift in his observations. Why? What conclusion did he then draw?

4 The ancient astronomers noticed that the stars moved around the earth but their relative positions stayed the same. How did they explain this? How do we explain this today?

5 The system introduced by Copernicus is no more accurate than that of Ptolemy. Why, then, is it considered a scientific revolution?

6 The Ptolemaic and the Copernican systems both explained most of the astronomical observations available to them. What main difference exists between these models?

7 By drawing appropriate diagrams, explain retrograde motion in the Ptolemaic and Copernican systems.

8 What was the main characteristic of Brahe's astronomical observations?

9 Consider a planet in elliptical orbit around the sun as shown in Figure E1.17. Use Kepler's second law to relate the ratio of the planet's speeds at the points nearest and furthest from the sun to the ratio of the distances of the planet from the sun at those points. More precisely, show that $\frac{v_P}{v_A} = \frac{SA}{SP}$.

10 In view of the result of question 9, can you explain why comets are rarely seen?

11 The asteroid Ceres orbits the sun at a distance that is 2.8 times as great as the distance from the earth to the sun. What is the period of revolution of Ceres?

12 The Martian year lasts for 687 earth days. What is the orbital radius of Mars in terms of that of earth?

13 What was the significance of Kepler's laws in the development of Newton's theory of gravitation?

14 Suppose that we hypothesize that the force of gravitation between two masses is given by the formula $F = \frac{GM_1M_2}{r^n}$, for some value of the parameter n. Apply this formula to the motion of a planet in a circular orbit around the sun and show that agreement with Kepler's third law requires that $n = 2$.

15 Suppose that planets moved around the sun in *circular orbits* but with the sun *not* at the centre of the circle (see Figure E1.18). Would this cause any problems?

Figure E1.18. For question 15.

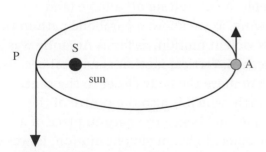

Figure E1.17 For question 9.

Mechanics

In this chapter we discuss Aristotle's ideas about force and motion, Galileo's discovery of the law of accelerated motion and parabolic projectile motion, and the beginning of the scientific method. Experiment, observations and measurement complement logic and mathematical reasoning in deriving the laws of the physical world. The chapter closes with a discussion of mechanical determinism – a discussion that will continue in Chapter E6, where we will look at determinism in the context of quantum theory.

Objectives

By the end of this chapter you should be able to:

- state the main points of *Aristotle's opinions* about force and motion;
- describe how *Galileo* arrived at his laws of motion;
- describe the differences in the methods of Aristotle and Galileo;
- appreciate the great synthesis created by *Newton*;
- state the meaning of the term *mechanical determinism* and describe how it applies to classical Newtonian mechanics.

Aristotle's views on motion and force

The Greek philosopher Aristotle (384–322 BC), in his books *Treatise on the Heavens* and *Physics*, provides perhaps the earliest written attempt at a systematic approach to motion and force and the relationship between them. Aristotle formulated what we might call in today's language a law of motion, which states:

> If a force *F* moves a given body a certain distance in a certain time, then the same force will move half the body the same distance in half the time. Equivalently, the same force will move half the body double the distance in the same time.

By 'half the body' we should understand half the mass. For Aristotle, a force is necessary for motion to take place in the first place and a force must be acting on the body as long as motion takes place. Aristotle also stated that 'a heavy body will fall faster than a lighter body'. If the heavy body is double the weight of the lighter body, then the time of fall for the heavy body will be half that of the lighter body.

Aristotle called falling vertically *natural motion* and contrasted this with all other kinds of motion, which he called *violent motions*. For example, a ball rolling off a table (and following, as we know, a parabolic path in the air) is violent motion, as far as Aristotle was concerned. Vertical motion is natural because it tends to move the body closer to the centre of the earth, which is also the centre of the universe, and hence the natural place of a heavy object to be. In violent motion, however, the air through which the projectile moves acquires the *motive agency* that set the ball in motion in the first place and now somehow pushes the projectile forward.

It is interesting that Aristotle mentioned elsewhere in his writings that a dense medium will offer a force of resistance to the motion of an object through it, this force being proportional to the density of the medium. This statement is in obvious contradiction to the previous paragraph.

It is also interesting to know that Aristotle thought that a vacuum could not exist, and his ideas on this topic are extremely illuminating. According to Aristotle, a vacuum cannot exist because in a vacuum natural motions cannot take place. If a body were to execute a natural motion in a vacuum, it could never come to stop anywhere, as there would be no *preferred* point for the body to stop. The body in a vacuum would then either have to remain at rest or move forever. This is a statement with astonishing similarities to the modern law of inertia or Newton's first law of mechanics.

It is also worth mentioning that Aristotle deduced that if two separate forces were to act on a body, the body would move in the direction of the diagonal of a parallelogram formed by the two forces. In other words, Aristotle essentially discovered the law of vector addition.

Galileo

Aristotle's ideas on force and motion went mainly unchallenged until the time of Galileo Galilei (1564–1642). Galileo himself started his academic career by writing comments on Aristotle's work, and, in his own early writings, the 'heaviness' of a body is defined as the 'natural inclination of the body to take itself to the centre of the earth', a completely Aristotelian point of view. He held the chair of Mathematics at the University of Pisa and began to show signs of departure from the scholastic tradition of his generation when he started to *experiment* with falling bodies and swinging pendulums.

Accelerated motion

By 1604, he seems to have deduced that a body in uniform acceleration starting from rest will cover a distance s in a time t such that

$$s \propto t^2$$

He had theoretical arguments for why this should be so, but while his conclusion was correct, many of the intermediate steps in his derivations were actually in error. There is also evidence that this fundamental result was known to others before Galileo, such as Dominic de Soto (1494–1560) and Nicole Oresme (1320–1382). The latter essentially derived this law in 1377.

Galileo's breakthrough, however, was that he demonstrated the validity of the law by careful experimentation – the beginning of the scientific method. In his book *Discorsi* (Dialogues), published in 1638, three characters, Salviati (representing Galileo himself), Sagredo and Simplicio (representing the old school of thought), discuss mechanics and motion. In one passage, Galileo described his experiments with a ball rolling down an inclined plane and his measurements of the distance travelled and the time taken. It is worthwhile reading the following short excerpts from *A History of Mechanics*, by R. Dugas (Dover Publications, New York, 1988, pp. 138–9).

Galileo described the measurement of the length and width of a ruler that was to serve as the inclined plane and how a groove was carved out in the middle so that a ball would roll down the length of the incline.

It was made quite straight and, in order that it should be polished and quite smooth, the inside was covered with a sheet of parchment as glazed as possible. A short ball of bronze that was very hard, quite round and well polished was allowed to move down the channel. The ruler, made as we have described, had one of its ends lifted to some height above the horizontal plane. As I have said, the ball was allowed to fall in the channel and the duration of its whole journey was observed in the way I have explained. The same trial was repeated many times in order to be quite sure of the length of this time. In this repetition, no difference greater than a tenth of a pulse was ever found. When this observation had been repeated and established with precision, we made the ball fall through only a quarter of length of the channel, and found that the measured duration of fall was always equal to half of the other.

Aware of experimental errors, Galileo realized the need to repeat his measurements many times:

When the observation had been repeated a hundred times, the distances travelled were always found to be in the ratio of the squares of the times, and this was true whatever the inclination of the plane, or that of the channel in which the ball fell, was made to be. We also observed that the durations of fall on differently inclined planes were in proportion assigned to them by our experiments.

He did not neglect to say how exactly each quantity was measured, in particular the very difficult measurement of time:

As for the measurement of the time, a large bucket filled with water was suspended in the air. A small hole in its base allowed a thin stream of water to escape, and this was caught in a small receptacle throughout the duration of the ball's descent of the channel, or of portions of it. The quantities of water caught in this way were weighed on a very accurate balance. The differences and relations of these weights gave the differences and relations of the times with such accuracy that, as I have said, these operations never gave a noticeable difference when repeated many times.

The motion of projectiles

Galileo also considered the problem of projectiles – a problem that had defied solution up to his time. Galileo imagined an object projected horizontally, and asked what the path of the subsequent motion would be. His genius was to recognize the independence of the horizontal and vertical motions of the body. He realized there would be a uniformly accelerated motion in the vertical direction, and therefore, from his previous work, he knew that the distance travelled in the vertical direction, y, would be proportional to the square of the time that went by. Horizontally, he appears to be introducing a version of the law of inertia by which he could claim that the motion would take place without acceleration (i.e. with constant velocity). Then, the distance travelled horizontally, x, would be proportional to the time. In other words

$$x \propto t$$
$$y \propto t^2$$

from which he concluded that

$$y \propto x^2$$

that is, the motion takes place on a parabola. There are interesting discussions in the *Discorsi* about the wisdom of combining the vertical and horizontal motions and whether this can be done so that 'neither alter each other, nor confuse each other, nor mutually hinder each other in mixing up'. Of course, Galileo used nothing more than the law of vector addition – a law that, as we have seen, was known to Aristotle.

Newton and Aristotle

Newton's laws of mechanics were discussed earlier in this book. For Newton, a force is required if a body is to change its velocity (i.e. if it has acceleration). When no force acts on a body, the body will either stay at rest or continue to move with uniform velocity in a straight line. For Aristotle, a force is necessary to keep the body moving. Aristotle's idea, as we also discussed earlier, is not unreasonable. We know that a force is required to push an object and keep it moving, for example a heavy piece of furniture. What Aristotle failed to appreciate was that the reason we must exert the force is because the motion is opposed by a frictional force. The force we exert simply cancels the opposing frictional force, leaving the body with a zero net force. Hence, the body moves with constant speed. (To get the body to move in the first place, of course, the pushing force must initially be greater than the opposing force. Once the body reaches a given speed, the pushing force becomes equal to the opposing force and the body continues with constant speed.)

It is interesting that Aristotle was close to appreciating this statement for bodies moving in a vacuum (where friction and opposing forces are absent). In fact, it was his faith in *his* laws of motion that led him to conclude that a vacuum could not exist.

Mechanical determinism

Newtonian mechanics is the perfect example of what has come to be called mechanical determinism. Given a system and its initial conditions, one can predict with absolute certainty the future evolution of that system by applying Newton's laws of mechanics to the system. The entire solar system, for example, is a finely tuned huge structure that runs with clockwork accuracy along its predetermined course. This picture of the universe as a 'machine' whose future state is determined once and for all by its present state and the laws of mechanics was expounded most forcefully by the French physicist and mathematician Pierre Simon Laplace (1749–1827).

As a trivial example, consider a ball with initial velocity 15 m s^{-1} that is launched vertically upward from a height of 20 m from the ground. The initial velocity and position of the ball are what we mean by initial conditions of the system. The application of Newton's laws tells us that the ball will move with an acceleration of (approximately) -10 m s^{-2}, so we can predict at any future time t what the position and velocity of the ball will be by using

$$y = 20 + 15t - 5t^2$$

and

$$v = 15 - 10t$$

Less trivial examples exist. For example, if a spacecraft is launched from earth at a specific time, from a specific position and with specific forces acting on it, then its future path will be completely determined simply by applying Newton's laws to the spacecraft. Similarly, knowledge of the position and velocity of a comet (or a planet) at any one time (the initial conditions) is enough to predict with extraordinary accuracy the position of the comet (or planet) hundreds of years into the future.

The notion of mechanical determinism has been eroded somewhat, however. Determinism (and the partial loss of it) within modern quantum theory is discussed separately in Chapter E6. Even within classical Newtonian mechanics, however, traditional determinism has suffered a blow in what is known as *chaos theory*. In 1890, the great French mathematician Henri Poincaré (1854–1912) showed that various differential equations arising in the study of the so-called *three-body problem* (the motion of three bodies under the action of each other's gravitation) gave rise to solutions that were so complicated that, for all practical purposes, predictability was lost. Poincaré's work went mostly unnoticed until the 1950s, when similar kinds of problem were discovered in the complicated equations describing the weather. Suppose we are given a system with a set of initial conditions. The equations are solved and the future state of the system is predicted. Naively one would expect that, if the initial conditions were changed by an infinitesimal amount, the future state of the system would also change by an infinitesimal amount. Alas, cases were discovered where the change in the final state was so great that its prediction based on the set of initial conditions was impossible. The word *chaos* has come to signify sensitivity to initial conditions – changing the initial conditions by a little bit results in a drastic and unpredictable change in the future state of the system.

Questions

1 A cart is being pulled with a rope and moves on a level road at constant speed. The rope is suddenly cut and the cart eventually comes to rest. What forces act on the cart while it is moving at constant speed? How do we explain that the cart stops moving? How would Aristotle describe the situation?

2 One heavy and one light ball are launched straight up with the same velocity. Which one climbs higher? What would Aristotle's answer be?

3 How would you compare the methods used by Galileo to obtain his results with those of Aristotle?

4 Could Aristotle perform *any* of the experiments that Galileo performed? What difficulties would he have had if he had attempted them?

5 Galileo is considered to be the father of the scientific method. Why?

6 Why was the church offended by the teachings of Copernicus and Galileo?

7 Read a bit more about the clash of Galileo and the church. Galileo actually recanted his views. Should this make us think less of him?

8 What do you understand by the term 'mechanical determinism'? Give one example.

9 Why does chaos theory violate mechanical determinism?

Heat

This chapter is a brief introduction to the phlogiston theory of combustion and the caloric theory of heat. Joule's experiment in which the nature of heat as another form of energy was revealed is also discussed.

Objectives

By the end of this chapter you should be able to:
- state the main facts about the *phlogiston theory* of combustion and describe how it was eventually replaced;
- state the main facts of the *caloric theory* of heat and describe how it was replaced;
- appreciate the contributions of Joule to our understanding of the nature of *heat as energy*.

The phlogiston and caloric theories of heat

The phlogiston theory of combustion

The *phlogiston* theory probably has its origins in the alchemy of the Middle Ages. It was revived in the seventeenth and eighteenth centuries by Johan Becher (1635–82) and Georg Stahl (1660–1734) as a theory to explain combustion. A material such as charcoal leaves very little residue behind when burned. It was natural to assume that charcoal contains a fluid, phlogiston, which is released from the charcoal in the process of burning. Initially the phlogiston was assumed to be a fluid without mass. When more quantitative studies became possible and it was found that the residues of a burned object actually weighed less than the original body, it became necessary to give mass to the fluid. When Antoine Lavoisier (1743–94) showed that in some cases the burning process left the body with an *increased* mass, it was necessary to invoke a *negative mass* for the

phlogiston. This convinced Lavoisier of the flaws of the phlogiston theory, which was subsequently abandoned. Lavoisier explained combustion in terms of oxidation, and found no need for the phlogiston fluid.

The caloric theory of heat

Having dismissed the phlogiston theory, Lavoisier proceeded with a new model for heat. He introduced the concept of the *caloric*, another fluid, which like the phlogiston could be found within ordinary bodies. A body was hot if it contained a lot of caloric and cold if it contained little caloric. Thus, when a hot body was placed in contact with a colder body, a certain quantity of caloric was supposed to flow from the hot to the colder body. The hot body would thus show a decrease in its temperature and the colder body an increase. The caloric fluid was supposed to be conserved so that the caloric lost by one body was always equal to that gained by another. There was no clear statement as to whether the caloric fluid had mass.

The caloric model of heat was a successful model in describing calorimetry experiments. However, if you rub your hands, heat will be generated. According to the caloric theory, caloric fluid must have flown into your hands from somewhere else where the temperature must have fallen. We do not observe anything else becoming colder when we rub our hands and this simple observation is enough to bring down the entire caloric model. Similarly, no one had ever observed an increase in the mass of a body that was heated. Such an increase should have been there if the caloric was supposed to be a fluid with mass.

Systematic observations of this nature were made by Benjamin Thompson (1753–1814) (later Count Rumford), a Massachusetts man who remained loyal to the British during the American War of Independence and went to England in 1776. While supervising the boring of cannons, he was impressed by the tremendous amount of heat generated – so much that the cannon and the drill had to be constantly cooled with water to avoid melting. The very large amount of heat would have required caloric fluid in large quantities to flow from some other body, reducing its temperature sharply. Thompson suspected that the heat was generated as a result of the mechanical work done by the drill but the connection between mechanical work and heat would be explained precisely somewhat later by James Joule (1818–89).

This led to the demise of the caloric theory and its replacement by the kinetic theory.

Heat as energy

It wasn't until the nineteenth century that heat was recognized as a form of energy. An experiment by Joule demonstrated the equivalence of heat and energy. The unit of heat had been the calorie, its definition being the quantity of heat needed to raise the temperature of 1 g of water by 1° Celsius. In his experiment, Joule used a set of weights, which were allowed to descend from a given height,

turning a paddle in a container of water as they did so (see Figure E3.1). The weights fell at a low speed, so very little kinetic energy was involved. The potential energy of the falling weights was converted into rotational energy of the paddle wheel and the water. This rotational energy became, through friction, internal energy of the water and the container (i.e. heat), which showed up as increased water temperature.

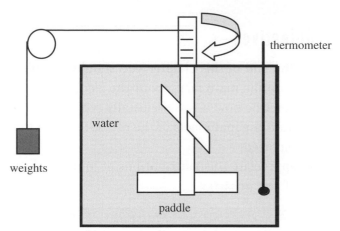

Figure E3.1 The descending weights do mechanical work, which is converted into heat, which raises the temperature of the water in the tank.

The amount of mechanical work done by the weights could be calculated from the distance they descend. Joule found the rise in the temperature of the water by equating the mechanical work done by the weights to the heat absorbed by the water. He thus found the equivalence of the calorie, the old unit of heat, to the joule, the conventional unit of energy. The result was 1 cal = 4.15 J, which compares very well with the present value of

$$1 \text{ cal} = 4.186 \text{ J}$$

This is quite remarkable for an experiment performed in 1845. Joule performed this experiment many times using different amounts of water, different weights and different heights of fall, always obtaining the same answer.

What we have seen here is mechanical work (the potential energy of the descending weights) being converted into a new form of energy, heat (or, more correctly, internal energy).

Questions

1 What is the phlogiston theory, and what brought about its demise?

2 What one important principle of physics is contained in the caloric theory of heat?

3 How does the caloric theory explain the fact that a hot body placed in contact with a colder body loses heat to it?

4 Does the caloric theory have an explanation as to why heat flows always from hot to colder bodies and not the other way?

5 What series of observations led to the rejection of the caloric theory?

OPTION E4

Electricity and magnetism

This chapter discusses the early theories of electric charge based on fluid models and the discovery of the inverse square law for the force between two electric charges. The material on electromagnetic induction and Ørsted's and Faraday's discoveries are presented as part of the core material in Chapters 5.6 and 5.7 and are only briefly touched upon here.

Objectives

By the end of this chapter you should be able to:

*   outline the early theories about the *nature of charge* based on *two fluids* and, later, on *one fluid*;
*   explain simple situations of *charging through the flow of a fluid*;
*   describe how the *inverse square law* was established experimentally;
*   understand that an electric current produces a *magnetic field*;
*   appreciate the importance of *magnetic flux* in producing an emf.

Electric and magnetic phenomena

Electric and magnetic phenomena were discovered very early. The ancient Greek philosopher Thales of Miletus (*c*.600 BC) knew that pieces of amber, when rubbed, developed the ability to attract pieces of straw. The word *electron* comes from the Greek word $\eta\lambda\epsilon\kappa\tau\rho\text{o}\nu$, the name for amber. It was also known then that lodestone (i.e. magnetite, Fe_2O_3) could attract pieces of iron. The word magnet comes from Magnesia, present-day Turkey, where magnetite was found. The earth has its own magnetic field with the geographic north pole near, but not exactly on, the earth's magnetic *south* pole. It was discovered that like poles repel and opposite poles attract. The Chinese discovered in the twelfth century that a small magnetic needle would align itself with the earth's magnetic field. This means that a magnetic needle's north pole is attracted to the earth's magnetic south pole, that is it points along the geographic north direction. The Chinese were the first to use this property for navigation.

Until the discovery in 1820 by Hans Ørsted (1777–1851) that an electric current produces a magnetic field, electric and magnetic phenomena were considered to belong to separate disciplines (even though many similarities were noted). As early as 1269, Petrus Peregrinus established that a magnet possesses two different kinds of magnetic poles and that a small magnet aligns itself with a north–south line. He even noted the very important fact that the poles cannot be separated. By 1600, William Gilbert (1540–1603) had compiled most of the available knowledge about magnetic phenomena in his book *De Magnete* and had added many of his own observations. So popular was the subject at the time that magnetic forces were firmly believed to be behind Kepler's newly discovered laws of planetary motion (an idea vehemently opposed by Newton).

The concept of electric charge

In 1729, Simon Gray (1666–1736) showed that materials fell into classes with respect to the newly discovered (and very fashionable) process of electrification. He noticed that when a piece of glass was electrified (i.e. charged) by friction and then connected by a damp piece of string (suspended by silk threads) to a small nail, pieces of straw were attracted to the nail. Gray thus realized that the effect of electricity could be transferred a large distance and that some materials had this ability while others did not. This gave rise to ideas of what we would call in today's language *conductors* and *insulators*. It also gave rise to the notion of electricity (i.e. electric charge) as a kind of fluid, which moved about carrying the effect of electricity.

In 1733, Charles du Fay (1698–1739) noticed that glass rubbed with silk became electrified. So did amber when rubbed with fur. Pieces of cork that came in contact with the charged glass were seen to *repel*, just as they did when they came in contact with the electrified amber. On the other hand, a piece of cork that was charged by contact with glass *attracted* a piece of cork that had come in contact with the amber. He was thus led to the discovery of *two kinds* of electric charge. Du Fay and, especially, Jean-Antoine Nollet (1700–70) established the *two-fluid model* of electric charge.

Excess of a fluid (*resinous electricity*) caused what we would call negative charge on a body. *Deficiency* of a fluid (*vitreous electricity*) caused positive charge on the body.

Thus, when glass (and materials like it) is rubbed with silk, it loses some of its vitreous fluid to silk and so becomes deficient in vitreous fluid – it is charged with what we call

today positive charge. The charging of a body by friction could then be explained by the flow of one or both kinds of fluid.

In 1751, Benjamin Franklin (1706–90) published his *Experiments and Observations on Electricity*, in which he proposed a *one-fluid* model of electric charge. Franklin had carefully established that when glass is rubbed with silk, not only is the glass rod charged, but so is the silk, with precisely the *opposite* amount. Franklin accepted one of the two fluids of the du Fay–Nollet theory and realized that the second fluid is superfluous – it is simply the *absence* of the first. Each body was assumed to have a certain quantity of this fluid.

If the body contained the *natural* amount of the fluid, the body was in a state of zero electrification (i.e. it had zero charge). If the body had more than its natural share of the fluid, the body was positively charged; if it had less than its natural share, the body was negatively charged. The assignment of positive and negative charge was natural given that Franklin had established that when glass is rubbed with silk, both glass rod and silk are charged with precisely opposite amounts.

In other words, according to Franklin, the fluid was the carrier of what we would call today positive charge. Franklin had no reason to call the fluid positive, and in fact he did not want to commit himself either way. The fact that he did assign the positive sign to the fluid of charge is the reason that, today, we use the convention that the direction of the electric current in a circuit (the 'flow of the fluid') is opposite to that of the motion of the electrons (see Figure E4.1).

Figure E4.1 The flow of electrons is opposite to the flow of Franklin's fluid.

Franklin's one-fluid model explains charging by friction very easily. A rubbed body acquires positive charge if fluid flows into the body. It acquires negative charge if the fluid moves out of the body. The one-fluid model also explains *conservation of electric charge*. If a certain amount of fluid leaves body A and enters body B, then body A will have a charge that is the same (apart from sign) as that of body B. The nature of the 'fluid' is, of course, left unclear but it was hypothesized to be essentially massless. Its constituent particles, whatever they might be, were supposed to repel each other. The one-fluid model could thus also account for charging by induction. Imagine bringing a charged rod near, but not touching, an electrically neutral insulated body. The neutral body contains its natural quantity of electric fluid. The particles of the fluid on the charged rod repel the particles of the fluid in the other body and thus force a redistribution of the fluid in the body (see Figure E4.2). The hypothesis of this repulsive force between the electric fluid particles was essential in understanding induction. However, no obvious mechanism could be found to transport the fluid from one body to another if they did not touch (as in the case of charging by friction).

Similarly, the one-fluid model could explain how two equally, but oppositely, charged objects neutralize their charges when they come in contact. The same amount of fluid leaves one body and enters the other.

It is interesting that most scientists in the eighteenth century preferred the two-fluid model because it was considered 'simpler'. In the nineteenth century, the issue became rather moot. Both models could explain the same phenomena and no experiment had been devised that could decide in favour of one and against the other. Choosing which model to take was more a question of taste than anything else. In the words of Michael Faraday (1791–1867), '[I] sought amongst the various experiments for any which might be considered as sustaining the theory of two electricities rather than of one . . . [but] could not find a single fact'. Later, James Maxwell (1831–79) would say that 'electricity may not belong to any known category of physical quantity'.

Earlier, Franklin had found out that, when charge was deposited on a metal cup, the charge stayed on the outside surface of the cup. Franklin suggested to his friend Joseph Priestley (1733–1804) that he look further into the matter. Priestley was an accomplished chemist and had discovered, among many other things, oxygen. In 1766, a few years before Cavendish and Coulomb performed their quantitative experiments (see later), Priestley was led to conclude that the distribution of charge on the *outside* surface of a conductor was the consequence of a repulsive force between similar charges that varied as the *inverse of the square of the separation of the charges*. In other words, Priestley discovered the inverse square law for the electrical force – the force we call today Coulomb's force.

It can be shown that the absence of charge *inside* the conductor can also be understood as the absence of an electric field inside the conductor. What kind of law leads to such a result?

Imagine charge of uniform density σ (that is charge per unit area) distributed on the surface of a sphere. Consider *any* point P inside the sphere (denoted by the black dot in Figure E4.3) and two cones starting at P and cutting areas A_1 and A_2 on the surface of the sphere. Assume that the electric field is given by the law $E \propto \frac{Q}{r^n}$,

neutral

charged
rod

Figure E4.2 The body on the left is electrically neutral because it contains its natural amount of electric fluid. When a charged rod is brought nearby, the fluid is redistributed so that its left side has more fluid relative to the natural amount. Thus, it appears positively charged. The right end has less fluid and so appears negatively charged.

for some value of n. Then the electric field at point P is

$$E \propto \frac{Q_1}{r_1{}^n} - \frac{Q_2}{r_2{}^n} = \frac{\sigma A_1}{r_1{}^n} - \frac{\sigma A_2}{r_2{}^n} = \sigma \left(\frac{A_1}{r_1{}^n} - \frac{A_2}{r_2{}^n} \right)$$

But, from geometry we know that $\frac{A_1}{r_1{}^2} = \frac{A_2}{r_2{}^2}$ (why?) and so, *if the electric field is to be zero*, we must have $n = 2$; that is, we have an inverse square law.

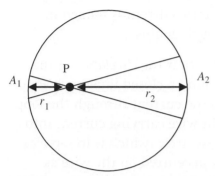

Figure E4.3 A sphere over whose surface a charge of uniform density σ is distributed.

Coulomb and Cavendish

The discovery of the force between two point charges is usually associated with the name of Charles Augustin de Coulomb (1736–1806), who published the results of his discovery in 1777. Unknown to Coulomb, the same results had been obtained earlier by the eccentric English physicist Henry Cavendish (1731–1810), who

never bothered to publish his discovery. (As we saw in the previous section, Priestley, too, had discovered the inverse square law.) Coulomb was a French military engineer who retired in provincial France (during the days of the French Revolution), where he conducted his now famous experiments on the force between electric charges. Coulomb used a *torsion balance* to measure the force between two charges (see Figure E4.4). When a load is suspended from a fine wire, the amount of torque required to twist the wire by a certain angle is proportional to the angle of twist. Coulomb used this method to discover that the force between two charges is given by

$$F = k \frac{Q_1 Q_2}{r^2}$$

(Cavendish had also used the torsion balance to measure the gravitational force between two spheres, from which he deduced the value of the gravitational constant G. Knowing G and the acceleration of gravity enabled him, for the first time, to calculate the mass of the earth.)

However, to establish the inverse square law, Cavendish used an ingenious method based on concentric spheres. Modern versions of what is essentially the Cavendish experiment show that if the exponent of the separation r in Coulomb's law differs from 2, it cannot do so by more than about 2.7×10^{-16}!

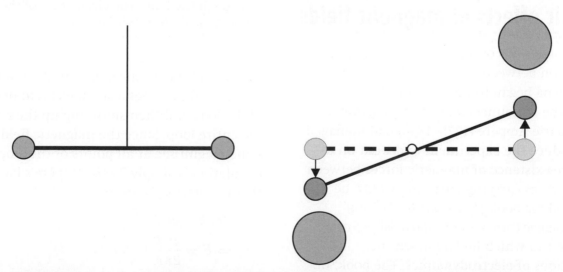

Figure E4.4 A torsion balance. The diagram on the right shows a view from the top. When charges are placed next to the charges on the balance, the rod joining them turns.

Note that the Coulomb and Cavendish methods were *direct* experimental attempts to *measure* the exponent of the separation of the charges. Priestley's method was an *indirect* method that used an apparently unrelated experimental fact (i.e. the distribution of charge on the outside surface of the body) to conclude mathematically that the law was an inverse square law.

The modern view of electric charge has come to us through the atomic model of matter in which electrons are the carriers of negative charge, with a unit of about -1.6×10^{-19} C. All the phenomena of electrification by friction are easily explained by the transfer of electrons from one body to the other, and induction is also explained by the forces between electrons. Interestingly, had Franklin not made the mistake of assigning positive charge to the electric fluid, we might be able to say today that the (essentially) massless Franklin fluid is nothing more than a collection of electrons. Just as Franklin could not explain the *nature* of the fluid, we, too, cannot explain the *nature* of the electric charge on the electron. We can only say that it is a *property* of the electron (and other particles) that happens to be conserved.

Magnetic effects of currents and electric effects of magnetic fields

With Ørsted's discovery (see Chapter 5.6), the connection between electric and magnetic phenomena began to grow serious roots. Within days of the announcement of the discovery, André Marie Ampère (1775–1836) had managed to reproduce the experiment and went on to show the existence of magnetic forces between parallel wires carrying current. In 1827, he published his book *Mathematical Theory of Electrodynamic Phenomena Deduced Solely from Experiment* in which he laid down the foundations of electrodynamics. The book, in the words of Maxwell, is one of the most brilliant achievements in science. 'The whole,

theory and experiment, seems as if to have leaped full grown and fully armed from the brain of the "Newton of electricity". It is perfect in form and unassailable in accuracy; and it is summed up in a formula from which all the phenomena may be deduced, and which must always remain the cardinal formula of electrodynamics.'

This is no small praise coming as it does from one of the giants of nineteenth-century physics. The SI unit for electric current is named in honour of this French genius.

Ampère's law states that the *circulation* of the magnetic field around a closed imaginary loop is proportional to the current through the loop. Consider a straight wire carrying current into the page. Imagine a circle (which is to serve as our imaginary loop) centred on the wire as shown in Figure E4.5.

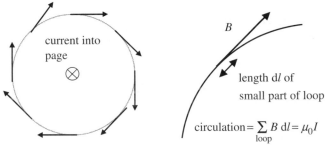

Figure E4.5 An imaginary loop (a circle of radius r) around a wire. A current of magnitude I goes through the loop. The circulation of the magnetic field is $2\pi r B$ and equals $\mu_0 I$.

By 'circulation' we mean the product of the magnetic field times a small element of length of the loop and then summing up the result for the entire loop. Since the magnetic field has the same magnitude at all points of the loop, the circulation is simply $2\pi r B$. Ampère's law states that it equals $\mu_0 I$ and so

$$2\pi r B = \mu_0 I$$
$$\Rightarrow B = \frac{\mu_0 I}{2\pi r}$$

The law can be used to calculate the magnetic field in a wide variety of situations.

Electromagnetic induction

In the meantime, the obvious question was posed: If electric currents could produce magnetic fields, could the reverse also happen – could magnetic fields produce electric currents? The answer turned out not to be so obvious. Placing a magnetic field near a wire produced nothing. It was only in 1831 that Michael Faraday succeeded in showing that a *changing magnetic flux* produced an emf in a coil (and hence a current). The discovery of electromagnetic induction and the importance of magnetic flux in the whole story are presented in Chapter 5.7.

Michael Faraday was one of ten children born to a poor family in England and had no means for any education. At age 14 he became an apprentice to a bookbinder in London, where he spent as much time reading the books as he did binding them. This self-educated genius spent most of his spare time doing experiments in physics and chemistry, and when he presented his notes to Humphry Davy (1778–1829), he was immediately taken on to be his assistant. We owe much of our electromechanical technology (electric motors and electric generators) to this modest man. His lack of mathematical sophistication was matched by an unparalleled physical intuition and experimental skill. His concept of electric and magnetic field lines was to develop, in the hands of mathematically minded physicists, into a powerful tool that pervaded almost all of physics. In 1846, some twenty years before Maxwell, Faraday conjectured that light had an electromagnetic origin. He was a man of principles, and refused to participate in a project to manufacture poison gas for use in the Crimean War.

Questions

1 What important principle is hidden behind the one-fluid theory of electric charge?

2 A charged rod is brought near to, but does not touch, a neutral conductor. Explain what will happen on the basis of:
(a) the two-fluid theory;
(b) the one-fluid theory;
(c) the modern theory of electric charge.

3 Do the same as in question 2 when a charged object is allowed to touch a neutral object and then separated from it.

4 Describe Coulomb's experiment that determined the inverse square law for the electric force.

5 An important fact about electric charge is that it is *quantized*, which means that the amount of charge on a body is an integral multiple of a basic unit (that being the charge of the electron). This was discovered by Millikan in the early part of the twentieth century. Could a fluid theory of charge, *in principle*, explain charge quantization?

6 We also have an inverse square law for gravitation. What is the gravitational field inside a hollow sphere? (Use Priestley's argument.)

7 A charged sphere is lowered into a metallic container resting on an insulated base without touching it. What do you expect to happen:
(a) to the *inside* surface of the container;
(b) to the *outside* surface of the container?

Atomic and nuclear physics

This part of Option E deals with the properties of cathode rays and the attempts made to identify them at the end of the nineteenth century. Cathode rays were identified to be electrons in a classic experiment by J.J. Thomson and this experiment is described in detail here. There follows a discussion of an early atomic model put forth by Thomson (the 'plum-pudding' model) and a comparison of this model with Rutherford's nuclear atom. The chapter closes with a discussion of the discovery of the neutron.

Objectives

By the end of this chapter you should be able to:
- discuss *cathode rays* and the attempts made to elucidate their nature;
- outline the contributions of *Hertz* and *Crookes*;
- describe *Thomson's* experiment that demonstrated the *nature of cathode rays* to be that of *negatively charged particles with definite mass*;
- appreciate the contributions of *Lenard*, who furthered our understanding of cathode rays;
- describe *Thomson's model of the atom* and its problems;
- describe the experiment in which *Chadwick* discovered the *neutron*.

The electron and cathode rays

A wire will emit electrons when heated, in a phenomenon known as *thermionic emission*. This is demonstrated with a device known as an electron gun. It consists of a small battery which heats a wire by running a current through it and two concentric metallic discs with a small hole at the centre of each. This creates a fine beam moving to the right, as shown in Figure E5.1. Before it was established that the emitted particles were electrons, the emissions from the hot wire were called *cathode rays*, because the rays originated from the negatively charged electrode, the cathode.

Early experiments by Heinrich Hertz (1857–1894) demonstrated that the cathode rays were deflected by magnetic fields but not by electric fields. This was a very puzzling

observation. The bending by magnetic fields indicated objects that were electrically charged. The direction of the deflection indicated further that the cathode rays were negatively

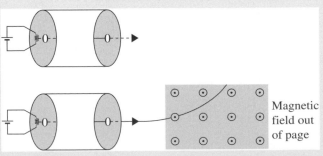

Figure E5.1 An electron gun. The wire is heated by a small battery and begins to glow. A fine beam of cathode rays is emitted through the two openings in the discs. If allowed to enter a region of magnetic field, the deflection indicates negatively charged objects.

charged. If so, they should have been bent by electric fields as well. The lack of such deflections in Hertz's investigations led him to believe that cathode rays were not charged particles, and this led further to speculation that they were a kind of radiation or wave. This was not a very satisfactory resolution, though, since the bending by magnetic fields then became inexplicable.

In 1879, Sir William Crookes (1832–1919) sent a beam of cathode rays through a glass tube containing a gas and observed that the gas in the path of the cathode rays began to glow. He interpreted this as a sign of the interaction of *particles* with the gas molecules. When a solid object was placed in the path of the cathode rays, a *sharp* shadow of the object was created (see Figure E5.2). This was another sign that he was dealing with particles and not waves (which might curve around the obstacle, creating a *fuzzy* shadow). The previous magnetic field deflection experiments had indicated that the particles must have been *negative*.

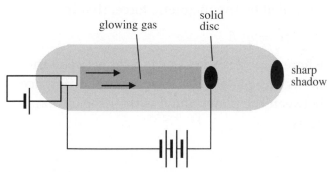

Figure E5.2 Crookes showed that cathode rays caused sharp shadows, indicating that they were particles.

It was up to Joseph John Thomson (1856–1940), however, to fully elucidate the nature of cathode rays and at the same time explain why Hertz could not detect any deflection of cathode rays by electric fields.

Thomson realized that the cathode rays ionized the atoms of the gases they travelled through.

Imagine a beam of cathode rays that passes through two parallel plates that are connected to a battery. There is an electric field in between the plates.

The ions are created because of the collisions of the cathode rays with the atoms of the gas between the plates. The positive ions move toward the negatively charged plate and the negative ions move toward the top, positive, plate (see Figure E5.3). In a very short time, the charge on the plates is neutralized and so the electric field between the plates becomes zero, causing no deflection of the cathode rays. Thomson had *actually observed a deflection by the electric field* but only for a *very* short time after the cathode rays had entered the region of the plates. This was before the ions had time to neutralize the charge on the plates and so eliminate the electric field.

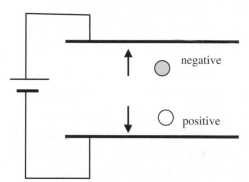

Figure E5.3 The ions created by the collisions of cathode rays with gas molecules neutralize the charge on the parallel plates, thus eliminating the electric field.

Convinced that he was dealing with negatively charged particles of definite mass, Thomson experimented with an apparatus from which he could evacuate all air before allowing cathode rays to enter it.

Thomson's *e/m* experiment

The properties of cathode rays can be investigated with a cathode-ray tube, which consists of an electron gun enclosed within an evacuated glass tube. A second source of voltage of a few hundred volts is connected as shown in

(a)   (b)

Figure E5.4 (a) The accelerated electrons pass through a region of electric and magnetic fields at right angles to each other. The electrons make a screen glow at the points where they impact. (b) A pair of Helmholz coils is used to give a uniform magnetic field.

Figure E5.4. It accelerates the cathode rays toward the right end of the tube, which is covered with fluorescent material, which glows when an object with electric charge falls on it.

On their way to the screen, the cathode rays pass through a region of electric and magnetic fields *at right angles to each other*. The electric field is created by two parallel plates connected to a source of potential difference. The magnetic field is created by current-carrying coils.

When the apparatus is turned on, it is observed that a point on the screen begins to glow. Putting a barrier in front of the hot wire, a piece of metal for example, eliminates the glow on the screen. The charge is therefore coming from the hot wire and the cathode rays cannot penetrate the metal. A small object in the path of the beam casts a sharp shadow of that object on the screen. This implies that cathode rays travel in straight lines; they do not bend around the obstacle. If the magnetic field is turned on, the point on the screen is deflected. A similar deflection is observed if the electric field between the plates is turned on. We are justified in suspecting that cathode rays are simply a stream of negatively charged particles emitted from the hot wire. Cathode rays are, in fact, a beam of fast-moving electrons.

In 1897, Thomson performed an experiment using a cathode-ray tube like the one described above in order to find out more about the nature of cathode rays. By arranging the voltage of the deflecting plates and the value of the magnetic field so that the cathode rays hit the fluorescent screen undeflected, Thomson could deduce that the electric force on the charge was cancelled by the magnetic force, that is

$$qE = qvB$$

where $E = \frac{V}{d}$ is the electric field between the deflecting plates, V is the potential difference between the plates and d is their separation. Thus

$$v = \frac{E}{B}$$

The speed of the particle could, however, also be determined from the fact that it had been accelerated from rest by the accelerating voltage V_a:

$$\frac{1}{2}mv^2 = qV_a$$

Thus

$$\frac{1}{2}m\frac{E^2}{B^2} = qV_a$$

$$\Rightarrow \frac{q}{m} = \frac{E^2}{2B^2V_a}$$

In other words, the *charge-to-mass ratio* is given in terms of measurable quantities and can be determined. Thomson substituted for q the value of electric charge that was known from electrolysis experiments (the charge of the hydrogen ion) and, using the value of q/m from his experiment, calculated the mass of the particle. He found $m = 9.1 \times 10^{-31}$ kg. This turned out to be smaller than any other mass known at that time. It had been determined in electrolysis experiments that the mass of the hydrogen atom is about 1840 times the number above, so the newly discovered particle was very light. It was called the electron, and is now considered to be a fundamental particle of physics, which means that it is believed to have no constituents (it is not made out of other more fundamental objects). Its radius is less than 10^{-18} m.

The discovery of the electron was to initiate a long and fruitful search for other particles that make up matter. This is a search that goes on to this day.

Example question

Q1

A proton and an electron of the same speed both enter a region of magnetic field B and are deflected into circular paths. What is the ratio of the radius of the electron's path to the proton's path?

Answer

We have (see page 317 for details)

$$\frac{q}{m} = \frac{v}{BR}$$

and so

$$\frac{R_{\mathrm{p}}}{R_{\mathrm{e}}} = \frac{m_{\mathrm{p}}}{m_{\mathrm{e}}}$$
$$= 1840$$

Additional studies of cathode rays were also undertaken by Philipp Lenard (1862–1947), who showed that the 'emissions' from a metallic surface when it was irradiated by ultraviolet light (the photoelectric effect) had an identical

e/m value to that established by Thomson for cathode rays. In other words, the particles emitted in the photoelectric effect were electrons. Lenard also investigated the penetrating power of cathode rays and showed that their absorption decreased as their velocity increased. The absorption was also found to be proportional to the density of the absorbing material but was not related to the nature of the material.

The Thomson model of the atom

An early model of the atom was provided by J.J. Thomson. He suggested that the positive charge of the atom was spread over its entire volume, with the electrons embedded in this 'fluid of positive charge', like raisins in a muffin or fruit in a plum pudding (this model is sometimes called the 'plum-pudding' model) (see Figure E5.5). For example, the hydrogen atom with its one electron would be thought of as a sphere of radius of order 10^{-10} m, filled with positive charge of $+e$, with the electron at the centre of this sphere.

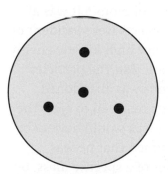

Figure E5.5 Thomson's model of the atom has the positive charge of the atom spread throughout the atomic volume and electrons peppered inside this volume.

At the centre, the electron would experience no electric force from the surrounding positive charge, but as soon as it was displaced from that equilibrium position, the electron would be forced to execute an oscillation with a specific frequency that could be calculated (simple harmonic motion). During these oscillations, the electron would radiate electromagnetic radiation (photons) of frequency equal to the frequency of oscillation. This frequency turns out to be a frequency corresponding to ultraviolet radiation. However, as we will see, the light emitted from atoms does not correspond to just one frequency (as the Thomson model suggests) but rather includes a large number of different frequencies. Thus, the Thomson model is a very inadequate description of the atom. An equally serious flaw of this model (and one that points the way to a more correct picture of the atom) was provided by an experiment of Geiger, Marsden and Rutherford in 1909, which is described in Chapter 6.1.

The discovery of the neutron

The neutron was discovered in 1932 by James Chadwick (1891–1974). It was known from earlier experiments that something very energetic was emitted when helium nuclei were directed towards a mass of beryllium. When the emitted particles or radiations were passed through a magnetic field, no deflection was observed, so it was shown that these objects had no electric charge. (Were they perhaps photons?) It was also known that, when these objects were incident on paraffin wax, protons of very high kinetic energy were emitted. The suspicion that the particles were very energetic photons was abandoned because the photon energy required to eject the protons from the paraffin wax would have to be enormous. Chadwick assumed that he was dealing with new particles of a specific mass, but electrically neutral.

In Chadwick's experiment, polonium was used as a source of alpha particles, which were allowed to fall on a sheet of beryllium. The ejected neutrons could easily travel through a thin sheet of lead and then fall on paraffin, from which they ejected protons. The protons then entered an ionization chamber, which is a container of gas that is ionized by the protons. The ionization current was detected by a galvanometer. Chadwick's apparatus is illustrated in Figure E5.6.

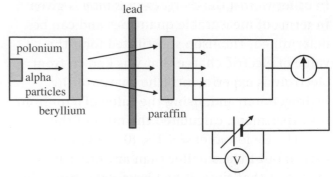

Figure E5.6 Apparatus used by Chadwick that allowed him to identify the neutron by measuring the speed of the ejected protons from paraffin that was hit by a neutron beam.

Chadwick used the fact that in an elastic collision between a neutron of mass m and a nucleus of mass M (with the nucleus initially at rest), application of the laws of conservation of energy and momentum leads to the result that M will recoil with a velocity

$$w = \frac{2m}{m + M} v$$

where v is the initial velocity of the incoming neutron. In Chadwick's original experiment, the speed of recoiling protons was measured first, and then that of recoiling nitrogen nuclei. Paraffin was then replaced by nitrogen. He found that the proton speed was about seven times larger than that of nitrogen. Thus

$$7 = \frac{w_P}{w_N} = \frac{m + M_N}{m + M_p} = \frac{m + 14\,\mathrm{u}}{m + 1\,\mathrm{u}}$$

This can be solved for the neutron mass to give $m = 1.16\,\mathrm{u}$. Later, more accurate measurements revealed a neutron mass that was only slightly larger than that of the proton. The neutron thus entered the set of known particles; together with protons, neutrons make up atomic nuclei.

The emission of neutrons when beryllium is bombarded with helium nuclei takes place according to the reaction

$$^4_2\mathrm{He} + {}^9_4\mathrm{Be} \rightarrow {}^{12}_6\mathrm{C} + {}^1_0\mathrm{n}$$

Being electrically neutral, neutrons do not ionize gases and so can be detected only indirectly by, for example, causing the emission of helium nuclei from nuclei of boron in the reaction

$$_0^1 n + {}_5^{10}B \rightarrow {}_3^7 Li + {}_2^4 He$$

The presence of the original neutron is then inferred from the ionization caused by the emitted helium nuclei.

Questions

1 Calculate the speed of an electron whose kinetic energy is 5.0 eV.

2 What is the speed of an electron that is accelerated through a potential difference of 150 V?

3 Explain why a magnetic field alone cannot change the kinetic energy of a beam of charged particles. Electrons are accelerated from rest by a potential difference of 125 V. They enter a region of magnetic field of magnitude 0.0014 T directed perpendicularly to the velocity of the electrons. Find the radius of the circular path the electrons will follow.

4 An electron of speed 2.0×10^6 m s^{-1} enters a region of electric field of magnitude 200 V m^{-1}. What magnetic field at right angles to the electric field is required in order to keep the electron moving undeflected?

5 Electrons from an electron gun are accelerated through a potential difference V_1 and enter a region of parallel plates of length L, separated by a distance d, moving very close to the bottom plate, which is negatively charged. The potential difference between the parallel plates is V_2. Beyond the parallel plates is a fluorescent screen at a distance D from the right end of the plates. (See Figure E5.7.)

(a) Show that the speed of the electron as it enters the plates is given by

$$v = \sqrt{\frac{2eV_1}{m}}$$

(b) Inside the plates, the electron experiences an electric force upwards. Show that this

force is given by $F = \frac{eV_2}{d}$ and hence that the acceleration of the electron is $a = \frac{eV_2}{md}$.

(c) Explain why the horizontal component of the electron's velocity will remain unchanged while the electron is between the plates.

(d) Show that by the time the electron is about to leave the plates, the vertical component of velocity is given by

$$v_y = \frac{V_2 L}{d}\sqrt{\frac{e}{2mV_1}}$$

(e) Hence, show that when the electron is about to leave the plates, its velocity makes an angle with the horizontal given by

$$\tan\theta = \frac{1}{2}\frac{V_2}{V_1}\frac{L}{d}$$

(f) When the electron is about to leave the plates, show that it has travelled a vertical distance given by

$$y_0 = \frac{1}{4}\frac{V_2}{V_1}\frac{L^2}{d}$$

(g) Finally show that the deflection of the beam when it hits the screen is given by

$$y = y_0 + \frac{1}{2}\frac{V_2}{V_1}\frac{LD}{d}$$

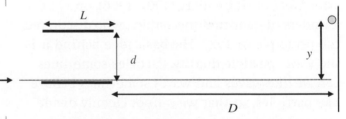

Figure E5.7 For question 5.

6 What principles of mechanics did Chadwick use in his determination of the mass of the neutron?

7 Why was Hertz led to believe that cathode rays were not charged particles?

8 Which crucial observation convinced Thomson that cathode rays were negatively charged particles?

9 Discuss and criticize the argument that the sharp shadow cast by cathode rays as they move past an obstacle is evidence that they are particles.

The uncertainty principle

Part E6 of Option E is for higher level students only. It includes the material on atomic spectra, the Bohr model, the Schrödinger theory and the de Broglie hypothesis. These topics are discussed in detail in Chapter 6.5. You should be familiar with that chapter before reading on. The only material that is not discussed there, as it is exclusively part of the option and not part of the AHL material, is Heisenberg's uncertainty principle. The discussion of this fundamental principle of physics is presented here.

Objectives

By the end of this chapter you should be able to:
*   understand the origin and significance of the *Heisenberg uncertainty principle*.

The Heisenberg uncertainty principle

The Heisenberg uncertainty principle is named after Werner Heisenberg (1901–1976), one of the founders of quantum mechanics, who discovered the principle in 1927. The basic idea behind it is the wave–particle duality. Particles sometimes behave like waves and waves sometimes behave like particles, so that we cannot cleanly divide physical objects as *either* particles *or* waves.

▶ The uncertainty principle states that it is not possible to simultaneously measure the position and momentum of something with absolute precision. This has nothing to do with imperfect measuring devices or experimental errors. It represents a fundamental property of nature.

The principle, applied to position and momentum, states that if we measure the position of an object with uncertainty Δx and the momentum with uncertainty Δp, then

$$\Delta x \cdot \Delta p \geq \frac{h}{4\pi}$$

where h is the Planck constant. This says that making momentum as accurate as possible makes position inaccurate, whereas accuracy in position results in inaccuracy in momentum.

Imagine that electrons are emitted from a hot wire in a cathode-ray tube and that we try to make them move in a horizontal straight line by inserting a metal plate with a small opening of size a. We can make the electron beam as thin as possible by making the opening as small as possible. Making the beam very thin means that we know fairly accurately the vertical position of the electron. The electron must be somewhere within the opening and so the uncertainty in its vertical position will be no bigger than a, that is $\Delta x \leq a$.

However, we will run into a problem as soon as the opening becomes of the same order as the de Broglie wavelength of the electrons. Recall that a wave of wavelength λ will *diffract* when going through an aperture of about the same size as the wavelength. Here, too, the electron will diffract through the opening, which means that a few electrons will emerge from the opening with a direction that is no longer horizontal.

We can describe this phenomenon by saying that there is an uncertainty in the electron's momentum in the vertical direction, of magnitude Δp. Figure E6.1 shows that there is a spreading of the electrons within an angular size 2θ.

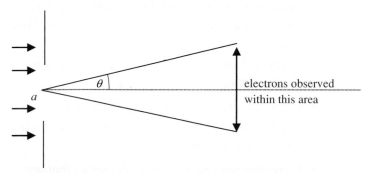

Figure E6.1 An electron passing through a slit suffers a deflection in the vertical direction.

The angle by which the electron is diffracted is given by (recall diffraction)

$$\sin \theta = \frac{\lambda}{a}$$

where a is the opening size. But from Figure E6.1, $\tan \theta = \frac{\Delta p}{p}$. Since the angle is small, the sine and the tangent are approximately equal, and thus

$$\frac{\lambda}{a} = \frac{\Delta p}{p}$$

If we now take the opening size a as the uncertainty in the electron's position in the vertical direction, we have

$$\Delta p \Delta x = \lambda p = h$$

This is a simple explanation of where the uncertainty formula comes from.

As an application of the uncertainty principle, consider an electron, which is known to be confined within a region of size L. Then the uncertainty in position must satisfy $\Delta x < L$, and the uncertainty in momentum must be

$$\Delta p \approx \frac{h}{4\pi \Delta x} \approx \frac{h}{4\pi L}$$

The electron must then have a kinetic energy of

$$E_k = \frac{p^2}{2m} > \frac{\Delta p^2}{2m} \approx \frac{h^2}{32\pi^2 m L^2}$$

If we apply this result to an electron in the hydrogen atom, we see that the size of the region within which the electron is confined is about $L \approx 10^{-10}$ m.

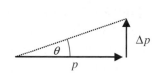

Then

$$E_k \approx \frac{h^2}{32\pi^2 m L^2}$$
$$= \frac{\left(6.6 \times 10^{-34}\right)^2}{32\pi^2 \left(9.1 \times 10^{-31}\right)\left(10^{-10}\right)^2}$$
$$= 1.5 \times 10^{-19} \text{ J}$$
$$\approx 1 \text{ eV}$$

which is, in fact, the correct order of magnitude value of the electron's kinetic energy.

The uncertainty principle also applies to measurements of energy and time. If a state is measured to have energy E with uncertainty ΔE, then there must be an uncertainty Δt in the time during which the measurement is made, such that

$$\Delta E \Delta t \geq \frac{h}{4\pi}$$

The Heisenberg uncertainty principle has many applications. It has been mentioned in the text that Coulomb's law is the consequence of the exchange of a massless photon between two charges. The photon in this case is what is called a *virtual* particle. Virtual particles are particles that exist for a short interval of time and during this time energy conservation may be violated. If the amount of energy violation is ΔE and the time it takes is Δt, then as long as $\Delta E \Delta t < \frac{h}{4\pi}$, the energy non-conservation is unobservable. In the general case where the emitted particle has mass m, then ΔE can be of order mc^2. In the time Δt for which this energy exists, the particle can move, at most, a distance $R = c \Delta t$. Thus,

$$R \approx \frac{h}{4\pi mc}$$

In the case of the photon, $m = 0$, and hence the range is infinite. It can be shown that the inverse square law in the electric force between two charges follows precisely from the fact that the exchanged particle in the electromagnetic interaction, the photon, is massless.

Determinism

As we have seen, the Heisenberg uncertainty principle forbids the knowledge of both momentum and position with absolute precision. This means that determinism in its classical sense is lost. To be able to predict the future state of a system we must know the initial conditions for the system, and this knowledge involves both the position and velocity (i.e. momentum). Heisenberg says that this knowledge is *in principle* not available.

Questions

1 The strong nuclear force has a range of about 1.5×10^{-15} m. If this is due to the exchange of a particle, find the mass of this particle. (This particle is the pion and the suggestion is that the pion mediates the strong nuclear force. This suggestion was made in 1935 by Hideki Yukawa. Pions were identified and studied in the late 1940s.)

2 Using the uncertainty principle, show that an electron in a hydrogen atom will have a kinetic energy of a few eV.

3 Using the uncertainty principle, show that an electron cannot be confined within a nucleus.

4 The electroweak interaction is mediated by the W and Z particles whose rest energy is very roughly 100 GeV. Use the uncertainty principle to deduce the range of the electroweak interaction.

5 Explain why the Bohr model is inconsistent with the uncertainty principle.

Introduction to the universe

This chapter is an introduction to the basic properties of the solar system and an account of the main celestial objects we meet in a study of astrophysics. The motion of the stars as they appear to an observer on the moving earth is also briefly discussed.

Objectives

By the end of this chapter you should be able to:

- describe the main features of the *solar system*;
- name the *main objects* making up the universe;
- give the definition of a *light year*;
- state the *average distances between stars and between galaxies*;
- outline the main facts about the *motion of stars* as they appear to an observer on earth.

The solar system

We live in a part of space called the solar system: a collection of nine planets bound in elliptical orbits around a star called the sun. The sun has a mass of 1.99×10^{30} kg and a radius of 6.96×10^8 m. The elliptical orbits of the planets have the sun at one of the two foci of the ellipse (see Figure F1.1a). The orbit of the earth is almost circular; those of Mercury and Pluto are the most elliptical. The planes of the orbits of the planets differ only slightly from the plane of the earth's orbit, with the exception of Mercury and Pluto, which have inclinations of about 7° and 17°, respectively (see Figure F1.1b). All planets revolve around the sun in the same direction. This is also true of the comets, with a few exceptions, the most famous being Halley's comet. The motion of the planets and comets around the sun is dictated by Kepler's laws, which we have met elsewhere in this book. Kepler's laws are also obeyed by the moons in their orbits around their respective planets. Characteristics of the planets are given in Tables F1.1–F1.3.

All the planets except Mercury and Venus have moons orbiting them. The earth's moon has a mass of 7.35×10^{22} kg, a radius of 1.74×10^6 m, an orbit radius around the earth of 3.84×10^8 m and an orbital period of 27.3 days. Jupiter has 16 moons, 4 of which are as big as earth's moon. Saturn has 17 moons and a spectacular ring system of millions of objects moving around the planet in circular, coplanar orbits. Uranus has 15 moons and a ring system. Pluto's moon, Charon, is almost as large as Pluto itself, so we may actually speak of a double planet system. The eccentricity of Pluto's orbit makes it cross the orbit of Neptune, and at times Pluto is actually closer to the sun than Neptune. These two planets might have a high probability of a collision were it not for the fact that the planes of their orbits are different.

In a region of space between the orbits of Mars and Jupiter is the *asteroid belt*. It consists of thousands of small objects (small planets) in orbit around the sun. The largest is called Ceres and has a diameter of 770 km; many are under 10 km

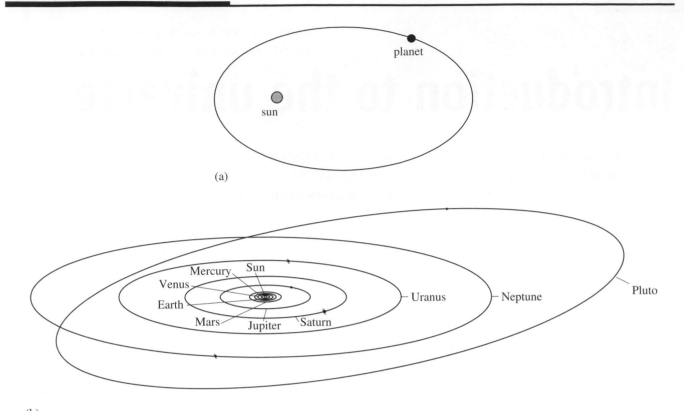

Figure F1.1 (a) Planets orbit the sun in elliptical orbits. The sun is at one of the two foci of the ellipse. (b) Planetary orbits. There is also a belt of small rocky asteroids between Mars and Jupiter.

Planet	Mass/kg	Radius/m	Orbit radius/m (average)	Orbital period
Mercury	3.30×10^{23}	2.44×10^6	5.79×10^{10}	88.0 days
Venus	4.87×10^{24}	6.05×10^6	1.08×10^{11}	224.7 days
Earth	5.98×10^{24}	6.38×10^6	1.50×10^{11}	365.3 days
Mars	6.42×10^{23}	3.40×10^6	2.28×10^{11}	687.0 days
Jupiter	1.90×10^{27}	6.91×10^7	7.78×10^{11}	11.86 yr
Saturn	5.69×10^{26}	6.03×10^7	1.43×10^{12}	29.42 yr
Uranus	8.66×10^{25}	2.56×10^7	2.88×10^{12}	83.75 yr
Neptune	1.03×10^{26}	2.48×10^7	4.50×10^{12}	163.7 yr
Pluto	1.5×10^{22}	1.15×10^6	5.92×10^{12}	248.0 yr

Table F1.1 The solar system. The distance between the sun and the earth (1.50×10^{11} m) is known as the astronomical unit (AU).

across. The asteroids revolve around their axes with periods under 12 h. There must have been many collisions between asteroids and the earth but traces of only a few such collisions remain. One theory about the asteroid belt involves the disruption of one planet into many pieces. Another invokes the effect of nearby Jupiter, whose large mass did not allow the material that was there at the time of the formation of the solar system to assemble into a planet.

Planet	
Pluto	(smallest)
Mercury	
Mars	
Venus	
Earth	
Neptune	
Uranus	
Saturn	
Jupiter	(largest)

Table F1.2 The planets listed in order of increasing size.

Planet	Radius	Mass	Acceleration due to gravity
Mercury	0.379	0.056	0.36
Venus	0.972	0.817	0.87
Earth	1.000	1.000	1.00
Mars	0.533	0.108	0.38
Jupiter	11.190	318	2.64
Saturn	9.470	95.2	1.13
Uranus	3.689	14.6	1.07
Neptune	3.496	17.3	1.41
Pluto	0.235	0.002	0.04

Table F1.3 The relative size, mass and acceleration of gravity of the planets compared with earth, which is assigned a value of 1 for all these properties.

Beyond the solar system

In the course of our study of the option on astrophysics, we will meet various objects making up the universe. Table F1.4 is an introduction to the meaning of the various terms. Most of these will be discussed in greater detail later on.

Example question

Q1

Take the density of interstellar space to be one atom of hydrogen per cubic centimetre of space. How much mass is there in a volume of interstellar space equal to the volume of the earth? Give an order-of-magnitude estimate without using a calculator.

Answer

The volume of the earth is

$$V = \tfrac{4}{3}\pi R^3$$
$$\approx \tfrac{4}{3} \times 3 \times (6 \times 10^6)^3 \text{ m}^3$$
$$\approx 4 \times 200 \times 10^{18}$$
$$\approx 10^{21} \text{ m}^3$$

Hence, the number of atoms in this volume is $10^{21} \times 10^6 = 10^{27}$ atoms of hydrogen. This corresponds to a mass of

$$10^{27} \times 1.6 \times 10^{-27} \text{ kg} \approx 1 \text{ kg}$$

The light year

As we move away from the solar system, we enter immense expanses of space. It is useful to have a more convenient unit of distance than the metre.

▶ We define the light year (ly) as the distance travelled by light in one year. Thus

$$1 \text{ ly} = 3 \times 10^8 \times 365 \times 24 \times 60 \times 60 \text{ m}$$
$$= 9.46 \times 10^{15} \text{ m}$$

Also convenient for measuring large distances is the *parsec* (pc), a unit that will be properly defined in Chapter F3: $1 \text{ pc} = 3.26 \text{ ly} = 3.09 \times 10^{16}$ m.

▶ The average distance *between stars* in a galaxy is about 1 pc, an easy number to remember. The distance to the nearest star (Proxima Centauri) is 4×10^{16} m, which is approximately $4.3 \text{ ly} = 1.3$ pc. A simple message sent to a civilization on Proxima Centauri would thus take 4.3 yr to reach it and an answer would arrive on Earth another 4.3 yr later.

The average distance *between galaxies* varies from about 100 kpc for galaxies within the same cluster to a few Mpc for galaxies belonging to different clusters.

Binary star	Two stars orbiting a common centre
Black dwarf	The remnant of a white dwarf after it has cooled down. It has very low luminosity
Black hole	A singularity in space-time; the end result in the evolution of a very massive star
Brown dwarf	Gas and dust that did not reach high enough temperatures to initiate fusion. These objects continue to compact and cool down
Cepheid variable	A star of variable luminosity. The luminosity increases sharply and falls off gently with a well-defined period. The period is related to the absolute luminosity of the star and so can be used to estimate the distance to the star
Clusters of galaxies	Galaxies close to each other and affecting each other gravitationally, behaving as one unit
Comet	A small body (mainly ice and dust) orbiting the sun in an elliptical orbit
Constellation	A group of stars in a recognizable pattern that *appear* to be near each other in space
Dark matter	Generic name for matter in galaxies and clusters of galaxies that is too cold to radiate. Its existence is inferred from techniques other than direct visual observation
Galaxy	A collection of a very large number of stars mutually attracting each other through the gravitational force and staying together. The number of stars in a galaxy varies from a few million in dwarf galaxies to hundreds of billions in large galaxies. It is estimated that 100 billion galaxies exist in the observable universe
Interstellar medium	Gases (mainly hydrogen and helium) and dust grains (silicates, carbon and iron) filling the space in between stars. The density of interstellar mass is very low. There is about one atom of gas for every cubic centimetre of space. The density of dust is a trillion times smaller. The temperature of the gas is about 100 K
Main sequence star	A normal star that is undergoing nuclear fusion of hydrogen into helium. Our sun is a typical main sequence star
Neutron star	If a red giant is very large (a supergiant), the end result of the explosion throwing off mass will be a star even smaller than a white dwarf (a few tens of kilometres in diameter) and very dense. This is a star consisting almost entirely of neutrons. The neutrons form a superfluid around a core of immense pressure and density. A neutron star is an astonishing macroscopic example of microscopic quantum physics
Nova	The sudden increase in luminosity of a white dwarf caused by material from a nearby star falling into the white dwarf
Planetary nebula	The ejected envelope of a red giant star
Pulsar	A rapidly rotating neutron star emitting electromagnetic radiation in the radio region. Pulsars have very strong magnetic fields. Periods of rotation vary from a few milliseconds to seconds
Quasars	Powerful energy emitters. These are very active cores of young galaxies. The name stands for quasi-stellar radio-emitting objects, a name given since the first observations of quasars indicated a small, stellar-like size. The energy output from a quasar is greater than that of hundreds of galaxies combined. From redshift measurements, quasars are known to move away from us at very high speeds
Red dwarf	A very small star with low temperature, reddish in colour
Red giant	A main sequence star evolves into a red giant – a very large, reddish star. There are nuclear reactions involving the fusion of helium into heavier elements
Stellar cluster	A group of stars that are physically near each other in space, created by the collapse of the same gas cloud
Supernova	The explosion of a red supergiant star. The amount of energy emitted in a supernova explosion can be staggering – comparable to the total energy radiated by our sun in its entire lifetime!
White dwarf	A red giant at the end stage of its evolution will throw off mass and leave behind a very small (the size of the earth), very dense star in which no nuclear reactions take place. It is very hot but its small size gives it a very low luminosity

Table F1.4 Definitions of terms.

Example questions

Q2

The Local Group is a cluster of some 20 galaxies, including our own Milky Way and the Andromeda galaxy. It extends over a distance of about 1 Mpc. Estimate the average distance between the galaxies of the Local Group.

Answer

Assume that a volume of

$$V = \tfrac{4}{3}\pi R^3$$
$$\approx \tfrac{4}{3} \times 3 \times (0.5)^3 \text{ Mpc}^3$$
$$\approx 0.5 \text{ Mpc}^3$$

is uniformly shared by the 20 galaxies. Then to each corresponds a volume of

$$\frac{0.5}{20} \text{ Mpc}^3 = 0.025 \text{ Mpc}^3$$

The linear size of each volume is thus

$$\sqrt[3]{0.025 \text{ Mpc}^3} \approx 0.3 \text{ Mpc}$$
$$= 300 \text{ kpc}$$

so we may take the average separation of the galaxies to be 300 kpc.

Q3

The Milky Way galaxy has about 2×10^{11} stars. Assuming an average mass equal to that of the sun, estimate the mass of the Milky Way.

Answer

The mass of the sun is 2×10^{30} kg and so the Milky Way galaxy has a mass of about

$$2 \times 10^{11} \times 2 \times 10^{31} = 4 \times 10^{41} \text{ kg}$$

Q4

The observable universe contains some 100 billion galaxies. Assuming an average mass comparable to that of the Milky Way, estimate the mass of the observable universe.

Answer

The mass is

$$100 \times 10^9 \times 4 \times 10^{41} \text{ kg} = 4 \times 10^{52} \text{ kg}$$

The motion of the stars

The observation of the motion of the stars is greatly complicated by the fact that the earth is itself moving. In the course of a night, stars and constellations appear to move across the sky from east to west. The ancient astronomers noticed, however, that the *relative* positions of the stars and constellations remained unchanged. That gave rise to the notion of the *celestial sphere*, a huge sphere surrounding and rotating around the earth on whose surface the stars and constellations were firmly embedded (see Figure F1.2). We know now that the rotation of the stars and constellations is a consequence of the rotation of the earth about its axis. If the axis of rotation of the earth is extended, it intersects the celestial sphere at the north and south celestial poles. The star Polaris (the North Star) is right on the celestial north pole and so appears not to move at all. The rest of the stars and constellations appear to rotate about it.

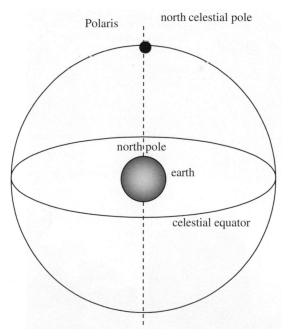

Figure F1.2 The celestial sphere upon which the stars seem to be embedded. The star Polaris is right on the celestial north pole.

As shown in Figure F1.3, the axis of rotation of the earth precesses in space. The axis of rotation that now points to the star Polaris will point to the star Vega in 12 000 years' time. Vega will then become the 'north star'.

Figure F1.3 The axis of rotation of the earth precesses in space tracing out a cone. Now it points at the star Polaris. In the year 14 000 AD it will point at the star Vega. The period of precession is about 26 000 yr.

A long time exposure of the night sky would show arcs traced by stars as the 'celestial sphere rotates' – that is, as the earth rotates about its axis (see Figure F1.4).

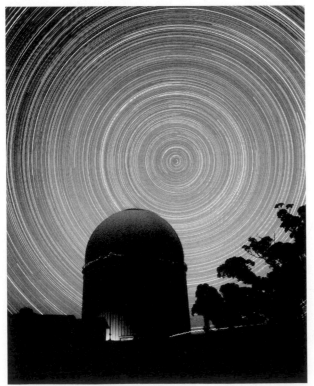

Figure F1.4 A photograph of the night sky over a long period of time shows stars moving along arcs. Copyright: Anglo-Australian Observatory. Photograph taken by David Malin.

As the earth rotates around the sun, the night sky appears to be changing. As can be seen from Figure F1.5, at different times of the year the night hemisphere points along different directions in the sky and hence the view of stars and constellations is different as well. Since the earth completes one revolution in one year, it follows that the change in the direction from one night to the next is $\frac{360°}{365} = 0.986°$, or about one degree. This is too small to be detected by the unaided eye but in the course of a few weeks the changes can easily be detected.

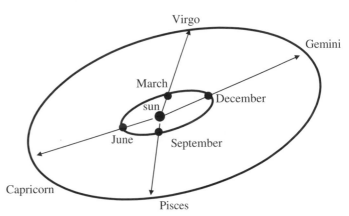

Figure F1.5 As the earth rotates around the sun, the earth's night hemisphere points at different constellations. Shown here are four of the twelve constellations making up the astrological zodiac.

Questions

1 The density of interstellar space is very low, yet light suffers significant absorption on its way to us from a distant star or galaxy. How can that be?

2 How would you distinguish the photograph of a star from that of a quasar?

3 A neutron star has an average density of about 10^{17} kg m^{-3}. Show that this is comparable to the density of an atomic nucleus.

4 A sunspot near the centre of the sun is found to subtend an angle of 4 arcseconds (1 arcsecond = 1/3600 of a degree). Find the diameter of the sunspot.

5 Draw appropriate diagrams to show how the phases of the Moon are created.

6 How many earth volumes fit into Jupiter?

7 Divide the planets among the students in your class and then calculate the density of each planet. List the planets in order of increasing density.

8 On which planet would you expect the escape velocity to be the greatest? Divide the planets among the students in your class and then calculate the escape velocity of each planet. List the planets in order of increasing escape velocity.

9 For the planets, make a graph of the logarithm of the period of revolution around the sun versus the logarithm of the distance to the sun. Draw a line of best fit and find the slope. What is the formula relating the period to the distance?

10 From Kepler's third law (see also question 9), it can be deduced that the distance of Venus from the sun is about 0.7 AU, where 1 AU is the distance of the earth from the sun. Assuming circular orbits, draw a diagram that shows Venus and the earth at their closest. A radar signal is emitted from earth, bounces off Venus, and is received back on earth 300 s later. From this information, find the value of 1 AU in metres.

11 The resolution of the Hubble Space Telescope is about 0.05 arcseconds (1 arcsecond = 1/3600 of a degree). What is the diameter of the smallest object on the moon that can be resolved by the telescope?

12 The moon never shows us its 'dark side'. What does this imply about its period of revolution about its axis and its period of revolution around the earth? Illustrate your answer by diagrams. Find out more about how this might come about.

13 Explain why the sun always rises in the east and sets in the west. Does the moon do the same? Do the stars do the same? Explain.

14 The speed of a body in orbit around another can be determined using Newton's law of gravitation. Let M be the mass of the body at the centre of a circular orbit and m the mass of the orbiting body. Then, the force on m is the force of gravity $F = \frac{GMm}{r^2}$. Equating this to mass times acceleration gives $v^2 = \frac{GM}{r}$. Use this to find the orbital speed of the earth around the sun.

15 Europa is a moon of Jupiter orbiting the planet in 3.55 days at a distance of 671 000 km. Find the mass of Jupiter.

16 The sun is at a distance of 28 000 ly from the centre of the Milky Way and revolves around the galactic centre with a period of 211 million years. Estimate from this information the orbital speed of the sun and the mass of the Milky Way. What assumption have you made in stating that your answer is indeed the mass of the galaxy? (See the two previous questions.)

17 Why are the planets Venus and Mercury always observed near the sun (for example, just after sunset or just before sunrise)?

Stellar radiation and stellar types

This chapter introduces two main tools in the study of stellar structure: the black-body radiation law and the related Wien displacement law. The significance of stellar spectra is discussed as well as the properties of a few special star systems, such as binary stars. The chapter closes with a discussion of another major tool in astrophysics: the Hertzsprung–Russell diagram.

Objectives

By the end of this chapter you should be able to:

*   understand that a star is in equilibrium under the action of two opposing forces, *gravitation* and the *radiation pressure of the star*;
*   appreciate that *nuclear fusion* provides the energy source of a star;
*   give the definitions of *luminosity*, $L = \sigma A T^4$, as the power radiated into space by a star and *apparent brightness*, $b = \frac{L}{4\pi d^2}$, as the power received per unit area on earth;
*   state the *Wien displacement law*, $\lambda_0 T = 2.90 \times 10^{-3}$ K m, and solve problems using it;
*   appreciate the kind of information a *stellar spectrum* can provide;
*   state the main properties of *main sequence stars*, *red giants*, *white dwarfs* and *binary stars*;
*   describe the structure of an *HR diagram* and place the main types of stars on the diagram.

The energy source of stars

A star such as our own sun radiates an enormous amount of energy into space – about 10^{26} J s^{-1}. The source of this energy is nuclear fusion in the interior of the star, in which nuclei of hydrogen fuse to produce helium and release energy in the process. Because of the *high temperatures* in the interior of the star, the electrostatic repulsion between protons can be overcome and hydrogen nuclei can fuse. Because of the *high pressure* in stellar interiors,

the nuclei are sufficiently close to each other to give a high probability of collision and hence fusion. The sequence of nuclear fusion reactions that take place is called the *proton–proton cycle* and consists of

$$^1_1H + {}^1_1H \rightarrow {}^2_1H + {}^0_1e^+ + {}^0_0\nu_e$$
$$^1_1H + {}^2_1H \rightarrow {}^3_2He + {}^0_0\gamma$$
$$^3_2He + {}^3_2He \rightarrow {}^4_2He + 2{}^1_1H$$

Energy is released at each stage of the cycle but most of it is released in the third and final stage. The energy produced is carried away by the photons and neutrinos produced in the reactions. As these particles move outwards they collide with surrounding protons and electrons and give them some of the energy. Thus, gradually, most of the particles in the star will receive some of the kinetic energy produced. The motion of the particles inside the star, as a result of the energy they receive, can stabilize the star against gravitational collapse. Note that the net effect of these reactions is to turn four hydrogen nuclei into one helium:

$$4^1_1\text{H} \rightarrow {}^4_2\text{He} + 2e^+ + 2\nu_e + 2\gamma$$

Helium, being heavier than hydrogen, collects in the core of the star. The energy released in the reactions above can be calculated by the methods of nuclear physics we studied earlier. The energy released per reaction is 26.7 MeV or 3.98×10^{-12} J.

> ▶ Nuclear fusion provides the energy that is needed to keep the star hot, so that the radiation pressure is high enough to oppose further gravitational contraction, and at the same time to provide the energy that the star is radiating into space (see Figure F2.1).

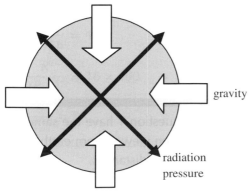

Figure F2.1 The stability of a star depends on equilibrium between two opposing forces: gravitation, which tends to collapse the star, and radiation pressure, which tends to make it expand.

Luminosity

> ▶ Luminosity is the amount of energy radiated by the star per second; that is, it is the power radiated by the star. As shown in the next section, luminosity depends on the surface temperature and surface area of the star.

Consider a star of luminosity L. Imagine a sphere of radius d centred at the location of the star. If the star is assumed to radiate uniformly in all directions, then the energy radiated in 1 s can be thought to be distributed over the surface of this imaginary sphere. A detector of area a placed somewhere on this sphere will receive a small fraction of this total energy (see Figure F2.2a). The fraction is equal to the ratio of the detector area a to the total surface area of the sphere; that is, the received energy per second will be $\frac{aL}{4\pi d^2}$.

> ▶ The received energy per second per unit area of detector is called the apparent brightness and is given by
>
> $$b = \frac{L}{4\pi d^2}$$
>
> The units of apparent brightness are W m^{-2}.

This shows that the apparent brightness is directly proportional to the intrinsic luminosity, and varies as the inverse square of the star's distance (see Figure F2.2b).

Apparent brightness is measured using a *charge coupled device* (CCD), which offers many advantages over the conventional photographic film method. A CCD has a photosensitive silicon surface that releases an electron when it is hit by a photon. The number of electrons released is proportional to the number of photons that hit the surface. Thus, the amount of charge is a direct measure of the brightness of the object

▶ Three clear features emerge from the HR diagram.

1 Most stars fall on a strip extending diagonally across the diagram from top left to bottom right. This is called the main sequence.

2 Some large stars, reddish in colour, occupy the top right – these are the *red giants* (large, cool stars).

3 The bottom left is a region of small stars known as *white dwarfs* (small and hot).

Also shown are some stars of variable luminosity. Cepheid variable stars occupy the black strip just above the position of the sun.

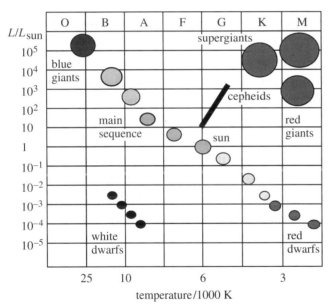

Figure F2.6 The Hertzsprung–Russell diagram. The (surface) temperature increases to the left. Note that the scales are not linear.

In fact, about 90% of all stars are main sequence stars, 9% are white dwarfs and 1% are red giants. Another feature of the HR diagram is that, as we move along the *main sequence* toward hotter stars, the mass of the stars increases as well. Thus, the right end of the main sequence is occupied by red dwarfs and the left by blue giants. Note that as we move up the main sequence (right to left) the mass of the stars increases.

Note that, once we know the temperature of a star (for example, through its spectrum), the HR diagram can tell us the luminosity of the star with an acceptable degree of accuracy, provided it is a main sequence star. (The main sequence is, after all, not a mathematical line but a broad band.) This observation is the basis for a method that determines the distance to a star called spectroscopic parallax (see Chapter F3).

Types of stars

As we have just seen, the HR diagram makes a clear division of stars into various types.

Main sequence stars

Our sun is a typical member of the main sequence. It has a mass of 2×10^{30} kg, a radius of 7×10^8 m, an average density of 1.4×10^3 kg m^{-3} and radiates at a rate of 3.9×10^{26} W. What distinguishes different main sequence stars is their mass. Main sequence stars produce enough energy in their core, from nuclear fusion of hydrogen into helium, to exactly counterbalance the tendency of the star to collapse under its own weight. The luminosity of stars on the main sequence increases as the mass increases.

Red giants

Red giants are another important class of stars. They are very large, cool stars with a reddish appearance. The luminosity of red giants is considerably greater than the luminosity of main sequence stars of the same temperature; they can, in fact, be a million or even a billion times bigger. Treating them as black bodies radiating according to the Stefan–Boltzmann law means that a luminosity of 10^6 times bigger corresponds to an area of 10^6 times bigger, which means a radius of 10^3 times bigger. This explains the name given to these stars. The mass of a red giant can be as much as 1000 times the mass of our sun, but their huge size also implies small densities. In fact, a red giant will have a central hot core surrounded by an enormous envelope of extremely tenuous gas.

White dwarfs

These are very common stars but their faintness makes them hard to detect. A well-known white dwarf is Sirius B, the second star in a binary star system (double star), the other member of which, Sirius A, is the brightest star in the evening sky. Sirius A and B have about the same surface temperature (about 10 000 K) but the luminosity of Sirius B is about 10 000 times smaller. This means that Sirius B has a radius that is 100 times smaller than that of Sirius A. Here is a star of mass roughly that of the sun with a size similar to that of the earth. This means that its density is about 10^6 times the density of the earth!

White dwarfs form when a star collapsing under its own gravitation stabilizes as a result of *electron degeneracy pressure*. This means that the electrons of the star are forced into the same quantum states. To avoid that, the Pauli exclusion principle forces them to acquire large kinetic energies. The large electron energies can then withstand the gravitational pressure of the star.

In addition, we may identify three other important star types.

Variable stars

Whereas the luminosity of our sun and other main sequence stars has remained constant over millions of years, stars exist that show a variation in their luminosity with time. These are called *variable stars*. The variation of luminosity with time (a graph showing the variation of luminosity with time is known as the *light curve* of the star) can be periodic or non-periodic. The reasons for the variable luminosity are mainly changes in the internal structure of the star. For example, a normal main sequence star will, as part of its evolutionary process, grow in size as its outer envelope expands. In doing so, it may eject mass from the outer layers, forming what is called a *planetary nebula*, with an ensuing increase in the star's luminosity. Similarly, if the star is substantially heavier than the sun, the release of mass and

energy from the outer envelope is even more dramatic, resulting in a *supernova* with luminosity increases by factors of a million. In the case of binary stars (see later), matter can be transferred from one star to the other and, on being heated, this matter can radiate, again increasing the star's luminosity.

Cepheids

Most prominent among the class of *periodic* variables are the Cepheid stars, because there exists a relationship between the period of the light curve and the peak luminosity of these stars. Thus, observation of a Cepheid over time allows the determination of its period and hence its peak luminosity. Knowledge of the luminosity is important since comparison with the apparent brightness yields the distance of the star. Cepheids have periods from 1 to 50 days.

The study of variable stars is important since it provides much information about the internal structure of the star and is a testing ground for theories about stellar structure.

Binary stars

A system of two stars that orbit a common centre is called a binary star system. Depending on the method used to observe them, binaries fall into three classes:

- visual
- eclipsing
- spectroscopic.

Binaries are important because they allow for the determination of stellar masses as explained below.

Visual binaries – These appear as two separate stars when viewed through a telescope. They are in orbit around a common centre, the centre of mass of the two stars, as shown in Figure F2.7 in the simplified case of circular orbits.

It is shown in the chapter on gravitation (Chapter 2.10) that the common period of rotation for a binary is given by

$$T^2 = \frac{4\pi^2 d^3}{G(M_1 + M_2)}$$

where d is the distance between the two stars. Thus we can conclude that:

> ▶ Measurement of the separation distance and period gives the *sum* of the masses making up the binary.

To determine the masses individually, we need information about the orbit of each star. Note that the inner star is the more massive of the two.

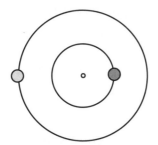

Figure F2.7 A binary star system. The stars rotate about their centre of mass. The two stars are always diametrically opposite each other.

Example question

Q7

A visual binary with a period of 50 yr is at a distance from earth of 8.79 ly. The distance

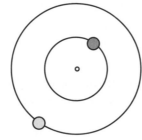

Figure F2.8 (Not to scale).

between the stars subtends an angle at earth (the 'angular diameter') of 7.56 arcseconds. Find the sum of the masses in the binary.

Answer

See Figure F2.8.

Figure F2.8 shows what is meant by 'angular diameter' – it is the angle θ that the separation of the stars subtends at earth. The distance

separating the stars is $d = r\theta$ where r is the distance to the binary. The angle must be expressed in radians, that is ($'' = $ arcseconds)

$$
\begin{aligned}
\theta &= 7.56'' \\
&= \frac{7.56°}{3600} \\
&= \frac{7.56°}{3600} \times \frac{\pi}{180°} \\
&= 3.665 \times 10^{-5} \text{ rad}
\end{aligned}
$$

The distance to the binary in metres is

$$
\begin{aligned}
r &= 8.79 \times 9.46 \times 10^{15} \\
&= 8.31 \times 10^{16} \text{ m}
\end{aligned}
$$

Hence the separation of the stars is $d = 3.05 \times 10^{12}$ m. From the formula for the period

$$
\begin{aligned}
M_1 + M_2 &= \frac{4\pi^2 d^3}{GT^2} \\
&= \frac{4\pi^2 (3.05 \times 10^{12})^3}{6.67 \times 10^{-11} \times (50 \times 365 \times 24 \times 60 \times 60)^2} \\
&= 6.75 \times 10^{30} \text{ kg}
\end{aligned}
$$

or 3.4 solar masses.

Eclipsing binaries – If the plane of the orbit of the two stars is suitably oriented relative to that of the earth, the light from one of the stars in the binary may be blocked by the other, resulting in an eclipse of the star, which may be total or partial. If a bright star (light grey circle) is orbited by a dimmer companion (dark circle), the light curve has the pattern shown in Figure F2.9. Such an example is provided by the system of AR Cassiopeia.

Figure F2.9 The light curve of AR Cassiopeia shows dips in brightness as the dimmer companion disappears behind the brighter star. When the dim star is in front, the dip is the largest.

Example question

Q8

Discuss the light curve of the eclipsing binary system Algol shown in Figure F2.10.

Figure F2.10.

Answer

This is an example of an eclipsing binary system in which the brighter of the two stars partially disappears from view every 3 days. The large dip in brightness occurs when the brighter star is behind the dimmer one. The small dip in brightness occurs when the brighter star is in front of the dimmer star.

Spectroscopic binaries – This system is detected by analysing the light from one or both of its members and observing that there is a periodic Doppler shifting of the lines in the spectrum. A blueshift is expected as the star approaches the earth and a redshift as it moves away from the earth in its orbit around its companion (Figure F2.11).

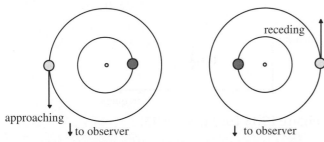

Figure F2.11 A binary star system. The stars rotate about their centre of mass. If the light grey star is the brighter, its light arrives at an observer blueshifted in the first diagram and redshifted in the second. In both positions shown, the stars are said to be in conjunction.

If λ_0 is the wavelength of a spectral line and λ the wavelength received on earth, the shift, z,

of the star is defined as

$$z = \left| \frac{\lambda - \lambda_0}{\lambda_0} \right|$$

If the speed of the source is small compared with the speed of light, it can be shown that

$$z = \frac{v}{c}$$

which shows that the shift is indeed directly proportional to the source's speed.

The top diagram in Figure F2.12 shows a spectrum with one line and the other two diagrams show what this line would look like if it were blue- or redshifted.

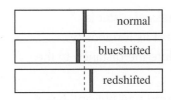

increasing wavelength

Figure F2.12 A normal spectral line (observed when the star's velocity is normal to the line of sight) is periodically blue- and redshifted as the star revolves in its orbit. In this example we are assuming that the second star is very dim so its light is not recorded. See questions 23 and 24 at the end of the chapter for the case in which light from both stars is analysed.

There is more discussion of the Doppler effect for light on page 544.

Example question

Q9

The blueshifts and redshifts of the bright star in Figure F2.12 are 3.4×10^{-5}. If it is known that the two stars are equal in mass and the distance separating them is 2.8×10^{12} m, what are these masses?

Answer

From the Doppler formula, $v = zc = 10\,200\ \mathrm{m\,s^{-1}}$. From

$$v^2 = \frac{GM_1^2}{d(M_1 + M_2)}$$
$$= \frac{GM}{2d}$$

it follows that

$$M = \frac{2v^2 d}{G}$$
$$= 4.4 \times 10^{30} \text{ kg}$$

Questions

1 The light from a star a distance of 70 ly away is received on earth with an apparent brightness of 3.0×10^{-8} W m^{-2}. Calculate the luminosity of the star.

2 The luminosity of a star is 4.5×10^{28} W and its distance from earth is 88 ly. Calculate the apparent brightness of the star.

3 The apparent brightness of a star is 8.4×10^{-10} W m^{-2} and its luminosity 6.2×10^{32} W. Calculate the distance to the star in light years.

4 Two stars have the same size but one has a temperature that is four times larger.
   (a) How much more energy per second does the hot star radiate?
   (b) The apparent brightness of the two stars is the same; what is the ratio of the distance of the cooler star to that of the hotter star?

5 Two stars are the same distance from earth and their apparent brightnesses are 9.0×10^{-12} W m^{-2} (star A) and 3.0×10^{-13} W m^{-2} (star B). Calculate the ratio of the luminosity of star A to that of star B.

6 Take the surface temperature of our sun to be 6000 K and its luminosity to be 3.9×10^{26} W. Find, in terms of the solar radius, the radius of a star with:
   (a) temperature 4000 K and luminosity 5.2×10^{28} W;
   (b) temperature 9250 K and luminosity 4.7×10^{27} W.

7 Two stars have the same luminosity. Star A has a surface temperature of 5000 K and star B a temperature of 10 000 K.
   (a) Which is the larger star and by how much?
   (b) If the apparent brightness of A is double that of B, what is the ratio of the distance of A to that of B?

8 Star A has apparent brightness 8.0×10^{-13} W m^{-2} and its distance is 120 ly. Star B has apparent brightness 2.0×10^{-15} W m^{-2} and its distance is 150 ly. The two stars have the same size. Calculate the ratio of the temperature of star A to that of star B.

9 Two stars A and B emit most of their light at wavelengths of 650 nm and 480 nm respectively. If it is known that star A has twice the radius of star B, find the ratio of the luminosities of the stars.

10 Explain how the surface temperature of a star determines the spectral class to which it belongs.

11 Describe how the colour of the light from a star can be used to determine the surface temperature of the star.

12 Explain why a star on the top left of the main sequence will spend much less time on the main sequence than another star on the lower right.

13 Describe the main features of the HR diagram. What quantities can be plotted on the vertical axis and which on the horizontal? Why are the scales non-linear?

14 Describe how a stellar absorption spectrum is formed.

15 Figure F2.13 shows the intensity of a particular spectral line emitted by a non-rotating star. On the same graph, draw what you would expect if the star were rotating.

Figure F2.13 For question 15.

16 Show that, if the stars in a binary star system have the same mass, they share the same orbit.

17 Make a sketch of the light curve of an eclipsing binary of period 20 yr in which:
   (a) both members are equally bright;
   (b) the inner star is much brighter than the other.

(Assume that the line of sight is in the orbital plane.) In each case draw diagrams to show the relative position of the two stars for significant times during the period.

18 From redshift measurements in a spectroscopic binary, it is known that the ratio of the masses is 1.20. If the period of the binary is 40 yr, and from parallax measurements it is known that the two stars are separated by a distance of 2.4×10^{12} m, find the individual masses of each star in the binary.

19 A visual binary system is at a distance of 5.0 pc. The distance between the two stars subtends an angle of 4.5 arcseconds.
   (a) What is this distance?
   (b) The period of the binary is 87.8 yr. What is the sum of the masses of the stars making up the binary?
   (c) The radius of the orbit of one of the stars subtends an angle of 1.91 arcseconds. What is the mass of each of the stars?

20 Describe what is meant by the term *white dwarf*. List two properties of the star. How does a white dwarf differ from a main sequence star of the same surface temperature?

21 A white dwarf, of mass half that of the sun and radius equal to one earth radius, is formed. What is the density of this white dwarf?

22 Where on the HR diagram would our sun lie at the time of its creation?

23 Figure F2.14 shows the spectrum of a spectroscopic binary.
   (a) Explain the structure of this spectrum.
   (b) Explain how it can be deduced that the stars are not equally massive.

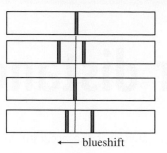

← blueshift

Figure F2.14 For questions 23 and 24.

   (c) Show by appropriate diagrams the relative positions of the two stars that give rise to each of the four spectra shown.

24 For the binary star system described in question 23, assume that the redshift in the second diagram of Figure F2.14 is 3.4×10^{-5} and the blueshift is 4.7×10^{-5}. Find the ratio of the masses of the two stars in the binary.

25 A binary star system consists of two stars that have a ratio of apparent brightness equal to 10. Explain carefully how we can deduce that the ratio of the luminosities of the stars is also 10.

26 (a) Find the temperature of a star whose spectrum is shown in Figure F2.15.
   (b) Assuming this is a main sequence star, what do you *estimate* its luminosity to be?

$I/10^{11}$ W m^{-3}

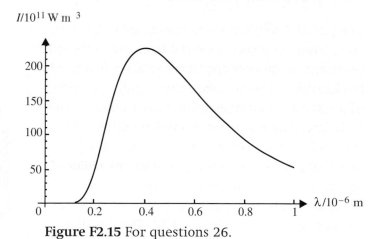

Figure F2.15 For questions 26.

Stellar distances

A major problem in astrophysics is the accurate determination of the distance to a star. This chapter discusses three methods for measuring distances: the parallax method, the spectroscopic parallax method and the Cepheid star method. The main tools in the study of stellar luminosity, such as absolute and apparent luminosities, and absolute and apparent magnitudes, are also discussed.

Objectives

By the end of this chapter you should be able to:

- describe the method of *parallax*, d (in parsecs) $= \frac{1}{p \text{ (in arcseconds)}}$, the method of *spectroscopic parallax* and the *Cepheids method* for determining distances in astronomy;
- define the *parsec*;
- state the definitions of *apparent brightness*, $b = \frac{L}{4\pi d^2}$, and *apparent* and *absolute magnitude*, $\frac{b}{b_0} = 2.512^{-m}$;
- solve problems using *apparent brightness* and *luminosity*.

The parallax method

The parallax method takes advantage of the fact that, when an object is viewed from two different positions, it appears displaced, relative to a fixed background. If we measure the angular position of a star and then repeat the measurement some time later, the two positions will be different, relative to a background of stars, because of the fact that in the intervening time the earth has moved in its orbit around the sun. We make two measurements of the angular position of the star six months apart; see Figure F3.1. The distance between the two positions of the earth is equal to $D = 2R$, the diameter of the earth's orbit around the sun ($R = 1.5 \times 10^{11}$ m). The distance to the star, d, is given by

$$\tan p = \frac{R}{d}$$

$$\Rightarrow d = \frac{R}{\tan p}$$

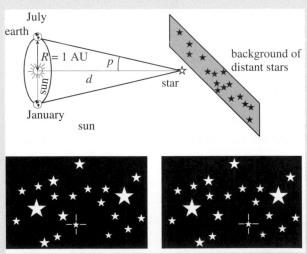

Figure F3.1 The parallax of a star. The second part shows two 'photographs' of the same region of the sky taken six months apart. The position of the star (indicated by a cross) has shifted, relative to the background stars, in the intervening six months.

Since the parallax angle is very small, $\tan p \approx p$ where the parallax p is measured in radians, and so

$$d = \frac{R}{p}$$

▶ The parallax angle is shown in Figure F3.1. It is the angle at the position of the star that subtends a distance equal to the radius of the earth's orbit around the sun, a distance known as one astronomical unit, $1\ \text{AU} = 1.5 \times 10^{11}$ m.

Parallaxes are measured quite accurately provided they are not too small. For example, parallaxes down to 1 arcsecond, symbol $1''$ (or 1/3600 of a degree), are easily measured.

▶ If the star is too far away, however, the parallax is too small to be measured and this method fails. Typically, distances up to 300 ly (roughly 100 parsec) can be measured with the parallax method, which is therefore mainly used for nearby stars.

The parallax method can be used to define a common unit of distance in astronomy, the parsec. One parsec (*parallax second*) is the distance to a star whose parallax is 1 arcsecond, as shown in Figure F3.2.

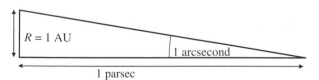

Figure F3.2 The definition of a parsec. A parsec is that distance at which 1 AU subtends an angle of 1 arcsecond.

In conventional units this means that

$$1\ \text{pc} = \frac{1.5 \times 10^{11}}{\left(\frac{2\pi}{360}\right)\left(\frac{1}{3600}\right)}\ \text{m}$$
$$= 3.09 \times 10^{16}\ \text{m}$$

(The factor of $2\pi/360$ converts degrees into radians.) In terms of a light year (1 ly $= 9.46 \times 10^{15}$ m), 1 pc = 3.26 ly. In summary:

- $1\ \text{AU} = 1.5 \times 10^{11}$ m
- $1\ \text{ly} = 9.46 \times 10^{15}$ m
- $1\ \text{pc} = 3.09 \times 10^{16}$ m $= 3.26$ ly

▶ This means that if the parallax of a star is known to be p arcseconds, the distance is $1/p$ parsecs, or

$$d\ (\text{in parsecs}) = \frac{1}{p\ (\text{in arcseconds})}$$

Table F3.1 shows the five nearest stars.

Star	Distance/ly
Proxima Centauri	4.3
Barnard's Star	5.9
Wolf 359	7.7
Lalande 21185	8.2
Sirius	8.6

Table F3.1 Distances to the five nearest stars.

Absolute and apparent magnitudes

The ancient astronomers devised a *relative* system of classifying stars according to how bright they *appeared* to an observer on earth. Each star was given a number called the *apparent magnitude m* – the higher the apparent magnitude, the dimmer the star. In the system of Hipparchos and Ptolemy, six classes of brightness were defined, and assigned numbers from 1 to 6. A magnitude 6 star was supposed to be 100 times *dimmer* than a magnitude 1 star. Thus, a magnitude 2 star is $100^{1/5} \approx 2.512$ times dimmer than a magnitude 1 star.

The modern system of assigning a measure to apparent brightness conforms roughly to that

Spectroscopic parallax

▶ The term *spectroscopic parallax* refers to a method of finding the distance to a star given the star's luminosity and apparent brightness. The term is misleading in that no use of parallax is being made.

Assume that we know the luminosity, L, and apparent brightness, b, of a star. Since these two quantities are related by

$$b = \frac{L}{4\pi d^2}$$

it follows that

$$d = \sqrt{\frac{L}{4\pi b}}$$

The question is then how to determine the luminosity of the star. This is done by examining its spectrum, from which, as we saw in the last chapter, the temperature can be deduced. Knowing the temperature and using the HR diagram (*assuming the star is a main sequence star*) allow us to determine the luminosity as well. Thus, the distance can be found. This method can be used to estimate distances to several thousand parsecs.

Example question

Q1

A main sequence star emits most of its energy at a wavelength of 3.87×10^{-7} m. Its apparent brightness is measured to be 4.3×10^{-9} W m^{-2}. How far is the star?

Answer

From Wien's law we find the temperature of the star to be

$$\lambda_0 T = 2.90 \times 10^{-3} \text{ K m}$$

$$\Rightarrow T = \frac{2.90 \times 10^{-3}}{3.87 \times 10^{-7}} \text{ K}$$

$$= 7500 \text{ K}$$

From the HR diagram in Chapter F2, we see that such a temperature corresponds to a luminosity of

about 10 times that of the sun, that is

$$L = 3.9 \times 10^{27} \text{ W}$$

Thus

$$d = \sqrt{\frac{L}{4\pi b}}$$

$$= \sqrt{\frac{3.9 \times 10^{27}}{4\pi \times 4.3 \times 10^{-9}}} \text{ m}$$

$$= 2.7 \times 10^{17} \text{ m}$$

$$\approx 28.4 \text{ ly}$$

$$\approx 8.7 \text{ pc}$$

The Cepheids

Cepheid variable stars are stars whose luminosity is not constant in time but varies from a minimum to a maximum *periodically*, the periods being typically from a couple of days to a couple of months. The brightness of the star increases sharply and then fades off more gradually, as shown in the light curve of a Cepheid in Figure F3.5.

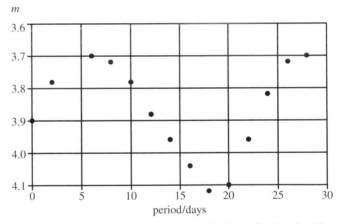

Figure F3.5 The apparent magnitude of a Cepheid star varies periodically with time.

The first Cepheid was discovered by the nineteen-year-old English astronomer John Goodricke in 1748, two years before his death.

The reason for the periodic behaviour of the brightness of Cepheid stars has to do with the interaction of radiation with matter in the atmosphere of the star. This interaction causes the outer layers of the star to undergo periodic expansions and contractions. The star is at its brightest when the surface of the star expands outward at high velocity. It is at its dimmest when the surface moves inward.

> ▶ At the beginning of the twentieth century, Henrietta Leavitt discovered a remarkable relationship between the peak luminosity of Cepheids and their period. The longer the period, the larger the luminosity (see Figure F3.6). This makes Cepheid stars 'standard candles' – observing a Cepheid and finding its period allows the determination of its luminosity. This, in turn, allows the determination of its distance, as explained below.

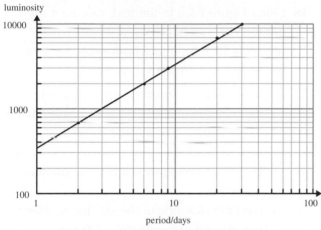

Figure F3.6 There is a relationship between the peak luminosity of a Cepheid star and its period. The luminosity is given in terms of the solar luminosity.

For example, the Cepheid whose light curve is shown in Figure F3.5 has a period of about 22 days. From Figure F3.6, this corresponds to a luminosity of about 720 solar luminosities, or about $L = 2.8 \times 10^{29}$ W. The peak apparent magnitude of the Cepheid from Figure F3.5 is about $m = 3.7$. The peak apparent brightness can be found from

$$\frac{b}{2.52 \times 10^{-8}} = 2.512^{-m}$$
$$\Rightarrow b = 2.52 \times 10^{-8} \times 2.512^{-3.7}$$
$$= 8.34 \times 10^{-10} \text{ W m}^{-2}$$

Now, using the relationship between apparent brightness, luminosity and distance,

$$b = \frac{L}{4\pi d^2}$$

$$\Rightarrow d = \sqrt{\frac{L}{4\pi b}}$$

$$= \sqrt{\frac{2.8 \times 10^{29}}{4\pi \times 8.37 \times 10^{-10}}}$$

$$= 5.17 \times 10^{18} \text{ m}$$

$$\approx 546 \text{ ly}$$

$$\approx 168 \text{ pc}$$

Thus, one can determine the distance to the galaxy in which the Cepheid is assumed to be. The Cepheids method can be used to find distances up to a few Mpc.

Figure F3.7 summarizes the distances at which each of the methods of determining stellar distance is effective.

Figure F3.7 The ordinary parallax method allows the determination of distances up to about 100 pc. The spectroscopic parallax method extends distance measurements to about 10 000 pc. The Cepheid variable star method extends the scale further to 15 Mpc.

Questions

1 Describe with the aid of a clear diagram what is meant by the parallax method in astronomy. Explain why the parallax method fails for stars that are very far away.

2 Give definitions of:
   (a) apparent magnitude of a star;
   (b) absolute magnitude of a star.

3 Find the distance to Procyon, which has a parallax of 0.285″.

4 The distance of Epsilon Eridani is 10.8 ly. What is its parallax?

5 Betelgeuse has an angular diameter of 0.016″ (i.e. the angle subtended by the star's diameter at the eye of an observer) and a parallax of 0.0067″.
   (a) What is the distance of Betelgeuse from the earth?
   (b) What is its radius in terms of the sun's radius?

6 The parallax of a star is 0.025″ and its absolute magnitude is $M = 0.8$. Is its apparent magnitude less than or greater than 0.8?

7 The parallax of Kapteyn's Star is 0.250″ and its apparent magnitude is 9.2.
   (a) How far is it?
   (b) Is this star visible to the human eye?

8 How many times brighter is a star of absolute magnitude 2 than a star of absolute magnitude 4?

9 Vega has an absolute magnitude of 0.5 and Capella an absolute magnitude of −0.6. Which is the brighter star and by how much?

10 Table F3.3 contains information on apparent magnitude and parallax for two stars.
   (a) Which star appears brighter?
   (b) Which star has the larger luminosity?

Star	Apparent magnitude	Parallax
A	4.82	0.022″
B	5.38	0.034″

Table F3.3 For question 10.

11 Table F3.4 contains information on absolute magnitude and parallax for two stars.
   (a) Which star has the larger luminosity?
   (b) Which star appears brighter?

Star	Absolute magnitude	Parallax
A	3.75	0.025″
B	3.75	0.040″

Table F3.4 For question 11.

12 The two stars making up a binary star system have apparent magnitudes of $m = 5.1$ (star A) and $m = 8.2$ (star B). Explain carefully how we can deduce that star A has the greater *luminosity*.

13 A main sequence star emits most of its energy at a wavelength of 2.42×10^{-7} m. Its apparent brightness is measured to be 8.56×10^{-12} W m^{-2}. How far is the star? (Use the HR diagram in Chapter F2.)

14 What is the apparent brightness and apparent magnitude of a star of luminosity 2.45×10^{28} W and a parallax of 0.034″?

15 (a) Altair has an apparent magnitude of $m = 1.0$. Calculate its apparent brightness.
   (b) Procyon has an apparent brightness of 1.78×10^{-8} W m^{-2}. Calculate its apparent magnitude.

16 Using Figure F3.6 in the text, calculate the distance of a Cepheid variable star whose period is 10 days and whose peak apparent brightness is 3.45×10^{-14} W m^{-2}.

17 (a) Show that the absolute and apparent magnitudes of a star, M and m, are related to the distance of the star through $m - M = 5 \log\left(\frac{d}{10}\right)$ or $d = 10^{\frac{m-M}{5}} \times 10$ pc. Use this formula to answer the following questions.
   (b) Find the distance of the star Rigel, which has absolute magnitude −7.0 and apparent magnitude 0.1.
   (c) Alpha Centauri has an apparent magnitude of −0.27 and a parallax of 0.760″. What is its absolute magnitude?
   (d) Our sun has an apparent magnitude of −26.74. What is the greatest distance from which this would be visible to the unaided human eye?

Cosmology

This chapter introduces the Olbers paradox and its resolution, and the monumental discovery by Edwin Hubble that the universe is expanding. The basic idea of the Big Bang theory is introduced and the difficulties in determining the future evolution of the universe are discussed.

Objectives

By the end of this chapter you should be able to:

- describe the *Olbers paradox* in Newtonian cosmology and how it is resolved;
- describe the main features of the *Big Bang* and the *expansion of the universe*;
- understand the significance of the *cosmic background radiation*;
- state the meaning of the terms *open universe* and *closed universe*;
- outline the theoretical possibilities for the *evolution of the universe*;
- state the meaning and significance of the term *critical density*;
- appreciate the importance of various forms of *dark matter*.

The Olbers paradox

The universe appears to be full of *structures*. There are planets and moons in our *solar system*, stars in our *galaxy*, our galaxy is part of a *cluster* of galaxies and our cluster is part of an even bigger *supercluster* of galaxies. If we look at the universe on a very large scale, however, we no longer see any structures. If we imagine cutting up the universe into cubes of side 300 Mpc across, the interior of any one of these cubes would look the same as the interior of any other cube, anywhere else in the universe. This has led to what is called the *homogeneity principle* in cosmology. On a *large scale*, the universe looks *uniform*.

Similarly, if we look in different directions, we see essentially the same thing. If we look far enough in any one direction, we will count the same number of galaxies. No one direction is

special in comparison with another. This has led to a second principle of cosmology, the *isotropy principle*.

▶ These two principles, homogeneity and isotropy, make up what is called the *cosmological principle* – a principle that has had a profound role in the development of cosmology.

The cosmological principle implies that the universe has no edge (for if it did, the part of the universe near the edge would look different from a part far from the edge, violating the homogeneity principle). Similarly, it implies that the universe has no centre (for if it did, observing from the centre would show a different picture from observing from any other point, violating the principle of isotropy).

Answer

From the Wien displacement law, $\lambda T = 2.9 \times 10^{-3}$ K m, it follows that most of the energy is emitted at a wavelength $\lambda = 1.07$ mm, which is a microwave wavelength.

The Big Bang: the creation of space and time

The discovery of the expanding universe by Hubble implies a definite beginning of the universe, some 14 billion years ago. The size of the universe at that time was infinitesimally small and the temperature and pressure enormous. These conditions create the picture of a gigantic explosion at $t = 0$, which set matter moving outwards. Billions of years later we see the remnant of this explosion in the receding motion of the distant galaxies. This is known as the Big Bang scenario in cosmology. It is important to understand that the Big Bang was not an explosion that took place at a specific time in the past somewhere in the universe. At the time of the Big Bang the space in which the matter of the universe resides was created as well. Thus, the Big Bang happened about 14 billion years ago everywhere in the universe (the universe then being a point).

The main experimental evidence in support of the Big Bang theory includes the following:

- **The expansion of the universe** – The universe is now observed to expand. Hence in the past the universe had a smaller size. Even further into the past the universe must have been a tiny object, which started to expand. This points to a picture of an 'explosion' that set the universe moving outward.

- **The cosmic background radiation** – Today we observe the background radiation at 2.7 K. This is consistent with a small, hot universe in the distant past, which began to cool down as it expanded.

- **Helium abundance** – It is a prediction of the Big Bang model that there should be an abundance of helium in the universe, of about 25% by mass. Measurements of helium abundance today, within our own galaxy, nearby galaxies and clusters of galaxies, as well as in newly born stars, give a number that is never less than 25%. It is very difficult to account for this lower bound on helium in such different measurements if we do not accept the cosmological explanation of helium formation.

The development of the universe

Mathematically, the expansion of the universe can be described in terms of a scale factor of the universe in the following way. If the distance between two galaxies was x_0 at some arbitrary time, then the separation of these two galaxies at some time t later is given by the expression

$$x(t) = R(t)x_0$$

The function $R(t)$ is called the *scale factor* of the universe and is of basic importance to cosmology. It is sometimes referred to loosely as the *radius of the universe*. Note that this is a scalar function, not a vector, indicating the standard assumption about the isotropy and homogeneity of the universe on a large scale.

It is a basic problem in cosmology to discover what this scale factor $R(t)$ is. Application of the laws of general relativity results in *three possibilities* for $R(t)$.

▶ The first possibility is that $R(t)$ starts from zero, increases to a maximum value and then decreases back to zero again. The universe collapses after an initial period of expansion. This is called a *closed universe*.

In the second possibility, the scale factor $R(t)$ increases without limit – the universe continues to expand forever. This is called an *open universe*.

The third possibility is that the universe does expand forever, but the rate of expansion decreases. This is called a *flat universe*.

These three possibilities are shown in Figure F4.3.

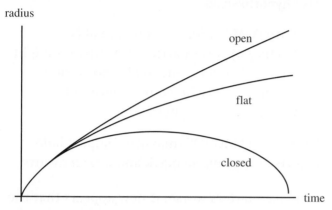

radius

open

flat

closed

time

Figure F4.3 The three solutions to Einstein's equations for the scale factor of the universe.

Which of the three possibilities is actually realized depends on the value of the mass density of the universe, ρ, relative to a *critical density* whose value (as shown later) is about $\rho_c \approx 10^{-26}$ kg m^{-3}.

- If $\rho < \rho_c$, the universe expands forever. The universe is called *open*.
- If $\rho = \rho_c$, the universe expands forever at a slowing rate. The universe is called *flat*.
- If $\rho > \rho_c$, the universe collapses after a period of expansion. The universe is called *closed*.

General relativity actually gives an additional interpretation to the three different scenarios for $R(t)$. General relativity says that the geometry of the universe (i.e. the rules of geometry) depend on the amount of mass in the universe. The mass in the universe bends or curves the space and time in the universe. The amount of bending depends on how much mass there is.

The case $\rho < \rho_c$ corresponds to an *open universe* of infinite volume, whose curvature is analogous to that of the surface of a saddle (a hyperboloid). The case $\rho > \rho_c$ corresponds to a *closed universe*, with a finite volume and a curvature similar to that of a sphere. This is a universe without edges. Finally, $\rho = \rho_c$ corresponds to an *open*, infinite, but *flat* universe, analogous to the surface of an ordinary plane.

These universes cannot be visualized. A closed universe means that its volume is finite and that it has no boundary. The *inside* of a sphere is a three-dimensional space of finite volume but it does have a boundary (the surface of the sphere). We therefore try to visualize these cases with two-dimensional analogies. For example, imagine dots on the surface of a balloon representing galaxies. As the balloon is inflated (the universe is expanding) the dots move further apart (the distance between the galaxies increases). (See Figure F6.5 later.)

Table F4.1 summarizes this information about these three possible types of universe.

Geometry	Density	Type	Volume	Expansion
Hyperbolic	$\rho < \rho_c$	Open	Infinite	For ever
Euclidean	$\rho = \rho_c$	Flat (open)	Infinite	For ever, but slows down
Spherical	$\rho > \rho_c$	Closed	Finite	Stops, followed by collapse

Table F4.1 Characteristics of different possible universes.

Supplementary material

Estimate of the critical density

The critical density can be calculated simply by using Newtonian mechanics. Consider a spherical cloud of dust of radius r and a mass m at the surface of this cloud which moves away from the centre with a velocity v that satisfies Hubble's law, $v = Hr$ (see Figure F4.4). Here the constant H stands for the Hubble constant. Its numerical value is 72 km s^{-1} Mpc^{-1}. This is discussed in detail in Chapter F6.

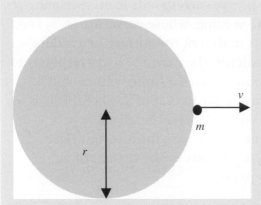

Figure F4.4 Estimating critical density.

The total energy of the mass is

$$E = \frac{1}{2}mv^2 - \frac{GMm}{r}$$

where M is the mass of the cloud. If we call the density of this cloud ρ, then $M = \rho\frac{4}{3}\pi r^3$ and using this together with $v = Hr$ we find

$$E = \frac{1}{2}mr^2\left(H^2 - \frac{8\pi\rho G}{3}\right)$$

The mass m will continue to move away if its total energy is positive. The expansion will halt at infinity if the energy is zero, and contraction will follow the expansion if the energy is negative.

▶ The criterion, therefore, is the value of the density relative to the quantity

$$\rho_c = \frac{3H^2}{8\pi G} \approx 10^{-26} \text{ kg m}^{-3}$$

Determining the mass density of the universe

To measure the mass density of the universe means measuring the mass of galaxies within a large volume of space and dividing that mass by the volume. There is an immediate problem in all of this in that we know there exists 'dark

matter', matter that we cannot see (because it is too cold to radiate). The determination of the density of the universe, ρ, is difficult. The problem is made worse by the fact that neutrino masses are not yet determined, so their contribution to the density of the universe is unknown. Dark matter could be in the form of brown dwarfs and other similar cold objects, but the existence of more exotic possibilities is also hypothesized.

First are WIMPS (non-baryonic, weakly interacting massive particles). Neutrinos might be classified as such but so also are various other particles predicted by theories of elementary particle physics.

Second are MACHOS (massive compact halo objects), for example black and brown dwarfs.

To make matters worse, it now appears that the universe also contains 'dark energy', which is a kind of vacuum energy associated with Einstein's famous cosmological constant Ω. So the question of what exactly is the mass and energy of the universe is far from having a definitive answer.

It is customary in cosmology to define the parameter Ω through

$$\Omega = \frac{\rho}{\rho_c}$$

Without any dark matter, Ω is about 0.01. Including the dark matter that is *known to exist* brings it to about 0.3. This is tantalizingly close to 1, the critical point between an open, forever expanding universe and a closed universe that one day will collapse to a point. This causes what is known as the 'flatness problem' in cosmology: if Ω were *exactly* 1 at the beginning of time it would remain 1 forever. But any initial deviation from 1 would, billions of years later, result in a huge deviation from 1. To have Ω so close to 1 now, means that Ω deviated from 1 at the beginning of time by no more than 10^{-15}. Why was Ω so finely tuned at the beginning of time?

Questions

1 State what you understand by the term *the Olbers paradox*. Why is this 'paradox' a problem for finite cosmologies? How is the paradox resolved in the Big Bang model of cosmology?

2 How many hydrogen atoms per m^3 does the critical density $\rho_c \approx 10^{-26}$ kg m^{-3} correspond to?

3 Discuss three pieces of evidence that support the Big Bang model of the universe.

4 The temperature of the cosmic background radiation measured from earth is about 2.7 K.
   (a) What is the significance of the cosmic background radiation?
   (b) What temperature for the cosmic background radiation would an observer in a very distant galaxy measure? Why?

5 What will happen to the temperature of the cosmic background radiation if:
   (a) the universe keeps expanding forever;
   (b) the universe starts to collapse?

6 It is said that the Big Bang started everywhere in space. What does this mean?

7 In the context of the Big Bang theory, explain why the question 'what existed before the Big Bang?' is meaningless.

8 Explain, with the use of two-dimensional examples if necessary, the terms *open* and *closed* as they refer to cosmological models.

Give an example of a space that is finite without a boundary and another that is finite with a boundary.

9 In the context of cosmology, what do you understand by the terms:
   (a) *critical density*;
   (b) *closed universe*;
   (c) *open universe*?

10 A student explains the expansion of the universe as follows: 'Distant galaxies are moving at high speeds into the vast expanse of empty space.' What is wrong with this statement?

11 Explain what a comparison of the mass density of the universe with the critical density allows us to determine.

12 What is the main difficulty in determining the value of the mass density of the universe?

13 What do you understand by the term *dark matter*? Give three examples of dark matter.

14 What was the temperature of the universe when the peak wavelength of the background radiation was equal to the wavelength of red light (7×10^{-7} m)?

15 (a) Draw a sketch graph to show the variation with wavelength of the intensity of the cosmic background radiation.
   (b) If the universe is in fact open, as recent evidence suggests, explain how the graph you drew in (a) will change many millions of years in the future.

Stellar processes and evolution

This chapter is a detailed account of the nuclear fusion reactions that can take place in the interior of a star, and how the sequence of these reactions determines the evolution and death of a star. The Hertzsprung–Russell (HR) diagram is used to show the evolutionary paths of stars.

Objectives

By the end of this chapter you should be able to:

- describe how a star is *formed*;
- state the main sequences of *nuclear reactions* taking place in a star and say how the *mass* of the star determines which sequences actually take place;
- describe the *main stages in the evolution of a star* and say how the *mass* plays a determining role;
- describe the *end stages* of stellar evolution and appreciate the significance of the *Chandrasekhar limit*;
- state the main properties of a *black hole*;
- state the main properties of *pulsars*;
- state the main characteristics of *quasars*;
- state the meaning of the term *gravitational lensing*.

Nucleosynthesis

Interstellar space (the space between stars) consists of gas and dust at a density of about 10^{-21} kg m^{-3}. This amounts to about one atom of hydrogen in every cubic centimetre of space. The gas is mainly hydrogen (about 74% by mass) and helium (25%), with other elements making up the remaining 1%. Whenever the gravitational energy of a given mass of gas exceeds the average kinetic energy of the thermal random motion of its molecules, the gas becomes unstable and tends to collapse:

$$\frac{GM^2}{R} \geq \frac{3}{2} NkT$$

where k = Boltzmann's constant, T = temperature and N = number of molecules.

This is known as the Jeans criterion. Stars formed and continue to be formed when rather cool gas clouds in the interstellar medium ($T \approx 10$–100 K) of sufficiently large mass (large enough to satisfy the Jeans criterion) collapsed under their own gravitation. In the process of contraction, the gas heated up. Typically, the collapsing gas would break up into smaller clouds, resulting in the creation of more than one star. When the temperature rises sufficiently for visible light to be emitted, the star so formed is called a *protostar* (see Figure F5.1).

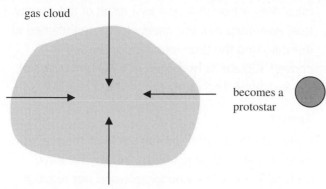

Figure F5.1 The formation of a protostar out of a collapsing cloud of gas.

Example questions

Q1

Show that the Jeans criterion can be rewritten as $M^2 = \frac{3}{4\pi\rho}\left(\frac{3kT}{2mG}\right)^3$, where ρ is the density of the gas and m is the mass of a molecule of the gas.

Answer

Cube each side of the Jeans criterion equation to find

$$\left(\frac{GM^2}{R}\right)^3 = \left(\frac{3kMT}{2m}\right)^3$$

$$\Rightarrow M^2 = \left(\frac{3}{4\pi\rho}\right)\left(\frac{3kT}{2mG}\right)^3$$

using the definition of density and $M = Nm$, where m is the mass of one molecule.

Q2

Take the density of interstellar gas to be about 100 atoms of hydrogen per cm^3. What is the smallest mass this cloud can have so that it becomes unstable and begins to collapse?

Answer

The density is

$$\frac{100 \times 1.67 \times 10^{-27} \text{ kg}}{10^{-6} \text{ m}^3} = 1.67 \times 10^{-19} \text{ kg}^{-3}$$

With $T = 100$ K in the Jeans criterion (see example question 1) we find

$$M \approx 3.0 \times 10^{33} \text{ kg}$$
$$= 1.5 \times 10^3 M_{sun}$$

This shows that the gas cloud is quite large and that it can break up, forming more than one star.

As the gas is compressed more (always under the action of gravity) its temperature rises and so does its pressure. The pressure in the core of the star is one way the star can become stable against gravity and stay at a fixed size. However, the core of the gas can get so hot ($T = 5 \times 10^6$ to 10^7 K) that nuclear fusion reactions take place, resulting in the release of enormous amounts of energy. The vast quantity of energy released can account for the sustained luminosity of stars such as our sun, for example, over the 4–5 billion years of its life so far. Thus, nuclear fusion provides the energy that is needed to keep the star hot, so that its pressure is high enough to oppose further contraction and at the same time to provide the energy that the star is radiating into space.

▶ While on the main sequence, the main nuclear fusion reactions taking place are those of the proton–proton cycle discussed in Chapter F2. The net effect of these reactions is to turn four hydrogen nuclei into one helium

$$4\,^1_1\text{H} \rightarrow \,^4_2\text{He} + 2e^+ + 2\nu_e + 2\gamma$$

with a release of about 26.7 MeV or 3.98×10^{-12} J of energy. Helium, being heavier than hydrogen, collects in the core of the star (see Figure F5.2).

A star on the main sequence will spend most of its time there (of the order of 10^{10} yr for a one solar mass star and a few million years for a star of mass equal to 10 solar masses). Nuclear physics predicts a direct relationship between luminosity and mass, of the form $L \propto M^\alpha$, where the exponent α is larger than 1 and depends on the mass. For main sequence stars, the exponent is between 3 and 4. We can find the lifetime T of a star by the following simple scaling argument. The total mass available for fusion is the mass M of the star. Since the luminosity is the amount of energy emitted per unit time, it follows that

$$M^\alpha = \frac{Mc^2}{T}$$
$$\Rightarrow T \propto M^{1-\alpha}$$

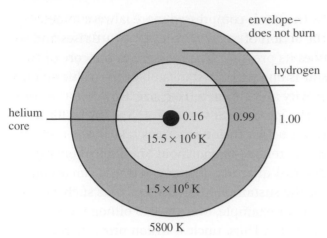

Figure F5.2 The structure of a main sequence star of one solar mass. The numbers 0.16, 0.99 and 1.00 represent the fraction of mass enclosed within each shell. The helium core consists of about 62% helium and 36% hydrogen, showing that nuclear fusion has already started converting hydrogen into helium. The rest of the star is predominantly hydrogen (73%) with 25% helium. The density in the core is about 164 kg m^{-3}, whereas in the outer levels the density falls to 90 kg m^{-3}.

Taking the exponent α to be equal to 4 for simplicity, it follows that $T \propto M^{-3}$. This shows that a star of mass 10 times that of the sun will have a lifetime that is 1000 times shorter than that of the sun. Taking the sun's lifetime to be 10^{10} yr, the massive star will thus have a lifetime of 10 million years. Massive stars burn their nuclear fuel too quickly.

> ▶ After the star has used about 12% of its hydrogen (the Schonberg–Chandrasekhar limit), its core will contract but its outside envelope will expand substantially, making it a very large star. The star will begin to leave the main sequence and move over to the red giant branch.

A more detailed calculation of the lifetime is given in the answer to the example question below.

Example question

Q3 ▬▬▬▬▬▬▬▬▬▬

The lifetime of the sun. Our sun emits energy at a rate (luminosity) of about 3.9×10^{26} W. How much mass does it lose in a year as a result of this energy loss? Assuming that the energy loss is maintained at this rate, find the time required for the sun to convert 12% of its hydrogen into helium. (Mass of sun = 1.99×10^{30} kg.)

Answer

Assuming the proton–proton cycle as the reaction releasing energy by fusing hydrogen, we have seen above that the energy released per reaction is about 3.98×10^{-12} J. Since the luminosity of the sun is 3.9×10^{26} W, it follows that the number of fusion reactions required per second is

$$\frac{3.9 \times 10^{26}}{3.98 \times 10^{-12}} = 9.8 \times 10^{37}$$

For every such reaction, four hydrogen nuclei turn into helium and thus the mass of the fused hydrogen is

$$9.8 \times 10^{37} \times 4 \times 1.67 \times 10^{-27} \text{ kg s}^{-1}$$
$$= 6.5 \times 10^{11} \text{ kg s}^{-1}$$

or 2×10^{19} kg per year.

At the time of its creation, the sun consisted of 75% hydrogen, corresponding to a mass of

$$0.75 \times 1.99 \times 10^{30} \text{ kg} = 1.5 \times 10^{30} \text{ kg}$$

The Schonberg–Chandrasekhar limit of 12% results in a hydrogen mass to be fused of 1.8×10^{29} kg. The time for this mass to fuse is thus

$$\frac{1.8 \times 10^{29}}{6.5 \times 10^{11}} \text{ s} = 2.8 \times 10^{17} \text{ s}$$
$$= 8.9 \times 10^{9} \text{ yr}$$

Since the sun has existed for about 5 billion years, it still has about 4 billion years left in its lifetime as a main sequence star.

Nuclear reactions beyond the main sequence

With the hydrogen in the core exhausted, nuclear reactions there stop and hence the core contracts under its own weight. The contraction of the core releases gravitational potential energy, which heats up the core and the surrounding envelope of hydrogen. The hydrogen continues to fuse and the released energy forces the outer layers of the star to expand. At the same time, though, the outer layers are getting cooler because of the rapid expansion. The star is thus getting bigger and cooler on the surface – it is becoming a *red giant*. In the meantime, the core temperature is increasing.

What happens next depends on the *mass* of the star.

Low-mass stars (mass less than 0.25 solar masses)
No further nuclear reactions take place. The core stays a core of helium.

Mass between 0.25 and 4 solar masses
The temperature of the core reaches the 10^8 K required for nuclear reactions in the core involving helium to start. Since a helium nucleus has two units of positive charge as opposed to one for hydrogen, higher temperatures are required for helium nuclei to fuse. This is because the larger electric charge implies a larger electric force of repulsion that has to be overcome.

The reactions involving helium produce nuclei of carbon and oxygen. Examples of such reactions are

$$_2^4\text{He} + {}_2^4\text{He} \rightarrow {}_4^8\text{Be} + \gamma$$
$$_2^4\text{He} + {}_4^8\text{Be} \rightarrow {}_6^{12}\text{C} + \gamma$$
$$_2^4\text{He} + {}_6^{12}\text{C} \rightarrow {}_8^{16}\text{O} + \gamma$$

The first two reactions occur in rapid succession and have the net effect of converting three helium nuclei into one of carbon. This is called the *triple alpha process*. No further nuclear reactions take place and the core now consists of carbon and oxygen.

Mass between 4 and 8 solar masses
In this mass range, the core temperature rises further and nuclear reactions involving carbon and oxygen take place, producing a core of oxygen, neon and magnesium.

Mass over 8 solar masses
The evolution of such a massive star is very different from that of less massive stars. Because of the large mass of the star, the oxygen, neon and magnesium core will contract further, reaching a temperature high enough for these core elements to fuse, producing heavier elements. In the outer layers helium continues to produce more carbon, and hydrogen more helium. This process repeats, with ever heavier elements settling in the central core. Eventually iron will be produced by the fusing of silicon, and once this happens, the iron will settle at the core. Fusion cannot produce elements heavier than iron, since the binding energy per nucleon peaks with iron and further fusion is not energetically possible. Thus, a massive star ends its cycle of nuclear reactions with iron at its core surrounded by progressively lighter elements, as shown in Figure F5.3. The outer layers of the star have since expanded to a very large size, making the star a *red supergiant*.

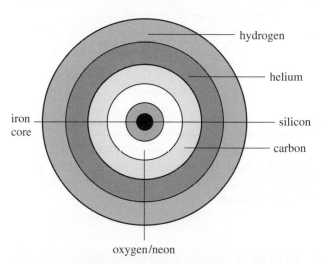

Figure F5.3 The central core of the star consists of iron with layers of lighter elements surrounding it.

Table F5.1 shows the temperatures at which various elements participate in fusion reactions.

Element	$T/10^6$ K	Where
Hydrogen	1–20	Main sequence
Helium	100	Red giant
Carbon	500–800	Supergiant
Oxygen	1000	Supergiant

Table F5.1 The temperatures at which elements participate in fusion reactions.

Evolutionary paths and stellar processes

Once a star is formed out of contracting gases, its surface temperature is not particularly high, but it has a large size, which means that the star starts out somewhere to the right of the main sequence in the HR diagram. As the star continues to contract, its temperature increases and the star moves toward the main sequence. The time spent moving toward the main sequence depends on the mass of the star. Heavier stars take less time. Our sun has taken about 20 to 30 million years to reach the main sequence. (See Figure F5.4.)

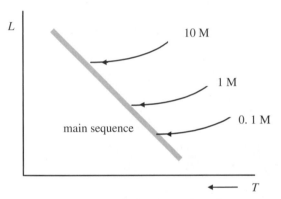

Figure F5.4 Evolutionary tracks of protostars as they approach the main sequence. M stands for one solar mass.

▶ The mass of the star is the factor that determines its final fate.

Table F5.2 shows the various outcomes for various stellar mass ranges. The table is explained in greater detail in what follows.

Case 1: Evolution of a star of mass under 8 solar masses

We saw in the last section that, depending on the mass of the star, nuclear reactions in the core stop when the core is made mainly out of helium or carbon/oxygen or oxygen/neon/magnesium. The energy released from the core contraction and the hydrogen or helium fusion

Initial mass of star (in terms of solar masses)	Outcome
<0.25	White dwarf with helium core
0.25–4	White dwarf with carbon/oxygen core
4–8	White dwarf with oxygen/neon/magnesium core
8–40	Neutron star
>40	Black hole

Table F5.2 The final fates of stars of various initial masses.

in the outer layers may force the tenuous outer layers to be ejected from the star in what is called a *planetary nebula* (see Figure F5.5). This leaves behind the small core of the star. The mass of the core may thus be substantially reduced compared with the original mass of the star.

But the core is still contracting under its own weight and getting smaller. The conditions in the core mean that the electrons behave as a gas and the pressure they generate is what keeps the core from collapsing further under its weight. This pressure is generated because of a quantum mechanical principle, Pauli's principle, which states that no two electrons may occupy the same quantum mechanical state.

The core has now become a *white dwarf star*. Now exposed, and with no further energy source, the star is doomed to cool down to practically zero temperature and will then become a *black dwarf*.

▶ The electron pressure can stop the further collapse of the core and the star will become a stable white dwarf only if the mass of the core is less than 1.4 solar masses. This important number in astrophysics is known as the Chandrasekhar limit. If the mass of the core is more than 1.4 solar masses, the star will become a neutron star or a black hole.

Figure F5.5 Helix: a planetary nebula. The star that produced this nebula can be seen at the exact centre. [Note: The name 'planetary nebula' is rather misleading, since it has no connection whatsoever with planets. Planetary nebulae were thought to resemble planets when first seen through a telescope, and the name has stuck.]

The Chandrasekhar limit is named after the great Indian (and later American) astrophysicist, Subrahmanyan Chandrasekhar. His work on collapsed stars was presented in 1935 at a meeting of the Royal Astronomical Society in England. His ideas were publicly ridiculed by Sir Arthur Eddington, his colleague and mentor at Cambridge University. For his work, Chandrasekhar shared the 1983 Nobel prize in physics.

Subrahmanyan Chandrasekhar.

The best known white dwarf is Sirius B, a star that accompanies the star Sirius. It has a mass of 1.02 solar masses, a radius of 5400 km and a surface temperature of 10 000 K. Although hot, it is hard to see, mainly because of the small surface area from which the light is emitted (i.e. the luminosity is low).

The transition from a white to a black dwarf may be uneventful, but occasionally something dramatic may take place. If the white dwarf is part of a binary system, it may attract material from the companion star, which may then be drawn into the white dwarf. As this material falls into the white dwarf, it heats up and emits light. In this way the luminosity of the white dwarf may, briefly, increase by tens of thousands of times. This temporary increase in luminosity is called a *nova* (see Figure F5.6).

Figure F5.6 A white dwarf star increasing in luminosity during a nova.

Case 2: Evolution of a star of mass over 8 solar masses

As we saw in the last section, the end of nuclear reactions has left a massive star with an iron core. The star is full of photons that have been produced in the various nuclear fusion reactions. They are so energetic that they rip the iron nuclei apart into smaller nuclei. The smaller nuclei are in turn ripped apart into individual protons and neutrons, so that in a very short time the star is composed mainly of protons, electrons, neutrons and photons. Because of the high densities involved, the electrons are forced into the protons, turning them into neutrons and producing neutrinos that escape from the star $(e^- + p \rightarrow n + \nu_e)$. The star's core is now made almost entirely of neutrons and it is still contracting rapidly. Pauli's principle is now applied to neutrons. The neutrons get too close to each other and a pressure develops to prevent them from getting any closer. But the neutrons have overshot. They have become too close together and the entire core will now rebound to a larger equilibrium size. The rebounding of the core is catastrophic for the star. It creates an enormous shockwave travelling outward that tears apart the outer layers of the star. The explosion that takes place is much more violent than a planetary nebula and is called a *supernova*. The core that is left behind is called a *neutron star*, and is more massive than the Chandrasekhar limit of 1.4 solar masses.

The first calculations showing the details of neutron star formation were performed by J.R. Oppenheimer (the 'father' of the American atomic bomb) and G.M. Volkoff in 1939. Neutron pressure keeps the star stable, provided the mass of the core is not more than about 3 solar masses – the Oppenheimer–Volkoff limit.

Black holes

If the mass of the collapsing star exceeds a few tens of solar masses, the gravitational collapse is unstoppable. The star will soon reach a radius at which the escape velocity from the surface of the sun equals the speed of light, and hence nothing can escape from the star. This radius is called the gravitational radius of the star, R_g, or the Schwarzschild radius or the event horizon radius. It can be found from

$$R_g = \frac{2GM}{c^2}$$

It can be readily calculated from this formula that for a star of one solar mass the gravitational radius is about 3 km. For the earth it is just 9 mm.

The fact that light cannot escape from a very massive object was known to Pierre Laplace as early as 1795. The first detailed calculations of how a star could actually collapse to form a black hole were performed by Oppenheimer and Snyder in 1939.

To summarize:

> ▶ If the mass of the core of a star is less than the Chandrasekhar limit of about 1.4 solar masses, the star will become a stable white dwarf in which electron pressure keeps the star from collapsing further.
>
> If the core is more massive than the Chandrasekhar limit, the core will collapse further until electrons are driven into protons, turning them into neutrons. Neutron pressure now keeps the star from collapsing further and the star has become a neutron star.
>
> If the core is substantially more massive than the Oppenheimer–Volkoff limit of 3 solar masses, neutron pressure will not be enough to oppose the gravitational collapse and the star will become a black hole.

Evidence for black holes

Even though a black hole cannot be seen directly, its effects are observable. If it happens to be in the vicinity of other stars, then the strong gravitational field of the hole will

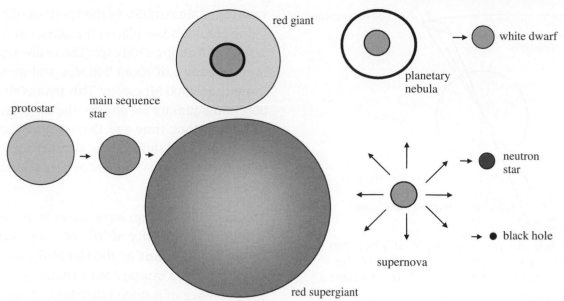

Figure F5.7 The birth and death of a star. The star begins as a protostar, evolves to the main sequence and then becomes a red giant or supergiant. After a planetary nebula or supernova explosion, the core of the star develops into one of the three final stages of stellar evolution, a white dwarf, a neutron star or a black hole.

influence the motion of nearby stars. Thus, one looks for binary star systems which are sources of X-rays and in which one star is invisible: gas forced into the black hole accelerates and becomes very hot, radiating X-rays on its way into the hole. There are now nine known examples of binary star systems in which the invisible member is a black hole. These include the oldest black hole candidate, the powerful X-ray binary Cygnus X-1, located near the centre of our galaxy. Much heavier black holes exist in other galactic centres. Fifteen of these are known and their masses are in the millions of solar masses.

Figure F5.7 shows a schematic summary of the life history of a star.

These evolutionary stages can be shown on an HR diagram (Figure F5.8).

Pulsars and quasars

Pulsars

A neutron star may have a magnetic field of quite large magnitude (10^8 T) and may rotate as well, with a period ranging from 30 ms to 0.3 s. Rotating neutron stars emit electromagnetic waves in the *radio* part of the spectrum and so neutron stars can be detected by radio telescopes. (They can also radiate in the X-ray part of the spectrum.) Rotating neutron stars that radiate in this way are called *pulsars*. Despite the name, it is rotation not pulsation that is responsible for the radiation. The

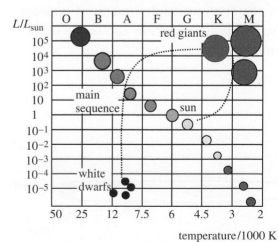

Figure F5.8 A star such as our sun leaves the main sequence on its way to the red giant branch. After a planetary nebula explosion leaves behind a white dwarf, the star moves rapidly to the white dwarf region on the diagram.

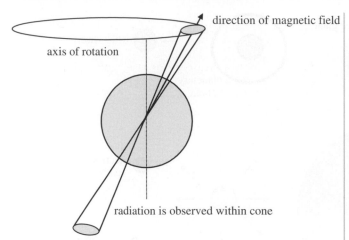

Figure F5.9 If the axis of rotation of a neutron star does not coincide with the direction of the magnetic field, the emitted radiation shows a beacon effect.

radiation emitted by the pulsar is in a narrow cone around the magnetic field direction. If the magnetic field is not aligned with the axis of rotation, then, as the star rotates, the cone containing the radiation *precesses* around the rotation axis (see Figure F5.9). An observer who can receive some of this radiation will then do so every time the cone sweeps past. This explains the pulse nature of this radiation. Pulsars were discovered by Jocelyn Bell (now Professor J. Bell-Burnell), a graduate student at Cambridge University, in 1967.

Quasars

In the early days of radio astronomy, a few radio sources were discovered for which there was no obvious optical counterpart. Finally, a star-like object was identified to be at the position of one of these radio sources and its emission spectrum was obtained. The spectrum was mysterious in that it contained lines that could not be identified with any known element. The puzzle was resolved when it was realized that the lines did belong to familiar elements but they were redshifted by amounts never seen before. The largest redshift for a quasar is just under 5, which corresponds to a recession

velocity of almost 95% of the speed of light. Using Hubble's law placed the quasar at a distance of about 4700 Mpc. The nearest quasar is at a distance of about 240 Mpc and most are more than 1000 Mpc away. This means that by observing quasars we observe the universe as it was a very long time ago. Quasars (the name stands for quasi-stellar radio sources) are believed to be the very active centres of very young galaxies.

The luminosity of quasars varies from 10^{38} W to 10^{42} W. A luminosity of 10^{42} W is equivalent to about 2×10^{15} suns or 100 000 Milky Ways! What powers a quasar? Most theories involve the presence of a huge black hole at the centre of the quasar that swallows up stars at a rate of perhaps 1000 each year. As the material falls into the black hole, it heats up and radiates, building the quasar's huge luminosity.

In 1979, two quasars were discovered in roughly the same region of space, raising hope for a binary quasar system. When the two were analysed further, they were found to have identical spectra. The 'two' quasars were in fact two images of just one quasar. The multiple images were created by gravitational lensing. Radio signals from the quasar travel past a massive galaxy on their way to earth and are bent by the galaxy in accordance with Einstein's theory of general relativity (see Figure F5.10). Such multiple images of quasars provide valuable information about the mass of the lensing body.

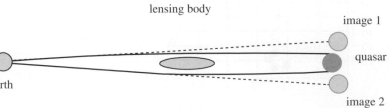

Figure F5.10 The radio signals from the distant quasar are bent as they travel past a massive galaxy. An observer on earth sees two images of the quasar.

Questions

1 What would the evidence be that a black hole exists at a particular point in space?

2 Using the known luminosity of the sun and assuming that it stays constant during the sun's lifetime, which is estimated to be 10^{10} yr, calculate the mass this energy corresponds to, according to Einstein's mass–energy formula.

3 A neutron star has a diameter of 20 km and makes 1000 revolutions per second.
(a) What is the speed of a point on its equator?
(b) What fraction of the speed of light is this?

4 Comparing two main sequence stars of mass 1 and 10 solar masses, which would you expect to stay longer on the main sequence? Why?

5 What is a planetary nebula? Why do most photographs show planetary nebulae as rings – doesn't the gas surround the core from all directions?

6 How would you react to a claim of the discovery of a star with a core of gold?

7 Assume that the luminosity of a main sequence star is given by $L \propto M^4$. Realizing that the available energy that can be radiated equals the rest mass of the star Mc^2, show that the lifetime of a star scales as $t \propto M^{-3}$. Hence show that a star that is twice as massive as the sun has a lifetime that is 8 times shorter than that of the sun.

8 How would you react to the discovery of a stellar cluster 100 million years old containing a large number of class O stars? (See question 7 and page 509.)

9 Assume that no stars of mass greater than about 2 solar masses could form. Would life as we know it on earth be possible?

10 Describe the evolution of a main sequence star of mass:
(a) 1 solar mass;
(b) 10 solar masses.

11 Calculate the energy released in the reactions:
(a) $^4_2He + ^8_4Be \rightarrow ^{12}_6C + \gamma$;
(b) $^4_2He + ^{12}_6C \rightarrow ^{16}_8O + \gamma$.

(Atomic masses: He = 4.00260 u, Be = 8.0053 u, O = 15.9941 u.)

12 Why is the temperature at which helium nuclei fuse higher than that for hydrogen?

13 What causes:
(a) a planetary nebula;
(b) a supernova?

14 Describe the significance of the Chandrasekhar limit in stellar evolution.

15 Describe the formation of a red giant star.

16 Show on an HR diagram the evolution of a star of 5 solar masses.

17 Consider the reaction $^4_2He + ^4_2He \rightarrow ^8_4Be + \gamma$ and look at Figure F5.11. The electrostatic repulsion of the positive helium nuclei prevents them from fusing unless the temperature is very high. Estimate this temperature by setting the kinetic energy of a helium nucleus equal to $\frac{3}{2}kT$, where k is Boltzmann's constant. At the point of closest approach the helium nuclei stop and if they are close enough the strong nuclear force will take over and force them to fuse. At this point, set the electrostatic potential energy of the nuclei equal to the sum of the kinetic energies, and thus show that the temperature can be found from

$$3kT = \frac{1}{4\pi\varepsilon_0}\frac{4e^2}{d}$$

Taking the distance of closest approach to be $d = 1.0 \times 10^{-14}$ m, calculate T numerically.

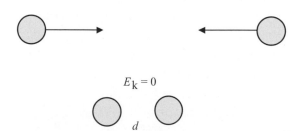

$E_k = 0$

Figure F5.11 For question 17.

18 Table F5.3 shows the luminosity L of a star and the corresponding mass M of the star. By plotting the logarithm of the luminosity versus the logarithm of the mass, find the relationship

Mass (in solar masses)	Luminosity (in solar luminosities)
1	1
3	42
5	238
12	4700
20	26500

Table F5.3 For question 18.

between these quantities assuming a power law of the kind $L = kM^\alpha$, giving the numerical value of the parameter α.

19 The light from a Cepheid star shows blue- and redshifts of varying magnitude. The blueshift is observed when the star is at its brightest and the redshift when at its dimmest. How can this be explained? When the shift is plotted against time, a periodic curve matching exactly the light curve of the Cepheid is obtained. How can this be explained? Theories of Cepheids as pulsating stars predict that the period and density are related by

$T^2 \rho = $ constant

Considering Cepheids of the same mass, show that this implies that the longer-period stars have larger luminosities.

20 Assume that the material of a main sequence star obeys the ideal gas law, $PV = NkT$. The volume of the star is proportional to the cube of its radius R, and N is proportional to the mass of the star, M. Show that $PR^3 \propto MT$. The star is in equilibrium under the action of its own gravity, which tends to collapse it, and the pressure created by the outflow of energy from its interior, which tends to expand it. It can be shown that this equilibrium results in the condition $P \propto \frac{M^2}{R^4}$. (Can you see how?) Combine these two proportionalities to show that $T \propto \frac{M}{R}$. Use this result to explain that, as a star shrinks, its temperature goes up. Conclude this rough analysis by showing that the luminosity of main sequence stars of the same density is given by $L \propto M^{3.3}$.

21 Compare the chemical composition of a young star with that of a star of similar mass but 10 billion years in age.

22 What is a mechanism for energy production in a quasar?

23 What was so unexpected in quasar spectra?

24 Why is the radiation observed from a pulsar pulsed and not continuous?

25 Is the energy emitted by a quasar much less than, about the same as or much larger than the energy emitted by a normal galaxy?

26 (a) Assuming a quasar swallows 1000 stars a year, how long would it take a quasar to consume the mass of the entire Milky Way galaxy?

   (b) What conclusion about a quasar's lifetime can you draw from your calculation?

Galaxies and the expanding universe

This chapter discusses Hubble's scheme for the classification of galaxies and provides more details about the expanding universe and Hubble's law. The main events in the lifetime of the universe are outlined.

Objectives

By the end of this chapter you should be able to:

*   understand the Hubble *classification scheme* of galaxies and describe the structure of the *Milky Way galaxy*;
*   state the *Hubble law* and solve problems using this law, $v = H d$;
*   state the meaning of the *Hubble constant*;
*   identify *significant epochs* in the life of the universe;
*   understand the term *inflationary universe*.

Types of galaxy

The Milky Way galaxy

Our sun is one of about 200 billion stars (2×10^{11}) making up the Milky Way, our galaxy, which is a spectacular object to scientist and non-scientist alike, that can be clearly seen on a clear, dark night. The Milky Way is a *spiral* galaxy with a central disc-like bulge (see Figure F6.1). The galaxy has a diameter of some 100 000 ly. At the edges it has a thickness of about 2000 ly. Our solar system occupies a position on one of the spiral arms a distance of about 30 000 ly from the centre, and orbits the galactic centre, completing one revolution every 225 million years. Assuming an average mass for stars equal to that of our sun $(2 \times 10^{30}$ kg) results in a mass for the galaxy of about 4×10^{41} kg.

Galaxies were classified by Edwin Hubble in 1924 into a scheme based mainly on

appearance. Hubble identified three basic types of galaxies, *spiral* (with a subdivision into *barred spirals*), *elliptical* and *irregular*. The original scheme has since been modified but it is still being used today.

Spiral galaxies

Our own Milky Way and our close neighbour Andromeda are examples of spiral galaxies. A spiral galaxy consists of a central nucleus, a flattened disc in which the spiral arms are found and a halo of older faint stars. A spiral galaxy contains old as well as young stars. Spirals range in diameter from 6000 pc to 30 000 pc and from 10^9 to 10^{12} solar masses. Our own galaxy is a large spiral in both size and mass. New stars are formed mainly in the spiral arms where the density of interstellar dust is the greatest. The presence of interstellar gas is seen from detailed photographs as well as from the observed radiation at a wavelength of 21 cm that is indicative of such gas. The central

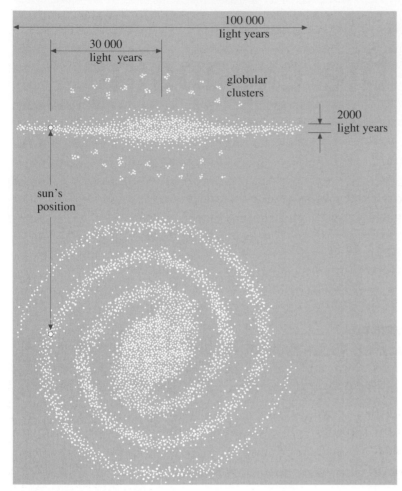

Figure F6.1 The size and structure of the Milky Way galaxy.

nucleus consists mainly of older stars. The subdivision called *barred spirals* is a class of galaxies that is a variation of the spirals; some astronomers believe that they are essentially spirals and therefore don't need a new class to describe them. Like spirals they have spiral arms, but a 'bar' of stars and gas runs through the central bulge and extends into the disc. The spiral arms appear to start from the ends of the bar and not from the central bulge as is the case in the ordinary spirals. Spirals are the most common galaxies; perhaps more than 50% of all galaxies fall into this class.

Elliptical galaxies

These galaxies have a spherical or ellipsoidal shape and consist almost entirely of old stars. There are giant elliptical galaxies containing very massive stars (stars of mass equal to 10^{12} solar masses) and extend in size to a few Mpc. A good example of such a galaxy is M87. The most common ellipticals, however, are small galaxies containing only a few million stars that can be as small as 1 kpc in diameter. A good example of such a dwarf elliptical is the Leo II system, which is so near our own galaxy as to be influenced by the Milky Way's gravity. Ellipticals differ from spirals in that they have no, or very little, interstellar gas. This means that there is very little star formation activity. About 45% of all galaxies are ellipticals.

Irregular galaxies

About 5% of all galaxies fall into the class of irregular galaxies. They have no definite symmetry and are irregular or even chaotic in appearance. Irregular galaxies seem to be undergoing intense star-making activity with many young star clusters. Our closest extragalactic neighbours, the Large and Small Magellanic Clouds, are irregular galaxies. The irregular shape of these galaxies is believed to be (in some but not all cases) due to the collision or close encounter of two regular galaxies.

The characteristics of the three types of galaxy are summarized in Table F6.1, and they are shown in Figure F6.2.

Galactic motion

As we leave our galaxy behind and enter intergalactic space, we find that our galaxy is part of a group of galaxies – the Local Group. There are about 20 galaxies in the Local Group, the nearest being the Large Magellanic Cloud at a distance of about 2 million light years. In this group, we find the Andromeda galaxy, a spiral galaxy like our own and the largest member of the Local Group. The Local Group extends over a distance of about 1 million light years.

	Spirals/barred spirals	**Ellipticals**	**Irregulars**
Shape	Flattened disc, central bulge from which spiral arms start. In barred galaxies, arms start from the ends of the bar. Halo	Spherical or ellipsoidal in shape with stars fairly uniformly distributed in the galaxy	No obvious structure
Star content	The disc contains both young and old stars. The halo has mainly old stars	Contain mainly old stars	Contain both young and old stars
Gas and dust	The disc contains significant amounts of both. The halo does not	Contain little or no gas and dust	Contain a lot of gas and dust
Star formation	Takes place in spiral arms	No significant new star formation in the last 10 billion years	Very significant star formation

Table F6.1 Properties of the three types of galaxy.

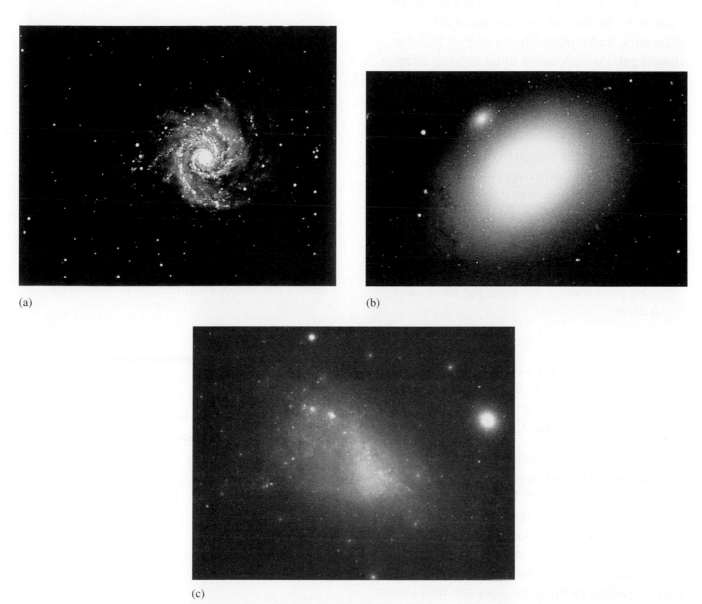

(a)

(b)

(c)

Figure F6.2 (a) Spiral galaxy. (b) Elliptical galaxy. (c) Irregular galaxy.

This grouping of galaxies into *clusters* is very common. As we move even further out, we encounter collections of clusters of galaxies, known as *superclusters*. It is believed that our Local Group cluster belongs to a supercluster (or supergalaxy) of size 15×10^6 pc across. Contrary to what was believed until recently, the distribution of clusters in space is not uniform but there seem to be areas of linear size 10^8 ly that are empty.

As early as 1914, V. M. Slipher announced his measurements on 15 spiral galaxies. Thirteen of these showed redshifted absorption lines, indicating that these galaxies were moving away from us. By 1925, the number of galaxies studied by Slipher and his assistant, M. Humason, had climbed to 45 and all but the closest galaxies appeared to be moving away at enormous speeds.

▶ The velocity of recession is found by an application of the Doppler effect to light. Light from galaxies arrives on earth redshifted. This means that the wavelength of the light measured upon arrival is longer than the wavelength at emission. According to the Doppler effect, this implies that the source of the light – the galaxy – is moving away from the observers on earth.

The redshift in the light from distant galaxies is, strictly speaking, an effect of general relativity (the expanding universe) and is not due to the Doppler effect.

Light emitted from galaxies comes from atomic transitions in the hot gas in the interior of the galaxies, which is mostly hydrogen. Galaxies are surrounded by cooler gas and thus light travelling through is absorbed at specific wavelengths, showing a characteristic absorption spectrum. The wavelengths corresponding to the dark lines are well known from experiments on earth but the observed wavelengths from the galaxies, when compared

to those measured on earth, were found to be a bit longer: they were redshifted. The same applies, of course, to the emission spectrum of the galaxy, but that is usually too faint to be seen.

If λ_0 is the wavelength of a spectral line and λ is the (longer) wavelength received on earth, the redshift, z, of the galaxy is defined as

$$z = \frac{\lambda - \lambda_0}{\lambda_0}$$

If the speed v of the receding galaxy is small compared with the speed of light c, then

$$z = \frac{v}{c}$$

which shows that the redshift is indeed directly proportional to the receding galaxy's speed (more correctly, the component of velocity along the line of sight – see Figure F6.3 and later).

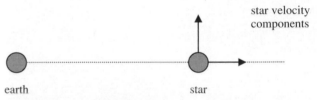

star velocity components

earth   star

Figure F6.3 Using the Doppler effect we can only measure the component of the star's velocity along the line of sight not the total velocity.

Example question

Q1

A hydrogen line has a wavelength of 434 nm. When received from a distant galaxy, this line is measured on earth at 486 nm. What is the speed of recession of this galaxy?

Answer

The redshift is

$$\frac{486 - 434}{434} = 0.12$$

hence

$$v = 0.12c$$
$$= 3.6 \times 10^7 \, \mathrm{m\,s^{-1}}$$

Hubble's law

In 1925, Edwin Hubble began a study to measure the distance to the galaxies for which Slipher and Humason had determined the velocities of recession. In 1929, Hubble (building on earlier work by V. M. Slipher, and C. Wirtz and K. Lundmark) could announce that galaxies move away from us with speeds that are proportional to their distance. This was a monumental discovery.

▶ Hubble studied a large number of galaxies and found that, the more distant the galaxy, the faster it moves away from us. This is Hubble's law, which states that the velocity of recession is directly proportional to the distance, or

$$v = Hd$$

where d is the distance between the earth and the galaxy, and v its velocity of recession (see Figure F6.4). The constant of proportionality, H, is the slope of the graph and is known as the Hubble constant.

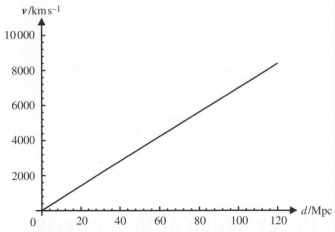

Figure F6.4 Hubble discovered that the velocity of recession of galaxies is proportional to their distance from us.

H is the constant of proportionality, known appropriately as the Hubble constant. (It is constant in space but it varies with time.) This was a dramatic discovery – it made the universe a dynamic, evolving, expanding universe. There is considerable debate as to the value of the Hubble constant. The uncertainties come mainly from the enormous difficulties in measuring distances to remote galaxies accurately. The graph in Figure F6.4 assumes a value of 72 km s^{-1} Mpc^{-1}. This is the most recent value of the Hubble constant, established after a Hubble Space Telescope study of Cepheid stars in 18 galaxies.

Hubble's discovery implies that, in the past, the distances between galaxies were smaller and, moreover, that at a specific time in the past the entire universe had the size of a point. This specific point in time is taken to be the beginning of the universe. Not only was time created then but also the space in which the matter and energy of the universe reside. As the space expanded, the distance between clumps of matter increased, leading to the receding galaxies that Hubble observed. It is conventional to describe this three-dimensional expansion of the universe by a two-dimensional model that can be visualized. If we draw two points on the surface of a balloon, they will move apart from each other as the balloon is inflated, as shown in Figure F6.5.

Figure F6.5 A two-dimensional model of Hubble's law. The points on the balloon move away from each other as the balloon is inflated.

This two-dimensional model can easily be visualized since we can observe the expansion of the balloon into the three-dimensional space in which the balloon is embedded. The expansion of the universe, on the other hand, is three-dimensional and could be visualized only if we could similarly view it as embedded in a four-dimensional space. We cannot.

Figure F6.6 shows how the 'radius' of the universe changes in an expanding universe.

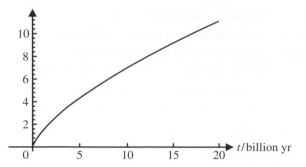

Figure F6.6 The 'radius' of the universe (in arbitrary units) as a function of time.

Hubble's law does not imply that the earth is at the centre of the universe even though the observation of galaxies moving away from us might lead us to believe so. An observer on a different star in a different galaxy would reach this (erroneous) conclusion about their location too. Suppose that a distant galaxy a distance r from the earth has speed v as measured by us. Let $\vec{r}$ be the vector joining the earth to the galaxy. Then $\vec{v} = H\vec{r}$. Now consider a different observer in a different galaxy a distance R from us and moving away at speed V (see Figure F6.7). Hubble's law applied to this galaxy states that $\vec{V} = H\vec{R}$.

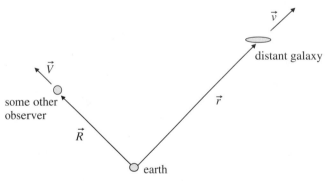

Figure F6.7 Observers on earth are not privileged when it comes to determining Hubble's law.

As far as this observer is concerned, the distant galaxy has velocity $\vec{v} - \vec{V}$, and position vector $\vec{r} - \vec{R}$. Clearly

$$\vec{v} - \vec{V} = H(\vec{r} - \vec{R})$$

that is, Hubble's law is satisfied by the other observer as well. Thus, all observers have the illusion that they are at the centre of the universe. The linear Hubble law is the only possible law for which this could happen.

▶ If we assume that the expansion of the universe has been constant up to now, then $1/H$ gives an upper bound to the age of the universe. This is only an upper bound since the expansion rate, having been faster at the beginning, implies a younger universe. The time $1/H$, known as the Hubble time, is about 14 billion years. The universe cannot be older than that. The more detailed argument that leads to this conclusion is as follows. Imagine a galaxy, which now is at a distance r from us. Its velocity is thus $v = Hr$. In the beginning the galaxy and the earth were at zero separation from each other. If the present separation of r is thus covered at the same *constant* velocity Hr, the time, T, taken to achieve this separation must be given by $v = \frac{r}{T} = Hr$, that is $T = \frac{1}{H}$. Time T is a measure of the age of the universe.

The numerical value of the Hubble time with $H = 72 \times 10^3 \text{ m s}^{-1} \text{ Mpc}^{-1}$ is

$$T_H = \frac{1}{H}$$

$$= \frac{1}{72 \times 10^3 \text{ m s}^{-1} \text{ Mpc}^{-1}}$$

$$= \frac{1}{72 \times 10^3 \text{ m s}^{-1}} \times 10^6 \text{ pc}$$

$$= \frac{1}{72 \times 10^3 \text{ m s}^{-1}} \times 10^6 \times 3.09 \times 10^{16} \text{ m}$$

$$= 4.29 \times 10^{17} \text{ s}$$

$$= \frac{4.29 \times 10^{17} \text{ s}}{365 \times 24 \times 60 \times 60 \text{ s yr}^{-1}}$$

$$= 13.6 \times 10^9 \text{ yr}$$

The evolution of the universe

If we extrapolate backwards in time, starting with the present temperature of 2.7 K, we can find the temperature of the radiation and the matter filling the universe at earlier times.

Out of the fundamental constants of G, c and h we may define a quantity with units of time. This is known as the *Planck time* and is assumed to mark that time in the history of the universe before which quantum gravitational effects were dominant. Since no quantum theory of gravity exists, the Planck time can be taken as the furthest one can extrapolate backwards in time. It is given by the combination

$$t_p = \sqrt{\frac{hG}{c^5}} \approx 10^{-43}\,\text{s}$$

At this early time after the Big Bang, the temperature was about 10^{32} K. The thermal energy associated with this temperature can be calculated from $E_k \approx \frac{3}{2}kT$, giving an energy of the order of 10^{19} GeV (1 GeV $= 10^9$ eV). Whatever particles existed then would have had a kinetic energy of this order of magnitude.

Forces are unified: time $= 10^{-43}$ s

The strong nuclear force presumably joined with the electroweak into one unified force. During this period, leptons (i.e. electrons, muons, neutrinos, etc.) were indistinguishable from quarks, and under the action of the unified force these particles turned into each other.

Strong nuclear force separates: time $= 10^{-35}$ s

The next milestone in the evolution of the universe occurred at a time of about 10^{-35} s, when the strong nuclear force decoupled from the electroweak force. The temperature by then had fallen to about 10^{27} K.

Inflation begins: time $= 10^{-35}$ s

There followed an extremely rapid period of expansion, called the inflationary epoch. It lasted for no more than 10^{-32} s but in this brief time the size of the universe increased by a factor of 10^{50}! See later for the necessity of inflation.

Forces separate: time $= 10^{-12}$ s

At a time of about 10^{-12} s after $t = 0$, the temperature was about 10^{16} K and the four fundamental forces, gravity, electromagnetism, strong nuclear and weak nuclear, behaved as separate forces. The size of the universe was about 10^{-16} of its present size.

Nucleons form: time $= 10^{-2}$ s

At $t = 10^{-2}$ s, the temperature had fallen sufficiently (to 10^{11} K) for quarks to bind together and to form protons and neutrons and their antiparticles. The universe had a size of about 10^{-10} of its present size. At $t = 1$ s after the Big Bang, $T = 10^{10}$ K, and protons, neutrons, electrons and their antiparticles were in thermal equilibrium with each other.

Example question

Q2 ▬▬▬▬▬▬▬▬▬▬▬▬▬▬
Show that at a temperature of $T = 10^{10}$ K there is enough thermal energy to create electron–positron pairs.

Answer

The thermal energy corresponding to $T = 10^{10}$ K is $E_k \approx \frac{3}{2}kT$, that is

$$1.5 \times 1.38 \times 10^{-13}\,\text{J} = 1.3\,\text{MeV}$$

The rest energy of an electron is about 0.5 MeV, which is enough to produce a pair.

Nuclei form: time $= 3$ min

At $t = 200$ s ('the first three minutes'), the temperature had fallen down to 10^9 K and the time was right for protons and neutrons to start combining, creating the nuclei of the light atoms. When the temperature was just over 10^9 K, the thermal motion of nucleons inside the nucleus was large enough to break the nucleus apart. Therefore, no nuclei could have existed prior to this time. This temperature sets the time when nuclei began to form – the period of *nucleosynthesis*. The relative numbers of protons, neutrons and electrons differ because of differences in mass, but can be determined by applying the laws of thermodynamic equilibrium. Using, in addition, the laws of nuclear physics, which determine how nucleons combine to form nuclei, one can predict the relative abundances of the nuclei so produced as the universe cools from 10^9 K to lower temperatures. For example, it can be shown that at this time there were seven protons for every neutron in the universe, or fourteen protons for every two neutrons. The two neutrons can combine with two protons to form one helium nucleus, the remaining twelve protons forming twelve hydrogen nuclei. The mass of twelve hydrogen nuclei is about 12 u and the mass of one helium nucleus about 4 u.

In this way, we can predict that there should exist an abundance of helium-4 in the universe of about 25% by mass. The fact that the measured abundance of helium is 25% is one of the strongest pieces of evidence in favour of the Big Bang scenario.

After the formation of light nuclei, 3 min or so after the Big Bang, the universe consisted mainly of electrons, photons and light nuclei (protons and deuterium and helium nuclei) up to a time of about 10^4 yr ($T = 10^4$ K). The universe then had a size of about 10^{-4} of its present size.

Atoms form: time = 3×10^5 yr

There followed a period of *recombination*, in which electrons joined with protons to form neutral atoms of hydrogen at about 3×10^5 yr, $T = 3000$ K. (The term *recombination* is misleading since atoms of hydrogen had not existed earlier.) The universe was cooling down sufficiently for matter and radiation to decouple. Previously, photons scattering off electrons kept the electrons (matter) in thermal equilibrium with radiation (photons). The fact that electrons were now in atoms and not free means that photons could move larger distances without being scattered by electrons. Earlier, the total energy carried by photons was greater than the energy carried by matter, but at these lower temperatures equality was reached. Soon afterwards, the energy carried by matter became the dominant energy in the universe; the universe became matter-dominated and continues to be so today.

First stars and galaxies form: time = 0.5×10^6 yr

About half a million years after $t = 0$, matter began to cool sufficiently to allow for the formation of stars and galaxies. Nuclear fusion

in the interior of stars provided their energy and heavier nuclei were formed. Our solar system formed just over a billion years from the Big Bang.

Matter and antimatter

The universe we observe is made out of matter and not antimatter. Yet in the very early universe there were *almost* equal numbers of particles and antiparticles. Note the word 'almost', for if the numbers of particles and antiparticles had been exactly the same, we would not be here – no matter would exist. Theories of elementary particles predict that in the very early universe an asymmetry in their interactions produced a very slight excess of particles over antiparticles (one extra particle for every 10^9 particle–antiparticle pairs in the universe). The particles constantly collided with the antiparticles and turned themselves into photons. But the reverse process also occurred, with photons turning themselves into pairs of particles and antiparticles. When the universe cooled down to below 10^{13} K, the energy of the photons was so reduced that they could no longer produce pairs of particles and antiparticles. The annihilation of particles and antiparticles into photons continued, however, until all particle–antiparticle pairs were turned into photons (permanently). This left behind the one particle, in the 10^9 pairs, that was unmatched. This is the matter that we see today.

Inflationary models

While successful in dealing with the observed properties of the universe (cosmic microwave radiation, helium abundance), the standard Big Bang model described here has serious technical difficulties. One of them is the observed isotropy of the background radiation. Radiation received on earth from two opposite directions is found to correspond to black-body radiation at the same temperature. These radiations were emitted from separate points in space a very long time ago. If we extrapolate back to the time of emission, it can be shown that the points of emission were so far apart that no information could have propagated from one point to the other in order to influence it in any way. Why, then, did these isolated points choose to emit radiation at the same temperature? This problem, among others, was solved in a model of cosmology that agrees with the Big Bang model for times after 10^{-32} s from the Big Bang but differs significantly from it at earlier times. Developed by Alan Guth, the characteristic feature of this *inflationary model*, as it is called, is a tremendous expansion of the universe in a very short interval of time. It is hypothesized that the scale factor R of the universe increased by a factor of 10^{50} over a time of only 10^{-32} s during the inflationary epoch! (See Figure F6.8.) The details of this model link in an intimate way the physics of cosmology (very large scale physics) with the physics of elementary particles (very small scale physics).

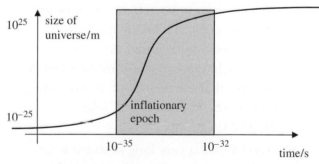

Figure F6.8 During the inflationary epoch the size of the universe increased by a factor of 10^{50} in a time interval of just 10^{-32} s.

Questions

1 What type of galaxy is the Milky Way according to Hubble's classification scheme.

2 Outline the structure of the Milky Way galaxy.

3 State and explain Hubble's law. Explain why this law is evidence for an expanding universe.

4 Some galaxies actually show a blueshift, indicating that they are moving toward us. Does this violate Hubble's law?

5 Galaxies are affected by the gravitational pull of neighbouring galaxies and this gives rise to

what are called *peculiar* velocities. Typically these are about 500 km s^{-1}. How far away should a galaxy be so that its velocity of recession due to the expanding universe equals its peculiar velocity?

6 Suppose that sometime a detailed study of the Andromeda galaxy and all the nearby galaxies in our Local Group will be possible. Would this help in determining Hubble's constant more accurately?

7 Figure F6.9 shows two lines due to calcium absorption in the spectrum of five galaxies, ranging from the nearby Virgo to the very distant Hydra. Each diagram gives the wavelength of the H line (hydrogen line). The wavelength of the H line in the lab is 656.3 nm. Use the Doppler shift formula (non-relativistic version) to find the velocity of recession of each galaxy. Using Hubble's law, find the distance to each galaxy. (Use $H = 72$ km s^{-1} Mpc^{-1}.)

Figure F6.9 For question 7.

8 Take Hubble's constant now to be $H = 72$ km s^{-1} Mpc^{-1}.
  (a) At what distance from the earth is the speed of a receding galaxy equal to the speed of light?
  (b) What happens to galaxies that are beyond this distance?
  (c) Is the theory of special relativity violated?

9 A spectral line, when measured on earth, corresponds to a wavelength of

4.5×10^{-7} m. When received from a distant galaxy, the wavelength of the same line is measured at 5.3×10^{-7} m.

(a) What is the redshift for this galaxy?

(b) How fast is this galaxy moving from us? Find the answer by using the non-relativistic formula

(c) How far is the galaxy?
(Take $H = 72$ km s^{-1} Mpc^{-1}.)

10 Explain why the inverse of the Hubble constant, $1/H$, is taken to be the 'age of the universe'. How old would the universe be if $H = 500$ km s^{-1} Mpc^{-1} (close to Hubble's original value)?

11 Explain how the Hubble constant sets an *upper bound* to the age of the universe.

12 Explain why the Hubble law does not imply that the earth is at the centre of the universe.

13 Consider a balloon and two points on its equator (see Figure F6.10). The radius of the balloon is R and is increasing with time. The distance between the two points is thus getting bigger. This distance is given by $r = R\theta$, where θ is the angle that the arc joining the two points subtends at the centre of the balloon. Assume that as the balloon expands the angle θ stays the same.

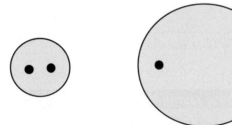

Figure F6.10 For question 13.

(a) Show that the velocity with which the two points move apart is proportional to their separation (i.e. show that $v = Hr$, where $H = \frac{1}{R}\frac{dR}{dt}$). This shows that Hubble's law is satisfied.

(b) Show that, if the radius of the balloon is expanding uniformly (i.e. if $R \propto t$),

then the Hubble 'constant' is actually decreasing with time as $H = \frac{1}{t}$.

(c) How should the radius be increasing in order that H be really constant in time?

14 What do you understand by the term *nucleosynthesis*?

15 What do you understand by the term *inflationary epoch*?

16 What significant event took place three minutes after the Big Bang?

17 The universe had almost equal quantities of matter and antimatter in its very early stages. Outline the reason why the universe today is made out of matter only.

18 All stars, regardless of age, contain *at least* 25% helium by mass. How is this significant?

19 An old theory of cosmology (the steady state theory) asserted that, as the universe expanded, matter was constantly being created so as to keep the density of the universe constant. Taking the density of the universe to be about 10^{-26} kg m^{-3}, find at what rate matter must be created in order that the density of an expanding universe be kept constant. Take $H = 72$ km s^{-1} Mpc^{-1}.

20 (The following very long problem is for mathematically inclined students who might enjoy it. It will certainly not be required in the IB examination!) Imagine space to be filled with gas of density ρ. A galaxy of mass m at a distance r from the earth is thus attracted toward the earth by the mass enclosed in a sphere of radius r centred on the earth. Newton's laws (second law and gravitation) then imply that

$$m\frac{dv}{dt} = \left(\frac{4\pi}{3}\rho r^3\right)\frac{Gm}{r^2}$$

where the quantity in brackets represents the mass of the gas in the sphere of radius r. Use $v = HRr_0 = \frac{dR}{dt}r_0$, where R is the scale factor of the universe and r_0 is the separation of two points at some arbitrary time t_0. Substituting into Newton's law we find

$$\frac{d^2 R}{dt^2} + \frac{4\pi}{3} G\rho R = 0$$

This is the equation obeyed by the scale factor $R(t)$, but it still cannot be solved because the density is also a function of time. But by the law of conservation of mass we must have (why?)

$$\rho R^3 = \rho_0 R_0^3$$

where the zero subscripts indicate the values of the density and the scale factor now. Thus, show that

$$2\frac{d^2 R}{dt^2} + \frac{C}{R^2} = 0$$

where the constant C has the value $C = \frac{8\pi G}{3}\rho_0 R_0^3$. Show that the differential equation for R just derived is equivalent to

$$\left(\frac{dR}{dt}\right)^2 - \frac{C}{R} + k = 0$$

where k is a new constant of integration. (Just differentiate this last equation and show that you get the old one.) This last equation is known as the Friedmann equation. It describes how the scale factor varies with time. It was derived by Newtonian mechanics but it turns out that

it is also valid in general relativity as well.

Solve this equation for the case of $k = 0$ to find $R(t) \propto t^{2/3}$. What does the rate of increase of R become as time gets large? Hence show that $H \propto \frac{1}{t}$. The expansion will stop if $\frac{dR}{dt} = 0$. Using the Friedmann equation, show that this requires that $k > 0$. Assuming that $k > 0$, show that the solution of the Friedmann equation is given in parametric form as

$$R(\theta) = \frac{C}{2k}(1 - \cos\theta)$$

$$t(\theta) = \frac{C}{2k^{3/2}}(\theta - \sin\theta)$$

where the parameter θ varies from 0 to 2π. This is the equation of a cycloid. Sketch this curve. Show that the largest value of the scale of the universe is then $R = \frac{C}{k}$ and that this takes place at a time given by $\frac{\pi C}{2k^{3/2}}$. Show that R becomes zero again at a time given by $\frac{\pi C}{2k^{3/2}}$. Show that, for small t, the solution for $k > 0$ of the previous problem agrees with the solution for $k = 0$, that is

$$R(t) \propto t^{2/3}$$

Why is there such an agreement? At which point in the lifetime of the universe was the expansion the fastest (i.e. largest rate of change of R)? What does this suggest? Attempt to perform the same analysis to the case $k < 0$. (*Hint:* You will have to replace sines and cosines by hyperbolic sines and cosines.) What do you guess k represents?

The principle of special relativity

At the end of the nineteenth century, it seemed that all the problems in physics had been solved and that scientists had a complete understanding of the laws of nature. Mechanics was triumphant, with daily applications in engineering as well as explanations of the motion of the heavenly bodies. Electricity and magnetism had been shown by James Maxwell to be two faces of the same thing (electromagnetism), thus unifying a large range of phenomena. The kinetic theory of gases provided an understanding of the workings of matter at the molecular level. Two problems defied solution, however, and they were about to bring down the entire structure of classical physics. The first was the attempt to understand the spectrum of the radiation emitted by a black body. The resolution to this problem came many years later. It involved the concept of a photon and the birth of quantum mechanics. The second problem had to do with the velocity of

light: it is said that Albert Einstein, as a boy, asked himself what would happen if he held a mirror in front of him and ran forward at the speed of light. With respect to the ground, the mirror would be moving at the speed of light. Rays of light leaving young Einstein's face would also be moving at the speed of light relative to the ground. This meant that the rays would not be moving relative to the mirror, hence there should be no reflection in it. This seemed odd to Einstein. He expected that looking into the mirror would not reveal anything unusual. Some years later, Einstein (left) would resolve this puzzle with a revolutionary new theory of space and time, the theory of special relativity.

Objectives

By the end of this chapter you should be able to:

• state the meaning of the term *frame of reference*;
• state what *Galilean relativity* means;
• solve problems of *Galilean relativity*;
• understand the significance of the *speed of light*;
• state the *two postulates of the principle of relativity*;
• appreciate that *absolute time does not exist* and that *simultaneity is a relative concept*.

Frames of reference

In a physics experiment, an observer records the occurrence of *events*: the time and place at which these events take place.

> ▶ The observer along with the rulers and clocks that he or she uses to measure distances and times constitute what is called a *frame of reference*. If the observer is *not accelerated*, the frame is called an *inertial frame of reference*. (See Figure G1.1.)

Figure G1.1 In this frame of reference the observer decides that lightning struck at time $t = 3$ s at position $x = 60$ m.

To discuss motion we must first specify the frame of reference with respect to which the motion is to be described. Thus, an observer with rulers and clocks who is firmly attached to the surface of the earth will conclude that a train travelling from one city to another moves, and the distances travelled and times taken can be calculated. The same events can also be viewed by another observer in a different frame of reference. Consider, therefore, the following situation involving one observer on the ground and another who is a passenger on the train. In Figure G1.2, a train moves past the observer on the ground (who is represented by a thin vertical line) at time $t = 0$ and is struck by lightning 3 s later. The observer on the train is represented by a thick vertical line. The train is travelling at a velocity of $v = 15$ m s^{-1} as far as the ground observer is concerned.

Let us see how the two observers view various events along the trip. Assume first that when the clocks carried by the two observers show zero, the origins of the rulers carried by the observers coincide. The stationary observer uses

Figure G1.2 The origins of the two frames of reference coincide when clocks in both frames show zero. The origins then separate. Lightning strikes a point on the train. The observer on the train measures the point where the lightning strikes and finds the answer to be x'. The ground observer measures that the lightning struck a distance x from his origin.

the symbol x to denote the distance of an event from the origin of his ruler. The observer on the train uses the symbol x'. As shown in Figure G1.2 these are related by

$$x' = x - vt$$
$$t' = t$$

since in the time of t s the train moves forward a distance vt. These equations express the relationship between the coordinates of the same event as viewed by two observers who are in relative motion.

Thus, to the event of Figure G1.2 ('lightning strikes') the ground observer assigns the coordinates $x = 60$ m and $t = 3$ s. The observer in the train assigns to this same event the coordinates $t' = 3$ s and $x' = 60 - 15 \times 3 = 15$ m.

We are assuming here what we know from everyday experience (a guide that, as we will see, may not always be reliable): that two observers always agree on what the time coordinates are; in other words, time is common to both observers. Or as Newton wrote:

> Absolute, true and mathematical time, of itself, and from its own nature, flows equably without any relation to anything external.

Of course, the train observer may wish to consider herself at rest and the ground below her to move away with velocity $-v$.

▶ It is impossible for one of the observers to claim that he or she is 'really' at rest and that the other is 'really' moving. There is no experiment that can be performed by the train observer, say, that will convince her that she 'really' moves (apart from looking outside the windows). If we consider instead a space station and a spacecraft as our two frames, out of earth's view, even looking out of the windows will not help. Whatever results the train observer gets out of her experiments, the ground observer also gets out of the same experiments performed in his ground frame of reference.

The equations

$$x' = x - vt$$
$$t' = t$$

reflect what is called a Galilean transformation: *the relation between coordinates of events when one frame moves past the other with uniform velocity on a straight line.* Frames moving with uniform velocity past each other on straight lines are called *inertial frames of reference*. These are non-accelerating frames. Both observers are equally justified in considering themselves to be at rest and the descriptions they give are equally valid.

A non-inertial frame, by contrast, is an accelerating frame, and in this case it is possible to distinguish the observer who is 'really' moving. An observer in an accelerating frame will feel forces pulling him back into his seat if he is accelerating, or thrown forward if he is decelerating. A mass hanging from a string will make an angle with the vertical in the accelerating frame but will hang vertically if the frame is inertial (i.e. moving with constant velocity). Similarly, in a rotating frame of reference, the surface of water in a bucket would not be level.

Galilean relativity has an immediate consequence for the *law of addition of velocities*: Consider a ball that rolls with velocity u' as measured by the train observer. Again assume that the two frames, train and ground, coincide when $t = t' = 0$ and that the ball first starts rolling when $t' = 0$. Then, after time t' the position of the ball is measured to be at $x' = u't'$ by the train observer (see Figure G1.3).

The ground observer records the position of the ball to be at $x = x' + vt = (u' + v)t$ (recall $t = t'$) and so as far as the ground observer is concerned the ball has a velocity (distance/time) given by

$$u = u' + v$$

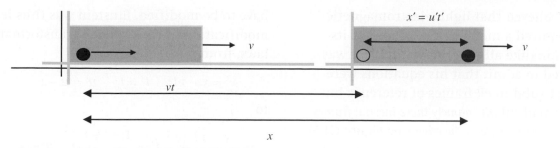

Figure G1.3 An object rolling on the floor of the 'moving' frame appears to move faster as far as the ground observer is concerned.

Example question

Q1

A ball rolls on the floor of a train at 2 m s^{-1} (with respect to the floor). The train moves with respect to the ground (a) to the right at 12 m s^{-1}, (b) to the left at 12 m s^{-1}. What is the velocity of the ball relative to the ground?

Answer

(a) The velocity is 14 m s^{-1}.
(b) The velocity is -10 m s^{-1}.

This apparently foolproof argument presents problems, however, if we replace the rolling ball in the train by a beam of light moving with velocity $c = 3 \times 10^8$ m s^{-1} as measured by the train observer. Using the formula above implies that light would be travelling at a higher speed relative to the ground observer. At the end of the nineteenth century, considerable efforts were made to detect variations in the speed of light depending on the state of motion of the source of light. The experimental result was that no such variations were detected!

The speed of light

In 1864, Maxwell corrected an apparent flaw in the laws of electromagnetism by introducing his famous 'displacement current' term in the electromagnetic equations. The result is that a changing electric flux produces a magnetic field just as a changing magnetic flux produces an electric field (as Faraday had discovered earlier). An immediate conclusion was

that accelerated electric charges produced a pair of self-sustaining electric and magnetic fields at right angles to each other, which eventually decoupled from the charge and moved away from it at the speed of light. Maxwell discovered *electromagnetic waves* and thus demonstrated the electromagnetic nature of light.

One prediction of the Maxwell theory was that the speed of light is a *universal constant*. Indeed, Maxwell was able to show that the speed of light is given by the expression

$$c = \frac{1}{\sqrt{\varepsilon_0 \mu_0}}$$

where the two constants are the electric permittivity and magnetic permeability of space (vacuum): two constants at the heart of electricity and magnetism.

> ► In other words, the speed of light does not have anything to do with the speed of the source that created it.

This results in a conflict with Galilean relativity. According to Galilean relativity, if the speed of light takes on the value c in the 'train' frame of reference then it will have the value $c + v$ in the 'ground' frame of reference (see Figure G1.4).

Figure G1.4 An observer in the train measures the speed of light to be c. An observer on the ground would then measure a different speed, $c + v$.

Maxwell believed that light (electromagnetic waves) required a medium (the ether) for its propagation (like all other waves did). He was thus forced to admit that his equations were not in fact valid in *all* frames of reference but only in a small subset, *namely those inertial frames that were at rest relative to the ether* (see Figure G1.5).

Figure G1.5 If the source is assumed to be at rest with respect to the ether, the speed of light is expected to be greater than when the source moves in the ether.

The ether, the medium for light waves, was hypothesized to be an all-pervading medium. If you moved in the ether, you would experience an 'ether wind', much the same as a car travelling in still air experiences an opposing wind. If while moving through the ether you were to emit a light signal in the direction of motion, the velocity of light was expected to be less than the velocity of light would be if you were at rest relative to the ether.

Experiments to detect these variations in the speed of light depending on the state of motion of the source failed, however, to produce any such difference. The most famous experiment in this regard was the Michelson and Morley experiment, which is discussed in Chapter G3. This puzzle of classical physics was resolved by Einstein in 1905, who simply threw away the entire notion of the ether. Light, as all other electromagnetic waves, does not require a medium and the speed of light in a vacuum is the *same for all observers*. The laws of physics (including Maxwell's electromagnetism) are the same in *all inertial frames of reference*. This means immediately that the laws of Galilean relativity

have to be modified. Einstein was thus led to a modification of the Galilean transformation laws, from

$$x' = x - vt; \quad t' = t; \quad u' = u - v$$

to

$$x' = \frac{x - vt}{\sqrt{1 - \frac{v^2}{c^2}}}; \quad t' = \frac{t - \frac{v}{c^2}x}{\sqrt{1 - \frac{v^2}{c^2}}}; \quad u' = \frac{u - v}{\left(1 - \frac{uv}{c^2}\right)}$$

The new transformation laws showed that the speed of light was the same for all inertial observers. The price to be paid, though, was that now Newton's laws of mechanics were not the same for all inertial observers if one used the new transformation equations! Einstein did not hesitate to change the laws of Newtonian mechanics as well, creating what is called *relativistic mechanics*. The laws of relativistic mechanics are presented in a later chapter (Chapter G4).

The principle of special relativity

The constancy of the speed of light for all observers is Einstein's first building block for the theory of relativity. The second is his observation that absolute motion does not exist. As we discussed earlier, it is impossible to perform any experiment within a closed box that moves with constant velocity relative to an inertial frame of reference, the purpose of which will be to let the occupants of the box find out whether they move or whether they are at rest. Further, if the occupants perform a series of experiments in order to discover the laws of physics, they will reach exactly the same laws as the occupants of any other box that is not accelerating. All inertial frames are equivalent. This leads to the principle of relativity with the two postulates:

- • The laws of physics are the same in all inertial frames.
- • The speed of light in a vacuum is the same for all inertial observers.

These two postulates of relativity, although they sound simple, have far-reaching consequences. The fact that the speed of light in a vacuum is the same for all observers means that absolute time does not exist. Consider a beam of light. Two different observers in relative motion to each other will measure different distances covered by this beam. But if they are to agree that the speed of the beam is the same for both observers, it follows that they must also measure different times of travel. Thus, observers in motion relative to each other measure time differently. The constancy of the speed of light means that space and time are now inevitably linked and are not independent of each other as they were in Newtonian mechanics.

A related consequence is the concept of simultaneous events. Imagine three rockets A, B and C travelling with the same constant velocity (with respect to some observer) along the same straight line. Imagine that rocket B is half-way between rockets A and C, as shown in Figure G1.6.

Figure G1.6 B emits signals to A and C. These are received at the same time as far as B is concerned. But the reception of the signals is not simultaneous as far as the ground observer is concerned.

At a certain time rocket B emits light signals that are directed toward rockets A and C. Which rocket will receive the signal first? The principle of relativity allows us to determine that as far as an observer in rocket B is concerned the light signals are received by A and C simultaneously (i.e. at the same time). This is obvious since we may imagine a big box enclosing all three rockets that moves with same velocity as the rockets themselves. Then, for any observer in the box, or in the rockets themselves, everything appears to be at rest. Since B is half-way between A and C, clearly the two rockets receive the

signals at the same time (light travels with the same speed). Imagine, though, that we look at this situation from the point of view of a different observer, outside the rockets and the box, with respect to whom the rockets move with velocity v. This observer sees that rocket A is approaching the light signal, while rocket C is moving away from it (again, remember that light travels with the same speed in each direction). Hence, it is obvious to this observer that rocket A will receive the signal *before* rocket C does.

We are thus forced to admit the following as a consequence of the principle of relativity:

▶ Events (i.e. occurrences) that are simultaneous for one observer *and* which take place at *different points in space*, are not simultaneous for another in motion relative to the first.

On the other hand, if two events are simultaneous for one observer *and* take place at the *same point in space*, they are simultaneous for all other observers as well.

Example question

Q2 ▆▆▆▆▆▆▆▆▆▆▆▆▆▆▆▆▆▆▆

Observer T is in the middle of a train carriage that is moving with constant speed to the right with respect to the train station. Two light signals are emitted at the same time as far as the observer, T, in the train is concerned (see Figure G1.7).

(a) Are the emissions simultaneous for observer G on the ground?

(b) The signals arrive at T at the same time as far as T is concerned. Do they arrive at T at the

Figure G1.7.

same time as far as G is concerned? According to G, which signal is emitted first?

Answer

(a) No, because the events (i.e. the emissions from A and B) take place at different points in space and so if they are simultaneous for observer T they will not be simultaneous for observer G.

(b) Yes, because the reception of the two signals by T takes place at the same time, so if they are simultaneous for T, they must also be simultaneous for G. From G's point of view, T is *moving away from the signal from A*. So the signal from A has a larger distance to cover to get to T. If the signals are received *at the same time*, and moved at the same speed (*c*), it must be that the one from A was emitted before that from B.

Simultaneity, like motion, is a relative concept. Our notion of absolute simultaneity is based on the idea of absolute time: events happen at specific times that all observers agree on. Einstein has taught us that the idea of absolute time, just like the idea of absolute motion, must be abandoned.

Questions

1 It was a very hotly debated subject centuries ago as to whether the earth goes around the sun or the other way around. Does relativity make this whole argument irrelevant since 'all frames of reference are equivalent'?

2 Give as many examples as you can of events that are simultaneous for one set of observers but not for others.

3 Two trains are travelling at constant speeds on two parallel straight lines. The first, A, is travelling at 5 m s^{-1}, the second, B, at 2 m s^{-1}. An observer at the station observes both trains. At a given instant of time, a passenger in A, a passenger in B and the observer at the station are all aligned along a line normal to the motion of the trains. At that point, a passenger in A drops an ice cube from his drink which he is holding at a height

of 1.40 m. Using Galilean relativity, where will the ice cube land as far as each of the three observers is concerned?

4 Discuss the approximations necessary in order to claim that the rotating earth is an inertial frame of reference.

5 Imagine that you are travelling in a train at constant speed in a straight line and that you cannot look at or communicate with the outside. Think of the first experiment that comes to your mind that you could do to try to find out that you are indeed moving. Then analyse it carefully to see that it will not work.

HL only

6 Here is another experiment that can be performed in the hope of determining whether you move or not.
The coil in Figure G1.8 is placed near a strong magnet and a galvanometer attached to the coil registers a current. Discuss whether we can deduce that the coil moves with respect to the ground.

Figure G1.8 For question 6.

7 What experiment might you perform in a train that is accelerating along a straight line that would convince you that it is accelerating? Could you also determine the direction of the acceleration?

8 How would you know that you find yourself in a rotating frame of reference? What experiment would convince you of that?

9 An electric current flows in a wire (see Figure G1.9). A proton moving parallel to the wire will experience a magnetic force due to

Figure G1.9 For question 9.

the magnetic field created by the current. From the point of view of an observer travelling along with the proton, the proton is at rest and so should experience no force. What do you say?

10 Imagine a 'train' that is 5400 000 km long travelling at 240 000 km s⁻¹ to the right. Two laser beams are emitted from the middle of the train toward the ends of the train, giving the signal to open the front and rear doors.

(a) When will the doors open according to an observer at the middle of the train?

(b) Which door will open first according to an observer on the platform? The platform observer is standing level with the train observer when the laser signals are emitted.

Relativistic kinematics

The principle of relativity has immediate consequences. Time runs differently for two observers who are in relative motion and these observers disagree about length measurements. This chapter discusses three basic relativity phenomena: time dilation, length contraction and velocity addition.

Objectives

By the end of this chapter you should be able to:

- give the definitions of *proper time interval* and *proper length*;
- describe the behaviour of the *gamma factor* $\gamma = \dfrac{1}{\sqrt{1-\frac{v^2}{c^2}}}$;
- state the meaning of *time dilation* and solve problems using time interval $= \gamma \times$ proper time interval;
- derive the *time dilation formula*;
- state the meaning of *length contraction* and solve problems using length $= \dfrac{\text{proper length}}{\gamma}$;
- use the law of *velocity addition* and appreciate its significance, $u = \dfrac{u'+v}{1+\frac{u'v}{c^2}}$ or, solving for u', $u' = \dfrac{u-v}{1-\frac{uv}{c^2}}$;
- appreciate that time dilation and length contraction are both *symmetrical* effects;
- describe and resolve the *twin paradox*.

Time dilation

A direct consequence of the principle of relativity is that observers who are in motion relative to each other do not agree on the interval of time separating two events. To see this, consider the following situation: a train moves with velocity v with respect to the ground as shown in Figure G2.1.

From point A on the train floor a light signal is sent toward point B directly above on the ceiling. The time it takes for light to travel from A to B and back to A is recorded and equals $\Delta t'$. Note that as far as the observers inside the train are concerned, the light beam travels along the straight-line segments AB and BA. From the

point of view of an observer on the ground, however, things look somewhat different. In the time it takes for light to return to A, B (which moves along with the train) will have

Figure G2.1 A signal is emitted at A, is reflected off B and returns to A again. The path shown is what the train observer sees as the path of the signal. The emission and reception of the signals happen at the same point in space.

moved forward. This means, therefore, that as far as this observer is concerned, the path of the light beam looks like that shown in Figure G2.2.

Figure G2.2 The ground observer sees things differently. In the time it takes the signal to return, the train has moved forward. Thus, the emission and reception of the signal do not happen at the same point in space.

Suppose that the stationary observer measures the time it takes light to travel from A to B and back to A to be Δt. What we will show now is that, if both observers are to agree that the speed of light is the same, then the two time intervals cannot be the same.

It is clear that

$$\Delta t' = \frac{2L}{c}$$

$$\Delta t = \frac{2\sqrt{L^2 + (v\,\Delta t/2)^2}}{c}$$

since the train moves forward a distance $v\,\Delta t$, in the time interval Δt that the stationary observer measures for the light beam to reach A. Thus, solving the first equation for L and substituting in the second (after squaring both equations)

$$(\Delta t)^2 = \frac{4\left(\frac{c^2(\Delta t')^2}{4} + \frac{v^2(\Delta t)^2}{4}\right)}{c^2}$$

$$c^2(\Delta t)^2 = c^2(\Delta t')^2 + v^2(\Delta t)^2$$

$$(c^2 - v^2)(\Delta t)^2 = c^2(\Delta t')^2$$

$$(\Delta t)^2 = \frac{c^2(\Delta t')^2}{c^2 - v^2}$$

So finally

$$\Delta t = \frac{\Delta t'}{\sqrt{1 - \frac{v^2}{c^2}}}$$

This is called the **time dilation** formula. It is customary to call the expression

$$\gamma = \frac{1}{\sqrt{1 - \frac{v^2}{c^2}}}$$

the gamma factor, in which case $\Delta t = \gamma\Delta t'$. Note that $\gamma > 1$. A graph of the gamma factor versus velocity is shown in Figure G2.3. We see that the gamma factor is approximately one for velocities up to about half the speed of light but approaches infinity as the speed approaches the speed of light.

Figure G2.3 The gamma factor as a function of velocity. The value of γ stays essentially close to one for values of the velocity up to about half the speed of light but approaches infinity as the velocity approaches the speed of light.

The time interval for the time of travel of the light beam is longer for the ground observer's clock. This is known as time dilation. If the train passengers measure a time interval of $\Delta t' = 6$ s and the train moves at a speed $v = 0.80c$, then the time interval measured by the ground observer is

$$\Delta t = \frac{6}{\sqrt{1 - 0.80^2}} \text{ s}$$

$$= \frac{6}{\sqrt{1 - 0.64}} \text{ s}$$

$$= \frac{6}{\sqrt{0.36}} \text{ s}$$

$$= \frac{6}{0.6} \text{ s}$$

$$= 10 \text{ s}$$

which is longer. It will be seen immediately that this large difference came about only because we chose the speed of the train to be extremely close to the speed of light. Clearly, if the train speed is small compared with the speed of light, then $\gamma \approx 1$, and the two time intervals agree, as we might expect them to from everyday experience. The reason that our everyday experience leads us astray is because the speed of light is enormous compared with everyday speeds. Thus, the relativistic time dilation effect we have just discovered becomes relevant only when speeds close to the speed of light are encountered. Otherwise, small speeds result in differences in time intervals that can only be measured with super-accurate atomic clocks, as indeed has been done in the Hafele–Keating experiment (see next page).

If an observer measures that two events take place at the *same point in space*, the time interval between the events is very special and is called a *proper time interval*. All other observers moving with respect to this observer will measure a *longer* time interval separating the *same* two events.

> ▶ A *proper time interval* is the time separating two events that take place at the *same point in space*:
>
> time interval = γ × proper time interval
>
> $$= \frac{1}{\sqrt{1 - \frac{v^2}{c^2}}} \times \text{proper time interval}$$

Note that there is no question as to which observer is right and which is wrong when it comes to measuring time intervals. Both are right. Two inertial observers moving relative to each other at constant velocity both reach valid conclusions according to the principle of relativity.

Example questions

Q1 ▮▮▮▮▮▮▮▮▮▮▮▮▮▮

The time interval between the ticks of a clock carried on a fast rocket is half of what observers on earth record. How fast is the rocket moving with respect to earth?

Answer

From the time dilation formula it follows that

$$2 = \frac{1}{\sqrt{1 - \frac{v^2}{c^2}}}$$

so

$$\sqrt{1 - \frac{v^2}{c^2}} = \frac{1}{2}$$

so

$$1 - \frac{v^2}{c^2} = \frac{1}{4}$$

so

$$\frac{v^2}{c^2} = \frac{3}{4}$$

so

$$v = 0.866c$$

Q2 ▮▮▮▮▮▮▮▮▮▮▮▮▮▮

A rocket moves past an observer in a laboratory with speed $v = 0.85c$. The observer in the laboratory measures that a radioactive sample of mass 50 mg (which is at rest in the laboratory) has a half-life of 2.0 min. What half-life do the rocket observers measure?

Answer

We have two events here. The first is that the laboratory observer sees a container with 50 mg of the radioactive sample. The second event is that the laboratory observer sees a container with 25 mg of the radioactive sample. These events are separated by 2.0 min as far as the laboratory observer is concerned. These two events take place at the same point in space as far as the laboratory observer is concerned and so *the laboratory observer has measured the proper time interval between these two events*. Hence the rocket observers will measure a longer half-life of

time interval = γ × proper time interval

$$= \frac{1}{\sqrt{1 - 0.85^2}} \times 2.0 \text{ min}$$

$$= 3.80 \text{ min}$$

The point of this example is that you must not make the mistake of thinking that proper time intervals are measured by 'the moving' observer. There is no such thing as 'the moving' observer.

The rocket observer is free to consider herself at rest and the laboratory observer moving with velocity $v = -0.85c$.

Q3

In the year 2010, a group of astronauts embark on a journey toward the star Betelgeuse in a spacecraft moving at $v = 0.75c$ with respect to the earth. Three years after departure from the earth (as measured by the astronauts' clocks) one of the astronauts announces that she has given birth to a baby girl. The other astronauts immediately send a *radio* signal to earth announcing the birth. When is the good news received on earth (according to earth clocks)?

Answer

When the astronaut gives birth, three years have gone by in the spacecraft's clocks. This is a proper time interval since the events 'departure from earth' and 'astronaut gives birth' happen at the same place as far as the astronauts are concerned (namely inside the spacecraft). Thus, the time between these two events according to the earth clocks is

$$\text{time interval} = \gamma \times \text{proper time interval}$$
$$= \frac{1}{\sqrt{1 - 0.75^2}} \times 3.0 \text{ yr}$$
$$= 4.54 \text{ yr}$$

This therefore is also the time for which the spacecraft has been travelling as far as the earth is concerned. The distance covered is (as far as earth is concerned)

$$\text{distance} = vt$$
$$= 0.75c \times 4.54 \text{ yr}$$
$$= 3.40c \times \text{yr}$$
$$= 3.40 \text{ ly}$$

This is the distance that the radio signal must then cover in bringing the message. This is done at the speed of light and so the time taken is

$$\frac{3.40 \text{ ly}}{c} = \frac{3.40c \times \text{yr}}{c}$$
$$= 3.40 \text{ yr}$$

Hence, when the signal arrives, the year on earth is

$2010 + 4.54 + 3.40 = 2018$ (approximately).

The time dilation effect just described is a 'real' effect. In the Hafele–Keating experiment, accurate atomic clocks taken for a ride aboard planes moving at ordinary speeds and then compared with similar clocks left behind show readings that are smaller by amounts consistent with the formulae of relativity. Time dilation is also a daily effect in the operation of particle accelerators. In such machines, particles are accelerated to speeds that are very close to the speed of light and thus relativistic effects must be taken into account when designing these machines. The time dilation formula has also been verified in muon decay experiments. This is discussed separately (see p. 574).

Time dilation is symmetric

Consider now the following situation. A rocket travelling at $0.80c$ starts from space station P and is directed to space station Q a distance of 864 million km away (as far as observers in both space stations are concerned – the stations do not move relative to each other). A passenger on the rocket sets his watch as the rocket leaves space station P by looking at the space station's clock. The time is zero. When the rocket arrives at space station Q, he checks his watch against the space station's clock. He will find that because of time dilation his clock is slow. Indeed, the trip lasted a time interval of

$$\Delta t = \frac{864 \times 10^9}{0.80 \times 3 \times 10^8} \text{ s}$$
$$= 3600 \text{ s}$$
$$= 60 \text{ min}$$

according to the space station clocks. Thus, the clock in space station Q shows 1 h when the rocket comes whizzing by. The traveller's watch measures the proper time interval between the events 'look at clock in space station P' and 'look at clock in space station Q' and since

$$\text{time interval} = \gamma \times \text{proper time interval}$$
$$1 \text{ h} = \frac{1}{\sqrt{1 - 0.80^2}} \times \text{proper time interval}$$

so

$$\text{proper time interval} = 1 \text{ h} \times \sqrt{1 - 0.80^2}$$
$$= 36 \text{ min}$$

The passenger's watch is slow by 24 min. Let us carefully review what the passenger actually did. First he compared his watch with the space station clock at P. Then he checked it again against the space station clock at Q. He found that the interval of time between leaving space station P and arriving in space station Q was 36 min. The interval of time was 60 min according to the stations' clocks. (See Figure G2.4.)

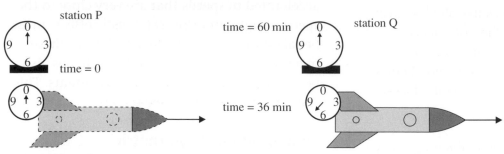

Figure G2.4 The passenger on the rocket records a time of travel from A to B of 36 min. The station clocks record 60 min.

What would happen, however, if the stationmaster at Q said that the rocket was at rest and that it was he (and the space station) that moved toward the rocket (as he is entitled to say)? Imagine that the rocket has a very long rod reaching from space station P to space station Q and that clocks are placed at regular intervals along the rod. The stationmaster at Q sets his watch by looking at the clock on the rod in front of him. The watch now shows zero. The stationmaster now thinks he is moving. Eventually, the stationmaster will see the rocket. He again compares his watch with a clock on the rocket. He will find that his watch shows 36 min while the rocket clock shows 60 min. (See Figure G2.5)

What we have described is that the time dilation effect is a *symmetric* effect. Both observers are free to call themselves at rest and the other moving and vice versa. Both are correct in their measurements of time since the principle of relativity states that all inertial observers make equally valid measurements.

The twin paradox

What if the rocket of the previous discussion moved, instead, on a long circular path. The rocket sets off from space station P and will eventually come back. The passenger in the rocket sets his clock by looking at the station's clock. The time is zero. When he returns, he looks at his watch and finds that it is slow compared with the station clock. Thus, if the trip lasted, say, 6 years by the passenger's watch, the passenger is 6 years older. However, the passenger's twin brother, who is the stationmaster, is older by 10 years. (We are assuming that the rocket moves at a speed of $v = 0.80c$ so that $\gamma = \frac{10}{6}$.)

By the previous argument, the stationmaster may claim that it was he who moved away. So when the stationmaster again meets the rocket passenger, he will claim that

Figure G2.5 The stationmaster is moving and the rocket is at rest. The stationmaster's watch shows 36 min when he sees the rocket. The rocket's clock shows 60 min.

his clock is slower than the passenger's. So the stationmaster is only 6 years older while the rocket passenger is 10 years older. How can that be? Which of the twins is the older when they meet again?

This is often referred to as the twin paradox. It is not a real paradox, though, because unlike the discussion of the previous section, the situation here is *not symmetric*. At all times the stationmaster was in an *inertial* frame. However, the rocket had been moving in a circle (thus experiencing centripetal acceleration) and so the rocket's frame had *not been inertial*. Careful application of the laws of relativity to this *asymmetric* situation leads to the conclusion that the stationmaster has aged by 10 years and the rocket twin by 6 years. Even if the rocket moves in a straight line and then reverses direction to return to the space station, this does not help because in this case the rocket must decelerate and then accelerate. So the rocket passenger again finds himself in a non-inertial frame for part of the time. This again ruins the symmetry of the situation; the rocket passenger is younger than his twin brother when they are reunited.

Length contraction

Suppose now that the observers inside a fast-moving train or rocket place a rod on the floor pointing in the direction of motion of the train (see Figure G2.6).

Figure G2.6 The rod is at rest in the moving frame. To an observer on the ground, the rod moves with the velocity of the frame.

They measure the length of this rod and find it to be L_0. What is the length of the rod when measured by the observers on earth with respect to whom the rod moves at speed v? To find the length of a rod means that one must record the positions of the ends of the rod simultaneously. The length L_0 for this rod was the result of a simultaneous measurement of the rod's ends in the frame of reference in which the rod is at rest (i.e. by the observers in the train). Measurements that are simultaneous in one frame of reference are not, however, necessarily simultaneous in others, as we saw earlier, and this will imply that an observer with respect to whom the rod moves will measure a different length for the rod.

Imagine that the observers on the train send a light signal from the left end of the train to the right end, where a mirror reflects the light back to its source (see Figure G2.7). The time taken for the return trip of the light beam is $\Delta t' = \frac{2L_0}{c}$, where L_0 is the length of the train as measured by the train observers. An observer with respect to whom the train moves with velocity v sees the light signal emitted at time zero, say, but in the time it takes for the signal to return to the emitter the emitter has moved forward along with the train. Let Δt_1 be the time interval for the light beam to reach the mirror for this observer and L the length of the train as far as this observer is concerned. Then, $c\Delta t_1 = L + v\Delta t_1$, giving $\Delta t_1 = \frac{L}{c - v}$. Similarly, if Δt_2 is the time for the light beam to reach the

Figure G2.7 Set-up for deriving the length contraction formula. A signal is emitted from the back of the box and is reflected back by a mirror on the front. The signal is thus emitted and received at the same point in space as far as the observer in the box is concerned.

emitter from the mirror, we have

$c\Delta t_2 = L - v\Delta t_2$ so that $\Delta t_2 = \frac{L}{c+v}$. Thus the total time for the return trip is

$$\Delta t = \Delta t_1 + \Delta t_2$$

$$= \frac{L}{c-v} + \frac{L}{c+v}$$

$$= \frac{2Lc}{c^2 - v^2}$$

$$= \frac{2L}{c\left(1 - \frac{v^2}{c^2}\right)}$$

Recall now that Δt and $\Delta t'$ are related by

$$\Delta t = \frac{\Delta t'}{\sqrt{1 - \frac{v^2}{c^2}}}$$ since $\Delta t'$ is a proper time interval

(why?). Thus

$$\frac{2L}{c\left(1 - \frac{v^2}{c^2}\right)} = \frac{2L_0}{c\sqrt{\left(1 - \frac{v^2}{c^2}\right)}}$$

giving

$$L = L_0\sqrt{1 - \frac{v^2}{c^2}}$$

or

$$L = \frac{L_0}{\gamma}$$

that is

$$\text{length} = \frac{\text{proper length}}{\gamma}$$

So, we can define proper length as follows:

▶ The length of an object measured by an inertial observer with respect to whom the object is at rest is called *proper length*.

The observers with respect to whom the rod moves at speed v measure a shorter length. This is called length contraction:

$$\text{length} = \frac{\text{proper length}}{\gamma}$$

Note that it is only lengths in the direction of motion that are contracted.

As with time dilation, length contraction is a real effect as well as a symmetric effect. Take two identical rods of proper length 1 m and put one on a rocket moving at high speed and keep the other on earth. The observers on the rocket measure the length of their rod and find 1 m. The observers on earth measure the length of the rocket rod and find it less than 1 m. The rocket people, on the other hand, measure the length of the earth rod and find it less than 1 m, whereas the earth observers will of course measure 1 m for their rod. Both sets of observers are correct according to the principle of relativity.

Example question

Q4 ▬▬▬▬▬▬▬▬▬▬▬▬

SLAC stands for the Stanford Linear Accelerator. In this accelerator, electrons of speed $v = 0.96c$ move down the 3.0 km long linear accelerator.

(a) How long does this take according to observers in the laboratory?

(b) How long does it take according to an observer travelling along with the electrons?

(c) What is the speed of the linear accelerator in the rest frame of the electrons?

Answer

(a) In the laboratory the electrons take a time of

$$\frac{3.0 \times 10^3}{0.96 \times 3 \times 10^8}\,\text{s} = 1.042 \times 10^{-5}\,\text{s}$$

(b) The arrival of the electrons at the beginning and the end of the accelerator track happens at the same point in space as far as the observer travelling along with the electrons is concerned and so that is a proper time interval. Thus

$$\text{time interval} = \gamma \times \text{proper time interval}$$

$$\gamma = \frac{1}{\sqrt{1 - 0.96^2}}$$

$$= 3.571$$

$$1.042 \times 10^{-5}\,\text{s} = 3.571 \times \text{proper time interval}$$

that is

$$\text{proper time interval} = \frac{1.0 \times 10^{-5}}{3.571}\,\text{s}$$

$$= 2.918 \times 10^{-6}\,\text{s}$$

(c) The speed of the accelerator is obviously
$v = 0.96c$ in the opposite direction. But this
can be checked as follows. As far as the
electron is concerned, the length of the
accelerator track is moving past it and so is
length-contracted according to

$$\text{length} = \frac{\text{proper length}}{\gamma}$$

$$= \frac{3.0\,\text{km}}{3.571}$$

$$= 0.8401\,\text{km}$$

and so has a speed of

$$\text{speed} = \frac{0.8401 \times 10^3}{2.918 \times 10^{-6}}\,\text{m s}^{-1}$$

$$= 2.879 \times 10^8\,\text{m s}^{-1}$$

$$\approx 0.96c$$

Addition of velocities

Consider a frame S' (for example a train) that
moves at constant speed v in a straight line
relative to another frame S (for example the
ground). An object slides on the train floor in
the same direction as the train (S') and its
velocity is measured *by the observers in S'* to be
u'. What is the speed of this object as measured
by the observers in S? (See Figure G2.8.)

Figure G2.8 The speed of the moving object is u'
in the frame S'. What is its speed when
measured from frame S?

In pre-relativity physics (i.e. Galilean–Newtonian
physics), the answer would be simply $u' + v$.
This cannot, however, be the correct relativistic
answer; if we replaced the fast particle by a
beam of light ($u' = c$), we would end up with
an observer (S) who measured a speed of light
different from that measured by S'. The correct
answer for the speed u of the particle relative to

S is given by

$$u = \frac{u' + v}{1 + \frac{u'v}{c^2}}$$

or, solving for u'

$$u' = \frac{u - v}{1 - \frac{uv}{c^2}}$$

It can be easily checked that, irrespective of how
close u' or v are to the speed of light, u is always
less than c. In the case in which $u' = c$, then
$u = c$ as well, as demanded by the principle of
the constancy of the speed of light (check this).
On the other hand, if the velocities involved are
small compared with the speed of light, then we
may neglect the term $\frac{u'v}{c^2}$ in the denominator, in
which case Einstein's formula reduces to the
familiar Galilean relativity formula $u = u' + v$.

Example questions

Q5 ▬▬▬▬▬▬▬▬▬▬▬▬▬▬▬▬
An electron has a speed of 2.00×10^8 m s^{-1}
relative to a rocket, which itself moves at a speed
of 1.00×10^8 m s^{-1} with respect to the ground.
What is the speed of the electron with respect to
the ground?

Answer

Applying the formula above with $u' = 2.00 \times 10^8$ m s^{-1} and $v = 1.00 \times 10^8$ m s^{-1} we find
$u = 2.45 \times 10^8$ m s^{-1}.

Q6 ▬▬▬▬▬▬▬▬▬▬▬▬▬▬▬▬
Two rockets move away from each other with
speeds of $0.8c$ and $0.9c$, with respect to the
ground, as shown in Figure G2.9. What is the
speed of each rocket as measured from the other?
What is the relative speed of the two rockets as
measured from the ground?

Figure G2.9.

Answer

Let us first find the speed of A with respect to B.
In the frame of reference in which B is at rest, the

ground moves to the left with speed $0.9c$ (i.e. a velocity of $-0.9c$). The velocity of A with respect to the ground is $-0.8c$. This is illustrated in Figure G2.10.

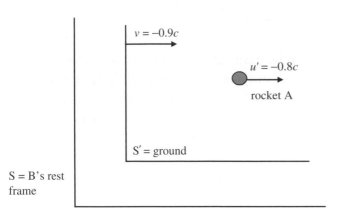

S = B's rest frame

Figure G2.10.

Applying the formula with the values given in Figure G2.10 we find

$$u = \frac{u' + v}{1 + \frac{u'v}{c^2}}$$

$$= \frac{-0.9c - 0.8c}{1 + \frac{(-0.9c)(-0.8c)}{c^2}}$$

$$= \frac{-1.70c}{1 + 0.72}$$

$$= -\frac{1.70c}{1.72}$$

$$= -0.988c$$

The minus sign means, of course, that rocket A moves towards the left of B. Let us now find the speed of rocket B as measured in A's rest frame. The appropriate diagram is shown in Figure G2.11.

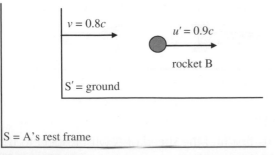

S = A's rest frame

Figure G2.11.

We thus find

$$u = \frac{u' + v}{1 + \frac{u'v}{c^2}}$$

$$= \frac{0.9c + 0.8c}{1 + \frac{(0.9c)(0.8c)}{c^2}}$$

$$= \frac{1.70c}{1 + 0.72}$$

$$= \frac{1.70c}{1.72}$$

$$= 0.988c$$

as expected.

The *relative speed* of the two rockets as measured from earth is $0.8c + 0.9c = 1.7c$. There is nothing to worry about here. This faster than light speed is not the speed of any material object, nor the speed of any inertial frame, nor can it be used to send a signal to anybody. It is simply a statement of how fast the distance between the rockets is increasing as seen from earth.

Q7

This question uses both the length contraction effect and the velocity addition formula. A rocket has a proper length of 200 m and travels with a speed $v = 0.95c$ relative to the earth. A missile is fired from the end of the rocket toward the front at a speed $u' = 0.90c$ relative to the rocket. When will the missile hit the front of the rocket as far as the rocket observers are concerned? When will this happen as far the earth observers are concerned?

Answer

Let L_0 stand for the proper length of the rocket and u for the speed of the missile relative to the earth. The time taken for the missile to hit the front end of the rocket is just L_0/u' for the rocket observers. For the earth observers the time will be different. Let this time be t. The length of the rocket as measured from earth is $L = \frac{L_0}{\gamma}$. In the time t it takes the missile to reach the front of the rocket, the rocket has moved forward a distance of vt. Thus, as far as the earth observers are concerned, the total distance the missile will cover is $L_0\sqrt{1 - \frac{v^2}{c^2}} + vt$. This distance is covered at a speed u and thus the time taken obeys

$$\frac{L_0\sqrt{1 - \frac{v^2}{c^2}} + vt}{u} = t$$

From the relativistic addition law for velocities

$$u = \frac{u' + v}{1 + \frac{u'v}{c^2}}$$

and so substituting for u and solving for t we find (after some algebra)

$$t = \frac{L_0}{u'} \frac{1}{\sqrt{1 - \frac{v^2}{c^2}}} \left(1 + \frac{u'v}{c^2}\right)$$

If instead of a missile a light signal is fired, then $u' = c$ and the formula above simplifies to

$$t = \frac{L_0}{c} \sqrt{\frac{\left(1 + \frac{v}{c}\right)}{\left(1 - \frac{v}{c}\right)}}$$

We can now put in the numbers to find numerical answers: $L_0 = 200$ m, $v = 0.95c$, $u' = 0.90c$, and so $L_0/u' = 7.4 \times 10^{-7}$ s. The time on earth is measured at 4.4×10^{-6} s.

Questions

1 An earthling sits on a bench in a park eating a sandwich. It takes him 5 min to finish it according to his watch. He is being monitored by planet Zenga invaders who are orbiting at a speed of $0.90c$.
   (a) How long do the aliens reckon it takes an earthling to eat a sandwich?
   (b) The aliens in the spacecraft get hungry and start eating their sandwiches. It takes a Zengan 5 min to eat her sandwich according to Zengan clocks. They are actually being observed by earthlings as they fly over earth. How long does it take a Zengan to eat a sandwich according to earth clocks?

2 An unstable particle has a lifetime of 5.0×10^{-8} s as measured in its rest frame. The particle is moving in a laboratory with a speed of $0.95c$ with respect to the lab.
   (a) Calculate the lifetime of the particle according to an observer at rest in the laboratory.
   (b) Calculate the distance travelled by the particle before it decays, according to the observer in the laboratory.

3 The star Vega is about 50 ly away from earth. A spacecraft moving at $0.995c$ is heading toward Vega.
   (a) How long will it take the spacecraft to get to Vega according to clocks on earth?
   (b) The crew of the spacecraft consists of 18-year-old IB graduates. How old are the graduates when they arrive at Vega?

4 A pendulum in a fast train is found by observers on the train to have a period of 1.0 s. What period would observers on a station platform measure as the train moves past them at a speed of $0.95c$?

5 A rocket travelling at $0.6c$ with respect to earth is launched toward a star. After 4 yr of travel (as measured by the rocket clocks) a radio message is sent to earth. When will it arrive on earth as measured by:
   (a) observers on earth;
   (b) observers on the rocket?
   (c) How far from earth was the rocket when the signal was emitted, according to observers on earth?

6 A spacecraft moves past you at a speed of $0.95c$ and you measure its length to be 100 m. What length would you measure if it were at rest with respect to you?

7 A spacecraft leaving the earth with a speed of $0.80c$ sends a radio signal to earth as it passes a space station 8.0 light years from earth (as measured by earth).
   (a) How long does the signal take to arrive on earth according to earth observers?
   (b) How long did it take the spacecraft to reach the space station (according to spacecraft clocks)?
   (c) As soon as the signal is received by earth, a reply signal is sent to the spacecraft. How long does the reply signal take to arrive at the spacecraft according to earth?
   (d) According to the spacecraft, how much time went by between the emission of their signal and the arrival of the reply?

8 Two *identical* fast trains move parallel to each other. An observer on train A tells an observer on train B that by her measurements (i.e. A's) train A is 30 m long and train B is 28 m long.

If the observer on train B takes measurements what will he find for:
(a) the speed of train A with respect to train B;
(b) the length of train A;
(c) the length of train B?

9 Two people meet at point A. They compare their watches and set them both to zero. They meet again at point B. Person P has been moving in a straight line at constant speed. Person Q has been moving on part of a circle with constant speed. Whose watch is slow when they meet at B? (See Figure G2.12.)

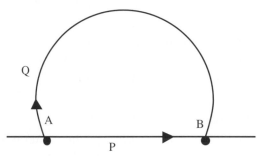

Figure G2.12 For question 9.

10 A rocket approaches a mirror on the ground at a speed of $0.90c$ as shown in Figure G2.13. The distance D between the front of the rocket and the mirror is 2.4×10^{12} m, as measured by the observers on the ground, when a light signal is sent toward the mirror from the front of the rocket. When is the reflected signal received by the rocket as measured by:
(a) the observers on the ground;
(b) the observers on the rocket?

Figure G2.13 For question 10.

11 Two objects move along the same straight line as shown in Figure G2.14. Their speeds are as measured by an observer on the ground. Find:
(a) the velocity of B as measured by A;
(b) the velocity of A as measured by B.

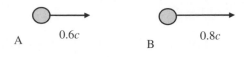

Figure G2.14 For question 11.

12 Repeat question 11 for the arrangement in Figure G2.15.

Figure G2.15 For question 12.

13 A particle A moves to the right with a speed of $0.60c$ relative to the ground. A second particle B moves to the right with a speed of $0.70c$ relative to A. What is the speed of B relative to the ground?

14 A particle A moves to the left with a speed of $0.60c$ relative to the ground. A second particle B moves to the right with a speed of $0.70c$ relative to A. What is the speed of B relative to the ground?

Effects of and evidence for special relativity

This chapter introduces the ideas of relativistic mass and energy. It closes with a discussion of the Michelson–Morley experiment – an experiment that failed to detect the motion of the earth through the ether.

Objectives

By the end of this chapter you should be able to:

* solve problems with *relativistic mass*, $m = \gamma m_0$ and *energy*, $E = \gamma m_0 c^2$;
* describe *muon decay experiments* as evidence for time dilation and length contraction;
* appreciate the significance of the *Michelson–Morley experiment*.

Relativistic mass and energy

One of the first consequences of Einstein's theories in mechanics is that the mass of a body is not constant. The mass of a body measured by an observer with respect to whom the body is at rest is called the *rest mass* and is denoted by m_0.

▶ An observer with respect to whom a particle moves with speed v measures what is called the *relativistic mass*, m, which is given by

$$m = \frac{m_0}{\sqrt{1 - \frac{v^2}{c^2}}} = \gamma m_0$$

and so it increases without limit as the speed approaches the speed of light.

It can be shown that it is necessary to have such a change from classical mechanics if the law of conservation of momentum is to remain true.

Figure G3.1 is a graph of the ratio of the mass to the rest mass versus speed. We see that, as the speed approaches the speed of light, the mass increases without limit. This is evidence

Figure G3.1 As the speed of the mass approaches the speed of light, its mass increases without limit.

that the speed of light cannot, in fact, be achieved by any material object.

Example questions

Q1

Find the speed of a particle whose relativistic mass is double its rest mass.

Answer

The observer who measures this relativistic mass sees the particle move at speed v where

$$m = \frac{m_0}{\sqrt{1 - \frac{v^2}{c^2}}}$$

$$\Rightarrow 2 = \frac{1}{\sqrt{1 - \frac{v^2}{c^2}}}$$

$$\Rightarrow \sqrt{1 - \frac{v^2}{c^2}} = \frac{1}{2}$$

$$\Rightarrow 1 - \frac{v^2}{c^2} = \frac{1}{4}$$

$$\Rightarrow \frac{v^2}{c^2} = \frac{3}{4}$$

$$\Rightarrow v = \frac{\sqrt{3}}{2} c = 0.866c$$

Q2

A constant force F is applied to a particle at rest. Find the acceleration of the particle. Find the acceleration again if the same force is applied to the same particle when it moves at speed $0.8c$ and comment on the result.

Answer

The acceleration is simply $a = \frac{F}{m_0}$ when the mass is initially at rest. If it moves at speed $0.8c$, we must use the relativistic mass of

$$m = \frac{m_0}{\sqrt{1 - \frac{v^2}{c^2}}}$$

$$= \frac{m_0}{\sqrt{1 - 0.8^2}}$$

$$= \frac{m_0}{0.6} = 1.67 m_0$$

and so the acceleration is

$$a = \frac{F}{m}$$

$$= \frac{F}{1.67 \times m_0}$$

that is, 1.67 times smaller than before. As the speed increases, the mass increases as well, thus decreasing the acceleration. The force cannot accelerate the mass to the speed of light.

Another result of relativity is that to every quantity of mass there corresponds a quantity of energy given by Einstein's famous formula

$$E = mc^2$$

$$= \frac{m_0 c^2}{\sqrt{1 - \frac{v^2}{c^2}}}$$

$$= \gamma m_0 c^2$$

If the object is at rest, then its mass is the *rest mass* and the total energy is given by $E_0 = m_0 c^2$ and is called the *rest energy*.

Example questions

Q3

Find:
(a) the rest energy of an electron;
(b) its total energy when it moves at a speed equal to $0.80c$.

Answer

(a) The rest energy is (using the *IBO Data Booklet*) 0.511 MeV or by direct calculation

$$E = m_0 c^2$$

$$= 9.1 \times 10^{-31} \times 9 \times 10^{16} \text{ J}$$

$$= 8.19 \times 10^{-14} \text{ J}$$

$$= \frac{8.19 \times 10^{-14}}{1.6 \times 10^{-19}} \text{ eV} = 0.511 \text{ MeV}$$

(b) The gamma factor at a speed of $0.8c$ is

$$\gamma = \frac{1}{\sqrt{1 - \frac{v^2}{c^2}}}$$

$$= \frac{1}{\sqrt{1 - 0.8^2}}$$

$$= \frac{1}{0.6} = 1.667$$

and so the relativistic mass is

$$m = \gamma m_0$$

$$= 1.667 \times 0.511 \text{ MeV } c^{-2}$$

$$= 0.852 \text{ MeV } c^{-2}$$

and so the total energy is

$$E = mc^2$$

$$= 0.852 \text{ MeV } c^{-2} \times c^2$$

$$= 0.852 \text{ MeV}$$

Q4

An electron has a total energy of 1.25 MeV. What is its speed?

Answer

The rest energy of the electron is 0.511 MeV (from the *IBO Data Booklet*). The total energy is given by

$$E = mc^2$$

$$= \frac{m_0 c^2}{\sqrt{1 - \frac{v^2}{c^2}}}$$

$$\Rightarrow 1.25 = \frac{0.511}{\sqrt{1 - \frac{v^2}{c^2}}}$$

$$\Rightarrow \sqrt{1 - \frac{v^2}{c^2}} = 0.4088$$

$$\Rightarrow 1 - \frac{v^2}{c^2} = (0.4088)^2$$

$$\Rightarrow \frac{v^2}{c^2} = 0.8329$$

$$\Rightarrow v = 0.91c$$

If a particle is accelerated by a potential difference of V volts, its total energy will *increase* by an amount qV where q is the charge of the particle. Thus, if a particle is initially at rest, its total energy is the rest energy $E_0 = m_0 c^2$. After going through the potential difference, the total energy will be $E = m_0 c^2 + qV$. We can then find the speed of the particle, as the next example question shows.

Example questions

Q5 ▇▇▇▇▇▇▇▇▇▇▇▇▇▇▇▇▇▇▇▇▇▇▇

An electron of rest energy 0.511 MeV is accelerated through a potential difference of 5.0 MV in a laboratory.
(a) What is its total energy with respect to the laboratory?
(b) What is its speed with respect to the laboratory?
(c) What is its mass with respect to the laboratory?

Answer

(a) The total energy of the electron will increase by

$$qV = 1\,\text{e} \times 5.0 \times 10^6\,\text{V}$$

$$= 5.0\,\text{MeV}$$

and so the total energy is

$$E = m_0 c^2 + qV$$

$$= 0.511\,\text{MeV} + 5.0\,\text{MeV}$$

$$= 5.511\,\text{MeV}$$

(b) We know that

$$E = mc^2$$

$$= \gamma m_0 c^2$$

$$\Rightarrow 5.511 = \gamma \times 0.511$$

$$\Rightarrow \gamma = \frac{5.511}{0.511}$$

$$= 10.785$$

Since

$$\gamma = \frac{1}{\sqrt{1 - \frac{v^2}{c^2}}}$$

it follows that

$$10.785 = \frac{1}{\sqrt{1 - \frac{v^2}{c^2}}}$$

$$\Rightarrow \sqrt{1 - \frac{v^2}{c^2}} = \frac{1}{10.785}$$

$$= 0.0927$$

$$\Rightarrow 1 - \frac{v^2}{c^2} = 0.008\,597$$

$$\Rightarrow v = 0.996c$$

(c) From

$$E = mc^2 = 5.511\,\text{MeV}$$

the mass is

$$m = 5.5\,\text{MeV } c^{-2}$$

To find the mass in kilograms

$$m = 5.511\,\text{MeV } c^{-2}$$

$$= \frac{5.511 \times 10^6 \times 1.6 \times 10^{-19}}{9 \times 10^{16}}\,\text{kg}$$

$$= 9.8 \times 10^{-30}\,\text{kg}$$

or

$$m = \gamma m_0$$

$$= 10.785 \times 9.1 \times 10^{-31}$$

$$= 9.8 \times 10^{-30}\,\text{kg}$$

Q6 ▇▇▇▇▇▇▇▇▇▇▇▇▇▇▇▇▇▇▇▇▇▇▇

A constant force is applied to a particle that is initially at rest. Sketch a graph that shows the variation of the speed of the particle with time for:
(a) Newtonian mechanics;
(b) relativistic mechanics.

Answer

In Newtonian mechanics a constant force produces a constant acceleration and so the speed increases uniformly without limit, exceeding the speed of light. In relativistic mechanics, the speed increases uniformly as long as the speed is substantially less than the speed of light and is in fact identical with the Newtonian graph. However, as the speed increases, so does the mass and hence the acceleration decreases. This means that the mass never reaches the speed of light. The speed approaches the speed of light asymptotically. Note that the speed is always less than the corresponding Newtonian value at the same time. Hence we have the graph shown in Figure G3.2.

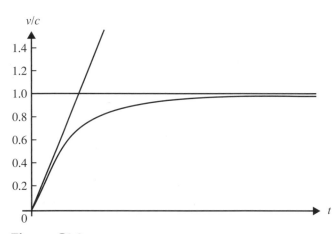

Figure G3.2.

Evidence for special relativity

Muon decay

Muons are particles with properties similar to those of the electron except that they are more massive, are unstable and decay into electrons; they have a lifetime of about 2.2×10^{-6} s. (The reaction is $\mu^- \rightarrow e^- + \bar{\nu}_e + \nu_\mu$.)

> ▶ This is the lifetime measured when the muon is at rest – this is the proper time interval between the creation of a muon and its subsequent decay.

From the point of view of an observer in the laboratory, however, with respect to whom the muons are moving at high speed, the lifetime is longer because of time dilation. Consider a muon created at a height of 3.0 km and moving toward the surface of the earth with a speed of $0.99c$. Its lifetime as measured by ground observers will be

$$\text{time interval} = \frac{\text{proper time}}{\sqrt{1 - \frac{v^2}{c^2}}}$$

$$= \frac{2.2 \times 10^{-6} \text{ s}}{\sqrt{1 - 0.99^2}}$$

$$= 1.56 \times 10^{-5} \text{ s}$$

In this time the muon travels a distance (as far as the laboratory observers are concerned)

$$0.99 \times 3 \times 10^8 \times 1.56 \times 10^{-5} \text{ m} = 4.63 \text{ km}$$

This means that the muon reaches the surface of the earth *before* decaying. Without the time dilation effect, the muon would have travelled a distance of only

$$0.99 \times 3 \times 10^8 \times 2.2 \times 10^{-6} \text{ m} = 0.653 \text{ km}$$

and thus would not make it to the surface.

> ▶ The fact that muons do make it to the surface of the earth in experiments based on what has just been discussed is evidence in favour of relativity.

The muon exists as a muon for only 2.2×10^{-6} s in the muon's rest frame. So how does an observer travelling along with the muon explain the arrival of muons (and not electrons) at the surface of the earth? The answer is that the distance of 3.0 km measured by the observers on earth is a proper length for them but not for the moving observer. The observer travelling along with the muon claims that it is the earth that is moving upward and so measures a length-contracted distance of

$$3.0 \times \sqrt{1 - 0.99^2} \text{ km} = 0.42 \text{ km}$$

to the surface of the earth. The earth's surface is coming up to this observer with a speed of $0.99c$ and so the time when they will meet is

$$\frac{0.42 \times 10^3}{0.99 \times 3 \times 10^8} \text{ s} = 1.4 \times 10^{-6} \text{ s}$$

that is, *before* the muon decays!

▶ In this sense, muon decay experiments are indirect confirmations of the length contraction effect.

The Michelson–Morley experiment

Nineteenth-century physics demanded that light, like all other waves, required a medium for its propagation. Just as water waves require water, waves on a string require a string, etc., it was presumed that light too required a medium in which its vibrations would take place and propagate. The medium for light waves was hypothesized to be an all-pervading medium called the *ether*. The problem with the ether was that an observer moving in it could not measure the same speed of light as one who was stationary in it. If an observer moved in the ether, they would experience an 'ether wind', much the same as a car travelling in still air experiences an opposing wind. If this observer were to emit a light signal in the direction of motion, the velocity of light was expected to be less than it would be if the observer were at rest relative to the ether (see Figure G3.3).

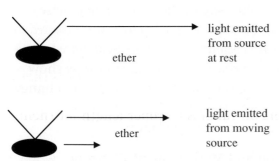

Figure G3.3 The speed of light would be less when emitted from a source that moved in the ether in the same direction as the light signal.

We have seen that neither mechanics nor electromagnetic experiments can help in deciding whether an inertial observer really is at rest or really moves. Could we use the ether in an attempt to define absolute rest and absolute motion? Consider an observer in a boat who looks at waves in the water. In the first instance,

the boat is at rest in the water (Figure G3.4). In the second, the boat moves smoothly at constant velocity relative to the water (Figure G3.5).

Figure G3.4 View from the boat at rest. The boat is at rest in the water and waves moving to the right and left move with the same speed relative to the boat. This velocity is u, the velocity of water waves relative to the water.

Figure G3.5 View from a moving boat. The boat moves with velocity v relative to the water. The speed of the waves is u relative to the water. Thus, the right-moving waves have velocity $U_R = u - v$ relative to the boat and the left-moving waves have a velocity $U_L = u + v$ relative to the boat.

▶ Observers in the boat thus *know* that they move and, in fact, can even measure their velocity relative to the water by finding the difference between the left- and right-moving waves and dividing by 2

$$\frac{U_L - U_R}{2} = \frac{(u + v) - (u - v)}{2} = v$$

So if the ether exists and pervades all space, we may refer all motions to the ether. If the velocity of a body relative to the ether is zero, we may say that the body is absolutely at rest. If the body has a velocity relative to the ether, then the body is in a state of absolute motion.

This was the idea behind the Michelson–Morley experiment: to find the speed of the earth relative to the ether as the earth rotated around the sun.

In 1881, Michelson, and later Michelson and Morley, performed an experiment to find the speed of the earth relative to the ether using an accurate interferometer designed by Michelson. The idea of the experiment appears to have been put forward a few years earlier by Maxwell himself. To their great disappointment, despite the accuracy of their experiment they found no speed at all. (One way out would be to say that this implies that the earth is in a state of absolute rest; this is not acceptable as the earth moves in different directions as it rotates around the sun and so could not be permanently at rest relative to the ether. This is why the experiment was repeated at different times of the year when the earth was in different points in its orbit around the sun.)

> ▶ This most famous of all 'null experiments' of classical physics was resolved in 1905 by Albert Einstein, who simply threw away the entire notion of the ether. Light, like all other electromagnetic waves, does not require a medium and the speed of light in a vacuum is the same for all observers. It is an interesting historical note that although Einstein knew of this experiment he was not particularly influenced by it in his formulation of the theory of relativity.

The experiment used Michelson's interferometer, which is shown in Figure G3.6.

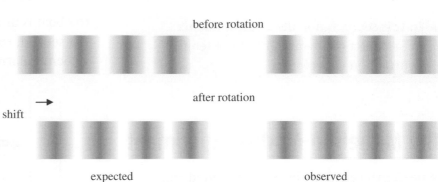

before rotation

after rotation

shift →

expected   observed

Figure G3.7 Expected and observed interference patterns before and after rotation in the Michelson–Morley experiment.

Light from a source S falls on a semitransparent mirror and the beam is split in two: the reflected part (dotted line) proceeds to mirror 1 from which it is reflected towards the microscope. The other part (solid line) goes through the mirror and proceeds towards mirror 2 from which it is reflected back towards the semitransparent mirror and from there into the microscope. The two beams are thus rejoined at the microscope. The two mirrors are not exactly perpendicular to each other, which means that as you look along the field of view of the microscope (F), interference fringes are observed. The interferometer floated in a container filled with mercury and could be rotated by 90°, say in the counter-clockwise direction. *Because the speed of light was expected to be different depending on whether light moved along or against the ether*, detailed calculations show that rotating the interferometer should change the interference pattern by shifting the interference fringes (see Figure G3.7).

Michelson and Morley saw no difference when they rotated their interferometer. Many physicists, including Fitzgerald and notably Lorentz, attempted to explain this result by various *ad hoc* assumptions. The simplest explanation, though, came from Einstein, who abandoned the ether idea and introduced the principle of the constancy of the speed of light in all directions and for all inertial observers.

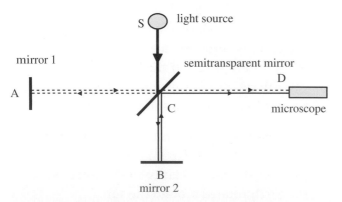

ether wind

F

Figure G3.6 The Michelson interferometer.

The constancy of the speed of light

The null result of the Michelson–Morley experiment is, of course, consistent with a constant speed of light, independent of the velocity of the source. However, the first conclusive experiment that demonstrated the constancy of the speed of light with great accuracy was performed at CERN (the European Centre for Nuclear Research) in 1964. In this experiment, neutral pions moving at $0.99975c$ decayed into a pair of photons moving in different directions. The speed of the photons in both directions was measured to be c with extraordinary accuracy. The speed of light does not depend on the speed of its source.

Questions

1 The rest mass of a proton is 1.67×10^{-27} kg. Find its rest energy.

2 What is the speed of a proton whose relativistic mass is 9 times its rest mass?

3 At what speed must a body move so that its total energy is 10 times its rest energy?

4 The rest energy of a particle is 135 MeV and its total energy is 200 MeV. What is its speed?

5 An electron is accelerated from rest through a potential difference of 0.80 MV.
   (a) What is its total energy?
   (b) What is its speed?

6 What is the total energy in MeV of a proton travelling at $0.80c$?

7 What happens to the density of a cube travelling past you at a relativistic speed?

8 A muon travelling at $0.95c$ covers a distance of 2.00 km (as measured by an earthbound observer) before decaying.
   (a) What is the muon's lifetime as measured by the earthbound observer?
   (b) What is the lifetime as measured by an observer travelling along with the muon?

9 The lifetime of the unstable pion particle is measured to be 2.6×10^{-8} s (when at rest). If this particle is to travel a distance of 20 m in the laboratory just before decaying, at what speed must it be moving?

10 Two islands in a river are separated by 12 km (see Figure G3.8). The current flows with a speed of 2 km per hour relative to the banks from A to B.
   (a) How long would a boat trip take from A to B if you can row with a speed of 4 km per hour with respect to the water?
   (b) How long would the return trip take?
   (c) How long would the entire trip take in still water?

Figure G3.8 For question 10.

11 Two barges, A and B, are opposite each other near the shores of a lake, 12 km apart (see Figure G3.9). A current of speed 3 km per hour relative to the shores flows as shown. You can row at 5 km per hour relative to the water and you want to get from A to B. How long will it take you?

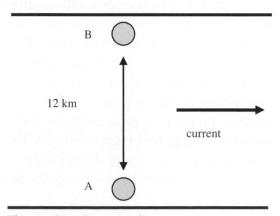

Figure G3.9 For question 11.

Relativistic mechanics

The familiar laws of mechanics based on Newton's laws of motion that we have studied earlier need to be modified whenever an object moves at speeds close to the speed of light. Relativistic mechanics introduces new relations between mass, energy and momentum.

Objectives

By the end of this chapter you should be able to:

- solve problems with *relativistic momentum*, $p = \frac{m_0 v}{\sqrt{1-\frac{v^2}{c^2}}} = \gamma m_0 v$, *relativistic*

  energy, $E = \frac{m_0 c^2}{\sqrt{1-\frac{v^2}{c^2}}}$, and *kinetic energy*, $E_k = (\gamma - 1)m_0 c^2$;

- solve problems with the formula relating *momentum*, *rest energy* and *total energy*, $E = \sqrt{m_0^2 c^4 + p^2 c^2}$;

- appreciate that a charge q that is accelerated from rest through a potential difference V *increases its kinetic energy* to E_k, where $qV = E_k$;

- use *relativistic units* for mass (e.g. MeV c^{-2}) and momentum (e.g. MeV c^{-1}).

Momentum and energy (or *momenergy*)

Consider a body of mass 1 kg initially at rest acted upon by a force of 1 N. The body will move with an acceleration of 1 m s^{-2} and thus in a time of 3×10^8 s the body will acquire a speed equal to the speed of light. Since this is impossible, modifications in the laws of mechanics are necessary to make them comply with the principle of relativity. These modifications make up what is called relativistic mechanics. As we will see, the concepts of energy and momentum are so interconnected in relativity that John A. Wheeler coined the word *momenergy* for both quantities.

Momentum

The first change involves the momentum of a particle. In classical mechanics, the momentum is given by the product of mass times velocity, but in relativity this is modified to

$$p = \frac{m_0 v}{\sqrt{1 - \frac{v^2}{c^2}}}$$
$$= \gamma m_0 v$$

We still have the usual law of momentum conservation, which states that, when no external forces act on a system, the total momentum is conserved. The symbol m_0 here stands for the rest mass of the particle and is a constant for all observers.

▶ This means that (unlike Newtonian mechanics) a *constant* force on the particle will produce a *decreasing* acceleration in such a way that the speed never reaches the speed of light.

Example question

Q1

A constant force F acts on an electron that is initially at rest. Find the speed of the electron as a function of time.

Answer

Initially, for small t, the speed increases uniformly, as in Newtonian mechanics. But as t becomes large, the speed tends to the speed of light but does not reach or exceed it. This is because as the speed increases so does the mass of the electron and so the acceleration becomes smaller and smaller, never achieving the speed of light. This results in the graph shown in Figure G4.1.

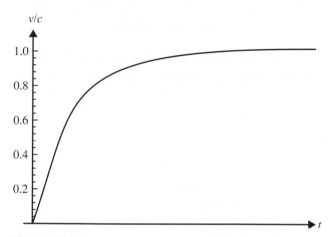

Figure G4.1.

HL Mathematics only

Begin with Newton's second law, $F = \frac{dp}{dt}$, where $p = \gamma m_0 v$ is the momentum of the electron. Since

$$\frac{dp}{dt} = \frac{d}{dt}\left(\frac{m_0 v}{\sqrt{1 - \frac{v^2}{c^2}}}\right)$$

$$= \frac{m_0}{\sqrt{1 - \frac{v^2}{c^2}}}\frac{dv}{dt} + \left(\frac{v}{c^2}\right)\frac{m_0 v}{\left(1 - \frac{v^2}{c^2}\right)^{3/2}}\frac{dv}{dt}$$

$$\frac{dp}{dt} = \frac{m_0}{\left(1 - \frac{v^2}{c^2}\right)^{3/2}}\frac{dv}{dt}$$

it follows that

$$\frac{dv}{dt} = \frac{F}{m_0}\left(-\frac{v^2}{c^2}\right)^{3/2}$$

---

or

$$\frac{dv}{\left(1 - \frac{v^2}{c^2}\right)^{3/2}} = \frac{F}{m_0}dt$$

Integrating both sides, we find that (assuming the mass starts from rest)

$$\frac{v}{\sqrt{1 - \frac{v^2}{c^2}}} = \frac{F}{m_0}t$$

Solving for the speed, we find

$$v^2 = \frac{(Ft)^2}{(m_0 c)^2 + (Ft)^2}c^2$$

The way the velocity approaches the speed of light is shown in Figure G4.1.

Energy

A mass moving with velocity v is said to have a total energy E given by

$$E = \frac{m_0 c^2}{\sqrt{1 - \frac{v^2}{c^2}}}$$

This means that even when the mass is at rest it has energy $E_0 = m_0 c^2$; this is called the rest energy of the mass. This is Einstein's famous formula from 1905. It states that mass and energy are equivalent and can be transformed into each other.

▶ The kinetic energy E_k is defined as the total energy minus the rest energy:

$$E_k = E - m_0 c^2$$

It can be rewritten as

$$E_k = \frac{m_0 c^2}{\sqrt{1 - \frac{v^2}{c^2}}} - m_0 c^2$$

$$= \gamma m_0 c^2 - m_0 c^2$$

$$= (\gamma - 1)m_0 c^2$$

This definition ensures that the kinetic energy is zero when $v = 0$, as can be easily checked. The familiar result from mechanics that the work done by the net force equals the change in kinetic energy holds in relativity as well.

This relativistic definition of kinetic energy does not look similar to the ordinary kinetic energy $\frac{1}{2}mv^2$. In fact, when v is small compared with c, we can approximate the value of the relativistic factor $\frac{1}{\sqrt{1-\frac{v^2}{c^2}}}$ using the binomial expansion for $\frac{1}{\sqrt{1-x}}$ for small x:

$$\frac{1}{\sqrt{1-x}} \approx 1 + \frac{1}{2}x + \cdots$$

Applying this to E_k with $x = \left(\frac{v}{c}\right)^2$ we find

$$E_k = m_0c^2\left(1 + \frac{1}{2}\frac{v^2}{c^2} + \cdots\right) - m_0c^2$$

that is

$$E_k \approx \tfrac{1}{2}m_0v^2$$

In other words, for low speeds the relativistic formula reduces to the familiar Newtonian version. For higher speeds, the relativistic formula must be used.

Total energy, momentum and mass are related: from the definition of momentum, we find that

$$p^2c^2 + m_0^2c^4 = \frac{m_0^2v^2c^2}{1-\frac{v^2}{c^2}} + m_0^2c^4$$

$$= \frac{m_0^2c^4}{1-\frac{v^2}{c^2}}$$

$$= E^2$$

that is

$$E = \sqrt{m_0^2c^4 + p^2c^2}$$

(This formula is the relativistic version of the conventional formula $E = \frac{p^2}{2m}$ in Newtonian mechanics.) This relation can be remembered by using the Pythagorean theorem in the triangle of Figure G4.2

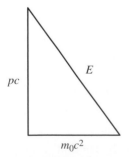

Figure G4.2 The rest energy, momentum and total energy are related through the Pythagorean theorem for the triangle shown.

The formula we just derived applies also to those particles that have zero mass, such as the photon, in which case $E = pc$. Remembering that for a photon $E = hf$, we find $p = \frac{hf}{c} = \frac{h}{\lambda}$.

A point about units

We have already seen that we can use units such as $\text{MeV}\,c^{-2}$ or $\text{GeV}\,c^{-2}$ for mass. This follows from the fact that the rest energy of a particle is given by $E_0 = m_0c^2$ and so allows us to express the mass of the particle in terms of the rest energy as $m_0 = E_0/c^2$. Thus, the statement 'the mass of the pion is 135 MeV c^{-2}' means that the rest energy of this particle is 135 MeV. (To find the mass in kg we would first have to convert the MeV into joules and then divide the result by the square of the speed of light.)

Similarly, the momentum of a particle can be expressed in units of $\text{MeV}\,c^{-1}$ or $\text{GeV}\,c^{-1}$. A particle of rest mass 5.0 MeV c^{-2} and total energy 13 MeV has momentum given by

$$E^2 = m_0^2c^4 + p^2c^2$$
$$\Rightarrow p^2c^2 = (169 - 25)\,\text{MeV}^2$$
$$= 144\,\text{MeV}^2$$
$$\Rightarrow pc = 12\,\text{MeV}$$
$$\Rightarrow p = 12\,\text{MeV}\,c^{-1}$$

The speed can be found from

$$E = \frac{m_0c^2}{\sqrt{1-\frac{v^2}{c^2}}}$$

$$\Rightarrow 13 = \frac{5}{\sqrt{1-\frac{v^2}{c^2}}}$$

$$\Rightarrow \sqrt{1-\frac{v^2}{c^2}} = \frac{5}{13}$$

$$\Rightarrow \frac{v^2}{c^2} = \frac{144}{169}$$

$$\Rightarrow v = \frac{12}{13}c$$

In conventional SI units, a momentum of 12 MeV c^{-1} is

$$12 \times 10^6 \times 1.6 \times 10^{-19}\,\frac{\text{J}}{3\times 10^8\,\text{m s}^{-1}}$$

$$= 6.4 \times 10^{-21}\,\frac{\text{kg m}^2\,\text{s}^{-2}}{\text{m s}^{-1}}$$

$$= 6.4 \times 10^{-21}\,\text{kg m s}^{-1}$$

Example questions

Q2

Find the momentum of a pion (rest mass 135 MeV c^{-2}) whose speed is $0.80c$.

Answer

The total energy is

$$E = \frac{m_0 c^2}{\sqrt{1 - \frac{v^2}{c^2}}}$$

$$= \frac{135}{\sqrt{1 - 0.80^2}}$$

$$= 225 \text{ MeV}$$

Using

$$E^2 = m_0^2 c^4 + p^2 c^2$$

$$\Rightarrow pc = \sqrt{225^2 - 135^2}$$

$$= 180 \text{ MeV}$$

$$\Rightarrow p = 180 \text{ MeV } c^{-1}$$

Q3

Find the speed of a muon (rest mass $= 105$ MeV c^{-2}) whose momentum is 228 MeV c^{-1}.

Answer

From $p = \gamma m_0 v$ we find

$$228 \text{ MeV } c^{-1} = \gamma \times 105 \text{ MeV } c^{-2} \times v$$

$$\Rightarrow \gamma \frac{v}{c} = 2.171$$

Hence

$$\frac{1}{1 - \left(\frac{v}{c}\right)^2}\left(\frac{v}{c}\right)^2 = 4.715$$

$$\Rightarrow \left(\frac{v}{c}\right)^2 = 4.715 - 4.715 \left(\frac{v}{c}\right)^2$$

$$\Rightarrow \left(\frac{v}{c}\right)^2 = \frac{4.715}{5.715}$$

$$= 0.8250$$

and so $v = 0.91c$.

Q4

Find the kinetic energy of an electron whose momentum is 1.5 MeV c^{-1}.

Answer

The total energy of the electron is given by

$$E^2 = m_0^2 c^4 + p^2 c^2$$

$$= 0.511^2 \text{ MeV}^2 + 1.5^2 \text{ MeV}^2 c^{-2} \times c^2$$

$$= 2.511 \text{ MeV}^2$$

$$\Rightarrow E = 1.58 \text{ MeV}$$

and so

$$E_k = E - m_0 c^2$$

$$= 1.58 \text{ MeV} - 0.511 \text{ MeV}$$

$$= 1.07 \text{ MeV}$$

A free electron cannot absorb a photon

The laws of relativistic mechanics forbid the absorption of a photon by a free electron. Assume for a minute that this is possible; that is, let a free electron initially at rest absorb a photon of energy ε (see Figure G4.3).

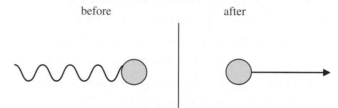

before   after

Figure G4.3 What would happen if a free electron could absorb a photon.

By conservation of momentum, the electron must then move in the same direction as that of the incident photon, with momentum ε/c, since this is the momentum the photon had before absorption,

$$p = \frac{\varepsilon}{c}$$

By conservation of energy, the total energy of the electron, E, after the photon absorption is $E = m_0 c^2 + \varepsilon$. But the electron's total energy E and momentum p are related by

$$E^2 = m_0^2 c^4 + p^2 c^2$$

and so this implies that

$$(m_0 c^2 + \varepsilon)^2 = m_0^2 c^4 + \frac{\varepsilon^2}{c^2}c^2$$

$$m_0^2 c^4 + \varepsilon^2 + 2m_0 c^2 \varepsilon = m_0^2 c^4 + \varepsilon^2$$

$$2m_0 c^2 \varepsilon = 0$$

which is an impossible relation. Hence the photon cannot be absorbed. In the photoelectric effect the absorption is possible, but only because the electron is not free but bound in an atom. The atom then participates in sharing energy and momentum so that the photon can be absorbed.

Questions

1 (a) Find the rest energy of an electron in MeV.
   (b) An electron is accelerated from rest by a potential difference of 1.00×10^9 V. Calculate the speed of the electron using (i) classical mechanics and (ii) relativistic mechanics.

2 What is the speed of a particle whose kinetic energy is 10 times its rest energy?

3 What is the momentum of a proton whose total energy is 5 times its rest energy?

4 What is the total energy of an electron with a speed equal to 0.9 times that of light?

5 What is the momentum, in conventional SI units, of a proton of momentum 685 MeV c^{-1}?

6 What is the kinetic energy of a proton whose momentum is 500 MeV c^{-1}?

7 The total energy of an electron is 10.0 GeV. What is its mass in kg?

8 (a) What is the speed of electrons accelerated to a total energy of 100.0 GeV?
   (b) What is it for protons?

9 What is the speed of an electron that has been accelerated from rest by a potential difference of 2.0 MV?

10 Through what potential difference must a proton be accelerated (from rest) so that its speed is 0.96c?

11 Find the kinetic energy of a proton whose speed is 0.99 times that of light.

12 What is the energy needed to accelerate an electron to a speed of:
   (a) 0.50c;
   (b) 0.90c;
   (c) 0.99c?

13 A proton initially at rest finds itself in a region of uniform electric field of magnitude 5.0×10^6 V m^{-1}. The electric field accelerates the proton over a distance of 1 km. Calculate:
   (a) the kinetic energy of the proton;
   (b) the speed of the proton.

14 (a) Show that the speed of a particle of rest mass m_0 and momentum p is given by

$$v = \frac{pc^2}{\sqrt{m_0^2 c^4 + p^2 c^2}}$$

An electron and a proton have the same momentum. What is the ratio of their speeds when the momentum is:
   (b) 1.00 MeV c^{-1};
   (c) 1.00 GeV c^{-1}?
   (d) What does the ratio become as the momentum gets larger and larger?

15 A particle at rest breaks apart into two pieces of masses 250 MeV c^{-2} and 125 MeV c^{-2}. The lighter fragment moves away at a speed equal to 0.85c.
   (a) What is the speed of the other fragment?
   (b) What is the rest mass of the particle that broke apart?
   (Use the laws of conservation of momentum and total energy.)

16 An electron and a positron (a particle of the same mass but opposite charge to the electron) each of kinetic energy 2.0 MeV collide head-on. The electron and positron annihilate each other into photons.
   (a) Explain why the electron–positron pair cannot create just one photon.
   (b) Assume that two photons are produced. Explain why the photons must be moving in opposite directions.
   (c) Calculate the energy of each photon.

17 *The Compton effect.* A photon of wavelength λ scatters off an electron initially at rest (see Figure G4.4).

Figure G4.4 For question 17.

(a) By treating the process as a collision and applying the laws of conservation of energy and momentum, show that the wavelength of the photon after the collision, λ', is given by

$$\lambda' - \lambda = \frac{h}{mc}(1 - \cos\theta)$$

(b) Explain why the scattered photon has a larger wavelength than that of the incoming photon.

(c) If the incoming photon has a wavelength of 3.00×10^{-12} m, find the wavelength of the scattered photon when the scattering angle is $60°$.

18 In the Compton effect (see question 17) an incoming photon of wavelength 5.00×10^{-12} m scatters off an electron initially at rest and goes back along the path it came from. With what kinetic energy and speed does the electron move off?

19 A neutral pion of mass 135 MeV c^{-2} travelling at $0.8c$ decays into two photons travelling in opposite directions, $\pi^0 \to 2\gamma$ (see Figure G4.5). What is the ratio of the frequency of photon A to that of photon B?

Figure G4.5 For question 19.

20 Two identical bodies with a rest mass of 3.0 kg are moving towards each other from opposite directions, each with a speed of $0.80c$. They collide and form one body. Determine the rest mass of this body.

General relativity

The theory of general relativity was formulated by Albert Einstein in 1916. It is a theory of gravitation that replaces the standard theory of gravitation of Newton and generalizes Einstein's special theory of relativity. Newton's theory of gravitation, while successful in dealing with planetary motion, cannot account for the effects of gravitation in very dense, massive objects and the behaviour of matter and energy in the universe as a whole. A number of physicists were close to discovering the laws of special relativity at the beginning of the twentieth century. The theory of general relativity, however, stands as the crowning achievement of Einstein's genius and is considered to be perhaps the most elegant and beautiful example of a physical theory ever constructed. The theory is a radical theory in that it relates the distribution of matter and energy in the universe to the structure of space and time. The geometry of space-time is a direct function of the matter and energy that space-time contains. In general, this geometry is not Euclidean, which means, among other things, that the angles of a triangle do not add up to 180°. Matter distorts the space-time in which it finds itself, in much the same way that a heavy ball would distort a rubber sheet on which it is placed.

Objectives

By the end of this chapter you should be able to:
- state the *equivalence principle* and appreciate its consequences;
- appreciate that the equivalence principle leads to the equality of *inertial mass* and *gravitational mass*;
- describe the tests of general relativity, in particular the *bending of light* by a massive object and the *gravitational redshift* or *Pound–Rebka experiment*;
- solve problems using $\frac{\Delta f}{f} = \frac{gH}{c^2}$;
- understand that general relativity is a theory that relates the *rules of geometry* to the *energy and mass* contained in space;
- appreciate that, in the absence of forces, objects in general relativity move along paths of shortest distance called *geodesics*;
- understand that general relativity predicts the existence of *black holes* whose event horizons have radius $R_S = \frac{2GM}{c^2}$;
- state the meaning of the term *event horizon*.

The principle of equivalence

We have already seen in Chapter 2.5 on Newton's second law that when a person stands on a scale inside a freely falling elevator ('Einstein's elevator') the reading of the scale is zero. It is as if the person is weightless. This is what the scale would read if the elevator were moving at constant velocity in deep space far from all masses. Similarly, consider an astronaut in a spacecraft in orbit around the earth. She too feels weightless and floats inside the spacecraft. But neither the person in the falling elevator nor the astronaut are really weightless. Gravity does act on both. We can say that the acceleration of the freely falling elevator or the centripetal acceleration of the spacecraft 'cancelled out' the force of gravity. The right acceleration can make gravity disappear and make the frame of reference under consideration look like one moving at constant velocity.

The right acceleration can also make gravity appear. Consider an astronaut in a spacecraft in deep space far from all masses that moves with constant velocity. The astronaut really is weightless. The spacecraft engines are now ignited and the spacecraft accelerates forward. The astronaut feels pinned down to the floor. If he drops a coin, it will hit the floor whereas previously it would have floated in the spacecraft. The coin falling to the floor and the sensation of being pinned down are what we normally associate with gravity.

We have seen two examples where the effects of acceleration mimic those of gravity. Another expression for 'the effects of acceleration' is 'inertial effects'. Einstein elevated these observations to a principle of physics – the equivalence principle:

▶ Gravitational and inertial effects are indistinguishable.

Applying this principle to the two examples we just discussed we may re-express it as:

▶ A frame of reference moving at constant velocity far from all masses is equivalent to a freely falling frame of reference in a uniform gravitational field.

Or:

▶ A frame of reference accelerating far from all masses is equivalent to a frame of reference at rest in a gravitational field.

You can use either one of these last two statements as a definition of the equivalence principle. But the original statement takes care of both.

Figure G5.1 shows a frame of reference, A, moving at constant velocity in deep space and a frame of reference, B, that is falling freely in a gravitational field. The principle of equivalence says that the two frames are equivalent. There is no experiment that the occupants of box A can perform that will give a different result from a similar experiment performed in box B. Nor can the occupants of either box decide which of the two states of motion they 'really' have.

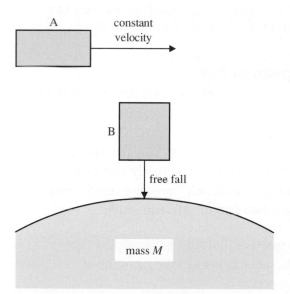

Figure G5.1 A frame of reference moving at constant velocity far from any masses (A) and a freely falling frame in a gravitational field (B) are equivalent.

Figure G5.2 shows a frame of reference, A, that accelerates in deep space and a frame of reference, B, that is at rest in a gravitational field. Again, there is no experiment that the occupants of box A can perform that will give a different result from a similar experiment performed in box B, nor can the occupants decide which is which.

This principle has immediate consequences.

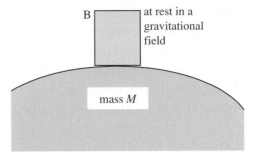

A — acceleration in deep space

B — at rest in a gravitational field

mass M

Figure G5.2 An accelerating frame of reference far from any masses (A) and a frame at rest in a gravitational field (B) are equivalent.

The speed of light

The first consequence is that *the speed of light is the same* whether in a gravitational field or not. An observer in box A of Figure G5.1 would measure $c = 3 \times 10^8$ m s^{-1} for the speed of light. An observer in the freely falling frame of box B must also reach the same conclusion since the two frames are equivalent.

▶ The speed of light in a gravitational field is the same as in any inertial frame of reference.

Inertial and gravitational mass

The second consequence is that *gravitational mass and inertial mass are the same.* Recall that inertial mass is the ratio of the net force on a body to the body's acceleration and gravitational mass is the ratio of the gravitational force on a body to the acceleration due to gravity.

In frame A of Figure G5.2, mass measurements are inertial mass measurements. In frame B at rest in a gravitational field, mass measurements are gravitational mass measurements. Since the two frames are equivalent, the equality of the two masses follows.

This is something that Galileo (and later Christiaan Huygens) checked experimentally when he showed that different objects fall at the same rate and that pendulums of equal lengths but with different masses have the same period. Modern, more accurate experiments by Dicke and Braginsky have verified this equality to an accuracy of 1 part in 10^{12}, that is

$$\frac{m_i - m_g}{m_i} < 10^{-12}$$

So there is good experimental evidence for the equivalence principle.

The bending of light

The third consequence of the equivalence principle is that *light bends toward a massive body.* Imagine a spacecraft orbiting a massive object. A ray of light is emitted from the back of the spacecraft toward the front. Where does it hit – at the front of the spacecraft at F or on the side at S (see Figure G5.3)? Remember that the frame of the spacecraft is freely falling (it is in orbit) and so is equivalent to a frame moving at constant velocity in a straight line (Figure G5.1). In this frame there is no doubt that the light will hit at F. So it must also hit at F in the spacecraft in orbit, since the two frames are equivalent.

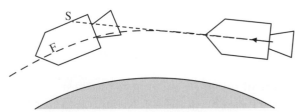

S

F

Figure G5.3 The ray of light will hit at F, indicating to an observer outside that the ray has bent toward the massive object.

But this means that from the point of view of an observer at rest on the surface of the massive body, light has bent towards it.

▶ A ray of light bends towards a massive body.

Massive objects can thus act as a kind of *gravitational lens*.

Time slows down

A final consequence of the equivalence principle is that *time slows down near a massive body*. Consider two rays on a wavefront AB, which are bent as they pass near a massive object (see Figure G5.4). A and B are thus points in phase.

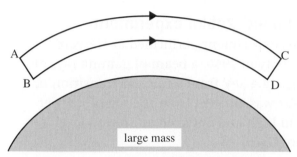

Figure G5.4 Ray BD appears to have covered a smaller distance than ray AC. Since the speed of light is the same for both rays, it follows that time must be 'running slower' near the massive object.

The ray at A moves to point C and that at B moves to point D. The wavefront AB has bent because the rays bend towards the massive object. If points C and D are to be in phase (they must be since they are on the same wavefront) the rays from A and B must take the same time to get to C and D. But ray BD covers a smaller distance than ray AC, yet travels at the same speed. The problem can be avoided if time runs slower for ray BD.

▶ Time slows down near massive objects.

Consider two identical clocks. One is placed near a massive body and the other far from it. When the clock near the massive body shows that 1 s has gone by, the far away clock will show that more than 1 s has gone by. This is the general relativity analogue of time dilation.

The tests of general relativity

The four main tests of the theory of general relativity are:

- the bending of light and radio signals near massive objects
- the gravitational frequency shift
- the precession of the perihelion of Mercury
- the time delay experiment

Of these, only the first two are required for examination purposes.

Test 1: The bending of light

The bending of light in the vicinity of a massive object (the sun, for example) was detected experimentally in a famous observation by F.W. Dyson, A.S. Eddington and C. Davidson in two separate eclipse expeditions to the islands of Principe and Sobral in 1919. News of their confirmation of Einstein's theory was telegraphed around the world and made Einstein known to the wider public. This is shown in Figure G5.5. The angle of bending is shown unrealistically large for clarity. When the sun is between the earth and the star, the sun's light would completely wipe out the light from the star. This is why such an observation is possible only during a total solar eclipse.

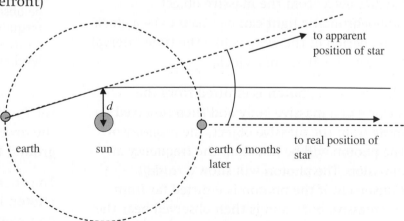

Figure G5.5 The star is observed during a solar eclipse and then 6 months later when the sun is not in the way. The angular position of the star is different in the two measurements. For a ray grazing the surface of the sun, the predicted angle of bending is about 1.75″ (arcseconds).

The bending of light that Eddington and his co-workers measured in 1919 was in agreement with the Einstein prediction, within experimental error, but the accuracy was not enough for this to constitute a test of the theory. The measurements have since been refined to include radio signals from distant galaxies, and these agree with general relativity predictions. Referring to Figure G5.5, if d is the distance of closest approach of a ray of light to the sun, the angle of deflection is predicted by general relativity to be

$$\theta = 1.75'' \frac{R}{d}$$

where R is the radius of the sun. (The angle is given in arcseconds – there are 3600 arcseconds in one degree.)

The bending of light is important to astronomers in the following way. Light from a distant star will be bent on its way to earth if it goes past a massive star or galaxy. This means that the star will not be observed to be at its true position. In some cases this leads to the formation of multiple images of the star. In this way massive objects act as a kind of *gravitational lens*.

Test 2: The gravitational frequency shift

General relativity predicts that clocks near a massive object run slower than similar clocks further away from the massive object. Monochromatic light can be taken to be a clock – the period of the wave is like the time interval between the 'ticks' of a clock.

Thus, when a photon is emitted from the surface of a massive body and then observed far away from the massive object, the *frequency* of the photon will be less than the frequency at emission. The photon will show a *redshift*. Conversely, if the photon is emitted far from the massive body and is then observed near the massive body, the photon will experience a *blueshift*.

This blueshift has actually been observed in the Pound–Rebka experiment in which the earth acts as the massive object (see Figure G5.6).

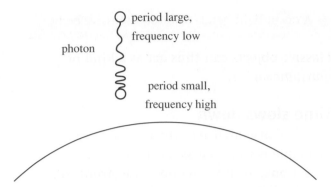

Figure G5.6 The photon has a larger frequency near the surface than at the point of emission far from the surface.

The Pound–Rebka experiment

In this experiment performed at Harvard University in 1960, a beam of gamma rays of energy 14.4 keV from a nuclear transition in iron-57 was emitted from the top of a tower 22.6 m high and detected at ground level (see Figure G5.7).

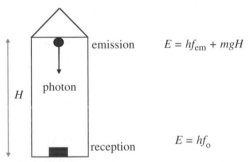

Figure G5.7 A photon emitted at ground level will be observed at the top of the tower with a lower frequency (redshift). Conversely, a photon emitted at the top will be observed at ground level at a higher frequency (blueshift).

Let f_{em} be the emitted frequency at the top of the tower and f_o the observed frequency at ground level.

The energy of the emitted photon is hf_{em}. This photon is received at a position lower than the emission point and energy conservation demands that

$$hf_{em} + mgH = hf_o$$

'Mass' here stands for the gravitational mass of the photon, that is its energy divided by c^2 (this is in effect the mass on which gravitation acts; it is not implied that the photon has a non-zero mass). This mass is thus (hf/c^2). Hence

$$hf_{em} + \frac{hf_{em}}{c^2}gH = hf_o$$

$$\Rightarrow f_o = f_{em}\left(1 + \frac{gH}{c^2}\right)$$

This means that the frequency shift $\Delta f = f_o - f_{em}$ is given by

$$\frac{\Delta f}{f} = \frac{gH}{c^2}$$

(Here, f stands for either the emitted or the observed frequency since they are almost equal.)

Example question

Q1 ▰▰▰▰▰▰▰▰▰▰▰▰▰▰▰▰

A photon of energy 14.4 keV is emitted from the top of a 30 m tall tower toward the ground. What shift of frequency is expected at the base of the tower?

Answer

On emission, the photon has frequency given by

$$E = hf$$

$$\Rightarrow f = \frac{E}{h}$$

$$= \frac{14.4 \times 10^3 \times 1.6 \times 10^{-19}}{6.63 \times 10^{-34}}$$

$$= 3.475 \times 10^{18} \text{ Hz}$$

The shift (it is a blueshift) is thus

$$\frac{\Delta f}{f} = \frac{gH}{c^2}$$

$$\Rightarrow \Delta f = f\frac{gH}{c^2}$$

$$= \frac{10 \times 30}{9 \times 10^{16}} \times 3.475 \times 10^{18} \text{ Hz}$$

$$= 1.16 \times 10^4 \text{ Hz}$$

Note how delicate this experiment actually is: the shift in frequency is only about 10^4 Hz compared with the emitted frequency of about 10^{18} Hz, a fractional shift of only

$$\frac{10^4 \text{ Hz}}{10^{18} \text{ Hz}} = 10^{-14}$$

Time slowing down near massive objects has also been detected directly in experiments. Atomic clocks carried on satellites have been compared with similar clocks on earth and the results have been consistent with general relativity. The clocks on earth are slow compared with those on satellites.

The structure of the theory

The theory of general relativity is a physical theory different from all others in that:

The mass and energy content of space determine the geometry of that space and time. The geometry of space-time determines the motion of mass and energy in the space-time.

That is

geometry ⇔ mass–energy

Space-time is a four-dimensional world with three space and one time coordinates. In the absence of any forces, a body moves in this four-dimensional world along paths of shortest length, called *geodesics*.

If a single mass M is the only mass present in the universe, the solutions of the Einstein equations imply that far from the mass the geometry of space is the usual Euclidean flat geometry with all its familiar rules (for example, the angles of a triangle add up to 180°). As we approach the neighbourhood of M, the space becomes curved as indicated by Figure G5.8. The rules of geometry then have to change. Large masses with small radii produce extreme bending of the space-time around them.

As an illustration of how the theory works, consider two balls that are made to move parallel to each other on a flat frictionless surface (see Figure G5.9a). The separation between the balls stays constant. In Newtonian mechanics we say that there is no force between the balls, no acceleration and hence no relative

Figure G5.8 Far from the mass, the space looks flat; near the mass, the deviation from flat geometry is large. This is only a two-dimensional diagram though; Einstein's theory demands a distortion in the geometry of four-dimensional space-time.

velocity. On the other hand, consider the same two balls on the curved surface of a sphere that also start out moving parallel to each other (see Figure 5.9b). The balls will start approaching each other and will actually meet at the north pole. In Newtonian mechanics we would have to invoke a force between the balls which brings them toward each other. In Einstein's relativity no force is required – the balls approach each other because of the geometry of space. The paths they follow are the 'straight' lines of the curved space.

Similarly, light retains its familiar property of travelling from one place to another in the shortest possible time. Since the speed of light is always constant, this means that light travels along paths of shortest length – *geodesics*. In the flat Euclidean geometry we are used to, geodesics are straight lines. In the curved non-Euclidean geometry of general relativity, something else replaces the concept of straight line. A ray of light travelling near the sun looks bent to us because we are used to flat space. But the geometry near the sun is curved and the 'bent' ray is actually the geodesic: it is the 'straight' line appropriate to that geometry.

Thus, the motion of a planet around the sun is, according to Einstein, not the result of a gravitational force acting on the planet (as Newton would have it) but rather due to the curved geometry in the space and time around the sun created by the large mass of the sun. The planet follows a geodesic in the curved space-time around the earth. This geodesic *appears* as a circular path if we view space-time as flat.

Black holes

The theory of general relativity also predicts the existence of objects that contract under the influence of their own gravitation, becoming ever smaller objects. No mechanism is known for stopping this collapse and the object is expected to become a hole in space-time, a point of infinite density. This creates an immense bending of space-time around this point. This is called a black hole – a name appropriately coined by John Archibald Wheeler, since nothing can escape from it. Massive stars can, under appropriate conditions, collapse under their own gravitation and end up as black holes (see Chapter F5 in the option on Astrophysics). Powerful theorems by Stephen Hawking and Roger Penrose show that the formation of black holes is inevitable and not dependent too much on the details of how the collapse itself proceeds.

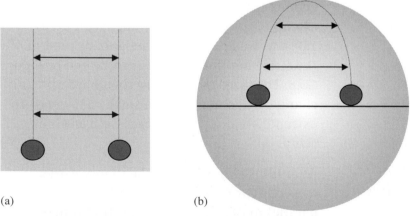

(a)   (b)

Figure G5.9 (a) On a flat surface the separation between the balls stays the same as the balls move parallel to each other. (b) On a curved surface the balls will approach each other even though no force acts between them.

The Schwarzschild radius and the event horizon

A distance known as the Schwarzschild radius of the black hole is of importance in understanding the behaviour of black holes. (Karl Schwarzschild was the German astronomer who provided the first solution of the Einstein equations.) The Schwarzschild radius is given by

$$R_S = \frac{2GM}{c^2}$$

where M is the mass and c the speed of light. This radius is not the actual radius of the black hole (the black hole is a point) – it is the distance from the hole's centre that separates space into a region from which an object can escape and a region from which no object can escape (see Figure G5.10).

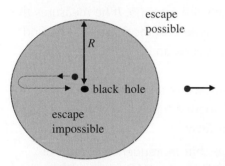

Figure G5.10 The Schwarzschild radius splits space into two regions. From within this radius nothing, not even light, can escape.

Any object closer to the centre of the black hole than R_S will fall into the hole; no amount of energy supplied to this body will allow it to escape from the black hole.

The escape velocity at a distance equal to R_S from the centre of the black hole equals the speed of light and hence nothing can escape from the star from within this radius. The Schwarzschild radius is also called the gravitational radius of the black hole, or the event horizon. The last name is apt since anything taking place within the event horizon cannot be seen by or communicated to the outside. The area of the event horizon is taken as the surface area of the black hole (but, remember, the black hole is a point).

The Schwarzschild radius can be derived in an elementary way without recourse to general relativity if we assume that a photon has a mass m on which the black hole's gravity acts. Then, as we did in the calculation of the escape velocity in Chapter 2.10 on gravitation,

$$\frac{1}{2}mc^2 = \frac{GM}{R_S}m$$

Thus m cancels and we can solve for R_S.

It can be readily calculated from this formula that for a star of one solar mass ($M \approx 2 \times 10^{30}$ kg) the gravitational radius is about 3 km:

$$\begin{aligned}
R_S &= \frac{2GM}{c^2} \\
&= \frac{2 \times 6.67 \times 10^{-11} \times 2 \times 10^{30}}{(3 \times 10^8)^2} \\
&\approx 3 \times 10^3 \text{ m}
\end{aligned}$$

For the earth it is just 9 mm. This means, for example, that if the sun were to become a black hole its entire mass should be confined within a sphere with a radius of 3 km or less.

Figure G5.11 shows that an observer on the surface of a star that is about to become a black hole would only be able to receive light

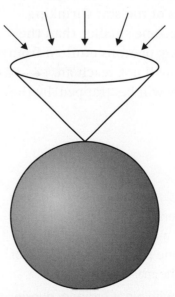

Figure G5.11 The horizon for observers on a collapsing star is rising; that is, only rays within a vertical cone can reach them.

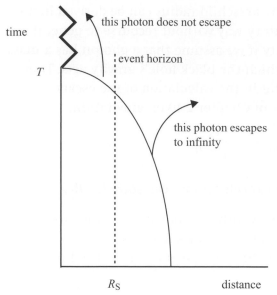

Figure G5.12 A space-time diagram of the formation of a black hole. As time goes on, the radius of the star is getting smaller. At $t = T$, the radius becomes zero and a singularity has been formed. A photon emitted from the surface of the star before the radius becomes less than the Schwarzschild radius will be received by an observer far from the hole. But once the star collapses beyond the event horizon, any photons emitted do not leave the black hole.

through a cone that is getting smaller and smaller as the star approaches its gravitational (Schwarzschild) radius. This is because rays of light coming 'sideways' will bend toward the star and will not reach the observer. Figure G5.12 shows the radius of the star shrinking. After the radius has become smaller than the gravitational radius, any photons emitted from the surface of the star will not reach an observer far away. They will be 'trapped' by the black hole.

Questions

1 Discuss the statement: 'a ray of light does not actually bend near a massive object but follows a straight-line path in the geometry of the space around the massive object'.

2 A spacecraft filled with air at ordinary density and pressure is far from any large masses. A helium-filled balloon floats inside the spacecraft which now begins to accelerate

towards the right. Which way (if any) does the balloon move?

3 The spacecraft from question 2 now has a lighted candle in it. When the craft begins to accelerate toward the right, what happens to the flame of the candle?

4 Describe what is meant by the equivalence principle. How does this principle lead to the predictions that:
    (a) light bends in a gravitational field;
    (b) the gravitational and inertial masses are the same;
    (c) time 'runs slower' near a massive object.

5 Describe what the general theory of relativity predicts about a massive object whose radius is getting smaller.

6 In a local inertial frame (i.e. one falling freely in a gravitational field) an observer attaches a mass m to the end of a spring, extends the spring and lets the mass go. If he measures the period of oscillation of the mass, will he find the same answer as an observer doing the same thing:
    (a) on the surface of a very massive star;
    (b) in a true inertial frame far from any masses?
    Explain your answer.

7 Calculate the shift in frequency of light of wavelength 500.0 nm that is emitted from sea level and is received at a height of 50.0 m.

8 If a photon of frequency f is emitted from the surface of a star, the frequency shift observed far from the star is given by

$$\Delta f \approx f \frac{R_g}{R}$$

where R_g is the gravitational radius of the star and R its radius. Use this formula to calculate the shift in frequency of a line in the sun's spectrum which has a wavelength of 548 nm at emission.

9 A collapsed star has a radius that is 5 times larger than its gravitational radius. An observer on the surface of the star carries a clock and a laser. Every second the observer sends a short pulse of laser light of duration 1.00 ms and wavelength 4.00×10^{-7} m (as measured by her instruments) toward another observer in a

spacecraft far from the star. Discuss *qualitatively* what the observer in the spacecraft can expect to measure for:
(a) the wavelength of the pulses;
(b) the frequency of reception of consecutive pulses;
(c) the duration of the pulses.

10 Two identical clocks are placed on a rotating disc. One is placed on the circumference of the disc and the other half-way toward the centre. Explain why the clock on the circumference will run slow relative to the other clock.

11 What would the density of the earth be if its entire mass were confined within a radius equal to its Schwarzschild radius?

12 What is the Schwarzschild radius of a black hole with mass equal to 10 solar masses?

13 Explain what is meant by *geodesic*.

14 A mass *m* moves past a massive body along the path shown in Figure G5.13. Explain the shape of the path according to:
(a) Newtonian gravity;
(b) Einstein's theory of general relativity.

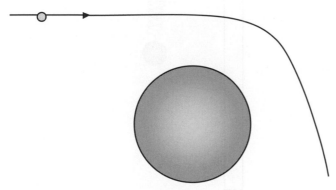

Figure G5.13 For question 14.

15 A ball is thrown with a velocity that is initially parallel to the floor of a spacecraft as shown in Figure G5.14. Draw and explain the shape of the ball's path when:
(a) the spacecraft is moving with constant velocity in deep space far from any large masses;
(b) the spacecraft is moving with constant acceleration in deep space far from any large masses.

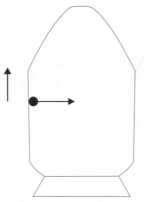

Figure G5.14 For question 15.

16 A ray of light moving parallel to the floor of a spacecraft enters the spacecraft through a small window as shown in Figure G5.15. Draw and explain the shape of the ray's path when:
(a) the spacecraft is moving with constant velocity in deep space far from any large masses;
(b) the spacecraft is moving with constant acceleration in deep space far from any large masses.

Figure G5.15 For question 16.

A problem just for fun

17 The curvature of a spherical surface of radius *R* can be defined in many ways. Two methods to calculate the curvature are as follows. Consider a circular patch (cap) of radius *r* centred at the 'north pole'. This radius is defined *along* the surface – in other words, it is the length of the arc from N to a point P on the sphere. (See Figure G5.16.)

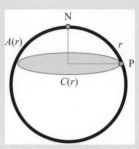

Figure G5.16 For question 17.

The curvature, K, is then defined by

$$K = 3 \lim_{r \to 0} \frac{2\pi r - C(r)}{\pi r^3} \quad \text{or}$$

$$K = 12 \lim_{r \to 0} \frac{\pi r^2 - A(r)}{\pi r^4}$$

where $C(r)$ and $A(r)$ are the circumference and area of the circular cap of radius r centred at N. Show that

$$C(r) = 2\pi R \sin \frac{r}{R} \quad \text{and}$$

$$A(r) = 2\pi R^2 \left(1 - \cos \frac{r}{R}\right)$$

Evaluate the two limits to find the curvature of the sphere. Hence explain why a large sphere is less curved than a smaller one. (You will find the following approximations useful: $\sin x \approx x - \frac{x^3}{6}$ and $\cos x \approx 1 - \frac{x^2}{2} + \frac{x^4}{24}$, which are valid if x (in radians) is small.)

18 An observer is standing on the surface of a massive object that is collapsing and is about to form a black hole. Describe what the observer sees in the sky:
   (a) before the object shrinks past its event horizon;
   (b) after the object goes past its event horizon.

19 A plane flying from southern Europe to New York City will fly over Ireland, across the North Atlantic, over the eastern coast of Canada and then south to New York. Why do you think such a path is followed?

20 *Einstein's birthday present.* A colleague of Einstein at Princeton presented him with the following birthday present. A long tube was connected to a bowl at its top end. A spring was attached to the base of the bowl and connected to a heavy brass ball that hung out of the bowl. (See Figure G5.17.) The spring was very 'weak' and could not pull the ball into the bowl. The exercise is to find a sure-fire method for putting the ball into the bowl without touching it. Einstein immediately found a way of doing it. Can you?

Figure G5.17 For question 20.

Light

This chapter describes Michelson's experiment to measure the speed of light, which is one of the most important physical constants. The various members of the large family of electromagnetic waves are introduced and their properties described. The dependence of the index of refraction on wavelength (the phenomenon of dispersion) is discussed and the chapter closes with a discussion of the laser and its applications.

Objectives

By the end of this chapter you should be able to:
- describe one experiment that measures the *speed of light*;
- understand the *nature of an electromagnetic wave* and how it is produced;
- name the *main members of the electromagnetic family of waves*;
- state the meaning of the term *dispersion* and calculate the *speed of light* from the *index of refraction* of the medium, $n = \frac{c_{vac}}{c_{med}}$;
- describe what the *laser* is and list a few of its uses;
- state the meaning of the terms *monochromatic* and *coherent*.

The speed of light

One of the most important physical constants is the speed of light in a vacuum. This is the limiting speed for all material objects according to Einstein's theory of relativity. A very early attempt to measure the speed of light was made by Galileo in 1600. A lantern was uncovered at a predetermined time and an observer some distance away was supposed to record the time that he first saw the lantern's light. Dividing his distance from the lantern by the time he recorded would give the speed of light. Obviously the experiment failed because the time taken by light to cover the known distance was so small that it could not be measured. The first measurement of the speed of light was made by the Danish astronomer Ole Roemer in 1676, who devised an ingenious method based on observations of eclipses of one of the moons of Jupiter. Roemer was thus the first to show that the speed of light is finite.

A very accurate terrestrial method to measure *c* was developed by the American physicist Albert Michelson in 1926. Michelson used a rotating octagonal prism whose rate of rotation could be very accurately controlled. A ray of light from a very strong source is reflected off face F_1 of the prism (see Figure H1.1) and allowed to travel a very large distance (about 35 km) to a spherical mirror, from which it is reflected back to the prism. A final reflection off face F_2 of the prism brings the light into an observing telescope. If the prism begins to rotate, the light in the telescope disappears, since the prism now has the wrong orientation relative to the rays from the mirror. As the speed of rotation is increased, light will again become visible in the telescope. This is because, in the time it has taken light to cover the distance from the prism to the spherical mirror and back, the prism has turned by exactly one-eighth of a revolution.

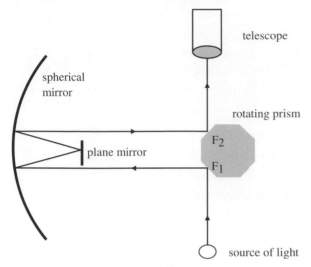

Figure H1.1 A simplified diagram of the arrangement used by Michelson to measure the speed of light. The distance of the prism to the spherical mirror was about 35 km so the diagram is very much out of scale.

Michelson saw light in the telescope with the prism rotating at a rate of 530 revolutions per second. Thus, he calculated the speed of light (in air) to be

$$c = \frac{2 \times 35}{(1/8) \times (1/530)} \frac{km}{s} = 2.97 \times 10^8 \text{ m s}^{-1}$$

Electromagnetic waves

There exists a very large family of waves called electromagnetic waves. This family has the following characteristics:

- they can travel in a vacuum;
- they travel at a speed of 3×10^8 m s^{-1} in a vacuum – the speed of light;
- they are transverse waves.

The displacement in electromagnetic waves is actually a pair of quantities: an electric and a magnetic field at right angles to each other, which vary with position and time. Both fields are at right angles to the direction of propagation of the wave, which makes electromagnetic waves *transverse*. In Figure H1.2 the electric field oscillates in the z–y plane and the magnetic field in the x–y plane. The direction of propagation is along the y

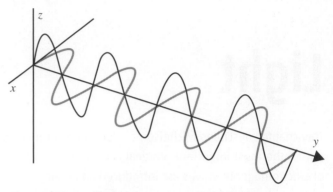

Figure H1.2 An electromagnetic wave has an electric and a magnetic field at right angles to each other and to the direction of motion of the wave.

direction (normal to both fields). As long as the plane along which the electric field oscillates stays the same, the wave is called plane *polarized*.

The theoretical prediction of electromagnetic waves was the crowning achievement of the Scottish theoretical physicist James Clerk Maxwell in 1867. The experimental verification of Maxwell's ideas came from the German physicist Heinrich Hertz in 1887, eight years after Maxwell's death.

The various members of this family of waves are distinguished by wavelength or frequency as well as their method of production. Electromagnetic waves include light, gamma and X-rays, ultraviolet and infrared light, microwaves, TV and radio waves. The wavelengths range from 10^{-14} m for very energetic gamma rays to 10^4 m for radio waves. Ordinary visible light occupies a small window in the electromagnetic spectrum: violet light at 400 nm (7.5×10^{15} Hz) to red light at 700 nm (4.3×10^{14} Hz) – see Table H1.1.

The entire electromagnetic spectrum is shown in Figure H1.3. The frequency increases as we move to the right. The photon energy increases from about 10^{-11} eV for a radio wave photon to 10^{-7} eV for an energetic gamma ray. This means that the photon, which represents the particle nature of light, becomes more dominant as we move toward the right in Figure H1.3.

Wavelength range/nm (= 10^{-9} m)	Frequency/ THz (= 10^{12} Hz)	Colour
390–455	659–769	Violet
455–492	610–659	Blue
492–577	520–610	Green
577–597	503–520	Yellow
597–622	482–503	Orange
622–780	384–482	Red

Table H1.1 Wavelengths and frequencies of visible light.

▶ Electromagnetic waves are produced when:
- an electric charge is accelerated;

or

- molecules, atoms or atomic nuclei make transitions to lower energy states.

Radio waves

These were the waves Hertz first observed. They are generally produced in various kinds of electrical circuits in which electrons are forced to accelerate. The emission antennas of radio and TV stations are typical examples of accelerated electron motion followed by radio wave emission.

Microwaves

Microwaves are now used extensively in communication, remote control devices and heating and cooking food. They are produced in molecular transitions. The energy associated with the rotational and vibrational motion of a molecule is quantized and the molecule finds itself in one of a number of energy levels, just as the electron's energy in a hydrogen atom is quantized, giving rise to molecular energy levels. When the molecule makes a transition from a high to a lower energy level, microwaves may be produced. Hydrogen gas emits microwave radiation with a wavelength of 21 cm – this has been detected from sources inside our galaxy, greatly increasing our knowledge of galactic structure. Microwave radiation with a wavelength of about 1 mm fills space and is a remnant of the Big Bang that created the universe.

Infrared

Just below the optical part of the spectrum (in frequency) is infrared (IR) radiation, first detected by Sir William Herschel in 1800. Commonly associated with this radiation is thermal radiation – the electromagnetic waves emitted by any object kept at some temperature of T kelvin. IR radiation is emitted by human bodies, hot pieces of coal, light-bulb filaments and the sun. Some nocturnal hunting animals, such as pit viper snakes, are sensitive to IR radiation. IR radiation is produced in molecular transitions.

Light

Occupying a tiny window in the huge electromagnetic spectrum is the all-important

Figure H1.3 The electromagnetic spectrum with wavelength expressed in metres and frequency in hertz.

visible light. The wavelengths range from (very roughly) 400 nm for violet light to about 700 nm for red. Light is produced in atomic transitions (for example in a discharge tube) or by accelerated electric charges (for example in the hot filament of a lamp where electrons are accelerated in constant collisions). The human eye is a detector of optical light and can record the arrival of as few as just 10 photons of light.

Ultraviolet

Ultraviolet (UV) radiation was discovered by Johann Ritter in 1801. UV radiation is very energetic and can ionize air (producing the ionosphere). UV radiation is harmful but most UV rays from the sun are absorbed by ozone (O_3) in the atmosphere. UV radiation is produced in atomic transitions.

X-rays

These were discovered by Wilhelm Conrad Röntgen in 1895. They are produced when electrons are rapidly decelerated as they collide with atoms (*Bremsstrahlung*), or when electrons make transitions from very excited states down to the ground state in high atomic number elements. They are very penetrating and have important applications in medicine. X-rays have been observed from galaxies, stars and black holes, greatly increasing our understanding of the universe by complementing knowledge derived from optical observations.

Gamma rays

These are the most energetic members of the electromagnetic spectrum with wavelengths of 10^{-12} m or less. They are produced when nuclei make transitions to lower nuclear energy levels or when particles annihilate in collisions with their antiparticles.

Dispersion

When a beam of white light falls on a triangular prism, the colours of the rainbow will emerge from the other side of the prism (see Figure H1.4). This is because the index of refraction of glass actually depends on the wavelength of light entering the glass. This is the phenomenon of dispersion. In fact, the index of refraction is slightly smaller for red light than it is for blue. This means that red light will be bent by a smaller amount than blue and so the beam that emerges splits into the colours of the rainbow. If the various colours are recombined, white light is again obtained. The graph in Figure H1.4 shows the variation with wavelength of the refractive index for two substances: acrylic plastic and flint glass. In both cases the refractive index is lower for red wavelengths.

The laser

Physicists for a long time searched for powerful yet concentrated, coherent sources of light over very narrow ranges of frequency (i.e. monochromatic). The emission of light from the hot filament of an ordinary light bulb is incoherent in the sense that the emissions of photons from different atoms in the filament are totally uncorrelated. We have no control over the emission times of photons from the various atoms. One way to make the source of radiation more coherent is to reduce the area from which radiation is being emitted. Reducing the area, though, in general means that the intensity of the light is also reduced. For example, the sun emits an enormous amount of energy per second, about 3.9×10^{26} W from its entire surface area, but this energy is emitted over all frequencies. The power radiated within 1 MHz around a wavelength of 500 nm (the wavelength at which most of the sun's energy is emitted) is only 7.5×10^{-2} W m^{-2}. Making the area 1 mm^2 means that the radiated power is an insignificant 7.5×10^{-8} W. The laser is the answer to this problem. The first laser was constructed by Theodore H. Maiman in 1960 following earlier work in the microwave region by Charles Townes in the USA and Aleksandr Prokhorov and Nikolai Basov in the USSR. The word laser is an acronym and stands for Light Amplification by Stimulated Emission of Radiation.

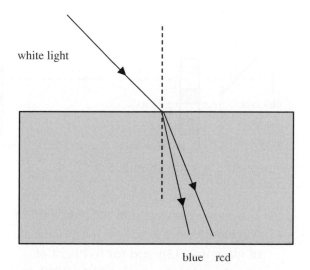

Figure H1.4 The index of refraction depends on wavelength and is smaller for red light. White light entering a prism splits into the colours of the rainbow in a phenomenon known as dispersion. The index of refraction for red light is smaller than that for blue and so a red ray has a larger angle of refraction.

▶ The laser is a source of very intense, very directional, monochromatic, coherent radiation.

Figure H1.5 shows a cross-section of a laser beam. All points in the cross-section have the same phase.

The introduction of lasers has revolutionized many areas of industry and medicine. In medicine, lasers are used to:

- destroy tumours;
- reattach damaged retinas (the laser damages part of the tissue so that the resulting scar welds the retina back into place);

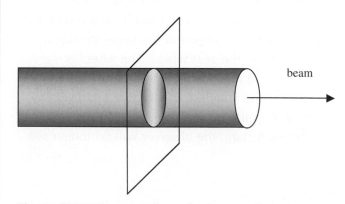

Figure H1.5 The meaning of coherent light: points on the same vertical plane through a laser beam have the same phase. The phase difference between widely separated points on the beam stays the same as time goes on.

- unblock arteries and heart valves (by destroying the plaque and other residues that clog them);
- cut and seal nerves in neurosurgery;
- correct vision defects such as myopia in cornea operations.

In industry and defence their uses include:

- welding;
- cutting and drilling metals;
- operating laser and compact discs;
- measuring distances accurately in surveying;
- measuring distances accurately between the earth and the moon by reflecting laser beams off mirrors left on the moon;
- reading barcodes;
- communication, where coded signals travel in optical fibres transmitting telephone conversations;
- sophisticated 'smart weapons', where a laser beam guides the weapon to its target.

Questions

1 In Galileo's attempt to measure the speed of light, the two lanterns were about 8 km apart.
   (a) How long would light take to travel this distance?
   (b) How does this time compare with a typical reaction time of 0.1 s?

2 In Armand Fizeau's measurement of the speed of light in 1849, a gear (toothed) wheel was used (see Figure H1.6). Light from a source falls on a plate P and part of it reflects through a hole H_1 in the gear wheel. The wheel is initially at rest. The light travels to a distant mirror and is reflected back through the same hole into the observer's eye. As the wheel begins to turn, the observer will no longer see

light. This is because on its return trip, the light ray hits a tooth and is intercepted. If, however, the speed of rotation is increased to a critical value, the observer again sees light. This is because it takes light as much time to travel the distance D *and back* as it takes hole H_2 to take up the position previously held by H_1. In Fizeau's experiment, a wheel with 720 teeth was used. Light was seen when the wheel revolved at 25.2 revolutions per second and the distance D to the mirror was 8.65×10^3 m. Find the speed of light obtained by Fizeau.

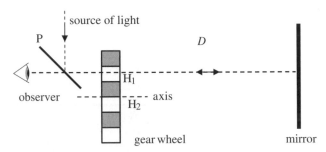

Figure H1.6 For question 2.

3 The index of refraction for blue light of wavelength 4.5×10^{-7} m for a particular kind of glass is 1.328 and for red light of wavelength 6.5×10^{-7} m it is 1.321. An equilateral prism is made out of this glass and white light is incident on it parallel to one of its bases. Find the angles the blue and red rays make with the normal as they emerge from the prism. What is the deviation of each ray?

4 What is the difference between light emitted from a light bulb and light from a laser?

5 Find out in detail how exactly a laser is used in:
   (a) a CD;
   (b) surveying;
   (c) reading a barcode.

Reflection and refraction

This chapter deals with the wave phenomena of reflection and refraction as they apply to light. In particular, we discuss image formation by reflection and refraction, and related phenomena such as total internal reflection and its applications.

Objectives

By the end of this chapter you should be able to:

- state the *law of reflection* and find *images* of objects placed in front of plane mirrors;
- state the difference between *specular* and *diffuse reflection*;
- state and use the *law of refraction*, $n_1 \sin \theta_1 = n_2 \sin \theta_2$;
- describe how refraction forms *images* of objects;
- state the meaning of *apparent depth*;
- understand what is meant by *total internal reflection* and calculate the *critical angle*, $\sin \theta_c = \frac{1}{n}$;
- state some *applications of internal reflection*, such as the endoscope and periscopes.

Scattering

The phenomena of reflection and refraction that we examined earlier in this book have been presented in a deceptively simple way. They both follow directly from Huygens' principle, and reflection, in particular, seems to be nothing more than a simple bouncing of a ray of light from a mirror, much like the bouncing of a ball from a wall. In reality, both phenomena are macroscopic manifestations of complicated interactions between light and the atoms of the reflecting surface (for reflection) or the interface of two media (for refraction). This microscopic interaction of light and matter is called *scattering of light* and the phenomena of reflection, refraction, absorption and transmission of light are macroscopic versions of this general phenomenon.

The topics covered in this chapter fall under the heading of *geometrical* optics. This means that phenomena such as diffraction and interference are *ignored* (but see Chapter H4). Light is then treated simply as rays of light that reflect or refract at various interfaces and its full wave nature is not taken into account.

Reflection

An object can be seen by an observer if rays of light from that object enter the eye of the observer. This means that either the object must produce its own light (such as a star, a light bulb, a candle, etc.) or light from another source falling on the object is reflected from the object and then enters the observer's eye.

▶ The law of reflection states that:

- the angle of incidence, θ_I (the angle between the ray and the normal to the reflecting surface at the point of incidence), equals the angle of reflection, θ_R (the angle between the normal and the reflected ray);

and

- the reflected and incident rays and the normal to the surface lie in the same plane, called the plane of incidence.

It applies to reflection from both plane and curved surfaces (see Figure H2.1). For a spherical surface, the normal is the direction toward the centre of the spherical surface. The experimental verification of this law has been discussed in Chapter 4.2.

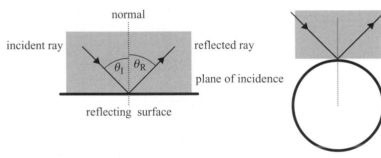

Figure H2.1 The incident and reflected rays make the same angle with the normal to the reflecting surface at the point of impact.

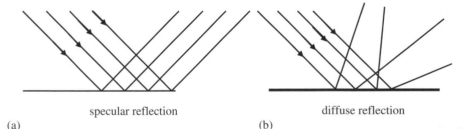

specular reflection   (a)   diffuse reflection   (b)

Figure H2.2 (a) Reflection from a smooth flat surface means that a parallel beam is reflected into another parallel beam. (b) Diffuse reflection occurs from surfaces that are not smooth.

When a parallel beam of light rays falls on a smooth surface such as a mirror, it will reflect into another parallel beam. We call such reflection *specular* reflection (see Figure H2.2a).

On the other hand, if the surface is not very smooth, a parallel beam of rays will not reflect into another parallel beam. We call this *diffuse* reflection (see Figure H2.2b). Specular reflection takes place when the wavelength of the incident wave is larger than the size of any irregularities of the reflecting surface.

Forming an image

Consider first a point object P that is placed in front of a plane mirror. A very large number of rays leaving the object will fall on the mirror and get reflected by it (Figure H2.3a). Figure H2.3b shows just two of those rays. Ray 1 hits the mirror at point N making an angle of incidence of 0° and so will be reflected with an angle of reflection of also 0°. Ray 2 hits the mirror at point M making an angle of incidence of θ and is reflected as shown. An observer on the same side of the mirror as the object may receive these two (and many other) reflected rays. If these reflected rays are projected backward as mathematical lines they will intersect at point P′. The brain of the observer is tricked into believing that the rays actually originated from point P′ (the human brain only knows about light rays travelling in straight lines). We call this the *image* of the object at P. Note that it is the mathematical extensions of the rays that have intersected, not the actual rays themselves. (Later we will see how images can be formed by intersections of rays themselves.)

▶ The image in a plane mirror is formed by extensions of rays and for this reason we call the image 'virtual'. No rays actually leave point P′, only the extensions of rays. At that point in space, behind the mirror where the virtual image is being formed, an eye, film or any other detecting device would record nothing. To see the image the eye must be put somewhere in front of the mirror.

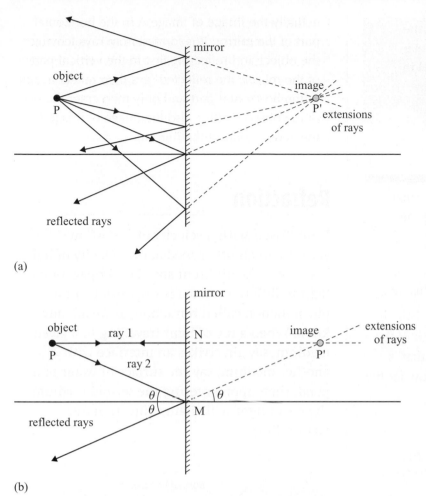

(a)

(b)

Figure H2.3 (a) The formation of an image by a plane mirror. (b) The formation of an image by a plane mirror. Two rays are shown leaving the top of the object. The reflected rays meet when extended backwards.

Consider now an *extended* object placed in front of the mirror. Its image can be found in a similar fashion by forming the image point by point. That is to say, we imagine the object to be made of a very large number of point objects, and we then find the image of each of those point objects. For most cases, it is sufficient to find the image of the top and bottom points of the object and then join the images to find the image of the entire object, as in Figure H2.4.

From simple geometry in Figure H2.4 and the law of reflection, we can now deduce the following general results about reflection from a plane mirror: note that triangles MNT and MNT′ are equal. This follows since they have one side common (MN), are right-angled (∠MNT and ∠MNT′) and ∠NMT = ∠NMT′. Hence NT = NT′, which means that the distance from the image to the mirror is the same as the distance from the object to the mirror. Also AT = BT′, which means that the height of the image equals that of the object.

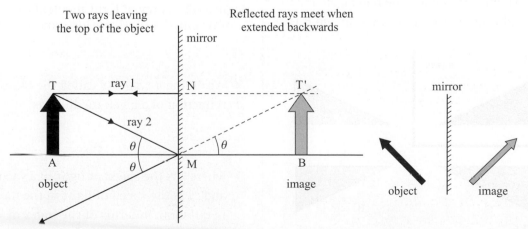

Figure H2.4 The formation of an image by a plane reflecting surface.

▶ This is a general result for images in plane mirrors: the image is at the same distance from the mirror as the object and equal in height. A plane mirror appears to reverse right and left but not top and bottom.

Example questions

Q1

How big must a plane mirror be so that a man can see all of himself in the mirror? Take the man's height to be 1.80 m.

Answer

The man must be able to see the top of his head and the bottom of his feet.

It follows from Figure H2.5 that the length of the required mirror is half the man's height, that is 0.90 m. The answer is independent of how far the man is standing from the mirror.

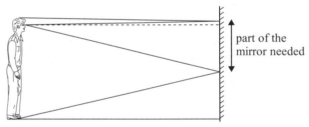

part of the mirror needed

Figure H2.5.

Q2

A black triangular object is placed in front of two plane mirrors at right angles to each other. How many images are formed?

Answer

There will be three images as shown in Figure H2.6. Images A and C are the obvious ones. Image B is

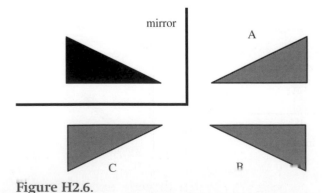

Figure H2.6.

actually the image of image A in the horizontal part of the mirror. It is formed from rays leaving the object and reflecting first in the vertical part of the mirror; the reflected rays then reflect again in the horizontal part and only then enter the eye of the observer. (It is also the image of image C in the vertical part of the mirror.)

Refraction

Light travels with a velocity of 3×10^8 m s^{-1} in a vacuum. In all other media, the velocity of light is smaller. The different speed of propagation of light in different media is responsible for a phenomenon called refraction, as we already know. When a ray of light travelling in a given medium, say air, strikes an interface with another medium, say the surface of water in a pond, then upon entering the second medium the ray of light will change direction (see Figure H2.7).

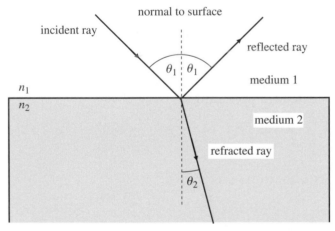

Figure H2.7 A ray of light incident on the interface of two media partly reflects and partly refracts.

▶ We define a quantity called the index of refraction of a given medium as:

$$n = \frac{c}{c_m}$$

where c is the speed of light in a vacuum and c_m is the speed of light in the medium in question. In terms of the index of refraction, Snell's law then reads

$$n_1 \sin \theta_1 = n_2 \sin \theta_2$$

(see Figure H2.7).

Since the speed of light is always largest in a vacuum, the index of refraction is always greater than 1. By definition, the index of refraction of a vacuum (and approximately of air) is 1. Thus, if we are given the index of refraction of a medium we can find the speed of light in that medium. For example in a glass with $n = 1.5$, the speed of light is

$$
\begin{aligned}
c_g &= \frac{c}{n_g} \\
&= \frac{3 \times 10^8}{1.5} \, \text{m s}^{-1} \\
&= 2 \times 10^8 \, \text{m s}^{-1}
\end{aligned}
$$

Example question

Q3 ▬▬▬▬

Light of wavelength 680 nm in air enters water making an angle of 40° with the normal. Find the angle of refraction and the wavelength of light in water. (The index of refraction of water is 1.33.)

Answer

By straightforward application of Snell's law we find

$$1 \times \sin 40° = 1.33 \times \sin \theta$$
$$\Rightarrow \theta = 28.9°$$

The wavelength in air is 680 nm and so the frequency in air is

$$
\begin{aligned}
f &= \frac{3.00 \times 10^8}{680 \times 10^{-9}} \\
&= 4.41 \times 10^{14} \, \text{Hz}
\end{aligned}
$$

The frequency cannot change as the wave moves into the second medium (can you explain why?) and since the speed of light in water is $2.26 \times 10^8 \, \text{m s}^{-1}$, it follows that

the wavelength in water is

$$
\begin{aligned}
\lambda &= \frac{2.26 \times 10^8}{4.41 \times 10^{14}} \\
&= 512 \, \text{nm}
\end{aligned}
$$

Looking at the sky from under water

If you lie down and look straight up with one eye, you can, theoretically, receive rays from objects within a hemisphere (with your eye at the centre). If, however, you do the same while swimming underwater, things change because of refraction. A ray moving parallel to the water surface (angle of incidence 90°) will refract and enter the water making an angle of refraction of about 49°. Thus, the eye perceives all rays that enter it to be within a vertical cone of opening angle 98° (see Figure H2.8).

Apparent depth

An object placed at the bottom of a glass of water, at point C in Figure H2.9, appears to an observer looking at it from above to be at a smaller depth, point B. This is a result of refraction.

We have drawn two rays: one goes straight up and makes an angle of incidence of zero; the second makes an angle of incidence of θ and an angle of refraction of ϕ. The refracted rays (actually their extensions) meet at B. This is where the object *appears* to be. Applying Snell's

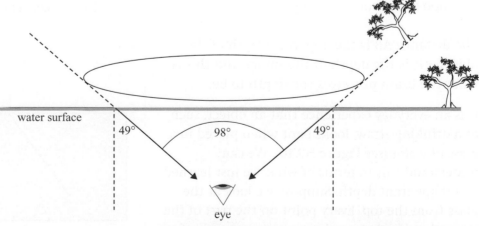

Figure H2.8 When looking at images above water from under water, the perceived field of vision is narrowed to a cone with an opening angle of 98°.

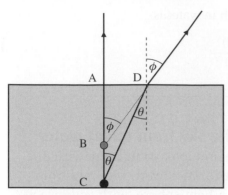

Figure H2.9 Diagram used in calculating the apparent depth of an object in a liquid.

law gives

$$n \sin\theta = \sin\phi$$

If the angles are small, then we may approximate their sines with their tangents and so

$$n \tan\theta \approx \tan\phi$$

But from Figure H2.9

$$\tan\theta = \frac{AD}{AC}$$

$$\tan\phi = \frac{AD}{AB}$$

and so

$$n\frac{AD}{AC} = \frac{AD}{AB}$$

$$\Rightarrow AB = \frac{AC}{n}$$

that is

$$\text{apparent depth} = \frac{\text{real depth}}{n}$$

The distance AB is the apparent depth of the object – it is the depth of the image and this is what the brain perceives the depth to be.

It is an everyday experience that an object, such as a drinking straw, looks bent when placed in a glass of water (see Figure H2.10). We can understand this in terms of what we just learned about apparent depth. Suppose we look at the glass from the top. Every point on the part of the straw that is submerged appears (as a result of refraction) to be at a smaller depth than its real depth. Thus, the straw appears bent.

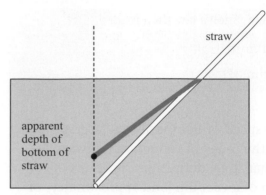

Figure H2.10 A straw in a glass of water appears to be bent.

Total internal reflection

An interesting phenomenon that follows from our discussion of refraction is total internal reflection. This effect occurs when a ray of light tries to enter a medium of smaller index of refraction than that of the medium in which it is already travelling. For example, total internal reflection can occur when light travels from water into air or from glass into air but not from air into water or from air into glass. We will see why shortly. Let us consider a ray of light travelling in glass of index of refraction $n_g = 1.5$. The ray hits a face of the glass surrounded by air and will therefore refract into air (see Figure H2.11).

Let the angle of incidence be $30°$. Then Snell's law says that the angle of refraction will be given by $1.5 \times \sin 30° = 1.0 \times \sin\theta$ and so $\theta = 48.59°$. Let us now increase the angle of

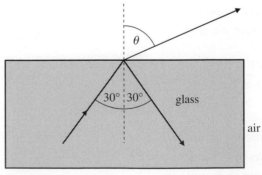

Figure H2.11 A ray entering a medium of lower index of refraction bends away from the normal.

incidence. If it becomes 35°, the angle of refraction works out to 59.36°, and if the angle of incidence becomes 39°, the angle of refraction is 70.73°. The angle of refraction increases as the angle of incidence increases. But there comes a point when for a specific angle of incidence the angle of refraction becomes 90°. For our example this happens when

$$1.5 \times \sin \theta_c = 1.0 \times \sin 90°$$

that is, when $\theta_c = 41.81°$. An angle of refraction of 90° means that the refracted ray travels along the interface of the two media, as in Figure H2.12.

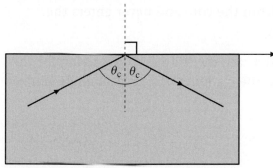

Figure H2.12 When the angle of incidence is the critical angle, the angle of refraction is 90°.

▶ The angle of incidence for which the angle of refraction is 90° is called the critical angle, θ_c.

In general it can be found for a ray trying to get into air from a medium with index of refraction n by

$$1.0 \times \sin 90° = n \times \sin \theta_c$$

that is

$$\sin \theta_c = \frac{1}{n}$$

or for a ray trying to get into some medium with index of refraction n' from a medium with index of refraction n by

$$n' \times \sin 90° = n \times \sin \theta_c$$

that is

$$\sin \theta_c = \frac{n'}{n}$$

(see Figure H2.13).

Figure H2.13 Diagram showing the calculation of the critical angle.

This shows that $n' < n$ for this to be possible. If the angle of incidence exceeds the critical angle, no refraction takes place. In our example, if the angle of incidence is, say, 45°, then the angle of refraction would be calculated from $1.5 \times \sin 45° = 1.0 \times \sin \theta$, which gives $\sin \theta = 1.061$, which is impossible. So what happens to the ray is that it is totally reflected from the glass–air interface and no light enters the air (see Figure H2.14).

This kind of reflection is called total internal reflection. It has applications in optical

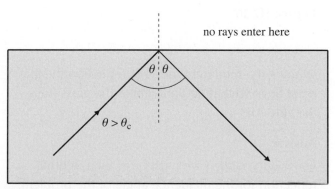

Figure H2.14 When the angle of incidence exceeds the critical angle, total internal reflection takes place. There is no refracted ray.

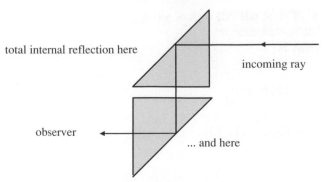

total internal reflection here

incoming ray

observer

... and here

Figure H2.15 An early application of total internal reflection has been in the periscope.

instruments, such as the periscope (see Figure H2.15).

Optical fibres, which are discussed in the next subsection, also rely on the phenomenon of total internal reflection.

Example question

Q4

A prism whose angles are 45°, 45° and 90° is illuminated by light entering it as shown in Figure H2.16.

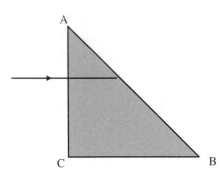

A

C   B

Figure H2.16.

What is the minimum index of refraction the glass must have so that no light leaves the glass from the side AB?

Answer

For this to happen we must have total internal reflection for the incidence angle of the problem, which happens to be 45°. Thus

$$n \times \sin 45° = 1.0 \times \sin 90°$$

so

$$n = 1.41$$

That is to say, the index of refraction must be bigger than 1.41.

Optical fibres

One important application of total internal reflection is a device known as an optical fibre. The optical fibre consists of a thin glass core whose diameter is about 0.01 mm or less and is surrounded by a material with a lower index of refraction (the cladding). Such a thin fibre can easily be bent and a ray of light can be sent down the length of the fibre core (see Figure H2.17). For most of the angles of incidence total internal reflection occurs so that the light ray stays within the core and never enters the cladding.

If n_1 and n_2 are the indices of refraction for the core and the cladding, the critical angle can be

cladding

core

cladding

(a)

at least 100 optic fibres

(b)

polyurethane sheath

Figure H2.17 (a) The path of a light beam in a thin optical fibre. (b) Cross-section through a fibre optical cable.

calculated as usual from

$$n_1 \sin\theta_c = n_2 \sin 90°$$

$$\Rightarrow \cos\theta_c = \sqrt{1 - \frac{n_2^2}{n_1^2}}$$

$$= \frac{\sqrt{n_1^2 - n_2^2}}{n_1}$$

The maximum angle of incidence a ray can make upon entering the fibre is Ω, which can be found as follows. Applying Snell's law at the entry point, we find (see Figure H2.18)

$$\sin\Omega = n_1 \sin\omega$$

but $\omega = 90° - \theta_c$, so

$$\sin\Omega = n_1 \sin(90° - \theta_c)$$
$$= n_1 \cos\theta_c$$
$$= \sqrt{n_1^2 - n_2^2}$$

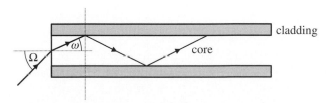

Figure H2.18 The maximum angle of incidence for total internal reflection in the fibre.

Optical fibres have many uses. A thin fibre can be inserted into the throat of a patient and from there into the stomach so that a doctor can examine it. Such a device is called an endoscope. A bundle of fibres can also transmit light signals upon which information has been encoded, for example telephone conversations or TV signals. Visible light has much higher frequency than radio waves and because the amount of information carried by a wave is proportional to the frequency, much more information can be transmitted by an optical fibre using visible light than by radio waves.

Questions

1 Photographic film is placed at the position of a real image. Will the film record the image? What if the image is virtual?

2 Two plane mirrors are at right angles to each other. If an object is placed in front of the mirrors, find out how many images are formed.

3 A plane mirror appears to reverse left and right. Show this with a diagram. Why does it not appear to reverse top and bottom?

4 An object is placed in front of two plane mirrors at right angles to each other, as shown in Figure H2.19. What images are formed in the mirrors?

Figure H2.19 For question 4.

5 The letter F is placed in front of two plane mirrors at right angles to each other, as shown in Figure H2.20. Draw the images that are formed.

Figure H2.20 For question 5.

6 An object is placed half-way between two parallel plane mirrors, as shown in Figure H2.21.
(a) What images are formed in the mirrors?
(b) What if the object is placed closer to one of the mirrors?
(c) Why are the distant images dimmer?

Figure H2.21 For question 6.

7 How many images will be formed when an object is placed in front of two plane mirrors that make an angle θ between them, as shown in Figure H2.22?

Figure H2.22 For question 7.

8 A coin is placed at the bottom of a swimming pool that is 1.50 m deep. A person looks down at the coin from directly above. What is the apparent depth of the coin? (The index of refraction of the water is 1.33.)

9 Light is emitted in a glass cube that is surrounded by air.
(a) If the index of refraction of the glass is 1.895, find the critical angle for which total internal reflection takes place.

(b) What would the critical angle be if the cube was surrounded by water with an index of refraction of 1.33?

10 The critical angle for a plastic–air interface is 47°. What would the critical angle be if the ray attempts to leave the plastic and enter a glass plate with an index of refraction of 1.29?

11 An optical fibre has a core index of refraction of 1.62 and a cladding index of refraction of 1.52. Determine the largest angle at which a ray of light can enter the fibre from air.

12 The angles of a glass prism are 45°, 45° and 90°.
(a) What must the minimum index of refraction be such that a ray of light entering the prism normally from one of the perpendicular sides gets totally internally reflected from the hypotenuse?
(b) What is the answer to the same question if the prism is immersed in water with an index of refraction of 1.33?

Lenses and optical instruments

In this chapter we discuss the formation of images by lenses and two optical instruments – the compound microscope and the refracting telescope. The chapter closes with brief remarks about lens aberrations.

Objectives

By the end of this chapter you should be able to:
- find *images* of objects placed in front of lenses using the graphical method;
- find *images* of objects placed in front of lenses using the algebraic method, $\frac{1}{u} + \frac{1}{v} = \frac{1}{f}$, $m = -\frac{v}{u}$, and appreciate the *conventions* being used;
- understand how a *simple magnifying glass* works and find its magnification;
- understand how a *compound microscope* works and find its magnification;
- understand how a *refracting telescope* works and find its magnification;
- describe the two main *lens defects* and how those defects are corrected.

Lenses

Just as the behaviour of mirrors is determined by the law of reflection, the behaviour of lenses is determined by the law of refraction. A ray of light that enters a lens will, in general, be deviated from its original path.

The amount of deviation depends on the index of refraction of the glass making up the lens, the radii of the two spherical surfaces that the lens is polished to and the angle of incidence of the ray.

We will make the approximation that the lens is always very *thin*, which allows for simplifications. The two sides of the lens are not necessarily cut from the same curvature glass surface and may be convex, concave or planar. Various types of lens are illustrated in Figure H3.1.

▶ The straight line that goes through the centre of the lens at right angles to the lens surface is known as the *principal axis* of the lens.

Converging lenses

Lenses that are thicker at the centre than at the edges are *converging* lenses, which means that a ray of light changes its direction towards the axis of the lens (see Figure H3.2a). Rays of a parallel beam of light converge towards each other after going through the lens.

A beam of rays parallel to the principal axis will, upon refraction through the lens, pass through the same point on the principal axis on the other side of the lens (see Figure H3.3a).

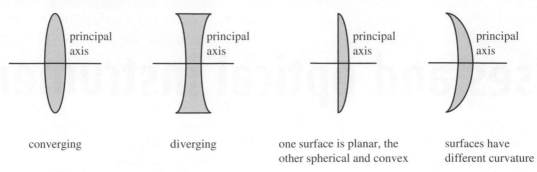

converging   diverging   one surface is planar, the   surfaces have
                                                other spherical and convex   different curvature

Figure H3.1 Various types of lens.

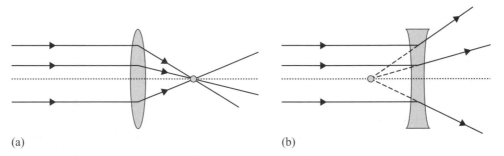

(a)   (b)

Figure H3.2 (a) A converging lens. (b) A diverging lens. A beam of rays parallel
to the principal axis converges toward the principal axis in the case of a
converging lens but diverges from it in the case of a diverging lens.

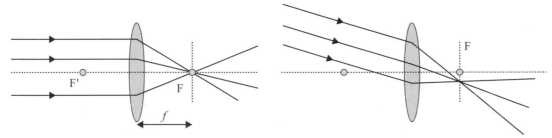

Figure H3.3 (a) Rays that are parallel to one another and are also parallel to the
principal axis pass through the focal point of the lens, a point on the principal
axis, after refraction. (b) If the rays are not parallel to the principal axis, the rays
will go through a common point that is in the same plane as the focal point.

▶ Rays that are parallel to the principal axis
will, after refraction in the lens, pass
through a point on the principal axis
called the *focal point*. The distance of the
focal point from the centre of the lens is
called the *focal length* and is denoted by *f*.

If the parallel beam of rays is not parallel
to the axis then the rays will again go
through a single point. This point and the
focal point of the lens are in the same
vertical plane.

(The point on the other side of the lens at a
distance *f* from the lens is also a focal point. A
ray parallel to the principal axis and entering
the lens from right to left will pass through F'.)

We now know how one set of rays will refract
through the lens. We may call a ray parallel to
the principal axis 'standard ray 1'.

Another set of rays whose refraction through
the lens is easy to describe is the set that first
pass through the left focal point of the lens.
They then emerge parallel to the principal axis
on the other side of the lens, as shown in Figure
H3.4. We may call such a ray 'standard ray 2'.

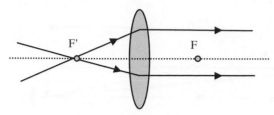

Figure H3.4 A ray passing through the focal point emerges parallel to the axis.

A third light ray whose behaviour we know something about is one that is directed at the centre of the lens. This ray will go through undeflected, as shown in Figure H3.5a. We may call such a ray 'standard ray 3'.

The reason for this behaviour is that near the mid-point of the lens the two lens surfaces are almost parallel. A ray of light going through glass with two parallel surfaces is shown in Figure H3.5b. The ray simply gets shifted parallel to itself. The amount of the parallel shift is proportional to the width of the glass block, which is the width of the lens. Since we

are making the approximation of a very thin lens, this displacement is negligible, which proves our result.

With the help of these three 'standard rays' we can find the image of any object placed in front of a converging lens. These rays are shown together in Figure H3.6.

We will get different kinds of images depending on the distance of the object from the lens. The distances of the object and the image are measured from the centre of the lens.

▶ An image can be real or virtual. A real image is one where actual rays of light pass through it. A real image can be projected and seen on a screen. A virtual image is one where no rays of light pass through, only their mathematical extensions. A virtual image cannot be projected onto a screen.

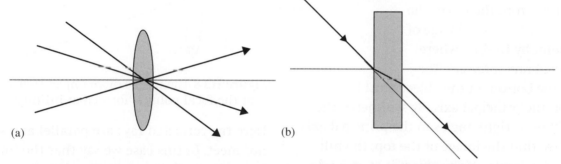

Figure H3.5 (a) A ray going through the centre of the lens is undeflected. (b) A ray entering a glass plate is shifted parallel to itself by an amount proportional to the thickness of the plate.

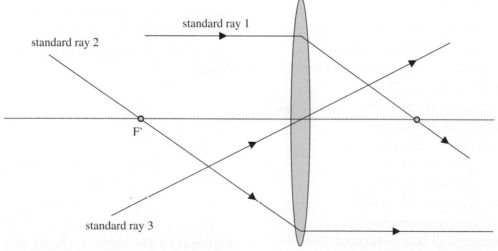

Figure H3.6 The refraction of the three standard rays in a converging lens.

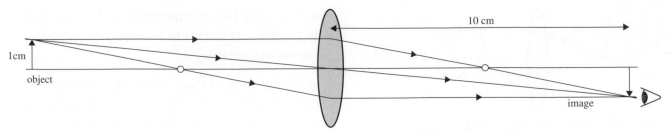

Figure H3.7 The image of an object that is further from the lens than the focal length.

In describing the image we would like to know:

- its distance from the lens;
- if it is real or virtual;
- if it is inverted or upright;
- if it is larger or smaller than the object and by how much.

We consider first an object of height 1 cm that is a distance of 10 cm from a lens of focal length 5 cm. Using all three standard rays, starting from the top of the object we construct the image of the top point by finding where the refracted rays intersect. The image of the bottom of the object must be formed on the principal axis. By symmetry, the image will be at right angles to the principal axis and so if we find the image of the top, the full image can be drawn. (If the object is at an angle to the principal axis then rays from the bottom must also be considered.) The full image is then as shown in Figure H3.7.

We see that the image is inverted. It is also real since rays of light actually pass through it. Measuring the distance from the lens to the image we find about 10 cm. The height of the image is about 1 cm. The image is the same size as the object. To see this image the eye must be put in a position where refracted rays enter the eye. Any position to the right of the lens will do. Note that if you cover any part of the lens, the image will still be formed. But because less light passes through the lens, the image will not be as bright. No other change in the image will be seen.

Consider next what happens when the object is placed at a distance from the lens equal to the focal length. Here we make use of standard rays 1 and 3 leaving the top of the object, as shown in Figure H3.8.

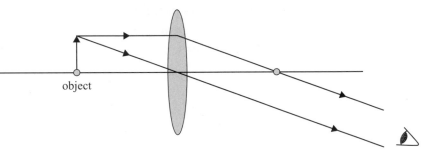

Figure H3.8 The image of an object that is placed at the focal point is formed at infinity.

Here the refracted rays are parallel and so do not meet. In this case we say that the image is formed at infinity.

For the final case, consider an object placed closer to the lens than the focal length, a distance of 3.5 cm from the lens. (The focal length is 5 cm). We again make use of standard rays 1 and 3 leaving the top of the object (see Figure H3.9).

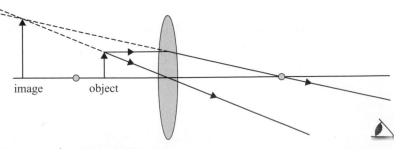

Figure H3.9 The object is placed closer to the lens than the focal length.

The refracted rays do not intersect. When extended backwards they do intersect to form a virtual image. The eye receiving the refracted rays is tricked into believing that they originated from the position where the extensions intersect. This is where the image is. The image is upright and larger than the object. Measuring the distance to the image we find about 11.7 cm. The height of the image is measured to be about 3.3 cm.

The methods described above are graphical methods for finding the image. These are very useful because they allow us 'to see the image being formed'. There is, however, also an algebraic method which is faster.

The algebraic method uses an equation that relates the object and image distances to the focal length of the lens. We derive this equation as follows. The object is placed in front of the lens as shown in Figure H3.10.

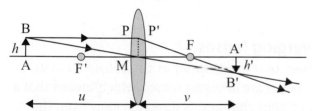

Figure H3.10 The image of an object placed in front of a converging lens.

Let u be the distance of the object from the lens and v that of the image. Triangles ABM and A′B′M are similar (angles are clearly equal) and so

$$\frac{h}{u} = \frac{h'}{v}$$

$$\Rightarrow \frac{h'}{h} = \frac{v}{u}$$

The lens is thin and so P and P′ may be considered to be the same point. Then, triangles MPF and A′B′F are also similar, so

$$\frac{h}{f} = \frac{h'}{v - f}$$

$$\Rightarrow \frac{h'}{h} = \frac{v - f}{f}$$

(note that MP = h). Combining the two equations gives

$$\frac{v}{u} = \frac{v - f}{f}$$

$$\Rightarrow vf = uv - uf$$

$$\Rightarrow vf + uf = uv \quad \text{(divide by } uvf)$$

$$\Rightarrow \frac{1}{u} + \frac{1}{v} = \frac{1}{f}$$

▶ The equation

$$\frac{1}{f} = \frac{1}{u} + \frac{1}{v}$$

is known as the thin lens equation and can be used to obtain image distances.

To examine whether the image is larger or smaller than the object we define the linear magnification, m, of the lens as the ratio of the image height to the object height:

$$m = \frac{\text{image height}}{\text{object height}}$$

Numerically, the linear magnification is $m = \frac{v}{u}$. It is much more convenient, though, to introduce a minus sign so that we define linear magnification as

$$m = \frac{\text{image height}}{\text{object height}}$$

$$= \frac{h'}{h}$$

$$= -\frac{v}{u}$$

The usefulness of the minus sign will be appreciated as soon as we look at an example.

The thin lens equation and the magnification formula allow a complete determination of the image without a ray diagram. But to do that a number of conventions must be followed.

The conventions used here are:

▶ • f is positive for a converging lens;
  • u is positive;
  • v is positive for real images (i.e. those formed on the other side of the lens from the object);

- v is negative for virtual images (i.e. those formed on the same side of the lens as the object);
- $m > 0$ means the image is upright;
- $m < 0$ means the image is inverted;
- $|m| > 1$ means the image is larger than the object;
- $|m| < 1$ means the image is smaller than the object.

Example questions

Q1

A converging lens has a focal length of 15 cm. An object is placed 60 cm from the lens. Determine the image.

Answer

The object distance is $u = 60$ cm and the focal length is $f = 15$ cm. Thus,

$$\frac{1}{v} = \frac{1}{f} - \frac{1}{u}$$
$$= \frac{1}{15} - \frac{1}{60}$$
$$= \frac{1}{20}$$
$$\Rightarrow v = 20 \text{ cm}$$

The image is real (positive v) and is formed on the other side of the lens. The magnification is

$$m = -\frac{20}{60}$$
$$= -\frac{1}{3}$$

The negative sign in the answer for magnification tells us that the image is inverted. This is why we defined magnification in the way we did. The magnitude of the magnification is less than one. The image is 3 times shorter than the object. (Construct a ray diagram for this example.)

Q2

An object is placed 15 cm in front of a converging lens of focal length 20 cm. Determine the image.

Answer

Applying the lens equation again we have

$$\frac{1}{v} = \frac{1}{f} - \frac{1}{u}$$
$$= \frac{1}{20} - \frac{1}{15}$$
$$= -\frac{1}{60}$$
$$\Rightarrow v = -60 \text{ cm}$$

The image is virtual (negative v) and is formed on the same side of the lens as the object. The magnification is

$$m = -\left(\frac{-60}{20}\right)$$
$$= +3$$

Thus, the image is 3 times taller than the object and is upright (positive m). The lens here is acting as a magnifying glass. (Construct a ray diagram for this example.)

▶ A converging lens can produce a real or a virtual image depending on the distance of the object relative to the focal length.

Diverging lenses

Lenses that are thinner at the centre than at the edges are *diverging* lenses, which means that a ray of light changes its direction *away* from the axis of the lens (see Figure H3.2b). Rays of a parallel beam of light diverge from each other after going through the lens.

With small but important changes, much of the discussion for converging lenses can be repeated for diverging lenses. We therefore need to know the behaviour of three standard rays in order to construct an image graphically.

First we need a definition of the focal point of a diverging lens. In a diverging lens, rays coming in parallel to the principal axis will, upon refraction, move away from the axis in such a way that their *extensions* go through a point on the principal axis called the focal point of the lens. The distance of the focal point from the centre of the lens is the focal length of the diverging lens (see Figure H3.11a). This is our 'standard ray 1' for diverging lenses.

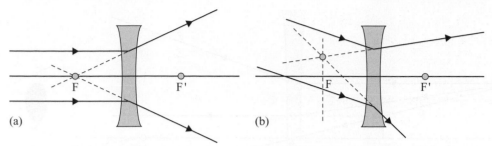

(a)

(b)

Figure H3.11 (a) Rays parallel to the principal axis diverge from the lens in such a way that the extensions of the rays pass through the focal point of the lens on the same side as the incoming rays. (b) Other parallel rays at an angle to the principal axis will appear to come from a point off the principal axis at a distance from the centre of the lens equal to the focal length.

If the beam is not parallel to the principal axis, the extensions of the refracted rays will all go through the same point a distance from the lens equal to the focal length (see Figure H3.11b).

The second standard ray is one that is directed at the focal point on the other side of the lens. This ray will refract parallel to the principal axis, as shown in Figure H3.12. This is 'standard ray 2'.

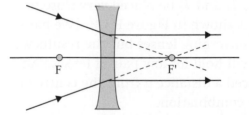

Figure H3.12 A ray directed towards the focal point on the other side of the lens emerges parallel to the principal axis.

Finally, a ray that passes through the centre of the lens is undeflected, as shown in Figure H3.13. This is 'standard ray 3'.

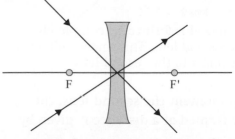

Figure H3.13 A ray directed at the centre of the lens passes through undeflected.

The behaviour of all three standard rays is shown in Figure H3.14.

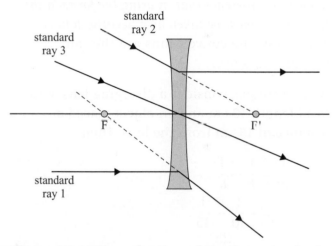

Figure H3.14 The refraction of the three standard rays in a diverging lens.

With this knowledge we can obtain the images of objects placed in front of diverging lenses. Consider an object placed a distance of 8 cm in front of a diverging lens of focal length 6 cm. The height of the object is 2 cm. Using all three standard rays (even though only two are required) we see that we form an image at a distance of about 3.4 cm from the lens. The image is virtual (it is formed by extensions of rays). It is upright and has a height of about 0.86 cm. (See Figure H3.15.)

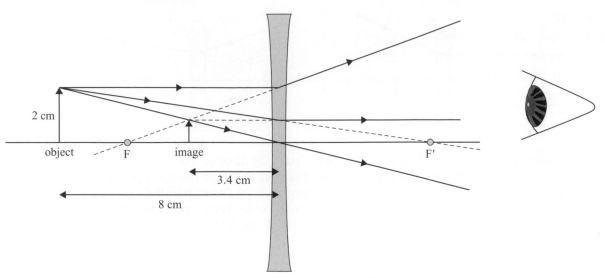

Figure H3.15 Formation of an image by a diverging lens. All three standard rays have been used here.

It can be shown that the same formula relating object and image distances and focal length that we used for converging lenses applies to diverging lenses as well, *with the very important difference that in using the formula the focal length must be taken as a negative number.* The rest of the conventions are the same as for converging lenses.

As an example, consider a diverging lens with focal length 10 cm and an object placed a distance of 15 cm from the lens. Then

$$\frac{1}{v} = \frac{1}{f} - \frac{1}{u}$$
$$= -\frac{1}{10} - \frac{1}{15}$$
$$= -\frac{25}{15 \times 10}$$
$$= -\frac{1}{6}$$
$$\Rightarrow v = -6 \text{ cm}$$

The negative sign for v implies that the object is virtual and is formed on the same side of the lens as the object. The magnification is

$$m = -\left(\frac{-6}{10}\right)$$
$$= +0.6$$

implying an image 0.6 of the height of the object and upright.

> ▶ When the object is real (i.e. $u > 0$), a diverging lens always produces a virtual image ($v < 0$). The magnification is then always positive implying an upright image.

Virtual objects

Let us finally consider an example involving non-real or virtual objects. Let two lenses of focal lengths f_1 and f_2 be placed very close to each other, as shown in Figure H3.16. (We have drawn two converging lenses but the results we will obtain will hold for any pair of lenses.) An object is placed a distance u from the centre of the two-lens combination.

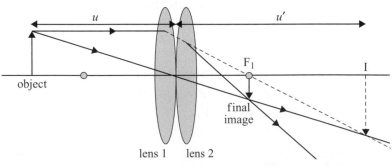

Figure H3.16 Image I is formed by completely ignoring the second lens. This image will act as the (virtual) object to the second lens.

Ignoring for a moment the second lens, the image will be formed at a distance v' given by

$$\frac{1}{v'} = \frac{1}{f_1} - \frac{1}{u}$$

This image serves as the object to the second lens. It is a virtual object, however. This is because the rays are actually entering the second lens from left to right but the 'object' is situated to the right of the second lens (i.e. on the 'wrong' side). As it is virtual, the distance of this object must be taken as negative, which means that u' of this virtual object is the negative of what we found for v'. Thus, the distance v of the final image is found from

$$\frac{1}{v} = \frac{1}{f_2} - \left[-\left(\frac{1}{f_1} - \frac{1}{u} \right) \right]$$

$$\Rightarrow \frac{1}{v} + \frac{1}{u} = \frac{1}{f_2} + \frac{1}{f_1}$$

Thus, the combination of the two lenses acts as a single lens of focal length f given by

$$\frac{1}{f} = \frac{1}{f_2} + \frac{1}{f_1}$$

Example questions

Q3

An object of length 9.5 cm lies on a table. A converging lens of focal length 75 cm is placed at a distance of 40 cm from the object. Determine the image formed by this lens. A second converging lens with the same focal length is now placed above the first lens at a distance of 6.5 cm from the first lens. Determine the image formed by this combination of lenses.

Answer

With just the first lens the image is formed at a distance found from

$$\frac{1}{v} + \frac{1}{u} = \frac{1}{f}$$

$$\Rightarrow \frac{1}{v} + \frac{1}{40} = \frac{1}{75}$$

$$\Rightarrow v = -85.7 \text{ cm}$$

The image is virtual and upright. This image acts as the object to the second lens. The distance of the object from the second lens is

$$85.7 + 6.5 = 92.2 \text{ cm}$$

The object is a real object for the second lens and so $u = +92.2$ cm. The new image is thus formed

at a distance found from

$$\frac{1}{92.2} + \frac{1}{v} = \frac{1}{75}$$

$$\Rightarrow v = 402 \text{ cm}$$

The final image is thus real. The first lens produces a magnification of

$$m_1 = \frac{h'}{h}$$

$$= -\left(\frac{-85.7}{40} \right)$$

$$\Rightarrow h' = +20.4 \text{ cm}$$

The second lens will magnify this image to a new size given by

$$m_2 = \frac{h''}{h'}$$

$$= -\left(\frac{402}{92.2} \right)$$

$$\Rightarrow h'' = -88.7 \text{ cm}$$

The overall magnification is given by

$$m = \frac{h''}{h}$$

$$= \frac{-88.7}{9.5}$$

$$= -9.34$$

The image is inverted. It can be checked that the overall magnification is the product of the magnifications of each lens.

Q4

Figure H3.17 shows the formation of an image in a converging lens of focal length 4.0 cm, ignoring the presence of the diverging lens (of focal length 6.0 cm). Determine the position of the image when the diverging lens is taken into account and complete the ray diagram.

Answer

Ignoring the diverging lens, the image is at a distance from the converging lens found from

$$\frac{1}{8} + \frac{1}{v} = \frac{1}{4}$$

$$\Rightarrow v = 8.0 \text{ cm}$$

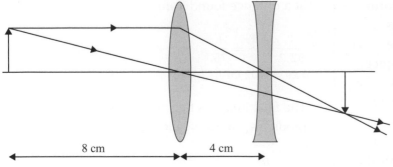

Figure H3.17.

Its distance from the diverging lens is therefore 4.0 cm. This image acts as the virtual object for the diverging lens. Hence $u = -4.0$ cm. The final image is therefore at a distance found from

$$\frac{1}{-4} + \frac{1}{v} = \frac{1}{-6}$$
$$\Rightarrow v = 12.0 \text{ cm}$$

The image is thus real. The magnification of the lens system is given by

$$-\frac{8}{8} \times -\frac{12}{-4} = -3$$

which implies that the final image is inverted and three times as large as the original object. Figure H3.18 is a ray diagram of the problem.

Optical instruments

Much of our knowledge about the natural world in which we live is owed to optical instruments based on mirrors and lenses. These have enabled the observation of very distant objects through telescopes and very small objects through microscopes. We have already seen how a single converging lens can produce an enlarged upright image of an object placed closer to the lens than the focal length, thus acting as a magnifying glass. The apparent size of an object depends on the size of the image that is formed on the retina. In turn, this size depends on the angle subtended by the object at the eye. This is why we bring a small object closer to the eye in order to view it – the angle subtended at the eye by the object increases.

▶ The closest point on which the human eye can focus without straining is known as the *near point* of the eye. This distance is taken to be about 25 cm for a normal eye, but it depends greatly on age. The largest distance the eye can focus on without straining is called the *far point*. The far point is taken to be infinity for a normal eye. In practice, infinity means anything larger than a few metres.

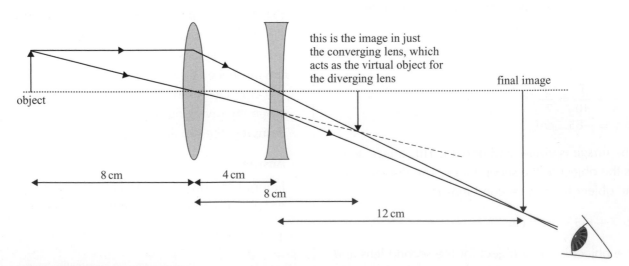

Figure H3.18 A ray diagram.

Thus, let an observer view a small object at a distance of 25 cm from the eye and let θ stand for the angle that the object subtends at the eye, as shown in Figure H3.19. Assuming the angle is small, we have approximately that $\theta = \frac{h}{25 \text{ cm}}$ (the approximation involved is $\theta \approx \tan\theta$).

Figure H3.19 The apparent size of an object depends on the angle subtended at the eye.

If the object is now viewed through a lens and is placed closer to the lens than the focal length, a virtual, upright, enlarged image will be formed (see Figure H3.20). Let θ' be the angle that the image subtends at the eye through the lens. We define the angular magnification by

$$M = \frac{\theta'}{\theta}$$

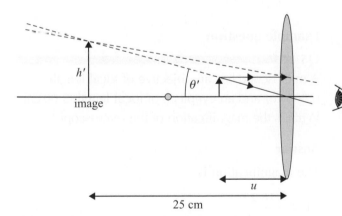

Figure H3.20 A converging lens acting as a magnifier.

Let the distance of the object to the lens be u. If the image is to be formed at a distance of 25 cm, then (remember the image is virtual, hence its distance is negative)

$$\frac{1}{f} = \frac{1}{u} + \frac{1}{-25}$$

$$\Rightarrow u = \frac{25 f}{25 + f}$$

From simple geometry we obtain

$$\theta' = \frac{h'}{25 \text{ cm}}$$

$$= \frac{h}{u}$$

$$= \frac{h(25 + f)}{25 f}$$

and, recalling $\theta = \frac{h}{25 \text{ cm}}$, the angular magnification is

$$M = \frac{\theta'}{\theta}$$

$$= \frac{h(25 + f)/25 f}{h/25}$$

$$= \frac{25 + f}{f}$$

$$= 1 + \frac{25}{f}$$

This is the magnification of the magnifying glass when the image is formed 25 cm from the lens. The lens is assumed to be very close to the eye.

If the object is placed at the focal length of the lens, the image is formed at infinity and the eye viewing this image is said to be relaxed. In this case, $u = f$, and so the angular magnification is

$$M = \frac{h/f}{h/25}$$

$$= \frac{25}{f}$$

(Here the lens need not be very close to the eye.)

In both cases, the magnification can be increased by decreasing the focal length of the lens. Lens defects known as aberrations (see later) limit the angular magnification to about 4.

The microscope

To increase the magnification more requires a microscope. A *compound microscope* (Figure H3.21) consists of two converging lenses. The object is placed at a distance from the first lens (the *objective*) slightly larger than the focal length f_o (the objective usually has a focal length that is less than 1 cm). A real inverted image is formed at a distance from the second lens (the *eyepiece*) that is equal to the focal length of the eyepiece (which is a few centimetres). This image acts as an object for the eyepiece and this lens now forms an enlarged, virtual, final image at infinity. The eyepiece thus acts as a simple magnifying glass on the image formed by the objective. The first image is formed a distance L to the right of the objective's focal point. Manufacturers arrange for this distance (known as the tube length) to be 16 cm. Let u be the distance of the object from the objective. The image formed by the objective is a distance of $f_o + 16$ from the objective and so (using the lens equation) u and f_o are related by

$$\frac{1}{u} + \frac{1}{f_o + 16} = \frac{1}{f_o}$$

$$\Rightarrow u = \frac{f_o(f_o + 16)}{16}$$

Thus, the objective produces a lateral magnification of

$$m = -\frac{16 + f_o}{u}$$

$$= -\frac{16 + f_o}{\left[\frac{f_o(16 + f_o)}{16}\right]}$$

$$= -\frac{16}{f_o}$$

The magnification of the microscope is the product of the magnification produced by the objective times the magnification produced by the eyepiece.

The eyepiece has an angular magnification of $M = \frac{25}{f_e}$ (f_e is the focal length of the eyepiece – the final image is at infinity).

▶ The final magnification of the microscope is therefore

$$M = -\frac{16}{f_o}\frac{25}{f_e}$$

Note: If the image by the objective lens is formed at a distance past the objective focal point other than 16 cm, the magnification is

$$M = -\frac{d}{f_o}\frac{25}{f_e}$$

where d is the distance of the image in the objective past the objective focal point. In this formula the focal lengths must be expressed in centimetres.

A compound microscope is illustrated in Figure H3.21.

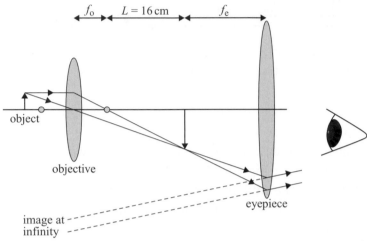

Figure H3.21 A compound microscope consists of two converging lenses.

Example question

Q5 ▮▮▮▮▮▮▮▮▮▮▮

A microscope has an objective of focal length 0.500 cm and an eyepiece of focal length 3.00 cm. What is the magnification of the microscope?

Answer

The magnification is

$$M = -\frac{16}{f_o}\frac{25}{f_e}$$

$$= -\frac{16}{0.500} \times \frac{25}{3.00}$$

$$= -267$$

The refracting telescope

The function of a telescope is to allow the observation of large objects that are very distant. A star is enormous but looks small because it is far away. The telescope is then used to increase the angle at which the star is observed relative to the angle at which the star is observed by the unaided eye. The telescope is

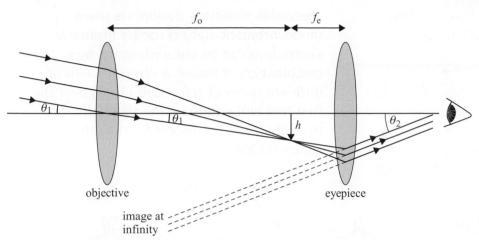

Figure H3.22 A refracting astronomical telescope. The final image is inverted.

thus not used to provide a *lateral* magnification of the star, since the image in that case would be many orders of magnitude larger than the earth. A refracting astronomical telescope (see Figure H3.22) consists of two converging lenses. Since the object observed is very far away, it follows that the image produced by the first lens (the objective) is at the focal plane of the objective lens. It is this image that is then magnified by the eyepiece, just as by a magnifying glass. The second lens (the eyepiece) forms a virtual, inverted image of the object. The final image is produced at infinity and so the distance between the two lenses is the sum of their focal lengths.

The angular magnification of the telescope is defined as the ratio of the angle the object subtends through the telescope divided by the angle subtended by the object at the unaided eye. Thus

$$M = \frac{\theta_2}{\theta_1}$$
$$= \frac{h/f_e}{h/f_o}$$
$$= \frac{f_o}{f_e}$$

The position of the eyepiece can be adjusted to provide clear images of objects other than very distant ones. The objective lens should be as large as possible in order to allow as much light as possible into the telescope. Because it is difficult to make very large lenses, telescopes have been designed to use mirrors rather than lenses.

Example question

Q6

A refracting telescope has a magnification of 70.0 and the two lenses are 60.0 cm apart when adjusted for a relaxed eye. What are the focal lengths of the lenses?

Answer

From

$$M = \frac{f_o}{f_e}$$
$$= 70$$
$$\Rightarrow f_o = 70\, f_e$$

and

$$f_o + f_e = 60 \text{ cm}$$
$$\Rightarrow 71\, f_e = 60 \text{ cm}$$
$$\Rightarrow f_e = 0.845 \text{ cm}$$
$$f_o = 59.2 \text{ cm}$$

Lens aberrations

Lenses do not behave exactly as described above – they suffer from *aberrations*. Two main types of aberration are important for lenses: *spherical* and *chromatic*.

> ▶ *Spherical aberrations* occur because rays that enter the lens far from the principal axis have a different focal length from rays entering near the axis.

In Figure H3.23, rays hitting the lens far from its mid-point refract through a point on the principal axis that is closer to the lens than rays that hit the lens closer to the middle. This means that the image of the point is not going to be a point image but a blurred patch of light. Spherical aberration can be reduced by

Figure H3.23 Spherical aberration. Rays from a distant point source are not brought to focus at a single point. The image is not a point image.

reducing the aperture of the lens (its diameter – this is called stopping down), but that means that less light goes through the lens, which results in a less bright image. A lens with a smaller diameter would also suffer from more pronounced diffraction effects.

The fact that the focal point varies for rays that are further from the principal axis means that the magnification produced by the lens also varies. This leads to a *distortion* of the image, as shown in Figure H3.24.

Figure H3.24 An example of distortion due to spherical aberration. The grid is distorted because the magnification varies as one moves away from the principal axis.

▶ The second aberration, *chromatic aberration*, arises because the lens has different refractive indices for different wavelengths. Thus, there is a separate focal length for each wavelength (colour) of light.

This makes images appear coloured – there are lines around the image in the colours of the rainbow (see Figure H3.25a). Chromatic

aberration obviously disappears when monochromatic light is used. Chromatic aberrations can be reduced, again, by a combination of lenses. A diverging lens of different index of refraction placed near the first lens will eliminate the aberration for two colours and reduce it for the others (see Figure H3.25b).

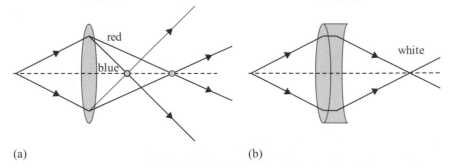

(a)   (b)

Figure H3.25 (a) Light of different colour bends by different amounts and hence different colours are focused at different places. (b) An achromatic doublet consists of a pair of lenses of different indices of refraction.

Questions

1 Define:
 (a) focal point of a converging lens;
 (b) focal length of a converging lens.

2 Define:
 (a) focal point of a diverging lens;
 (b) focal length of a diverging lens.

3 Explain what is meant by:
 (a) a real image formed by a lens;
 (b) a virtual image formed by a lens.

4 Explain why a real image can be projected on a screen but a virtual image cannot.

5 A mirror appears to reverse left and right. Does a lens do the same? Explain your answer.

6 A student wants to buy lenses for a homemade telescope. Should she look for a short or long focal length objective lens?

7 A converging lens has a focal length of 6.0 cm. Determine the distance x in Figure H3.26.

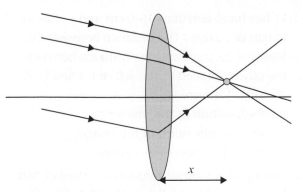

Figure H3.26 For question 7.

8 Figure H3.27 shows the real image of an object in a converging lens. Complete the rays drawn.

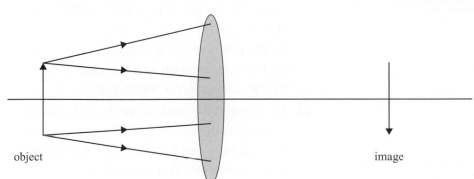

Figure H3.27 For question 8.

9 An object 2 cm tall is placed in front of a converging lens of focal length 10 cm. Using ray diagrams, construct the image when the object is at a distance of:
   (a) 20 cm;
   (b) 10 cm;
   (c) 5 cm.
   Confirm your ray diagrams by using the lens equation.

10 Repeat the previous problem for the case of a diverging lens. Confirm your ray diagrams by using the lens equation.

11 Using the graphical method, determine the image characteristics of an object of height 2.5 cm that is placed a distance of 8.0 cm in front of a converging lens of focal length 6.0 cm. Confirm your ray diagram by using the lens equation.

12 Using the graphical method, determine the image characteristics of an object of height 4.0 cm that is placed a distance of 6.0 cm in front of a converging lens of focal length 8.0 cm. Confirm your ray diagram by using the lens equation.

13 An object 5.0 cm tall is placed 2.0 cm in front of a diverging lens of focal length 4.0 cm. Determine the image characteristics using the graphical method. Confirm your ray diagram by using the lens equation.

14 Consider a converging lens of focal length 5.00 cm. An object of length 2.236 cm is placed in front of the lens as shown in Figure H3.28 (not to scale) so that the middle of the object is on the principal axis. By drawing appropriate rays, determine the image in the lens. Is the angle the image makes with the principal axis the same as that of the object?

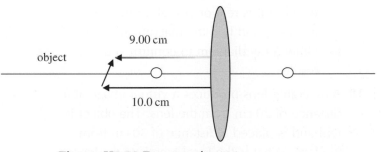

Figure H3.28 For question 14.

15 A student finds the position of the image created by a converging lens for various positions of the object. She constructs a table of object and image distances (Table H3.1).
   (a) Explain how these data can be used to determine the focal length of the lens.
   (b) Determine the focal length quoting the uncertainty in its value.

u/cm $\pm$ 0.1 cm	12.0	16.0	20.0	24.0	28.0
v/cm $\pm$ 0.1 cm	60.0	27.2	19.9	17.5	16.8

Table H3.1 For question 15.

16 An object is placed in front of a converging lens which rests on a plane mirror as shown in Figure H3.29. The object is moved until the image is formed exactly at the position of the object. Draw rays from the object to form the image in this case. Explain how the focal length of the lens can be determined from this arrangement.

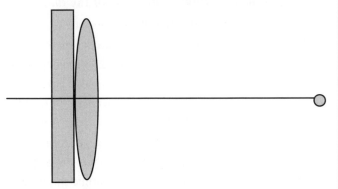

Figure H3.29 For question 16.

17 A converging lens has a focal length of 15 cm. An object is placed 20 cm from the lens.
  (a) Determine the image (i.e. its position and whether it is real or virtual, upright or inverted) and find the magnification.
  (b) Draw a ray diagram to confirm your results.

18 A diverging lens produces a virtual image at a distance of 20 cm from the lens. The object is real and is placed a distance of 30 cm from the lens. What is the focal length of the lens?

19 An object is at a distance of 5.0 m from a screen. A converging lens of focal length 60 cm is placed between the object and the screen so that an image of the object is formed on the screen.
  (a) At what distance(s) from the screen should the lens be placed?
  (b) Which choice results in the larger image?

20 Two converging lenses each of focal length 10.0 cm are 4.00 cm apart. Find the focal length of this lens combination.

21 An object is viewed through a system of two converging lenses L_1 and L_2 (to the right of L_1).

L_1 has focal length of 15.0 cm and L_2 has focal length of 2.0 cm. The distance between the lenses is 25.0 cm and the distance between the object (placed to the left of L_1) and L_1 is 40.0 cm. Determine:
  (a) the position of the image;
  (b) the magnification of the image;
  (c) the orientation of the image.

22 An object is viewed through a system of two lenses L_1 and L_2 (to the right of L_1). L_1 is converging and has a focal length of 35.0 cm; L_2 is diverging and has a focal length of 20.0 cm. The distance between the lenses is 25.0 cm and the distance between the object (placed to the left of L_1) and L_1 is 30.0 cm. Determine:
  (a) the position of the image;
  (b) the magnification of the image;
  (c) the orientation of the image.

23 The pupil of the human eye through which light enters the eye is about 3 mm in radius. Find out how much more light a telescope with a radius of 5.0 m can collect.

24 A converging lens of focal length 10.0 cm is used as a magnifying glass. An object whose size is 1.6 mm is placed at some distance from the lens so that a virtual image is formed a distance of 25 cm in front of the lens.
  (a) What is the distance between the object and the lens?
  (b) Where should the object be placed if the image is to form at infinity?
  (c) When the image is at infinity, find its angular size.

25 Your *IBO Data Booklet* lists the formula for the angular magnification of the simple magnifying glass as $M = \frac{\theta'}{\theta}$.
  (a) By drawing suitable diagrams, show the angles that are entered into this formula.
  (b) A simple magnifying glass produces an image at the near point. Explain what is meant by near point.
  (c) Show that when a simple magnifying glass produces an image at the near point, the magnification is given by $M = 1 + \frac{25}{f}$, where f is the focal length of the lens.

26 The normal human eye can distinguish two objects a distance of 0.12 mm apart when they are placed at the near point. If a simple magnifying glass of focal length 5.00 cm is used to view the images at the near point, how close can the objects be and still be distinguished as distinct?

27 The objective of a microscope has a focal length of 0.80 cm and the eyepiece has a focal length of 4.0 cm. Find the magnification of the microscope. (The final image is at infinity.)

28 The moon is at a distance of about 3.8×10^8 m and its diameter is about 3.5×10^6 m.
   (a) Determine that the angle subtended by the diameter of the moon at the eye of an observer on earth is about $0.53°$.
   (b) A very large telescope objective lens has a focal length of about 20 m. Calculate the diameter of the image of the moon formed by such a lens.

29 A telescope consists of an objective, L_1, which is a converging lens of focal length 80.0 cm and an eyepiece of focal length 20.0 cm. The object is very far from the objective (effectively an infinite distance away) and the image is formed at infinity.
   (a) What is the angular magnification of this telescope?
   (b) The telescope is used to view a building of height 65.0 m a distance of 2.50 km away. What is the angular size of the final image?

30 A refracting telescope has an eyepiece focal length of 3.0 cm and an objective focal length of 67.0 cm.
   (a) What is the magnification of the telescope?
   (b) What is its length? (Assume that the final image is produced at infinity.)

31 A refracting telescope has a distance between the objective and the eyepiece of 60 cm. The focal length of the eyepiece is 3.0 cm. The eyepiece has to be moved 1.5 cm further from the objective to provide a clear image of an object some finite distance away. What is this distance? (Assume that the final image is produced at infinity.)

32 (a) Describe the two main lens aberrations and indicate how these can be corrected.
   (b) In an attempt to understand the distortion caused by spherical aberration, a student considers the following model. She places an object of height 4.00 cm at a distance of 8.00 cm from a converging lens. One end of the object is 1.00 cm below the principal axis and the other 3.00 cm above. She assumes that rays leaving the bottom of the object will have a focal length of 4.00 cm and the rays from the top a focal length of 3.50 cm. (See Figure H3.30.) (i) Under these assumptions, draw rays from the bottom and top of the object to locate the image. (ii) Draw the image again by using the 4.00 cm focal length for all rays and compare.

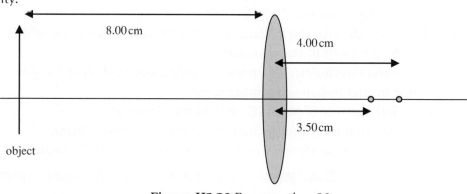

object

Figure H3.30 For question 32.

33 An object is placed in front and to the left of a converging lens, and a real image is formed on the other side of the lens. If the distance of the object from the left focal point is x and the distance of the image from the right focal point is y, prove that $xy = f^2$.

Interference and diffraction

In the previous two chapters, we saw the behaviour of light in the *geometrical approximation*, which is when the important phenomena of diffraction and interference are neglected so that we can treat light propagation along straight lines. This chapter deals in detail with the problem of single-slit diffraction, the effect of slit width in the interference pattern, the limits to resolution imposed by diffraction, and interference due to thin films.

Objectives

By the end of this chapter you should be able to:

- understand *diffraction* and draw the *diffraction patterns* from a rectangular slit, a sharp edge, a thin tube and a circular aperture;
- appreciate that the *first minimum* in single-slit diffraction past a slit of width b is approximately at an angle $\theta = \frac{\lambda}{b}$;
- draw the *intensity patterns* for a *single slit* of finite width and for *two slits* of negligible width;
- show the effect of *slit width* on the intensity pattern of two slits;
- understand what is meant by *resolution* and apply the *Rayleigh criterion*;
- show the effect on the intensity of light of adding *more narrow slits* with the same slit separation;
- solve problems with the *diffraction grating formula*, $d \sin \theta = n\lambda$, which gives the positions of the maxima;
- understand interference by division of amplitude such as in *thin-film interference* and *thin-air-wedge interference*;
- appreciate the role of *phase difference* in interference;
- appreciate that *phase changes* may be introduced upon *reflection*;
- appreciate that interference may be used to *measure small distances*.

Diffraction

Diffraction, as we have seen earlier, is the spreading of a wave as it goes past an obstacle or through an aperture.

Let us consider a plane wave of wavelength λ propagating toward the right, where an aperture of size b is waiting. What will the wavefronts look like after the wave has gone through the aperture? The answer is not so straightforward. As we will see, the value of the wavelength in relation to the aperture size will be crucial in determining what answer we get. In the first case let us assume that the wavelength is very, very small compared with b (see Figure H4.1).

That part of the wave which is blocked by the screen does not propagate through and only that part which is free to go through does so. If the wave in question is light, this picture says

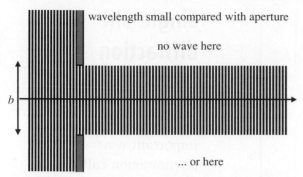

Figure H4.1 When the wavelength is small compared with the size of the opening of the aperture, the amount of diffraction is negligible.

that light goes through the opening, so that if we put a screen beyond the aperture we will see light on an area of the screen identical to the opening and darkness around it. Light travels in straight lines and does not bend as it goes through the aperture. There is no diffraction.

On the other hand, if the wavelength is comparable to or bigger than b, the new wavefronts are curved and the wave manages to go around the edges (see Figure H4.2).

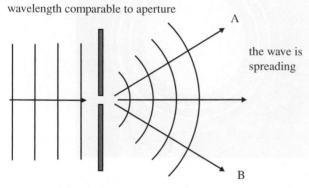

Figure H4.2 When the wavelength is comparable to the opening of the aperture, diffraction takes place.

If we put a screen some distance away from the aperture, we would see light in places where we would not expect any, such as points A and B, for example. This is the phenomenon of diffraction. It takes place whenever a wave whose wavelength is comparable to or bigger than the size of an aperture or an obstacle

attempts to move through or past the aperture or obstacle. (Note that here 'comparable to' means that the wavelength can be a few times smaller than the aperture size.)

Diffraction explains how we can hear, but not see, around corners. For example, a person talking in the next room can be heard through the open door because sound diffracts around the opening of the door; the wavelength of sound for speech is roughly the same as the door size. On the other hand, light does not diffract around the door since its wavelength is much smaller than the door size.

Other examples of diffraction are shown in Figures H4.3–H4.5.

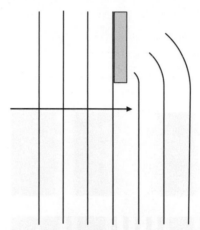

Figure H4.3 Diffraction also takes place when a wave moves past an obstacle.

If the wavelength is much smaller than the obstacle size, no diffraction takes place, as seen in Figure H4.4a. Diffraction does takes place if the wavelength is comparable to the obstacle size, as seen in Figure H4.4b.

Figure H4.5 shows interference patterns due to (a) a single slit, (b) two slits, (c) a sharp edge, (d) a circular aperture and (e) a thin cylindrical tube. Notice the wide central maximum in (a) and the secondary maxima in (b). In (c) the pattern consists of bright and dark strips and in (d) of bright and dark rings. In (e) notice the presence of a bright fringe right behind the tube.

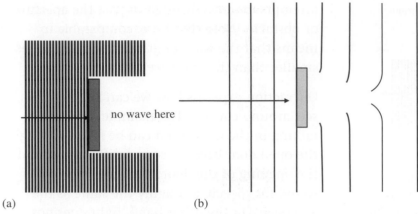

(a) (b)

Single-slit diffraction

When a wave of wavelength λ falls on an aperture whose opening size is b, an important wave phenomenon called diffraction takes place. As we saw earlier:

Figure H4.4 (a) If the wavelength is much smaller than the obstacle, no diffraction takes place and a shadow of the object is formed. (b) If the wavelength is comparable to the obstacle size, diffraction takes place and the wave appears far from the object in the region where the shadow was expected.

▶ Diffraction is appreciable if the wavelength is of the same order of magnitude as the opening or bigger, i.e. when
$$\lambda \geq b$$
Diffraction is negligible, however, if the wavelength is much smaller than the opening size, i.e. when
$$\lambda \ll b$$

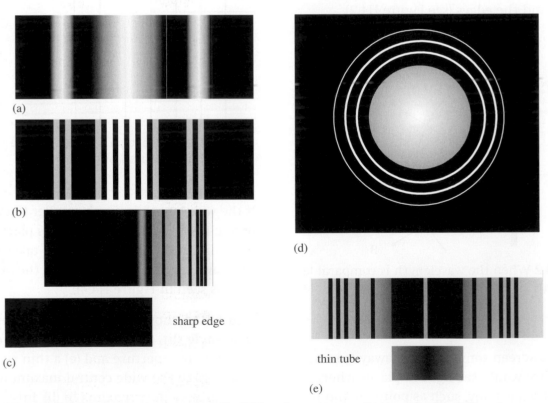

Figure H4.5 (a) Single-rectangular-slit diffraction pattern. (b) Double-slit diffraction pattern. (c) Sharp-edge diffraction pattern. Note that light extends on the inside of the sharp edge. (d) Diffraction pattern from a circular aperture. (e) Diffraction pattern due to a very thin tube with sharp edges. Note that there is light even directly behind the tube.

To investigate this phenomenon we use Huygens' principle and say that every point on the wavefront that hits the slit will act as a source of secondary coherent radiation. Then what we see at a point P on a screen a large distance away will be the result of the interference of the waves arriving at P from each of the points on the wavefront. Figure H4.6 shows 10 such points labelled A_1, A_2, A_3, A_4, A_5 and B_1, B_2, B_3, B_4 and B_5. We choose the Bs in such a way that they are symmetrically placed relative to the As.

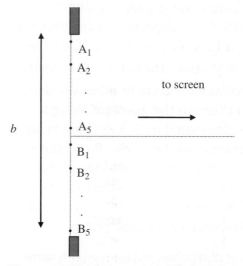

Figure H4.6 In the case of finite slit width each point on the wavefront entering the slit acts as a source of waves according to Huygens' principle and so interference will, in general, result on a screen some distance away.

All these points are on the same wavefront and therefore are coherent. But, in general, the wave from A_1 will travel a different distance in order to get to P than the wave from B_1 (see Figure H4.7). This path difference will, as in our discussion of interference, result in a phase difference between these two waves at P.

If the path difference is half a wavelength, the two waves arrive at P with a 180° phase difference, so the maxima of one wave match the minima of the other. The result is destructive interference, or no wave at P. But remember, we still have to consider the other points, not just A_1 and B_1. What about A_2 and B_2? Triangles $A_1B_1C_1$ and $A_2B_2C_2$ are equal since they are right angled, that is $A_1B_1 = A_2B_2$ and

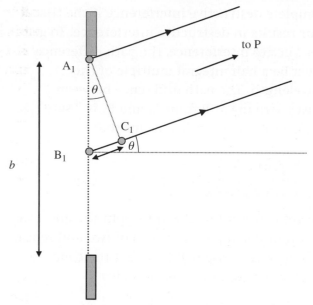

Figure H4.7 Diagram used to calculate the path difference. The path difference equals the distance B_1C_1. Lines A_1P and B_1P are approximately parallel since P is far away. Thus, triangle $A_1B_1C_1$ is approximately right angled and angle $B_1A_1C_1$ equals θ. The path difference is the length B_1C_1.

$\angle B_1A_1C_1 = \angle B_2A_2C_2$ (see Figure H4.8). Thus, we see that whatever phase difference exists at P from A_1 and B_1, the same will be true for A_2 and B_2, and so on.

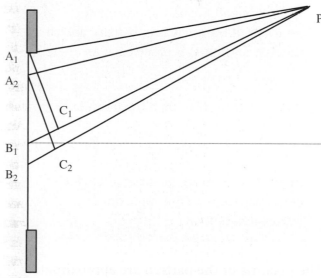

Figure H4.8 Triangles $A_1C_1B_1$ and $A_2C_2B_2$ are equal.

Thus, if we get zero wave at P from the first pair, we will get the same from the second as well. Continuing this argument we see that all the points on the wavefront will result in complete destructive interference if the first pair results in destructive interference. To get destructive interference, the path difference must be a half-integral multiple of the wavelength. The path difference between waves arriving at P from A_1 and B_1 is $\frac{b}{2} \sin \theta$ (see Figure H4.7) and so this means that if

$$\frac{b}{2} \sin \theta = \frac{\lambda}{2}$$
$$\Rightarrow b \sin \theta = \lambda$$

we get a minimum at P. If we split the aperture into four equal pieces instead of two and repeat this argument, we will find that the condition for destructive interference is also

$$\frac{b}{4} \sin \theta = \frac{\lambda}{2}$$
$$\Rightarrow b \sin \theta = 2\lambda$$

▶ In general, in interference from a single slit we get *destructive* interference at points P if

$$b \sin \theta = n\lambda \qquad n = 1, 2, 3, \ldots$$

This equation gives the angle θ at which minima are observed on a screen behind the aperture of size b on which light of wavelength λ falls. Since the angle is typically small, we may approximate $\sin \theta \approx \theta$ (if the angle is in radians) and so the first minimum is observed at an angle

$$\theta \approx \frac{\lambda}{b}$$

If the slit is circular, then the formula above becomes

$$\theta \approx 1.22 \frac{\lambda}{b}$$

In practice, it makes no difference which one is used as both are approximate expressions anyway.

The maxima of the pattern are approximately half-way between minima. This equation is very important in understanding the phenomenon of diffraction, so let us take a closer look.

The first minimum ($n = 1$) occurs at $b \sin \theta = \lambda$. If the wavelength is comparable to or bigger than b, appreciable diffraction will take place, as we said earlier. How do we see this from this formula? If $\lambda > b$, then $\sin \theta > 1$ (i.e. θ does not exist). The wave has spread so much around the aperture, the central maximum is so wide, that the first minimum does not exist. (Remember that diffraction is the spreading of the wave around the aperture, not necessarily the existence of interference maxima and minima.)

If now the wavelength is comparable to b, then again appreciable diffraction takes place and a number of minima and the intervening maxima are visible (comparable means that the wavelength can be a bit less than b). If, on the other hand, $\lambda \ll b$, then from $\theta \approx \frac{\lambda}{b}$ it follows that θ is approximately zero. In other words, the wave goes through the aperture along a straight line represented by $\theta = 0$. There is no wave at any point P on the screen for which θ is not zero. This means that the passage of the wave leaves a shadow of the aperture on the screen. There is no spreading of the wave and hence no diffraction, as we expected.

The intensity of light observed on a screen some distance from the slit is shown in Figure H4.9a for the case $b = 2\lambda$ and in Figure H4.9b for $b = 3\lambda$ (the vertical units are arbitrary).

Note that the narrower slit (a) has a *wider* central maximum.

The effect of slit width

At this point it is worth reminding you that in our previous discussion of the Young's two-slit interference experiment, we never talked about the size of the slit width, only the separation d of the two slits entered in the formula. This is because we assumed that the slit width was much smaller than the wavelength. As we discussed above, in this case ($\lambda \gg b$) there is no interference pattern from points within the individual slit. The wave just spreads past the slit. The interference pattern we got on the screen in that case was the interference of the two waves after each had spread through each

(a)

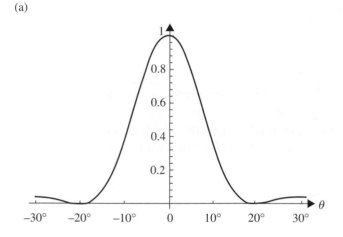

(b)

Figure H4.9 The single-slit intensity pattern for (a) a slit of size $b = 2\lambda$, and (b) a slit of size $b = 3\lambda$.

slit. Thus, in this limiting case, if one of the two slits were covered, the interference pattern would disappear.

On the other hand, the case of two slits whose widths cannot be so neglected will result in a more complicated pattern on the screen. This pattern will be the combined effect of (a) the interference pattern from one slit alone and (b) the interference from waves coming from different slits. Let us consider the intensity pattern for two very narrow slits separated by $d = 16\lambda$ shown in Figure H4.10.

The intensity pattern for a single slit of width $b = 3\lambda$ was shown in Figure H4.9.

Finally, the intensity pattern for two slits separated by $d = 16\lambda$ as before, but whose width is not negligible, $b = 3\lambda$, is shown in Figure H4.11.

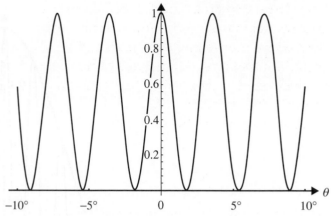

Figure H4.10 The two-slit interference intensity pattern for slits of negligible width separated by $d = 16\lambda$.

We have shown the single-slit pattern again, which is in fact the envelope curve for the two-slit pattern. The position of the maxima is the same as in the case of the narrow slits but the effect of the slit width is to *modulate* the intensity by the single-slit diffraction pattern.

Missing orders

If the slit width is ignored in a Young-type two-slit interference pattern, we observe a number of equally bright maxima, as in Figure H4.10. If the slit width is not ignored, this intensity pattern will be modulated by the diffraction effects of the slits. It sometimes happens that the first diffraction minimum in the one-slit diffraction pattern coincides with one of the maxima in the two-slit interference pattern. If that happens, the maximum will be reduced to a point of zero intensity and we then speak of a missing order. Suppose that the first diffraction minimum occurs at an angle θ. Then $b \sin \theta = 1 \times \lambda$. Suppose that the nth maximum of the two-slit pattern coincides with the first diffraction minimum. Then $d \sin \theta = n\lambda$. Combining the two equations we see that

$$\begin{array}{l} d \sin \theta = n\lambda \\ b \sin \theta = \lambda \end{array} \Rightarrow d = nb$$

that is, the slit separation is n times the slit width, where n is the missing order. Figure H4.12 is an example of this where the missing order is $n = 4$.

Figure H4.11 The modulated two-slit intensity pattern when the slit width is not negligible. Shown here is the case for $b = 3\lambda$ and $d = 16\lambda$. The thick grey curve is the one-slit diffraction curve for a slit width of $b = 3\lambda$.

Figure H4.12 The fourth maximum in the two-slit pattern is missing because it coincides with the first diffraction minimum of the one-slit pattern. We can conclude that $d = 4b$.

Resolution

In the previous section, we discussed in some detail the diffraction of a wave through a slit of linear size b. One application of diffraction is in the problem of the resolution of the images of two objects that are close to each other.

The Rayleigh criterion

Light from a distant star will, upon passing through a lens, diffract around the circular aperture of the lens. The image of a star is an extended disc with diffraction rings around it. Two distant objects that are very close to each other will, in general, produce diffraction patterns that will merge with each other, making it difficult to distinguish the pattern as one belonging to two separate objects (see Figure H4.13).

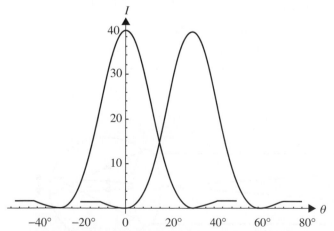

Figure H4.13 Diffraction limits our ability to distinguish two separate sources. In the first diagram the diffraction patterns have merged.

Figure H4.14 The Rayleigh criterion states that two sources are just resolved if the central maximum of the diffraction pattern of one source falls on the first minimum of the other.

Rayleigh suggested that a useful criterion for deciding whether the two objects can be resolved is that the central maximum of one of the sources is formed at the position of the first minimum in the diffraction pattern of the other (see Figure H4.14).

Figure H4.15 shows two unresolved and two well-resolved sources.

▶ Recall that the first minimum in the diffraction pattern through a circular aperture of size b is formed at an angle θ given by

$$\theta = 1.22\frac{\lambda}{b}$$

and for a square aperture of side b by

$$\theta = \frac{\lambda}{b}$$

It then follows that the two objects can be resolved if their angular separation is larger than the θ given by the diffraction formulae above.

(a)

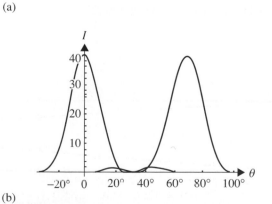

(b)

Figure H4.15 (a) Two unresolved sources. (b) Two well-resolved sources.

Figure H4.16 To see the two objects as distinct we need a lens that can resolve the angle θ.

In Figure H4.16 the two objects are separated by a distance s and their distance from the observer is d. Their angular separation θ is given by $\theta = s/d$ in radians.

Example questions

Q1 ▬▬▬▬▬▬▬▬▬▬▬▬

The camera of a spy satellite orbiting at 200 km has a diameter of 35 cm. What is the smallest distance this camera can resolve on the surface of the earth? (Assume a wavelength of 500 nm.)

Answer

Using Rayleigh's criterion and a wavelength of 5.0×10^{-7} m, we find that the distance s that can be resolved is given by $s = r\theta$ where

$$\theta \approx \frac{1.22 \times 5 \times 10^{-7}}{0.35}$$
$$\approx 1.74 \times 10^{-6} \text{ rad}$$
$$\Rightarrow s = r\theta$$
$$= 2 \times 10^5 \times 1.74 \times 10^{-6} \text{ m}$$
$$= 0.34 \text{ m}$$

Q2 ▬▬▬▬▬▬▬▬▬▬▬▬

The headlights of a car are 2 m apart. The human eye has a lens with a diameter of about 2 mm and suppose that light of wavelength 500 nm is being used. What is the maximum distance at which the two headlights are seen as distinct?

Answer

The resolution of the eye is

$$\theta \approx \frac{1.22 \times 5 \times 10^{-7}}{2 \times 10^{-3}}$$
$$\approx 3 \times 10^{-4} \text{ rad}$$
$$\Rightarrow r = \frac{s}{\theta}$$
$$= \frac{2}{3 \times 10^{-4}}$$
$$= 0.67 \times 10^4$$
$$\approx 700 \text{ m}$$

The car should be no more than this distance away.

Q3 ▬▬▬▬▬▬▬▬▬▬▬▬

The human eye has a lens with a diameter of about 2 mm and the distance between the eye lens and the back of the eye (the retina) where the image is formed is about 20 mm. Suppose the eye uses light of wavelength 500 nm. Use this information to estimate the distance between the receptors in the eye.

Answer

The angular separation, θ, of two objects that can be resolved is, from the answer above, 3×10^{-4} rad. From Figure H4.17 this is also the angular separation between two receptors on the retina. Thus, the linear separation of the two receptors must be *smaller* than about

$$l = r\theta$$
$$= 20 \times 10^{-3} \times 3 \times 10^{-4}$$
$$= 6 \times 10^{-6} \text{ m}$$

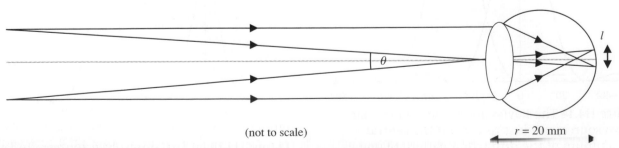

(not to scale)

Figure H4.17. The point here is that if the two receptors had a separation larger than 6 μm, the two images would fall on the same receptor and would then appear as one.

Multiple-slit diffraction

As the number of slits increases, the interference pattern increases in complexity. We will consider here the simplified case in which the width of each slit is very small compared with the wavelength being used. Consider the case of four slits separated by a distance d, as shown in Figure H4.18. If the path difference between the ray leaving slit 1 and the ray leaving slit 2 is an integral number of wavelengths, then by similar triangles the path difference between *any* two rays is also an integral number of wavelengths. The path difference between the rays from slits 1 and 2 is $d \sin \theta$ and so constructive interference takes place whenever

$$d \sin \theta = n\lambda, \quad n = 0, \pm 1, \pm 2, \pm 3, \ldots$$

that is, the same condition as in the two-slit case. Here d is the separation of two successive slits.

> ▶ Thus the maxima of the multiple-slit interference pattern are observed at the same angles as the corresponding two-slit pattern with the same slit separation.

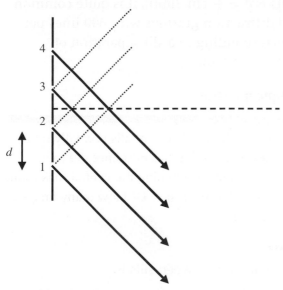

Figure H4.18 The path difference between the first slit and any other slit is an integral multiple of the path difference between the first and second slit. Thus, if the path difference between the first and second slit is an integral multiple of a wavelength, constructive interference from all slits takes place.

At points for which the condition above is *not* satisfied, there is cancellation of the waves from the four slits, but the cancellation is not always complete, giving rise to secondary maxima.

The number of secondary maxima is $N - 2$ where N is the number of slits. The intensity of the principal maxima is proportional to N^2 and their width is proportional to $1/N$. Thus, as N increases, the intensity of the secondary maxima decreases and becomes completely negligible (see Figures H4.19 and H4.20). This means, therefore, that for large N the primary maxima are bright and thin, making the measurement of their separation easy.

The minima are observed at

$$d \sin \theta = \frac{m}{N}\lambda$$

where $m = 1, 2, 3, \ldots$, but $m = N, 2N, 3N, \ldots$ are excluded. Here N stands for the number of slits.

(a)

(b)

Figure H4.19 (a) The intensity distribution for two slits. (b) The intensity distribution for four slits. Note how the width of the maxima decreases but their position stays the same.

(a)

(b)

Figure H4.20 (a) The intensity distribution for six slits. Note how the width of the maxima decreases but their position stays the same. Note also how the relative importance of the secondary maxima decreases with increasing slit number. (b) The intensity pattern for two slits (top), four slits (middle) and very many slits (bottom). Note that the principal maxima are observed at the same positions. For $N = 4$ there are two secondary maxima. As N increases, the secondary maxima become unimportant and the primary maxima become very narrow. In all cases we assume the slit width to be negligible.

Example question

Q4

What is the slit separation for the intensity distribution patterns of Figure H4.20a?

Answer

The first primary maximum occurs at $\theta = 30°$ and since

$$d \sin \theta = \lambda$$

$$\Rightarrow d = \frac{\lambda}{\sin 30°}$$

$$= 2\lambda$$

The diffraction grating

The diffraction grating is an important device in spectroscopy (the analysis of light) whose main purpose is the measurement of the wavelength of light. A grating is simply a large number of parallel slits whose width we take to be negligible. Instead of actual slits, modern gratings consist of a transparent slide on which lines or grooves have been precisely cut. The first diffraction gratings were constructed by the American astronomer David Rittenhouse in 1785 and a few years later by the German Joseph von Fraunhofer, who made significant discoveries with it. The advantage of a large number of slits, N, is that the maxima in the interference pattern are sharp and bright and can easily be distinguished from their neighbours. This makes measurement of their separation easier. The maxima of the pattern are observed at angles given by the formula

$$d \sin \theta = n\lambda, \quad n = 0, 1, 2, 3, \ldots$$

In practice, a diffraction grating is stated by its manufacturer to have 'X lines per centimetre (millimetre)'. This means that the separation of the slits is $d = \frac{1}{X}$ cm (mm). It is quite common to find diffraction gratings with 600 lines per mm corresponding to a slit separation of $d = 1.67 \times 10^{-6}$ m.

Example question

Q5

Light of wavelength 680 nm falls normally on a diffraction grating that has 600 lines per mm. What is the angle separating the central maximum ($n = 0$) from the next ($n = 1$)? How many images can be seen?

Answer

The separation between slits is

$$d = \frac{1}{600} \times 10^{-3} \, \text{m}$$

With $n = 1$ we find

$$\sin \theta = 1 \times 680 \times 10^{-9} \times 600 \times 10^{3}$$

$$= 0.408$$

Hence

$$\theta = 24.1°$$

For $n = 2$ we find $\theta = 54.7°$ and no solution can be found for $n = 3$; the sine of the angle becomes larger than 1. Thus, we can see the central maximum and two orders on either side.

Thin-film interference

This phenomenon is commonly seen as the coloured patches on thin layers of leaked oil floating on water on streets, on thin layers of grease floating on water in a cup and in soap bubbles. To understand this phenomenon we must first realize that, upon reflection, a ray of light may undergo a phase change (see Figure H4.21).

Consider now a thin film with parallel sides surrounded by air (see Figure H4.22).

Let d be the thickness of the film of oil. Then the path difference is $2d$ assuming we view the film normally from above. There will be a phase change of π at the first reflection at the air–oil interface since oil has a larger index of refraction than air. At the second reflection at

Figure H4.22 Thin-film interference in oil is explained by the phase difference due to the extra distance covered by one of the rays and by the phase change upon reflection at the top surface.

the oil–air interface there is no phase change. Using the condition for *constructive interference* in the presence of a phase difference $\phi = \pi$ (with λ_o the wavelength in oil) we get

$$\text{path difference} = k\lambda_o + \frac{\phi}{2\pi}\lambda_o$$
$$k = 0, 1, 2, 3, \ldots$$

that is

$$\text{path difference} = \left(k + \frac{1}{2}\right)\lambda_o$$
$$k = 0, 1, 2, 3, \ldots$$

which means we get a maximum if this path difference is a half-integral multiple of the wavelength. However, the wavelength of light in oil (λ_o) is not the same as that in air. Rather, in oil $\lambda_o = \lambda/n$, where n is the index of refraction of oil and λ the wavelength of light in air.

> ▶ Thus, constructive interference takes place when
> $$2d = \left(k + \frac{1}{2}\right)\frac{\lambda}{n}$$
> that is
> $$2dn = \left(k + \frac{1}{2}\right)\lambda, \quad k = \text{integer}$$

The wavelength that shows constructive interference for a particular thickness of the film will lend its colour to the film.

low index of refraction

higher index of refraction

there is a phase change here of π

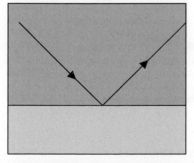

high index of refraction

lower index of refraction

there is no phase change here

Figure H4.21 A ray of light reflecting off a medium with higher index of refraction will undergo a phase change of π.

Example question

Q6 ▪▪▪▪▪▪▪▪▪▪

A solar cell must be coated in order that as little as possible of the light falling on it is reflected. A solar cell has a very high index of refraction (about 3.50). A coating of index of refraction 1.50 is placed on such a cell. What should its minimum thickness be in order to minimize reflection of light of wavelength 524 nm?

Answer

We will have phase changes of 180° at *both* reflections (from the top of the coating and the solar cell surface), hence the condition for a minimum is

$$2dn = \tfrac{1}{2}\lambda$$

$$\Rightarrow d = \frac{\lambda}{4n}$$

$$= \frac{524 \times 10^{-9}}{4 \times 1.50}$$

$$= 87.3 \text{ nm}$$

Thin air wedges

Another example of interference is provided by an arrangement in which two flat glass plates are put on top of each other with a thin piece of paper (of width D) in between them so that a very small angle is formed between the plates (see Figure H4.23). Air is trapped between the glass plates, forming an air wedge of variable thickness. Fringes are seen when the glass plates are observed from above after being illuminated by light from an extended source. The problem is essentially that of interference in thin films except that here the thickness of the film is variable.

We assume that the glass plates are coated so that no reflection takes place from the top surface of the top plate and the bottom surface of the bottom plate.

A ray of light coming vertically down will then partly reflect from point A (the interface of the top plate and the air wedge underneath it) and partly continue to point B. Point B is at the top face of the bottom plate. It will reflect from this point and move up where it will interfere with the ray that reflected from A. The path difference is thus $2d$, where d is the thickness of the air wedge at the point of impact of the light ray. The ray undergoes no phase change at A (A is on the inside of the top plate) but there is a phase change of π at B. Applying the condition for *constructive* interference we find

$$2d = \left(k + \frac{1}{2}\right)\lambda$$

that is

$$2d = \left(k + \frac{1}{2}\right)\lambda, \qquad k = \text{integer}$$

Thus the *bright fringes* occur for thicknesses given by

$$d = \frac{\lambda}{4}, \frac{3\lambda}{4}, \frac{5\lambda}{4}, \text{ and so on}$$

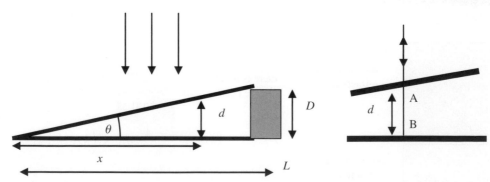

Figure H4.23 The two plates have a thin wedge of air in between them. A ray of light coming down vertically splits at A (the interface of the top plate and the air wedge underneath it). Part of it reflects upward and part traverses the air gap twice after having reflected at B.

We see that the fringes are equally separated (see Figure H4.24).

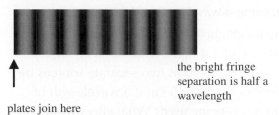

↑

plates join here

the bright fringe separation is half a wavelength

Figure H4.24 The fringe pattern of the air-wedge system.

Measuring small distances

The air wedge can be used to measure small distances such as D in Figure H4.23. To do that we need to find the angle of the wedge. From Figure H4.23, $d = x \tan\theta$ and so the difference of air-wedge thicknesses corresponding to successive bright bands, Δd, obeys $\Delta d = \Delta x \tan\theta$. Since $\Delta d = \lambda/2$ it follows that

$$\frac{\lambda}{2} = \Delta x \tan\theta$$

$$\Rightarrow \tan\theta = \frac{\lambda}{2\Delta x}$$

But Δx is the bright fringe separation, which can be measured (by measuring the separation of many fringes and dividing appropriately), and hence the angle of the wedge can be determined. Having determined the angle, measurement of the length L allows the determination of the small distance D (see Figure H4.23).

Example question

Q7

A wire of diameter D is placed between two glass plates of length 4 cm forming a thin air wedge as described in the text. When the plates are illuminated with light of wavelength 590 nm, 20 dark fringes are observed across the top plate. Find the diameter of the wire.

Answer

The separation of the dark fringes is the same as that of the bright fringes. It is simply

$$\frac{4\ \text{cm}}{20} = 0.20\ \text{cm}$$

The angle of the wedge is thus found from

$$\tan\theta = \frac{\lambda}{2\Delta x}$$

$$= \frac{590\ \text{nm}}{2 \times 0.20\ \text{cm}}$$

$$= \frac{590 \times 10^{-9}\ \text{m}}{2 \times 0.20 \times 10^{-2}\ \text{m}}$$

$$= 1.48 \times 10^{-4}$$

that is

$\theta = 1.48 \times 10^{-4}$ rad (since the angle is small, $\theta \approx \tan\theta$)

Hence

$$D = L \tan\theta$$

$$= 4\ \text{cm} \times 1.48 \times 10^{-4}$$

$$= 5.92 \times 10^{-4}\ \text{cm}$$

(see Figure H4.23).

Questions

1 A single slit of width 1.50 μm is illuminated with light of wavelength 500.0 nm. Find the angular width of the central maximum.

2 Microwaves of wavelength 2.80 cm fall on a slit and the central maximum at a distance of 1.0 m from the slit is found to have a half-width (i.e. distance from middle of central maximum to first minimum) of 0.67 m. Find the width of the slit.

3 The intensity pattern for single-slit diffraction is shown in Figure H4.25. (The vertical units are arbitrary.)

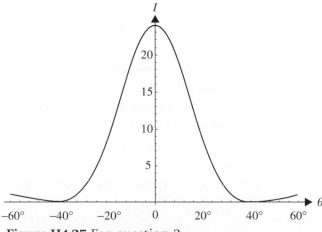

Figure H4.25 For question 3.

(a) Find the width of the slit in terms of the wavelength used.

(b) Draw on the same diagram the intensity pattern for two such slits placed parallel to each other and separated by a distance equal to 10 wavelengths. How many interference maxima fall within the central diffraction maximum?

4 From the information in Figure H4.26, determine the wavelength used to obtain the single-slit diffraction pattern shown. The screen is 0.60 m from the slit and the slit width is 2.30 cm. What kind of wave is most likely being used?

1.40 m

Figure H4.26 For question 4.

5 In a two-slit interference experiment with slits of negligible width, five maxima are observed on each side of the central maximum. When the slits are replaced by two slits of finite width separated by the same distance as before, the third maximum on either side of the central maximum is missing (i.e. the intensity of light there is zero). Calculate the width of the slits in terms of their separation, d.

6 Two *very narrow*, parallel slits separated by a distance of 1.4×10^{-5} m are illuminated by coherent, monochromatic light of wavelength 7.0×10^{-7} m.

(a) Describe what is meant by coherent and monochromatic light.

(b) Draw a graph to show the intensity of light observed on a screen far from the slits.

(c) By drawing another graph on the same axes, illustrate the effect on the intensity distribution of increasing the width of the slits to 2.8×10^{-6} m.

7 Could a telescope with an objective lens of diameter 20 cm resolve two objects a distance of 10 km away separated by 1 cm? (Assume we are using a wavelength of 600 nm.)

8 The headlights of a car are separated by a distance of 1.4 m. At what distance would these be resolved as two separate sources by a lens of diameter 5 cm if a wavelength of 500 nm is being used? What effect would decreasing the wavelength used have on the distance you just found?

9 A diffraction grating with 350 lines per mm produces first-order maxima at angles 8.34° and 8.56° for two separate wavelengths of light.

(a) What are these wavelengths?

(b) What angle separates the second-order maxima of these wavelengths?

10 A grating with 400 lines per mm is illuminated with light of wavelength 600.0 nm.

(a) At what angles are maxima observed?

(b) What is the largest order that can be seen with this grating and this wavelength?

11 Visible light ranging in wavelength from 400.0 nm to 700.0 nm falls on a grating with 400 lines per mm. Describe the spectrum that is observed.

12 (a) Draw a graph to show the variation with angle of the intensity of light observed on a screen some distance from two very narrow, parallel slits when coherent monochromatic light falls on the slits.

(b) Illustrate by a graph on the same axes the effect on the intensity of light of replacing the two slits by five very narrow slits whose separation is the same as that of the original two slits.

13 When a thin soap film of uniform thickness is illuminated with white light, it appears purple in colour. Explain this observation carefully.

14 A piece of glass of index of refraction 1.50 is coated with a thin layer of magnesium fluoride of index of refraction 1.38. If it is illuminated with light of wavelength 680 nm, what is the minimum thickness of the coating that will result in no reflection?

15 A thin soap bubble of index of refraction 1.33 is viewed with light of wavelength 550.0 nm and appears very bright. What is a possible value of the thickness of the soap bubble?

16 A soap film will appear dark if it is very thin and will reflect all colours when thick. Carefully justify these statements using interference from thin films.

17 In the thin-air-wedge interference pattern, how would the separation of the bright fringes change if the angle of the wedge is made smaller?

18 In a thin-air-wedge interference experiment, 12 maxima are observed within a length of 5 cm when the plates are illuminated with light of wavelength 500 nm. Calculate the angle between the plates.

Physics and the theory of knowledge (TOK)

This is a brief introduction to the role of physics in the context of the theory of knowledge (TOK) class, which all IB students must take. We will begin with a very short discussion of the developments and changes that have taken place in the theories used to explain phenomena in three areas of physics: the motion of the planets; gas pressure; and the nature of light. We will then take a closer look at the nature of theories and why they need to change.

Those who chose to study Option E on The history and development of physics will recall that in ancient times the prevailing model of the solar system was a *geocentric* one. In the Ptolemaic system, the earth was at the centre of the solar system and all other celestial bodies orbited it. The practising scientists of the time embraced this model and used it for many purposes. When observations began to accumulate showing disagreement with the model, Ptolemy, among others, modified the model to make it fit the new observations. One such famous alteration was the introduction of *epicycles*. Originally, planets were supposed to move in perfect circles around the earth. With epicycles, the planets now had to complete smaller circles at the same time as they completed the large circular orbit around the earth. When even newer observations showed yet more deviations from the model, more epicycles were introduced with the express purpose of making the model again fit the data. Eventually, more than 50 epicycles were needed to account for the motion of the five known planets, the sun and the moon, resulting in an extremely complicated and cumbersome model. Interestingly, this model lasted for 1400 years before it was replaced (through the efforts of Copernicus, Kepler and Newton) by the modern heliocentric system. The planets orbit the sun in elliptical orbits according to well-defined

physical principles summarized in Newton's laws of mechanics and gravitation.

A few centuries later, experimenters looking into the properties of gases realized that the pressure of a gas increased as its volume was slowly compressed. Robert Boyle (one of the gas laws bears his name) thought that a gas consists of tiny springs. When the gas is compressed, the springs are also compressed and the tension of these springs is what gives rise to the pressure of the gas. Newton thought instead that the gas consists of tiny particles between which a force of repulsion exists. The force was hypothesized by Newton to be inversely proportional to their separation. Thus, when the gas was compressed, the repulsive forces between the molecules grew larger, giving rise to the pressure of the gas. Bernoulli, on the other hand, did not find the need to introduce forces between the molecules. The gas, he said, consisted of an extremely large number of particles that moved about and constantly collided with each other and the container walls. It was the momentum exchanged in the collisions that was responsible for the pressure as far as Bernoulli was concerned. Boyle's model is an unnatural model. Why should a gas consist of something as artificial as a spring? Newton's idea is much more reasonable, but it requires the introduction of a new force. What is the origin of the force and where else is it operating? Bernoulli's model is by far the simplest. It requires nothing new, just the application of the laws of mechanics to a very large number of material particles making up the gas.

By the end of the nineteenth century, a very large amount of data had been collected indicating that, when light fell on certain metallic surfaces, negative charges (electrons) were emitted from the surface. The puzzling thing about those observations was that, despite every expectation, increasing the intensity of light did not result in any increase in the energy of the emitted electrons. The puzzling features of the many experiments on this effect (the photoelectric effect) were explained by Albert Einstein in 1905. He proposed a revolutionary theory in which light should be viewed as a stream of massless particles and not as a wave, as had been the practice since the time of Christiaan Huygens. The theory of light as a wave could not account for its behaviour in the photoelectric effect and thus that theory had to be abandoned in favour of a better theory. If the new theory were correct, it should be in a position to predict new phenomena; phenomena that would not be possible within the old theory. Indeed, Einstein's theory of *photons* (the particles of light) predicted that, when light of very short wavelength hit electrons, the light would bounce off the electrons with an *increased* wavelength. Soon afterwards, Arthur Compton observed this scattering of light off electrons in precise agreement with the new theory of light as photons.

We may extract a number of observations from the previous three paragraphs, which may help us in our discussion. Knowledge in physics accumulates when observations of physical phenomena must be explained. To explain these phenomena, a *model* is constructed. The model is a set of rules, usually accompanied by a set of pictures, describing how a few basic ingredients are supposed to work so that the phenomena are explained at some level. In

Ptolemy's model of the solar system, the ingredients were the earth, the sun and the planets, and his rules stated that these objects moved in circular paths around the earth. This model could explain some rough features of the observations about the motion of celestial bodies. When the observations did not exactly agree with Ptolemy's predictions based on circular orbits, epicycles were introduced. There was no other reason to introduce the epicycles other than to make the model fit the data. Epicycles were *ad hoc* statements made to save a model. Fourteen centuries later, Kepler, using much more accurate data than was available to Ptolemy, deduced that planets move in elliptical orbits around the sun. His model was a better model than Ptolemy's. For one thing, it was simpler. It agreed with observations very well and could explain things that Ptolemy's model could not, such as why the brightness of the planets varies at different times of the year. Kepler could state that planets covered equal areas in equal times and could calculate the time of revolution of a planet around the sun if he knew the distance between the planet and the sun. Ptolemy's model could not even handle these questions let alone answer them, but even Kepler could not explain *why* the planets moved in elliptical paths. To answer such a detailed question more knowledge was required; this was supplied by Newton, who realized that the key behind it all was a force of attraction between the sun and the planets – the force of gravity. Newton thus made a new and simpler model whose premise was a force of attraction between *any* two masses, not just those of celestial bodies. It could be shown that all the observations that Kepler had made were simple *consequences* of the law of gravitation and the laws of mechanics.

The development of the models of the motion of the planets from Ptolemy to Newton was not a gradual evolution, with a few details of the original model changing as it was refined into a better one. It involved an abrupt and fundamental change – a change in *paradigm* and, as philosopher Thomas Kuhn says, a 'scientific revolution'. Newton's ideas about the motion of the planets were a fundamental and different reconsideration of the entire problem, not an attempt to fix some of the original model's flaws.

The signs that the original model was wrong were many and obvious. First because observations did not agree with the model and second because the model was getting too complicated, too cumbersome and too *ad hoc*. Newton's model was simpler, more elegant, more general and agreed with the data. Newton's model passed many tests. Detailed predictions based on the model were found to be true by observation. By the early part of the nineteenth century, anomalies (i.e. deviations from Newtonian behaviour) were observed in the motion of the planet Uranus. The astronomers J.C. Adams in England and U. Le Verrier in France assumed that an unknown planet was affecting the orbit of Uranus. By applying Newton's law of gravitation, the two independently showed that the anomalies in the Uranus orbit could be explained by the presence of this planet. Calculations showed the position of the planet and the very night Le Verrier's letter arrived at the Berlin observatory the planet Neptune was discovered exactly where Le Verrier said it should be. More detailed calculations, however, showed that the effect of Neptune explained most, but not all, of the anomaly in the Uranus orbit. More work again showed that a smaller planet was responsible for that bit of the anomaly. After several decades of intensive search, the planet Pluto was discovered at the edge of the solar system. Newtonian gravitation was triumphant. These were tremendous successes for physics and showed the *universality* of physical laws – they could be applied anywhere not just on earth. Even though many other disciplines have tried to imitate and copy the methods of physics (with varying success), no other discipline has been able to produce the universality of its laws.

At about the same time as Adams and Le Verrier were discovering new planets, more anomalies were observed, this time in the motion of the planet Mercury. Did this imply that Newton's theory was wrong or would it imply more incredible discoveries within the theory? The problem was that Mercury's orbit was not exactly a closed ellipse. Within the Newtonian model attempts were made to account for this anomaly. Mercury's orbit is influenced not only by the sun but also by the other planets. The orbit would be a perfect ellipse if the sun and only the sun influenced Mercury. Taking into account the effects of the other planets *almost* eliminated the anomaly. That is, one could understand the observed orbit of Mercury and its deviations from a perfect ellipse in terms of the Newtonian model itself. The model did not have to change – it could account for the new phenomena without the need to change the model in any way and without the need for new assumptions. The paradigm held.

Note that we said that the Newtonian model *almost* accounted for the anomaly, about 92% of it to be precise. The remaining 8% proved disastrous for the Newtonian model of gravitation. Countless experiments had confirmed the Newtonian theory. As philosopher Karl Popper stresses, however, no number of successful experiments (no matter how large the number) can convince us that a theory is right. But just one experiment is enough to *falsify* the theory. In the case of Mercury's orbit, the 8% that could not be accounted for were to lead in 1915 into another change of paradigm: the fall of Newtonian gravitation and the introduction of Einstein's general theory of relativity. But models do not change so easily and not before all ways to resolve the problem within the model are exhausted. Was there no way out of the problem with Mercury's orbit within the Newtonian theory? There was if one assumed that the shape of the sun was not exactly spherical and hence its gravitational field was not exactly an inverse square field. The shape of the sun could not then be measured sufficiently accurately, however, to settle the question. Die-hards of the Newtonian theory could thus claim not to be worried about Mercury and could also hope that one day Mercury's abnormalities could be settled by a few details within the Newtonian theory itself. But as soon as Einstein convincingly demonstrated the solution to Mercury's problems within the new theory (general relativity), new areas were discovered where the Newtonian theory had not been tested before. General relativity predicted that light would bend as it went past a very massive object (such as the sun). Newtonian gravity predicted a deflection also but of the wrong magnitude. Experiments in 1919 favoured relativity. The physics of very dense stars demanded relativity and not Newtonian gravity for their correct description. Even the Newtonian die-hards would have to concede defeat (and the issue of the precise shape of the sun became a minor detail concerning only the experts on the shape of the sun!).

The story of the second example mentioned at the beginning of this chapter (the ideas behind the pressure of a gas) is not as dramatic as that of the motion of the planets, but it shares many of the same features. Bernoulli's ideas are simpler, more elegant, more general and more natural (even though we could debate for a long time what exactly more 'elegant' or 'natural' or even 'simpler' really means).

The third example mentioned (the photoelectric effect) also has a fascinating story. Einstein's explanation of the photoelectric effect is another scientific revolution. The wave theory of light cannot account for this effect and a particle view of light had to be introduced that does explain it. But here things are a bit stranger. The 'old' paradigm (light as a wave) cannot just be thrown away because the 'new' paradigm (light as particles) cannot explain everything by itself. The introduction of photons revealed the particle nature of light, but in other experiments light most definitely exhibited a wave nature. Soon it was to be discovered that electrons, protons and neutrons, which are normally thought to be particles, behave in

certain situations like waves. A stream of electrons directed at a crystal diffracts (i.e. suffers the most tell-tale wave phenomenon of all). The sharp distinction between particles and waves of the nineteenth century gave rise to the *duality* of matter and waves. Everyday language, based on our limited experience with the microscopic world, fails to provide an adequate description of objects that sometimes behave like particles and sometimes like waves. Our sense of 'reality', which in the nineteenth century conveniently classified objects as particles or waves, had to give way to the new reality of duality and the corresponding loss of determinism that the uncertainty principle introduced.

In the preceding pages, we have conveyed the prejudice that exists among physicists who believe that the main virtues of a theory are that it be simple and elegant and the belief that, ultimately, nature will be described by such a theory. It is this prejudice, and much less the adherence to the conventional 'scientific method', that is the guiding principle in the discovery of new knowledge about the natural world. Whether this prejudice is correct and whether nature will be described in such a way, only time will tell.

Discussion questions

1 An ichthyologist wants to study the fish in a lake. She catches the fish using a net with a spacing between the net threads of about 5 cm. She observes that she never catches fish of length smaller than 5 cm and so deduces that no fish of length less than 5 cm live in that lake. What can you say to this claim?

2 Procrustes was a thug living outside ancient Athens who stopped travellers and made them lie in a bed by the road. If they were too short for the bed he stretched them until they fitted just right. If they were too tall he cut off their legs so they again would fit. In what sense (other than the obvious!) is this story a parable of unethical scientific practice?

3 A student says that physics is just one wrong theory after the other. We start by learning Newton's laws of mechanics only to find out later that these are wrong and have to be replaced by Einstein's theory of relativity. Similarly, Rutherford's model of the atom is replaced by the Bohr model, which in turn is replaced by Schrödinger's theory. Write a response to this student.

4 An experiment can overthrow a theory but can never completely confirm a theory. Discuss this statement using specific situations in physics.

5 Traditionally much of the new knowledge in basic physics has come from experiments with high-energy accelerators that have been able to probe matter at ever smaller scales. To investigate matter at even smaller distances requires accelerators that are far too big and far too costly ever to have a chance of being built. What does that imply about the future of fundamental physics?

6 A professional astrologer says: 'Physicists are simply prejudiced. There is so much unknown stuff out there, so how do they know that there isn't something to astrology?' What do you think?

7 Newton would not have been able to apply his theory of gravitation to the motion of the planets had he not developed a branch of mathematics called calculus. How close is the relationship between physics and mathematics? Does physics need mathematics or could we arrive at the same level of knowledge of the physical world without it? How has physics influenced the development of mathematics?

8 Practically every area of mathematics, including such highly esoteric fields as number theory, has eventually found an application in physics. Is this a sign that knowledge in mathematics is essentially governed by the need to understand the physical world around us?

9 Mathematicians of the nineteenth century developed theories of geometry that follow different rules from those of the ordinary Euclidean geometry taught at school. Where in physics are the ideas on non-Euclidean geometry used? Were these geometries developed to solve problems of the physical world?

10 Physics tries to find the ultimate laws that govern the behaviour of the physical world. Is there any evidence that ultimate laws exist?

11 Discuss whether and to what degree the methods used in the acquisition of knowledge in physics can be used in other disciplines as well. Discuss in particular biology and economics.

12 Many people use the second law of thermodynamics to explain phenomena that do not fall in the realm of physics, such as economics, the stock market, etc. Is this justified?

13 A student says: 'Chemistry is part of physics. If you know physics you automatically know chemistry.' Do you agree?

14 A student says: 'The underlying laws of biology are basically those of physics. When we discover those laws, biology will become a part of physics.' Do you agree?

15 The wave–particle duality of modern quantum theory introduces via the uncertainty principle a lack of determinism. Write an essay discussing determinism and the loss of it in modern physics. What impact, if any, has modern physics had on the issue of free will and choice of an individual?

16 We are aware of three space dimensions but no more. How can we talk about higher dimensions when we cannot even visualize them?

17 A student says 'I got a 7 on my physics higher level exam and I still don't know what mass or electric charge *really* are!' If the student takes a three-year university course in physics will she know what mass and electric charge *really* are?

18 Electric and magnetic field lines are useful concepts when thinking about electric and magnetic fields, yet they do not exist. How exactly are these concepts useful and how do they influence the way we think about electric and magnetic fields?

19 We have a picture in our minds when we speak of electrons and that picture often influences the way we think about electrons. Most people see a tiny round ball when they think of an electron. Richard Feynman sees 'a vector and a ψ written somewhere, sort of mixed with it somehow, and an amplitude all mixed up with x's … a mathematical expression wrapped into and around, in a vague way, around the object'. Do you know of any examples where a particular visualization of an object or process has been instrumental in the understanding of that object or process?

20 J.R. Oppenheimer, the physicist in charge of the Manhattan project that developed the American nuclear bomb during the Second World War, said after the completion of the project that 'physicists have known sin'. What did he mean? Do you agree that knowledge that can prove dangerous should be contained? *Can* knowledge be contained and if so, by whom?

21 At the time of Kepler, five planets were known (excluding the earth) – Mercury, Venus, Mars, Jupiter and Saturn. In his book *Mysterium cosmographicum* Kepler suggests that only five planets *could* exist because there are only five Platonic solids. Find out what a Platonic solid is. Kepler then went on to say that the orbit radius of each of the five planets was proportional to the radius of the sphere in which the Platonic solid was inscribed. (He assumed that each Platonic solid was fitted into the next in the same order as the planets.) What do you think of this theory? How scientific is it? It is obviously false since there are more than five planets, but if only five planets did exist, what would its merits be then? Steven Weinberg says of Kepler's idea that where he went wrong was not in the kind of conjectures he made but in assigning too much importance to the planets. What does Weinberg mean?

Physical constants

The values quoted here are those usually used in calculations and problems. The constants are known with a much better precision than the number of significant digits quoted here implies.

Atomic mass unit	$1\,u = 1.661 \times 10^{-27}\,kg = 931.5\,MeV\,c^{-2}$
Avogadro constant	$N_A = 6.02 \times 10^{23}\,mol^{-1}$
Boltzmann constant	$k = 1.38 \times 10^{-23}\,J\,K^{-1}$
Coulomb's law constant	$\frac{1}{4\pi\varepsilon_0} = 8.99 \times 10^9\,N\,m^2\,C^{-2}$
Electric permittivity	$\varepsilon_0 = 8.85 \times 10^{-12}\,N^{-1}\,m^{-2}\,C^2$
Gravitational constant	$G = 6.67 \times 10^{-11}\,N\,kg^{-2}\,m^2$
Magnetic permeability	$\mu_0 = 4\pi \times 10^{-7}\,T\,m\,A^{-1}$
Magnitude of electronic charge	$e = 1.60 \times 10^{-19}\,C$
Mass of the electron	$m_e = 9.11 \times 10^{-31}\,kg = 5.49 \times 10^{-4}\,u = 0.511\,MeV\,c^{-2}$
Mass of the neutron	$m_n = 1.675 \times 10^{-27}\,kg = 1.008\ 665\,u = 940\,MeV\,c^{-2}$
Mass of the proton	$m_p = 1.673 \times 10^{-27}\,kg = 1.007\ 276\,u = 938\,MeV\,c^{-2}$
Planck constant	$h = 6.63 \times 10^{-34}\,J\,s$
Speed of light in a vacuum	$c = 3.00 \times 10^8\,m\,s^{-1}$
Stefan–Boltzmann constant	$\sigma = 5.67 \times 10^{-8}\,W\,m^{-2}\,K^{-4}$
Universal gas constant	$R = 8.31\,J\,mol^{-1}\,K^{-1}$

A few unit conversions

astronomical unit	$1\,AU = 1.50 \times 10^{11}\,m$
atmosphere	$1\,atm = 1.01 \times 10^5\,N\,m^{-2} = 101\,kPa$
degree	$1° = \frac{\pi}{180°}\,rad$
electronvolt	$1\,eV = 1.60 \times 10^{-19}\,J$
kilowatt–hour	$1\,kW\,h = 3.60 \times 10^6\,J$
light year	$1\,ly = 9.46 \times 10^{15}\,m$
parsec	$1\,pc = 3.26\,ly$
radian	$1\,rad = \frac{180°}{\pi}$

Tables of the elements

Table A2.1 gives atomic masses, including the masses of electrons, in the neutral atom. The masses are averaged over the isotopes of each element. In the case of unstable elements, numbers in brackets indicate the approximate mass of the most abundant isotope of the element in question. The masses are expressed in atomic mass units, u. Table A2.2 gives the atomic masses of a few selected isotopes

Table A2.1 Atomic numbers and atomic masses of the elements.

Atomic number	Name and symbol	Atomic mass/u	Atomic number	Name and symbol	Atomic mass/u
1	Hydrogen, H	1.0080	30	Zinc, Zn	65.37
2	Helium, He	4.0026	31	Gallium, Ga	69.723
3	Lithium, Li	6.941	32	Germanium, Ge	72.59
4	Beryllium, Be	9.012 18	33	Arsenic, As	74.921
5	Boron, B	10.811	34	Selenium, Se	78.96
6	Carbon, C	12.000 000	35	Bromine, Br	79.91
7	Nitrogen, N	14.007	36	Krypton, Kr	83.80
8	Oxygen, O	15.999	37	Rubidium, Rb	85.467
9	Fluorine, F	18.998	38	Strontium, Sr	87.62
10	Neon, Ne	20.180	39	Yttrium, Y	88.906
11	Sodium, Na	22.999	40	Zirconium, Zr	91.224
12	Magnesium, Mg	24.31	41	Niobium, Nb	92.906
13	Aluminium, Al	26.981	42	Molybdenum, Mo	95.94
14	Silicon, Si	28.086	43	Technetium, Tc	(99)
15	Phosphorus, P	30.974	44	Ruthenium, Ru	101.07
16	Sulphur, S	32.066	45	Rhodium, Rh	102.906
17	Chlorine, Cl	35.453	46	Palladium, Pd	106.42
18	Argon, Ar	39.948	47	Silver, Ag	107.868
19	Potassium, K	39.102	48	Cadmium, Cd	112.40
20	Calcium, Ca	40.078	49	Indium, In	114.82
21	Scandium, Sc	44.956	50	Tin, Sn	118.69
22	Titanium, Ti	47.90	51	Antimony, Sb	121.75
23	Vanadium, V	50.942	52	Tellurium, Te	127.60
24	Chromium, Cr	51.996	53	Iodine, I	126.904
25	Manganese, Mn	54.938	54	Xenon, Xe	131.30
26	Iron, Fe	55.847	55	Caesium, Cs	132.91
27	Cobalt, Co	58.933	56	Barium, Ba	137.34
28	Nickel, Ni	58.71	57	Lanthanum, La	138.91
29	Copper, Cu	63.54	58	Cerium, Ce	140.12

Table A2.1 (Continued)

Atomic number	Name and symbol	Atomic mass/u	Atomic number	Name and symbol	Atomic mass/u
59	Praseodymium, Pr	140.907	82	Lead, Pb	207.2
60	Neodymium, Nd	144.24	83	Bismuth, Bi	208.980
61	Promethium, Pm	(144)	84	Polonium, Po	(210)
62	Samarium, Sm	150.4	85	Astatine, At	(218)
63	Europium, Eu	152.0	86	Radon, Rn	(222)
64	Gadolinium, Gd	157.25	87	Francium, Fr	(223)
65	Terbium, Tb	158.92	88	Radium, Ra	(226)
66	Dysprosium, Dy	162.50	89	Actinium, Ac	(227)
67	Holmium, Ho	164.93	90	Thorium, Th	(232)
68	Erbium, Er	167.26	91	Protactinium, Pa	(231)
69	Thulium, Tm	168.93	92	Uranium, U	(238)
70	Ytterbium, Yb	173.04	93	Neptunium, Np	(239)
71	Lutetium, Lu	174.97	94	Plutonium, Pu	(239)
72	Hafnium, Hf	178.49	95	Americium, Am	(243)
73	Tantalum, Ta	180.95	96	Curium, Cm	(245)
74	Tungsten, W	183.85	97	Berkelium, Bk	(247)
75	Rhenium, Re	186.2	98	Californium, Cf	(249)
76	Osmium, Os	190.2	99	Einsteinium, Es	(254)
77	Iridium, I	192.2	100	Fermium, Fm	(253)
78	Platinum, Pt	195.09	101	Mendelevium, Md	(255)
79	Gold, Au	196.97	102	Nobelium, No	(255)
80	Mercury, Hg	200.59	103	Lawrencium, Lr	(257)
81	Thallium, Tl	204.37			

Table A2.2 Atomic masses of a few selected isotopes.

Atomic number	Name	Atomic mass/u	Atomic number	Name	Atomic mass/u
1	Hydrogen, H	1.007 825	7	Nitrogen-14	14.003 074
1	Deuterium, D	2.014 102	7	Nitrogen-15	15.000 109
1	Tritium, T	3.016 049	8	Oxygen-16	15.994 915
2	Helium-3	3.016 029	8	Oxygen-17	16.999 131
2	Helium-4	4.002 603	8	Oxygen-18	17.999 160
3	Lithium-6	6.015 121	19	Potassium-39	38.963 708
3	Lithium-7	7.016 003	19	Potassium-40	39.964 000
4	Beryllium-9	9.012 182	92	Uranium-232	232.037 14
5	Boron-10	10.012 937	92	Uranium-235	235.043 925
5	Boron-11	11.009 305	92	Uranium-236	236.045 563
6	Carbon-12	12.000 000	92	Uranium-238	238.050 786
6	Carbon-13	13.003 355	92	Uranium-239	239.054 291
6	Carbon-14	14.003 242			

Astronomical data

Body	Mass/kg	Radius/m	Orbit radius/m (average)	Orbital period
Sun	1.99×10^{30}	6.96×10^{8}	–	–
Moon	7.35×10^{22}	1.74×10^{6}	3.84×10^{8}	27.3 days
Mercury	3.30×10^{23}	2.44×10^{6}	5.79×10^{10}	88.0 days
Venus	4.87×10^{24}	6.05×10^{6}	1.08×10^{11}	224.7 days
Earth	5.98×10^{24}	6.38×10^{6}	1.50×10^{11}	365.3 days
Mars	6.42×10^{23}	3.40×10^{6}	2.28×10^{11}	687.0 days
Jupiter	1.90×10^{27}	6.91×10^{7}	7.78×10^{11}	11.86 yr
Saturn	5.69×10^{26}	6.03×10^{7}	1.43×10^{12}	29.42 yr
Uranus	8.66×10^{25}	2.56×10^{7}	2.88×10^{12}	83.75 yr
Neptune	1.03×10^{26}	2.48×10^{7}	4.50×10^{12}	163.7 yr
Pluto	1.5×10^{22}	1.15×10^{6}	5.92×10^{12}	248.0 yr

Luminosity of the sun $\qquad$ $L = 3.9 \times 10^{26}$ W

Distance to nearest star (Proxima Centauri) $\qquad$ 4×10^{16} m (approx. 4.3 ly)

Diameter of the Milky Way $\qquad$ 10^{21} m (approx. 100 000 ly)

Mass of the Milky Way $\qquad$ 4×10^{41} kg

Distance to nearest galaxy (Andromeda) $\qquad$ 2×10^{22} m (approx. 2.3 million ly)

Mathematical results

In physics problems, the following are useful.

$$a^{-x} = \frac{1}{a^x} \qquad a^x a^y = a^{x+y} \qquad \frac{a^x}{a^y} = a^{x-y}$$

$$\log a = x \Rightarrow 10^x = a \qquad \ln a = x \Rightarrow e^x = a$$

$$\ln(ab) = \ln a + \ln b \qquad \ln\left(\frac{a}{b}\right) = \ln a - \ln b$$

$$\ln(a^x) = x \ln a \qquad \ln(1) = 0 \qquad e^0 = 1$$

$$\sin 2x = 2 \sin x \cos x$$
$$\cos 2x = 2 \cos^2 x - 1 = 1 - 2 \sin^2 x = \cos^2 x - \sin^2 x$$

The quadratic equation $ax^2 + bx + c = 0$ has two roots given by

$$x = \frac{-b \pm \sqrt{b^2 - 4ac}}{2a}$$

In approximations, the binomial theorem

$$(1 + x)^n = 1 + nx + \frac{n(n-1)}{2!}x^2$$
$$+ \frac{n(n-1)(n-2)}{3!}x^3 + \cdots$$

is extremely useful. Here $-1 < x < 1$ and n can be any real number, not necessarily integer.

Also very useful are the approximations

$$\sin x \approx x - \frac{x^3}{6} + \cdots$$

and

$$\cos x \approx 1 - \frac{x^2}{2} + \cdots$$

valid when x in radians is small.

From geometry, we must know the following expressions for lengths, areas and volumes.

Property	Formula
Circumference of a circle of radius R	$2\pi R$
Area of a circle of radius R	πR^2
Surface area of a sphere of radius R	$4\pi R^2$
Volume of a sphere of radius R	$\frac{4\pi R^3}{3}$
Volume of a cylinder of base radius R and height h	$\pi R^2 h$

The length of an arc of a circle of radius R that subtends an angle θ at the centre of the circle is $s = R\theta$. In this formula the angle must be expressed in radians. An angle of 2π radians is equivalent to an angle of $360°$, so

$$1 \text{ radian} = \frac{360°}{2\pi} = 57.3°$$

Nobel prize winners in physics

No awards were made in years not listed.

2004: The prize was awarded jointly to D.J. Gross, H.D. Politzer and F. Wilczek (all USA) for their discovery of asymptotic freedom in quantum chromodynamics.

2003: The prize was awarded jointly to Alexei Abrikosov (Russia and USA), Vitaly Ginzburg (Russia) and Anthony Leggett (UK and USA) for pioneering contributions to the theory of superconductors and superfluids.

2002: Half the prize was awarded jointly to Raymond Davis Jr (USA) and Masatoshi Koshiba (Japan), and the other half was awarded to Riccardo Gianconi (USA) for pioneering contributions to astrophysics, particularly for the detection of cosmic neutrinos.

2001: The prize was awarded jointly to Eric Cornell (USA), Wolfgang Ketterle (Germany) and Carl Wieman (USA) for the achievement of Bose–Einstein condensation in dilute alkali gases and for early fundamental studies of the properties of the condensates.

2000: Half the prize was awarded jointly to Zhores I. Alferov (Russia) and Herbert Kroemer (USA) for developing semiconductor heterostructures used in high-speed and opto-electronics, and the other half was awarded to Jack St. Clair Kilby (USA) for his part in the invention of the integrated circuit.

1999: The prize was awarded jointly to Gerardus 't Hooft and Martinus J.G. Veltman (both Netherlands) for elucidating the quantum structure of electroweak interactions in physics.

1998: The prize was awarded jointly to Robert B. Laughlin (USA), Horst L. Stormer (Germany) and Daniel C. Tsui (USA) for their discovery of a new form of quantum fluid with fractionally charged excitations.

1997: The prize was awarded jointly to Steven Chu (USA), Claude Cohen-Tannoudji (France) and William D. Phillips (USA) for development of methods to cool and trap atoms with laser light.

1996: The prize was awarded jointly to David M. Lee, Douglas D. Osheroff and Robert C. Richardson (all USA) for their discovery of superfluidity in helium-3.

1995: The prize was awarded for pioneering experimental contributions to lepton physics, with half to Martin L. Perl (USA) for the discovery of the tau lepton, and the other half to Frederick Reines (USA) for the detection of the neutrino.

1994: The prize was awarded jointly to Bertram N. Brockhouse (Canada) and Clifford G. Shull (USA) for pioneering contributions to the development of neutron scattering techniques for studies of condensed matter: Brockhouse for the development of neutron spectroscopy, and Shull for the development of the neutron diffraction technique.

1993: The prize was awarded jointly to Russell A. Hulse and Joseph H. Taylor Jr (both USA) for the discovery of a new type of pulsar – a discovery that has opened up new possibilities for the study of gravitation.

1992: Georges Charpak (France) for his invention and development of particle detectors, in particular the multiwire proportional chamber.

1991: Pierre-Gilles de Gennes (France) for discovering that methods developed for studying order phenomena in simple systems can be generalized to more complex forms of matter, in particular to liquid crystals and polymers.

1990: The prize was awarded jointly to Jerome I. Friedman, Henry W. Kendall (both USA) and Richard E. Taylor (Canada) for their pioneering investigations concerning deep inelastic scattering of electrons on protons and bound neutrons, which have been of essential importance for the development of the quark model in particle physics.

1989: Half of the prize was awarded to Norman F. Ramsey (USA) for the invention of the separated oscillatory fields method and its use in the hydrogen maser and other atomic clocks, and the other half was awarded jointly to Hans G. Dehmelt (USA) and Wolfgang Paul (Germany) for the development of the ion trap technique.

1988: The prize was awarded jointly to Leon M. Lederman, Melvin Schwartz and Jack Steinberger (all USA) for the neutrino beam method and the demonstration of the doublet structure of the leptons through the discovery of the muon neutrino.

1987: The prize was awarded jointly to J. Georg Bednorz (Germany) and K. Alexander Müller (Switzerland) for their important breakthrough in the discovery of superconductivity in ceramic materials.

1986: Half of the prize was awarded to Ernst Ruska (Germany) for his fundamental work in electron optics and for the design of the first electron microscope, and the other half was awarded jointly to Gerd Binnig (Germany) and Heinrich Rohrer (Switzerland) for their design of the scanning tunnelling microscope.

1985: Klaus von Klitzing (Germany) for the discovery of the quantized Hall effect.

1984: The prize was awarded jointly to Carlo Rubbia (Italy) and Simon van der Meer (Netherlands) for their decisive contributions to the large project that led to the discovery of the field particles W and Z, communicators of the weak interaction.

1983: The prize was divided equally between Subrahmanyan Chandrasekhar (USA) for his theoretical studies of the physical processes of importance to the structure and evolution of the stars, and William A. Fowler (USA) for his theoretical and experimental studies of the nuclear reactions of importance in the formation of the chemical elements in the universe.

1982: Kenneth G. Wilson (USA) for his theory for critical phenomena in connection with phase transitions.

1981: Half the prize was awarded jointly to Nicolaas Bloembergen and Arthur L. Schawlow (both USA) for their contribution to the development of laser spectroscopy, and the other half was awarded to Kai M. Siegbahn (Sweden) for his contribution to the development of high-resolution electron spectroscopy.

1980: The prize was divided equally between James W. Cronin and Val L. Fitch (both USA) for the discovery of violations of fundamental symmetry principles in the decay of neutral K-mesons.

1979: The prize was divided equally between Sheldon L. Glashow (USA), Abdus Salam (Pakistan) and Steven Weinberg (USA) for their contributions to the theory of the unified weak and electromagnetic interaction between elementary particles, including, among other things, the prediction of the weak neutral current.

1978: Half the prize was awarded to Pyotr Leonidovich Kapitsa (USSR) for his basic inventions and discoveries in the area of low-temperature physics, and the other half was divided equally between Arno A. Penzias and Robert W. Wilson (both USA) for their discovery of cosmic microwave background radiation.

1977: The prize was divided equally between Philip W. Anderson (USA), Sir Nevill F. Mott (UK) and John H. van Vleck (USA) for their fundamental theoretical investigations of the electronic structure of magnetic and disordered systems.

1976: The prize was divided equally between Burton Richter and Samuel C.C. Ting (both USA) for their pioneering work in the discovery of a heavy elementary particle of a new kind.

1975: The prize was awarded jointly to Aage Bohr, Ben Mottelson (both Denmark) and James Rainwater (USA) for the discovery of the connection between collective motion and particle motion in atomic nuclei, and the development of the theory of the structure of the atomic nucleus based on this connection.

1974: The prize was awarded jointly to Sir Martin Ryle and Antony Hewish (both UK) for their pioneering research in radio astrophysics: Ryle for his observations and inventions, in particular of the aperture synthesis technique, and Hewish for his decisive role in the discovery of pulsars.

1973: Half the prize was equally shared between Leo Esaki (Japan) and Ivar Giaever (USA) for their experimental discoveries regarding tunnelling phenomena in semiconductors and superconductors, respectively, and the other half was awarded to Brian D. Josephson (UK) for his theoretical predictions of the properties of a supercurrent through a tunnel barrier, in particular those phenomena that are generally known as the Josephson effects.

1972: The prize was awarded jointly to John Bardeen, Leon N. Cooper and J. Robert Schrieffer (all USA) for their jointly developed theory of superconductivity, usually called the BCS theory.

1971: Dennis Gabor (UK) for his invention and development of the holographic method.

1970: The prize was divided equally between Hannes Alfvén (Sweden) for fundamental work and discoveries in magneto-hydrodynamics with fruitful applications in different parts of plasma physics, and Louis Néel (France) for fundamental work and discoveries concerning antiferromagnetism and ferromagnetism, which have led to important applications in solid state physics.

1969: Murray Gell-Mann (USA) for his contributions and discoveries concerning the classification of elementary particles and their interactions.

1968: Luis W. Alvarez (USA) for his decisive contributions to elementary particle physics, in particular the discovery of a large number of resonance states, made possible through his development of the technique of using a hydrogen bubble chamber and data analysis.

1967: Hans Albrecht Bethe (USA) for his contributions to the theory of nuclear reactions, especially his discoveries concerning energy production in stars.

1966: Alfred Kastler (France) for the discovery and development of optical methods for studying hertzian resonances in atoms.

1965: The prize was awarded jointly to Sin-Itiro Tomonaga (Japan), Julian Schwinger and Richard P. Feynman (both USA) for their fundamental work in quantum electrodynamics, with far-reaching consequences for the physics of elementary particles.

1964: Half the prize was awarded to Charles H. Townes (USA) and the other half was awarded jointly to Nicolay Gennadiyevich Basov and Aleksandr Mikhailovich Prokhorov (both USSR) for fundamental work in the field of quantum electronics, which has led to the construction of oscillators and amplifiers based on the maser–laser principle.

1963: Half the prize was awarded to Eugene P. Wigner (USA) for his contributions to the theory of the atomic nucleus and the elementary particles, particularly through the discovery and application of fundamental symmetry principles, and the other half was awarded jointly to Maria Goeppert-Mayer (USA) and J. Hans D. Jensen (Germany) for their discoveries concerning nuclear shell structure.

1962: Lev Davidovich Landau (USSR) for his pioneering theories for condensed matter, especially liquid helium.

1961: The prize was divided equally between Robert Hofstadter (USA) for his pioneering studies of electron scattering in atomic nuclei and for his thereby achieved discoveries concerning the structure of the nucleons, and

Rudolf Ludwig Mössbauer (Germany) for his researches concerning the resonance absorption of gamma radiation and his discovery in this connection of the effect which bears his name.

1960: Donald A. Glaser (USA) for the invention of the bubble chamber.

1959: The prize was awarded jointly to Emilio Gino Segre and Owen Chamberlain (both USA) for their discovery of the antiproton.

1958: The prize was awarded jointly to Pavel Alekseyevich Cherenkov, Il'ja Mikhailovich Frank and Igor Yevgenyevich Tamm (all USSR) for the discovery and the interpretation of the Cherenkov effect.

1957: The prize was awarded jointly to Chen Ning Yang and Tsung-Dao Lee (both China) for their penetrating investigation of the so-called parity laws, which has led to important discoveries regarding the elementary particles.

1956: The prize was awarded jointly, one-third each, to William Shockley, John Bardeen and Walter Houser Brattain (all USA) for their researches on semiconductors and their discovery of the transistor effect.

1955: The prize was divided equally between Willis Eugene Lamb (USA) for his discoveries concerning the fine structure of the hydrogen spectrum and Polykarp Kusch (USA) for his precision determination of the magnetic moment of the electron.

1954: The prize was divided equally between Max Born (UK) for his fundamental research in quantum mechanics, especially for his statistical interpretation of the wavefunction, and Walther Bothe (Germany) for the coincidence method and his discoveries made using this method.

1953: Frits (Frederik) Zernike (Netherlands) for his demonstration of the phase contrast method, especially for his invention of the phase contrast microscope.

1952: The prize was awarded jointly to Felix Bloch and Edward Mills Purcell (both USA) for their development of new methods for nuclear magnetic precision measurements and discoveries made using these methods.

1951: The prize was awarded jointly to Sir John Douglas Cockcroft (UK) and Ernest Thomas Sinton Walton (Ireland) for their pioneering work on the transmutation of atomic nuclei by artificially accelerated atomic particles.

1950: Cecil Frank Powell (UK) for his development of the photographic method of studying nuclear processes and his discoveries regarding mesons made with this method.

1949: Hideki Yukawa (Japan) for his prediction of the existence of mesons on the basis of theoretical work on nuclear forces.

1948: Lord Patrick Maynard Stuart Blackett (UK) for his development of the Wilson cloud chamber method, and his discoveries using this method in the fields of nuclear physics and cosmic radiation.

1947: Sir Edward Victor Appleton (UK) for his investigations of the physics of the upper atmosphere, especially for the discovery of the so-called Appleton layer.

1946: Percy Williams Bridgman (USA) for the invention of an apparatus to produce extremely high pressures, and for the discoveries he made using this apparatus in the field of high-pressure physics.

1945: Wolfgang Pauli (Austria) for the discovery of the exclusion principle, also called the Pauli principle.

1944: Isidor Isaac Rabi (USA) for his resonance method for recording the magnetic properties of atomic nuclei.

1943: Otto Stern (USA) for his contribution to the development of the molecular ray method and his discovery of the magnetic moment of the proton.

1939: Ernest Orlando Lawrence (USA) for the invention and development of the cyclotron and for results obtained with it, especially with regard to artificial radioactive elements.

1938: Enrico Fermi (Italy) for his demonstrations of the existence of new radioactive elements produced by neutron irradiation, and for his related discovery of nuclear reactions brought about by slow neutrons.

1937: The prize was awarded jointly to Clinton Joseph Davisson (USA) and Sir George Paget Thomson (UK) for their experimental discovery of the diffraction of electrons by crystals.

1936: The prize was divided equally between Victor Franz Hess (Austria) for his discovery of cosmic radiation, and Carl David Anderson (USA) for his discovery of the positron.

1935: Sir James Chadwick (UK) for the discovery of the neutron.

1933: The prize was awarded jointly to Erwin Schrödinger (Austria) and Paul Adrien Maurice Dirac (UK) for the discovery of new productive forms of atomic theory.

1932: Werner Heisenberg (Germany) for the creation of quantum mechanics, the application of which has, among other things, led to the discovery of the allotropic forms of hydrogen.

1930: Sir Chandrasekhara Venkata Raman (India) for his work on the scattering of light and for the discovery of the effect named after him.

1929: Prince Louis-Victor de Broglie (France) for his discovery of the wave nature of electrons.

1928: Sir Owen Willans Richardson (UK) for his work on the thermionic phenomenon, and especially for the discovery of the law named after him.

1927: The prize was divided equally between Arthur H. Compton (USA) for his discovery of the effect named after him, and Charles Thomson Rees Wilson (USA) for his method of making the paths of electrically charged particles visible by condensation of vapour.

1926: Jean B. Perrin (France) for his work on the discontinuous structure of matter, and

especially for his discovery of sedimentation equilibrium.

1925: The prize was awarded jointly to James Franck and Gustav Hertz (Germany) for their discovery of the laws governing the impact of an electron upon an atom.

1924: Karl Manne Georg Siegbahn (Sweden) for his discoveries and research in the field of X-ray spectroscopy.

1923: Robert Andrews Millikan (USA) for his work on the elementary charge of electricity and on the photoelectric effect.

1922: Niels Bohr (Denmark) for his services in the investigation of the structure of atoms and of the radiation emanating from them.

1921: Albert Einstein (Germany) for his services to theoretical physics, and especially for his discovery of the law of the photoelectric effect.

1920: Charles Edouard Guillaume (Switzerland) in recognition of the service he has rendered to precision measurements in physics by his discovery of anomalies in nickel–steel alloys.

1919: Johannes Stark (Germany) for his discovery of the Doppler effect in canal rays and the splitting of spectral lines in electric fields.

1918: Max Karl Ernst Ludwig Planck (Germany) in recognition of the services he rendered to the advancement of physics by his discovery of energy quanta.

1917: Charles Glover Barkla (UK) for his discovery of the characteristic Röntgen radiation of the elements.

1915: The prize was awarded jointly to Sir William Henry Bragg and Sir William Lawrence Bragg (both UK) for their services in the analysis of crystal structure by means of X-rays.

1914: Max von Laue (Germany) for his discovery of the diffraction of X-rays by crystals.

1913: Heike Kamerlingh-Onnes (Netherlands) for his investigations on the properties of matter at low temperatures, which led, among other things, to the production of liquid helium.

1912: Nils Gustaf Dalén (Sweden) for his invention of automatic regulators for use in conjunction with gas accumulators for illuminating lighthouses and buoys.

1911: Wilhelm Wien (Germany) for his discoveries regarding the laws governing the radiation of heat.

1910: Johannes Diderik van der Waals (Netherlands) for his work on the equation of state for gases and liquids.

1909: The prize was awarded jointly to Guglielmo Marconi (Italy) and Carl Ferdinand Braun (Germany) in recognition of their contributions to the development of wireless telegraphy.

1908: Gabriel Lippmann (France) for his method of reproducing colours photographically based on the phenomenon of interference.

1907: Albert Abraham Michelson (USA) for his optical precision instruments and the spectroscopic and metrological investigations carried out with their aid.

1906: Sir Joseph John Thomson (UK) in recognition of the great merits of his

theoretical and experimental investigations on the conduction of electricity by gases.

1905: Philipp Eduard Anton Lenard (Netherlands) for his work on cathode rays.

1904: Lord John William Strutt Rayleigh (UK) for his investigations of the densities of the most important gases and for his discovery of argon in connection with these studies.

1903: Half the prize was awarded to A. Henri Becquerel (France) in recognition of the extraordinary services he has rendered by his discovery of spontaneous radioactivity, and the other half was awarded jointly to Pierre and Marie Curie (France) in recognition of the extraordinary services they rendered by their joint researches on the radiation phenomena discovered by Henri Becquerel.

1902: The prize was awarded jointly to Hendrik A. Lorentz and Pieter Zeeman (both Netherlands) in recognition of the extraordinary service they rendered by their researches into the influence of magnetism upon radiation phenomena.

1901: Wilhelm K. Röntgen (Germany) in recognition of the extraordinary services he rendered by the discovery of the remarkable rays subsequently named after him.

Answers to questions

1 Physics and physical measurement

Chapter 1.1
Many of the calculations in the problems of this chapter have been performed without a calculator and are estimates. Your answers may differ.

1 3.3×10^{-24} s.

2 3.6×10^{51}.

3 3.3×10^{60}.

4 6.4×10^{41}.

5 2.6×10^{9}.

6 2×10^{11}.

7 6.7×10^{11}.

8 1.0×10^{25}.

9 2.0×10^{27}.

10 3×10^{79}.

11 4×10^{17} kg m^{-3}.

12 8.3 min.

13 16 000 (assuming a 4000 kg elephant).

14 Assume a 200 m^2 house with 100 m^2 on each floor (10×10). Take the height of a floor to be 3 m. Divide each floor into four rooms. The wall area is thus $10 \times 3 \times 6 \times 2 = 360$ m^2. Subtract about 80 m^2 for windows and doors and we are left with 280 m^2 of wall area. Assuming a brick of size 20 cm $\times$ 5 cm, i.e. of area 10^{-2} m^2, gives as the number of bricks 2.8×10^4. No corridors etc. have been taken into account.

15 (a) 5.356×10^{-9} m; (b) 1.2×10^{-15} m; (c) 3.4×10^{-3} m.

16 (a) 4.834×10^{6} J; (b) 2.23×10^{-12} J; (c) 3.64×10^{11} J.

17 (a) 4.76×10^{-9} s; (b) 2.4×10^{-2} s; (c) 8.5×10^{-18} s.

18 1.792×10^{5} m s^{-1}.

19 (a) 4×10^{-19} J; (b) 54 eV.

20 2.2×10^{-5} m^3.

21 8.4×10^{-3} m.

22 32 ft/s^2.

25 (a) 200 g; (b) 2 kg; (c) 400 g.

26 100 000 years.

27 5×10^{9} kg m^{-3}.

28 About 0.7.

29 2×10^{28}.

30 2×10^{-7} N.

31 4×10^{42}.

33 (a) $\dfrac{243}{43} \approx \dfrac{250}{50} = 5$;

(b) $2.80 \times 1.90 \approx 3 \times 2 = 6$;

(c) $\dfrac{312 \times 480}{160} \approx \dfrac{3 \times 10^2 \times 5 \times 10^2}{1.5 \times 10^2}$

$\qquad = \dfrac{15}{1.5} \times 10^2 = 10^3$;

(d) $\dfrac{8.99 \times 10^9 \times 7 \times 10^{-6} \times 7 \times 10^{-6}}{(8 \times 10^2)^2}$

$\approx \dfrac{10 \times 10^9 \times 5 \times 10^{-6} \times 5 \times 10^{-6}}{64 \times 10^4}$

$\approx \dfrac{25 \times 10^{-2}}{64 \times 10^4} \approx 3 \times 10^{-7}$;

(e) $\dfrac{6.6 \times 10^{-11} \times 6 \times 10^{24}}{(6.4 \times 10^6)^2}$

$\approx \dfrac{7 \times 10^{-11} \times 6 \times 10^{24}}{(6 \times 10^6)^2}$

$\approx \dfrac{40 \times 10^{13}}{36 \times 10^{12}} \approx 10$.

Chapter 1.2
1 No.

2 Systematic.

3 The line of best fit intersects the vertical axis at about 4 mA, which is within the uncertainty in the current. A line within the error bars can certainly be made to pass through the origin.

4 The line of best fit intersects the vertical axis at about 10 mA, which is outside the uncertainty in current. A line within the error bars can be made to pass through the origin.

5 The line of best fit intersects at 12 mA. The extreme line within the error bars intersects at 6 mA. So no line can be made to go through the origin for this data. A systematic error of about 12 mA is required.

6 $2.4\,\mathrm{m\,s^{-2}}$; $3.1\,\mathrm{m\,s^{-1}}$.

Chapter 1.3

1 16 atm.
2 4.
3 By $\sqrt{2}$.
4 4 times as large.
5 (a) By 4; (b) increased by 2.
6 Increase by 9.
7 By $\sqrt{2}$.
8 Decreased by 16.
9 By a factor of 16.
10 2.83 yr.
11 (a) 1.00 m; (b) 0.714 Hz; (c) 0.30 m.
12 (a) $1/a$ against $1/b$; (b) intercept equals $1/f$.
13 (a) A straight line through the origin; (b) a straight line intersecting the temperature axis at -273.
14 $R^{3/2}$.
15 A straight line of slope ma.
16 (a) From the negative of the vertical intercept; (b) from the slope; (c) they are parallel.

Chapter 1.4

1 See Figure A1.

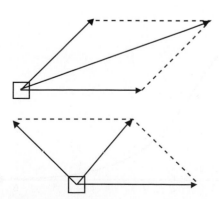

Figure A1.

3 (a) $\vec{A}+\vec{B}$: magnitude $= 18.2$, direction $= 49.7°$; (b) $\vec{A}-\vec{B}$: magnitude $= 9.2$, direction $= -11.8°$; (c) $\vec{A}-2\vec{B}$: magnitude $= 12.4$, direction $= -52.0°$.

4 7.79 km at 34.5°.

5 (a) 5.66 at 225°; (b) 200.8 at $-51.9°$; (c) 5 at $-90°$; (d) 8 at 0.0°.

6 (a) $\vec{A}$: magnitude 3.61, direction 56.31°;
   (b) $\vec{B}$: magnitude 5.39, direction 111.8°;
   (c) $\vec{A}+\vec{B}$: magnitude 8, direction 90°;
   (d) $\vec{A}-\vec{B}$: magnitude 4.47, direction $-26.57°$;
   (e) $2\vec{A}-\vec{B}$: magnitude 6.08, direction 9.46°.

7 $\vec{C}=(-4,1)$.

8 (2, 6).

9 Magnitude $14.1\,\mathrm{m\,s^{-1}}$, direction south-west (225°).

10 $\Delta p = 0.518\,p$.

11 (a) (x_2-x_1, y_2-y_1); (b) (x_1-x_2, y_1-y_2);
   (c) $\sqrt{x_1^2+y_1^2}$.

12 (a) $8\,\mathrm{m\,s^{-1}}$ at 0.0°; (b) $5.66\,\mathrm{m\,s^{-1}}$ at 135°;
   (c) $5.66\,\mathrm{m\,s^{-1}}$ at 45°. It is the sum of the answers to (a) and (b).

13 (a) $704\,\mathrm{m\,s^{-1}}$ in magnitude; (b) zero.

14 (a) $(-7.66, 6.43)$; (b) $(-8.19, -5.74)$; (c) $(3.75, -9.27)$; (d) $(7.43, -6.69)$; (e) $(-5.00, -8.66)$.

15 C has magnitude 6.00 and direction 270° to the positive x-axis.

16 (a) 25.1 N at 36.2° to the positive x-axis;
   (b) 22.7 N at 64.4° to the positive x-axis;
   (c) 25.0 N at direction 3.13° to the positive x-axis.

Chapter 1.5

1 Circle.
2 Sphere.
3 $\dfrac{x^2}{2}$.
4 (a) 54.6 V s; (b) 6.93 s; (c) $R = 2\,\mathrm{M\Omega}$.
5 $v = 0.2(1 - e^{-0.5t})$.
6 $\alpha = 3.4$.
7 $c = 2$.
8 Logarithm of y against x^2.
9 Sum $= 180 \pm 8$ N; difference $= 60 \pm 8$ N.
10 (a) 2.0 ± 0.3; (b) 85 ± 13; (c) 2 ± 2; (d) 100 ± 6; (e) 25 ± 7.5.
11 $F = 68 \pm 24$ N.
12 $(18.3 \pm 3.9) \times 10^3\,\mathrm{kg\,m^{-3}}$.

13 (a) 1.5 cm²; (b) 0.6 cm.
14 (a) 114 cm²; (b) 1295 cm³.
15 Area = 37 ± 3 cm²; perimeter = 26 ± 1 cm.
16 Increases by $\sqrt{2}$.
17 1%.
18 1.7%.

2 Mechanics

Chapter 2.1

1 166.7 m s⁻¹.
2 15 km h⁻¹.
3 (a) 1.67 km h⁻¹; (b) 1.20 km h⁻¹ at 33.7° south of east.
4 See Figure A2.

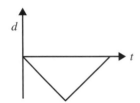

Figure A2.

5 (a) 88 m; (b) 68 m; (c) speed = 8.33 m s⁻¹; velocity = 5.0 m s⁻¹.
6 (a) 30 km; (b) 60 km.
7 (a) vt; (b) $d\sqrt{N}$.
8 (a) −130 km h⁻¹; (b) 130 km h⁻¹.
9 (a) −2 m s⁻¹; (b) −5 m s⁻¹.
10 8 m s⁻¹ to the right.
11 (a) 1.75 m s⁻¹; (b) −6.0 m s⁻¹.
12 (a) Speed = 4.0 m s⁻¹; (b) velocity = 0 m s⁻¹.

Chapter 2.2

1 3.0 m s⁻².
2 60 m s⁻¹.
3 4.0 s.
4 126 m.
5 −1.6 m s⁻².
6 8.0 s.
7 3.0 s.
8 278 m s⁻².
9 (a) 220 m; (b) 200 m; (c) 20 m; (d) less.
10 (a) 1.2 s; (b) 3.6 s; (c) 21.6 m; (d) 9.0 m s⁻¹; (e) 28.8 m.
11 (a) 4.32 s; (b) 33.2 m s⁻¹; (c) 60 m.

12 (a) 1.79 s; (b) 22.9 m s⁻¹.
13 0.324 s.
14 −15 m s⁻¹.
15 (a) 12.7 m s⁻¹; (b) 1.1.
16 25 m.
17 (a) 20 m s⁻¹.
18 2.0 m s⁻².
19 See Figure A3.

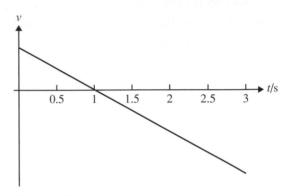

Figure A3.

20 See Figure A4.

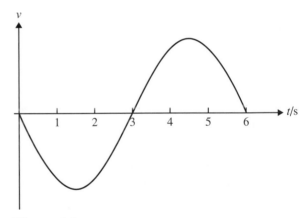

Figure A4.

21 See Figure A5.

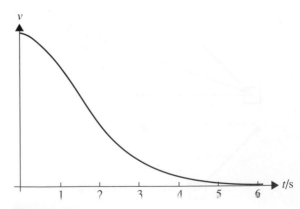

Figure A5.

22 See Figure A6.

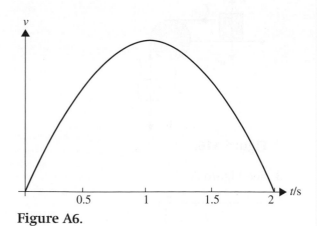

Figure A6.

23 See Figure A7.

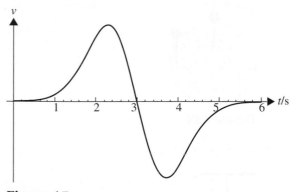

Figure A7.

24 See Figure A8.

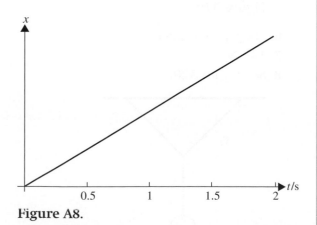

Figure A8.

25 See Figure A9.

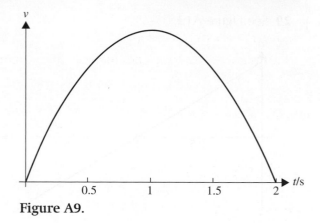

Figure A9.

26 See Figure A10.

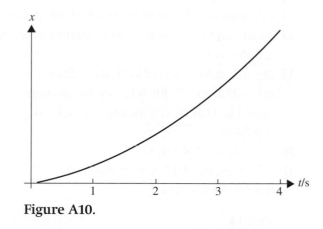

Figure A10.

27 See Figure A11.

Figure A11.

28 See Figure A12.

Figure A12.

29 See Figure A13.

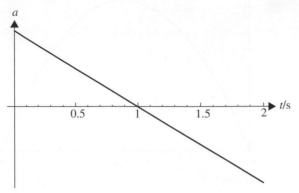

Figure A13.

30 5.8 s.
31 (a) Negative; (b) zero; (c) positive; (d) positive.
32 Make graphs of displacement against time; the graphs must cross.
35 (a) 3.2 m from top of cliff; (b) 3.56 s; (c) -27.6 m s^{-1}; (d) 41.4 m; (e) average speed = 11.6 m s^{-1}; average velocity = -9.83 m s^{-1}.
36 (a) 60 m; (b) 40 m s^{-1}.
37 (a) 70 m; (b) 10.7 s from the start.
  (c) See Figure A14.

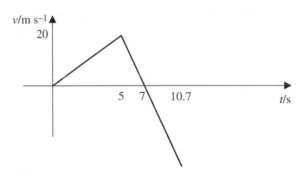

Figure A14.

38 (a) 115 m s^{-1}; (b) 660 m; (c) -60.5 m s^{-1}.

Chapter 2.3

1 See Figure A15.

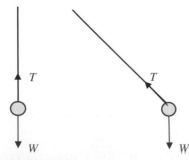

Figure A15.

2 See Figure A16.

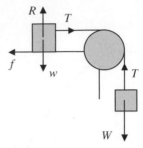

Figure A16.

3 See Figure A17.

Figure A17.

4 See Figure A18.

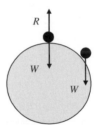

Figure A18.

5 See Figure A19.

Figure A19.

6 They are the same.
7 143 N.
8 See Figure A20.

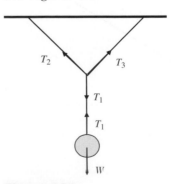

Figure A20.

9 See Figure A21.

Figure A21.

10 See Figure A22.

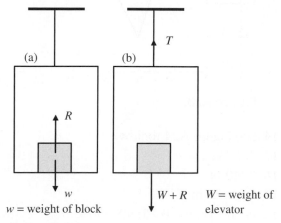

w = weight of block

$W + R$ W = weight of elevator

Figure A22.

Chapter 2.4

1 (a) 30 N to the right; (b) 6 N to the right;
   (c) 8 N to the left; (d) 15 N to the right;
   (e) 10 N down; (f) 20 N up.
2 28.28 N up.
3 7.57 N at 57.5°.
4 The weight cannot be balanced.
5 (a) Top; (b) bottom.
6 5.57 N at 162.12°.
7 4.89 N.
8 62.5 N.
9 1.2 kg.
10 $T_1 = 50$ N; $T_2 = 70.7$ N; $T_3 = 50$ N.
11 20.2 N and 47.1 N.
12 1343 N.
13 (a) 25 980 N; (b) 25 585 N.
14 $\sin\theta = \dfrac{m}{M}$.
15 $x = \dfrac{mg}{2k\cos\theta}$.

Chapter 2.5

1 (a) Decreasing mass; (b) increasing mass.
2 0.425 m s^{-2}.
3 1 m s^{-1}.
4 7 m s^{-2} and 3 m s^{-2}.

5 (a) mg; (b) mg; (c) $mg - ma$; (d) 0; the man is hit by the ceiling.
6 (a) mg; (b) mg; (c) greater than mg; (d) less than mg; (e) mg.
8 96 N.
10 210 N.
11 They experience the same force.
12 800 N.
13 Apart from weights and vertical reaction forces we have: 16 N left on the 2 kg as a reaction from the 3 kg mass; 16 N right on the 3 kg as a reaction from the 2 kg and 10 N left as a reaction from the 5 kg mass; 10 N right on the 5 kg as a reaction from the 3 kg mass.
14 100 N.
15 200 N.
16 On the 10 kg mass: weight 100 N down, reaction from bottom block 100 N up. On the 20 kg mass: weight 200 N down, reaction from top block of 100 N down and so reaction of 300 N up from table.
17 On the 10 kg mass: weight 100 N down, external force of 50 N down, reaction from bottom block 150 N up. On the 20 kg mass: weight 200 N down, reaction from top block of 150 N down and so reaction of 350 N up from table.
19 5 m s^{-2}.
20 (a) 15 N; (b) yes.
21 40 N.
22 3 m s^{-2}.
23 20 N; 2 m s^{-1}.
24 (a) 40 N (b) 56 N; (c) 60 N in (a) and 84 N in (b).

Chapter 2.6

1 6.00 N.
2 (a) -0.900 N s; (b) 7.20 N.
3 Zero.
4 7.00 m s^{-1}.
5 1.04 m.
6 (a) 1.41 N s down.
7 (a) -5.00 N s; (b) -25.0 N.
10 (a) Yes; (b) no.
11 (b) The order of magnitude is about 10^{-23} m.
12 (a) 96.0 N s; (b) 32.0 m s^{-1}; (c) -32.0 m s^{-1}.
13 50.0 kg.
14 7.0 m s^{-1} to the right.

15 0.46 m s^{-1} in the direction of the 1200 kg car.
16 5.05 N s at 56.3°.
17 A: 7.37 m s^{-1}; B: 6.80 m s^{-1}.
18 (a) 2 m s^{-1}.
19 (a) 50 kg; (b) 15 m s^{-2}; (c) 0.8 s; (d) 0.80 m (note that the net impulse is exactly 200 N s).
20 (b) 20.3 N.
22 (a) 2.5 m s^{-2}; (b) 12.5 m s^{-1}; (c) 1 m s^{-2}; (d) 18.8 m s^{-1}.
23 (a) 0.83 m s^{-1}.
24 (a) 1 m s; (b) about 50 N s; (c) about 50 N.

Chapter 2.7

1 1.2 × 10^2 J.
2 −7.7 J.
3 3.5 × 10^2 J.
4 (a) Work done by weight and reaction force is zero. Work done by F is 240.0 J and by friction is –168.0 J.
(c) The kinetic energy increases by 72.0 J.
5 (a) −1900 J; (b) +1900 J; (c) zero.
6 7.3 N.
7 0.16 J.
8 0.49 m s^{-1}.
9 (a) 8.94 m s^{-1}; 6.32 m s^{-1}; (b) 8.0 m s^{-1}; 10.2 m s^{-1}.
10 7.75 m s^{-1}; 11.8 m s^{-1}.

11 22 N.
12 2.45 m s^{-1}; 2.35 m s^{-1}.
13 (a) See Figure A23; (b) 58.0 J; (c) 7.62 m s^{-1}.

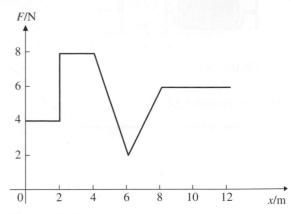

Figure A23.

14 See Figure A24 (below).
15 305 W.
16 3240 N.
17 (a) 0.21 m s^{-1}.
18 (a) 60 W; (b) 0.75; (c) 250 s.
19 $F \propto v^2$.
20 3750 N.
21 (a) The potential energy the mass has at the top is converted into kinetic energy. As the mass lands, all its potential energy has been converted to kinetic energy. (b) Some of the initial potential energy has been converted to

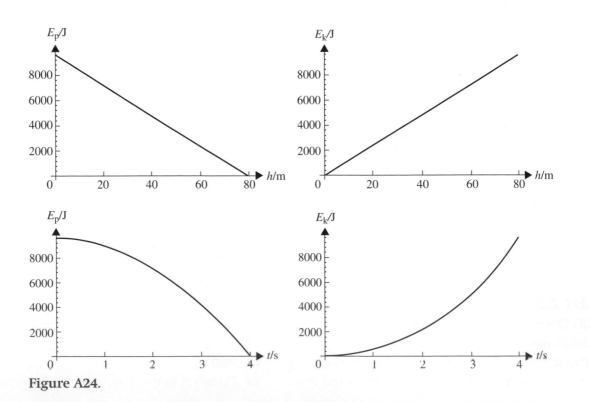

Figure A24.

kinetic energy. The kinetic energy remains constant during the fall. The remaining potential energy decreases as the mass falls and gets converted into thermal energy. As the mass lands, all the initial potential energy gets converted into thermal energy (and perhaps a bit of sound energy and deformation energy during impact with the ground). (c) The kinetic energy remains constant. The potential energy is increasing at a constant rate equal to the rate at which the pulling force does work.

23 (a) 2900 N; (b) 5.8 kW; (c) 500 N; (d) 2.0 kW; (e) 700 N.

24 27.4 J.

25 13.5 J.

26 (a) 2.42 m s^{-1}; (b) 93%.

27 5.77 m s^{-1}.

28 See Figure A25.

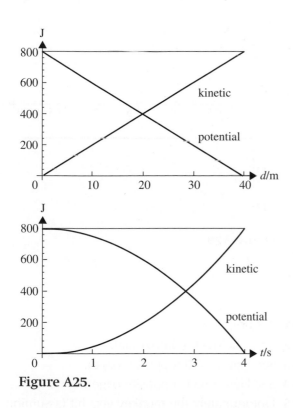

Figure A25.

30 Light to heavy = 2.

31 (a) $T = mg \sin \theta$; (b) $W = mgd \sin \theta$; (c) $W = -mgd \sin \theta$; (d) zero; (e) zero.

32 30.7 N.

33 (a) 1.36 m s^{-2}; 0.51 m s^{-2}. (c) The ratio of the accelerations is the ratio of the forces (i.e. 2.67). The ratio of the average speeds

when squared becomes 2.62. This suggests that the force is proportional to speed squared; (d) 218 m; 135 m; (e) 3.8×10^5 J; 8.5×10^4 J.

34 (a) 200 N m^{-1}.

35 (a) 15.5 m s^{-1}; (b) 16.4 m s^{-1}; (d) See Figure A26.

Figure A26.

36 (b) 38 400 N on both; (c) 4800 N s; (d) the force would be larger but the impulse would be the same; (e) 4000 J; the final kinetic energy is 10 000 J.

38 The 8.0 kg mass moves at 5.45 m s^{-1}; other rebounds at 4.55 m s^{-1}.

39 The 6.0 kg ball moves at 4 m s^{-1} and the 4.0 kg ball rebounds at 1 m s^{-1}. Collisions take place at the vertices of a regular pentagon inscribed in the circle; the initial position of the 6.0 kg mass is a vertex of this pentagon.

40 (a) $\dfrac{v^2}{2g}$; (b) $\dfrac{v^2}{2g} \dfrac{M}{m + M}$.

41 (a) 50 m; (b) 90 m; (c) 15 s from start; (d) See Figure A27. (e) See Figure A28 (next page). (f) from 5 s on; (g) 22.5 W; (h) 45 W.

Figure A27.

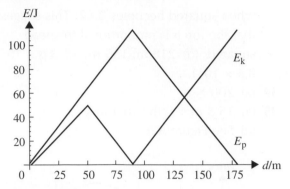

Figure A28.

Chapter 2.8

1 (a) 7.20 m s^{-2} north-west; (b) 8.0 m s^{-2}.
2 (a) 10 N; (b) 2.83 m s^{-1}; (c) 0.80 m.
3 21.4 rpm.
5 (a) 29.9 km s^{-1}; (b) 5.95 × 10^{-3} m s^{-2};
(c) 3.56 × 10^{22} N.
6 (a) 5.07 s^{-1}; (b) 0.81 Hz.
7 1.18 × 10^3 m s^{-2}.
8 84.49 min.
9 (a) 30 m s^{-1}; (b) 13.42 m s^{-1}.
10 3.6 × 10^{22} N.
11 0.02169 m s^{-2}, 0.097°.
12 $v = \sqrt{\dfrac{Mgr}{m}}$.
13 (a) 594 N; 523 N; (b) 3.16 m s^{-1}; (c) 23.7°.
14 A: 5 m s^{-2} at 278.13°; B: 5 m s^{-2} at 261.87°.
15 (a) 48.99 m s^{-1}; (b) 1800 N; (c) 30 m s^{-2}.
16 (a) 6.32 m s^{-1}; (b) 20 m s^{-2}; (d) 150 N.
17 3.2 × 10^9 m s^{-2}.
18 About 12.
19 48.2°.

Chapter 2.9

1 (a) 5.0 cm; (b) 200 m s^{-1}.
2 1.02 m.
3 (a) 0.77 s; (b) 9.22 m s^{-1}.
4 (a) 2.0 s; (b) 12.8 m s^{-1}; (c) −51.3°;
(d) 21.5 m s^{-1} at −68.2°.
5 1.48 m.
6 5.66 m s^{-1}.
7 316.2 m.
8 $L/2$.
9 7.59 m.
10 See Figure A29.

(a)

(b)

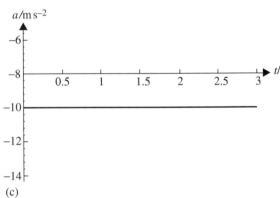

(c)

Figure A29.

11 0.33 m.
12 53.2° below the horizontal.
13 See Figure A30 (opposite page).
14 See Figure A31 (opposite page).
15 Unfortunately the monkey gets hit (assuming the bullet can get that far).
16 (a) 10 m s^{-1}; (b) the weight, vertically down.
(c) See Figure A32 (opposite page).
17 (a) $v_x = 30$ m s^{-1}, $v_y = 20$ m s^{-1}; (b) 34°;
(c) $g = 20$ m s^{-2}; (d) horizontal arrow for velocity, vertical for weight; (e) range and maximum height half as large, as shown in Figure A33 (opposite page).

(a)

(b)

Figure A30.

(a)

(b)

Figure A31.

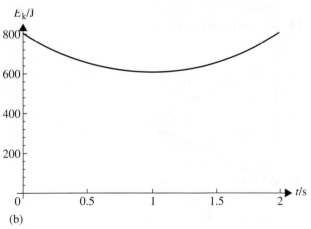

18 18.27 m s⁻¹ at 57.99°.

19 40.0 m s⁻¹.

21 0.45 m.

22 36° at 34 m s⁻¹.

Chapter 2.10

1 (a) 1.99×10^{20} N; (b) 4.17×10^{23} N;
(c) 1.0×10^{-47} N.

Figure A32.

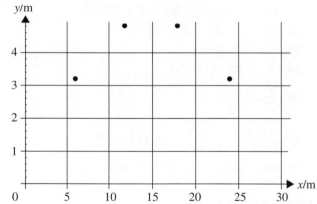

Figure A33.

2 (a) Zero; (b) zero; (c) $\dfrac{Gm^2}{4R^2}$; (d) $\dfrac{Gm(m+M)}{4R^2}$.

3 1/81.

4 1/2.

5 3.

6 Twice as large.

9 7.61 km s⁻¹; 94.6 min.

10 About 35 870 km (i.e. about 42 250 km from the earth's centre).

11 0.9.

12 (a) -7.63×10^{28} J; (b) -1.04×10^6 J kg^{-1};
(c) 1019 m s^{-1}.

13 See Figure A34.

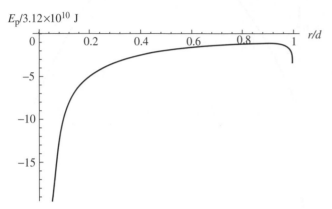

Figure A34.

14 (a) -1.25×10^7 J kg^{-1}; (b) -6.25×10^9 J.

15 P: $g = 0$; Q: $g = 1.41 \times 10^{-6}$ N kg^{-1}.

16 To the left.

17 Orbit 1 is not possible, orbit 2 is.

18 The normal reaction force from the spacecraft floor is zero.

20 The work required to move the mass on which the force is acting from $r = a$ to $r = b$.

21 (a) 1.5×10^{28} kg; (c) 3.2×10^6 m s^{-1};
(d) 6.0×10^{15} J; (e) 2.4×10^6 m s^{-1}.

22 (a) $9 : 1$; (b) 3.6×10^6 m s^{-1}.

23 -5.29×10^{33} J.

24 (a) B; (b) A; (c) A.

26 $\dfrac{5R}{2}$.

27 $\sqrt{\dfrac{GM}{R}} - \sqrt{\dfrac{GM}{2R}} = 2.32$ km s^{-1}.

28 Run them backwards to slow down.

Chapter 2.11

1 $d = \dfrac{2\mu L}{\sqrt{1 + \mu^2}}$.

2 (a) Just over 45 N; (b) 1.5 m s^{-2}.

3 $a = g/\mu$.

4 Between 10.95 m s^{-1} and 18.26 m s^{-1}.

5 (a) 29.1 m s^{-1}; (b) 31.9 m s^{-1}.

6 (b) 0.18.

7 (a) 3.0 m s^{-2} for both; (b) 3.0 m s^{-2} for top;
5.0 m s^{-2} for bottom.

8 (a) 18 N; (b) 81 N.

9 (a)

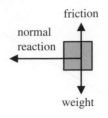

(b) $N = \sqrt{\dfrac{g}{4\pi^2 r \mu}}$.

Chapter 2.12

1 (a) 30 N m; (b) 23.0 N m; (c) 26.0 N m.

2 $\tau_1 = 0$; $\tau_2 = 106$ N m counter-clockwise;
$\tau_3 = 75$ N m counter-clockwise; $\tau_4 = 0$;
$\tau_5 = 150$ N m, clockwise.

3 (a) $T \times (L \sin \theta)$; (b) $(T \sin \theta) \times L$.

4 (a) $T = 1000$ N; (b) $R = 866$ N.

5 (a) $T = 1200$ N; (b) $R = 1044$ N at 5.50° to the horizontal.

6 (a) $3L/4$; (b) four books.

7 (a) $W = 45$ N; (b) $F = 36$ N.

8 39.8°.

9 Reaction from floor = 100 N; friction = 37.5 N; reaction from vertical wall = 37.5 N.

10 Reaction from floor = 750 N; friction = 330 N; reaction from vertical wall = 330 N; coefficient of friction = 0.44.

11 (a) see Figure A35.

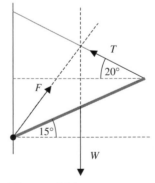

Figure A35.

(b) 126 N; (c) 160 N; (d) 42° to the horizontal.

3 Thermal physics

Chapter 3.1

3 (a) No; (b) 300 K; (c) 4×10^6 J.

4 (a) 3.72×10^{-26} m^3; (b) 3.04×10^{-29} m^3;
(c) 1124.

5 (a) 4.49×10^{-26} kg; (b) 6.02×10^{28} m^{-3}.

× 10²² ; (c) 0.07 m³.

× 10²⁴ ; (c) 358.5 K.

...nol.

² ; (c) 0.87 g.

m⁻³ ; (c) 1.43 kg m⁻³.

⁶ m³ ; water: 2.99 ×

× 10⁻²⁹ m³ ;

× 10⁻¹⁰ m;

f 2.

gas.

K.

00 K; (c) 3.6 × 10⁶ J;

× 10⁵ Pa; (c) 2493 J;

temperatures by the same
easing the cold reservoir

J.

W; (c) 7.6 min.

00 W; (c) 3.

Page 1 of 1

Reminder:
Caltech Alumni Opera In The Park

Date: Tuesday, August 22

Time: 6:30 pm (performance begins at 8:00 pm)

Join Caltech alumni and friends to meet Caltech's incoming students from the Tri-State area. The group will meet on the Great Lawn at 6:30 pm, followed by a performance by the Metropolitan Opera at 8:00 pm.

Bring a blanket to sit on and share. You may also want to bring a jacket or sweater as it gets cool in the evening.

We will provide:
- Food and drink
- Candles
- Insect repellent
- Plastic lining for under blankets

Contact Sonny Arcilla '95 at Sonny_Arcilla@ML.com or 201/723-6363 to RSVP and get information on the meeting place.

Directions to the Great Lawn:
The Great Lawn is located mid-park from 79th to 85th Street. The band shell is located in the northern portion of Great Lawn.

Take the 4/5/6 to 86th Street. Walk West 3 blocks to 5th Avenue and enter the park at the entrance between 85th/86th Streets.

Figure A36.

9 (a) At B, 1200 K; at C, 600 K; at D, 150 K;
(b) At B.

10 10 atm.

Figure A37.

(b) 750 K; (c) +911.7 J (for both);
(d) (i) −607.8 J; (ii) −911.7 J; (iii) 1519.5 J out.

4 Waves

Chapter 4.1

3 (a) 1.29 m; (b) 1.32×10^{-2} m.

5 25.3 m s^{-1}.

6 (a) $\lambda = 3.33$ m; (b) the same.

7 (a) $v = 3.0$ m s^{-1}; (b) $T = 1.5$ s;
   $f = 0.667$ Hz; (c) $\lambda = 4.5$ m; $A = 12$ cm.

8 (a) $\lambda = 0.66$ m; (b) $\lambda = 2.98$ m.

9 3.16 m s^{-1}.

11 $d = 2400$ m; $\lambda = 0.050$ m; number of waves
   = 30.

12 From left to right: down, down, up.

13 From left to right: up, up, down.

14 See Figure A38.

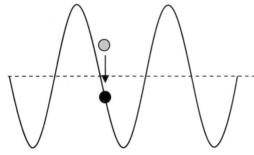

Figure A38.

15 (a) 0.6 cm; (b) 4.0 m; (c) 5.0 m s^{-1}
   (d) 1.25 Hz; (e) no.

16 See Figure A39.

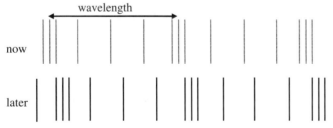

Figure A39.

17 See Figure A40.

Figure A40.

Chapter 4.2

1 See Figure A41.

Figure A41.

2 See Figure A42.

Figure A42.

3 See Figure A43.

4 See Figure A44.

5 (a) 22.89°; (b) 1.895×10^8 m s^{-1};
   (c) 4.3×10^{-7} m.

6 (a) 1.0×10^{-8} s; (b) 6×10^6.

7 1.06 cm.

8 See Figure A45.

10 13.1°.

11 See Figure A46.

Figure A43.

Figure A44.

Figure A45.

Figure A46.

Chapter 4.3

1 See Figure 3.2 in text.
2 See Figure 3.1 in text.
3 Reflection and diffraction of sound. Absence of these for light. By using a mirror at the corner.
4 8.0 m.
5 400 m.
6 0.83 m.
7 (a) The path difference is two wavelengths, so the observer hears a loud sound because of constructive interference. (b) The path difference is one and a half wavelengths, so the observer hears no sound because of destructive interference.
8 See Figure 3.10 in text.
9 See Figure 3.12 in text.
10 The car receives a higher frequency because it is approaching. The car now acts as a source. Since the source is approaching, the frequency received will be *even* higher.
11 It is approaching.

Chapter 4.4

1 $n = 3$.
2 0.33 m.
3 8.5 mm.
8 (a) 3.86 mm in air; (b) 2.91 mm in water.
9 105 m.
10 (a) 2.143 km; (b) 114.3 km.
11 $d = 2.92\lambda$
12 See Figure A47.

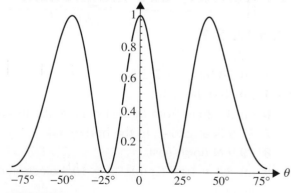

Figure A47.

Chapter 4.5

2 566 Hz.
3 439 Hz.
4 497 Hz.
5 674 Hz.

6 7 m s^{-1}.

7 4.1 m s^{-1}.

8 489.3 to 511.2 Hz.

Chapter 4.6

7 354 Hz.

8 0.500.

9 548 Hz.

10 (a) 225 Hz; (b) 1.47 m.

12 0.81 m; 1.35 m.

13 (a) 321.1 m s^{-1}; (b) 1.4 cm.

14 (a) 2.75 m; (b) $n = 5$ and $n = 6$.

15 (a) 122.5 Hz; (b) 12.25 m.

Chapter 4.7

1 453 Hz and 447 Hz.

2 1.935 s or 2.069 s.

3 See Figure A48.

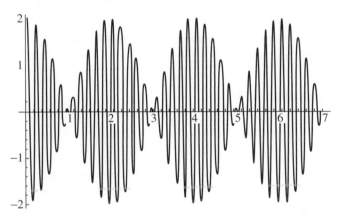

Figure A48.

5 Electricity and magnetism

Chapter 5.1

3 −2 C.

4 (a) 28.8 N; (b) 7.2 N.

5 90 N to the right.

6 (a) 3.22 cm from the left charge; (b) unstable.

7 77.9 N at 228.3° to the horizontal.

8 29.9 N north-east.

9 (a) 8.1×10^{-9} C; (b) 5.1×10^{10} electronic charges.

11 (a) 2×10^{28}; (b) 10^{27} N. (c) One assumption is the number of electrons through the assumption of water as the material of the body, but a more significant assumption is the use of Coulomb's law for bodies which are fairly close to each other and are not point charges. (d) The net charge of a person is zero because of the protons that have been neglected in this estimate. This leads to zero force.

Chapter 5.2

4 (a) 8.0×10^{-16} N; (b) 8.0×10^{-16} N; (c) 8.0×10^{-16} N; (d) 4.8×10^{-17} J.

5 1.60×10^{-17} N left; 1.76×10^{13} m s^{-2}.

6 6.0 N C^{-1}.

7 3.84×10^5 N C^{-1} to the right.

8 5.77×10^5 N C^{-1} at 3.2° below the horizontal.

9 (a) 500 J; (b) 1000 J; (c) 500 J.

10 (a) 5.93×10^6 m s^{-1}; (b) 1.38×10^5 m s^{-1}.

11 170 N C^{-1} at 137.4° to the horizontal for each.

12 (a) Zero; (b) zero; (c) 1.60×10^6 N C^{-1}; (d) 9.0×10^5 N C^{-1}.

Chapter 5.3

2 (a) 2.55×10^6 V; (b) $E = 0$.

3 (a) $\frac{4Q}{4\pi\varepsilon_0 d}$; (b) zero.

4 −15 kV.

5 3.6×10^7 J.

6 1.44×10^{-7} J.

7 5.93×10^6 m s^{-1}.

8 (a) 11.8 N at 75.4° below the horizontal; (b) 5.1×10^5 V; (c) 5.1×10^{-4} J.

9 (a) 3.875×10^{-11} m; (b) zero; (c) 1.24×10^{-23} N m.

10 (a) 0.8 μC (small sphere) and 1.2 μC; (b) 6.37×10^{-6} C m^{-2} (small sphere) and 4.24×10^{-6} C m^{-2}; (c) 7.2×10^5 N C^{-1} (small sphere) and 4.8×10^5 N C^{-1}.

12 (a) 0.30×10^{-3} J; (b) -0.30×10^{-3} J; (c) -0.60×10^{-3} J.

13 (a) 7.19 V; (b) 1.6×10^{-19} C.

14 (a) $\frac{2Qa}{4\pi\varepsilon_0(d^2+a^2)^{3/2}}$ vertically down; (b) $\frac{2Qd}{4\pi\varepsilon_0(d^2+a^2)^{3/2}}$ horizontally to the left.

15 $\frac{8Q}{36\pi\varepsilon_0 d^2}$ up.

16 (d) $\frac{q^2}{16\pi\varepsilon_0 r}$.

Chapter 5.4

5 Decreases by a factor of 4.

6 5.9×10^{28} m^{-3}.

7 4.29×10^{-5} m s^{-1}.

8 (a) 3.6×10^4 C; (b) 2.25×10^{23} electrons.

9 (a) Yes.

10 14 V.

11 No.

12 12 Ω.

13 14.7 Ω.

14 40 Ω.

15 (a) 8 V for the 4 Ω resistor and 12 V for the
6 Ω resistor; (b) 16 V; 16 V; 4 V.

16 (a) See Figure A49.

(b) 8.5 V

Figure A49.

17 (a) 0.27 A; (b) 0.136 A, (c) 15 W.

18 (a) 403.3 Ω, (b) 57 cm.

19 (a) 0.1 kW h; (b) 3.6×10^5 J.

20 Cost is the same.

Chapter 5.5

1 2.67 Ω; 12.4 Ω; 1.0 Ω.

2 38.75 Ω.

3 4.0 Ω.

4 0.01 Ω, 100 Ω.

5 $R/4$.

6 See Figure A50.

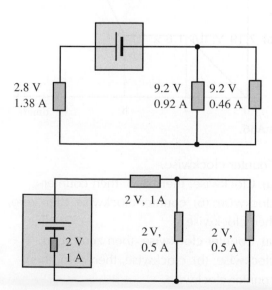

Figure A50.

7 2.0 Ω.

8 The same.

9 (a) 5.45 A and 2.27 A; (b) 1.7 kW h.

10 See Figure A51.

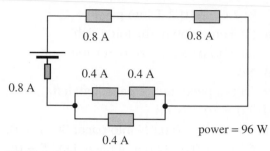

Figure A51.

11 (a) 9.09 A; (b) 24.2 Ω; (c) 315 s; (d) $0.0175.

12 (a) 0.14 A and 0.17 A; (b) Costs more at
220 V by a factor of 4.

13 No.

14 No.

15 (a) 30 kΩ; (b) 0.20 mA.

16 The power in the lamp will increase by a
factor of 2.4.

17 (a) 4.4 kW; (b) 19 min.

18 6.48 V.

19 18.5 W; 14.8 W.

20 293.

21 (a) 4 V; (b) 40 mA; (c) 6 V, 30 mA.

22 5.0 A.

23 (a) 15.94 W; (b) 598 J.

24 (a) A and B are the same, C is brighter by a
factor of 4; (b) the same; (c) A goes out, C
stays the same.

25 (a) 0.5 V (3 kΩ), 1.0 V; (b) 0.25 V.

26 See Figure A52.

Figure A52.

27 $R\left(1 + \sqrt{3}\right)$.

28 6.0 A.

Chapter 5.6

2 (a) *B* into page; (b) *F* into page; (c) *B* out of page; (d) force zero; (e) force zero.

3 5.4×10^{-6} T into page.

4 P: 3.75×10^{-4} T out of page; Q: zero; R: 2.67×10^{-4} T into page.

6 (a) Force down; (b) force right.

7 (a) Into page; (b) zero; (c) force up.

8 No.

9 Out of page; out of page; left; left.

10 3.0×10^{-7} N up.

11 (a) AB: $F = 0.02$ N into page; BC: $F = 0$; CD: $F = 0.02$ N out of page; DA: $F = 0$; (b) net force = 0.

12 27.1 m.

13 P: out of page; Q: into page.

14 (a) 8.0 cm from 2 A wire, in between wires; (b) 40.0 cm above 2 A wire.

15 (a) 0.012 T into page; (b) yes; (c) no.

16 (a) No; (b) yes, it will rotate counter-clockwise.

17 2.25 N.

18 Will attract.

19 See Figure A53.

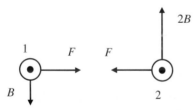

Figure A53.

20 $f = \frac{eB}{2\pi m}$.

21 (b) 2.71 cm; (c) 7.62×10^{6} per second; (d) 7.5×10^{5} m s^{-1}; (e) 0.098 m.

22 5.96×10^{-12} s.

23 2.67μT up.

24 2.86×10^{-5} T at 2.8° to the horizontal.

25 28.28μN m^{-1} at 225° with the positive *x* axis.

26 $B = \frac{\mu_0 ev}{(2\pi r)^2}$

28 (a) $B = \frac{\mu_0 I}{2\pi} \left(\frac{1}{r+d/2} + \frac{1}{r-d/2} \right)$;
(b) $B = \frac{\mu_0 I}{2\pi} \left(\frac{1}{r-d/2} - \frac{1}{r+d/2} \right)$.

29 (d) 1.40×10^{10} per second; (e) 3.84×10^{-12} J.

30 0.05 N m^{-1}, left.

31 (a) Out of paper; (b) left.

Chapter 5.7

1 See Figure A54.

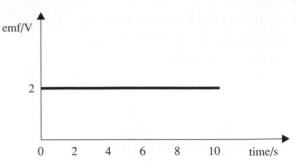

Figure A54.

2 See Figure A55.

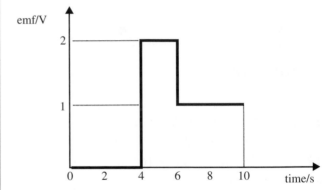

Figure A55.

3 (a) See Figure A56.

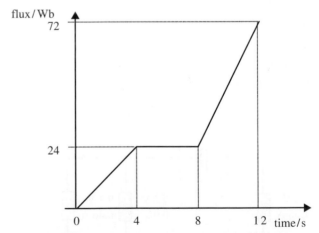

Figure A56.

4 Counter-clockwise.

5 (a) Clockwise, then zero, then counter-clockwise; (b) counter-clockwise, then zero, then clockwise.

6 (a) Counter-clockwise, then zero, then clockwise; (b) clockwise, then zero, then counter-clockwise.

7 (a) Force is upward; (b) force is upward.

8 Right end is positive.

9 (a) Clockwise; (b) counter-clockwise.

10 0.0592 V.

12 It will move to the right.

13 Part A: (a) flux = $BA\cos\theta$; (b) emf = $BLv\cos\theta$; (c) counter-clockwise as we look down on the loop from above; (d) $F = \frac{B^2L^2v\cos\theta}{R}$, horizontal to the right; (e) $v_T = \frac{mgR\sin\theta}{B^2L^2\cos^2\theta}$.

Part B: the dependence of velocity on time is $v = \frac{mgR\sin\theta}{B^2L^2\cos^2\theta}[1 - \exp(-\frac{B^2L^2\cos^2\theta}{mR} t)]$. As time gets large the velocity approaches the value found in (e).

14 (a) Clockwise, $I = Bav/R$ where v is the speed of the loop; (b) acceleration $= g - B^2a^2v/(mR)$.

15 (a) Points on the rim; (c) clockwise looking at the diagram.

Chapter 5.8

1 (a) 88 V; 50 Hz; (b) 10.5 A.

2 (a) 23.4%; (b) 15%.

3 0.0825 T.

4 4.9×10^4 V.

5 (a) 30%; (b) 1.2%.

7 (a) 2 A; (b) 5 V; (c) 1 s; (d) see Figure A57.

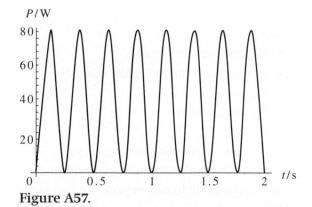

Figure A57.

8 (b) The graph for flux is the same as Figure 8.12 in the text. (a) and (c) The emf has double the amplitude at the high speed but the dependence on angle is otherwise the same. See Figure A58. Note that no numbers have been put on the emf axis as we do not know the rate of rotation.

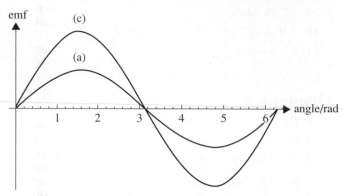

Figure A58.

6 Atomic and nuclear physics

Chapter 6.1

1 (a) 2.29×10^{17} kg m^{-3}; (b) 2.9×10^{13} times larger; (c) 14.3 km.

6 0; 2; 20; 128.

7 $2|e|$.

12 $\frac{F_e}{F_g} = 4 \times 10^{42}$.

Chapter 6.2

1 Plot d against $\frac{1}{\sqrt{c}}$.

2 Plot ln I against x.

3 0.5 mg.

4 8 h.

5 $^4_2$He.

7 3.6×10^3 (alpha to electron).

8 $^3_1$H $\rightarrow$ $^0_{-1}$e $+ \bar{\nu}_e + ^3_2$He.

9 $^{14}_6$C $\rightarrow$ $^0_{-1}$e $+ \bar{\nu}_e + ^{14}_7$N.

10 $^{210}_{83}$Bi $\rightarrow$ $^0_{-1}$e $+ \bar{\nu}_e + ^0_0\gamma + ^{210}_{84}$Po.

11 $^{239}_{94}$Pu $\rightarrow$ $^4_2\alpha + ^{235}_{92}$U.

12 ^A_ZX $\rightarrow$ 2^0_{-1}e $+ ^4_2\alpha + ^{A-4}_{Z}$X.

13 $^{22}_{11}$Na $\rightarrow$ $^0_{+1}$e $+ \nu_e + ^{22}_{10}$Ne.

15 2.88 MeV.

Chapter 6.3

1 545.3 MeV; 8.79 MeV.

2 8.029 MeV; 12.37 MeV.

3 0.783 MeV.

4 (a) 2.44×10^{-11} m; (b) gamma ray.

5 3.65 MeV.

6 (c) 179.4 MeV.

7 (a) Seven electrons; (b) 207.8 MeV.

8 183.8 MeV.

9 17.59 MeV.

10 8.9×10^9 yr.

11 17.5 MeV.

Chapter 6.4

1 (b) 7.24×10^{14} Hz.

2 (b) 0.671 V.

3 (b) 1.6×10^{-4} A; (c) 0.20 eV; (d) 2.1 eV;
(e) 3.2×10^{-4} A.

4 (b) 2.7×10^{-7} m.

5 (b) 3.90 eV.

6 (a) 16 min.

7 (a) 5.0×10^{14} Hz; (b) 2.08 eV; (c) 1.25 eV;
(d) the graph is parallel to the original graph.

8 (a) 2.65×10^{-34} m.

9 (b) 1071 m s^{-1}.

10 $E_k = \frac{h^2}{8mL^2} n^2$.

Chapter 6.5

3 11.5 eV or 1.3 eV.

4 (b) (i) No excitation; (ii) 4; (iii) 6.

5 (b) 4.37×10^5 m s^{-1}.

6 (b) 4.88×10^{-7} m.

7 8.2×10^{14} s^{-1}.

8 (b) 1.51 eV.

9 (b) $n = 4$.

10 (a) 9.14×10^{-8} m; (b) 2.19×10^6 m s^{-1}.

12 1.05×10^5 K.

13 (b) 7.29×10^5 m s^{-1}; (c) 6.58×10^{-7} m;
(d) optical.

14 (a) 2.03×10^{-15} m; (b) 6.66×10^{-10} m.

15 (b) 1.86×10^{-11} m.

16 (b) 1.0×10^8 m s^{-1}; (c) 7.2×10^{18} Hz.

18 (a) 1.11×10^{-11} m; (b) 796 W.

Chapter 6.6

1 6.6×10^7 m s^{-1}.

2 See Figure A59 (next column).

3 (a) 3.0×10^4 N C^{-1}; (b) 0.083 m;
(c) 0.091 m.

6 (a) 0.231 s^{-1}; (b) (i) 4.78×10^{21};
(ii) 3.79×10^{21}; (iii) 3.01×10^{21}.

7 (a) 0.5; (b) 0.875; (c) 0.5.

8 3.66×10^{10} Bq.

9 1.10×10^6 Bq.

10 4.20×10^{11}.

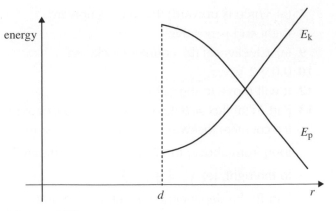

Figure A59.

11 3.8×10^9 yr.

12 4.11×10^9 yr.

13 (b) About 7.2 min.

14 (a) 0.75; (b) 0.95; (c) 1.50.

18 (a) 1.5×10^{-15} m; (b) 4000 N; (c) 230.4 N;
(d) 1.86×10^{-34} N; (e) 1.24×10^{36}.

20 (a) $^{226}_{88}\text{Ra} \rightarrow {}^{226}_{88}\text{Ra} + {}^{0}_{0}\gamma$; (b) 1.83×10^{-11} m.

Chapter 6.7

1 (a) 1.04×10^{-12} m; (b) 0.689 MeV.

2 1707 MeV.

3 $\overline{u}\,\overline{d}\,\overline{d}$.

5 $\overline{u}$ s.

6 No.

7 $|e|$.

8 Zero.

9 Electron lepton number.

10 Electron and muon lepton numbers.

11 Electric charge.

12 Baryon number.

13 Energy.

14 Baryon number and electric charge.

15 None, it would violate baryon number.

16 No, the particle is a meson.

17 -1.

18 A photon.

19 A d quark turns into a u quark.

22 Yes in both cases. The particles contain quarks.

23 (a) Yes; (b) no.

24 Yes, since it consists of electrically charged quarks.

25 They have opposite lepton numbers.

Option C: Energy

Chapter C1

1 (a) 5×10^8 J; (b) 138.9 kW h;
(c) 0139 MW h; (d) 1.576 × 10^{16} J;
(e) 4.38×10^9 kW h; (f) 4.38×10^6 MW h.

2 2.50%.

3 12.24 m².

4 6.53 m².

5 6.6×10^6 kg.

6 (a) 926 MW; (b) 1389 MW;
(c) 6.6×10^4 kg s⁻¹.

8 3.6×10^{11} J.

9 200 kW.

10 (a) 126.5 MeV; (b) 1.73×10^6 kg.

11 (a) 3.76×10^{19} nuclei per second;
(b) 14.7 mg s⁻¹.

15 (a) 14.4 kg; (b) 30.7 °C; (c) 425 kJ K⁻¹;
(e) 0.75×10^{-3} K s⁻¹; (f) 237 min.

Option D: Biomedical physics

Chapter D1

1 86.8 g.

2 2.04.

3 (a) 3.375; (b) 2.25; (c) 1.5.

4 L^{-1}.

6 2.828.

7 L^{-1}.

10 L.

Chapter D2

1 3.14×10^3 W.

2 79.77 dB.

3 74 dB.

4 31.6.

5 10.

6 3.16×10^{-5} W⁻².

7 1.58×10^{-10} W⁻².

Chapter D3

1 (a) 4 mm and 6 mm; (b) the one with
HVT = 6 mm has the larger energy.

2 (a) 0.139 mm⁻¹; (b) 11.5 mm.

3 12.6 mm.

4 0.794.

5 1.40.

6 (a) 1.12 kW m⁻²; (b) 0.396 kW m⁻².

7 5350 cm³.

8 0.31 mm.

Chapter D4

1 (a) 595 N; (b) 589 N at 8.9°.

2 297 N.

3 229 N.

4 Reaction from floor = 300 N; bone reaction
= 1071 N; tendon = 771 N.

5 (a) 2164 N; (b) 2117 N horizontal.

6 420 N (at head); 280 N (at feet).

7 Muscle force = 265 N; reaction = 522 N.

8 (a) 131 N; (b) 244 N; (c) 79.5° to the
horizontal.

9 (a) 4924 N; (b) 5112 N; (c) 1.58° below the
spine.

10 (a) 286 N (hands); (b) 414 N (feet).

11 35.6 L h⁻¹.

12 14.5 h.

14 (a) 87.16 W; (b) 450 W; (c) 2.3%.

16 (a) 2100 W; (b) 10 582.5 W; (c) 17 g.

Chapter D5

1 14.0 J.

2 4.67 J.

3 (a) 10 Gy of alpha particles; (b) they do the
same damage.

4 166.

5 (a) 0.4 mGy; (b) 0.3 mJ; (c) 3.75×10^{10}.

6 15 mSv (assuming a constant activity in the
30 min interval – justified since 30 min is
short compared with the half-life).

7 2.8 mSv.

8 (a) 1.07×10^{-6} W m⁻²; (b) 2.4×10^{-8} J;
(c) 2.47 μGy; (d) 2.47 μSv.

9 About 0.31 mm.

Option E: The history and development of physics

Chapter E1

11 4.685 yr.

12 1.52 AU.

Chapter E5

1 $1.3 \times 10^6 \, \text{m s}^{-1}$.
2 $7.3 \times 10^7 \, \text{m s}^{-1}$.
3 2.69 cm.
4 $1.0 \times 10^{-4} \, \text{T}$.

Chapter E6

1 $100 \, \text{MeV} \, c^{-2}$.
2 Confining the electron within a region of about 10^{-10} m gives it a kinetic energy of about $E_k \approx \frac{\Delta p^2}{2m} \approx \frac{1}{2m} \frac{h^2}{16\pi^2 \Delta x^2} \approx 16 \, \text{eV}$.
3 Confining the electron in a region of 10^{-15} m gives it a kinetic energy of $4 \times 10^4 \, \text{MeV}$. Such an energy would break the nucleus apart.
4 About 1×10^{-18} m.

Option F: Astrophysics

Chapter F1

3 Do an order-of-magnitude calculation without calculator: mass of a helium nucleus $4 \times 1.6 \times 10^{-27} \, \text{kg} \approx 6 \times 10^{-27} \, \text{kg}$. The radius of helium nucleus is $1.2 \times 10^{-15} \times 4^{1/3}$ m so the volume is about
$\frac{4\pi}{3} \left(1.2 \times 10^{-15} \times 4^{1/3} \right)^3 \, \text{m}^3$
$\approx 4 \times 1.5 \times 4 \times 10^{-45} \, \text{m}^3$
$\approx 2 \times 10^{-44} \, \text{m}^3$ so the density of the nucleus is $\frac{6 \times 10^{-27} \, \text{kg}}{2 \times 10^{-44} \, \text{m}^3}$
$= 3 \times 10^{17} \, \text{kg m}^{-3}$.
4 5.3×10^8 m.
6 1000.
8 Jupiter.
10 1.5×10^{11} m.
11 93 m.
14 $29.7 \, \text{km s}^{-1}$.
15 1.9×10^{27} kg.
16 $250 \, \text{km s}^{-1}$; 2.48×10^{41} kg (mass enclosed within a radius of 28 000 ly).

Chapter F2

1 1.7×10^{29} W.
2 $5.2 \times 10^{-9} \, \text{W m}^{-2}$.

3 2.6×10^4 ly .
4 (a) 256 times; (b) 1/16.
5 30.
6 (a) 26; (b) 1.5.
7 (a) $\frac{R_A}{R_B} = 4$; (b) $\frac{d_A}{d_B} = 0.71$.
8 $\frac{T_A}{T_B} = 4$.
9 1.2.
18 2.34×10^{30} kg and 2.80×10^{30} kg.
19 (a) 3.37×10^{12} m; (b) 2.95×10^{30} kg; (c) 1.70×10^{30} kg; 1.25×10^{30} kg.
21 $9.2 \times 10^8 \, \text{kg m}^{-3}$.
23 (c) See Figure A60.

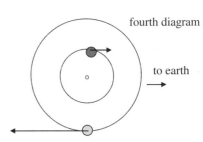

Figure A60.

24 1.4.
26 (a) $T = 7250$ K; (b) about 5 to 8 times that of the sun (by looking at the HR diagram).

Chapter F3

3 3.51 pc.
4 0.30 arcseconds.
5 (a) 149.3 pc; (b) 257 solar radii.
6 The distance to the star is 40 pc. Hence the star appears dimmer than a magnitude 0.8; its apparent magnitude is thus greater than 0.8.
7 (a) 4 pc.
8 6.3 times.
9 Capella by a factor of 2.75.

10 (a) Star A; (b) star A because it appears brighter even though it is further away.

11 (a) They both have the same luminosity; (b) star B appears brighter because it is closer.

13 6.3×10^3 ly (used a luminosity of 1000 solar luminosities).

14 2.37×10^{-9} W m^{-2}; 2.57.

15 (a) 1.0×10^{-8} W m^{-2}; (b) 0.38.

16 1.8×10^5 ly (used a luminosity of 3500 solar luminosities).

17 (b) 263 pc; (c) 4.13; (d) 17 pc.

Chapter F4

2 About 6.

3 Expansion of the universe; helium abundance; cosmic background radiation.

4 (a) Evidence for the Big Bang; (b) the same.

5 (a) Will approach absolute zero; (b) will reach minimum and then begin to increase.

6 All of space was a point at the time of the Big Bang.

8 Open means that the universe is expanding forever. Closed means that it will recollapse. The surface of a sphere is finite but has no boundary. The surface of a sheet of paper is finite and has a boundary.

10 The galaxies are not moving into empty space. Space is being created in between them.

14 Just above 4000 K.

15 (b) Same black-body spectrum curve with a peak that is shifted to the right (longer wavelengths).

Chapter F5

2 1.37×10^{27} kg.

3 (a) 6.28×10^7 m s^{-1}; (b) 21%.

4 The 1 solar mass star. The heavier the star, the faster evolution proceeds.

6 Cannot produce elements heavier than iron in core.

8 Most O type stars would have evolved past the supernova stage.

9 No. Elements crucial for life would not have been produced.

11 (a) 7.36 MeV; (b) 7.92 MeV.

12 Larger nuclear charge leads to larger repulsion.

17 2.2×10^9 K.

18 3.4.

26 (a) 2×10^8 yr. (b) Implies quasar active life must be very short.

Chapter F6

5 6.94 Mpc.

7 (a) 1.2×10^6 m s^{-1}; 16.53 Mpc; (b) 1.5×10^7 m s^{-1}; 208.3 Mpc; (c) 2.2×10^7 m s^{-1}; 308 Mpc; (d) 3.9×10^7 m s^{-1}; 541.7 Mpc; (e) 6.1×10^7 m s^{-1}; 847.2 Mpc.

8 (a) 4167 Mpc; (b) they are unobservable. (c) No, this speed is due to the expanding space between the galaxies. It cannot be used to send a signal.

9 (a) 0.178; (b) 5.33×10^7 m s^{-1}; (c) 741 Mpc.

10 1.96 billion years.

13 (c) $R = R_0 \exp[c(t - t_0)]$.

19 7×10^{-44} kg m^{-3} s^{-1}.

20 *Long problem.* Small time means small θ. The replacement by hyperbolic functions means that the scale factor increases forever. The parameter k is related to the curvature of space.

Option G: Relativity

Chapter G1

3 A: $x = 0$; B: $x = 1.59$ m; (c) $x = 2.65$ m.

6 Assuming the coil is at rest and the magnet moving gives *exactly identical* results.

10 (a) Both open 9 s later; (b) the rear door will open first.

Chapter G2

1 (a) 11.5 min; (b) 11.5 min.

2 (a) 1.6×10^{-7} s; (b) 45.6 m.

3 (a) 50.3 yr; (b) 5.0 yr older.

4 3.20 s.

5 (a) 3 yr; (b) 6 yr; (c) 3 ly.

6 320.3 m.

7 (a) 8.0 years; (b) 6.0 years; (c) 72 years; (d) 48 years.

8 (a) $0.359c$; (b) 28 m; (c) 30 m.

9 Q's clock is slow.

10 (a) 8.42×10^3 s; (b) 3.67×10^3 s.

11 (a) $0.385c$; (b) $-0.385c$.

12 (a) $0.946c$; (b) $-0.946c$.

13 $0.915c$.

14 $0.172c$.

Chapter G3

1 939.4 MeV.

2 $0.994c$.

3 $0.995c$.

4 $0.738c$.

5 (a) 1.31 MeV; (b) $0.921c$.

6 1566 MeV.

7 It increases.

8 (a) 7.02×10^{-6} s; (b) 2.19×10^{-6} s.

9 2.796×10^8 m s^{-1}.

10 (a) 2 h; (b) 6 h; (c) 6 h.

11 3 h.

Chapter G4

1 (a) 0.511 MeV; (b) (i) 1.88×10^{10} m s^{-1}; (ii) $0.999\,999\,87c$.

2 $0.9959c$.

3 4595 MeV c^{-1}.

4 1.17 MeV.

5 3.66×10^{-19} kg m s^{-1}.

6 124.9 MeV.

7 1.78×10^{-26} kg.

8 (a) $0.999\,999\,999\,987c$; (b) $0.999\,956c$.

9 $0.979c$.

10 2412 MV.

11 5711 MeV.

12 (a) 0.079 MeV; (b) 0.66 MeV; (c) 3.11 MeV.

13 (a) 500 MeV; (b) $0.758c$.

14 (b) 835; (c) 1.37; (d) 1.

15 (a) $0.628c$; (b) 558.5 MeV.

16 (c) 2.5 MeV.

17 (c) 4.2×10^{-12} m.

18 0.122 MeV; $0.59c$.

19 9.

20 10 kg.

Chapter G5

2 In the direction of acceleration.

3 Bends toward the right.

6 (a) Yes; (b) yes.

7 3.27 Hz.

8 2.33×10^9 Hz.

9 (a) 500 nm; (b) 1.25 s; (c) 1.25 ms.

10 The acceleration there is larger and so by the equivalence principle it finds itself in a larger gravitational field.

11 2.05×10^{30} kg m^{-3}.

12 2.96×10^4 m.

17 $\dfrac{1}{R^2}$.

Option H: Optics

Chapter H1

1 (a) 50 μs.

2 3.14×10^8 m s^{-1}.

3 Red: 53.989°, deviation = 23.981°; blue: 54.632°, deviation = 24.632°.

Chapter H2

2 Three.

4 See Figure A61.

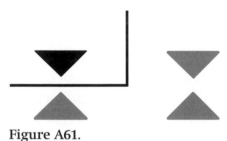

Figure A61.

5 See Figure A62.

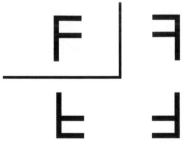

Figure A62.

7 $\frac{360}{\theta} - 1$, *if* this is an integer.

8 1.13 m.

9 (a) 31.85°; (b) 44.6°.

10 70.6°.

11 34.1°.

12 (a) 1.414; (b) 1.881.

Chapter H3

7 6.0 cm.

9 (a) $v = 20$ cm; $h' = -2$ cm; (b) image is at infinity; (c) $v = -10$ cm; $h' = 4$ cm.

10 (a) $v = -6.67$ cm; $h' = 0.67$ cm;
  (b) $v = -5$ cm; $h' = 1.0$ cm;
  (c) $v = -3.33$ cm; $h' = 1.33$ cm.

11 $v = 8.0$ cm, real, inverted, image height 7.5 cm.

12 $v = -24$ cm, virtual, upright, image height 16 cm.

13 $v = -4.0$ cm, virtual, upright, image height 10 cm.

15 (b) 10.1 cm ± 0.3 cm.

17 (a) $v = 60$ cm, real, inverted, 3 times larger.

18 -60 cm.

19 (a) 430 cm and 70 cm. (b) The distance 430 cm results in the larger image.

20 3.75 cm from right lens.

21 (a) 2 cm to the left of L_2; (b) -1.2;
  (c) inverted.

22 (a) 18.4 cm to the left of L_2; (b) 0.55;
  (c) upright.

23 2.8×10^6 times more.

24 (a) 7.14 cm; (b) 10 cm; (c) 0.160 rad.

26 0.02 mm.

27 -125.

28 (b) 18.5 cm.

29 (a) 4; (b) 0.104 rad.

30 (a) 22.3; (b) 70 cm.

31 22.2 m.

Chapter H4

1 $38.9°$.

2 5.03 cm.

3 (a) 1.556λ; (b) 13 maxima. See Figure A63.

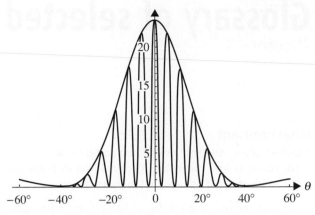

Figure A63.

4 1.746 cm; microwave.

5 3λ.

7 No, can resolve 3.6 cm.

8 115 km.

9 (a) 4.14×10^{-7} m; 4.25×10^{-7} m; (b) $0.462°$.

10 (a) $0.0°$; $13.89°$; $28.69°$; $46.05°$; $73.74°$.
  (b) $n = 4$.

14 0.123 μm.

15 103.4 nm.

17 Will increase.

18 6×10^{-5} rad.

Glossary of selected terms

Measurement

Random error An error due to inexperience of the observer and the difficulty of reading instruments. It can be reduced by repeated measurements.

Systematic error An error due to incorrectly calibrated instruments — it is the same for all data points and cannot be reduced by repeated measurements.

Mechanics

Acceleration The rate of change with time of the velocity vector. It is a vector. It is the gradient of a velocity versus time graph.

Centrifugal force There is no such thing. Students incorrectly assume such a force pushing a body away from the centre of a circular path to claim that the body is in equilibrium. But the body is not in equilibrium, and so no such force is required.

Centripetal acceleration The acceleration due to a changing velocity direction. It points towards the centre of the circular path.

Centripetal force A force, or component of a force or the resultant of forces, which points towards the centre of a circular path.

Coefficient of dynamic friction The ratio of the frictional force between two bodies to the normal force between them when one body moves relative to the other.

Coefficient of static friction The ratio of the largest possible frictional force between two bodies to the normal force between them when there is no relative motion between the bodies.

Displacement The distance in a given direction from a fixed origin. It is a vector.

Efficiency The ratio of the output work (or power) to the input work (or power).

Escape speed The minimum speed of an object (at the surface of a planet) so that it can move an infinite distance away, $v = \sqrt{\dfrac{2GM}{r}}$.

Gravitational field strength The gravitational force per unit mass experienced by a small point mass. For a spherical or point mass, $g = \dfrac{GM}{r^2}$. It is a vector.

Gravitational potential The work done per unit mass in bringing a small point mass from infinity to a point in a gravitational field. For a spherical or point mass, $V = -\dfrac{GM}{r}$. It is a scalar.

Gravitational potential energy of two masses (Numerically) the work that must be done in order to bring two masses an infinite distance apart, $E_G = -\dfrac{GMm}{r}$. For objects moving near the earth's surface, it is sufficient to use just $E_G = mgh$.

Hooke's law The tension in a spring is proportional to its extension, $F = kx$.

Impulse The total momentum change of a system as a result of a force acting on it. It is given by the area under a force versus time graph. It is a vector.

Inertial/gravitational mass Inertial mass is the ratio of the net force on the body to its acceleration; and gravitational mass is the ratio of the gravitational force on the body to the gravitational field strength. Inertial and gravitational masses are equal to each other.

Law of gravitation There is an attractive force between any two point masses, given by $F = G\dfrac{m_1 m_2}{r^2}$, where r is their separation.

Momentum conservation When the net external force on a system is zero, the total momentum of the system stays the same.

Newton's first law When the net force on a system is zero, the system remains at rest or moves with constant velocity.

Newton's second law The (average) net force on a body equals the rate of change of the body's momentum, $F_{NET} = \dfrac{\Delta p}{\Delta t}$. When the mass is constant, this reduces to $F_{NET} = ma$.

Newton's third law If body A exerts a force on body B, then body B will exert an equal and opposite force on body A.

Orbit The path of an object when under the influence of just the force of gravitation.

Orbital speed The speed of a body in orbit, $v = \sqrt{\dfrac{GM}{r}}$.

Power The rate at which work is being performed, $P = \dfrac{\Delta W}{\Delta t} = Fv$. It is a scalar.

Velocity The rate of change with time of the displacement vector. It is a vector. It is the gradient of a displacement versus time graph.

Work It is the product of the force times the distance moved by its point of application in the direction of the force. It is given by the area under the graph of force versus distance. It is a scalar.

Work done in a gravitational field The work done in moving a mass m from one point to another in a gravitational field is $W = m\Delta V$. It is independent of the path followed.

Work–kinetic energy relation The net work done on a body (i.e. the work of the net force or the sum of the work done by individual forces) equals the change in kinetic energy of the body, $W_{NET} = \Delta E_k$.

Thermal physics

Adiabatic A thermodynamic process in which no thermal energy is exchanged.

Carnot cycle A thermodynamic cycle consisting of two adiabatics and two isotherms.

Entropy A measure of the disorder of a thermodynamic system.

Ideal gas A gas with no intermolecular forces obeying the ideal gas law, $PV = nRT$ (T in kelvin) at all temperatures, pressures and volumes.

Internal energy The total kinetic and potential energy of the molecules of a substance. By `potential energy' we understand the energy due to intermolecular forces.

Irreversible A process in which the entropy increases. Natural processes are irreversible.

Isothermal A thermodynamic process in which the temperature stays the same.

Pressure The force normal to an area per unit area.

Reversible Idealized processes in which the entropy stays the same.

Second law The entropy of an isolated system (a system on which no work is being done from the outside) never decreases.

Specific heat capacity The energy needed to raise the temperature of a unit mass by one degree.

Specific latent heat of fusion/vaporization The energy required to melt/vaporize a unit mass at constant temperature.

Temperature A measure of the average kinetic energy of the molecules of a substance.

Work It equals the area under the graph of pressure versus volume. For constant pressure, it equals $W = P\Delta V$. The net work done in a cyclic process is the area of the loop in a pressure versus volume graph.

Waves

Amplitude The maximum displacement of a wave. It is a measure of the energy carried by the wave (energy per unit wavefront length or area).

Coherent Two sources of identical waves are said to be coherent if there is a constant phase difference between them. Two sources must be coherent for interference to be observed. (Coherence implies that the frequencies of the sources are the same.)

Diffraction A general wave phenomenon shown by all waves. It is the spreading of a wave as it passes through an aperture or past an obstacle. It is substantial only when the wavelength and the aperture size are comparable. The minima of single-slit diffraction are given by $b\sin\theta = n\lambda$, where b is the aperture size.

Doppler effect The frequency received by an observer is different from that emitted if there is relative motion between the receiver and the source of the waves.

Electromagnetic waves Transverse waves travelling in vacuum with the speed of light. They range from low-wavelength gamma rays to long-wavelength radio waves. The visible spectrum ranges from blue light at about 400 nm wavelength, to red light at 750 nm.

Frequency The number of full waves emitted per second.

Huygens' principle Every point on a wavefront acts a source of secondary spherical wavefronts called wavelets. The next wavefront is tangent to all the wavelets. It explains reflection and refraction and partly diffraction.

Index of refraction The ratio of the speed of light in vacuum to the speed of light in a given medium.

Interference When two similar coherent waves meet, the resulting wave will have a large (maximum) amplitude if the waves meet crest to crest or zero (minimum) amplitude if the waves meet crest to trough.

Longitudinal wave A wave in which the displacement is parallel to the direction of energy transfer of the wave. Sound is a longitudinal wave.

Path difference The difference in distance from each of two sources to the observer. If the path difference (p.d.) is an integral multiple of the wavelength, constructive interference takes place, p.d. $= n\lambda$. If it is an integral multiple and one-half wavelength, interference is destructive, p.d. $= (n + \frac{1}{2})\lambda$.

Period The time to create a full wave.

Ray A line at right angles to a wavefront along the direction of energy transfer of a wave.

Snell's law The angles of incidence and refraction are related to the wave speeds in two media through $\dfrac{\sin\theta_1}{c_1} = \dfrac{\sin\theta_2}{c_2}$, where the angles are defined to be those between the rays and the normal or the wavefronts and the surface.

Standing wave A wave formed by the superposition of two identical waves moving in opposite directions. A standing wave does not transfer energy.

Superposition When two waves meet, the resulting displacement is the sum of the individual displacements.

Transverse wave A wave in which the displacement is normal to the direction of energy transfer of the wave. Electromagnetic waves are transverse waves.

Two-slit interference The maxima are given by $d\sin\theta = n\lambda$. The separation of two consecutive maxima on a screen a distance D away from the slits is $s = \dfrac{\lambda D}{d}$.

Wave speed The speed at which energy is transferred by the wave, $v = f\lambda$.

Wavefront A surface at right angles to the direction of energy transfer of the wave consisting of points in phase.

Wavelength The length of a full wave, or the distance from a crest to the next crest.

Electricity and magnetism

Coulomb's law There is an electric force between two point charges given by $F = k\dfrac{Q_1 Q_2}{r^2}$, where r is their separation. The law also holds for two spherical charges, far apart, in which case r is the centre-to-centre separation. The force is attractive for unlike charges, and repulsive for like charges.

Current The amount of charge per unit time that passes through the cross-sectional area of a conductor.

Electric field The electric force per unit charge experienced by a positive test charge. It is a vector. A point or spherical charge Q produces an electric field $E = k\dfrac{|Q|}{r^2}$. The electric field is zero inside a conductor.

Electric potential The work per unit charge performed in bringing a positive test charge from infinity to a given point in an electric field. It is a scalar. A point or spherical charge Q produces an electric potential $V = k\dfrac{Q}{r}$. The electric potential is constant inside a conductor and equals its value at the surface.

Electric power The rate at which electrical energy is dissipated in a conductor, given by $P = VI = RI^2 = \dfrac{V^2}{R}$.

Emf The work per unit charge in moving a positive test charge across the terminals of a battery. When the battery sends out a current I into a circuit, the quantity $\mathcal{E}I$ is the total power dissipated in the circuit, where $\mathcal{E}$ is the emf.

Faraday's law The induced emf in a loop is the rate of change with time of the magnetic flux linkage through the loop, $\text{emf} = N\dfrac{\Delta\Phi}{\Delta t}$.

Lenz's law The direction of the induced current is such as to oppose the change in flux that created it.

Magnetic field Produced by currents and magnets. The magnetic field of a long straight current is $B = \mu_0\dfrac{I}{2\pi r}$ and inside a solenoid $B = \mu_0\dfrac{NI}{L}$.

Magnetic flux The product of magnetic field magnitude multiplied by the area of a loop and the cosine of the angle between the normal to the area and B, that is $\Phi = BA\cos\theta$. It is a scalar.

Magnetic force A moving charged particle or a current in a magnetic field will experience a force $F = qvB\sin\theta$ or $F = BIL\sin\theta$. The force is always at right angles to the velocity or the current.

Ohm's law The current in a conductor at constant temperature is proportional to the voltage across it.

Path in electric field The path of a charge in an electric field can be (1) a parabola or (2) a straight line.

Path in magnetic field The path of a charge in a magnetic field can be (1) a circle or (2) a helix or (3) a straight line. The radius of the circular path is $R = \dfrac{mv}{qB}$.

Resistance The ratio of voltage across a conductor to the current through it, $R = \dfrac{V}{I}$.

Rms current The peak current divided by $\sqrt{2}$. It is the square root of the average of the square of the current.

Rms voltage The peak voltage divided by $\sqrt{2}$. It is the square root of the average of the square of the voltage.

Atomic and nuclear physics

Activity The number of decays per second of a radioactive sample. The activity after time t is $A = A_0 e^{-\lambda t} = A_0\left(\dfrac{1}{2}\right)^{t/T_{1/2}}$. The unit of activity is the becquerel (1 Bq = 1 decay per second).

Antiparticles Particles with the same mass but opposite other properties, such as electric charge. The antiparticle of the electron is the positron.

Atomic/nuclear transitions When an electron makes a transition to a lower atomic state, a photon is emitted whose energy equals the difference in energy of the levels involved, $hf = \Delta E$. The same is true when a nucleus makes a nuclear transition between nuclear energy levels. The photon in that case is a gamma ray photon.

Atomic number The number of protons in a nucleus.

Baryon number Particles made out of three quarks. They are assigned a quantum number of $+1$ called baryon number. Antibaryons then have a baryon number of -1.

Binding energy The energy required to completely separate the nucleons of a nucleus.

Conservation laws At the elementary particle level , energy, momentum, electric charge, baryon number and lepton number are always conserved in all reactions.

Critical frequency (threshold frequency) The lowest frequency of electromagnetic radiation that results in electrons being emitted from the surface.

De Broglie wavelength To a particle of momentum mv there corresponds a wavelength $\lambda = \dfrac{h}{mv} = \dfrac{h}{p}$. For example, electrons can show wave behaviour, e.g. diffraction when shot at a crystal.

Decay constant The probability of decay per unit time of a given nucleus. It is related to half-life through $\lambda T_{1/2} = \ln 2$.

Exchange particles Interactions are described in terms of the exchange of (virtual) particles. These are the photon (electromagnetic), graviton (gravitational), $W^{\pm}$, Z^0 (weak) and gluons (strong).

Hadrons Particles made out of quarks. There are baryons (e.g. protons and neutrons), which are made of three quarks, and mesons (e.g. pions and kaons), which are made of one quark and one antiquark.

Half-life The time for the initial activity of a radioactive sample to decrease by a factor of 2.

Isotopes Nuclei with the same atomic number but different mass number (due to a different number of neutrons).

Lepton number Leptons are assigned a quantum number called lepton number of $+1$. Antileptons have a lepton number of -1.

Leptons The known leptons are the electron, muon and tau, with their antiparticles and their respective neutrinos and antineutrinos.

Mass defect The difference between the mass of the separated nucleons and the mass of the nucleus made of these nucleons.

Mass number The number of nucleons in a nucleus.

Minimum X-ray wavelength The lowest wavelength emitted when X-rays are produced. It is given by $\lambda = \dfrac{hc}{eV}$, where V is the accelerating voltage.

Neutrino Low-mass, neutral, very weakly interacting particle. Postulated by W. Pauli and E. Fermi to explain why the energy of electrons in beta decay is not

unique. With only two particles produced, momentum conservation demands the two move oppositely and so each have a fixed share of the available kinetic energy. With three, there is a range of energies for the electron, as is observed in experiments. Neutrinos are leptons.

Nuclear fission The splitting of a large nucleus into two smaller ones plus neutrons, radiation and energy.

Nuclear fusion The joining of two light nuclei into a larger nucleus plus radiation and energy.

Photoelectric effect The emission of electrons from a surface when electromagnetic radiation is incident on the surface. The maximum emitted electron energy is $E_k = hf - \phi$, where ϕ is the work function of the surface. The intensity of the radiation does not affect the electron kinetic energy, only the number of electrons emitted per second.

Photon A zero rest-mass neutral particle, the quantum of electromagnetic radiation. The energy of a photon is $E = hf$ and its momentum is $p = \dfrac{hf}{c} = \dfrac{h}{\lambda}$.

Quarks Elementary particles making up hadrons. There are six quarks (flavours): up, down, strange, charm, bottom and top. They have fractional charges, e.g. $Q_u = \frac{2}{3}|e|$ and $Q_d = -\frac{1}{3}|e|$. The proton is uud and the neutron ddu. Quarks are confined — they cannot appear as free particles. Attempting to extract a quark from a hadron results in another hadron being formed.

Radioactive decay law The rate of decay is proportional to the number of radioactive nuclei present, $\dfrac{dN}{dt} \propto N$, leading to $N = N_0 e^{-\lambda t} = N_0 \left(\dfrac{1}{2}\right)^{t/T_{1/2}}$.

Rutherford's experiment An experiment in which alpha particles were directed at a thin foil of gold. Most went through slightly deflected by the electric force between the positive charges of the alphas and the atom, but occasionally a few were turned back, indicating the existence of a massive, tiny, positive charge in the atom, the atomic nucleus.

Schrödinger's theory The modern quantum theory of atoms and molecules. It applies to many-electron atoms and assigns a wavefunction to electrons. The absolute value squared of the wavefunction is a probability density function that gives the probability of finding the electron somewhere. Unlike Bohr's theory, it predicts relative intensities of spectral lines and is consistent with Heisenberg's uncertainty principle.

Strong nuclear force Attractive force between nucleons in a nucleus keeping them together and overcoming the electrical force of repulsion between the protons. The force has very short range.

Weak nuclear force Short-range force acting within the nucleus, responsible for beta decay.

Work function The minimum energy required to free an electron from a metal.

Astrophysics

Absolute magnitude The apparent magnitude a star would have if observed from a distance of 10 pc.

Apparent brightness The received energy per second per unit area of detector. It equals $b = \dfrac{L}{4\pi d^2}$. Its units are $W\,m^{-2}$.

Apparent magnitude A measure of brightness of a star as seen from earth in a relative system of classification. The higher the numerical value of apparent magnitude, the dimmer the star.

Big Bang The singular point at which space, time, matter and energy were created. The universe has been expanding ever since.

Cepheid variables Stars with a periodically changing luminosity due to contractions and expansions of its surface. There is a definite relationship between the period of variation of the luminosity and the peak luminosity allowing determination of distances.

Chandrasekhar limit The largest mass a white dwarf can have. It is about 1.4 solar masses.

Cosmic background radiation Microwave, blackbody radiation filling the universe at a temperature of about 2.7 K. It is the remnant of the high temperatures at the time of the Big Bang. It is one of the strongest pieces of evidence in favour of the Big Bang model.

Critical density The density of the universe that separates a universe that will expand forever (open universe) and one that will re-collapse (closed universe). A universe with a density equal to the critical density is called flat (and will expand forever at a slowing rate).

Dark matter Matter that is too cold to radiate and so cannot be seen. Has been invoked to solve the puzzle of the missing mass of the universe.

HR (Hertzsprung–Russell) diagram A plot of stars according to luminosity or absolute magnitude (vertical axis) and temperature or spectral class (horizontal axis, temperature increasing to the left).

Hubble classification scheme Galaxies are grouped according to their shape as (1) spiral, (2) elliptical and (3) irregular.

Hubble constant The slope of a graph of galaxy speed versus distance.

Hubble time The inverse of the Hubble constant, giving an estimate for the age of the universe.

Hubble's law Distant galaxies are moving away from the earth with a speed that is proportional to their distance.

Luminosity The amount of energy radiated by the star per second, i.e. the power radiated by the star. Luminosity depends on the surface temperature and surface area of the star, $L = \sigma A T^4$. The constant σ is called the Stefan–Boltzmann constant ($\sigma = 5.67 \times 10^{-8}\,W\,m^{-2}\,K^{-4}$).

Main sequence Stars undergoing nuclear fusion of hydrogen into helium. They lie on a strip on the HR diagram from top left to bottom right.

Olbers' paradox The night sky should have been bright if there were an infinite number of stars in an infinite and eternal universe. There is (1) a finite number of stars and (2) they will not live forever, so the night sky is dark.

Parallax method A method to measure the distance of nearby stars (up to 100 pc), which relies on the fact that the star appears displaced relative to the background of distant stars when viewed from two different positions in space.

Pulsars Rotating neutron stars emitting radio waves.

Spectral class A classification of stars according to surface temperature and colour. The classes are OBAFGKMN, with O being hot and blue, and N cool and red. The sun is a class G star (yellow/orange at 6000 K).

Spectroscopic parallax A method to measure distances to stars. It uses the spectrum of the star to estimate its temperature and then through the HR diagram to estimate the luminosity. Knowledge of luminosity and apparent brightness allows determination of distance.

Stellar evolution The evolution of a star from its birth, to its life on the main sequence, to its life as a red giant or red supergiant and its death. The way the star dies is determined by its mass. If the star is not too massive (under 10 solar masses), a planetary nebula ejects most of the mass of the star and leaves behind a dense, hot core, a white dwarf, of maximum mass 1.4 solar masses (the Chandrasekhar limit). If the star is more massive, a supernova ejects most of the star's mass, leaving behind a neutron star, of maximum mass 3 solar masses (the Oppenheimer–Volkoff limit). If the star is even more massive, it ends up as a black hole.

Wien displacement law The wavelength at which most of the energy from a star is emitted is related to surface temperature through $\lambda_0 T = 2.90 \times 10^{-3}\,K\,m$. This implies that the higher the temperature, the lower the wavelength at which most of the energy is emitted. The peak wavelength determines the colour of the star; thus there is a connection between the colour and the surface temperature of the star.

Relativity

Bending of light Light `bends' near a massive body. In reality, light follows the geodesic of the space-time that has been curved by the massive body.

Black hole A singularity of space-time. A point of infinite density and curvature.

Equivalence principle It is impossible to distinguish between gravitational and inertial effects. Acceleration can make gravity appear (e.g. when an elevator accelerates upwards, you feel heavier) as well as disappear (e.g. in free fall or in orbit, you feel weightless).

Event horizon A surface separating space into two regions such that nothing within the event horizon can escape or be communicated to the outside.

Frame of reference An array of rulers and clocks used by an observer to record the positions and times of events.

Gamma factor (Lorentz factor) The quantity $\gamma = \dfrac{1}{\sqrt{1 - \frac{v^2}{c^2}}}$.

Gamma is always bigger than 1, but becomes appreciably bigger than 1 only for speeds larger than $0.5c$. Given gamma, the speed is found from $\dfrac{v}{c} = \sqrt{1 - \dfrac{1}{\gamma^2}}$.

General relativity The theory according to which mass and energy curve space-time. The geometry of space-time determines the motion of light and particles in the space-time.

Geodesic Curve of least length, corresponds to the `straight' line, in a curved space-time. Light and bodies on which no forces act move on geodesics.

Gravitational lensing Rays of light from a distant object passing near a very massive body will bend, creating multiple images of the object.

Gravitational redshift The frequency of electromagnetic radiation observed far from a massive body is less than the frequency emitted at the surface. If H is small, $\dfrac{\Delta f}{f} = \dfrac{gH}{c^2}$.

Inertial observer An observer who is not accelerating.

Kinetic energy The quantity $E_k = (\gamma - 1)m_0 c^2$. It is approximately equal to $E_k = \frac{1}{2}mv^2$ only for speeds that are small compared to c.

Length contraction The length of an object in the direction of motion is contracted relative to that observer with respect to whom the body moves, $\text{length} = \dfrac{\text{proper length}}{\gamma}$.

Michelson–Morley experiment An experiment designed to measure the speed of the earth relative to the ether. No such velocity was measured — and this led to the abandonment of the ether idea.

Momentum energy relation The relation $E^2 = (m_0 c^2)^2 + (pc)^2$ between total energy and momentum. It allows the definition of momentum for particles of zero rest mass (like the photon).

Newtonian limit At low speeds, results of relativity and those of Newtonian mechanics agree.

Postulates of special relativity (1) The speed of light in vacuum is the same for all inertial observers. (2) The laws of physics are the same for all inertial observers.

Proper length The length of an object in its rest frame.

Proper time interval The time interval between two events that occur at the same point in space.

Rest energy The energy needed to create a particle, $E = m_0 c^2$.

Rest frame The frame of reference in which a given object is at rest.

Rest mass The mass of an object in its rest frame.

Schwarzschild radius The radius at which a star becomes a black hole. Nothing can escape from the star if its distance from the centre is less than this radius.

Simultaneity This is relative. If two events taking place at different points in space according to an observer are simultaneous, then they will not be simultaneous according to any other observer in relative motion with respect to the first observer.

Time dilation The time interval between any two events is shortest in the frame of reference in which the two events occur at the same point in space. In all other frames, time interval = $\gamma \times$ proper time interval.

Total energy The rest energy plus all other forms of energy a body may have, e.g. kinetic energy, $E = mc^2 = \gamma m_0 c^2$.

Velocity addition If frame A has velocity u' with respect to frame B and frame B has velocity v with respect to frame C, then the velocity of A with respect to C is $u = \dfrac{u' + v}{1 + \frac{u'v}{c^2}}$.

Index